Operation	Step Sequence	Page
	or ↵ Modify Structure/Order ↵ Organize/**E**rase Marked Records [↵] **Y** **Ctrl-End**	
SORTING THE DATABASE		
For simple sorts:	Highlight the database name in the Data panel Design (**Shift-F2**) **Esc** Move the cursor to the index column of the field to sort by **Y** **Ctrl-End**	86
For more complex sorts:	Highlight the database name in the Data panel Design (**Shift-F2**) Organize/**C**reate New Index [↵] **N**ame of Index [↵] Type a name for the index ↵ **I**ndex Expression [↵] Type the field name to index on ↵ *or* **Shift-F1** highlight the field name ↵ **O**rder of Index [↵] Ascending or Descending **Ctrl-End** Data (**F2**)	90
SEARCHING THE DATABASE		
Searching for Particular Records		
From the browse or edit screen:	Menus (**F10**)/Go To Top Record *or* Last Record *or* Record Number *n* ↵ *or* Skip *n* ↵	113
Isolating Records with Queries		
Accessing the Query Design Screen	Highlight <create> in the Queries panel with database open ↵	125
Searching for a Value from the Query Design Screen	Highlight the field to search Type the condition to find ↵ Data (**F2**)	127
Searching Memo Fields		
In query design screen condition box:	"*search string*" **$** *field name*	151
DESIGNING FORMATTED REPORTS		
Accessing the Reports Design Screen	Open the database file Highlight <create> in the Reports panel ↵	227

dBASE IV USER'S DESKTOP COMPANION

SYBEX READY REFERENCE SERIES

dBASE IV™
USER'S DESKTOP COMPANION

Alan Simpson

SAN FRANCISCO • PARIS • DÜSSELDORF • LONDON

Acquisitions Editor: Dianne King
Developmental Editor: James A. Compton
Copy Editor: Judith Ziajka
Technical Editor: Jeff Green
Word Processors: Christine Mockel, Scott Campbell
Book and Cover Designer: Thomas Ingalls + Associates
Pasteup and Layout: Evelyn Ong-Sy
Technical Art: Rick van Genderen
Screen Graphics: Sonja Schenk
Typesetter: Robert Myren
Proofreaders: Sylvia Townsend, Vanessa Miller, Hilda van Genderen
Indexer: Anne Leach
Cover Photographer: David Bishop
Screen reproductions produced by XenoFont

dBASE III, dBASE III PLUS, dBASE IV, RunTime +, RapidFile, and Framework II are registered trademarks of Ashton-Tate.
EPSON is a registered trademark of Epson Corporation.
IBM, PC/AT, PC/XT, PC-DOS, and PS/2 are registered trademarks of International Business Machines Corporation.
Lotus, Symphony, and 1-2-3 are registered trademarks of Lotus Development Corporation.
MS-DOS, Microsoft, Multiplan, SYLK, and OS/2 are registered trademarks of Microsoft Corporation.
PFS and PFS:File are trademarks of Software Publishing Corporation.
Quattro is a trademark of Borland International, Inc.
UNIX is a trademark of AT&T.
VisiCalc is a trademark of VisiCorp, Inc.
WordPerfect is a trademark of WordPerfect Corporation.
WordStar and MailMerge are trademarks of WordStar International Corporation.
XenoFont is a trademark of XenoSoft.

SYBEX is a registered trademark of SYBEX, Inc.

SYBEX is not affiliated with any manufacturer.

Every effort has been made to supply complete and accurate information. However, SYBEX assumes no responsibility for its use, nor for any infringements of patents or other rights of third parties which would result.

Copyright ©1989 SYBEX Inc., 2021 Challenger Drive #100, Alameda, CA 94501. World rights reserved. No part of this publication may be stored in a retrieval system, transmitted, or reproduced in any way, including but not limited to photocopy, photograph, magnetic or other record, without the prior agreement and written permission of the publisher.

Library of Congress Card Number: 89-61320
ISBN 0-89588-523-9
Manufactured in the United States of America
10 9 8 7 6 5 4 3 2 1

To Susan and Ashley

Table of Contents

Preface   x

PART I: Setting Up the Database

Chapter 1: Starting and Using dBASE IV   3
Chapter 2: Creating a Database File   23

PART II: Manipulating the Data

Chapter 3: Adding, Changing, and Deleting Data   57
Chapter 4: Sorting the Database   83
Chapter 5: Searching the Database   111
Chapter 6: Performing Calculations   173

PART III: Displaying and Printing the Data

Chapter 7: Designing Formatted Reports   225
Chapter 8: Designing Mailing Labels   265
Chapter 9: Printing Reports and Labels   287
Chapter 10: Creating Custom Forms   317

PART IV: Managing the Database

Chapter 11: Managing Groups of Records   355
Chapter 12: Managing Multiple Related Databases   397
Chapter 13: Using Keystroke Macros   435
Chapter 14: Managing Files and the Workspace   459

PART V: Developing Applications

Chapter 15: Creating Application Objects   515
Chapter 16: Assigning Actions to Application Objects   569
Chapter 17: Generating and Using an Application   637

PART VI: PROGRAMMING AND CONFIGURING DBASE IV

Chapter 18: Introduction to the Programming Language	661
Chapter 19: Using DBSETUP	679
Chapter 20: Protecting Data	721

APPENDICES

Appendix A: Installing dBASE IV	757
Appendix B: Using DOS	773
Appendix C: Summary of Changes from dBASE III PLUS to dBASE IV	789
Appendix D: dBASE IV Functions	799
Appendix E: dBASE IV Commands	811
Appendix F: Designing and Developing an Application	833
Appendix G: ASCII Table	907
Index	914

PREFACE

dBASE IV is a truly enormous program with a vast array of features and options. Few people can memorize the details of every screen, menu option, and special key, or the exact steps required to achieve a goal. This book is designed to provide quick and easy access to all those easily forgotten (or previously unknown) details and steps.

The basic idea behind this book is straightforward: Whenever you feel stuck, lost, or unsure of how to get dBASE IV to do something, use this book as a quick resource for finding answers. Its overall structure, organization, and extensive index are all designed to provide easy access to the information you need.

WHO THIS BOOK IS FOR

This book is written for the dBASE IV *user* who prefers to interact with dBASE through the Control Center rather than the dot prompt or by programming. The book discusses all features and capabilities available from the Control Center, including the Applications Generator.

Readers who are more interested in the dBASE programming language may prefer this author's *dBASE IV Programmer's Reference Guide* (SYBEX, 1990), which focuses exclusively on the programming language.

HOW TO USE THIS BOOK

This book is organized into chapters that deal with specific topics, such as creating a database, sorting a database, designing reports, and so on. Each chapter discusses its topic in depth, with discrete sections that present specific topics.

To make information easy to find, section headings describe a task to be performed, such as "Getting Help," rather than a dBASE feature, like "Using the F1 Key." The index at the back of the book and the small table of contents at the beginning of each chapter also help you focus on specific tasks to be performed.

Most chapter sections are divided into three subsections, titled Sequence of Steps, Usage, and Examples, described in the following paragraphs. Chapters conclude with a Tips and Traps section and a summary.

The Sequence of Steps Section

The Sequence of Steps section for a topic quickly summarizes the exact steps, menu options, and keys required to perform a task or access a particular screen. The step sequences are intentionally brief and assume that you have some basic knowledge of how to use the dBASE IV menus. For example, the following sequence of steps is used to create a new catalog:

From the Control Center:

>Menus (**F10**)
>Catalog/**U**se a Different Catalog [◄─┘]
><create>
>type a name for the catalog ◄─┘

Notice that the key sequence begins with the starting point of the operation: the Control Center in this example. Names of keys are presented in **boldface**. Menu names and options to select are separated by a slash. In the preceding example, the step sequence is as follows: Press the **F10** key to access the Catalog pull-down menu. Then select the Use a Different Catalog option. The bracketed ◄─┘ (Return or Enter on some keyboards) symbol and boldface indicate that you can select the option either by highlighting it and pressing ◄─┘, or by typing the letter U. From the next menu that appears, select <create>. Then type a new name for the catalog and press ◄─┘. When the ◄─┘ symbol appears without brackets, it means the ◄─┘ key must be used; there is no alternative keystroke.

These brief step sequences are provided for those situations where you simply need a reminder about the exact steps required to achieve a goal. If you need more information, refer to the Usage section that follows the Sequence of Steps.

The Usage Section

The Usage section describes the step sequence and the task at hand in detail. Figures, diagrams, and tables are used liberally in the Usage sections to illustrate concepts and provide easy access to all the details.

The Examples Section

The Examples section, where applicable, provides a specific example illustrating how to perform a task and the results of performing that task. Most examples refer to a sample database that you can create in Chapter 2. If you create this database, you can try the examples yourself right at your keyboard.

Tips and Traps and Summary Sections

Each chapter closes with a Tips and Traps section and a Summary. The Tips and Traps section summarizes useful tips and potential traps that relate to the entire chapter. The Summary section summarizes the chapter discussion and provides references to related topics in other chapters.

THE STRUCTURE OF THIS BOOK

This book is not designed to be read in any particular order. Instead, each chapter, and each section within each chapter, is designed to be as self-contained as possible. But of course not many dBASE IV capabilities can be used in a vacuum. (For example, you can't print data from a database if you don't have a database to work with yet.)

Therefore, chapters are grouped into parts. Chapters in each part start at the most introductory level and progress to those topics that require more experience and knowledge. The parts are summarized here:

Part 1, "Setting up the Database," consists of two chapters that describe how to run dBASE IV and how to create a database.

Part 2, "Manipulating Data," describes the techniques involved in performing common database management functions, such as adding new data; changing and deleting data; and sorting, searching, and performing calculations.

Part 3, "Displaying and Printing the Data," consists of four chapters that discuss how to print your data on neatly formatted reports and labels. Techniques for creating your own custom screens for entering, displaying, and editing data are also discussed in this part.

Part 4, "Managing the Database," contains four chapters that focus on managing all the various components that make up a complete database, including the actual data, report formats, and label formats. Database design and techniques for managing multiple related database files are also discussed here.

Part 5, "Developing Applications," contains three chapters that focus on the dBASE IV Applications Generator. For those readers who need a little further help making the jump from a dBASE user to an applications developer, Appendix F provides an added hands-on tutorial that demonstrates the entire application design and development process.

Part 6, "Advanced Topics," contains three chapters describing dBASE IV operations that, while accessible through the Control Center, have traditionally been considered too esoteric for the user who is not a programmer. Chapter 18 provides an introduction to the dBASE IV programming language for readers who would like to "get their feet wet" in this area, or who just want to gain a little more insight into what's going on "behind the screens" when they use dBASE

IV. Chapter 19 describes the DBSETUP program, which lets you customize dBASE IV to your computer equipment, your country, and your tastes. Chapter 20 shows how to establish a file security system using the Tools menu's Protect program. File protection is a necessity whenever dBASE is used in a network, and it may also be an important concern when several people within an office use the program on a single machine.

The appendices provide additional support, including specific instructions for installing dBASE IV, an overview of DOS techniques relevant to dBASE IV, and a summary of changes from dBASE III PLUS to dBASE IV (for experienced dBASE III PLUS users). Also included are summaries of all dBASE commands and functions, and an ASCII table.

It is our hope that you will keep this book near the computer whenever you use dBASE IV, and that it will answer your questions and solve your problems, as they arise.

Acknowledgments

Although only one author's name appears on the cover, this book is the result of the combined skills and talents of many people. Much credit (and my sincere thanks) are owed to the following people:

To Valerie Robbins and Cliff Philip, who actually produced much of the material in this book.

To the entire editorial and production staff at SYBEX, who converted the original first draft manuscript into the polished work you now hold in your hands.

To Bill and Cynthia Gladstone of Waterside Productions, my literary agents.

And to Susan and Ashley, wife and daughter, for their patience and support through yet another long and demanding project.

Alan Simpson

PART 1

SETTING UP THE DATABASE

Chapter 1: Starting and Using dBASE IV
Chapter 2: Creating a Database File

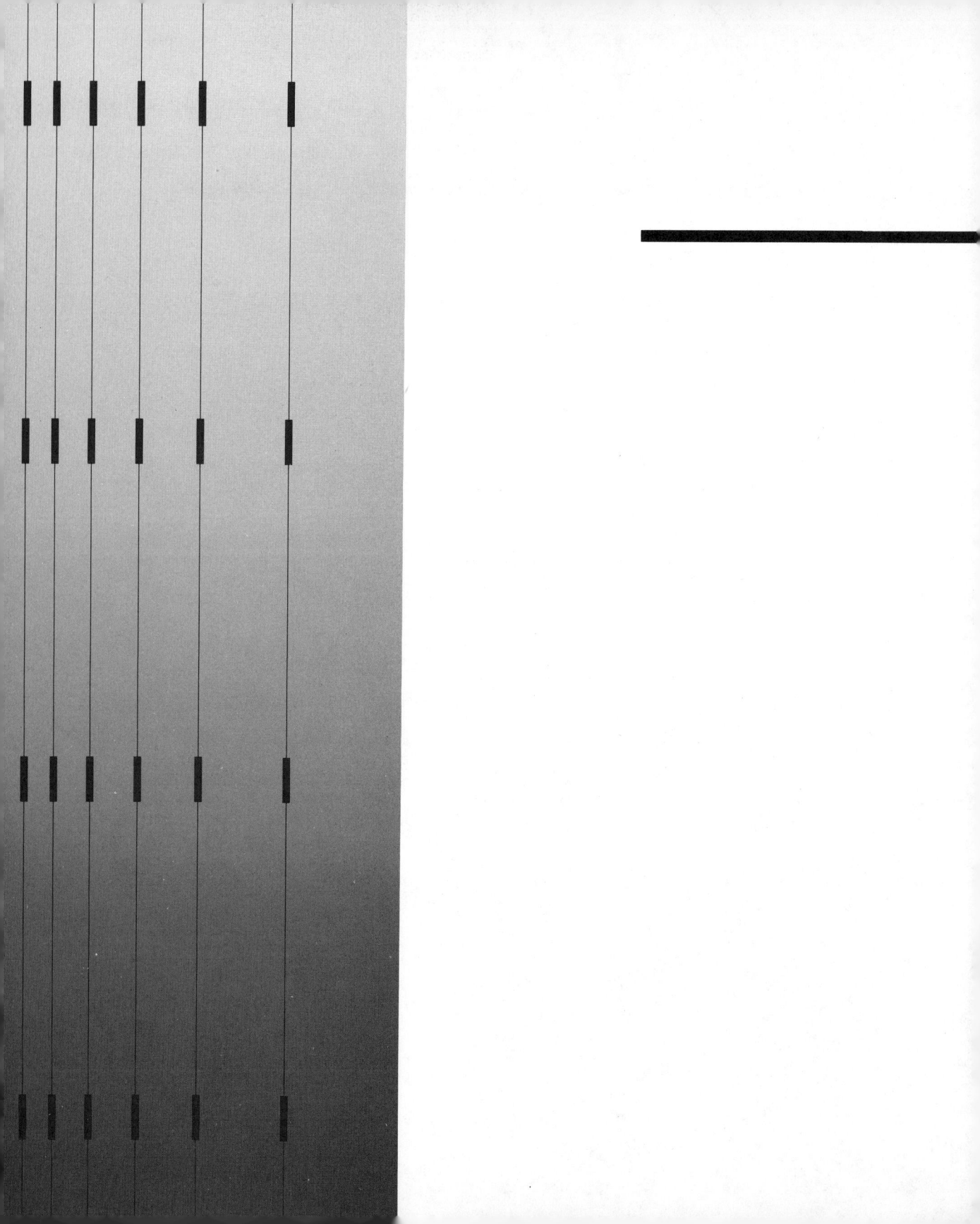

CHAPTER 1

STARTING AND USING dBASE IV

Starting dBASE IV. 5
Control Center Components. 6
    Menu Bar. 6
    Current Catalog. 7
    Work Space Panels. 7
    Current File. 8
    Navigation Line. 8
Using the Pull-Down Menus. 9
    Options with Submenus. 9
    Unavailable Options. 9
    Navigating through the Menu Options. 10
Using the Help System. 11
    Getting Help with the Current Task. 11
Help Window Options. 12
    Using the Help System Table of Contents. 13
Creating a Catalog. 15
The Dot Prompt. 18
Exiting dBASE IV. 19
Tips and Traps. 20
Summary. 20

STARTING AND USING dBASE IV

Before you can use dBASE IV on your computer, it needs to be installed (as described in Appendix A). If you followed the recommended installation procedure, you should be able to start dBASE from any directory on your hard disk. If someone else installed your copy of the program, or if you are using dBASE IV on a network, you may need to ask a knowledgeable person for the exact startup procedure for your computer.

STARTING dBASE IV

SEQUENCE OF STEPS

At the DOS prompt:

    DBASE ←┘

USAGE

First, turn on your computer. You will see the *DOS prompt*, which is *C>*, or something similar. Enter the DOS command **CD** to log on to the directory that you want to use to store your dBASE files. (If you are unfamiliar with such terms as *DOS prompt* and *directory*, now is a good time to read Appendix B).

Type **DBASE** and press ←┘. After a brief display of the dBASE IV logo, the dBASE IV copyright screen shown in Figure 1.1 appears. If you wait a few seconds, the copyright screen disappears, and the screen displays the dBASE IV Control Center. Instead of waiting, you can press ←┘ to display the Control Center more quickly.

If instead of running dBASE, your screen simply displays the message *Bad command or file name*, then dBASE is either not installed on your computer or not available from the current directory. Try logging on to the \DBASE directory by entering the command **CD \DBASE** (followed by a press on the ←┘ key). If DOS displays the error message *Invalid directory*, chances are that dBASE is not installed yet (see Appendix A). Otherwise, next type **DBASE** and press ←┘.

If dBASE IV is installed on the \DBASE directory, your screen should display the dBASE copyright notice, indicating that the program is running. (You may want to use the DBSETUP program described in Chapter 19 to reconfigure DOS so you can run dBASE from any directory.) If dBASE IV is not installed on

```
┌─────────────────────────────────────────────────────────────────┐
│  ┌──────────────────────────────┬──────────────────────────┐   │
│  │                              │              Ashton-Tate │   │
│  │  This software is licensed to:│            Ashton-Tate │   │
│  │                              │            Ashton-Tate   │   │
│  │         Alan Simpson         │            Ashton-Tate   │   │
│  │            Author            │            Ashton-Tate   │   │
│  │         0937737-36           │            Ashton-Tate   │   │
│  │                              │            Ashton-Tate   │   │
│  ├──────────────────────────────┴──────────────────────────┤   │
│  │   Copyright (c) Ashton-Tate Corporation 1985,1986,1987,1988. All │
│  │   Rights Reserved. dBASE, dBASE IV and Ashton-Tate are trademarks│
│  │                   of Ashton-Tate Corporation.           │   │
│  │   You may use the software and printed materials in the dBASE IV│
│  │   package under the terms of the Software License Agreement;    │
│  │   please read it.  In summary, Ashton-Tate grants you a paid-up,│
│  │   non-transferable, personal license to use dBASE IV on one     │
│  │   computer work station.  You do not become the owner of the    │
│  │   package nor do you have the right to copy (except permitted   │
│  │   backups of the software) or alter the software or printed     │
│  │   materials.  You are legally accountable for any violation of the│
│  │   License Agreement and copyright, trademark, or trade secret law.│
│  ├─────────────────────────────────────────────────────────┤   │
│  │   Press ◄┘ to assent to the License Agreement and begin dBASE IV│
│  └─────────────────────────────────────────────────────────┘   │
└─────────────────────────────────────────────────────────────────┘
```

FIGURE 1.1: The copyright screen appears every time you run dBASE IV. If you wait a few seconds, the copyright screen will be replaced by the Control Center. You can press ◄┘ to move to the Control Center more quickly.

the \DBASE directory, then you will again see the message *Bad command or file name*. You need to refer to Appendix A for installation instructions.

CONTROL CENTER COMPONENTS

The dBASE IV *Control Center* is shown in Figure 1.2. (Your screen may show the names of various files in the rectangular panels, particularly if you share a computer with others, but the basic structure should be the same.) The screen components are labeled in the figure and discussed here.

Menu Bar

At the upper-left corner of the Control Center is the *menu bar*. The Control Center menu bar options are Catalog, Tools, and Exit. Each option has a pull-down menu associated with it.

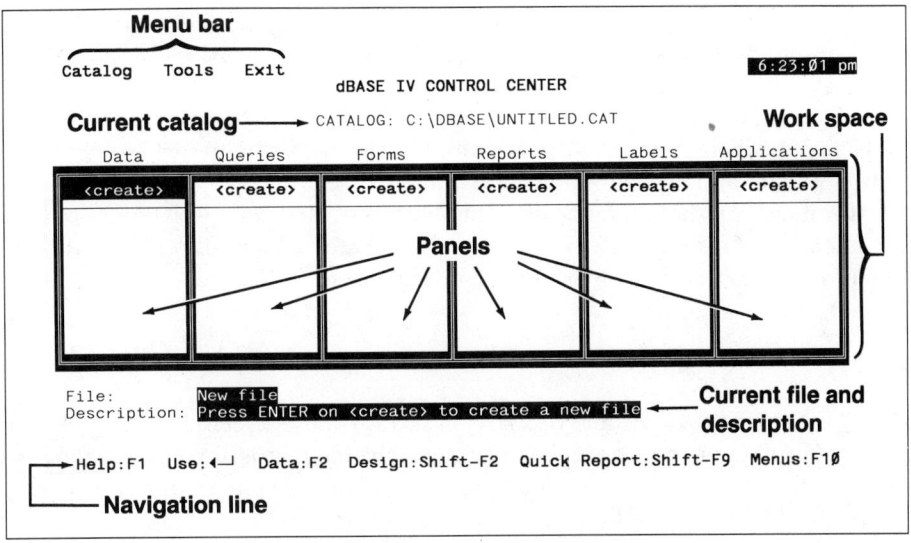

FIGURE 1.2: The Control Center is the center of operations for dBASE IV. You can use the Control Center as the starting point for every dBASE activity.

Current Catalog

Centered beneath the title of the Control Center screen is the name of the current catalog. A *catalog* is simply a tool for organizing related information in a database; it is like a department in a corporation. For example, you might store accounts receivable information in one catalog and inventory information in another.

The catalog name consists of several parts. In Figure 1.2, *C:* is the name of the disk drive that contains the catalog, *\DBASE* is the name of the directory on the hard disk where the catalog is stored, and *UNTITLED.CAT* is the name of the catalog. (Your screen may show something different if you are using a different directory, or if you are not using your version of dBASE IV for the first time.)

Work Space Panels

In the center of the screen is the Control Center *work space,* which consists of six *panels*. Each panel holds the names of various objects within the current catalog. An *object* is simply one piece of the overall collection of information. For example, in an accounts receivable system, the credit application for collecting data may be one object, the file of existing customers may be a second object, and the invoices produced from the file may be a third object. When you first use dBASE IV, the panels may not display any object names.

The leftmost panel, titled Data, holds the names of *database files* that store data. The panels labeled Forms, Reports, and Labels hold the names of *formats* used to display forms and to print reports and mailing labels. The panels labeled Queries and Applications hold the names of other objects, discussed in later chapters.

Each panel also includes the option <create>, which allows you to create your own database file, form, report, or whatever.

Current File

The current file name and description section of the screen, beneath the work space, displays the name and description of the file that is currently highlighted in the panel. If <create> is highlighted instead of a file name, this area displays *New file* and *Press ENTER on <create> to create a new file*.

Navigation Line

The navigation line at the bottom of the screen lists some of the special keys currently available to you. For example, *Help:F1* tells you that you can get help by pressing the function key labeled **F1**.

USING THE PULL-DOWN MENUS

The pull-down menus are attached to the menu bar at the top of the screen. You can access the pull-down menus in two ways. Both methods work at any time.

- Press the Menus (**F10**) key. The cursor will jump to the first menu on the menu bar for that screen. Once the cursor is on the menu bar, you can access another menu on the bar by pressing the → and ← keys.
- Hold down the **Alt** key and type the first letter of the menu you want.

The first time you access the menus, pressing Menus (**F10**) pulls down the Catalog menu, shown in Figure 1.3. You can leave the menus and return to the Control Center at any time by pressing the **Esc** key until the pull-down menu is removed from the screen.

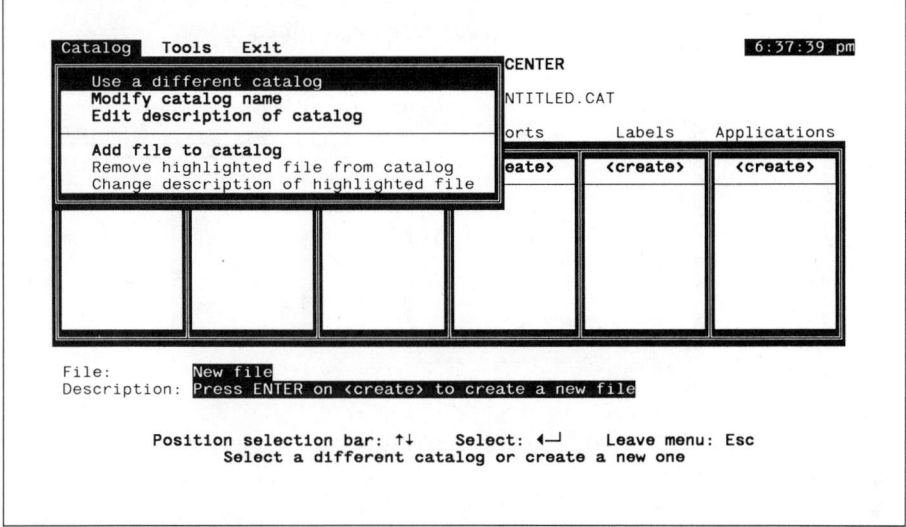

FIGURE 1.3: You can access the pull-down menu for the Catalog option by pressing Menus (**F10**), highlighting Catalog, and pressing ←; or by pressing **Alt-C**.

Options with Submenus

On some pull-down menus, you will see a pointer (a right-pointing triangle) to the left of some options. This symbol means that a *submenu* (another menu containing more options) is available after you select the option.

For example, if you press **Alt-T** to pull down the Tools menu, you will see that the options Macros, Import, and Export each have a pointer to the left of them. If you press ← while Macros is highlighted, the submenu of macro options shown in Figure 1.4 will appear.

Unavailable Options

Whenever you access a pull-down menu, some options on the menu are shaded (that is, they appear darker than other options). The shaded options are not available at the moment, usually because they make no sense in the current situation. Even though you cannot use shaded options at a particular moment, they may be available later in a different situation.

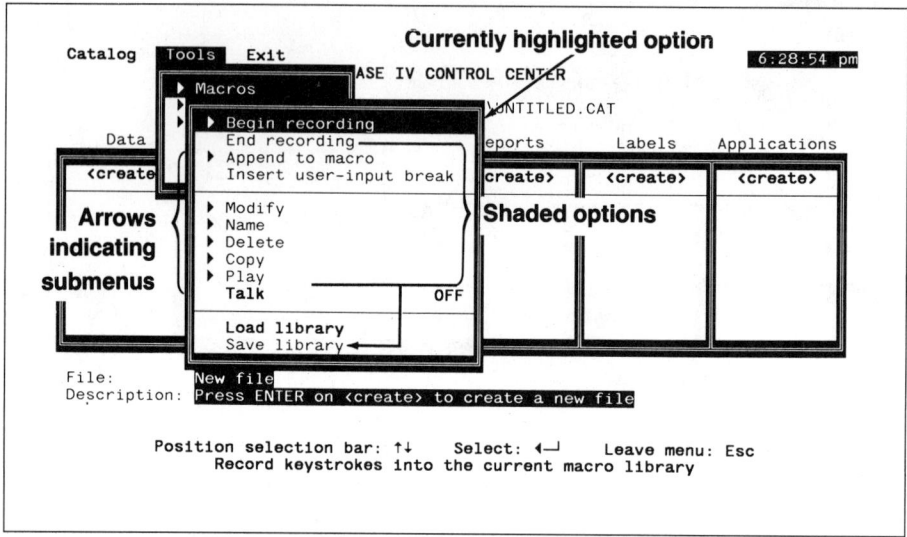

FIGURE 1.4: Macros is a menu option that presents a submenu when you select it. The pointer beside Macros on the Tools menu indicates that this is an option with submenus.

Navigating through the Menu Options

Regardless of whether you use the Menus (**F10**) key or an **Alt-key** combination to access the pull-down menus, you can use the keys listed in Table 1.1 to navigate through the menus and make selections.

Notice that, when any pull-down menu is displayed, pressing ← or → moves the highlight over to the next menu. Pressing ↑ and ↓ moves the highlight up and down through each option on the menu. Whenever any option is highlighted, a brief description of that option appears at the bottom of the screen. (If your arrow keys don't work at all, press the **NumLock** key once and then try the arrow keys again.)

On most keyboards you can hold down a key to repeat a keystroke. This is called the *typematic* feature. To try this feature at the Control Center, press Menus (**F10**) to pull down a menu. Then hold down the → key for a few seconds. You should see the highlight move quickly across Catalog, Tools, and Exit on the menu bar. (If your computer starts to beep, just release the key that you are holding down. The highlight may take a few seconds to stop moving.)

Remember that any time you want to leave a particular menu, you can just press the **Esc** key.

KEY	EFFECT
→	Moves to the menu bar option on the right
←	Moves to the menu bar option on the left
↓	Moves down to the next available (unshaded) menu option on the current pull-down menu
↑	Moves up to the next available (unshaded) menu option on the current pull-down menu
PgDn	Moves to the last available option on the current pull-down menu
Home	Same as PgUp
PgUp	Moves to the first available option on the current pull-down menu
End	Same as PgDn
↵	Selects the currently highlighted option
First letter of any option	Selects that option
Esc	Backs up to the previous menu or to the Control Center

Table 1.1: Keys Used to Navigate through the Pull-Down Menus

USING THE HELP SYSTEM

You can use the Help key at any time to get help with dBASE IV. The help screens are *context sensitive*, which means they provide help that is relevant to the operation you are currently performing. If you want help with a task that you are not currently performing, or if you want more general help with dBASE, you need to access the help system table of contents and choose the topic from there.

Getting Help with the Current Task

SEQUENCE OF STEPS

From anywhere in dBASE IV:

    Help (**F1**)
    Next (**F4**) *or* Previous (**F3**)
    Esc

USAGE

When the Control Center first appears, the <create> option in the Data panel is highlighted. If you press the Help (**F1**) key, you will see a help screen (also called a *help window*) titled Create Database Files, shown in Figure 1.5.

The navigation line at the bottom of the screen says that you can press **F4** to see the next screen or **F3** to see the previous screen. If you press **F4**, you will see the second "page" of help for creating database files. Press **F3** to scroll back to the previous page. Press **Esc** to leave the help screen and return to the Control Center.

Help Window Options

The options Contents, Related Topics, Backup, and Print are displayed at the bottom of every help window, with the Contents option highlighted. You press the ← or → key to move the highlight from one option to the next, and ↵ to select the option. Each of these options is briefly described here.

Contents   Displays a table of contents for the current topic. When a table of contents is displayed, you can use

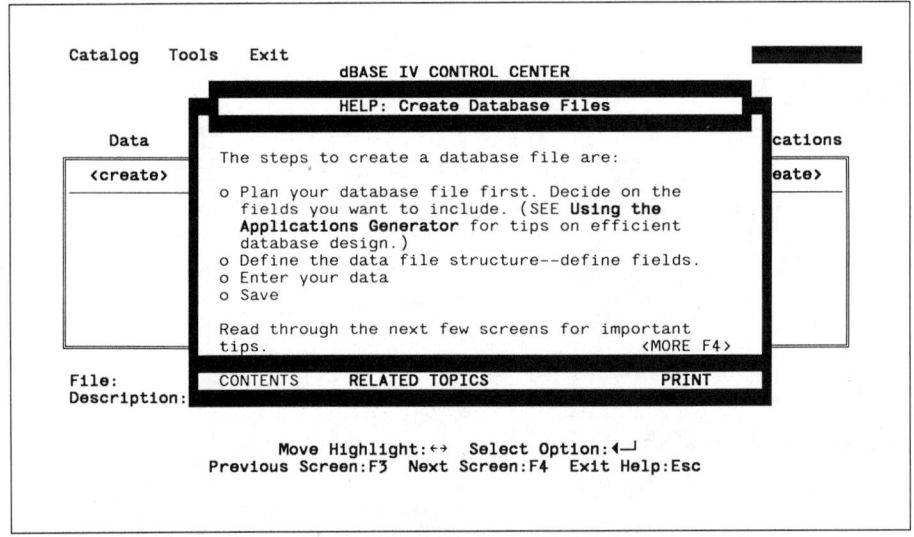

FIGURE 1.5: The help screen for creating database files is an example of the many help screens available to you at any time by pressing Help (**F1**). Note that because this is the first screen available from the Control Center, the Backup option does not appear.

	the More General (**F3**) and More Specific (**F4**) keys to change to more general or more specific tables of contents.
Related Topics	Displays a list of topics related to the current topic.
Backup	Scrolls back to the previous screen. This option appears only if there is a previous screen. Thus, it does not appear in the Create Database Files help window, which is the first screen available.
Print	Prints a copy of the current help window.

Using the Help System Table of Contents

SEQUENCE OF STEPS

From anywhere in dBASE IV:

>Help (**F1**)
>highlight the Contents option in the help window ↵
>More General (**F3**) *or* More Specific (**F4**)
>highlight the help topic you want ↵
>**Esc**

USAGE

If you want help with some dBASE topic other than the current task, you use the help system table of contents to find and display the help window you need.

EXAMPLE

Suppose you have just accessed the Control Center and you press Help (**F1**). You will see the help screen shown in Figure 1.5. But you do not want help with creating database files. Instead, you want more general help with the Control Center. To locate the appropriate help area, you need to check the help system table of contents.

If necessary, move the highlight to the Contents option in the help window and then press ↵ to select it. The help screen shown in Figure 1.6 appears. Notice the options More General (**F3**) and More Specific (**F4**) on the navigation line at the bottom of the screen.

To see a more general table of contents, press **F3**. Figure 1.7 shows the table of contents that appears. The first entry on this screen offers information about the

14 ━━ **CH. 1** STARTING AND USING dBASE IV

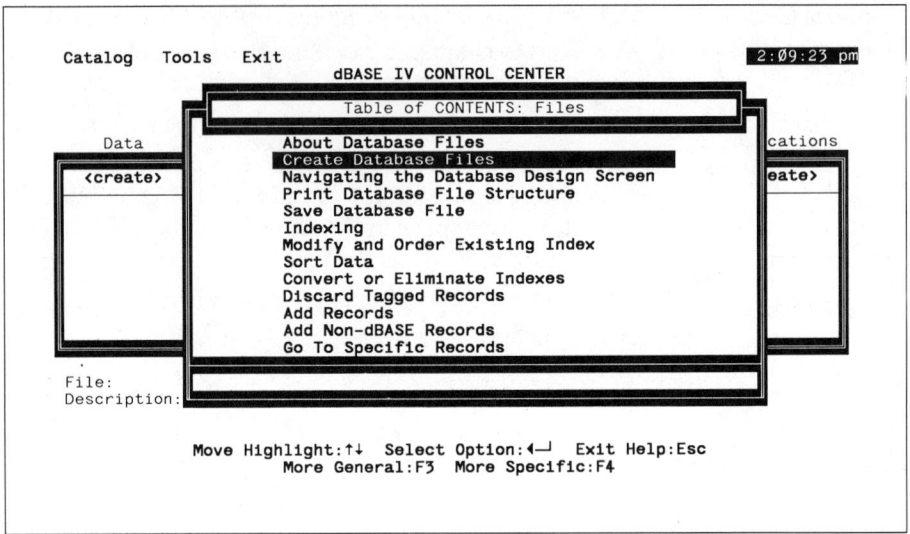

FIGURE 1.6: The help table of contents for files presents a list of the help screens available on the subject of files.

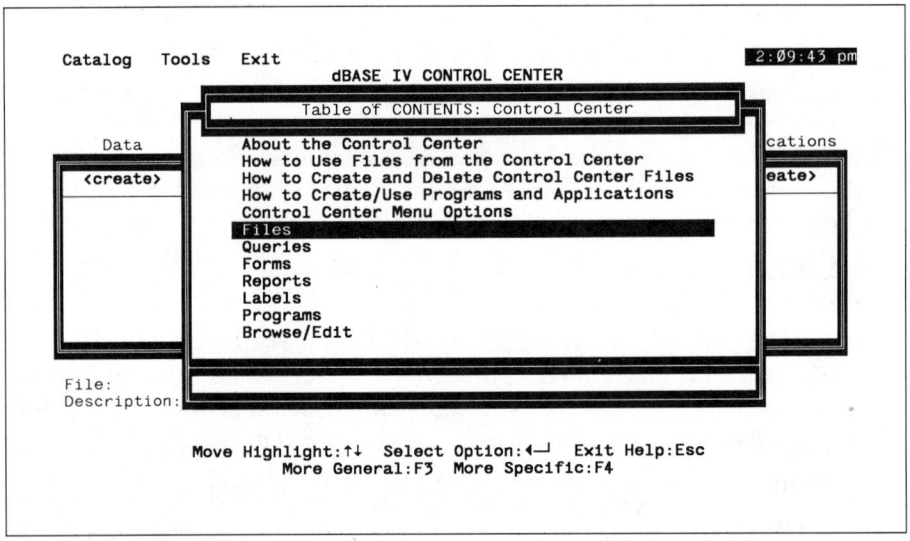

FIGURE 1.7: You can get help using the Control Center by accessing this table of contents and selecting from the list of help screens.

Control Center. Press **PgUp** once to move the highlight to the About the Control Center option and press ↵ to select it.

The help screen for the Control Center now appears, as shown in Figure 1.8. As the navigation line reminds you, you can use the Previous Screen (**F3**) and Next Screen (**F4**) keys to scroll through additional pages of help. Press **Esc** to return to the Control Center.

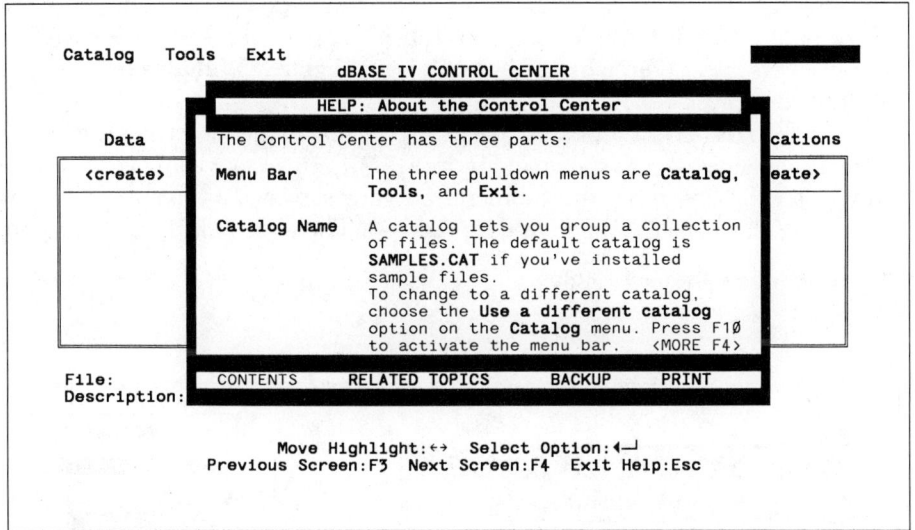

FIGURE 1.8: This help screen appears when you select About the Control Center from the Control Center table of contents.

CREATING A CATALOG

SEQUENCE OF STEPS

To reach the Catalog menu from the Control Center:

    Menus (**F10**) *or* **Alt-C**

    From the Catalog menu: **U**se a Different Catalog [↵]

    <create>

    type a name for the catalog ↵

USAGE

A catalog is a dBASE tool for grouping together the various components of a database, such as the database files, forms, and report formats. Catalogs help you organize your databases. dBASE IV provides one catalog, called UNTITLED.CAT, to get you started. You can also create your own catalogs.

To create a new catalog, first press Menus (**F10**) or **Alt-C** to access the Catalog menu on the Control Center screen. The first option on the Catalog pull-down menu is Use a Different Catalog, which should now be highlighted. Press ⏎ or type **U** to select it. (As noted in Table 1.1, pressing the first letter of an option selects the option, whether or not it is highlighted. With this method you don't have to press ⏎.)

The screen displays a submenu of existing catalog names as well as the option to create a new catalog, as shown in Figure 1.9. (If you are not using your copy of dBASE for the first time, the submenu on your screen may list other catalog names.) With <create> highlighted, press ⏎. The screen displays the prompt

   Enter name for new catalog:_

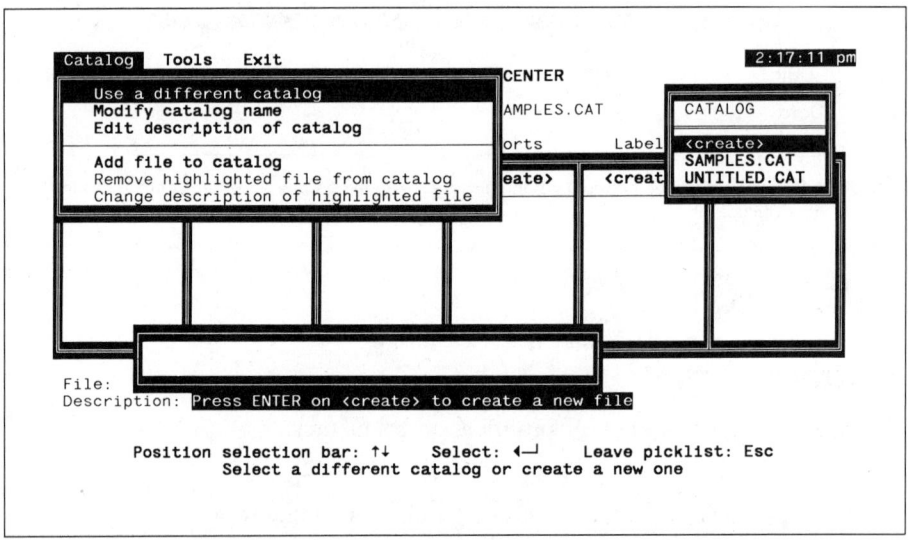

FIGURE 1.9: When you select Use a Different Catalog from the Catalog menu, dBASE presents a submenu of the available catalogs.

The name you enter for a catalog must be a valid DOS file name. Follow these rules, which also apply to the names of most of the objects you create in dBASE IV:

- A name can be no more than eight characters long.
- A name can contain numbers (0 to 9) but *cannot* contain any blank spaces or punctuation marks (such as ? * . $: or ;). The underline character (_) is the only special character allowed.
- A name can contain upper- or lowercase letters, but lowercase letters are automatically converted to uppercase.

Table 1.2 shows examples of valid and invalid catalog names.

After you enter a name for the new catalog, you press ↵. (If you make a mistake while typing the catalog name, press the **Backspace** key to back up and make corrections.)

FILE NAME	VALID/INVALID
LEARN	Valid
MyData	Valid
June89	Valid
1989Qtr1	Valid
My_Data	Valid
My Data	Invalid; contains a space
Qtr1:89	Invalid; contains a colon
January1989	Invalid; too long
LEARN DBASE	Invalid; too long and contains a space

Table 1.2: Examples of Valid and Invalid Catalog Names

EXAMPLE

To create a catalog named LEARN, press Menus (**F10**) from the Control Center to pull down the Catalog menu. Press ↵ to select Use a Different Catalog. Press ↵ to select the <create> option. In response to the prompt for a catalog name, type **LEARN** and press ↵. Your screen should look like Figure 1.10.

Notice that the current catalog is now the one you just created. dBASE has included the .CAT extension, and the catalog name has become LEARN.CAT. (See Appendix B if you need more information about DOS and dBASE file name extensions.)

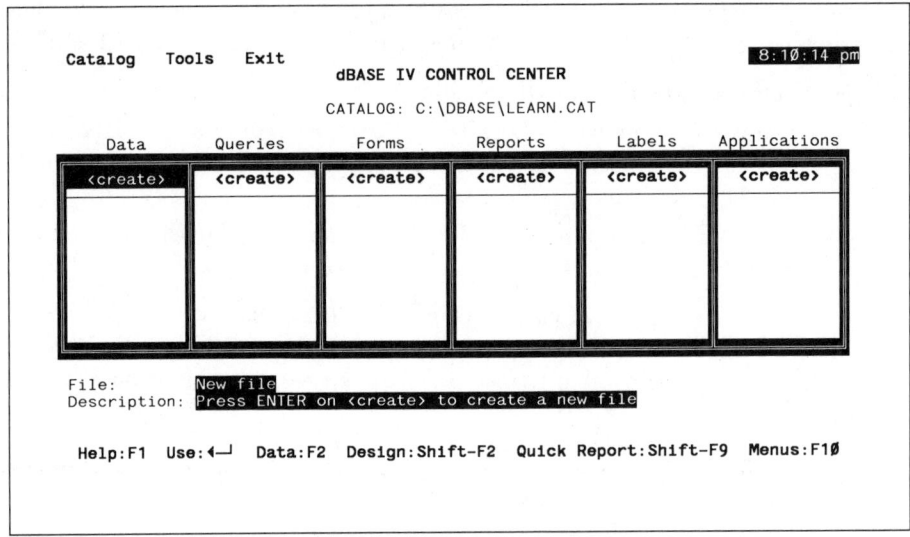

FIGURE 1.10: After you have created a new catalog (called LEARN in this example), the Control Center display looks like this.

THE DOT PROMPT

You can use dBASE IV in two ways: from the Control Center or from the *dot prompt*. Earlier versions of dBASE did not include the Control Center. dBASE II, for example, offered only the dot prompt mode for interacting with dBASE. To make the program easier to use, dBASE IV provides the Control Center. When you use dBASE from the dot prompt, you type *commands* rather than selecting options from pull-down menus. From the Control Center, you can select options from menus to perform most of the available dBASE activities, and you may never need to use the dot prompt mode.

However, if you develop large, complex business applications, you will want to use dBASE commands from the dot prompt to take advantage of dBASE's most advanced capabilities.

At the dot prompt, you see only a highlighted bar, a period (dot), and the blinking cursor, as shown in Figure 1.11. To leave the dot prompt at any time and return to the Control Center, type the word **ASSIST** and press ← (or just press the **F2** key).

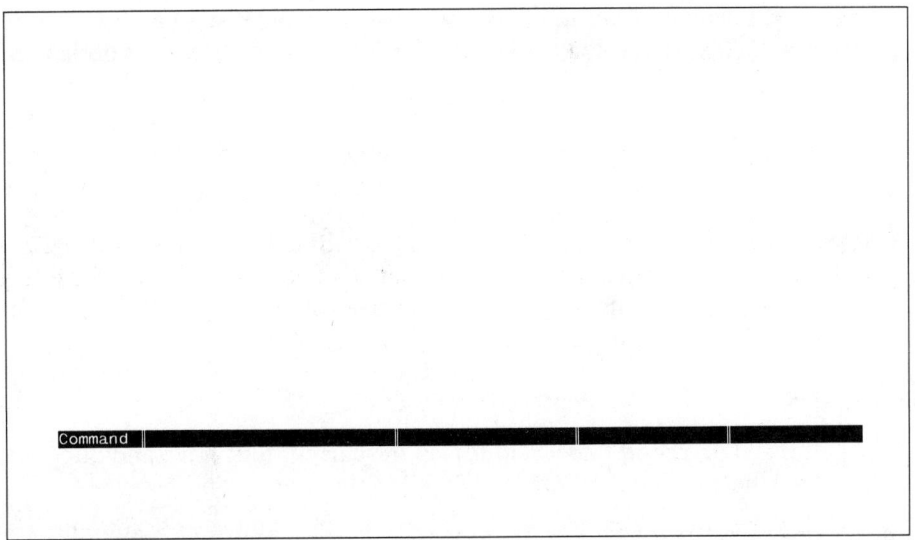

FIGURE 1.11: The dBASE IV dot prompt offers an alternative means of accessing every dBASE IV activity. Chapter 18 discusses dot prompt use.

This book focuses on using dBASE from the Control Center. If you want to use dBASE commands from the dot prompt, see Chapter 18.

EXITING dBASE IV

SEQUENCE OF STEPS

From anywhere in dBASE IV:

    Esc, as necessary, to return to the Control Center

    Menus **(F10)**/Exit   *or*   **Alt-E Q**uit to DOS [↵]

USAGE

Whenever you finish a dBASE IV session, you should exit (or quit) dBASE IV before you turn off your computer. If you do not remember to do so, you will probably find that dBASE IV is not saving all of your work.

To exit dBASE IV, first return to the Control Center. (You can press **Esc** as many times as necessary to back out of the menus.) Press Menus **(F10)** to access the pull-down menus. Press → or ← as necessary to highlight the Exit pull-down menu. You can also reach the Exit menu by simply pressing **Alt-E**, bypassing the

Menus key. Highlight Quit to DOS (by pressing ↓ if necessary) and select it by pressing ↵. (If you simply type **Q**, you don't need to highlight the option and press ↵.)

You should *always* quit dBASE IV before turning off your computer. You will see the message

*** END RUN   dBASE IV

followed by the DOS prompt, which looks something like *C:\DBASE>*. Once you see this prompt, dBASE has safely stored all of your information for future use. You can then turn off your computer or use another program.

TIPS AND TRAPS

- If the DOS prompt does not display the current disk drive and directory, type the command **PROMPT PG** at the prompt and press ↵.
- If, when you try to access the Control Center, you see the message *Bad command or file name*, either dBASE is not installed on the computer at all, or it is not available from the current drive and directory.
- If the arrow keys on your keyboard do not move the highlight on the screen, press the **NumLock** key once to turn the numeric keypad off.
- If you want to exit to DOS, but you exit to the dot prompt by mistake, press Data (**F2**) to return to the Control Center.
- If you are experimenting with the menu system and do not know how to exit from the menu you are in, press **Esc** as many times as necessary until you are back at the Control Center.

SUMMARY

This chapter presented the commands necessary to access and exit dBASE along with the basic skills you need to use the dBASE IV Control Center. Studying the various components of the Control Center is worthwhile because the Control Center screen provides much information that you will find useful as you work with dBASE IV.

This chapter also presented the techniques for accessing and navigating through the pull-down menu system, as well as the methods for displaying on-screen help about any dBASE topic. The chapter also discussed how to create a catalog. You can use any catalog of your choice as you follow the examples in later chapters.

The next chapter presents all the information you need to build a database.

For help installing dBASE IV:

- Appendix A, "Installing dBASE IV"

For instructions on using DOS:

- Appendix B, "Commonly Used DOS Commands"

For a detailed discussion of catalogs:

- Chapter 12, "Managing Multiple Related Databases"

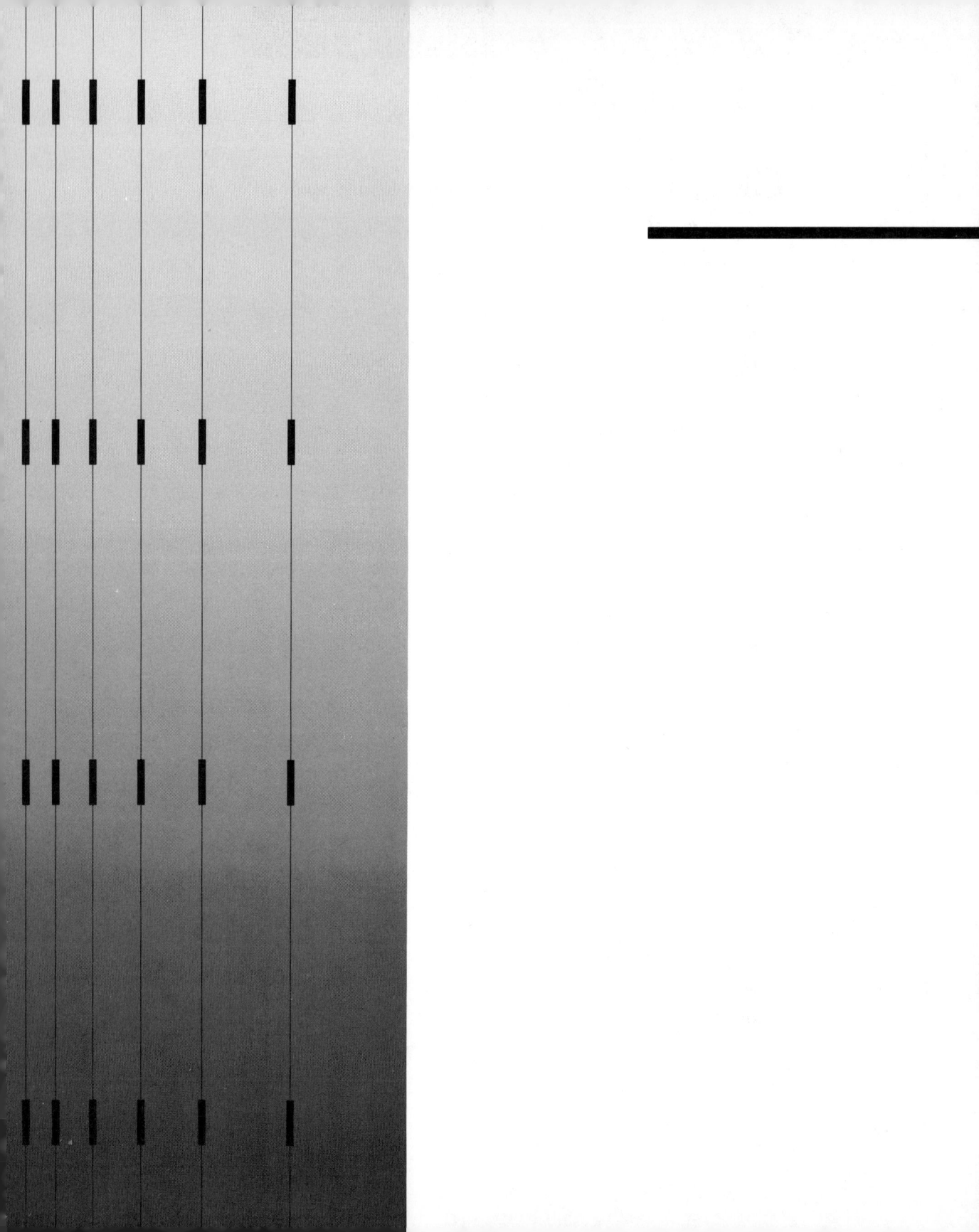

CHAPTER 2

CREATING A DATABASE FILE

Records and Fields. 25
Naming Fields. 26
Field Data Types. 27
Designing a Database. 29
    Making Corrections. 31
    Entering Field Names. 31
    Selecting Data Types. 31
    Specifying Field Widths. 32
    Specifying Decimal Precision. 32
    Indexing a Field. 32
Adding a Database Description. 33
Saving the Database Structure. 35
Entering Records. 36
    Using the Edit Screen. 37
    Using the Browse Screen. 40
Saving the Records. 43
Reading the Status Bar. 43
Modifying an Existing Database Structure. 44
    Adding a Field. 45
    Deleting a Field. 46
    Moving a Field. 47
    Renaming a Field. 48
    Changing the Width of a Field. 49
    Changing the Type of a Field. .49
Opening and Closing Database Files. 50
Using the dBASE IV Screens. 50
Tips and Traps. 52
Summary. 52

CREATING A DATABASE FILE

When you create a database file, you can put anything you want into it. But remember that dBASE can handle many database files simultaneously, so there is no need to put every bit of information that your business uses into a single file. For example, you would not want to mix customer names and addresses with parts inventory and accounts receivable. Rather than combine all of this information into a single database file, you should create separate files for each type of information and group them into a catalog, as discussed in Chapter 1.

Before you can store information in a database file, you need to create a *structure* for the file, where you specify the field names and the type of data stored in each *field*.

The most important point to keep in mind when you are structuring a database is that each unique item of information should be stored in its own field. Try not to be influenced by how you want the information to look when it is printed. The manner in which you *store* information in a database file in no way limits the manner in which you can print it later.

RECORDS AND FIELDS

A database file consists of *records* (or *rows*) of information. Each record is divided into separate *fields* (or *columns*) of information. For example, Figure 2.1 shows a database file that contains names and addresses.

As you can see, the names are stored in two fields, called LASTNAME and FIRSTNAME. Because the last name and first name are separated from each other, you can isolate the last name for both sorting and searching. For example, dBASE can sort the names into alphabetical order by last name. Similarly, you can tell dBASE to search for the last name Mahoney, because dBASE can isolate the last name as something to search for.

If you want to include titles, such as Mr. and Ms., and middle initials, you can break the name into four different fields as follows:

TITLE	LASTNAME	FIRSTNAME	MI
Mr.	Smith	John	J.
Ms.	Adams	Annie	T.
Dr.	Watson	Wilbur	H.

CH. 2 CREATING A DATABASE FILE

```
         LASTNAME    FIRSTNAME   ADDRESS            CITY        STATE   ZIP      PHONE
         ...........................................................................
         Smith       John        123 A St.          San Diego   CA      92122    (619)555-1212

         Adams       Annie       345 C St.          Malibu      CA      92001    (714)555-0123

         Watson      Wilbur      P.O. Box 987       New York    NY      12345    (212)555-9988

         Mahoney     Mary        211 Seahawk St.    Seattle     WA      88977    (206)555-8673

         Newell      John        734 Rainbow Dr.    Butte       MT      54321    (303)555-6739

         Beach       Sandy       11 Elm St.         Portland    OR      76543    (717)555-0898
```

FIGURE 2.1: A dBASE IV database file of names and addresses. The information is arranged into fields (columns) and records (rows).

Mrs.	Mahoney	Mary	
Mr.	Newell	John	J.
Miss	Beach	Sandy	B.

This structure gives you maximum flexibility in using the names. For example, if you were printing form letters, you could join the four fields together to create an entire name, such as Mr. John J. Smith, and you could just as easily isolate the first name for the greeting in a letter (Dear John:). And, of course, you could still isolate the last name for sorting and searching.

In a name-and-address database, be sure to place the city, state, and zip code in separate fields, as shown in the figure. (You need not worry about including a comma between the city and state. You can add that to your printed reports without storing it in the database file.) With this arrangement of fields, you can sort the information into zip code order for bulk mailing, because dBASE can isolate the zip codes. You can also isolate all of the records for a particular state, such as California (CA), or sort the data into state order.

A single database record can contain a maximum of 255 fields, or 4000 characters (bytes) of information, whichever limit it reaches first. The contents of Memo fields are not included in this maximum character count; Memo field text can contain over 64,000 characters.

NAMING FIELDS

Each field in a database file must have a unique name (that is, no two fields within a single file can have the same name). The name assigned to a field must conform to the following rules:

- It can include no more than ten characters.
- The first character must be a letter, but numbers can be used after the first letter.
- Blank spaces and punctuation marks are *not* allowed.
- The underscore character (_) is the only special symbol allowed.

You need not memorize all these rules; the message line at the bottom of the database design screen reminds you of them. Also, when you enter a field name, dBASE makes sure the name adheres to the rules. If you attempt to break a rule, dBASE beeps, and whatever you typed will not appear on the screen.

FIELD DATA TYPES

Each field in a dBASE IV database file must be categorized by *data type* (or *field type*). dBASE offers six data types to choose from. They are listed in Table 2.1. The correct data type for a particular field is usually obvious, though not always. For example, when storing phone numbers and zip codes, your first impulse may be to use a Numeric data type field. However, doing so could cause problems later.

To dBASE, a true number is a quantity, such as the number of items purchased, a price, or a test score. These quantities can be numbers only: numeric digits (0 through 9) and, optionally, a decimal point (.) and a leading minus sign (−). Other characters—such as letters, commas, parentheses, hyphens, and blank spaces—are not allowed in Numeric fields. (When you print reports from this data, you may want to add dollar signs, commas to separate thousands, and perhaps other nonnumeric characters. You can do so later by including them as part of the print format; see Chapter 7.)

Thus, storing phone numbers and zip codes in Numeric fields can lead to problems. Phone numbers usually contain nonnumeric characters such as parentheses and hyphens, as in the phone number (213)555-1212. Some zip codes contain hyphens (for example, 92038-2802), and foreign postal codes contain letters and blank spaces (for example, H3X 3T4). If you tried to store these in a Numeric field, dBASE would not allow you to enter the nonnumeric characters.

Before you assign the Numeric or Float data type to a field, ask yourself this question: "Is this an item for which I might want to calculate totals?" Certainly, you would not need to total a group of phone numbers or all the zip codes in a database. In general, you should use the Numeric and Float data types only for fields on which you need to perform mathematical calculations. (Don't be concerned about sorting zip codes or phone numbers; dBASE will sort them properly whether they are stored in Numeric or Character fields.)

DATA TYPE	CONTENTS	EXAMPLES
Character	Any textual information that has no true numeric value and has a maximum length of 254 characters	Jones Spark plug 123 Oak St.
Numeric	Any true numeric value on which you may want to perform arithmetic operations; usually used for quantities and prices	10 −123.45 100 1234.567
Float	Basically the same as Numeric, except that the number of decimal places is not fixed	10.0 −123.45 100.00 1234.567
Date	Any date stored in the format *mm/dd/yy*; always use this option to store dates	1/1/90 12/31/89 6/12/90
Logical	Either a true (T) or false (F) value and no other information; for example, a Logical data type field named PAID might contain T when a charge has been paid and F when it has not been paid	T F
Memo	Large volumes of text, perhaps including several paragraphs, such as abstracts of journal articles or long descriptions	Abstracts, comments

Table 2.1: The dBASE IV Data Types

The Numeric and Float (short for *floating point*) data types are both used to store numbers, but each uses a slightly different storage technique. Basically, you use the Numeric data type for "business" (as opposed to scientific) types of numbers, which usually have a fixed number of decimal places. For example, a quantity such as 10 has no decimal places, and a dollar amount such as $123.45 always has two decimal places. Any calculations that you perform on such numbers will be most accurate if you store the numbers in a Numeric field (because there will be few, or no, rounding errors).

The Float data type is best used for storing scientific data with no fixed number of decimal places: for example, when one record contains the number 1.0030203, and another record contains the number 232123.2. Storing such numbers in a Float data type field ensures the most accuracy when you later perform calculations with these numbers.

DESIGNING A DATABASE

SEQUENCE OF STEPS

From the Control Center Data panel:

> highlight <create> ←┘

To create a field (repeat for each field):

> type a field name in the Field Name column ←┘
> Character *or* Numeric *or* Float *or* Date *or* Logical *or* Memo ←┘
> for Character, Numeric, and Float only: type a width for the field ←┘
> for Numeric and Float only: type the number of decimal places ←┘
> in the Index column: **N** *or* **Y**

USAGE

To create a database structure, you use the *database design screen*, shown in Figure 2.2, where you tell dBASE the name, data type, and so forth for each field that you want in your database. To access the database design screen for a new database, make sure that the <create> option in the Control Center Data panel is highlighted and then press ←┘ (see Figure 2.3). Use the arrow keys or the **Tab** key, if necessary, to move the highlight to the <create> option.

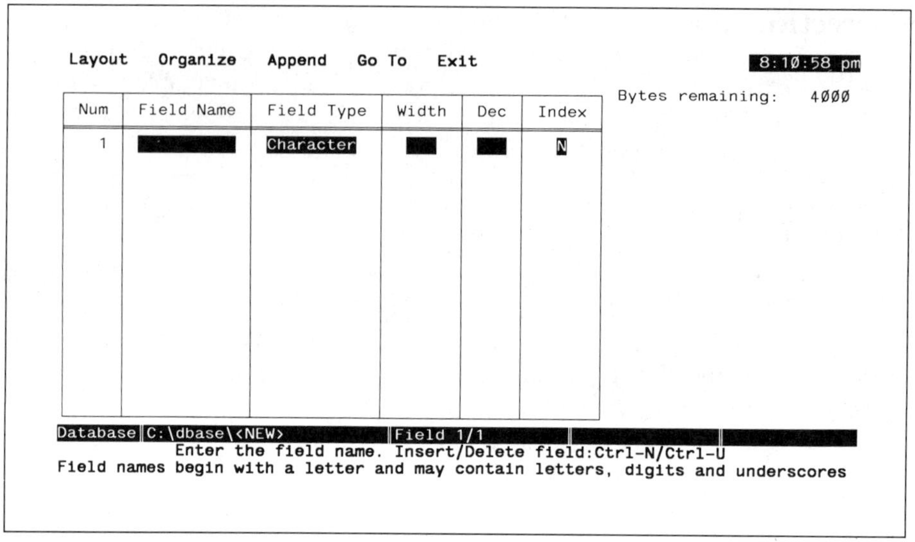

30 —— **CH. 2** CREATING A DATABASE FILE

FIGURE 2.2: The database design screen is where you specify the design of the fields in your database. You must give each field a name and assign it one of the dBASE IV data types.

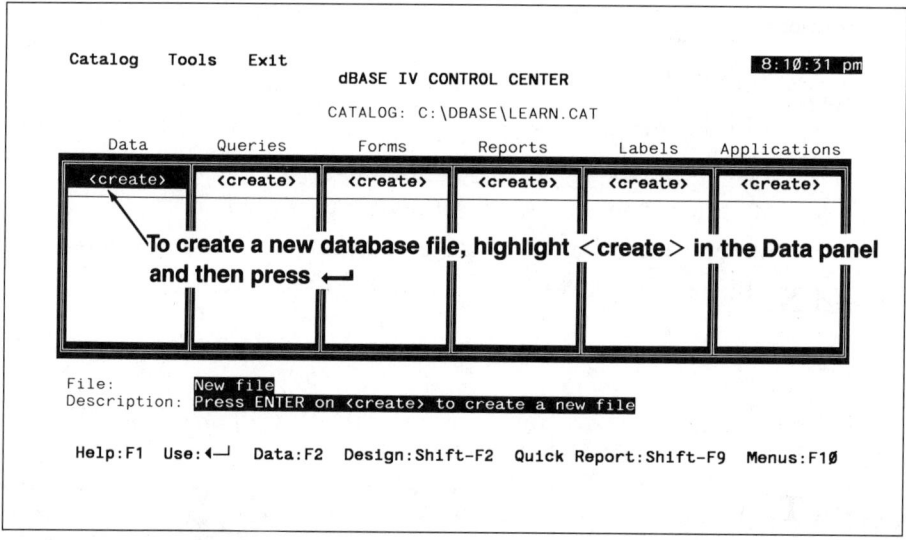

FIGURE 2.3: You create a new database file from the Control Center Data panel by highlighting <create> and pressing ⏎.

Making Corrections

You can use a number of keys to move the highlight and cursor around the database design work area to make changes. These keys are listed in Table 2.2. Note that some keys do not work if you attempt to leave a row that has incomplete or invalid data. You may have to experiment with several of the keys from Table 2.2 or press **Ctrl-U** to completely delete an incomplete or invalid row and get the cursor moving in the direction you want.

KEY	EFFECT
↑	Moves the highlight up one row
↓	Moves the highlight down one row
←	Moves the cursor one character to the left
→	Moves the cursor one character to the right
Tab	Moves the cursor one column to the right (only if valid information is already present in the column you are moving to)
Shift-Tab	Moves the cursor one column to the left (only if valid information is already present in the column you are moving to)
Backspace	Moves the cursor one space back, erasing along the way
↵	Completes an entry and moves to the next column or row
Ctrl-N	Inserts a blank row between two existing rows
Ctrl-U	Deletes the entire current row

TABLE 2.2: Keys Used to Make Changes on the Database Design Screen

Entering Field Names

To enter a field name, first make sure that the blinking cursor is in the Field Name column on the screen. Type a name for the field and press ↵. The cursor jumps to the Field Type column.

Selecting Data Types

Notice that dBASE provides Character as the default data type. While the blinking cursor is in the Field Type column, you can press the space bar to scroll through the various data types before making a selection. Each time you press the space bar, the name of a data type appears within the highlight, and a brief description of the data type appears at the bottom of the screen. To select the currently displayed data type, just press ⏎. The cursor will jump to the Width column.

A shortcut for entering a data type is simply to type the first letter of its name; for example, type **F** for Float or **D** for Date. If you make a mistake, press ← or **Shift-Tab** to move back to the Field Type column and try again.

Specifying Field Widths

The next step in creating a database structure is to specify a maximum *width* for the field. This value sets the number of characters that you can use for an entry in that field. The rule of thumb here is to select a reasonable maximum width, but not to make the field wider than you are likely to need. (The wider a field is, the more disk space it consumes.) Type a number for the field width and press ⏎.

For some data types, dBASE automatically fills in the field width, and the cursor jumps to the Index column. When you enter Date data types, dBASE provides a field width of 8; for Logical data types, a width of 1; and for Memo fields, a width of 10. You cannot (and need not) change the widths for these field types.

Specifying Decimal Precision

When you define a field as the Numeric or Float data type, the cursor jumps to the Dec column. In the Dec column, you specify the number of decimal places that the field requires. Type a number for the decimal places and press ⏎.

For data types other than Numeric and Float, the cursor bypasses the Dec column and jumps straight to the Index column after you type the field width.

Indexing a Field

In the rightmost column, labeled Index, you can enter either **Y** (for yes) or **N** (for no) to indicate whether the field should be indexed. dBASE provides N, for no, as the default entry. You can press ⏎ to accept this setting initially; you can then change it later if you prefer. (Chapter 4 discusses indexing in detail.)

At this point, you have fully defined a field. Now the highlight jumps down to the next blank row, and you can enter information for the next field. You can also move around the work area and make corrections or changes.

EXAMPLE

The database created in this example contains the field names LASTNAME, FIRSTNAME, COMPANY, ADDRESS, CITY, STATE, ZIP, PHONE, STARTDATE, and PAID. In the next section, we will save this database under the name CUSTLIST (for customer list). You can think of CUSTLIST as a database of customers who subscribe to a newsletter.

To create a new database, highlight <create> in the Data panel and press ↵. On the database design screen, with the cursor blinking on the Field Name column, type the first field name **LASTNAME** and press ↵. The cursor then jumps to the Field Type column, where you need to select a data type for the LASTNAME field.

To assign the Character data type to the LASTNAME field, just press ↵ with the Character data type displayed. If necessary, press the space bar repeatedly until the Character option appears. As soon as you press ↵, the cursor jumps to the Width column.

For the LASTNAME field, a width of 15 should be sufficient. Type **15** and press ↵. The cursor jumps to the Index column. Press ↵ to leave the index option for LASTNAME set to N.

Enter the rest of the database file structure shown in Figure 2.4. Notice that ZIP and PHONE both use the Character data type. Because the STARTDATE and PAID fields use the Date and Logical data types, respectively, dBASE automatically fills in their widths as 8 and 1. Again, you cannot (and need not) change the widths of these data types.

ADDING A DATABASE DESCRIPTION

SEQUENCE OF STEPS

From the Control Center:

    highlight the database name in the Data panel
    Design (**Shift-F2**)
    Layout/**E**dit Database Description [↵]
    type a description ↵

From the database design screen:

    Menus (**F10**)/Layout   *or*   **Alt-L**
    Edit Database Description [↵]
    type a description ↵

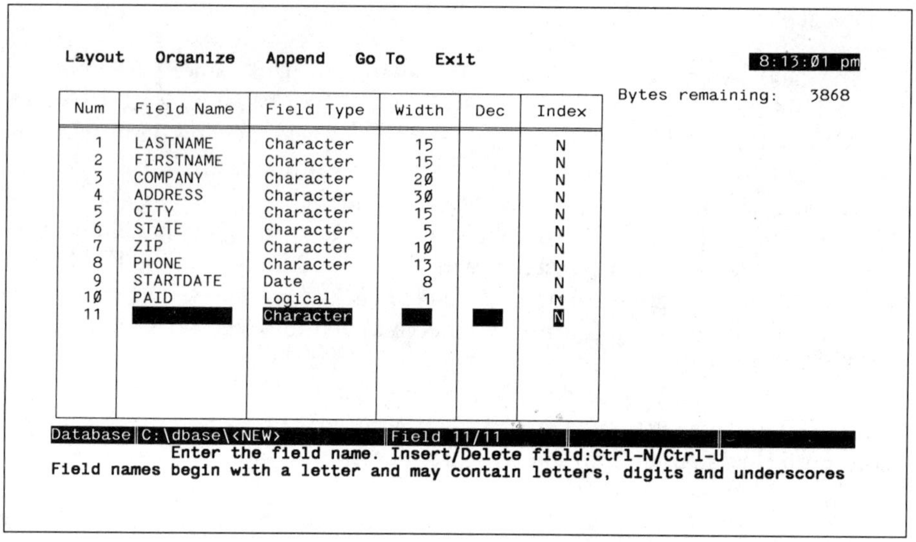

34 — CH. 2 CREATING A DATABASE FILE

```
Layout    Organize    Append    Go To    Exit                    8:13:01 pm
                                                      Bytes remaining:  3868
 Num   Field Name   Field Type   Width   Dec   Index
  1    LASTNAME     Character     15            N
  2    FIRSTNAME    Character     15            N
  3    COMPANY      Character     20            N
  4    ADDRESS      Character     30            N
  5    CITY         Character     15            N
  6    STATE        Character      5            N
  7    ZIP          Character     10            N
  8    PHONE        Character     13            N
  9    STARTDATE    Date           8            N
 10    PAID         Logical        1            N
 11                 Character

Database  C:\dbase\<NEW>           Field 11/11
        Enter the field name. Insert/Delete field:Ctrl-N/Ctrl-U
  Field names begin with a letter and may contain letters, digits and underscores
```

FIGURE 2.4: The completed CUSTLIST database file structure entered on the database design screen. Note that Date data types always have a width of 8, and Logical data types always have a width of 1.

USAGE

A database *description* is simply a sentence that describes, in plain English, what is stored in a database. Whenever you highlight the name of the database in the Data panel, this brief description appears beneath the Control Center panels.

From the database design screen, first press Menus (**F10**) to access the pull-down menus. Highlight the Layout option on the top menu. (If necessary, use the → or ← key to do so.) As a shortcut, you can simply press **Alt-L** from the database design screen. Use the ↓ key to highlight the Edit Database Description option on the Layout menu and then press ↵ to select it.

dBASE displays the message *Edit the description of this .dbf file* and a highlighted bar for you to type in. (dBASE always adds the extension .DBF to a database file name.) Type a description for your database and press ↵ when you are done.

EXAMPLE

To add a description to the CUSTLIST database, press Menus (**F10**) from the database design screen to access the pull-down menus. If necessary, use the → or ← key to highlight the Layout option on the top menu. Use the ↓ key to highlight Edit Database Description on the pull-down menu and then press ↵ to select it.

The screen displays the message *Edit the description of this .dbf file*, and dBASE presents a highlighted bar for you to type in. Type the following description:

Customer names and addresses

Press ⏎ after typing the description.

SAVING THE DATABASE STRUCTURE

SEQUENCE OF STEPS

From the database design screen:

    Menus (**F10**)/Exit [⏎]   *or*   **Alt-E**
    Save Changes and Exit [⏎]

or simply

    Ctrl-End
        type a name for the database ⏎

USAGE

When you have entered all the fields in your database structure and supplied a description for your new database, you need to save your work. First, press Menus (**F10**) to access the pull-down menus. Use the ← or → key to highlight the Exit option on the top menu. If necessary, use the ↑ key to highlight the Save Changes and Exit option. Press ⏎. When you see the prompt *Save as:*, type the name of your database and press ⏎.

dBASE returns you to the Control Center. The name of your new database file is displayed in the Data panel and also near the bottom of the Control Center screen, where dBASE IV automatically adds the extension .DBF to the name you provide, to identify the file as a database file. The screen may also display the names of the disk drive and directory on which the file is stored. The database description appears beneath the file name.

If you attempt to save a database file using a name that already exists, dBASE beeps and displays the message *File already exists*. The program also gives you two options: Overwrite, to replace the existing database with the new structure, and Cancel, to stop and use a different file name.

Selecting Overwrite in response to the *File already exists* prompt completely erases all data in the existing database file, replacing it with the empty database structure currently on the screen. Make sure you want to do this before you select the Overwrite option.

EXAMPLE

When your screen looks like Figure 2.4, you are ready to save the new CUSTLIST database file structure. To do so, press Menus (**F10**) to access the pull-down menus. Use the ← or → key to highlight the Exit option on the top menu. If necessary, use the ↑ key to highlight the Save Changes and Exit option. Press ↵. When you see the prompt *Save as:*, type the name **CUSTLIST** and press ↵.

dBASE returns you to the Control Center. Here, you can see the name of the new database file in the Data panel, as shown in Figure 2.5. (If CUSTLIST is not currently highlighted on your screen, use the ↓ or → key to move the highlight to CUSTLIST, as in Figure 2.5.)

Near the bottom of the Control Center, you can see the file name *CUSTLIST.DBF*. The screen in the figure also displays the names of the disk drive and directory on which the file is stored (*C:\DBASE*). The database description, *Customer names and addresses*, appears beneath the file name.

ENTERING RECORDS

When you have created the database structure, you are ready to enter records. You can enter records on the *edit screen* or on the *browse screen*. You can also use

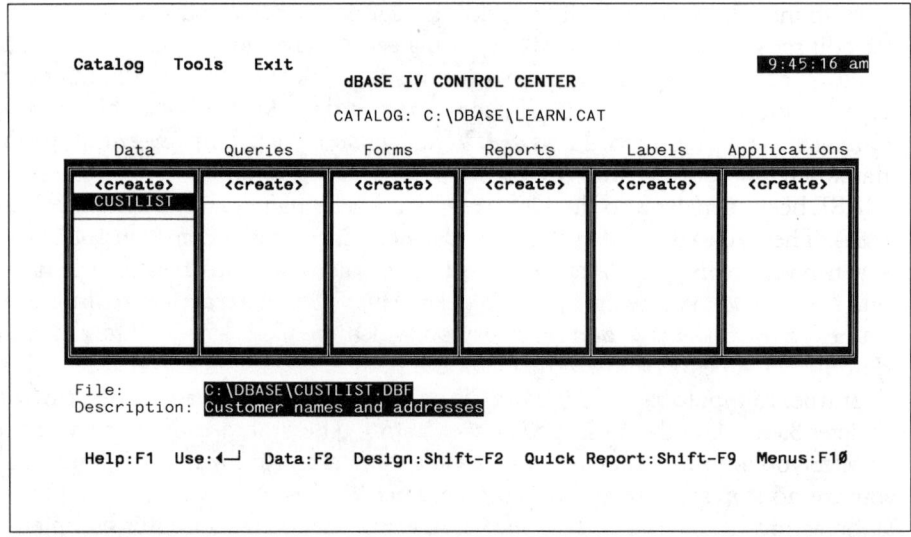

FIGURE 2.5: After you have created a database file (designing it by using the database design screen), dBASE displays its file name in the Data panel.

either of these two screens later when you need to add more records, delete records, or change information in the database (see Chapter 3).

Using the Edit Screen

SEQUENCE OF STEPS

From the Control Center:

>highlight the database name in the Data panel
>Data (**F2**)
>Data (**F2**) again, if necessary
>enter data

USAGE

To enter records in a database from the edit screen, first move the highlight in the Control Center Data panel to the name of the database for which you are entering records. Use ←, →, **Tab**, or **Shift-Tab** as necessary to move the highlight to the Data panel. To highlight the database name, you can use ↑ or ↓, or you can begin typing the database name until dBASE moves the highlight to it.

With the database name highlighted, press the Data (**F2**) key. You should see the edit screen for the database, like the one shown in Figure 2.6. (If a different screen appears, press Data (**F2**) again.) As you can see, the edit screen is a blank form for a single record.

Enter your first record, typing the entry for each field and pressing ↵. Notice that when your entry completely fills the field, you do not need to press ↵. dBASE beeps when you have filled the space provided (if your system is set up to beep). The cursor automatically moves to the next field.

When you enter a date into a Date field, dBASE enters the slashes for you. To enter a date, just type the numbers (for example, type **123190** for 12/31/90). To enter a date such as January 5, 1991, you can either type **010591** or **1/5/91**. When entering data into a Logical field, you can type the letter **f**, **F**, **n**, or **N** for false, or the letter **t**, **T**, **y**, or **Y** for true. Memo fields require an extra step and the use of an *editor*, as discussed in Chapter 3.

After you fill in the last field and press ↵, dBASE does one of two things: If you are adding records for the first time, dBASE automatically creates a new blank record and allows you to add more data. If you are adding records to a database that already contains data, dBASE displays the prompt = = = > *Add new records? (Y/N)*_. Whenever you see *Y/N*, dBASE is waiting for a yes or no answer. To answer yes, press **Y**; to answer no, press **N**.

38 ——— **CH. 2** CREATING A DATABASE FILE

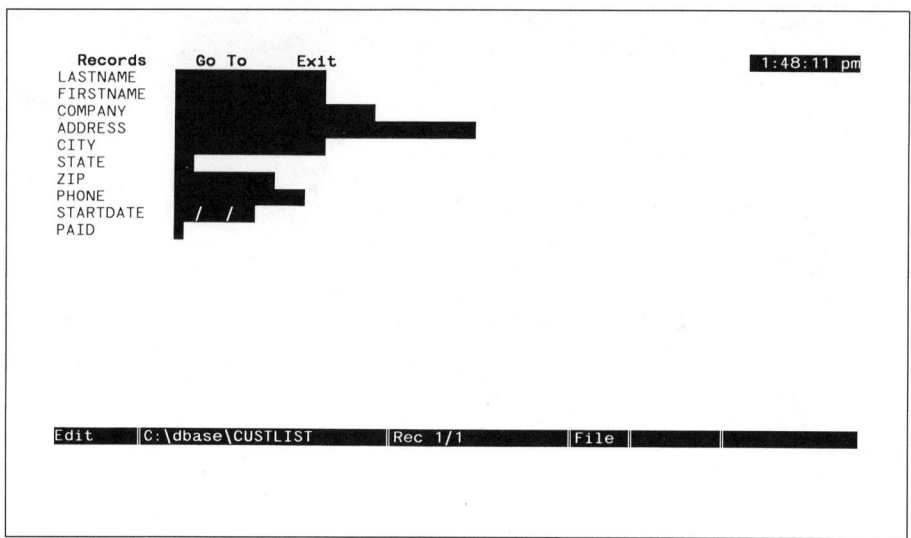

FIGURE 2.6: A blank edit screen for the CUSTLIST database. Notice that the fields are in the same order as specified in the database design. Also notice that dBASE provides the slashes for the Date field.

EXAMPLE

Follow this example to enter the first record on the edit screen and the next example to enter the second record on the browse screen for the CUSTLIST database. You can then enter all the records shown in Figure 2.7 into the CUSTLIST database (for which we created the structure in the first part of this chapter).

With the edit screen displayed, begin entering the first record by typing the last name **Smith** and pressing ←. Type the first name **John** and press ←. Type the company name **ABC Co.** and press ←. Type the address **123 A St.** and press ←. Type the city **San Diego** and press ←. Type the state **CA**. Type the zip code **92067** and press ←. Type the phone number **(619)555-1234**. The highlight jumps to the STARTDATE field.

Notice that in the STARTDATE field, the slashes are already entered for you. To enter the date November 15, 1989, type **11**, then **15**, then **88**. At this point, your screen should look like Figure 2.8.

To indicate that John Smith has paid his dues (or membership fee, subscription, or whatever the PAID field represents), type the letter **T** while the cursor is in the Logical PAID field. dBASE then displays a new, blank record. The indicator at the bottom of the screen, which shows *Rec 2/2*, tells you that you are now positioned on the second record in a database that contains two records.

USING THE EDIT SCREEN — 39

LASTNAME	FIRSTNAME	COMPANY	ADDRESS	CITY	STATE	ZIP	PHONE	STARTDATE	P
Smith	John	ABC Co.	123 A St.	San Diego	CA	92067	(619)555-1234	11/15/88	T
Adams	Annie		345 C St.	Malibu	CA	92001	(714)555-0123	01/01/89	F
Watson	Wilbur	HiTech Co.	P.O. Box 987	New York	NY	12345	(212)555-9988	11/15/88	T
Mahoney	Mary		211 Seahawk St.	Seattle	WA	88977	(206)555-8673	12/01/88	T
Newell	John	LoTech Co.	734 Rainbow Dr.	Butte	MT	54321	(303)555-6739	12/15/88	T
Beach	Sandy	American Widget	11 Elm St.	Portland	OR	76543	(717)555-0898	12/15/88	T
Kenney	Ralph		1101 Rainbow Ct.	Los Angeles	CA	96607	(213)555-9988	12/30/88	F
Schumack	Susita	SMS Software	47 Broad St.	Philadelphia	PA	45543	(202)555-9720	12/30/88	T
Smith	Anita	Zeerocks, Inc.	2001 Engine Dr.	Hideaway	CA	92220	(415)555-9854	01/01/89	T

FIGURE 2.7: Some sample records for the CUSTLIST database. If you enter these records into the database, you will have some data on which to try out many of the examples in this book.

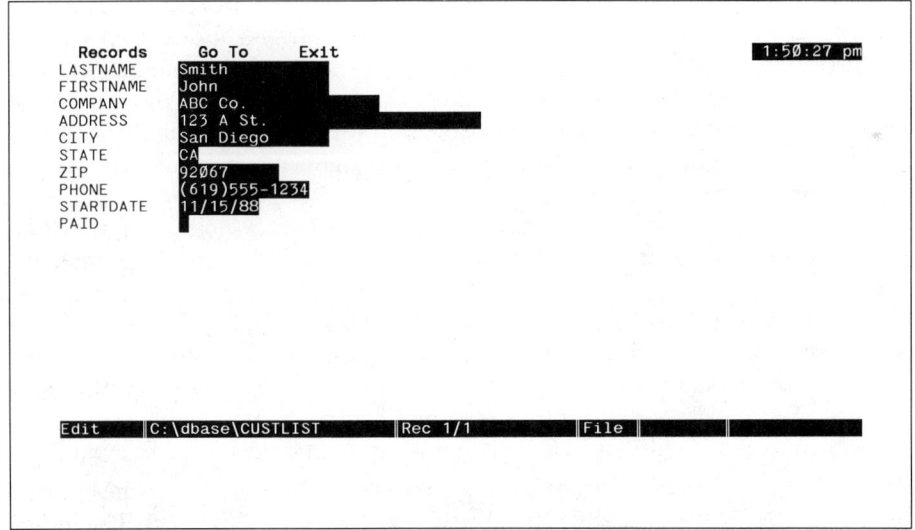

FIGURE 2.8: The first database record filled in on the edit screen. Notice that the status bar displays *Rec 1/1*, indicating that John Smith's record is number 1 out of a total of 1 record.

If you need to back up and make corrections to John Smith's record, just press the **PgUp** key. To move back down, press the **PgDn** key. In this case, dBASE displays the prompt = = = > *Add new records? (Y/N)*_. (Type **N** to answer no if you are following this example.)

Using the Browse Screen

SEQUENCE OF STEPS

From the Control Center:

> highlight the database name in the Data panel
> Data (**F2**)
> Data (**F2**), if necessary

From the edit screen:

> Data (**F2**)

USAGE

You can also enter data using the browse screen. On the browse screen, you can see several records at once, though usually not all the fields for each record. To switch between the edit screen and the browse screen, you simply press Data (**F2**).

By pressing **Tab** or ↵, you can scroll the browse screen to the right to see the fields that are currently hidden. Each time you press **Tab**, the highlight moves one field to the right. To scroll all the way to the right, you can either press **Tab** several times or just press **End**.

To scroll to the left one column at a time, press **Shift-Tab** (hold down the **Shift** key while pressing the **Tab** key). To quickly scroll all the way to the leftmost field, press **Home**.

To add a new record while the current record is still displayed on the browse screen, press ↓ to move down to the next row. If that row currently contains no record, dBASE displays the prompt = = = > *Add new records? (Y/N)*. To add records, type **Y**. The cursor jumps to the first field of the next blank row.

You can use Ditto (**Shift-F8**) to copy information into the current record from the same field in the previous record. For example, suppose that the STATE field in the previous record contains CA. With the cursor in the STATE field of the current record, press Ditto (**Shift-F8**) to enter CA into that field. Then press ↵.

dBASE provides the slashes for Date fields. To enter the date January 1, 1990, you can type **1/1/90** or **010190**; dBASE automatically converts either entry to 01/01/90.

USING THE BROWSE SCREEN — 41

EXAMPLE

If you entered the record on the edit screen in the example for the last section, when you press Data (**F2**), you will see part of that record at the top of the database file, as shown in Figure 2.9.

To scroll the browse screen all the way to the right, to the PAID field, which is not currently visible, you can either press the **Tab** key nine times or just press the **End** key. Figure 2.10 shows the browse screen scrolled all the way to the right.

Type the second record shown in Figure 2.7 (for Annie Adams). Make sure the highlight is in the LASTNAME field. Type the last name **Adams** and press ←⎯. Type the first name **Annie** and press ←⎯. Annie has no company affiliation, so press ←⎯ to leave the COMPANY field blank. Type the address **345 C St.** and press ←⎯. Type the city **Malibu** and press ←⎯.

Press Ditto (**Shift-F8**) to copy the state (CA) from the previous record to the current one. You'll see CA entered as the state in the current record. Press ←⎯. Type the zip code **92001** and press ←⎯. Type the phone number **(714)555-0123**. Type **1/1/89** for the date. When the cursor gets to the PAID field, type the letter **F** to indicate that Annie has not paid.

As shown in Figure 2.11, dBASE scrolled to the right as you filled in fields. After you type an **F** into the PAID field (to indicate that Annie has not paid), dBASE automatically scrolls back to the left side of the browse screen.

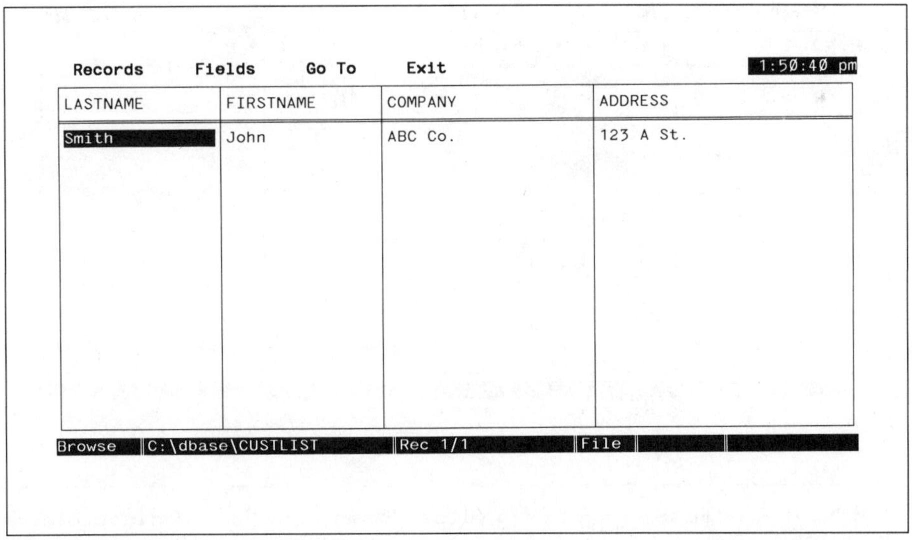

FIGURE 2.9: When you press Data (**F2**), you will see the first four fields of John Smith's record displayed on the browse screen.

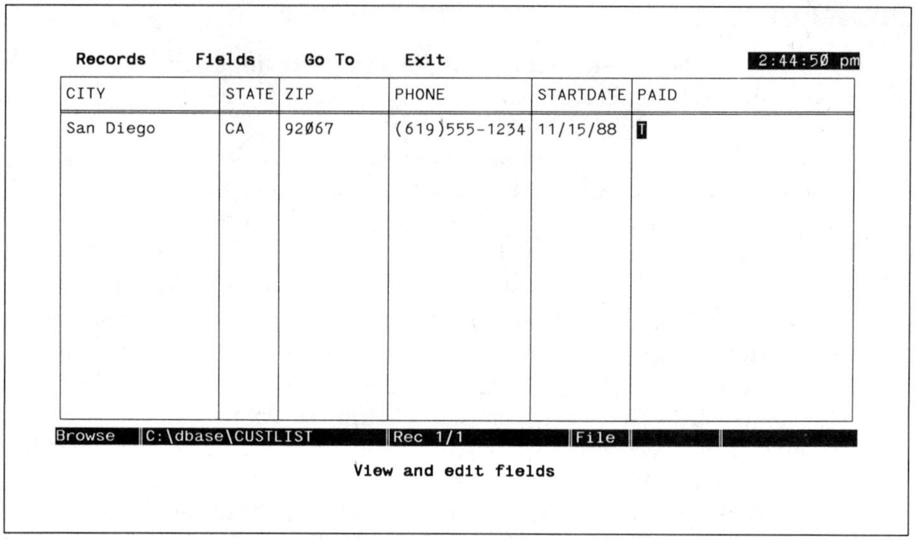

CH. 2 CREATING A DATABASE FILE

```
    Records    Fields    Go To    Exit                      2:44:50 pm
   CITY              STATE ZIP     PHONE          STARTDATE PAID
   San Diego         CA    92067   (619)555-1234  11/15/88  T




   Browse    C:\dbase\CUSTLIST       Rec 1/1        File
                          View and edit fields
```

FIGURE 2.10: You can scroll the browse screen to the right (by pressing **Tab** a few times or by pressing **End**) to see the other six fields of the first record.

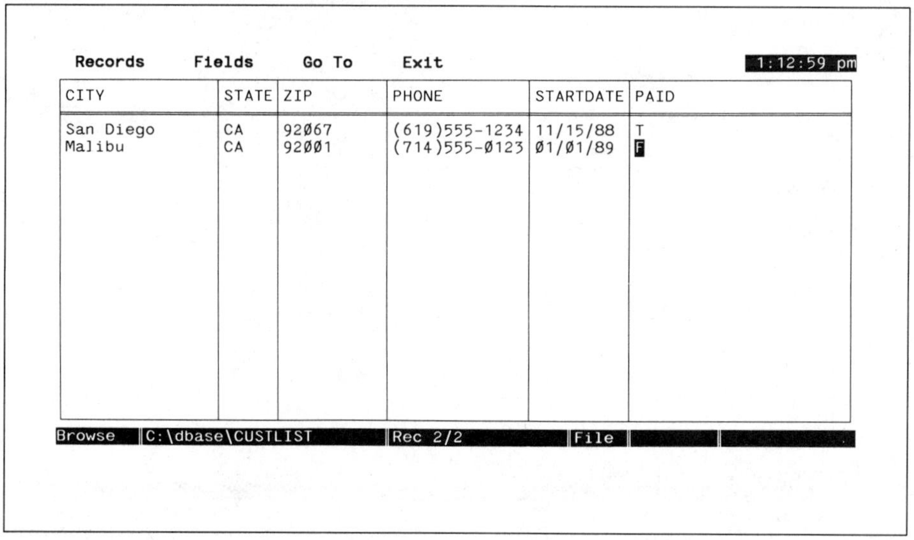

```
    Records    Fields    Go To    Exit                      1:12:59 pm
   CITY              STATE ZIP     PHONE          STARTDATE PAID
   San Diego         CA    92067   (619)555-1234  11/15/88  T
   Malibu            CA    92001   (714)555-0123  01/01/89  F




   Browse    C:\dbase\CUSTLIST       Rec 2/2        File
```

FIGURE 2.11: Part of the second record displayed on the browse screen. (The browse screen is scrolled to the right.)

SAVING THE RECORDS

SEQUENCE OF STEPS

From the browse or edit screen:

    Menus (**F10**)/Exit [⏎]   *or*   **Alt-E**
    Exit [⏎]

or simply

    Ctrl-End

USAGE

You can enter as many records as you want in your database. (A dBASE database can contain approximately a billion records, or two billion characters, whichever limit dBASE reaches first.) You can enter records using either the edit screen or the browse screen—or switching back and forth between them with the Data (**F2**) key. You can also add records later—you do not have to enter them all at once.

To save the records and return to the Control Center (from either the edit or the browse screen), press either **Alt-E** or Menus (**F10**) to access the pull-down menus and then ← or →, as necessary, to highlight the Exit option on the menu bar. After reaching the Exit menu by either method, select Exit by typing **E** or by pressing ⏎ while this option is highlighted. As a shortcut, you can simply press **Ctrl-End** from either screen.

READING THE STATUS BAR

On both the browse and edit screens, dBASE displays a highlighted *status bar* at the bottom of the screen to help you with your work. Figure 2.12 shows the location of the following information on the status bar:

- The type of screen in use (such as the edit screen or the browse screen).
- The drive, directory, and name of the database file currently in use.
- The current record in the database and the total number of records. For example, the message *Rec 1/2* means that you are currently viewing record number 1 in a database containing two records.
- The source of the data currently on the screen (for example, the name of the database file).

CH. 2   CREATING A DATABASE FILE

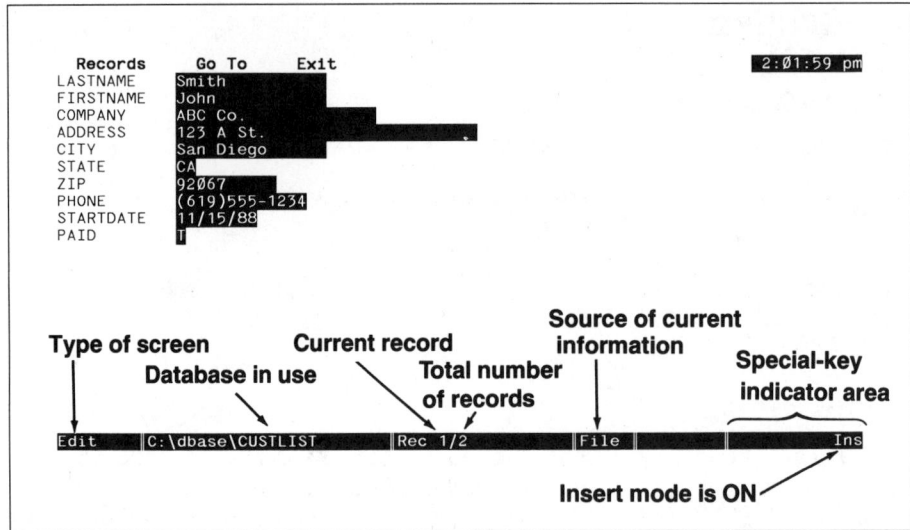

FIGURE 2.12: The status bar provides a lot of information about the current dBASE activity. From the status bar you can determine such things as the current database, which record is displayed, and whether insert mode is on.

- The settings of various *toggle keys*. For example, if *Num* is displayed, the **NumLock** key is on. If *Caps* is displayed, the **CapsLock** key is on. If *Ins* is displayed, you are in insert mode rather than overwrite mode. Pressing the **NumLock**, **CapsLock**, or **Ins** key turns these settings (and the appropriate indicators) on and off.

MODIFYING AN EXISTING DATABASE STRUCTURE

You can change the structure of a database at any time, regardless of how many records are in the database. To do so, you can highlight the name of the database in the Control Center Data panel and press Design (**Shift-F2**) (or press ⏎ and type **M** to select Modify Structure/Order). The database design screen will display the structure of the database. You can change any field definitions, add new fields, delete fields, change the positions of existing fields, and so forth.

As soon as you enter the database design screen, dBASE IV makes a temporary copy of the records in the current database. After you save your changes, dBASE attempts to copy the records from the temporary database back into your new database structure. It will be successful at doing so only if you are careful when you change the database structure.

It is a good idea to make a backup copy of your database structure before modifying the structure in any way. Then if anything goes wrong, you can start again with the original structure. (See Chapter 14 for instructions on backing up the database structure.)

Adding a Field

SEQUENCE OF STEPS

From the Control Center:

> highlight the database name in the Data panel
> Design (**Shift-F2**) *or* ⏎ Modify Structure/Order ⏎
> **Esc**
> move the cursor to the field name preceding the new field location
> **Ctrl-N**
> enter the field information
> Menus (**F10**)/E**x**it [⏎] *or* **Alt-E**
> **S**ave Changes and Exit [⏎]

or simply

> **Ctrl-End**
> **Y** *or* **N**

USAGE

To add a new field to an existing database structure, press Design (**Shift-F2**) with the highlight on the database name in the Control Center Data panel. Press **Esc** to remove the Organize pull-down menu from the database design screen work surface. Use the arrow keys to move the cursor to the Field Name column for the field before which you want to insert a new field; then press **Ctrl-N**. dBASE provides a new row for the field entry. Enter the specifications for the new field.

After you have filled in the new field, you can save the new structure by selecting Save Changes and Exit from the Exit pull-down menu or simply by pressing **Ctrl-End**. dBASE will display the prompt *Input data records now? (Y/N)*. (Look at the bottom of the screen for any additional messages.) Type **N** to return to the Control Center or type **Y** to go to the edit or browse screen to add new records.

EXAMPLE

To add a field to the CUSTLIST database created in the examples in this chapter, first highlight CUSTLIST in the Control Center Data panel and press ↵. Type **M** to select Modify Structure/Order and press **Esc** to clear the work surface. Press ↓ ten times to move to the Field Name column of the first blank row.

To add a Memo field called COMMENTS to the end of the CUSTLIST database structure, type **COMMENTS** and press ↵. The cursor jumps to the Field Type column. Press the space bar five times until *Memo* appears and then press ↵. dBASE enters a field width of ten characters, skips the Dec column, enters N in the Index column, and moves the cursor down to the next row. Your screen should look like Figure 2.13.

Press **Ctrl-End** to save the new structure. dBASE prompts *Input data records now? (Y/N)*. Type **Y** again to use the edit or browse screen or **N** to return to the Control Center.

Deleting a Field

SEQUENCE OF STEPS

From the Control Center:

>highlight the database name in the Data panel
>Design (**Shift-F2**)   *or*   ↵ Modify Structure/Order ↵
>**Esc**
>move the cursor to the field to be deleted
>**Ctrl-U**
>Menus (**F10**)/Exit [↵]   *or*   **Alt-E**
>**S**ave Changes and Exit [↵]

or simply

>**Ctrl-End**
>**Y** *or* **N**

USAGE

When you delete a field from a database structure, keep in mind that you are also deleting all the data in that field. For example, if you had a database with

```
Layout   Organize   Append   Go To   Exit              10:41:21 pm
                                                  Bytes remaining:   3861
 Num  | Field Name  | Field Type | Width | Dec | Index
  1   | LASTNAME    | Character  |  15   |     |   N
  2   | FIRSTNAME   | Character  |  15   |     |   N
  3   | COMPANY     | Character  |  20   |     |   N
  4   | ADDRESS     | Character  |  30   |     |   N
  5   | CITY        | Character  |  15   |     |   N
  6   | STATE       | Character  |   2   |     |   N
  7   | ZIP         | Character  |  10   |     |   N
  8   | PHONE       | Character  |  13   |     |   N
  9   | STARTDATE   | Date       |   8   |     |   N
 10   | PAID        | Logical    |   1   |     |   N
 11   | COMMENTS    | Memo       |  10   |     |   N
 12   |             | Character  |       |     |   N

Database  C:\dbase\CUSTLIST          Field 12/12
          Enter the field name.  Insert/Delete field:Ctrl-N/Ctrl-U
Field names begin with a letter and may contain letters, digits and underscores
```

FIGURE 2.13: A Memo field called COMMENTS added to the CUSTLIST database structure. dBASE automatically assigns a width of ten characters to Memo fields, but this does *not* mean that you can enter only ten characters in Memo fields.

10,000 names and addresses in it and you deleted the CITY field from that database structure, you would lose all the city names that were in that field. To get them back you would have to type each name again.

To delete a field from a database structure, first highlight the name of the database in the Data panel and then press Design (**Shift-F2**). Press **Esc** to remove the Organize pull-down menu. Use the arrow keys to move the cursor to anywhere in the field you want to delete and then press **Ctrl-U**. Press **Ctrl-End** to save the modified structure. Type **Y** to use the edit or browse screen or **N** to return to the Control Center.

Moving a Field

When you have been entering data on the edit screen for a while, you may find that changing the order of the fields would make data entry easier or more efficient. You may therefore want to move a field. Before you change the position of a field in the database structure, first note the exact spelling of its name, the data type, the width, and the number of decimal places.

To move a field, you combine the techniques for deleting and adding a field. Delete the field from its current position by pressing **Ctrl-U**. Press **Ctrl-N** to insert a new blank field (or just add the new field after the existing field names). Be sure to use the same spelling, data type, width, and number of decimal places as before. Do not perform any other operations at this time; save your changes and exit immediately.

Renaming a Field

SEQUENCE OF STEPS

From the Control Center:

> highlight the database name in the data panel
> Design (**Shift-F2**)   *or*   ⏎ Modify Structure/Order ⏎
> **Esc**
> move the cursor to the field name to be changed
> type the new field name
> Menus (**F10**)/**E**xit   *or*   **Alt-E**
> **S**ave Changes and Exit [⏎]

or simply

> **Ctrl-End**
> **Y** *or* **N**

USAGE

You can change the name of a field *only* if you do not add, change, move, or delete any fields during the same operation. If you change field names and rearrange fields in the same operation, dBASE will become confused, and there is no telling how things might be arranged after you save your changes.

To rename an existing field, move the cursor to the field name on the database design screen. Type a new name for the field. If you are in overwrite mode, the new name will write over the old one, and you can use the space bar to delete characters from the old name. If you are in insert mode, you can use any of the editing keys to change one name to the other, including deleting the old name with the **Backspace** key. When you have the new name in place, press **Ctrl-End** to save the changed structure.

Changing the Width of a Field

SEQUENCE OF STEPS

From the Control Center:

    highlight the database name in the data panel
    Design (**Shift-F2**)   *or*   ⏎ Modify Structure/Order ⏎
    Esc
    move the cursor to the field width column to be changed
    type the new field width
    Menus (**F10**)/Exit [⏎]   *or*   **Alt-E**
    Save Changes and Exit [⏎]

or simply

    Ctrl-End
    Y *or* **N**

USAGE

You may find that a field width you provided when you first created your database no longer meets your needs. You may want to widen it, or you may have no need for as wide a field as you anticipated and now want to narrow the field and save some disk storage space.

If you make a field narrower than some data you have already entered in that field, be aware that dBASE will *truncate* (cut off) the data to fit the new field width.

To change the width of a field, use the arrow keys to move the cursor to the Field Width column for that field on the database design screen. Type a new width for the field and press ⏎. Press **Ctrl-End** or use one of the other methods described earlier to save the modified database structure.

Changing the Type of a Field

You can also change the data type of a field, but keep in mind that fields with different data types hold different kinds of data, and therefore changing the data type may make no sense. For example, if you've already stored many records in a Logical field and you change that field to the Date data type, dBASE will not know how to convert the .F.'s and .T.'s in the Logical field to dates.

You can, however, reliably convert any field type to the Character data type. This is the most common type of change. For example, suppose you create a field named PARTNUMBER using the Numeric data type. Later you discover that you cannot enter the part number XLT-212 into this field. In this case, you can simply change the Numeric field to the Character data type. You will then be able to add part numbers with letters, hyphens, and blank spaces. Any part numbers that you've already entered will be converted to the Character data type, but their values will not change.

If you plan to change a field's data type while modifying the database structure, you should *not* change any field names during the same operation. Instead, go to the database design screen, change a single field's data type, and save your changes. Saving your changes immediately prevents dBASE from becoming confused when trying to copy the temporary database back into the new structure. You can then return to the database design screen and make other changes if you wish.

OPENING AND CLOSING DATABASE FILES

Once you highlight a database file name and press either Design (**Shift-F2**) or Data (**F2**), dBASE *opens* that database file and keeps it open. You can also open (or close) a database file at any time by highlighting its name in the Data panel and pressing ↵. A *prompt box* appears displaying either Use File, to open the database, or Close File, to close the database if it already open.

The prompt box also displays the options Modify Structure/Order (which takes you to the database design screen) and Display Data (which transfers you to the browse or edit screen). Use the highlight and ↵ technique to select either of these options. You can use these two options as alternatives to pressing the Design (**Shift-F2**) and Data (**F2**) keys.

USING THE dBASE IV SCREENS

dBASE IV uses three major types of screens:

- The *Control Center*. The Control Center is the central workplace in dBASE IV; from it you can access all dBASE IV operations.
- The *design screen*. The database design screen provides access to the design (that is, to the *structure*) of a database file, including field names, indexes, and available sort orders. The database design screen does *not* show the data (contents) that the database holds.

- The *data screens*. The edit and browse screens are data screens; they show the actual data (contents) of a database (such as names and addresses).

To move from screen to screen,

- Press Design (**Shift-F2**) to go to the database design screen from a data screen. (This keystroke returns you to the database design screen only if that is the design screen you left most recently. Otherwise, pressing Design (**Shift-F2**) takes you to the queries design screen; see Chapter 5.)
- Press Data (**F2**) to go to a data screen, such as the browse screen or edit screen.
- Press Menus (**F10**) to access the pull-down menus.
- To exit any screen, press Menus (**F10**) and highlight the Exit option (always the last option on the right). Selecting Exit from the Control Center takes you either out of dBASE or to the dot prompt.

Figure 2.14 summarizes these keystrokes. The navigation line reminds you of the keystrokes that are available. These same keystrokes are used in other panels of the Control Center to move into and out of design and data screens.

You can use these alternative keystrokes to exit from a screen:

- Pressing **Ctrl-End** saves any changes and exits the current screen. This is a shortcut for selecting Exit or Save Changes and Exit from the Exit pull-down menu.

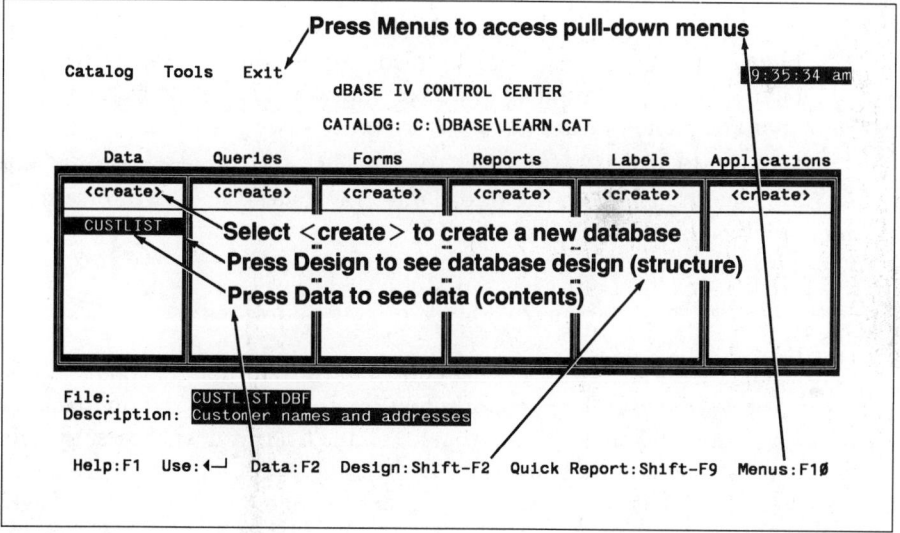

FIGURE 2.14: The message line at the bottom of the screen describes the keys that you can use from the Control Center.

- Pressing **Esc** also exits the current screen, but does not save any recent changes. This is a shortcut for selecting Abandon Changes and Exit from the Exit pull-down menu.

If you press **Esc** while a pull-down menu is displayed, dBASE leaves the current menu and keeps you in the current screen. If you press **Esc** when no pull-down menu is displayed, dBASE leaves the current screen without saving any changes. Before leaving the current screen, dBASE double-checks your intentions by displaying the message

```
Are you sure you want
to abandon operation?
Yes   No
```

If you have not made any changes on the current screen, select Yes (by highlighting the word and pressing ⏎ or by typing **Y**). If you have made changes, select No. If you select No, you can then save your changes and exit by pressing **Ctrl-End** or by selecting an option from the Exit pull-down menu.

TIPS AND TRAPS

- When you save a revised database file structure, before selecting overwrite in response to the *File already exists* prompt, be sure you want to completely erase all data in the existing database file. dBASE will replace the existing database with the empty database structure currently on the screen.

- To avoid accidental data loss, make a backup copy of your database before changing its structure. Also, when you make one structural change, save the modified structure and exit. Do not make a variety of changes at one time.

- If you press Data (**F2**) from the edit screen and the browse screen does not appear, enter at least one record into your database. The browse screen will then appear.

SUMMARY

This chapter concludes Part I, which provides the information you need to set up a dBASE IV database file. You must first create a structure for your database, providing names and other information for all the fields you will be using. Then you can enter data into those fields.

The CUSTLIST database created in the examples in this chapter is used again in later chapters for sorting, searching, creating queries, and so forth. If you want to follow the examples for those techniques, you need to create CUSTLIST. You can use the example sections in this chapter to do so.

Part II focuses on data manipulation. The next chapter—which presents techniques for adding, changing, and deleting data—provides further discussion and examples using the edit and browse screens.

For more information about Numeric and Float fields:

- Chapter 6, "Performing Calculations"

To find out how to make a backup copy of the database structure:

- Chapter 14, "Managing Files and the Workspace"

To create better forms than the edit screen provides:

- Chapter 10, "Creating Custom Forms"

To use the database design screen Index column to index a database:

- Chapter 4, "Sorting the Database"

Part II

Manipulating the Data

Chapter 3: Adding, Changing, and Deleting Data
Chapter 4: Sorting the Database
Chapter 5: Searching the Database
Chapter 6: Performing Calculations

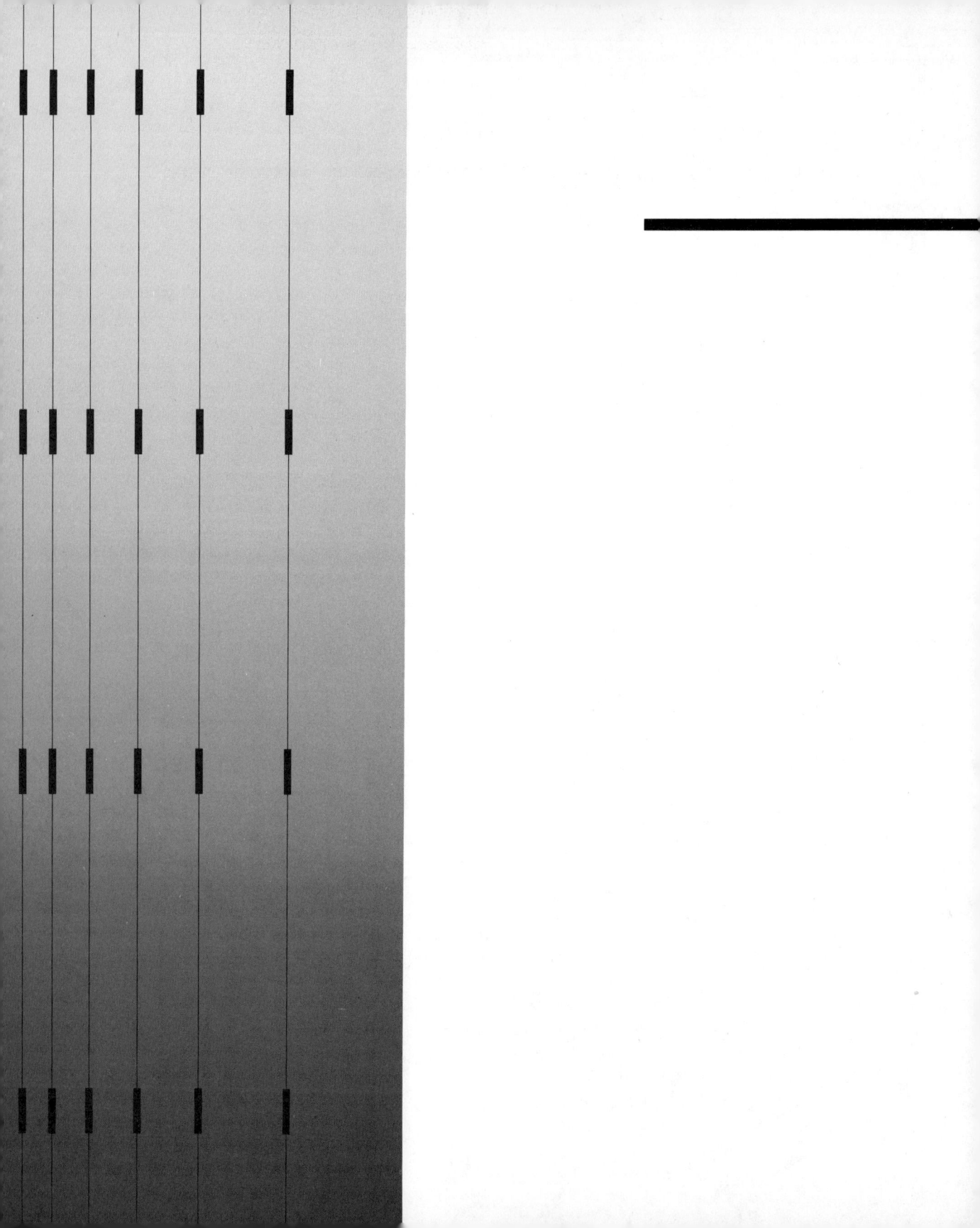

CHAPTER 3

Adding, Changing, and Deleting Data

How to Edit Data. 59
    Undoing an Edit. 62
Using Memo Fields. 63
    The Memo Field Editor. 64
Adding More Records. 68
Deleting Records. 69
    Marking a Record for Deletion. 69
    Hiding Deleted Records. .71
    Removing a Deletion Mark. 72
    Removing Deleted Records. 74
Customizing the Browse Screen. 77
    Locking a Field. 77
    Freezing a Field. 78
    Blanking a Field or Record. 79
    Sizing Columns. 79
    Preventing Automatic Cursor Repositioning. 80
    Locking Records. 80
Tips and Traps. 81
Summary. 81

Adding, Changing, and Deleting Data

To select a database file and access its data (to add, view, or change information), highlight the database name in the Data panel by positioning the highlight with the arrow keys. (If the highlight is already in the Data panel, you can also position the highlight by typing the first few letters of the name of the database file.) Press Data (**F2**) when the database name is highlighted.

You will be taken to the edit or browse screen, depending on which screen you last used. You can make changes from either the edit screen or the browse screen, and you can press Data (**F2**) to switch from one screen to the other. If you highlight a record on the browse screen and then press Data (**F2**), the same record appears on the edit screen.

How to Edit Data

You can use the keys listed in Table 3.1 to move around on the edit and browse screens and make changes in the data. The **Ins** (insert) key acts as a *toggle* for the insert and overwrite modes. Each time you press **Ins**, dBASE switches from the current mode to the other mode. The *Ins* indicator appears in the lower-right corner of the screen when you are in *insert mode*. In this mode, anything you type is inserted at the cursor location, and the existing text moves to the right. Press **Ins** once to turn off the *Ins* indicator. When the indicator does not appear on the screen, you are in *overwrite mode*. In this mode, anything you type replaces the existing text.

You can use any combination of editing keys to make your changes. The changes you make are saved when you either scroll to a new record using the **PgUp** or **PgDn** key or exit from the edit or browse screen.

EXAMPLE

(This and other examples in this chapter use the sample CUSTLIST database introduced in Chapter 2. Use the instructions there to create it, if necessary.) Suppose you want to change Annie Adams's address from 345 C St, Malibu, to 3456 Ocean St., Santa Monica. From the edit screen, press **PgDn** or **PgUp** until Annie Adams's data appears as in Figure 3.1.

KEY	EFFECT
↓	Moves the cursor down
↑	Moves the cursor up
→	Moves the cursor right one character
←	Moves the cursor left one character
↵	Completes the entry and moves the cursor to the next field
PgDn	Moves down one record on the edit screen and one screenful on the browse screen
PgUp	Moves up one record on the edit screen and one screenful on the browse screen
Del	Deletes the character at the cursor
Backspace	Moves left one character, erasing along the way
Ditto (Shift-F8)	Carries data from the previous record to the same field in the current record
Ctrl-Y	Deletes all characters to the right of the cursor
Ins	Switches between insert and overwrite modes
Home	Moves to the first field on the browse screen and to the first character in the current field on the edit screen
End	Moves to the last field on the browse screen and to the end of the current field on the edit screen
Tab	Moves to the next field
Shift-Tab	Moves to the previous field
Esc	Leaves the current record without saving changes
Help (F1)	Displays help
Data (F2)	Switches between the browse and edit screens
Previous (F3)	Scrolls back to the previous field
Next (F4)	Scrolls to the next field
Menus (F10)	Accesses the pull-down menus

Table 3.1: Navigation and Editing Keys for the Browse and Edit Screens

To change the address, press ↓ three times to move the cursor into the ADDRESS field, like this:

345 C St.

Press → three times to move the cursor to the right of 345, like this:

345_C St.

HOW TO EDIT DATA — 61

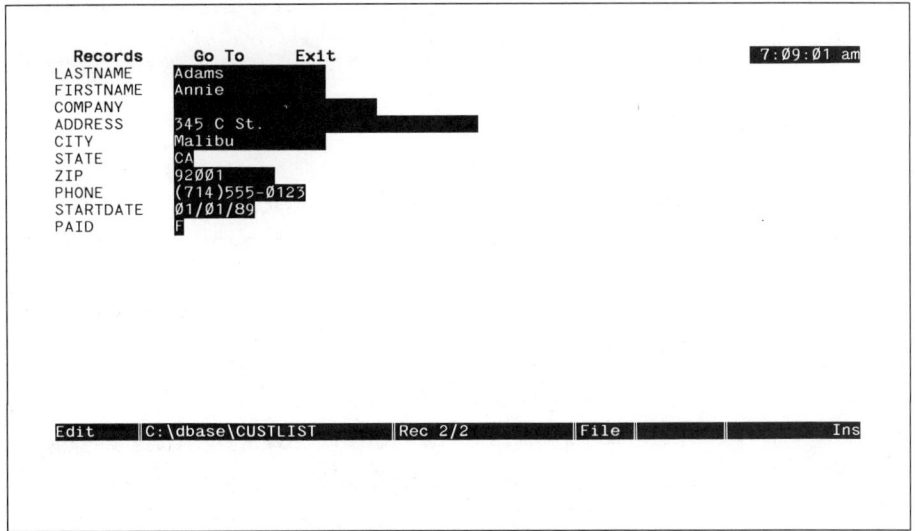

FIGURE 3.1: The second record from the CUSTLIST database on the edit screen.

Look at the lower-right corner of your screen to see if the indicator *Ins* appears (as it does in Figure 3.1). If it does not, press **Ins**. Now you are in insert mode. Type **6 Ocean**, so the entry looks like this:

3456 Ocean_C St.

Notice that the new text you typed was inserted into the existing text. That is because insert mode (controlled by the **Ins** key) is currently on.

Press **Del** (the delete key) twice to get rid of the unnecessary characters. The address should look like this:

3456 Ocean St.

To change the city, press ↵ to move down to the CITY field. You will see the cursor at the start of the name Malibu, like this:

Malibu

This time, you want to completely type over the existing city name, so press **Ins** once to turn off insert mode. The *Ins* indicator at the bottom-right corner of the screen disappears. Type **Santa Monica**, which completely overwrites Malibu.

Once you have changed the address and city for Annie's record, your screen should look like Figure 3.2. Save these changes in Annie's record by pressing **PgUp** to move up a record. The record for John Smith should appear on the edit screen. You can now edit this or another record or return to the Control Center.

62 — **CH. 3** ADDING, CHANGING, AND DELETING DATA

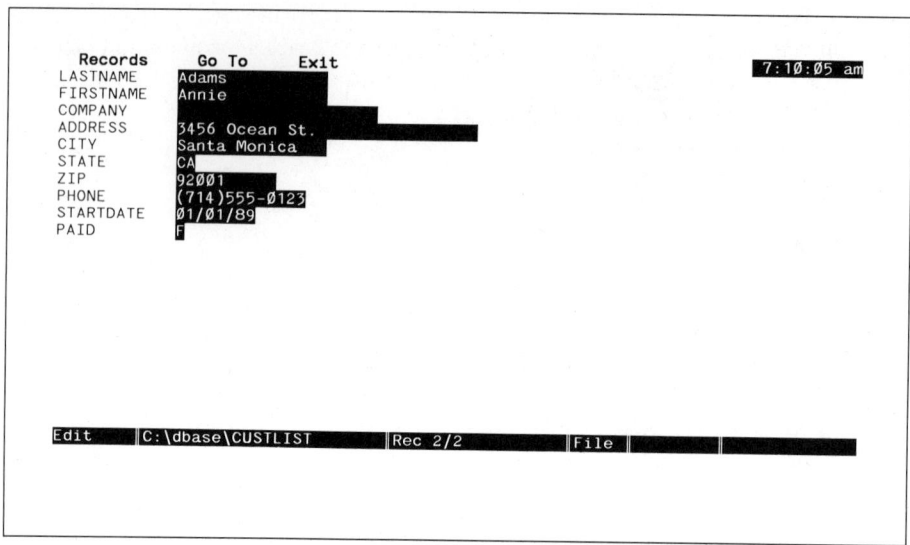

FIGURE 3.2: Annie Adams's record after editing with a new address and city.

Undoing an Edit

SEQUENCE OF STEPS

From the edit or browse screen:

    Menus (**F10**)/Records *or* **Alt-R**

    Undo Changes to Record [↵]

USAGE

    Once in a while, you will make the common mistake of changing or erasing a field's contents without paying enough attention to what you are doing. Suddenly, you realize that you have changed the wrong information and do not remember what the old information was.

    Fortunately, you can easily undo accidental changes made in a record, so long as you have not yet moved to the next record. When you realize that you have incorrectly edited a record, undo your changes by pressing Menus (**F10**) to access the pull-down menus. Use ← or →, as necessary, to highlight the Records option on the menu bar. Press ↑, if necessary, to highlight Undo Change to Record and press ↵ to select it. You will see the previous contents of the record restored.

Note that selecting Undo Change to Record undoes *all* of the changes you have made in the current record, not just the last field you changed. If you have not made any changes in the record currently on the screen, the Undo Change to Record option is shaded when you call up the Records menu, indicating that it is not available since there are no changes to undo. This will be the case when you have moved on from the record where you made mistakes.

EXAMPLE

To see how undoing an edit works, you can change one field and delete the contents of another and then reverse those changes. Using the CUSTLIST database, bring the data to the edit or browse screen (as usual, using the Data (**F2**) key). Then position the cursor on John Smith's record.

Move the cursor to the COMPANY field. Type **HA HA HO HO** (or any other nonsense that suits your fancy) and press ↵. With the cursor in the ADDRESS field, press **Ctrl-Y** (hold down the **Ctrl** key and press **Y**) to erase everything to the right of the cursor, thereby emptying the ADDRESS field.

Suppose that you now realize you are making a mess of things. *Do not* move to another record (thereby saving your changes). Instead, undo your changes by pressing Menus (**F10**) to access the pull-down menus and using ← or →, as necessary, to highlight the Records option on the menu bar. Press ↑, if necessary, to highlight Undo Change to Record and press ↵ to select it. You will see John Smith's record back on the screen, exactly as it was before you made your erroneous changes.

USING MEMO FIELDS

In some databases, you might want to store an entire written document with each database record. For example, you might want to store resumes in a personnel database. In a real estate office database, you might want to store descriptions of each property. You might want to store abstracts of journal articles in a database of scientific research references, and reviews of performances in a music-collection database.

To store a large body of text in a dBASE IV database, you use a *Memo field*. (Figure 2.13 in Chapter 2 showed a database structure with a Memo field.) A Memo field can hold over 64,000 characters, or about 18 single-spaced pages of text. dBASE offers many features for managing Memo fields, including the *word-wrap editor*, which provides tools for creating, changing, and formatting the text in a Memo field.

When you include a Memo field in your database, the edit screen displays the Memo field with the word *memo* inside it, as shown in Figure 3.3. The word *memo* is used as a *marker* to remind you that this field can actually contain a much larger memo.

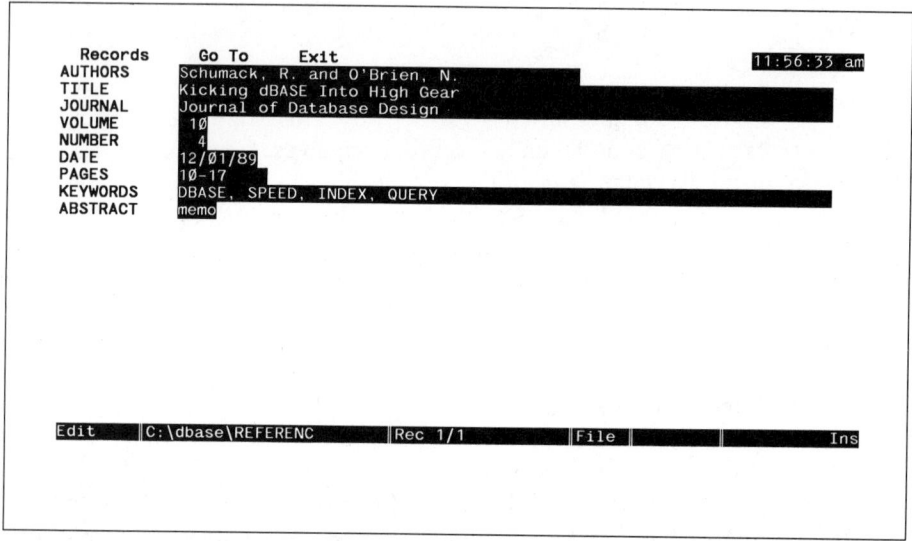

FIGURE 3.3: Edit screen a for bibliographical database with a Memo field named ABSTRACT. Notice that the Memo field displays *memo*, indicating that the field is empty.

The Memo Field Editor

To enter text into a Memo field, you must first access the Memo field editor. You can use any one of three techniques to do so:

- Move the cursor to the Memo field marker and press **Ctrl-Home**.
- Move the cursor to the Memo field marker and press Zoom (**F9**).
- If the cursor is in the field directly before the Memo field, pressing Next (**F4**) moves the cursor into the Memo field, automatically preparing the screen for data to be added or modified. If the cursor is in the field directly after the Memo field, pressing Previous (**F3**) automatically takes you to the Memo field editor.

Like a word processor, the Memo field editor automatically *word-wraps* the text you enter, so that you do not press ⏎ at the end of each line, but only at the end of each paragraph. If you change something in a paragraph, dBASE reformats the entire paragraph automatically.

The editing keys that you can use in the Memo field editor are listed in Table 3.2. Notice that many operations provide alternative keystrokes. For example, to move the cursor right one space, you can press either → or **Ctrl-D**. The alternative keystrokes are identical to those in the WordStar word processing program.

KEYS	ALTERNATIVE	EFFECT
→	Ctrl-D	Moves the cursor right one character.
←	Ctrl-S	Moves the cursor left one character.
↓	Ctrl-X	Moves the cursor down one line.
↑	Ctrl-E	Moves the cursor up one line.
Ins	Ctrl-V	Toggles between Insert and Overwrite modes: in Insert mode, the cursor appears as a blinking square; in Overwrite mode, the cursor appears as a blinking underline.
Del	Ctrl-G	Deletes the character at the cursor, or the block of text that is currently selected with the F6 key.
Ctrl-T		Deletes characters to the right of the cursor up to the first letter of the next word.
Ctrl-Y		Deletes the entire line.
Backspace	Ctrl-H	Moves the cursor left one character, erasing along the way.
↵	Ctrl-M	Marks the end of a paragraph; adds a new blank line if Insert mode is on.
Ctrl-N		Inserts a blank line, regardless of whether Insert mode is on.
Home	Ctrl-Z	Moves the cursor to the beginning of the line.
End	Ctrl-B	Moves the cursor to the end of the line.
Ctrl-→	Ctrl-F	Moves the cursor to the beginning of the next word.
Ctrl-←	Ctrl-A	Moves the cursor to the beginning of the previous word.
PgDn	Ctrl-C	Scrolls down one screen or to the bottom of the existing text on the current page.
PgUp	Ctrl-R	Scrolls up one screen or to the top of the existing text on the current page.

TABLE 3.2: Editing Keys Used in the dBASE IV Editor.

KEYS	ALTERNATIVE	EFFECT
Tab		Moves the cursor to the next tab stop, or if used when the cursor is on the first character of a paragraph, indents the entire paragraph.
Shift-Tab		Moves the cursor to the previous tab stop, or if used when the cursor is on the first character of a paragraph, "outdents" the entire paragraph.
Select (F6)		Begins the process of making a block of text to work with in a Memo field. Use the arrow keys to select a block of text and ⏎ to complete your selection.
Move (F7)		Moves a block of text that has been selected with the **F6** key to the current cursor position.
Copy (F8)		Copies a block of text that has been selected with the **F6** key to the current cursor position.
Ctrl-End	Ctrl-W	Saves changes and exits.
Ctrl-Q	Esc	Abandons changes and exits. If a block of text is currently selected (with the **F6** key), pressing **Esc** "unselects" the block.

TABLE 3.2: Editing Keys Used in the dBASE IV Editor (continued).

The top of the editor screen displays a menu bar and a ruler (see Figure 3.4). Within the ruler, the left bracket ([ ) shows the left margin and the right bracket ( ]) shows the right margin. By default, the left margin is set at 0 and the right margin is set at 65, about the right width for printing on 8½-by-11 inch paper (assuming that your printer has a default 1-inch left margin; if it does not, you should change this margin as discussed in Chapter 9). The triangles show tab stops.

After you have finished entering the text for your Memo field, you can use either of the following techniques to save your work:

- Select Save Changes and Exit from the Exit pull-down menu.
- Press **Ctrl-End**.

You will be returned to the edit screen. Notice that the marker in the Memo field now reads *MEMO*. When a Memo field contains information, its marker is shown in uppercase letters, so you can tell when a Memo field contains data without going to the editor.

```
  Layout   Words   Go To   Print   Exit                    12:06:26 pm
[.......▼1......▼..2....▼....3..▼.....4▼.█.....▼5......▼..6....]....7..▼.......
  The authors discuss several techniques for maximizing dBASE IV
  processing speed.  Numerous alternative techniques for sorting
  and searching a large database are discussed, and relative
  processing times are compared.  The authors recommend three
  techniques for maximizing the speed of dBASE IV:

  Any database field that will be used heavily for sorting or
  searching should be indexed.

  Always include complex indexes in all queries.

  Be sure to store one-to-many related database fields in separate,
  related database files.

  The authors also provide additional tips for maximizing the speed
  of dBASE IV command files.




  Edit   │ C:\dbase\REFERENC  │ Line:17 Col:43 │ File │           │  Ins
```

FIGURE 3.4: Paragraphs of text typed into a Memo field. Notice that insert mode is on. When entering the text, press ↵ to end paragraphs and to insert blank lines.

Most of the editing keys used with the Memo field editor are identical to those for the word-wrap editor used in the reports design screen to create form letters and design reports. (For examples of creating paragraphs with fancy formats, see Chapter 7.) Many of the alternative keystrokes shown in Table 3.2 are available in other dBASE editing modes as well.

You can import text from foreign files into a Memo field, as well as export Memo field data to external files (see Chapter 14). You can also search a database for words or phrases embedded in Memo fields (see Chapter 5).

EXAMPLE

Figure 3.3 shows the edit screen for a database of journal article references. ABSTRACT is a Memo field, for which *memo* is displayed on the edit screen. Of course, you do not need to create this database to practice using the Memo field editor. You can use any database that has a Memo field.

First access the edit screen for the database you are using. Move the cursor to the Memo field and press Zoom (**F9**). dBASE displays the Memo field editor, where you can enter the text for the memo.

When you type paragraphs of text into a Memo field, the main point to keep in mind is that you do not press ↵ until you get to the end of a paragraph; like word processors, dBASE automatically word-wraps text within a paragraph when you attempt to type past the right margin.

To enter the Memo field text shown in Figure 3.4, type the first paragraph without pressing ⏎ until you get to the colon at the end of the paragraph; then press ⏎ twice before typing the next two lines of text. Type the entire memo, pressing ⏎ twice at the end of each paragraph (wherever you see a blank line in the figure). Press **Ctrl-End** to return to the edit screen. Notice that the Memo field marker now reads *MEMO*.

ADDING MORE RECORDS

SEQUENCE OF STEPS

From the Control Center:

    Menus (**F10**)/Records *or* **Alt-R**
    Add New Records [⏎]
    enter your new records

To save and exit:

    Menus (**F10**)/Exit *or* **Alt-E**
    Exit [⏎]

or simply

    Ctrl-End

From the edit or browse screen:

    PgDn
    Y
    enter your new records

To save and exit:

    Menus (**F10**)/Exit *or* **Alt-E**
    Exit [⏎]

or simply:

    Ctrl-End

USAGE

When you have created a database structure but have not entered any records, you have created an empty database for which dBASE assumes you will be adding new data. However, once you have some data in a database, you are then adding new records.

There are two ways to add more records to an existing database. The first is to use the Add New Records option. Press **Alt-R** or select Menus (**F10**) from the Control Center to access the pull-down menus and use → or ←, as necessary, to highlight the Records menu. Type **A** or press ⏎ to select the highlighted Add New Records option. Then enter your new records.

The other method is pressing **PgDn** from the edit screen or ↓ from the browse screen until you see the prompt = = > *Add new records? (Y/N)*. Then type **Y** and enter your new records.

To save your work after you have finished entering records, use any of the methods of saving and editing introduced in Chapter 2. The simplest method is pressing **Ctrl-End**. You can also first press Menus (**F10**) to access the pull-down menus. Press ← or → to move to the Exit option. Select Exit by typing **E** or by pressing ⏎ while Exit is highlighted. dBASE returns you to the Control Center, where you will again see the database name in the Data panel.

DELETING RECORDS

There are two major steps to deleting database records. First, you must *mark* the record. This does not actually remove the record from the database, but allows you to hide, or temporarily delete, it. You can bring marked records out of hiding and unmark them at any time.

The second step is often called *packing*. Packing a database permanently removes all records currently marked for deletion. Any records following a deleted record move up a notch to fill the void left by the deleted record (hence the term *packing*). There is no way to recover deleted records once you have packed the database.

Marking a Record for Deletion

SEQUENCE OF STEPS

From the edit screen:

    move the cursor to the record to be deleted
    Ctrl-U

From the browse screen:

    move the cursor to the record to be deleted
    Menus (**F10**)/Records *or* **Alt-R**
    Mark Record for Deletion [⏎]

USAGE

Whether you are using the edit or browse screen or a custom form, you use the same techniques to mark a record for deletion. First, use the arrow, **PgUp**, and **PgDn** keys to move the cursor to the record you want to mark. Then use one of the following ways to mark the record: select Mark Record for Deletion from the Records pull-down menu or press **Ctrl-U**.

EXAMPLE

Suppose Wilbur Watson has not placed an order in many months, so you decide to delete him from the CUSTLIST database. (The complete CUSTLIST database is shown in Chapter 2, where you will also find instructions for creating it. Depending on whether you carry out this and some or all of the subsequent examples in this book, the state of your CUSTLIST database may differ in minor details from that shown in particular examples. It is not assumed that you will work through all of the examples in this reference in sequence, and the differences do not affect the essential content of any example.)

Move to Watson's record on the browse screen and type **Ctrl-U** to mark his record for deletion. The only indication that the record has been marked is the word *Del* in the status bar at the bottom of the screen. Figure 3.5 shows Wilbur Watson's record marked for deletion on the browse screen.

```
 Records    Fields     Go To     Exit                         2:21:22 pm
┌──────────────┬──────────────┬─────────────────┬──────────────────────┐
│ LASTNAME     │ FIRSTNAME    │ COMPANY         │ ADDRESS              │
├──────────────┼──────────────┼─────────────────┼──────────────────────┤
│ Smith        │ John         │ ABC Co.         │ 123 A St.            │
│ Adams        │ Annie        │                 │ 3456 Ocean St.       │
│ Watson       │ Wilbur       │ HiTech Co.      │ P.O. Box 987         │
│ Mahoney      │ Mary         │                 │ 211 Seahawk St.      │
│ Newell       │ John         │ LoTech Co.      │ 734 Rainbow Dr.      │
│ Beach        │ Sandy        │ American Widget │ 11 Elm St.           │
│ Kenney       │ Ralph        │                 │ 1101 Rainbow Ct.     │
│ Schumack     │ Susita       │ SMS Software    │ 47 Broad St.         │
│ Smith        │ Anita        │ Zeerocks, Inc.  │ 2001 Engine Dr.      │
│ Jones        │ Fred         │ American Sneaker│ P.O. Box 3381        │
│              │              │                 │                      │
│              │              │                 │  Current record is   │
│              │              │                 │  marked for deletion │
│              │              │                 │           ↓          │
├──────────────┴──────────────┴─────────────────┴──────────────────────┤
│ Browse │ C:\dbase\CUSTLIST │ Rec 3/10 │ File │             │ Del     │
└──────────────────────────────────────────────────────────────────────┘
```

FIGURE 3.5: The *Del* indicator on the status bar shows that the current record is marked for deletion. The highlight is on Watson's record; therefore, his record is marked for deletion.

Hiding Deleted Records

SEQUENCE OF STEPS

From the Control Center:

    Menus (**F10**)/Tools *or* **Alt-T**
    Settings [⏎]
    Deleted On
    Esc

To exit:

    Menus (**F10**)/Exit *or* **Alt-E**
    Exit to Control Center [⏎]

or simply

    Ctrl-End

USAGE

You can hide marked records without permanently deleting them. At the Control Center, press **Alt-T** or Menus (**F10**) and → as necessary to highlight Tools on the menu bar. Select Settings. Highlight the Deleted option and press the space bar to change the option from off to on. Your screen should look like Figure 3.6. Press **Esc**. Select Exit to Control Center from the Exit pull-down menu.

Assuming that you marked a record for deletion in the previous section, if you now highlight the same database in the Data panel and press Data (**F2**) to view its records, you will see that the record you marked no longer appears. If you use the ↓ key to scroll through the records, you will notice that the *Rec* indicator skips the number for that record. The record still exists; it is just hidden for the time being.

When the Deleted option is on, marked records are excluded from *all* dBASE operations, as though the records do not exist. Always remember to turn the Deleted option off when you no longer need to hide marked records.

To bring marked records out of hiding, return to the Control Center and follow the same steps that you used to hide the records, but change the Deleted setting from on back to off. If you then return to the browse screen, you will see the record once again. If you move the cursor to that record, you will see that it is still marked for deletion.

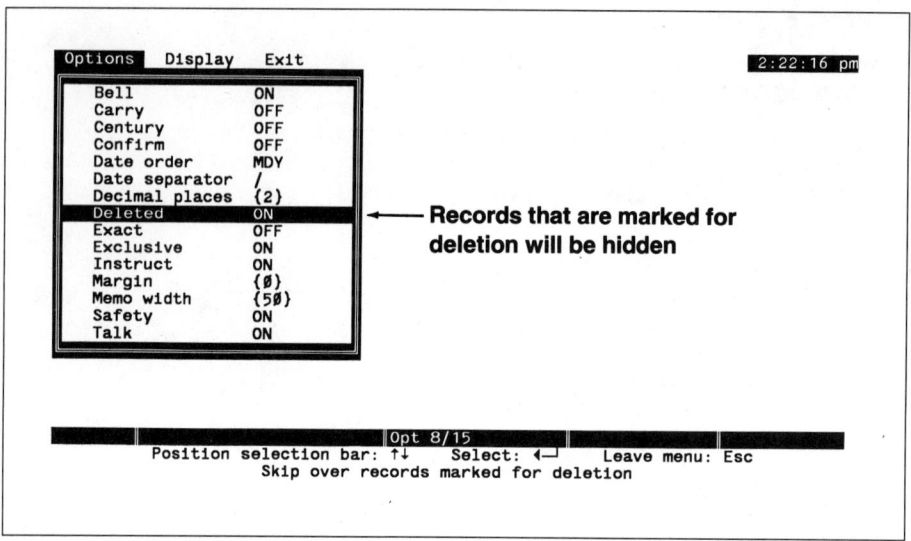

FIGURE 3.6: Deleted option turned on.

Removing a Deletion Mark

From the browse screen:

> move the cursor to the record to be unmarked
>
> Menus (**F10**)/Records   *or*   **Alt-R**
>
> Clear Deletion Mark [⏎]   *or*   **Ctrl-U**

USAGE

To remove the mark for deletion from a record, first make sure that the Deleted option is off. (Otherwise, you will not be able to see the marked record that you are trying to unmark.) Then move the cursor to the record that you want to unmark and use one of these techniques: select Clear Deletion Mark from the Records pull-down menu or press **Ctrl-U**.

Note that the Clear Deletion Mark option appears on the Records pull-down menu *only* if the current record is already marked for deletion. Otherwise, the option reads *Mark Record for Deletion*.

Notice that Ctrl-U acts as a toggle. That is, each time you press **Ctrl-U**, the current record's status changes from marked to unmarked. You will see the *Del* indicator in the status bar appear or disappear each time you press **Ctrl-U**.

EXAMPLE

Continuing from the previous example, you can hide Wilbur Watson's marked record without permanently deleting it. First, select Exit from the Exit pull-down menu to return to the Control Center if you are not there already. At the Control Center, press Menus (**F10**) and → to highlight Tools on the menu bar. Press ⏎ to select Settings. Highlight the Deleted option and press the space bar to change the option from off to on. Select Exit to Control Center from the Exit pull-down menu.

If you now highlight CUSTLIST in the Data panel and press Data (**F2**) to view its records, you will no longer see Wilbur Watson's record, as Figure 3.7 shows. Use ↓ to scroll through the records; notice that the *Rec* indicator skips from 2 to 4 when you scroll from Adams to Mahoney. Wilbur's record (number 3) still exists, but it is hidden.

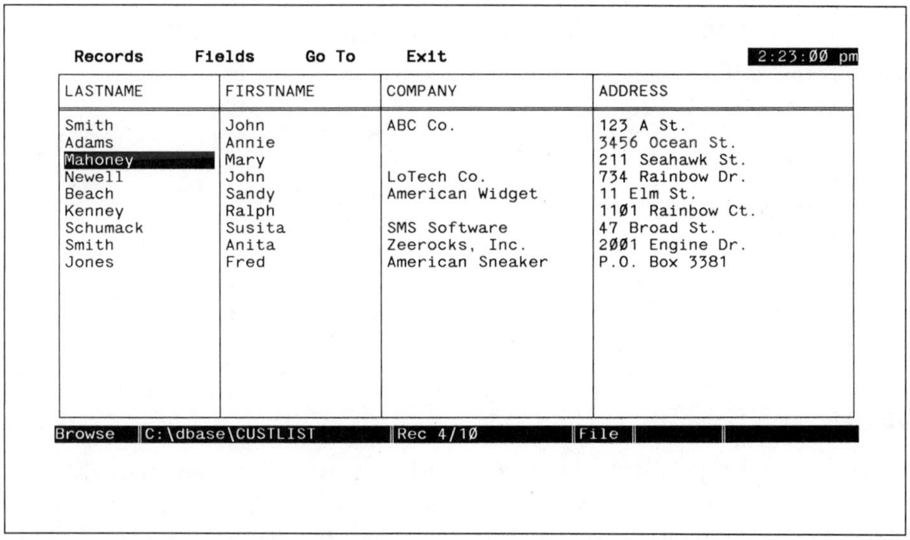

```
 Records    Fields    Go To    Exit                          2:23:00 pm
┌──────────────┬──────────────┬──────────────────┬────────────────────┐
│ LASTNAME     │ FIRSTNAME    │ COMPANY          │ ADDRESS            │
├──────────────┼──────────────┼──────────────────┼────────────────────┤
│ Smith        │ John         │ ABC Co.          │ 123 A St.          │
│ Adams        │ Annie        │                  │ 3456 Ocean St.     │
│ Mahoney      │ Mary         │                  │ 211 Seahawk St.    │
│ Newell       │ John         │ LoTech Co.       │ 734 Rainbow Dr.    │
│ Beach        │ Sandy        │ American Widget  │ 11 Elm St.         │
│ Kenney       │ Ralph        │                  │ 1101 Rainbow Ct.   │
│ Schumack     │ Susita       │ SMS Software     │ 47 Broad St.       │
│ Smith        │ Anita        │ Zeerocks, Inc.   │ 2001 Engine Dr.    │
│ Jones        │ Fred         │ American Sneaker │ P.O. Box 3381      │
└──────────────┴──────────────┴──────────────────┴────────────────────┘
 Browse   C:\dbase\CUSTLIST         Rec 4/10      File
```

FIGURE 3.7: To hide records marked for deletion, turn on Deleted on the Options menu. Those records will no longer be displayed in the database. To bring the records out of hiding, turn Deleted off.

To bring Wilbur's record out of hiding, return to the Control Center and follow the same steps that you followed to hide the records, but change the Deleted setting from on back to off. If you then return to the browse screen, you will see Wilbur's record once again. If you move the cursor to his record, you will see that it is still marked for deletion.

To remove the mark for deletion from Wilbur's record, first make sure that the Deleted option is off. Then move the cursor to Wilbur's record and press **Ctrl-U**.

Removing Deleted Records

SEQUENCE OF STEPS

To view marked records from the Control Center:

> highlight <create> in the Queries panel ←┘
> Menus (**F10**)/Condition   *or*   **Alt-C**
> Add a Condition Box [←┘]
> DELETED( ) ←┘
> Data (**F2**)

To delete marked records from the Control Center:

> highlight the database name in the Data panel
> Design (**Shift-F2**)   *or*   ←┘ Modify Structure/Order ←┘
> Organize/**E**rase Marked Records [←┘]
> **Y**

To save and exit:

> Menus (**F10**)/Exit   *or*   **Alt-E**
> **S**ave Changes and Exit [←┘]

or simply

> **Ctrl-End**

USAGE

Because packing the database permanently removes all marked records, you should do so with caution. A good approach is to isolate all marked records and look at them on the browse screen before you pack the database. Use **Ctrl-U** or the Clear Deletion Mark option to unmark any records that you do not want permanently removed; *then* pack the database.

To isolate records marked for deletion, you use a *query*, but you place the *filter condition* in the *condition box* rather than in a specific field. The condition box is like any other box on the query design screen, except that it takes into consideration the record as a whole, rather than just a specific field. (See Chapter 5 for information about queries and filter conditions.) You then place the dBASE DELETED( ) function in the condition box, which isolates the records marked for deletion.

With the database you want to use displayed on the browse screen, mark a record for deletion. Return to the Control Center by selecting Exit from the Exit pull-down menu (or by pressing **Ctrl-End**). Select <create> from the Queries panel. Press Menus (**F10**) and select Add Condition Box from the Condition pull-down menu. Enter the DELETED( ) function into the condition box by typing **DELETED( )**, as shown in Figure 3.8. Press Data (**F2**) to execute the query.

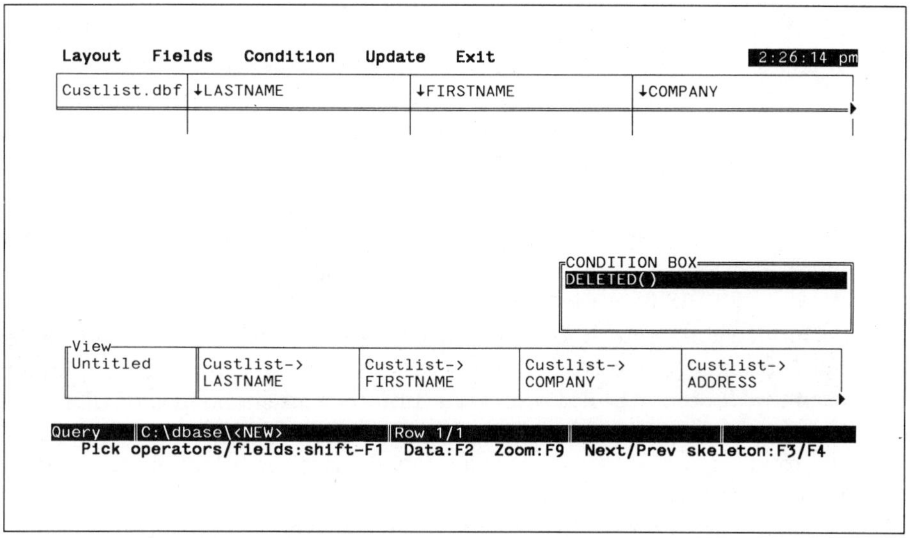

FIGURE 3.8: A condition box on the query design screen with the DELETED( ) function entered to isolate records marked for deletion.

The browse screen reappears, showing only those records that are marked for deletion. You can scroll through the records and use **Ctrl-U** or the Clear Deletion Mark option to unmark any records that you do not want permanently removed.

Note that unmarking a record (the procedure is discussed in the previous section) may not immediately remove the record from the browse screen, though the *Del* indicator will disappear from the status bar. To be safe, you can switch back and forth from the query to the browse screen until you are certain that only records you want permanently removed are marked.

Move the cursor to the marked record and press **Ctrl-U** (so that the *Del* indicator disappears). Select Transfer to Query Design from the Exit pull-down menu or just press Design (**Shift-F2**) to return to the query design screen. Execute the same query again, to double-check the marked record, by pressing Data (**F2**).

Now no marked records should appear on the browse screen, because you have removed the deletion mark. Select Exit from the Exit pull-down menu. When dBASE asks if you want to save the query that displays marked records, select no. You will be returned to the Control Center.

To delete all marked records from the database permanently, you need to return to the database design screen and select Erase Marked Records. From the Control Center, highlight the database you are using in the Data panel and press Design (**Shift-F2**). Select Erase Marked Records from the Organize pull-down menu. When dBASE asks for confirmation, type **Y** to select yes. When the job is complete, you will see an indicator beside the marked records that were erased. Press **Ctrl-End** to return to the Control Center.

If you view the database data now, you will see that the records you deleted are indeed gone (press **PgUp** to view all preceding records). All records following the one you deleted have moved up a number to fill the void left by the deletion; there is no longer a gap in the record numbers.

EXAMPLE

Suppose that you want to delete both Watson and Kenney from the customer list. With CUSTLIST on the browse screen, mark both Watson and Kenney's records for deletion. Return to the Control Center by pressing **Ctrl-End**. Select <create> from the Queries panel. Press Menus (**F10**) and select Add Condition Box from the Condition pull-down menu. Enter the function **DELETED( )** into the condition box, as shown in Figure 3.8. Press Data (**F2**) to execute the query.

The browse screen appears, showing only those records that are marked for deletion, as shown in Figure 3.9. You can scroll through the records and use the Clear Deletion Mark option to unmark any records that you do not want permanently removed.

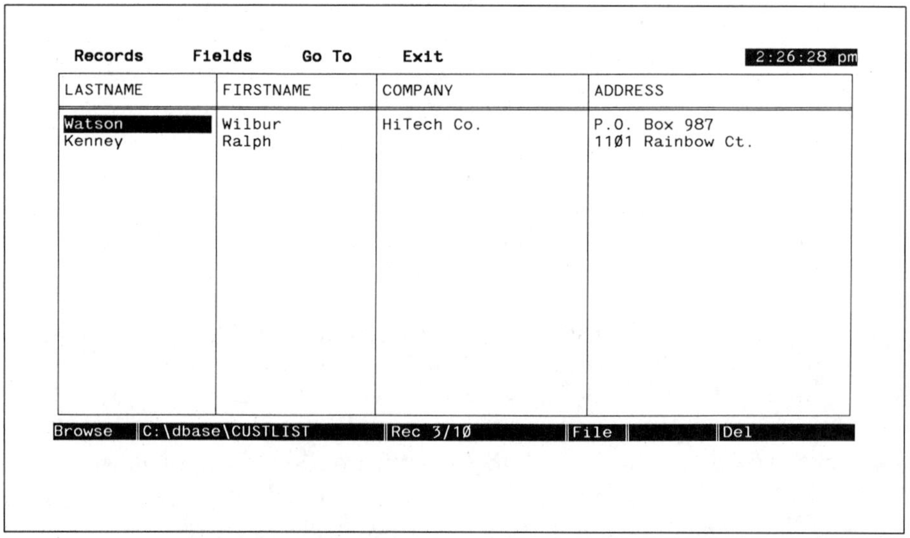

```
  Records     Fields      Go To      Exit                          2:26:28 pm
 ┌──────────────┬──────────────┬──────────────┬────────────────────────────┐
 │ LASTNAME     │ FIRSTNAME    │ COMPANY      │ ADDRESS                    │
 ├──────────────┼──────────────┼──────────────┼────────────────────────────┤
 │ Watson       │ Wilbur       │ HiTech Co.   │ P.O. Box 987               │
 │ Kenney       │ Ralph        │              │ 1101 Rainbow Ct.           │
 │              │              │              │                            │
 └──────────────┴──────────────┴──────────────┴────────────────────────────┘
  Browse   C:\dbase\CUSTLIST       Rec 3/10        File            Del
```

FIGURE 3.9: When you press Data (**F2**) from the screen shown in Figure 3.8, dBASE displays only the records marked for deletion on the browse screen.

Now only Wilbur Watson's record should appear in the browse screen because you have removed the deletion mark from Kenney's record. Assuming that you do indeed want to leave both Kenney's and Watson's records marked for deletion, select Exit from the Exit pull-down menu. When dBASE asks if you want to save the query that displays marked records, select No to return to the Control Center.

To permanently erase all marked records from the database, highlight CUSTLIST in the Data panel and press Design (**Shift-F2**). Select Erase Marked Records from the Organize pull-down menu. When dBASE asks for confirmation, select Yes. When the job is complete, you will see an indicator after the marked records that you erased. Press **Ctrl-End** to return to the Control Center.

If you view the data for the CUSTLIST database now, you will see that both Ralph Kenney's and Wilbur Watson's records are gone (press **PgUp** to view all preceding records). If you move the highlight to Mahoney's record, you will see that it is now number 2, rather than number 4. All records following Watson's have moved up by two numbers to fill the void. (Again, because you will probably not use this reference book as a tutorial, working through all the examples in sequence, subsequent examples may not assume that you have made these or any other deletions or additions.)

CUSTOMIZING THE BROWSE SCREEN

The browse screen offers several features to help you manipulate your view of the data. These features are particularly useful when you work with large databases because it is much faster to scroll through hundred of records on the browse screen than it is on the edit screen. All of these features are available from pull-down menus from the browse screen.

Locking a Field

SEQUENCE OF STEPS

From the browse screen:

    Menus (**F10**)/Fields   *or*   **Alt-F**
    Lock Fields on Left [↵]
    type the number of fields ↵

USAGE

Select the Lock Fields on Left option on the Fields pull-down menu to lock one or more fields at the left of the database so that they do not disappear when you scroll to the right. When you select this option, dBASE asks how many fields you want to remain stationary. Enter a number and press ←.

Figure 3.10 shows the CUSTLIST database on the browse screen with the two fields, LASTNAME and FIRSTNAME, locked. Notice that the cursor is scrolled all the way to the PAID field, but the two locked fields, LASTNAME and FIRSTNAME, are still on the screen. (Note that your CUSTLIST database will be in sorted order if you have not exited from dBASE since sorting it.)

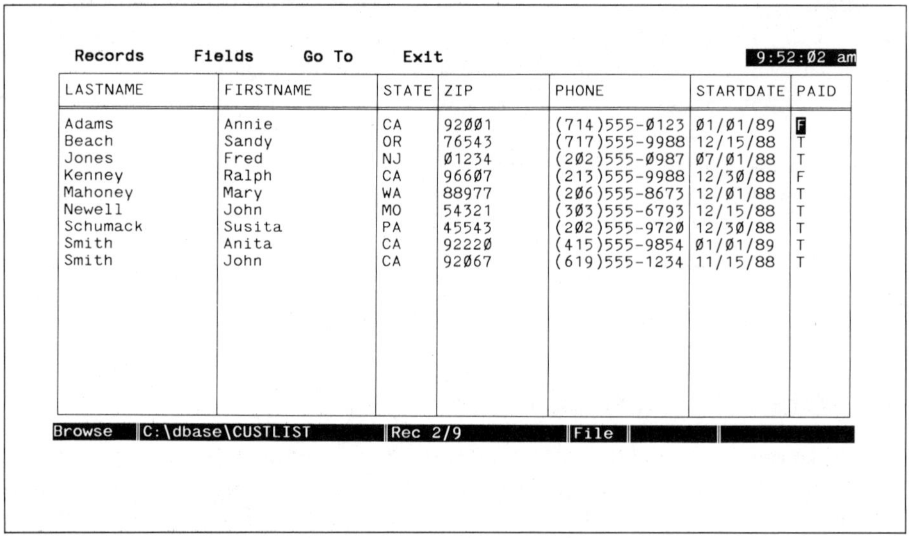

```
  Records      Fields     Go To      Exit                      9:52:02 am
  LASTNAME     FIRSTNAME       STATE  ZIP      PHONE           STARTDATE  PAID
  Adams        Annie           CA     92001    (714)555-0123   01/01/89   F
  Beach        Sandy           OR     76543    (717)555-9988   12/15/88   T
  Jones        Fred            NJ     01234    (202)555-0987   07/01/88   T
  Kenney       Ralph           CA     96607    (213)555-9988   12/30/88   F
  Mahoney      Mary            WA     88977    (206)555-8673   12/01/88   T
  Newell       John            MO     54321    (303)555-6793   12/15/88   T
  Schumack     Susita          PA     45543    (202)555-9720   12/30/88   T
  Smith        Anita           CA     92220    (415)555-9854   01/01/89   T
  Smith        John            CA     92067    (619)555-1234   11/15/88   T




  Browse   C:\dbase\CUSTLIST          Rec 2/9        File
```

FIGURE 3.10: With the LASTNAME and FIRSTNAME fields locked on the browse screen, you can view the rightmost fields of the database along with the customer names.

Freezing a Field

SEQUENCE OF STEPS

From the browse screen:

    Menus (**F10**)/Fields   *or*   **Alt-F**
    Freeze Field [←]
    type the field name ←

USAGE

Select the Freeze Field option on the Fields pull-down menu to isolate a particular field on the browse screen. When you select this option, dBASE asks for the name of the field to freeze. Type the field name and press ←.

The highlight moves to the field you named and cannot be moved out of that field. Pressing ← and → moves the highlight up and down, rather than across fields. To unfreeze the field, select the Freeze Field option again and press the **Backspace** key to remove the field name.

Blanking a Field or Record

SEQUENCE OF STEPS

From the browse screen (fields):

    Menus (**F10**)/Fields   *or*   **Alt-F**
    Blank Field [↵]

From the browse screen (records):

    move the highlight to the record you want to blank
    Menus (**F10**)/Records   *or*   **Alt-R**
    Blank Record [↵]

USAGE

To empty the contents of a field, move the cursor to the appropriate field and select Blank Field from the Fields pull-down menu. To empty all the fields in a record, move the cursor to the record and select Blank Record from the Records pull-down menu. If you accidentally blank the wrong field or record, select Undo Change to Record from the Records pull-down menu. Note that the Blank Record option leaves an empty record in a database. It does not mark or delete the record.

Sizing Columns

SEQUENCE OF STEPS

From the browse screen:

    move the cursor to the column you want to size
    Menus (**F10**)/Fields   *or*   **Alt-F**
    Size Field [↵]
    ← *or* →, as necessary ↵

USAGE

You can expand or contract the size of a column on the browse screen by moving the highlight to the appropriate column and selecting Size Field from the Fields pull-down menu. After selecting the option, use the ← or → key to widen or narrow the field; then press ↵.

Preventing Automatic Cursor Repositioning

SEQUENCE OF STEPS

From the browse screen:

    Menus (**F10**)/Records *or* **Alt-R**
    Follow Record to New Position [↵]
    No

USAGE

When you are using an index to maintain a sort order on the browse screen, changing values in the index field causes the records to be re-sorted. Usually, the cursor follows a modified record to its new location in the sort order. If you do not want dBASE to follow edited records while you are editing, select Follow Record to New Position on the Records pull-down menu and press ↵ to change its setting from Yes to No.

Locking Records

SEQUENCE OF STEPS

From the browse screen:

    Menus (**F10**)/Records *or* **Alt-R**
    Lock Record [↵]

If you are using dBASE IV on a network, other users working on the same database may change information in the database while you are viewing it. To prevent other users from changing the data in a record while you are viewing it, select Lock Record from the Records pull-down menu. The record will remain locked until you move the highlight to a different record.

Tips and Traps

- To view the contents of a database, highlight the database file name in the Data panel and then press Data (**F2**). Do not use the pull-down menus.
- If you accidentally change the wrong data while editing a record, you can select Undo Change to Record from the Records pull-down menu. Your previous version of that record will become current again.
- You can tell whether a Memo field contains data by checking its appearance on the browse screen. If the browse screen displays *memo*, the field is empty; if it displays *MEMO*, in the field contains data.
- So you do not delete records you would rather keep, it is good idea to isolate marked records and look at them on the browse screen before you pack the database.
- Locking fields on the browse screen obviates scrolling back and forth to see the information you need.
- When the Deleted option is on, marked records are excluded from *all* dBASE operations, as though the records do not exist. Always remember to turn the Deleted option off when you no longer need to hide marked records.

Summary

This chapter presented many techniques for working with the edit and browse screens. The chapter discussed editing, deleting, and adding records, as well as using Memo fields and customizing the browse screen.

You can use the navigation and editing keys listed in Table 3.1 and the dBASE IV editor keys listed in Table 3.2 for many activities. They work for designing a database structure, creating forms, and creating report formats, as well as in many other situations.

For using queries and condition boxes:

- Chapter 5, "Searching the Database"

For examples of more decorative paragraph formats that can be used with the Memo field editor:

- Chapter 7, "Designing Formatted Reports"

To find out about edits and deletions that are global in scope:

- Chapter 11, "Managing Groups of Records"

For a summary of dBASE IV functions:

- Appendix D, "dBASE IV Functions"

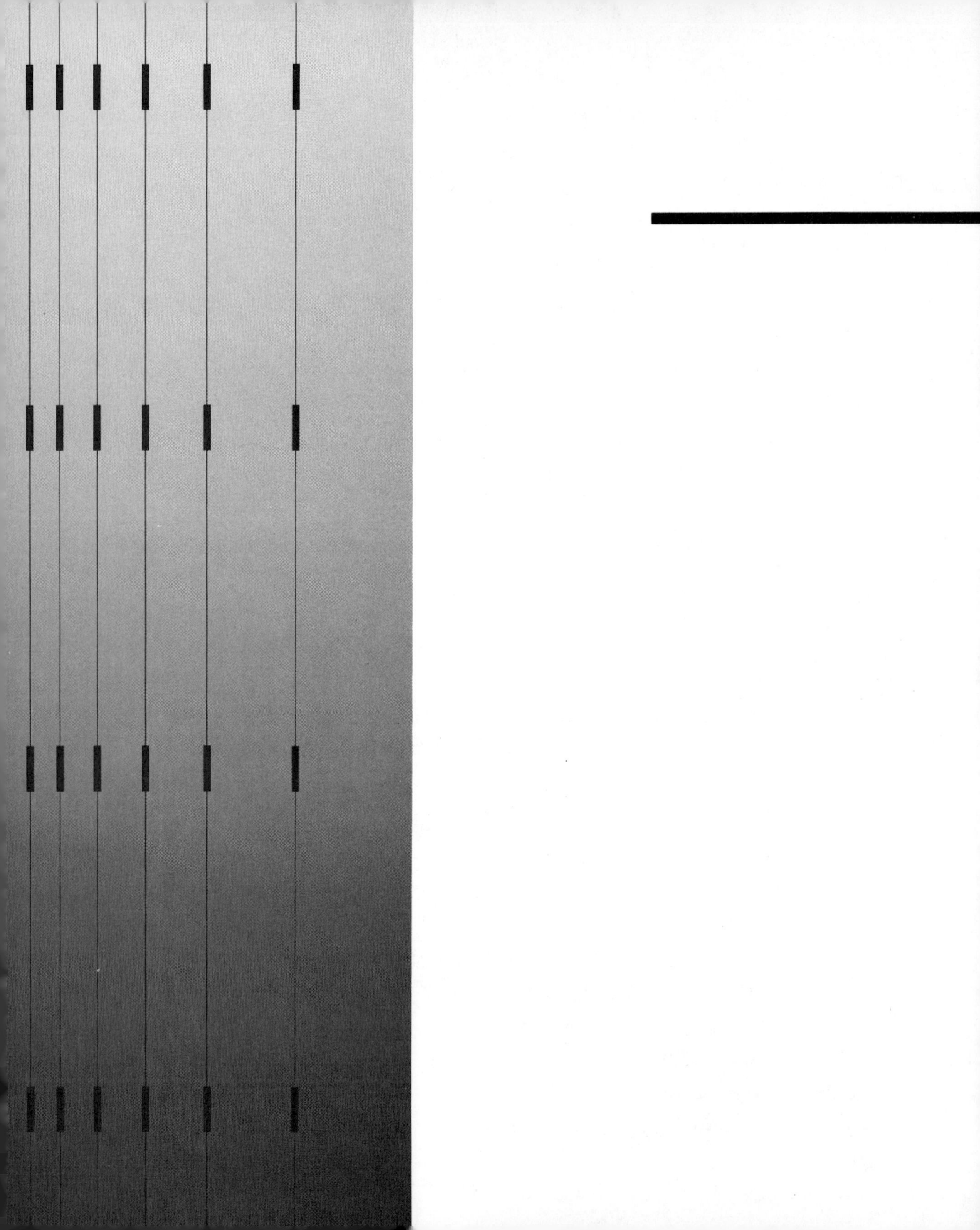

CHAPTER 4

SORTING THE DATABASE

What Is an Index?. 85
Sorting an Index on a Single Field (Quick Method). 86
    Activating an Index. 87
Sorting an Index on a Single Field (Second Method). 90
Performing Index Sorts within Sorts. 91
    Index Expressions. 93
    Indexing Fields of Various Data Types. .95
    Performing Sorts within Sorts with Numbers. 97
Modifying an Existing Index. 98
Controlling Uppercase/Lowercase Distinctions. 100
Combining Ascending and Descending Sort Orders. 100
Effects of Indexes on Editing. 102
Making a Sorted Copy of a Database. 103
    Viewing the Sorted Copy. 106
    Deleting the Sorted Copy. 106
Tips and Traps. 108
Summary. 108

Sorting the Database

Most likely, you enter information into a database as it becomes available to you. Very often, you need to rearrange, or *sort*, that information into a more useful order, such as alphabetical order by name or zip code order for bulk mailing. This chapter provides examples of typical database sort operations.

dBASE IV offers two ways to sort database files. By far the fastest and most efficient method is *indexing*. An alternative, but slower, way to sort a database is by making a sorted copy of the database file. This chapter discusses both methods of sorting.

What Is an Index?

A dBASE IV index is similar to the index in the back of a book. A book index lists topics in alphabetical order and the numbers of the pages where the topic appears. The purpose of a book index is to help you find information about a certain topic.

dBASE uses indexes in two different ways. First, when you activate an index, dBASE automatically *displays* the records in the sort order specified by the index. Note that the actual records in the database are still in their original order; the index just tells dBASE the order in which to display information on the screen (or printer), though it *appears* as though the database has actually been sorted.

Second, dBASE uses the index to quickly locate items of information in the database, just as you use the index in the back of a book. Chapter 5 discusses this "lookup" aspect of dBASE IV indexes in detail.

The most important fact to remember about indexes is that once you create an index, dBASE automatically manages the index behind the scenes. You will never see the contents of an index, nor do you ever need to interact directly with the contents of an index. In fact, you can add, change, and delete data from your database without giving a second thought to the index files. dBASE automatically adjusts them all.

You can create up to 47 indexes for any given database. However, indexes do take up disk space and require some time for dBASE to manage, so you should create indexes only on fields that you use often for sorting (or for certain types of searches; see Chapter 5). You can create or modify an index at any time; it does not matter whether the database contains no records or thousands of records.

Sorting an Index on a Single Field (Quick Method)

SEQUENCE OF STEPS

From the Control Center:

>highlight the database name in the Data panel
>Design (**Shift-F2**)
>**Esc**
>move the cursor to the index column of the field to sort by
>**Y**
>Menus (**F10**)/Exit [◄─┘]   *or*   **Alt-E**
>**S**ave Changes and Exit [◄─┘]

or simply

>**Ctrl-End**

USAGE

You can create indexes while you are creating or modifying a database structure simply by changing the Index option in the rightmost column to *Y*. dBASE assigns the name of the field as the name of the index, and it actually creates the index when you save the database structure.

To quickly sort a database on a single field, first highlight the database name in the Control Center Data panel. Press Design (**Shift-F2**) to access the database design screen. Press **Esc** to remove the Organize pull-down menu. Highlight the name of the field to sort by. Press **End** to move to the Index column. Type **Y** (or press the space bar until *Y* is displayed) to change the Index setting to Yes. To save your changes and exit, press **Ctrl-End** or use any of the methods introduced in Chapter 2. Press ◄─┘ to confirm the change.

EXAMPLE

(This and other examples in this chapter use the CUSTLIST database introduced in Chapter 2. Use the instructions there to create it, if necessary. Note that some of the records in your database may differ from the ones shown in this chapter, but such differences do not affect the content of the examples.)

Databases often need to be sorted into zip code order for bulk mailing. Using the CUSTLIST database, you can sort the database into zip code order by first highlighting the database name CUSTLIST in the Data panel of the Control Center and pressing Design (**Shift-F2**) to gain access to the database design screen.

When you reach the database design screen, dBASE automatically displays the Organize pull-down menu, as shown in Figure 4.1. Press **Esc** to remove the pull-down menu. Next, press ↓ six times until the field name ZIP is highlighted. Then press **End** to move the cursor to the Index column. Type **Y**, or press the space bar until a *Y* appears in the highlighted box. At this point, the ZIP field is marked *Y* for indexing, as shown in Figure 4.2.

To save your work, you can either press **Ctrl-End** or press Menus (**F10**) and select Save Changes and Exit from the Exit pull-down menu. When dBASE asks for confirmation (at the bottom of the screen), press ←.

If you press Data (**F2**) to view your data at this point, the records will be in sorted order (as you can best see if you switch to the browse screen, scroll to the ZIP field, and use the **PgUp** key to go to the beginning of the database).

Activating an Index

SEQUENCE OF STEPS

From the Control Center:

>highlight the database name in the Data panel
>Design (**Shift-F2**)
>**O**rganize/**O**rder Records by Index [←]
>highlight the index name ←
>Data (**F2**)

USAGE

In many situations, you will have more than one index associated with a database file. Only one index at a time, however, controls the sort order of the database records. The index that is currently controlling the sort order is often called the *master index*.

To select an existing index as the master index, you first need to go to the database design screen by highlighting the database name in the Data panel and pressing Design (**Shift-F2**). The Organize menu appears automatically when you enter the database design screen. At any other time, you can press Menus (**F10**) and use the ← or → key to highlight Organize and then press ← to select it.

Next, you need to select Order Records by Index from the Organize menu. A submenu with a list of existing index names appears. Highlight the name of the

CH. 4 SORTING THE DATABASE

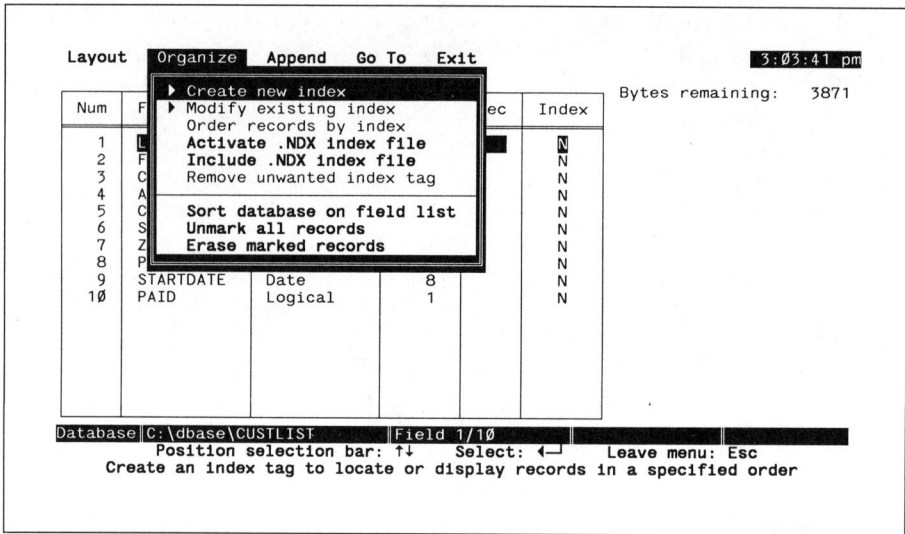

FIGURE 4.1: When you first access your database structure, the database design screen is partially obscured by the Organize pull-down menu. Press **Esc** to remove the menu and view the database structure.

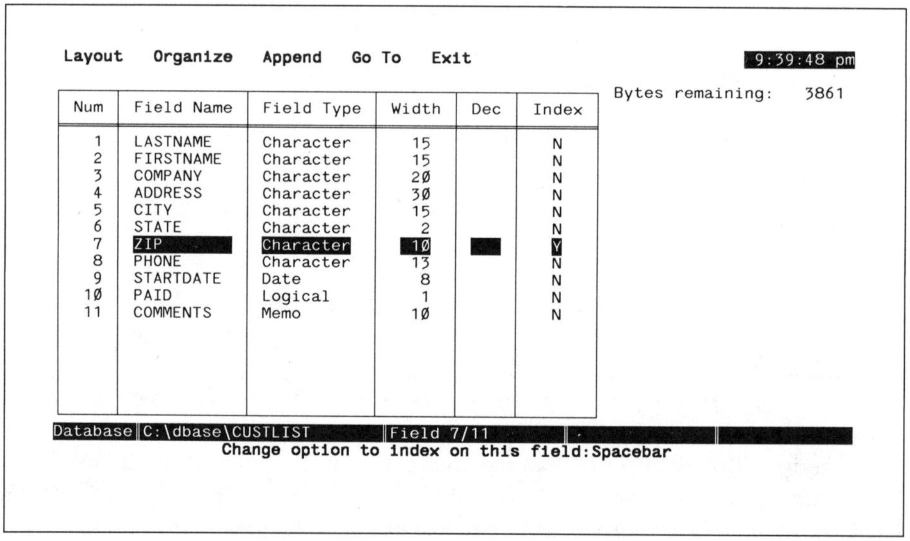

FIGURE 4.2: Database design screen with the ZIP field marked for indexing (that is, with *Y* in the Index column).

index that you want to control the sort order and press ↵ to select it. To quickly check the current sort order, press Data (**F2**) to go to the edit or browse screen.

The sort order is best viewed on the browse screen. If the edit screen appears instead, press Data (**F2**) again to switch to the browse screen. If necessary, press **Ctrl-PgUp** to scroll up to the first record.

To select a different sort order, press **Shift-F2** to get back to the database design screen and then select Order Records by Index from the Organize menu again and repeat the general procedure for selecting an index. (Using the Data (**F2**) and Design (**Shift-F2**) keys, you can switch back and forth between the database design screen and browse screen as often as you wish.)

EXAMPLE

To select the ZIP index for the CUSTLIST database as the master, first go to the database design screen by highlighting CUSTLIST in the Data panel and pressing Design (**Shift-F2**). Highlight Order Records by Index and press ↵. A submenu with a list of existing index options appears. Highlight ZIP and press ↵ to select that index. Then press Data (**F2**) to see the database sorted into ascending order, from lowest to highest zip code, as shown in Figure 4.3.

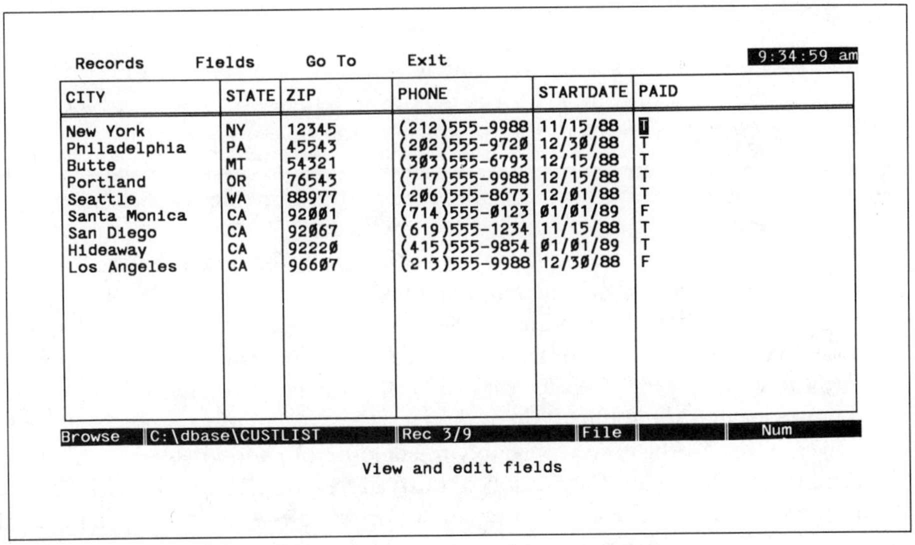

```
  Records      Fields      Go To     Exit                              9:34:59 am
 ┌─────────────┬──────┬──────┬──────────────┬───────────┬──────┐
 │ CITY        │STATE │ZIP   │ PHONE        │ STARTDATE │PAID  │
 ├─────────────┼──────┼──────┼──────────────┼───────────┼──────┤
 │ New York    │ NY   │12345 │(212)555-9988 │ 11/15/88  │ T    │
 │ Philadelphia│ PA   │45543 │(202)555-9720 │ 12/30/88  │ T    │
 │ Butte       │ MT   │54321 │(303)555-6793 │ 12/15/88  │ T    │
 │ Portland    │ OR   │76543 │(717)555-9988 │ 12/15/88  │ T    │
 │ Seattle     │ WA   │88977 │(206)555-8673 │ 12/01/88  │ T    │
 │ Santa Monica│ CA   │92001 │(714)555-0123 │ 01/01/89  │ F    │
 │ San Diego   │ CA   │92067 │(619)555-1234 │ 11/15/88  │ T    │
 │ Hideaway    │ CA   │92220 │(415)555-9854 │ 01/01/89  │ T    │
 │ Los Angeles │ CA   │96607 │(213)555-9988 │ 12/30/88  │ F    │
 └─────────────┴──────┴──────┴──────────────┴───────────┴──────┘
 Browse  C:\dbase\CUSTLIST       Rec 3/9       File             Num
                        View and edit fields
```

FIGURE 4.3: If you press Data (**F2**) from the screen in Figure 4.2, you will see the records sorted into zip code order on the browse screen.

Sorting an Index on a Single Field (Second Method)

SEQUENCE OF STEPS

From the Control Center:

>highlight the database name in the Data panel
>Design **(Shift-F2)**
>Organize/**C**reate New Index [↵]
>**N**ame of Index [↵]
>type a name for the index ↵
>**I**ndex Expression [↵]
>type the field name to index on ↵   *or*   **Shift-F1**
>highlight the field name ↵ **O**rder of Index [↵]
>Ascending *or* Descending
>**Ctrl-End**
>Data **(F2)**

USAGE

A second method for sorting on a single field that also uses the index method lets you perform more complex sorts. To use this method, first move the highlight in the Control Center to the database name in the Data panel and press Design (**Shift-F2**). This takes you to the database design screen, where you will see the database structure partially obscured by the Organize pull-down menu. From the Organize menu, select Create New Index.

A submenu appears, asking for information about the index. Select Name of Index by pressing ↵. You can assign any name to the index that you wish, following the same basic guidelines as for creating field names (the name can include up to ten characters, must start with a letter, and can contain no spaces or punctuation). However, to keep track of your indexes, it is advisable to use the field name itself as the name of the index.

Type a name for the index (probably the field name) and press ↵. The highlight moves to the Index Expression option. Here you define the field that the index is to be based on. Select Expression by pressing ↵ and then type the field name to index on and press ↵ again. If you can't remember how a field name is spelled, you can instead press **Shift-F1** to get a list of field names. Highlight the field you want and press ↵. The highlight moves to the Order of Index option, where you can choose either Ascending or Descending by pressing the space bar.

Choosing Ascending orders items from lowest to highest (that is, from A to Z, smallest number to largest number, or earliest date to latest date). Choosing Descending orders records in the opposite sequence. Select a sort order by pressing ← when the order you want is displayed. Then press **Ctrl-End**.

dBASE IV creates the index and shows its progress on the screen briefly. When it is done, the database design screen reappears. Notice that the option in the Index column for the field is changed from N (for no) to Y (for yes), because that field is now indexed.

Pressing Data (**F2**) now immediately displays the records in the new sort order. But remember, in future sessions with dBASE IV, you will need to select this or another index as the master, as described in the preceding section, "Activating the Index."

EXAMPLE

To sort the CUSTLIST database into alphabetical order by last name, highlight CUSTLIST in the Control Center Data panel. Press Design (**Shift-F2**). From the Organize menu select Create New Index.

A submenu appears, asking for information about the index. Select Name of Index by pressing ←. Type **LASTNAME** and press ←. The highlight moves to the Index Expression option. Here you define the field that the index is to be based on. Press ← and either type **LASTNAME** or press **Shift-F1** and highlight the name on the list. Then press ← again.

The highlight moves to the Order of Index option, where you can choose either Ascending or Descending. Leave the option set to Ascending (press the space bar if necessary). Your screen should look like Figure 4.4. Press **Ctrl-End**.

dBASE IV creates the index and shows its progress on the screen briefly. When it is done, the database design screen again appears. Notice that the option in the Index column for the LASTNAME field is changed from N (for no) to Y (for yes), because the LASTNAME field is now indexed.

To view the data in the sorted order, press Data (**F2**). The sort order is best viewed on the browse screen. If the edit screen appears instead, press Data (**F2**) again to switch to the browse screen. If necessary, press **Ctrl-PgUp** to scroll to the first record. You will see the CUSTLIST database sorted into alphabetical order by last name, as shown in Figure 4.5.

PERFORMING INDEX SORTS WITHIN SORTS

SEQUENCE OF STEPS

From the Control Center:

>   highlight the database name in the Data panel

92 ── **CH. 4** SORTING THE DATABASE

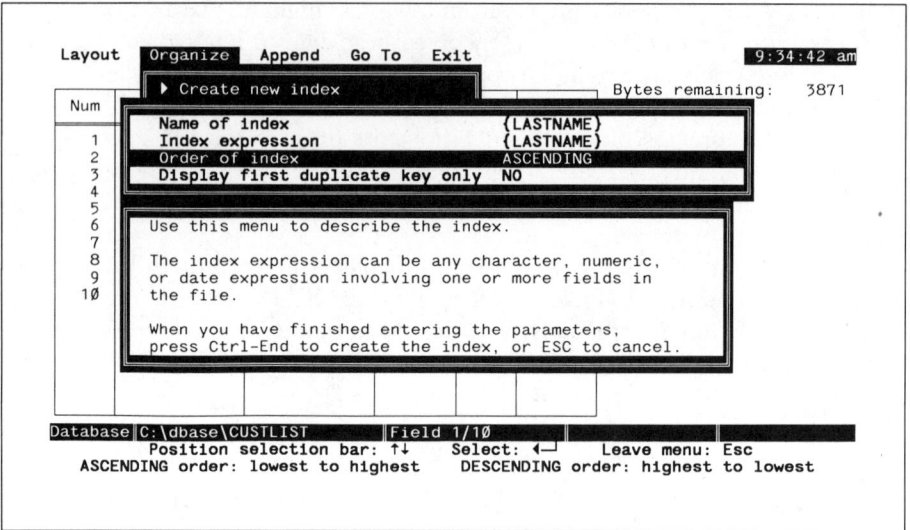

FIGURE 4.4: Creating a new index called LASTNAME that indexes on the LASTNAME field in ascending order. Press *Ctrl-End* to create the index.

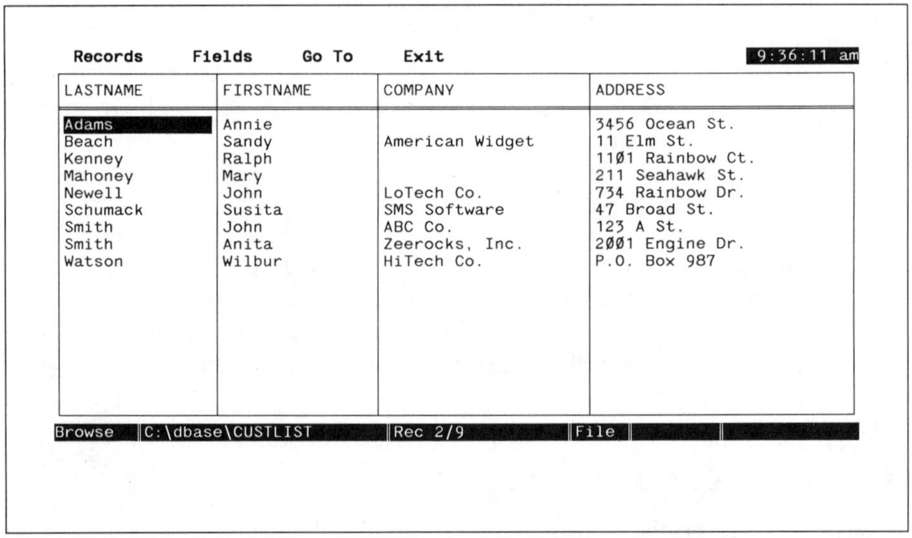

FIGURE 4.5: Records displayed on the browse screen sorted into alphabetical order by last name. Note that the two Smiths are displayed in the order their records were entered.

Design (**Shift-F2**)

Organize/**C**reate New Index

Name of Index [⏎]

type a name for the index ⏎

Index Expression [⏎]

type the index expression   *or*   Pick (**Shift-F1**)/select from the Expression Builder menu

⏎

Ctrl-End

Data (**F2**)

USAGE

Sometimes, sorting a database on a single field is not sufficient. For example, if a database contains people's names divided into two fields called LASTNAME and FIRSTNAME, a sort based on the LASTNAME field alone might place a name such as John Smith before Anita Smith. In a small database this does not create a problem, but if the database contained several hundred Smiths, you would be hard pressed to find John Smith's record if all the Smiths were in random first-name order. (In fact, the sort order in these cases is based on the order of data entry.)

The ideal way to sort people's names is not simply by last name, but by first name within last name, as the telephone book does:

Smith	Anita
Smith	Barbara
Smith	Carla
Smith	Charles
Smith	John
Smith	Karen

To sort database records into this kind of an order, you use an *index expression* that lists the fields to sort on. You list the fields in order of priority, with a plus sign between each field name.

Index Expressions

A sort within a sort uses an *index expression*. Although dBASE IV expressions are usually formulas, such as 1 + 1 or LASTNAME + FIRSTNAME, an index expression can be a single field name, such as DATEPAID or ZIP. You can create an index expression by typing it when prompted, or you can use the dBASE IV *Expression Builder* to create it.

The Expression Builder menu is shown in Figure 4.6. It is available whenever you see the message *Expression Builder: Shift-F1* on the navigation line, which appears whenever you select Index Expression.

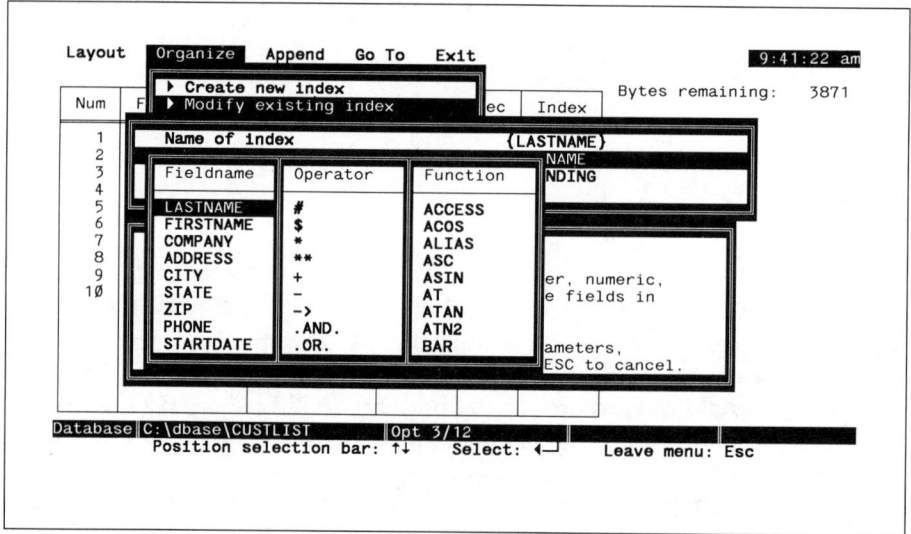

FIGURE 4.6: The Expression Builder menu, from which you can select field names, operators, and functions to include in your index expressions. Use the arrow keys to move around the menu. Press ⏎ to select the highlighted item for inclusion in your index expression.

To sort records into alphabetical order by LASTNAME, with names alphabetized by FIRSTNAME within identical last names, you use the index expression LASTNAME + FIRSTNAME. If this database included a field for middle initials, named MI, you could use the index expression LASTNAME + FIRSTNAME + MI to sort the database into last-name order, with names alphabetized by first name and then middle initial within identical last names (for example, Smith, John A., would precede Smith, John B.).

In the example LASTNAME + FIRSTNAME, where records are sorted first by last name and then by first name within identical last names, LASTNAME is called the *primary* index field, and FIRSTNAME is called the *secondary* index field. (A third field after FIRSTNAME would be called a tertiary index field, and so on.) The + sign is a dBASE *operator* that you use to combine two or more fields in an index expression.

You need to follow a few basic rules when building index expressions. First, you cannot index on Memo fields (but you can search them with queries; see Chapter 5). Second, you can use the + key by itself only to join fields that use the Character data type. For example, the index expression STATE+CITY+ LASTNAME+FIRSTNAME is acceptable because all four fields use the Character data type. (The resulting sort order would show records alphabetized by state; within each state, records would be alphabetized by city; and within each city, records would be alphabetized by last and then first name.)

EXAMPLE

You can create an index of the CUSTLIST database with a primary sort on the LASTNAME field and a secondary sort on the FIRSTNAME field. We will name the index FIRSTNAME. This example also demonstrates using the Expression Builder.

From the Control Center, highlight CUSTLIST in the Data panel and press Design (**Shift-F2**) to get to the database design screen. Press ↵ to select Create New Index from the Organize menu. Press ↵ to select Name of Index. Type **FIRSTNAME** and press ↵. The highlight moves to the line for entering the Index Expression. Press ↵ to select it.

Press **Shift-F1** to call up the Expression Builder. Highlight **LASTNAME** and press ↵ to select it; LASTNAME appears on the Index Expression line. Press **Shift-F1** again. Use → and ↓ to highlight the + operator and press ↵ to select it. The Index Expression now reads LASTNAME+. Press Pick (**Shift-F1**) again to bring back the Expression Builder menu. Use ← and ↓ to highlight FIRSTNAME and press ↵ to select it. The index expression now reads LASTNAME+FIRSTNAME. Press ↵ to indicate that the expression is complete. Press ↵ again to accept Ascending as the sort order and **Ctrl-End** to create the index. Press Data (**F2**) to view the records in order. Anita Smith now comes before John Smith.

Indexing Fields of Various Data Types

You cannot directly mix data types in index expressions. For example, although STARTDATE can be used as an index field to display the records in date order, the index expression STARTDATE+LASTNAME+FIRSTNAME is invalid, because STARTDATE uses the Date data type and therefore cannot be mixed directly with the LASTNAME and FIRSTNAME Character fields. However, there are ways to get around these limitations.

To mix fields of various data types in an index expression, you can use dBASE *conversion functions* to change non-Character data to the Character data type. The

DTOS( ) (date to string) function converts the Date data type to the Character data type, in the format *yyyymmdd* (for example, it converts 12/31/90 to 19901231). You need to convert the data type only within the index, not in the actual database. So to sort records by last name and by date within each last name, you enter the index expression **LASTNAME + DTOS(STARTDATE)**. To sort records into date order and by last and first names within each date, you enter the index expression **DTOS(STARTDATE) + LASTNAME + FIRSTNAME**.

The STR( ) (string) function converts Numeric and Float data to the Character data type. Within the STR( ) function, you define the width and number of decimal places for the number. (If you do not define these, dBASE assumes a width of 10, with no decimal places.) It is advisable to use the same width and number of decimal places as you defined in the database structure.

Suppose you want to sort the ORDERS database, shown in Figure 4.7, by part number and then by quantity within each part number. You cannot use the index expression PARTNO + QTY because PARTNO uses the Character data type and QTY uses the Numeric data type. Instead, you enter the index expression **PARTNO + STR(QTY,3)**, where 3 is the width of the QTY field. Similarly, if you want to sort the records by part number and by unit price within each part number, you enter the index expression **PARTNO + STR(UNITPRICE,9,2)** when creating the index at the database design screen. In this expression, 9 is the width of the UNITPRICE field and 2 is the number of decimal places in UNITPRICE.

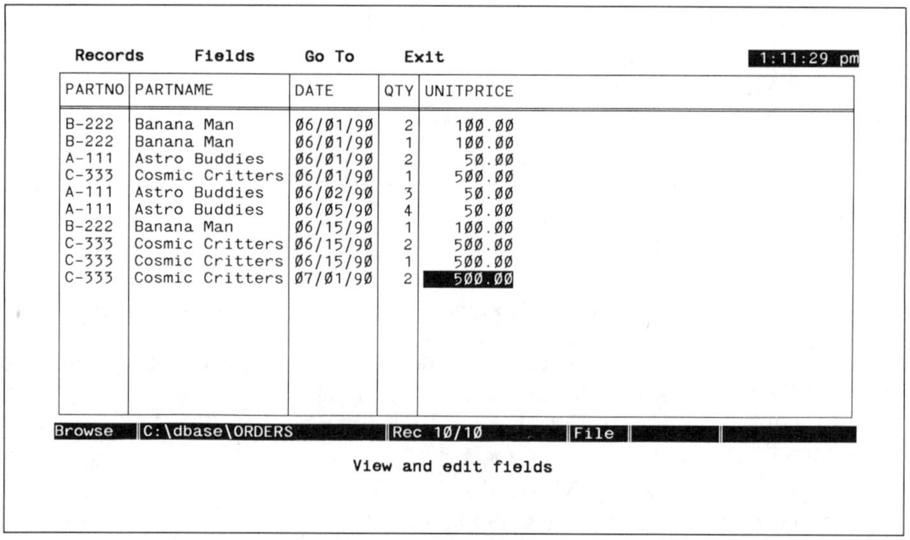

```
    Records     Fields     Go To     Exit                    1:11:29 pm
   ┌──────┬───────────────┬────────┬───┬─────────┐
   │PARTNO│PARTNAME       │DATE    │QTY│UNITPRICE│
   ├──────┼───────────────┼────────┼───┼─────────┤
   │B-222 │Banana Man     │06/01/90│ 2 │  100.00 │
   │B-222 │Banana Man     │06/01/90│ 1 │  100.00 │
   │A-111 │Astro Buddies  │06/01/90│ 2 │   50.00 │
   │C-333 │Cosmic Critters│06/01/90│ 1 │  500.00 │
   │A-111 │Astro Buddies  │06/02/90│ 3 │   50.00 │
   │A-111 │Astro Buddies  │06/05/90│ 4 │   50.00 │
   │B-222 │Banana Man     │06/15/90│ 1 │  100.00 │
   │C-333 │Cosmic Critters│06/15/90│ 2 │  500.00 │
   │C-333 │Cosmic Critters│06/15/90│ 1 │  500.00 │
   │C-333 │Cosmic Critters│07/01/90│ 2 │  500.00 │
   └──────┴───────────────┴────────┴───┴─────────┘
   Browse │C:\dbase\ORDERS     │Rec 10/10     │File
                     View and edit fields
```

FIGURE 4.7: Sample data for the ORDERS database displayed on the browse screen. If you enter this data, you can use the ORDERS database to try out many of the examples in this book.

If you are combining both dates and numbers in an index expression, you need to convert both to the Character data type. For example, to sort records in the ORDERS database in date order and then by quantity within each date, you enter the index expression **DTOS(DATE) + STR(QTY,3)**. Suppose you want to sort the records by date, by part number within each date, and then by quantity within each part number. To do so, you enter the index expression **DTOS(DATE) + PARTNO + STR(QTY,3)**.

Note that you can also convert the data in Logical fields to Character data, using the IIF( ) function, so that you can index on Logical fields as well. The technique for using IIF( ) is presented in Chapter 18. All of the dBASE functions are summarized in Appendix D.

When you use a field name as part of an index expression rather than as the sole field for the index, dBASE does not mark the field as Y, for indexed, in the Index column on the database design screen.

Performing Sorts within Sorts with Numbers

If you want to combine numbers in an index to obtain a sort within a sort, convert both numeric fields to the Character data type. Otherwise, the index will contain the sum of the two numeric fields—that is, the result of a calculation—rather than a combination of the two fields.

For example, suppose you had a database with the following floor numbers and office numbers stored in two fields named FLOOR and ROOM:

FLOOR	ROOM
1	1
1	2
1	3
1	4
2	1
2	2
2	3

If you created an index based on the expression **FLOOR + ROOM**, the index would contain the *sums* of the room and floor numbers and would therefore display the floor and room numbers in the order shown here:

ROOM + FLOOR	FLOOR	ROOM
2	1	1
3	1	2

3	2	1
4	1	3
4	2	2
5	1	4
5	2	3

To obtain a correct sort-within-a-sort order, you must convert both numeric fields to character strings using the index expression **STR(FLOOR,1,0) + STR(ROOM,1,0)**. The resulting index would contain character strings that combine the numeric digits (shown in quotation marks) and would produce the appropriate sort order, as shown here:

STR(FLOOR,1,0) + STR(FLOOR,1,0)	FLOOR	ROOM
"11"	1	1
"12"	1	2
"13"	1	3
"14"	1	4
"21"	2	1
"22"	2	2
"23"	2	3

Modifying an Existing Index

SEQUENCE OF STEPS

From the Control Center:

>highlight the database name in the Data panel
>Design (**Shift-F2**)
>Organize/**M**odify Existing Index [◄┘]
>highlight the index name ◄┘
>select modification option ◄┘
>specify change
>**Ctrl-End**

USAGE

Sometimes after creating an index you discover that you need to change it in some way. The Organize menu's Modify Existing Index submenu offers the

MODIFYING AN EXISTING INDEX — 99

same four options as the Create New Index submenu:

- Name of Index
- Index Expression
- Order of Index
- Display First Duplicate Key Only

The last option allows you to instruct dBASE to display only the first record that matches your index expression if there are duplicates. For example, a LASTNAME + ADDRESS expression would find any two family members at the same address, and you might not want to send them both the same mailing.

To use this submenu, first highlight the database name in the Control Center's Data panel, press Design (**Shift-F2**), pull down the Organize menu and select Modify Existing Index. You'll see a list of the active index names. The highlighted name will be accompanied by its index expression. Highlight the index you want to modify and press ↵. The submenu appears and you can make your changes. Press **Ctrl-End** when you are finished.

EXAMPLE

Suppose that you have created an index of the CUSTLIST database on the LASTNAME field, following the example in the section "An Index Sort on a Single Field (Second Method)" earlier in this chapter. You now decide to modify the index, which you named LASTNAME, to include a secondary sort on the FIRSTNAME field.

From the Control Center, highlight CUSTLIST in the Data panel and press Design (**Shift-F2**) to go to the database design screen. Type **M** for Modify Existing Index from the Organize menu. Use the arrow keys, as necessary, and press ↵ to select LASTNAME as the index to modify. Press ↓ to highlight Index Expression and ↵ to select it.

Press Pick (**Shift-F1**) to call up the Expression Builder menu. Press → once and ↓ four times to highlight the + operator. Press ↵ to select it. Press Pick (**Shift-F1**) again to bring back the Expression Builder menu. Press ← once and ↓ once to highlight FIRSTNAME. Press ↵ to select it. The index expression now reads *LASTNAME + FIRSTNAME*. Press ↵ to complete the change.

To change the name, select Name of Index and backspace over the existing name. Type **NAMES** as the new name. Press ↵ and then **Ctrl-End**.

To view the results of the new index expression, press the Data (**F2**) key. If the edit screen appears, press **F2** to switch to the browse screen. Press the **Home** and **Ctrl-PgUp** keys to scroll to the upper-left corner of the database. (Remember, to use this new index in future sessions of dBASE, you need to make it the master index using the technique described in the section "Activating the Index" earlier in this chapter.)

Controlling Uppercase/Lowercase Distinctions

Indexes use the ASCII sorting method, in which all lowercase letters are considered to be "larger" than all uppercase letters. Hence, an index of the LASTNAME field puts a name such as van der Pool after Zastrow in a sort order.

To get around this problem, you can convert all values in a Character field to uppercase using the UPPER( ) function in the index expression. For example, the index expression **UPPER(LASTNAME)** creates the following sort order (even though the names in the actual database are stored with both uppercase and lowercase letters):

ADAMS
BAKER
CARLSON
MILLER
VAN DER POOL
WILSON
ZASTROW

Remember that only the index contains words converted to uppercase; the names in the actual database are still in their original format. If you want to combine first and last names in the sort order, place the index expression in the UPPER( ) function, like this: **UPPER(LASTNAME + FIRSTNAME)**.

Combining Ascending and Descending Sort Orders

Whenever you create an index by the second method presented earlier in this chapter, dBASE lets you specify the entire sort in either ascending or descending order. In some situations, you might want to combine ascending and descending sort orders. For example, suppose you want to display records from the ORDERS database shown in Figure 4.7 in *ascending* part number order, but in *descending* quantity order (largest to smallest) within each part number, like this:

A-111	4
A-111	3
A-111	2
B-222	2
B-222	1
B-222	1

COMBINING ASCENDING AND DESCENDING SORT ORDERS

```
C-333    3
C-333    2
C-333    1
```

You need to index on the *inverse* of the quantity by subtracting each quantity from the largest possible quantity.

The structure for the ORDERS database is shown in Figure 4.8. Notice that the QTY field has a width of 3, with no decimal places, so the largest possible number in QTY is 999. Because you are combining this value with PARTNO, the result has to be converted to the Character data type. Hence, the appropriate index expression is **PARTNO + STR(999 − QTY,3)**. (You still select Ascending as the overall sort direction, to make sure the part numbers are in ascending order.)

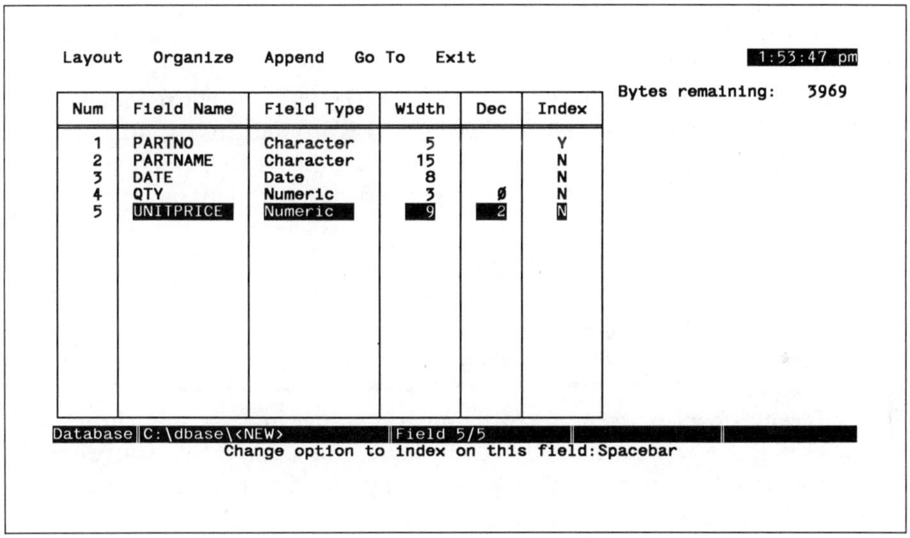

```
 Layout   Organize   Append   Go To   Exit              1:53:47 pm

                                                Bytes remaining:  3969
 ┌─────┬────────────┬────────────┬───────┬─────┬───────┐
 │ Num │ Field Name │ Field Type │ Width │ Dec │ Index │
 ├─────┼────────────┼────────────┼───────┼─────┼───────┤
 │  1  │ PARTNO     │ Character  │   5   │     │   Y   │
 │  2  │ PARTNAME   │ Character  │  15   │     │   N   │
 │  3  │ DATE       │ Date       │   8   │     │   N   │
 │  4  │ QTY        │ Numeric    │   3   │  0  │   N   │
 │  5  │ UNITPRICE  │ Numeric    │   9   │  2  │   N   │
 └─────┴────────────┴────────────┴───────┴─────┴───────┘

 Database │C:\dbase\<NEW>          │Field 5/5│
          Change option to index on this field:Spacebar
```

FIGURE 4.8: The structure of the ORDERS database defined on the database design screen. If you create the ORDERS database, you can use it for many of the examples in this book.

The UNITPRICE field has a width of 9 and two decimal places. Hence, the largest possible number in the UNITPRICE field is 999999.99. Therefore, to display the unit price field in descending order within an ascending index, you invert the unit prices with the basic formula **999999.99 − UNITPRICE**. To convert this to a Character string, use the STR function with a width of 9 and two decimal places, like this: **STR(999999.99 − UNITPRICE,9,2)**.

You can reverse the order of dates within an ascending index order by subtracting each date from the latest possible date in the field. For example, suppose you want to list records in ascending part number order, but in descending order by date, as follows:

A-111	07/01/90
A-111	06/15/90
A-111	06/01/90
B-222	07/01/90
B-222	06/15/90
B-222	06/14/90
C-333	06/15/90
C-333	06/10/90
C-333	06/01/90

Assuming that the latest possible date is 12/31/1999, the entire index expression is **PARTNO + STR({12/31/99} – DATE)**—again using an ascending order for the overall index. Note that, in this case, the STR( ) function is used to convert the numeric result of subtracting two dates to the Character data type.

There is no reliable technique for inverting Character data. For example, you cannot subtract people's last names from ZZZZZZ to invert the sort order. To display records in descending order in a Character field, you must select Descending as the overall sort order for the index.

An inverted Numeric or Date field is always displayed in the opposite order of the overall index. That is, the expression **PARTNO + STR(999 – QTY,3)** displays part numbers in ascending order and quantities in descending order when the overall index order is ascending. However, this same index expression displays part numbers in descending order and quantities in *ascending* order when the overall sort order is descending.

EFFECTS OF INDEXES ON EDITING

Whenever you change the contents of a database record, the change is not made permanent until you move to another record. You can undo changes to a record so long as the cursor is still on that record. Re-sorting is based on a similar principle. dBASE does not re-sort the database according to existing indexes until you move to a new record.

Suppose you are working on the browse screen and you change somebody's last name (suppose you change the name Adams to Zastrow, for example). With an existing index on the LASTNAME field, dBASE re-sorts the database to put Zastrow in its proper alphabetical position as soon as you move the highlight to a new record, thereby completing the edit. After you scroll down and back up, you will see the display re-sorted.

Note that the Records pull-down menu on both the edit and browse screens provides the option Follow Records to New Position. When left at its default setting, Yes, the cursor automatically follows a modified record to its new position in the database when you make a change. If you change this option to No, dBASE still re-sorts a changed record into its proper position in the database, but the highlight does not follow the record to its new position.

MAKING A SORTED COPY OF A DATABASE

SEQUENCE OF STEPS

From the Control Center:

    highlight the database name in the Data panel
    Design (**Shift-F2**)
    Organize/**S**ort Database on Field List [↵]
    Pick (**Shift-F1**)
    highlight the field name to sort on ↵
    ↵
    highlight the type of sort ↵
    Ctrl-End
    Type a name for the sorted database ↵

To return to the Control Center:

    Menus (**F10**)
    Exit/**S**ave Changes and Exit [↵]

Besides indexing a database file, dBASE IV offers *sorting* as an alternative method of displaying data in sorted order. However, sorting is generally slower and less efficient than indexing. Another important difference between indexing and sorting is that when sorting, dBASE always makes a copy of the database (which could cause a problem if the database is large and storage space is limited). The new copy has the new file name you provide. The original database remains unsorted, and the new database contains the same information in the sort order you specify.

The four available sort orders are listed, with examples, in Table 4.1. The basic difference between the dictionary technique and the ASCII technique is that an ASCII sort considers uppercase letters "smaller" than lowercase letters. For example, an ASCII sort places Zeppo before aardvark in an ascending sort. (Indexes use the ASCII technique to display sort orders. Unless you convert lowercase letters to uppercase with the UPPER( ) function, as discussed earlier in this chapter, an index of names places names beginning with lowercase letters—for example, van der Pool—at the end of the list—for example, after Zeppo.)

ORDER	EXAMPLE SORT
Ascending ASCII (0..9, A..Z, a..Z)	123 999 Albert Zeppo van der Pool
Descending ASCII (z..a, Z..A, 9..0)	van der Pool Zeppo Albert 999 123
Ascending Dictionary (0..9, Aa..Zz)	123 999 Albert van der Pool Zeppo
Descending Dictionary (Zz..Aa, 9..0)	Zeppo van der Pool Albert 999 123

Table 4.1: Options for Sorting a Database

Both ASCII and dictionary sorts consider numeric characters to be "smaller" than alphabetic characters. Therefore, if you sort a list of addresses in ascending order, all addresses beginning with numbers (for example, 123 A St. to 999 Z St.) will be listed before addresses beginning with letters (for example, P.O. Box 2802).

If you are sorting a Character field that does not use consistent capitalization, you should use the dictionary technique. If you are sorting any other data type, you can use an ASCII sort instead.

To make a sorted copy of a database from the Control Center, first highlight the database name in the Data panel and press Design (**Shift-F2**) to display the database design screen. Type **S** for Sort Database on Field List from the Organize menu. Press Pick (**Shift-F1**) to see a list of valid field names. Type ↓, as necessary, to highlight the field name to sort on and press ← to select it. Press ← again to complete the entry.

After you choose a field to sort on, the highlight moves down to let you put more fields into the sort. These are sort-within-a-sort fields, as discussed under indexing. For example, selecting LASTNAME as the first sort field and FIRSTNAME as the second sort field sorts the records in the same way as the index expression LASTNAME + FIRSTNAME.

In the Type of Sort column, you can select from the sorts listed in Table 4.1. Press the **space bar** to display the various sorts and press ← to select the one you want. Press **Ctrl-End**.

dBASE prompts *Enter name of sorted file*. You can enter any valid file name (eight characters maximum length, with no spaces or punctuation). Type a name for the sorted database and press ←. dBASE creates the new database, showing its progress briefly on the screen. To return to the Control Center, press Menus (**F10**) to access the pull-down menus and highlight **Exit**. Press ←.

EXAMPLE

To make a sorted copy of the CUSTLIST database from the Control Center, first highlight CUSTLIST in the Data panel. Press Design (**Shift-F2**) to display the database design screen with the Organize menu pulled down. Type **S** to select Sort Database on Field List from the Organize menu. Press Pick (**Shift-F1**) to see a list of valid field names. Type ↓ six times to highlight STARTDATE as the field name to sort on and press ← to select it. Press ← again to complete the entry.

In the Type of Sort column, press the space bar once to display Descending ASCII and press ← to select it. Then press **Ctrl-End**.

dBASE prompts *Enter name of sorted file*. Type **DATEORD** and press ←. dBASE creates DATEORD, showing its progress briefly on the screen. To return to the Control Center, press Menus (**F10**) to access the pull-down menus. Highlight Exit and press ←.

If you press Data (**F2**) and **End** after sorting the CUSTLIST database to scroll to the STARTDATE field on the browse screen, you will see that the records are *not* sorted into date order. This is because the sorted records are in the database file named DATEORD; the original database (CUSTLIST) has not been sorted.

Viewing the Sorted Copy

The new database file is listed in the Control Center Data panel. To view the sorted copy, highlight the new database name and press Data (**F2**). Scroll the browse screen to see all the fields under the new sort. Press Menus (**F10**) and select Exit to return to the Control Center.

EXAMPLE

The new DATEORD database file is listed in the Control Center Data panel, as shown in Figure 4.9. Figure 4.10 shows the DATEORD database on the browse screen with the records in descending date order (from January 1, 1989, to November 15, 1988).

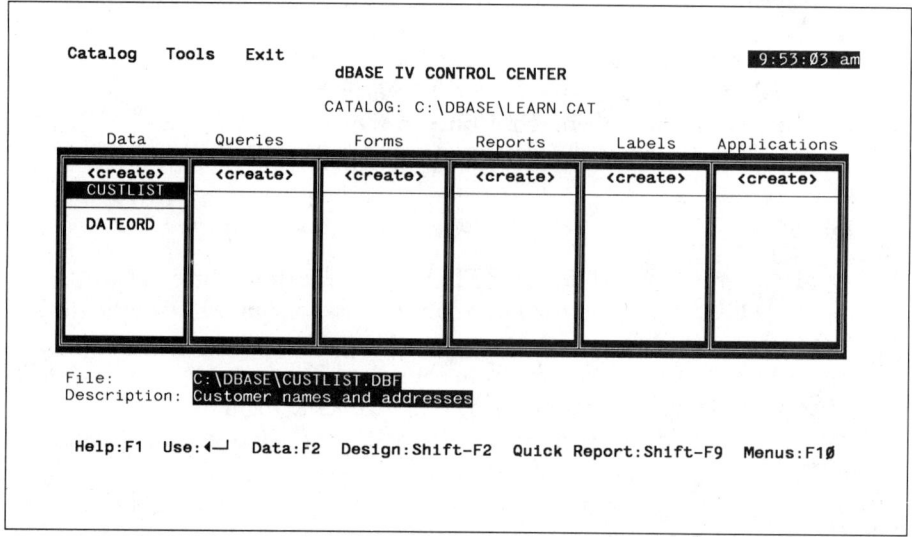

FIGURE 4.9: A new database named DATEORD displayed in the Control Center Data panel. If you follow the example for creating a sorted copy of a database, you will create DATEORD from ORDERS.

Deleting the Sorted Copy

SEQUENCE OF STEPS

From the Control Center:

    highlight the sorted database name in the Data panel ↵

    Close File [↵]

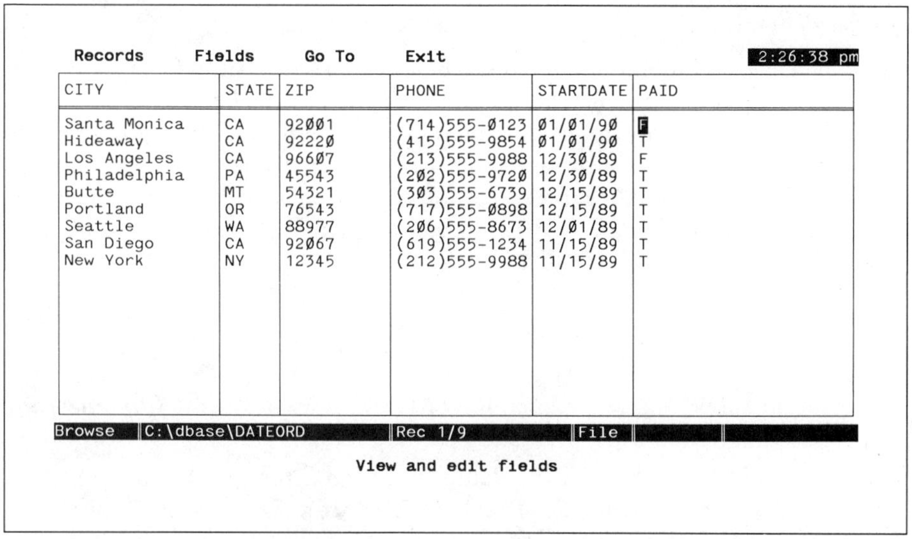

```
  Records    Fields    Go To    Exit                          2:26:38 pm
 CITY          STATE ZIP     PHONE         STARTDATE PAID
 Santa Monica  CA    92001   (714)555-0123 01/01/90  F
 Hideaway      CA    92220   (415)555-9854 01/01/90  T
 Los Angeles   CA    96607   (213)555-9988 12/30/89  F
 Philadelphia  PA    45543   (202)555-9720 12/30/89  T
 Butte         MT    54321   (303)555-6739 12/15/89  T
 Portland      OR    76543   (717)555-0898 12/15/89  T
 Seattle       WA    88977   (206)555-8673 12/01/89  T
 San Diego     CA    92067   (619)555-1234 11/15/89  T
 New York      NY    12345   (212)555-9988 11/15/89  T

 Browse  C:\dbase\DATEORD        Rec 1/9         File
                        View and edit fields
```

FIGURE 4.10: The DATEORD database on the browse screen. Notice that the records are sorted into descending date order.

highlight the sorted database name in the Data panel

Menus (**F10**)

Catalog/**R**emove Highlighted File from Catalog [←]

Y

Y

Whenever you create an index, dBASE automatically manages it for you, updating it when you add, change, or delete information. This is *not* the case for sorted copies of files. Any changes you make to the CUSTLIST database have no effect on the DATEORD database (and vice versa).

Because of this, it is not a good idea to keep sorted copies of database files. You might accidentally use the wrong database file, and your work could quickly become confused.

To delete the sorted database, highlight its name in the Control Center Data panel and press ←. Type **C** for Close File. Highlight the database name in the Data panel once more. Press Menus (**F10**) to pull down the Catalog menu. Type **R** for Remove Highlighted File from Catalog. dBASE prompts: *Are you sure you want to remove this file from the catalog?* Type **Y** for yes. dBASE prompts: *Do you also want to delete this file from the disk?*. Type **Y** for yes. The sorted copy of your database no longer exists, so you cannot confuse it with the original database.

EXAMPLE

To delete DATEORD, highlight DATEORD in the Control Center and press ←┘. Type **C** for Close File. Highlight DATEORD in the Data panel. Press Menus (**F10**) to pull down the Catalog menu. Type **R** for Remove Highlighted File from Catalog. dBASE prompts: *Are you sure you want to remove this file from the catalog?* Type **Y** for yes. dBASE prompts: *Do you also want to delete this file from the disk?*. Type **Y** for yes. DATEORD does not exist anymore, so you need not worry about confusing it with CUSTLIST.

TIPS AND TRAPS

- Remember to select Order Records by Index from the Organize pull-down menu to use a previously created index.
- To quickly move from the database design screen to the browse or edit screen, press Data (**F2**). Press Design (**Shift-F2**) to switch back to the database design screen.
- Do not keep sorted copies of your databases where you could accidentally use them instead of the original database for updating your data. Otherwise, you will have multiple, different versions of your database.

SUMMARY

This chapter discussed the two methods for sorting database files with dBASE IV: creating a sort index and making a sorted copy. It presented the steps required for the index method—creating and then activating the index—and described how to view the various sort orders. Sorts within sorts and the Expression Builder were also discussed, as well as how and when dBASE IV updates its sort indexes.

For information about using indexes for quickly locating data:

- Chapter 5, "Searching the Database"

To find out how to index a Logical field:

- Chapter 11, "Managing Groups of Records"

To see how to use indexes to print subtotals:

- Chapter 6, "Performing Calculations"

For more about using dBASE functions, including the required function syntax:
- Chapter 18, "Introduction to the Programming Language"
- Appendix D, "dBASE IV Functions"

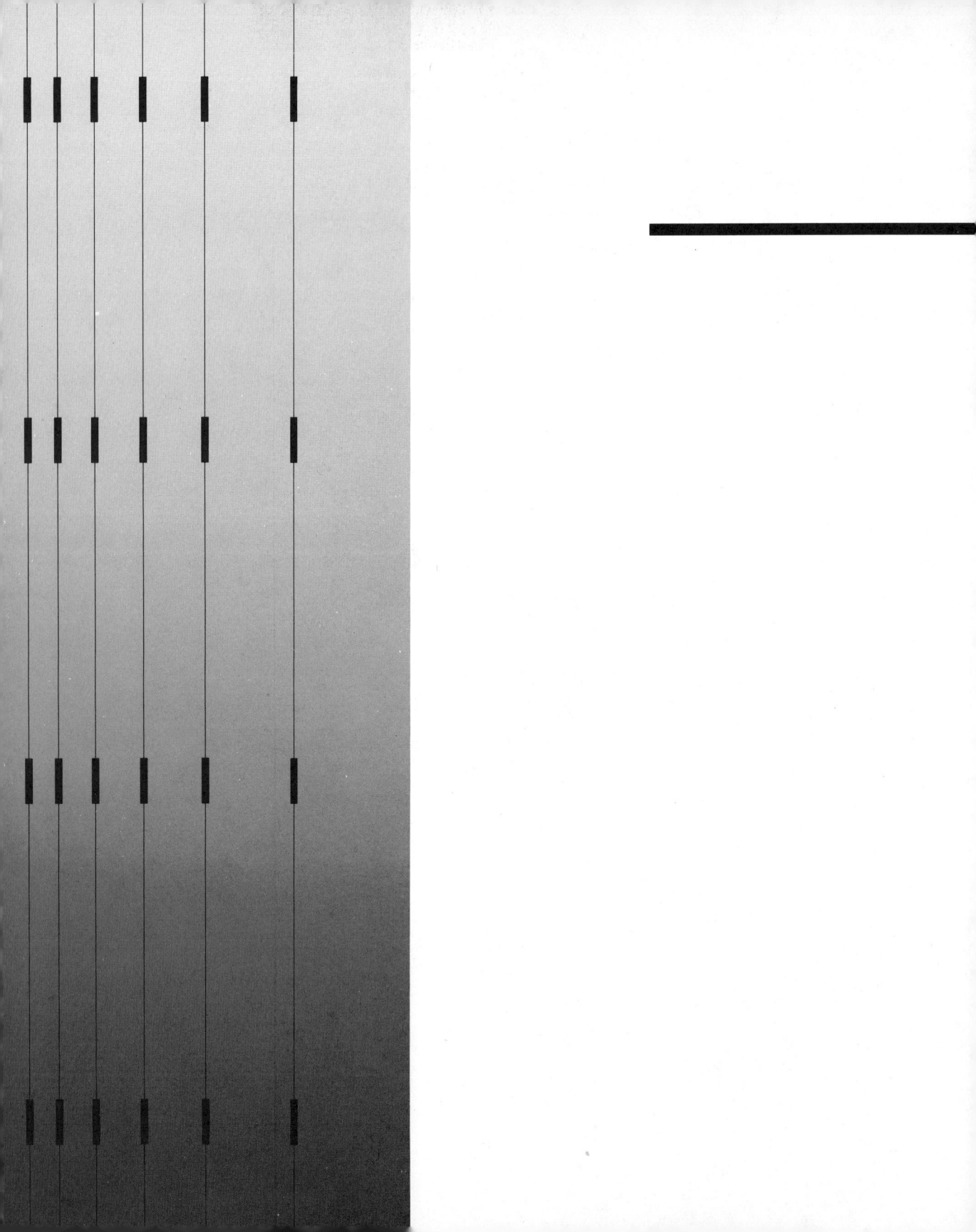

CHAPTER 5

SEARCHING THE DATABASE

Searching for Particular Records. 113
Searching for Specific Information. 114
    Performing Forward Searches. 115
    Performing Backward Searches. 117
    Matching Capitalization. 118
    Using Wildcards in Searches. 118
Using Indexes for Quick Lookups. 119
    Activating the Search Index. 120
    Performing the Search. 121
    Searching Multiple Fields. 122
    Searching Complex Indexes. 122
Using Queries to Isolate Records. 123
    Designing a Query. 125
        The File Skeleton. 125
        The View Skeleton. 126
    Using the Query Design Screen. 126
    Searching for a Value. 127
        Querying Character Fields. 127
        Querying Date Fields. 130
        Querying Logical Fields. 130
    Searching with Operators. 132
        Searching for Near Spellings. 133
        Searching for Patterns. 135
        Searching for Embedded Text. .136
        Searching for Exceptions. 136
    Searching with AND Logic. 137
    Searching with OR Logic. 140
    Searching Multiple Fields. 143
    Searching for Ranges. 144

Creating Complex Queries.	145
Using Condition Boxes.	150
Searching Memo Fields.	151
Sorting the Results of Queries.	151
Sorting to a Separate Database File.	152
Sorting Multiple Fields.	155
Combining Filter and Sort Conditions.	156
Using Indexes to Sort Query Results.	156
Using Complex Indexes.	158
Using Queries to Find a Record.	160
Selecting Fields for Display.	162
Moving Fields in the View Skeleton.	164
Selecting Groups of Fields.	165
Saving a Query.	166
Using Views.	167
Changing a View.	168
Deactivating a View.	169
Options for Using the Queries Panel.	169
Tips and Traps.	169
Summary.	170

Searching the Database

Regardless of the contents or size of your database, dBASE can always help you find the information you need. In some cases, you may simply want to look up a piece of information, such as a person's address and phone number. In other cases, your searches might be more complex, such as for "all customers who live on the West Coast, subscribed before January 1, and still have not paid." This chapter presents the many available techniques for searching your databases.

Searching for Particular Records

Both the browse and edit screen menu bars include an option titled Go To, which performs some simple, basic searches. From the browse or edit screen, press Menus (**F10**) and highlight Go To to see the pull-down menu shown in Figure 5.1.

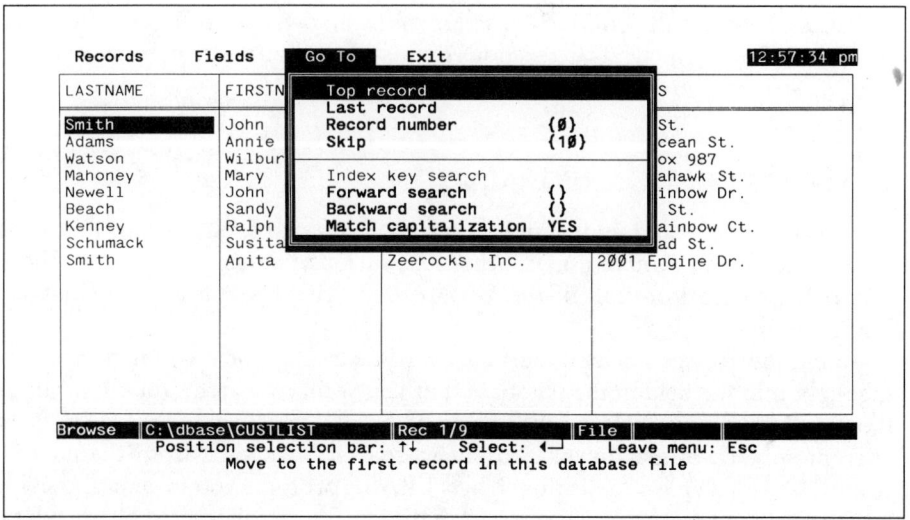

FIGURE 5.1: You can use the Go To pull-down menu to move around the records on the browse screen and to perform basic searches.

The first four Go To options allow you to position the highlight on a particular record on the browse screen (or to display the record on the edit screen) based on the record's position in the database file. Your options are as follows:

Top Record	Highlights or displays the top record
Last Record	Highlights or displays the bottom record
Record Number	Highlights or displays a particular record based on its position in the database
Skip	Highlights or displays a record that is a specified number of records from the current record

If you select Record Number, dBASE asks you to enter a record number. The record number indicates the record's position in the database (not the index order if you are using an index). Type a number between 1 and the total number of records in your database and then press ⏎. The highlight jumps to the appropriate record.

The Skip option moves the highlight a certain number of records up or down in the database. For example, if you select Skip, type **2**, and press ⏎, the highlight (or edit screen) skips forward two records (if possible). If you enter a negative number, such as −**3**, the highlight (or screen) jumps backward three records.

These four searches assume that you know the location of the record you want to access. Basically, they mimic the action of the arrow, **PgUp**, **PgDn**, and other navigation keys. The next two sections discuss the other, more useful options on the Go To menu.

SEARCHING FOR SPECIFIC INFORMATION

In most cases, you do not simply want to go to a particular record in a database. Instead, you want to find information, such as a person's address or phone number. The bottom half of the Go To menu displays options for locating information.

To use the Forward Search and Backward Search options, you first move the highlight into the field in the database that you want to search. You then call up the Go To menu and select either Forward Search, to search forward from the current record, or Backward Search, to search backward from the current record. Once you have made this choice, dBASE prompts you to enter the string (series of characters) it should attempt to find in the specified field of your database. (The Go To menu does not allow you to search for information that spans more than one field. Use the querying techniques discussed later in this chapter for those more complex searches.)

After dBASE finds the first record that matches the search requirement, you can use the Find Next (**Shift-F4**) or Find Previous (**Shift-F3**) key to search forward or backward for other matching records. If no match is found, dBASE displays the message **Not Found** and waits for you to press any key to continue.

When you search a database, dBASE looks for information that exactly matches your request. A record that contains any characters not in your search string is not an exact match, even if your entire string appears in the field. This characteristic can be inconvenient at times. For example, if you are looking for the record of the person who lives at 1101 Rainbow Ct., a search that specifies only **Rainbow** in the address field will not locate the record you want, because the addresses contain the street number as well as the street name. Similarly, if you are searching for a name but are not sure whether it is spelled Smith, Smyth, or Smythe, a search for **Smith** will not locate the other spellings. Techniques for overcoming these problems are presented in the section "Using Wildcards in Searches" later in this chapter.

Performing Forward Searches

SEQUENCE OF STEPS

From the browse screen:

> Menus (**F10**)
> Go To/**T**op Record [↵]
> Menus (**F10**)
> Go To/**F**orward Search [↵]
> type the search string ↵
> Find Next (**Shift-F4**), as necessary

USAGE

On the browse screen, use the **Tab** key to move the highlight to the field you want to search. Press Menus (**F10**) and →, as necessary, to move to the Go To option. To start the search from the beginning of the database file, type **T** to select Top Record. Press Menus (**F10**) again to bring back the Go To menu. Type **F** to select Forward Search.

When dBASE displays the prompt *Enter search string:* type what it is you want to search for and press ↵. (*String* simply means "a string of characters." In this context, a string can be any letter, number, date, or word or group of words; for example, *X* or *123.45* or *12/31/90* or *Smith* or *123 Oak Tree Lane*.)

116 ── **CH. 5** SEARCHING THE DATABASE

The highlight moves to the first record that contains the search string you entered in the field you selected. If this is not the specific record you were looking for and you want to find the next record that matches your search string, press Find Next (**Shift-F4**). The highlight will move to the next matching record.

Press Find Next (**Shift-F4**) as many times as necessary to have dBASE scroll forward in the database to the next matching record. Press the Find Previous key (**Shift-F3**) to move back to the previous matching record.

EXAMPLE

Using the CUSTLIST database (introduced in Chapter 2), press the **Tab** key to move the highlight to the STATE field on the browse screen. (Note that various earlier CUSTLIST examples have added and deleted fields and records. If you have worked through any or all of those examples, the state of your database may differ slightly from that shown here. The differences are not significant.) Press Menus (**F10**) and move to the Go To option. To start from the beginning of the database file, press **T** to select Top Record. Press Menus (**F10**) again to bring back the Go To menu. Type **F** to select Forward Search.

To search for records with CA as the state, when dBASE displays the prompt *Enter search string:* type **CA** as shown in Figure 5.2. Press ↵. The highlight moves to the first record that has CA in the STATE field.

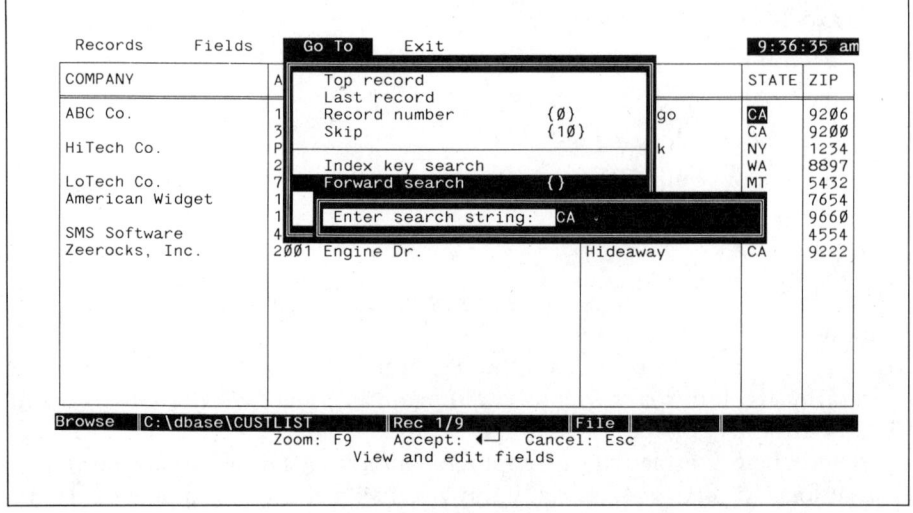

FIGURE 5.2: An example of using the Go To menu. The search string **CA** is used to find records with CA in the STATE field.

Suppose that this is not the specific record you were looking for, and you want to find the next record with CA in the STATE field. Press Find Next (**Shift-F4**). The highlight moves to the next record with CA in the STATE field. Each time you press Find Next (**Shift-F4**), dBASE scrolls forward to the next record in the database that has CA in the STATE field. Each time you press Find Previous (**Shift-F3**), the highlight scrolls back to the previous record with CA in the STATE field.

Performing Backward Searches

SEQUENCE OF STEPS

From the browse screen:

    Menus (**F10**)
    Go To/**L**ast Record [↵]
    Menus (**F10**)
    Go To/**B**ackward Search [↵]
    type the search string ↵
    Find Previous (**Shift-F3**), as necessary

USAGE

The Backward Search option can be handy for making changes after you enter a group of new records. For example, suppose you entered a hundred new records and wanted to double-check one of them. Since new records are always appended (added to the end) of a database file, you will want to begin your search from the bottom.

Move the highlight to the field you want to search. Press Menus (**F10**) and →, as necessary, to highlight Go To. Type **L** to select Last Record. Press Menus (**F10**) again to bring back the Go To menu. Type **B** to select Backward Search. If a previous search value is displayed next to the *Enter search string:* prompt, press **Backspace** a few times to erase it. Enter the string to search for and press ↵.

As with forward searches, during backward searches you can use the Find Next (**Shift-F4**) and Find Previous (**Shift-F3**) keys to find other matching values.

Matching Capitalization

SEQUENCE OF STEPS

From the browse screen:

    Menus (**F10**)
    Go To/Match Capitalization [⏎]
    Yes

USAGE

At the bottom of the Go To pull-down menu is the Match Capitalization option. When you move the highlight to this option and press the space bar, the option setting changes from Yes to No. When Yes is selected, a forward or backward search is *case sensitive*, meaning that the upper- and lowercase letters in the search string must match those in the database. When No is selected, upper- and lowercase distinctions do not matter.

For example, if Match Capitalization is set to No, then a search for SMITH locates Smith, SMITH, or smith. However, if Match Capitalization is set to Yes, then a search for **SMITH** finds only SMITH, not Smith, smith, or SmItH, because the upper- and lowercase letters do not match.

Using Wildcards in Searches

Whenever you type a string to search for, you can include *wildcard characters* to locate record entries that match a pattern. Use the wildcard character ? to match a single character and the wildcard character * to match any group of characters.

For example, searching a name field for **Sm*** would find Smith, Smyth, Smythe, Smartalec, and any other name in the field that begins with the letters *Sm*. A search for **Sm?t*** would locate Smith, Smyth, Smythe, and any other name that has the pattern *Sm* followed by any single letter, followed by a *t* and any number of other letters.

In a Date field, a search for **11/??/89** would locate any record with a date in November 1989. In a field for zip codes, a search for either **92???** or **92*** would locate a zip code beginning with the numbers 92 (that is, any zip code in the range 92000 to 92999). In an address field, a search for ***Rainbow*** would locate any record with the word *Rainbow* in the address (such as 734 Rainbow Dr. and 1101 Rainbow Ct.). In a phone number field, a search for **(213)*** would locate all the records with 213 as the area code.

USING INDEXES FOR QUICK LOOKUPS

When you are working with large databases, you will find that the Forward Search and Backward Search options on the Go To menu are quite slow. As an alternative you can use the Index Key Search option, also on the Go To menu. This option uses an index to search for data and can usually find information in a database of any size in less than a second.

Although index key searches are very fast, they are not as flexible as forward searches and backward searches. You cannot use the Match Capitalization setting with index searches, which work only when upper- and lowercase letters match exactly. A search for **SMITH** would not find Smith, for example. Nor can you use wildcard characters with index searches. A search for **Sm?th** or **Smi*** will not find any matching database records.

When dBASE searches an index, it considers a longer value to match a shorter search value if the first characters of the longer value match all the characters in the search value. For example, an index search for the letters **Sm** will match Smith, Smythe, Smart, or Sm, but not Sampson or Samuels (because these begin with *Sa*, not *Sm*).

Therefore, if you want to search for somebody named Smith, but are not sure if the name is spelled Smith or Smyth, you could just search for **Smith**. When dBASE displays the first last name beginning with the letters *Sm*, you can just use the **PgDn** key (on the edit screen) or ↓ key (on the browse screen) to search through all names that begin with *Sm*.

Because dBASE compares only the leftmost characters in the indexed field to the search value (that is, the same number of characters as in your search string), you cannot search the index for an embedded field. For example, if you created your index with the expression LASTNAME + FIRSTNAME, the index will contain both first- and last-name fields, as follows:

```
"Adams Annie"
"Smith John"
"Beach Sandy"
```

If you tried to use an index search to locate Annie, dBASE would find no match, because none of the example names have "Annie" as the leftmost five characters.

Note that these limitations affect the index-search method only. You can set up a search using multiple fields in a database or characters embedded within fields by using queries (discussed later in this chapter).

Activating the Search Index

SEQUENCE OF STEPS

From the Control Center:

> highlight the database name in the Data panel
> Design (**Shift-F2**)
> Organize/**O**rder Records by Index [↵]
> highlight the index name ↵
> Data (**F2**)

USAGE

To use the Index Key Search option, you need to activate the index that contains the field you want to search. For example, to search a field called LASTNAME using an index, you need to activate an index that uses LASTNAME either as the only key or as the first field in the index expression (such as a LASTNAME + FIRSTNAME index).

To activate an index, first highlight the database name in the Control Center Data panel and press Design (**Shift-F2**). (If an appropriate index does not exist, you can create one using the techniques discussed in Chapter 4.)

From the Organize pull-down menu, type **O** to select Order Records by Index. From the submenu, select the index by highlighting its name and pressing ↵. Now the index is activated, and you can go straight to the edit or browse screen to conduct your search. To do so, press Data (**F2**).

EXAMPLE

Suppose that you want to use an index to search the CUSTLIST database records by people's last names. To do so, you must first activate the existing LASTNAME index. (A LASTNAME index for CUSTLIST was created in an example in Chapter 4.)

If the browse or edit screen is displayed, press **Esc** or select Exit from the Exit pull-down menu to return to the Control Center. With CUSTLIST highlighted in the Data panel, press Design (**Shift-F2**). From the Organize pull-down menu, type **O** to select Order Records by Index. From the submenu, select the LASTNAME index by highlighting LASTNAME and pressing ↵. The index is now activated. You can use either the browse or edit screen for this search. Press Data (**F2**).

Performing the Search

SEQUENCE OF STEPS

From the edit or browse screen:

>Menus (**F10**)
>Go To/Top Record [↵]
>Menus (**F10**)
>Go To/Index Key Search [↵]
>type the search string ↵

To perform the search from the edit (or browse) screen, press Menus (**F10**) and use →, as necessary, to move to the Go To option on the menu bar. Press ↵ (or type **T**) to select Top Record. Record 1 will appear (or the highlight will move to it). To execute the index search, press Menus (**F10**) again, and again move to the Go To menu option. Type **I** to select Index Key Search.

dBASE presents the prompt

>Enter search string for
>*INDEXNAME*

to tell you what field or fields you can currently search.

To find the record you want, type the search string appropriate for the active index (remembering that the search is case sensitive) and then press ↵.

dBASE will immediately locate and display (or highlight) the first record in the database that matches the string you provided. You *cannot* use the Find Next (**Shift-F4**) or Find Previous (**Shift-F3**) key with an index search to scroll through records for other occurrences. However, because the records are presented in order, you can use the **PgDn** and **PgUp** keys to scroll through nearby matching records.

EXAMPLE

For this example, the active index must be NAMES, an index for the CUST-LIST database created in Chapter 4 in the section "Modifying an Existing Index." It uses the expression LASTNAME + FIRSTNAME.

From the edit screen, press Menus (**F10**) and use →, as necessary, to move to the Go To option on the menu bar. Type **T** to select Top Record. Annie Adams's record will appear (because the LASTNAME + FIRSTNAME index sort order is in effect). To execute the index search, press Menus (**F10**) again, and again

move to the Go To menu option. Type **I** to select Index Key Search.
dBASE presents the prompt

> Enter search string for
> LASTNAME + FIRSTNAME:

LASTNAME + FIRSTNAME is the expression for the current index. dBASE displays this to tell you what fields you can currently search.

To find the record for Smith, type **Smith** (using the upper- and lowercase letters shown) and then press ↵. dBASE will immediately locate and display the first record for Smith in the database. Because the index groups all the Smiths together (in alphabetical order), you can use the **PgDn** and **PgUp** keys to scroll through nearby Smith records.

Searching Multiple Fields

If you want to search multiple fields, you can take advantage of the fact that an index field always has the same width as that field in the database structure. For example, in the CUSTLIST database, the LASTNAME field has a width of 15 characters (see the CUSTLIST structure in Chapter 2). Therefore, in the index based on the expression LASTNAME + FIRSTNAME, the LASTNAME field still has a fixed width of 15 characters.

Thus, although a search for

> Smith Anita

will not find a matching record in the database, a search for

> Smith   Anita

with ten spaces between Smith and Anita, *will* find Anita Smith's record. Since Smith is five letters long, the ten blank spaces *pad* the last name to the width of the database field.

As discussed later in this chapter, however, dBASE offers many other ways to search multiple fields, and you may not use this particular method very often.

Searching Complex Indexes

When you are using an index to display records on the browse or edit screen, you can use the Index Key Search option on the Go To menu to quickly look up a value. However, keep in mind that this option searches the *index,* not the actual database file. Therefore, any special techniques that you used in creating the index must also be used in searching the index.

Suppose you have organized records in the ORDERS database (introduced in Chapter 4) into descending DATE order and ascending PARTNO order within each date, using the index expression **STR({12/31/1999} – DATE) + PARTNO**. If you want to search this index for a particular date, you need to convert that date in exactly the same manner as you converted the dates in the index. That is, to search for the first record with 06/01/90 in the date field, you need to enter **STR({12/31/1999} – {06/01/90})** as the Index Key Search value.

Unfortunately, the Index Key Search option may not provide enough space for entering such a large, complex expression. To overcome this problem, you could create one index with the complex expression **STR({12/31/1999} – DATE) + PARTNO** to define a sort order only and another index with the simple field name **DATE** for searching. Then, when searching for dates, you could use the index with the simpler expression so that you would not need to convert the date.

EXAMPLE

Suppose you sorted the CUSTLIST database using the index expression UPPER(LASTNAME + FIRSTNAME) and that index is in effect while you are at the browse screen. You want to quickly locate the first Smith record, so you select Index Key Search from the Go To pull-down menu. dBASE displays the index expression and allows you to type a value to search for.

When you see the expression UPPER(LASTNAME + FIRSTNAME), remember that all the values in the index are in uppercase letters, so you must specify whatever you want to search for in uppercase letters. Therefore, you must enter **SMITH** (as shown in Figure 5.3), rather than **Smith**, to locate the first Smith record.

USING QUERIES TO ISOLATE RECORDS

The searches discussed so far are all alike in one way: They help you *locate* a particular item of information in a database. In some situations, you may instead want to *isolate* or *filter* some type of information. For example, if you want to send a form letter to all California residents in your customer database, you will want to isolate records that have CA in the state field, filtering out all other records.

These kinds of searches are called *queries,* because you query (ask) dBASE for some information, and dBASE answers by displaying only records that meet your requirements. You do not use the Go To pull-down menu to enter queries. Instead, you enter them on the *query design screen,* using the Queries panel in the Control Center.

You can use queries to print mailing labels and form letters, perform calculations, make copies of database files, and simplify editing, as well as for many other tasks. In fact, you will probably find that you use queries more than any other feature of dBASE IV.

When you simply want to view the results of a query, you do not need to save the query to do so. After you view the query on the browse screen, you can just continue working with dBASE.

When you create a query for the purpose of printing a report, mailing labels, and so forth, you need to save the query and give it a name. A saved query is called a *view*, because a query provides a particular view of the data in a database.

Unlike a database file, a view does not actually contain data. Instead, it contains instructions that dBASE IV reads to see how you want to view the data in a database. Therefore, any changes you make to the original database will indeed be reflected in the view the next time you use it.

The reverse is also true: Because the view file shows data that is actually from another database, if you change any data in the view, that change actually occurs in the original database.

The technique that you use to construct a query is called *query by example*, often abbreviated as QBE. In this method, dBASE presents a skeleton of the database file in use, and you give examples of the kinds of information you want dBASE IV to display.

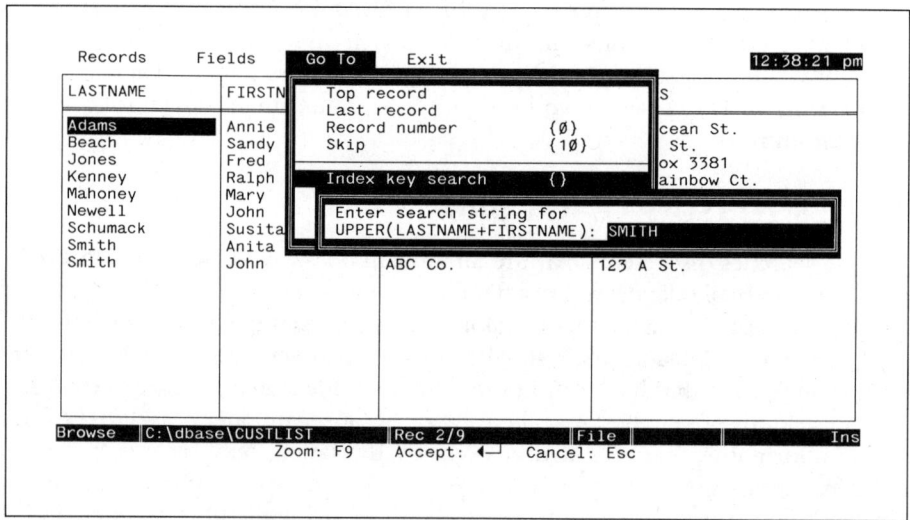

FIGURE 5.3: Using the Index Key Search option on the Go To menu to search for the first Smith record.

Designing a Query

Before you query a database, check to see whether the database is currently *open* (in use). You can easily see if a database file is in use by looking at its position in the Data panel of the Control Center. If the name of the database file appears above the thin line in the panel, the database is open and ready for action. Figure 5.4 indicates that the CUSTLIST database is currently in use.

To design a query for the currently open database file, use the arrow keys to highlight <create> in the Queries panel of the Control Center and press ↵ to select it.

You will find yourself at the query design screen (or *surface*, as it is also called), shown in Figure 5.5. Like other dBASE IV work areas, the query design screen includes a menu bar at the top of the screen and a status bar and navigation line at the bottom. The query design screen also includes a file skeleton and a view skeleton.

THE FILE SKELETON

The file skeleton is near the top of the screen. In the leftmost column is the name of the database file that the skeleton represents (CUSTLIST.DBF in Figure 5.5). The field names in the database are listed in boxes to the right of the database name. You can use the **Home, End, Tab,** and **Shift-Tab** keys to scroll

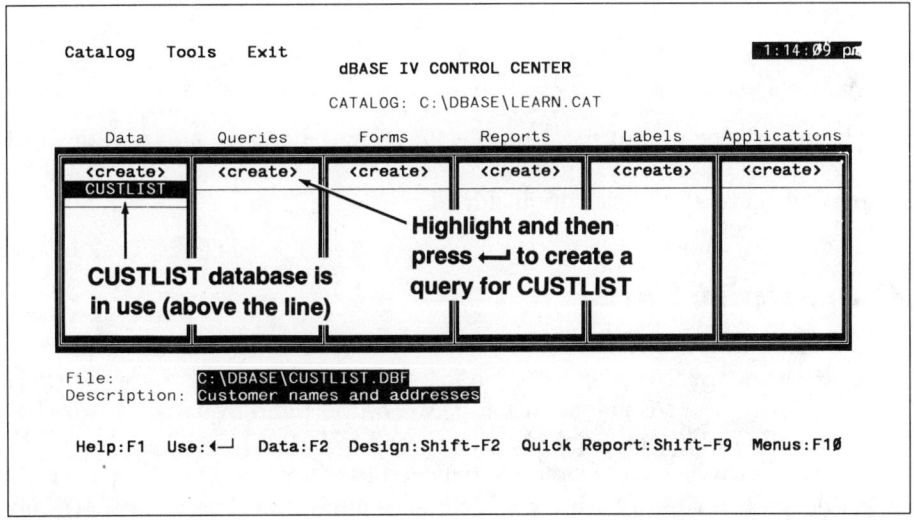

FIGURE 5.4: To access the query design screen, press <create> in the Queries panel when the database is open (that is, active).

126 — CH. 5 SEARCHING THE DATABASE

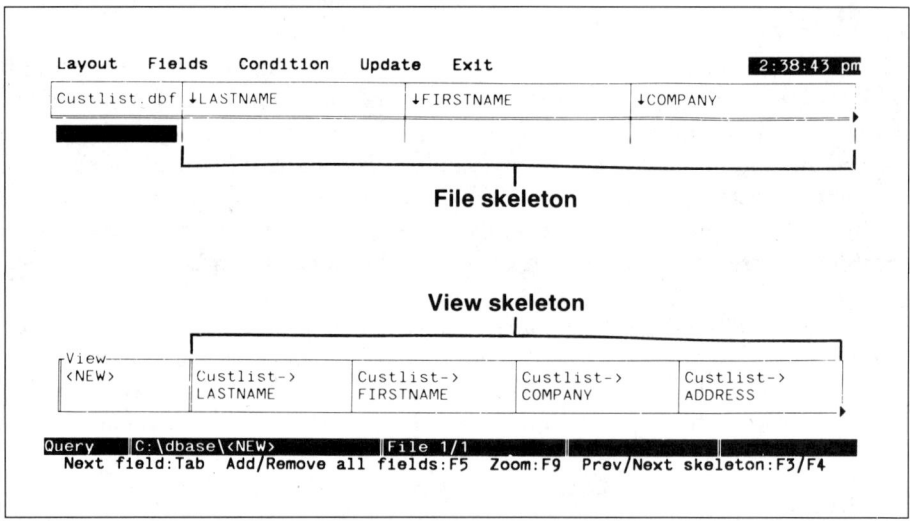

FIGURE 5.5: On the query design screen, dBASE provides a box in the file skeleton and a box in the view skeleton for each of the fields in the database.

left and right through these field names and to view those that are off the right edge of the screen. You use the file skeleton to specify search criteria.

THE VIEW SKELETON

The view skeleton, near the bottom of the screen, shows the names of the fields that the query will display. Initially, the query feature assumes that you want to display all fields, so all fields are included.

Using the Query Design Screen

You can edit information on the query design screen using the same techniques that you use to edit information in a database. Use the arrow keys to position the cursor, the **Ins** key to switch between insert and overwrite modes, the **Backspace** or **Del** key to delete characters, and so forth.

After you have viewed or worked with the results of a query, you can return to the query design screen from the browse or edit screen either by pressing Design (**Shift-F2**) or by selecting Transfer to Query Design from the Exit pull-down menu.

Searching for a Value

SEQUENCE OF STEPS

From the query design screen:

>   highlight the field you want to query
>
>   type the condition you want to find ↵
>
>   Data (**F2**)

To return to the query design screen:

>   Design (**Shift-F2**)

USAGE

To specify which records you want a query to display, you enter *filter conditions* in the file skeleton near the top of the query design screen. You type the filter conditions under the appropriate box. The filter displays only records that have the entry you specify in the field you specify. Press Data (**F2**) to see the results.

A filter condition can be a simple string, a date, or a logical value, as discussed in the following sections. These are simple filter conditions. More complex conditions—involving relational operators, multiple fields, and so forth—are discussed later in the chapter.

QUERYING CHARACTER FIELDS

When you are querying a field that uses the Character data type, you must enclose filter conditions in quotation marks.

To query a Character field, first access the query design screen for the database you are using. On the query design screen, highlight the field you want to query by tabbing to it in the file skeleton. Type the condition you want to find for that field *inside double quotation marks* and press ↵.

To view the results of your query, press Data (**F2**) to switch to the browse screen. dBASE will take a few seconds to complete the filtering. You will see the message *Processing query* . . . .

If the edit screen appears, press Data (**F2**) again. As necessary, press **Tab** until the queried field appears. Only records that match your filter condition will appear. Press Design (**Shift-F2**) to return to the query design screen.

128 — **CH. 5** SEARCHING THE DATABASE

EXAMPLE

Using the CUSTLIST database, create a filter condition for records that have CA in the STATE field. First access the query design screen for the CUSTLIST database.

Press the **Tab** key six times, so that the highlight moves to the STATE field in the file skeleton. Type the condition **"CA"** (including the double quotation marks) and press ←┘. Your screen should look like Figure 5.6. Press Data (**F2**) to see the results of the query (which might take a few seconds to appear).

If the edit screen appears after you press Data (**F2**), press this key again to switch to the browse screen. Press **Tab** a few times until the STATE field appears. This will give you a better view of the query results. As you can see on your screen (and in Figure 5.7), only records that have CA in the state field appear.

You can also isolate records that have Smith in the LASTNAME field. To do so, remove "CA" from the STATE field on the query design screen by using the **Del** (delete) key or by pressing **Ctrl-Y**. Press **Home** and then **Tab** to move the highlight to the LASTNAME field.

Type **"Smith"**, including the quotation marks, and press ←┘. Press Data (**F2**) to see the results of the query. As shown in Figure 5.8, only records that have Smith in the LASTNAME field are displayed.

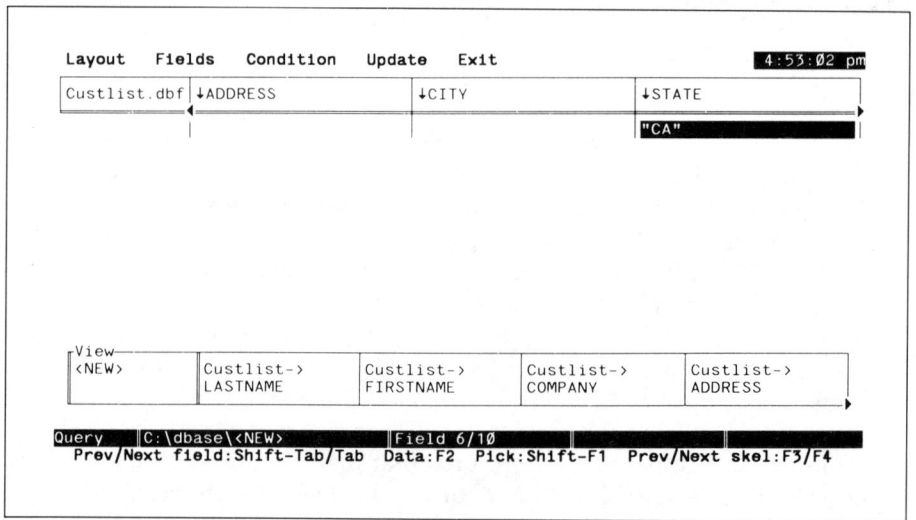

FIGURE 5.6: Using the query design screen to find records with CA in the state field. The search string is enclosed in quotation marks (**"CA"**) because it is a character string.

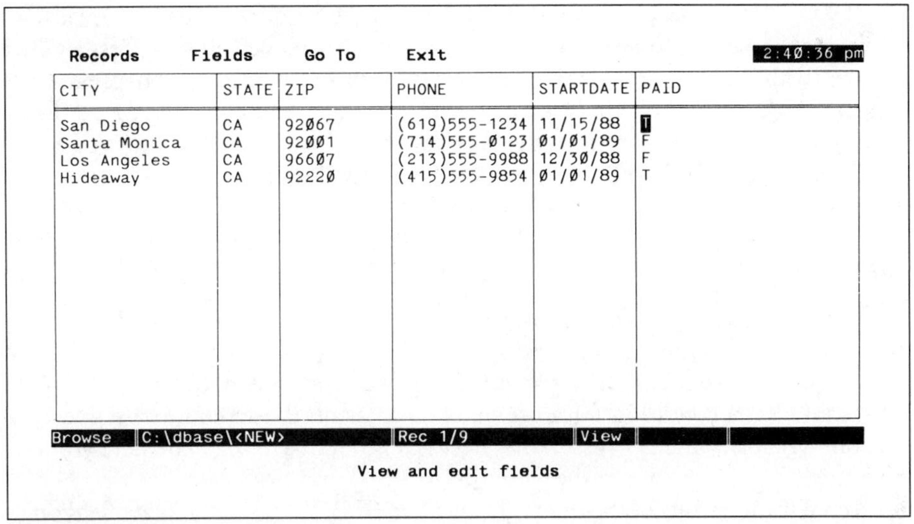

```
    Records    Fields    Go To    Exit                          2:40:36 pm
   ┌─────────────┬──────┬─────┬──────────────┬──────────┬─────┐
   │CITY         │STATE │ZIP  │PHONE         │STARTDATE │PAID │
   ├─────────────┼──────┼─────┼──────────────┼──────────┼─────┤
   │San Diego    │CA    │92067│(619)555-1234 │11/15/88  │ T   │
   │Santa Monica │CA    │92001│(714)555-0123 │01/01/89  │ F   │
   │Los Angeles  │CA    │96607│(213)555-9988 │12/30/88  │ F   │
   │Hideaway     │CA    │92220│(415)555-9854 │01/01/89  │ T   │
   │             │      │     │              │          │     │
   └─────────────┴──────┴─────┴──────────────┴──────────┴─────┘
    Browse    C:\dbase\<NEW>           Rec 1/9       View
                      View and edit fields
```

FIGURE 5.7: Results of the query in Figure 5.6 for records with CA in the STATE field, displayed on the browse screen.

```
    Records    Fields    Go To    Exit                          2:41:13 pm
   ┌──────────────┬───────────────┬──────────────┬──────────────┐
   │LASTNAME      │FIRSTNAME      │COMPANY       │ADDRESS       │
   ├──────────────┼───────────────┼──────────────┼──────────────┤
   │Smith         │John           │ABC Co.       │123 A St.     │
   │Smith         │Anita          │Zeerocks, Inc.│2001 Engine Dr.│
   │              │               │              │              │
   └──────────────┴───────────────┴──────────────┴──────────────┘
    Browse    C:\dbase\<NEW>           Rec 1/9       View
                      View and edit fields
```

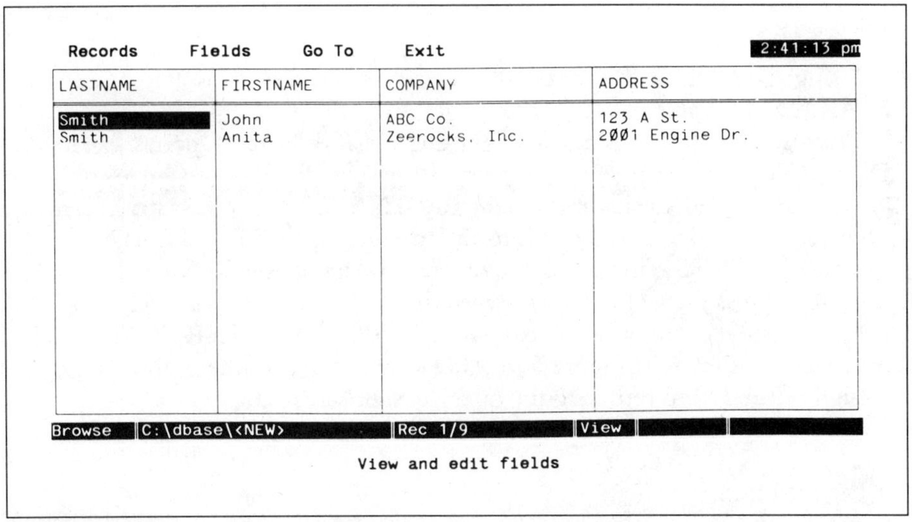

FIGURE 5.8: Results of a query for records with Smith in the LASTNAME field, displayed on the browse screen.

If you now press Data (**F2**), you will notice that the query is carried over to the edit screen, where the record for the first Smith is displayed. If you press **PgDn** to move to the next record, the next Smith record appears. If you press **PgDn** again, dBASE displays the prompt = = = > *Add new records? (Y/N)*, as though there were no other records in the database file.

Press Design (**Shift-F2**) to return to the query design screen.

QUERYING DATE FIELDS

When querying a field of the Date data type, you must enclose the date you are searching for in curly braces ({}).

To query a Date field, first access the query design screen for the database you are using. (If a condition for a previous query is on the screen, erase that entry before typing another.) Press **Tab** as necessary to move to the Date field you want to query. Type the date in the form {02/05/90} and press ↵.

To view the results of the query, press Data (**F2**). Scroll to the Date field on the browse screen, and you will see only records with the date you specified displayed. After viewing the results of the query, press Design (**Shift-F2**) to return to the query design screen.

EXAMPLE

Using the CUSTLIST database, construct a query to isolate records with STARTDATE values of 12/15/88.

From the Control Center, highlight CUSTLIST in the Queries panel. Press Design (**Shift-F2**) to move to the query design screen. (If you completed the previous example, with the highlight in the LASTNAME field, press **Ctrl-Y** to remove "Smith".) Press **End** and then **Shift-Tab** to move to the STARTDATE field.

Type **{12/15/88}** (including the braces) and press ↵. To view the results of the query, press Data (**F2**). If you scroll the browse screen to the STARTDATE field, you will see that only records with 12/15/88 in the STARTDATE field are displayed, as shown in Figure 5.9. After viewing the results of the query, press Design (**Shift-F2**) to return to the query design screen.

QUERYING LOGICAL FIELDS

Logical fields can have one of only two possible values: true or false. You can use .T., .t., .Y., or .y. for true; and .F., .f., .N., or .n. for false. The periods are required by dBASE to distinguish these entries from regular characters. When you query a field that uses the Logical data type, you enter either .T. or .F. as the value to search for.

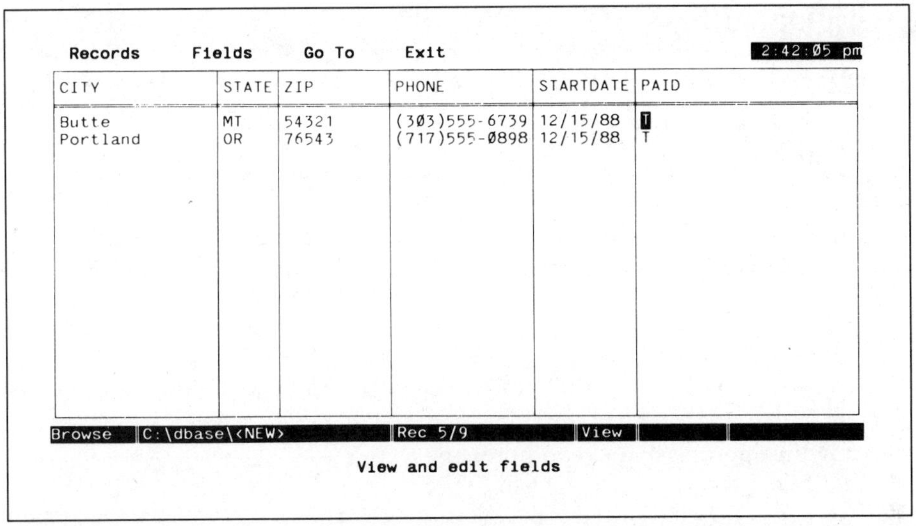

```
       Records      Fields      Go To    Exit                             2:42:05 pm
      CITY               STATE  ZIP       PHONE         STARTDATE  PAID
      Butte              MT     54321     (303)555-6739 12/15/88   T
      Portland           OR     76543     (717)555-0898 12/15/88   T




      Browse   C:\dbase\<NEW>            Rec 5/9        View
                              View and edit fields
```

FIGURE 5.9: Results of a query for records with STARTDATE {12/15/88}, displayed on the browse screen.

To query a Logical field, first access the query design screen for the database you are using. (If a condition for a previous query is on the screen, erase that entry before typing another.) Press **Tab** as necessary to move to the Logical field you want to query. Type either **.T.** or **.F.** (including the periods on each side) and press ←.

To view the results of the query, press Data (**F2**). Scroll to the Logical field on the browse screen, and you will see only records with the value you specified displayed. After viewing the results of the query, press Design (**Shift-F2**) to return to the query design screen.

EXAMPLE

To query the PAID field in the CUSTLIST database for those records that are marked true (that is, that contain *T*), first access the query design screen for CUSTLIST. Remove any existing filter conditions; if you completed the previous example, move to the STARTDATE field and press **Ctrl-Y** to remove the date.

Press **Tab** to move to the PAID field. Type **.T.** and press ←. Press Data (**F2**) to execute the query. When the browse screen appears, press **End** to scroll to the PAID field. Notice that only records marked true (T) are displayed. After viewing the records, press Design (**Shift-F2**) to return to the query design screen.

Searching with Operators

dBASE IV includes many *relational operators* that you can use to refine your queries. Table 5.1 lists and defines these operators. If you do not use an operator in a query, dBASE uses the default operator, equals (=). Therefore, for example, putting "CA" in the STATE field tells dBASE that you want to see records where STATE *equals* "CA".

You can type the operators you want to use as part of the filter condition, or you can select operators from the Expression Builder menu, shown in Chapter 4.

EXAMPLE

To create a query of the CUSTLIST database, first access the query design screen. If any existing filter conditions are on the screen, remove them by highlighting the appropriate field and pressing **Ctrl-Y**.

To display records for people whose last names begin with a letter between A and M, press **Tab**, if necessary, to move the highlight to the LASTNAME field. Type the filter condition <"N", including the quotation marks, and press ↵.

To see the results of the query, press Data (**F2**). The browse screen, as Figure 5.10 shows, displays only records with the appropriate last names. The filter condition <"N" told dBASE to display only records with last names that are less than N, so only records with last names beginning with the letters A though M are displayed.

Press Design (**Shift-F2**) to return to the query design screen. To change the filter condition in the LASTNAME field to > = "N" (greater than or equal to N) using the Expression Builder, first delete <"N" from the LASTNAME field with **Ctrl-Y**.

OPERATOR	MEANING
=	Equal to
>	Greater than
<	Less than
> =	Greater than or equal to
< =	Less than or equal to
< > or #	Not equal to
$	Contains
Like	Pattern match using wildcard characters
Sounds like	Soundex search for words that sound alike

Table 5.1: The dBASE IV Relational Operators

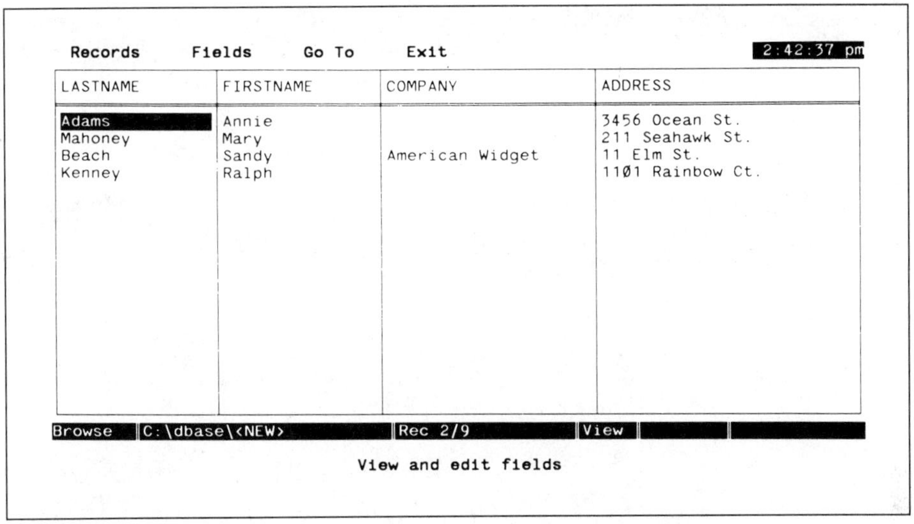

```
Records     Fields    Go To    Exit                          2:42:37 pm
LASTNAME         FIRSTNAME      COMPANY          ADDRESS
Adams            Annie                           3456 Ocean St.
Mahoney          Mary                            211 Seahawk St.
Beach            Sandy          American Widget  11 Elm St.
Kenney           Ralph                           1101 Rainbow Ct.




Browse   C:\dbase\<NEW>       Rec 2/9        View
                        View and edit fields
```

FIGURE 5.10: Results of a query for records with last names "less than" N (<"N").

With the highlight still on the LASTNAME field, press Pick (**Shift-F1**) to use the Expression Builder. Move the highlight to the Operator panel in the Expression Builder and use ↓ to highlight > = . Press ↵. Type **"N"** and press ↵ again. Press Data (**F2**) to display records that have last names beginning with the letters N through Z.

SEARCHING FOR NEAR SPELLINGS

Suppose you want to look up Ralph Kenney's address, but you misspell the last name as *Kinny*. When you perform the lookup operation, dBASE informs you that there is no Kinny. This is an instance when you might want to use the *sounds like* operator. "Sounds like" uses a technique called *soundex* to locate words that sound alike, regardless of how they are spelled.

EXAMPLE

To query the CUSTLIST database for a name that sounds like *Kinny*, first access the query design screen. Move the highlight to the LASTNAME field, pressing **Ctrl-Y** to empty the field if it already contains data. Type the filter condition **Sounds like "Kinny"**, including the quotation marks (as shown in Figure 5.11), and press ↵.

134 — **CH. 5** SEARCHING THE DATABASE

Press Data (**F2**) to view the results of the query. The query located the record for Kenney, as Figure 5.12 shows. Press Design (**Shift-F2**) to return to the query design screen.

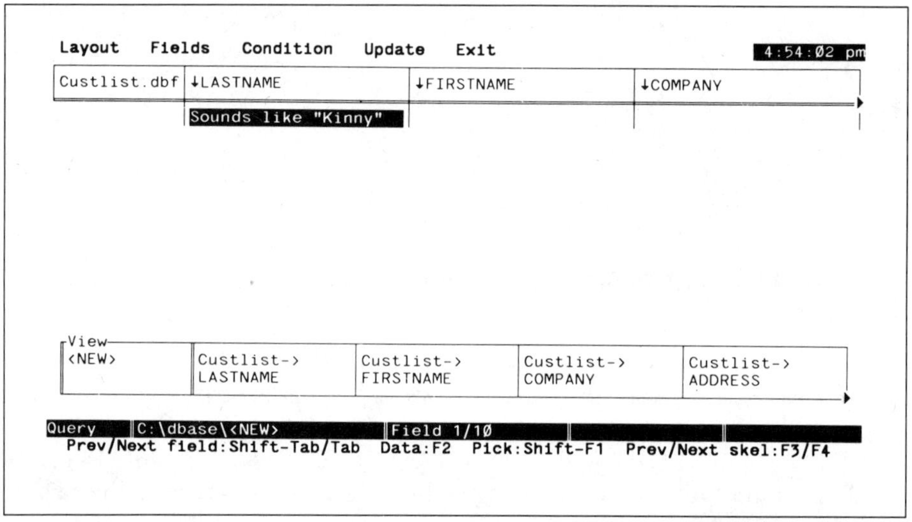

```
 Layout   Fields   Condition   Update   Exit                    4:54:02 pm
┌─────────────┬──────────────────┬──────────────────┬──────────────────┐
│Custlist.dbf │↓LASTNAME         │↓FIRSTNAME        │↓COMPANY          │
│             │Sounds like "Kinny"│                 │                  │
│             │                  │                  │                  │
└─────────────┴──────────────────┴──────────────────┴──────────────────┘

┌View─────────┬──────────┬──────────┬──────────┬──────────┐
│<NEW>        │Custlist->│Custlist->│Custlist->│Custlist->│
│             │LASTNAME  │FIRSTNAME │COMPANY   │ADDRESS   │
└─────────────┴──────────┴──────────┴──────────┴──────────┘
 Query   C:\dbase\<NEW>        Field 1/10
    Prev/Next field:Shift-Tab/Tab  Data:F2  Pick:Shift-F1  Prev/Next skel:F3/F4
```

FIGURE 5.11: A search for records with names that sound like *Kinny*, using the *sounds like* operator.

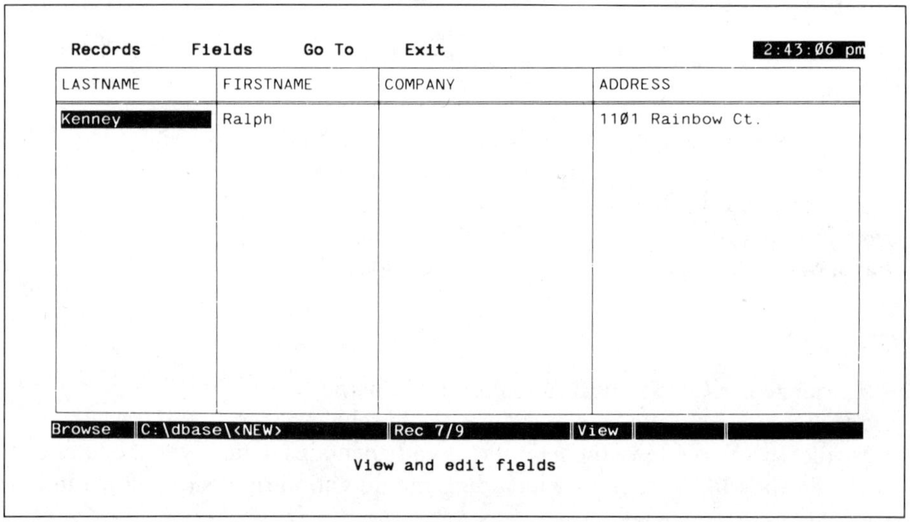

```
 Records   Fields   Go To   Exit                              2:43:06 pm
┌──────────────┬──────────────┬──────────────┬──────────────────────┐
│LASTNAME      │FIRSTNAME     │COMPANY       │ADDRESS               │
│Kenney        │Ralph         │              │1101 Rainbow Ct.      │
│              │              │              │                      │
└──────────────┴──────────────┴──────────────┴──────────────────────┘
 Browse   C:\dbase\<NEW>         Rec 7/9         View
                        View and edit fields
```

FIGURE 5.12: Results of the query in Figure 5.11 for names that sound like *Kinny*.

Searching for Patterns

As discussed earlier in this chapter, you can use wildcards in dBASE IV searches. Wildcards are also available for queries involving character fields. The wildcard character **?** stands for any single character, and the wildcard character ***** stands for any group of characters. To use these two wildcards characters with queries, you first use the *like* operator.

Suppose you want to search a zip code field for zip codes that begin with 92. First access the query design screen for the database you want to use. Erase any existing filter conditions on the query design screen (using **Ctrl-Y**). Type the filter condition **Like "92*"**, including the quotation marks, in the zip code field.

When you press Data (**F2**) to see the results of the query, you will find that only records with zip codes that start with 92 appear on the browse screen. (Scroll the browse screen, if necessary, to see the zip code field.) Press Design (**Shift-F2**) to return to the query design screen.

EXAMPLE

You can search the CUSTLIST database using the filter condition **Like "92*"**, as shown in Figure 5.13.

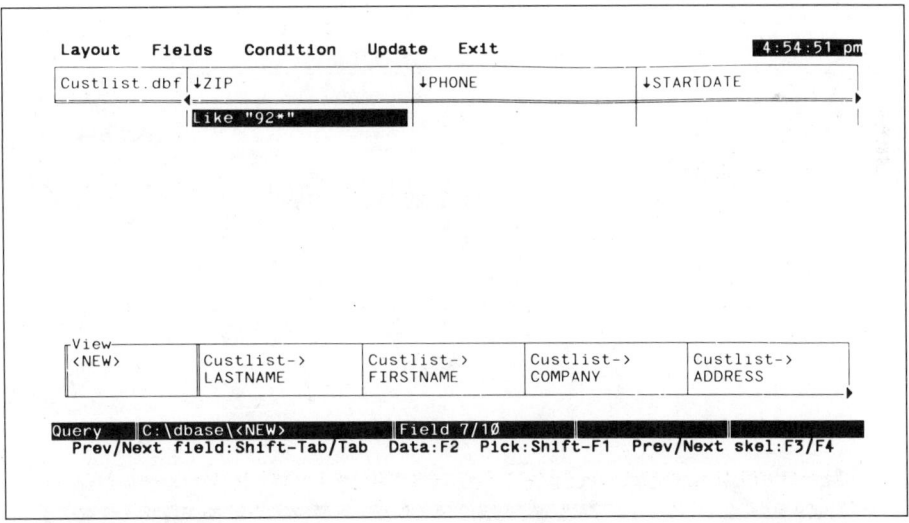

FIGURE 5.13: Using the *like* operator with the * wildcard to search for records with zip codes beginning with 92.

Searching for Embedded Text

You can use the *contains* operator, **$**, to search for text embedded in a Character field.

For example, suppose you want to view all the records in a database with *Rainbow* in the street address. First delete any previous filter conditions from the query design screen. Move the highlight to the ADDRESS field. Type the filter condition **$ "Rainbow"**, including the quotation marks, and press ↵. Press Data (**F2**) to view the results. Press Design (**Shift-F2**) to return to the query design screen.

EXAMPLE

Using the CUSTLIST database, enter the filter condition **$ "Rainbow"** in the ADDRESS field of the query design screen. Figure 5.14 shows how the query design screen should look. Press Data (**F2**) to view the records. You will see only records with *Rainbow* in the ADDRESS field displayed, as shown in Figure 5.15.

Searching for Exceptions

You can use the not-equal-to operator, **#** or **< >**, to execute a query that shows all records *except* those that meet some condition.

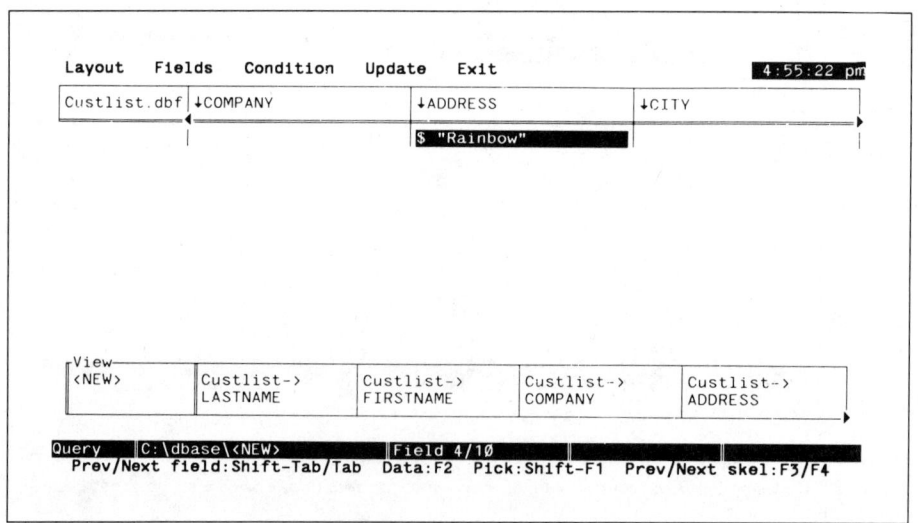

FIGURE 5.14: A query for records with addresses that have *Rainbow* in them, using the *Contains* ($).

EXAMPLE

To view all the records in the CUSTLIST database except those with CA in the STATE field, first access the query design screen and remove any filter conditions.

Move the highlight to the STATE field and type the filter condition # **"CA"**, as in Figure 5.16. Press ↵. When you press Data (**F2**) and then scroll to the STATE field on the browse screen, you will see that none of the records displayed has CA in the STATE field (see Figure 5.17).

Searching with AND Logic

If you develop large databases, you may want to use some sophisticated queries. For example, you might want to ask dBASE to display records for customers who live in California *and* began subscribing in 1988 *and* have not yet paid. To ask such questions, you create queries that use *AND logic*.

You must remember one simple rule when creating AND queries: You must put all filter conditions for the query *on the same row* in the query design screen.

Suppose you want to isolate all records for a customer named Anita Smith. To do so, you enter **"Smith"** in the LASTNAME field and **"Anita"** in the FIRSTNAME field on the same row of the query design screen, as shown in Figure 5.18.

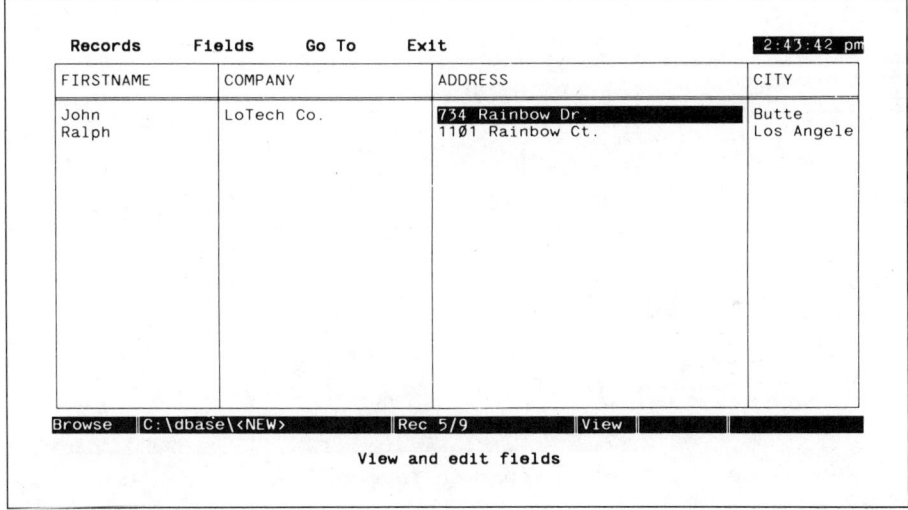

FIGURE 5.15: Results of the query in Figure 5.14 for *Rainbow* embedded in the ADDRESS field.

When you press Data (**F2**) to execute the query, only Anita Smith's records will appear on the browse screen. Press Design (**Shift-F2**) to return to the query design screen.

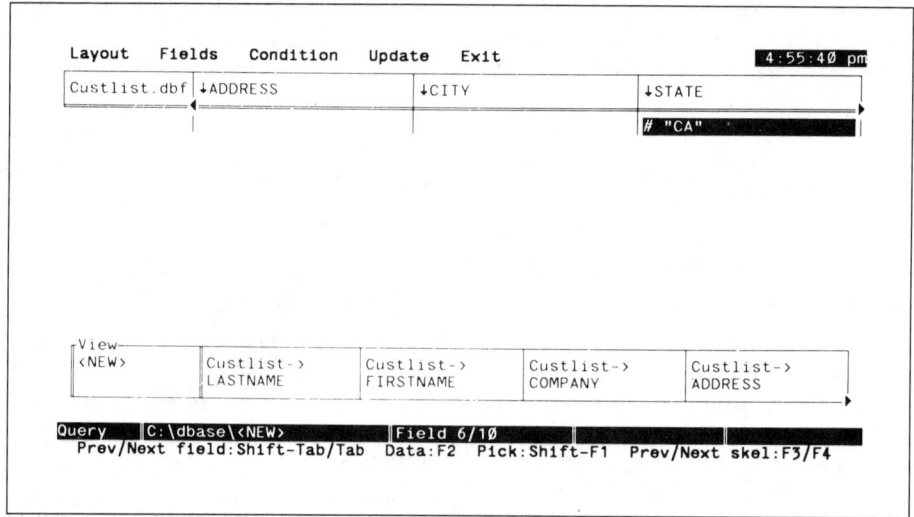

FIGURE 5.16: Query for records that do *not* have CA in the STATE field, using the not-equal-to operator (#).

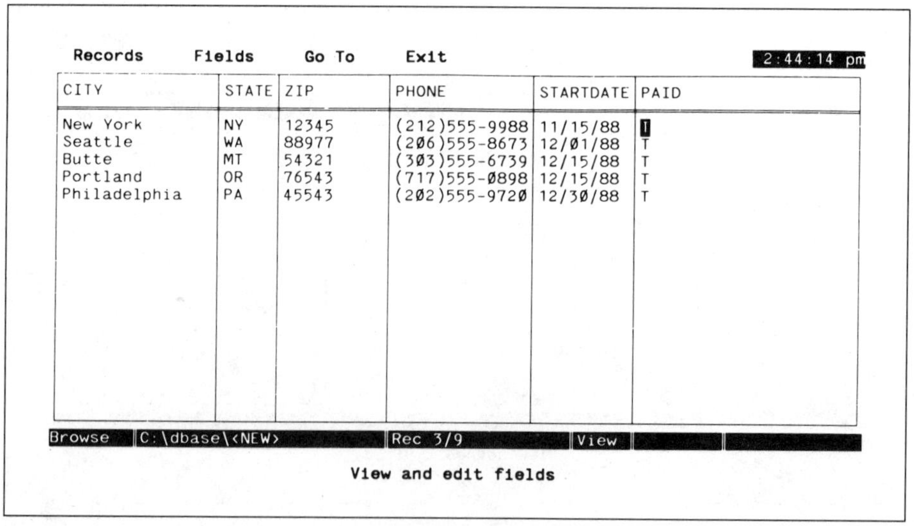

FIGURE 5.17: Results of the query in Figure 5.16 for records that do *not* have CA in the STATE field.

SEARCHING WITH AND LOGIC —— **139**

Suppose you want to list all customers who live on Broad St. in Philadelphia. That is, you want to display all records with the name Broad St. embedded in the ADDRESS field *and* the name Philadelphia embedded in the CITY field. You need to set up your query as shown in Figure 5.19.

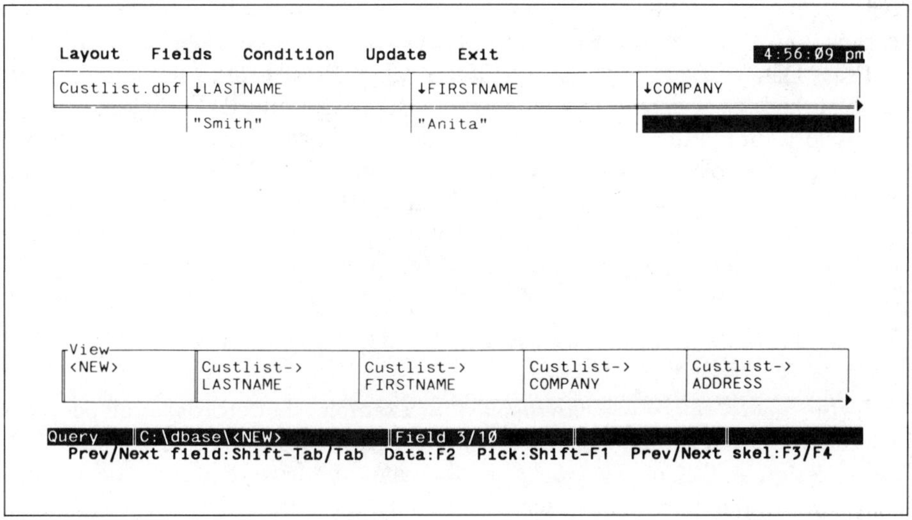

FIGURE 5.18: Query for records containing the name Anita Smith.

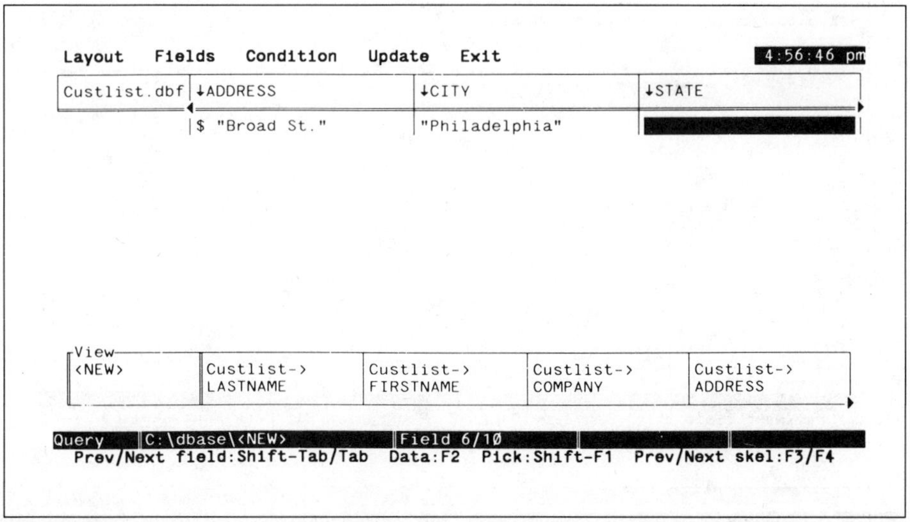

FIGURE 5.19: Query for records of customers living on Broad St. in Philadelphia, using the *Contains* operator ($).

Notice that the two filter conditions are on the same row within the query. Pressing Data (**F2**) displays the record for Susita Schumack, the only customer in the CUSTLIST database who lives on Broad St. in Philadelphia.

Figure 5.20 shows how to set up another query of the CUSTLIST database. This query lists all customers who have not yet paid, and who began subscribing before January 1, 1989 (that is, customers with .F. in the PAID field and dates earlier than 1/1/89 in the STARTDATE field).

Press Data (**F2**) to see the results of the query. Press **End** to scroll to the right edge of the browse screen to view the STARTDATE and PAID fields.

If you want to limit the preceding query to California residents who have not paid yet and who began subscribing before January 1, 1989, you just need to add **"CA"** (with quotation marks) to the STATE field on the query design screen. Make sure that "CA" is in the top row of the query screen (the same row as the other filter conditions). Then press Data (**F2**) to execute the query.

Searching with OR Logic

Using an OR query you can display, for example, the records for all people in the database who live in Washington *or* Oregon *or* California.

To design an OR query, you *stagger* the values you are searching for on separate rows on the query design screen. Initially, the query design screen displays

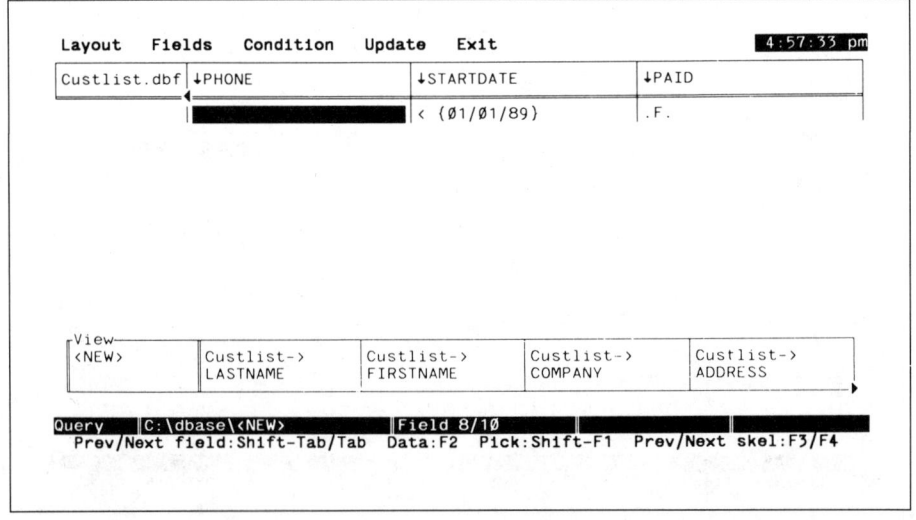

FIGURE 5.20: Query for records of customers who began subscribing before 1/1/89 and have not paid, using the less-than operator to query the STARTDATE field and .F. to query for F in the logical PAID field.

only a single row. You create more rows by pressing ↓. You can use ↓ to create as many rows as you wish. For example, the query in Figure 5.21 displays records for residents of Pennsylvania (PA), New York (NY), Montana (MT), or Washington (WA) (that is, for people who live in PA *or* NY *or* MT *or* WA).

EXAMPLE

To create a query of the CUSTLIST database, start with an empty query design screen (use the **Tab** key to scroll from field to field and use **Ctrl-Y** to delete any existing filter conditions).

To display the records of customers who live in either California or Washington, move the highlight to the STATE field on the query design screen. Type **"CA"**, including the quotation marks, to specify California as a state to search for. Press ↓ to add a new row. Type **"WA"** to specify Washington as another state to search for. Press ←┘. Your query design screen should look like Figure 5.22.

Staggering the filter conditions onto two separate rows tells dBASE that you want records that have *either* CA or WA in the STATE field. Press Data (**F2**) to view the results of the query. Press **End** to scroll to the right of the browse screen, which should look like Figure 5.23.

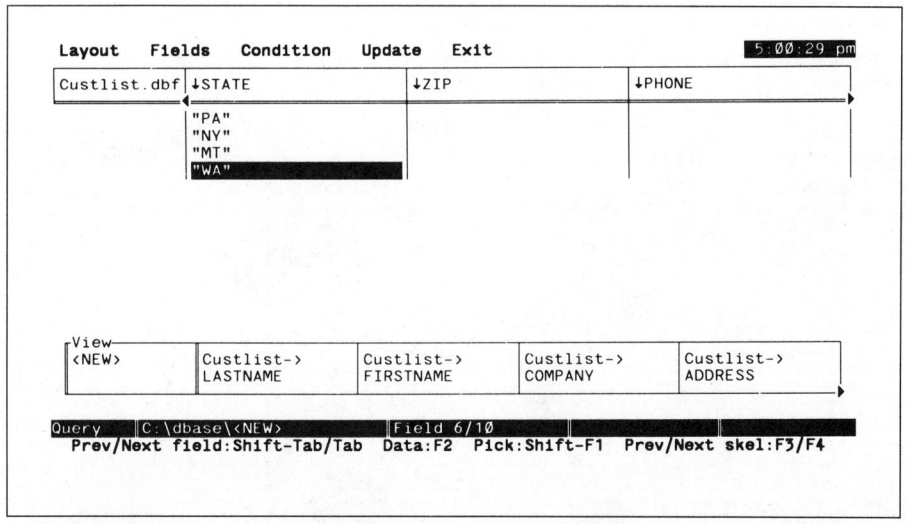

FIGURE 5.21: Query for records of Pennsylvania, New York, Montana, or Washington residents. This query uses OR logic for one field.

After viewing the results of the query, return to the query design screen by pressing Design (**Shift-F2**). To erase both filter conditions, first press **Ctrl-Y** to erase the last filter condition. Then press ↑ to move to the first filter condition (the second row will disappear, because it is now empty) and press **Ctrl-Y** to erase the first filter condition.

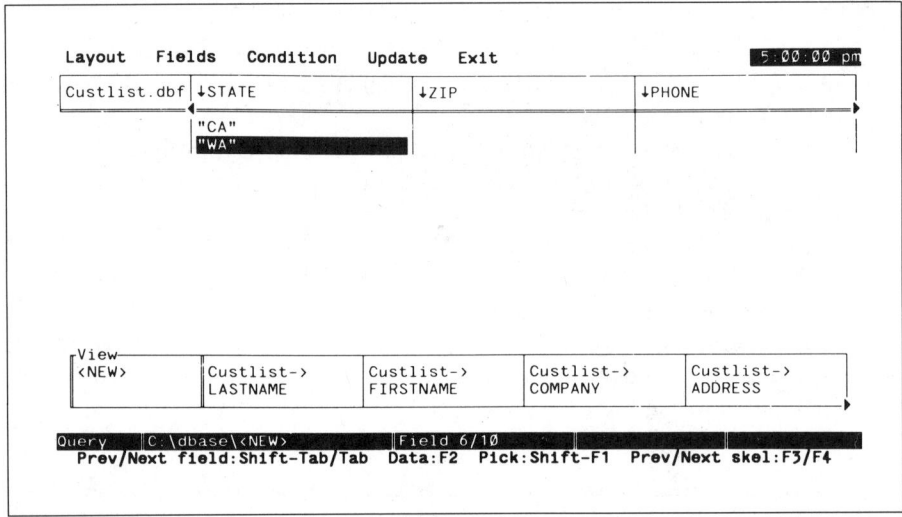

FIGURE 5.22: Query for records of California or Washington residents. This query uses OR logic for one field.

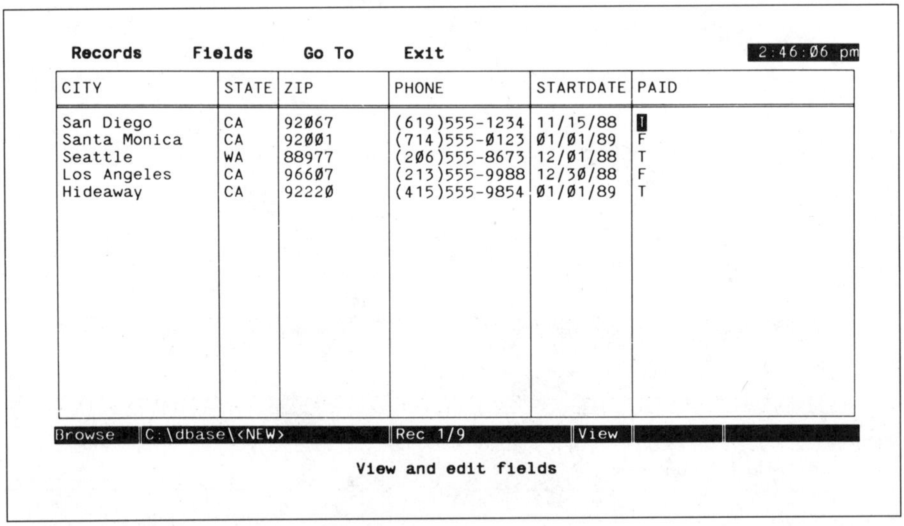

FIGURE 5.23: Results of the query in Figure 5.22 for records of California or Washington residents.

Searching Multiple Fields

Suppose you want to view records that have a particular value in one field *or* some other value in another field. For example, suppose you are a salesperson who works primarily on the phone, and you have been assigned a territory that includes the entire state of California, plus the entire 717 telephone area code (which includes, but extends outside of, the state of California).

You cannot find the appropriate records for your customers by executing a query for records that have CA in the STATE field *and* (717) in the PHONE field, because that query would limit the display to records with the 717 area code within the state of California. What you want to display are records that have CA in the STATE field (regardless of the area code) *or* 717 in the PHONE field (regardless of the state).

To execute such a query, you need to stagger the STATE and PHONE filter conditions onto two separate rows, to tell dBASE that you want records meeting one condition *or* the other. Placing the two fields on two different rows on the query design screen tells dBASE that you are requesting OR logic in the query.

EXAMPLE

Figure 5.24 shows a query for records with either CA in the STATE field or 717 in the PHONE field, using the CUSTLIST database. Press ↓ to create a second row on the query design screen before entering **$ "(717)"** in the PHONE

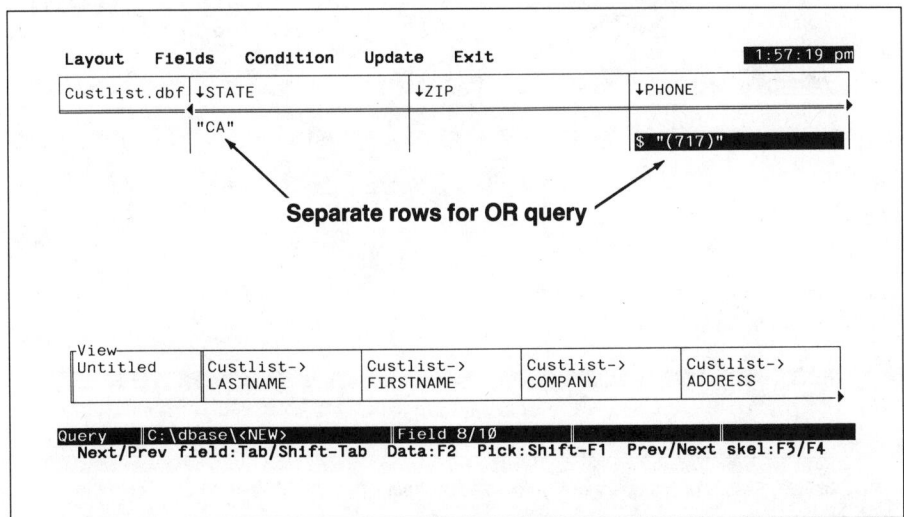

FIGURE 5.24: Query for records with either CA in the STATE field or (717) in the PHONE field. This is an OR query of two different fields. The filter conditions are entered on different lines in the file skeleton.

field. When you press Data (**F2**), the browse screen displays records that have either CA in the STATE field or (717) embedded ($) in the PHONE field, as shown in Figure 5.25.

Searching for Ranges

You may need to search for data that falls within some range of values, such as zip codes in the range 92000 to 92555 or names in the alphabetical range A through J. You might want to search for records that fall within a particular range of dates, such as November 15, 1989, to December 15, 1989. Range searches can be particularly useful in Numeric fields: for example, "Display all employees with salaries in the range $20,000 to $30,000." (Chapter 6 discusses Numeric fields further.)

To perform a range search, use an AND query within a single field. Use the > = operator before the low end of the range and the < = operator before the high end of the range, separating the two with a comma.

For example, the filter condition > = "A", < = "J" translates to "greater than or equal to A AND less than or equal to J"—in other words, "between A and J."

```
  Records     Fields     Go To     Exit                          2:46:44 pm
 CITY          STATE ZIP        PHONE         STARTDATE PAID
 San Diego     CA    92067      (619)555-1234 11/15/88  T
 Santa Monica  CA    92001      (714)555-0123 01/01/89  F
 Portland      OR    76543      (717)555-0898 12/15/88  T
 Los Angeles   CA    96607      (213)555-9988 12/30/88  F
 Hideaway      CA    92220      (415)555-9854 01/01/89  T




 Browse   C:\dbase\<NEW>          Rec 1/9       View
                        View and edit fields
```

FIGURE 5.25: Results of the query in Figure 5.24 for either CA in the STATE field or (717) in the PHONE field.

EXAMPLE

Suppose you want to view customers in the CUSTLIST database in the zip code range 80000 through 97000: that is, records with zip codes that are greater than or equal to 80000 AND also less than or equal to 97000. To do so, you place the filter condition > = "80000", < = "97000" in the ZIP field, as shown in Figure 5.26. Figure 5.27 shows the results of this query.

Or suppose you want to view customers who began subscribing on dates between 11/15/88 and 12/15/88. You use exactly the same kind of filter condition as in the previous example, but you use curly braces to indicate the Date data type. Figure 5.28 shows > = {11/15/88}, < = {12/15/88}, the appropriate filter condition, in the STARTDATE field of the query form (although part of the filter condition is hidden because the box that contains it is too narrow).

CREATING COMPLEX QUERIES

You can create very complex queries. You can combine AND and OR logic and include many additional conditions. For example, you can design a single query with 15 rows of AND and OR logic, with many *sounds like* operators, range searches, and *like* pattern matches. dBASE imposes no limitations on your queries, but they will work only when the query makes sense.

For example, entering **"CA","WA"** in the STATE field of the CUSTLIST query design screen will not display any records because the query asks for records that have both CA *and* WA in the STATE field. But a single person can (presumably) live in only one state. That is, no single record can possibly have both CA and WA in the STATE field at the same time. (To display records with *either* CA or WA in the STATE field, you need to stagger the two filter conditions onto two separate rows.)

dBASE considers each row in a query to be a single question. Thus, you describe your query using a separate row for each question, as explained in the example that follows.

EXAMPLE

Suppose you want to see records from the CUSTLIST database for all people in the states of California, New York, and Washington who have paid. At first you might think that the logic for this requires the query "Locate customers who have paid AND live in Washington OR California OR New York." If so, you might set up the query incorrectly, as in Figure 5.29.

146 —— **CH. 5** SEARCHING THE DATABASE

```
 Layout   Fields   Condition   Update   Exit                    4:58:43 pm
┌─────────────┬──────────────────────┬──────────────┬──────────────────┐
│Custlist.dbf │↓ZIP                  │↓PHONE        │↓STARTDATE        │
│             │>="80000",<="97000"   │              │                  │
└─────────────┴──────────────────────┴──────────────┴──────────────────┘




 ┌View──┬──────────┬──────────┬──────────┬──────────┐
 │<NEW> │Custlist->│Custlist->│Custlist->│Custlist->│
 │      │LASTNAME  │FIRSTNAME │COMPANY   │ADDRESS   │
 └──────┴──────────┴──────────┴──────────┴──────────┘
 Query   C:\dbase\<NEW>       Field 7/10
     Prev/Next field:Shift-Tab/Tab  Data:F2  Pick:Shift-F1  Prev/Next skel:F3/F4
```

FIGURE 5.26: Query for records in the 80000 to 97000 zip code range, using the greater-than-or-equal-to operator and the less-than-or-equal-to operator. Notice the use of the comma in the filter condition.

```
 Records   Fields   Go To   Exit                                2:45:20 pm
┌────────────────┬──────────────┬─────┬──────┬─────────────┐
│ADDRESS         │CITY          │STATE│ZIP   │PHONE        │
├────────────────┼──────────────┼─────┼──────┼─────────────┤
│123 A St.       │San Diego     │ CA  │92067 │(619)555-1234│
│3456 Ocean St.  │Santa Monica  │ CA  │92001 │(714)555-0123│
│211 Seahawk St. │Seattle       │ WA  │88977 │(206)555-8673│
│1101 Rainbow Ct.│Los Angeles   │ CA  │96607 │(213)555-9988│
│2001 Engine Dr. │Hideaway      │ CA  │92220 │(415)555-9854│
│                │              │     │      │             │
└────────────────┴──────────────┴─────┴──────┴─────────────┘
 Browse   C:\dbase\<NEW>        Rec 1/9       View
                            View and edit fields
```

FIGURE 5.27: Results of the zip code range query in Figure 5.26.

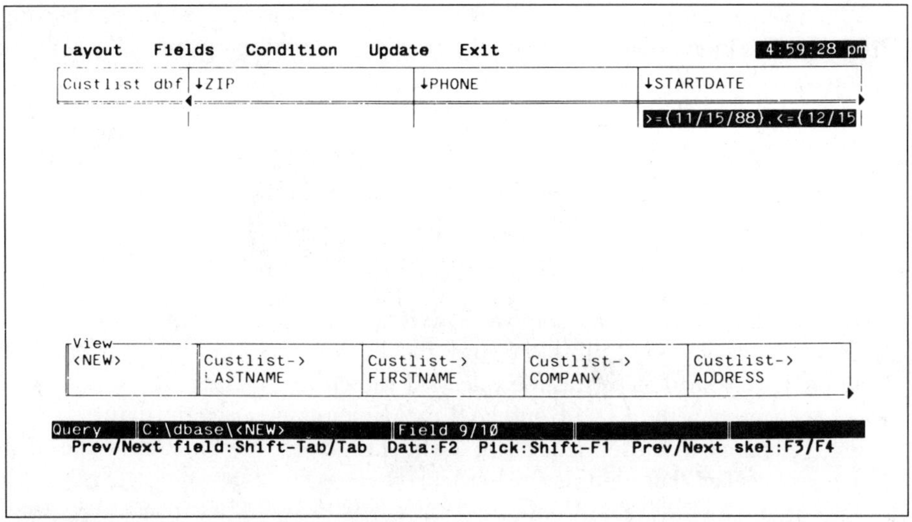

```
Layout   Fields   Condition   Update   Exit              4:59:28 pm
Custlist.dbf │↓ZIP          │↓PHONE         │↓STARTDATE
                                            │>=(11/15/88),<=(12/15
```

```
┌View─────
│<NEW>    │Custlist->│Custlist-> │Custlist-> │Custlist->
│         │LASTNAME  │FIRSTNAME  │COMPANY    │ADDRESS
```
Query   C:\dbase\<NEW>   Field 9/10
Prev/Next field:Shift-Tab/Tab   Data:F2   Pick:Shift-F1   Prev/Next skel:F3/F4

FIGURE 5.28: A query for records with STARTDATE values between 11/15/88 and 12/15/88, using the greater-than-or-equal-to operator and the less-than-or-equal-to operator. Notice the use of the comma in the filter condition. (Part of the filter condition is scrolled off the screen.)

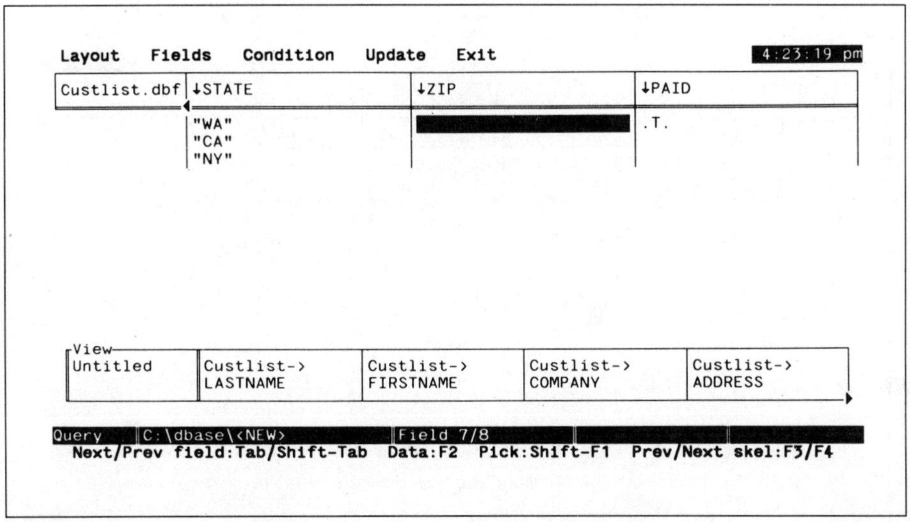

```
Layout   Fields   Condition   Update   Exit              4:23:19 pm
Custlist.dbf │↓STATE      │↓ZIP          │↓PAID
             │"WA"        │              │.T.
             │"CA"        │              │
             │"NY"        │              │
```

```
┌View─────
│Untitled │Custlist->│Custlist-> │Custlist-> │Custlist->
│         │LASTNAME  │FIRSTNAME  │COMPANY    │ADDRESS
```
Query   C:\dbase\<NEW>   Field 7/8
Next/Prev field:Tab/Shift-Tab   Data:F2   Pick:Shift-F1   Prev/Next skel:F3/F4

FIGURE 5.29: Example of how *not* to set up a query to display records for California, New York, and Washington residents who have paid. (Note that this figure is a composite. The STATE and PAID fields are actually too far apart to be viewed simultaneously.)

148 —— **CH. 5** SEARCHING THE DATABASE

When you execute the query shown in Figure 5.29, the results will look like Figure 5.30. The intent of the query in Figure 5.29 was to display only CA, NY, and WA records with .T. in the PAID field, but as you can see in Figure 5.30, some records with .F. in the PAID field are displayed.

The incorrect query in Figure 5.29 asked these questions:

- Does this record have WA in STATE and .T. in PAID?
- Does this record have CA in STATE?
- Does this record have NY in STATE?

The results displayed by the query were accurate for these questions. However, this is not what was intended. To see records for all WA, CA, and NY residents who have paid, you need to set up the query as shown in Figure 5.31. (Again, your screen will not show the STATE and PAID fields simultaneously; the figure is a composite. To change the order of fields on the browse screen, see the section "Selecting Fields for Display" later in this chapter.)

The query in Figure 5.31 meets your needs exactly, because it asks these questions:

- Does this record have WA in STATE and .T. in PAID?

```
  Records     Fields      Go To       Exit                              2:47:58 pm
 CITY                STATE  ZIP      PHONE           STARTDATE  PAID
 San Diego           CA     92067    (619)555-1234   11/15/88   T
 Santa Monica        CA     92001    (714)555-0123   01/01/89   F
 New York            NY     12345    (212)555-9988   11/15/88   T
 Seattle             WA     88977    (206)555-8673   12/01/88   T
 Los Angeles         CA     96607    (213)555-9988   12/30/88   F
 Hideaway            CA     92220    (415)555-9854   01/01/89   T




 Browse   C:\dbase\<NEW>            Rec 1/9          View
                        View and edit fields
```

FIGURE 5.30: Results of the incorrect query in Figure 5.29. Records are displayed for residents of the three states, but the condition of having paid has not been met.

- Does this record have CA in STATE and .T. in PAID?
- Does this record have NY in STATE and .T. in PAID?

It then displays only records that meet all these criteria, as Figure 5.32 shows.

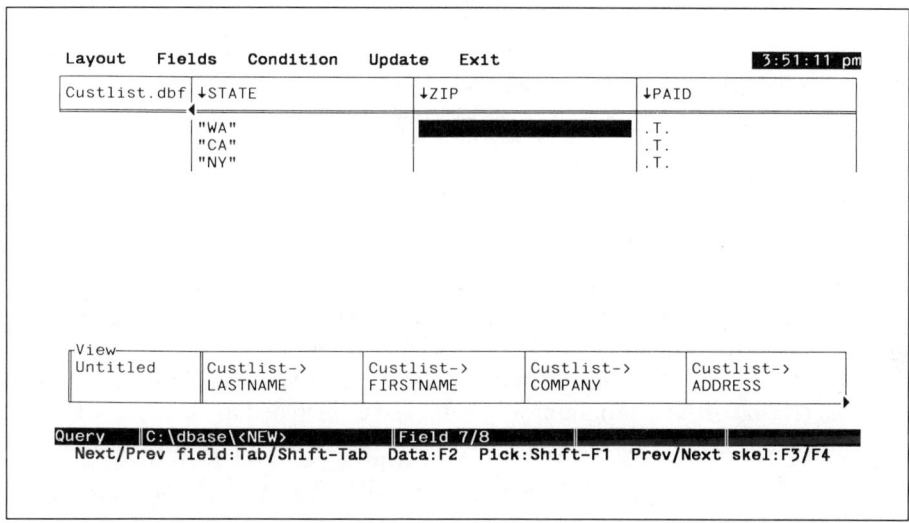

FIGURE 5.31: The correct way to set up a query to display records for California, New York, and Washington residents who have paid. This query combines AND and OR logic.

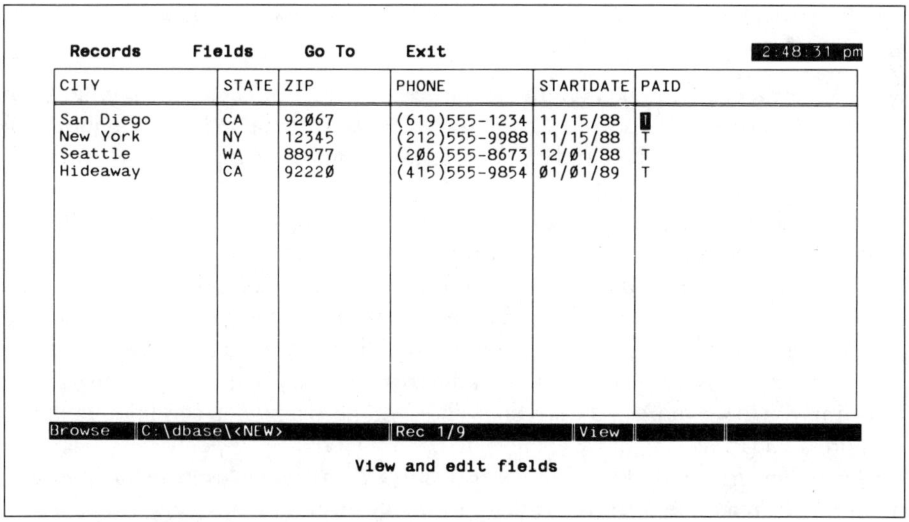

FIGURE 5.32: Results of the query in Figure 5.31 combining AND and OR logic.

Using Condition Boxes

SEQUENCE OF STEPS

To create a condition box on the query design screen:

    Menus (**F10**)

    Condition/Add Condition Box [↵]

    type a condition ↵   *or*   press Pick (**Shift-F1**) to select a condition from a menu

USAGE

Condition boxes can be used to enter search queries using the dBASE programming language, rather than the query-by-example method. The box is provided mainly as an alternative to the new dBASE IV query-by-example search technique, as a convenience for users who are already familiar with earlier versions of dBASE, such as dBASE III (the dBASE programming language is discussed in Chapter 18).

However, all users will need to use condition boxes in a few circumstances:

- When using a global function, such as DELETED( ), to search for records (see Chapter 3 for an example).
- When searching for text embedded in a Memo field (see the section that follows).
- When using multiple related databases with complex AND and OR combinations (see Chapter 12).

To create a condition box on the query design screen, select Add Condition Box from the Condition pull-down menu. You can enter a condition by typing it into the condition box. To use AND and OR queries, surround the AND and OR with periods (.AND. and .OR.).

As an alternative to typing the condition, you can press Pick (**Shift-F1**) and choose from a menu of condition options, including field names, operators, and functions. When using a condition box to create filter conditions, you can press Zoom (**F9**) to expand the condition box and make room for your entry.

The Show Condition Box option on the Condition menu is a toggle, which can be set to Yes or No. When you set it to No, the condition box is hidden (not displayed), allowing you to see more of the screen. When you need a hidden condition box, you can press **F3** (Previous) and **F4** (Next) to open the box.

After filling in the condition box, press Data (**F2**) as usual to execute the query. To return to the query design screen after viewing the results of the query, press Design (**Shift-F2**).

Searching Memo Fields

On the query design screen, you can use the **$** (*contains*) operator to isolate records that have a particular word or group of words in a Memo field. The **$** is the only operator that makes sense for a Memo field, since a Memo field usually contains a large body of text. For example, Figure 5.33 shows a query that searches a bibliographic database called REFERENC for records with the character string "dBASE IV" embedded in the ABSTRACT field. Notice that this query uses a condition box.

You can use AND and OR queries in Memo fields. For example, the query in Figure 5.34 uses a condition box to search the REFERENC database for records that have the character string "dBASE IV" in the KEYWORDS or ABSTRACT field. Notice that the query uses .OR. You must include periods for AND and OR queries when you use a condition box.

Sorting the Results of Queries

You may want the results of your queries sorted. For example, you may want to send form letters to California residents and to print them in zip code order for bulk mailing. For this, you need a *query* to isolate records with CA in the state field and a *sort* to arrange the records into zip code order.

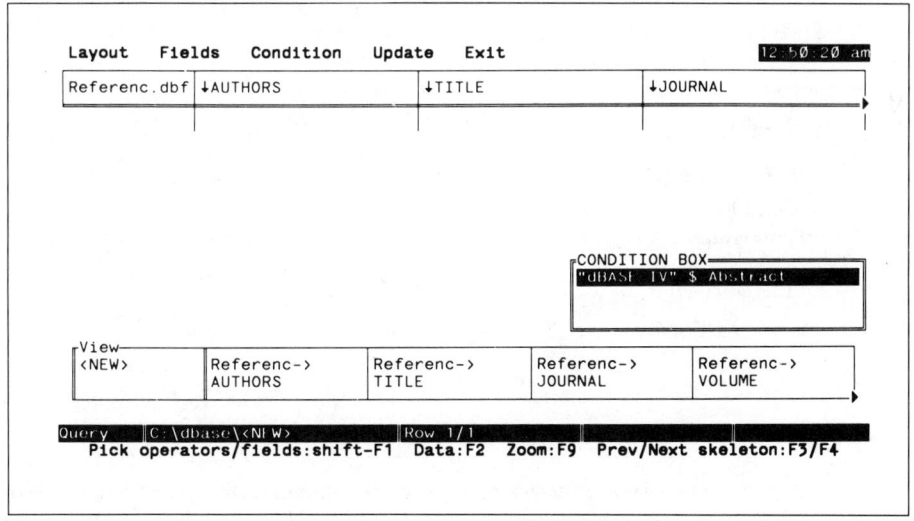

FIGURE 5.33: Query for records with the character string "dBASE IV" in the ABSTRACT field, using a condition box.

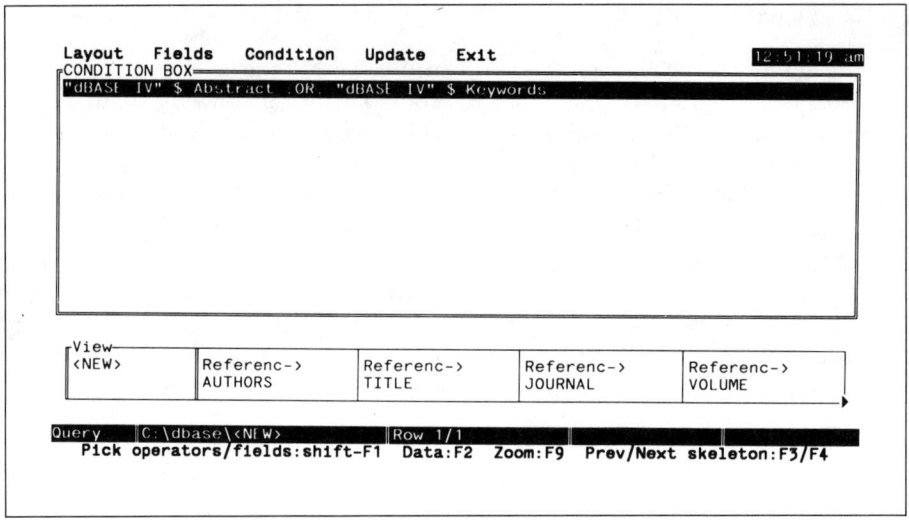

FIGURE 5.34: A complex query involving a Memo field. The query uses a condition box to search for the character string "dBASE IV" in the ABSTRACT field (which is a Memo field) or in the KEYWORDS field.

Sorting to a Separate Database File

SEQUENCE OF STEPS

From the query design screen:

> highlight the query field
> type the filter condition ↵
> highlight the sort field
> Menus (**F10**)
> Fields/**S**ort on This Field [↵]
> select a sort order
> Data (**F2**)

USAGE

To sort the results of a query to a separate database file, first erase any old filter conditions on the query design screen. Move the highlight to the field to query.

Type the filter condition and press ↵. Move the highlight to the field to sort on. Press Menus (**F10**) and → to move to the Fields option on the menu bar. Type **S** to select Sort on This Field.

From the submenu of sorting options, make a selection. (These sorting options are the same as those presented in Table 4.1.) Press Data (**F2**) to execute the query. If you are sorting a large database, dBASE will take some time to execute the query.

If you scroll to the field you sorted using the browse screen, you will see that only records meeting your search criteria are displayed. The browse screen displays the data from a separate, sorted file (not from the original file). The status bar at the bottom of the screen shows the name of the sorted database. The word *ReadOnly* appears in the status bar, because you can only read (look at) the data on this browse screen—you cannot write (change) any data.

If dBASE allowed you to change the data in the sorted browse screen, your changes would *not* be reflected in the original database file. Therefore, dBASE simply does not permit you to change the results of a sorted query.

EXAMPLE

Using the CUSTLIST database, you can isolate records that have CA in the STATE field and sort those records into alphabetical order by city. From the query design screen, use **Ctrl-Y** to erase any existing filter conditions.

Move the highlight to the STATE field. Type the filter condition **"CA"** and press ↵. Press **Shift-Tab** to move to the CITY field. Press Menus (**F10**) and → to move to the **Fields** option on the menu bar. Type **S** to select Sort on This Field.

From the submenu of sorting options, press ↓ twice to highlight Ascending Dictionary and press ↵ to select it. The CITY field now contains the sort condition *AscDict1*, which stands for "ascending dictionary order—first field." Figure 5.35 shows the completed query.

Press Data (**F2**) to execute the query. If you scroll to the CITY and STATE fields on the browse screen, you will see that the screen displays only records with CA in the STATE field, and that the cities are in alphabetical order, as Figure 5.36 shows.

The browse screen displays the data from the separate, sorted file (not from the original CUSTLIST file). The name *C:\dbase\<NEW>* in the status bar (at the bottom of Figure 5.36) shows that a new, unnamed database is displaying the results of the query. The word *ReadOnly* appears in the status bar, because you can only read (look at) the data on this browse screen—you cannot write (change) any data.

154 — CH. 5 SEARCHING THE DATABASE

```
  Layout    Fields    Condition   Update    Exit            5:03:06 pm
 ┌─────────────┬──────────┬──────────────┬──────────────┬──────────────┐
 │Custlist.dbf │↓ADDRESS  │    ↓CITY     │              │ ↓STATE       │
 │             │          │   AscDict1   │              │  "CA"        │
 └─────────────┴──────────┴──────────────┴──────────────┴──────────────┘

  ┌View─────┬──────────┬──────────┬──────────┬──────────┐
  │<NEW>    │Custlist->│Custlist->│Custlist->│Custlist->│
  │         │LASTNAME  │FIRSTNAME │COMPANY   │ADDRESS   │
  └─────────┴──────────┴──────────┴──────────┴──────────┘
  Query    C:\dbase\<NEW>         Field 5/10                        Ins
    Prev/Next field:Shift-Tab/Tab  Data:F2  Pick:Shift-F1  Prev/Next skel:F3/F4
```

FIGURE 5.35: Query for records of California residents, sorted alphabetically by city.

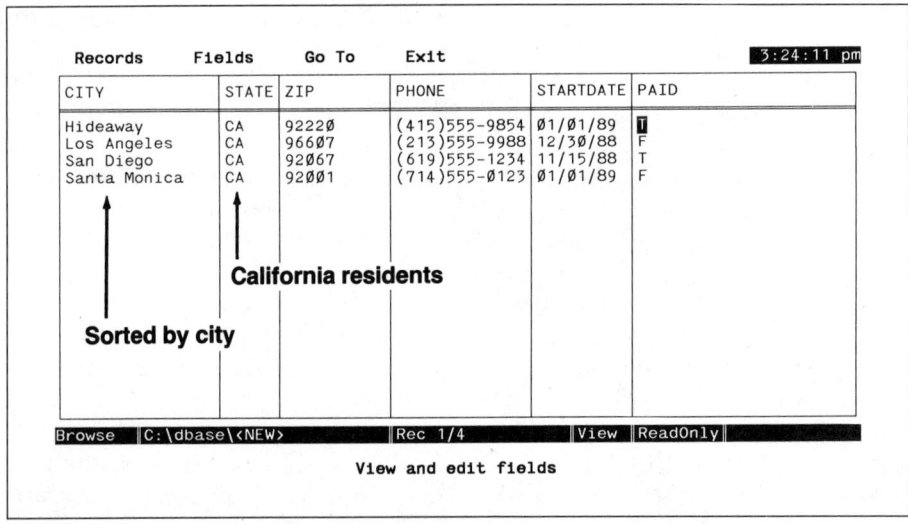

FIGURE 5.36: Results of the query in Figure 5.35 for records of California residents, sorted alphabetically by city.

Sorting Multiple Fields

You can perform sorts within sorts in a query form simply by selecting fields to sort on in most-important to least-important order. For example, if you want to sort the results of a query alphabetically by last name and then alphabetically by first name within last names, you move the highlight to the LASTNAME field, select Sort on This Field, move the highlight to the FIRSTNAME field, and select Sort on This Field again.

dBASE includes a number in the sort condition so that you can see the field's position in the sort order. For example, in Figure 5.37, *AscDict1* indicates that LASTNAME is the first (primary) sort field, and *AscDict2* indicates that FIRSTNAME is the secondary sort field. (The sorted result is the same as when you use LASTNAME + FIRSTNAME in an index; see Chapter 4.)

dBASE continues to add 1 to the AscDict symbol each time you select Sort on This Field from the Fields menu, so long as you are still in the same query session. (A query session ends when you exit the query design screen and return to the Control Center.) Therefore, your queries might show *AscDist3, AscDict4,* and so on. Nevertheless, the sorting precedence remains the same.

For example, if the LASTNAME field contains *AscDict1* and the FIRSTNAME field contains *AscDict2,* the records are sorted by first name within last names. If LASTNAME contains *AscDict3* and FIRSTNAME contains *AscDict4,* you get the same results; first names are still sorted within last names.

```
  Layout    Fields   Condition   Update   Exit              2:25:02 pm
 ┌─────────────┬──────────────────┬──────────────────┬──────────────────┐
 │Custlist.dbf │↓LASTNAME         │↓FIRSTNAME        │↓COMPANY          │
 │             │AscDict1          │AscDict2          │                  │
 └─────────────┴──────────────────┴──────────────────┴──────────────────┘




 ┌View─┬──────────┬──────────┬──────────┬──────────┐
 │Untitled│Custlist->│Custlist->│Custlist->│Custlist->│
 │        │LASTNAME  │FIRSTNAME │COMPANY   │ADDRESS   │
 └────────┴──────────┴──────────┴──────────┴──────────┘
 Query   C:\dbase\<NEW>        Field 3/10                          Ins
  Next/Prev field:Tab/Shift-Tab  Data:F2  Pick:Shift-F1  Prev/Next skel:F3/F4
```

FIGURE 5.37: Query to sort records alphabetically by last name and by first name within last names.

Combining Filter and Sort Conditions

Any field on the query design screen can contain both a filter condition and a sort condition. First enter your filter conditions for all the fields by which you want to sort, and then select the fields to sort on. dBASE will automatically place the sort condition, preceded by a comma, after the filter condition.

Figure 5.38 shows an example in which CITY is the primary sort field, and ADDRESS is the secondary sort field. The filter condition **$ "Rainbow"** limits the resulting display to database records with *Rainbow* embedded in the ADDRESS field. The records are sorted in alphabetical order by city.

If you were to execute this query on a larger database, you would see the addresses sorted so that, for example, 123 Rainbow Dr. would precede 124 Rainbow Dr. in each city.

Using Indexes to Sort Query Results

SEQUENCE OF STEPS

From the query design screen:

>Menus (**F10**)
>Fields/Include Indexes [◄─┘]
>Yes
>highlight the query field
>type the filter condition ◄─┘
>highlight the sort field
>Menus (**F10**)
>Fields/**S**ort on This Field [◄─┘]
>select a sort order
>Data (**F2**)
>Design (**Shift-F2**)

USAGE

If you use an index to sort the results of a query, you will get your results more quickly than if you create a sorted database file—and you will be able to make changes on the resulting browse screen.

You can sort the results of a query using an existing index that you have created. To include an index in your query, press Menus (**F10**) and → to move to

USING INDEXES TO SORT QUERY RESULTS — 157

```
  Layout   Fields   Condition   Update   Exit              5:04:18 pm
 Custlist.dbf │↓ADDRESS            │↓CITY            │↓STATE
              │$ "Rainbow", AscDict2│AscDict1






  ┌View─────┬──────────┬──────────┬──────────┬──────────
  │<NEW>    │Custlist->│Custlist->│Custlist->│Custlist->
  │         │LASTNAME  │FIRSTNAME │COMPANY   │ADDRESS
 Query  │C:\dbase\<NEW>      │Field 6/10                    Ins
   Prev/Next field:Shift-Tab/Tab  Data:F2  Pick:Shift-F1  Prev/Next skel:F3/F4
```

FIGURE 5.38: A filter condition combined with a sort in the ADDRESS field. Notice that the filter condition precedes the sort order.

the Fields menu and then use ↓ to highlight the Include Indexes option. Press ↵ to change the setting to Yes. To isolate records, press the **Tab** key, if necessary, to get to the field you want to query. Enter the filter condition and press ↵. Notice that a pound sign (#) appears next to any field name for which an index exists.

Move the highlight to the field to sort on. Press Menus (**F10**) and → to pull down the Fields menu. Type **S** to select Sort on This Field. From the submenu, select the sort order you want.

To execute the query, press Data (**F2**). You will see the browse screen display only filtered records, sorted according to the index. Press Design (**Shift-F2**) to return to the query design screen.

EXAMPLE

Suppose you want dBASE to display the records only of California residents in zip code order. You can use the ZIP index of the CUSTLIST database (created in Chapter 4) to sort the results of a query.

On the query design screen, press Menus (**F10**) and → to select the Fields menu. Move the highlight to the Include Indexes option and press ↵ to change the setting to Yes, so you can include indexes in your query.

To isolate records for California residents, press **Tab** until you get to the STATE field, enter the filter condition **"CA"** (including the quotation marks), and press ↵.

158 ── **CH. 5** SEARCHING THE DATABASE

Press **Tab** to move to the ZIP field. Notice that a pound sign (#) appears next to the ZIP field name. This symbol tells you that ZIP is an index field and that dBASE will use the ZIP index to speed the sort.

Press Menus (**F10**) and → to select the Fields pull-down menu. Type **S** to select Sort on This Field. From the submenu, select Ascending ASCII and press ←⎯. Notice in Figure 5.39 that the ZIP field now contains the sort operator *Asc1*, which is the same sort operator you would use if no index file were involved.

To execute the query, press Data (**F2**). As you can see in Figure 5.40, the browse screen displays California residents only, sorted into zip code order. Press Design (**Shift-F2**) to return to the query design screen.

USING COMPLEX INDEXES

A *complex index* uses more than one field. Complex indexes are always displayed to the right of database fields on the query design screen. In the preceding example, dBASE marked the ZIP field with a pound sign (#) to indicate that it was an index field. For a complex index such as LASTNAME + FIRSTNAME, dBASE displays an addition field on the query design screen. You can use this field both for sorting and for querying, just like any other field on the query design screen.

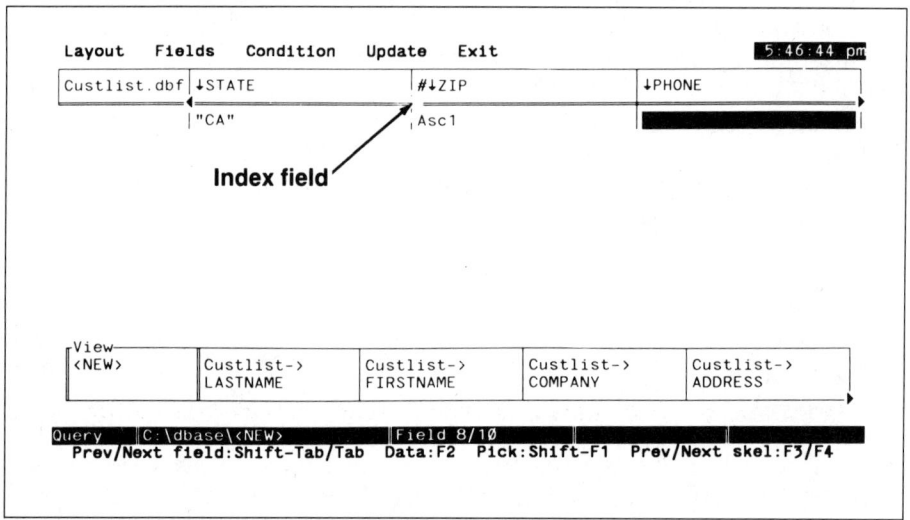

FIGURE 5.39: Query to display records of California residents, sorted by zip code. The ZIP field is indexed, as you can see by the # sign that precedes its name in the file skeleton.

USING INDEXES TO SORT QUERY RESULTS — 159

In a complex index field such as LASTNAME + FIRSTNAME, you cannot search for a first name or even for a last and first name unless you *pad* the last name with enough blank spaces to match the width of the field in the database, as discussed earlier in this chapter.

EXAMPLE

You must have an existing index named LASTNAME + FIRSTNAME to follow this example. This index was created in Chapter 4.

Suppose you want to display records from the CUSTLIST database for California residents only, in alphabetical order by last and first name. On the query design screen, press Menus (**F10**) and → to select the Fields menu. Move the highlight to the Include Indexes option and press ↵ to change the setting to Yes, so you can include indexes in your query.

Remove the Asc1 operator from the ZIP field, if it is there from the previous example. Leave the filter condition "CA" in the STATE field, or enter **"CA"** in the STATE field (including the quotation marks) if it is not there already. Press **End** to move to the rightmost column. You will see the additional field # *LASTNAME + FIRSTNAME*, with the # symbol again indicating that this is an index field.

```
  Records     Fields     Go To     Exit                          2:52:05 pm
 ┌──────────────┬───────┬───────┬───────────────┬───────────┬──────┐
 │ CITY         │ STATE │ ZIP   │ PHONE         │ STARTDATE │ PAID │
 ├──────────────┼───────┼───────┼───────────────┼───────────┼──────┤
 │ Santa Monica │ CA    │ 92001 │ (714)555-0123 │ 01/01/89  │      │
 │ San Diego    │ CA    │ 92067 │ (619)555-1234 │ 11/15/88  │ T    │
 │ Hideaway     │ CA    │ 92220 │ (415)555-9854 │ 01/01/89  │ T    │
 │ Los Angeles  │ CA    │ 96607 │ (213)555-9988 │ 12/30/88  │ F    │
 └──────────────┴───────┴───────┴───────────────┴───────────┴──────┘

 Browse  │C:\dbase\<NEW>│          │ Rec 2/9 │     │View│
                          View and edit fields
```

FIGURE 5.40: Results of the query in Figure 5.39. Records for California residents are displayed, sorted by zip code.

160 — CH. 5 SEARCHING THE DATABASE

With the highlight on # LASTNAME + FIRSTNAME, select Sort on This Field from the Fields pull-down menu. Select Ascending ASCII as the sort order. You have now specified that you want to search the index for California residents and to use the index to control the sort order of the display. Figure 5.41 shows a composite of how the query design screen looks. (Your screen will not show all of these fields at the same time, though you can change the order of fields on the browse screen—see the section "Selecting Fields for Display" later in this chapter.)

Press Data (**F2**) to execute the query. The browse screen displays only CA records, listed in alphabetical order by last and first name. Press Design (**Shift-F2**) to return to the query design screen after viewing the results of the query.

Using Queries to Find a Record

SEQUENCE OF STEPS

From the query design screen:

> highlight the query field
> type a filter condition ⏎

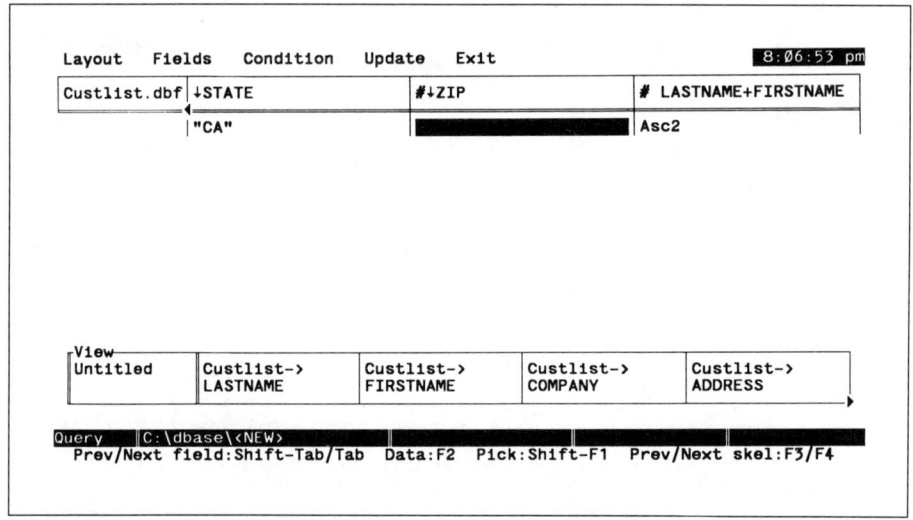

FIGURE 5.41: Search for California residents, with the LASTNAME + FIRSTNAME sort specified.

USING QUERIES TO FIND A RECORD 161

highlight the database name in the file skeleton
Find ↵
Data (**F2**)

USAGE

You can also use queries to *find* a particular record in the database. This is a handy way to locate a specific record in a database, without filtering out any other records. It is also a valuable alternative to the Forward Search option on the Go To menu, because it allows you to search multiple fields, using all the capabilities of the query design screen.

To use a query to locate a particular record, you enter the filter conditions on the query design screen. Move the highlight to the database name in the file skeleton (press **Home** to do this.) Type the word **Find** beneath the database file name, and press ↵.

When you press Data (**F2**) to execute the query, the highlight will be positioned on the record you specified in the query. All the other database records are still accessible; use the arrow, **PgUp** and **PgDn** keys to get them.

Figure 5.42 shows an example of a query that locates the first record with Mahoney in the LASTNAME field and Mary in the FIRSTNAME field.

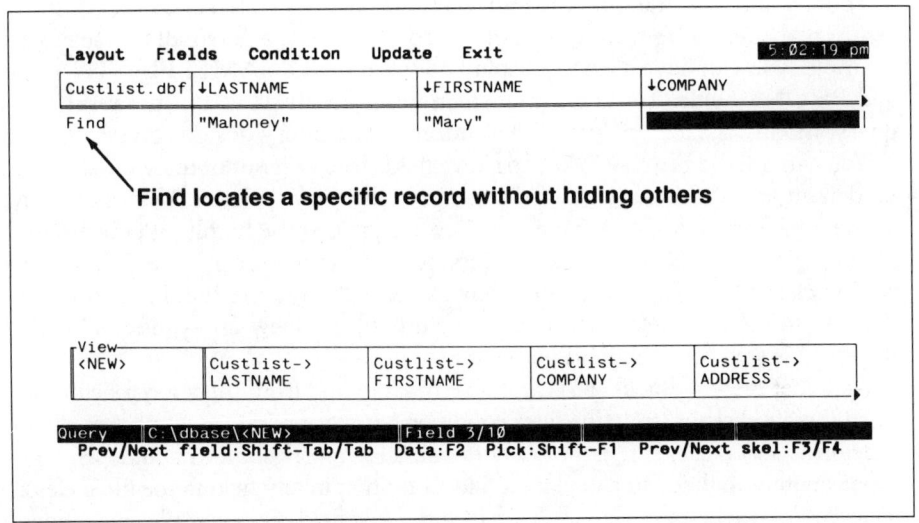

FIGURE 5.42: Query using the Find operator to locate Mary Mahoney's record.

Selecting Fields for Display

SEQUENCE OF STEPS

From the Control Center:

> highlight the database name in the Data panel ↵
> Use File
> highlight <create> in the Queries panel ↵
> highlight the database file name in the file skeleton
> Field (**F5**)

To copy fields into the view (repeat as necessary):

> highlight the field name in the file skeleton
> Field (**F5**)

To see the results:

> Data (**F2**)

USAGE

You can also use the query design screen to display only certain fields in the results of a query, rather than certain records. To create a personal phone list, for example, you can have dBASE display only the LASTNAME, FIRSTNAME, and PHONE fields. To determine which fields are displayed in the results of a query, modify the *view skeleton* at the bottom of the query design screen.

You can use the Field (**F5**) key to move fields into and out of the view skeleton. By default, dBASE includes all field names in the view skeleton. You can remove all the field names (and put them back) by positioning the highlight beneath each file name in the file skeleton and pressing Field (**F5**) (see Figure 5.43). Once you've cleared all fields from the view skeleton, move the highlight in the file skeleton to the first field you want to include in the view and press Field (**F5**). Repeat this step for each field you want to display.

Note that pressing Field (**F5**) can move fields to and from the view skeleton only when the file skeleton contains filter conditions or sort operators. However, the file skeleton and view skeleton in the query design screen work somewhat independently of one another in that you can place a filter condition in any field in the file skeleton, regardless of whether the view skeleton includes that field. For example, even though you can create a view skeleton to display only the PHONE, FIRSTNAME, and LASTNAME fields, you can still enter **"CA"** into the STATE field of the file skeleton to limit the phone number list to California residents.

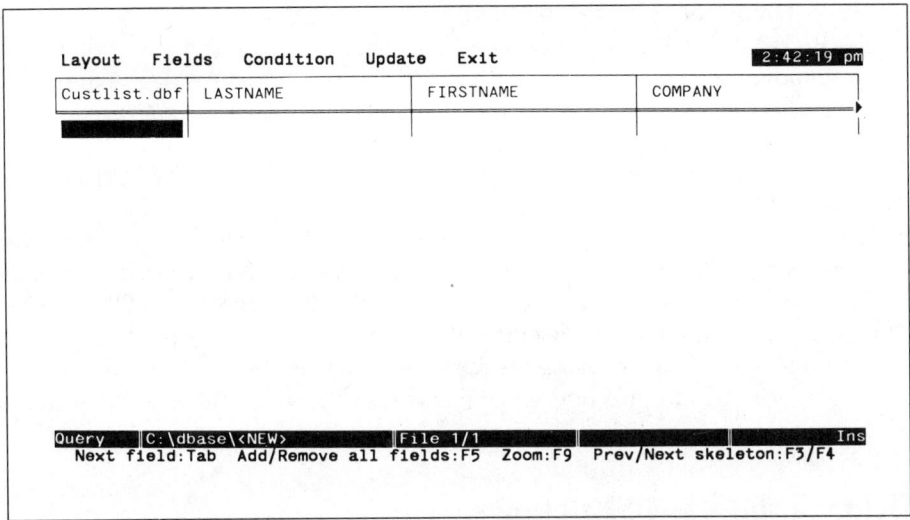

FIGURE 5.43: How to remove all fields from the view skeleton. Once you have removed all the fields, you can place them back in the view skeleton in the order you want to display them.

When you have created several view skeletons, you can see the next view skeleton by pressing Next (**F4**). When you press **F4**, a new set of navigation key options appears at the bottom of the screen. One of the options, *Prev/Next skeleton:F3/F4*, tells you that you can move back to the previous skeleton by pressing Previous (**F3**) and forward to the next skeleton by pressing Next (**F4**).

EXAMPLE

To create a view skeleton displaying only the PHONE, FIRSTNAME, and LASTNAME fields, begin at the Control Center. Highlight the CUSTLIST database in the Data panel and press ←. Select Use File by pressing ←. Move the highlight to <create> in the Queries panel and press ← to get to the query design screen and create a new query.

Press **Home**, if necessary, to move the highlight beneath the file name CUSTLIST.DBF. Then press Field (**F5**) until the view skeleton is empty (no field names appear at the bottom of the screen). Move the highlight to the PHONE field.

Press Field (**F5**) to copy this field into the view skeleton. You will notice two things: *Custlist->PHONE* now appears in the view skeleton, and the ↓ symbol appears to the left of the field name PHONE in the file skeleton. Both changes serve as reminders that the field will be displayed in the results of the query.

Press **Home** and then **Tab** twice to move the highlight to the FIRSTNAME field. Press Field (**F5**) to move a copy of the field to the view skeleton. Press **Shift-Tab** to move the highlight to the LASTNAME field. Press Field (**F5**) to move a copy of the LASTNAME field to the view skeleton.

As Figure 5.44 shows, the view skeleton now displays the three fields that will be displayed as a result of the query: PHONE, FIRSTNAME, and LASTNAME.

Now you can press Data (**F2**) to see the results. You will see that the browse screen displays the PHONE, FIRSTNAME, and LASTNAME fields for all the records in the database, as shown in Figure 5.45. If you press Data (**F2**) to switch to the edit screen, it too will display only these three fields. Press Design (**Shift-F2**) to return to the query design screen after viewing the results of the query.

If you want to save this query, see the section "Saving a Query" later in this chapter.

Moving Fields in the View Skeleton

SEQUENCE OF STEPS

In the view skeleton:

>highlight the field you want to move
>Move (**F7**)

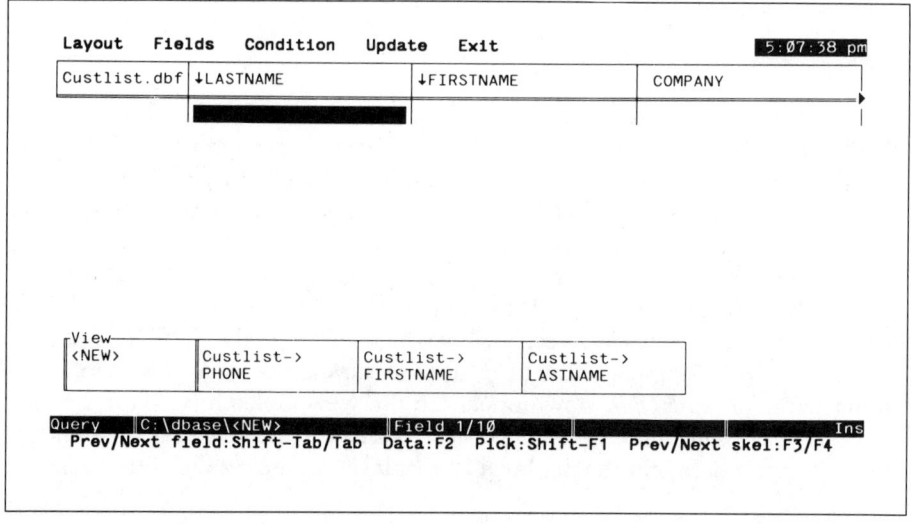

FIGURE 5.44: PHONE, FIRSTNAME, and LASTNAME fields are moved into the view skeleton so that the resulting query will display only those fields and in that order.

highlight the new location for the field

↵

USAGE

To move a field in the view skeleton, thereby rearranging the order in which fields are displayed, first make sure that the highlight is in the view skeleton. Then use the **Tab** or **Shift-Tab** key to highlight the field that you want to move. Finally, press Move (**F7**). dBASE will highlight the frame around the field and present the instructions *TAB or BACKTAB to move fields. <Return> to end*. This means that you use the **Tab** or **Shift-Tab** key to move the highlighted box to the new location for the field. When the field is in its new location, press ↵.

Selecting Groups of Fields

SEQUENCE OF STEPS

In the view skeleton:

> highlight the leftmost or rightmost field in the group
> Select (**F6**)
> highlight the other end of the group
> ↵

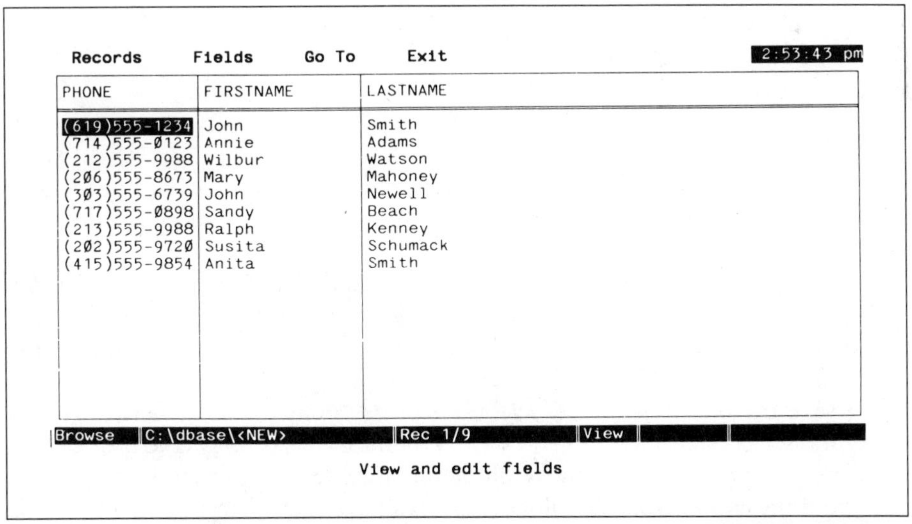

```
  Records      Fields      Go To     Exit              2:53:43 pm
 PHONE          FIRSTNAME   LASTNAME
 (619)555-1234  John        Smith
 (714)555-0123  Annie       Adams
 (212)555-9988  Wilbur      Watson
 (206)555-8673  Mary        Mahoney
 (303)555-6739  John        Newell
 (717)555-0898  Sandy       Beach
 (213)555-9988  Ralph       Kenney
 (202)555-9720  Susita      Schumack
 (415)555-9854  Anita       Smith

 Browse   C:\dbase\<NEW>         Rec 1/9      View
                       View and edit fields
```

FIGURE 5.45: Browse screen of the view created by the query in Figure 5.44. The PHONE, FIRSTNAME, and LASTNAME fields are displayed.

USAGE

While at the view skeleton, you can use Select (**F6**) to highlight a group of adjacent fields to work with. To use Select (**F6**), move the highlight to the leftmost or rightmost field in the group you want to select. Press Select (**F6**) and press the **Tab** or **Shift-Tab** key to extend the highlight to the left or right, as instructed on the screen. (Do not highlight *all* the fields, or you will not be able to move them.)

Press ↵ after highlighting a group of fields. Press Field (**F5**) to remove all those fields from the view. Press Move (**F7**) to move that entire group of fields to a new location. After you complete your job, the highlighting disappears.

SAVING A QUERY

SEQUENCE OF STEPS

To provide a description:

> Menus (**F10**)
> Layout/Edit Description of Query [↵]
> type a description ↵

To save the query and its description:

> Menus (**F10**)
> Exit/Save Changes and Exit [↵]
> type a name ↵

USAGE

You can save any query that you create. You can then use that query again later without having to reenter all the keystrokes for filter conditions and so forth. In dBASE IV, a saved query is called a *view*.

Before you save a query, first assign a description to it by pressing Menus (**F10**) from the query design screen, highlighting Layout in the menu bar, and selecting Edit Description of Query. When prompted, type a description and then press ↵.

To save the query and its description, press Menus (**F10**) again, highlight Exit, and select Save Changes and Exit. When dBASE displays the prompt *Save as:*, type a valid DOS file name (eight letters maximum, no spaces or punctuation) and press ↵. dBASE will add the extension .QBE to the file name you provide.

You will be returned to the Control Center, where the Queries panel will list the new query. When you highlight the name of the query, its description will also appear.

EXAMPLE

To save the query created in the last example (and shown in Figure 5.44), first provide a description for the query. Press Menus (**F10**) from the query design screen, highlight Layout in the menu bar, and select Edit Description of Query. When prompted, type **California phone numbers** and press ↵.

To save the query and its description, press Menus (**F10**) again, highlight Exit, and select Save Changes and Exit. When dBASE displays the prompt *Save as:*, type **PHONELST** and press ↵. dBASE will add the extension .QBE. You will be returned to the Control Center, where the Queries panel will list PHONELST.QBE. When you highlight the query name, its description will also appear, as shown in Figure 5.46.

USING VIEWS

Figure 5.46 shows the three basic techniques that you can use with a view (or saved query).

To look at (or edit) database data through a view, highlight the name of the query in the Queries panel and press Data (**F2**). This sequence is similar to the one you use

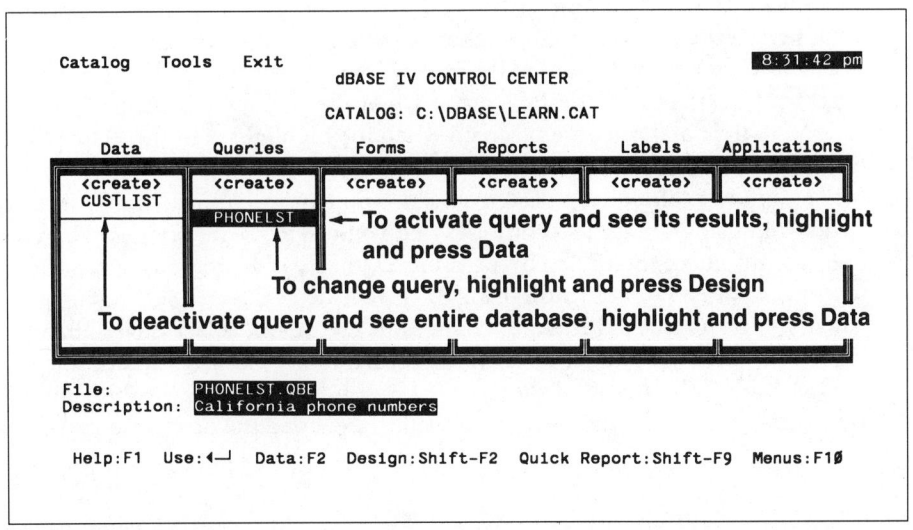

FIGURE 5.46: When you save and name a query, its name (PHONELST in this example) appears in the Queries panel.

to view the contents of the entire database, where you highlight the name of the database in the Data panel and press Data (**F2**).

When you have finished looking at (or editing) the data through the view, select Exit from the Exit pull-down menu to return to the Control Center. At the Control Center, you will see the name of the view above the line in the Queries panel, indicating that the row is still in use. (So long as the view is in use, you can access the database from which you created it only through this view.)

EXAMPLE

If you created the PHONELST view in the previous examples, highlight its name in the Queries panel and press Data (**F2**). You will see the edit or browse screen with entries from the LASTNAME, FIRSTNAME, and PHONE fields of the CUSTLIST database. From there, you can use Data (**F2**) to switch between the edit and browse screens.

When you have finished looking at (or editing) the data through the view, select Exit from the Exit pull-down menu to return to the Control Center. At the Control Center, you will see the PHONELST name above the line in the Queries panel, indicating that this view is still in use. So long as the PHONELST view is in use, you can access the CUSTLIST database only through this view.

Changing a View

If you want to change a query, highlight its name in the Queries panel and press Design (**Shift-F2**). You will be taken to the query design screen, where you can make any changes you want to the query. (Note that pressing Design (**Shift-F2**) takes you to the query design screen when the highlight is in the Queries panel, and to the database design screen when the highlight is in the Data panel of the Control Center.)

While you are at the query design screen, you can modify the query in any way you want using the same techniques that you use to create queries. You can also see the results of the query by pressing Data (**F2**). To return to the query design screen, press Design (**Shift-F2**).

When you have finished making changes to the query, select Save Changes and Exit from the Exit pull-down menu to return to the Control Center (or just press **Ctrl-End**). The name of the query will still be accessible in the Control Center, and any changes you have made will be included the next time you activate the query.

Deactivating a View

When you want to stop using a query and regain access to all the records and fields in your database file, simply open the database file, which deactivates the query. For example, to deactivate the PHONELST query of the CUSTLIST database and regain access to all the records and fields in that CUSTLIST database, highlight CUSTLIST in the Data panel and press Data (**F2**). dBASE will send you to the browse (or edit) screen for the entire CUSTLIST database.

To leave the edit or browse screen and return to the Control Center, select Exit from the Exit pull-down menu (or just press **Esc**). When you return to the Control Center, the CUSTLIST database name will be above the line in the Data panel, indicating that the CUSTLIST database is open and ready for use. The PHONELST query name will be below the line, indicating that it is no longer active (that is, no longer affecting your view of the CUSTLIST database).

Options for Using the Queries Panel

Just as the Data panel offers alternatives to the Data and Design keys, so does the Queries panel. If you highlight the name of a saved query in the Queries panel and press ←┘, you will see three options. If the query is not active, the three options will be

    Use View   Modify Query   Display Data

If the highlighted query is active when you press ←┘, the three options will be

    Close View   Modify Query   Display Data

Selecting Use View puts the view name above the line in the queries panel. Selecting Close View deactivates the query, putting its name below the line. Selecting Modify Query takes you to the query design screen—exactly as though you had pressed Design (**Shift-F2**)—and lets you make changes to the query. Selecting Display Data activates the view and takes you to the edit or browse screen—as though you had pressed Data (**F2**).

TIPS AND TRAPS

- The wildcard characters, ? and *, can be used in several contexts within dBASE (and outside of dBASE as well), so you should at least be familiar with them.

- Remember to move the highlight to the field you want to search before using the Search Forward or Search Backward options on the Go To menu.
- If you forget to put quotation marks around the filter condition in a Character field search, dBASE will still accept the value and execute the query. However, the results of the query will probably not be what you had in mind.
- If you forget to remove the previous filter condition from the query design screen before you enter a new one, the old filter condition will affect the new query. Therefore, if your query does not produce the results you expected when you press Data (**F2**), press Design (**Shift-F2**) to return to the query design screen. Then use the **Tab** key to scroll through the fields to see if you forgot to erase any filter conditions from the previous query. If you find a filter condition, remove it (using **Ctrl-Y** or **Del**) and try the query operation again.
- When you are querying a field of the Date data type, you must enclose the date you are searching for in curly braces ({}).
- The most common error people make in queries is entering filter conditions that do not make sense, such as looking for records with one state AND another, instead of OR another as intended.
- One simple rule to remember when you are creating AND queries: You must put all filter conditions for the query *on the same row* of the query design screen.
- One simple rule to remember when you are creating OR queries: You must put all filter conditions for the query *on different rows* of the query design screen.

SUMMARY

This chapter discussed the techniques for searching a database and for combining sorting and searching. If you are working with large databases, you will want to use indexes to handle your sorting and searching, because indexes provide the fastest, most efficient means for performing these tasks.

Later chapters describe how to use saved queries (views) to isolate records for printing information such as mailing labels and form letters. Such tasks are where saved queries really come in handy. Saved queries allow you to isolate targeted records (those of New York residents, for example) and then print letters and labels in zip code order to take advantage of bulk-mailing rates.

For techniques for using the Expression Builder menu:

- Chapter 4, "Sorting the Database"

For discussion of using queries with Numeric fields:
- Chapter 6, "Performing Calculations"

For printing formatted reports from the results of queries:
- Chapter 9, "Printing Reports and Labels"

For discussion of using queries with multiple datatabases and printing reports from queries of multiple databases:
- Chapter 10: "Managing Multiple Related Databases"

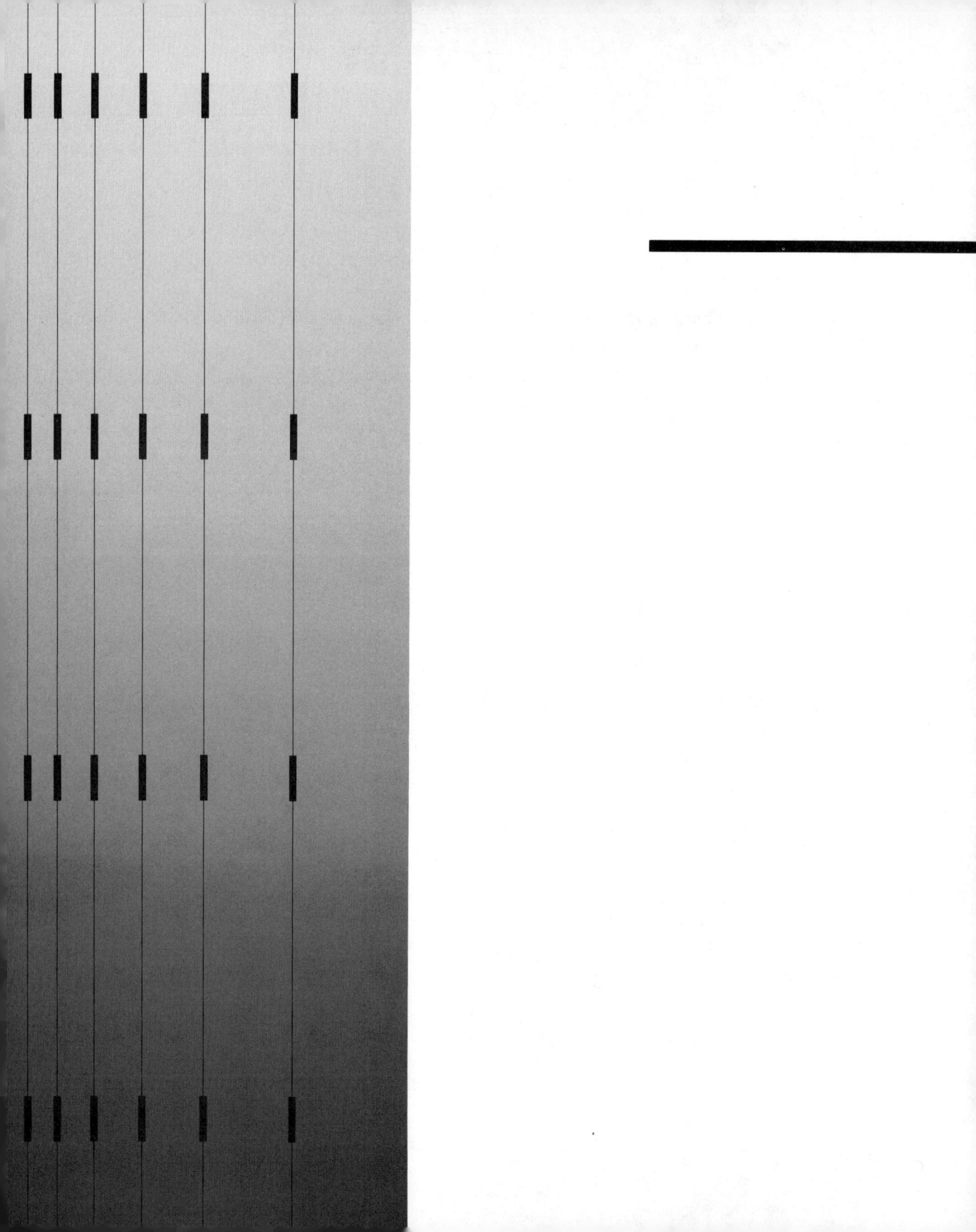

CHAPTER 6

PERFORMING CALCULATIONS

Using Numeric Fields. 175
    Numeric and Float Data Types. 175
    Arithmetic Operators. 175
    Order of Precedence. 176
    Negative Numbers. 176
    Sizing Numbers. 176
Using Numeric Templates. 177
Using Numeric Picture Functions. 177
Performing Calculations in Reports. 178
    Printing Quick Reports with Totals. 179
    Creating a Report Format. 181
    Adding Calculated Fields. 183
    Calculating Totals. 185
        Adding a Row of Equal Signs. 188
    Calculating Subtotals. 190
        Printing Subtotaled Reports. 195
Adding Calculated Fields to Forms. 196
Using Queries to Perform Calculations. 198
    Creating Calculated Fields. .199
        Removing All Calculated Fields. 201
    Using Filter Conditions with Numbers. 202
    Using Summary Operators. .203
    Performing Calculations on Groups of Records. 207
        Changing the Sort Order. .208
    Calculating Frequency Distributions. 209
    Calculating Dates. 211
    Comparing Fields. 212
        Using Placeholders to Compare Dates. 213

    Performing Conditional Calculations. 214
Indexing on the Results of Calculations. .219
Tips and Traps. 220
Summary. 221

Performing Calculations

dBASE IV offers great power and flexibility for performing calculations in reports, forms, and queries. Whether you need to add 6.5 percent tax to sales transactions, print a subtotaled report of outstanding orders, list accounts receivable over 30 days past due, or count the customers in each state in a customer list, dBASE can help you get the information you need.

Using Numeric Fields

dBASE IV offers two different types of numeric fields: Float (floating point) and Numeric. You can use all of the techniques discussed in this chapter with either type of number. The only difference between the two is the way dBASE handles them behind the scenes, which affects the type of number you use for a particular application.

Numeric and Float Data Types

You can use the Numeric data type for most business applications, where numbers usually have a fixed number of decimal places. For example, sales quantities, such as 10 or 190 units, usually have no decimal places. Dollar amounts, such as $1.98, always have two decimal places. The Numeric data type is the most accurate for performing calculations with such numbers.

You should use the Float data type for scientific applications that involve extremely large or extremely small numbers with no fixed number of decimal places. If a single field has a very large number, such as 789,876.1, in one record and a very small number, such as 0.00012, in another, and you need to perform calculations on these numbers, then you should use the Float data type.

Arithmetic Operators

dBASE IV offers the arithmetic operators shown in Table 6.1 for performing calculations. You can also use relational operators—such as < (less than), > (greater than), < = (less than or equal to), > = (greater than or equal to), = (equal to), and # or < > (not equal to)—to compare numbers.

OPERATOR	PERFORMS	EXAMPLE
+	Addition	2 + 2 = 4
−	Subtraction	5 − 3 = 2
*	Multiplication	3*5 = 15
/	Division	10/2 = 5
^ or **	Exponentiation	3^2 = 9 3**2 = 9
( )	Grouping	(1 + 2)*5 = 15 1 + (2*5) = 11

Table 6.1: dBASE IV Arithmetic Operators

Order of Precedence

dBASE IV follows the standard mathematical order of precedence when performing calculations. That is, parenthetical operations take place first, followed by exponentiation, then multiplication and division, then addition and subtraction. Therefore, the formulas 2*5 + 1 and 1 + 2*5 both produce the same result, 11, because the multiplication takes place first.

When in doubt about order of precedence, use parentheses to group operations. For example, the formula (1 + 2)*5 results in 15, because the parentheses force the addition to take place before the multiplication. When using parentheses in a mathematical formula, you must make sure that the formula contains an equal number of opening and closing parentheses. Otherwise, dBASE responds with an error message, such as *Syntax error* or *Unbalanced parentheses*.

Negative Numbers

To enter a negative number into a field, precede the number with a minus sign. (You can use the hyphen on the keyboard.) For example, −10 is negative 10 (or minus 10).

Sizing Numbers

When you create a database with Numeric or Float fields, you need to define both a width and a number of decimal places for those fields. If you need only whole numbers, then you can set the number of decimal places to zero. For example, a numeric field with a width of four characters and zero decimal places can handle any number in the range −999 to 9999 (the minus sign requires a place in the width you specify).

When you are sizing numbers that require decimal places, remember that the decimal point takes up one digit in the width you assign. Therefore, if you assign a width of nine characters and two decimal places to a field, then the field can hold any number in the range −99999.99 to 999999.99.

Using Numeric Templates

When you place a numeric field (Numeric or Float) in a report or form design, you will see a *template* that reflects the width and number of decimal places assigned to the number in the database. For example, if a number is assigned a width of eight characters and two decimal places, the template for that field will automatically be 99999.99.

Unlike Character data, numeric data is never truncated to fit within the space provided by a template. When a number is too large for the space allotted, dBASE displays only asterisks. For example, the template 999 displays only numbers with three or fewer digits. It displays any larger number, such as 1,000, as asterisks (***). Therefore, if you change a template on a form or report format, be sure to specify enough digits to accommodate the largest possible number for the field or calculation.

To specify the number of decimal places displayed in printed numbers, insert a decimal point in the appropriate position in the template. dBASE will round the number to fit the template. For example, the template 99999 displays the value 12345.678 as 12346 (no decimal places displayed). The template 99999.99 displays the same value as 12345.68. The template 99999.9999 displays the value as 12345.6780.

To display numbers with embedded commas, such as 12,345 (rather than 12345), insert commas into the template wherever you want them to appear in the printed number. If you use the template 999,999.99 to display extended prices, then the value 3850.00 will be displayed as 3,850.00. The number 123.45 will still be displayed as 123.45, because it is not large enough to require a comma.

Using Numeric Picture Functions

Numeric picture functions let you refine the format of printed numbers. Whenever you select Add Field or Modify Field from the Fields menu and then select Picture Functions, you will see the options shown in Figure 6.1. This same menu appears when you use the Fields menu from the reports, labels, or forms

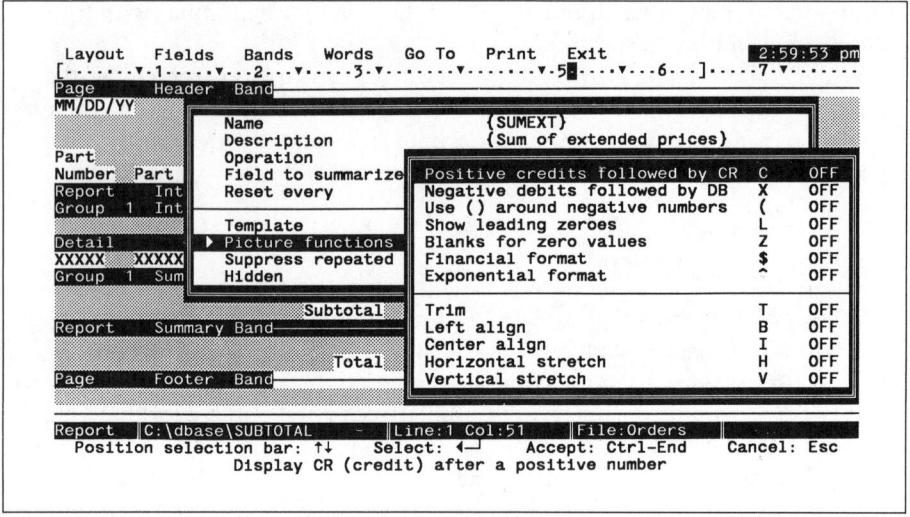

FIGURE 6.1: Numeric picture functions menu. This menu appears when you select Add Field or Modify Field from the Fields pull-down menu and then select Picture Functions on the report, labels, and forms design screens. These picture functions are explained with examples in Table 6.2.

design screen. You can move the highlight to any option and press the space bar to turn it on or off.

Table 6.2 lists the picture functions on the menu, with examples of how those functions affect the numbers 0, −123, and 98765.43. The examples all use 999,999.99 as the template.

You can combine picture functions. For example, combining the C and X functions places CR after positive numbers and DB after negative numbers. Combining the Z and (functions prints positive numbers normally, negative numbers in parentheses, and zeros as blank spaces (rather than as 0 or 0.00). Combining the (and $ functions places parentheses around negative dollar amounts: for example, ($123.45).

PERFORMING CALCULATIONS IN REPORTS

You can create reports for databases that include calculated data. dBASE displays the results of calculated fields, and it calculates totals and subtotals for you. This discussion assumes that you know how to set up and generate dBASE reports, as discussed in Chapter 7. If you have never worked with reports before, you should read that chapter first.

It is not a good idea to *store* the results of calculations in a database, for two reasons. First, any calculations can easily be performed while you are displaying

PICTURE FUNCTION	SYMBOL	EXAMPLES
Follow positive credits by CR	C	0.00 CR − 123.00 98,765.43 CR
Follow negative debits by DB	X	0.00 123.00 DB 98,765.43
Use ( ) around negative numbers	(	0.00 (123.00) 98,765.43
Show leading zeroes	L	000000.00 000 − 123.00 098,765.43
Use blanks for zero values	Z	 − 123.00 98,765.43
Use financial format	$	$0.00 $ − 123.00 $98,765.43
Use exponential format	^	.00000000000E + − .123 .123000000000000E + 3 .987654300000000E + 5

Table 6.2: Numeric Picture Functions

data, so storing the results of calculations in the database file wastes disk space. Second, if you store the results of calculations in a field, then any time you change a number in another field that affects the calculation, you will have to make sure that all other calculated fields are also changed accordingly. This wastes time and increases the likelihood of errors.

Printing Quick Reports with Totals

SEQUENCE OF STEPS

From the Control Center:

>highlight the database name in the Data panel
>Quick Report (**Shift-F9**)
>**B**egin Printing [⏎]

USAGE

You can print a quick report of a database with numeric fields, and dBASE will automatically total those fields. A *quick report* uses exactly the same structure as the database it is derived from, and it does not allow any data formatting, such as adding dollar signs. As their name suggests, quick reports are intended more for your own review than for presentation to others. See "Creating a Report Format" later in this chapter for information about using the report design screen to specify exactly what you want your report to look like.

To print a quick report, highlight the database name in the Data panel and press Quick Report (**Shift-F9**). Select Begin Printing from the submenu by pressing ↵. You will see that the report contains totals of the numeric fields in the database.

EXAMPLE

Figure 6.2 shows the structure of a database named ORDERS. As you can see, the QTY field has a width of three characters and zero decimal places, and the UNITPRICE field has a width of nine characters and two decimal places.

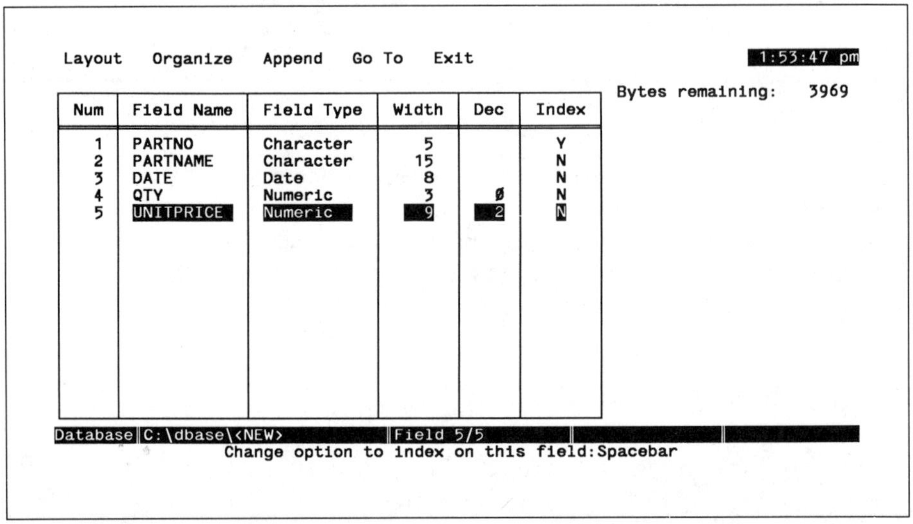

FIGURE 6.2: Structure of the ORDERS database. If you create this database, you will be able to follow many of the examples in this book.

Notice that the database includes fields for the quantity and unit price of each order, but not for the extended price (that is, the quantity times the unit price).

CREATING A REPORT FORMAT — 181

This is because the extended price is the result of a calculation. The section "Adding Calculated Fields" later in this chapter shows how to include such a field in reports you design; also see "Adding Calculated Fields to Forms" and "Using Queries to Perform Calculations" later in this chapter.

Figure 6.3 shows ten records entered into the ORDERS database. Enter the records as shown to follow the examples in this chapter. (Note that you may have already created this database if you followed the examples in Chapter 4.)

```
    Records     Fields     Go To     Exit                    1:41:26 pm
    ┌───────┬───────────────┬─────────┬─────┬──────────┐
    │PARTNO │PARTNAME       │DATE     │ QTY │UNITPRICE │
    ├───────┼───────────────┼─────────┼─────┼──────────┤
    │B-222  │Banana Man     │06/01/90 │  2  │  100.00  │
    │B-222  │Banana Man     │06/01/90 │  1  │  100.00  │
    │A-111  │Astro Buddies  │06/01/90 │  2  │   50.00  │
    │C-333  │Cosmic Critters│06/01/90 │  1  │  500.00  │
    │A-111  │Astro Buddies  │06/02/90 │  3  │   50.00  │
    │A-111  │Astro Buddies  │06/05/90 │  4  │   50.00  │
    │B-222  │Banana Man     │06/15/90 │  1  │  100.00  │
    │C-333  │Cosmic Critters│06/15/90 │  2  │  500.00  │
    │C-333  │Cosmic Critters│06/15/90 │  1  │  500.00  │
    │C-333  │Cosmic Critters│07/01/90 │  2  │  500.00  │
    └───────┴───────────────┴─────────┴─────┴──────────┘
    Browse  C:\dbase\ORDERS       Rec 10/10    File
                         View and edit fields
```

FIGURE 6.3: Sample data in the ORDERS database for use in the examples in this chapter.

Highlight ORDERS in the Data panel and press Quick Report (**Shift-F9**) to print a quick report of its data. Select Begin Printing from the submenu by pressing ↵. You will see that the report contains totals of the numeric fields QTY and UNITPRICE, as Figure 6.4 shows.

Creating a Report Format

SEQUENCE OF STEPS

From the Control Center:

    highlight <create> in the Reports panel ↵
    Layout/**Q**uick Layouts [↵]
    Column Layout [↵]

```
            Page No.   1
            07/08/90
            PARTNO   PARTNAME         DATE        QTY     UNITPRICE
            B-222    Banana Man       06/01/90     2        100.00
            B-222    Banana Man       06/01/90     1        100.00
            A-111    Astro Buddies    06/01/90     2         50.00
            C-333    Cosmic Critters  06/01/90     1        500.00
            A-111    Astro Buddies    06/02/90     3         50.00
            A-111    Astro Buddies    06/05/90     4         50.00
            B-222    Banana Man       06/15/90     1        100.00
            C-333    Cosmic Critters  06/15/90     2        500.00
            C-333    Cosmic Critters  06/15/90     1        500.00
            C-333    Cosmic Critters  07/01/90     2        500.00
                                                  19       2450.00
```

FIGURE 6.4: Quick report of the ORDERS database. dBASE creates this report when you press Shift-F9 from the Control Center.

USAGE

To create a quick, generic report with totals, you can use the generic report layout option, which creates a report format that is identical to the format used for quick reports. Templates for all fields are spread across the Detail band, and templates for the totals of numeric fields appear in the Report Summary band. The names of the database fields, which appear as column headings in the printed report, appear within the Page Header band. (Report bands and field templates are discussed in Chapter 7. Briefly, *bands* are the areas on a design screen in which you specify what will appear in corresponding areas of the report that dBASE generates; the Detail band corresponds to the body of the report, where the specified values from the database will appear. *Templates* are series of characters showing how and where data from corresponding fields will appear.)

The advantage of using this option is that you can use the basic layout as a starting point for your report, and then you can modify the design from the reports design screen.

First make sure the database you want to use is open (with its name above the line in the Control Center Data panel). Use the **Tab** key to move the highlight to <create> in the Reports panel and then press ←┘. Select Quick Layouts from the Layout pull-down menu. Then select Column Layout.

EXAMPLE

To create a generic report layout for the ORDERS database (shown in Figure 6.2), first make sure the ORDERS database is open (with its name above the line in the Control Center Data panel). Use the **Tab** key to move the highlight to the Reports panel and select <create>. Select Quick Layouts from the Layout pull-down menu. Then select Column Layout.

dBASE creates a report format that is identical to the format used for quick reports, as Figure 6.5 shows. To modify the report layout, proceed to the next example.

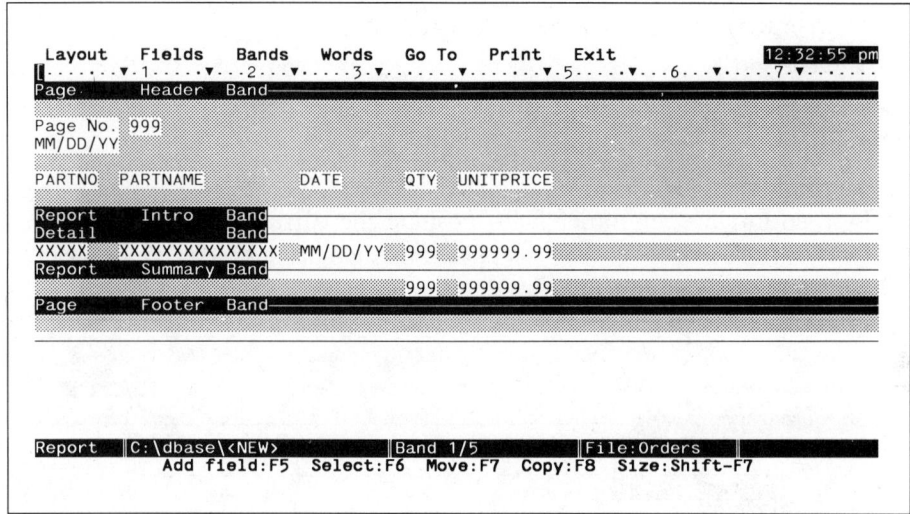

FIGURE 6.5: Initial column layout provided by dBASE for a report of the ORDERS database. You can modify this layout.

The example here uses a database with very few fields, so all the data easily fits across one row on the screen and on one printed page. When you create columnar reports with larger databases, the fields might extend well beyond the right margin of the screen and printed page. You can move field templates (or remove them) using the basic techniques discussed in Chapter 7.

Adding Calculated Fields

SEQUENCE OF STEPS

On the reports design screen:

    move the cursor to where you want the field to appear
    Field (**F5**)
    highlight <create> in the CALCULATED column ↵
    Name [↵]

184 — CH. 6 PERFORMING CALCULATIONS

enter a name

Description [↵]

enter a description

Expression [↵]

enter the expression for this calculated field

Ctrl-End

USAGE

The basic steps for adding a calculated field to a report format are the same as those used to place any other field. Position the cursor on the reports design screen where you want the field to appear and then press Field (**F5**). You will see the menu of options shown in Figure 6.6.

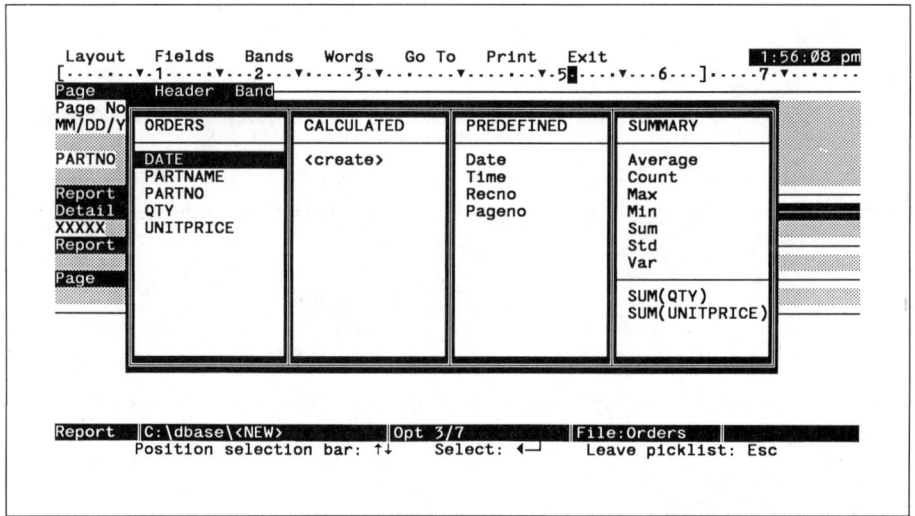

FIGURE 6.6: Options for fields to place in the report format. On the reports design screen, press Field (**F5**) with the cursor at the position where you want the field to appear. Select <create> from the CALCULATED column to create a calculated field. See Chapter 7 for information about the predefined fields.

Select <create> in the CALCULATED column, because you want to create a calculated field. At this point, you are given options to define a name, description, and expression and to display attributes for the calculated field.

You need to enter a name for the new calculated field. Select Name and enter a name. Select Description to enter a plain-English description. The description is optional, but you may find it useful for future reference. Select Expression and enter the expression for this calculated field.

You can also change the display attributes (that is, the template and picture functions) for the calculated field, as discussed earlier in this chapter.

Press **Ctrl-End** to place the new calculated field template in the report format. Notice that when the cursor is in the calculated field template, the bottom line of the screen describes the field. This information can be helpful in the future, when you need to know what a field template contains.

EXAMPLE

Add a calculated field to the report format for the ORDERS database shown in Figure 6.5. The new field will display the extended price (the quantity times the unit price).

On the reports design screen, move the cursor to column 55 in the Detail band (two spaces to the right of all other field templates within the Detail band). Press Field (**F5**). You will see the menu of options shown in Figure 6.6.

Select <create> in the CALCULATED column, because you want to create a calculated field. At this point, you are given options to define a name, description, and expression and to display attributes for the calculated field.

Select Name and enter **EXTPRICE** as the name for this new calculated field. Select Description and enter **Extended price**. Select Expression and enter the expression **Qty * UnitPrice** to multiply the quantity by the unit price in this calculated field.

Your screen should now look like Figure 6.7. Press **Ctrl-End** to place the new calculated field template in the report format, as shown in Figure 6.8. Note that in this figure the Page Header band has been modified, the column titles have been changed, and a title has been added for the new field. (Chapter 7 tells how to make modifications such as these.)

Notice that when the cursor is in the calculated field template in the Detail band, the bottom line of the screen describes the field, as follows:

EXTPRICE Expression: Qty * UnitPrice

This information can be helpful in the future, when you need to know what a field template contains.

Calculating Totals

SEQUENCE OF STEPS

On the reports design screen:

    move the cursor to the column to display the total in the Report Summary band

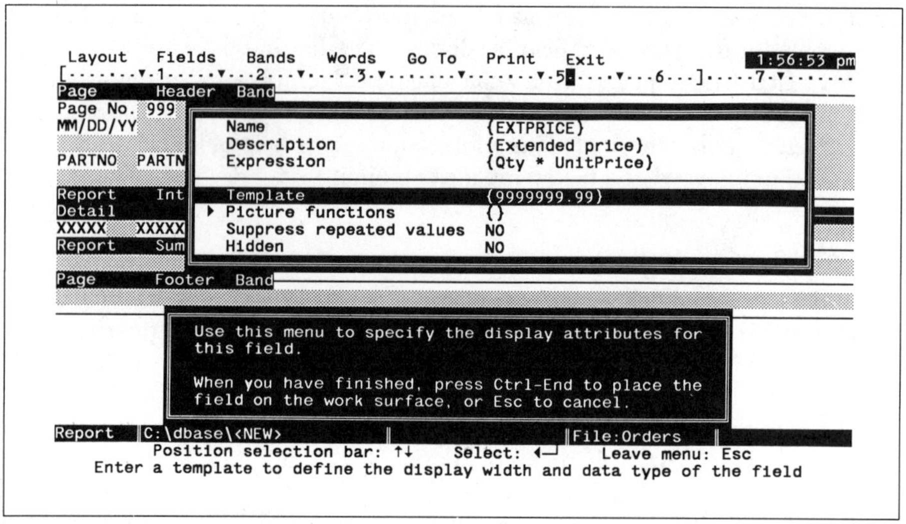

186 —— **CH. 6** PERFORMING CALCULATIONS

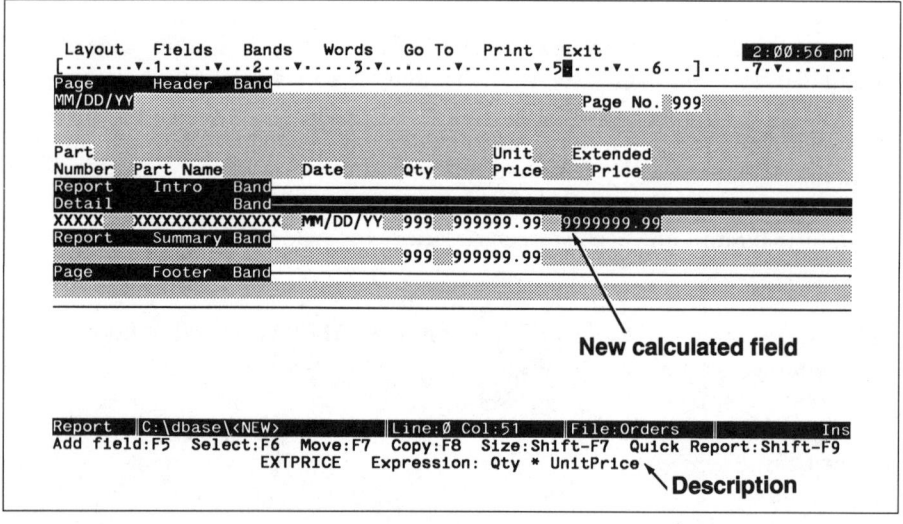

FIGURE 6.7: Calculated field defined by name, description, and expression. Press **Ctrl-End** to place the field on the report form.

FIGURE 6.8: Calculated field added to the report format.

       Field (**F5**)
       Sum in SUMMARY column [←]
       Name [←]
       enter a name for the field
       Description [←]
       enter a description for the field
       Field to Summarize On [←]
       select the field to total
       Ctrl-End

To describe the report:

       Layout/**E**dit Description of Report [←]
       type a description ←

To save the report format:

       Exit/**S**ave Changes and Exit [←]
       type the report name ←

From the Control Center, to print the report:

       highlight the report name in the Reports panel ←
       Print Report [←]
       Begin Printing [←]

USAGE

To display totals in custom reports, you need to use a *summary field*. A summary field summarizes the information in a group of records. The summary might be a total or subtotal, an average, a count, or some other calculation. Table 6.3 lists the summary options. You can use as many of these options as appropriate; for example, a statistical report might include the maximum, minimum, standard deviation, and variance.

To display the total once at the end of a report, you need to place it in the Report Summary band. In the Report Summary band, move the cursor to the column where you want the total to appear and press Field (**F5**). You will see the menu of options shown in Figure 6.6.

You want a summary field that calculates a total (sum), so move the cursor to the SUMMARY column and select Sum. You can select Name and enter a name for the field (such as **SUMEXT**) and select Description and enter

OPTION	OPERATION
Average	Displays the average for a group of numbers
Count	Counts the number of records in a group
Max	Displays the largest value in a group
Min	Displays the smallest value in a group
Sum	Displays the total of the values in a group
Std	Displays the standard deviation (a statistical measure) for a group
Var	Displays the variance (a statistical measure) for a group

Table 6.3: Summary Field Options

a description. The name and description are optional in summary fields. If you do not name the field, the Operation and Summarize information still appears at the bottom of the screen. In the Add Field menu that appears when you press Field (**F5**), unnamed summary fields are displayed in the format SUM(QTY), SUM(UNITPRICE), and so on.

Select Field to Summarize On and then select the field you want to total from the submenu that appears. Press **Ctrl-End**. The template for the summary field will appear on the screen.

Adding a Row of Equal Signs

To improve the report format, you can use a row of equal signs to create a double line between the Detail band and the totals. To do so, first press **Home** to move the cursor to column 0 in the Report Summary band. Press **Ctrl-N** to insert a blank line above the totals templates.

Type a string of equal signs above the 9s in the field templates, as was done in Figure 6.9, which shows a report format with a summary field and equal signs. Notice that when the cursor is within the template for the summary field, its name, the operation it performs, and the name of the field it summarizes are displayed at the bottom of the screen.

To save the report format, first select Edit Description of Report from the Layout pull-down menu and enter a description. Then select Save Changes and Exit from the Exit pull-down menu. When asked to name the report, enter a valid name. After dBASE creates a program for printing the report, it returns you to the Control Center. From there, you can print the report by selecting its name from the Reports panel and then selecting Print Report and Begin Printing.

CALCULATING TOTALS   189

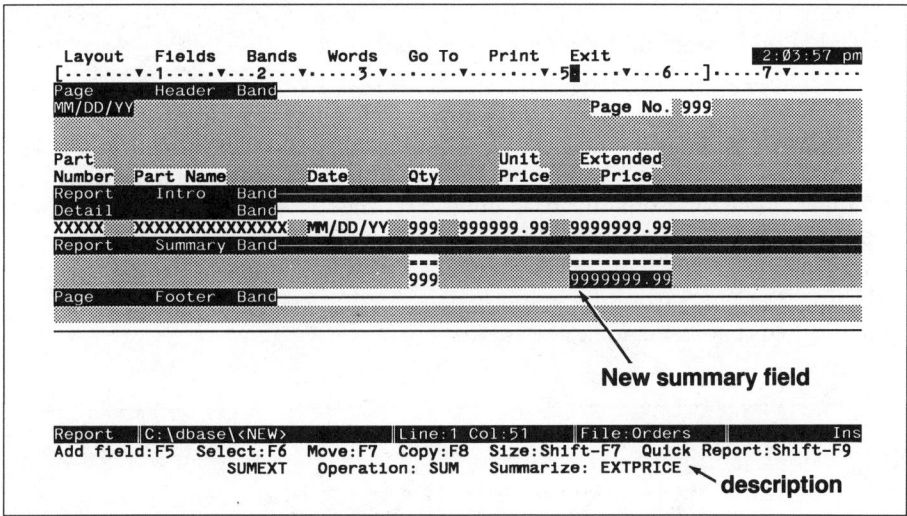

FIGURE 6.9: Summary field added to the report format.

EXAMPLE

Suppose you want to create a summary field to total all the extended prices in the ORDERS database. You want this total to appear once at the end of the report, so you need to place it in the Report Summary band. (If the total of the UNITPRICE field is currently in the format, remove it now by moving the cursor to the summary field template for the UNITPRICE field and pressing **Del** to remove the template. The description at the bottom of the screen will show *Operation: SUM Summarize: UNITPRICE* when the cursor is in the correct template.)

Staying within the Report Summary band, use the arrow keys to move the cursor to column 55. Press Field (**F5**). You want a summary field that calculates a total (sum), so move the cursor to the SUMMARY column and select Sum. Select Name and enter **SUMEXT** as the name for the field. Select Description and enter **Sum of extended prices**. Select Field to Summarize On and then select EXTPRICE from the submenu that appears (because you want to total the EXTPRICE field). Press **Ctrl-End**. The template for the summary field will be displayed.

Now use equal signs to create a double line between the Detail band and the totals. To do so, first press **Home** to move the cursor to column 0 in the Report Summary band. Press **Ctrl-N** to insert a blank line.

Type a string of equal signs above the 99999 and 9999999.99 templates. Figure 6.9 shows the report format with the new summary field and the equal signs. Notice that when the cursor is within the template for the summary field, its name, the operation it performs, and the name of field it summarizes are displayed at the bottom of the screen, as follows:

SUMEXT Operation: SUM Summarize: EXTPRICE

To save the report format, first select Edit Description of Report from the Layout pull-down menu and enter the description **Total sales**. Then select Save Changes and Exit from the Exit pull-down menu. When asked to name the report, enter **TOTALS**. After dBASE creates a program for printing the report, it returns you to the Control Center. From there, you can print the report by selecting TOTALS from the Reports panel, Print Report, and Begin Printing. The printed report will look like Figure 6.10.

```
07/08/90                                          Page No.    1

Part                                     Unit      Extended
Number   Part Name     Date      Qty     Price     Price
B-222    Banana Man    06/01/90   2      100.00    200.00
B-222    Banana Man    06/01/90   1      100.00    100.00
A-111    Astro Buddies 06/01/90   2       50.00    100.00
C-333    Cosmic Critters 06/01/90 1      500.00    500.00
A-111    Astro Buddies 06/02/90   3       50.00    150.00
A-111    Astro Buddies 06/05/90   4       50.00    200.00
B-222    Banana Man    06/15/90   1      100.00    100.00
C-333    Cosmic Critters 06/15/90 2      500.00   1000.00
C-333    Cosmic Critters 06/15/90 1      500.00    500.00
C-333    Cosmic Critters 07/01/90 2      500.00   1000.00
                                 =====             ==========
                                  19               3850.00
```

FIGURE 6.10: The printed TOTALS report, with quantity and extended price totals.

Calculating Subtotals

SEQUENCE OF STEPS

From the Control Center:
   To modify an existing report format to include subtotals:

      highlight the report name in the Data panel

      Design
      (**Shift-F2**)

      move the cursor to the Report Intro band border

      Menus (**F10**)

      Bands/**A**dd a Group Band [↵]

      Field Value [↵]

highlight the field to group by [↵]

move the cursor to the blank line between the Group 1 Summary band and the Report Summary band

Field (**F5**)

Sum in the SUMMARY column [↵]

Name [↵]

enter a field name

Description [↵]

enter a description

Field to Summarize On [↵]

select the field name you want

Reset Every [↵]

select the field name to group by

Ctrl-End

Menus (**F10**)

Exit/**S**ave Changes and Exit [↵]

USAGE

Suppose you want to print a report that shows not only overall totals, but also subtotals of groups of records. To display subtotals, you need to add *group bands* to the report format. (Group bands are discussed in detail in Chapter 11.) The Group Summary band displays its contents once at the bottom of each group. This is where you place summary fields to display subtotals.

To add a group band that subtotals records to an existing report format, first make sure that the database you want to use is active. Move the highlight to the name of the report you want to modify and press Design (**Shift-F2**) to access the reports design screen.

To insert a group band, move the cursor to the Report Intro band border. Press Menus (**F10**) and select Add a Group Band from the Bands pull-down menu. Select Field Value from the submenu and then select the field to group by from the fields displayed.

You will see the new group band appear in the report format. While the cursor is still on the group band, the message *Group by <fieldname>* appears centered at the bottom of the screen. If you were to print the report now, however, you would not see any subtotals, because the Group Summary band is still empty.

To add summary fields, move the cursor to the blank line between the Group 1 Summary band and the Report Summary band. Type a row of hyphens beneath the templates displayed there (directly above the Report Summary band).

Press **Ctrl-N** to insert a blank line. Move the cursor to directly below the hyphens you just entered. Press Field (**F5**) and select Sum in the SUMMARY column. Select Name and enter a name for the field. Select Description and enter a description. Select Field to Summarize On, and then select the field name you want from those displayed.

Select Reset Every and then select the field to group by. This step is required so that dBASE will reset the subtotal to zero each time it encounters a new entry for the field to group by while printing the report. (dBASE will suggest the current group band field as the Reset Every value, which in most cases will be the correct selection.)

Select Template and modify the existing template to your needs (make it match the template for the field to group by). Press **Ctrl-End**. Now your report will print subtotals as well as grand totals. You might want to add the words **Subtotal** and **Total** to the report format as well, as was done in Figure 6.11.

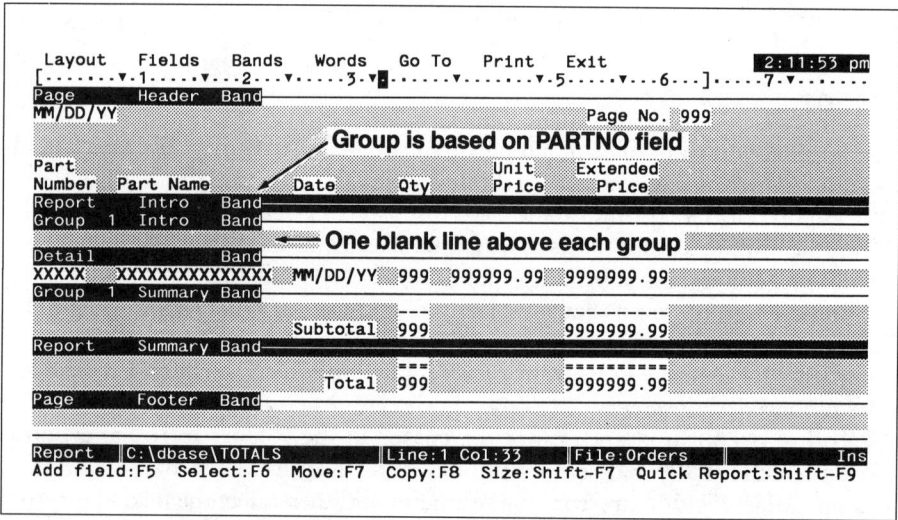

FIGURE 6.11: Report format for subtotals. The report will be grouped by part number.

To save your new report format without overwriting the one you have modified, press Menus (**F10**) and select Save This Report from the Layout pull-down menu. Remove the existing file name, type a new name, and press ↵. When dBASE finishes saving the report format, select Abandon Changes and

Exit from the Exit pull-down menu (because you have already saved the new report format).

You will be returned to the Control Center, where both the original report that you modified and the new report you created will be displayed in the Reports panel. You can use this technique whenever you design a report that is similar to an existing report, so that you do not have to rebuild each report format from scratch.

EXAMPLE

Suppose you want to add a group band to the TOTALS report created in the last example for the ORDERS database. Your goal is to subtotal records by part number and make the report format look something like Figure 6.11.

First make sure that the ORDERS database is in use. (If not, highlight its name in the Data panel, press ←, and press ← again to select Use File.) Move the highlight to TOTALS in the Reports panel and press Design (**Shift-F2**). To insert a group band, move the cursor to the Report Intro band border (the indicator in the status bar will read *Band 2/5*).

Press Menus (**F10**) and select Add a Group Band from the Bands pull-down menu. Select Field Value from the submenu. Select PARTNO as the field to group by.

You will see the new group band appear in the report format. While the cursor is still on the group band, the message *Group by PARTNO* appears centered at the bottom of the screen. If you were to print the report now, however, you would not see any subtotals, because the Group Summary band is still empty.

Press ↓ five times to move the cursor to the blank line between the Group 1 Summary band and the Report Summary band. Move the cursor to column 35 and type hyphens beneath the QTY (99999) and EXTPRICE (9999999.99) templates (directly above the equal signs in the Report Summary band).

Press **Ctrl-N** to insert a blank line. Move the cursor to line 1, column 35, directly below the hyphens you just entered. Press Field (**F5**) and select Sum in the SUMMARY column.

Select Name and enter **SUBQTY** as the name for the field. Select Description and enter **Subtotal of Qty field**. Select Field to Summarize On and select QTY. If the Reset Every option is not already set to the PARTNO field, select Reset Every and then select PARTNO. Select Template and press **Backspace** until the template reads 99999. Then press ← and **Ctrl-End**.

To add another subtotal field for the extended price, press → until the cursor is in column 55 (above the equal signs). Press Field (**F5**). Select Sum in the SUMMARY column. Select Name and enter **SUBEXT**. Select Description and enter **Subtotal of extended price**. Select Field to Summarize On and then select EXTPRICE from the submenu.

Select Reset Every and then select PARTNO if it is not already selected. Your screen will look like Figure 6.12. Press **Ctrl-End**. Now this report will print subtotals as well as grand totals. You might want to add the words **Subtotal** and **Total** to the report format as well, as shown in Figure 6.11.

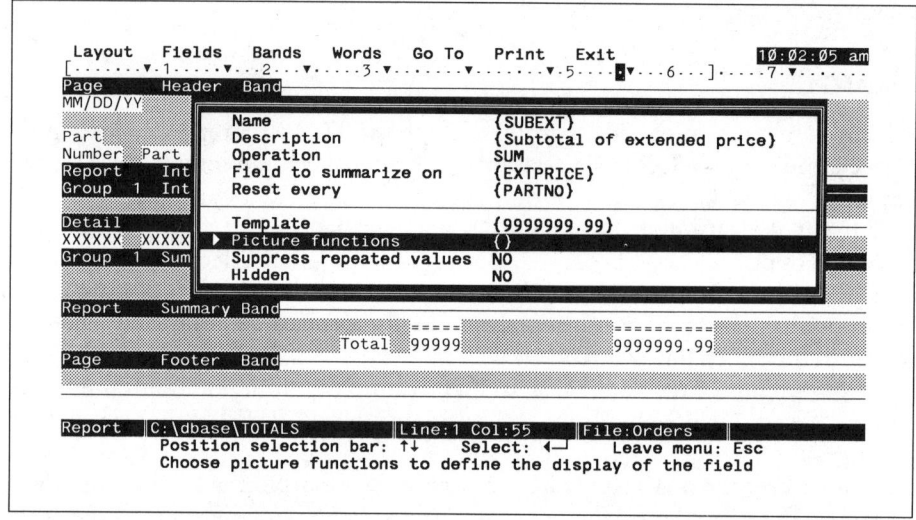

FIGURE 6.12: Information entered to create extended-price subtotals for records grouped by part number.

Rather than using this format to *replace* the previous TOTALS report, you can save this format as a new, separate file. That way, you will still be able to use the TOTALS report format.

Press Menus (**F10**) and select Edit Description of Report from the Layout menu. Press **Home** and then **Ctrl-Y** to erase the previous description. Enter the description **Subtotals by part number (requires PARTNO index)**. Press Menus (**F10**) and select Save This Report from the Layout pull-down menu. Press **Backspace** ten times to remove the TOTALS.FRM file name. Type the new name **SUBTOTAL** and press ⏎.

When dBASE is done, select Abandon Changes and Exit from the Exit pull-down menu, because you have already saved your changes under a new file name. You are returned to the Control Center, where the original TOTALS report remains unchanged and the new format is displayed with the name SUBTOTAL.

Printing Subtotaled Reports

SEQUENCE OF STEPS

From the Control Center:

>highlight the database name in the Data panel Design (**Shift-F2**)
>
>Organize/**O**rder Records by Index [↵]
>
>highlight the index to use ↵
>
>**Ctrl-End**
>
>highlight the report name from the Reports panel ↵
>
>**P**rint Report [↵]
>
>**B**egin Printing [↵]

USAGE

Before you print the new subtotaled report, you need to ensure that records will be displayed in sorted order, based on the field (or fields) used to group the subtotal values. Otherwise, each time dBASE encounters a new item for that field while printing the report, it will consider that record to be the start of a new group. Hence, it would print the records from the example SUBTOTAL report as shown in Figure 6.13.

You can use an index to presort the records before printing the report. To activate an existing index, highlight the database name in the Data panel and press Design (**Shift-F2**). Select Order Records by Index from the Organize pull-down menu. Select the index to use. Press **Ctrl-End** to return to the Control Center. Now you can print the subtotaled report by selecting it from the Reports panel, pressing ↵, and then selecting Print Report and Begin Printing. (If an appropriate index does not yet exist, you can create one using the techniques discussed in Chapter 5. Also see the section "Sorting by the Results of Calculations" later in this chapter).

EXAMPLE

You need to organize the records in the ORDERS database into PARTNO order before printing the SUBTOTAL report. If you created the index called PARTNO following the examples in Chapter 5, you just need to put that index into action.

```
07/08/90                                          Page No.    1

Part                                        Unit      Extended
Number   Part Name    Date      Qty         Price     Price

B-222    Banana Man   06/01/90    2         100.00    200.00
B-222    Banana Man   06/01/90    1         100.00    100.00
                                 -----                ----------
                      Subtotal    3                   300.00

A-111    Astro Buddies 06/01/90   2         50.00     100.00
                                 -----                ----------
                      Subtotal    2                   100.00

C-333    Cosmic Critters 06/01/90 1         500.00    500.00
                                 -----                ----------
                      Subtotal    1                   500.00

A-111    Astro Buddies 06/02/90   3         50.00     150.00
A-111    Astro Buddies 06/05/90   4         50.00     200.00
                                 -----                ----------
                      Subtotal    7                   350.00

B-222    Banana Man   06/15/90    1         100.00    100.00
                                 -----                ----------
                      Subtotal    1                   100.00

C-333    Cosmic Critters 06/15/90 2         500.00    1000.00
C-333    Cosmic Critters 06/15/90 1         500.00    500.00
C-333    Cosmic Critters 07/01/90 2         500.00    1000.00
                                 -----                ----------
                      Subtotal    5                   2500.00
                                 =====                ==========
                      Total      19                   3850.00
```

FIGURE 6.13: Result of printing the SUBTOTAL report without first activating the index. This is *not* what you need.

To do so, first highlight ORDERS in the Data panel. Press Design (**Shift-F2**). Select Order Records by Index from the Organize pull-down menu. Select PARTNO. Press **Ctrl-End** to return to the Control Center.

Now you can print the SUBTOTAL report by selecting it from the Reports panel, pressing ↵, and then selecting Print Report and Begin Printing. The results should look something like Figure 6.14.

ADDING CALCULATED FIELDS TO FORMS

SEQUENCE OF STEPS

On the forms design screen:

>move the cursor to where you want the field
>Field (**F5**)
>highlight <create> in the CALCULATED column ↵

```
07/08/90                                    Page No.    1
Part                                    Unit      Extended
Number  Part Name       Date    Qty     Price     Price

A-111   Astro Buddies   06/01/90   2    50.00     100.00
A-111   Astro Buddies   06/02/90   3    50.00     150.00
A-111   Astro Buddies   06/05/90   4    50.00     200.00
                                 -----           ----------
                        Subtotal   9              450.00

B-222   Banana Man      06/01/90   2   100.00     200.00
B-222   Banana Man      06/01/90   1   100.00     100.00
B-222   Banana Man      06/15/90   1   100.00     100.00
                                 -----           ----------
                        Subtotal   4              400.00

C-333   Cosmic Critters 06/01/90   1   500.00     500.00
C-333   Cosmic Critters 06/15/90   2   500.00    1000.00
C-333   Cosmic Critters 06/15/90   1   500.00     500.00
C-333   Cosmic Critters 07/01/90   2   500.00    1000.00
                                 -----           ----------
                        Subtotal   6             3000.00
                                 =====           ==========
                        Total     19             3850.00
```

FIGURE 6.14: Correctly subtotaled report with records grouped and subtotaled by part number.

>   **Name** [◄┘]
>   type a name for the field ◄┘
>   **Description** [◄┘]
>   type a description for the field ◄┘
>   **Expression** [◄┘]
>   type an expression ◄┘
>   **Ctrl-End**

USAGE

You can create calculated fields in custom forms using techniques similar to those used in reports. The calculated fields will be displayed on the form whenever you scroll through existing records in the database. However, the calculations are *not* updated on the screen automatically as you add new data, so calculated fields on a custom form are of limited value.

To create a custom form, see Chapter 10. To add a calculated field to a custom form, position the cursor where you want the field to appear and then press Field (**F5**). Select <create> in the CALCULATED column of the submenu that appears. You will see a menu of options for the new field. You need to name the calculated field; the description is optional. Select Expression and type an expression.

198 — **CH. 6** PERFORMING CALCULATIONS

You can then select the Template and Picture Function options to improve the display of the field, just as when you place a calculated field in a report format. Press **Ctrl-End** to place the field on the form.

EXAMPLE

Figure 6.15 shows a form design for the ORDERS database. Notice that the form has three calculated fields, each with its own expression. The expression **Qty*UnitPrice** displays the extended price. The expression **0.065*(Qty*UnitPrice)** displays the sales tax at 6.5 percent. The expression **1.065*(Qty*UnitPrice)** displays the total sale (the extended price with 6.5 percent tax added).

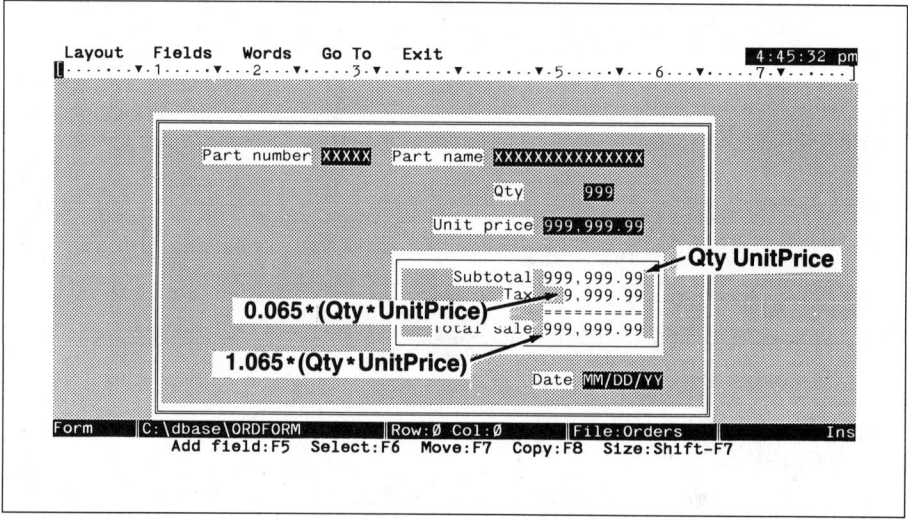

FIGURE 6.15: A form design with calculated fields.

Figure 6.16 shows how the form design in Figure 6.15 appears when you use it to view records in the ORDERS database. As you can see, the form calculates and displays the subtotal, tax, and total sale for each record. As you scroll through records with the **PgDn** and **PgUp** keys, the calculations adjust to new quantity and unit-price values.

USING QUERIES TO PERFORM CALCULATIONS

You can use the queries design screen to perform some quick calculations without going through all the steps involved in creating a form or report format.

CREATING CALCULATED FIELDS — 199

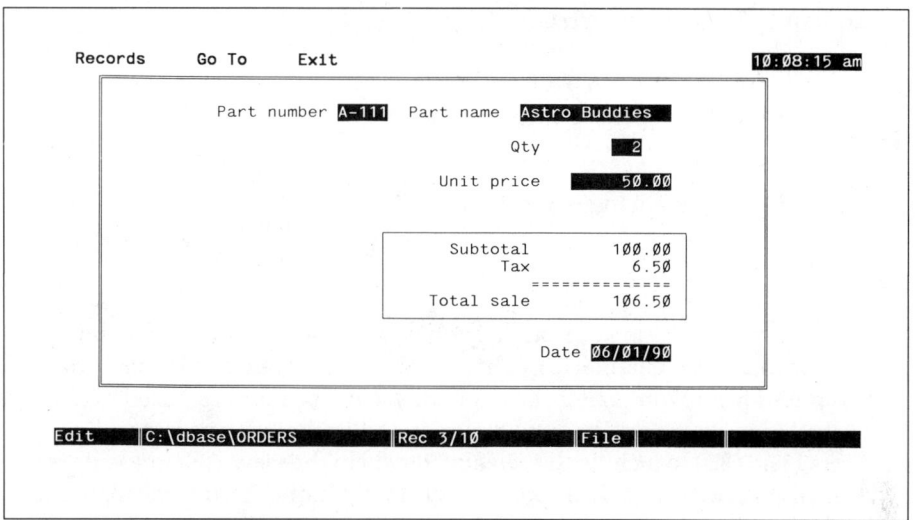

FIGURE 6.16: Custom form displaying calculations.

Quick calculations are useful when you just want to experiment with data and do not need a neatly formatted report.

Creating Calculated Fields

SEQUENCE OF STEPS

With the database name above the line in the Control Center Data panel:

    highlight <create> in the Queries panel ⏎
    Menus (**F10**)
    Fields/**C**reate Calculated Field [⏎]
    type the expression to perform the calculation ⏎
    Field (**F5**)
    type a name for the calculated field ⏎

To view the results of the query:

    Data (**F2**)

To print a report of the query:

    Quick Report (**Shift-F9**)

200 —— **CH. 6** PERFORMING CALCULATIONS

To return to the design screen:

Design (**Shift-F2**)

To return to the Control Center:

Menus (**F10**)

Exit/Abandon Changes and Exit [←]

USAGE

To perform calculations through queries, first create a query for the appropriate database (see Chapter 5). Then select Create Calculated Field from the Fields pull-down menu. Enter the expression (the formula) required to perform the calculation, using database field names and arithmetic operators.

Press Field (**F5**) to include the calculated field in the view skeleton so its results will be displayed. When prompted, enter a field name for the calculated field. Press Data (**F2**) to see the results of the query.

You can add up to 20 calculated fields to a query, simply by selecting Create Calculated Field from the Fields menu. Each new calculated field that you create will be added to the right of existing calculated fields. Use the Previous (**F3**) and Next (**F4**) keys to move up and down from one skeleton to the next.

Press Data (**F2**) to see the results. Press Quick Report (**Shift-F9**) to print the data. Press Design (**Shift-F2**) to return to the queries design screen. There you can elect to Abandon Changes and Exit, using the Exit menu.

EXAMPLE

This example uses the ORDERS database shown throughout this chapter. First make sure that the ORDERS database is open (that its name appears above the line in the Data panel). Select <create> from the Queries panel to display the queries design screen.

Press Menus (**F10**) and select Create Calculated Field from the Fields pull-down menu. The screen displays a skeleton titled *Calc'd Flds*. Type the formula **Qty*UnitPrice** into the Calc'd Flds box (the cursor is already in position). Press ← after typing the formula.

Press Field (**F5**) to move the calculated field to the view skeleton at the bottom of the screen. When you are prompted with *Enter field name*, type **ExtPrice** and press ←. Figure 6.17 shows the completed query. If the calculated field in the view skeleton is scrolled off the right side of your screen, you can press Next (**F4**) and then **End** to view the right side of the view skeleton.

CREATING CALCULATED FIELDS — 201

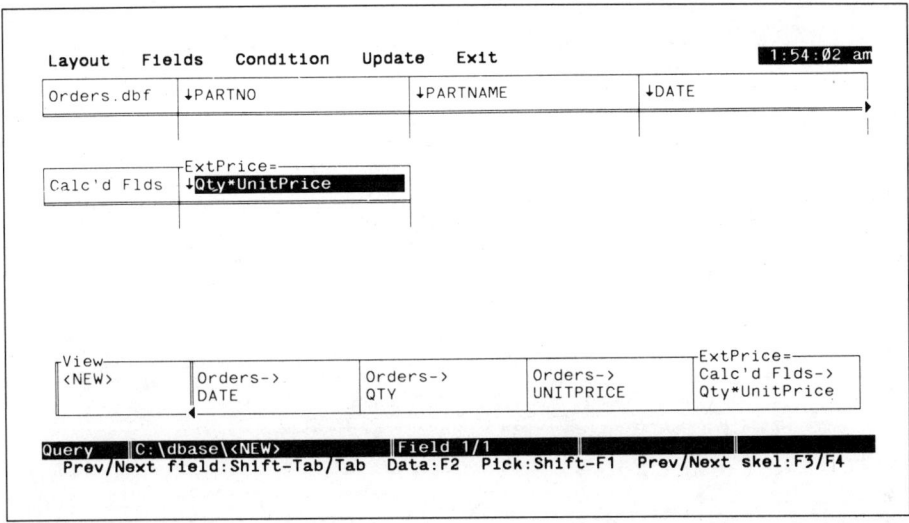

FIGURE 6.17: You can include calculated fields in queries. Notice the ExtPrice calculated field in both the file skeleton and the view skeleton.

When you press Data (**F2**) to execute the query, the results will include a copy of the calculated field, as shown in Figure 6.18. The calculated field will appear in both the browse and edit screens. You can print the results of this or any other query simply by pressing Quick Report (**Shift-F9**) while the results are on the screen. Press Design (**Shift-F2**) to return to the queries design screen, where you can save and name the query or select Abandon Changes and Exit, using the Exit menu.

REMOVING ALL CALCULATED FIELDS

SEQUENCE OF STEPS

On the queries design screen:

>   move the cursor to any calculated field
>   Layout/**R**emove File from Query [⏎]

USAGE

To remove all of the calculated fields from a query, move the cursor into any calculated field and select Remove File from Query from the Layout menu.

```
Records      Fields      Go To      Exit                          10:10:31 am
PARTNO  PARTNAME        DATE      QTY  UNITPRICE  EXTPRICE
B-222   Banana Man      06/01/90   2    100.00      200.00
B-222   Banana Man      06/01/90   1    100.00      100.00
A-111   Astro Buddies   06/01/90   2     50.00      100.00
C-333   Cosmic Critters 06/01/90   1    500.00      500.00
A-111   Astro Buddies   06/02/90   3     50.00      150.00
A-111   Astro Buddies   06/05/90   4     50.00      200.00
B-222   Banana Man      06/15/90   1    100.00      100.00
C-333   Cosmic Critters 06/15/90   2    500.00     1000.00
C-333   Cosmic Critters 06/15/90   1    500.00      500.00
C-333   Cosmic Critters 07/01/90   2    500.00     1000.00

Browse  C:\dbase\<NEW>          Rec 1/10     View
                    View and edit fields
```

FIGURE 6.18: Results of the query in Figure 6.17.

Using Filter Conditions with Numbers

You can use filter conditions freely in queries containing calculated fields. Here are four examples of queries of the ORDERS database, used throughout this chapter.

The first query, in Figure 6.19, uses two filter conditions to display records that have A-111 in the PARTNO field *and* a value greater than 100 in the calculated EXTPRICE field. (Both filter conditions are in the top row of their respective skeletons, so dBASE assumes that they have an AND relationship.) The results of the query are shown in Figure 6.20.

Figure 6.21 shows a query that isolates records with extended price values in the range $100 to $200. Figure 6.22 shows a query for records that have a number greater than 3 in the QTY field *or* an extended price of $500 or more. This query uses a condition box because of the complexity of the query. The query is complicated because the QTY field is in the file skeleton for the ORDERS database, whereas the calculated field for the extended price is in the Calc'd Flds skeleton. You cannot stagger an OR query across two different skeletons, but instead must enter an expression using the .OR. operator in the condition box. (See Chapter 5 for additional information and examples.)

USING SUMMARY OPERATORS 203

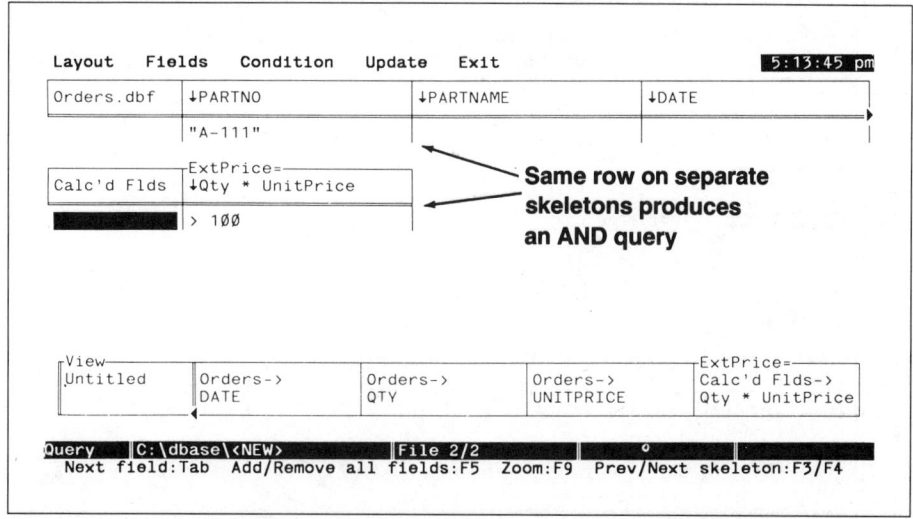

FIGURE 6.19: Filter conditions added to a calculated field query. This query isolates records for part number A-111 that have an extended price greater than $100.

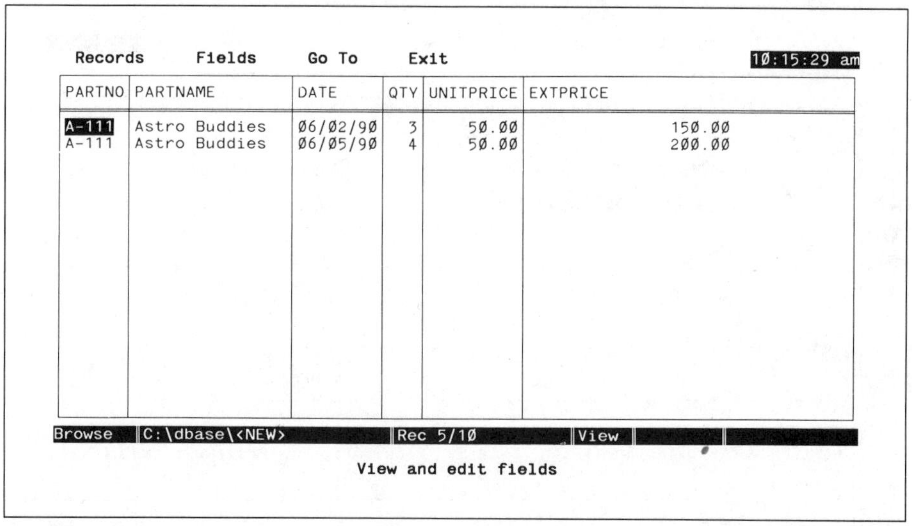

FIGURE 6.20: Results of the query in Figure 6.19.

Using Summary Operators

As with reports, you can use summary operators in queries. To use a summary operator in a query, you place its name beneath the box in the appropriate

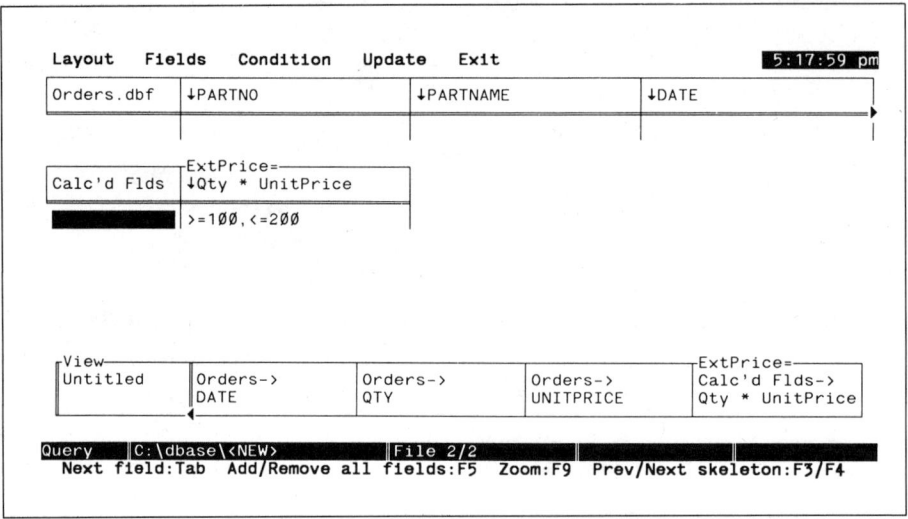

FIGURE 6.21: Query for records with extended prices in the range $100 to $200.

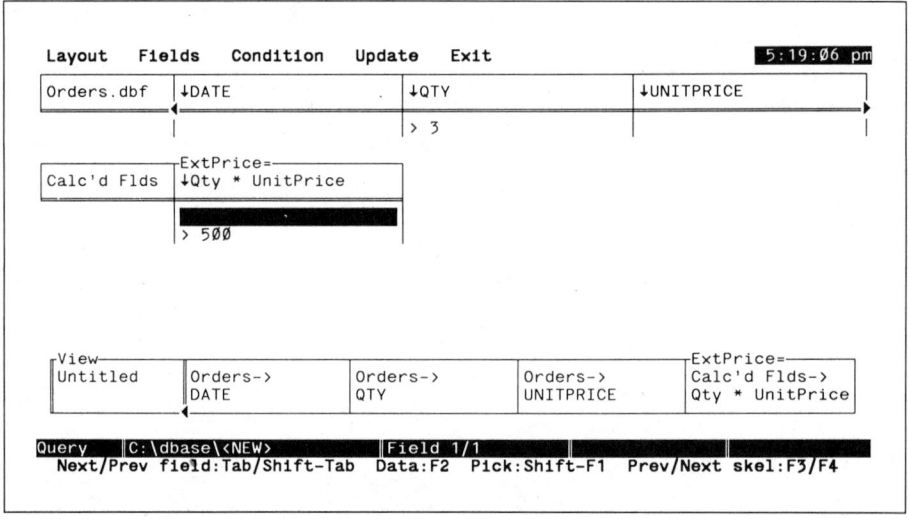

FIGURE 6.22: An OR query entered into a condition box. This query will locate orders for quantities less than 3 or with extended prices less than $500.

field. You must spell the summary operator correctly, as in the left column of Table 6.4. The table also lists the data types with which each summary operator can be used.

USING SUMMARY OPERATORS — 205

SUMMARY OPERATOR	CALCULATES	DATA TYPES
AVG or AVERAGE	Average	Numeric, Float
CNT or COUNT	Count	Numeric, Float, Character, Date, Logical
MAX	Highest value	Numeric, Float, Character, Date
MIN	Lowest value	Numeric, Float, Character, Date
SUM	Total	Numeric, Float

Table 6.4: Summary Operators Used in Query Forms

You can use summary operators with regular fields (though not with calculated fields). Here are three examples from the ORDERS database used throughout this chapter.

Figure 6.23 shows a query that displays the sum of the QTY field. Figure 6.24 shows the results of this query. As you can see, only the summed field is displayed. It would not make much sense to display any other fields, because the sum includes all records, not just those for a particular part number or part name.

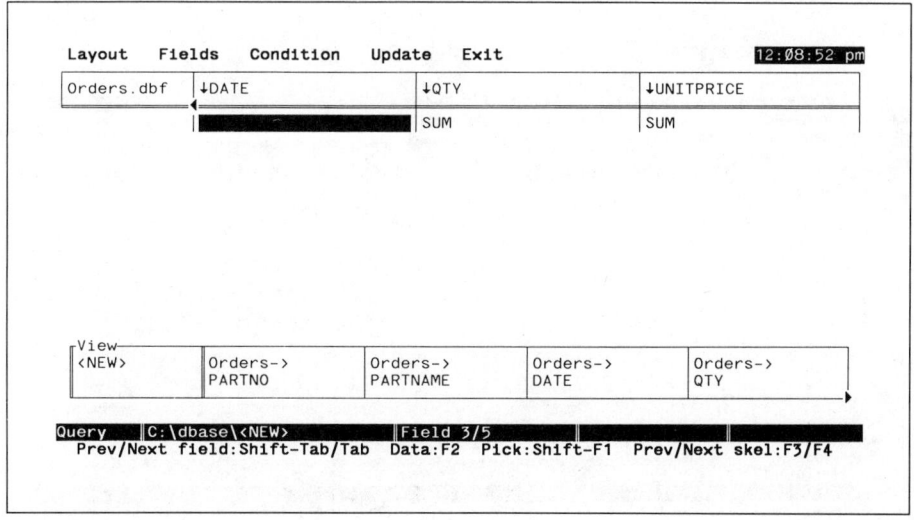

FIGURE 6.23: Query to sum the QTY field.

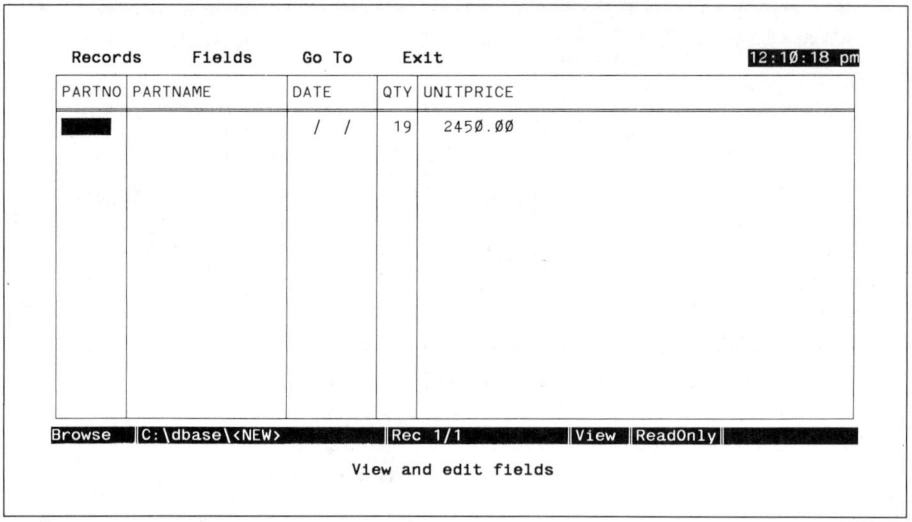

FIGURE 6.24: Results of the query in Figure 6.23.

You can combine filter conditions and summary operators in separate fields or in the same field. When combining the two in a single field, separate them with a comma, as in Figure 6.25. (The query counts the number of records in the database with part number A-111.)

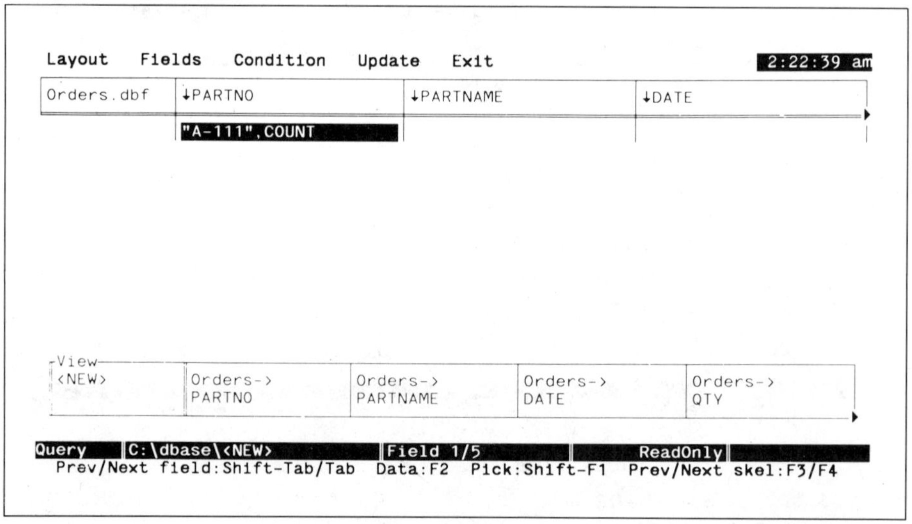

FIGURE 6.25: Query to count the number of records with A-111 in the PARTNO field. Notice that the filter condition comes first and is separated from the COUNT summary operator by a comma.

You can combine different summary operators in a single query. For example, the query in Figure 6.26 displays the "highest" (most recent) date, the average quantity, and the lowest unit price. You could also use a filter condition, such as **A-111** in the PARTNO field, to limit the calculation to a single record.

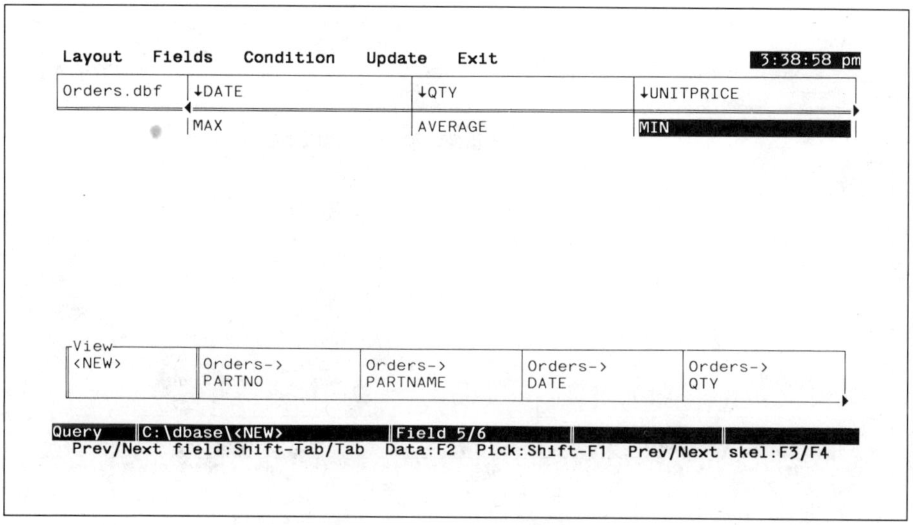

```
Layout   Fields   Condition   Update   Exit                    3:38:58 pm
┌─────────────┬──────────────┬──────────────┬──────────────────┐
│ Orders.dbf  │ ↓DATE        │ ↓QTY         │ ↓UNITPRICE       │
│             │ MAX          │ AVERAGE      │ MIN              │
└─────────────┴──────────────┴──────────────┴──────────────────┘

┌View──────────────────────────────────────────────────────────────────┐
│ <NEW>        Orders->      Orders->     Orders->      Orders->       │
│              PARTNO        PARTNAME     DATE          QTY            │
└──────────────────────────────────────────────────────────────────────┘
Query   C:\dbase\<NEW>        Field 5/6
Prev/Next field:Shift-Tab/Tab  Data:F2  Pick:Shift-F1  Prev/Next skel:F3/F4
```

FIGURE 6.26: Summary operators combined in a query to locate the latest date, the average quantity, and the lowest unit price.

Performing Calculations on Groups of Records

SEQUENCE OF STEPS

On the queries design screen file skeleton:

    type **GROUP BY** under the field you want to group ↵

    type **SUM** under the field you want to sum ↵

USAGE

Queries can generate quick calculations that involve groups or subtotals, without the use of report formats or indexes. To group the results of a query, place the GROUP BY operator in the field that you want records grouped by and include at least one summary operator to perform a calculation.

Figure 6.27 shows an example query of the ORDERS database used throughout this chapter. The query groups records by the PARTNAME field and sums the QTY field for each group. The results of the query are shown in Figure 6.28. Note that the results of the query show *only* the resulting summaries and not the individual details within each group.

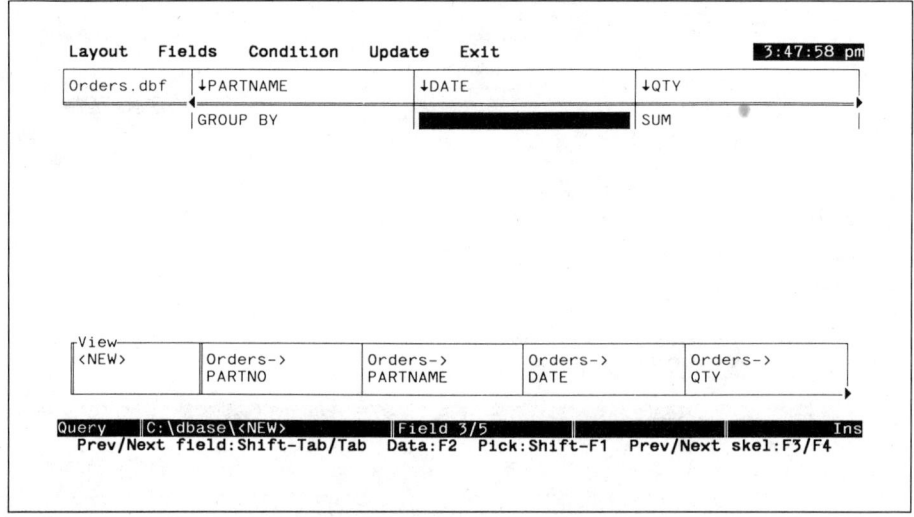

FIGURE 6.27: Query to subtotal quantities by part name. The GROUP BY operator groups the report by part name, and the SUM operator subtotals the QTY field.

Changing the Sort Order

SEQUENCE OF STEPS

On the queries design screen file skeleton:

    type **GROUP BY** under the field you want to group ↵

    type **SUM** under the field you want to sum ↵

    move the cursor to the field to group by

    Menus (**F10**)

    Fields/Sort on This Field [↵]

USAGE

By default, dBASE will sort the results of queries that use the GROUP BY operator into ascending order, based on the GROUP BY field. You can override

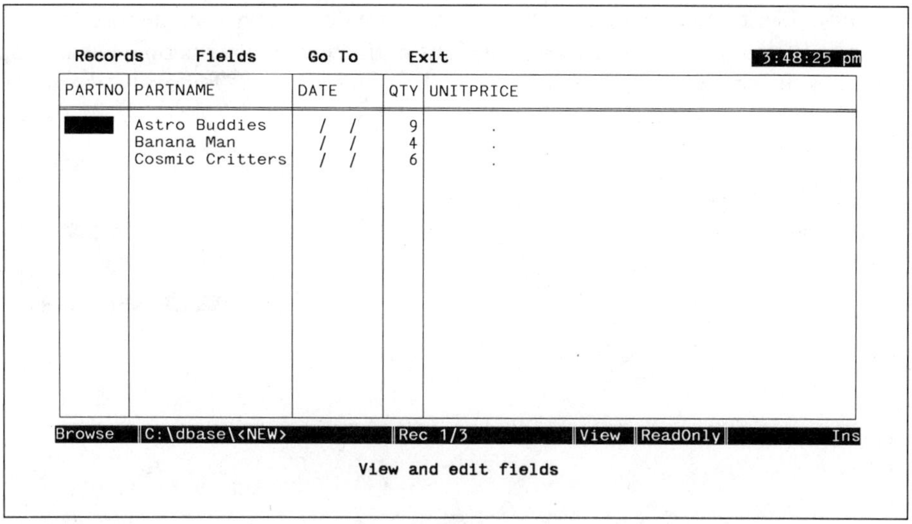

```
Records     Fields      Go To       Exit                    3:48:25 pm
PARTNO  PARTNAME        DATE     QTY UNITPRICE
▓▓▓▓▓▓  Astro Buddies    /  /      9     .
        Banana Man       /  /      4     .
        Cosmic Critters  /  /      6     .


Browse  C:\dbase\<NEW>          Rec 1/3      View  ReadOnly         Ins
                        View and edit fields
```

FIGURE 6.28: Results of the query in Figure 6.27.

this default sort order by using the Sort on This Field option from the Fields pull-down menu in the query design screen. For example, if the query in Figure 6.27 contained **GROUP BY, Dsc1** in the PARTNO field, the results would have been displayed in descending order.

Calculating Frequency Distributions

You can combine the GROUP BY and COUNT summary functions in a query to calculate a *frequency distribution* (a count of all records that have a specific value). To perform frequency distributions, you place the GROUP BY operator, as opposed to the COUNT operator, in the field of interest.

For example, to count the number of people who live in each city listed in a database of names and addresses, place the GROUP BY operator in the city field on the queries design screen. To count the number of people in each zip code area, place the GROUP BY operator in the zip code field. Include the GROUP BY field in the view skeleton.

EXAMPLE

Suppose that in the CUSTLIST database (introduced in Chapter 2; note that your records may differ from those shown here) you want to know how many customers live in each state. First, select the CUSTLIST database from the

Control Center Data panel to open it. Then create a query like the one shown in Figure 6.29. Figure 6.30 shows the results of the query. Four people live in California, and one person lives in each of the other states. (Obviously, the results would be more impressive with a larger database.)

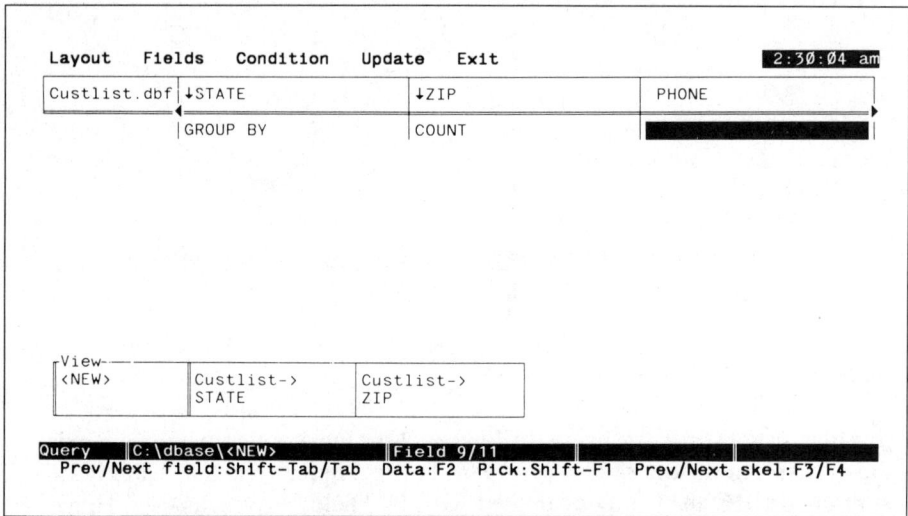

FIGURE 6.29: Frequency distribution query using the COUNT and GROUP BY operators.

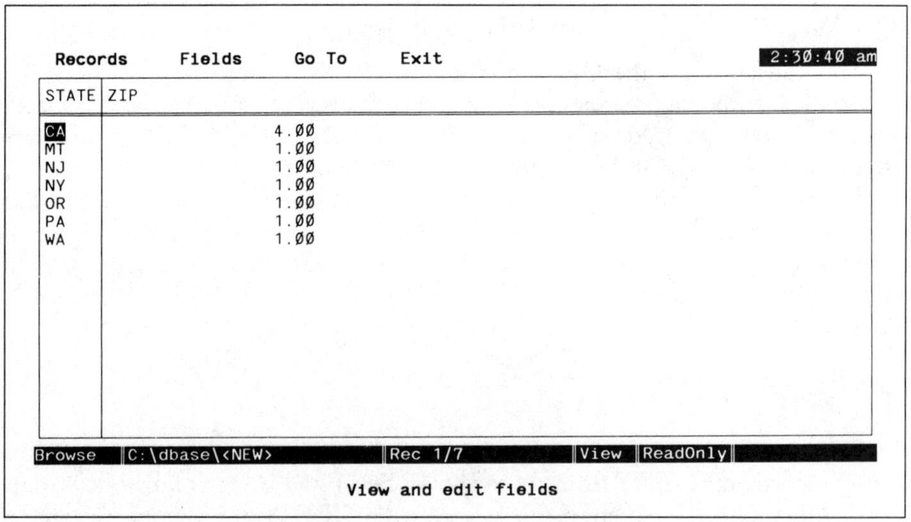

FIGURE 6.30: Results of the frequency distribution query in Figure 6.29.

Calculating Dates

You can add a number to a date, or subtract a number from a date, to determine the date a certain number of days away. For example, the formula **{01/01/89} + 90** results in the date 04/01/89, the date that is 90 days past January 1, 1989. The formula **{12/15/88} – 60** results in 10/16/88, the date 60 days prior to December 15, 1988.

You can use this basic *date arithmetic* in queries. The query in Figure 6.31 uses a filter condition in the DATE field of the ORDERS database (shown throughout this chapter) to display records with dates "less than or equal to 9/12/89 minus 90 days." In English, this translates to dates that are 90 or more days before 9/12/89.

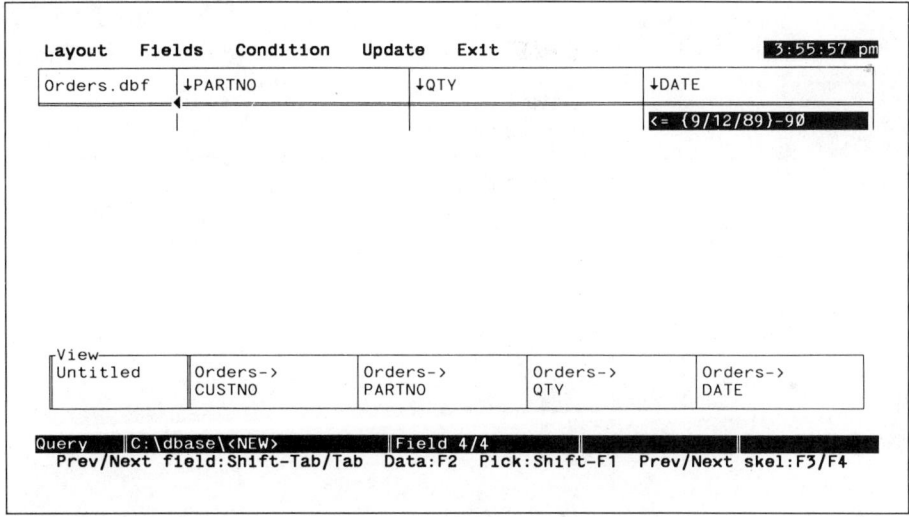

FIGURE 6.31: Query for records with dates 90 or more days before 9/12/89.

You can use the dBASE DATE( ) (today's date) function in place of a specific date in a query. If you replace the formula < = {9/12/89} – 90 in Figure 6.31 with the formula < = **DATE( ) – 90**, the query will display records with dates that are 90 or more days before today. If you then save that query, you can simply select it from the Control Center at any time in the future to see records with dates 90 or more days before the current date. This feature is very handy for accounts receivable.

You can also subtract one date from another to determine the number of days between two dates. For instance, the formula **{12/15/89} – {12/01/89}** results in the number 14, because 12/15/89 is 14 days "larger than" (that is, after) 12/01/89. The formula {01/01/89} − {03/01/89} results in −59, because 1/1/89 is 59 days "smaller than" (that is, before) 3/1/89.

This kind of date arithmetic can be very useful in databases that store starting and ending dates for projects. For instance, suppose a database contains two fields, named STARTDATE and ENDDATE, and both use the Date data type. You can create a calculated field (either in a report or query) that uses the expression **ENDDATE − STARTDATE** to quickly display the number of days between each starting and ending date.

Comparing Fields

You can create a query that compares values in one field to values in another field. Suppose, for example, that you want to isolate records from the database of stock prices shown in Figure 6.32. The isolated records will have closing stock prices at least three dollars higher than their opening prices.

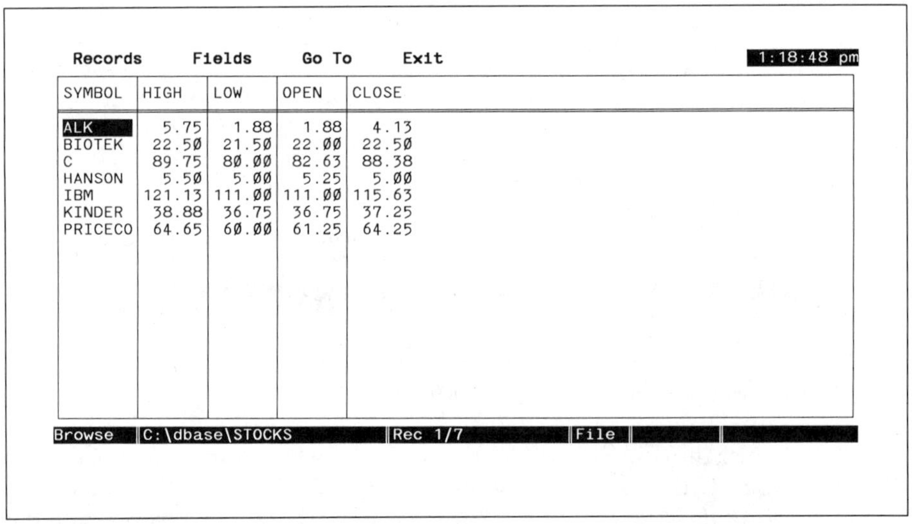

```
     Records    Fields    Go To    Exit                          1:18:48 pm
   ┌────────┬───────┬───────┬───────┬───────┐
   │ SYMBOL │ HIGH  │ LOW   │ OPEN  │ CLOSE │
   ├────────┼───────┼───────┼───────┼───────┤
   │ ALK    │   5.75│   1.88│   1.88│   4.13│
   │ BIOTEK │  22.50│  21.50│  22.00│  22.50│
   │ C      │  89.75│  80.00│  82.63│  88.38│
   │ HANSON │   5.50│   5.00│   5.25│   5.00│
   │ IBM    │ 121.13│ 111.00│ 111.00│ 115.63│
   │ KINDER │  38.88│  36.75│  36.75│  37.25│
   │ PRICECO│  64.65│  60.00│  61.25│  64.25│
   └────────┴───────┴───────┴───────┴───────┘
   Browse   C:\dbase\STOCKS        Rec 1/7        File
```

FIGURE 6.32: Database of stock prices.

To create such a query, you need to use an *example*, or *placeholder*, in the query. The placeholder can be any letter or word (such as X, Y, or Zookie). Type the placeholder into one of the fields in the comparison and then use the placeholder in the filter condition of the other field in the comparison.

Figure 6.33 shows the design of the stock prices database query. Notice that the word *Open* is used as the placeholder for the OPEN field (though the placeholder could just as easily be X or YooHoo). The CLOSE field uses the filter condition > = **Open + 3** to isolate records that have a value in the CLOSE field that is greater than or equal to the value in the OPEN field plus 3.

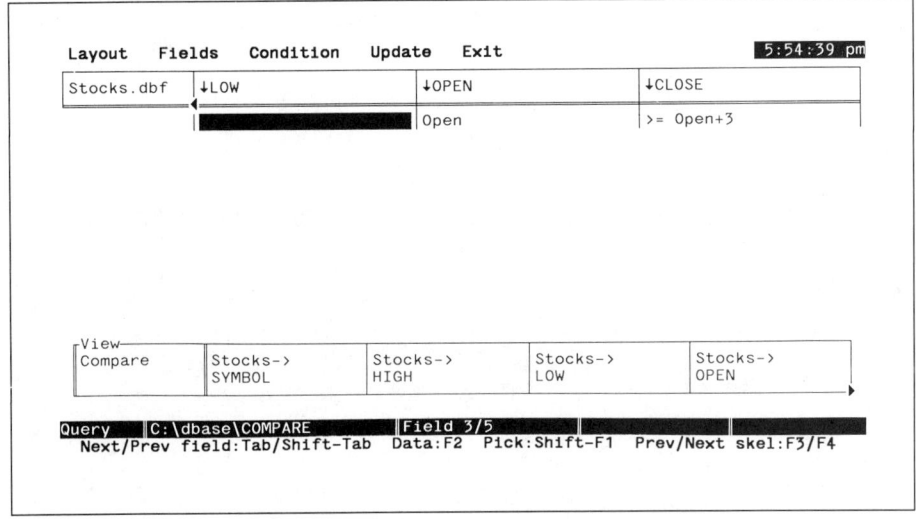

FIGURE 6.33: Query comparing two fields in the stock prices database.

The results of this query are shown in Figure 6.34. As you can see, only records for stocks that closed three or more dollars above their opening prices are displayed.

Using Placeholders to Compare Dates

Suppose you want to isolate database records with 90 or more days between their starting and ending dates, and your database has fields named STARTDATE and ENDDATE. You can type a placeholder into the STARTDATE field and a filter condition into the ENDDATE field. The condition isolates records with ending dates that are 90 or more days "greater than" the starting dates. Figure 6.35 shows such a query for a database of projects, and Figure 6.36 shows the results.

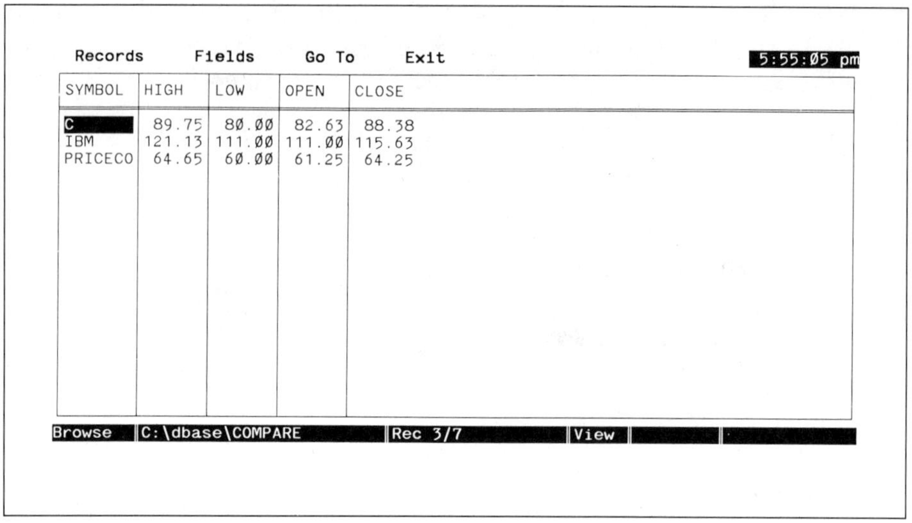

214 — **CH. 6** PERFORMING CALCULATIONS

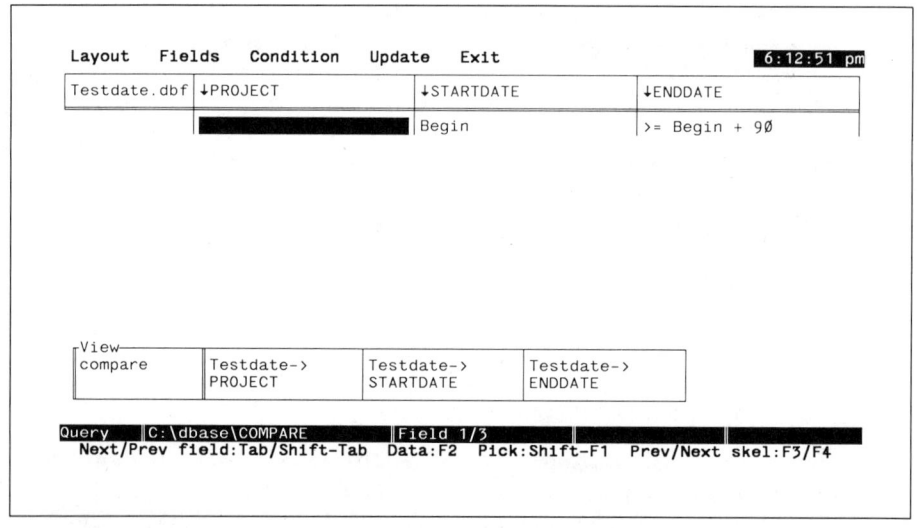

FIGURE 6.34: Results of the query for comparing opening and closing stock prices in Figure 6.33.

FIGURE 6.35: Query of a database of projects locating records with ending dates 90 or more days past their starting dates.

Performing Conditional Calculations

In some situations, you may want to have a report, custom screen, or query "decide" whether or not to perform a calculation based upon a given situation.

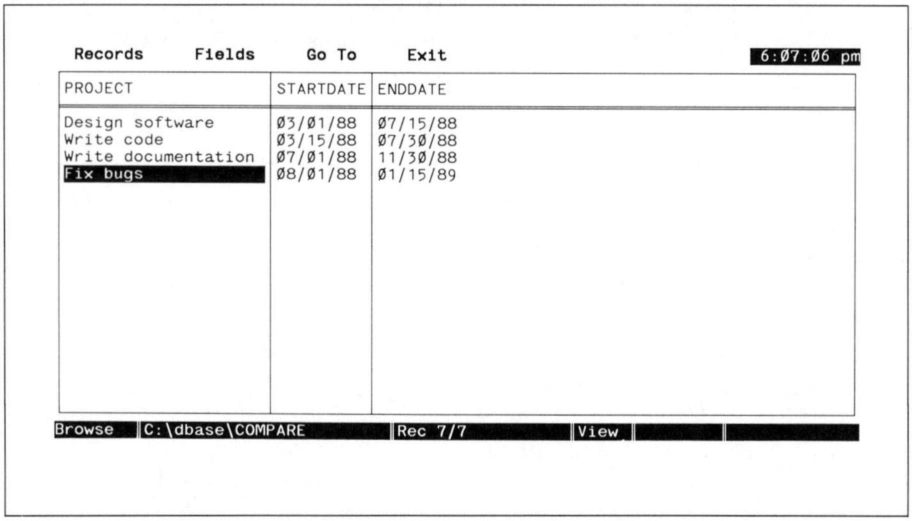

FIGURE 6.36: Results of the query for projects of 90 days or more in Figure 6.35.

For example, if your product line includes both taxable and nontaxable items, you'll need a calculation formula that adds tax only to taxable items.

First, you'll need to identify which items are and are not taxable. Figure 6.37 shows a modified version of the ORDERS database with a Logical field named TAXABLE added.

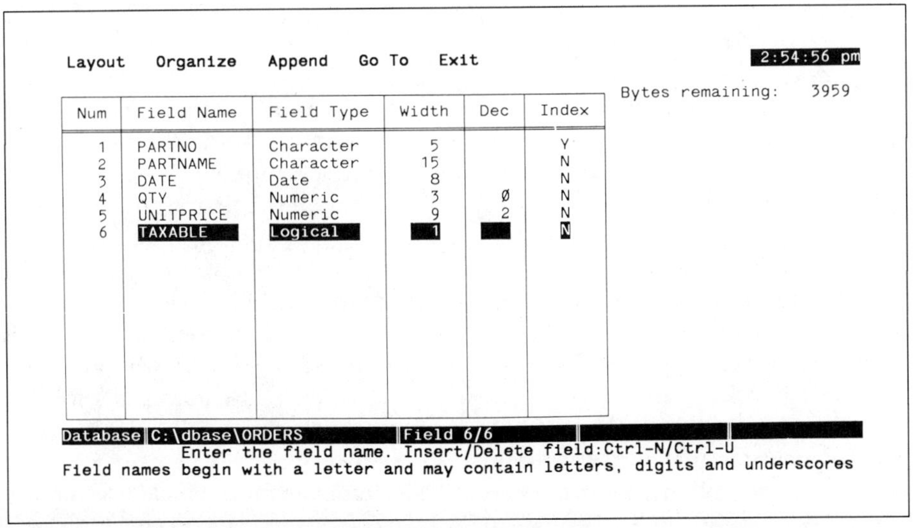

FIGURE 6.37: Field named TAXABLE added to the ORDERS database.

Figure 6.38 shows the modified ORDERS database with some transactions marked as taxable (T), and others marked as nontaxable (F).

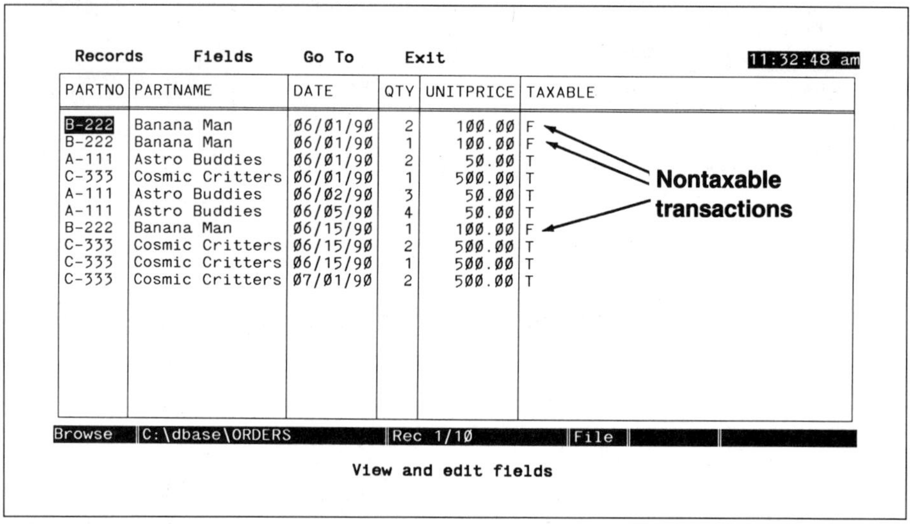

```
 Records      Fields      Go To       Exit                          11:32:48 am
 PARTNO PARTNAME        DATE     QTY  UNITPRICE  TAXABLE
 B-222  Banana Man      06/01/90   2    100.00   F
 B-222  Banana Man      06/01/90   1    100.00   F
 A-111  Astro Buddies   06/01/90   2     50.00   T
 C-333  Cosmic Critters 06/01/90   1    500.00   T
 A-111  Astro Buddies   06/02/90   3     50.00   T
 A-111  Astro Buddies   06/05/90   4     50.00   T
 B-222  Banana Man      06/15/90   1    100.00   F
 C-333  Cosmic Critters 06/15/90   2    500.00   T
 C-333  Cosmic Critters 06/15/90   1    500.00   T
 C-333  Cosmic Critters 07/01/90   2    500.00   T

 Browse  C:\dbase\ORDERS        Rec 1/10        File
                    View and edit fields
```

(Arrows indicate Nontaxable transactions)

FIGURE 6.38: Transactions marked as taxable or nontaxable.

To have dBASE "decide" whether or not to add tax to a calculated extended price, use the IIF( ) (immediate if) function, which requires the following general syntax:

   IIF(*this-is-true,do-this,otherwise-do-this*)

The first *argument* in the function, *this-is-true*, must be either the name of a Logical field or a comparison that results in a true or false result. The second argument is a formula that is calculated only if the first argument proves true. The third argument is a formula that is calculated only if the first argument proves false. See Chapter 18 and Appendix D for more information about IIF( ) and other functions.

Figure 6.39 shows an example report format that includes calculated fields in the Detail band. The calculated Extended Price field, named EXTPRICE, uses the formula **Qty*UnitPrice** to calculate the extended price without tax.

The Tax column is a calculated field named TAX that contains the formula **IIF(Taxable,0.065*ExtPrice,0)**. In English, this formula says "If the TAXABLE field for this record contains .T., then display 6.5 percent times the extended price; otherwise, display zero." The template for that field was reduced

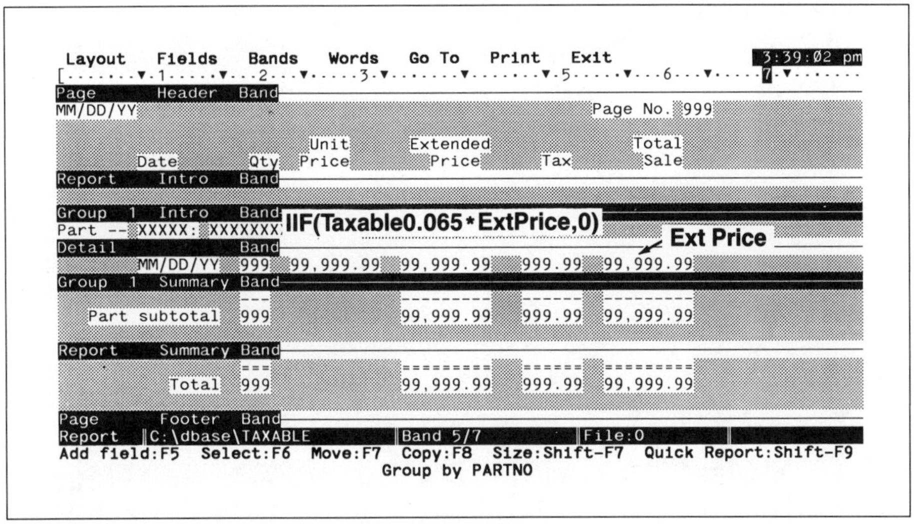

PERFORMING CONDITIONAL CALCULATIONS — 217

FIGURE 6.39: Report format that calculates tax on taxable items.

to 999.99, and the Blanks for Zero Values function was set to On so that nontaxable items display blanks, rather than zeroes, in the column.

The column labeled Total Sale uses the formula **ExtPrice + Tax** to calculate the total amount of the transaction. Figure 6.40 shows a report printed from the report format (after using an index to put the records into PARTNO order to properly sort for subtotals). Note that the total sale for nontaxable items (part number B-222) does not include any tax, and totals for the other (taxable) items include tax.

Figure 6.41 shows a custom form that uses the IIF( ) function in calculated fields to perform tax calculations. In this example, all expressions use actual field names, rather than the names of calculated fields, to calculate values. The result is the same: Only taxable items display a tax amount and include that amount in the total sale. (Remember, though, that dBASE does not update the screen while you add new records, only when you edit existing records.)

The first argument in the IIF( ) function need not be the name of a Logical field. It can be any comparison that results in a true or false result. For example, suppose you have a database that includes a numeric field named AMOUNTDUE and a date field named DATEDUE. The following formula adds 10 percent to the AMOUNTDUE field if the due date is 90 or more days earlier than the current date (DATE( )); otherwise, it simply displays the amount due:

IIF(DATE( ) − DateDue >90,1.10*AmountDue,AmountDue)

218 — CH. 6 PERFORMING CALCULATIONS

```
04/18/89                                              Page No.   1
                         Unit    Extended              Total
           Date    Qty   Price   Price      Tax        Sale
    Part-- A-111: Astro Buddies
           06/01/90  2   50.00   100.00     6.50       106.50
           06/02/90  3   50.00   150.00     9.75       159.75
           06/05/90  4   50.00   200.00    13.00       213.00
                   ---          --------  ------      --------
           Subtotal  9          450.00    29.25       479.25

    Part-- B-222: Banana Man
           06/01/90  2  100.00   200.00                200.00
           06/01/90  1  100.00   100.00                100.00
           06/15/90  1  100.00   100.00                100.00
                   ---          --------  ------      --------
           Subtotal  4          400.00                 400.00

    Part-- C-333: Cosmic Critters
           06/01/90  1  500.00   500.00    32.50       532.50
           06/15/90  2  500.00 1,000.00    65.00     1,065.00
           06/15/90  1  500.00   500.00    32.50       532.50
           07/01/90  2  500.00 1,000.00    65.00     1,065.00
                   ---          --------  ------      --------
           Subtotal  6         3,000.00   195.00     3,195.00

                   ===         ========= ======     =========
           Total   19         3,850.00   224.25     4,074.25
```

FIGURE 6.40: Sample report with tax calculations.

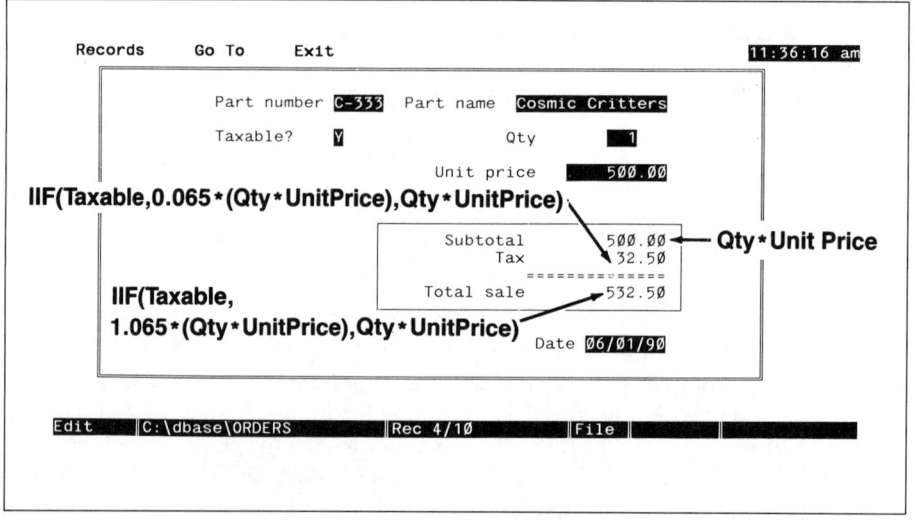

FIGURE 6.41: Custom form with tax calculations.

As with all calculations, you can place this expression in any report, custom screen, or query design as a calculated field, so long as the database includes fields named DATEDUE and AMOUNTDUE.

You can even *nest* IIF functions to make several decisions, so long as you make certain that each IIF function has an opening and closing parenthesis. For example, the following expression adds 15 percent to the charges (AMOUNTDUE) that are more than 90 days past due, 10 percent to amounts more than 60 days past due, 5 percent to amounts more than 30 days past due, and nothing to charges that are less than 30 days past due:

```
IIF(DATE( ) - DateDue >90,AmountDue*1.15,
IIF(DATE( ) - DateDue >60,AmountDue*1.10,
IIF(DATE( ) - DateDue >30,AmountDue*1.05,
AmountDue)))
```

Note that the expression is divided into separate lines only to fit into this book. When entering this expression in a report, screen, or query design, you would need to enter it as one long line without blank spaces. Note also that the three closing parentheses each close one IIF function.

INDEXING ON THE RESULTS OF CALCULATIONS

Chapter 4 discussed techniques for sorting a database by using an index expression (that is, by first selecting Create New Index from the Organize menu of the database design screen). Index expressions may also contain expressions that perform calculations. This means that even if your database does not contain a field for storing the extended price of each sale, you can still display records in extended price order by indexing on the expression **Qty*UnitPrice**.

EXAMPLE

Suppose you want to display records in the ORDERS database used throughout this chapter in extended-price order (that is, from the smallest total sale to the largest, or vice versa). To do so, you index on a calculated field, just as you display the extended price as a calculated field.

To display records in extended-price order from smallest to largest total sale, you use the index expression **QTY*UNITPRICE** and Ascending as the overall sort order. To display records in order from largest to smallest extended price, you use the same index expression, but Descending as the overall sort order. To see the results of the index, you need to use a query or report format—such as TOTALS shown earlier in this chapter—that includes a calculated field to display the extended price.

What if you want to display records sorted by part number and by extended price within each part number? You need to convert the results of the calculation **QTY*UNITPRICE** to the Character data type, because the results of the calculation are numeric, but the PARTNO field is a Character field. To ensure an adequate width in the Character field, use the sum of the widths within the STR( ) function. QTY has a width of 3, and UNITPRICE has a width of 9, so within the STR( ) function, you specify a width of 12.

For example, to display records in ascending part number and extended-price order, you use the index expression

PARTNO + STR(QTY*UNITPRICE,12,2)

To display records in ascending part-number order and descending extended-price order, you use the following index expression instead:

PARTNO + STR(999999999.99 − QTY*UNITPRICE,12,2)

This index produces the sort order shown here, where part numbers are sorted into ascending order, and extended prices are sorted into descending order within each part number:

A-111	220.00
A-111	165.00
A-111	100.00
B-222	200.00
B-222	200.00
B-222	100.00
C-333	1000.00
C-333	1000.00
C-333	500.00
C-333	500.00

Tips and Traps

- Remember that you *always* need to press ↵ after entering a value in dBASE IV.
- Before you can print a subtotaled *report*, the records in the database must be sorted into the grouping order, using either an index or a query.

- dBASE automatically displays extremely large numbers in scientific notation; for example, it might display a 30-digit number as .37789318629576E+30.
- To change the format of an existing numeric template in a form or report design, move the cursor into the field template and press Field (**F5**).
- You must name *calculated* fields. However, providing a description is optional.
- Naming a *summary* field is optional. If you do not provide a name, the Operation and Summarize information will still appear at the bottom of the screen.
- When placing a summary field to calculate subtotals in a Group Summary band, make sure that the Reset Every option specifies the field that defines the groups (for example, when displaying subtotals by part number, the Reset Every field should be PARTNO).
- Use placeholders (also called *examples*) when comparing fields in filter conditions.
- Use the dBASE IV IIF( ) function to perform conditional calculations.

SUMMARY

You will find more features and options for reports and forms in the chapters that follow. This chapter presented most of dBASE IV's math capabilities, as well as specific considerations for using numeric data in queries.

For information about sorting with indexes:

- Chapter 4, "Sorting the Database"

To learn more about designing queries:

- Chapter 5, "Searching the Database"

To find out how to create a variety of custom reports:

- Chapter 7, "Designing Formatted Reports"

For more discussion and examples of grouping records:

- Chapter 11, "Managing Groups of Records"

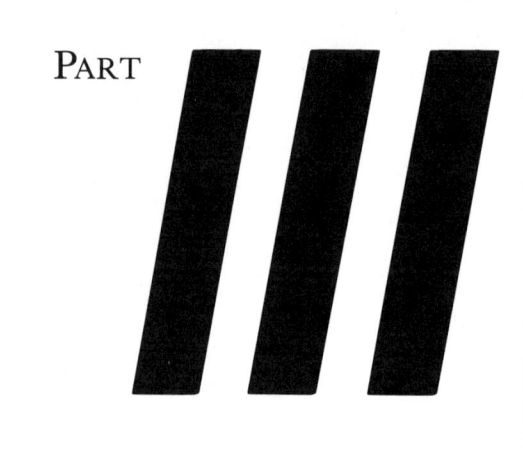

PART III

DISPLAYING AND PRINTING THE DATA

Chapter 7: Designing Formatted Reports
Chapter 8: Designing Mailing Labels
Chapter 9: Printing Reports and Labels
Chapter 10: Creating Custom Forms

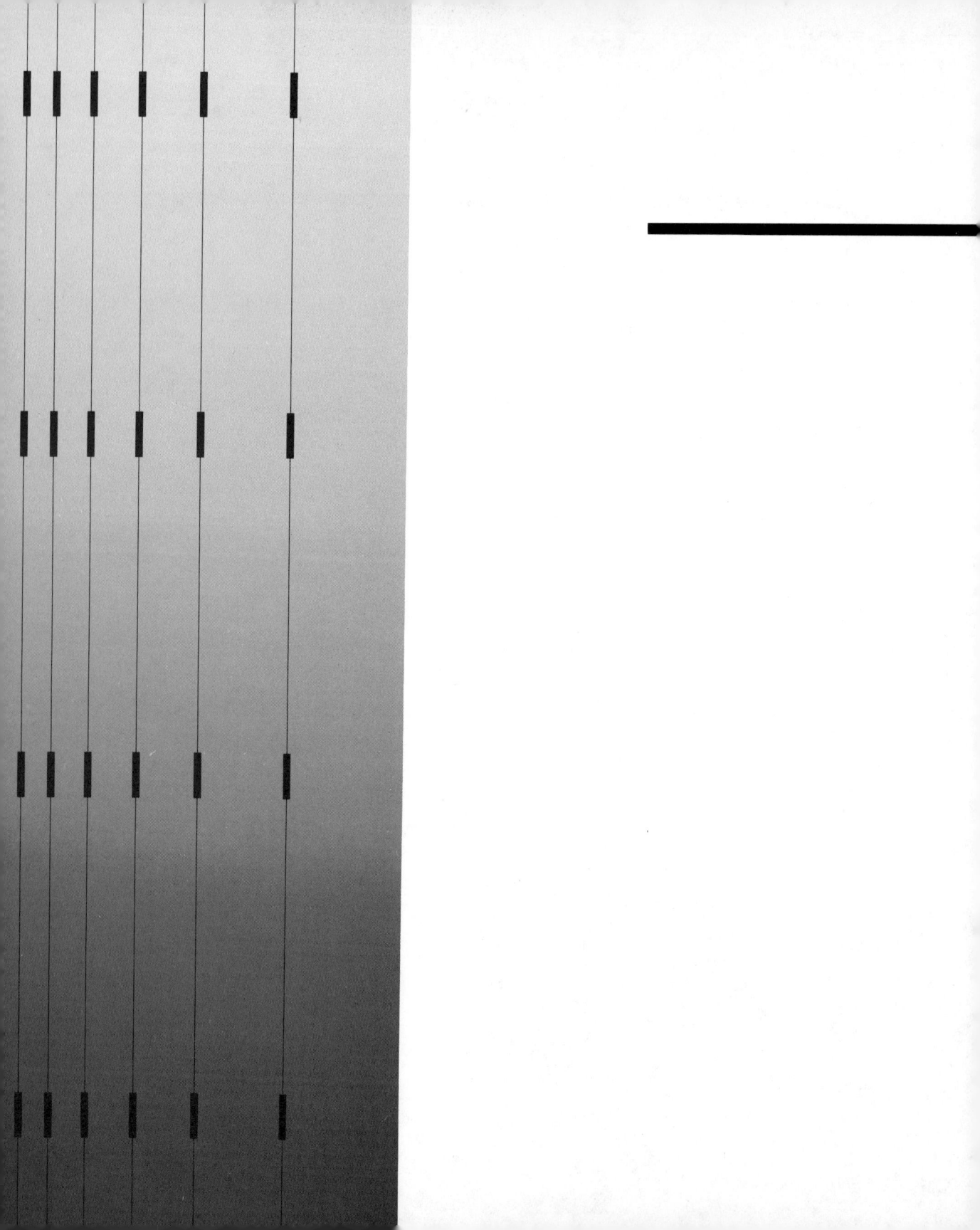

CHAPTER 7

DESIGNING FORMATTED REPORTS

Accessing the Reports Design Screen. 227
Generic Report Formats. 228
    Column Layout. 230
    Form Layout. 230
    Mailmerge Layout. 230
Specifying Report Margins. 232
The Reports Design Screen Bands. 233
Modifying Report Bands. 235
    Page Header Band. 235
    Report Intro Band. 235
    Detail Band. 236
    Report Summary Band. 238
    Page Footer Band. 239
Saving a Report Format. 240
Viewing the Report. 241
Making Design Changes. 241
    Opening and Closing Bands. 242
    Formatting Report Bands. 243
    Moving and Copying. 244
    Adding Fields. 245
    Deleting Fields. 245
    Adding and Deleting Text. 246
    Adding and Deleting Lines. 246
    Formatting Fields. 246
        Changing a Field's Picture Functions. 247
        Changing a Field's Width. 249
    Drawing Lines and Boxes. 251
    Saving Your Changes. 251

Displaying Memos in Reports. 252
Creating Form Letters. 253
      Setting Margins. 255
      Writing the Text of the Letter. 256
      Working with Blocks of Text. 257
      Reformatting Paragraphs. 258
      Adding Database Fields. 258
      Saving Your Form Letter. 261
      Viewing Your Form Letter. 262
Tips and Traps. 262
Summary. 263

Designing Formatted Reports

This chapter presents techniques for formatting your dBASE IV information into a variety of useful reports, such as customer lists and form letters. You use the *reports design screen* to specify how the report data should be printed on a full page. Full printed pages might consist of many different sections of text, such as page headings, page numbers, totals sections, and subtotals sections.

Chapter 9 presents the printing options for formatted reports. If you create the example report design in this chapter, use the information in Chapter 9 to print it.

Accessing the Reports Design Screen

SEQUENCE OF STEPS

From the Control Center:

> open the database file
> highlight <create> in the Reports panel
> **Esc**

USAGE

To access the reports design screen, open the database file for which you want to design a report. Then select <create> from the Reports panel. You will see the reports design screen, partially obscured by the Layout menu. Press **Esc** to remove the Layout menu. Your screen will look like Figure 7.1.

Table 7.1 lists the keys you can use on the reports design screen. Many of these keys are similar to those used on the edit and browse screens.

The reports design screen has many of the same characteristics as other dBASE IV design screens. The menu bar at the top of the screen has pull-down menus associated with it, which you access by pressing Menus (**F10**). The ruler just below the menu bar shows margins and tab stops. At the bottom of the screen, the navigation line displays special keys that you can use to format your report.

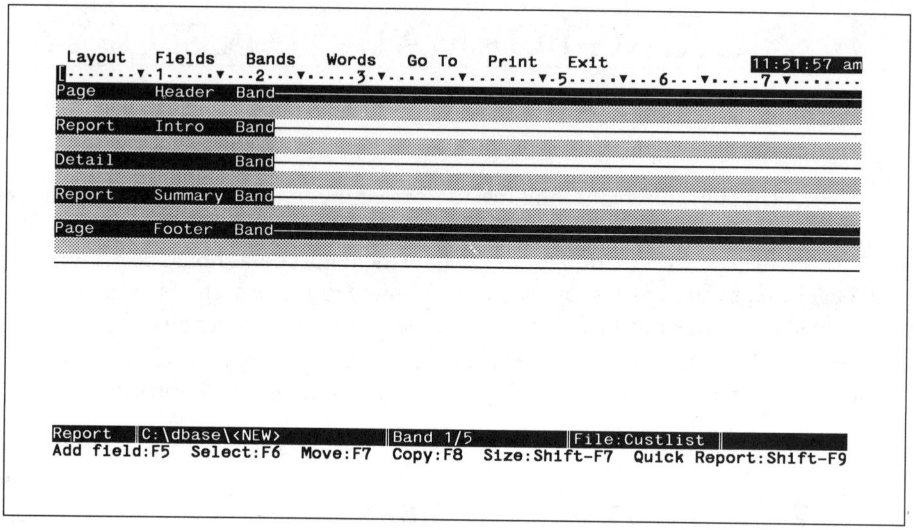

228 — CH. 7 DESIGNING FORMATTED REPORTS

```
Layout   Fields   Bands   Words   Go To   Print   Exit            11:51:57 am
|......▼.1.....▼...2...▼......3.▼......▼.....5....▼...6....▼.....7.▼.....
 Page       Header   Band
 Report     Intro    Band
 Detail              Band
 Report     Summary  Band
 Page       Footer   Band




 Report  |C:\dbase\<NEW>        |Band 1/5       |File:Custlist
 Add field:F5  Select:F6  Move:F7  Copy:F8  Size:Shift-F7  Quick Report:Shift-F9
```

FIGURE 7.1: The reports design screen as it first appears, with five empty report bands.

EXAMPLE

(This and other examples in this chapter use the CUSTLIST database, introduced in Chapter 2. Use the instructions there to create it, if necessary. Note that some of the records in your database may differ from the ones shown in this chapter, but these differences do not affect the content of the examples.)

If you have created the CUSTLIST database, you can develop a report of its data. First, you need to get to the reports design screen. If CUSTLIST is not currently in use, highlight CUSTLIST in the Data panel, press ⏎, and select Use File. Highlight <create> in the Reports panel and press ⏎. The reports design screen now appears. You can press **Esc** if you want to remove the Layout menu from it; however, you may want to use that menu to select a generic report format, as discussed next.

GENERIC REPORT FORMATS

SEQUENCE OF STEPS

On the reports design screen:

    Menus (**F10**)
    Layout/**Q**uick Layouts [⏎]
    Column Layout *or* **F**orm Layout *or* **M**ailmerge Layout [⏎]

KEY	EFFECT
↓	Moves down one row
↑	Moves up one row
→	Moves right one character or to the end of a field template
←	Moves left one character or to the beginning of a field template
PgUp	Moves to the top of the screen
PgDn	Moves to the bottom of the screen
End	Moves to the end of the line
Home	Moves to the beginning of the line
Ins	Toggles insert mode on and off
↵	If insert mode is off, moves down one row; if insert mode is on, inserts a new line
Help (F1)	Provides help on the current task
Field (F5)	Adds a new field template or changes the currently highlighted one
Select (F6)	Selects a field template or block
Move (F7)	Moves the field or block selected with **F6**
Copy (F8)	Copies the field or block selected with **F6**
Size (Shift-F7)	Changes the size of the currently selected field template
Ctrl-N	Inserts a new line
Backspace	Erases the character to the left
Del	Deletes the character, field template, or block selected with **F6**
Ctrl-T	Removes the word or field to the right
Ctrl-Y	Removes the entire line
Tab	Moves to the next tab setting (reformats the paragraph in the word-wrap editor)
Shift-Tab	Moves to the previous tab setting (reformats the paragraph in the word-wrap editor)
Esc	Abandons the current format without saving changes

Table 7.1: Keys Used on the Reports Design Screen

To help you design your reports, dBASE provides three generic report layouts: the column layout, the form layout, and the mailmerge layout. You can use any of these general layouts as the starting point for designing your own report. These formats are summarized here.

To create a general report format for your database, first press Menus (**F10**) and highlight Layout on the menu bar. Select Quick Layouts and then one of the three layout options. dBASE immediately creates a general report for the currently active database.

Column Layout

If you select Column Layout, data is printed in evenly aligned columns. You can use the column layout for reports that present data in lists or that include totals or subtotals. The sample report in Figure 7.2 uses a column layout to print names and phone numbers.

```
                       Phone Numbers


            Last name      First name     Phone number
            ------------------------------------------

            Adams          Annie          (714)555-0123
            Beach          Sandy          (717)555-0898
            Kenney         Ralph          (213)555-9988
            Mahoney        Mary           (206)555-8673
            Newell         John           (303)555-6739
            Schumack       Susita         (202)555-9720
            Smith          Anita          (415)555-9854
            Smith          John           (619)555-1234
            Watson         Wilbur         (212)555-9988
```

FIGURE 7.2: Report of the CUSTLIST database using the Column Layout option. You can use this layout as a starting point for a custom report of this type.

Form Layout

If you select Form Layout, data is not presented in columns, but is instead stacked or arranged in some other free-form format that you specify. The printed customer list report shown in Figure 7.3 uses the form layout. Notice that the information appears in blocks, not columns.

Mailmerge Layout

You usually select Mailmerge Layout when you want to combine a large body of text with information from a database. This is the layout you use to create form letters. (*Mailmerge* refers to the procedure in which you *merge* the text of a typewritten letter with names and addresses from a database to create form letters, or *mail*.)

```
                    06/01/89



                                    Customer List

                Adams, Annie
                     3456 Ocean St.
                     Santa Monica, CA    92001
                     Phone: (714)555-0123
                     Starting date: 01/01/89   Paid: N

                Smith, Anita    Zeerocks, Inc.
                     2001 Engine Dr.
                     Hideaway, CA    92220
                     Phone: (415)555-9854
                     Starting date: 01/01/89   Paid: Y

                Kenney, Ralph
                     1101 Rainbow Ct.
                     Los Angeles, CA    96607
                     Phone: (213)555-9988
                     Starting date: 12/30/88   Paid: N

                Schumack, Susita    SMS Software
                     47 Broad St.
                     Philadelphia, PA    45543
                     Phone: (202)555-9720
                     Starting date: 12/30/88   Paid: Y

                Newell, John    LoTech Co.
                     734 Rainbow Dr.
                     Butte, MT    54321
                     Phone: (303)555-6793
                     Starting date: 12/15/88   Paid: Y

                Beach, Sandy    American Widget
                     11 Elm St.
                     Portland, OR    76543
                     Phone: (717)555-9988
                     Starting date: 12/15/88   Paid: Y

                Mahoney, Mary
                     211 Seahawk St.
                     Seattle, WA    88977
                     Phone: (206)555-8673
                     Starting date: 12/01/88   Paid: Y




                                        Page:   1
```

FIGURE 7.3: Customer list report generated with the Form Layout option. Today's date is printed at the top left, the Customer List heading is centered over the list, and a page number is printed at the bottom of the page.

EXAMPLE

To create a form layout for the CUSTLIST database, select Quick Layouts from the Layout menu and then select Form Layout. (If the Layout menu is not displayed, press Menus (**F10**) from the reports design screen and highlight Layout on the menu bar.)

dBASE creates the general report format shown in Figure 7.4. Notice the page number and date template at the top of the page. The name of each field in the CUSTLIST database is displayed with a template for each field.

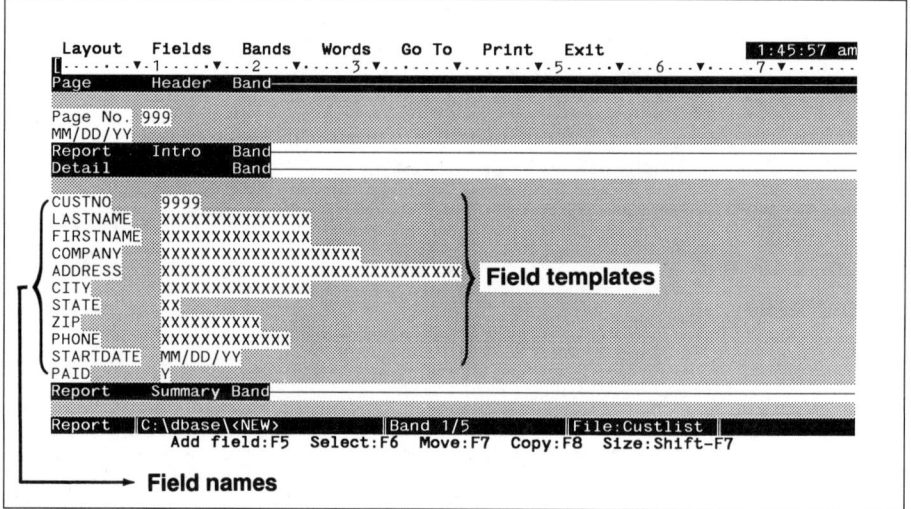

FIGURE 7.4: dBASE suggests this layout when you use the Form Layout option for the CUSTLIST database. You can then modify this initial layout.

SPECIFYING REPORT MARGINS

SEQUENCE OF STEPS

From the reports design screen:

    Menus (**F10**)

    Words/**M**odify Ruler [↵]

    move the cursor to the column where you want the left margin

    [

move the cursor to the column where you want the right margin

]

↵

USAGE

After you have selected a general format for your report, you should then select margins so that you can more easily center titles and other information in your report. When printing on 8½-by-11-inch paper, a right margin setting of about 64 will provide adequate left and right margins on the printed page.

You may not need to adjust the left margin, because although the left margin is set at column 0 (as you can see by the [symbol on the ruler), many printers still leave about a 1-inch margin on the left. Note that you can also adjust the left margin from the Print menu (see Chapter 9).

EXAMPLE

To set the margins for the customer list, first press Menus (**F10**) to access the pull-down menus on the reports design screen. Use ← or → to scroll to the Words option on the menu bar. Select Modify Ruler from the Words menu. The cursor will move to the ruler. Press **Tab** eight times to move to column 64. Type] to mark the right margin. (The] key is near the ↵ key on most keyboards.) Press ↵ to finish adjusting the position of the right margin.

THE REPORTS DESIGN SCREEN BANDS

In Figure 7.1, earlier in this chapter, you can see that the center of the screen, where you design the format of the report, is initially divided into five *bands*. (You can modify the screen to include additional bands.) Each band corresponds to a section of the printed report. Anything that you place within a band is printed only in the corresponding section of the report.

The *Page Header band* contains text to be printed at the top of each page. The *Report Intro band* contains the report introduction, which is printed once at the beginning of the report. The *Detail band* contains the body of the report. Typically, this section displays the database file records. The *Report Summary band* contains text to be printed once at the end of the report; you can use it to display totals or closing information about the report. The *Page Footer band* contains text to be printed at the bottom of each page; you can use it to display page numbers, for example. Figure 7.5 shows a sample printed report with the various bands pointed out on each of two pages.

234 — **CH. 7** DESIGNING FORMATTED REPORTS

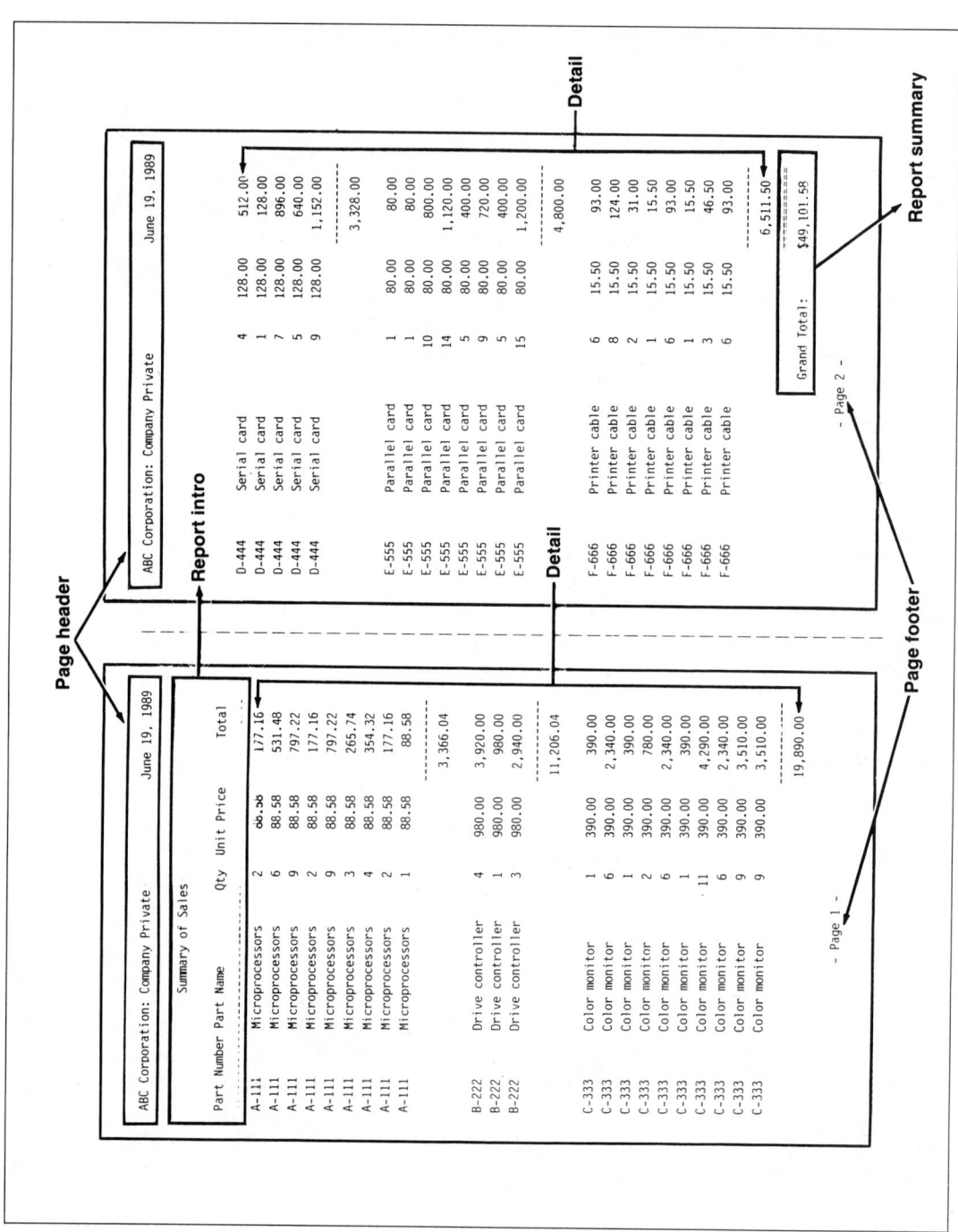

FIGURE 7.5: A dBASE IV report, showing the positioning of data in the five report bands.

Modifying Report Bands

You can modify the format and content of any of the five bands on the reports design screen, using the keys listed in Table 7.1. This section is an extended example that shows how to modify each of the report bands to produce the customer report shown earlier in Figure 7.3. When you have completed the modifications outlined in this section, your reports design screen should look like Figure 7.7 later in this chapter. You can use this figure as a guide while you are modifying the report bands.

The general technique for modifying the report band is to move the cursor into that band, delete any default text that you do not want (such as the field names in the Detail band), and add any information (either as literal text or as field name templates) that you do want to include. The specific techniques used in this section—opening bands, adding lines, deleting text, and so forth—are explained in the section "Making Design Changes" later in this chapter.

Page Header Band

Use the Page Header band to specify the information that should appear at the top of each page in your report. By default, this band includes the page number and date. You can delete the page number from the Page Header band. You can then put the page number at the bottom of each page, instead of at the top. (See "Page Footer Band" later in this chapter for instructions on adding the page number at the bottom of each page.)

On the reports design screen, first press ↓ to move the cursor to the *P* in *Page No.* in the Page Header band (line 1, column 0). Press **Ctrl-Y** to delete the entire line. Then press the **End** key to move the cursor to the end of the date template (MM/DD/YY). Press **Ctrl-N** twice to insert two blank lines.

The page header now consists of the current date and two blank lines. dBASE will print this page header at the top of every page.

Report Intro Band

A report introduction, which will appear on the first printed page of the report, may consist of simply a report title, as in Figure 7.3; it may also include column heads, as in Figure 7.5. An introductory paragraph or a distribution list could also appear here. To add a report introduction, first press ↓ three times to move the cursor to the Report Intro band border. (The line position at the bottom of the screen will show *Band 2/5*.)

Press ↵ to open the band. Press ↓ to move the cursor into the band. (The cursor position will be line 0, column 8.) Make sure that insert mode is on. (If the *Ins* indicator does not appear in the lower-right corner of the status bar, press **Ins** until it does.)

Press ↵. Notice that this adds a new blank line to the Report Intro band, which will print a blank line on the printed report. Type the report heading **Customer List**. To center the heading, press Menus (**F10**) and select Position from the Words pull-down menu. Then select Center from the submenu that appears, as shown in Figure 7.6. To move to the end of the heading, press **End**. Press ↵ to add another blank line.

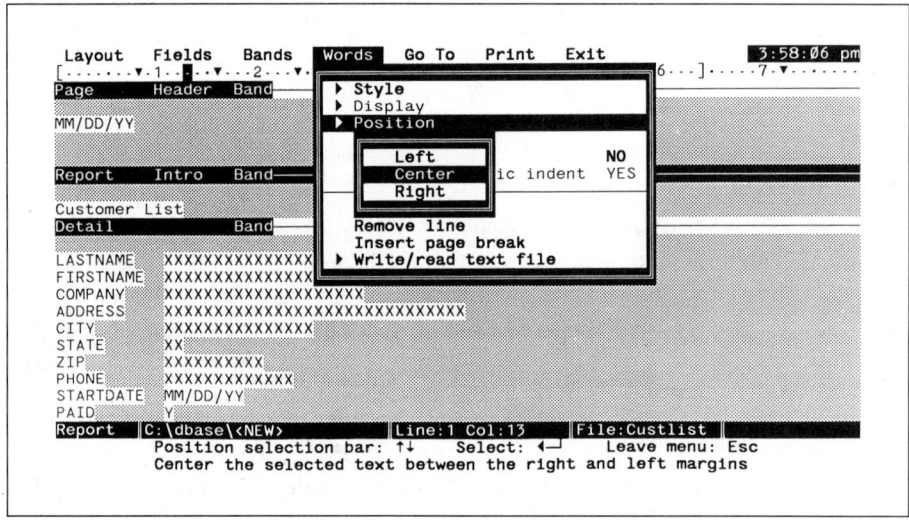

FIGURE 7.6: To center text on the report, select Position and Center from the Words pull-down menu.

Detail Band

The detail area of a report is the body of the report; it presents the values for fields you specify in the Detail band. You also use the Detail band to specify the layout of the data in the printed report. The left side of the Detail band contains the database *field names* (such as LASTNAME and FIRSTNAME). The field names appear in the report exactly as they do on the screen (unless you remove or change the names). The right side of the Detail bands contains the *field templates* (the X's, MM/DD/YY, and Y), indicating where the data from the database will appear. For example, the name Smith will appear in place of the X's to the right of LASTNAME, and the start date will appear in place of MM/DD/YY to the right of STARTDATE. The number of characters that appear in a field template is the maximum length allocated to that field in the database structure.

When you move the cursor around the screen, you will find that whenever the cursor is in a field template, it jumps to the first character of the template. The name of the field associated with the current template appears near the bottom of the screen.

Reformatting the field templates, as explained in this section, requires many steps. Like many real-world databases, CUSTLIST has numerous fields, and you must reformat them one at a time. But remember that you have to design a report format only once. You can then use that format over and over again to print data. Therefore, time spent designing a report is time well spent.

Press ↓ three times to move the cursor to the *L* in the LASTNAME field name. Press **End** to move the cursor to line 1, column 26. Type a comma (,) and then press the space bar to ensure that a comma and blank space appear after the last name on the printed report.

Use the ↓ and ← keys to move the cursor to the FIRSTNAME template (line 2, column 11). Press Select (**F6**) and then ← to select that template. (It will be highlighted on your screen.) Press Move (**F7**) to begin to move the template. Use the ↑ and → keys to move the image of the template to line 1, column 28, of the Detail band. Press ← to complete the move.

Press **End** to move to the end of the template. Press the space bar three times to insert three blank spaces. Use the ↓ and ← keys to move the cursor to the COMPANY field template (line 3, column 11). Press Select (**F6**) and ← to select the template. Press Move (**F7**) and use the arrow keys to move the template image to line 1, column 46. Press ← to complete the move.

Use the arrow keys to move the cursor to the ADDRESS field template (line 4, column 11). Press Select (**F6**), **End**, ↓, and then ← to select the ADDRESS and CITY field templates. Press Move (**F7**) and use the arrow keys to move the template image to line 2, column 16. Press ← to complete the move.

Press ↓ and then **End** to move to the end of the CITY field template (line 3, column 31). Type a comma (,) and then press the space bar, so that the printed report will show a comma and blank space. Use the arrow keys to move the cursor to the STATE field template (line 6, column 11). Press Select (**F6**) and then ← to select the template. Press Move (**F7**) and use the arrow keys to move the template image to the right of the comma and space (line 3, column 33). Press ← to complete the move.

Press **End** to move to the end of the STATE template (line 3, column 35). Press the space bar three times to insert three blank spaces. Use the arrow keys to move the cursor to the ZIP template (line 7, column 11). Press Select (**F6**) and

238 ——— **CH. 7** DESIGNING FORMATTED REPORTS

then ↵ to select the template. Press Move (**F7**), move the template image to line 3, column 38, and then press ↵ to complete the move.

Move the cursor to line 4, column 16. Type **Phone:** and then press the space bar. Move the cursor into the PHONE field template (line 8, column 11). Press Select (**F6**) and then ↵ to select the template. Press Move (**F7**), use the arrow keys to move the template image to line 4, column 23, and then press ↵ to complete the move.

Move the cursor to line 5, column 16. Type **Starting date:** and press the space bar. Move the cursor to the STARTDATE field template (line 9, column 11). Press Select (**F6**) and then ↵ to select the template. Press Move (**F7**), move the template image to line 5, column 31, and press ↵.

Press **End** and then press the space bar twice to move the cursor to line 5, column 41. Type **Paid:** and then press the space bar. Move the cursor into the PAID field template (line 10, column 11). Press Select (**F6**) and then press ↵. Press Move (**F7**), move the template image to line 5, column 47, and then press ↵.

Press **Home** and then press ↑ four times (until the cursor moves to the *L* in the LASTNAME field name, at line 1, column 0). Press Select (**F6**), press → eight times, and press ↓ to highlight all the field names (but *not* any of the field templates).

Press ↵ to finish highlighting the field names. Press **Del** to delete all the field names.

To move all the field templates up and to the left, first move the cursor to line 1, column 11 (to the LASTNAME field template). Press Select (**F6**), press **End**, and press ↓ four times to highlight all the field templates and text. Then press ↵. Press Move (**F7**), press **Home**, and press **PgUp** to move the upper-left corner of the template image to line 0, column 0. Press ↵ to complete the move.

dBASE displays the message *Delete all covered text and fields? (Y/N)* because the template image is overlapping other text and fields. Type **Y** to answer yes.

Press ↓ six times to go to line 6, column 0. Press **Ctrl-Y** five times to delete blank lines beneath the cursor position, leaving a single blank line at the bottom of the Detail band.

Report Summary Band

Report summary bands are used, in reports that present numeric information, to display information such as column totals. The summary appears only once, at the end of the report. See Figure 7.5 for an example and Chapter 6 for more information.

The customer list report does not include a report summary, so you need to *close* the report summary band. To do so, first press ↓ to move to the Report Summary band border. (The center of the status bar will show *Band 4/5* when you get there.) Press ↵ to close the band.

Page Footer Band

Use the Page Footer band to specify the information you want to display at the bottom of each page. The customer list report has page numbers centered at the bottom of each page. To modify the design to achieve this, first press ↓ twice to move into the Page Footer band. (The status bar will show that you are at line 0, column 0.)

Press **Ctrl-N** to insert a blank line. Press ↓ once to move to line 1, column 0, in the Page Footer band. Type **Page:** and then press the space bar. Press Field (**F5**) to place the page number.

A menu appears showing all of the fields that you can place in the current report format. Select Pageno from the Predefined column. Press **Ctrl-End** to place the field on the report. Notice that the page number template appears as *999* on the report format, indicating that dBASE is saving space for three digits in the page number.

To center the page number, press Menus (**F10**) and select Position from the Words pull-down menu. Select Center from the submenu. You are now finished designing the report. Your screen should look like Figure 7.7.

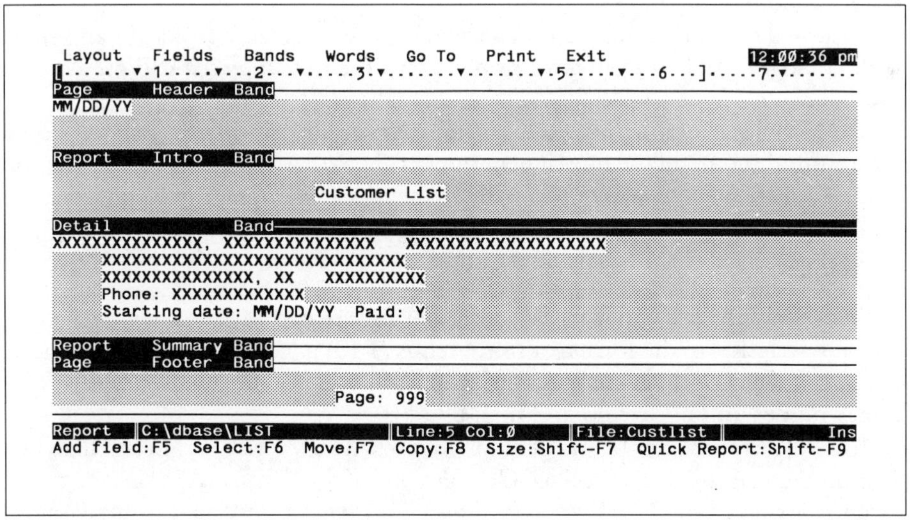

FIGURE 7.7: The completed format for the customer list report. Field templates show where the data will print on the report.

SAVING A REPORT FORMAT

SEQUENCE OF STEPS

On the reports design screen:
  To provide a description:

  Menus (**F10**)
  Layout/**E**dit Description of Report [◄─┘]
  type a description of the report ◄─┘

  To save the report format:

  Menus (**F10**)
  Exit/**S**ave Changes and Exit [◄─┘]
  type a file name ◄─┘

USAGE

Before you save the report design you have created, you should provide a description of the format, so you will know in the future what kind of report you can create with it. To add a description, press Menus (**F10**) and highlight Layout on the menu bar. Select Edit Description of Report. Type a description for the report and then press ◄─┘.

To save the report format and description, press Menus (**F10**) again and select Save Changes and Exit from the Exit pull-down menu. When dBASE presents the prompt *Save as:*, type a valid file name and press ◄─┘.

dBASE will take some time to write a program for printing the report. You'll see a running count of the lines it generates. When dBASE is done, it returns you to the Control Center, where you will see the report name in the Reports panel.

EXAMPLE

Before saving the format for the customer list created in the previous section, add a description to the format. Press Menus (**F10**) and highlight Layout on the menu bar. Select Edit Description of Report. Type the description **List of customer names and addresses** and then press ◄─┘.

To save the report format and description, press Menus (**F10**) again and highlight Exit on the menu bar. Select Save Changes and Exit. When dBASE presents the prompt *Save as:*, type **LIST** and press ◄─┘. You will be returned to the Control Center, where you will see the LIST report name in the Reports panel.

VIEWING THE REPORT

SEQUENCE OF STEPS

From the Control Center:

    highlight the report name in the Reports panel ⏎
    Print Report [⏎]
    View Report on Screen   *or*   **B**egin Printing [⏎]
    press the space bar as necessary   *or*   **Esc**

USAGE

To view a report you have saved, highlight the report name in the Reports panel and press ⏎. Select Print Report from the options that appear. When the print submenu appears, select View Report on Screen to preview the printed report on your screen or Begin Printing to print the report. (See Chapter 9 for additional instructions and options for printing the report on paper.)

EXAMPLE

To view the customer list report, highlight LIST in the Reports panel of the Control Center and press ⏎. Select Print Report and View Report on Screen from the submenu. Press the space bar to view more records in the report. Press **Esc** to return to the Control Center.

MAKING DESIGN CHANGES

SEQUENCE OF STEPS

From the Control Center:
  To access an existing report format:

    highlight the report name in the Reports panel
    Design (**Shift-F2**)

    or

    highlight the report name in the Reports panel ⏎
    Modify Layout [⏎]

USAGE

Once you have saved a report format, you can easily return to the design screen when you want to make some changes. Just highlight the name of the format in the Reports panel of the Control Center and press Design (**Shift-F2**). (Alternatively, after highlighting the format name, you can press ↵ and then select Modify Layout from the submenu that appears.)

This section discusses several modifications that you might want to make to a report design. Note that you can make such changes at any time from the reports design screen.

Opening and Closing Bands

SEQUENCE OF STEPS

On the reports design screen:
  To open a band:

    move the cursor to the band border ↵

  To close a band:

    move the cursor to the band border ↵

  To open all bands:

    Menus (**F10**)
    Bands/**O**pen All Bands [↵]

USAGE

As you add new bands to your report format, your screen may become increasingly cluttered and difficult to read. You can close bands that you are not using at the moment by moving the cursor to the band border and pressing ↵. Just remember to reopen the band before you print the report, because closed bands do not print.

To open a closed band, move the cursor to the band border and press ↵ again. You also can select Open All Bands from the Bands pull-down menu (shown in Figure 7.8) to open all closed bands. The options above the line on the Bands menu concern group bands, which are discussed in Chapter 11.

FORMATTING REPORT BANDS

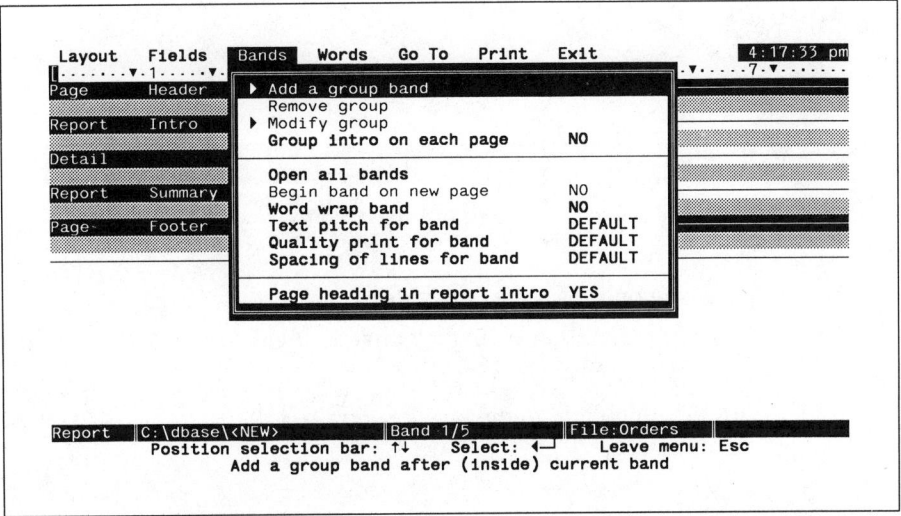

FIGURE 7.8: From the options below the line on the Bands pull-down menu, you can open and close bands; elect to begin bands on a new page; choose to word-wrap the text in a band; and select text pitch, quality, and line spacing.

Formatting Report Bands

SEQUENCE OF STEPS

On the reports design screen:

>   Menus (**F10**)
>   Bands/**T**ext Pitch *or* **Q**uality *or* **S**pacing of Lines [↵]
>   **Ctrl-End**

USAGE

You can specify the pitch, quality, and spacing of lines for an individual band by moving the cursor to the band border and selecting the appropriate option from the Bands menu. Press the space bar to view or change the options. Press **Ctrl-End** to save your new settings. These three options are also available from the Print menu, as discussed in Chapter 9. Use these options from the Bands menu when you want to affect only the current band.

Moving and Copying

SEQUENCE OF STEPS

On the reports design screen:
  To move:

      move the cursor to a corner of the area to move
      Select (**F6**)
      If moving only a field template: ⏎
      If moving more than a single template: highlight the area to move ⏎
      Move (**F7**)
      move the highlight to the new location ⏎

  To copy:

      move the cursor to a corner of the area to copy
      Select (**F6**)
      If copying only a field template: ⏎
      If copying more than a single template: highlight the area to copy ⏎
      Copy (**F8**)
      move the highlight to the new location ⏎

USAGE

To move or copy any part of a report format, first move the cursor to a corner of the area you want to move and press Select (**F6**). If you are moving only a field template, press ⏎. If you are moving more than a single template, use the arrow keys to highlight the entire area that you want to move or copy and then press ⏎.

Press either Move (**F7**) or Copy (**F8**), depending on which operation you want to perform. Move the highlight to the new location and press ⏎.

If you attempt to move or copy selected text to a place where it overlaps existing text or templates, dBASE presents the message *Delete covered text and fields? (Y/N)*. If you select yes, dBASE deletes any covered text or field template. If you select no, the covered text or field is not deleted; you can then press **Esc** to stop copying or moving or to move to another location.

If you press Select (**F6**) and then make a mistake while highlighting, you can press **Esc** to cancel the selection.

Adding Fields

SEQUENCE OF STEPS

From the reports design screen:

> move the cursor to where you want the field template
> Field (**F5**)   *or*   Menus (**F10**) Fields/**A**dd Field [←┘]
> select a field
> **Ctrl-End**

USAGE

To add a new field to a report format, first position the cursor where you want the leftmost character of the field template to appear. Then either press Field (**F5**) or press Menus (**F10**) and select Add Field from the Fields pull-down menu. You will see a submenu of possible fields to add to the format, including database, calculated, and predefined fields.

Database fields are those available from the current database file or query. Predefined fields are those that dBASE IV provides and handles automatically. (Calculated fields are discussed in Chapter 6.)

Select a field by moving the highlight to the option you want and pressing ←┘. You will be given an opportunity to change the Template and Picture Functions options assigned to the field. (These options are discussed later in this chapter in the section "Formatting Fields." Because they are also available for forms design, they also are discussed in detail in Chapter 10.) Press **Ctrl-End** to place the field and return to the reports design screen.

Deleting Fields

SEQUENCE OF STEPS

From the reports design screen:

> move the cursor to the field template
> **Del**   *or*   Fields/**R**emove Field [←┘]

USAGE

To delete a field from the format, move the cursor to the field template and press **Del** or select Remove Field from the Fields submenu.

Adding and Deleting Text

You can place text—such as words, punctuation marks, and blank spaces—anywhere in a report format. To *insert* text into an existing format, position the cursor where you want the new text to appear. Make sure that insert mode is on (the *Ins* indicator will appear in the bottom-right corner of the screen) and then type your text. To *change* existing text, position the cursor on the text to be changed and activate overwrite mode (press **Ins** until the *Ins* indicator disappears). When you type your changes, the new characters will overwrite (replace) the existing characters.

To delete text from the format, position the cursor on the character you want to delete and press **Del**. You can delete an entire section of text and fields by using Select (**F6**) to highlight the area that you want to delete. After pressing ⏎ to complete the selection, press **Del** to delete the entire highlighted block.

Adding and Deleting Lines

SEQUENCE OF STEPS

On the reports design screen:
   To insert a new line in a report format:

      move the cursor to where you want the new line to appear

      Words/**A**dd Line [⏎]   *or*   **Ctrl-N**   *or*   (in insert mode) ⏎

   To delete a line from a report format:

      move the cursor to the line to delete

      Words/**R**emove Line [⏎]   *or*   **Ctrl-Y**

USAGE

dBASE provides three methods for adding a line on the reports design screen and two methods for deleting a line. Be sure to use only one of these methods.

Note that any blank lines in a report band appear as blank lines in the printed report. You can include blank lines in your report formats to make your reports easier to read. Figure 7.9 shows blank lines in a report format.

Formatting Fields

dBASE IV automatically assigns certain *display attributes* to field templates used in report formats. If these automatic attributes do not fit your needs, you can

FORMATTING FIELDS — 247

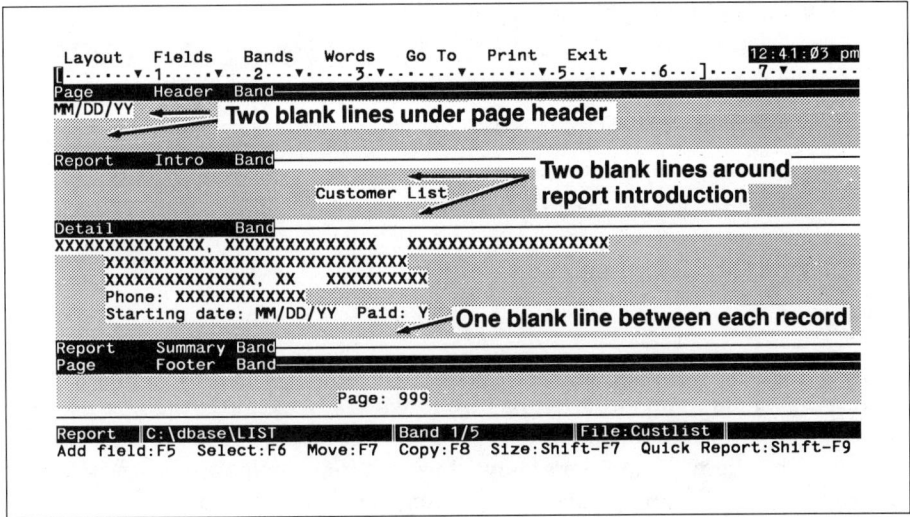

FIGURE 7.9: When you include blank lines in a report format, you improve the appearance of the report and clarify grouping of data.

change them. You can change the display attribute of a field template in a report format by moving the cursor to the appropriate field template on the reports design screen and accessing the display attributes menu. To do so, press Field (**F5**) or select Modify Field from the Fields pull-down menu. Either technique displays a submenu that describes the field and presents the Template and Picture Functions options.

CHANGING A FIELD'S PICTURE FUNCTIONS

SEQUENCE OF STEPS

On the reports design screen:

    move the cursor to the field template
    Field (**F5**)
    Picture Functions [⏎]
    highlight the option to be changed
    press the space bar to select On or Off
    Ctrl-End

or

move the cursor to the field template
Menus (**F10**)
Fields/**M**odify Field [⏎]
Picture Functions [⏎]
highlight the option to be changed
press the space bar to select On or Off
Ctrl-End

USAGE

A *picture function* is a code that tells dBASE how to display a piece of information. dBASE offers many different picture functions, which are listed on a submenu when you select Picture Functions while adding or changing a field template. The Picture Functions menu for Character fields is shown in Figure 7.10. (Numeric picture functions are discussed in Chapter 6.)

You can turn any available function on or off by highlighting that option and pressing the space bar. Press **Ctrl-End** to save the change. The options you will use most often with report formats are summarized in Table 7.2.

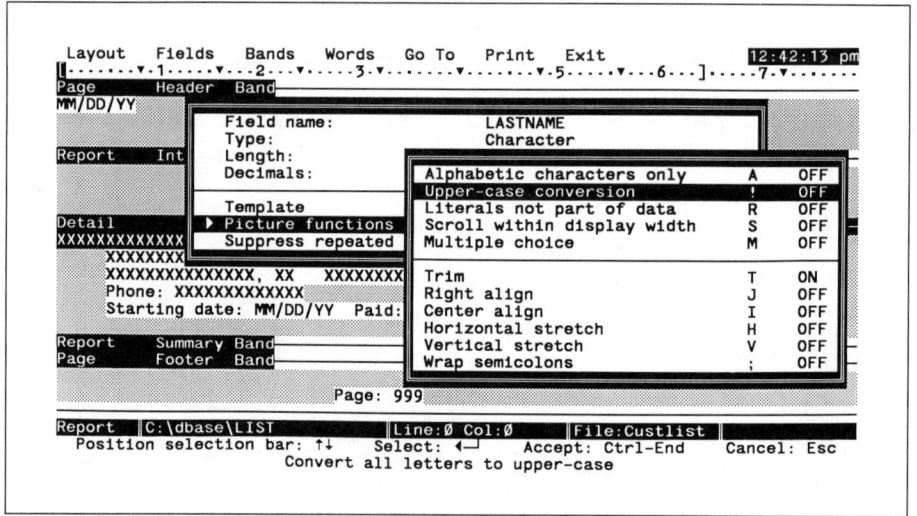

FIGURE 7.10: Picture function options for Character fields. These options are explained with examples in Table 7.2.

PICTURE FUNCTION	SYMBOL	EFFECT
Uppercase Conversion	!	Displays all letters (a–z) in uppercase (A–Z)
Trim	T	Removes leading and trailing blanks
Right Align	J	Right-aligns text within the space allotted for the field
Center Align	I	Centers text within the space provided
Horizontal Stretch	H	Adjusts template width to the width of data
Vertical Stretch	V	Wraps text onto several lines within the allotted width

Table 7.2: Picture Functions Commonly Used for Reports

Changing a Field's Width

SEQUENCE OF STEPS

On the reports design screen:
  To widen or narrow a field:

    move the cursor to the field template
    Size (**Shift-F7**)
    → or ←, as necessary ↵

or

    move the cursor to the field template
    Field (**F5**)
    Template [↵]
    Backspace or **Del** as necessary   *or*   type **X**'s

    Many picture functions affect the display of data within the width provided by the field template. You can control the width of a field on a printed report by changing the size of the field template. By default, dBASE assigns a width that matches the field's width in the database.

For example, given a LASTNAME field that is 15 characters wide, dBASE automatically places the template

XXXXXXXXXXXXXXX

in the report format to display data from that field.

To widen or narrow a field, you can use either of these two techniques:

- Move the cursor to the field template, press Size (**Shift-F7**), and use → and ← to widen or narrow the field; then press ↵.
- Move the cursor to the field template, press Field (**F5**), and select Template. Press **Backspace** or **Del** to narrow the template, or type **X**'s to widen the template.

Note that if you use the latter technique, dBASE displays a submenu of *character input symbols*. These are more relevant to custom forms than they are to reports and so are discussed in Chapter 10.

The way dBASE fits data from the database into the space allotted by the field template on the report depends on three picture functions: Trim, Horizontal Stretch, and Vertical Stretch. For example, suppose your database contains a field named ADDRESS that is 30 characters wide, but on your report you narrow the template to 15 characters (that is, to XXXXXXXXXXXXXXX). How would dBASE display the address 3456 Rancho Santa Fe Dr.?

If you assign the Trim picture function to the ADDRESS field, dBASE will *truncate* the data to fit it within the template. That is, dBASE will display only the first 15 characters, as follows:

3456 Rancho San

If you assign the Vertical Stretch picture function to the ADDRESS field, dBASE will word-wrap the address within the width allotted. Hence, if you print the example address using a template that is 15 characters wide and you use the Vertical Stretch picture function, the sample address will appear on the report as

3456 Rancho
Santa Fe Dr.

If you assign the Horizontal Stretch picture function, dBASE will automatically adjust the size of the template to fit the data being displayed. Thus, it will not matter what size you make the template. (In fact, you cannot alter the size of a field template that has the Horizontal Stretch function assigned to it.) Hence, regardless of the size of the template, the Horizontal Stretch picture function always displays the full address—in this case

3456 Rancho Santa Fe Dr.

The Horizontal Stretch function also trims off any leading or trailing blanks when it prints data.

Note that when you assign the Vertical Stretch picture function to a field, the template appears as V's rather than X's. When either V's or X's appear, you can use the Size (**Shift-F7**) key to size the template. When you assign the Horizontal Stretch picture function to a field, the template appears as H's, and you cannot resize the field.

You can also use the Center and Right Align picture functions to specify how data is displayed within the width provided by the field template. If you assign the Center picture function, dBASE will center text within the width, as in these examples:

```
   123 Appleton Court
     34 Reposo Alto
       123 A St.
      P.O. Box 3384
```

If you assign the Right Align attribute to a field, dBASE will right-align text within the width allotted by the field template, as follows:

```
   123 Appleton Court
       34 Reposo Alto
            123 A St.
        P.O. Box 3384
```

Drawing Lines and Boxes

You can draw lines and boxes on a report format using the Box and Line options from the Layout pull-down menu. However, not all printers can print the lines and boxes. Chapter 10 discusses the techniques for drawing lines and boxes.

Saving Your Changes

SEQUENCE OF STEPS

From the reports design screen:
  To save and exit:

   Menus (**F10**)

   Exit/**S**ave Changes and Exit [⏎]

To exit without saving:

> Menus (**F10**)
> Exit/**A**bandon Changes and Exit [⏎]

To save as a new file:

> Menus (**F10**)
> Layout/**S**ave This Report [⏎]
> enter a file name
> Menus (**F10**)
> Exit/**A**bandon Changes and Exit [⏎]

After you have modified your report format, you must save your changes. To save the report under the last name you used, select Save Changes and Exit from the Exit pull-down menu. If you do *not* want to save your changes, select Abandon Changes and Exit from the menu instead.

If you want to save your modified format as a new file—leaving the original, unmodified format file intact—select Save This Report from the Layout pull-down menu and provide a new file name. Then select Abandon Changes and Exit from the Exit pull-down menu.

DISPLAYING MEMOS IN REPORTS

You can place Memo fields in report formats just as you can in any other database field. By default, a Memo field is displayed in a template 50 characters wide, using the Vertical Stretch picture function so that all text is word-wrapped within the allotted width.

Figure 7.11 shows a sample report format, which was created by selecting Form Layout from the Quick Layouts submenu and then modified to arrange the field templates into a more pleasing layout. Notice that the Abstract field template is displayed as a series of 50 V's.

You cannot change the template assigned to a Memo field; it must be V (for Vertical Stretch). However, you can widen or narrow the field. To do so, move the cursor into the field template and then press Size (**Shift-F7**). Use the ← and → keys to narrow or widen the template and then press ⏎ when you are done. Later, when you print the report, all text in the memo field will be word-wrapped within the width of the field template on the report.

Because Memo fields use the Vertical Stretch picture function, the text within the margin extends downward when the report is printed. Place at least one blank line beneath the Memo field template in the Detail band if you want to print a blank line at the bottom of the memo. Figure 7.12 shows a single record

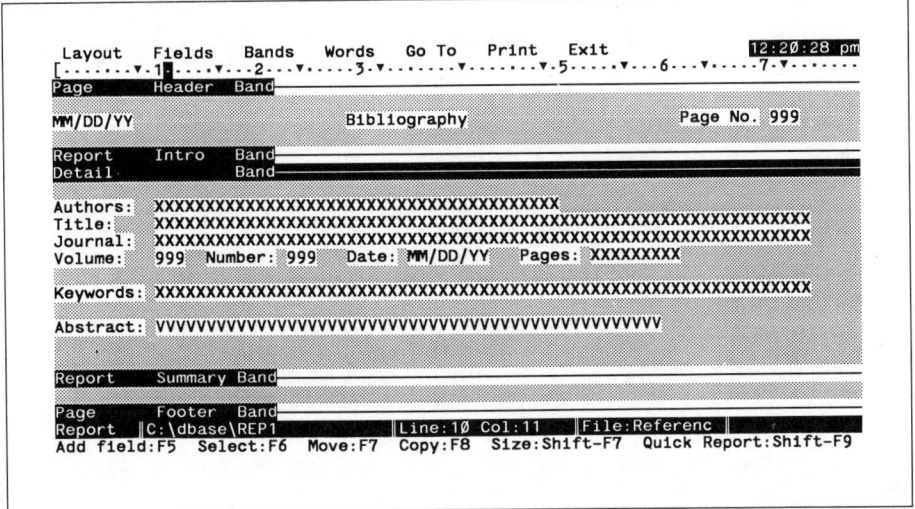

FIGURE 7.11: Sample report format for a bibliographical database with a Memo field named ABSTRACT. Notice that dBASE uses a template of V's for the Memo field.

printed from the sample report format. Notice that the text in the Memo field is word-wrapped within the default width of 50 characters.

CREATING FORM LETTERS

SEQUENCE OF STEPS

From the Control Center:

> highlight <create> in the Reports panel ↵
> Layout/**Q**uick Layouts
> **M**ailmerge Layout

USAGE

To create form letters with dBASE IV, you can take advantage of a special feature called the *word-wrap editor*, so called because it automatically wraps paragraphs inside of any margins, always breaking sentences between words rather than within words. This capability gives you much of the power and flexibility of a word processor—you can easily create, change, delete, and add text to perfect

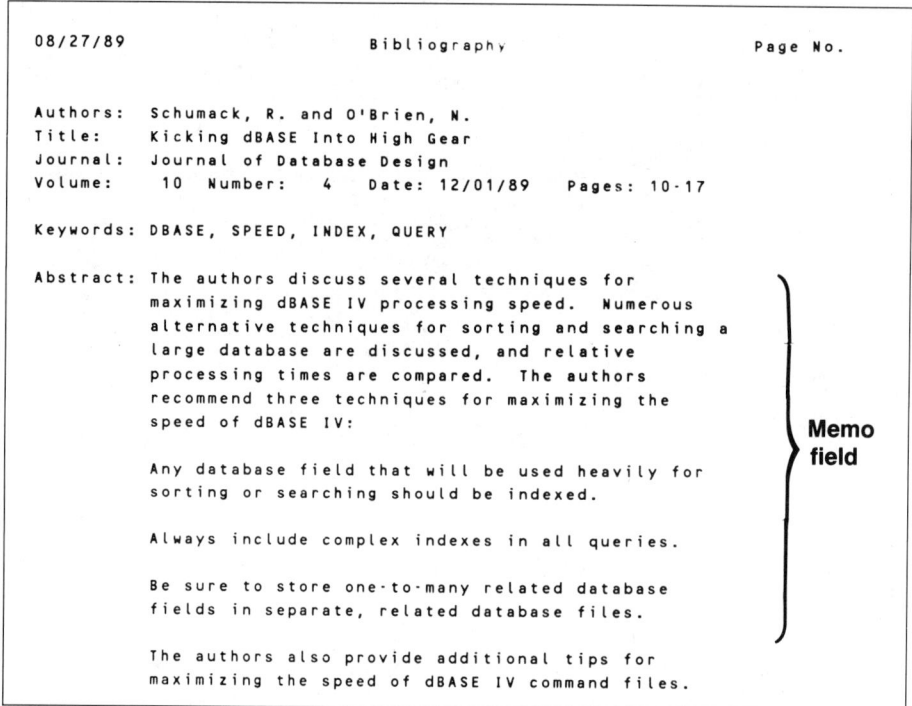

FIGURE 7.12: A printed record from the bibliographical database, using the report format in Figure 7.11.

your letter, and the word-wrap editor takes care of the formatting automatically. If you need more of the capabilities modern word processors offer, see the discussion of exchanging files with other software in Chapter 14.

Even though the word-wrap editor offers special features, keep in mind that a form letter is like any other report in dBASE. You create the form letter through the reports design screen. After you have saved it, its name appears in the Reports panel of the Control Center, and you can print it at any time using the same techniques you use to print other reports.

The name and address on the letter—and possibly other information, such as a current balance due—come directly from the database. dBASE will print a letter for every record in the database or for records you specify in a query (for example, for New York residents only or for people who are late in paying).

To begin creating a form letter, first make sure that the database you want to use is active. Then highlight <create> in the Reports panel and press ⏎. On the reports design screen, select Quick Layouts from the Layout pull-down menu. Select Mailmerge Layout to start creating your form letter.

dBASE automatically closes all report bands except the Detail band, which lengthens to accommodate a large body of text. But you are not limited to the space initially displayed in the Detail band; the Detail band will lengthen to accommodate as much text as you enter.

EXAMPLE

Figure 7.13 shows a form letter created from the CUSTLIST database.

To get started, make sure that the CUSTLIST database name is active (above the line in the Data panel). If it is not, highlight CUSTLIST, press ↵, and select Use File to open it.

Highlight <create> in the Reports panel and press ↵. From the reports design screen, select Quick Layouts from the Layout pull-down menu. Select Mailmerge Layout to start creating your form letter.

```
09/01/89

Anita Smith
2001 Engine Dr.
Hideaway, CA  92220

Dear Anita:

Believe it or not, this is a form letter!  My new dBASE IV
program lets me add text, delete it, make changes and
corrections.

Not only can I type up a storm, but I can also use dBASE IV's
many other capabilities with my form letters, including:

         Sorting form letters and matching mailing labels
         into zip code order for bulk mailing.

         Selecting particular people to print letters and
         mailing labels for, such as yourself, Anita.

Sincerely,

Alfred Winstein
```

FIGURE 7.13: Sample form letter created with the MailMerge Layout option and the dBASE IV editor.

Setting Margins

SEQUENCE OF STEPS

From the reports design screen:

    Menus (**F10**)

    Words/**M**odify Ruler [↵]

move the cursor to the column where you want the left margin
[
move the cursor to the column where you want the right margin
]
←┘

USAGE

It is a good idea to decide on the margins for your form letter before you start typing. Follow these steps to set the right margin to 64 (a good setting for 8½-by-11-inch paper): Press Menus (**F10**) and move to the Words pull-down menu. Select Modify Ruler. Press **Tab** eight times to move the cursor to column 64 on the ruler. Type] to mark the right margin. Press ←┘ to set the margin. See Chapter 9 if you need to set the left margin; many printers offer a 1-inch default setting, which you can accept.

Writing the Text of the Letter

You can now type the text of the letter. Because you selected mailmerge layout as the general format for the report, the cursor is in the Detail band, and dBASE is already in word-wrap mode, which means that you can take advantage of the word-wrap editor. When using the word-wrap editor, keep one important point in mind: Do not press the ←┘ key until you get to the end of a paragraph. If you are accustomed to word processing, the principal is the same. The program takes care of formatting lines and sentences within paragraphs.

EXAMPLE

Type the first paragraph of the letter, as shown here, but type as though it were one long line (do not press ←┘):

> Believe it or not, this is a form letter! My new dBASE IV program lets me type up a storm. I can add text, delete it, and make changes and corrections.

Notice that dBASE automatically word-wraps the entire paragraph to the margins you specified. The paragraph is a single *block* of text now. Press ←┘ twice to start a new paragraph (block) and add a blank line. Then type the next block of text (again, without pressing ←┘):

> Not only can I type up a storm, but I can also use dBASE IV's many other capabilities with my form letters, including:

Press ↵ twice and type the following sentence, again without pressing the ↵ key:

> Sorting form letters and matching mailing labels into zip-code order for bulk mailing.

Press ↵ twice. Then type the following sentence (without pressing ↵):

> Selecting particular people to print letters and mailing labels for, such as yourself,

Now press ↵ twice and type **Sincerely,** (including the comma). Then press ↵ twice again and type the name **Alfred Winstein**.

At this point, the Detail band on your reports design screen should look something like Figure 7.14. You have created the *body* of the letter.

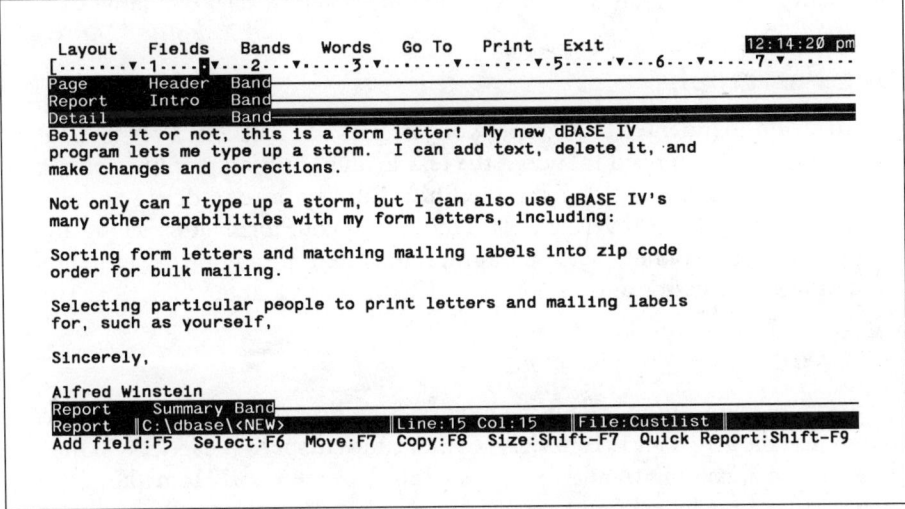

FIGURE 7.14: The text of the form letter in the report format Detail band.

Working with Blocks of Text

You can use all the editing keys listed in Table 7.1 to make changes and corrections to your form letter, including the arrow keys to position the cursor, the **Del** key to delete characters, the **Backspace** key to move backward or delete characters, and the **Ins** key to switch between insert and overwrite modes. You can also use any of the special keys listed in the navigation line, and you can mark blocks of text to copy, move, or delete.

EXAMPLE

Suppose you want to remove the words *type up a storm. I can* from the first paragraph of the example letter. Follow these steps to do so.

Use the arrow keys to move the cursor to the blank space in front of the letter *t* in *type* (at line 1, column 15). Then press Select (**F6**).

Press → until the highlight covers the words *type up a storm. I can.* (If you go too far, press ← to back up.) Press ↵ to complete the selection (which will be highlighted). Press **Del** to delete the highlighted text. The prompt *Press y to perform the block deletion* will appear at the bottom of the screen to double-check your intentions. Press **Y**, for yes.

Instantly, dBASE removes the highlighted text and automatically reformats the entire paragraph so that it still fits perfectly within the margins. Keep in mind that once you highlight a block of text with the Select (**F6**) key, you can also move or copy that text using the Move (**F7**) or Copy (**F8**) key. The navigation line at the bottom of the screen reminds you that these features are available.

Reformatting Paragraphs

To create an indented paragraph, you just press the **Tab** key. Press the **Tab** key several times if you need to indent the text further. Subsequent lines of text that you type are also indented. Press the **Shift-Tab** key once to delete an indent or several times to delete several levels of indent. (If your form letter is long and you want only the first line of each paragraph indented, it may be easier to create it with a word processor and import it to dBASE; see Chapter 14.)

EXAMPLE

Suppose you want to indent the last two sentences (or blocks) in the letter. To do so, use the arrow and **Home** keys to move the cursor to the letter *S* in the word *Sorting* (line 7, column 0) and then press **Tab**. Use the ↓ and **Home** keys to move the cursor to the letter *S* in the word *Selecting* (line 10, column 0) and then press **Tab** again. Both blocks of text are now indented, and dBASE has reformatted each one accordingly, as shown in Figure 7.15.

Adding Database Fields

SEQUENCE OF STEPS

On the reports design screen in the Detail band (repeat as necessary):

    move the cursor to where you want the field to begin
    Field (**F5**)

ADDING DATABASE FIELDS — 259

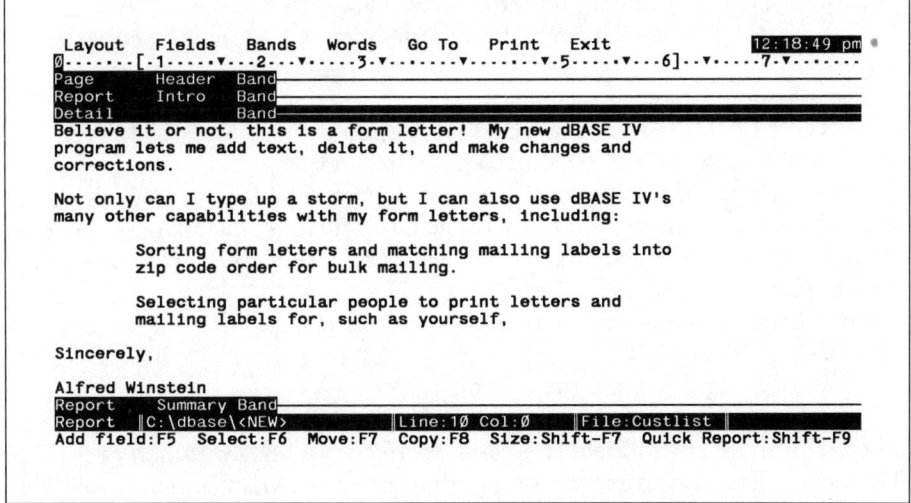

FIGURE 7.15: Two blocks of indented text. Use the Tab key to indent text—subsequent text that you type in that paragraph will align with the indented first line.

select the name of the field

Ctrl-End

USAGE

You need to place field templates from the database in the form letter to show dBASE where to place names and addresses when it prints the letter.

To place field templates in the letter, use the same techniques that you used to place field templates on mailing labels and reports. That is, position the cursor where you want the field to begin and press Field (**F5**). Then select the name of the field you want to display by highlighting its name and pressing ⏎. Press **Ctrl-End** to place the field in the letter.

EXAMPLE

To add database fields to the example letter, first press **Home** and ↑ until the cursor gets to the letter *B* in the word *Believe* (line 0, column 0, in the Detail band). Press **Ctrl-N** eight times to make room for the fields.

To place the current date at the top of the form letter, press Field (**F5**) and select Date from the Predefined column of the submenu that appears. Press **Ctrl-End** to place the date field in the letter.

Move the cursor to line 2, column 0. Press Field (**F5**) and select FIRSTNAME from the first panel of the submenu that appears. Press **Ctrl-End** to place the field on the letter.

Press **End** and then press the space bar to insert a blank space. Press Field (**F5**), select LASTNAME, and press **Ctrl-End**. Press ↓, press Field (**F5**), and select ADDRESS. Press **Ctrl-End** to place the address.

Press ↓, press Field (**F5**), and select CITY. Press **Ctrl-End** to place the CITY field. Press **End** to move to the end of the CITY field template. Type a comma (,) and then press the space bar. Press Field (**F5**) and select STATE. Press **Ctrl-End** to place the STATE field beside the CITY field.

Press **End** to move to the end of the STATE field template (line 4, column 19). Press the space bar twice to insert two blank spaces. Press Field (**F5**), select ZIP, and press **Ctrl-End** to place the ZIP field.

Press ↓ twice to move to line 6, column 21. Type **Dear** and press the space bar to insert a space. Press Field (**F5**), select FIRSTNAME, and then press **Ctrl-End**. Press **End** to move to the end of the FIRSTNAME field template. Then type a colon (:).

The form letter now includes a greeting at the top, such as **Dear John:**. At this point, your letter should look like Figure 7.16. (Some of the text is scrolled off the bottom of the screen.)

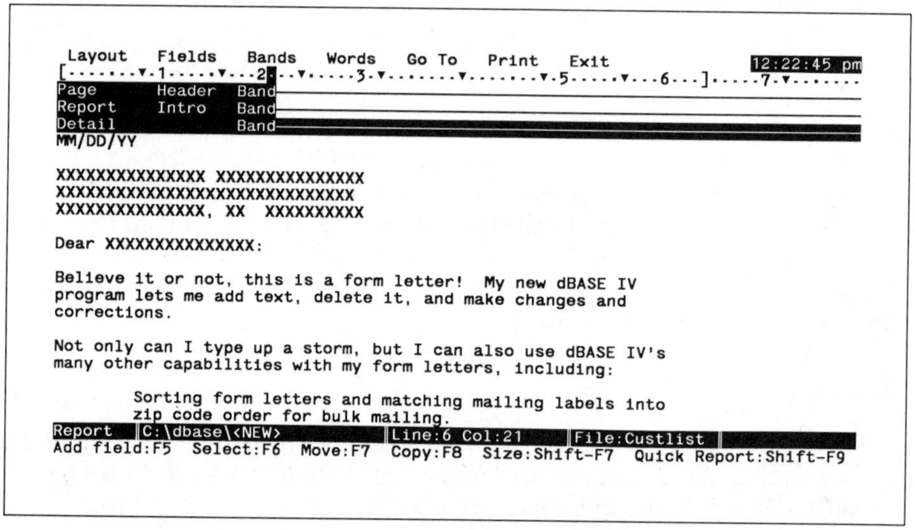

FIGURE 7.16: Form letter with field templates added. This format will print letters for each of the people in the database. The letters will look like Figure 7.13.

The example form letter also prints the recipient's first name again near the bottom of the letter. Follow these steps to place the FIRSTNAME template accordingly: Press ↓ about 15 times and then press **End** to move the cursor to the right of the words *such as yourself,*.

Press the space bar to insert a blank space. Press Field (**F5**) and select FIRSTNAME as the field to place. Press **Ctrl-End**. Press **End** to move past the end of the FIRSTNAME field template (about line 19, column 61) and type a period (.).

Saving Your Form Letter

SEQUENCE OF STEPS

On the reports design screen:
  To add a description:

  Menus (**F10**)
  Layout/**E**dit Description of Report [↵]
  type a description ↵

  To save and name the form letter:

  Menus (**F10**)
  Exit/**S**ave Changes and Exit [↵]
  type a file name ↵

USAGE

It is a good idea to add a description of the form letter before you save it, so that months later you will know what it contains. To add a description, press Menus (**F10**) and select Edit Description of Report from the Layout pull-down menu. When prompted, type a description and press ↵.

To save and name the form letter, press Menus (**F10**) and select Save Changes and Exit from the Exit pull-down menu. When prompted, type a file name and press ↵.

dBASE will take a few seconds to prepare a program for the form letter. When it is done with this task, it will return you to the Control Center, where the name of the form letter will appear in the Reports panel.

EXAMPLE

To add a description of the example form letter, press Menus (**F10**) and select Edit Description of Report from the Layout pull-down menu. When prompted, type the description **Example form letter** and then press ↵.

To save the file, press Menus (**F10**) again and select Save Changes and Exit from the Exit pull-down menu. When prompted, type the name **FORMLET** and press ↵. After a few seconds, dBASE returns you to the Control Center, where the name of the form letter FORMLET appears in the Reports panel.

Viewing Your Form Letter

SEQUENCE OF STEPS

From the Control Center:

> highlight the form letter name in the Reports panel ↵
>
> **P**rint Report [↵]
>
> **V**iew Report on Screen [↵]
>
> press the space bar, if necessary
>
> **Esc**

To view the form letter on the screen, follow the same steps as for viewing any report. That is, highlight the form letter name in the Reports panel and then press ↵. Select Print Report from the options that appear and then select View Report on Screen. Press the space bar to view additional screens of the report and **Esc** to return to the Control Center.

Figure 7.12 earlier in this chapter showed how the example letter appears on your screen (or printer). To print your form letters, see Chapter 9.

TIPS AND TRAPS

- The line and column position of the cursor does not appear on the reports design screen until the cursor is inside a band.
- When the cursor is inside a field template, it always jumps to the first position in that template. The name of the associated field appears near the bottom of the screen.
- Pressing ↵ adds new blank lines on the reports design screen *only* when insert mode is on. Pressing **Ctrl-N** adds a new blank line regardless of whether insert mode is on.

- When you press Select (**F6**) or Move (**F7**), the navigation line provides instructions regarding what to do next.
- Any field template that is only partially highlighted (selected) will not be deleted when you press **Del**.
- You cannot alter the width of fields that use the Date data type.

Summary

You can create a great variety of reports with dBASE IV. You begin by selecting one of the three generic report formats provided and then modify that format through menu options until the report meets your requirements. This chapter discussed creating form letters because dBASE IV treats form letters as reports. Chapter 9 presents the printing options for reports.

For information about reports with totals and subtotals, including examples:

- Chapter 6, "Performing Calculations"

For information about drawing lines and boxes, and for further discussion of the Template and Picture Functions options:

- Chapter 10, "Creating Custom Forms"

For a discussion of group bands in reports:

- Chapter 11, "Managing Groups of Records"

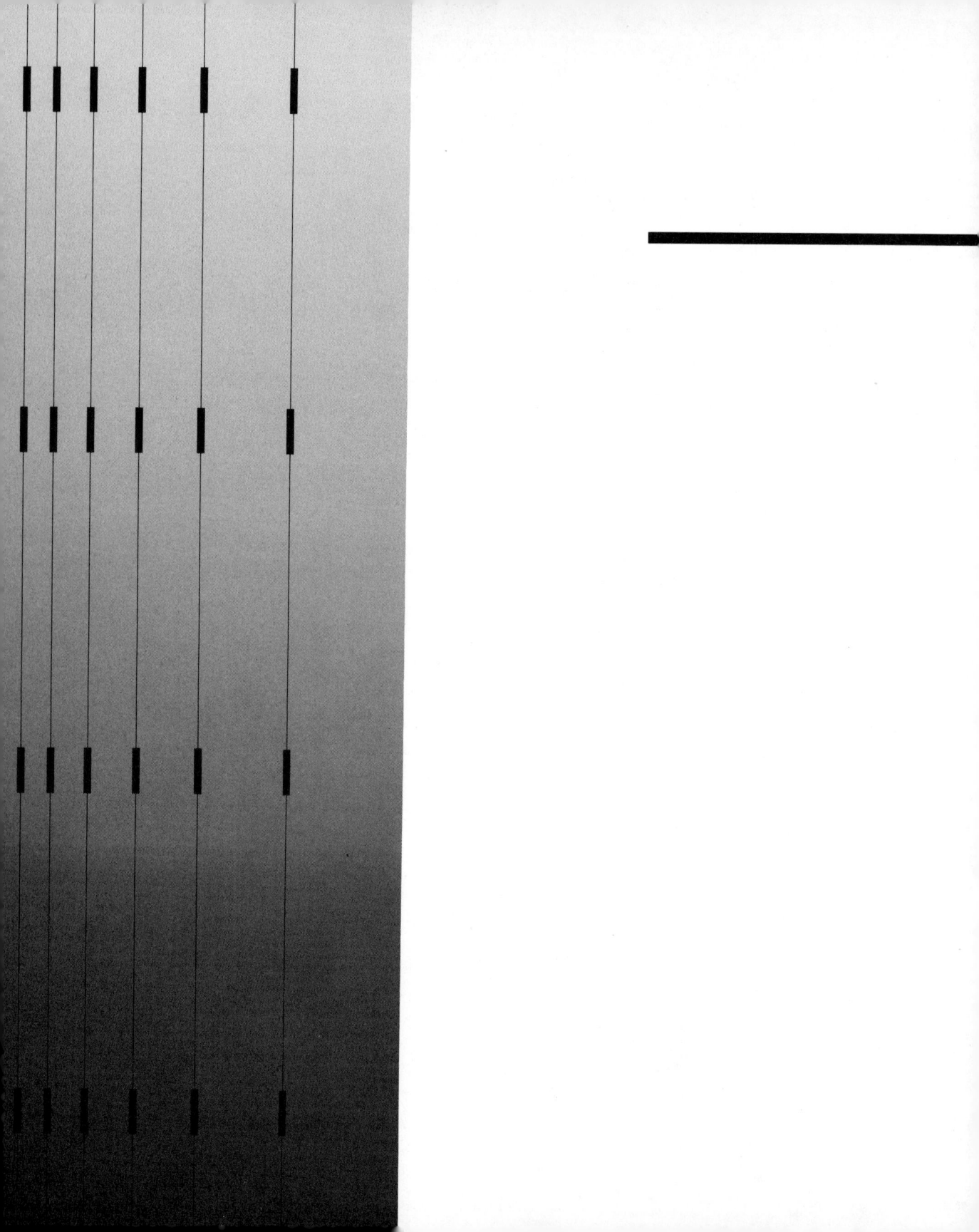

CHAPTER 8

DESIGNING MAILING LABELS

Accessing the Labels Design Screen. 267
Selecting a General Label Format. 269
Placing Fields on a Label. 271
Saving a Label Format. 275
Using Label Files. 276
Viewing a Label Design. 278
Editing on the Labels Design Screen. 278
    Moving and Copying. 280
    Adding Fields. 281
    Deleting Fields. 281
    Adding and Deleting Text. 282
    Formatting Fields. 283
        Using Picture Functions. 283
        Changing Field Widths. 284
Tips and Traps. 285
Summary. 285

Designing Mailing Labels

dBASE IV provides many options for the design of mailing labels. To design, or *format,* the labels, you use the *labels design screen* (or *labels design work surface*). dBASE IV uses the term *labels* loosely. You can use the labels design screen to print any type of mailing label, as well as to print envelopes, Rolodex cards, and general-purpose labels such as identification stickers.

Accessing the Labels Design Screen

SEQUENCE OF STEPS

From the Control Center:
   To open the database file, if necessary:

      highlight the database name in the Data panel ↵

      Use File

Then:

      <create> in the Labels panel ↵

USAGE

Before you begin to design a label format, you need to choose the database file or query for which you want to print labels. If the database or query is currently in use (open), its name appears above the line in the Data or Queries panel. If this is not the case, you need to open the database or query by highlighting its name in the Data or Queries panel and pressing ↵. You press ↵ again to select Use File.

After you have specified the database file or query from which you want to print labels, you need to access the labels design screen. To do so, move the highlight to the <create> option in the Labels panel and press ↵. Figure 8.1 shows both steps. You will then see the labels design screen shown in Figure 8.2.

The labels design screen has the same components as most other dBASE IV screens: a menu bar at the top and a status bar and navigation line at the bottom. The box in the center of the screen represents a blank label; this is where you design your label format. The ruler above the box shows you the width of the label in inches.

268 — **CH. 8**   DESIGNING MAILING LABELS

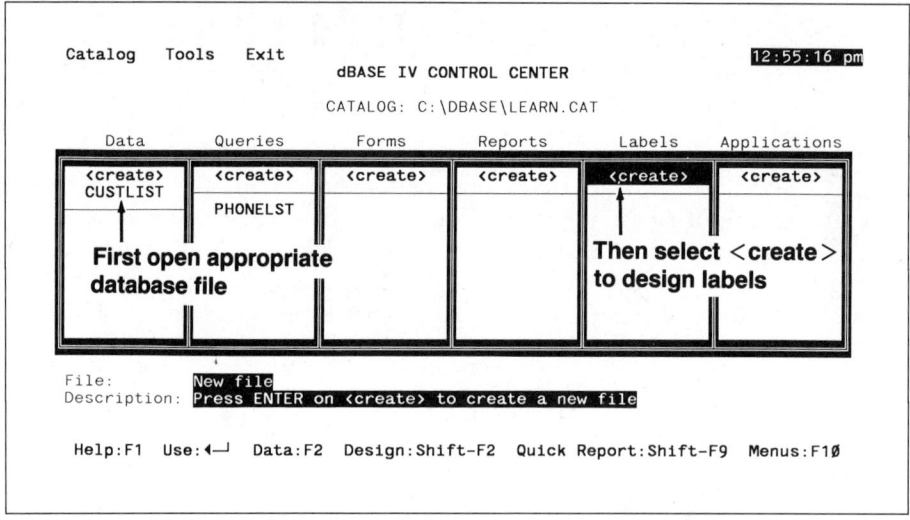

FIGURE 8.1: Steps to take to begin designing labels. Make sure that the database file is open (above the line in the Data panel) before selecting <create>.

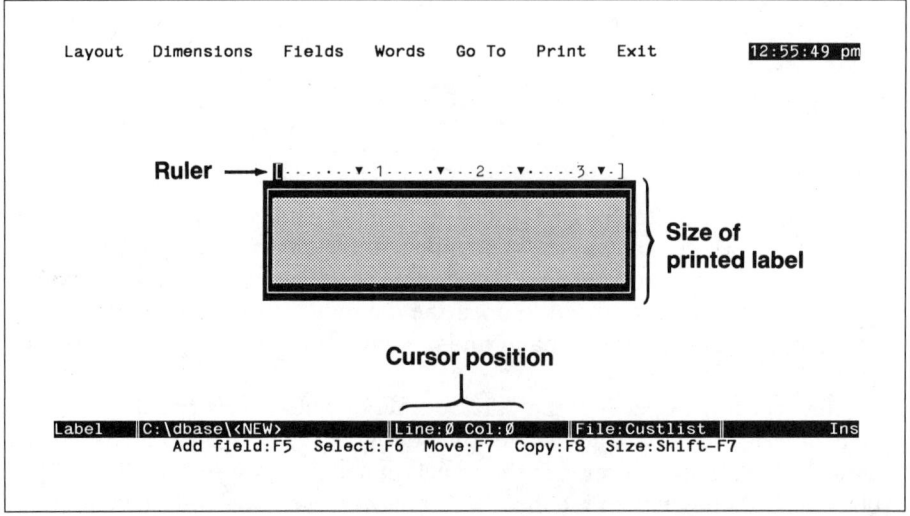

FIGURE 8.2: The labels design screen. Use the line and column indicator on the status line to check the cursor position as you design your label.

EXAMPLE

You can design a label format for the CUSTLIST database. (CUSTLIST was introduced in Chapter 2. Use the instructions there to create this database, if necessary. Note that some of the records in your database may differ from the ones shown in this chapter.) If necessary, open the CUSTLIST database by highlighting CUSTLIST in the Data panel and pressing ←┘. Then press ←┘ again to select the Use File option. To begin designing a label format, highlight <create> in the Labels panel and press ←┘.

SELECTING A GENERAL LABEL FORMAT

SEQUENCE OF STEPS

From the labels design screen:

> Menus (**F10**)
> **D**imensions [←┘]
> Predefined Size/select a size   *or*   select and change individual settings as necessary

USAGE

The window in the center of the labels design screen is sized to show the space available on the printed label. Before you design the label format, you should select the overall label size you want to use. To do so, press Menus (**F10**) and move the highlight to Dimensions on the menu bar. You'll see the submenu shown in Figure 8.3. On this menu, you can select one of dBASE IV's predefined label sizes, or you can change individual settings to specify your own label size. If you select Predefined Size, you will see the submenu of common label sizes shown in Figure 8.4.

On the Predefined Size submenu, the label sizes are described by their height and width in inches and by the number of labels that print across each page. For example, the option 15/16 × 3½ by 3 prints labels that are 15/16 inch (or about 1 inch) tall, 3½ inches wide, and printed three across a page. Select an option by highlighting it and then pressing ←┘.

If the label size you want is not available on the Predefined Size submenu, select individual settings for the label format from the Dimensions pull-down menu. To change any of the settings, highlight the setting to change and press ←┘; then type the new setting and press ←┘ again.

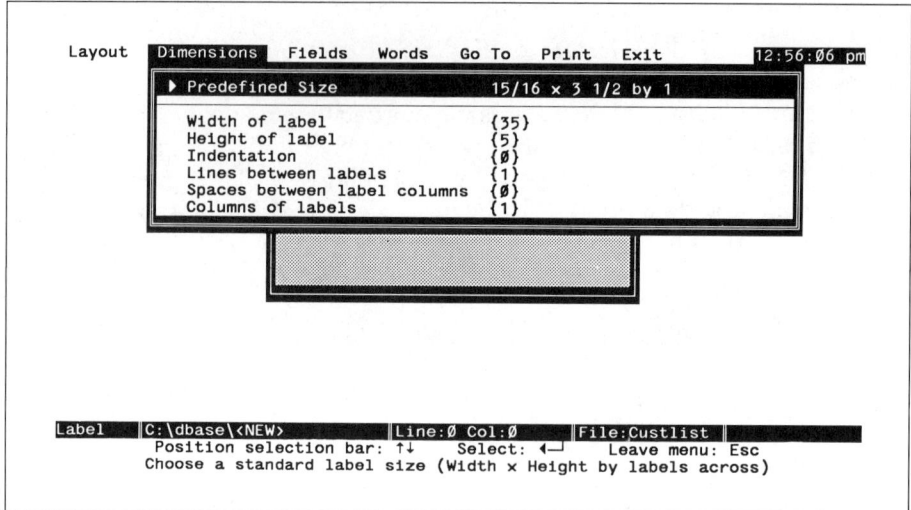

FIGURE 8.3: Label Dimensions menu, where you can select the Predefined Size submenu or change the individual default settings displayed.

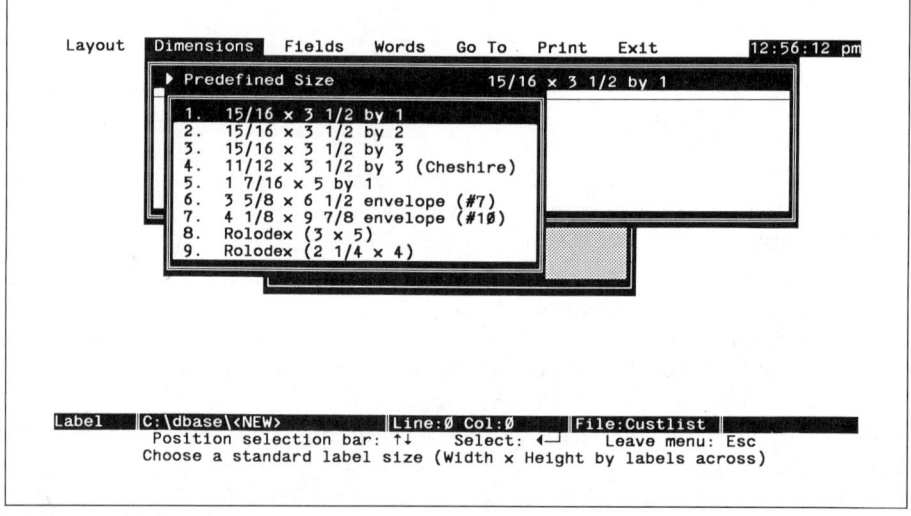

FIGURE 8.4: You can choose from nine predefined label sizes, including sizes for mailing labels, envelopes, and Rolodex cards.

The Width of Label option specifies the number of total characters across the width of the label. You specify the Height of Label option in number of printed lines. The maximum size for either of these options is 255.

The Indentation setting specifies the number of character spaces between the left margin and the first label. You also specify the Spaces between Label Columns option in number of characters. The Lines between Labels setting specifies the number of blank lines between one label (or row of labels) and the next. The Columns of Labels option specifies the number of labels to print across the page. The maximum setting is 15 across, which is more than you are likely to need.

Note that the Width of Label option assumes that your printer is using the standard print size of ten characters per inch (*pica* type). Similarly, the Height of Label option assumes the common print size of six lines per inch. If your printer uses different print sizes, you will want to adjust these settings from the Print menu, which is discussed in Chapter 9.

EXAMPLE

To select an overall label size for the CUSTLIST database labels, from the labels design screen press Menus (**F10**). Move the highlight to the Dimensions pull-down menu. Press ↵ to display the Predefined Size submenu. Press ↓ to highlight option 2, for two labels across, and press ↵ to select it.

PLACING FIELDS ON A LABEL

SEQUENCE OF STEPS

On the labels design screen (repeat for each field on the label):

    move the cursor to where you want the data printed

    Field (**F5**)   *or*   Menus (**F10**)/**F**ields/**A**dd Field [↵]

    select a field to appear on the label

    Ctrl-End

USAGE

After you have selected a label size, you need to place *field templates* on the empty label on the screen. These templates serve essentially the same role as in other design screens; here they show dBASE what information from the database is to be printed and where it will appear on the label.

Notice that the message *Line:0 Col:0* appears centered on the status line near the bottom of the screen. This line tells you the line and column position of the cursor at any given moment, which is helpful information when you are placing the field templates.

To place a field template, you first move the cursor to where you want the data to be printed on the label. Then either press Field (**F5**), or press Menus (**F10**) and select Add Field from the Fields pull-down menu. You will see a submenu of items that you can place on the label, similar to that shown in Figure 8.5. These items include the fields for the database you are using, calculated fields (discussed in Chapter 6), and certain predefined fields.

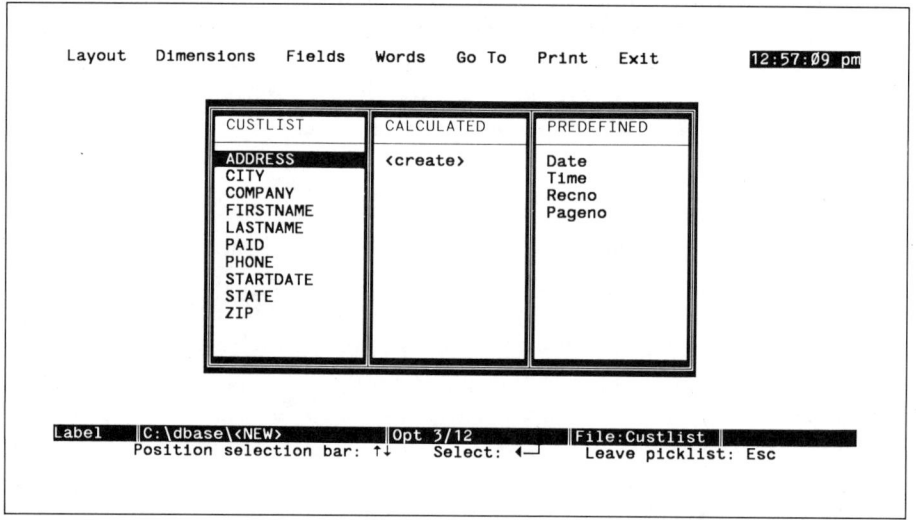

FIGURE 8.5: Submenu of fields that can be placed on a label. The options on this submenu are similar to those for reports.

dBASE provides these four predefined fields:

Date	The date the labels were printed
Time	The time the labels were printed
Recno	The record number (position) of the record
Pageno	The page number

To select a predefined field, use the same technique as for selecting any field: Move the highlight to the option you want and press ←┘.

Position the cursor where you want the first field on the label to begin. Press Field (**F5**) and use ↓ to move to the first field that you want to appear on the label and press ←┘ to highlight and select it; then press **Ctrl-End**. Position the cursor on the label where you want the second field to begin. Press Field (**F5**) again and select the second field from the list by using ↓ and pressing ⏎; then again press **Ctrl-End**. Continue in this way until you have selected all the fields you need.

Each time you press **Ctrl-End**, a series of X's appear on the previously blank label. These X's comprise the *field template*. They show the maximum amount of space that the database information in that field will occupy on the printed label. This is the maximum length for the field as defined in the database structure.

You can also include *text* on each label. You can add any text to a label format by typing it at the place where you want it to appear.

EXAMPLE

You can create a mailing label format to print labels for the CUSTLIST database that look like this:

```
John Smith
ABC Co.
123 A St.
San Diego, CA 92067
```

With the cursor at line 0, column 0, press Field (**F5**) to add a new field. You will see the submenu of items that you can place on the label (shown in Figure 8.5). This menu includes all the fields in the CUSTLIST database, the four predefined fields, and the option of creating a calculated field. Use ↓ to highlight FIRSTNAME; then press ⏎. Press **Ctrl-End** to place the FIRSTNAME field on the label. You will see a series of X's fill in a portion of the screen, as shown in Figure 8.6. These X's are the field template. They show the maximum amount of space that the information in the FIRSTNAME field will occupy on the printed label. You can, if you want, add *Attn:* before the FIRSTNAME field; see "Adding and Deleting Text" later in this chapter.

To add the LASTNAME field to the label format, press the space bar to insert a space between the FIRSTNAME and LASTNAME fields. (The space will appear as a solid box.) Press Field (**F5**) again. Use ↓ and press ⏎ to select LASTNAME. Press **Ctrl-End**. The LASTNAME field template is added to the sample label. Notice the blank space between the first and last names (see Figure 8.7).

Press ⏎ to move the cursor down to the next row (line 1, column 0). To place the COMPANY field, press Field (**F5**), select COMPANY, and press **Ctrl-End**. Press ⏎ to move the cursor to line 2, column 0. Press Field (**F5**) and select ADDRESS. Press **Ctrl-End**. Press ⏎ to move the cursor to line 3, column 0. To place the CITY field, press Field (**F5**), select CITY, and press **Ctrl-End**.

To place a comma and a space after the city name, type a comma and then press the space bar. The comma and space in the format are *text* that will appear on each label. You can add *any* text to a label format simply by typing it at the place where you want it to appear on each label.

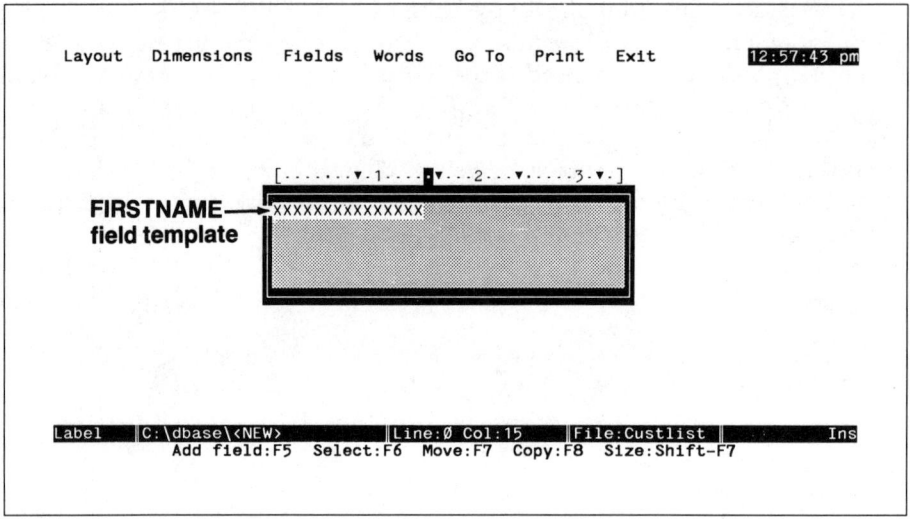

FIGURE 8.6: FIRSTNAME field added to the sample label. Because FIRSTNAME is a Character field, dBASE uses X's for the field template.

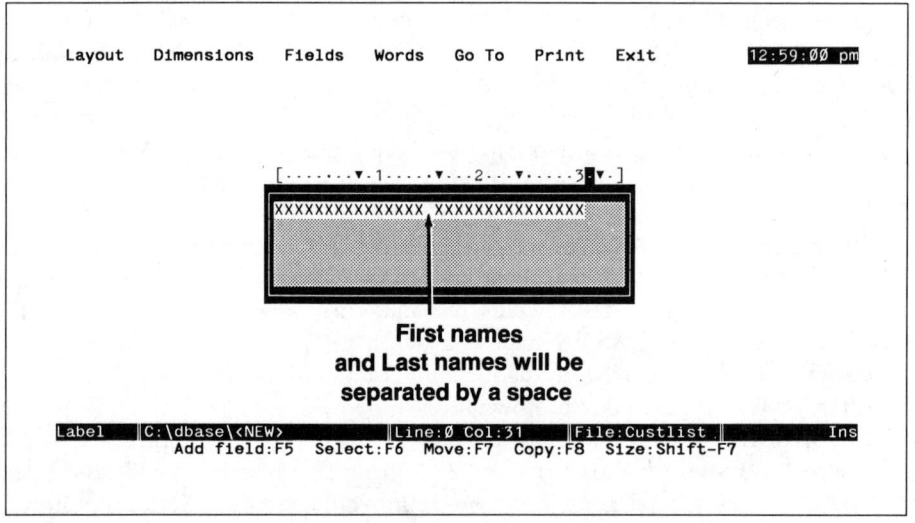

FIGURE 8.7: FIRSTNAME and LASTNAME fields separated by a space. Spaces that you enter into the design will be reproduced exactly on the printed labels.

To place the STATE field, press Field (**F5**), select STATE, and press **Ctrl-End**. To leave two spaces between the STATE and ZIP code fields, press the space bar twice. To place the ZIP field, press Field (**F5**), select ZIP, and press **Ctrl-End**. Your label format should now look like Figure 8.8.

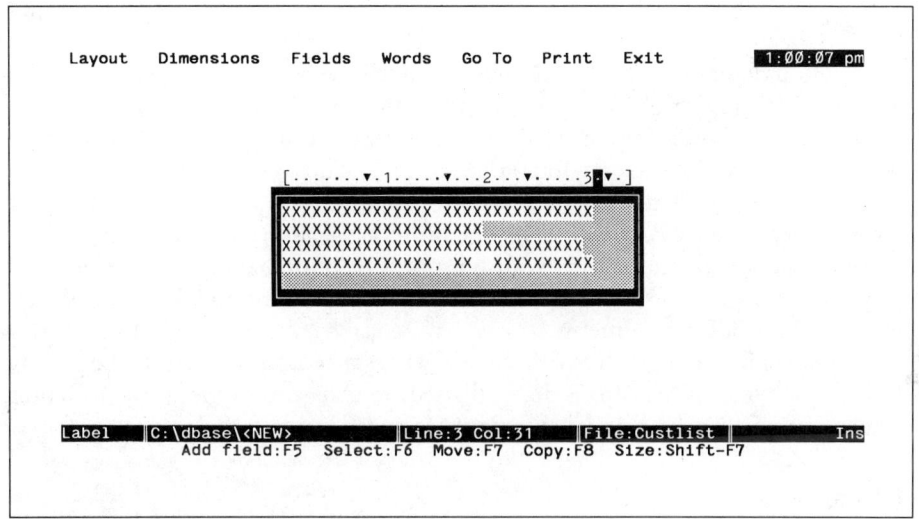

FIGURE 8.8: Completed mailing label with seven Character field templates, appropriate spaces, and a comma.

Saving a Label Format

SEQUENCE OF STEPS

To add a description to the label format:

    Menus (**F10**)
    Layout/**E**dit Description of Label Design [←]
    type a description ←

To save the format:

    Menus (**F10**)
    Exit/**S**ave Changes and Exit [←]
    type a file name ←

To start over:

>Menus (**F10**)
>
>**E**xit/**A**bandon Changes and Exit [⏎]

USAGE

To add a description to the label format and save it for future use, first press Menus (**F10**) and highlight the Layout option on the menu bar. Select Edit Description of Label Design and type any description you like. (This step is optional; you do not have to add a description.) Then press ⏎.

Press Menus (**F10**) again and select Save Changes and Exit from the Exit pull-down menu. When dBASE presents the prompt *Save as:*, type a valid file name of no more than eight characters, with no spaces or punctuation. Then press ⏎. (If you do not want to save your label format, select Abandon Changes and Exit from the Exit pull-down menu.)

There will be a delay while dBASE IV writes a program to print labels in the format you wish. When this is done, dBASE returns you to the Control Center, where you will see the new label format file name in the Labels panel.

EXAMPLE

To add a description to the label format for the CUSTLIST database and save it for future use, first press Menus (**F10**) and highlight the Layout option on the menu bar. Select Edit Description of Label Design, type **2-across mailing labels**, and press ⏎.

Press Menus (**F10**) again and select Save Changes and Exit from the Exit pull-down menu. When dBASE presents the prompt *Save as:*, type **Mailing** and press ⏎. After a short delay, dBASE returns you to the Control Center, where the Labels panel displays the MAILING file name, as shown in Figure 8.9.

USING LABEL FILES

SEQUENCE OF STEPS

From the Control Center:
  To return to the labels design screen:

>highlight the label file in the Labels panel
>
>Design (**Shift-F2**)

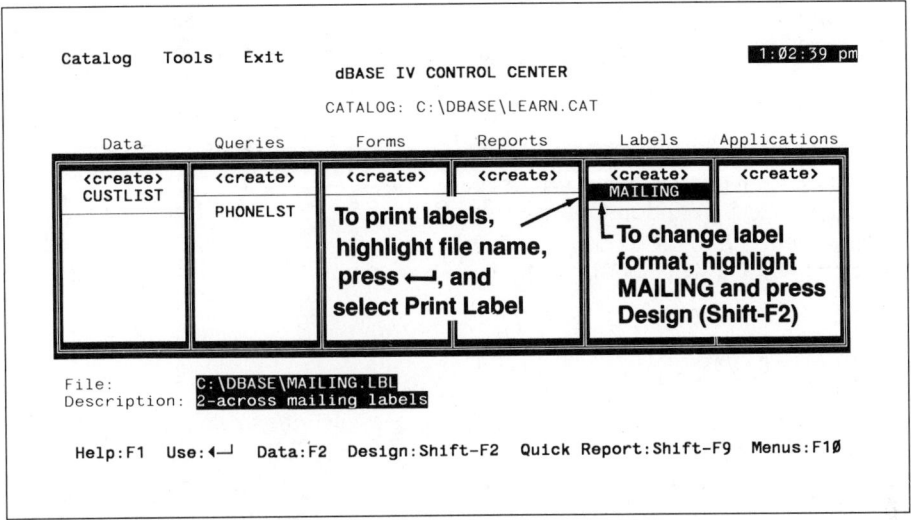

FIGURE 8.9: The MAILING label format in the Control Center Labels panel, with steps for printing labels or changing the label format.

or

> highlight the label file in the Labels panel ⏎
> Modify Layout

To save the design under the same name:

> Menus (**F10**)
> **E**xit/**S**ave Changes and Exit [⏎]

To save as a new design:

> Menus (**F10**)
> **L**ayout/**S**ave This Label Design [⏎]
> type a name for the label file ⏎
> **E**xit/**A**bandon Changes and Exit [⏎]

USAGE

You can make changes to your label format by returning to the label file you have saved. To do so, highlight the name of the mailing label format in the Labels panel and press Design (**Shift-F2**) (or press ⏎ and select Modify Layout from the options that appear).

If you want to save the modified format under the same name, select Save Changes and Exit from the Exit pull-down menu. You will be returned to the Control Center.

If you want to save the modified format under a new name (and thus be able to use the original format as well), select Save This Label Design from the Layout menu. Type a new name for this design when dBASE prompts *Save as:*. Press ⏎ and then select Abandon Changes and Exit from the Exit pull-down menu. You will be returned to the Control Center, where you will see the new label file listed below the previous label file in the Labels panel.

VIEWING A LABEL DESIGN

SEQUENCE OF STEPS

From the Control Center:

>highlight the label file name in the Labels panel ⏎
>
>**P**rint Label [⏎]
>
>**V**iew Labels on Screen [⏎]
>
>press the space bar, if necessary
>
>**Esc**

USAGE

To view a label design that you have saved, highlight the label file name in the Labels panel and press ⏎. Select Print Label from the options that appear. When the print submenu appears, select View Labels on Screen to preview the printed labels. Press the space bar to view subsequent screens of labels. Press **Esc** to return to the Control Center.

It may seem strange that the View Labels on Screen option is on the Print Label menu, but when dBASE IV displays the label design on the screen, it is in fact printing the file to the screen. (See Chapter 9 for instructions and options for printing hard copies of the labels.)

EDITING ON THE LABELS DESIGN SCREEN

You can use the editing keys listed in Table 8.1 to move around and make changes on the labels design screen. Many of the keys are similar to those used in the edit and browse screens.

KEY	EFFECT
↓	Moves down one row
↑	Moves up one row
→	Moves right one character or to the end of the field template
←	Moves left one character or to the beginning of the field template
PgUp	Moves to the top of the screen
PgDn	Moves to the bottom of the screen
End	Moves to the end of the line
Home	Moves to the beginning of the line
Ins	Toggles insert mode on and off
↵	If insert mode is off, moves down one row; if insert mode is on, inserts a new line
Help (F1)	Provides help
Field (F5)	Adds a new field template or changes the currently highlighted one
Select (F6)	Selects a field template or block
Move (F7)	Moves a field or block selected with **F6**
Copy (F8)	Copies a field or block selected with **F6**
Size (Shift-F7)	Changes the size of the currently selected field template
Ctrl-N	Inserts a new line
Backspace	Erases the character to the left of the cursor
Del	Deletes the character, field template, or block selected with **F6**
Ctrl-T	Deletes the word or field to the right of the cursor
Ctrl-Y	Removes the entire line
Tab	Moves to the next tab setting
Shift-Tab	Moves to the previous tab setting
Esc	Abandons the current format without saving changes

TABLE 8.1: Keys for Use on the Labels Design Screen

Although the labels design screen shows only templates (X's) indicating where data will be printed on the label, you can easily determine which database field is associated with each template. Just use the arrow keys to move the cursor into the template of interest and look at the status bar at the bottom of the screen. The status bar indicates the database and field represented by that template, along with the data type, width, and number of decimal places for that field, as defined in the database structure.

Moving and Copying

SEQUENCE OF STEPS

On the labels design screen:
  To move:

  move the cursor to a corner of the area to be moved

  Select (**F6**)

  If moving only a field template: ↵

  If moving more than a single template: highlight the area to move ↵

  Move (**F7**)

  move the highlight to the new location ↵

  To copy:

  move the cursor to a corner of the area to be copied

  Select (**F6**)

  If copying only a field template: ↵

  If copying more than a single template: highlight the area to copy ↵

  Copy (**F8**)

  move the highlight to the new location ↵

USAGE

To move or copy any part of a label format, first move the cursor to a corner of the area you want to move and press Select (**F6**). If you are moving only a field template, press ↵. If you are moving more than a single template, use the arrow keys to highlight the entire area that you want to move or copy and then press ↵.

Press either Move (**F7**) or Copy (**F8**), depending on the operation you want to perform. Move the highlight to the new location and press ↵.

If you attempt to move or copy selected text to a place where it overlaps existing text or templates, dBASE will present the message *Delete covered text and fields? (Y/N)*. If you select Yes, dBASE deletes any text and field templates that are covered. If you select No, dBASE does not delete covered text or fields; you can then press **Esc** to stop the copy or move operation and then move to another location.

DELETING FIELDS — 281

If you press Select (**F6**) and then make a mistake while highlighting, you can press **Esc** to cancel the selection.

Adding Fields

SEQUENCE OF STEPS

On the labels design screen:

    move the cursor to where you want the field template
    Field (**F5**) *or* Menus (**F10**)/Fields/Add Field [↵]
    select a field
    Ctrl-End

USAGE

To add a new field to a label format, first position the cursor where you want the leftmost character of the field template to appear. Then either press Field (**F5**), or press Menus (**F10**) and select Add Field from the Fields pull-down menu. You will see a submenu of possible fields to add to the format, including database, calculated, and predefined fields.

Database fields are those fields available from the current database file or query. Predefined fields are those that dBASE IV provides and handles automatically; they are discussed earlier in this chapter in the section "Placing Fields on a Label." (Calculated and summary fields are discussed in Chapter 6.)

Select a field by moving the highlight to the option you want and pressing ↵. You will be given an opportunity to change the Template and Picture Functions options assigned to the field (as discussed later in this chapter in the section "Formatting Fields"). Press **Ctrl-End** to place the field on the labels design screen.

Deleting Fields

SEQUENCE OF STEPS

On the labels design screen:
    To delete a field:

        move the cursor to the field template
        Del *or* Menus (**F10**)/Fields/**R**emove Field [↵]

To delete a line:

> move the cursor to the line to be deleted
> **Ctrl-Y**

USAGE

To delete a field from your label format, move the cursor to the field template and either press **Del** or press Menus (**F10**) and select Remove Field from the Fields submenu. To delete an entire line, including all fields and text, move the cursor to the appropriate line and press **Ctrl-Y**.

Adding and Deleting Text

SEQUENCE OF STEPS

On the labels design screen:
To insert text:

> position cursor at insertion point
> in insert mode, type the new text

To overwrite text:

> position cursor at beginning of text to be overwritten
> in overwrite mode, type the new text

To delete a character:

> position cursor at character to be deleted
> **Del**

To delete a block:

> position cursor at beginning or end of block to be deleted
> Select (**F6**)
> highlight block to delete ←┘
> **Del**

USAGE

You can place text—such as words, punctuation marks, and blank spaces—anywhere in a label format. To *insert* text into an existing format, position the cursor where you want the new text to appear. Make sure insert mode is on and then type your text. To *change* existing text, position the cursor on the text to be changed and activate overwrite mode (press **Ins** until the *Ins* indicator disappears). When you type your changes, the new characters will overwrite (replace) the existing characters.

To delete text from your label format, position the cursor on the character you want to delete and press **Del**. To delete an entire section of text and fields, first use Select (**F6**) to highlight the area that you want to delete. Then press ← to complete the selection and press **Del** to delete the entire highlighted block.

Formatting Fields

dBASE IV automatically assigns certain *display attributes* to the field templates used in label formats. You can change these display attributes by moving the cursor to the appropriate field template on the labels design screen and pressing Field (**F5**), or by selecting Modify Field from the Fields pull-down menu.

Either technique displays a submenu that describes the field and presents the Template and Picture Functions options.

USING PICTURE FUNCTIONS

SEQUENCE OF STEPS

On the labels design screen:

> move the cursor to the field template
> Field (**F5**) *or* Menus (**F10**)/Fields/Modify Field [←]
> **P**icture Functions
> move the cursor to the picture function
> press the space bar to turn the picture function on or off

USAGE

A *picture function* is a code that tells dBASE how to display a piece of information. dBASE IV offers many picture functions, which are discussed fully in Chapter 7. You can turn any available function on or off by highlighting that option and pressing the space bar. Table 8.2 summarizes the options you are likely to use for label formats.

Many of the picture functions affect the display of data within the width provided by the field template, as the next section explains.

PICTURE FUNCTION	SYMBOL	EFFECT
Uppercase conversion	!	Displays all letters (a–z) in uppercase (A–Z)
Trim	T	Removes leading and trailing blanks
Right Align	J	Right-aligns text within the space allotted for the field
Center Align	I	Centers text within the space allotted
Horizontal Stretch	H	Adjusts the template width to the width of the data
Vertical Stretch	V	Wraps text onto several lines within the allotted width

TABLE 8.2: Common Picture Functions for Labels

Changing Field Widths

SEQUENCE OF STEPS

On the labels design screen:

>move the cursor to the field template

either

>Size (**Shift-F7**)
>→ and ←, as necessary, to widen or narrow the field ↵

or

>Field (**F5**) *or* Menus (**F10**)/**F**ields/**M**odify Field [↵]
>**T**emplate [↵]
>To narrow template: **Backspace** *or* **Del**
>To widen template: type **X**'s

USAGE

You can control the width of a field on a label by changing the size of the field template. By default, dBASE assigns a width that matches the width of the field in the database. To widen or narrow a field, you can use either of two techniques:

- Move the cursor to the field template, press Size (**Shift-F7**), and use the → and ← keys to widen or narrow the field. Then press ↵.

- Move the cursor to the field template, press Field (**F5**), and select Template. Press **Backspace** or **Del** to narrow the template, or type **X**'s to widen the template.

Note that if you use the latter technique, dBASE displays a submenu of *character input symbols*. These are more relevant to custom forms than they are to labels and so are discussed in Chapter 10.

TIPS AND TRAPS

- When you create a custom label format, press Help (**F1**) while selecting label dimensions for explanations of the various settings.
- To guarantee that a space separates two fields on a printed label or report, go to the report or label design screen, make sure insert mode is on, move the cursor to where you want the blank space to appear, and then press the space bar.
- You can press Move (**F7**) or Copy (**F8**) either before or after moving the cursor to the move or copy destination.
- Pressing **Del** does not delete a field template that is only partially contained in a highlighted (selected) area.
- You cannot alter the width of fields that use the Date or Logical data type.
- You can add *any* text to a label format simply by typing it at the place where you want it to appear on each label.

SUMMARY

Once you have designed a label format to your satisfaction, you are ready to print your labels. The next chapter discusses the options available for printing labels (and for printing reports as well).

To print labels:

- Chapter 9, "Printing Reports and Labels"

For a complete discussion of picture functions available from both the labels design screen and the reports design screen:

- Chapter 7, "Designing Formatted Reports"

For help with choosing character input symbols for picture functions:

- Chapter 10, "Creating Custom Forms"

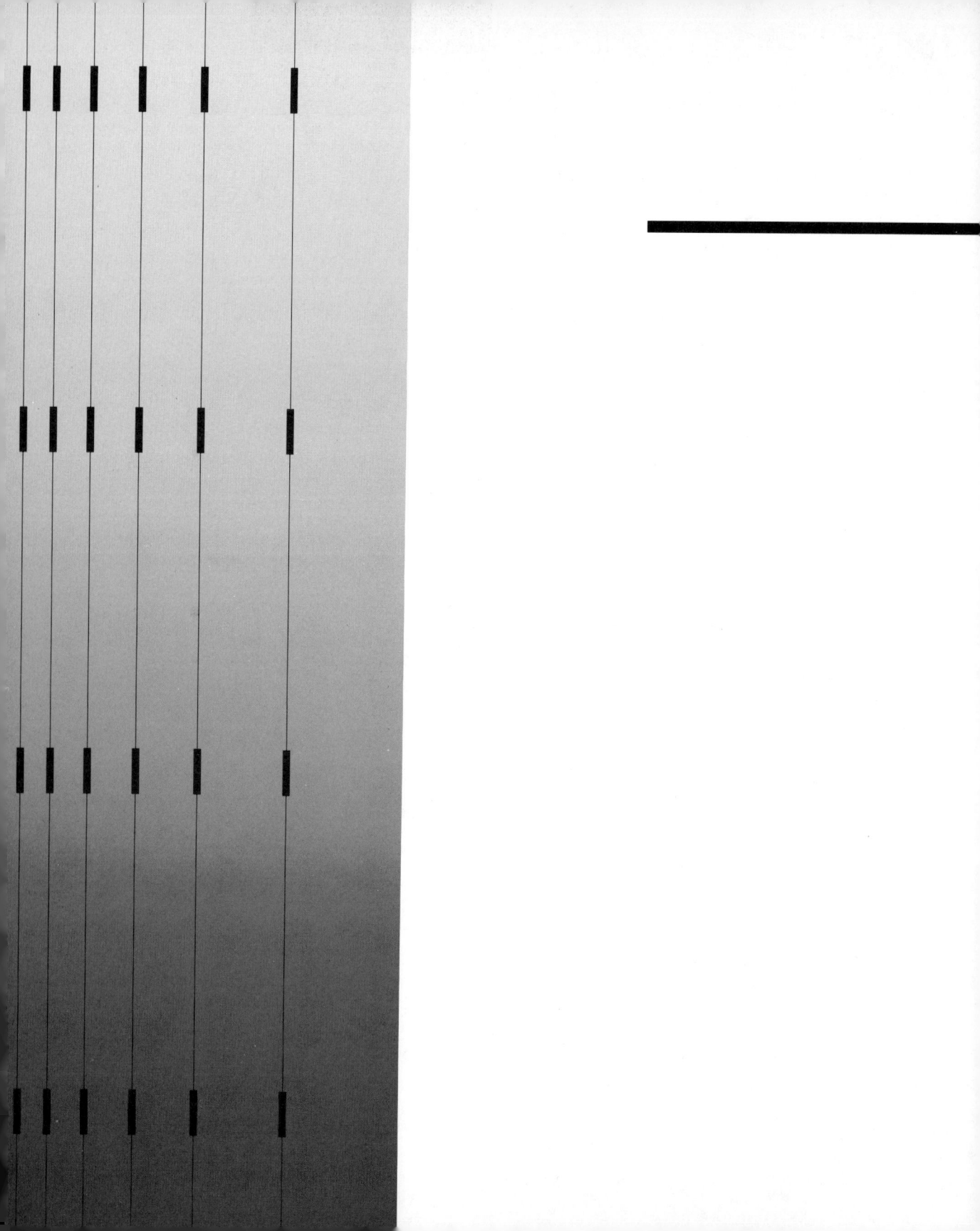

CHAPTER 9

PRINTING REPORTS AND LABELS

Printing a Quick Report. 289
Printing a Formatted Report. 290
Printing Mailing Labels. 291
Sorting Reports and Labels for Printing. 293
    Presorting Records with an Index. 293
    Using a Query to Presort Records. 294
Selecting Records to Print. 296
    Printing from a Query. 297
Controlling the Printer. 298
    Setting the Top of the Page. 299
    Determining the Print Destination. 300
    Controlling Print Size. 301
    Controlling Print Quality. 302
    Controlling Page Breaks. 303
    Printing Single Sheets. 304
    Using Special Printer Features. .304
        Epson- and IBM-Compatible Printers. 305
        Hewlett-Packard LaserJet Printers. 305
    Controlling Page Numbers. 306
    Printing Multiple Copies. 308
    Controlling Page Length and Margins. 309
    Saving Printer Settings. 311
Pausing and Canceling Printing. 311
Tips and Traps. 312
Summary. 312

Printing Reports and Labels

dBASE IV provides many options for printing reports and labels. The simplest method is printing a quick report, but it creates the least pleasing report. As discussed in Chapter 7, you can also choose one of the three generic report formats. However, the most professional and impressive dBASE reports are those that you customize yourself, using the features of the reports design screen presented in Chapter 7. This chapter provides the information you need to print your reports (including form letters) and labels on paper.

Printing a Quick Report

SEQUENCE OF STEPS

From the Control Center:

> highlight the database name or query name
> Quick Report (**Shift-F9**)
> **B**egin Printing [⏎]

USAGE

The quickest and easiest way to get a printed copy of your information is to use the Quick Report option (**Shift-F9**) from the Control Center. This technique simply dumps data from your database to the printer, without much regard for formatting. To use Quick Report, you highlight the name of the database file or query that you want to print from, press **Shift-F9**, and select Begin Printing from the menu that appears.

Before printing starts, dBASE IV generates a program that it uses to print the report. This task may take a few seconds. As dBASE prints the report, it displays a submenu that allows you to cancel or pause printing. This submenu disappears when printing is complete.

EXAMPLE

In this example, you print the results of the PHONELST query created in Chapter 5. Figure 9.1 shows the printed report. The PHONELST query includes the LASTNAME, FIRSTNAME, and PHONE fields for California residents of the CUSTLIST database, so the quick report displays only this information.

Move the highlight to the PHONELST query in the Queries panel and press Quick Report (**Shift-F9**). If dBASE asks whether you want to use the current view or PHONELST.QBE, select PHONELST.QBE. From the submenu that appears, press ⏎ to select Begin Printing.

You can highlight CUSTLIST rather than PHONELST to print a quick report that displays all the information in the CUSTLIST database file, probably spread across a few pages.

```
Page No.   1
06/30/90

PHONE            LASTNAME      FIRSTNAME
(619)555-1234    Smith         John
(714)555-0123    Adams         Annie
(213)555-9988    Kenney        Ralph
(415)555-9854    Smith         Anita
```

FIGURE 9.1: Quick report printed from the PHONELST query. With the query highlighted in the Control Center, press **Shift-F9** to print a quick report.

Printing a Formatted Report

SEQUENCE OF STEPS

From the Control Center:

> highlight the report name in the Reports panel ⏎
> **P**rint Report [⏎]
> **B**egin Printing [⏎]

USAGE

To print a formatted report, highlight the report name in the Reports panel and press ⏎. Select Print Report from the options that appear. When the Print menu appears, select Begin Printing.

EXAMPLE

If you created the customer list report called LIST in Chapter 7, you can print it now. First, if the associated database, CUSTLIST, is not already open (if its name is not above the line in the Data panel), open that database by highlighting

CUSTLIST, pressing ←, and selecting Open File. Then highlight the report name, LIST, in the Reports panel and press ←. Select Print Report to bring up the Print menu and then select Begin Printing. The results should look like the report in Chapter 7, Figure 7.3.

If you are using a laser printer, you may need to eject the page from the printer. To do so, repeat the initial steps for printing the report to access the Print menu. That is, highlight LIST in the Reports panel, press ←, select Print Report, and then select Eject Page Now. Then press **Esc** to return to the Control Center. (See the section "Controlling Page Breaks" later in this chapter to avoid having to repeat this step in the future.)

PRINTING MAILING LABELS

SEQUENCE OF STEPS

From the Control Center:

    highlight the labels file in the Labels panel ←
    Print Label [←]
    Generate Sample Labels [←]
    N

or

    highlight the labels file in the Labels panel ←
    Print Label [←]
    Begin Printing [←]

To return to the Control Center:

    Esc

USAGE

Getting text to line up properly on mailing labels can be tricky. To help you, dBASE offers the Generate Sample Labels option on the Print menu. When you select this option, dBASE prints a row of sample labels as X's and displays the message *Do you want more samples? (Y/N)*. You can realign the labels in the printer and select Yes (by typing **Y**) until your labels are lined up properly. Then select No (**N**) when the query appears, and dBASE will print your labels.

When you are sure that the data is aligned to your satisfaction, you can print the labels without generating samples. Highlight the labels file you want to use

292 ── **CH. 9** PRINTING REPORTS AND LABELS

in the Labels panel and press ←┘. From the options that appear, select Print Label. From the menu that appears next, select Begin Printing to print the labels.

EXAMPLE

If you designed the format of the CUSTLIST database labels as described in the examples in Chapter 8, you can use that format to print the names and addresses from the CUSTLIST database.

Highlight MAILING in the Labels panel of the Control Center and press ←┘. From the options that appear, select Print Label. From the Print menu that appears next, select Generate Sample Labels. If the data in the resulting sample printing is aligned properly on the label stock, type **N** when asked if you want to see more samples. dBASE will print the labels as shown in Figure 9.2.

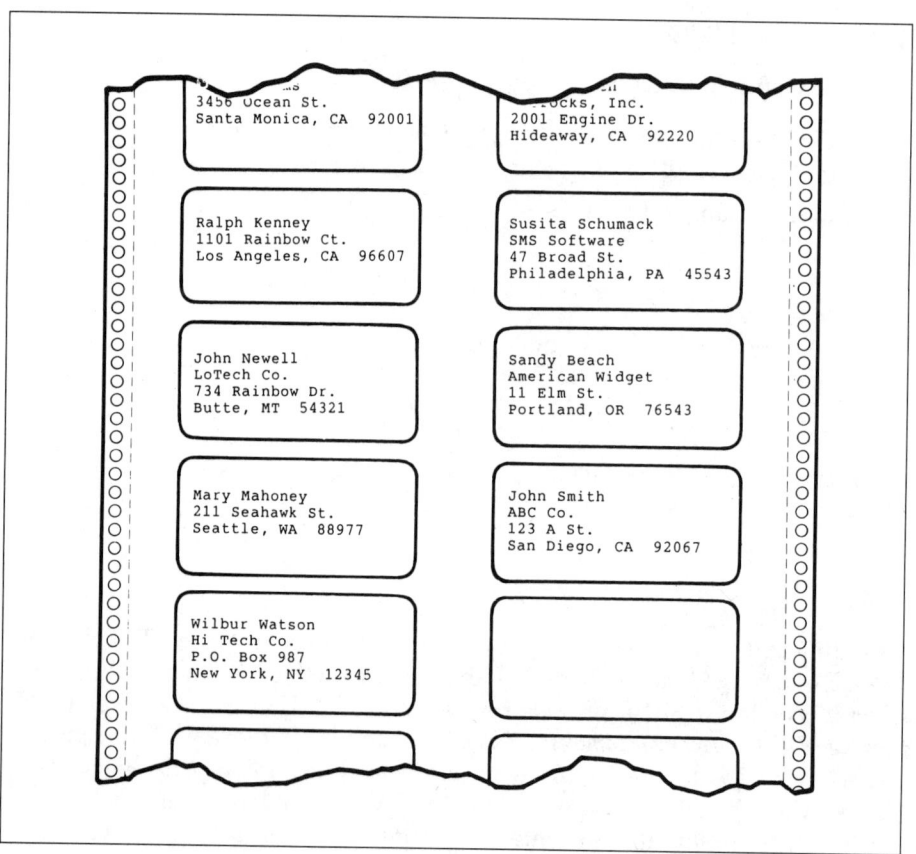

FIGURE 9.2: Mailing labels printed from the CUSTLIST database.

If you want to print mailing labels using a laser printer, be sure to use labels that are specifically designed for use on laser printers. Most stationery stores carry, or can order, such labels (Avery Label Company offers laser printer labels). Note that three-across labels may require you to use compressed print, whereas two-across labels do not.

If you use a laser printer to print labels, you may need to eject the last page of printed labels from your printer. See the section "Controlling Page Breaks" later in this chapter for information.

SORTING REPORTS AND LABELS FOR PRINTING

You can use either of two techniques to presort data to be printed on reports into the desired sort order. You can order records using an index you previously created on the database design screen, or you can create a query that presorts the database records and then use that query (rather than the database file) to print the report or labels. Each method is discussed and demonstrated in the sections that follow.

Presorting Records with an Index

The quickest way to presort data for printing is to use an existing index. (Chapter 4 discusses how to create an index.)

SEQUENCE OF STEPS

From the Control Center:

>   highlight the database name in the Data panel
>   Design (**Shift-F2**)
>   **O**rganize/**O**rder Records by Index [⏎]
>   select the index name you want
>   **E**xit/**S**ave Changes and Exit [⏎]
>   highlight the report name in the Reports panel   *or*   highlight the label name in the Labels panel ⏎
>   **P**rint Report   *or*   **P**rint Labels [⏎]
>   **B**egin Printing [⏎]

USAGE

To print reports or mailing labels in sorted order, activate the appropriate index and then print the report or labels.

From the Control Center, highlight the database name in the Data panel and press Design (**Shift-F2**) to get to the database design screen. Select Order Records by Index from the Organize menu. Select the index you want to use. Select Save Changes and Exit from the Exit pull-down menu. If prompted to press **Enter** to confirm exiting (the prompt will appear near the bottom of the screen), press ← to return to the Control Center.

Now use the usual techniques to print the report or labels. That is, highlight the name of the report in the Reports or Labels panel and press ←. Select Print Report (or Print Labels) and then select Begin Printing. The printed data will be sorted in the order specified by the index you selected.

EXAMPLE

This example prints the customer list in alphabetical order. To follow this example, you must have created the CUSTLIST database, an index of CUST-LIST called LASTNAME (see Chapter 4), and a report format for CUSTLIST called LIST (see Chapter 7).

From the Control Center, highlight CUSTLIST in the Data panel and press Design (**Shift-F2**) to get to the database design screen. Select Order Records by Index from the Organize menu. Select the LASTNAME index. Select Save Changes and Exit from the Exit pull-down menu.

In the Reports panel, highlight LIST and press ←. Select Print Report and then Begin Printing. The report will be sorted in alphabetical order by customer's last name. (If you created the ZIP index in Chapter 4, you can print mailing labels and form letters in zip code order by following the same basic steps, but selecting ZIP as the index for organizing records.)

Using a Query to Presort Records

As an alternative to using an index to presort records in a database for printing, you can use a query. Assuming you have already created the appropriate query (as in the following example), you can use the basic key sequence listed here.

SEQUENCE OF STEPS

From the Control Center:

> highlight the query in the Queries panel ←
>
> highlight the report name in the Reports panel *or* highlight the label name in the Labels panel ←
>
> **C**urrent View [←]
>
> **P**rint Report *or* **P**rint Labels [←]
>
> **B**egin Printing [←]

USAGE

The following example demonstrates how to print the LIST report (designed in Chapter 7), with records sorted by last and first name. The first steps show how to create the query. These are followed by techniques for printing a report or labels using the sort order specified in the query.

EXAMPLE

First make sure the CUSTLIST database is open (that its name is above the line in the Data panel). If the database is not open, highlight its name, CUSTLIST, in the data panel, press ↵, and select Use File.

Next highlight <create> in the Queries panel and press ↵. Use the general techniques discussed in the section "Sorting the Results of Queries" in Chapter 5 to create a sort order. In this example, you move the highlight to the LASTNAME field, press **F10**, select Sort on This Field from the Fields pull-down menu, and then select Ascending Dictionary sort order. Then you move the highlight to the FIRSTNAME field and again press **F10**, select Sort on This Field from the Layout pull-down menu, and select Ascending Dictionary sort order. Figure 9.3 shows the finished query.

Now you need to save the query. Press **F10**, select Save Changes and Exit, and enter a valid file name; for this example, use **NAMESORT**. Press ↵ after typing the file name.

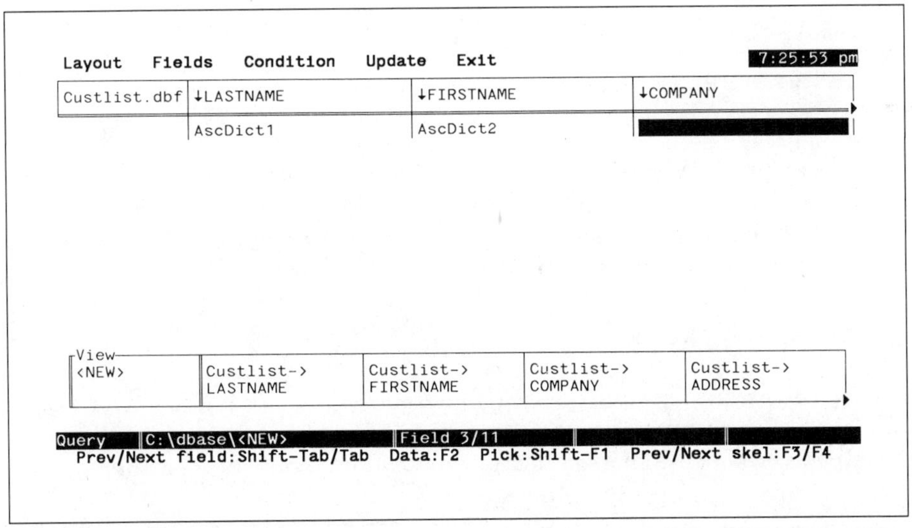

FIGURE 9.3: Query to sort records by last name and by first name within common last names.

296 — CH. 9 PRINTING REPORTS AND LABELS

To use the NAMESORT query at any later time to print a report or labels, first activate the query. If its name does not appear above the line in the Queries panel, highlight NAMESORT, press ←┘, and select Use View.

To begin printing, highlight the name of the report or label format you want to use (LIST in this example) in the Reports or Labels panel. Press ←┘ and select Print Report. dBASE will double-check to make sure that you actually intend to use the current query (view), rather than the original database, by presenting a prompt box like the one shown in Figure 9.4.

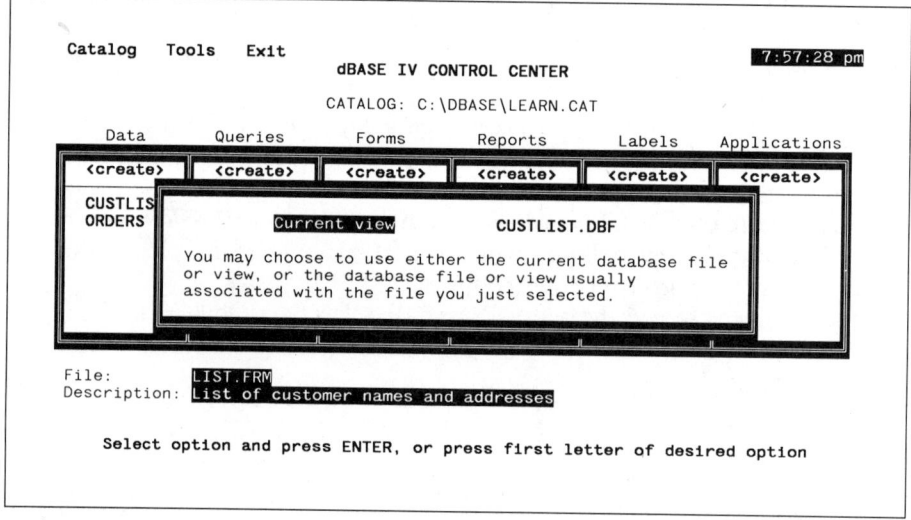

FIGURE 9.4: Prompt box for verifying that you want to use the current view, rather than the entire database.

Select Current View to proceed. To print your report, select Begin Printing from the Print menu that appears. Records will be displayed in the sort order specified in the current view. (Read the next section for additional advice on using queries to print reports and labels.)

SELECTING RECORDS TO PRINT

You can use any existing query to filter records that are printed in a report or on labels. For example, you can use a query to print form letters and mailing labels for certain customers in the state of California only or for customers with outstanding balances over 90 days past due. If an appropriate query does not exist yet, use the techniques described in Chapter 5 to create one, and be sure to save the query for future use.

When you use a query to print reports or labels, the view skeleton in the query form must contain all the fields that the report or label format is designed to print. Typically, when you first design a query, the view skeleton already contains all the fields in the database, so if you do not remove any fields from the view skeleton, the report or labels will print fine. (However, as discussed in Chapter 10, queries that operate on multiple related database files require some extra steps.)

Printing from a Query

SEQUENCE OF STEPS

From the Control Center, with the appropriate database open:

    highlight the query file name in the Queries panel ↵

    Print Report   *or*   **P**rint Labels [↵]

    Current View [↵]

    Begin Printing [↵]

EXAMPLE

This example demonstrates both how to create a query and how to use that query to print a report. The query in this example isolates CUSTLIST customers in the state of California and presorts them into zip code order by using an existing index.

If necessary, first open the CUSTLIST database by highlighting its name in the Data panel, pressing ↵, and selecting Use File.

Highlight <create> in the Queries panel and press ↵. Tab to the STATE field and enter the filter condition **"CA"** (including the quotation marks). Press ↵.

Press Menus (**F10**) and highlight Include Indexes from the Fields pull-down menu. Press ↵ to change the setting to Yes. Tab to the ZIP field, press Menus (**F10**), and select Sort on This Field from the Fields pull-down menu. Select Ascending ASCII as the sort order. *Asc1* will appear in the ZIP field, as shown in Figure 9.5.

Press Menus (**F10**) and select Edit Description of Query from the Layout pull-down menu. Type the description **California customer names and addresses** and press ↵. Press Menus (**F10**). Select Save Changes and Exit from the Exit pull-down menu. When prompted with *save as:*, type the file name **CALCUST** and press ↵.

When you return to the Control Center, you can use the query to print reports (including form letters) or mailing labels by activating the query and then

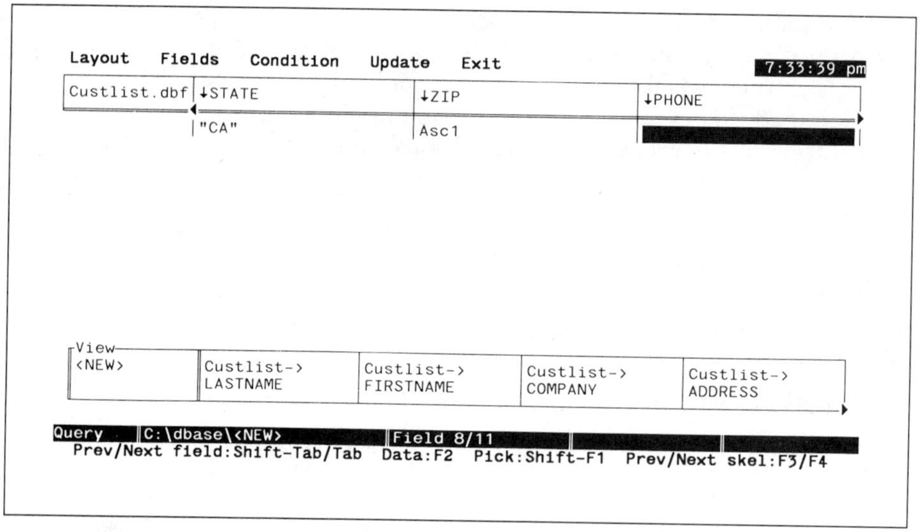

```
Layout    Fields   Condition   Update   Exit                    7:33:39 pm
Custlist.dbf ↓STATE          ↓ZIP              ↓PHONE
             │"CA"            Asc1

┌View─────────────────────────────────────────────────────────────────
│<NEW>      │Custlist->   │Custlist->   │Custlist->   │Custlist->
│           │LASTNAME     │FIRSTNAME    │COMPANY      │ADDRESS
Query  │C:\dbase\<NEW>          │Field 8/11
  Prev/Next field:Shift-Tab/Tab  Data:F2  Pick:Shift-F1  Prev/Next skel:F3/F4
```

FIGURE 9.5: Query to isolate California customers and sort them into zip code order.

printing the appropriate reports. If the query (view) you have just created is not already in use (if its name does not appear above the line in the Queries panel), highlight its name in the Queries panel, press ←┘, and select Use View.

Highlight the name of a report or label format in the Reports or Labels panel and press ←┘. Select Print Label or Print Report. When dBASE double-checks your intentions, select Current View. Select Begin Printing.

The query will stay in effect for any other reports that you print until you deactivate it either by opening another query or database file or by selecting the current query name from the Queries panel and choosing Close View.

CONTROLLING THE PRINTER

SEQUENCE OF STEPS

From the Control Center:
  For reports:

   highlight the report name in the Reports panel ←┘
   Print Report [←┘]

  For labels:

   highlight the label name in the Labels panel ←┘
   Print Labels [←┘]

USAGE

When you are printing reports, form letters, or labels, you will see the Print menu shown in Figure 9.6. This menu appears for reports and form letters when you highlight the report name in the Reports panel, press ←┘, and select Print Report; for labels, you reach this menu when you highlight the label name in the Labels panel, press ←┘, and select Print Labels.

Note that the Print menu is also available from the reports and labels design screens. From either design screen, press **F10** and select Print to pull down the Print menu.

Setting the Top of the Page

SEQUENCE OF STEPS

From the Control Center, with the report or label name highlighted:

    Print Report   *or*   **P**rint Labels [←┘]
    Eject Page Now

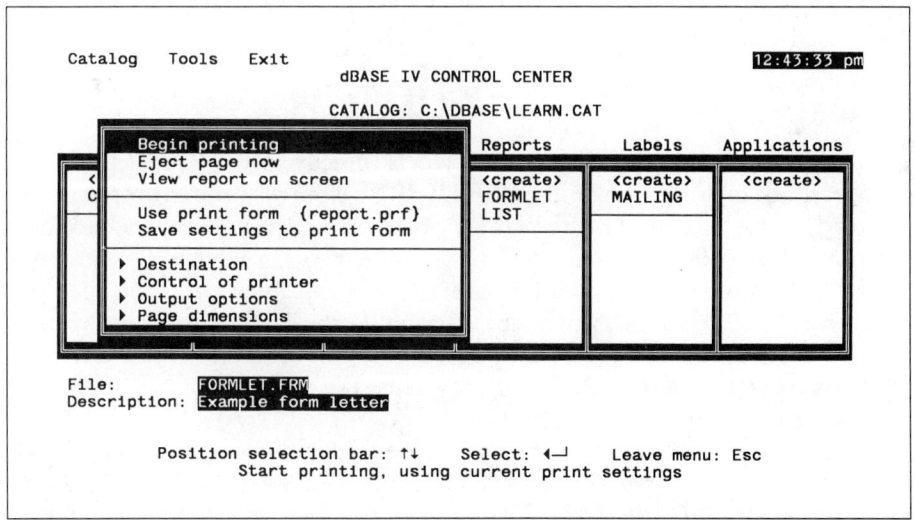

FIGURE 9.6: You can access the Print menu for reports and labels by highlighting the report or label name in the Control Center, pressing ←┘, and selecting Print Report or Print Labels. Alternatively, from the reports or labels design screen, select the Print pull-down menu.

USAGE

To ensure that printing starts at the top of a new page, you can select Eject Page Now. Note that this option works only if the paper is aligned in your printer. If you select Eject Page Now and the paper does not move to the top of a page, turn off your printer, hand crank the paper up to the top of a new page, and turn the printer on again. So long as you do not hand crank the paper in the printer again, your pages will stay aligned.

Determining the Print Destination

SEQUENCE OF STEPS

From the Control Center, with the report or label name highlighted:

Print Report   *or*   **P**rint Labels [◄┘]
Destination [◄┘]
Printer   *or*   **D**OS File [◄┘]
Printer Model [◄┘]
press the space bar to scroll through the list of installed printers
Echo to Screen [◄┘]
press the space bar to scroll through Yes/No options
Ctrl-End   *or*   ←

USAGE

dBASE sends the printed report or labels directly to the default printer (as defined during installation or in DBSETUP). To store the printed output in a file instead, select Destination from the Print menu. You will see the submenu shown in Figure 9.7.

To send printed output to a file rather than the printer, press the space bar while the Write To option is highlighted to change the destination from Printer to DOS File. dBASE will suggest naming the DOS file with the same name as the database plus the extension .PRT. Press ↓ to use this suggested name or press ◄┘ to enter a new name.

If you have installed several printers, move the highlight to the Printer Model option and press the space bar to scroll through the options.

If you want to use the DOS PRINT command to print the file later, select ASCII Text File as the printer model. The advantage of using this technique is that it allows you to continue to use your computer as the printer is working (see your DOS manual for details). If you use a different printer model for output to a

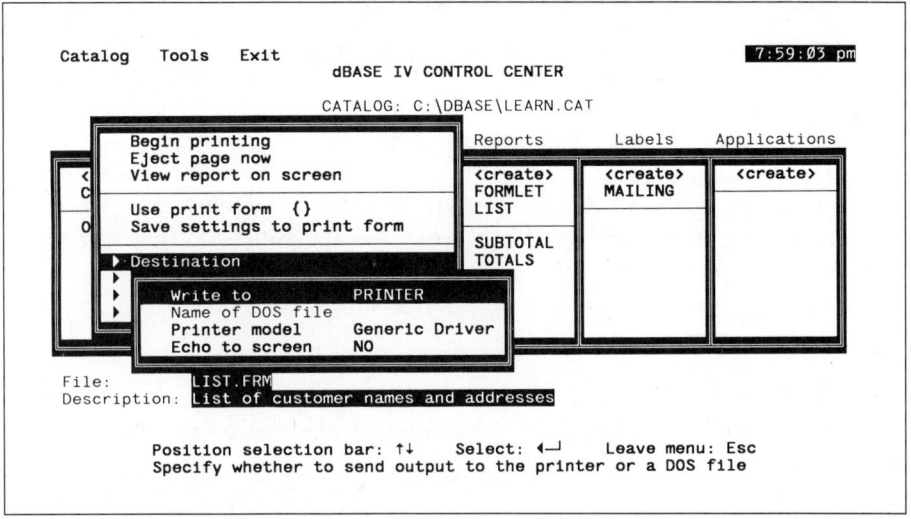

FIGURE 9.7: Destination submenu of the Print menu.

DOS file, use the DOS COPY command rather than the DOS PRINT command. For example, if you save the file as CUSTLIST.PRT, you enter the command **COPY CUSTLIST.PRT /B PRN** to print to a DOS file. Again, refer to your DOS manual for details.

You can also import a report or label that has been printed to a file into most word processing software packages, either for further editing and refinement or for inclusion in a larger document. (See Chapter 14 for details.)

If you change the Echo to Screen option to Yes, dBASE displays the report on the screen as it is being sent to the printer or file. Leave this option set to No if you do not want to see the printed report or labels on the screen.

Press **Ctrl-End** after defining the print destination. You can then continue to select other options from the Print menu or select Begin Printing to start printing.

Controlling Print Size

SEQUENCE OF STEPS

From the Control Center, with the report or label name highlighted:

    Print Report   *or*   **P**rint Labels [←]
    Control of Printer [←]
    Text Pitch [←]

        Pica   *or*   **E**lite *or* **C**ondensed *or* **D**efault [↵]
        Ctrl-End   *or*   ←

USAGE

Some printers can print in a variety of letter sizes. If you have such a printer, you can select the Control of Printer option from the Print menu to choose a print size. Highlight the Text Pitch option on the submenu that appears, as shown in Figure 9.8.

Press the space bar to scroll through the options, listed here:

Pica	Prints 10 characters per inch
Elite	Prints 12 characters per inch
Condensed	Prints very small letters (their exact size is determined by your printer)
Default	Uses whatever size the printer is set to

After selecting a print size, press ← or **Ctrl-End** to return to the Print menu.

Controlling Print Quality

SEQUENCE OF STEPS

From the Control Center, with the report or label name highlighted:

        Print Report   *or*   **P**rint Labels [↵]
        Control of Printer [↵]
        Quality Print [↵]
        Yes *or* **N**o *or* **D**efault [↵]
        Ctrl-End   *or*   ←

USAGE

Some printers offer two or more options for print quality: *draft* quality (for faster printing) and *near letter quality* (for neater—but slower—printing). If your printer supports these features, you can specify a print quality by selecting Control of Printer from the Print menu. Highlight Quality Print on the submenu that appears and press the space bar to scroll through the options. Select Yes to use the best-quality print, select No to use the draft-quality print, and select Default to use whatever quality the printer itself is currently set for.

CONTROLLING PAGE BREAKS

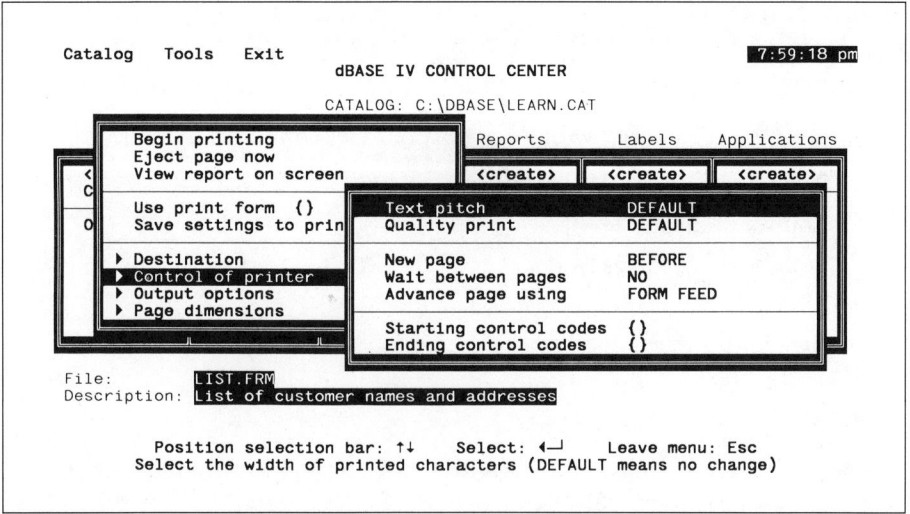

FIGURE 9.8: Control of Printer submenu of the Print menu.

Controlling Page Breaks

SEQUENCE OF STEPS

From the Control Center, with the report or label name highlighted:

    Print Report   *or*   **P**rint Labels [←┘]
    Control of **P**rinter [←┘]
    New Page [←┘]
    After *or* **B**efore *or* **B**oth *or* **N**one [←┘]
    Ctrl-End   *or*   ←

USAGE

You can determine when dBASE ejects the page currently in the printer: before printing a report, after printing a report, both before and after printing a report, or not at all (no blank or incomplete pages are ejected). On most tractor-feed printers, the Before option is preferred, so that printing always begins on a new page. On most laser printers, the After option is preferred, so that the printer automatically ejects the last printed page.

Select Control of Printer from the Print submenu and highlight New Page on the submenu that appears. Then press the space bar until the option you want is displayed. Press **Ctrl-End** to return to the Print menu.

Printing Single Sheets

SEQUENCE OF STEPS

From the Control Center, with the report or label name highlighted:

    Print Report *or* **P**rint Labels [◄┘]
    Control of Printer [◄┘]
    Wait between Pages [◄┘]
    Yes [◄┘]
    Ctrl-End *or* ←

USAGE

When you need to hand-feed individual sheets into your printer, you can have dBASE pause between each printed page. Select Control of Printer from the Print menu, highlight Wait between Pages on the submenu that appears, and press the space bar to set the option to Yes. Then press ← or **Ctrl-End** to return to the Print menu.

Using Special Printer Features

SEQUENCE OF STEPS

From the Control Center, with the report or label name highlighted:

    Print Report *or* **P**rint Labels [◄┘]
    Control of Printer [◄┘]
    Starting Control Codes *or* **E**nding Control Codes [◄┘]
    enter code ◄┘
    Ctrl-End *or* ←

USAGE

To activate special features that your printer may offer, such as compressed or expanded print, you need to send a special *control code* to the printer. Different printers use different control codes, so you will need to refer to your printer manual for most specific codes. This chapter lists the IBM/Epson special features and their codes and the HP LaserJet modes and codes.

Typically, printer codes are either **Ctrl-*key*** sequences, with an ASCII value less than 32, or *escape code* sequences, which begin with an escape key. You can enter **Ctrl-*key*** sequences in the setup string as two-digit numbers enclosed in curly braces. For example, you enter **Ctrl-O** as {15} (because O is the fifteenth letter of the alphabet). Your printer manual may show the ASCII decimal number rather than the **Ctrl-*key*** sequence. For example, if your printer manual states that the code for starting a feature is ASCII 15, then you enter {15} as the printer code.

You can use either {27} or {ESC} to send an escape key to the printer. For example, if your printer uses the code Esc-4 or Esc+4 to start printing in italics, the control code to send from dBASE is **{ESC}4**.

Keep in mind that when you send a starting control code from dBASE to the printer, it stays in effect for the entire printed report. To reset the printer to its normal settings, enter a value in the Ending Control Codes box.

Note that if you use compressed print to print many characters across the page, you will want to change the right margin to about column 120 (depending on your printer and print size) in your report format. As discussed in Chapter 7, you adjust the right margin in the reports design screen by selecting Modify Ruler from the Words pull-down menu. Mark the right margin with the] symbol. (Even though the screen displays only 80 columns, you can scroll further to the right using the → and **Tab** keys.)

EPSON- AND IBM-COMPATIBLE PRINTERS

Table 9.1 shows codes for activating special features of many IBM and Epson printers (and compatibles). The exact codes that you enter as the starting control code are presented to the right of each feature (note, however, that on many printers expanded print affects one line only).

HEWLETT-PACKARD LASERJET PRINTERS

The Hewlett-Packard LaserJet printer offers four print modes. The codes that you send from dBASE to use these print modes are listed in Table 9.2. Note that the character sequence lOO is the lowercase letter *l* followed by a zero, followed by the uppercase letter *O*. The sequence l1O is the lowercase letter *l* followed by the number 1 followed by the uppercase letter *O*.

Typically, for the ending control code you use whatever code resets your printer to its default settings or the codes necessary to stop the specified printer features. Figure 9.9 shows an example in which the code to start printing in LaserJet landscape mode is entered as the starting control code, and the code to reset the printer is entered as the ending control code.

FEATURE	CODE TO SEND FROM dBASE
Start compressed print	{15}
End compressed print	{18}
Start expanded print	{ESC}W1
Stop expanded print	{ESC}W0
Start boldface	{ESC}E
Stop boldface	{ESC}F
Start double-strike	{ESC}G
Stop double-strike	{ESC}H
Start underline	{ESC}-1
Stop underline	{ESC}-0
Start italics	{ESC}4
Stop italics	{ESC}5

TABLE 9.1: Codes Used with IBM- and Epson-compatible Printers

MODE	CODE TO SEND FROM dBASE
Portrait	{ESC}E{ESC}&l0O
Compressed portrait	{ESC}E{ESC}&l0O{ESC}&k2S
Landscape	{ESC}E{ESC}&l1O
Compressed landscape	{ESC}E{ESC}&l1O{ESC}&k2S
Reset to default mode	{ESC}E

Table 9.2: HP LaserJet Modes and Codes to Send from dBASE

Controlling Page Numbers

SEQUENCE OF STEPS

From the Control Center, with the report or label name highlighted:
To print part of a report:

    Print Report   *or*   **P**rint Labels [↵]
    Output Options [↵]
    Begin on Page [↵]

CONTROLLING PAGE NUMBERS

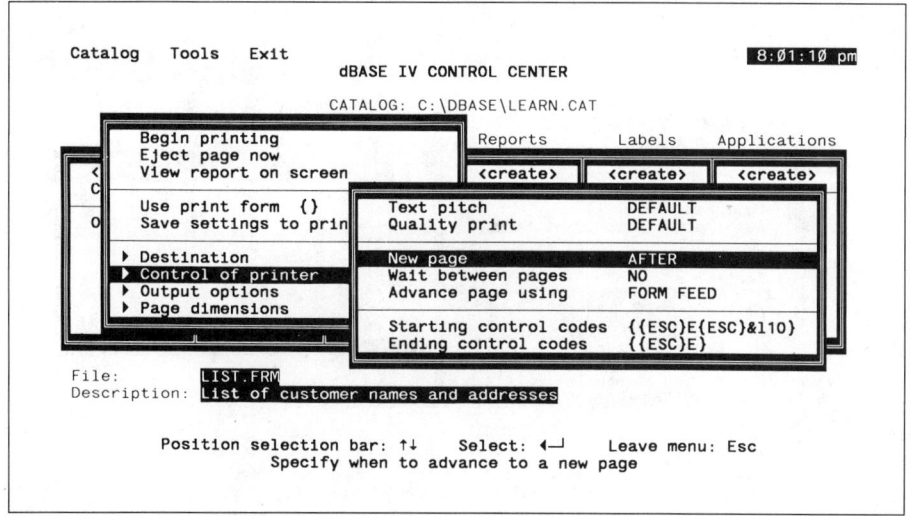

FIGURE 9.9: Codes to print a report on the HP LaserJet in landscape mode.

enter a page number

End after Page [←]

enter a page number

To begin page numbering at a number other than 1:

Output Options [←]

First Page Number [←]

enter a page number

Ctrl-End *or* ←

USAGE

Suppose you notice an error on page 39 of a long printed report. After correcting the error, you need not reprint the entire report. Instead, you can select Output Options from the Print menu and then set the Begin on Page and End after Page options to print only those pages that need reprinting. For example, if you begin printing on page 39 and end printing after page 39, only page 39 will be printed.

The Output Options submenu is shown in Figure 9.10. When you press ← to select an option from this submenu, dBASE prompts *Enter an integer*. Type a number and press ←.

CH. 9 PRINTING REPORTS AND LABELS

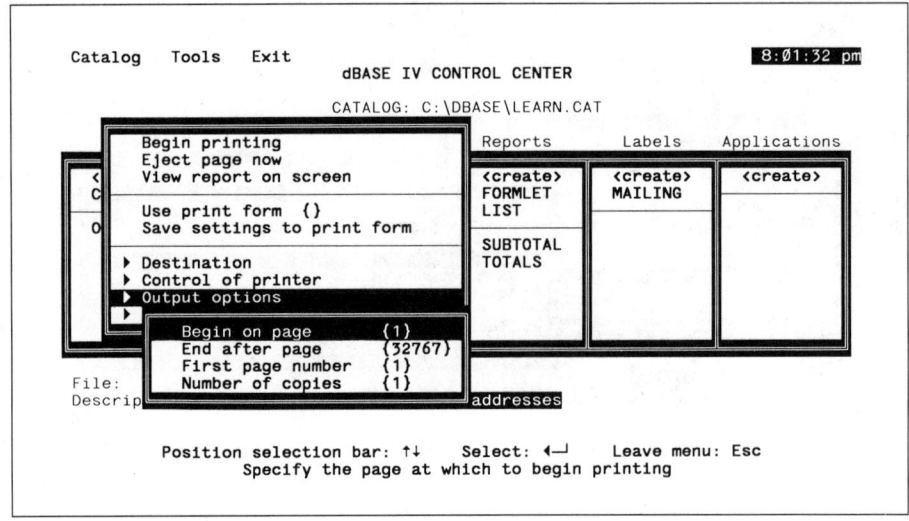

FIGURE 9.10: Output Options submenu of the Print menu.

The First Page Number option on the Output Options submenu lets you choose the starting page number for the entire report. This option prints every page in the report, but starts numbering pages at the value you set. For example, if you set this value to 100, dBASE numbers the first page of the report as page 100 and remaining pages as 101, 102, and so forth. This feature is useful when you combine several reports into a single document and you want the pages to be numbered consecutively.

Printing Multiple Copies

SEQUENCE OF STEPS

From the Control Center, with the report or label name highlighted:

Print Report   *or*   **P**rint Labels [←]
Output Options [←]
Number of Copies [←]
enter the number of copies
Ctrl-End   *or*   ←

USAGE

If you want to print multiple copies of a report, select Output Options from the Print menu and Number of Copies from the submenu. Enter the number of copies that you want to print and press ⏎. Press **Ctrl-End** or ← to return to the Print menu.

Controlling Page Length and Margins

SEQUENCE OF STEPS

From the Control Center, with the report or label name highlighted:
To change the page length:

    Print Report   *or*   **P**rint Labels [⏎]
    Page Dimensions [⏎]
    Length of Page [⏎]
    enter a number for the page length

or

    Print Report   *or*   **P**rint Labels [⏎]
    Control of Printer [⏎]
    Advance Page Using [⏎]
    Line Feeds [⏎]

To change the left margin:

    Print Report   *or*   **P**rint Labels [⏎]
    Page Dimensions [⏎]
    Offset from Left [⏎]
    enter a number for the offset

To change line spacing:

    Print Report   *or*   **P**rint Labels [⏎]
    Page Dimensions [⏎]
    Spacing of Lines [⏎]
    Single *or* **D**ouble *or* **T**riple [⏎]

To return to the Print menu:

    Ctrl-End   *or*   ←

USAGE

When you select Page Dimensions from the Print menu, dBASE gives you three options for formatting the printed page, as shown in the box at the bottom of Figure 9.11. When you press ⏎ to select from the Page Dimensions submenu, dBASE prompts *Enter an integer*. Type a number and press ⏎.

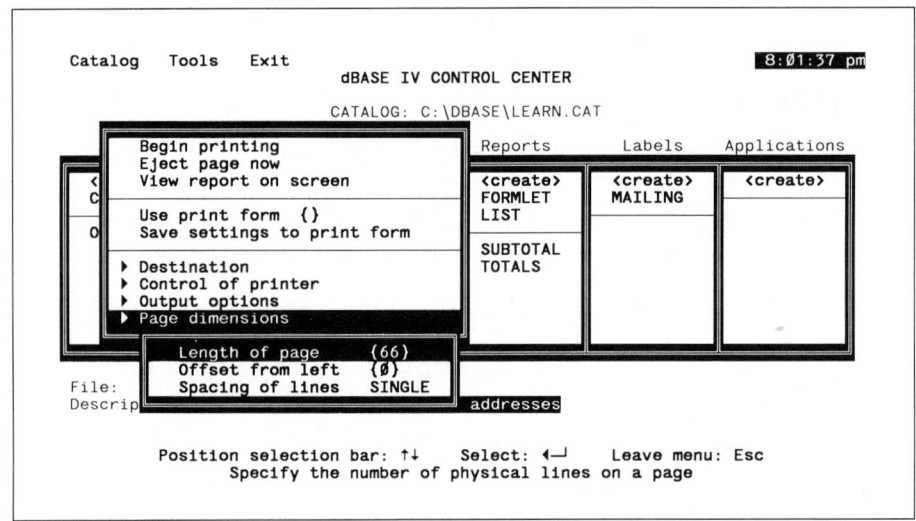

FIGURE 9.11: Page Dimensions submenu of the Print menu.

The Length of Page option is preset to 66 lines (for 6 lines to the inch on an 11-inch sheet of paper). You can change this number to print a different page length. If you want to use an unusual size of page and you cannot set your printer to the new page height, then select the Control of Printer option from the Print menu and the Advance Page Using option from the submenu. Change the setting from Form Feed to Line Feeds by pressing the space bar. dBASE will calculate the number of lines required to get to the top of the next page based on the Length of Page option setting.

The Offset from Left option lets you decide how many blank spaces are printed at the left of each page. The larger this number, the wider the left margin on the printed page. Most printers print ten characters to the inch, so an entry of 10 will leave a 1-inch margin at the left of the page. (You can change this setting in the DBSETUP program as well, so that all printed output uses the same basic margin; see Chapter 19.)

The Spacing of Lines option lets you choose among single, double, and triple spacing for the printed report. (Note that numerous dBASE IV users have found difficulties using double and triple spacing on their printers. This problem should be rectified in the version 1.1 release of dBASE IV.)

Saving Printer Settings

SEQUENCE OF STEPS

From the Control Center, with the report or label name highlighted:
To save settings:

    Print Report *or* **P**rint Labels [⏎]

    Save Settings to Print Form [⏎]

    ⏎ *or* enter a file name

To use saved settings:

    Print Report *or* **P**rint Labels [⏎]

    Use Print Form [⏎]

    select the file name

USAGE

If you find that you use the same printer settings for many different reports and labels, you will want to save those settings for use with future reports and labels. To save your printer settings, select Save Settings to Print Form from the Print menu. If you have already saved the report or label format, dBASE will suggest using that same name, with the extension .PRF. Press ⏎ if you wish to use the suggested file name. If dBASE does not suggest a name, enter any valid file name.

When you later want to reuse your print settings, select Use Print Form from the Print menu and select the appropriate file name from the submenu that appears.

PAUSING AND CANCELING PRINTING

While dBASE IV is printing, it displays the following instructions:

    Cancel printing: ESC
    Pause printing: CTRL-S

Resume printing with any key

Note that printing might not stop or
pause immediately if your printer has
a buffer

This means that you can cancel printing altogether by pressing **Esc**. To pause printing temporarily, press **Ctrl-S** and then press any key later to resume printing. Any characters that were already transmitted and are stored in your printer's buffer when you give the order to cancel or pause will be printed before printing stops.

TIPS AND TRAPS

- Most tractor-feed printers allow you to slide the paper to the left or right to set the left margin.
- To define a standard left margin for all printed reports in dBASE IV, you can set the page offset in the DBSETUP program (see Chapter 19).
- If you are using a tractor-feed printer, make sure that a page perforation is aligned just above the print head before you turn on the printer. Then printing will always start at the top of a new page.
- If your printer has a buffer (a storage area for text that is waiting to be printed), pausing or canceling printing will not take effect until the buffer is empty.
- It is a good idea to select Generate Sample Labels before printing mailing labels for an entire database.
- If you change the Print menu settings for a particular report or label format, save those settings using the same file name as the report or label format, but with the .PRF extension (as dBASE will suggest). This will help you easily find and reactivate those settings in the future.

SUMMARY

You can use the options on the Print menu for printing reports, form letters, and labels. You may need to experiment with the available print settings to find out which work with your printer. You can also print databases, queries, or quick reports by using the dBASE IV Quick Report option.

For information about indexing your databases:
- Chapter 4, "Sorting the Database"

For information about creating queries (views) and using filter conditions:
- Chapter 5, "Searching the Database"

For tips on importing reports that were printed to files into other software products:
- Chapter 12: "Managing Multiple Related Databases"

To find out how to print a database structure:
- Chapter 2, "Creating a Database File"

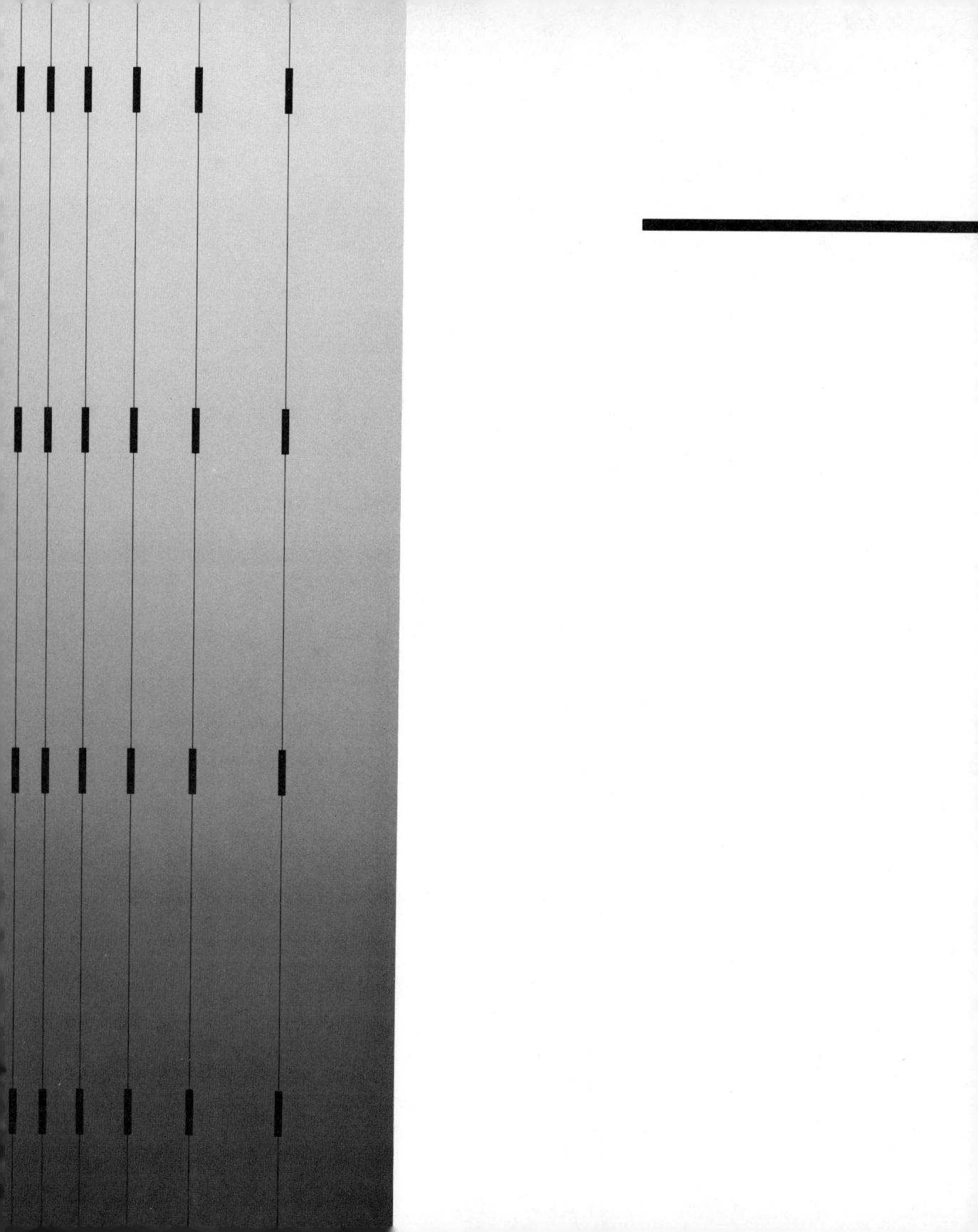

CHAPTER 10

CREATING CUSTOM FORMS

Using the Forms Design Screen. 317
Creating a Quick Layout. 319
Moving Text and Fields. 319
Adding Boxes and Lines. 322
Adding Graphics Characters. 323
Controlling Input. 325
    Specifying Template Characters. 325
        Changing Field Templates. 327
    Specifying Picture Functions. 328
        Assigning a Picture Function to a Field. 328
            Alphabetic Characters Only. .330
            Uppercase Conversion. 330
            Literals Not Part of Data. 330
            Scroll within Display Width. .331
            Multiple Choice. 331
            Trim, Right Align, and Center Align. 332
    Specifying Edit Options. 333
        Assigning Edit Options. 334
            Editing Allowed. 334
            Permit Edit If. 334
            Message. 335
            Carry Forward. 336
            Default Value. 336
            Smallest and Largest Allowed Value. 337
            Accept Value When. 338
            Unaccepted Message. 338
Saving Your Custom Form. 339
Using Your Custom Form. 340

Using Memo Fields in Custom Forms	342
Building a Memo Window	344
Modifying Your Form	345
Coloring Custom Forms	346
Creating Multiple-Page Custom Forms	347
Tips and Traps	348
Summary	350

USAGE

The dBASE IV *forms design screen* lets you be as creative as you wish when developing custom forms for your database files. To create a custom form, you first open the database file for which you want to design the form and then select <create> from the Forms panel of the Control Center (by highlighting and pressing ⏎).

You will see the forms design screen, with the Layout menu pulled down, as shown in Figure 10.2. The forms design screen is very similar to the reports design screen, except that the word *Form* appears in the lower-left corner of the screen and the menus are slightly different.

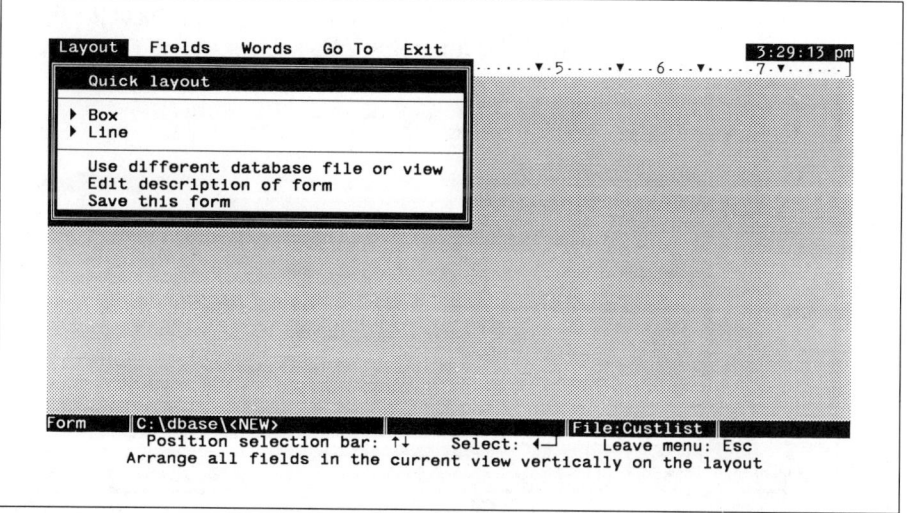

FIGURE 10.2: Whenever you access the forms design screen, the Layout menu is displayed pulled down. Press **Esc** if you do not want to choose from the Layout menu right away.

The current row and column position of the cursor is displayed in the center of the status bar near the bottom of the screen. A custom form can be as wide as the screen (from column 0 to column 79).

When you use the form later to enter or change data, the top row of the screen (row 0 on the form) will display the menu bar, and rows 22, 23, and 24 at the bottom of the screen will display the status bar and other messages. Therefore, when designing a form, try to use only rows 1 through 21.

CREATING CUSTOM FORMS

For entering and editing data, custom forms have several advantages over the dBASE IV edit screen. Besides looking better, custom forms can actually do some of the work involved in entering data, and they can trap and correct errors before those errors are stored in the database.

Figure 10.1 shows a custom form for the CUSTLIST database. (This form will be developed through the examples in this chapter.) Field names (such as LASTNAME) have been replaced with plain-English descriptions (such as Last Name). The box at the top of the screen provides information about the purpose of the form (in this case, Enter/Edit Customer Information), and the box at the bottom of the screen lists important keys. In addition, the Paid field accepts the more natural Y and N (for yes and no), rather than T and F (for true and false).

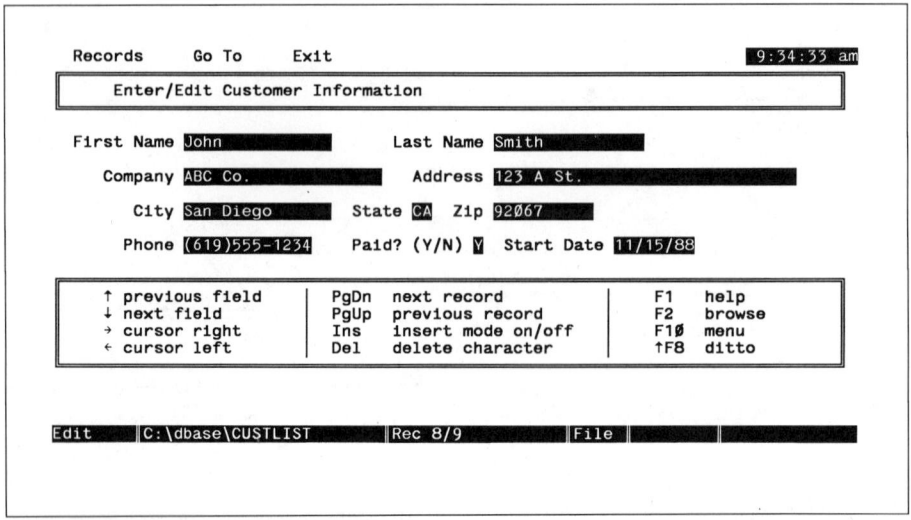

FIGURE 10.1: Custom form for the CUSTLIST database. If you follow the examples in this chapter you can refer to this figure, which shows the layout you are aiming for.

USING THE FORMS DESIGN SCREEN

SEQUENCE OF STEPS

From the Control Center:
    highlight <create> in the Forms panel ←┘

EXAMPLE

To begin creating the form in Figure 10.1, make sure that the CUSTLIST database is active. (If it is not, highlight CUSTLIST in the Data panel, press ↵, and select Use File.) Highlight <create> in the Forms panel and press ↵. You will see a blank forms design screen with the Layout menu pulled down, as shown in Figure 10.2.

(This and other examples in this chapter use the CUSTLIST database, introduced in Chapter 2. Use the instructions there to create it, if necessary. Note that some of the records in your database may differ from the ones shown in this chapter, but these differences do not affect the content of the examples.)

CREATING A QUICK LAYOUT

SEQUENCE OF STEPS

On the forms design screen:

>   Layout/Quick Layout [↵]

USAGE

The best way to create a form is to have dBASE create a simple form similar to the standard edit screen and to then modify that design to suit your purposes. To do so, select Quick Layout from the Layout pull-down menu. Your screen will look similar to Figure 10.3.

EXAMPLE

With CUSTLIST selected as the active database, press ↵ to select Quick Layout from the forms design screen's Layout pull-down menu. Your screen should look like Figure 10.3. As in the Quick Layout report design screen, each field in the active database (in this case CUSTLIST) is followed by a template showing the field's assigned width.

MOVING TEXT AND FIELDS

The basic editing keys you can use for rearranging and designing a custom form are the same as those used for report and label design. (See Table 7.1 in Chapter 7.) As you move the cursor around the screen, whenever you move to a field template, the cursor jumps to the first position in that template.

CH. 10 CREATING CUSTOM FORMS

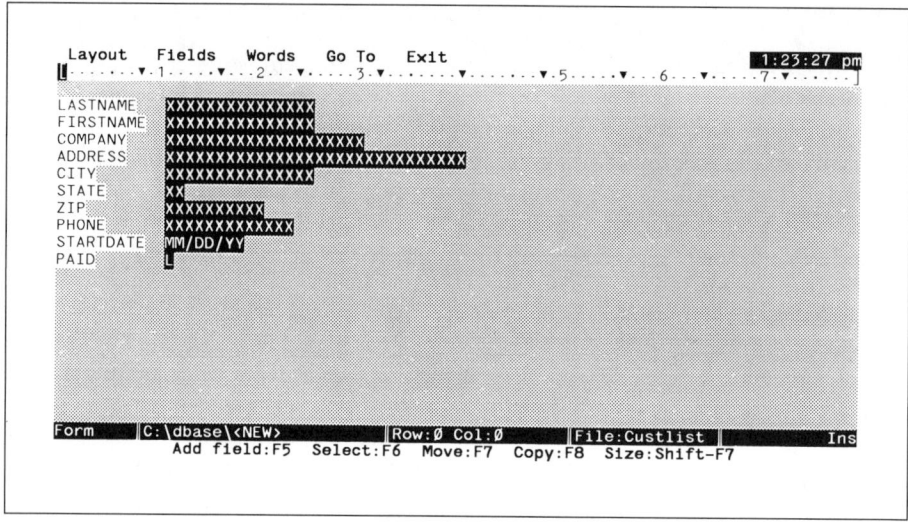

FIGURE 10.3: Quick layout form for the CUSTLIST database. You can use Quick Layout as a starting point for creating your custom form.

For each field for which you want to provide a prompt and template, do the following:

1. Place the cursor where you want the prompt to appear and type the prompt.
2. Select the appropriate field name and template and place them immediately after your prompt.
3. If you want to place another prompt and template on the same line, do so now before deleting the first field name from the form.

EXAMPLE

To design the form shown in Figure 10.1, first make sure that insert mode is on (press **Ins** until the *Ins* indicator appears in the status bar). With the cursor at row 0, column 0, press ↵ six times to insert six blank lines at the top of the form. Use the arrow keys to move the cursor to row 2, column 6, and then type **Enter/Edit Customer Information**.

Use the ↓ and ← keys to move the cursor to row 5, column 2, and type **First Name**. Press ↓ three times to move the cursor to the FIRSTNAME template (row 8, column 11). Press Select (**F6**) and then ←. Press Move (**F7**), move the cursor to row 5, column 13, and press ←.

Use → to move the cursor to row 5, column 34, and type **Last Name**. Move the cursor inside the LASTNAME template (row 7, column 11). Press Select (**F6**) and then ←. Press Move (**F7**), move the template image to row 5, column 44, and then press ←.

Move the cursor to the *L* in *LASTNAME* (row 7, column 0) and press **Ctrl-T** to remove the LASTNAME field name. Press ↓ to move to row 8, column 0, and then press **Ctrl-T** again to remove the FIRSTNAME field name.

Move the cursor to row 7, column 5, and type **Company**. Press ↓ to move the cursor to the COMPANY template (row 9, column 11), press Select (**F6**), and press ←. Press Move (**F7**), move the cursor to row 7, column 13, and press ←.

Move the cursor to row 7, column 36, and type **Address**. Move the cursor inside the ADDRESS template (row 10, column 11). Press Select (**F6**) and then ←. Press Move (**F7**), move the template image to row 7, column 44, and press ←. Move the cursor to row 9, column 0, and press **Ctrl-T** to erase COMPANY. Press ↓ to move the cursor to row 10, column 0, and press **Ctrl-T** to erase ADDRESS.

Move the cursor to row 9, column 8, and type **City** (which will be right-aligned with the text above). Press ↓ twice to move to the CITY template, press Select (**F6**), and press ←. Press Move (**F7**), move the template image to row 9, column 13, and press ←. Move the cursor to row 9, column 30, and type **State**. Move the cursor to the STATE template (row 12, column 11), press Select (**F6**), and press ←. Press Move (**F7**), move the template image to row 9, column 36, and press ←. Move the cursor to row 9, column 40, and type **Zip**. Move the cursor to the ZIP template (row 13, column 11), press Select (**F6**), and press ←.

Press Move (**F7**), move the template image to row 9, column 44, and press ←. Move the cursor to row 11, column 0 (the *C* in *CITY*). Press Select (**F6**), press ↓ five times, press → eight times so that all remaining field names are highlighted, and then press ←. Press **Del** to delete the highlighted block.

Move the cursor to row 11, column 7, and type **Phone**. Move the cursor to the PHONE template (row 14, column 11), press Select (**F6**), and then press ←. Press Move (**F7**), move the template image to row 11, column 13, and press ←.

Move the cursor to row 11, column 30, and type **Paid? (Y/N)**. Move the cursor to the PAID template (the *L* in row 16, column 11), press Select (**F6**), and press ←. Press Move (**F7**), move the template image to row 11, column 42, and press ←.

Move the cursor to row 11, column 45, and type **Start Date**. Move the cursor to the STARTDATE template (MM/DD/YY in row 15, column 11). Press Select (**F6**) and then ←. Press Move (**F7**), move the template image to row 11, column 56, and press ←. Your screen should look like Figure 10.4.

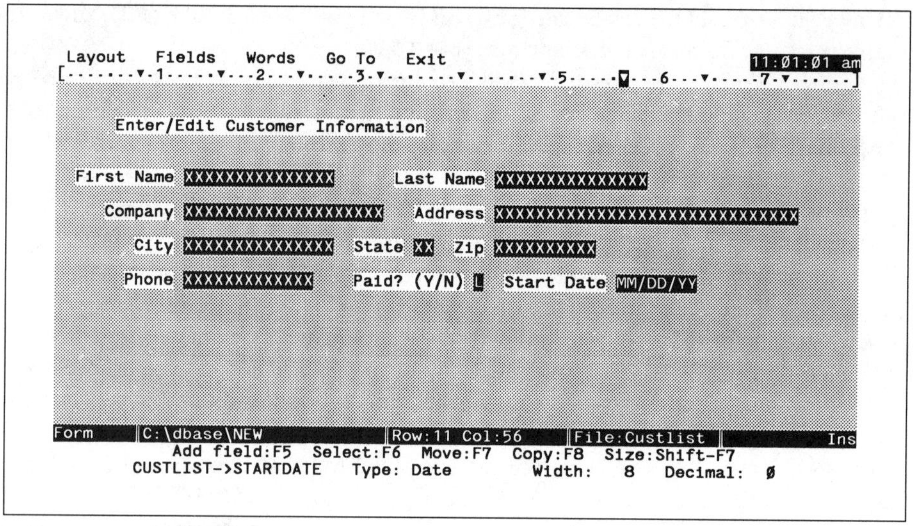

FIGURE 10.4: Fields rearranged on the form in a new layout.

Adding Boxes and Lines

SEQUENCE OF STEPS

From the forms design screen:

    Layout/Box   *or*   Line [↵]
    Single Line   *or*   Double Line [↵]
    move cursor to start of box or line ↵
    use arrow keys to draw box or line
    ↵

USAGE

Boxes and lines will make your forms look more professional. Options for drawing boxes and lines are on the Layout pull-down menu. Box drawing and line drawing use the same basic techniques. You select either Box or Line from the Layout pull-down menu, and then you select a style: either single line or double line. You then mark the starting point for the box or line by pressing ↵, draw the box or line using the arrow keys, and complete the box or line by pressing ↵ again. The bottom of the screen provides instructions to help you as you work.

The only difference between drawing boxes and lines is that the Box option always draws an even, rectangular box. The Line option is generally used to draw straight lines, but it can actually be used to draw any shape or even a single special graphics character, as explained in the next section.

Notice that while the cursor is within the box, the box frame is highlighted. So long as the frame is highlighted, you can manipulate the box. For example, you can use the Select (**F6**) key to select the box and then press the Move (**F7**) or Copy (**F8**) key to move or copy the box. You can press **Del** to delete the box, or you can press Size (**Shift-F7**) to resize the box, using the arrow keys.

EXAMPLE

Placing a double-line box around the form title is easy. First press Menus (**F10**) and select Box from the Layout menu. Select Double Line from the submenu. At the bottom of the screen, dBASE displays the instructions *Position upper left of box with cursor keys, complete with ENTER*. Move the cursor to row 1, column 0 (the upper-left corner of the box), and press ←.

The instructions now read *Stretch box with cursor keys, complete with ENTER*. Press ↓ twice, hold down the → key until the lower-right corner moves to row 3, column 78, and then press ←. You have drawn a double-line box around the form title.

To draw the box at the bottom of the form, first move the cursor to row 13, column 0. Select Box from the Layout pull-down menu and Double Line from the submenu. Press ← to mark the upper-left corner of the box. Use the ↓ and → keys to extend the box to row 18, column 78, and press ←.

To add a vertical line to the lower box, first move the cursor to row 14, column 25. Select Line from the Layout pull-down menu and Single Line from the submenu. Press ← to mark the current cursor position as the start of the line. Press ↓ four times to move the cursor to row 18, column 25. Press ← to complete the line.

To copy the line to column 55, move the cursor back to row 14, column 25 (the top of the line), and press Select (**F6**). Press ↓ three times to highlight the entire line. Press ←. Press Copy (**F8**). Move the cursor to row 14, column 55, and press ←. Your double-line box is now subdivided into three smaller boxes by the two lines.

ADDING GRAPHICS CHARACTERS

SEQUENCE OF STEPS

From the forms design screen:

    Layout/Line/Using Specified Character [←]
    select character with ← when highlighted

USAGE

You can use characters other than the single line and double line to draw boxes. You access these *graphics characters* with the Using Specified Character option on the Line submenu of the Layout menu. (You can also use this option to individually place graphics characters on the screen.) Selecting Using Specified Character presents a submenu of graphics characters and ASCII numbers assigned to those characters. Use the **PgDn** and **PgUp** keys to scroll through this menu. When the character you want is highlighted, press ← to select it.

EXAMPLE

To add some arrows to the form, first move the cursor to row 14, column 5. From the Layout pull-down menu, select line and then Using Specified Character. Press **PgDn** and then press ↓ seven times until you get to the ↑ symbol (number 24 in the leftmost column of the submenu). Press ← to select the ↑ symbol.

You need to draw a line that is one character long. To do so, press ← to mark the start of the line, press → once to draw the short line, and press ← again to complete the line. The arrow now appears on the screen. Move the cursor to row 15, column 5. From the Layout menu, first select Line and then Using Specified Character. Use ↓ to highlight character number 25 (the ↓) on the submenu and ← to select it. Press ←, →, and then ← again to place the down-pointing arrow on the screen.

Move the cursor to row 16, column 5. From the Layout menu, first select Line and then Using Specified Character. Use ↓ to highlight character number 26 on the submenu (the →) and ← to select it. Press ←, then →, and then ← again to place the right-pointing arrow on the screen. Move the cursor to row 17, column 5. From the Layout menu, first select Line and then Using Specified Character. Use ↓ to highlight character number 27 (the ←) on the submenu and ← to select it. Press ←, then →, and then ← again to place the left-pointing arrow on the screen.

In the form, ↑ stands for the **Shift** key next to **F8** (because there is not enough room to spell out *Shift*). To copy the ↑ arrow to the appropriate place, first move the cursor to row 14, column 5 (the ↑ symbol). Press Select (**F6**) and ←. Press Copy (**F8**), move the cursor to row 17, column 60, and press ←.

The form is nearly complete now. You just need to add the text inside the box at the bottom of the screen. To type the text, turn insert mode off (press **Ins** until the *Ins* indicator disappears from the lower-right corner of the screen). Position the cursor, using the arrow keys, to where you want the text to begin. Then type the text. Use the completed form shown in Figure 10.5 as a guide to help you position the cursor and enter the text.

SPECIFYING TEMPLATE CHARACTERS —— **325**

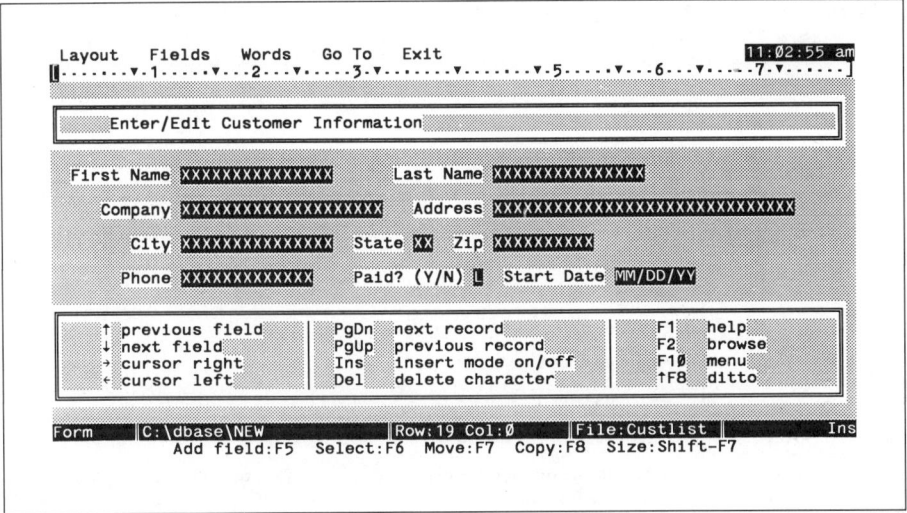

FIGURE 10.5: The custom form with text entered. The text provides a "menu box" for data entry, making the custom form more useful than the edit screen for novice users.

CONTROLLING INPUT

dBASE provides three ways for you to control what is actually entered into a field on the form and thus trap errors as they occur, before they are actually stored in the database. The same techniques can also ensure that data in a field is consistent: for example, that all phone numbers are entered with an area code, in the format (999)999-9999. You can control input using template characters, picture functions, and edit options. The following sections discuss these methods.

Specifying Template Characters

A *field template* marks the place where actual database data will appear. Initially, Character fields use templates such as XXXXXXXXXXXXX, Date fields use the template MM/DD/YY, and Logical fields use the template L. There are other template characters that you can use, as summarized in Table 10.1.

Here are some examples of templates and template characters:

!XXXXXXXXXXXXX   Accepts any characters, but capitalizes the first character; for example, entering **smith** produces Smith.

AAAAAAAAAAAAA   Accepts only letters, such as **Smith** or **SMITH**, but will not accept **123 A St**.

SYMBOL	DESCRIPTION
A	Accepts alphabetic characters (A–Z and a–z), but no numbers, spaces, or punctuation
N	Accepts alphabetic and numeric characters (A–Z, a–z, and 0–9), but no spaces or punctuation
Y	Accepts either Y or N
#	Accepts numeric digits (0–9), spaces, periods (.), and plus (+) and minus (−) signs
L	Accepts T, F, Y, or N
X	Accepts any character
!	Accepts any character and converts letters to uppercase
9	Accepts real numbers only, including plus and minus signs
Other	Any other characters are *literal* characters and are actually stored in the database

TABLE 10.1: Characters for Use in Field Templates

(because of the numbers) or **Tom Jones** (because of the space).

(999)999-9999   Accepts any numbers, 0–9, and automatically adds parentheses and hyphens; hence, entering **2139876543** produces (213)987-6543.

999-99-9999   Accepts any number and inserts hyphens; for example, entering **123456789** produces 123-45-6789.

!-!!!   Accepts any characters, but converts letters to uppercase and inserts a hyphen; for example, entering **a1j3** produces A-1J3.

!-999   Accepts a character followed by any three numbers, converting the character to uppercase; hence, entering **x555** produces X-555 (you cannot enter a1j3 into this field, because the *j* appears where a number is required).

Changing Field Templates

SEQUENCE OF STEPS

On the forms design screen:

> highlight the field template you want to change
> Field (**F5**)
> make your changes
> **Ctrl-End**

You cannot actually see the effects of field template changes until after you have saved the form.

EXAMPLE

To include some new template characters in the example form, first make sure that insert mode is off. Move the cursor to the FIRSTNAME field template (row 5, column 13). Press Field (**F5**). From the menu of options that appears, select Template. A list of template characters appears, and the cursor is readied to make changes, as shown in Figure 10.6.

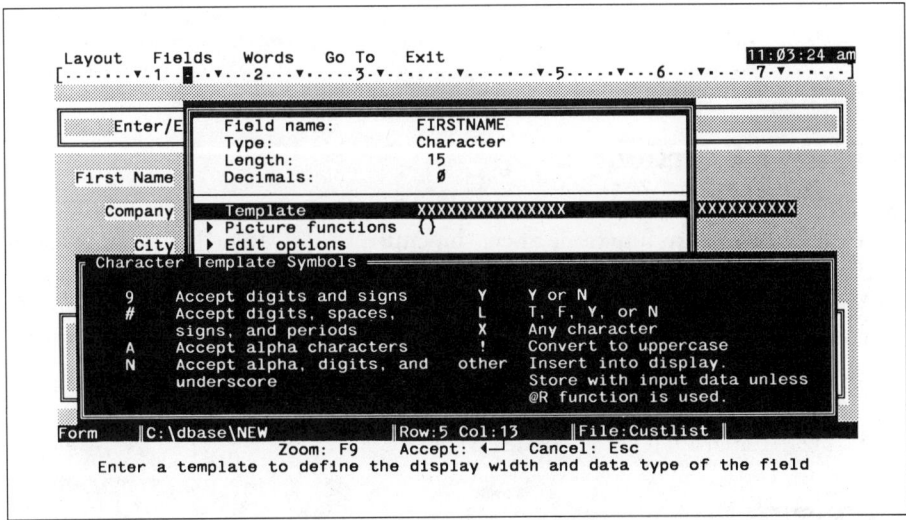

FIGURE 10.6: Template characters available for custom forms. Table 10.1 describes the effects of these characters.

Press **Home** to move to the first character in the template. Type ! (for Convert to Uppercase) and then press ↵. Press **Ctrl-End** to save the change. The template for the FIRSTNAME field now looks like this:

!XXXXXXXXXXXXX

To change the template for the LASTNAME field, move the cursor to the LASTNAME field template (row 5, column 44) and repeat the same steps.

To add a template to the PHONE field that will insert parentheses and hyphens, first move the cursor to the PHONE field template (row 11, column 13). Press Field (**F5**) and select Template. Press **Home**. Type the new template **(999)999-9999** and press ↵. Press **Ctrl-End**.

Notice that the PHONE field template includes parentheses and a hyphen, which are not special characters. These "other" characters are called *literal characters*, or just *literals*. Literal characters actually become part of the data stored in the field.

The (999)999-9999 template allows you to type any ten numeric digits into the PHONE field. The form automatically displays the literal characters like this:

( ) -

These characters will actually be stored in the database after you type a phone number.

To change the PAID field template so that it accepts only a Y (yes) or N (no) entry, move the cursor to the PAID field template (row 11, column 42). Press Field (**F5**) and select Template from the options. Press ← and type the letter **Y**. Press ↵ and then **Ctrl-End**. You will see the new template characters in their fields, as shown in Figure 10.7.

Specifying Picture Functions

Whereas template characters control the individual characters that are typed into a field, picture functions affect the entire field. Table 10.2 summarizes the picture functions. Picture functions operate on data as it is entered into or changed in a custom form. The picture functions available for the Character data type are discussed in the following sections. (Picture functions for the Numeric data type are discussed in Chapter 6.)

ASSIGNING A PICTURE FUNCTION TO A FIELD

SEQUENCE OF STEPS

On the forms design screen:

    highlight the field

SPECIFYING PICTURE FUNCTIONS — 329

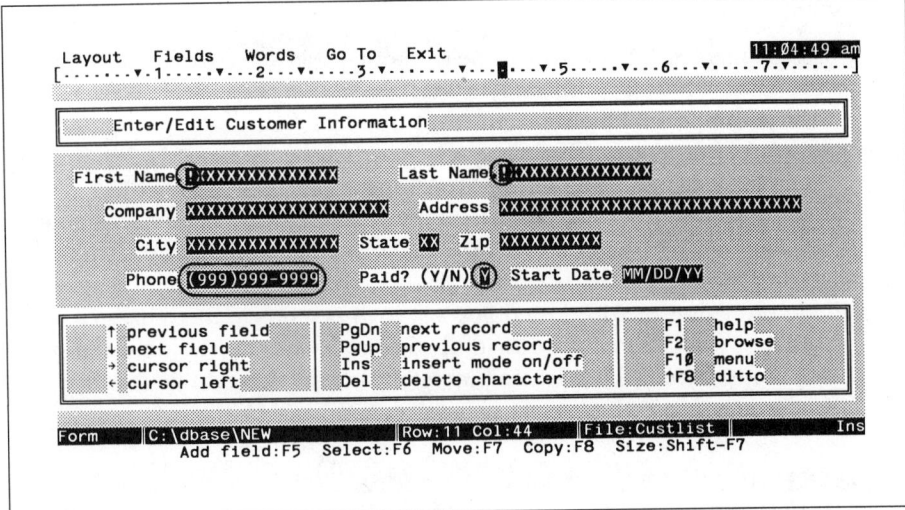

FIGURE 10.7: New template characters on the form. The !'s in the name fields will convert letters to uppercase, the 9's will accept only numbers in the PHONE field, and the PAID field will now accept only Y or N.

FUNCTION	EFFECT
A	Accepts alphabetical characters only
!	Accepts any data, but converts all letters to uppercase
R	Removes literal characters from entry before storing them in the database
S	Allows long text to be entered into short field displays
M	Allows multiple-choice options to be displayed in a form and selected by pressing ⏎
T	Removes leading and trailing blank spaces
J	Right-aligns data in the field template
I	Centers data in the field template

TABLE 10.2: Picture Functions for Custom Forms

Field (**F5**)
Picture Functions [⏎]
select the functions you want

USAGE

To assign picture functions to a field template on the forms design screen, move the cursor to the appropriate field template and press Field (**F5**). The Picture Function option on the menu that appears will display the currently assigned picture functions (if any) between curly braces. To add or change picture functions, highlight the Picture Functions option and press ⏎.

You will see a menu of the picture function options that are available for the current data type. Each option can be turned on or off by highlighting the option and pressing the space bar.

When you assign picture functions, you will not notice any changes on the design screen, because picture functions do not appear in the field templates. However, you can see what picture functions are assigned to a field template by moving the cursor into the template and pressing Field (**F5**).

EXAMPLE

You can assign the ! (uppercase) function to the STATE field in the example form. Move the cursor to the STATE template (row 9, column 36). Press Field (**F5**) and select Picture Functions. Highlight Upper-case Conversion and press the space bar to turn the option on. Press **Ctrl-End** to leave the submenu. You will see the picture function displayed as {!}. Press **Ctrl-End** again to save the change.

Alphabetic Characters Only   If you assign the Alphabetic Characters Only picture function to a field template, the field will accept only letters (A to Z and a to z) when you use the completed form later. The field will not even accept blank spaces or hyphens. Thus, a field template that has this picture function turned on could not accept **123 Appleton Way** or **Pulver-Smith** as an entry.

Uppercase Conversion   The Uppercase Conversion picture function, when turned on, converts all lowercase letters entered in the field to uppercase. For example, suppose you assign this picture function to a database field named PARTCODE. When you later use the form to add or edit data, dBASE will convert an entry such as **Ak7-7jl** to **AK7-7JL**.

Literals Not Part of Data   The Literals Not Part of Data picture function, when turned on, removes all *literals* from data typed in a form before storing the data in the database. For example, suppose you specify the field template **(999)999-9999** for entering data into a field named PHONE. When you type a phone number into the field, dBASE will fill in the literals (the parentheses and hyphen) and store your entry in the database with these characters included. But if you turn on the Literals Not Part of Data picture function for the PHONE field, dBASE will remove the literals after you enter a phone number. That is, the form will still *display* the phone number with the parentheses and hyphen inserted, but dBASE will store only the numbers in the database. Hence, if you enter **(213)555-1212** as the phone number, the actual database record will contain 2135551212.

The only advantage of using the Literals Not Part of Data picture function is that it saves a small amount of disk space by not storing the repetitive parentheses and hyphen. However, when designing a form (or report), you should always include the literal text—for example, you should use the (999)999-9999 template to display data from the PHONE field (otherwise, phone numbers will be printed without the parentheses and hyphen).

Scroll within Display Width   You can define a width of up to 254 characters for the Character data type when you create a database. However, a standard screen is only 80 characters wide. Suppose you create a database with a Character field named REMARKS and a width of 100 characters. How would you place such a field in a custom form?

Your best bet is to modify the field template to whatever size best fits on your custom form. You could use the full 80-character width of the screen or any smaller width.

Assume that you use a field template that consists of 40 X's to display the REMARKS field on your custom form. To ensure access to the full 100 characters that the REMARKS field offers, you need to turn on the Scroll within Display Width picture function. Later, when you use the completed custom form, the form will display a highlight that is 40 characters wide for entering data into the REMARKS field. But when the cursor gets to that field in the form, you can still type up to 100 characters into the field. As you type beyond the fortieth character, the text in the field scrolls to the left to make more room.

When you are viewing existing data on the completed form, you will see only the first 40 characters stored in the REMARKS field. But once the cursor gets to the REMARKS field, you will be able to use the ← and → keys to scroll to the left and right within the field and thereby view all 100 characters.

Multiple Choice   The Multiple Choice picture function allows you to create a multiple-choice field on your custom form. A multiple-choice field is one that allows only certain entries. For example, suppose you create a database of members in a club, and that database includes a Character field named STATUS. Any given member can have the status Regular, Officer, Honorary, or Expired. Because these are the only four acceptable entries for the field, there is no need even to allow the field to accept other data.

When you use a completed custom form that has a multiple-choice field in it, the form initially displays one of the acceptable values in the field. When the cursor gets to that field on the form, you can press ↵ to use the displayed value or press the space bar to view other possible options. When the option that you want to enter in the field is displayed on the form, you press ↵ to accept it.

Example To see a multiple-choice field in action, follow these steps to modify the example form (in Figure 10.1). On the forms design screen, move the cursor to the STATE field template (row 9, column 36). Press Field (**F5**) and select Picture Functions. Highlight Multiple Choice and press ↵. The screen displays the prompt *Enter multiple choices:*.

Type all the possible entries for the field, separating entries with a comma. (It is a good idea to type the entries in alphabetical order.) For this example, type the two-letter state abbreviations shown here. Do not include any blank spaces and do not press ↵ until you have typed all the two-letter abbreviations. Use the **Backspace** key to make corrections.

**AK,AL,AR,AZ,CA,CO,CT,DC,DE,FL,GA,GU,HI,IA,ID,IL,IN,KS,
KY,LA,MA,MD,ME,MI,MN,MO,MS,MT,NC,ND,NE,NH,NJ,NM,NY,
OH,OK,OR,PA,RI,SC,SD,TN,TX,UT,VA,VI,VT,WA,WI,WV,WY**

After typing all the abbreviations, press ↵. Press **Ctrl-End** twice to leave the menus. Select Save Changes and Exit from the Exit pull-down menu to save the change.

You have now provided error-trapping for the STATE field, as explained later in this chapter in the section "Using Your Custom Form."

Trim, Right Align, and Center Align The Trim, Right Align, and Center Align picture functions determine how data is displayed within the field template. Normally, character data is left-aligned within the width provided by the field template. If you turn on the Trim option along with the Right Align or Center Align picture function, you can align character strings in different ways. Some examples follow (where the | characters mark the width of the field highlight on the form):

```
| Smith          | Left-aligned (default setting)
|     Smith      | Centered
|         Smith  | Right-aligned
```

Chapter 7 explains these three options in more detail.

Specifying Edit Options

Another way that you can control what is entered into a field is through *edit options*. These options are summarized in Table 10.3. This section discusses all of the edit options available for custom forms.

EDIT OPTION	EFFECT
Editing Allowed	If Yes, field contents can be changed; if No, field contents can be viewed but not changed
Permit Edit If	Allows you to enter a logical formula to determine when a field can be changed
Message	Allows you to enter a message, which is displayed at the bottom of the screen when the field is highlighted
Carry Forward	If Yes, data entered into the current field for one record is automatically carried over to the next record when you add new records
Default Value	Allows you to place a value into a field; you can accept or change the value when you are entering data
Smallest Allowed Value	Specifies the smallest allowable value for the field
Largest Allowed Value	Specifies the largest allowable value for the field
Accept Value When	Allows you to define a logical formula, which determines whether a value can be entered into a field
Unaccepted Message	Allows you to define a message, which is displayed on the screen whenever an unacceptable value is entered into that field

TABLE 10.3: Edit Options for Custom Forms

Assigning Edit Options

The general technique you use to assign or change an edit option for a field is similar to the technique you use to change templates and picture functions. You need to get to the forms design screen and move the cursor inside the appropriate field template. Then you press Field (**F5**) and select Edit Options from the menu that appears. The Edit Options submenu will appear on the screen, where you can highlight and press ↵ to select any option.

Note that selecting an edit option does not produce any immediate effect on the form you are designing. However, you will see the edit options in action when you use the completed form.

Editing Allowed   The Editing Allowed edit option lets you determine whether a particular field can be edited. By default, all fields on a custom form can be changed when the completed form is used. If you change the Editing Allowed option to No, the form will display the contents of a field, but you will not be able to change those contents.

Permit Edit If   The Permit Edit If option lets you enter an expression that defines when a field can be edited. The expression you enter can take the form of any filter condition that you would use in a query, except that it must be a *complete expression*. For example, in the query design screen, you can place the *incomplete expression* "**CA**" in the STATE box to limit the display to California residents. But when creating an expression for the Permit Edit If edit option, you need to use the complete expression **STATE = "CA"**.

Use the Permit Edit If option when you want your custom form to permit a field to be edited only when some other field's contents meet a particular condition. For example, suppose you have a database with two Character fields named PARTCODE and PARTNAME. To ensure that a part is assigned a part code before the part name is entered on the custom form, you could use the Permit Edit If expression

   PARTCODE < > " "

(part code does not equal blank) in the PARTNAME field.

Table 10.4 shows examples of expressions that you could use in the Permit Edit If edit option (though, as mentioned, you can use any valid expression, and dBASE poses virtually no limitations).

Remember that when you use your custom form in the future, dBASE will always move the cursor from field to field from left to right and from top to bottom. Therefore, when placing a field on your custom form, place any field that depends

EXPRESSION	MEANING
LASTNAME <> " "	True when the first character in a Character field named LASTNAME is not a blank space
STARTDATE <= DATE( ) + 30	True when the Date field named STARTDATE contains a date that is no more than 30 days beyond the current date
"-" $ PARTCODE	True when the Character field named PART-CODE has a hyphen (-) embedded in it
PAID	True when the Logical field named PAID contains .T
.NOT. PAID	True when the Logical field named PAID contains .F

TABLE 10.4: Examples of Valid Expressions for Permit Edit If

on the contents of another field below (or to the right of, if the fields are on the same line) the field that it depends on. This placement allows the independent field to be filled before the dependent field decides whether to permit editing.

For example, to use the Permit Edit If option with the PARTCODE and PARTNAME fields as discussed previously, you need to make certain that the field template for the PARTNAME field—which depends on the PARTCODE field—is either to the right of (if it is on the same row) or below the PARTCODE field template when you design the form. That way, when you use the form later to enter data, the cursor will first land in the PARTCODE field, screening for a valid part code before letting you fill in a part name. Figure 10.8 illustrates this placement.

Message The Message edit option lets you create a *custom message* for any field. This message appears centered at the bottom of the screen whenever the cursor is in that field. You can create a separate and unique message for each field in your custom form. The message can be no more than 79 characters wide and cannot contain double quotation marks (").

Example You can add a message to the STARTDATE field on the example form, so that a message appears whenever the STARTDATE field is highlighted. To do so, first move the cursor to the STARTDATE template (row 11, column 56) on the forms design screen. Press Field (**F5**) and select Edit Options.

Select Message from the submenu and type **Press Enter to accept suggested date, or type in a new date**. (Notice how the text scrolls in the highlight bar as you type.) Press ⏎ after typing the entire message. Press **Ctrl-End** to leave the submenu and then press **Ctrl-End** again to save your selections.

CH. 10 CREATING CUSTOM FORMS

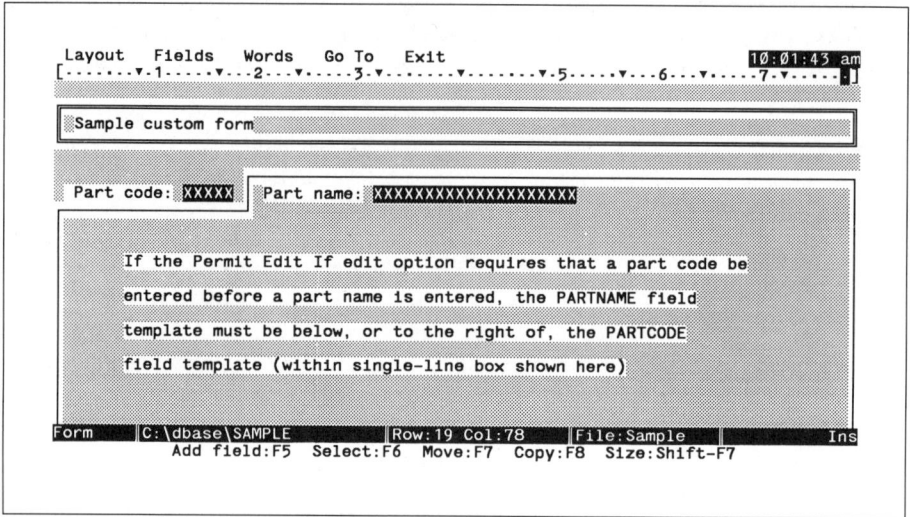

FIGURE 10.8: Placement of dependent fields on a custom form.

See the section "Using Your Custom Form" later in this chapter to see how the message works on the form.

Carry Forward When you enter new records into a database, each new record is normally displayed with empty fields (except those that use a default value—see the next section). If you prefer, you can have dBASE carry the value entered into one field in a new record to the next new record. In the next new record, you can accept the value carried forward by pressing ↵ when the cursor gets to that field, or you can type a new value.

For example, suppose you set the Carry Forward option to Yes for the STATE field in the CUSTLIST database. Then when you use the form to enter new records, you enter **CA** as the state for the first new record. When you finish entering all the data for that record and dBASE scrolls to the next new record, you will see *CA* in the STATE field, because the previous entry was carried forward.

Each new record that you add will display *CA* in the STATE field, until you enter a new state for a particular record. From that point on, the *new* state will be carried forward to additional new records. Each time you change the state in a particular record, that new value will be carried forward to the ensuing new records.

Default Value You can provide a default value for a database field. When you use the completed form, dBASE provides the default value for that field when you add new records in the database. You can either accept the suggested value as is (by pressing ← when the cursor is in the field) or type a new value.

You can enter any value as a default value, so long as you use the correct data type. For example, if most of the records in a database of addresses will have Los Angeles as the city, then you can assign **"Los Angeles"** as the default value for that field. (The quotation marks are required for Character fields.) To use a specific date as the default value for a Date field, enclose the date in curly braces: for example **{01/01/90}**. You can also specify **.T.** or **.F.** as the default value for a Logical field.

Example   On the CUSTFORM custom form, you can use the dBASE DATE( ) function to display the current date in the STARTDATE field. Later, when you add new records to the database, dBASE will provide the current date in the STARTDATE field. You can either accept the suggested value as is (by pressing ← when the cursor is in the field) or type a new value.

Move the cursor to the STARTDATE template (row 11, column 56). Press Field (**F5**) and select Edit Options. From the submenu, select Default Value. Type **DATE( )**—a dBASE function, which displays the current date—and press ←. Press **Ctrl-End** once to leave the submenu and again to save your selections.

To see the DATE( ) function at work, follow the example later in this chapter in the section "Using Your Custom Form."

Smallest and Largest Allowed Value   You can use the Smallest Allowed Value and Largest Allowed Value edit options independently or together to define ranges of acceptable values for a specific field in a database. Remember to use the proper delimiters for the data type of the field (for example, quotation marks for Character fields and curly braces for dates).

For example, suppose the current year is 1989 and you want your custom form to accept only date values in the range January 1, 1989, to December 31, 1989. To restrict the data entered in the Date field, you specify **{01/01/89}** as the lowest acceptable value for the field and **{12/31/89}** as the highest acceptable value.

Later, when you use the custom form to enter data in the database, entering an invalid date causes dBASE to beep and display the message

Range is 01/01/89 to 12/31/89 (press SPACE)

Or suppose you have a database of part codes, part names, and so forth. The field named PARTCODE in this database uses the Character data type, and all codes in your business begin with a letter between *M* and *P* (for example, M-000 to P-999). To ensure that no part numbers outside this range are entered into the database, you can specify **"M-000"** (including the quotation marks) as the lowest acceptable value for the field and **"P-999"** as the highest acceptable value.

Later, when you use the custom form to enter data in the database, entering an invalid part number causes dBASE to beep and display the message

> Range is M-000 to P-999 (press SPACE and then re-enter value)

at the bottom of the screen. You must then press the space bar and enter a new, valid value before proceeding.

Accept Value When   The Accept Value When edit option is similar to the Smallest and Largest Allowed Value options just discussed, but provides a little more flexibility. You can use any valid expression (such as the expressions discussed in the section "Permit Edit If" earlier in this chapter) to test data as soon as it is entered in a field. Then when you use the completed form to enter and edit data, the field will accept only entries that cause the expression to evaluate to true. Any other entry will be rejected and will need to be reentered.

For example, suppose you create a database for storing accounts receivable. This database includes a field named DATEPAID, which uses the Date data type. You want to ensure that no back-dated payments are entered into the database, so you want the DATEPAID field to accept only dates that are greater than or equal to the current date.

To make dBASE do so, you enter **DATEPAID > = DATE( )** as the Accept Value When expression for the DATEPAID field. (DATE( ) is a dBASE IV *function* that always represents the current date.) Later, when you use the form to enter or edit data, any date that you enter into the DATEPAID field will have to be greater than (later than) or equal to the current date. Any earlier date will be rejected.

Note that the example expressions displayed in Table 10.4 work with both the Accept Value When edit option and the Permit Edit If edit option.

Unaccepted Message   The Unaccepted Message edit option lets you define a message that will be displayed whenever an invalid value is entered into a field that uses the Accept Value When edit option. For example, if you created the DATEPAID field and Accept Value When edit option discussed in the previous section, you could also add an Unaccepted Message such as *Date must be today's date, or later.*

When you use the custom form to enter or edit data, an unacceptable entry in the DATEPAID field will cause dBASE to reject the entry and display the message *Date must be today's date, or later (press SPACE)* at the bottom of the screen. You will need to press the space bar and enter a new date.

Note that you can use any character other than the double quotation mark (") in your message.

Saving Your Custom Form

SEQUENCE OF STEPS

On the forms design screen:
To add a description:

Menus (**F10**)

Layout/Edit Description of Form [←]

type a description ←

To save the form:

Menus (**F10**)

Exit/Save Changes and Exit [←]

type a file name ←

USAGE

It is a good idea to add a description to your form before you save it. The description will appear in the Control Center when the form name is highlighted, reminding you of the form's use. To add a description, press Menus (**F10**) and select Edit Description of Form from the Layout pull-down menu. Type a description and press ←. To save the form, press Menus (**F10**) and select Save Changes and Exit from the Exit pull-down menu. When prompted, type a file name and press ←.

After dBASE creates the appropriate form (in its own language), it will return you to the Control Center, where you will see the name of the new form in the Forms panel.

EXAMPLE

To add a description to the custom form for the CUSTLIST database and save the form design, follow these steps. Press Menus (**F10**) and select Edit

Description of Form from the Layout pull-down menu. Type the description **Form for entering/editing customer information** and press ↵. Press Menus (**F10**) again and select Save Changes and Exit from the Exit pull-down menu. When prompted, type the file name **CUSTFORM** and press ↵.

After dBASE creates the appropriate form, it returns you the Control Center, where the name of the new form, CUSTFORM, appears in the Forms panel.

USING YOUR CUSTOM FORM

SEQUENCE OF STEPS

From the Control Center:

    highlight the form name in the Forms panel
    Data (**F2**)

or

    highlight the form name in the Forms panel ↵
    Display Data [↵]

To add new records:

    Menus (**F10**)
    Records/**A**dd New Records [↵]

or

    (from the bottom of the form)
    Y

To return to the Control Center:

    Exit/**E**xit   *or*   **Ctrl-End** [↵]

USAGE

To use a custom form, first make sure that the database is active (its name appears above the line in the Data panel). Highlight the form name in the Forms panel of the Control Center and press Data (**F2**) (or press ↵ and select Display Data). Using a custom form is essentially the same as using the edit screen. Use Data (**F2**) to switch back and forth between the custom form and the browse screen.

You can use the arrow keys, **PgDn**, **PgUp**, and so forth to scroll through records. You can enter and change information with the usual editing keys. To add new

USING YOUR CUSTOM FORM — 341

records, press Menus (**F10**) and select Add New Records from the Records menu, or respond to the *Add New Records?* prompt following the last record.

When you are done adding records, you can return to the Control Center by selecting Exit from the Exit pull-down menu or by pressing **Ctrl-End**.

EXAMPLE

To view the CUSTFORM form from the Control Center, highlight CUSTFORM in the Forms panel and press Data (**F2**). If the browse screen is displayed, press Data (**F2**) again to get to the custom form. To add new records using the custom form, press Menus (**F10**) and select Add New Records from the Records menu.

If you made the modifications in the previous examples in this chapter, your custom form will look like Figure 10.9. Notice that the STARTDATE field already displays the current date. The PHONE field displays parentheses and a hyphen for the general format of a phone number. Also, if you were to fill in the form, you would see that the PAID field displays either Y or N, as opposed to T or F, because you changed the template for that field.

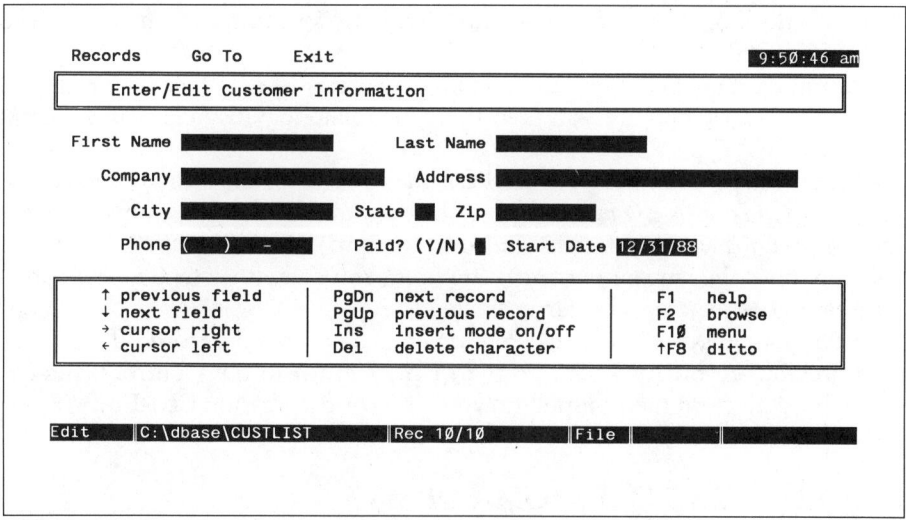

FIGURE 10.9: Completed custom form, ready to accept data for a new record.

You can use this section to test the modifications and error-checking features of the CUSTFORM form. Remember that when you enter data, you need to press ↵ except when your entry fills the field.

Type **fred** in the FIRSTNAME field. Notice that your entry is immediately converted to *Fred*. Type **jones** in the LASTNAME field. Your entry is converted to *Jones*. dBASE performs both of these instant conversions because you included the ! picture function in the respective field templates in the form design.

For COMPANY, enter **American Sneaker**. For ADDRESS, enter **P.O. Box 3381**. For CITY, enter **Newark**. When you get to the STATE field, you can experiment with the following techniques to select a state:

- Type the first letter of a state abbreviation (such as *M*) to see the first option that begins with that letter.
- Type any letter repeatedly to see all state abbreviations that start with that letter.
- Press the space bar to scroll through state abbreviations without regard to the first letter in the abbreviation.

Type **nj**. You will see the entry immediately converted to **NJ**, because of the ! picture function you assigned to that field. In the ZIP field, enter **01234**.

When you get to the PHONE field, first try typing **ABC**. dBASE will reject the letters, because you specified the field template (999)999-9999, and the 9 template character does not accept letters. Now type **2025550987**. dBASE already displays the parentheses and hyphen, so the phone number reads (202)555-0987.

In the PAID field, try entering a letter such as **J** or **Q**. Once again, dBASE rejects the entry, because you used the Y template for this field, which accepts only Y or N. Type **Y** now.

When you get to the STARTDATE field, you will see the message *Press Enter to accept suggested date, or type in a new date* at the bottom of the screen. (This is the custom message that you entered in the forms design.) The STARTDATE field will already have the current (system) date in it. You can either type a new date or just press ← to accept the current date.

After you press ←, dBASE scrolls down to a new blank record. (To return to the previous record, you can press **PgUp**.) Return to the Control Center by selecting Exit from the Exit pull-down menu (or by pressing **Ctrl-End**).

USING MEMO FIELDS IN CUSTOM FORMS

The standard edit and browse screens always indicate Memo fields with markers. When you create custom forms, any Memo fields will be displayed initially with markers. The marker *memo* appears when there is no memo text; it changes to *MEMO* when there is text (exactly as on the standard browse and edit screens). An example is shown in Figure 10.10.

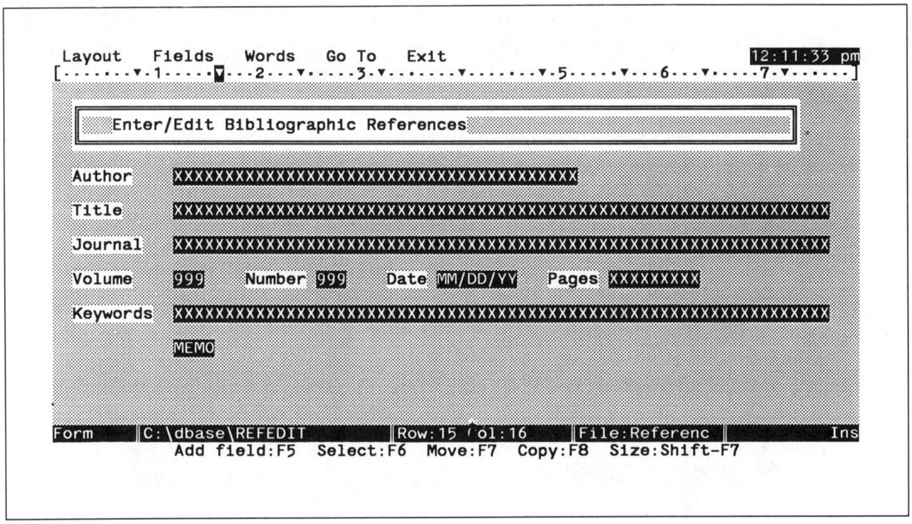

USING MEMO FIELDS IN CUSTOM FORMS —— 343

FIGURE 10.10: Custom form for a bibliographical database with the marker *MEMO* positioned where the Memo field text will appear.

On custom forms, you can alternatively display parts of Memo fields in a *memo window*. The window technique is very handy because it lets you see at least a portion of the Memo field while still viewing other fields in the database.

Figure 10.11 shows a record in a database called REFERENC displayed on a custom form, with a Memo field displayed in a memo window. The memo

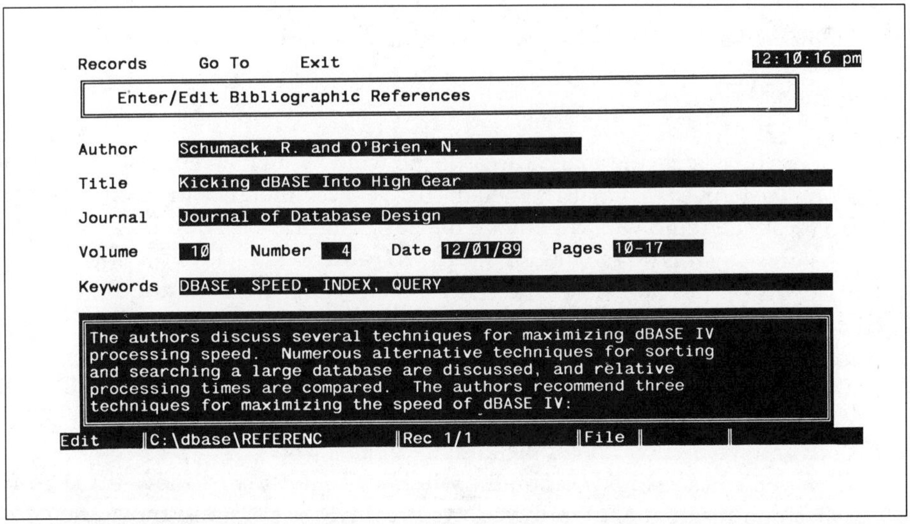

FIGURE 10.11: Memo field displayed in a memo window on the custom form.

window in this example shows just the first few lines of the Memo field text (which is in the ABSTRACT field). However, you can make a memo window any size you wish.

Building a Memo Window

SEQUENCE OF STEPS

On the forms design screen:
   To create a memo window:

      move the cursor inside the Memo field template to the first *M*

      Field (**F5**)

      Display as Window [↵]

      Border Lines [↵]

      select a border type

      Ctrl-End

   To size and position the window:

      move the cursor into the memo window

      Move (**F7**)

      move the cursor to where you want the upper-right corner ↵

      Size (**Shift-F7**)

      move the cursor to where you want the lower-right corner ↵

USAGE

Before you change the marker to a memo window, first arrange all of the other fields on the form so that there is enough space to accommodate the memo window.

To create a memo window, move the cursor inside the Memo field template (so that the cursor is on the first *M* in *MEMO*) and press Field (**F5**). Highlight the Display As option and press the space bar to change the setting to Window. Select Border Lines. Select any border type you wish. Press **Ctrl-End** to leave the submenu.

When you return to the forms design screen, a large memo window filled with X's will appear. (The bottom of the window may be partially obscured by the status bar and navigation line of the design screen.)

Now you can size and position the window. To do so, first move the cursor to any position inside the memo window. Press Move (**F7**) and move the cursor to where you want the upper-right corner of the window. Press ⏎ to complete the move. Press Size (**Shift-F7**). Use the ↑ and → keys to position the lower-right corner of the memo window. Press ⏎ to finish sizing the window.

Figure 10.12 shows the memo window for the REFERENC database on the forms design screen. A double-line border has been chosen for this window.

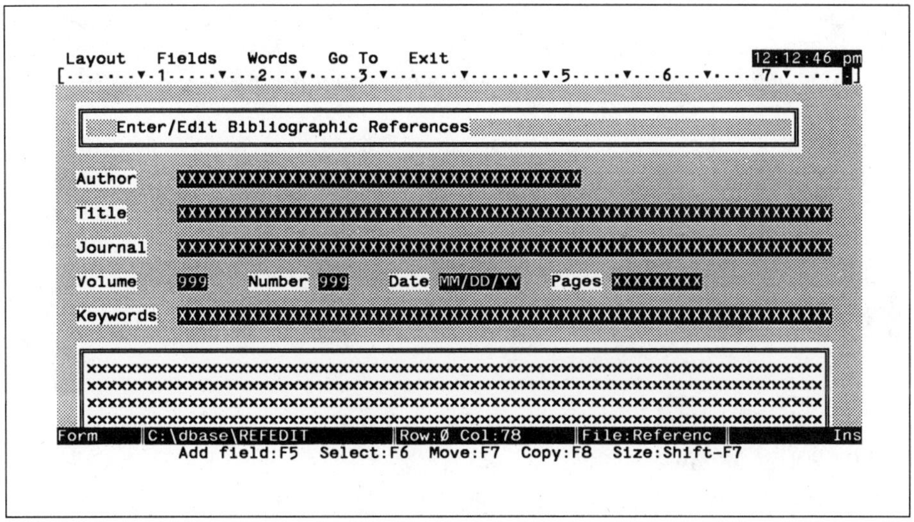

FIGURE 10.12: Memo window on the forms design screen.

Modifying Your Form

SEQUENCE OF STEPS

From the Control Center:

    highlight the form name ⏎
    Modify Layout [⏎]

or

    highlight the form name
    Design (**Shift-F2**)

When you are done making changes:

    Menus (**F10**)
    Exit/**S**ave Changes and Exit [⏎]

If you do not want to save your changes:

>Menus (**F10**)
>
>**E**xit/**A**bandon Changes and Exit [⏎]

USAGE

To change an existing form design, first make sure the appropriate database file is open (that its file name is above the line in the Data panel). Then highlight the name of the form that you want to edit and either press ⏎ and select Modify Layout or press Design (**Shift-F2**).

You can use the same techniques that you used to create the form to make changes to it. When you are done making changes, select Save Changes and Exit from the Exit pull-down menu. (If you do *not* want to save your changes, select Abandon Changes and Exit instead.) You will be returned to the Control Center.

COLORING CUSTOM FORMS

SEQUENCE OF STEPS

On the forms design screen:

>move the cursor to the upper left of the area to color
>
>Select (**F6**)
>
>move the cursor to the lower right of the area to color ⏎
>
>Menus (**F10**)
>
>**W**ords/**D**isplay [⏎]
>
>select from the menu

USAGE

You can color any selected area of your custom form by selecting Display from the Words pull-down menu on the forms design screen. (First, choose the area to color: move the cursor to the upper left of the area and press Select (**F6**); then move the cursor to the lower right of the area and press ⏎.)

If you are using a monochrome monitor, you will be given the options Intensity (to display letters in a bright boldface), Underline (to underline words), Reverse Video (to reverse the light and dark shades used for letters and their background), and Blink (to cause letters to blink on and off).

If you are using a color monitor, you will see the dBASE IV *electronic palette* for selecting a foreground and background color combination, as well as an option for blinking. (See the section "Changing the Display Colors" in Chapter 14 for information about selecting foreground and background colors.)

Note that after you select a display attribute or color combination, the selected area that you colored will still be highlighted, so your selection might not be readily apparent. To unselect the area and see the effects of your selection, press Select (**F6**) and then **Esc**.

CREATING MULTIPLE-PAGE CUSTOM FORMS

A single dBASE IV database file can contain up to 255 fields per record. Needless to say, if you were to create a database with that many fields in it, you would be hard pressed to squeeze all those fields onto a single screen. To solve this problem, dBASE IV lets you divide any custom form into several pages (or screens) of fields.

Figure 10.13 shows a portion of the structure for a database named TAXES.DBF that contains 112 fields for entering income tax data. An accountant or tax preparer might create such a database to store income tax information. Each record in the database can hold enough data to fill in an income tax form for each client.

To enter and edit information in this database would require several pages of custom forms. For example, Figure 10.14 shows how the first page of the form might look on the screen, and Figure 10.15 shows how the second page on the form might appear. For convenience, the fields on each page are roughly organized to resemble the fields on the paper form.

Initially, the forms design screen displays only enough space to create a single page (on which you would use rows 1 through 21). To create multiple-page custom forms, just use the **PgDn** and **PgUp** keys to scroll through additional pages on the forms design screen. A single custom form can actually contain over 1600 screen pages.

When using a completed form that contains multiple pages, you use the **PgUp** and **PgDn** keys to scroll forward and backward through individual pages. When you are at the last page of the form, pressing **PgDn** scrolls to the next record in the database. When you are at the first page, pressing **PgUp** scrolls back to the previous database record.

When you create your own multiple-page custom forms, it is a good idea to display useful identifying information on each page of the form. For example, Figure 10.15 displays the customer number and name from page 1 of the form so that you can see at a glance to which client the information on the screen refers.

You can repeat any field or fields on any page of a multiple-page form by positioning the cursor, pressing Field (**F5**), and selecting the field name from the menu that appears. Note that because the field is repeated, there is no need to

```
Structure for database: TAXES.DBF

Field  Field Name  Type       Width  Dec  Index
    1  CLIENT_NO   Character      4         Y
    2  LASTNAME    Character     15         N
    3  FIRSTNAME   Character     15         N
    4  MI          Character      1         N
    5  ADDRESS     Character     25         N
    6  CITY        Character     20         N
    7  STATE       Character      2         N
    8  ZIP         Character     10         N
    9  PHONE       Character     13         N
   10  SSN         Character     12         Y
   11  SPOUSESSN   Character     12         N
   12  OCCUPATION  Character     30         N
   13  SPOUSEOCC   Character     30         N
   14  ELECT_FUND  Logical        1         N
   15  SP_ELECFND  Logical        1         N
   16  FILESTATUS  Character     25         N
   17  SP_DE__
                                           N
       ____CU_YR   Numeric        2         N
  100  IRADEDUCT   Numeric       10    2    N
  101  IRAPAY      Numeric       10    2    N
  102  KEOGH       Numeric       10    2    N
  103  PENALTY     Numeric       10    2    N
  104  ALIMONYPD   Numeric       10    2    N
  105  COUPLEWRK   Numeric       10    2    N
  106  TAXWITHELD  Numeric       10    2    N
  107  ESTPAYMNTS  Numeric       10    2    N
  108  EARNEDINC   Numeric       10    2    N
  109  EXTEN_PD    Numeric       10    2    N
  110  EXCESS_SSN  Numeric       10    2    N
  111  FUEL_CRDIT  Numeric       10    2    N
  112  RIC_CREDIT  Numeric       10    2    N
```

FIGURE 10.13: Printout of a portion of the TAXES database. Note that this figure is a composite.

edit it on every page in the form. Therefore, you can set the Editing Allowed edit option to No for repeated fields and prevent the cursor from moving into the field highlight on page 2 and subsequent pages.

TIPS AND TRAPS

- When changing template characters, make sure that insert mode is off so you do not change the size of the template.

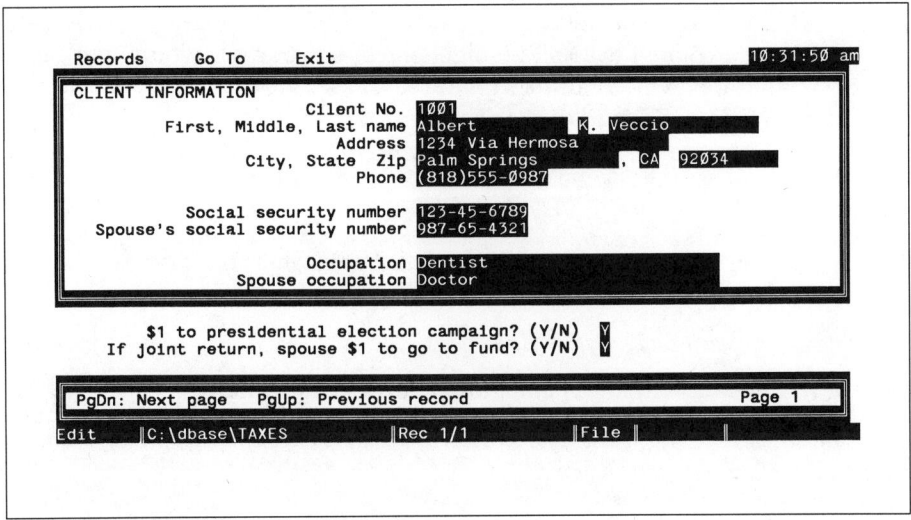

FIGURE 10.14: First page of a two-page custom form for entering tax data.

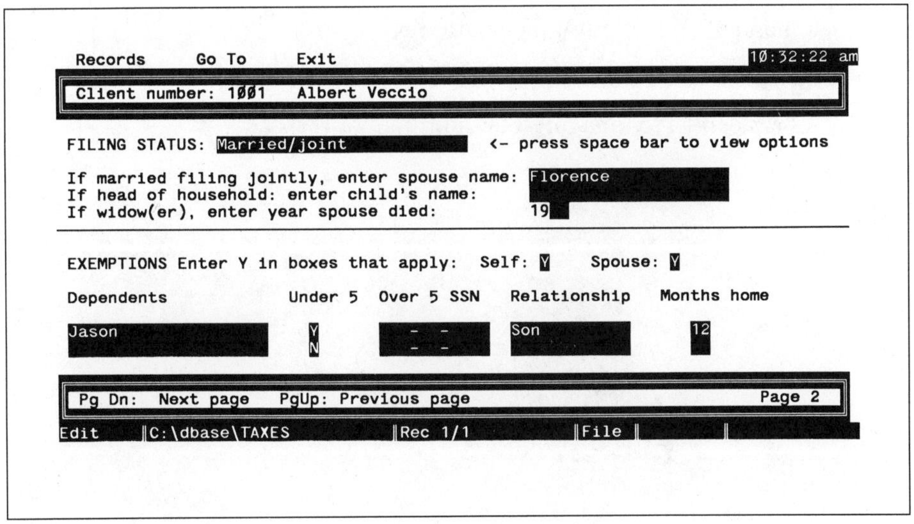

FIGURE 10.15: Second page of a two-page custom form for entering tax data.

- You cannot assign picture functions to field templates for the Date or Logical data types.
- Never use double quotation marks (") when listing options for a multiple-choice field or in custom-designed messages.

- After you select a display attribute or color combination, the selected area that you colored will still be highlighted, so your selection might not be readily apparent. To unselect the area and see the effects of your selection, press Select (**F6**) and then **Esc**.

SUMMARY

This chapter concludes the third part of the book, which has discussed displaying and printing your data in reports, on mailing labels, and on custom forms.

For information about data entry for Memo fields:

- Chapter 3, "Adding, Changing, and Deleting Data"

For a discussion of picture functions for the Numeric data type and techniques for performing on-screen calculations with custom forms:

- Chapter 6, "Performing Calculations"

For more information about and examples of the Trim, Right Align, and Center Align options:

- Chapter 7, "Designing Formatted Reports"

For information about selecting foreground and background custom screen colors:

- Chapter 14, "Managing Files and the Workspace"

Part IV

MANAGING THE DATABASE

Chapter 11: Managing Groups of Records
Chapter 12: Managing Multiple Related Databases
Chapter 13: Using Keystroke Macros
Chapter 14: Managing Files and the Workspace

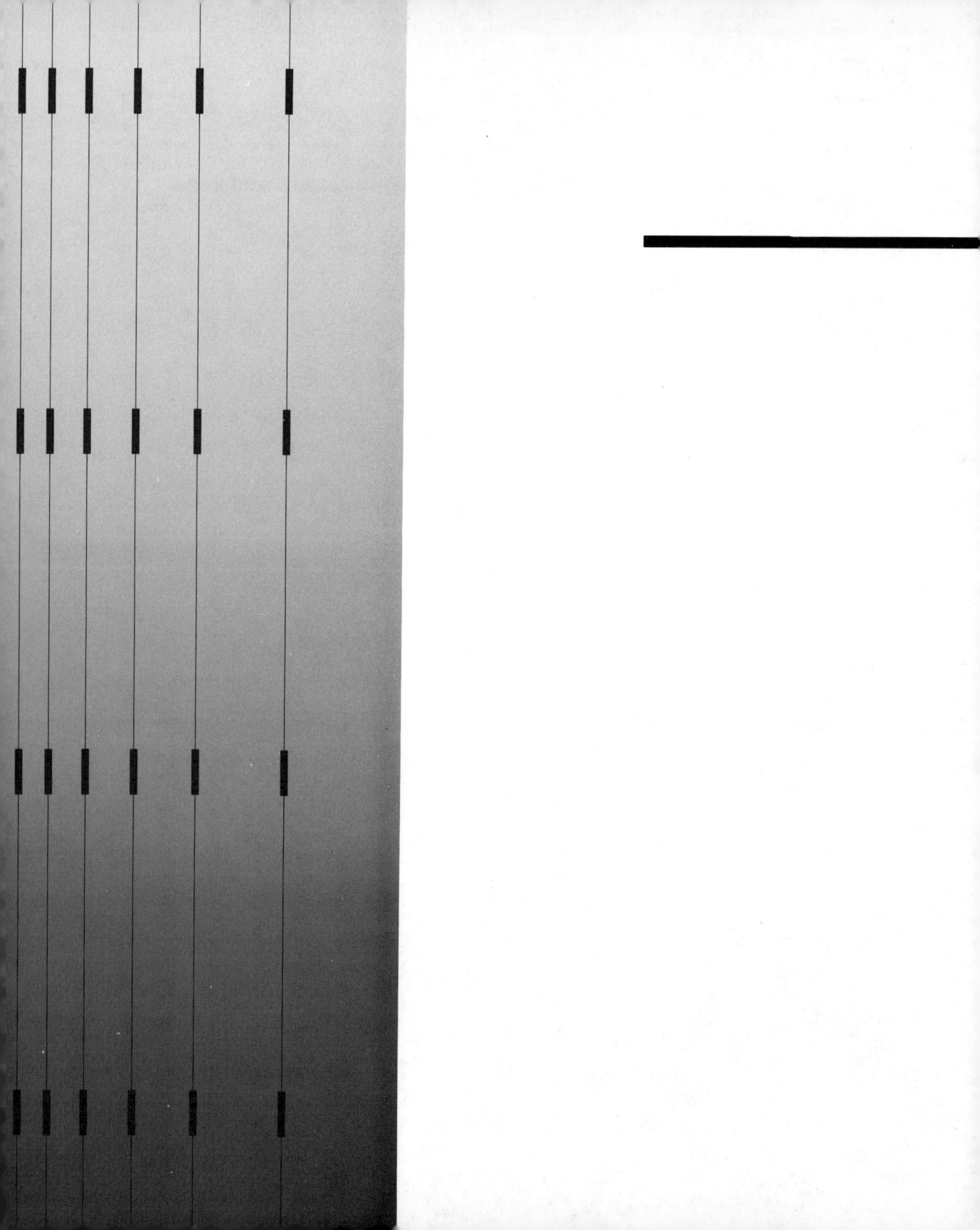

CHAPTER 11

MANAGING GROUPS OF RECORDS

Using Group Bands in Reports. 357
    Adding Group Bands. 357
    Indexing on Report Groups. 359
    Grouping by Expression Value. 359
        Grouping by Date. 360
        Grouping by First Letter. 361
        Grouping by Record Count. 362
    Changing Group Bands. 364
    Handling Groups and Page Breaks. .365
    Removing Redundant Fields. 365
    Nesting Groups within Groups. 368
Hiding Duplicate Records. 373
Global Editing with Update Queries. 376
    Replacing Character Data. 377
    Changing Numeric Data. 381
    Marking Records for Deletion. 384
    Unmarking Marked Records. 387
    Appending Groups of Records. 390
Tips and Traps. 394
Summary. 395

Managing Groups of Records

In managing your database, you may sometimes need to perform an operation on an entire group of records. For example, if you want to raise the unit price of part B-222 by 10 percent, this change should be reflected in all records that contain the part number. To change all records in this way, you use an update query, discussed in this chapter.

You may also sometimes want to hide individuals within groups, treating each group as an individual. For example, suppose you have a database of employees that includes the department in which each employee works. If you want to send just a single memo to each department, you can hide records with duplicate departments, leaving only one unique record for each department in the database. You can then use these records to print one memo for each department.

You may also want to create reports to present records grouped in a variety of ways. Managing groups of records in reports is the first topic of this chapter.

Using Group Bands in Reports

A *group band* tells dBASE to group similar items in a report. You can group records in any manner you wish. For instance, in the CUSTLIST database you can group customers by city, state, or zip code. As discussed in Chapter 6, to display subtotals you must add group bands to the report format.

A group band consists of a Group Intro band and a Group Summary band. Information in the *Group Intro band* is displayed once at the top of each group. For example, a report grouped by part number might display the group heading *Part number: A-111* for one group and *Part number: B-222* for the next group. The *Group Summary band* displays its contents once at the bottom of each group. This band is where you place summary fields to display subtotals, record counts, or any summary information about the group.

Adding Group Bands

SEQUENCE OF STEPS

From the Control Center:

> highlight the report name in the Reports panel
> Design (**Shift-F2**)

On the reports design screen:

> move the cursor to the Report Intro band border
> Menus (**F10**)
> **B**ands/**A**dd a Group Band [↵]
> **F**ield Value *or* **E**xpression Value *or* **R**ecord Count [↵]

USAGE

To add a group band to an existing report format, first make sure that the database you want to use is active. Move the highlight to the name of the report you want to modify and press Design (**Shift-F2**) to access the reports design screen.

To insert a group band, move the cursor to the Report Intro band border. Press Menus (**F10**) and select Add a Group Band from the Bands pull-down menu. dBASE displays three options: Field Value, Expression Value, and Record Count. Selecting Field Value lets you specify a particular field to group by from a list of the fields in the database, as shown in Figure 11.1.

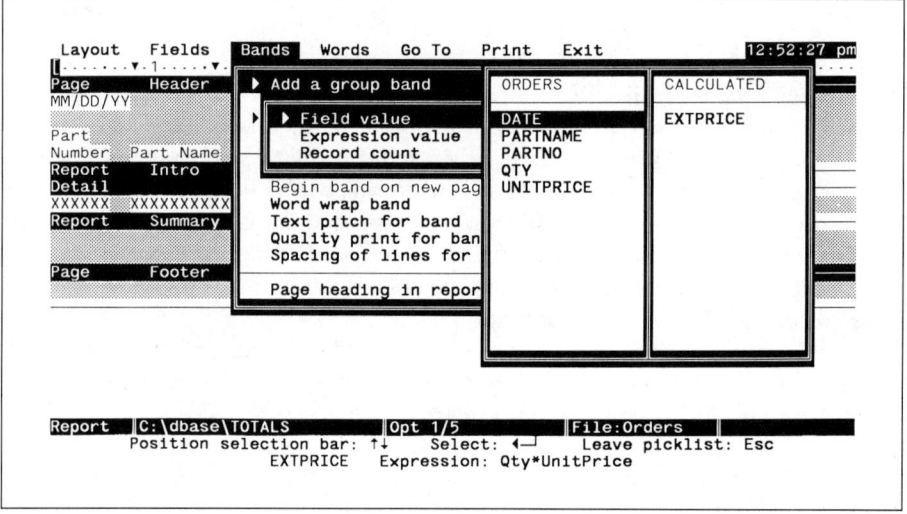

FIGURE 11.1: When you select Field Value for a group band, dBASE displays a list of the fields in the database from which you can select.

Selecting Expression Value lets you group records according to a dBASE IV expression, rather than by a field. Grouping by Record Count produces a report in groups of whatever number of records you specify: 5, 10, 12, or whatever.

Indexing on Report Groups

SEQUENCE OF STEPS

On the database design screen:
To create an index:

Menus (**F10**)
Organize/**C**reate New Index [⏎]
select a field   *or*   type an index expression ⏎
enter a name for the index

To activate the index:

Organize/**O**rder Records by Index [⏎]
select from the available indexes

USAGE

The group bands in the report format do not *create* groups; they simply tell dBASE when to print summaries and introductions. Therefore, before you print a report using groups, you need to *index* the records in the database. If you do not first index the database, each time dBASE encounters a new item for that field while printing the report, it will consider that record to be the start of a new group.

For Field Value groups, index on the field you are using to group by. For groups based on expression values, you must create and activate an appropriate index (as explained in the following sections).

If you need to create an index to match your report grouping, select Create New Index from the Organize menu on the database design screen. Select a field or type an index expression. Give the index a name.

Before finally printing the report, you must activate the index. To do so, select Order Records by Index from the Organize menu and select from the available indexes.

Grouping by Expression Value

The Expression Value option on the Add a Group Band menu lets you group records by a dBASE IV *expression*. The expression you enter can be a combination of Character fields joined with a plus sign, such as LASTNAME +FIRSTNAME. However, you can also use expressions that contain dBASE IV *functions*. The functions that are especially useful for report groupings are summarized in Table 11.1. Appendix D summarizes all the dBASE functions.

360 — CH. 11 MANAGING GROUPS OF RECORDS

FUNCTION	RETURNS	DATA TYPE USED WITH
CMONTH( )	The month of a date	Date
YEAR( )	The year of a date	Date
CDOW( )	The day of the week	Date
LEFT( )	The leftmost characters	Character

Table 11.1: Functions Used in Grouping

GROUPING BY DATE

Suppose you want to group records in a report by month, regardless of the particular day. If you use DATE alone as the grouping field, your report will display a separate group for each specific date. However, if you use the expression value CMONTH(DATE) to determine groups, all of the records for January will be grouped together, followed by all of the records for February, and so forth. Figure 11.2 shows a sample report format that uses the CMONTH( ) function for grouping.

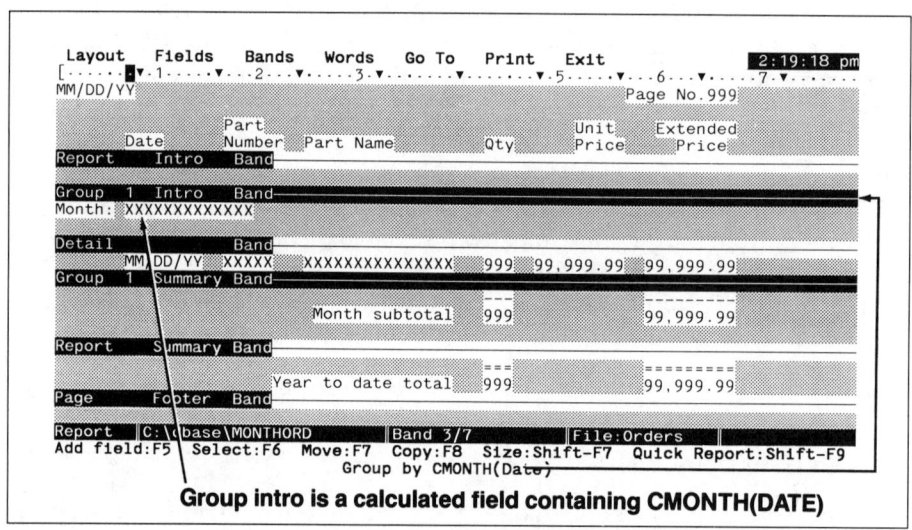

FIGURE 11.2: Report format for grouping records by month, using the CMONTH( ) function.

Before printing the report, you need to activate an index that puts the records in date order. This can be a simple index of the DATE field or a complex index using DTOS(DATE) combined with another field, so long as the records are presorted into date or month order. Figure 11.3 shows a sample report printed using this format, with DATE as the field for the index.

```
07/08/90                                                    Page No.   1

                    Part                         Unit       Extended
            Date    Number   Part Name    Qty    Price      Price

  Month: January

            01/01/90  A-111  Astro Buddies   2    50.00       100.00
            01/05/90  B-222  Banana Man      2   100.00       200.00
            01/09/90  B-222  Banana Man      1   100.00       100.00
            01/11/90  C-333  Cosmic Critters 1   500.00       500.00
            01/12/90  A-111  Astro Buddies   3    50.00       150.00
            01/15/90  A-111  Astro Buddies   4    50.00       200.00
            01/20/90  B-222  Banana Man      1   100.00       100.00
            01/21/90  C-333  Cosmic Critters 2   500.00     1,000.00
            01/30/90  C-333  Cosmic Critters 1   500.00       500.00
                                             ---             --------
                          Month subtotal    17               2,850.00

  Month: February

            02/02/90  C-333  Cosmic Critters 2   500.00     1,000.00
            02/11/90  C-333  Cosmic Critters 1   500.00       500.00
            02/12/90  A-111  Astro Buddies   3    50.00       150.00
            02/15/90  A-111  Astro Buddies   4    50.00       200.00
            02/20/90  B-222  Banana Man      1   100.00       100.00
            02/21/90  C-333  Cosmic Critters 2   500.00     1,000.00
            02/30/90  C-333  Cosmic Critters 1   500.00       500.00
                                             ---             --------
                          Month subtotal    14               3,450.00

  Month: March

            03/03/90  A-111  Astro Buddies   2    50.00       100.00
            03/05/90  B-222  Banana Man      2   100.00       200.00
            03/09/90  B-222  Banana Man      1   100.00       100.00
            03/11/90  C-333  Cosmic Critters 1   500.00       500.00
            03/12/90  A-111  Astro Buddies   3    50.00       150.00
                                             ---             --------
                          Month subtotal     9               1,050.00
                                             ===             ========
                       Year to date total   40               7,350.00
```

FIGURE 11.3: Report of orders subtotaled by date within each part number.

GROUPING BY FIRST LETTER

With Character fields, you can use the LEFT( ) function to group records by the leading characters in each field. To use the LEFT( ) function, you must include both the field name and the number of characters within the parentheses.

For example, suppose you want to print a customer list grouped by the first letter in people's last names (that is, all the A's, then all the B's, and so forth). To do so, you need to base the grouping on the expression LEFT(LASTNAME,1), with the 1 indicating that only the first letter is to be used for grouping. Figure 11.4 shows a sample report format that groups records by the first letter in the LASTNAME field.

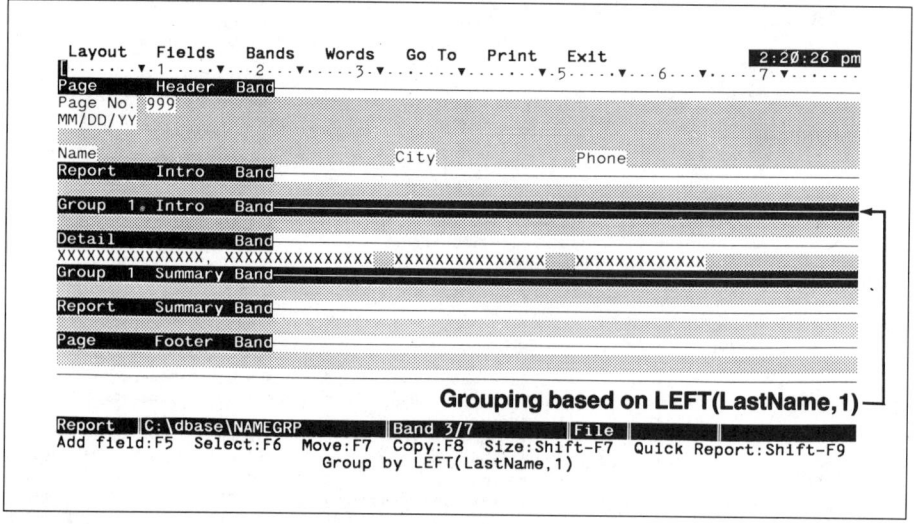

FIGURE 11.4: Report format to group records by the first letter of last names, using the expression LEFT(LASTNAME, 1). The grouping expression is shown in the message line centered at the bottom of the screen.

Before printing the report, you need to once again put the records into alphabetical order. You can use any appropriate index expression, such as LASTNAME or LASTNAME + FIRSTNAME. Figure 11.5 shows a sample printed report that uses the LASTNAME + FIRSTNAME index expression and the format shown in Figure 11.4.

Suppose you want to group customers by general zip code area, such as all zip codes beginning with 91 followed by those beginning with 92, then 93, and so forth. If the zip codes are stored as the Character data type in a field named ZIP, then the expression for grouping is LEFT(ZIP,2). In this case, you need to activate an index of the ZIP field before printing the report.

GROUPING BY RECORD COUNT

You can group records by record count, which simply separates printed rows into equal-sized blocks. To do so, select Record Count from the Add a Group Band submenu and enter the number of records you want within each group. Figure 11.6 shows a sample report format with records divided into groups of five.

```
               Phone List                              01/01/90

               Name               City                 Phone

               Adams, Annie       Santa Monica         (714)555-0123
               Adroit, Bob        Palm Springs         (714)555-9987
               Agajanian, Roo     Oakland              (415)787-5233
               Amanda, Rhonda     Newark               (217)555-0990
               Anastasie, Steve   Hatboro              (215)543-9283
               Atritia, Ted       Buffalo              (208)756-9320

               Beach, Sandy       Portland             (717)555-9988
               Boon, Lenny        New Orleans          (606)551-1212
               Byers, Bob         Torrance             (213)675-9090

               Caruthers, Candy   Ocean Beach          (619)465-3968
               Carlyle, Tim       Glendora             (818)550-3345
               Casanova, Juan     Azusa                (818)776-5464
               Coulter, Lou       San Diego            (619)225-0998
               Cuisine, Zeke      Carmel               (404)649-2453

               Davis, Randi       Newport Beach        (714)564-3648
               Delorrio, Maria    Orange               (818)555-0989
               Devine, Deedra     Santa Ana            (714)557-0295
               Dillon, Jack       Indianapolis         (317)800-5434
               Divin, Adam        Los Angeles          (213)655-8956
```

FIGURE 11.5: Printed report from the format in Figure 11.4. The records are grouped by the first letter of the last names.

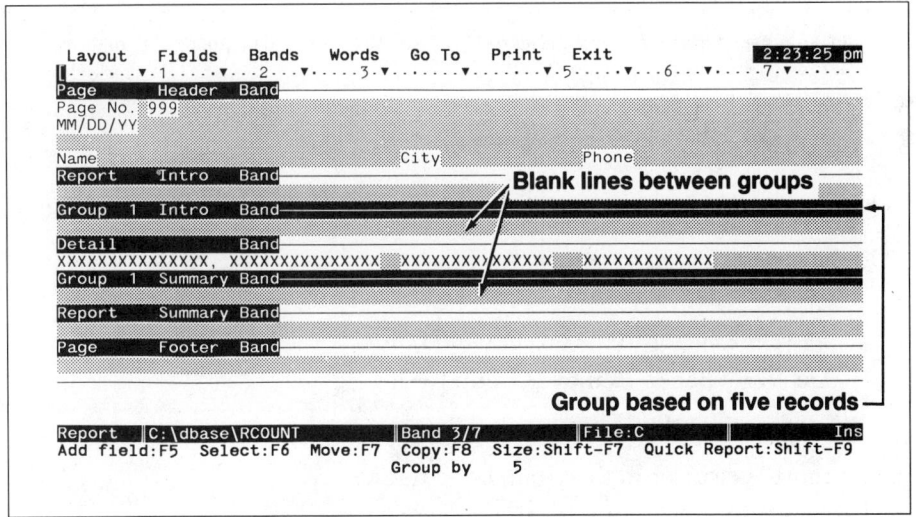

FIGURE 11.6: Report format for records grouped by count. The record count is five, as indicated in the message line centered near the bottom of the screen.

Figure 11.7 shows a sample report printed with this format. Notice that the records are organized into groups of five, regardless of their contents. The number of blank spaces that appears between each group is determined by the number of blank lines in the group band in the report design.

```
Phone List                                01/01/90

Name                City              Phone

Adams, Annie        Santa Monica      (714)555-0123
Adroit, Bob         Palm Springs      (714)555-9987
Agajanian, Roo      Oakland           (415)787-5233
Amanda, Rhonda      Newark            (217)555-0990
Anastasie, Steve    Hatboro           (215)543-9283

Atritia, Ted        Buffalo           (208)756-9320
Beach, Sandy        Portland          (717)555-9988
Boon, Lenny         New Orleans       (606)551-1212
Byers, Bob          Torrance          (213)675-9090
Caruthers, Candy    Ocean Beach       (619)465-3968

Carlyle, Tim        Glendora          (818)550-3345
Casanova, Juan      Azusa             (818)776-5464
Coulter, Lou        San Diego         (619)225-0998
Cuisine, Zeke       Carmel            (404)649-2453
Davis, Randi        Newport Beach     (714)564-3648

Delorrio, Maria     Orange            (818)555-0989
Devine, Deedra      Santa Ana         (714)557-0295
Dillon, Jack        Indianapolis      (317)800-5434
Divin, Adam         Los Angeles       (213)655-8956
```

FIGURE 11.7: Report from the format in Figure 11.6. Records are printed in groups of five.

Changing Group Bands

SEQUENCE OF STEPS

On the reports design screen:
  To remove a group band:

    move the cursor to the group band border
    Del *or* **Bands/R̲emove Group [←┘]**

  To change the field for a group band:

    move the cursor to the group band border
    Bands/M̲odify Group [←┘]

USAGE

To permanently remove a group band from a report format, place the cursor in the band's border and press **Del** or select Remove Group from the Bands pull-down menu. To change the field that a group band is based on, move the cursor to the group band border and select Modify Group from the Bands menu.

Handling Groups and Page Breaks

SEQUENCE OF STEPS

On the reports design screen:
    To print the current Group Intro at the top of each page:

        Menus (**F10**)
        Bands/**G**roup Intro on Each Page **Y**es [←⎯]

    To print each new group on a new page:

        move the cursor to the group band border
        Menus (**F10**)
        Bands/**B**egin Band on New Page **Y**es [←⎯]

USAGE

If a particular group in a report continues to the next printed page, dBASE does not automatically repeat the Group Intro on the new page. To have the Group Intro repeated on the new page, change the Group Intro on Each Page option on the Bands menu from No to Yes.

You can print groups successively, as in the examples in this chapter, or you can print each new group on a separate page. Move the cursor to the appropriate group band border and then highlight Begin Band on New Page on the Bands menu. Change the setting to Yes to start each printed group on a new page.

Removing Redundant Fields

SEQUENCE OF STEPS

On the reports design screen:

    move the cursor to the field templates for the group
    Select (**F6**) ←⎯

move the cursor to the Group Intro Band
Move (**F7**) ←┘

USAGE

Reports that group data need not display redundant data. For example, the SUBTOTAL report (created in Chapter 6 and shown again in Figures 11.8 and 11.9) repeats part numbers and part names within each group. You can change the report format so that this redundant data is displayed (and printed) only once.

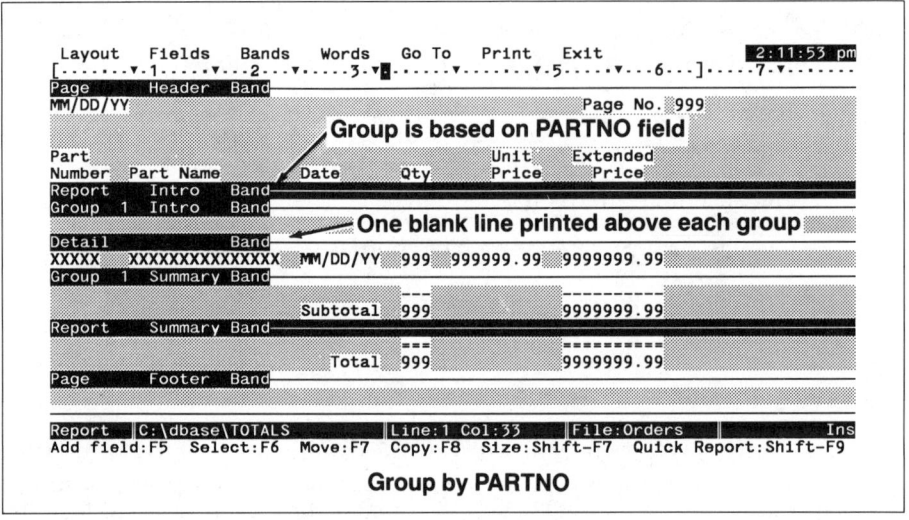

FIGURE 11.8: Report format grouping records by part number and then subtotaling them. (See Chapter 6 to create this format.)

To modify an existing report format so that groups print without repeating data, first access the appropriate reports design screen. Move the cursor to the Group Intro Band and type any text that you want to appear in the group introduction. Move the cursor to the field templates for the group. Press Select (**F6**) and ←┘ to highlight the templates. Move the cursor back to the Group Intro Band and press Move (**F7**) and then ←┘.

Now you can save the new format. When you return to the Control Center, activate the appropriate index and then print the report.

EXAMPLE

If you followed the steps in Chapter 6 to create the SUBTOTAL report for the ORDERS database, you can modify it by following this example.

REMOVING REDUNDANT FIELDS — 367

```
07/08/90                                    Page No.   1

Part                                 Unit      Extended
Number   Part Name      Date   Qty   Price     Price

A-111    Astro Buddies  06/01/90  2  50.00     100.00
A-111    Astro Buddies  06/02/90  3  50.00     150.00
A-111    Astro Buddies  06/05/90  4  50.00     200.00
                                  -----        ----------
                        Subtotal  9            450.00

B-222    Banana Man     06/01/90  2  100.00    200.00
B-222    Banana Man     06/01/90  1  100.00    100.00
B-222    Banana Man     06/15/90  1  100.00    100.00
                                  -----        ----------
                        Subtotal  4            400.00

C-333    Cosmic Critters 06/01/90 1  500.00    500.00
C-333    Cosmic Critters 06/15/90 2  500.00   1000.00
C-333    Cosmic Critters 06/15/90 1  500.00    500.00
C-333    Cosmic Critters 07/01/90 2  500.00   1000.00
                                  -----        ----------
                        Subtotal  6           3000.00
                                  =====        ==========
                        Total    19           3850.00
```

FIGURE 11.9: Printed subtotaled report from the format in Figure 11.8. Notice that part numbers and names are repeated within the groups.

At the Control Center, make sure the ORDERS database is open (that its name appears above the line in the Data panel). Highlight SUBTOTAL in the Reports panel and press Design (**Shift-F2**). Use ↓ to move the cursor into the Group 1 Intro band. Type **Part:** (including the colon).

Press ↓ and ← until the cursor is in the PARTNO field template. (The bottom of the screen will show *ORDERS->PARTNO* when the cursor is properly positioned.) Press Select (**F6**). Press → until both the PARTNO and PARTNAME field templates are highlighted (the highlight should extend to column 22). Press ↵ to complete the selection. Press ↑ and ← to move the cursor to the right of the word **Part:** (in column 6). Press Move (**F7**) and then ↵. The move is now complete.

To add a colon between the part number and the part name, press → twice and type the colon (:). Press **End** to move to the end of the field templates. Press ↵ to insert a blank line in the Group 1 Intro band. Your screen should look like Figure 11.10.

To save the new report design, select Save This Report from the Layout pull-down menu. When dBASE displays the original file name, you can press ↵ to accept it, or you can enter a new name, thereby keeping the orginal report format as well. Select Abandon Changes and Exit from the Exit pull-down menu.

When you return to the Control Center, you must activate the appropriate index to sort the data into part-number order before you print the report.

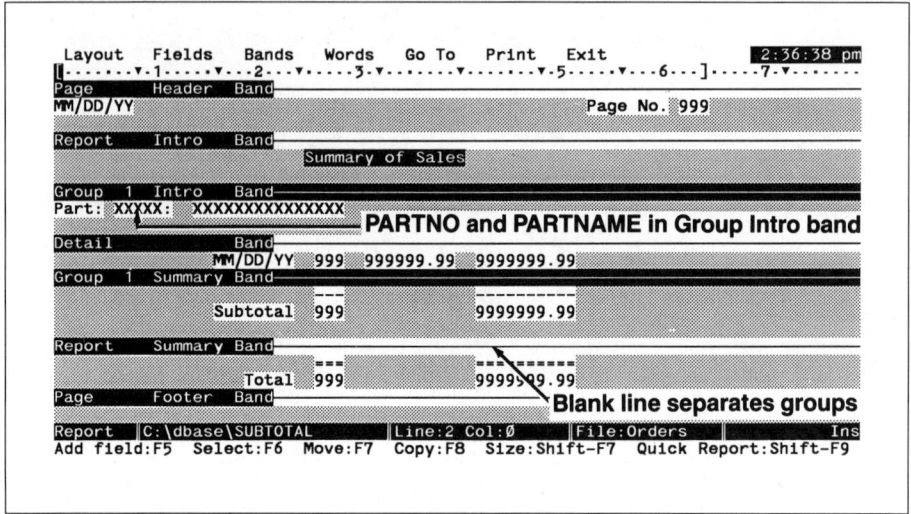

FIGURE 11.10: Report format with PARTNO and PARTNAME fields in the Group Intro band.

The index for the sort is PARTNO + PARTNAME, which you may have created if you followed the examples in Chapter 6. Figure 11.11 shows a printed copy of the new report.

Nesting Groups within Groups

You can *nest* group bands inside one another to produce groups within groups. For instance, suppose you place a group band for part numbers in a report format and then a group based on the DATE field within that group. You can then print a report that subtotals sales for particular part numbers and, for each part number, that subtotals sales by date.

Groups within groups require an index that matches the grouping. For example, if group 1 is based on the PARTNO field and group 2 is based on the DATE field, then the index expression needed is PARTNO + DATE. However, you cannot combine different data types in an index expression.

This problem is easily solved by using a dBASE IV type-conversion function in your index expression. Even though you cannot use the index expression PARTNO + DATE, you can use the DTOS( ) function to index on PARTNO + DTOS(DATE) to create the index that the report grouping requires.

Figure 11.12 shows a report format that prints records from the ORDERS database grouped by part number and by date within each part number. The

NESTING GROUPS WITHIN GROUPS — 369

```
07/08/90                                           Page No.   1

                         Summary of Sales

    Part: A-111: Astro Buddies

                06/01/90        2       50.00         100.00
                06/02/90        3       50.00         150.00
                06/05/90        4       50.00         200.00
                                -----                 ----------
                Subtotal:       9                     450.00

    Part: B-222: Banana Man

                06/01/90        2      100.00         200.00
                06/01/90        1      100.00         100.00
                06/15/90        1      100.00         100.00
                                -----                 ----------
                Subtotal:       4                     400.00

    Part: C-333: Cosmic Critters

                06/01/90        1      500.00         500.00
                06/15/90        2      500.00        1000.00
                06/15/90        1      500.00         500.00
                07/01/90        2      500.00        1000.00
                                -----                 ----------
                Subtotal:       6                    3000.00

                                =====                 ==========
                Grand total:   19                    3850.00
```

FIGURE 11.11: Report printed using the format in Figure 11.10. Notice that the part number and part name are printed only once at the top of each subtotal group and that a single blank line beneath each subtotal separates the groups.

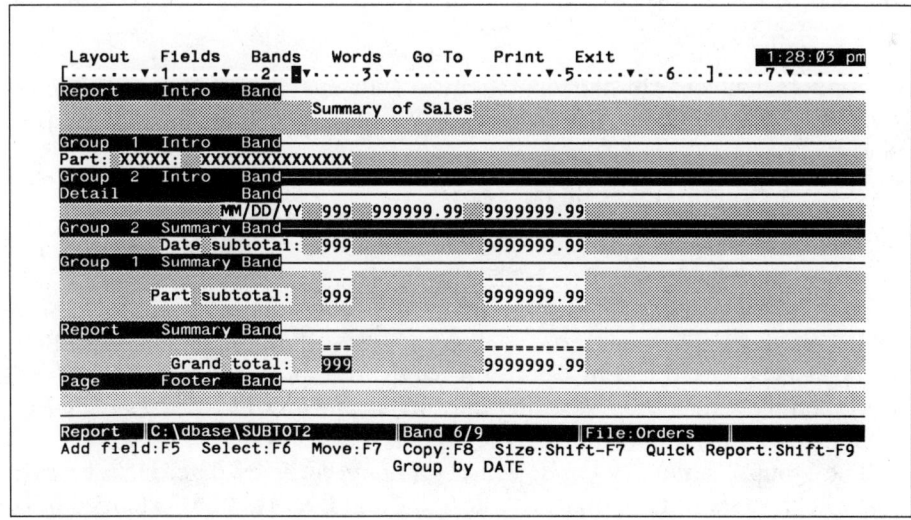

FIGURE 11.12: Report format to subtotal by date within parts.

group 2 summary band displays the subtotal for each date within each part number. The group 1 summary band prints a subtotal for each part number.

Before printing the report, you create an index with the expression PARTNO + DTOS(DATE), as shown in Figure 11.13. After activating the index, you can print the report. Figure 11.14 shows a sample printed report, using some hypothetical data to illustrate the subtotal groups.

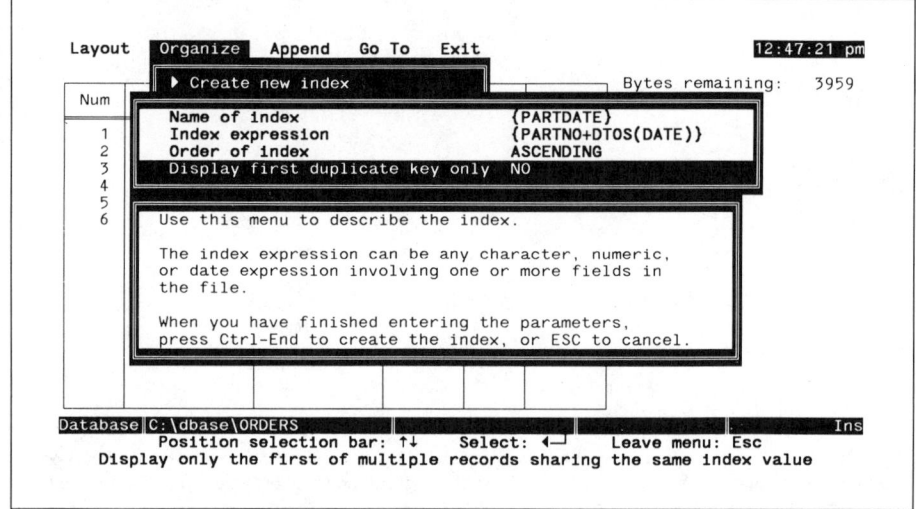

FIGURE 11.13: Index for report with part number and date subtotals, using the DTOS( ) function in the index expression to combine different data types.

Suppose that you want the report printed with part numbers in ascending sort order and dates in descending sort order. You need to change the index expression to

PARTNO + STR({12/31/1999} – DATE)

If you print the report with this modified index activated, the subtotals all will be displayed, but the dates will be in descending order, as shown in Figure 11.15.

As you can see in the figure, the outermost group, group 1, is based on the PARTNO field. The inner group, group 2, is based on the DATE field. Summary fields are used within the group bands to display subtotals. These were placed on the screen by positioning the cursor, pressing **F5**, and selecting Sum from the SUMMARY column of the options that appear.

The group 2 summary band, which groups records by date, includes summary fields to show the subtotals of the QTY and EXTPRICE (extended price)

```
                        Summary of Sales
      Part: A-111: Astro Buddies
                 06/01/90           2        50.00         100.00
                 06/01/90           4        50.00         200.00
                 06/01/90           2        50.00         100.00
                 06/01/90           4        50.00         200.00
                 06/01/90          10        50.00         500.00
             Date subtotal:        22                     1100.00
                 06/15/90           3        50.00         150.00
                 06/15/90           4        50.00         200.00
                 06/15/90           5        50.00         250.00
                 06/15/90           3        50.00         150.00
             Date subtotal:        19                      950.00
                                  ---                  ----------
             Part subtotal:        37                     1850.00

      Part: B-222: Banana Man
                 06/01/90           2       100.00         200.00
                 06/01/90           2       100.00         200.00
                 06/01/90           8       100.00         800.00
                 06/01/90          10       100.00        1000.00
                 06/01/90           1       100.00         100.00
             Date subtotal:        23                     2300.00
                 06/15/90           1       100.00         100.00
                 06/15/90           5       100.00         500.00
                 06/15/90           1       100.00         100.00
                 06/15/90           1       100.00         100.00
                 06/15/90           6       100.00         600.00
             Date subtotal:        14                     1400.00
                                  ---                  ----------
             Part subtotal:        37                     3700.00

      Part: C-333: Cosmic Critters
                 06/01/90           1       500.00         500.00
                 06/01/90           2       500.00        1000.00
                 06/01/90           1       500.00         500.00
                 06/01/90           1       500.00         500.00
                 06/01/90           2       500.00        1000.00
                 06/01/90           1       500.00         500.00
                 06/01/90           3       500.00        1500.00
             Date subtotal:        11                     5500.00
                 06/15/90           2       500.00        1000.00
                 06/15/90           6       500.00        3000.00
                 06/15/90           4       500.00        2000.00
                 06/15/90           8       500.00        4000.00
                 06/15/90           2       500.00        1000.00
                 06/15/90           1       500.00         500.00
             Date subtotal:        23                    11000.00
                                  ---                  ----------
             Part subtotal:        34                    16500.00

                                  ===                  ==========
               Grand total:       108                    22050.00
```

FIGURE 11.14: Printed report with records grouped by part number and date.

fields. While placing these fields on the report, the Reset Every option was set to the DATE field to ensure that the subtotals were reset to zero as soon as a new date was encountered in the DATE field.

```
                    Summary of Sales

   Part: A-111: Astro Buddies
              06/15/90         3       50.00         150.00
              06/15/90         4       50.00         200.00
              06/15/90         5       50.00         250.00
              06/15/90         3       50.00         150.00
         Date subtotal:       19                     950.00
              06/01/90         2       50.00         100.00
              06/01/90         4       50.00         200.00
              06/01/90         2       50.00         100.00
              06/01/90         4       50.00         200.00
              06/01/90        10       50.00         500.00
         Date subtotal:       22                    1100.00
                              ---                 ----------
         Part subtotal:       37                    1850.00

   Part: B-222: Banana Man
              06/15/90         1      100.00         100.00
              06/15/90         5      100.00         500.00
              06/15/90         1      100.00         100.00
              06/15/90         1      100.00         100.00
              06/15/90         6      100.00         600.00
         Date subtotal:       14                    1400.00
              06/01/90         2      100.00         200.00
              06/01/90         2      100.00         200.00
              06/01/90         8      100.00         800.00
              06/01/90        10      100.00        1000.00
              06/01/90         1      100.00         100.00
         Date subtotal:       23                    2300.00
                              ---                 ----------
         Part subtotal:       37                    3700.00

   Part: C-333: Cosmic Critters
              06/15/90         2      500.00        1000.00
              06/15/90         6      500.00        3000.00
              06/15/90         4      500.00        2000.00
              06/15/90         8      500.00        4000.00
              06/15/90         2      500.00        1000.00
              06/15/90         1      500.00         500.00
         Date subtotal:       23                   11000.00
              06/01/90         1      500.00         500.00
              06/01/90         2      500.00        1000.00
              06/01/90         1      500.00         500.00
              06/01/90         1      500.00         500.00
              06/01/90         2      500.00        1000.00
              06/01/90         1      500.00         500.00
              06/01/90         3      500.00        1500.00
         Date subtotal:       11                    5500.00
                              ---                 ----------
         Part subtotal:       34                   16500.00

                              ===                 ==========
         Grand total:        108                   22050.00
```

FIGURE 11.15: Report with records grouped by part number and date, with parts in ascending order and dates in descending order.

The group 1 summary band, which is based on the PARTNO field, also contains summary fields for the QTY and EXTPRICE fields. However, the Reset Every option for these summary fields is set to PARTNO, because the subtotals displayed by these fields need to be reset to zero when a new part number is encountered in the PARTNO field.

The number of group bands that you can place in a report format is unlimited. Just be certain to use the appropriate index expression to print the report. For example, suppose you have a database that includes fields named SALESREP, PARTNUMBER, DATE, QTY, and UNITPRICE, and you want to print a report with subtotals by sales representative, by date within each sales representative, and by part number within each date. Furthermore, you want records displayed in descending order by quantity within each date.

In the report format, SALESREP would be the group 1 field, DATE would be the group 2 field, PARTNUMBER would be the group 3 field, and QTY would be the group 4 field.

To create the sort order required to print the report, the order of the fields in the index must match the order of the group band fields: SALESREP, DATE, PARTNUMBER, and QTY. DATE is a date field and QTY is a numeric field, so you need to use type-conversion functions to convert their data types.

Also, because you want the QTY field displayed in descending order, you need to subtract the quantities from some large constant. The actual index expression (entered at the database design screen) used to print the report is

SALESREP + DTOS(DATE) + PARTNUMBER + STR(9999 – QTY)

HIDING DUPLICATE RECORDS

SEQUENCE OF STEPS

From the Control Center:

> highlight the database name in the Data panel
> Design (**Shift-F2**)
> Create New Index   *or*   Modify Existing Index
> enter or select an index name
> Display First Duplicate Key Only
> press the space bar to select Yes
> **Ctrl-End**

USAGE

A feature that you may find useful for managing groups of data is dBASE IV's ability to hide duplicate records—that is, records with the same value in a given field. Instead of grouping such records together, you may sometimes want to work with only one of several records that match your index key. For example, suppose you have a database named EMPLOYEE.DBF that contains personnel data for employees in your company, and you want to print only one memo for each department. The memos will be addressed to the departments, not to particular individuals. Figure 11.16 shows a portion of such a database, with existing data displayed on the browse screen.

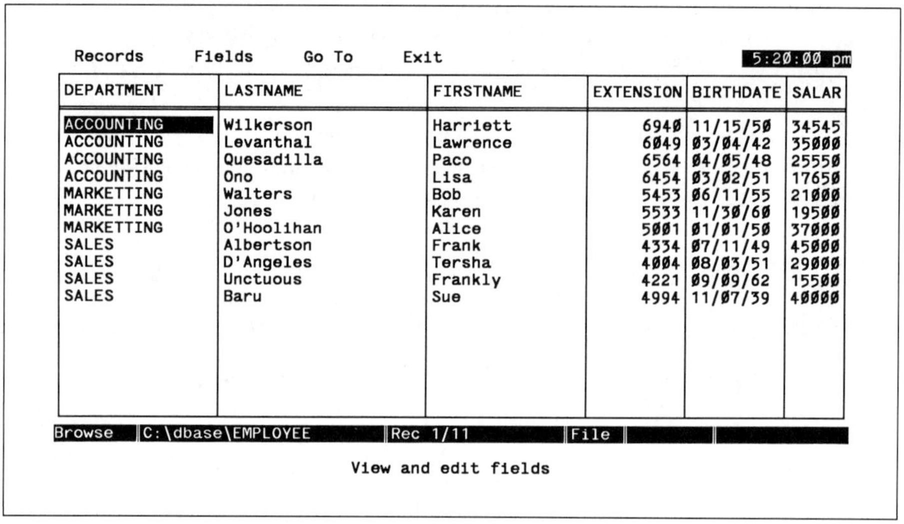

```
 Records     Fields    Go To    Exit                       5:20:00 pm
┌────────────┬────────────┬────────────┬─────────┬─────────┬──────┐
│DEPARTMENT  │LASTNAME    │FIRSTNAME   │EXTENSION│BIRTHDATE│SALAR │
├────────────┼────────────┼────────────┼─────────┼─────────┼──────┤
│ACCOUNTING  │Wilkerson   │Harriett    │  6940   │11/15/50 │34545 │
│ACCOUNTING  │Levanthal   │Lawrence    │  6049   │03/04/42 │35000 │
│ACCOUNTING  │Quesadilla  │Paco        │  6564   │04/05/48 │25550 │
│ACCOUNTING  │Ono         │Lisa        │  6454   │03/02/51 │17650 │
│MARKETING   │Walters     │Bob         │  5453   │06/11/55 │21000 │
│MARKETING   │Jones       │Karen       │  5533   │11/30/60 │19500 │
│MARKETING   │O'Hoolihan  │Alice       │  5001   │01/01/50 │37000 │
│SALES       │Albertson   │Frank       │  4334   │07/11/49 │45000 │
│SALES       │D'Angeles   │Tersha      │  4004   │08/03/51 │29000 │
│SALES       │Unctuous    │Frankly     │  4221   │09/09/62 │15500 │
│SALES       │Baru        │Sue         │  4994   │11/07/39 │40000 │
└────────────┴────────────┴────────────┴─────────┴─────────┴──────┘
Browse │C:\dbase\EMPLOYEE    │Rec 1/11    │File│
                        View and edit fields
```

FIGURE 11.16: EMPLOYEE database on the browse screen.

EXAMPLE

Assume that you have a database like EMPLOYEE, and you want to print one memo for each department. You first need to create an index that displays each department only once. The index expression is the DEPARTMENT field name. To ensure that the index displays only unique department names, set the Display First Duplicate Key Only option to Yes, as shown in Figure 11.17.

Press Data (**F2**) to view the database while the index is active. You will see only one record per department, as in Figure 11.18. All other database records remain hidden until you return to the database design screen and select a different index from the Organize menu, select a different database, or exit dBASE IV.

To print a memo for each unique department, select the Mailmerge option from the Quick Layouts submenu on the reports design screen. This lets you access the word-wrap editor (as discussed in Chapter 7).

HIDING DUPLICATE RECORDS — 375

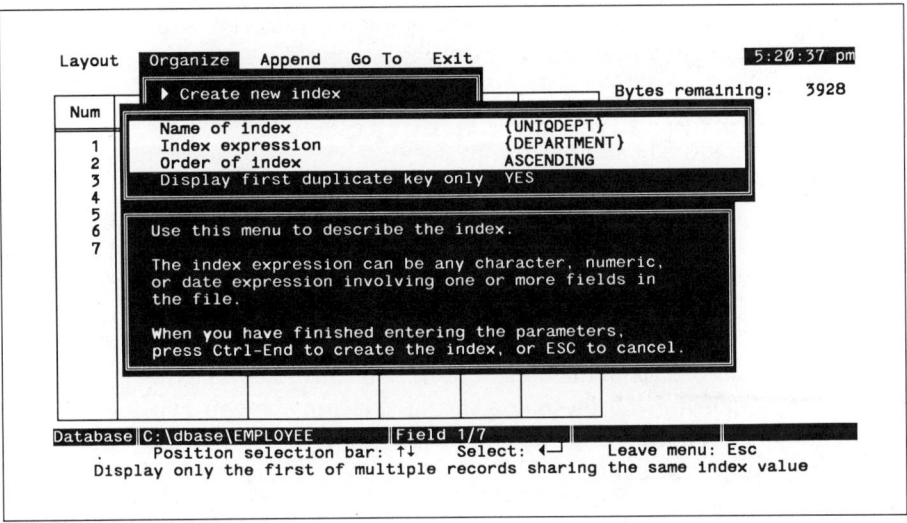

FIGURE 11.17: Index for displaying unique department names. To hide duplicate records, set the Display First Duplicate Key Only option to Yes.

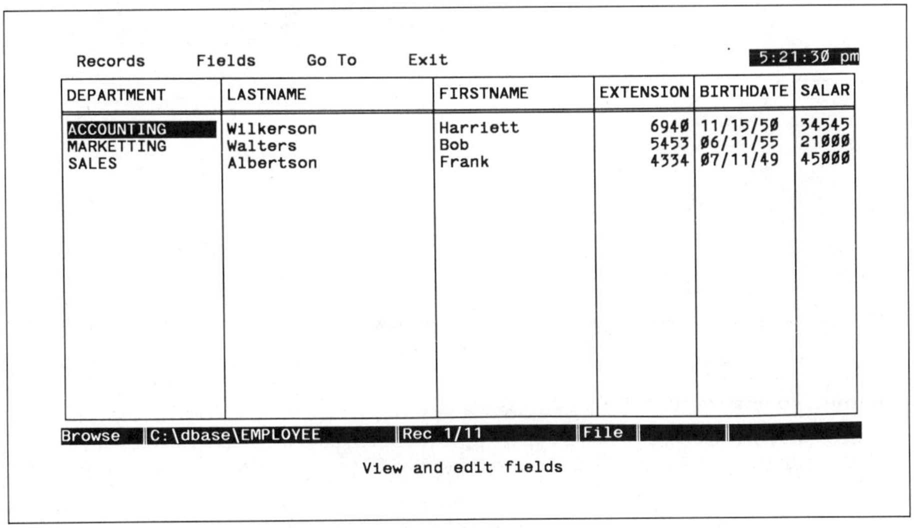

FIGURE 11.18: Unique departments in the EMPLOYEE database.

Use Field (**F5**) to place the DEPARTMENT field from the EMPLOYEE database anywhere in the report format and then type the rest of your memo. Save your memo in the usual way, assigning a name to it when prompted. When you print, only one memo per department will be output (so long as the index of unique department names is in control).

GLOBAL EDITING WITH UPDATE QUERIES

With dBASE IV's *global editing* capability, you can change several records simultaneously. For example, for a sales order database, you can increase or decrease the unit price of all orders for part A-111 by 10 percent in a single operation. You can also add or subtract 30 days from shipping dates for part number C-333.

The tool for performing global editing is the *update query.* You use the usual query design screen and filter conditions for the query (see Chapter 5), but you specify an *update operator* in the file skeleton. You can either type the update operator directly beneath the file name in the skeleton, or you can select Specify Update Operation from the Update pull-down menu (as shown in Figure 11.19) and select from the menu.

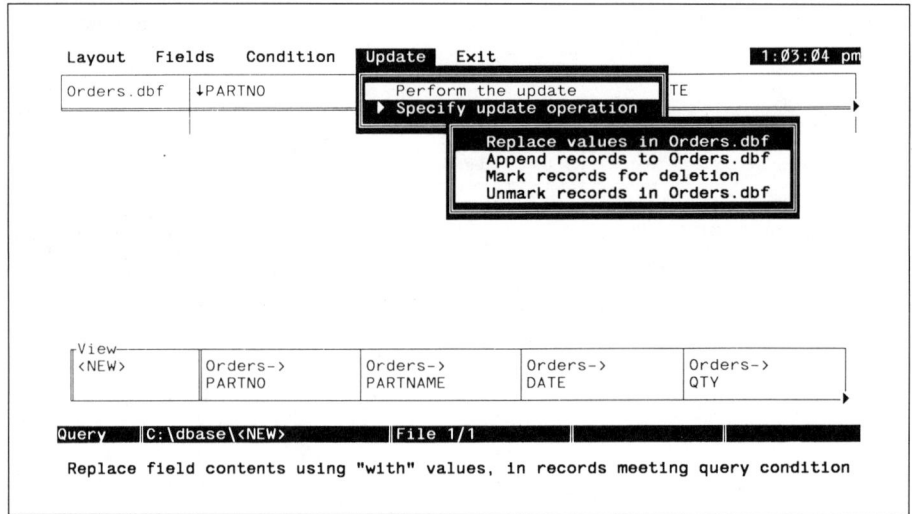

FIGURE 11.19: Menu of update operations for update queries. Selecting Replace Values in ORDERS.DBF achieves the same result as entering REPLACE under the file name in the file skeleton.

The REPLACE update operator replaces the contents of fields that meet the filter condition with some new value. You use the MARK and UNMARK update operators with filter conditions to mark records—for deletion or to hide them from display—and to unmark those records. The APPEND option, discussed later in this chapter, reads records from an external database into the current database.

Unlike other queries, where you can press Data (**F2**) to see the results, update queries require you to select Perform the Update from the Update pull-down menu on the query design screen.

Replacing Character Data

SEQUENCE OF STEPS

From the Control Center:
   To create a query:

      with the database open, highlight <create> in the Queries panel ⏎

   To isolate the data to be changed:

      enter a filter condition under the appropriate field in the file skeleton

   To test the filter:

      Data (**F2**)

   To return to the query design screen:

      Design (**Shift-F2**)

   To replace data:

      enter **REPLACE** under the file name in the file skeleton
      Proceed [⏎]
      enter **WITH** and the replacement character string (in quotation marks) under the field name in the file skeleton
      Menus (**F10**)
      Update/**P**erform the Update [⏎]

   To view the replacement:

      press any key
      Menus (**F10**)
      Exit/**A**bandon Changes and Exit [⏎]
      Yes [⏎]
      Data (**F2**)

USAGE

You can use an update query to make global changes in a database, replacing one character string with another. First create a regular query to isolate the data to be changed. After entering the appropriate filter condition, press Data (**F2**) to view the filtered records on the browse screen. Make sure that only the records that you want to change are displayed.

This step may seem superfluous, but when performing update queries, it is highly recommended that you test your filter condition. Otherwise, you might inadvertently change the wrong records.

For example, suppose you created an update query to change the part name Banana Man to Mondo Man and forgot to include the filter condition that would limit changes to only those records with the appropriate part number. dBASE would not filter out other part numbers from the query. Hence, the update query would change *all* part names in the database to Mondo Man, and there would be no easy way to undo the erroneous (and extensive) change.

In this example, the filter condition is not complex, so you can easily be sure that the appropriate records are displayed. But when you start using REPLACE operators with complex filter conditions, you will find that making a mistake is easy.

If the appropriate records are not displayed, be sure to adjust the filter condition accordingly. Switch back to the query design screen by pressing Design (**Shift-F2**), modify the filter condition, and test the condition again by pressing Data (**F2**). Repeat this procedure until the browse screen displays only the records that you want to change.

To change your basic query into an update query, press Design (**Shift-F2**) to return to the query design screen. Press **Shift-Tab** to move the highlight to the space beneath the database name in the file. Type the update operator **REPLACE** and press ↵, or select Replace Values in *filename*.DBF from the Specify Update Operation submenu of the Update pull-down menu, where *filename* is the currently selected database.

When dBASE tells you that it will delete the view skeleton, select Proceed. You do not need the view skeleton because it is used to display data, and update queries do not *display* data—they *change* it.

Tab to the field where you want to replace data. Type **WITH** and the new character string in the highlighted area. Be sure to enter quotation marks on each side of the character string. Press ↵.

Now you are ready to actually execute the update query. Press Menus (**F10**) to access the pull-down menus. Use ← or → to display the Update pull-down menu. Select Perform the Update from the Update pull-down menu. dBASE will take a few seconds to make the change. Update queries do not show any immediate results—you need to return to the browse screen to see what happened.

You need not save this update query, because its job is done. When prompted, press any key to continue. Select Abandon Changes and Exit from the Exit pull-down menu and select Yes to confirm abandoning the query. You will be back at the Control Center, where you can highlight the database name in the Data panel and press Data (**F2**). The browse screen will display the replaced data. The change is complete and permanent. To return to the Control Center, select Exit from the Exit pull-down menu.

EXAMPLE

This example uses the ORDERS database (its structure and data are shown in Chapter 4). Suppose that product number B-222, Banana Man, is not doing well in the marketplace. A corporate decision is made to change the product's name to Mondo Man. Your job is to change all references to Banana Man in the ORDERS database to Mondo Man. You can use an update query to change all the records without retyping them.

Open the ORDERS database by selecting ORDERS from the Data panel in the Control Center and Use File from the submenu. Highlight <create> in the Queries panel and press ←┘.

To limit the update operation to part number B-222, enter the filter condition **"B-222"** (including the quotation marks, because the part number is a character field) under the PARTNO field name in the file skeleton, as shown in Figure 11.20.

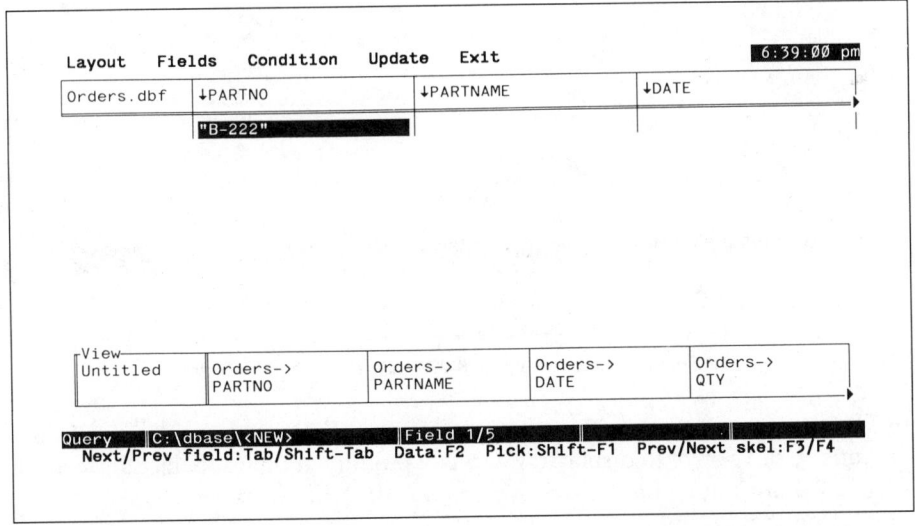

FIGURE 11.20: Filter condition for part number B-222. You must filter the database for the records you want to change before you enter the replacement character string.

CH. 11 MANAGING GROUPS OF RECORDS

Press Data (**F2**) to make sure you have isolated the appropriate records. The browse screen should show only records with part number B-222 in the PARTNO field.

To change your basic query into an update query, press Design (**Shift-F2**) to return to the query design screen. Press **Shift-Tab** to move the highlight to the space beneath the database name in the file. Type the update operator **REPLACE** and press ↵ (or select Replace Values in ORDERS.DBF from the Specify Update Operation submenu of the Update pull-down menu).

When dBASE tells you that it will delete the view skeleton, select Proceed. Move the highlight to the PARTNAME field. Type **WITH "Mondo Man"** (including the quotation marks) in the highlighted area and press ↵.

Your query should now look like Figure 11.21. Notice that the query is quite descriptive. The word *Target* above the file name tells which database file is about to be changed (ORDERS.DBF in this case). The filter condition specifies records with B-222 in the PARTNO field. The update operation is to replace PARTNAME with Mondo Man.

```
 Layout    Fields    Condition    Update    Exit                    6:42:11 pm
─Target──────────────────────────────────────────────────────────────────────
 Orders.dbf │ PARTNO      │ PARTNAME          │ DATE        │
            │             │                   │             │
            │ "B-222"     │ WITH "Mondo Man"  │             │
 REPLACE    │             │                   │             │




 Query  │ C:\dbase\<NEW>   │ Field 2/5 │              │              │
  Next/Prev field:Tab/Shift-Tab  Data:F2  Pick:Shift-F1  Prev/Next skel:F3/F4
```

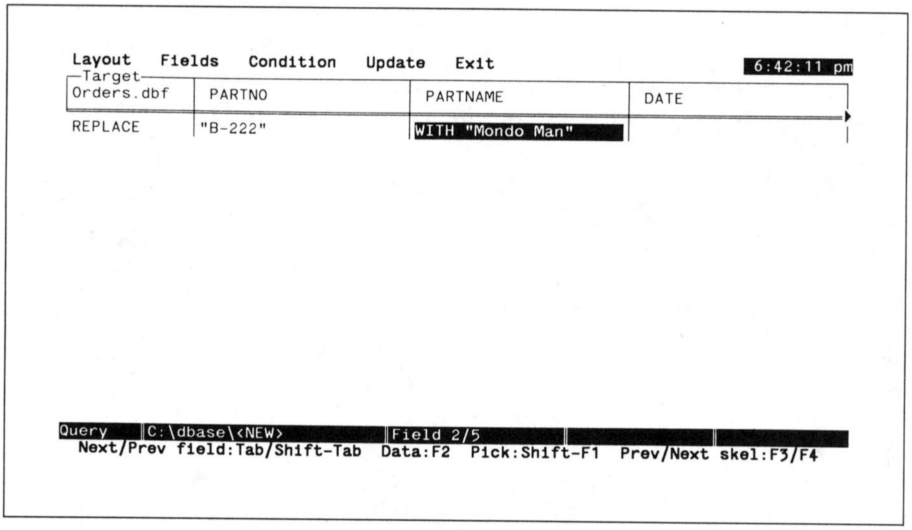

FIGURE 11.21: Query to replace the part number B-222 part name with Mondo Man.

To execute the update query, press Menus (**F10**) to access the pull-down menus. Use ← or → to display the Update pull-down menu. Select Perform the Update from the Update pull-down menu. dBASE will take a few seconds to make the change.

You do not need to save this query because its job is done. When prompted, press any key to continue. Select Abandon Changes and Exit from the Exit pull-down menu. Select Yes to confirm abandoning the query. dBASE returns you to the Control Center, where you can highlight ORDERS in the Data panel and press Data (**F2**).

On the browse screen (as Figure 11.22 shows) you will see that all part names for records with part number B-222 have been changed to Mondo Man. The change is complete and permanent. To return to the Control Center, select Exit from the Exit pull-down menu.

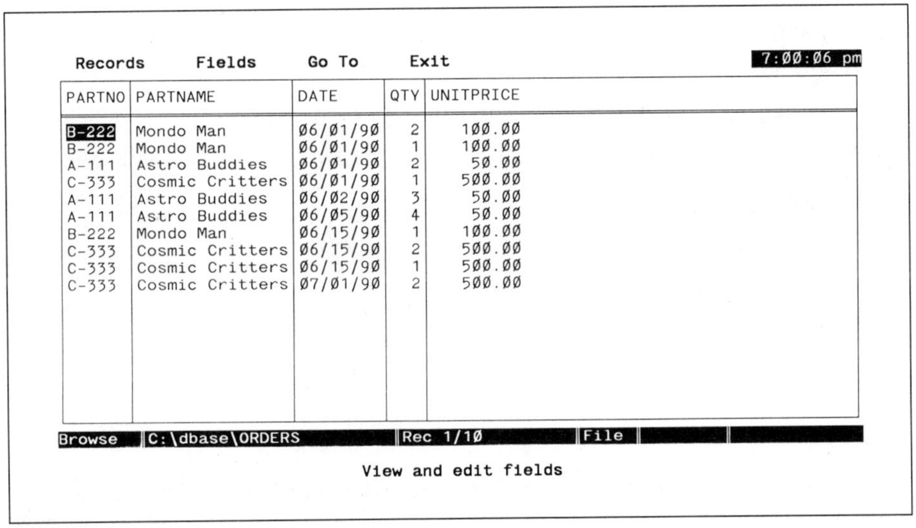

```
   Records     Fields      Go To      Exit                    7:00:06 pm
  PARTNO PARTNAME         DATE     QTY UNITPRICE
  B-222  Mondo Man        06/01/90  2    100.00
  B-222  Mondo Man        06/01/90  1    100.00
  A-111  Astro Buddies    06/01/90  2     50.00
  C-333  Cosmic Critters  06/01/90  1    500.00
  A-111  Astro Buddies    06/02/90  3     50.00
  A-111  Astro Buddies    06/05/90  4     50.00
  B-222  Mondo Man        06/15/90  1    100.00
  C-333  Cosmic Critters  06/15/90  2    500.00
  C-333  Cosmic Critters  06/15/90  1    500.00
  C-333  Cosmic Critters  07/01/90  2    500.00

  Browse  C:\dbase\ORDERS      Rec 1/10     File
                    View and edit fields
```

FIGURE 11.22: Results of the update query for character data displayed on the browse screen. Banana Man has been changed to Mondo Man.

Changing Numeric Data

SEQUENCE OF STEPS

From the Control Center:
  To create a query:

  with the database open, highlight <create> in the Queries panel ⏎

  To isolate the data to be changed:

  enter a filter condition under the appropriate field in the file skeleton

To test the filter:

   Data (**F2**)

To return to the query design screen:

   Design (**Shift-F2**)

To replace data:

   enter **REPLACE** under the file name in the file skeleton

   Proceed [←]

   enter **WITH** and the replacement expression under the field name in the file skeleton

   Menus (**F10**)

   Update/**P**erform the Update [←]

To view the replacement:

   press any key

   Menus (**F10**)

   Exit/**A**bandon Changes and Exit [←]

   Yes [←]

   Data (**F2**)

USAGE

You can use update queries to change numeric data in the database globally. For example, suppose that the price of Astro Buddies (part number A-111) is increased by 10 percent on June 1, 1990. Your job is to add 10 percent to any orders for Astro Buddies that come in after June 1. To perform this task, you need to isolate records that have order dates later than 06/01/90 in the Date field *and* that have part number A-111 in the PARTNO field. For this task, you use a regular query with filter conditions. You then need to increase the UNITPRICE value by 10 percent for those records. For this task, you use the REPLACE update operator.

If the field that you are changing in an update query is the same field that you are using for the filter condition, then enter the filter condition into the field first, test the basic query, and return to the query design screen. Then enter **WITH** and a replacement expression to the right of the filter condition, preceded by a comma.

For example, to add 30 days to the date 06/01/90 in the ORDERS database, first enter the filter condition **{06/01/90}** into the Date field on the query design

CHANGING NUMERIC DATA 383

screen. Press Data (**F2**) to test the query and then Design (**Shift-F2**) to return to the query. Then enter the REPLACE operator under the file name and the expression **,WITH Date + 30** next to the filter condition in the Date box, as shown in Figure 11.23.

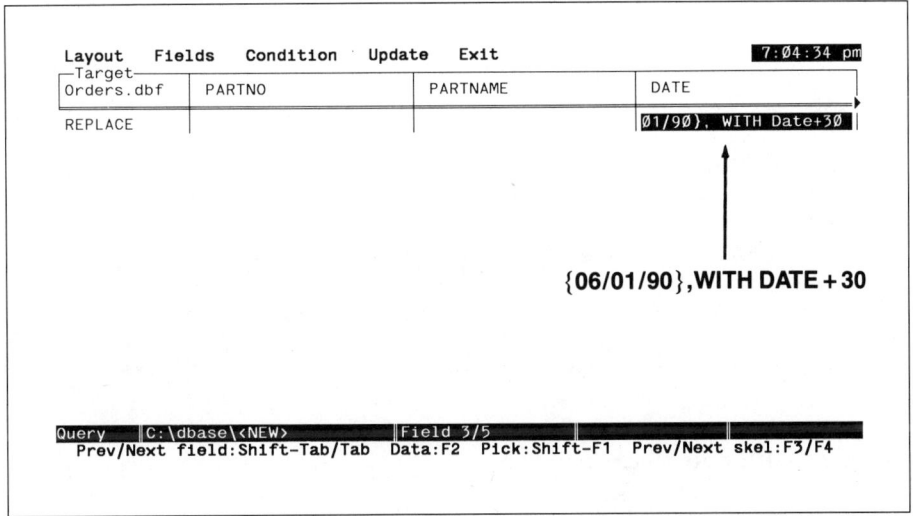

FIGURE 11.23: Filter condition and replacement value in one box, separated by a comma. Part of the filter condition is obscured in this figure.

EXAMPLE

Using the ORDERS database, you can globally increase the price of Astro Buddies by 10 percent for orders after June 1.

To begin, you need to set up the basic filter condition for the query as shown in Figure 11.24. Notice that the query isolates records that have A-111 in the PARTNO field *and* dates greater than 6/1/90 in the DATE field. Press Data (**F2**) to make sure that the filter conditions isolate the appropriate records. After testing the query, press Design (**Shift-F2**) to return to the query design screen.

Next you need to enter the REPLACE update operator under the file name in the query design screen file skeleton. Press **Home**, type the word **REPLACE**, and then press ←┘. Select Proceed when dBASE reminds you that the view skeleton will be removed.

Now tell dBASE to replace the current unit price with the current unit price plus 10 percent. Once again, you need to enter the keyword **WITH** to perform the replacement. In this case you are not just entering in a new value. Instead,

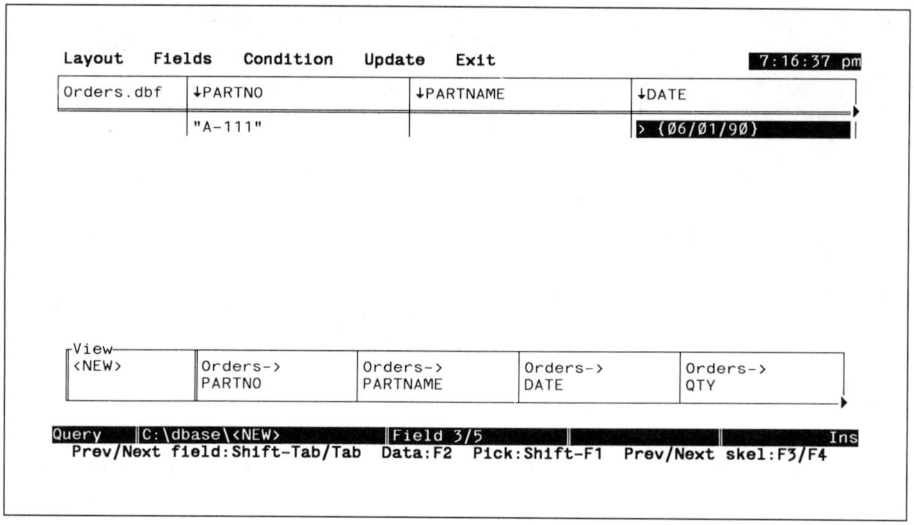

384 — CH. 11 MANAGING GROUPS OF RECORDS

```
 Layout   Fields   Condition   Update   Exit                        7:16:37 pm
┌──────────┬──────────────┬─────────────────┬────────────────────────────────┐
│Orders.dbf│↓PARTNO       │↓PARTNAME        │↓DATE                           │
│          │"A-111"       │                 │> {06/01/90}                    │
└──────────┴──────────────┴─────────────────┴────────────────────────────────┘

┌View────┬──────────┬──────────┬──────────┬──────────┐
│<NEW>   │Orders->  │Orders->  │Orders->  │Orders->  │
│        │PARTNO    │PARTNAME  │DATE      │QTY       │
└────────┴──────────┴──────────┴──────────┴──────────┘
Query    C:\dbase\<NEW>       Field 3/5                                    Ins
Prev/Next field:Shift-Tab/Tab  Data:F2  Pick:Shift-F1  Prev/Next skel:F3/F4
```

FIGURE 11.24: Query to isolate orders for part number A-111 that were placed after June 1.

you are increasing a value by 10 percent, so you want to multiply the current unit price by 1.10. Enter the expression

    WITH 1.10 * UNITPRICE

under the UNITPRICE field name, as shown in Figure 11.25.

Select Perform the Update from the Update pull-down menu to make the change. If you press Data (**F2**) to view the results, you will see that the appropriate unit prices have been increased by 10 percent, as Figure 11.26 shows.

Marking Records for Deletion

SEQUENCE OF STEPS

From the Control Center:
    To create a query:

        with the database open, highlight <create> in the Queries panel ↵

    To isolate the records to be marked for deletion:

        enter a filter condition under the appropriate fields in the file skeleton

    To test the filter:

        Data (**F2**)

MARKING RECORDS FOR DELETION — 385

To return to the query design screen:

Design (**Shift-F2**)

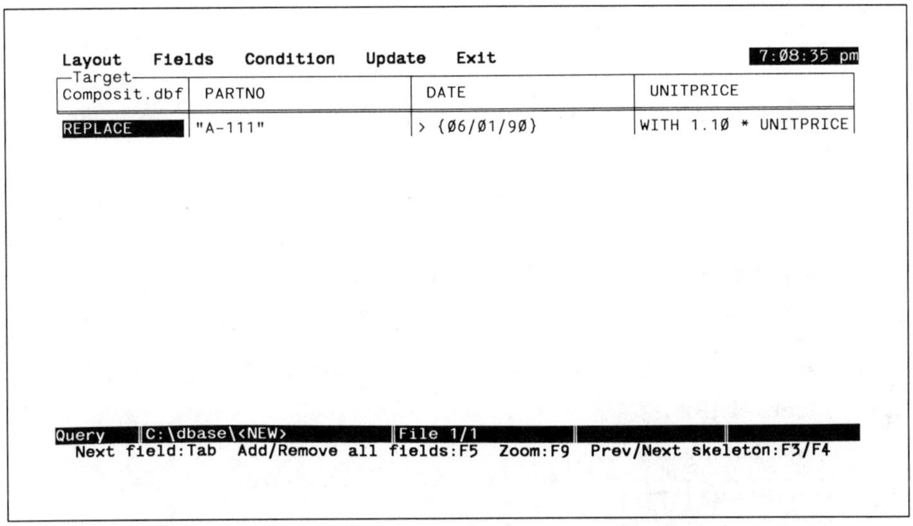

```
 Layout   Fields   Condition   Update   Exit                    7:08:35 pm
┌Target─────────┐
│Composit.dbf│ PARTNO         │ DATE          │ UNITPRICE            │
│ REPLACE    │ "A-111"        │ > {06/01/90}  │ WITH 1.10 * UNITPRICE│




 Query  │C:\dbase\<NEW>      │File 1/1
   Next field:Tab  Add/Remove all fields:F5  Zoom:F9  Prev/Next skeleton:F3/F4
```

FIGURE 11.25: Query to increase the price of orders for part number A-111 after 6/1/90 by 10 percent. Note that this figure is a composite; your screen cannot show the PARTNO, DATE, and UNITPRICE fields simultaneously.

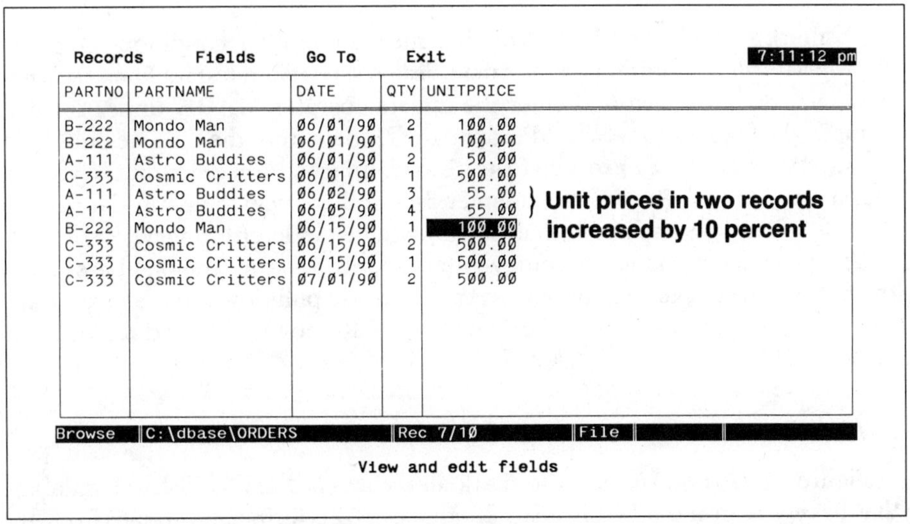

```
    Records    Fields    Go To    Exit                7:11:12 pm
   │PARTNO│PARTNAME      │DATE    │QTY│UNITPRICE│
    B-222  Mondo Man      06/01/90  2   100.00
    B-222  Mondo Man      06/01/90  1   100.00
    A-111  Astro Buddies  06/01/90  2    50.00
    C-333  Cosmic Critters 06/01/90  1   500.00
    A-111  Astro Buddies  06/02/90  3    55.00  ⎫ Unit prices in two records
    A-111  Astro Buddies  06/05/90  4    55.00  ⎬ increased by 10 percent
    B-222  Mondo Man      06/15/90  1   100.00  ⎭
    C-333  Cosmic Critters 06/15/90  2   500.00
    C-333  Cosmic Critters 06/15/90  1   500.00
    C-333  Cosmic Critters 07/01/90  2   500.00




 Browse │C:\dbase\ORDERS    │Rec 7/10      │File
                         View and edit fields
```

FIGURE 11.26: Results of the update query in Figure 11.25.

To mark records for deletion:

> enter **MARK** under the file name in the file skeleton
> Menus (**F10**)
> **U**pdate/**P**erform the Update [↵]

To view marked records:

> press any key
> Menus (**F10**)
> **E**xit/**A**bandon Changes and Exit [↵]
> **Y**es [↵]
> Data (**F2**)

To hide marked records:

> **Esc**
> Menus (**F10**)
> **T**ools/**S**ettings [↵]
> **D**eleted ON [↵]
> **Esc**
> **E**xit/**E**xit to Control Center [↵]

USAGE

To mark for deletion all records that meet some filter condition, enter the appropriate filter condition on the query design screen and test it. Then return to the query design screen and enter the update operator **MARK** under the field name in the file skeleton. Select Perform the Update from the Update pull-down menu. Press Data (**F2**) to view the records marked for deletion. If you set Deleted to On (as described in Chapter 3) and then view the data, the marked records will not be displayed; that is, they will be hidden from view.

You can also permanently remove marked records from the database, using the Erase Marked Records option on the Organize pull-down menu in the database design screen, as discussed in the section "Removing Deleted Records" in Chapter 3.

EXAMPLE

Figure 11.27 shows a query to mark all records in the CUSTLIST database that have CA in the STATE field. If you select Perform the Update from the

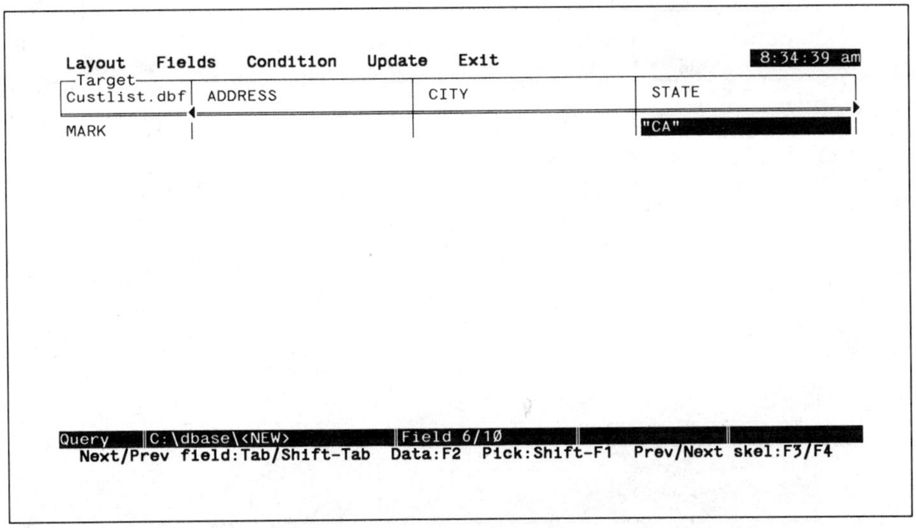

```
Layout    Fields   Condition   Update   Exit              8:34:39 am
─Target──
 Custlist.dbf│ ADDRESS        │ CITY          │ STATE         │
             ◄                                                       ►
              MARK                                            "CA"



Query    C:\dbase\<NEW>         Field 6/10
   Next/Prev field:Tab/Shift-Tab  Data:F2  Pick:Shift-F1  Prev/Next skel:F3/F4
```

FIGURE 11.27: Query to mark all records that have CA in the STATE field. Because this is an update query, it needs to be executed by selecting Perform the Update from the Update pull-down menu

Update pull-down menu after setting up the query shown in Figure 11.27 and then press Data (**F2**), you will still see California residents in the database.

However, as you scroll through the records, you will notice that all the records for California residents are marked for deletion. If you set Deleted to On and then view the data, the records for all California residents will be hidden, as in Figure 11.28.

Unmarking Marked Records

SEQUENCE OF STEPS

From the Control Center:
    To unmark certain records:

        with the database open, highlight <create> in the Queries panel ↵

    To isolate the records to be unmarked:

        enter a filter condition under the appropriate field in the file skeleton

    To test the filter:

        Data (**F2**)

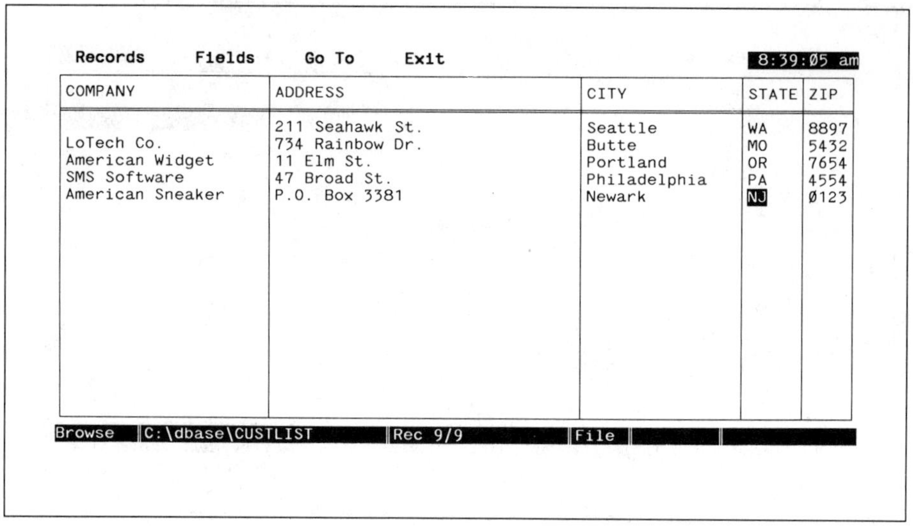

CH. 11 MANAGING GROUPS OF RECORDS

```
 Records     Fields      Go To     Exit                      8:39:05 am
 COMPANY          ADDRESS              CITY          STATE  ZIP

 LoTech Co.       211 Seahawk St.      Seattle       WA     8897
 American Widget  734 Rainbow Dr.      Butte         MO     5432
 American Widget  11 Elm St.           Portland      OR     7654
 SMS Software     47 Broad St.         Philadelphia  PA     4554
 American Sneaker P.O. Box 3381        Newark        NJ     0123




 Browse  │C:\dbase\CUSTLIST        │Rec 9/9    │File│
```

FIGURE 11.28: Records for California residents are hidden.

To return to the query design screen:

    Design (**Shift-F2**)

To unmark the filtered records:

    enter **UNMARK** under the file name in the file skeleton
    Menus (**F10**)
    Update/**P**erform the Update [↵]

To view the database:

press any key
Menus (**F10**)
Exit/**A**bandon Changes and Exit [↵]
Yes [↵]
Data (**F2**)

On the database design screen:
  To unmark all marked database records:

    Organize/**U**nmark All Records [↵]

USAGE

You can unmark some or all of the database records that are marked for deletion. Before you do, you should first make sure that the marked records are not hidden, because hidden records are hidden from all dBASE IV operations, including unmarking.

To ensure that no records are hidden, set the Deleted option on the Setting pull-down menu to Off. To make sure this option is off, starting from the Control Center, press **F10** and select Settings from the Tools pull-down menu. Move the highlight to the Deleted option and press the space bar until the option setting is Off. Then select Exit to Control Center from the Exit pull-down menu.

To unmark only certain records, you can use the Unmark update operator in the queries design screen. To unmark all database records, you can either use the query design screen with no filter conditions or the Unmark All Records option on the Organize pull-down menu on the database design screen, as shown in the examples that follow.

EXAMPLE

Suppose that you previously marked several groups of records in the CUSTLIST database for deletion, including those for California residents. Now you want to unmark the records for California residents. First, as discussed, make sure that the Deleted setting on Settings pull-down menu is set to Off, so that marked records are no longer hidden. Then, starting from the Control Center, make sure that the CUSTLIST database is open and select <create> from the Queries panel. When you get to the query design screen, enter the filter condition **"CA"** in the STATE field. Press **F10** and select Specify Update Operation from the Update pull-down menu. From the submenu, select Unmark Records in Custlist.dbf.

Select Proceed when prompted, and you will see the Unmark operator in the first column of the file skeleton, as in Figure 11.29. Then, to execute the query so that the records are unmarked, press **F10** and select Perform the Update from the Update pull-down menu.

When updating is finished, you will be prompted to press any key to return to the query design screen. After pressing any key, you can press **F2** to switch to the browse screen and view the results of the update. (The highlight on the browse screen will be positioned beneath the last record. Press **PgUp** to move up through the records.)

Suppose that, rather than unmarking records only of California residents, you want to unmark all marked records in the database. Again, if you are not sure whether any records currently are hidden, check the Deleted setting on the Settings pull-down menu and set it to Off if it is set to On.

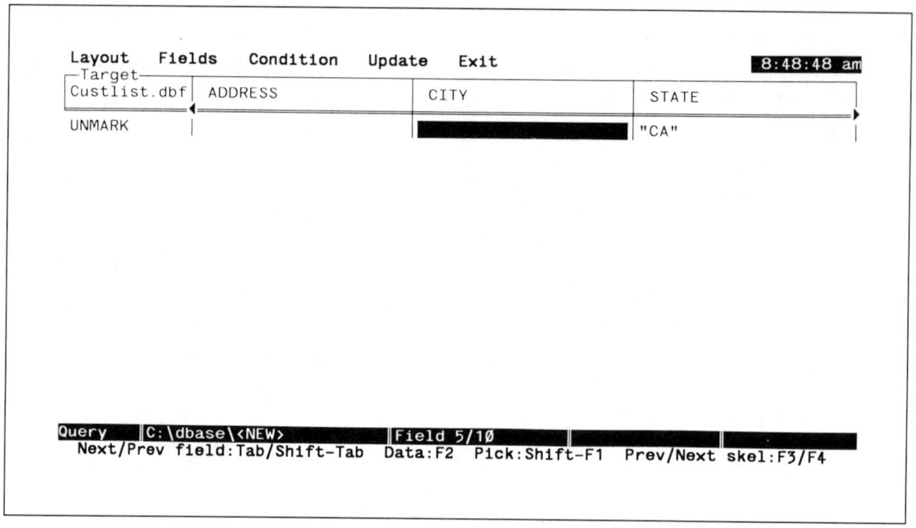

```
Layout   Fields   Condition   Update   Exit              8:48:48 am
┌Target─────────┬─────────────┬──────────────┬──────────────────┐
│Custlist.dbf│ ADDRESS     │ CITY         │ STATE            │
│            │             │              │                  │
│ UNMARK     │             │ ██████████   │ "CA"             │
└────────────┴─────────────┴──────────────┴──────────────────┘




Query  C:\dbase\<NEW>        Field 5/10
Next/Prev field:Tab/Shift-Tab  Data:F2  Pick:Shift-F1  Prev/Next skel:F3/F4
```

FIGURE 11.29: A sample update query to unmark records that have CA in the STATE field. After creating an update query, you must select Perform the Update from the Update pull-down menu to execute the update.

Next you can perform the basic operation just discussed to create and perform an update query, but without using any filter conditions. Alternatively, you can use the database design screen.

First highlight CUSTLIST in the Data panel in the Control Center and press Design (**Shift-F2**). Then select Unmark All Records from the Organize pull-down menu. When dBASE IV asks for permission to unmark, select Yes to proceed with the unmarking. When the unmarking is done, press **Ctrl-End**, or select Save Changes and Exit from the Exit pull-down menu, to return to the Control Center.

Appending Groups of Records

SEQUENCE OF STEPS

From the Control Center:

> with the database to receive records open, highlight <create> in the Queries panel
>
> ↵
>
> **F10**

APPENDING GROUPS OF RECORDS — 391

    Update/**S**pecify Update Operation [←]
    Append Records to *filename*.DBF
    Proceed
    F10
    Layout/**A**dd File to Query [←]
    select the name of the file to append records from

To limit appended records to those that match a filter condition:

    enter filter conditions in the bottom file skeleton

To specify fields to copy:

    enter examples (placeholders) in the bottom file skeleton
    F3
    enter examples (placeholders) in the top file skeleton

To perform the operation

    F10
    Update/**P**erform the Update [←]

USAGE

The Append update operation lets you copy some or all records from one database file to the bottom of another database file. The database receiving the records is referred to as the *target*, and the database containing the records you want to copy is referred to as the *source*.

File skeletons for both the target and source databases must be on the query design screen. If you want to limit the append operation to certain records in the source database, enter filter conditions in its file skeleton.

To specify the fields to copy, enter examples (placeholders) in both file skeletons. You can also use expressions to modify the data as it is copied. If the data type of the field in the target database does not match the data type of the corresponding field in the source database, you must use a type conversion function in the target file skeleton to convert the data type.

For example, suppose you want to append records from a database named JOESCUST to a database named MYCUST. The JOESCUST database specifies zip codes as numeric data, whereas the MYCUST database stores zip codes as character data. To convert the numeric zip codes to character data during the Append operation, the ZIP field in the MYCUST file skeleton needs to include an expression like **STR(ZIP)**.

EXAMPLE

Suppose you have a database of phone numbers, named PHONES, that contains only two fields: NAME and PHONE. Both fields are the character data type. You also have another database named CUSTLIST, which includes several fields, including LASTNAME, FIRSTNAME, and PHONE. You want to copy the names and phone numbers for all California residents from the CUSTLIST database into the PHONES database.

Your first step is to open the PHONES database by highlighting its name in the Data panel, pressing ←┘, and selecting Use File. Then you need to select <create> from the Queries panel to get to the query design screen.

Next, since you want to perform an Append operation, press F10 and select Specify Update Operation. From the submenu, select Append Records to Phone.dbf. When the screen asks for permission to remove the view skeleton, select Proceed. You will see the word *append* appear in the first column of the file skeleton and the word *Target* appear above the file name (because this is the database that will receive incoming records).

Your next step is to bring a file skeleton for the source database to the design screen. To do so, press **F10**, select Add File to Query from the Layout pull-down men, and select the name of the source database, CUSTLIST.DBF in this example, from the list of file names that appears.

If you want to limit the records appended from CUSTLIST, enter filter conditions into its file skeleton. For example, to append only CUSTLIST records with CA in the STATE field, enter the filter condition **"CA"** (including the quotation marks) in the STATE field box of the CUSTLIST file skeleton.

Now place an example (placeholder) in each field of the source file skeleton that you want to copy to the target. The placeholder can be the same as the field name, or it can be any arbitrary word (so long as it begins with a letter and does not contain any blanks).

For example, if you want to copy data from the LASTNAME, FIRSTNAME, and PHONE fields into the target database, you can place the examples **LName** in the LASTNAME field, **FName** in the FIRSTNAME field, and **PNumber** in the PHONE field.

Now you need to enter the same placeholders in the appropriate fields of the target database. In this example, however, the target has only a single field for storing names, so you need to use an expression to join the data from the LASTNAME and FIRSTNAME fields in CUSTLIST into a single field in PHONES.

For this example, enter the expression

TRIM(LName) + ", " + FName

into the NAME field of the PHONES file skeleton. This tells dBASE to store the LASTNAME with blanks trimmed off, followed by a comma and a blank, followed by a first name, in the NAME field. (Note that the formula uses the placeholders, rather than the field names.)

You also need to enter the PNumber placeholder in the PHONE field for the PHONES file skeleton, so that dBASE will know to copy that field as well. Figure 11.30 shows the completed update query. You can see the "CA" filter condition and the PNumber placeholder in the bottom query. The LASTNAME and FIRSTNAME fields are scrolled off the screen, but these contain the placeholders LName and FName.

```
 Layout    Fields    Condition    Update    Exit              7:42:47 pm
 ┌Target─┐
 │Phones.dbf│ NAME                    │ PHONE                │
 │       │                         │                      │
 │Append │ TRIM(LName)+", "+FNam   │ PNumber              │

 │Custlist.dbf│ STATE      │ ZIP        │ PHONE                │
 │            │ "CA"       │            │ PNumber              │




 Query   C:\dbase\<NEW>         Field 7/10
      Prev/Next field:Shift-Tab/Tab   Data:F2   Pick:Shift-F1   Prev/Next skel:F3/F4
```

FIGURE 11.30: An update query to append records from the CUSTLIST database to the PHONES database. The expression in the NAME box is cut off. It reads **TRIM(LNAME) + ", " + FName**. The LASTNAME and FIRSTNAME fields in the bottom skeleton (currently scrolled off the screen) contain the examples LName and FName, respectively.

After completing the query, press **F10** and select Perform the Update to execute the update query. When the operation is done, you will be prompted to press any key to continue. After pressing any key, you can press **F2** to view the contents of the target database.

Figure 11.31 shows the contents of the PHONE.DBF database (which was previously empty) after records were appended from CUSTLIST.DBF. Notice the format of the data in the NAME field: Each last name is separated from the first name by a comma and a single blank space.

394 — CH. 11 MANAGING GROUPS OF RECORDS

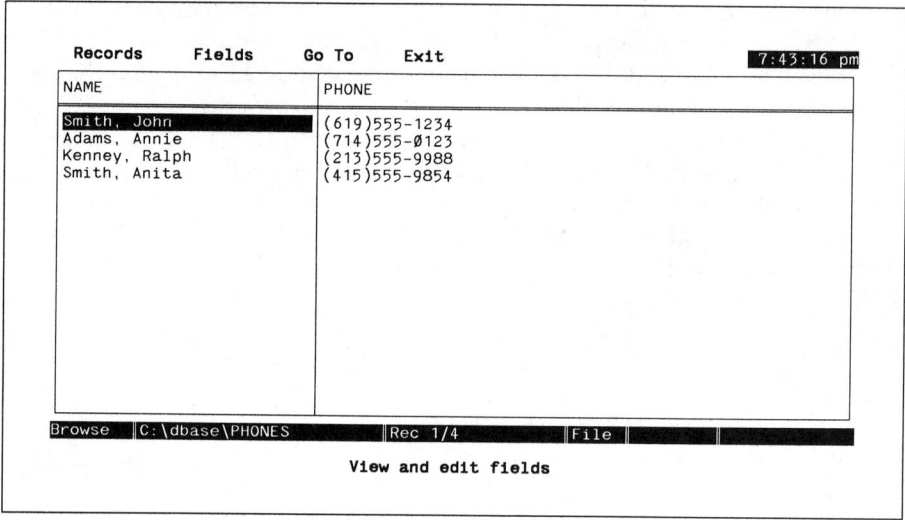

FIGURE 11.31: Contents of the PHONES database, which was previously empty, after appending records from the CUSTLIST database. The LASTNAME and FIRSTNAME fields from the CUSTLIST database are combined into a single field named NAMED.

Note that even if the PHONES database had not been empty before the Append operation, the operation would still have been successful. The new records would simply have been placed beneath the existing records in PHONES.

The records appended from the CUSTLIST database are still in the CUSTLIST database. The Append update operator simply copies records from the source to the target; it does not change the source database in any way.

TIPS AND TRAPS

- When executing update queries on your own important data, take the extra precaution of backing up your original database before making global changes. Chapter 14 tells you how to make backup copies.
- Whenever you execute an update query, *always* enter the filter condition first and test that filter condition by pressing Data (**F2**). Scroll through the browse screen and make sure that it displays *only* the records that you want to change.
- Use Zoom (**F9**) as a toggle on the query design screen to zoom into and out of the current box.

SUMMARY

This chapter discussed report groups and update queries. With these features of dBASE IV, you can isolate groups of records to delete or hide them and to create reports to make global changes (updates).

For more about deleting records:

- Chapter 3, "Adding, Changing, and Deleting Data"

For more about indexing:

- Chapter 4, "Sorting the Database"

For examples of report grouping used to create subtotaled reports:

- Chapter 5, "Searching the Database"

For more about report formats:

- Chapter 6, "Performing Calculations"

For more about using queries and filter conditions:

- Chapter 7, "Designing Formatted Reports"

For more about sorting before printing reports:

- Chapter 9, "Printing Reports and Labels"

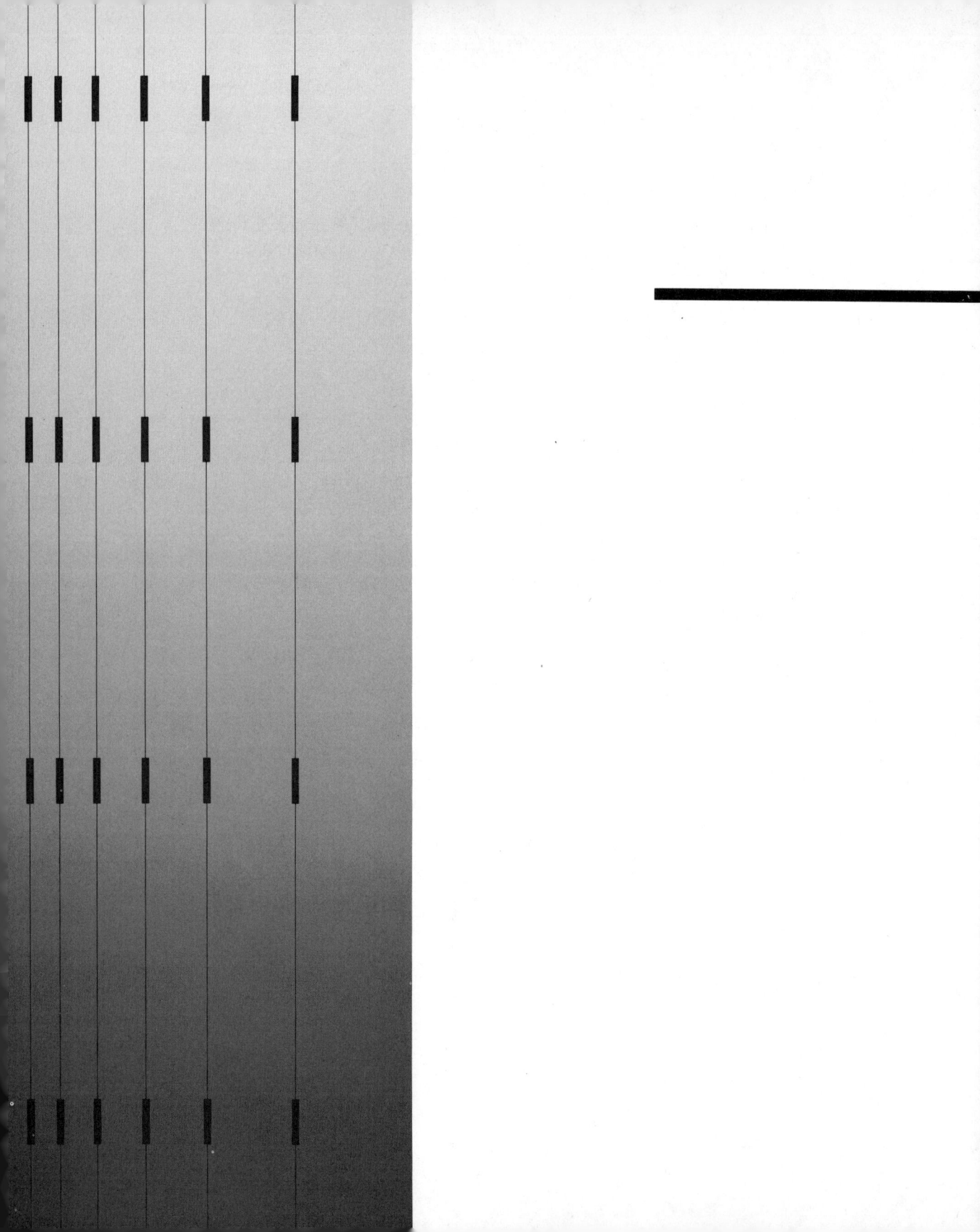

CHAPTER 12

MANAGING MULTIPLE RELATED DATABASES

One-to-Many Database Designs. 400
    Using Common Fields. 400
    Creating a Field of Record Numbers. 402
Many-to-Many Database Designs. 406
Creating Views of Multiple Databases. .409
    Creating Many-to-Many Database Views. 413
    Viewing Every Record. 416
    Combining Filter Conditions and Links. 419
Using Views to Print Reports. 420
Using Forms with Related Files. 424
Tips and Traps. 431
Summary. 432

Managing Multiple Related Databases

In most business applications, storing all information in a single database file simply is not practical. Suppose, for instance, that you want to store accounts receivable information for customer charge-account transactions. If you store all the information in a single database file that uses one record per transaction, as shown in Figure 12.1, the database would store the correct information. However, the database would not be efficient or convenient to use for these reasons:

- The repetition of names and addresses wastes disk space.
- The person entering the information has to retype the name and address for every order, which wastes time.
- When a customer moves, the address change must be made in many different records.

LastName	FirstName	Address	City	State	Zip	Amount	Date
Smith	John	123 A St.	San Diego	CA	92067	$276.69	01/01/90
Smith	John	123 A St.	San Diego	CA	92067	$600.26	01/01/90
Smith	John	123 A St.	San Diego	CA	92067	$962.91	01/01/90
Smith	John	123 A St.	San Diego	CA	92067	$291.88	02/02/90
Smith	John	123 A St.	San Diego	CA	92067	$972.70	02/02/90
Beach	Sandy	11 Elm St.	Portland	OR	76543	$331.77	01/01/90
Beach	Sandy	11 Elm St.	Portland	OR	76543	$100.63	01/01/90
Beach	Sandy	11 Elm St.	Portland	OR	76543	$698.52	01/01/90
Beach	Sandy	11 Elm St.	Portland	OR	76543	$183.15	02/02/90
Beach	Sandy	11 Elm St.	Portland	OR	76543	$217.41	02/02/90

FIGURE 12.1: A poorly designed accounts receivable database: first example.

If, instead, you use one record per customer and multiple fields for charge transactions, you eliminate the problem of repeated names and addresses. Figure 12.2 shows a second design for the accounts receivable database in which fields named Amount1, Amount2, Amount3, and so on store charge amounts; and fields named Date1, Date2, Date3, and so on store dates. This second design, however, has a different set of problems:

- The number of fields that a database record can have is limited, so the number of charges per customer this database can record is also limited.
- If you wanted to query for all charge transactions that occurred on a certain date—for example, on 01/01/90—you would need to include each Date field in the query (Date1 = 01/01/90, Date2 = 01/01/90, Date3 = 01/01/90, and so on).
- You cannot easily distinguish charges that have been invoiced or paid from those that have not.

LastName	FirstName	Address	City	State	Zip	Amount1	Date1	Amount2	Date2	Amount3	Date3	AmountN	DateN
Smith	John	123 A St.	San Diego	CA	92067	$468.39	01/01/90	$926.61	01/01/90	$54.66	01/01/90	$595.54	01/01/90
Adams	Annie	345 Ocean St.	Santa Monica	CA	92001	$702.02	01/01/90	$253.07	01/01/90	$684.76	01/01/90	$458.14	01/01/90
Mahoney	Mary	211 Seahawk	Seattle	WA	88977	$632.50	01/01/90	$351.02	01/01/90	$702.53	01/01/90	$402.11	01/01/90
Newell	John	734 Rainbow	Butte	MT	54321	$665.33	01/02/90	$892.19	01/02/90	$294.24	01/02/90	$894.41	01/02/90
Beach	Sandy	11 Elm St.	Portland	OR	76543	$75.96	01/02/90	$970.92	01/02/90	$99.69	01/02/90	$806.65	01/02/90
Kenney	Ralph	1101 Rainbow	Los Angeles	CA	96607	$582.68	01/02/90	$307.47	01/02/90	$523.95	01/02/90	$63.38	01/02/90
Schumack	Susita	47 Broad St.	Philadelphia	PA	45543	$990.16	01/03/90	$598.00	01/03/90	$943.32	01/03/90	$534.35	01/03/90

FIGURE 12.2: A poorly designed accounts receivable database: second example.

ONE-TO-MANY DATABASE DESIGNS

At the heart of the accounts receivable problem discussed in the previous section is the fact that there is a natural *one-to-many* relationship between customers and their charges. Any *one* customer may have *many* charges, and in fact may have an unpredictable number of charges.

The best way to store information when a one-to-many relationship is involved is to place the information in separate databases in such a way that repetition of information is minimized. Hence, the best way to store information about customers and their charges is to use two separate database files: one for names and addresses (perhaps named CUSTOMER) and another for charge transactions (perhaps named CHARGES). With these two databases you will not need to repeat information unnecessarily, and the number of charge transactions that a customer can make will not be limited.

Using Common Fields

If you store customer information in one database and charges in another, you need some way to *relate* each charge to the appropriate customer. To do this, you create a *common field*: a field that exists in both databases. This field contains *linking* information, which must be unique to each customer.

If you used the customer's last name to link charges to customers, dBASE could look at any single charge and link it to a specific customer, such as Smith. But what if the database contained two or more Smiths? Even if you used the two fields LastName and FirstName in the CHARGES database, you would run into the same problem when the database contained two customers named John Doe. You could further specify the customer by adding the Address field to the CHARGES database, but then you would be repeating too much information from the CUSTOMER database in the CHARGES database.

The best way to relate the two databases is to assign each customer a unique customer number, or code, and to store this code with each record in the CHARGES database. So long as no two customers have the same customer number, there can be no confusion about to whom each charge transaction belongs.

When you create a common field to relate two (or more) files, you may be tempted to put some additional meaning into the data in that field. For example, you might assign each customer a code in which each element says something about the customer; that is, you might assign the code SD41289, where SD stands for San Diego, 4 stands for an excellent credit rating, and 1289 stands for a starting date. But if you try to use a scheme like this and end up with two or more San Diego residents with credit ratings of 4 and starting dates of 12/89, you have a problem on your hands. When you enter a charge transaction for customer number SD41289, dBASE will not know to which customer SD41289 the transaction belongs.

Using an arbitrary and meaningless number is the best way to relate two files. For example, if you have fewer than 9000 customers, you can assign each customer a number in the range 1001 to 9999. Starting at 1001 ensures that each customer has a four-digit number, which adds consistency to the numbering scheme.

Figure 12.3 shows a linking field named CustNo in both the CHARGES and CUSTOMER databases. Notice that each customer has a unique customer number, so there is no doubt about who gets billed for charges to customer number 1002 or to any other number.

Of course, the design shows only a basic structure for the accounts receivable application. Realistically, you would probably want to store more information about each charge, such as the item purchased, the quantity, and the unit price. You could certainly add such fields to the CHARGES database.

In an accounts receivable system, you also need to keep track of payments. For this, you could create a third database, perhaps named Payments, and use the CustNo field to identify the customer number to which each payment belongs.

```
CUSTOMER database

       CustNo  LastName   FirstName  Address        City          State  Zip
       1001    Smith      John       123 A St.      San Diego     CA     92067
  ---> 1002    Adams      Annie      345 Ocean St.  Santa Monica  CA     92001
  |    1003    Mahoney    Mary       211 Seahawk    Seattle       WA     88977
  |    1004    Newell     John       734 Rainbow    Butte         MT     54321
  |    1005    Beach      Sandy      11 Elm St.     Portland      OR     76543
  |    1006    Kenney     Ralph      1101 Rainbow   Los Angeles   CA     96607
  |    1007    Schumack   Susita     47 Broad St.   Philadelphia  PA     45543
  |
  |
  |          CHARGES database
  |
  |           CustNo   Amount1    Date1
  |           1001     $468.39    01/01/90
  |           1001     $702.02    01/01/90
  |           1001     $632.50    01/01/90
  |           1001     $665.33    01/02/90
  |--------> 1002     $75.96     01/02/90
  |--------> 1002     $582.68    01/02/90
  |--------> 1002     $990.16    01/03/90
  |--------> 1002     $926.61    01/03/90
             1003     $253.07    01/01/90
             1003     $351.02    01/01/90
```

FIGURE 12.3: A practical design for an accounts receivable database system. A one-to-many database design was needed because one customer can have many charges. The two databases are linked by the common field CustNo.

Here is an example database, where the CustNo field clearly links each payment to a specific customer:

CustNo	CheckNo	AmtPaid	DatePaid
1001	285	$100.00	01/30/89
1002	998	$300.00	01/29/89
1003	335	$50.00	02/01/89

Creating a Field of Record Numbers

SEQUENCE OF STEPS

From the Control Center:

    highlight <create> in the Queries panel ↵

    enter **REPLACE** beneath the file name in the file skeleton ↵

    Proceed [↵]

Tab, as necessary
enter **WITH RECNO( )** beneath the field in the file skeleton
Menus (**F10**)
Update/**P**erform the Update [⏎]
Data (**F2**)

USAGE

You can easily assign a unique number to each database record by using the update querying technique discussed in Chapter 11 and the dBASE function RECNO( ). Select <create> from the Queries panel of the Control Center. Type the update operator **REPLACE** beneath the file name in the file skeleton and press ⏎. Select Proceed when dBASE warns you about removing the view skeleton. Press **Tab** and enter the update expression **WITH RECNO( )** under the appropriate field name. This update query tells dBASE to replace the current (empty) contents of the field with the record number, using the RECNO( ) function.

Press Menus (**F10**) and select Perform the Update from the Update pull-down menu. When the update is complete, press Data (**F2**) to see the results. Each record will have a unique number, starting at **1**. To start numbering records at a number other than 1, you modify the RECNO( ) function. For example, to start numbering at 101, enter **RECNO( ) + 100**. The records will be numbered 101, 102, 103, and so forth.

EXAMPLE

To see how multiple related databases work, you can modify the CUSTLIST and ORDERS databases to link orders to customers. The relationship between customers and orders is basically the same as the relationship between customers and charges. Any given customer can order one or several items. That is, for every *one* customer, there may be *many* orders. So to simplify matters, we will just modify the existing CUSTLIST and ORDERS databases to explore techniques for managing one-to-many relationships. (The structure and data for ORDERS are shown in Chapter 4; the CUSTLIST database is shown in Chapter 2.) Both databases need a common field. Follow the instructions here to add a field named CustNo to both databases, to assign unique numbers to customers, and to include customer numbers in transactions.

Highlight CUSTLIST in the Control Center Data panel and press Design (**Shift-F2**). Press **Esc** to leave the Organize menu and then press **Ctrl-N** to insert a new field above the existing fields. Enter a new field named **CustNo**, with the **Numeric** data type, a width of **4** digits, **0** decimal places, and **Y** in the index column, as shown in Figure 12.4. Press **Ctrl-End** to complete the addition. When dBASE verifies your change, select Yes.

The next step is to assign a number to each customer. Select <create> from the Queries panel of the Control Center. Type the update operator **REPLACE** beneath the file name in the file skeleton and press ↵. Select Proceed when dBASE warns you about removing the view skeleton. Press **Tab** and enter the update expression **WITH RECNO( ) + 1000** under the CustNo field name, so your screen looks like Figure 12.5. Press Menus (**F10**) and select Perform the Update from the Update pull-down menu. When the update is complete, press Data (**F2**) to see the results. Your screen should look like Figure 12.6, where each customer has a unique number, with numbers starting at 1001.

```
 Layout    Organize   Append    Go To   Exit                    6:36:02 pm
                                                   Bytes remaining:   3867
 Num   Field Name   Field Type   Width   Dec   Index
  1    CUSTNO       Numeric       4       0     Y
  2    LASTNAME     Character     15            N
  3    FIRSTNAME    Character     15            N
  4    COMPANY      Character     20            N
  5    ADDRESS      Character     30            N
  6    CITY         Character     15            N
  7    STATE        Character     2             N
  8    ZIP          Character     10            Y
  9    PHONE        Character     13            N
 10    STARTDATE    Date          8             N
 11    PAID         Logical       1             N

 Database C:\dbase\CUSTLIST        Field 2/11                      Num
          Enter the field name.  Insert/Delete field:Ctrl-N/Ctrl-U
 Field names begin with a letter and may contain letters, digits and underscores
```

FIGURE 12.4: The CustNo field added to the CUSTLIST database. CUSTNO is the common field that links CUSTLIST to the ORDERS database, thus linking each customer to his or her orders.

Now you need to modify the ORDERS database. Leave the current browse screen by pressing **Esc** and selecting No when dBASE asks if you want to save the query. When you get back to the Control Center, highlight ORDERS in the Data panel and press Design (**Shift-F2**) to get to the database design screen. Press **Esc** to leave the Organize pull-down menu. Press **Ctrl-N** to add a new field. Add the CustNo field, using the exact same field name, data type, width, decimal places, and index option you used in the CUSTLIST database, as shown in Figure 12.7. Press **Ctrl-End** after adding the field and select Yes when dBASE asks for verification.

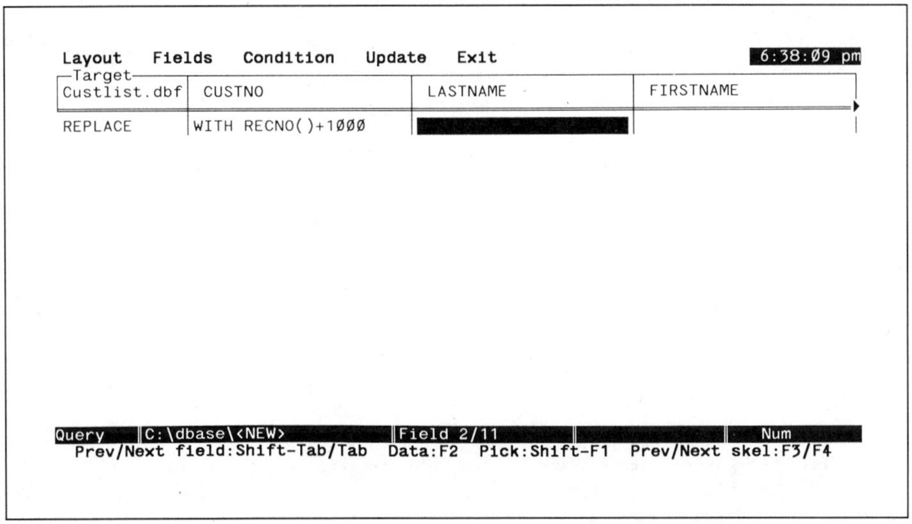

CREATING A FIELD OF RECORD NUMBERS — 405

```
 Layout    Fields   Condition   Update   Exit              6:38:09 pm
 ┌Target─────────┐
 │Custlist.dbf│ CUSTNO              LASTNAME         FIRSTNAME
 ├────────────┼─────────────────────────────────────────────────────
 │REPLACE     │ WITH RECNO()+1000




 Query    C:\dbase\<NEW>        Field 2/11                  Num
 Prev/Next field:Shift-Tab/Tab  Data:F2  Pick:Shift-F1  Prev/Next skel:F3/F4
```

FIGURE 12.5: Query to fill the CUSTNO field with record numbers. On the query design screen, *REPLACE* is entered under the database name and *WITH RECNO( ) + 1000* is entered under the CustNo field. This query creates consecutive numbers, beginning at 1001, in the CustNo field.

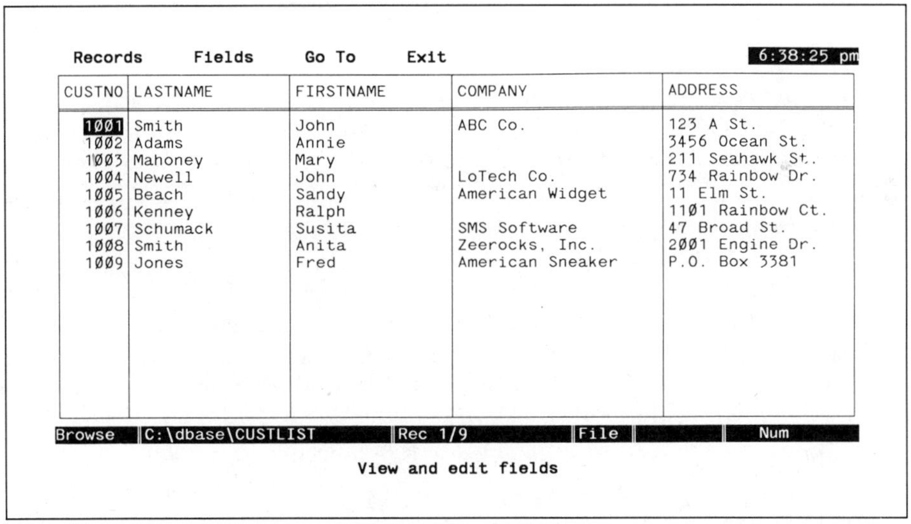

```
 Records    Fields   Go To    Exit                         6:38:25 pm
 CUSTNO LASTNAME    FIRSTNAME   COMPANY           ADDRESS
 ┌────┐
 │1001│ Smith       John        ABC Co.           123 A St.
 └────┘
  1002  Adams       Annie                         3456 Ocean St.
  1003  Mahoney     Mary                          211 Seahawk St.
  1004  Newell      John        LoTech Co.        734 Rainbow Dr.
  1005  Beach       Sandy       American Widget   11 Elm St.
  1006  Kenney      Ralph                         1101 Rainbow Ct.
  1007  Schumack    Susita      SMS Software      47 Broad St.
  1008  Smith       Anita       Zeerocks, Inc.    2001 Engine Dr.
  1009  Jones       Fred        American Sneaker  P.O. Box 3381




 Browse   C:\dbase\CUSTLIST    Rec 1/9       File            Num
                          View and edit fields
```

FIGURE 12.6: Results of the query in Figure 12.5. dBASE assigned a unique number to each customer.

Now you need to assign a customer number to each order in the ORDERS database. Again, since we are simply developing a sample database here, you

```
Layout    Organize    Append    Go To    Exit                        6:38:59 pm
                                                         Bytes remaining:   3955
  Num   Field Name    Field Type   Width   Dec   Index
   1    CUSTNO        Numeric        4      0     Y
   2    PARTNO        Character      5            Y
   3    PARTNAME      Character     15            N
   4    DATE          Date           8            N
   5    QTY           Numeric        3      0     N
   6    UNITPRICE     Numeric        9      2     N
   7    TAXABLE       Logical        1            N




  Database  C:\dbase\ORDERS          Field 2/7                         Num
          Enter the field name.  Insert/Delete field:Ctrl-N/Ctrl-U
   Field names begin with a letter and may contain letters, digits and underscores
```

FIGURE 12.7: The CUSTNO field added to the ORDERS database. CUSTNO is the common field that links ORDERS to the CUSTLIST database, thus linking customers to their orders.

can assign these numbers arbitrarily, using the browse screen. In actual practice, however, you could develop a custom form to greatly simplify assigning customer numbers to orders. (See "Using Forms with Related Files" later in this chapter for more information.)

For now, assign customer numbers to orders using the browse screen. To do so, press Data (**F2**) to get to the browse screen. (If the edit screen appears instead, press **F2** again.) Press **PgUp** to make sure you are at the topmost record in ORDERS. Type the customer numbers shown in Figure 12.8. When the *Add New Records* prompt appears after you enter the last customer number, type **N** for No. Select Exit from the Exit pull-down menu.

At this point, you have assigned each customer in the CUSTLIST database a unique customer number. You have also assigned transactions in the ORDERS database to individual customers. You have not yet related the CUSTNO field in ORDERS to the CUSTNO field in CUSTLIST. To do this, you use the common CUSTNO field to create a *view* that links records from the two databases (see "Creating Views of Multiple Databases" later in this chapter).

MANY-TO-MANY DATABASE DESIGNS

Another common database design is based on a *many-to-many* relationship. Linking three or more files is no more difficult than linking two. Just be sure that you include common fields so that you can set up links.

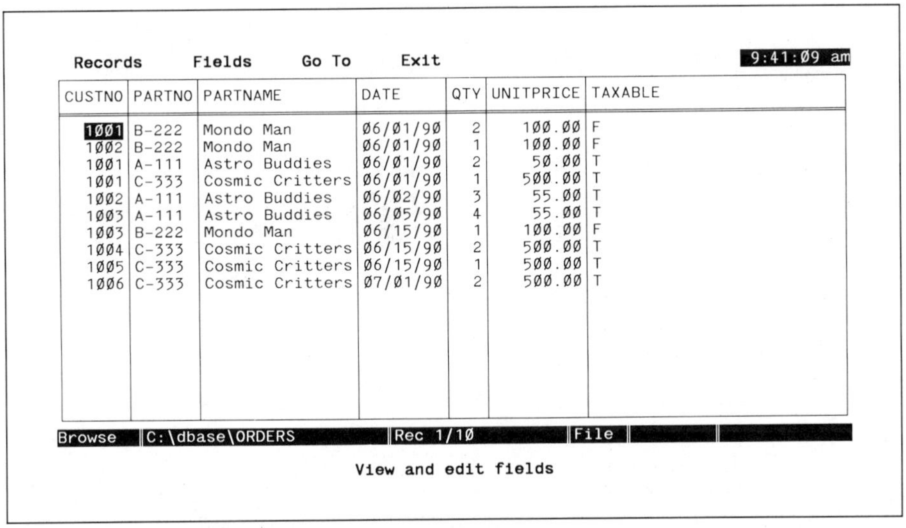

```
Records      Fields     Go To    Exit                         9:41:09 am
CUSTNO PARTNO PARTNAME       DATE     QTY UNITPRICE TAXABLE
 1001  B-222  Mondo Man      06/01/90  2   100.00    F
 1002  B-222  Mondo Man      06/01/90  1   100.00    F
 1001  A-111  Astro Buddies  06/01/90  2    50.00    T
 1001  C-333  Cosmic Critters 06/01/90 1   500.00    T
 1002  A-111  Astro Buddies  06/02/90  3    55.00    T
 1003  A-111  Astro Buddies  06/05/90  4    55.00    T
 1003  B-222  Mondo Man      06/15/90  1   100.00    F
 1004  C-333  Cosmic Critters 06/15/90 2   500.00    T
 1005  C-333  Cosmic Critters 06/15/90 1   500.00    T
 1006  C-333  Cosmic Critters 07/01/90 2   500.00    T

Browse   C:\dbase\ORDERS        Rec 1/10        File
                       View and edit fields
```

FIGURE 12.8: To try out the example, you need to add customer numbers to the ORDERS database.

The ORDERS database contains repeated information: PARTNAME and UNITPRICE are repeated for each part number. You could create a third database with information about parts, including part number, part name, and unit price, and then include only the part number in the ORDERS database to avoid repetition.

For example, Figure 12.9 shows a modified version of the CUSTLIST and ORDERS databases with a third database, named PARTLIST, added. The PARTLIST database contains information about the product inventory. PartNo is the common field that links the PARTLIST database to the ORDERS database. As is required when creating a common field, the PartNo field in the PARTLIST database has the same name, data type, width, number of decimal places, and index option as the PartNo field in the ORDERS database. (See "Creating Views of Multiple Databases" later in this chapter for an example view.)

Whereas there is a one-to-many relationship between customers and orders (each customer can place many orders) and a one-to-many relationship between orders and parts (each part can appear in many different orders), there is a many-to-many relationship between customers and parts—that is, many customers can order many different parts.

Many-to-many relationships often occur in applications that involve scheduling. For example, a school offers many different courses, and each course is attended by many different students. To set up a database design for such an application, you need three database files: one to list students, one to list courses,

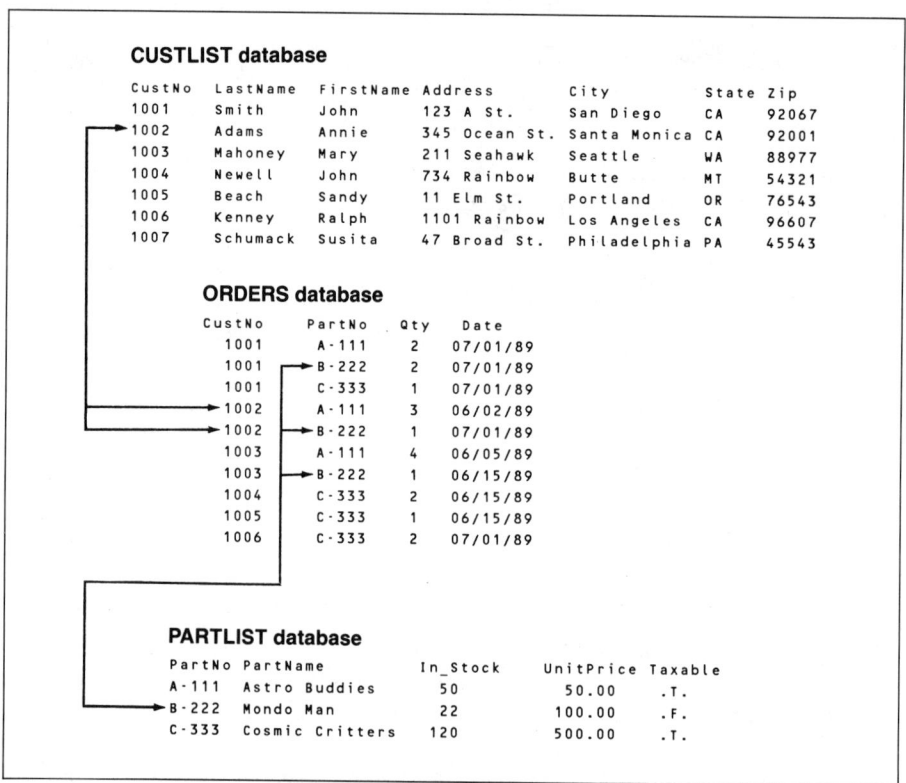

FIGURE 12.9: An example of a many-to-many database design. Customer numbers in CUSTLIST and part numbers in PARTLIST are linked to customer orders in ORDERS.

and one to list student's numbers and the courses in which each student is enrolled. The design assumes that each student and each course has a unique number.

Figure 12.10 shows these three databases and the links among them. The common field between STUDENTS and LINKER is StudentID, a Character field that is 11 spaces wide in both databases. The common field linking COURSES to LINKER is CourseID, a Character field with a width of 5 spaces in both databases.

In Figure 12.10, you can see that course identifiers use a department abbreviation combined with a number (for example, Bi101). In a sense, this identification scheme goes against earlier advice about using arbitrary identifiers in common fields. However, in this particular case, so long as the school makes certain that each department has a unique abbreviation, and that each course in

CREATING VIEWS OF MULTIPLE DATABASES — 409

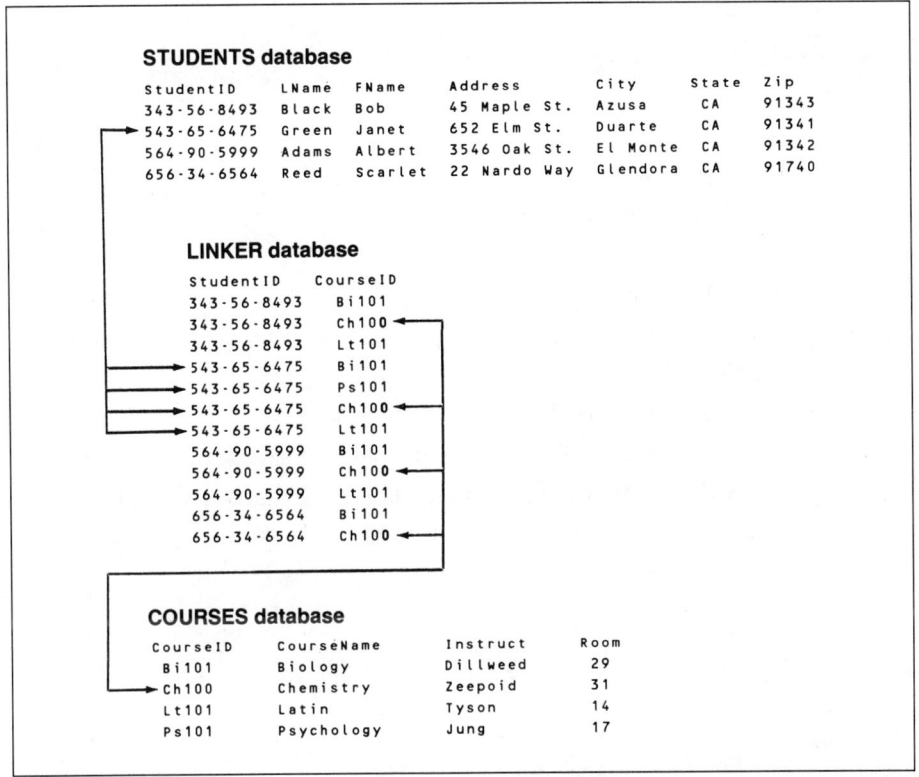

FIGURE 12.10: A second example of a many-to-many database design. Three related databases are used for scheduling. Student numbers in STUDENT and course numbers in COURSES are linked to the LINKER database of student course enrollment.

each department has a unique number, then each course will be ensured a unique code.

To set up a query to link the three files for student enrollment, see the next section, "Creating Views of Multiple Databases." You can save the query and use it as a basis for creating a report format. (See "Using Views to Print Reports" later in this chapter.)

CREATING VIEWS OF MULTIPLE DATABASES

SEQUENCE OF STEPS

From the Control Center, with the first database open:

   highlight <create> in the Queries panel ↵

Menus (**F10**)

Fields/Include Indexes [⏎]

Yes

Menus (**F10**)

Layout/**A**dd File to Query [⏎]

select the second database from the list

menus (**F10**)

Fields/Include Indexes [⏎]

Tab, as necessary, to the common field in one database file skeleton

Menus (**F10**)

Layout/**C**reate Link by Pointing [⏎]

Previous (**F3**) *or* Next (**F4**) to go to the new file skeleton

Tab, as necessary, to the common field in the second database file skeleton

⏎

Field (**F5**), as necessary, to add fields to the view skeleton

Data (**F2**)

To save, name, and describe the view:

Design (**Shift-F2**)

Menus (**F10**)

Layout/**E**dit Description of Query [⏎]

enter a description

Menus (**F10**)

Exit/**S**ave Changes and Exit [⏎]

enter a name for the view

USAGE

Once you have created two or more databases with common fields and appropriate indexes (as explained in the preceding sections of this chapter), you can create a *view* to query the databases. The view can contain information gleaned from each of the databases.

A multiple-database view is a query that includes two or more file skeletons and an *example* (or *placeholder*) to relate the common fields. The placeholder that you use on the query design screen must show dBASE that records with identical values in the common field in all databases are related. Thus, you create *links* between the common fields.

Before you execute the query, you need to adjust the view skeleton that defines the fields that will be displayed in the results of the query. (See Chapter 5 for more information about creating views.)

When a browse or edit screen is displaying a view, you cannot make changes. That is why the message *ReadOnly* appears in the status bar near the bottom of the screen. If you attempt to make changes from a view, dBASE ignores your keystrokes.

EXAMPLE

Suppose you want to view all the records in the ORDERS database, along with the names of the customers who placed the orders. You need some information from ORDERS and some from CUSTLIST to accomplish this. The view created in this example links the two databases by their common field, CUSTNO, which we created in the example in the section "One-to-Many Database Designs" earlier in this chapter.

When you want to link two related databases, you should start with the database on the "many" side of the one-to-many relationship. In this example, there are many orders for each one customer, so we will start the linking procedure by opening the ORDERS database.

If the ORDERS database is not currently open (if it does not appear above the line in the Data panel), highlight its name and press ←. Then select Open File to open the database. Highlight <create> in the Queries panel and press ←, which brings you to the query design screen. Press Menus (**F10**). Then highlight Include Indexes on the Fields pull-down menu and press ← to change its setting to Yes. (A # symbol will appear next to the indexed CUSTNO field.)

Now you need to bring a file skeleton of the CUSTLIST database into the design screen. Press Menus (**F10**) and select Add File to Query from the Layout pull-down menu. From the submenu that appears, select CUSTLIST.DBF. Activate the CUSTLIST index by selecting Include Indexes from the Fields pull-down menu.

To tell dBASE that the two databases are related through the CUSTNO field, press **Tab** to move the highlight to the CUSTNO field in the CUSTLIST file skeleton. Then press Menus (**F10**) and select Create Link by Pointing from the Layout pull-down menu. The placeholder *LINK1* appears in the box, and instructions appear at the bottom of the screen telling you to move the cursor to another file and then press ←.

In this example, press Previous (**F3**) and **Tab** to move the highlight to the CUSTNO field in the ORDERS database file skeleton. Press ← to complete the link. dBASE adds the placeholder *LINK1* to the CUSTNO field of the ORDERS skeleton.

The view skeleton includes only fields from the ORDERS database. To view the customer's name with each order, you need to include the LASTNAME and FIRSTNAME fields from the CUSTLIST database in the view skeleton. To include fields from both databases, you need to rearrange the view skeleton.

Press Next (**F4**) to move the highlight to the CUSTLIST database file skeleton. Press **Tab** to move the highlight to the LASTNAME box. Press Field (**F5**) to copy the LASTNAME field to the view skeleton. (An arrow appears next to the field, indicating that it is now included in the view skeleton.) Press **Tab** to move the highlight to the FIRSTNAME box. Press Field (**F5**) to copy FIRSTNAME to the view skeleton.

To display the customer names next to the customer numbers, you need to rearrange the view skeleton. Press Next (**F4**) to move the highlight to the view skeleton. Press **End** to move to the end of the view skeleton. Press Select (**F6**) and then press **Shift-Tab** to highlight the LASTNAME and FIRSTNAME boxes. Press ← to finish highlighting.

Press **Home** to move back to the beginning of the view skeleton. Press Move (**F7**) and then press ← to move the LASTNAME and FIRSTNAME boxes to the right of the CUSTNO box. At this point, your query should look like Figure 12.11.

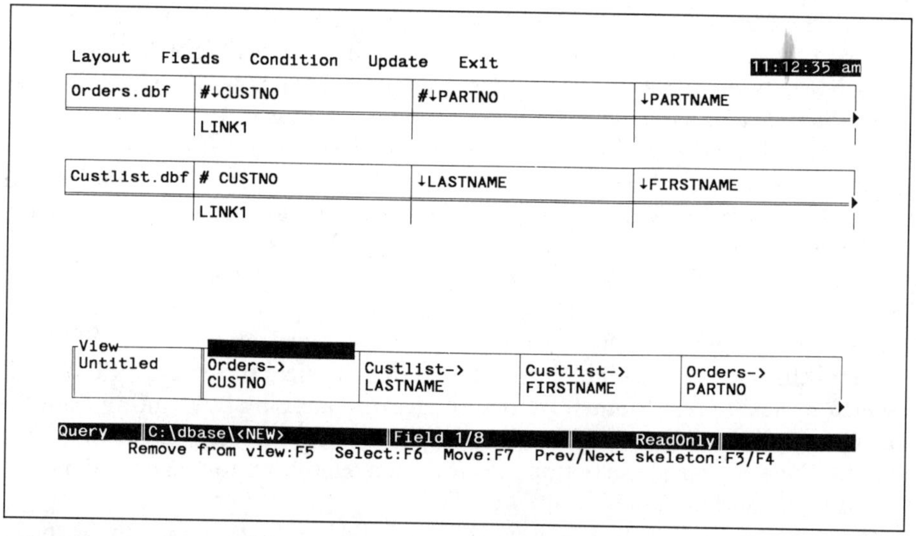

FIGURE 12.11: Query to create the link between ORDERS and CUSTLIST. dBASE provides the placeholder LINK1 when you select Create Link by Pointing from the Layout pull-down menu.

Notice that the view skeleton shows both the database and field names in each box. The Orders->CUSTNO box will display the CUSTNO field from the Orders database. The Custlist->LASTNAME and Custlist->FIRSTNAME boxes will display the LASTNAME and FIRSTNAME fields from the CUSTLIST database. (Some additional fields are beyond the right edge of the display.)

At this point, you can press Data (**F2**) to execute the query. The browse screen will show all the fields that you specified in the view skeleton in the order you specified them. Figure 12.12 shows a view with LASTNAME and FIRSTNAME from the CUSTLIST database, and CUSTNO, PARTNO, PARTNAME, QTY, and UNITPRICE from the ORDERS database.

Records Fields Go To Exit 1:04:03 am

CUSTNO	LASTNAME	FIRSTNAME	PARTNO	PARTNAME	QTY	UNITPRICE	TA
1001	Smith	John	B-222	Mondo Man	2	100.00	F
1002	Adams	Annie	B-222	Mondo Man	1	100.00	F
1001	Smith	John	A-111	Astro Buddies	2	50.00	T
1001	Smith	John	C-333	Cosmic Critters	1	500.00	T
1002	Adams	Annie	A-111	Astro Buddies	3	55.00	T
1003	Mahoney	Mary	A-111	Astro Buddies	4	55.00	T
1003	Mahoney	Mary	B-222	Mondo Man	1	100.00	F
1004	Newell	John	C-333	Cosmic Critters	2	500.00	T
1005	Beach	Sandy	C-333	Cosmic Critters	1	500.00	T
1006	Kenney	Ralph	C-333	Cosmic Critters	2	500.00	T

Browse | C:\dbase\<NEW> | Rec 1/10 | View | ReadOnly

View and edit fields

FIGURE 12.12: Data from CUSTLIST and ORDERS combined in a view. Some fields from ORDERS have been deleted from the view. (Use the **Tab** key to scroll horizontally through the browse screen and view other fields.)

Creating Many-to-Many Database Views

Figure 12.9 showed three databases (CUSTLIST, ORDERS, and PARTLIST) set up with PARTNO as a common field. To create a query to link the three files, you need to include file skeletons for all three files, using Add File to Query from the Layout pull-down menu to add each new skeleton. Select Create Link by Pointing to set up the link between CUSTLIST and ORDERS and then select Create Link by Pointing a second time to set up the link between

ORDERS and PARTLIST. (dBASE will automatically use *LINK2* as the placeholder for the second link.)

Figure 12.13 shows the completed query. (To place the ASC1 operator in the query, move the highlight to the CUSTNO field in the ORDERS file skeleton, press **F10**, and select Sort on This Field from the Fields pull-down menu. Then select Ascending ASCII.) The view skeleton includes selected fields from all three files.

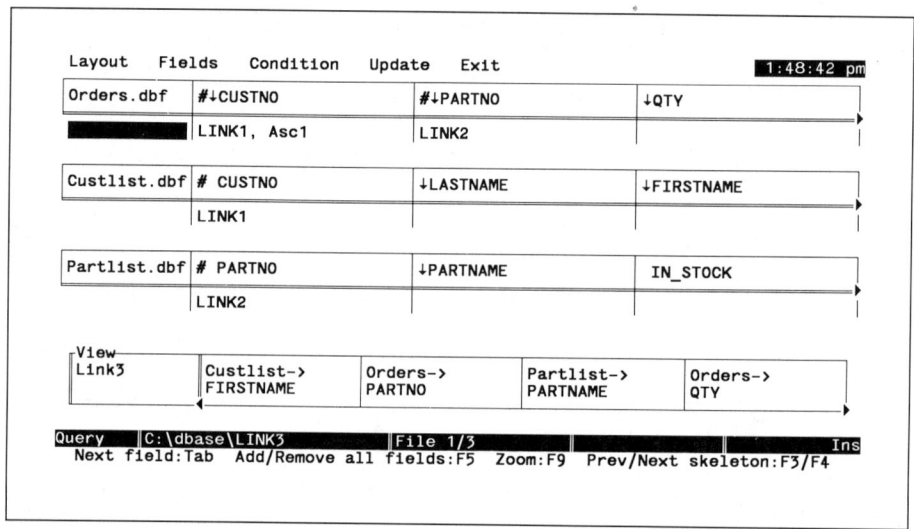

FIGURE 12.13: View linking the three files in Figure 12.9. Notice the placeholders: LINK1 links ORDERS to CUSTLIST, and LINK2 links ORDERS to PARTLIST. (Note that some fields are beyond the left and right edges of the screen.)

Figure 12.14 shows the results of the query. The customer name, the part number, the part name, the unit price, and other information for each order is readily available and appears to be in one database. You could save this query and use it as the basis for developing report formats. See "Using Views to Print Reports" later in this chapter.

Figure 12.10 showed three databases for student enrollment in college courses. The fields common to more than one of the databases are STUDENTID and COURSEID. Figure 12.15 shows a query to display information from the three databases, with records sorted by the STUDENTID field in the LINKER database. The view skeleton includes some fields from all three files (and several more fields exist beyond the right edge of the screen). Notice that all of the linking fields are indexed, as indicated by the # symbol.

CREATING MANY-TO-MANY DATABASE VIEWS — 415

```
 Records      Fields      Go To      Exit                        1:50:19 pm
 CUSTNO LASTNAME   FIRSTNAME        PARTNO PARTNAME         QTY UNITPRICE
 1001   Smith      John             B-222  Mondo Man          2    100.00
 1001   Smith      John             A-111  Astro Buddies      2     50.00
 1001   Smith      John             C-333  Cosmic Critters    1    500.00
 1002   Adams      Annie            B-222  Mondo Man          1    100.00
 1002   Adams      Annie            A-111  Astro Buddies      3     50.00
 1003   Mahoney    Mary             A-111  Astro Buddies      4     50.00
 1003   Mahoney    Mary             B-222  Mondo Man          1    100.00
 1004   Newell     John             C-333  Cosmic Critters    2    500.00
 1005   Beach      Sandy            C-333  Cosmic Critters    1    500.00
 1006   Kenney     Ralph            C-333  Cosmic Critters    2    500.00

 Browse  C:\dbase\LINK3        Rec 1/10       View ReadOnly          Ins
                          View and edit fields
```

FIGURE 12.14: Results of the view linking three databases in Figure 12.13. The data is in ascending customer number order because we placed the *Asc1* operator in the CUSTNO field of the view.

```
 Layout    Fields    Condition    Update    Exit                 2:08:14 pm
 Students.dbf | # STUDENTID    | ↓LNAME          | ↓FNAME           |
              | LINK1          |                 |                  |

 Linker.dbf  | #↓STUDENTID    | #↓COURSEID      |
              | LINK1, Asc1    | LINK2           |

 Courses.dbf | # COURSEID     | COURSENAME      | INSTRUCT         |
              | LINK2          |                 |                  |

 ┌View─────────────────────────────────────────────────────────────────
 │ StList  | Linker->       | Students->  | Students->  | Linker->    |
 │         | STUDENTID      | FNAME       | LNAME       | COURSEID    |

 Query  C:\dbase\STLIST       File 3/3
     Next field:Tab  Add/Remove all fields:F5  Zoom:F9  Prev/Next skeleton:F3/F4
```

FIGURE 12.15: Query to link three databases as shown in Figure 12.10. The data will be sorted by the STUDENTID field.

You can press Data (**F2**) to see the immediate results of the query. You can also save and name the query and then use it for printing a report. (See "Using Views to Print Reports" later in this chapter.)

To create a list of courses and the students enrolled in each, you can set up the links in the query design screen as shown in Figure 12.16, basing the sort order on the COURSEID field in the LINKER database. You can use this query as the basis for a report design. (See "Using Views to Print Reports" later in this chapter.)

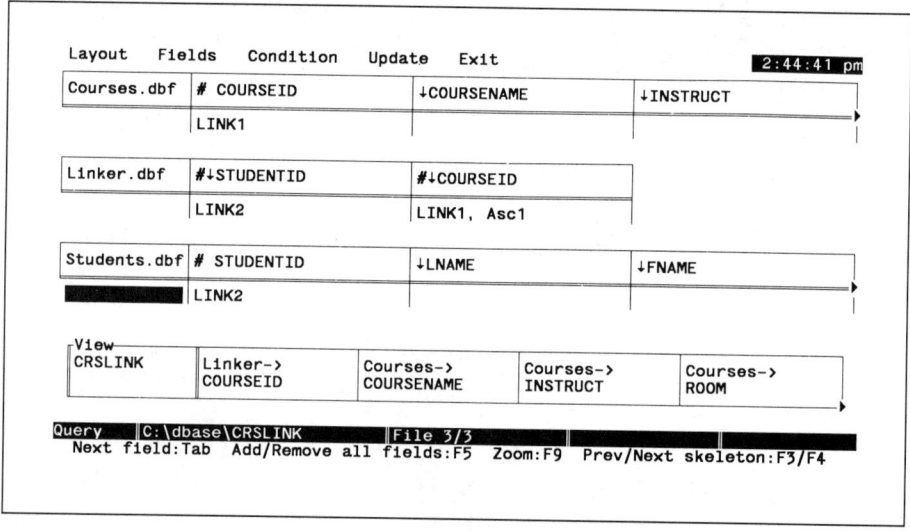

FIGURE 12.16: Query to list the course schedule in COURSEID order. (Some of the fields in the view skeleton are scrolled off the right edge of the screen.)

Viewing Every Record

The views presented so far in this chapter do not include records that are not common to both, or all, of the databases involved. For example, Figure 12.12 showed a view that presents only records with a common customer number in both the CUSTLIST and ORDERS databases. Customers who have no records in the ORDERS database are not included in the view. However, in some situations you might want to include all records from a database file, even if the related files contain no information for some of the records.

To include all records from a file in a view, use the *every* operator in the query, placing it in the file skeleton for the database for which you want to display all records. The *every* operator should appear *before* the linking placeholder.

EXAMPLE

You can modify the view shown in Figures 12.11 and 12.12 to include all of the records in the CUSTLIST database. On the query design screen, move the highlight to the CUSTNO field in the CUSTLIST file skeleton. Change the entry to **Every LINK1**, as shown in Figure 12.17. (You can type over the existing entry or insert the word *Every* in insert mode.) Press Data (**F2**) to execute the query.

```
 Layout    Fields   Condition   Update    Exit              12:35:37 pm
 Orders.dbf  │#↓CUSTNO       │#↓PARTNO        │↓PARTNAME
             │LINK1          │                │

 Custlist.dbf│# CUSTNO       │↓LASTNAME       │↓FIRSTNAME
             │Every LINK1    │▓▓▓▓▓▓▓▓▓▓▓▓▓▓▓▓│



 ┌View────────┬──────────┬──────────┬──────────┬──────────┐
 │Untitled    │Orders->  │Custlist->│Custlist->│Orders->  │
 │            │CUSTNO    │LASTNAME  │FIRSTNAME │PARTNO    │
 └────────────┴──────────┴──────────┴──────────┴──────────┘
 Query  │C:\dbase\<NEW>    │Field 2/11│                  Ins
    Prev/Next field:Shift-Tab/Tab  Data:F2  Pick:Shift-F1  Prev/Next skel:F3/F4
```

FIGURE 12.17: Query to include all the records from CUSTLIST in the view. Notice the placement of the *every* operator—to include every customer in CUSTLIST.

Figure 12.18 shows the results of the query. Notice that even though there are no orders for Susita Schumack, Anita Smith, and Fred Jones, the view includes their records. Fields in the ORDERS database for these customers are empty, because no information has yet been entered. (Even though these customers actually have customer numbers assigned to them in the CUSTLIST database, the view is showing the CUSTNO field from the ORDERS database).

Figure 12.19 shows another example query. This query designs a report to print the invoices in the section "Using Views to Print Reports" later in this chapter. The *every* operator ensures that all customers are included in the view. You can omit this operator to print invoices for only those individuals who have outstanding orders.

Using the *Asc1* operator in the Orders->CUSTNO field ensures that the orders are sorted into customer-number order. (The sort is particularly important in this case because, when printing invoices, a group band based on customer number is needed to print each customer's charges on a single invoice.)

All fields from both database file skeletons, except Orders->CUSTNO, are included in the view skeleton. Orders->CUSTNO is not included because this

CH. 12 MANAGING MULTIPLE RELATED DATABASES

```
 Records      Fields      Go To      Exit                         9:57:57 am
 CUSTNO  LASTNAME     FIRSTNAME    PARTNO  PARTNAME          DATE      QTY  UNI
 1001    Smith        John         B-222   Mondo Man         06/01/90   2
 1001    Smith        John         A-111   Astro Buddies     06/01/90   2
 1001    Smith        John         C-333   Cosmic Critters   06/01/90   1
 1002    Adams        Annie        B-222   Mondo Man         06/01/90   1
 1002    Adams        Annie        A-111   Astro Buddies     06/02/90   3
 1003    Mahoney      Mary         A-111   Astro Buddies     06/05/90   4
 1003    Mahoney      Mary         B-222   Mondo Man         06/15/90   1
 1004    Newell       John         C-333   Cosmic Critters   06/15/90   2
 1005    Beach        Sandy        C-333   Cosmic Critters   06/15/90   1
 1006    Kenney       Ralph        C-333   Cosmic Critters   07/01/90   2
         Schumack     Susita                                  /  /
         Smith        Anita                                   /  /
         Jones        Fred                                    /  /

 Browse  C:\dbase\<NEW>             Rec 1/9           View  ReadOnly
                         View and edit fields
```

FIGURE 12.18: Results of the query in Figure 12.17. The CUSTNO field contains blanks because the view skeleton shows *Orders->CUSTNO*. If you changed the view skeleton to show *CustList->CUSTNO*, then customer numbers for these three individuals would be displayed.

```
 Layout   Fields   Condition   Update   Exit                    12:56:09 pm
 Orders.dbf  │ # CUSTNO         │ #↓PARTNO      │ ↓PARTNAME
             │ LINK1, Asc1      │               │

 Custlist.dbf│ #↓CUSTNO         │ ↓LASTNAME     │ ↓FIRSTNAME
             │ Every LINK1      │               │


 ┌View──────────────────────────────────────────────────────────────────
 │Untitled │ Custlist->  │ Custlist->  │ Custlist->   │ Custlist->
 │         │ CUSTNO      │ LASTNAME    │ FIRSTNAME    │ COMPANY

 Query  C:\dbase\<NEW>         Field 2/11                           Ins
  Prev/Next field:Shift-Tab/Tab  Data:F2  Pick:Shift-F1  Prev/Next skel:F3/F4
```

FIGURE 12.19: In this query, the *LINK1* placeholder sets up the link between CUSTLIST and ORDERS based on the common CUSTNO field. The *every* operator includes all customers in the view.

field is blank when records for customers with no charge transactions are displayed. To print a customer number on each invoice, the query uses the

CUSTNO field from the CUSTLIST database (which contains all of the customer numbers).

After creating the query and testing it by pressing the Data (**F2**) key, press Design (**Shift-F2**) to return to the query design screen. Then select Edit Description of Query from the Layout pull-down menu and enter a description such as **View to link ORDERS and CUSTLIST**. Then select Save Changes and Exit from the Exit pull-down menu. When prompted, enter the file name **JOIN1**.

Combining Filter Conditions and Links

You can place any filter condition in a query to isolate records that meet some search criterion (as explained in Chapter 5). You also can combine filter conditions with database links. If the filter condition is based on one of the linking fields, enter the LINK example first, followed by a comma and the filter condition. For example, the query shown in Figure 12.20 limits the display to orders for customer number 1002. Figure 12.21 shows the results of this query.

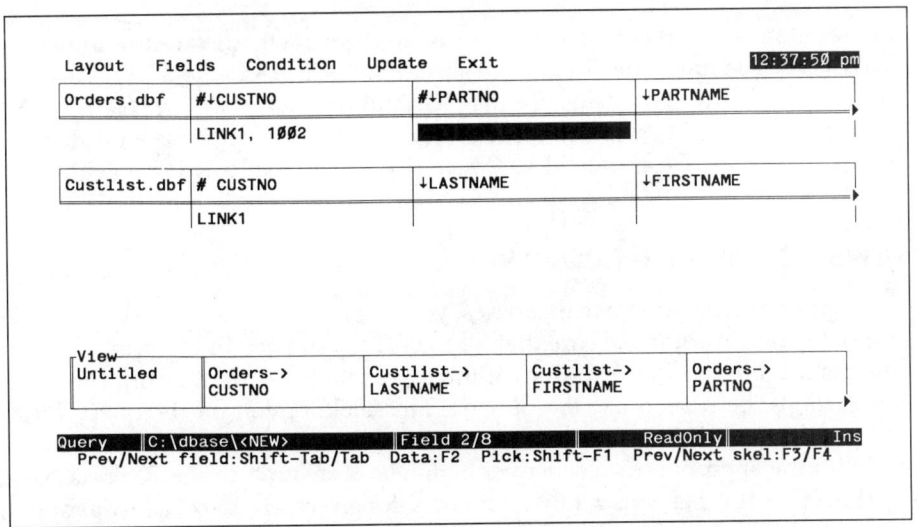

FIGURE 12.20: Query combining a filter condition (for orders by customer 1002) and a link.

You can place filter conditions in any other field boxes and use the rows from each skeleton to create AND and OR relationships. For example, placing **"CA"** (with the quotation marks) in the STATE field of the CUSTLIST database limits output to California residents. Placing **"CA"** in the top row of the CUSTLIST

```
    Records     Fields     Go To     Exit                              12:43:13 pm
   ┌─────────┬──────────┬───────────┬───────┬──────────────┬─────┬──────────┐
   │ CUSTNO  │ LASTNAME │ FIRSTNAME │ PARTNO│ PARTNAME     │ QTY │ UNITPRICE│
   ├─────────┼──────────┼───────────┼───────┼──────────────┼─────┼──────────┤
   │  1002   │ Adams    │ Annie     │ B-222 │ Mondo Man    │  1  │  100.00  │
   │  1002   │ Adams    │ Annie     │ A-111 │ Astro Buddies│  3  │   55.00  │
   └─────────┴──────────┴───────────┴───────┴──────────────┴─────┴──────────┘

   Browse   C:\dbase\ORDERS        Rec 2/10        File  ReadOnly          Ins
                            View and edit fields
```

FIGURE 12.21: Results of the query in Figure 12.20.

file skeleton and **"A-111"** in the top row of the ORDERS skeleton under the PARTNO field limits the display to records that have CA in the STATE field *and* A-111 in the PARTNO field. Placing **"CA"** in the first row of the CUSTLIST skeleton and **"A-111"** in the second row of the ORDERS skeleton displays records that have CA in the STATE field *or* A-111 in the PARTNO field.

USING VIEWS TO PRINT REPORTS

To print a report from two databases, you first need to create a query that links the databases. Also, make sure that all the fields you need in the printed report are included in the view skeleton. If the report that you want to print involves any groups, be sure to use the Sort on This Field option on the query Fields menu to arrange the records into proper order for grouping.

With the appropriate view active, highlight <create> in the Reports panel and press ←┘. When you get to the reports design screen, select a layout option from the Quick Layout submenu to start your report design. The initial layout will include all fields that are in the view (though some may be off the right edge of your screen). To the reports design screen, a view is the same as a database file, so you can use the same techniques that you use with single database file views to design a report format to your liking.

You can create reports from the student enrollment queries shown previously, in Figures 12.15 and 12.16. These reports illustrate the importance of selecting

USING VIEWS TO PRINT REPORTS — 421

```
   Layout    Fields    Bands   Words    Go To    Print    Exit              8:10:20 pm
 ......▼.1.....▼...2.....▼....3.▼......▼......▼.5.....▼...6...▼...7.▼.......
  Page        Header    Band
 MM/DD/YY
                                   Student Schedules
  Report      Intro     Band
  Group  1    Intro     Band ◄─────────────── Grouped by Student ID ──────
  Student ID: XXXXXXXXXXX  XXXXXXXXX XXXXXXXXX
  Detail                Band
              XXXXX        XXXXXXXXXXXXXX XXXXXXXXXXXXXX 999
  Group  1    Summary   Band
  Report      Summary   Band
  Page        Footer    Band


  Report   C:\...invent\STUDLIST    Line:0 Col:0    File:Qbe    12           Ins
  Add field:F5  Select:F6  Move:F7  Copy:F8  Size:Shift-F7  Quick Report:Shift-F9
```

FIGURE 12.22: Student enrollment example: a report format to list students and courses.

```
    07/21/90
                              Student Schedules

    Student ID: 343-56-8493   Bob Black

                Bi101     Biology        Dillweed      29
                Ch100     Chemistry      Zeepoid       31
                Lt101     Latin          Tyson         14

    Student ID: 543-65-6475   Janet Green

                Bi101     Biology        Dillweed      29
                Ps101     Psychology     Jung          17
                Ch100     Chemistry      Zeepoid       31
                Lt101     Latin          Tyson         14

    Student ID: 564-90-5999   Albert Adams

                Bi101     Biology        Dillweed      29
                Ch100     Chemistry      Zeepoid       31
                Lt101     Latin          Tyson         14

    Student ID: 656-34-6564   Scarlet Reed

                Bi101     Biology        Dillweed      29
                Ch100     Chemistry      Zeepoid       31
```

FIGURE 12.23: Report showing courses grouped by students. This report is based on the format in Figure 12.22. Because the query sorts records into STUDENTID order, student numbers are printed in ascending order and grouped according to the group band field, STUDENTID.

an appropriate sort field from the queries design screen if you want to print the results in a grouped report. To print a report with records grouped by students, the results of the query must be sorted by student number. To print a report with records grouped by courses, the results of the query must be sorted by course number.

The report format shown in Figure 12.22 is from the query in Figure 12.15, with a group band based on the STUDENTID field. Figure 12.23 shows the output from the report format. Figure 12.24 shows a report format produced by the query in Figure 12.16, with a group band based on the COURSEID field. The report printed by this format is shown in Figure 12.25.

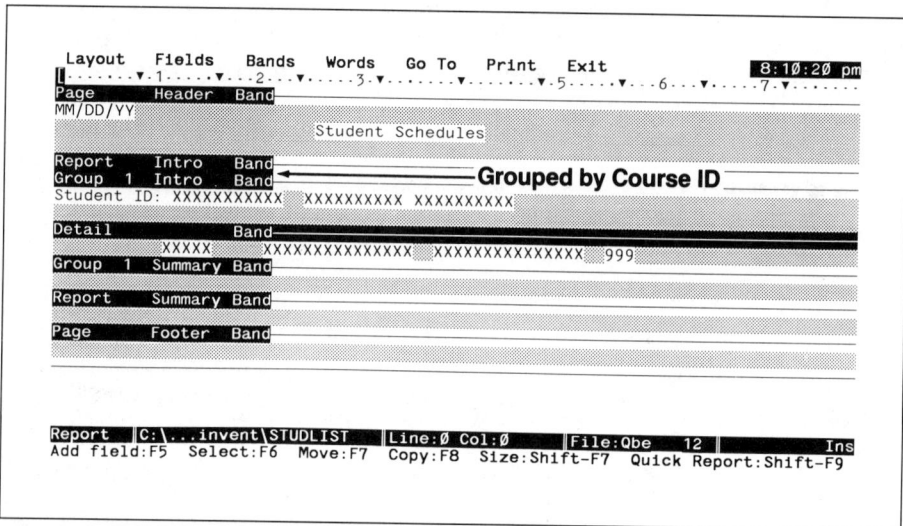

FIGURE 12.24: Student enrollment example: a report format to print a course list.

EXAMPLE

You can use the query in Figure 12.19 to design a report to print invoices. If JOIN1 is not already above the line in the Queries panel, highlight its name, press ↵, and select Use View. Highlight <create> in the Reports panel and press ↵. When you get to the reports design screen, select the Column Layout option from the Quick Layout submenu to start with a column layout.

To ensure that charges for a single customer are grouped together on one invoice, move the cursor to the Report Intro band (Band 2/5) and select Add a Group Band from the Bands pull-down menu. Select Field Value and then CUSTNO as the field to base the groups on.

```
07/21/90                      Course Enrollments

Course number: Bi101    Course name: Biology
Instructor: Dillweed            Room: 29

         564-90-5999   Adams      Albert    3546 Oak St.    El Monte
         343-56-8493   Black      Bob       45 Maple St.    Azusa
         543-65-6475   Green      Janet     652 Elm St.     Duarte
         656-34-6564   Reed       Scarlet   22 Nardo Way    Glendora

Course number: Ch100    Course name: Chemistry
Instructor: Zeepoid             Room: 29

         564-90-5999   Adams      Albert    3546 Oak St.    El Monte
         343-56-8493   Black      Bob       45 Maple St.    Azusa
         543-65-6475   Green      Janet     652 Elm St.     Duarte
         656-34-6564   Reed       Scarlet   22 Nardo Way    Glendora

Course number: Lt101    Course name: Latin
Instructor: Tyson               Room: 14

         564-90-5999   Adams      Albert    3546 Oak St.    El Monte
         543-65-6475   Green      Janet     652 Elm St.     Duarte
         343-56-8493   Black      Bob       45 Maple St.    Azusa

Course number: Ps101    Course name: Psychology
Instructor: Jung                Room: 17

         543-65-6475   Green      Janet     652 Elm St.     Duarte
```

FIGURE 12.25: Report showing enrollment grouped by courses. This report is based on the format in Figure 12.24.

To print each invoice on a separate page, move the cursor to the Group 1 Intro band border and change the Begin Band on New Page option on the Bands pull-down menu to Yes.

Figure 12.26 shows a sample report format with some field templates added, rearranged, or deleted. The field template furthest to the right in the Detail band is a calculated field named EXTPRICE, based on the expression QTY * UNITPRICE. The template below that one is a summary field that sums the EXTPRICE field. Be sure to set Reset Every to CUSTNO for this summary field so that the total is reset to zero for each customer.

After creating the report format, use the Save Changes and Exit option on the Exit pull-down menu to save it. When prompted, enter **INVOICES** as the file name. When you get back to the Control Center, you can select INVOICES from the Reports panel to print the invoices. Figure 12.27 shows an invoice printed from the report format.

USING FORMS WITH RELATED FILES

You can use a view that links two or more databases as the basis for creating custom forms (just as you can for creating report formats). However, keep in

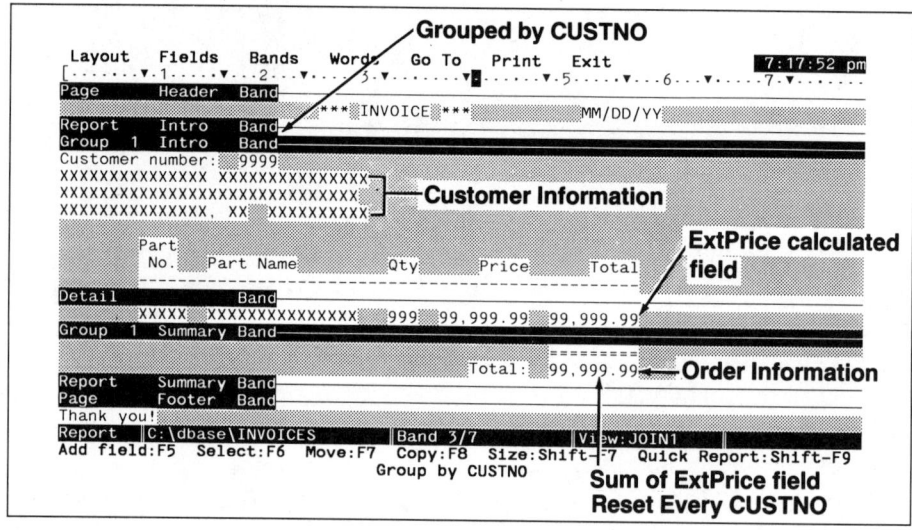

FIGURE 12.26: Report format for printing invoices from the query in Figure 12.19.

```
                        *** INVOICE ***              06/30/90

    Customer number: 1003
    Mary Mahoney
    211 Seahawk St.
    Seattle, WA    88977


         Part
          No.    Part Name          Qty      Price        Total
         -----------------------------------------------------------
         A-111  Astro Buddies        4       55.00       220.00
         B-222  Mondo Man            1      100.00       100.00
                                                       =========
                                              Total:    320.00


    Thank you!
```

FIGURE 12.27: An invoice printed from the view in Figure 12.19 and the report format in Figure 12.26.

mind that whenever you display data from two or more files in a view, all of the data has read-only status. Therefore, although the form would allow you to view data from multiple related databases, it would not allow you to add new data or change existing data. Hence, there is little reason to create forms that are based on views.

You may think that this is a weakness in dBASE IV, but actually, it is a means of protecting your data. If dBASE allowed you to create custom forms that display data from multiple related files, it would need to have some built-in rules about how to handle certain situations that arise.

For example, suppose you have a single form that displays a customer's name and address from the CUSTLIST database and the same person's outstanding orders from the ORDERS database. If, while using this form, you purposely (or accidentally) delete a customer record, how should dBASE handle this deletion? Should it assume that you are deleting the customer from the CUSTLIST database? If so, should it also delete all the current (and perhaps even fulfilled) orders for this customer? Or should it leave the customer in the CUSTLIST database, but just delete the person's outstanding orders?

Then again, perhaps dBASE should not allow you to delete the customer at all. Or maybe it should warn you that the customer has outstanding orders and then allow you to decide whether you want to proceed with the deletion.

These are a few questions that arise when dealing with a fairly simple pair of related databases: customers and their orders. Suppose that a custom form displays data from three or five or even ten related database files, and you change or delete an item in one field. There are literally hundreds of ways that this change or deletion and its effects on related databases could be interpreted.

Because dBASE cannot possibly know exactly what you mean when you change or delete data from one field among many related database files, it simply does not allow you to do so. Therefore, create a form for each database and then add and change data individually for each database, rather than trying to manage multiple related databases through a single form. You can still use queries and views to analyze or print related data, as preceding examples in this chapter demonstrate.

Actually, it *is* possible to create forms for managing data in multiple related database files; it is just not possible to do so using the query design screen and forms design screen. You need more precise control than the design screens offer, and the only way to get this control is by programming, using the built-in dBASE IV programming language.

Using the programming language, you can set up your own rules to handle the kinds of situations and problems that arise when you simultaneously manage data from multiple database files. To see just how specific the programming language allows you to be, let's look at a custom form used for entering and editing orders. Unfortunately, this book cannot show how to *create* this form, because the programming techniques are too advanced. (A more advanced book that is dedicated to the programming language, such as *dBASE IV Programmer's Reference Guide* by this same author and also published by SYBEX, can help you create forms such as the one demonstrated here.)

First keep in mind that this example uses three databases. These are similar to the CUSTLIST, ORDERS, and MASTER databases used in preceding examples in this chapter: One stores information about existing customers, another stores information about orders, and another stores information about inventory.

When the user wants to add new orders, he or she first sees the screen shown in Figure 12.28. The invoice number at the top of the screen is calculated and displayed automatically (by the program that manages the entire form).

Notice that the cursor is in the field for the customer number. The message line at the bottom of the screen describes actions that the user can take. If the user

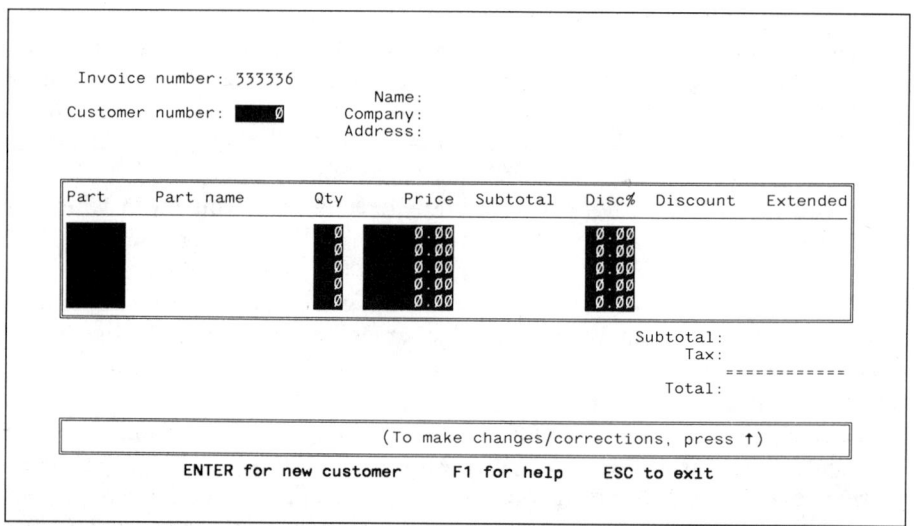

FIGURE 12.28: Form for entering new orders. This sample form was created using the dBASE IV programming language. It manages data from three related databases simultaneously.

presses ⏎, leaving the field blank, the form assumes that the order is for a new customer. Immediately the form assigns the next available customer number to this customer, and the cursor moves to the right and allows the user to type the customer name and address.

Alternatively, the user can press **F1** to see a list of existing customer names, addresses, and numbers (from the CUSTLIST database). These are displayed in alphabetical order. When the user types a part of the customer's last name, the cursor immediately jumps to the area in the database where similarly spelled names are stored. For example, in Figure 12.29 the user has pressed **F1** and typed the letters **SM**; the window now displays customers whose names begin with the letters *SM*.

The user can now move the highlight to the appropriate customer name and press ⏎. The window of customer names then disappears from the screen, and the customer's number is automatically entered into the Customer Number field on the form. In addition, the customer's name and address is displayed on the form, and the cursor jumps to the square box where order details are entered.

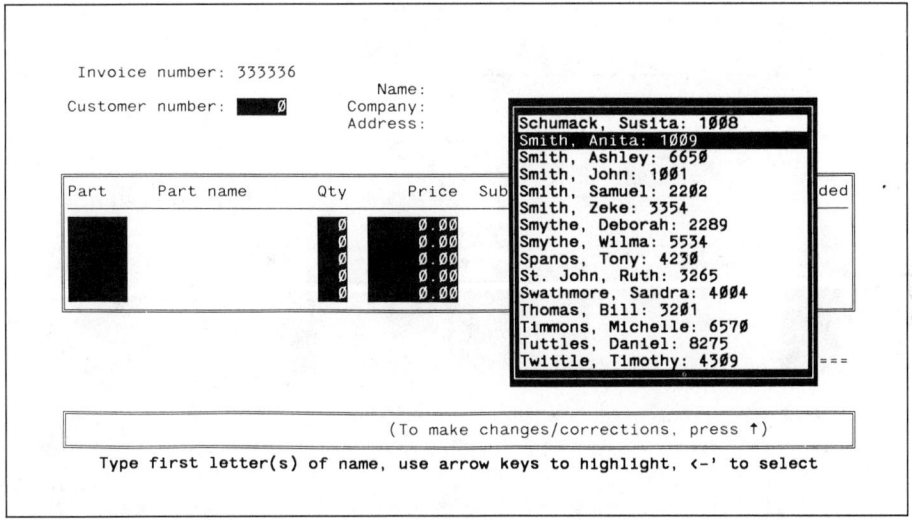

FIGURE 12.29: The user has asked for help in locating a customer number by pressing **F1** and typing the letters **SM**. The window lists customers whose last names begin with *SM*. The user can now move the highlight to the appropriate customer, if any, and press ⏎ to select that customer.

The user can also simply type a customer number (if he or she knows it) while the cursor is in the Customer Number field on the form. If the user enters a valid customer number, the customer's name and address are displayed on the screen. If the user enters an invalid customer number, then dBASE beeps, reports that no such customer number exists, and asks the user to enter a different number (or to press **F1** to look up the customer by name).

Of course, should the user make a mistake, such as typing the wrong customer number, the user can simply change the customer number. The customer name and address on the form will be updated immediately. Optionally, to exit and stop entering orders, the user can press **Esc** while the cursor is in the customer number field.

After the user has entered a valid customer number, the cursor moves down to the area for entering order details, as shown in Figure 12.30. Notice that the selected customer name and number are now on the screen, and the window of existing customers has been removed.

Entering order information is similar to entering a customer number. While the cursor is in the Part field, the user can enter a part number (if the user knows it) or press **F1** to see a list of existing part names. When the window displaying

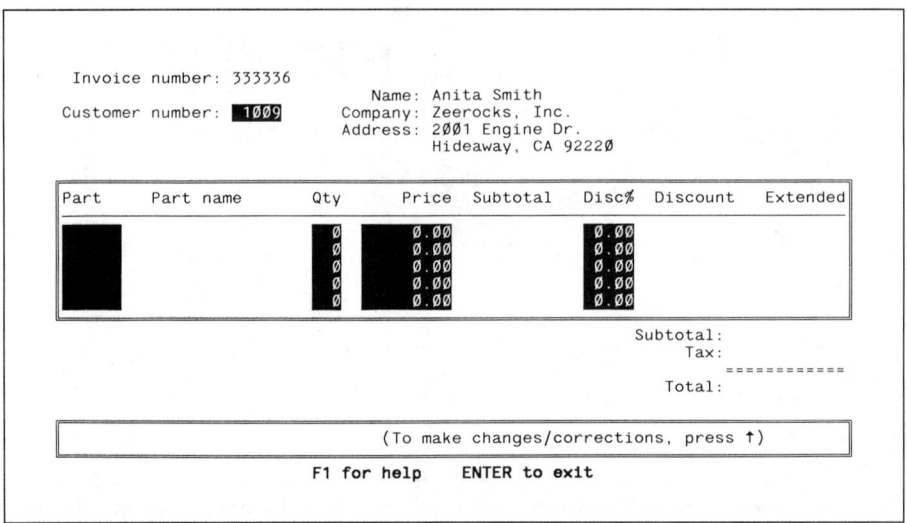

FIGURE 12.30: A valid customer number has been entered on the screen, and that customer's name and address are displayed. The user can now enter order information.

part names appears on the screen, the user can scroll through names (using the ↑, ↓, **PgDn**, and **PgUp** keys) or type the first letter or letters of the part name to quickly move the highlight to the appropriate general area (part names that begin with that letter or letters).

In Figure 12.31, the user has pressed **F1** and typed **Amp** to move to the general area of parts that begin with the letters *Amp*. The user can now move the highlight to any part name and press ↵ to select that part name.

After the user selects a part number, the part name, unit price, and item discount rate appear on the screen. (Actually, in this particular form the CUST-LIST database provides a field for the maximum discount rate that the customer can receive. If the customer's discount rate is less than the item discount rate, the customer's discount rate is displayed instead.)

Now the user can enter the quantity ordered. dBASE offers several techniques to handle back orders should the amount ordered exceed the quantity in stock. Because different businesses handle back orders in different ways, again some programming will probably be required.

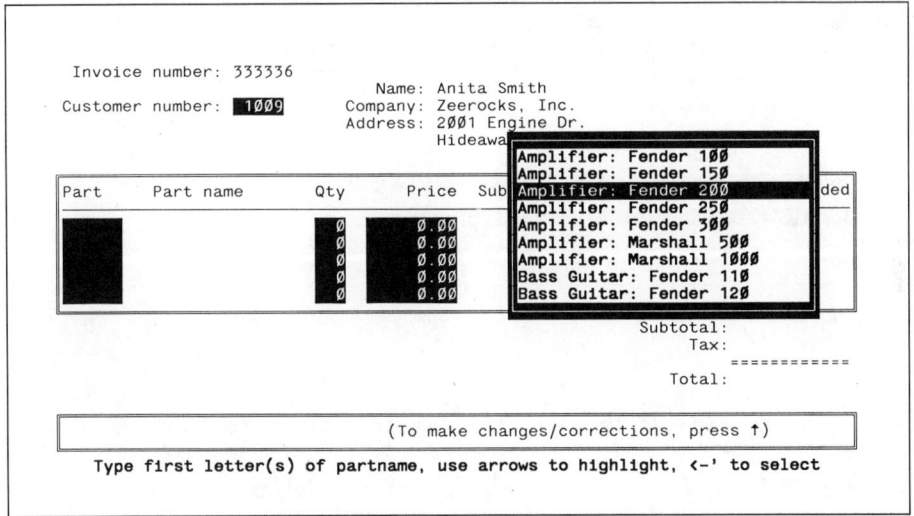

FIGURE 12.31: A window displaying a list of existing part names and part numbers appears on the screen, because the user pressed **F1** for help. The user can select any part name from this window by highlighting the name and pressing ↵.

The user can also modify the unit price and discount rate or leave them as suggested on the form. (On your own screens, you may not want the user to be able to modify these fields.) The user can add any number of items to the customer's order. If there are too many items to fit into the box, existing orders scroll upward to make room for new ones (as on the dBASE browse screen).

When the entire order has been filled in, the subtotal, tax, and total are calculated. The user has one more chance to change anything on the order form. Figure 12.32 shows a completed order on the screen, with a prompt asking the user if the order is now ready for entry.

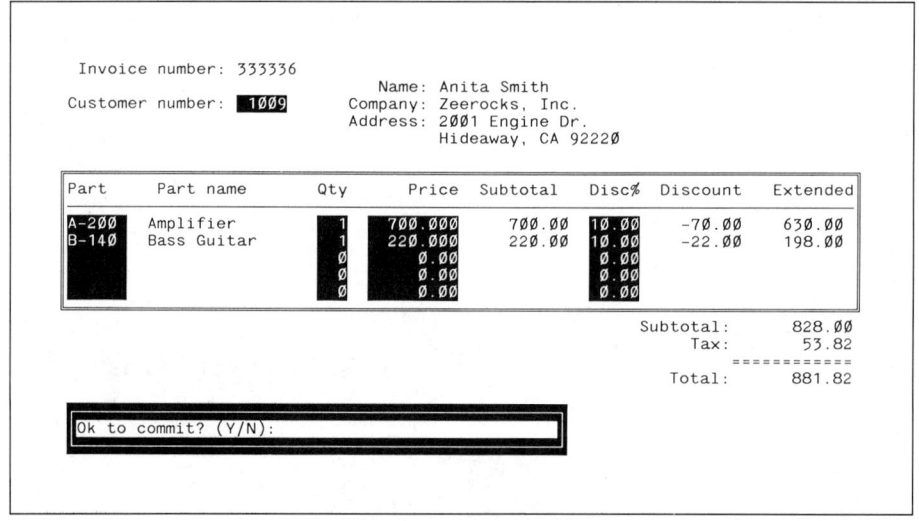

FIGURE 12.32: A completed order on the screen. The user has one last chance to check the order and make changes if necessary.

If the user opts to enter the order (to not make any more changes), the order is accepted as valid and goes into the database for future processing. You might, however, prefer to have a program like this immediately print the invoice or, in some cases, a receipt. If so, yet another situation arises where only the precise control of a programming language can give you the power to instantly take the data displayed on the screen and send it to the printer as an invoice or receipt.

The preceding example demonstrates techniques for entering new orders. Another screen, practically identical to this screen, allows the user to modify existing orders (so long as they have not already been fulfilled). The editing screen is programmed to handle various situations. For example, if the user deletes the customer number, the program "knows" that the user actually wants to delete only this order, not necessarily to delete the customer from the CUST-LIST database (a different form allows the user to delete customers).

If the user deletes or changes a part number in the order, the system "knows" that the change refers only to the current order, not to the MASTER database part number or to other orders. In other words, the entire form is specifically designed according to the manner in which a particular business handles its orders. A different business might use entirely different techniques and options, but the programming language could almost certainly handle the job.

Though programming requires a great deal of study and experience to fully master, doing so is not necessarily an unpleasant task. If you take the time to look into Chapter 19 of this book, which introduces programming concepts, you will probably find that programming in dBASE is much easier than you had expected. But again, a book this size cannot possibly discuss dBASE programming in the depth required to create a custom form like the one presented in this chapter.

TIPS AND TRAPS

- On the queries design screen, use **Tab** and **Shift-Tab** to move back and forth in the file and view skeleton boxes. Use Previous (**F3**) and Next (**F4**) to move the highlight from one skeleton to the next. Use Field (**F5**) to move fields into and out of the view skeleton. Use Select (**F6**) and Move (**F7**) to rearrange the order of fields in the view skeleton.

- On the queries design screen, dBASE uses # to indicate indexed fields and ↓ to indicate fields included in the view skeleton.

- On the reports design screen, to move the cursor to field templates that are off the right edge of the screen, move the cursor into the Detail band and press **End** to move to the rightmost template or **Ctrl-→** to move to the next template.

- When you use the Create Link by Pointing menu option for linking fields, dBASE uses LINK1 as the placeholder. Instead of using this option, you can just type any letter or word into the common fields (so long as you use the same letter or word in both file skeletons).

Summary

You will sometimes need to create several linked databases for your database management tasks. This chapter discussed one-to-many and many-to-many database designs, how to create views from multiple-database designs, and the requirements for printing reports from multiple-database views.

For more information about creating views from queries:

- Chapter 5, "Searching the Database"

For more information about report design:

- Chapter 7, "Designing Formatted Reports"

For more discussion and examples of update queries:

- Chapter 11, "Managing Groups of Records"

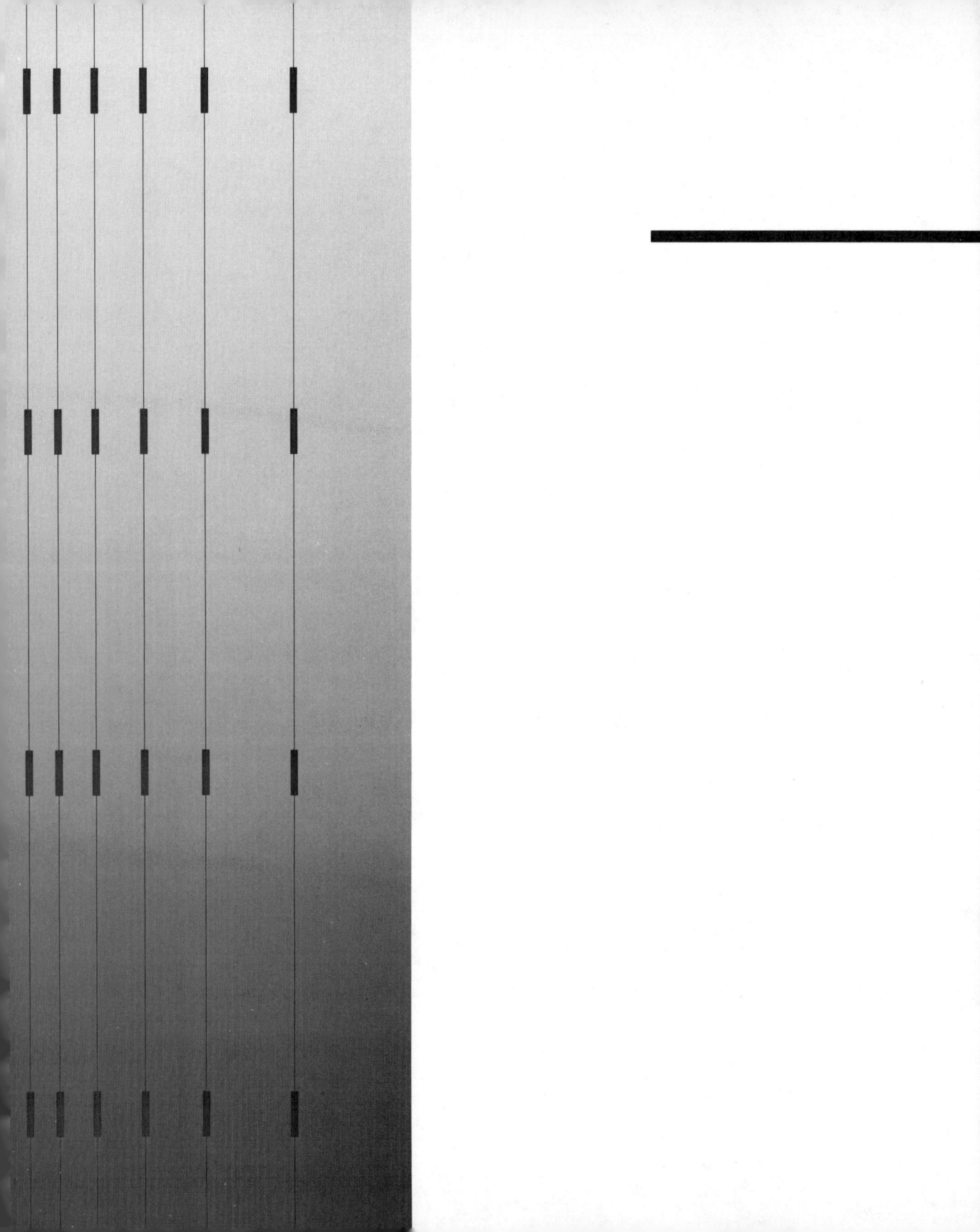

CHAPTER 13

USING KEYSTROKE MACROS

Recording Keystroke Macros from the Control Center. 437
Recording Keystrokes from Anywhere in dBASE. 438
Typing Macro Keystrokes. 440
Playing Back Recorded Keystrokes. 442
Canceling Macro Playback. 444
Entering Macro Names. 445
Saving Keystroke Macros. 445
Loading a Macro Library. 446
Pausing a Macro. 447
Editing Keystroke Macros. 448
    Making One Macro Play Another. 452
    Adding to an Existing Macro. 452
Viewing Macro Keystrokes during Playback. 453
Copying a Macro. 454
Deleting a Macro. 454
Sending Commands to DOS from a Macro. 455
Tips and Traps. 456
Summary. 456

Using Keystroke Macros

Some dBASE IV operations require many keystrokes to accomplish. As an alternative to reentering these keystrokes each time you want to perform an operation, you can record all the necessary keystrokes in a keystroke macro and then play them back at any time in the future. You can also use keystroke macros for blocks of text that you type often. For example, if you regularly type your company name and address in form letters, you can record the required keystrokes in a keystroke macro. To type your company name and address in the future, you need only play back the macro.

Macro means large (the opposite of *micro*); a *keystroke macro* is a single keystroke that plays back many keystrokes—that is, a "large keystroke." The general steps for creating and saving keystroke macros are summarized here:

1. Select Begin Recording from the macros menu.
2. Assign a key name to the macro.
3. Type the keystrokes to be recorded.
4. Select End Recording from the macros menu.

There are several ways to begin recording keystrokes in a macro, depending on whether you start from the Control Center or from a design screen. To save recorded keystrokes for use in future sessions with dBASE IV, you must take the additional step of storing the macro in a macro library.

Recording Keystrokes from the Control Center

To begin recording keystrokes, when starting at the Control Center, you can use the Macros option on the Tools pull-down menu.

SEQUENCE OF STEPS

From the Control Center:

    Menus (**F10**)
    Tools/**M**acros [↵]
    Begin Recording [↵]

USAGE

To record a set of keystrokes as a macro, starting at the Control Center, press Menus (**F10**), move to the Tools pull-down menu, and select Macros. You will see the submenu shown in Figure 13.1. Select Begin Recording from this menu. The submenu shown in Figure 13.2 will appear, instructing you to choose the key that will activate the macro once it is recorded.

You can name your macro with any letter key (a through z) or function key (**F1** through **F10**). You will later use this letter or function key to play back your macro.

Type a letter key or press a function key. The navigation line informs you that keystrokes are now being recorded, so you can type the keystrokes that you want to save (see "Typing Macro Keystrokes" later in this chapter).

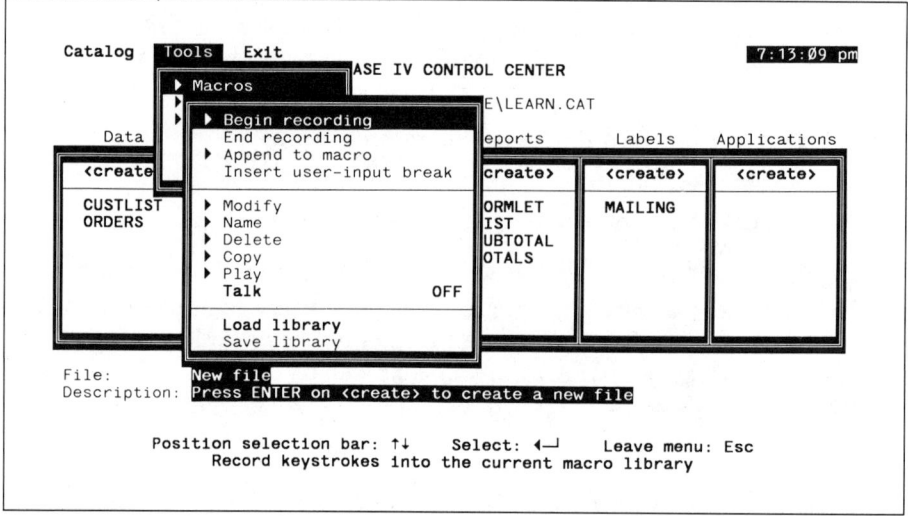

FIGURE 13.1: To access the Macros submenu, select Macros from the Tools pull-down menu at the Control Center.

RECORDING KEYSTROKES FROM ANYWHERE IN dBASE

As an alternative to using the macros option on the Tools pull-down menu to record keystrokes, you can use the macros prompt box. This alternative allows you to start recording macro keystrokes from anywhere within dBASE, including any design screen.

RECORDING KEYSTROKES FROM ANYWHERE IN dBASE — 439

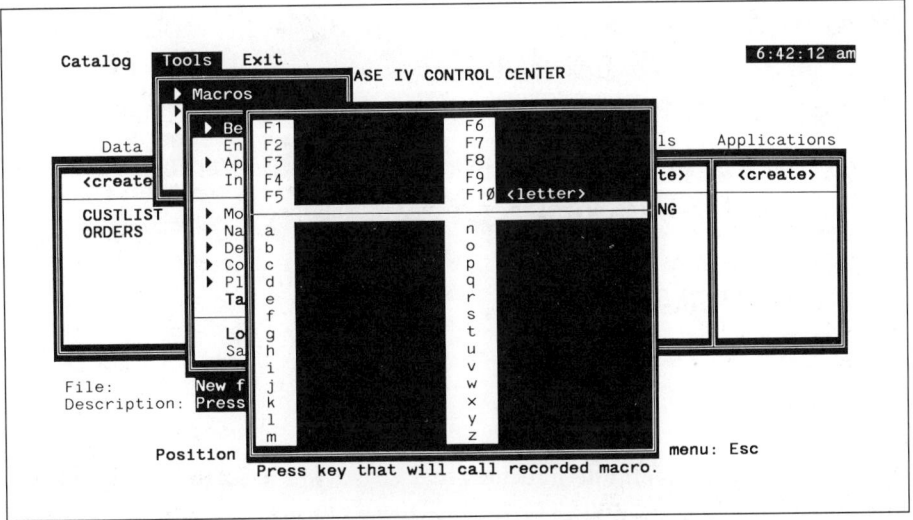

FIGURE 13.2: Submenu for naming keystroke macros. You can choose any of the letters or function keys on the menu to name your macro. (Later you can add a descriptive name, to help you remember what the macro does.)

SEQUENCE OF STEPS

From anywhere in dBASE IV:

> Macros (**Shift-F10**)
> Begin Recording [↵]

USAGE

To access the macros prompt box, press **Shift-F10**. Then, to name your macro, select Begin Recording. dBASE will display the message *Press the key that will call this macro*. Type a single-letter name (a through z) or press a function key (**F1** through **F10**).

If you select a key name that is already assigned to a macro, the screen displays the message *Do you really want to overwrite <key name>? (Y/N)*. If you select No, the operation is canceled, and you can start over. If you select Yes, dBASE begins recording keystrokes immediately.

The navigation line will remind you that dBASE is now recording your keystrokes, and that you can press **Shift-F10** when you want to stop recording.

Typing Macro Keystrokes

SEQUENCE OF STEPS

While dBASE is recording keystrokes:

    type the keystrokes necessary to perform the operation

To end recording:

    Macros (**Shift-F10**)

    End Recording [↵]

USAGE

When the navigation line indicates that keystrokes are being recorded, type the keystrokes necessary to perform the operation that you want to save as a macro. To make your keystroke macros as accurate as possible, use the most explicit method of selecting any menu or option; avoid using any method that depends on context. You may not always run the macro with the same menu in effect as when you recorded it or with the highlight in the same position.

If your keystroke macro accesses the pull-down menus, use **Alt**-*key* combinations, rather than Menus (**F10**), when you record the keystrokes. For example, **Alt-T** always pulls down the Tools menu, whereas Menus (**F10**) pulls down whichever menu was used last. If you use Menus (**F10**) to pull down a menu while recording keystrokes, dBASE may pull down a different menu when you play back the macro.

Similarly, select options from pull-down menus by typing the first letter of the option, rather than by moving the highlight with an arrow key and pressing ↵. In this way, you ensure that the macro will not select the wrong option because the highlight is in a different position during playback than it was when you recorded the macro.

If you want the macro to select an option from a submenu of file names or field names, type the file name or field name rather than selecting it from the submenu. Submenus of file and field names change as you add and delete objects, so the position of a field or file name in a submenu may vary. If you type the file or field name while recording keystrokes, you need not be concerned about its position in a submenu when you later use the macro.

To stop recording keystrokes, press Macros (**Shift-F10**) and select End Recording. The navigation line informs you that macro recording has finished.

EXAMPLES

Suppose you want to record the keystrokes necessary to view the names and sizes of your dBASE database files. You need to record the keystrokes required to access the DOS Utilities file list and to limit the display to only database (.DBF) files. To do so, follow these steps:

1. From the Control Center, press Menus (**F10**) and select Macros from the Tools pull-down menu.
2. Select Begin Recording.
3. Type a name for the macro, such as the letter **D**. dBASE reminds you that keystrokes are now being recorded.
4. Press **Alt-T** to access the Tools pull-down menu.
5. Type **D** to select DOS Utilities.
6. Press **Alt-F** to access the Files pull-down menu.
7. Type **D** to select Display Only.
8. Press **Ctrl-Y** to erase the current entry.
9. Type *.**DBF** and press ↵ to display the names of database files only.
10. If necessary, press **PgDn** and ↓ to scroll past subdirectory names to where the file names appear.
11. To stop recording keystrokes, press Macros (**Shift-F10**) and select End Recording.

The navigation line now informs you that macro recording has stopped. To return to the Control Center, press **F10** and select Exit to Control Center from the Exit pull-down menu. See "Playing Back Recorded Keystrokes" later in this chapter to play back the macro keystrokes. To save the recorded macro in the current macro library, see "Saving Keystroke Macros" later in this chapter.

Suppose now that you want to record another keystroke macro that types your company name and address to help you create form letters. Since you will always use this macro from the reports design screen, you may want to begin recording the keystrokes from that screen. Follow these steps:

1. From the Control Center, open a database, such as CUSTLIST (introduced in Chapter 2), by selecting its name from the data panel and selecting Use File from the prompt box.
2. Select <create> from the Reports panel to go to the reports design screen.
3. Select Quick Layouts.
4. Select Mailmerge layout.

442 — **CH. 13** USING KEYSTROKE MACROS

5. Press **Shift-F10** and select Begin Recording.
6. Enter a name for the macro, such as **C**.
7. Type the keystrokes that you want to record, using the exact format in which you want them entered, as in Figure 13.3, which displays a company name and address.
8. To stop recording keystrokes, press **Shift-F10** and select End Recording.
9. To return to the Control Center without saving the report format, press **F10**, select Abandon Changes and Exit, and then select Yes when asked to confirm your selection.

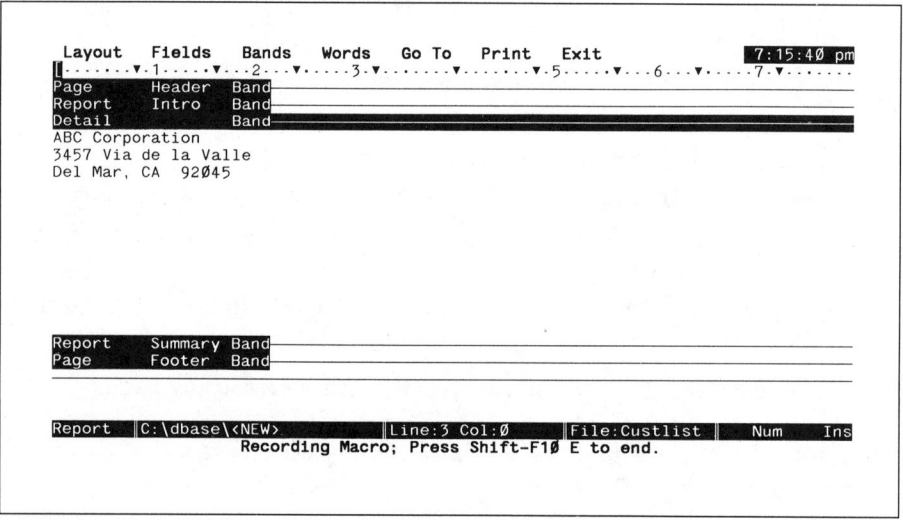

FIGURE 13.3: A company name and address typed into the mailmerge editor on the reports design screen. Recording these keystrokes while typing them will allow you to retype the company name and address in the future simply by playing back the macro.

PLAYING BACK RECORDED KEYSTROKES

SEQUENCE OF STEPS

From the Control Center:

    Menus (**F10**)
    Tools/**M**acros [↵]

Play [⏎]
   type the letter or function key

From any place in dBASE (for letter keys):

Alt-F10
   press the letter key

From any place in dBASE (for function keys):

Alt-*function key*

USAGE

To play back your recorded keystrokes from the Control Center, press Menus (**F10**) and select Macros from the Tools pull-down menu. Select Play from the submenu that appears. Type the letter or function key that is the name of your macro. dBASE automatically performs the recorded keystrokes, doing whatever you set up that macro to do.

To play back a macro recorded with a letter key from any place in dBASE where the Tools menu is not available, press **Alt-F10**. dBASE displays the prompt *Press an alphabetic key of the macro to play back.* Type the letter name you assigned to the keystroke macro to start playing it back.

When you have assigned one of the function keys **F1** through **F9** to a macro, you can play back the macro from anywhere in dBASE at any time by holding down the **Alt** key and pressing the appropriate function key. For example, if you assign **F5** as the macro name when you begin recording a macro, you can play back the macro simply by pressing **Alt-F5**. (**Alt-F10** cannot be the name of a keystroke macro, because this is the keystroke combination necessary to play back macros with single-letter names.)

Note that you must be at the same starting point that you used to begin recording keystrokes when you play back the keystrokes. Otherwise, the keystrokes may not make any sense. For example, suppose that from the word-wrap editor you record the keystrokes necessary to type a paragraph. If you try to play back this macro from the Control Center or from another design screen, the keystrokes will not make any sense to dBASE. They will have unpredictable results and probably cause a lot of beeping.

EXAMPLES

To use the D macro to view the names of all .DBF files in the current directory, first make sure that you are at the Control Center. Then press Menus (**F10**) and

444 ——— CH. 13   USING KEYSTROKE MACROS

select Macros from the Tools pull-down menu. Select Play from the submenu and type the name of the macro, **D**. dBASE IV plays back the recorded keystrokes, leaving you at the DOS Utilities screen with the names of all the .DBF files displayed, as shown in Figure 13.4.

Once the recorded keystrokes are all played back, you can either do more work on the DOS Utilities screen or select Exit to Control Center from the Exit pull-down menu.

To use the macro that types the company name and address, you must first get to the mailmerge editor in the reports design screen. Open a database file and then select <create> from the Reports pull-down menu. Select Quick Layouts and Mailmerge from the Layout pull-down menu.

Next, position the cursor where you want the company name and address to be typed. To play back the macro, press **Alt-F10**. The screen displays the message *Press an alphabetic key of the macro to play back*. In this example, type the letter **C**, and the macro will type the company name and address.

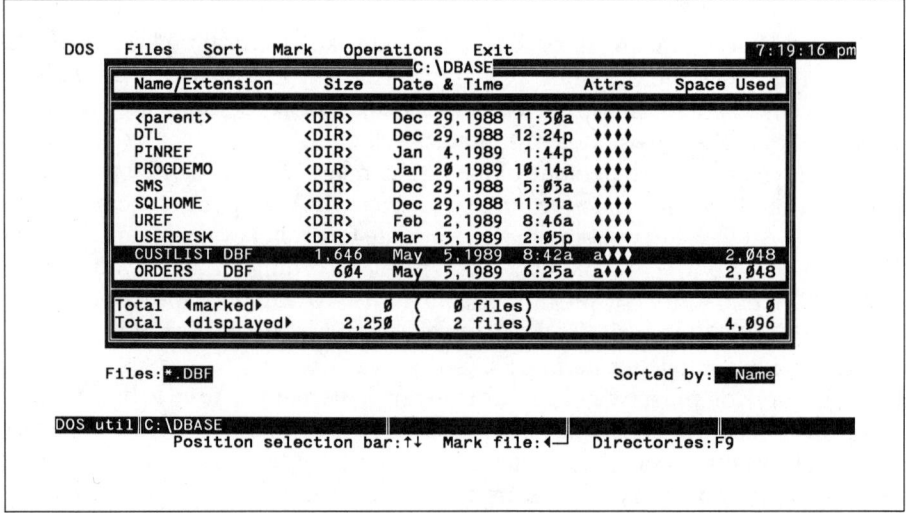

FIGURE 13.4: The DOS utilities screen displaying information about the dBASE IV database (.DBF) files in the current directory. This screen was displayed by playing back a series of recorded keystrokes, stored under the macro name D.

CANCELING MACRO PLAYBACK

To interrupt a macro as it is typing, press the **Esc** key. dBASE will display the message *Escape pressed. End macro? (Y/N)*. Type **Y** and press ↵ to stop the macro or **N** and ↵ to resume the macro.

Entering Macro Names

SEQUENCE OF STEPS

From the Control Center:

> Menus (**F10**)
> Tools/**M**acros [↵]
> **N**ame [↵]
> type a name ↵

USAGE

When you create a macro, you initially give it the same name as the key used to play it back. You can enter a more descriptive name to help you remember what each macro does.

To name a macro, starting from the Control Center, press Menus (**F10**) and select the Macros option from the Tools pull-down menu. Then select Name, and the screen will display the names of all current macros. Press the key that you use to play back the macro. For example, to rename macro C, type **C**.

dBASE will prompt you to enter a new name for the macro. The name can be up to ten characters long, but cannot contain any blank spaces. Type a name and press ↵. Figure 13.5 shows an example, where macro C is named COMPANY, and macro D is named FILENAMES.

Renaming macros does not affect the way in which you execute them. Regardless of the longer descriptive name that you assign a macro, you still use the single-letter name to play back the macro.

Saving Keystroke Macros

SEQUENCE OF STEPS

From the Control Center:

> Menus (**F10**)
> Tools/**M**acros [↵]
> **S**ave Library [↵]
> enter a file name ↵

USAGE

When you first save recorded keystrokes in a macro, dBASE stores them in RAM (temporary memory), not on disk. This means that when you exit

446 — CH. 13 USING KEYSTROKE MACROS

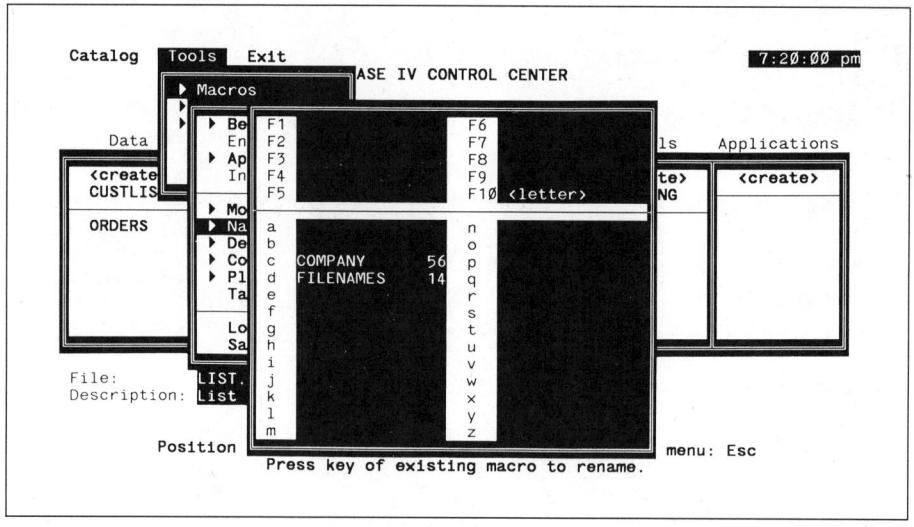

FIGURE 13.5: The Name option on the Macros menu allows you to assign more descriptive names to your keystroke macros. In this example, macro C has been renamed COMPANY, and macro D has been renamed FILENAMES.

dBASE, the macro will be erased. If you want to save a keystroke macro for future use, you must save it on disk in a *macro library*.

To do so, Press Menus (**F10**) and select Macros from the Tools pull-down menu from the Control Center. Select Save Library from the menu (shown in Figure 13.1). Type a valid DOS file name, with no extension (such as MYMACROS), and press ←⏎.

A single macro library can contain up to 36 macros. When you want to use one of the macros in the library or to add more macros to an existing macro library, you must first be sure that the appropriate macro library is loaded.

You can create as many macro libraries as you wish, each with a maximum of 34 macros. For convenience, you may want to create a separate macro library for each database application, such as one for inventory management and one for producing form letters.

LOADING A MACRO LIBRARY

SEQUENCE OF STEPS

From the Control Center:

    Menus (**F10**)
    Tools/Macros [←⏎]

Load Library [↵]
select the macro library name

USAGE

To load a macro library from the Control Center, press Menus (**F10**), select the Macros option from the Tools pull-down menu, and then select Load Library from the macro menu (shown in Figure 13.1). Select the macro library name from the submenu that appears.

The macro library stays loaded for the duration of the current dBASE session or until you load a different macro library. You can play any macro in the current library using the usual techniques for playing a macro. Any new macros that you create are stored in the current library as well. However, if you add new macros to the library, you must save the entire library again. Otherwise, your new macros will not be saved.

If you load more than one macro library, the incoming macros will replace any current macros that have the same name. For example, suppose a macro library named MACLIB1 contains macros named A, B, and C, and a macro library named MACLIB2 contains macros named C, D, and E. If you have already loaded MACLIB1 and then load MACLIB2, macros named A through E will be available for use. However, since both MACLIB1 and MACLIB2 contain a macro named C, and MACLIB2 was loaded second, the current macro named C will be the one from the MACLIB2 macro library.

PAUSING A MACRO

SEQUENCE OF STEPS

At any time while recording macro keystrokes:

Macros (**Shift-F10**)
Insert User-Input Break [↵]
↵
type remaining keystrokes to complete the macro
Macros (**Shift-F10**)
End Recording [↵]

USAGE

You can make a macro pause so you can enter text or select menu options directly. For example, suppose that you create a macro to enter your company name and address, but you want the macro to pause to allow you to enter a department name.

To create such a macro, you follow the same steps as presented earlier to create the macro named C in the mailmerge editor. However, after typing the company name and pressing ←, you press **Shift-F10** and select Insert User-Input Break. You then press ← again and type the company address. When you have finished recording keystrokes, you press **Shift-F10** and select End Recording to stop recording keystrokes.

When you play back the macro, it will type the company name and move the cursor to the next line. The screen then will display the message *Macro playback suspended, press* **Shift-F10** to resume playback. During this pause, you can type the department name. When you are done typing, you press **Shift-F10** to have the macro resume playing back the rest of the recorded keystrokes.

You can insert any number of user-input breaks into a keystroke macro.

EDITING KEYSTROKE MACROS

SEQUENCE OF STEPS

From the Control Center:

> Menus (**F10**)
> Tools/Macros [←]
> Modify [←]
> enter the macro letter or function key name
> edit macro using same keys as in the Memo field editor (see Table 3.2)
> Menus (**F10**)
> Exit/Save Changes and Exit [←]

USAGE

You can modify a series of recorded keystrokes in a keystroke macro. To do so, start from the Control Center. Press **F10** and select Macros from the Tools pull-down menu. Then select Modify and dBASE will display the names of all macros. Type the letter, or press the function key, that you use to play back the macro. The macro will appear on the screen in a special version of the word-wrap editor, as in Figure 13.6.

The word-wrap editor for editing macros is similar to the editor used to create and edit data in Memo fields (see Table 3.2 in Chapter 3). The arrow keys move

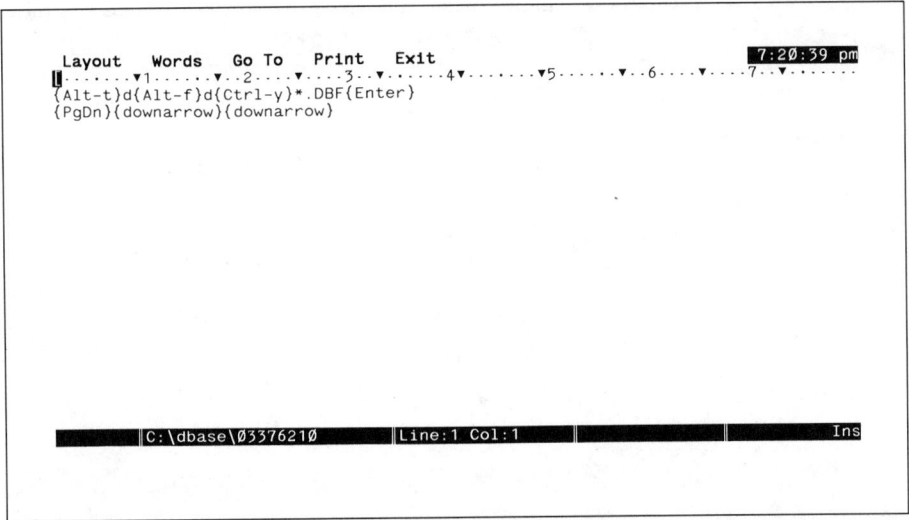

FIGURE 13.6: A keystroke macro in the word-wrap editor, ready for editing. The word-wrap editor for modifying keystroke macros works much like the editor for entering and editing memo fields.

the cursor, **F10** pulls down menus, and **F6** lets you select a block of text to work with. To move a selected block of text, move the cursor to the new location for the text and press ←┘. To copy a selected block of text, move the cursor to the destination for the copy and press **F8**. To delete a selected block of text, press **Del** and type **Y** when prompted for permission to delete.

Remember that literal keys, such as letters, numbers, and blank spaces, in a macro are typed directly when you play back the macro. When you are using the macro editor, to have a macro play back special keys such as ←┘ and ↑, you must enter the key names enclosed in curly braces. You can use either uppercase or lowercase letters for the key names. Table 13.1 lists the special key names used in keystroke macros.

You must also enclose function key names **F1** through **F10** in curly braces. For example, **{F2}** presses the **F2** key when you play back the macro. You can combine **Alt**, **Ctrl**, or **Shift** with any function key name. For example, **{Alt-F1}** presses the **Alt-F1** combination when you play back the macro.

You can combine **Alt** with any lowercase letter (a–z) or number (0–9). For example, **{Alt-t}** presses **Alt-t** when you play back the macro. You can combine **Ctrl** with any letter (a–z). For example, **{Ctrl-y}** presses **Ctrl-y** when you play back the macro.

While working in the macro editor, you can press ←┘ or **Tab** at any time to format a keystroke macro. These keystrokes are not played back later when you

SPECIAL KEY	NAME USED IN MACRO EDITOR
↑	{Uparrow}
↓	{Downarrow}
←	{Leftarrow}
→	{Rightarrow}
↵	{Enter}
Backspace	{Backspace}
Tab	{Tab}
Shift-Tab	{Shift-Tab}
PgUp	{PgUp}
PgDn	{PgDn}
Home	{Home}
End	{End}
Ins (or Insert)	{Ins}
Del (or Delete)	{Del}
Esc	{Esc}
PrtSc	{PrtSc}
function key	{*function key*}
Alt-*key*	{Alt-*key*}
Ctrl-*key*	{Ctrl-*key*}
Shift-*function key*	{Shift-*function key*}
Alt--	{Alt-hyphen}
Ctrl--	{Ctrl-hyphen}
User-Input Break	{InpBreak}

Table 13.1: Names for Special Keys in the Macro Editor

use the macro. A macro presses the **Tab** and ↵ keys only where you specify the {**Tab**} and {**Enter**} key names.

When you have finished editing your macro, press **F10** and select Save Changes and Exit from the Exit pull-down menu. To abandon the current changes, select Abandon Changes and Exit from the Exit menu.

EXAMPLE

Suppose that while recording a macro named B, which types a boilerplate paragraph that you use in many communications, you make a mistake and use the **Backspace** key to back up and make corrections. Later, when you play back the recorded macro, it will first type the mistake and then back up and make your corrections.

To remove the error and **Backspace** keystrokes, press Menus (**F10**) and select Macros from the Tools pull-down menu. Then select Modify and type the name of the keystroke macro: **B** in this example.

When the macro appears on the editor screen, move the cursor to the beginning of the text you want to delete. Press **F6** and then use the → key to highlight the block of text that you want to delete, as in Figure 13.7. After highlighting the entire block, press ←┘.

Once the block to delete is highlighted, press **Del**. dBASE presents the message *Press y to perform the block deletion*. When you press **Y**, the block is deleted immediately, and all text to the right and below moves left and up to fill the void.

To save the edited version of the macro, press **F10** and select Save Changes and Exit from the Exit pull-down menu. Note that the edited version of the macro is saved only in RAM at this point. To save the edited version of the macro for future use, you must resave the entire macro library, just as you do when you save a new macro.

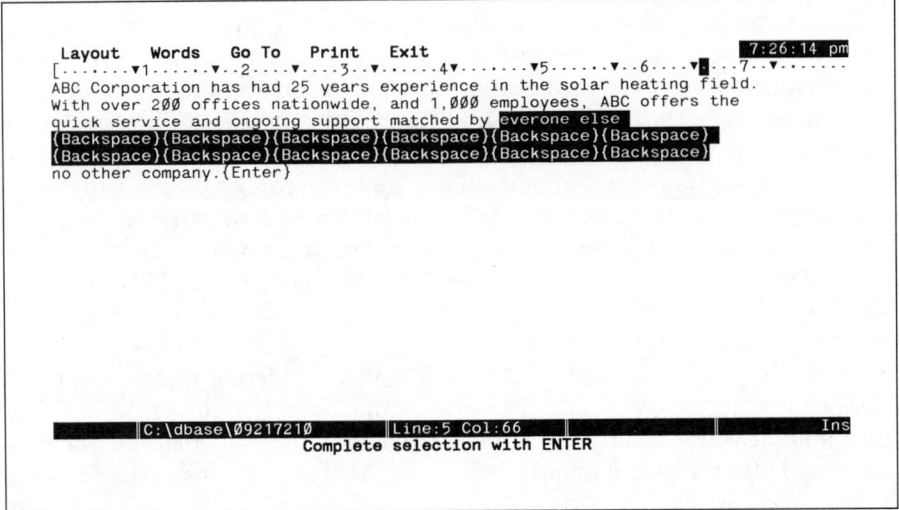

FIGURE 13.7: A block of text in a keystroke macro is highlighted in the macro editor, using the **F6** key. You can press **Del** to delete the highlighted block, or you can move the cursor to a new location and press **F7** to move, or **F8** to copy the block to the new destination.

Making One Macro Play Another

SEQUENCE OF STEPS

From anywhere in dBASE IV:

    Macros (**Shift-F10**)
    Begin Recording [↵]
    enter the letter or function key name for the new macro
    Alt-F10
    enter the name of the macro to play

USAGE

By including in one macro the keystrokes that call up another macro, you can tell dBASE to play back the second macro during its creation of the first. This feature, along with the related capability to duplicate a macro within its library, allows you to use individual macros as building blocks for larger, more sophisticated macros. For example, suppose you have a boilerplate sentence that sometimes appears on its own in your reports and sometimes is included in other boilerplate paragraphs. In the macro for the boilerplate paragraph, you would insert the keystrokes to play the sentence macro at the point where you want that sentence to appear and then continue typing your paragraph. Of course, for this technique to work, the nested macro must be in the current macro library.

You can embed one macro within another either when you create the "outer" macro or while you are editing it.

To make one macro play another macro while recording a macro, simply press the keys necessary to play the second macro (which must be in the current macro library). For example, if you are currently recording a macro named N, and you want it to play a macro named M, press **Alt-F10** then the letter **M** to play the M macro. When the M macro is finished, you can continue recording keystrokes for the N macro in the usual way.

If you are editing a macro and want it to play a different macro, include the keystrokes necessary to play the second macro in the current macro. For example, if you are currently editing a macro named X, and you want that macro to play the macro named Z, include {**Alt-F10**}Z in the current macro.

Adding to an Existing Macro

SEQUENCE OF STEPS

From the Control Center:

    Menus (**F10**)

Tools/**M**acros/**A**ppend to Macro [↵]
select the name of macro to append to
enter the new keystrokes for the macro
Macros (**Shift-F10**)
End Recording [↵]

USAGE

To add more keystrokes to an existing macro, starting from the Control Center, press Menus (**F10**) and select Macros from the Tools pull-down menu. Select Append to Macro and the name of the macro that you want to add keystrokes to.

Type the new keystrokes in the usual manner. When you are done typing new keystrokes, press Macros (**Shift-F10**) and select End Recording. Remember to save the entire macro library after adding new keystrokes to a macro.

The Append to Macro option is available only through the Tools pull-down menu from the Control Center. If you want to add to a macro that works on a design or edit screen, you will need to start from the Control Center. Then go to the design screen and record the additional keystrokes. The macro will contain the keystrokes that you pressed to leave the Control Center and go to the design screen. If necessary, you can edit the macro to remove these keystrokes.

When you are done recording keystrokes, press Macros (**Shift-F10**) and select End Recording. Remember to save the entire macro library after making changes to an existing macro.

VIEWING MACRO KEYSTROKES DURING PLAYBACK

SEQUENCE OF STEPS

From the Control Center:

> Menus (**F10**)
> Tools/**M**acros [↵]
> **T**alk [↵]
> press the space bar to select On *or* Off

USAGE

If a macro contains an error and you have difficulty finding it, you can have dBASE display each keystroke before typing it when you play back the macro. You can then see exactly where the macro goes awry during playback.

To use this feature, starting from the Control Center, press **F10** and select Macros from the Tools pull-down menu. Move the highlight to the Talk option and press the space bar to change its setting from Off to On.

Next select Play and the name of the macro to play back. You will see each keystroke as it is played at the bottom of the screen. You can also control the speed at which the macro is played back. Press > repeatedly (you do not need to hold down the **Shift** key) to increase playback speed or < to slow it down.

COPYING A MACRO

SEQUENCE OF STEPS

From the Control Center:

> Menus (**F10**)
> Tools/Macros [↵]
> Copy [↵]
> enter the name of macro to copy
> type a name for the copy

USAGE

You can copy keystroke macros to use as building blocks in constructing larger macros to automate complex tasks. To copy a keystroke macro to another name in the current macro library, starting from the Control Center, press Menus (**F10**), and select Macros from the Tools pull-down menu. Select Copy; the message *Press key for source macro* appears at the bottom of the screen. Press the single-letter or function key name of the macro you want to copy.

The message *Press key of destination* then appears at the bottom of the screen. Type the single letter or function key that you want to assign to the copied macro. The screen will prompt you to enter a new name for the macro. Type a new name and then press ↵.

Remember to save the entire library to make the copy permanent.

DELETING A MACRO

SEQUENCE OF STEPS

From the Control Center:

> Menus (**F10**)

Tools/Macros [↵]
Delete [↵]
type the name of the macro to delete
Y *or* **N**
↵

USAGE

To delete a macro from the current library, starting from the Control Center, press Menus (**F10**) and select Macros from the Tools pull-down menu. Select Delete from the submenu. The message *Press key of macro to delete* appears at the bottom of the screen. Press the single-letter or function key name of the macro that you want to delete. dBASE will ask for permission before deleting the macro. Type **Y** to delete the macro or **N** if you change your mind. Then press ↵.

If you want the deletion to be permanent, save the entire macro library after deleting a macro.

SENDING COMMANDS TO DOS FROM A MACRO

SEQUENCE OF STEPS

From the Control Center:

Macros (**Shift-F10**)
Begin Recording [↵]
enter a name for the macro
Alt-T
D
Alt-D
P
type a DOS command ↵
Macros (**Shift-F10**)
End Recording [↵]

USAGE

DOS file-management operations often involve relatively long but unvarying keystroke sequences, which makes them good candidates for recording in a macro. To send commands to DOS from a keystroke macro, you must use the Perform DOS Command option (as opposed to the Go to DOS option) on the DOS Utilities screen. Starting from the Control Center, press Macros (**Shift-F10**) and select Begin Recording. Enter a name for the macro.

Next, type **Alt-T** to access the Tools pull-down menu. Then type D to select DOS Utilities. From the DOS Utilities screen, press **Alt-D** to access the DOS pull-down menu and then type **P** to select Perform DOS Command. Type a valid DOS command and then press ←.

If you want to send additional commands to DOS from the current macro, press any key to return to dBASE. Then type **Alt-D** and **P** to select Perform DOS Command again. Type the DOS command and press ←. You can repeat this series of steps as many times as you wish to send multiple commands to DOS.

After DOS executes your command, it displays its messages (if any) on your screen before returning you to dBASE. If you want your keystroke macro to leave these messages on the screen, press **Shift-F10** and select End Recording while the DOS messages are on the screen. If you do not want your macro to leave the DOS messages on the screen, press any key to return to dBASE. You can then record additional keystrokes, or you can press **Shift-F10** and select End Recording to stop recording.

Do not forget to save the entire macro library after creating a new macro.

TIPS AND TRAPS

- Give each macro a recognizable name in addition to its single-letter name to help you—and other users—remember what it does.
- When recording macro keystrokes, always use **Alt-**_key_ combinations to pull down menus, select menu options by typing their first letters, and type complete file names rather than selecting file names from lists.
- When you run a keystroke macro, make sure that you start from the same screen in dBASE that you were in when you recorded the keystrokes. Otherwise, the keystrokes may make no sense.
- New and modified macros are automatically saved only in RAM. To save macros permanently, you must save the entire macro library.

SUMMARY

dBASE IV macros are easy to create and use, and they can increase efficiency dramatically, particularly when your applications require you to access the same menu options over and over again. Any text that you type often is also a good candidate for a macro.

For specific keystrokes available in the macro editor:

- Table 3.2 in Chapter 3, "Adding, Changing, and Deleting Data"

For information about other options on the Tools menu:

- Chapter 14, "Managing Files and the Workspace"

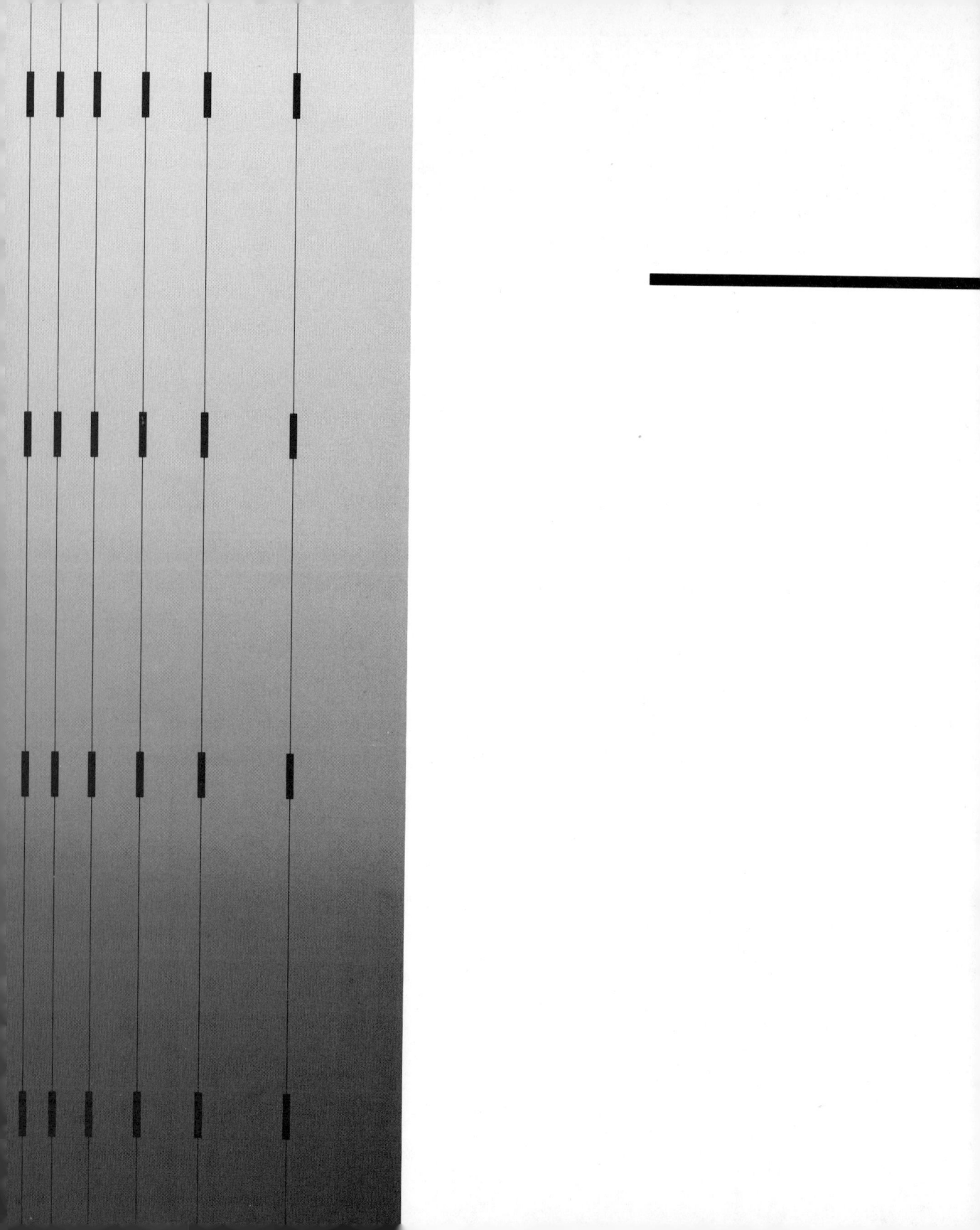

CHAPTER 14

MANAGING FILES AND THE WORKSPACE

Managing Catalogs. 461
    Creating a New Catalog. 462
    Selecting a Catalog. 462
    Changing a Catalog Description. 463
    Adding File Names to a Catalog. 463
    Removing File Names from a Catalog. 464
    Changing a File Description. .465
    Changing the Name of the Current Catalog. 466
Managing Files. 466
    Accessing the DOS Utilities Screen. 467
    Temporarily Changing Directories. 469
    Selecting Files to Display. 471
    Sorting File Names. 471
    Marking Files. 472
    Deleting, Copying, Moving, and Renaming Files. 473
        Deleting Files. 474
        Copying Files. 475
        Moving Files. 476
        Renaming Files. 477
    Viewing and Editing ASCII Text Files. 478
    Making Backup Copies of Files. 479
    Changing the Default Drive and Directory. 482
Accessing DOS Commands. 482
Importing Data into dBASE IV. 483
    Importing Data from Supported Software. 484

    Importing Data from Lotus 1-2-3. . . . .**484**
        Isolating Data to Import. **485**
        Importing the Spreadsheet Data. **486**
        Redefining the Data Types. **487**
        Renaming Fields. **488**
    Importing ASCII Text Files. **490**
        Creating the ASCII Text File. **490**
        Ascertaining the File Structure. **490**
        Planning the dBASE IV Database Structure. **491**
        Copying and Renaming the Text File. **492**
        Creating the Database Structure. **492**
    Importing WordStar MailMerge Data. **493**
Exporting Data from dBASE IV. **495**
    Exporting Data to Supported Software. **495**
    Exporting Data to Lotus 1-2-3. . . . .**496**
    Exporting Data as ASCII Text Files. **499**
        Creating the Text File. **500**
        Reading the Report into WordStar. **501**
        Reading the Report into WordPerfect. **501**
    Exporting to WordStar MailMerge Files. **502**
Changing Environment Settings. **504**
    Options for Changing the Display. **504**
    Changing the Display Colors. **507**
Tips and Traps. **509**
Summary. **509**

MANAGING FILES AND THE WORKSPACE

This chapter presents general techniques for managing catalogs, files, and settings, as well as techniques for interfacing with DOS. Many of the tasks discussed in this chapter are referred to as *housekeeping chores,* because they help you keep the files on your disk in order.

MANAGING CATALOGS

A *catalog* is a dBASE tool for helping you keep the names of files that belong together visible in the Control Center. Any time you create a file (a database file, report format, custom screen, or whatever), dBASE automatically adds the file name that you assign to the file to the *current catalog,* and that name appears in the Control Center.

Because a catalog consists of only the names of files, you can include the same file in more than one catalog. As you create and work with multiple catalogs, you may sometimes want to add, change, or delete file names in a catalog. The Catalog pull-down menu is shown in Figure 14.1.

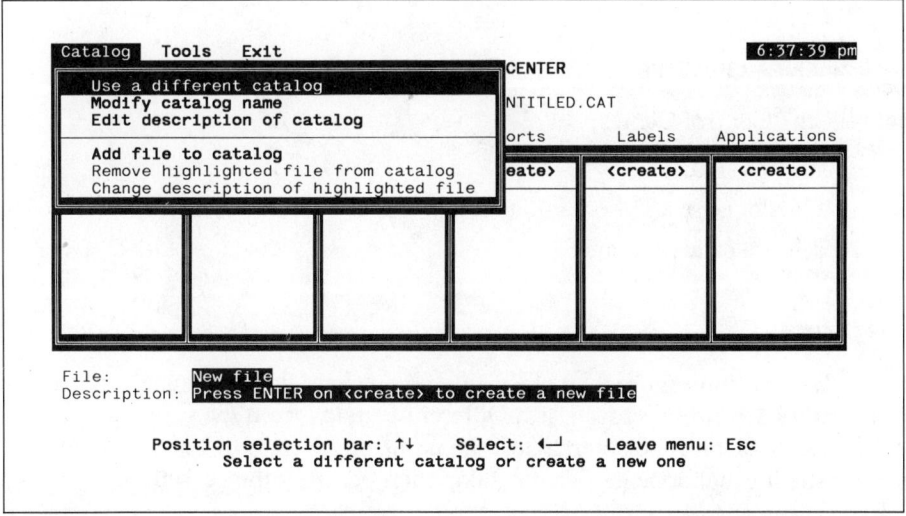

FIGURE 14.1: You access the Catalog pull-down menu from the Control Center. This menu provides all the techniques for managing catalogs.

Creating a New Catalog

SEQUENCE OF STEPS

From the Control Center:

    Menus (**F10**)
    Catalog/**U**se a Different Catalog [⏎]
    <create>
    type a file name ⏎

USAGE

To create a new catalog, press Menu (**F10**) at the Control Center, select Use a Different Catalog from the Catalog pull-down menu, and then select <create> from the submenu that appears. When you are prompted for a name, type a valid file name (eight letters maximum, with no spaces) and press ⏎. This new catalog becomes the current catalog, and the panels in the Control Center are empty. Any new files that you create while using the new catalog will be listed in that catalog.

Selecting a Catalog

SEQUENCE OF STEPS

From the Control Center:

    Menus (**F10**)
    Catalog/**U**se a Different Catalog [⏎]
    select a catalog name

USAGE

When you have more than one catalog, you can switch from one to another by pressing **F10** and selecting Use a Different Catalog from the Catalog pull-down menu at the Control Center. Select the name of the catalog that you want to use from the list that appears. That catalog then becomes the current one.

Changing a Catalog Description

SEQUENCE OF STEPS

From the Control Center, with the appropriate catalog current:

>Menus (**F10**)
>Catalog/**E**dit Description of Catalog [◄─┘]
>change the description or type a new description ◄─┘

USAGE

When you select Use a Different Catalog and then scroll through catalog names, you see the catalog descriptions. To change the description of a catalog or to provide a description for an existing catalog, first make sure that the catalog is current. Press **F10** and select Edit Description of Catalog from the Catalog pull-down menu. dBASE displays the message *Edit the description of this .cat file*. Use the usual editing keys to change the description (or type a new description). Then press ◄─┘.

Adding File Names to a Catalog

SEQUENCE OF STEPS

From the Control Center:

>Menus (**F10**)
>Catalog/**U**se a Different Catalog [◄─┘]
>select the appropriate catalog
>move the highlight to the appropriate Control Center panel
>Menus (**F10**)
>Catalog/**A**dd File to Catalog [◄─┘]
>highlight the file name ◄─┘
>◄─┘

USAGE

Suppose you create a file while using one catalog and want that file name to appear in a different catalog. To add a file name to a catalog, first make current the catalog where you want the file to appear. (Press **F10** and select the catalog from the list that appears when you choose Use a Different Catalog from the Catalog menu.) Move the highlight to the Control Center panel that describes the type of file you want to add. For example, if you want to add a database file name to the current catalog, move the highlight to the Data panel.

Next, press **F10** and select Add File to Catalog from the Catalog pull-down menu. A submenu will list all files in the current directory that match the type of file you are adding (for example, the submenu will list all .DBF files if the highlight is in the Data panel). The submenu will also list options for changing to a different disk drive, to the parent directory, or to another subdirectory. If necessary, switch to the appropriate directory to locate the file name. Then select the file name from the submenu.

You can either edit the description of the file or just press ↵ to use the current description. The name of the file will appear in the appropriate Control Center panel.

If you are adding a query, form, report, or label file name to the current catalog, the submenu will display every file name with every extension (such as CUSTFORM.FRM and CUSTFORM.SCR). You need select only one of these multiple names, using the appropriate extension, as listed here:

FILE TYPE	EXTENSION TO SELECT
Query	.QBE
Update query	.UPD
View query	.VUE
Form	.SCR
Report	.FRM
Labels	.LBL
Application	.APP

If you add the name of a file stored on a floppy disk to a particular catalog, that disk must be in its drive whenever you use that catalog; adding a file name to a catalog does not copy the file to the current drive or directory. If you do want to copy the file from the floppy disk onto your hard disk, use the copying techniques discussed later in this chapter and then add the file name to the hard disk catalog.

Removing File Names from a Catalog

SEQUENCE OF STEPS

From the Control Center:

    highlight the file name to remove

Menus (**F10**)
Catalog/**R**emove Highlighted File from Catalog [↵]
Yes
Yes *or* No

USAGE

To remove a file name from the current catalog, first highlight the file name that you wish to remove and press Menus (**F10**). Then select Remove Highlighted File from Catalog from the Catalog pull-down menu. dBASE will double-check your request by asking

> Are you sure you want to remove
> this file from the catalog?
> Yes No

Select Yes if you do want to delete the file. Next, dBASE will ask,

> Do you also want to delete
> this file from the disk?
> Yes No

If you select No, then dBASE removes the file name from the catalog, but the file itself remains intact on the disk. (You can later add the file name to some other catalog by selecting its name from the list that appears when you choose Add File to Catalog.) If you select Yes, then dBASE permanently removes the file from the disk, and you cannot recover it. Use this option with caution.

Changing a File Description

SEQUENCE OF STEPS

From the Control Center:

> highlight the file name
> Menus (**F10**)
> Catalog/**C**hange Description of Highlighted File [↵]
> type or edit the description ↵

USAGE

To change the description that you assigned to a file, first highlight the file name in the Control Center. Then press **F10** and select Change Description of

Highlighted File from the Catalog pull-down menu. Use the arrow and **Backspace** keys to position the cursor and erase as needed. Then save the new description by pressing ←┘.

You can also use this option to provide a description for a file that does not yet have a description. The new description will appear below the Control Center panels whenever the file name is highlighted.

Changing the Name of the Current Catalog

SEQUENCE OF STEPS

From the Control Center:

    Menus (**F10**)
    Catalog/**M**odify Catalog Name [←┘]
    edit the catalog name ←┘

USAGE

To change the name of the current catalog, press Menus (**F10**) and select Modify Catalog Name from the Catalog pull-down menu. Press **Backspace** to erase the current name and then enter the new name. (You need not enter the .CAT extension; dBASE will add it automatically. Do not enter a different extension.)

If you start dBASE IV from a directory that contains no catalogs, dBASE will automatically create a catalog named UNTITLED.CAT that includes all dBASE IV database files in the current directory. You might want to change UNTITLED.CAT to something more descriptive of your applications.

MANAGING FILES

The computer's disk operating system (DOS) handles all basic file-management tasks, including saving, retrieving, copying, moving, and deleting files, as well as managing directories. dBASE IV lets you interact with DOS to manage files via the *DOS Utilities screen*. With this utility, you do not need to exit from dBASE IV to the DOS prompt to perform any DOS activities or commands.

Whereas the Catalog pull-down menu lets you manage the file *names* that appear in a catalog, the DOS Utilities screen offers options for manipulating *files*, including commands for copying, moving, deleting, and renaming files.

Accessing the DOS Utilities Screen

SEQUENCE OF STEPS

From the Control Center:

> Menus (**F10**)
> Tools/**D**OS Utilities [↵]

To return to the Control Center:

> Menus (**F10**)
> Exit/**E**xit to Control Center [↵]

USAGE

To get to the DOS Utilities screen, press **F10** and select DOS Utilities from the Tools pull-down menu at the Control Center, as shown in Figure 14.2. You will see a box containing a *file list* that includes the names of all subdirectories (directories under the current directory) and files, as shown in Figure 14.3. You can use the arrow, **PgUp**, **PgDn**, **Home**, and **End** keys to scroll through the file list.

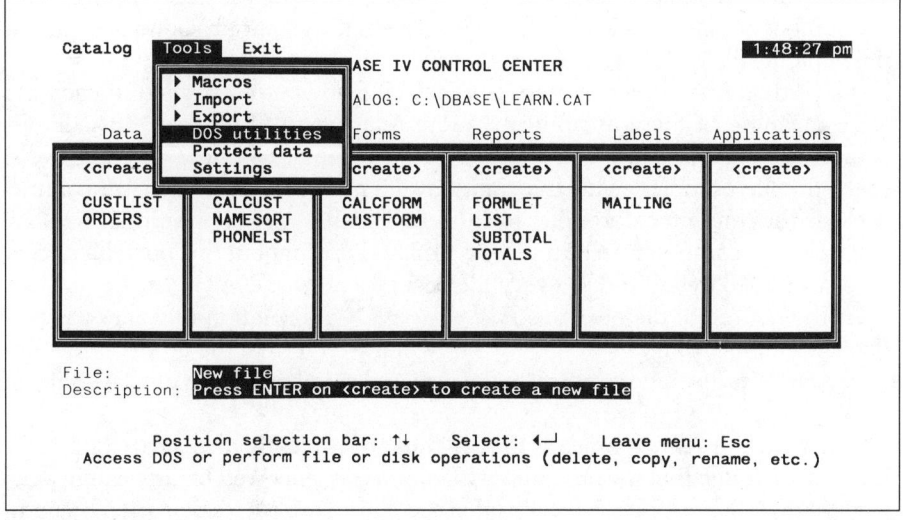

FIGURE 14.2: Selecting DOS Utilities from the Tools pull-down menu.

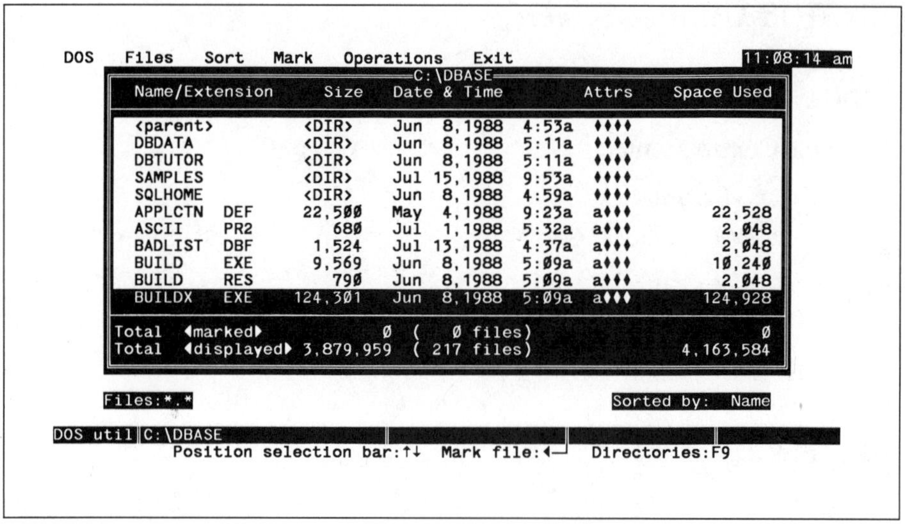

CH. 14 MANAGING FILES AND THE WORKSPACE

```
DOS    Files    Sort    Mark    Operations    Exit            11:08:14 am
                         ─────C:\DBASE─────
    Name/Extension       Size    Date & Time        Attrs    Space Used
    <parent>             <DIR>   Jun  8,1988  4:53a  ♦♦♦♦
    DBDATA               <DIR>   Jun  8,1988  5:11a  ♦♦♦♦
    DBTUTOR              <DIR>   Jun  8,1988  5:11a  ♦♦♦♦
    SAMPLES              <DIR>   Jul 15,1988  9:53a  ♦♦♦♦
    SQLHOME              <DIR>   Jun  8,1988  4:59a  ♦♦♦♦
    APPLCTN   DEF       22,500   May  4,1988  9:23a  a♦♦♦       22,528
    ASCII     PR2          680   Jul  1,1988  5:32a  a♦♦♦        2,048
    BADLIST   DBF        1,524   Jul 13,1988  4:37a  a♦♦♦        2,048
    BUILD     EXE        9,569   Jun  8,1988  5:09a  a♦♦♦       10,240
    BUILD     RES          790   Jun  8,1988  5:09a  a♦♦♦        2,048
    BUILDX    EXE      124,301   Jun  8,1988  5:09a  a♦♦♦      124,928
    Total  ◄marked►           0  (    0 files)                       0
    Total  ◄displayed► 3,879,959 (  217 files)                4,163,584

    Files:*.*                                       Sorted by:    Name
 DOS util  C:\DBASE
          Position selection bar:↑↓    Mark file:◄┘   Directories:F9
```

FIGURE 14.3: The DOS Utilities screen provides information about the files on a disk. From this screen you can access DOS files and file commands without exiting to DOS.

The names of the current drive and directory, C:\DBASE in the figure, are displayed at the top of the box. Within the file list, the Name/Extension column lists subdirectory names followed by <DIR> and file names. The Size column displays the number of characters in each file. The Date & Time column shows the date and time that the file was created or last changed.

The Attrs (Attributes) column lists the DOS attributes assigned to each file. (The meaning of these attributes is more relevant to DOS than dBASE. For details, see Appendix B. The Space Used column shows how much real disk space the file occupies. This information differs from that in the Size column, because the computer stores files in clusters, which have some minimal size. For example, the computer used in Figure 14.3 and throughout this book has a cluster size of 2048 bytes, and so every file occupies at least 2048 bytes.

At the bottom of the box, the *Total <marked>* information indicates the total size and number of files that are currently marked (zero in the figure). The *Total <displayed>* information indicates the size and number of files displayed in the file list.

The indicator *Files:* *.* means that all files are currently displayed. The *.* is the *wildcard pattern* that means "files with any name, followed by any extension." The *Sorted by: Name* indicator means that file names are currently sorted by name (although subdirectory names are listed before file names).

Temporarily Changing Directories

SEQUENCE OF STEPS

From the DOS Utilities screen:

    highlight the directory or subdirectory name ⏎

or

    Zoom (**F9**)
    highlight the directory or subdirectory name ⏎

or

    Menus (**F10**)
    Files/Change Drive:Directory [⏎]
    enter a new drive and directory   *or*   Pick (**Shift-F1**) and select a drive and directory

USAGE

You can use the ↑ and ↓ keys to move the highlight through the file list. To switch to a subdirectory, select the subdirectory name using the usual technique of highlighting and pressing ⏎. To switch to the parent directory, select <parent>.

To get a better view of the overall directory structure, press Zoom (**F9**). dBASE will present the directory structure in a tree format, as in Figure 14.4. Notice that subdirectory names are indented below the name of their parent directory. A pointer to the left of the directory name indicates the current directory (DBASE in the figure).

To switch to any directory or subdirectory while the directory tree is displayed, highlight the appropriate name and press ⏎. The file list will appear, showing the names of files on the new current directory.

You can also switch to a new drive and directory by selecting Change Drive:Directory from the Files pull-down menu, as shown in Figure 14.5. When you select this option, you will be given the opportunity to enter a new drive and directory. Alternatively, you can press Pick (**Shift-F1**) to choose from the directory tree.

Note that these temporary changes affect only the DOS Utilities screen display. When you return to the Control Center, the directory that was in effect before you went to the DOS Utilities screen will still be in effect.

470 —— **CH. 14** MANAGING FILES AND THE WORKSPACE

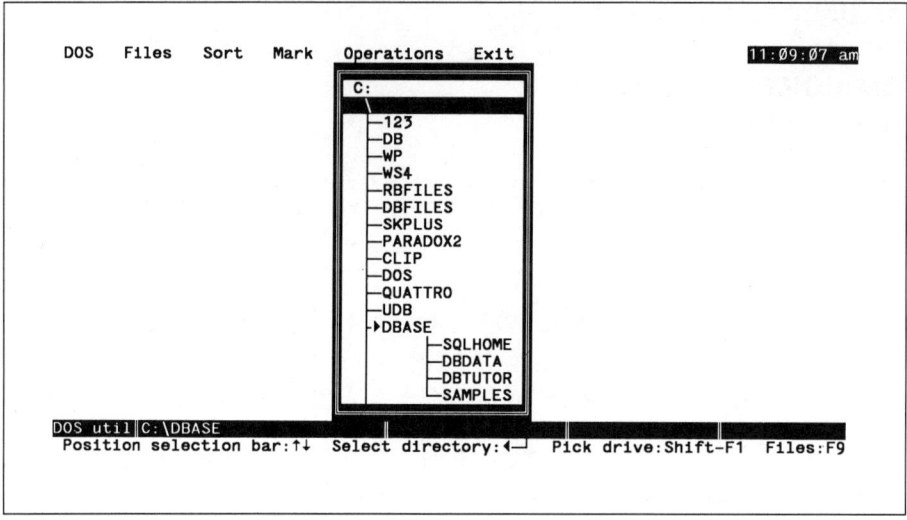

FIGURE 14.4: Press Zoom (**F9**) from the DOS Utilities screen to access the directory tree, which displays the structure of your directory. Each subdirectory is displayed as a branch of its parent directory.

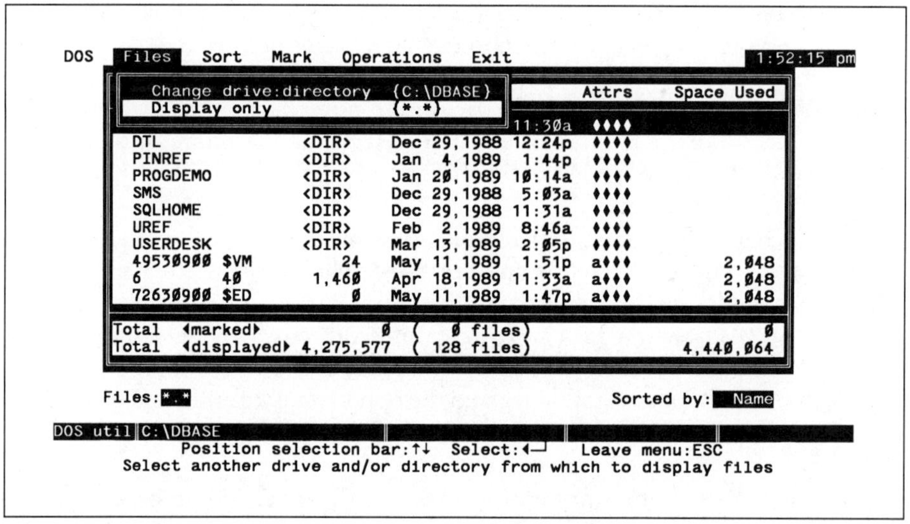

FIGURE 14.5: Selecting Change Drive:Directory from the DOS Utilities Files submenu.

Selecting Files to Display

SEQUENCE OF STEPS

From the DOS Utilities screen:

> Menus (**F10**)
> Files/**D**isplay Only [⏎]
> enter the new wildcard pattern

USAGE

You can limit the file names displayed on the DOS Utilities screen to only those that match some wildcard pattern. As with searches, you can use **?** to stand for any single character and ***** to stand for any group of characters. To change the wildcard pattern, press Menus (**F10**), select Display Only from the Files pull-down menu, and type the new wildcard pattern.

For example, changing the wildcard pattern to ***.DBF** displays only database file names (those with the extension .DBF). Changing the wildcard pattern to **CUST*.*** displays only file names that begin with the letters *CUST.* Note that the screen still displays the subdirectory names and the <parent> option, regardless of the wildcard pattern you use.

Sorting File Names

SEQUENCE OF STEPS

From the DOS Utilities screen:

> Menus (**F10**)
> Sort
> **N**ame *or* **E**xtension *or* **D**ate & Time *or* **S**ize [⏎]

USAGE

You can use the Sort pull-down menu, shown in Figure 14.6, to select a sort order for viewing file names. The file list is initially displayed sorted by name (the default setting), except that subdirectories appear at the top of the list, before the file names. You can view the file list alphabetically by extension, in ascending order by date and time, or by size (from smallest to largest).

CH. 14 MANAGING FILES AND THE WORKSPACE

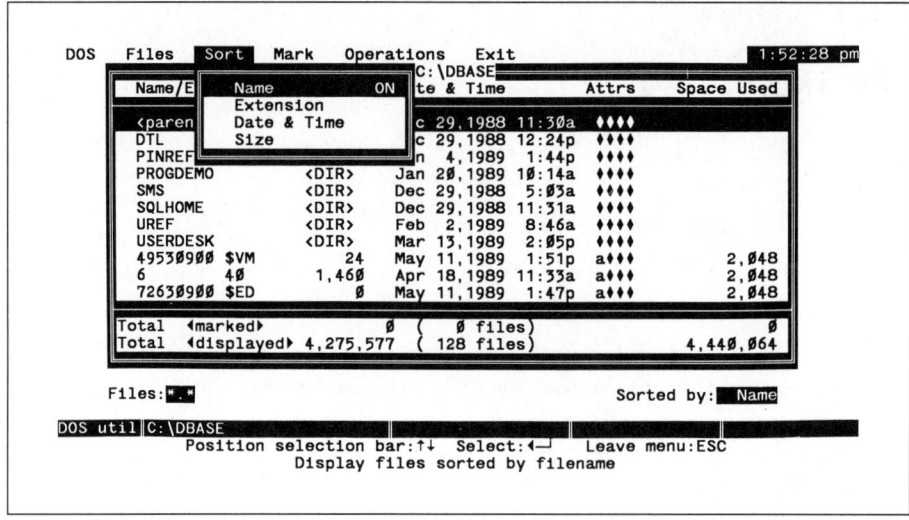

FIGURE 14.6: From the DOS Utilities Sort submenu, you can sort the file list so that you can view it in name, extension, date and time, or size order.

Marking Files

SEQUENCE OF STEPS

From the DOS Utilities screen:

>Menus (**F10**)
>
>Mark/**M**ark All *or* **U**nmark All *or* **R**everse Marks [↵]

or

>menus (**F10**)
>
>highlight file name ↵ (repeat as necessary)

USAGE

To perform operations on groups of files, first you need to *mark* the files in the group. The simplest way to mark files is to scroll the highlight on the DOS Utilities screen to the file that you want to mark and then press ↵. You can mark as many files as you wish in this manner. (Note that in this context, ↵ works as a toggle: Each time you press it, it either marks or unmarks the current file name.) A pointer appears next to each marked file.

Another way to mark files is by using the DOS Utilities Mark pull-down menu. The Mark All option marks all currently displayed file names. Hence, if the wildcard pattern CUST*.* is in effect and you select Mark All, then dBASE will mark all files beginning with the letters *CUST*. Changing the wildcard pattern does not affect the marks, so you can mark several groups of files by changing the wildcard pattern and selecting Mark All.

The Unmark All option on the Mark pull-down menu unmarks all currently displayed file names. The Reverse Marks option swaps the file marks, so that unmarked files are marked, and marked files become unmarked. For example, you can use this option to copy two groups of files to two floppy disks. You can mark one set of files and copy those files to one floppy disk. Then you can reverse the marks and copy the rest of the files to another floppy disk.

Deleting, Copying, Moving, and Renaming Files

SEQUENCE OF STEPS

From the DOS Utilities screen:

    mark files, as necessary

    Menus (**F10**)

    Operations/**D**elete *or* **C**opy *or* **M**ove *or* **R**ename [↵]

    Single File *or* **M**arked Files *or* **D**isplayed Files [↵]

USAGE

To copy, delete, move, or rename files, first mark the appropriate files, press **F10**, and select the appropriate option from the Operations pull-down menu. You will see a submenu of options, as shown in Figure 14.7. Choose Single File to perform the operation on the currently highlighted file. Choose Marked Files to include all currently displayed marked files in the operation. Choose Displayed Files to include all currently displayed files. (Note that *currently displayed* here refers to all files that match the current wildcard pattern. Hence, any file names that are not visible at the moment simply because they are scrolled off the bottom of the screen are still included in the operation.)

If the highlight is on a directory name when you choose a group of files for an operation and you select Single File, then the operation will be performed for all files in that directory.

After you have selected the files to include in the operation, you will be given further information and options relevant to that operation, as discussed in the following sections.

474 — CH. 14 MANAGING FILES AND THE WORKSPACE

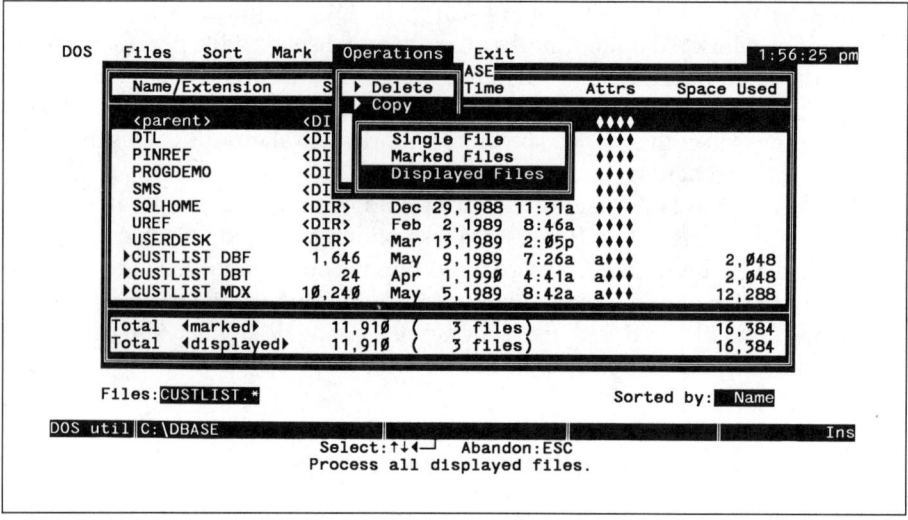

FIGURE 14.7: Submenu of options for files to include in file operations. dBASE displays this submenu when you select Delete, Copy, Move, or Rename from the DOS Utilities Operations menu.

DELETING FILES

SEQUENCE OF STEPS

From the DOS Utilities screen:

> mark files to delete
> Menus (**F10**)
> Operations/**D**elete [↵]
> **S**ingle File *or* **M**arked Files *or* **D**isplayed Files [↵]
> **P**roceed [↵]

To delete a single file (quick method):

> highlight the file name in the file list
> **Del**
> **P**roceed [↵]

USAGE

Before deleting all marked or displayed files, use **PgDn** and **PgUp** to scroll through the file list to make certain that you know exactly which files will be deleted.

DELETING, COPYING, MOVING, AND RENAMING FILES — **475**

When you press Menus (**F10**) and select Delete from the operations menu, dBASE displays the options Proceed and Cancel. If you are sure you want to delete all the files described, select Proceed. Use this option with caution, because once you delete a file, you cannot retrieve it. If you are unsure about deleting the files, select Cancel.

You can also delete any single file by moving the highlight to the appropriate file name in the file list and pressing **Del**. You will be given the option to Proceed or Cancel.

COPYING FILES

SEQUENCE OF STEPS

From the DOS Utilities screen:

    mark files to copy

    Menus (**F10**)

    Operations/**C**opy [⏎]

    Single File *or* **M**arked Files *or* **D**isplayed Files [⏎]

    enter the destination drive and directory   *or*   Pick (**Shift-F1**) and select from the directory tree

    enter the destination file name or wildcard pattern

    Ctrl-End

To copy a single file (quick method):

    highlight the file name in the file list

    Copy (**F8**)

    enter the destination drive and directory   *or*   Pick (**Shift-F1**) and select from the directory tree

    change the file name, if appropriate

    Ctrl-End

USAGE

When you select Copy as the file operation, you are prompted to specify the destination and file names for the copied files. Enter the disk drive and directory where you want to store the copy and press ⏎ to use the existing file names. For example, to copy files to a floppy disk in drive A, delete the suggested destination and type the new destination **A:** (be sure to type the colon). Then press ⏎.

If you are copying a single file, its name will be displayed as the name for the copied file. You can change that name (so that the copied file has a different name than the original file) or press ⏎ to use the same name. If you are copying a group of files, enter ***.*** as the destination file name to ensure that copied files have the same names as the original files.

If you prefer, you can assign new names to the copied files. In the destination file name, use a combination of the new name (for that part of the file name that you want to change) and a wildcard (for the part of the file name that you want to remain the same). For example, suppose you mark the files CUSTLIST.DBF and CUSTLIST.MDX as the file group to copy. If you enter **CUSTBAK.*** as the destination file name, the copied files will have the names CUSTBAK.DBF and CUSTBAK.MDX.

If you want to place copied files in the same directory as the original files, you must specify a new name for the copied files (because a directory cannot have two files with the same name). For example, say you want to copy C:\DBASE\-ORDERS.DBF and C:\DBASE\ORDERS.MDX to two backup files in the same directory. You would keep C:\DBASE as the copy destination but enter a file name with a wildcard character, such as **OLDORDER.***, so that the copies would have the file names OLDORDER.DBF and OLDORDER.MDX.

When you have finished filling in the destination and file name for the copy, press **Ctrl-End** to begin the copy operation. Note that you can also copy a single file by highlighting its name in the file list and pressing Copy (**F8**).

See "Making Backup Copies of Files" later in this chapter for more information about copying files.

Moving Files

SEQUENCE OF STEPS

From the DOS Utilities screen:

> highlight or mark files, as necessary
>
> Menus (**F10**)
>
> Operations/**M**ove [⏎]
>
> **S**ingle File *or* **M**arked Files *or* **D**isplayed Files [⏎]
>
> enter the destination drive and directory   *or*   Pick (**Shift-F1**) and select from the directory tree
>
> ***.***
>
> **Ctrl-End**

MAKING BACKUP COPIES OF FILES — 477

To move a single file (quick method):

>highlight the file name
>
>Move (**F7**)
>
>enter the destination drive and directory *or* Pick (**Shift-F1**) and select from the directory tree
>
>←┘
>
>**Ctrl-End**

USAGE

The Move option lets you move a file from one disk drive or directory to another. This option works in the same manner as the Copy option, except that the original file is deleted from its original drive and directory after being copied to its new destination. The general technique used is identical to that used for copying. After you select the option and specify whether you are moving a single file, the marked files, or all displayed files, you specify a disk drive or directory to move the file to or press Pick (**Shift-F1**) to select a new directory from the directory tree.

After you specify the disk drive and directory to move the file to, you will be prompted to enter a new name for the moved file. If you are moving a single file, its name will be displayed, and you can just press ←┘ to retain the name. If you are moving a group of files, enter the wildcard pattern ***.*** to move all files and retain their current names. Press **Ctrl-End** after responding to both prompts (or press **Esc** to abort the operation).

You can move a single file by highlighting its name in the file list and pressing Move (**F7**).

RENAMING FILES

SEQUENCE OF STEPS

From the DOS Utilities screen:

>mark the files to rename
>
>Menus (**F10**)
>
>Operations/**R**ename [←┘]
>
>**S**ingle File *or* **M**arked Files *or* **D**isplayed Files [←┘]
>
>enter a new file name or wildcard pattern

USAGE

The Rename option lets you change the name of a file, a group of files, or a subdirectory. When you select this option, you will be prompted to enter the new name. If you are renaming a group of files, be sure to use a wildcard character in the new file name. For example, if you want to rename all files named CUSTBAK to OLDCUST, enter **OLDCUST.*** as the new file name. Each file previously named CUSTBAK will be renamed OLDCUST, but will still have the original extension. (Hence, CUSTBAK.DBF becomes OLDCUST.DBF, and CUSTBAK.MDX becomes OLDCUST.MDX.)

If the new name that you assign to a file is the same as an existing file name, dBASE will warn you that the existing file will be erased. The screen will display options to overwrite the existing file or to skip the renaming operation. Unless you are absolutely sure that you wish to replace the currently named file with the new one, select Skip.

Viewing and Editing ASCII Text Files

SEQUENCE OF STEPS

On the DOS Utilities screen:

    Menus (**F10**)
    Operations/**V**iew *or* **E**dit [⏎]
    edit file as necessary
    Menus (**F10**)
    Exit/**S**ave Changes and Exit [⏎]

USAGE

You can view or edit any DOS text file (also called an ASCII text file, or just a text file) using the View or Edit option on the Operations menu on the DOS Utilities screen. ASCII text files are files that contain only standard characters, such as the letters A through Z, the numbers 0 through 9, and punctuation marks that are on your keyboard. DOS batch (.BAT) files, dBASE program (.PRG) and print (.PRT or .TXT) files, and message files that contain notes and upgrades (often named READ.ME or README.) are examples of ASCII text files that can be viewed and edited. The DOS CONFIG.SYS file, which configures your computer during startup, is also a text file.

When you have finished viewing or editing the file, select Save Changes and Exit from the Exit pull-down menu, or simply press Ctrl-End.

EXAMPLE

Suppose while using dBASE IV you keep receiving the error message *Too many files are open*. The solution to this problem is to change your CONFIG.SYS file (which must be stored in the root directory of your hard disk) so that the DOS FILES setting is at least 40, and the BUFFERS setting is at least 15. To change that file, starting from the DOS Utilities screen, you first need to press **F9** to view the directory tree and then switch to the root directory by highlighting its name (which is simply \) and pressing ↵.

Next, move the highlight to the name of the file, CONFIG.SYS in this example, and press **F10**. Move the highlight to the Operations pull-down menu and select View to view the current contents of the file or Edit to change the current contents of the file.

If you select View, dBASE will display as much of the file as will fit on the screen along with a message indicating the percentage of the file that is currently displayed (for example, 25 percent for each page of a four-page file). You can press the space bar to scroll through the file one page at a time or press ↵ to start and stop rapid scrolling. Press **Esc** to stop viewing the file and return to the DOS Utilities screen.

If you select Edit, DOS will display the file in an editor similar to the word-wrap editor that you use to edit memo fields. Use the arrow keys and **PgUp** and **PgDn** keys to move the cursor. Press **Ctrl-N** to insert a new line at the current cursor position or **Ctrl-Y** to delete a line. You can also press **F10** to access the pull-down menus, which provide the usual options for editing, printing, searching, and saving the file.

In this particular example, you add the commands

```
FILES = 40
BUFFERS = 15
```

to your CONFIG.SYS file (or if these commands already exist, change the settings to **40** and **15**). To save your changes, press **F10** and select Save Changes and Exit from the Exit pull-down menu (or select Abandon Changes and Exit to abandon your changes). You will be returned to the DOS Utilities screen. (The new settings in the CONFIG.SYS file, however, will not take effect until the next time you start your computer.)

Making Backup Copies of Files

SEQUENCE OF STEPS

On the DOS Utilities screen:
    mark the files to copy

Menus (**F10**)

Operations/**C**opy [⏎]

Single File *or* **M**arked Files [⏎]

enter the destination drive and directory *or* **P**ick (**Shift-F1**) and select from the directory tree

enter the destination file name or wildcard pattern

Ctrl-End

USAGE

You can use the DOS Utilities screen to make backup copies of your files. First mark the files that you want to copy. To begin the copy operation, select Copy from the Operations menu and Marked Files from the submenu. (If you are backing up to a floppy disk, place the disk in drive A.) Press **Ctrl-Y** if the current drive and directory names suggested by the prompt are not what you need and enter the appropriate destination drive and directory. Enter a wildcard pattern or the file names to copy. (The copied files will retain their same names and extensions.) To perform the copy operation, press **Ctrl-End**.

dBASE will copy the files. Note that if the disk already contains copies of these files, you will be given the option to overwrite (replace) the current file or skip (not copy) the file with the currently displayed name.

EXAMPLE

To see how to use the DOS Utilities screen as a tool for making backup copies of files, you can copy the CUSTLIST and ORDERS databases to a formatted disk in drive A. (This example assumes that you have a formatted disk with at least 51K of blank space on it readily available, and that your floppy disk drive is named A. If you need help creating a formatted floppy disk, see the FORMAT command in your DOS manual. But be careful when using the FORMAT command, because it permanently erases any files already on the disk.)

As a first step to backing up the files, you need to mark the files that you want to back up. From the Control Center, select DOS Utilities from the Tools pull-down menu. When the file list appears, select Display Only from the Files pull-down menu and change the wildcard pattern to **CUSTLIST.** *. Then select Mark All from the Mark pull-down menu to mark the files named CUSTLIST.DBF and CUSTLIST.MDX (the .MDX file contains the indexes for CUSTLIST.DBF).

Next, select Display Only from the Files pull-down menu and change the wildcard pattern to **ORDERS.** *. Once again, select Mark All from the Mark pull-down menu. Select Display Only from the Files pull-down menu again and change the wildcard pattern to **.*** (or just press **Ctrl-Y** to blank the option; dBASE will change it to **.*** after you press ←).

If you use the **PgDn** and **PgUp** keys now to scroll through the file list, you will see that the CUSTLIST and ORDERS files are the only ones marked. Also, beneath the file list you can see the total amount of space used by the marked files. (If you divide this figure by 1024, you can determine the number of kilobytes the files take up.)

To begin the copy operation, first place the floppy disk in drive A. Then press **F10** and select Copy from the Operations menu and Marked Files from the submenu. Press **Ctrl-Y** to erase the current drive and directory names suggested by the prompt and then enter **A:** as the destination drive. Press ← and enter **.*** as the file name, so that copied files retain their same names and extensions. Your screen will look like Figure 14.8. To perform the copy operation, press **Ctrl-End**. dBASE will copy all the marked files onto the disk in drive A.

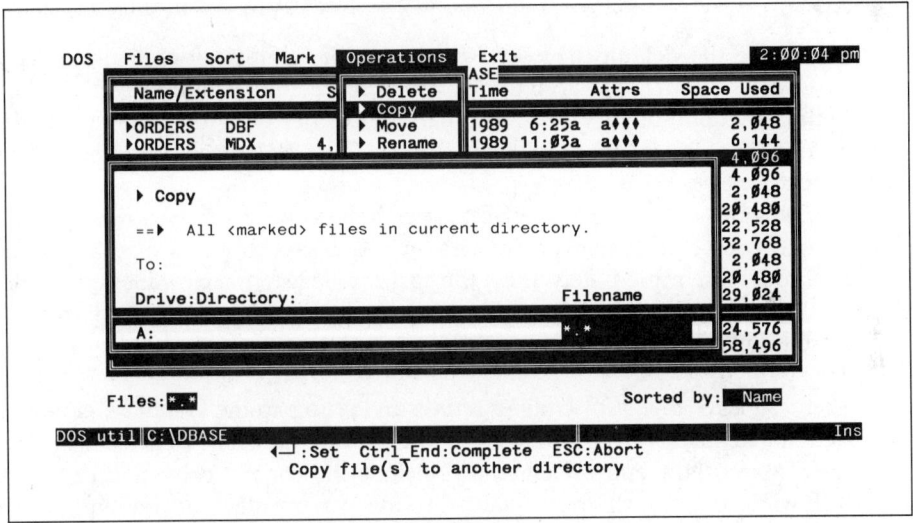

FIGURE 14.8: Backing up a group of files to the disk in drive A. After filling in the screen as shown here, press **Ctrl-End** to perform the copy operation.

To verify the copy operation, select Change Drive:Directory from the Files pull-down menu and change the setting to **A:**. After you press ←, you should see the names of the copied files on the disk in drive A. (If the floppy disk in drive A, also contains other files, you may need to use **PgDn** and **PgUp** to scroll through the file list.)

To return to the C:\DBASE directory, select Change Drive:Directory from the Files pull-down menu once again and replace A: with **C:\DBASE**. Then press ⏎.

Changing the Default Drive and Directory

SEQUENCE OF STEPS

From the DOS Utilities screen:

    Menus (**F10**)

    DOS/**S**et Default Drive:Directory

    enter the name of the new drive and directory *or* Pick (**Shift-F1**) and select from the directory tree

USAGE

To change the default drive and directory for *all* operations in the current dBASE session from the DOS Utilities screen, select Set Default Drive:Directory from the DOS pull-down menu. You can then either type the name of the new drive and directory to log on to or press Pick (**Shift-F1**) to select an option from the directory tree.

Note that this change tells dBASE to search the new drive and directory for all files you request during the current session and to save any new or changed files there. It does not immediately affect the current file list. (To view files on the new default drive and directory, you need to select Change Drive:Directory from the Files pull-down menu and type or select the name of the new default drive and directory.)

After you leave the DOS Utilities screen and return to the Control Center, you will see that dBASE is logged on to the new drive and directory. (The catalog name centered above the Control Center will include the current drive and directory.) dBASE will search only this new default directory for any files that you request. Any new files that you create will be saved on the new drive and directory.

ACCESSING DOS COMMANDS

SEQUENCE OF STEPS

From the Control Center:

    Menus (**F10**)

Tools/**D**OS Utilities [◄─┘]
DOS/**P**erform DOS Command [◄─┘]
enter a DOS command

or

DOS/**G**o to DOS [◄─┘]
Proceed [◄─┘]
enter a DOS command
type **EXIT** ◄─┘

USAGE

dBASE IV offers two techniques for accessing DOS commands without quitting dBASE. Both are available by selecting DOS Utilities from the Tools menu at the Control Center and DOS from the DOS Utilities menu.

The Perform DOS Command option lets you enter a single DOS command. When the DOS command completes its job, you will be prompted to press any key to return to dBASE IV.

The Go to DOS option on the DOS pull-down menu temporarily leaves dBASE IV and displays the DOS prompt. If any marked files are currently in the file list, dBASE will warn you that all marked files will be unmarked and will ask you whether you want to proceed or to cancel the operation.

If you select Proceed, you will be taken to the DOS prompt, with dBASE IV suspended in memory. You then can enter whatever DOS commands you wish. (Commonly used DOS commands are presented in Appendix B.) To return to dBASE IV, type the command **EXIT** at the DOS prompt and press ◄─┘.

IMPORTING DATA INTO dBASE IV

dBASE IV can read dBASE III and dBASE III PLUS database files directly, without translating the file formats. However, if you want to use dBASE IV with files that were created with other software products, you will need to *import* those files into dBASE in a format that dBASE can use.

If you need to transfer data from software products that dBASE IV does not *support* (that is, the product is not listed on the Import menu), you have several alternatives for managing the transfer.

If the software product itself is capable of transferring files in dBASE IV, dBASE III, or dBASE III PLUS database format, you can use this capability to *export* data to dBASE IV. If such a capability is not available, most likely the product will be able to export *ASCII text files*. You can use these files as intermediary files in the transfer.

Importing Data from Supported Software

SEQUENCE OF STEPS

From the Control Center:

> Menus (**F10**)
> Tools/Import [⏎]
> select supported software from list
> enter name of external file to import
> If prompted for permission to overwrite existing dBASE file of that name: Overwrite

To view database contents, with database selected in the Control Center:

> Data (**F2**)

USAGE

To access dBASE IV's Import menu, shown in Figure 14.9, select Import from the Tools pull-down menu at the Control Center. If the file that you want to import was created with one of the software products listed, select that product. Then type the name of the file to import.

If a file of that name already exists in dBASE, you will be asked for permission to overwrite it. Select Overwrite to proceed (and lose any data currently in that file). You will be returned to the Control Center, with the name of the new database above the line in the Data panel. Press Data (**F2**) to see the contents of the database. dBASE assigns the simple field names A, B, C, D, and so on to the fields. (You will probably want to change these names to more descriptive ones.)

Importing Data from Lotus 1-2-3

If you want to import data from a spreadsheet to a dBASE IV database, you should be aware that spreadsheets store data differently than databases. Database files store data in even rows and columns, whereas spreadsheets allow data to be stored in any format. You should import only the portion of the spreadsheet

IMPORTING DATA FROM LOTUS 1-2-3 — 485

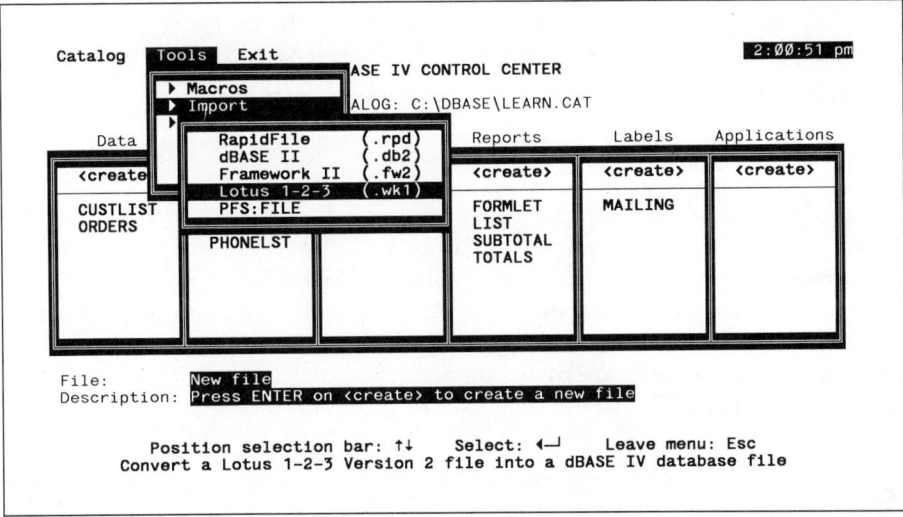

FIGURE 14.9: Menu displayed by the Tools menu Import option. If you are importing files from one of the software products listed, the import procedure is straightforward.

that stores data in even rows and columns. The example given here demonstrates importing a Lotus 1-2-3 spreadsheet, but many of the procedures involved apply to importing spreadsheets in general.

EXAMPLE

Suppose you have a Lotus 1-2-3 spreadsheet that stores data for invoices, and you wish to switch to dBASE IV to manage the database. Suppose that the invoices are stored in a Lotus 1-2-3 spreadsheet file named INVOICES.WK1, which is stored in a directory named C:\123, and that you want to import the spreadsheet data to a dBASE IV database named INVOICES.DBF on the C:\DBASE directory. The following sections detail the stages of the importation process.

ISOLATING DATA TO IMPORT

The first phase of the importation process is isolating the data to be imported. With both Lotus 1-2-3 and the file to import on the C:\123 directory, from the DOS prompt enter the command **CD\123** to log on to the 123 directory. Enter the command **123** to start Lotus 1-2-3. Type **/FR** (File Retrieve) and select the name of the file that you want to copy to dBASE IV (**INVOICES** in this example).

Move the cell pointer to the upper-left corner of the range. Type **/FXV** (File Xtract Values) to begin extracting data. Enter a drive, directory, and file name for the exported file. To simplify matters, be sure to specify the drive and directory where you want the imported database file to be stored. For example, in this case you want to store the imported data on the C:\DBASE directory, so press **Esc** twice to erase the suggested drive and directory and then enter **C:\DBASE\TRANSFER** as the file name. (Version 2.0 of 1-2-3 automatically adds the .WK1 extension. If you are using an earlier version, include the .WK1 extension; that is, enter **C:\DBASE\TRANSFER.WK1**.)

Highlight the data to export to dBASE IV, excluding column titles, underscores, totals, or any other spreadsheet embellishments. Figure 14.10 shows an example. Press ↵ after specifying the range to export. You will be prompted for a file name. Type **/QY** (Quit Yes) to leave 1-2-3 and return to DOS.

```
F16: (D1) [W13] +D16+30                                              POINT
Enter xtract range: A4..F16

     A        B              C           D            E           F
1  Customer invoices                                Date:       11-May-89
2
3  Invoice Customer        InvAmt      InvDate      PdAmt       DatePaid
4    10001 Smith Electric  $412.96    06-Oct-89    $412.96     05-Nov-89
5    10002 Toy World       $208.23    06-Oct-89    $208.23     05-Nov-89
6    10003 CompuGames       $39.89    06-Oct-89     $39.89     05-Nov-89
7    10004 Rainbird        $228.60    06-Oct-89    $228.60     05-Nov-89
8    10005 SMS Software    $591.30    06-Oct-89
9    10006 DEK Video       $248.89    06-Oct-89    $248.89     05-Nov-89
10   10007 CompuGames      $643.37    06-Oct-89    $643.37     05-Nov-89
11   10008 Rainbird         $98.36    07-Oct-89     $98.36     06-Nov-89
12   10009 SMS Software    $352.77    07-Oct-89    $352.77     06-Nov-89
13   10010 DEK Video       $985.48    07-Oct-89
14   10011 Toy World       $736.70    07-Oct-89    $736.70     06-Nov-89
15   10012 CompuGames      $261.75    07-Oct-89    $261.75     06-Nov-89
16   10013 Rainbird        $659.24    07-Oct-89    $659.24     06-Nov-89
17 --------               ----------              ----------
18 Totals                $5,467.55                $3,890.76
19
20
```

FIGURE 14.10: Range of data to export to dBASE IV highlighted on a 1-2-3 spreadsheet.

Importing the Spreadsheet Data

To import the spreadsheet data to dBASE IV, you need to get dBASE up and running and then use the Import submenu of the Tools pull-down menu. Enter the command **CD\DBASE** to log on to the dBASE directory. Enter the command **DBASE** to run dBASE IV.

At the Control Center, press Menus (**F10**) and select Import from the Tools pull-down menu. Select Lotus 1-2-3. Select the name of the extracted spreadsheet file

(TRANSFER.WK1 in this example). If a database file named TRANSFER.DBF already exists, dBASE will ask for permission to overwrite it. Select Overwrite to proceed (and lose any data currently in TRANSFER.DBF). You will be returned to the Control Center, with the name of the new database, TRANSFER, above the line in the Data panel.

With the highlight on TRANSFER in the Data panel, press Data (**F2**) to see the contents of the database. You can use Data (**F2**) and **PgUp** to switch back and forth between browse and edit mode and to scroll through records. Figure 14.11 shows how the sample file appears on the browse screen after importation.

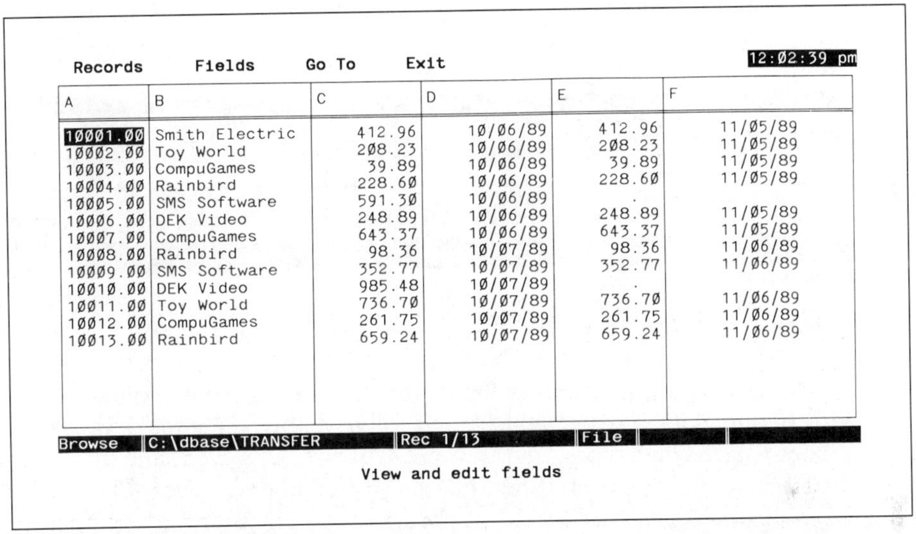

```
 Records    Fields    Go To    Exit                      12:02:39 pm

 A          B                  C         D           E          F

 10001.00   Smith Electric     412.96    10/06/89    412.96     11/05/89
 10002.00   Toy World          208.23    10/06/89    208.23     11/05/89
 10003.00   CompuGames          39.89    10/06/89     39.89     11/05/89
 10004.00   Rainbird           228.60    10/06/89    228.60     11/05/89
 10005.00   SMS Software       591.30    10/06/89
 10006.00   DEK Video          248.89    10/06/89    248.89     11/05/89
 10007.00   CompuGames         643.37    10/06/89    643.37     11/05/89
 10008.00   Rainbird            98.36    10/07/89     98.36     11/06/89
 10009.00   SMS Software       352.77    10/07/89    352.77     11/06/89
 10010.00   DEK Video          985.48    10/07/89
 10011.00   Toy World          736.70    10/07/89    736.70     11/06/89
 10012.00   CompuGames         261.75    10/07/89    261.75     11/06/89
 10013.00   Rainbird           659.24    10/07/89

 Browse  C:\dbase\TRANSFER         Rec 1/13        File
                         View and edit fields
```

FIGURE 14.11: Data imported from Lotus 1-2-3 displayed on the browse screen. Notice that dBASE assigned the simple field names A, B, C, D, and so on to the fields. (You will probably want to change these names to more descriptive ones.)

REDEFINING THE DATA TYPES

To see what data types dBASE has assigned to the imported fields, you need to access the database design screen. If the browse or edit screen is displayed, press **Esc** to return to the Control Center. With the highlight still on TRANSFER, press Design (**Shift-F2**) to switch to the database design screen. Press **Esc** to remove the Organize pull-down menu.

Figure 14.12 shows the structure of the imported file. dBASE automatically assigned two decimal places to Numeric fields and specified fields containing dates as Character fields.

```
   Layout   Organize   Append   Go To   Exit                    12:03:16 pm
                                                   Bytes remaining:    3932
   Num   Field Name   Field Type   Width   Dec   Index
    1    A            Numeric         8     2     N
    2    B            Character      15           N
    3    C            Numeric        10     2     N
    4    D            Character      12           N
    5    E            Numeric        10     2     N
    6    F            Character      13           N

   Database C:\dbase\TRANSFER           Field 1/6
              Enter the field name. Insert/Delete field:Ctrl-N/Ctrl-U
        Field names begin with a letter and may contain letters, digits and underscores
```

FIGURE 14.12: Structure initially assigned by dBASE IV to the sample file imported from 1-2-3. Notice that all Numeric fields, including the invoice number (an integer), have been assigned two decimal places, and that the fields containing dates have been designated as Character fields.

You can change the data types of any fields and also mark fields for indexing. However, during this phase you should not perform any other operations, such as renaming, adding, or deleting fields. (dBASE may become confused when copying backup data into the database and will probably lose some of your data.) After changing the data types, save the new structure (**Ctrl-End**) and then return to the database design screen (**Shift-F2**) and make other changes. Figure 14.13 shows a suggested structure for the imported database. After making appropriate changes, select Save Changes and Exit from the Exit pull-down menu and Yes when dBASE asks for confirmation.

When you get back to the Control Center, you can press Data (**F2**) and **PgUp** to view the data and verify that the changes are correct. Press **Esc** to return to the Control Center.

RENAMING FIELDS

You will want to use field names that are more descriptive than the single-letter names that dBASE assigned. With the highlight on TRANSFER in the Control Center, press Design (**Shift-F2**) to get to the database design screen. Press **Esc** to leave the Organize pull-down menu.

Enter new field names, but do not make any other changes to the database structure. (Figure 14.14 shows some suggested field names for this example.)

```
Layout   Organize   Append   Go To   Exit                    12:03:41 pm
                                                   Bytes remaining:  3936
 Num  Field Name   Field Type   Width   Dec   Index
  1   A            Numeric        8      0     N
  2   B            Character     15            N
  3   C            Numeric       10      2     N
  4   D            Date           8            N
  5   E            Numeric       10      2     N
  6   F            Date           8            N

Database C:\dbase\TRANSFER    Field 6/6
         Change option to index on this field:Spacebar
```

FIGURE 14.13: More accurate data types assigned to the imported database. The dates have been assigned the Date data type (with a corresponding change in width), and no decimal places have been allocated to the invoice numbers.

```
Layout   Organize   Append   Go To   Exit                    12:05:09 pm
                                                   Bytes remaining:  3941
 Num  Field Name   Field Type   Width   Dec   Index
  1   INVOICE      Numeric        8      0     N
  2   CUSTOMER     Character     15            N
  3   INVAMT       Numeric       10      2     N
  4   INVDATE      Date           8            N
  5   AMTPAID      Numeric       10      2     N
  6   DATEPAID     Date           8            N

Database C:\dbase\TRANSFER    Field 6/6
         Enter the field name.  Insert/Delete field:Ctrl-N/Ctrl-U
Field names begin with a letter and may contain letters, digits and underscores
```

FIGURE 14.14: Suggestions for new field names to assign to the imported database.

Select Save Changes and Exit from the Exit pull-down menu. Answer Yes to the prompts that appear until you get back to the Control Center. To view the database and verify your changes, press Data (**F2**) and **PgUp**.

The database will appear on the edit or browse screen with the new field names. To return to the Control Center after viewing your data, press **Esc**. At this point, the entire importation is complete, and you can use the imported data just as you would any dBASE IV database file. If you wish to change the name of the imported database, use the Rename option on the Operations pull-down menu of the DOS utilities screen (discussed earlier in this chapter).

Importing ASCII Text Files

If neither dBASE IV nor the other software product provides built-in options for interfacing between the two programs, you can use an ASCII text file as an intermediary for the transfer operation. Most software products, even those with very limited interfacing capability, have some means of storing data in ASCII text files. The chances are good that you can import that text file into a dBASE IV database.

CREATING THE ASCII TEXT FILE

You need to look in the software product's manual for information about creating ASCII text files, either by using a file exporting option or by storing printed reports or data in disk files. (*Text file* is a synonym for ASCII text file, or DOS text file.) Use whatever means are available to create the ASCII text file. Note the disk drive, directory, and complete file name of the text file you create.

ASCERTAINING THE FILE STRUCTURE

The next step is to look at the ASCII text file and ascertain its structure. To do so, starting from the DOS prompt, log on to the directory where the file is stored and use the DOS command TYPE to look at the contents of the file. For example, if the ASCII text file is stored in C:\FBASE\EXPORTED.DAT, you enter the following commands at the DOS prompt to view the contents of the file:

```
CD\FBASE
TYPE EXPORTED.DAT
```

Most likely, the file will be in one of three formats: delimited, blank delimited, or fixed field length (also called structured data format, or SDF). *Delimited* ASCII files generally place a comma between each field and surround character strings with quotation marks or some other characters. *Blank-delimited* files separate each field with a single blank space, and individual fields contain no blank spaces. *Fixed-field-length* files place each field in evenly aligned columns. Figure 14.15 shows examples of these three formats.

```
Delimited (with ") format:

1001,"Smith","John","ABC Co.","123 A St.","San Diego","CA"
1002,"Adams","Annie","","3456 Ocean St.","Santa Monica","CA"

Blank-delimted format:

1001 Smith John CA 92067 (619)555-1234 19881115 Y
1002 Adams Annie CA 92001 (714)555-0123 19890101 F

Fixed field-length (SDF) format:

1001 Smith      John      ABC Co.
1004 Newell     John      LoTech Co.
```

FIGURE 14.15: You can use these examples of ASCII file formats to determine which type of format has been used by the software product you are using to create ASCII files.

Notice that the delimited file in Figure 14.15 uses double quotation marks as delimiters. Not all delimited files use quotation marks, however. For example, the file might use apostrophes (') to delimit character strings, as follows:

1001,'Smith','John','ABC Co.','123 A St.','San Diego'
1002,'Adams','Annie','','3456 Ocean St.','Santa Monica'

Make a note of the character used to delimit character strings, to remind yourself later.

If you find that the ASCII file you have created uses none of the formats discussed in this section, you may need to write a program to perform the conversion. WordPerfect mailmerge files, for example, use a very unusual format that cannot easily be imported into or exported from dBASE IV database files.

Planning the dBASE IV Database Structure

While viewing the contents of the ASCII text file on your screen, you need to plan a structure for the dBASE IV database. Assign a name, data type, width, and number of decimal places (for numbers) to each field. Be sure to list field names in the same order that they are displayed, from left to right, in the text file.

If the fields in the file are separated by commas or single blank spaces, then you can assign any width that you wish to each field. However, if the file has the fixed field-length (SDF) structure, the width you assign to each field in your dBASE IV database must match exactly the width of the corresponding field in the ASCII text file.

COPYING AND RENAMING THE TEXT FILE

Next you need to copy the file to the C:\DBASE directory and change the extension to .TXT. (If you have a DOS redirect or move utility, you can move the file instead.) For example, to copy the C:\FBASE\EXPORTED.DAT file to C:\DBASE\EXPORTED.TXT, you enter this command at the DOS prompt:

COPY C:\DBASE\EXPORTED.DAT C:\DBASE\EXPORTED.TXT

CREATING THE DATABASE STRUCTURE

Now you can log on to the \DBASE directory and run dBASE. When the Control Center appears, select <create> from the Data panel and design a database with the field names and data types that you noted earlier. Save the database structure using the Save This Database File Structure option on the Database Design screen Layout pull-down menu.

While you are still at the database design screen, select Copy Records from Non-dBASE file from the Append pull-down menu. Then select the appropriate file format from the submenu (shown in Figure 14.16) that appears.

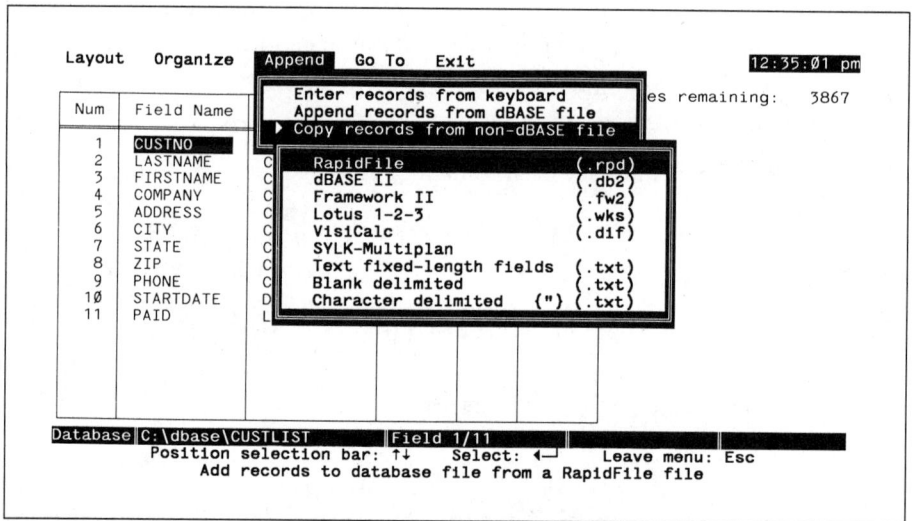

FIGURE 14.16: Append menu import options. This menu has the same options as the Import submenu of the Tools menu, but also includes Multiplan files and the three types of ASCII text files.

The importation is now complete. When you press Data (**F2**) to view your new database on the browse screen, you should find all the records correctly placed in the fields you created.

Importing WordStar MailMerge Data

This section demonstrates how to import data from a WordStar MailMerge file into a dBASE IV database. WordStar MailMerge files are already in ASCII delimited format, so you need not take any intermediate steps to import them into dBASE IV.

EXAMPLE

Suppose you used WordStar to create a long list of names and addresses for WordStar MailMerge operations. Now you want to import those names and addresses to a dBASE IV database file and use dBASE to manage them.

Suppose you have stored the names and addresses in a text file named C:\WS4\NAMES.MRG. From the DOS prompt, enter the command **CD\WS4** to log on to the \WS4 directory. To view the contents of the file, enter the command **TYPE NAMES.MRG** at the DOS prompt.

Suppose now that the screen displays the contents of the NAMES.MRG file, as shown in Figure 14.17. Because commas separate fields in this example, you can assign any widths that you wish to each field. You might jot down notes about the file and define field names and data types, as follows:

Format:	Delimited (with ")
LastName	Character 15
FirstName	Character 15
Company	Character 20
Address	Character 30
City	Character 20
State	Character 2
Zip	Character 10

Copy the text file to the \DBASE directory and change its extension to .TXT by entering the command

COPY C:\WS4\NAMES.MRG C:\DBASE\NAMES.TXT

at the DOS prompt.

Log on to the dBASE directory (by entering the command **CD\DBASE** at the DOS prompt) and run dBASE. Select <create> from the Data panel in the Control Center. Design the database structure according to your earlier notes, as shown in Figure 14.18.

494 — **CH. 14** MANAGING FILES AND THE WORKSPACE

```
C:\WS4>TYPE Names.MRG
"Smith","John","ABC Co.","123 A St.","San Diego","CA",92067
"Adams","Annie","","3456 Ocean St.","Santa Monica","CA",92001
"Mahoney","Mary","","211 Seahawk St.","Seattle","WA",88977
"Newell","John","LoTech Co.","734 Rainbow Dr.","Butte","MT",54321
"Beach","Sandy","American Widget","11 Elm St.","Portland","OR",76543
"Kenney","Ralph","","1101 Rainbow Ct.","Los Angeles","CA",96607
"Schumack","Susita","SMS Software","47 Broad St.","Philadelphia","PA",45543
"Smith","Anita","Zeerocks, Inc.","2001 Engine Dr.","Hideaway","CA",92220
"Jones","Fred","American Sneaker","P.O. Box 3381","Newark","NJ",01234


C:\WS4>
```

FIGURE 14.17: Contents of the sample WordStar MailMerge file.

```
Layout    Organize    Append    Go To    Exit              12:38:40 pm
                                                   Bytes remaining:   3898
 Num   Field Name   Field Type   Width   Dec   Index

  1    LASTNAME     Character      15            Y
  2    FIRSTNAME    Character      15            N
  3    COMPANY      Character      20            N
  4    ADDRESS      Character      30            N
  5    CITY         Character      20            N
  6    STATE        Character       2            N
  7    ZIP          Character      10            N








 Database  C:\dbase\<NEW>            Field 7/7
            Change option to index on this field:Spacebar
```

FIGURE 14.18: Suggested structure for the database that will receive the sample imported WordStar MailMerge records.

Select Save This Database File Structure from the Layout pull-down menu and assign the file a valid name (such as **NAMES**). Select Copy Records from non-dBASE File from the Append pull-down menu. Select Character Delimited from the submenu. The submenu that appears suggests using quotation marks as delimiters. The text file uses this character, so just press ↵.

Select the name of the text file (NAMES.TXT in this example) from the submenu that appears. Select Save Changes and Exit from the Exit pull-down menu.

The importation is now complete. You can press Data (**F2**) to switch to the edit and browse screens and use the **PgUp**, **PgDn**, and arrow keys to scroll through the database and verify that all the records were imported appropriately.

EXPORTING DATA FROM dBASE IV

To export data from a dBASE IV database to a format used by another program, select the Export option from the Tools pull-down menu. You will see the submenu of exporting formats shown in Figure 14.19.

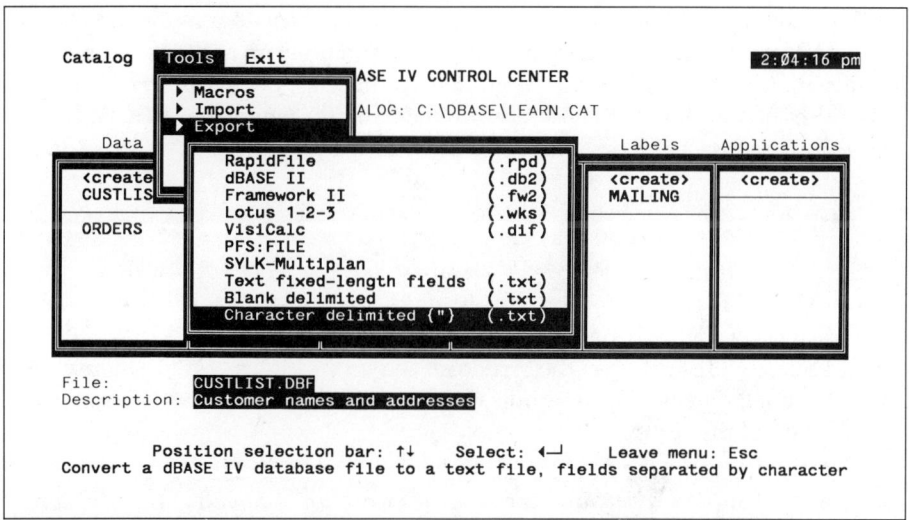

FIGURE 14.19: The Export submenu of the Tools menu provides a straightforward method for exporting to any of the seven supported products, as well as to three different types of ASCII text files.

If you are exporting to one of the seven software products listed on the Export menu, see the following section, "Exporting Data to Supported Software." Otherwise, you can export your dBASE IV databases as ASCII text files. You must first determine which of the three ASCII file types you should use. See "Exporting Data as ASCII Text Files" later in this chapter.

Exporting Data to Supported Software

The dBASE II option copies data to the dBASE II format and assigns the original file name plus the extension .DB2 to the exported file. Do not change the

.DB2 extension to .DBF until you have moved the file to another directory, disk drive, or computer. If you change the .DB2 extension to .DBF while the file is still on the same directory as the dBASE IV database, you may overwrite your original dBASE IV database.

The Export menu also supports a number of other software formats. Each option copies data to the format used by the software named. Files created for RapidFile are assigned the extension .RPD. Framework II files are given the extension .FW2. VisiCalc files become .DIF files. PFS:FILE files and Multiplan SYLK files are not given any extension.

Exporting Data to Lotus 1-2-3

The Lotus 1-2-3 option copies a dBASE IV database to a file with the extension .WKS, which can be used by Symphony and Quattro as well as Lotus 1-2-3. Different versions of 1-2-3 and Symphony require files with different extensions (for example, version 2 of 1-2-3 requires files with the extension .WK1). If necessary, you can use 1-2-3 or Symphony to change a .WKS file to a .WK1 file.

EXAMPLE

Suppose you have a dBASE IV database file named PARTSORD.DBF on the C:\DBASE directory, and you want to use Lotus 1-2-3 to print a graph of total orders for each part number stored in the database. Assume that the PARTSORD.DBF file has the structure shown in Figure 14.20. Figure 14.21 shows a small portion of the sample database (additional records are scrolled off the bottom of the screen).

Before you export the database to Lotus 1-2-3, you need to generate total sales for each part number, because that is the information that you want to graph. To do so, you need to set up a query to total the QTY field for each part number, as shown in Figure 14.22.

The next step is to create a database file from the results of the query—by selecting Write View as Database File from the Layout pull-down menu. When prompted, enter a file name (such as **ORDTOTS** in this example) for the new database file. Press Menus (**F10**) and select Abandon Changes and Exit from the Exit pull-down menu and Yes when prompted for verification.

When you get back to the Control Center, you are ready to export the totaled data in ORDTOTS.DBF to Lotus 1-2-3. To do so, press Menus (**F10**), select Export from the Tools pull-down menu, and select Lotus 1-2-3 from the Export menu. Select ORDTOTS.DBF from the submenu that appears.

To move the exported ORDTOTS.WKS file to the C:\123 directory (where Lotus 1-2-3 is stored), press Menus (**F10**) and select DOS Utilities from the

EXPORTING DATA AS ASCII TEXT FILES ——— 497

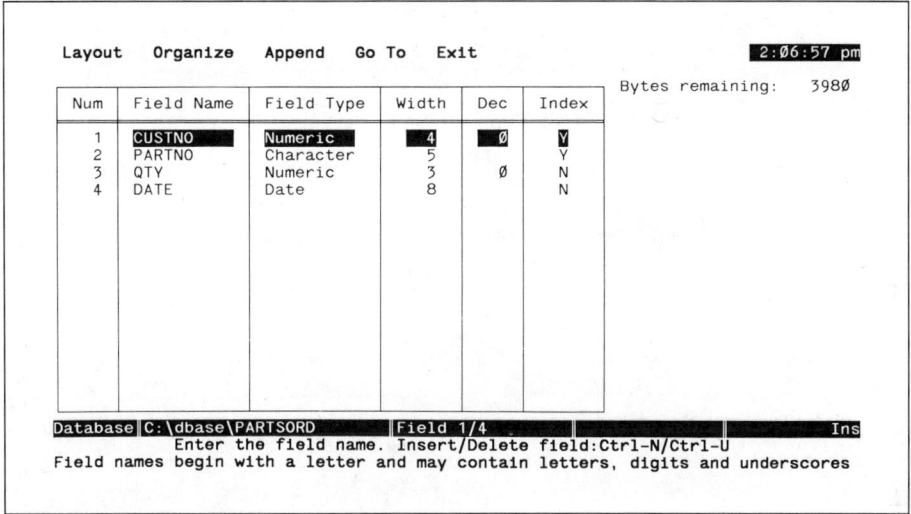

FIGURE 14.20: Structure of the PARTSORD database.

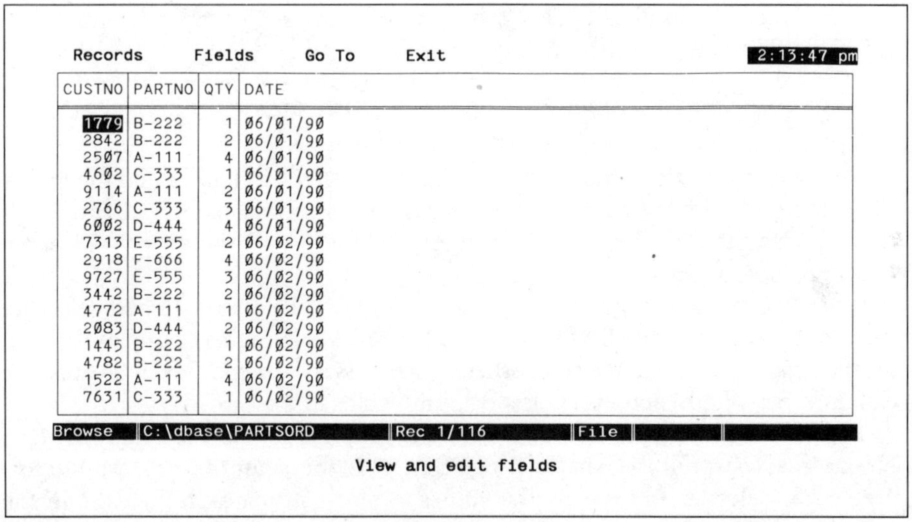

FIGURE 14.21: Sample data in the PARTSORD database.

Tools pull-down menu. Press Menus (**F10**) again and select Display Only from the Files pull-down menu. Change the setting to ***.WKS** and press ↵.

Use the **PgDn** and arrow keys to locate and highlight ORDTOTS.WKS in the files list. Press Menus (**F10**) and select Move from the Operations pull-down

CH. 14 MANAGING FILES AND THE WORKSPACE

```
Layout   Fields   Condition   Update   Exit                    2:15:39 pm
Partsord.dbf  #↓CUSTNO              #↓PARTNO              ↓QTY
                                    GROUP BY              SUM




┌View─────────────────────────────────────────────────────────────────────
│<NEW>        Partsord->    Partsord->    Partsord->    Partsord->
│             CUSTNO        PARTNO        QTY           DATE
Query    C:\dbase\<NEW>        Field 1/4
   Prev/Next field:Shift-Tab/Tab   Data:F2   Pick:Shift-F1   Prev/Next skel:F3/F4
```

FIGURE 14.22: Query to total orders by part number. The results of this query will provide the data from which to generate a 1-2-3 graph.

menu. Select Single File. Press **Ctrl-Y** to erase the suggested destination and type **C:\123** as the new destination. Press **Ctrl-End**.

When the move is complete, press Menus (**F10**) and select Exit to Control Center from the Exit pull-down menu. Leave dBASE IV by selecting Quit to DOS from the Exit pull-down menu.

Now you need to load the exported data into Lotus 1-2-3 and build the graph. First, log on to the appropriate directory (C:\123 in this example), run 1-2-3, and retrieve the file. (Enter the command **CD\123** and then type **123** at the DOS prompt to run 1-2-3.)

When the blank spreadsheet appears, type **/FR** (File Retrieve) and select the name of the exported dBASE IV file (ORDTOTS.WKS in this example). You will see the exported totals on the spreadsheet. As necessary, use the **/WCS** (Worksheet, Column, Set-Width) options to alter column widths in the spreadsheet.

Type **/GTB** (Graph Type Bar) to select a graph type. Select X and highlight X-axis titles (part numbers in the range B2..B7 in this example) as shown in Figure 14.23. Select A and specify the values to plot on the graph (C2..C7 in this example). Select View.

The graph will appear on the screen. You can use other 1-2-3 graph options to add titles or other features, as was done in Figure 14.24. After viewing the graph, press any key to return to the spreadsheet. You can treat the imported data as you would any other spreadsheet data. If you wish to save any changes in the spreadsheet, use the 1-2-3 **/FS** (File Save) options. To leave 1-2-3, type **/QY** (Quit Yes).

EXPORTING DATA AS ASCII TEXT FILES ━━ **499**

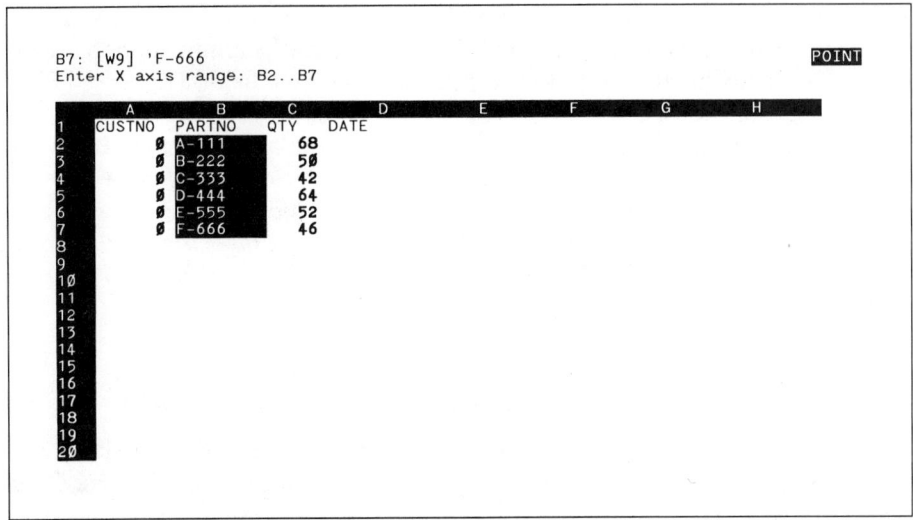

FIGURE 14.23: Part names selected as the X-axis titles in a 1-2-3 spreadsheet.

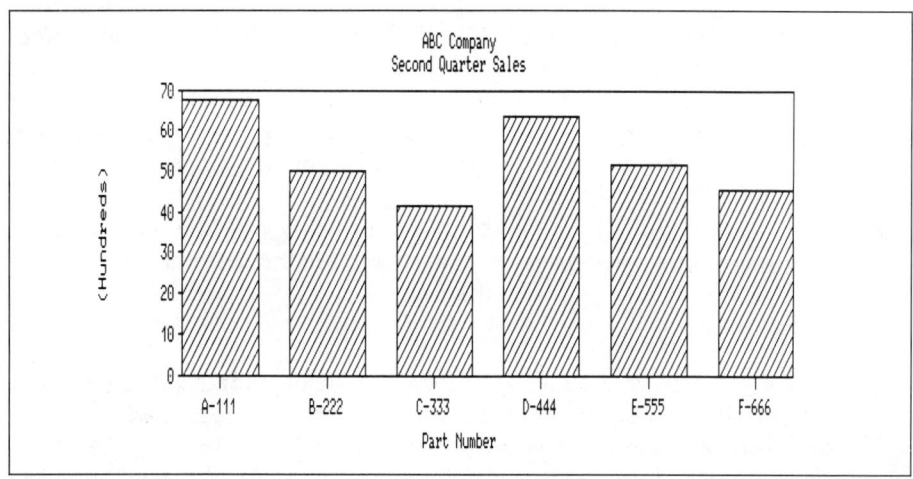

FIGURE 14.24: Sample graph printed by 1-2-3. The graph is the result of a view exported from dBASE IV.

Exporting Data as ASCII Text Files

You can use the three ASCII text files options on the Export menu (shown in Figure 14.19) to copy a dBASE IV database to an ASCII text file (also called a disk file, or DOS file). The Text Fixed-Length Fields option lists fields in evenly aligned columns (earlier versions of dBASE called this the SDF format). The copied file will have the extension .TXT. The Blank Delimited option creates a text file that includes a single blank space between each field. The copied file will have the extension .TXT.

The Character Delimited option creates a file with a general format that most software products can import. When you select this option, you can specify a delimiter other than the default quotation marks. (Quotation marks are the most common delimiter, however.) You can find examples of these three file formats in Figure 14.15 and in the section "Importing ASCII Text Files" earlier in this chapter.

CREATING THE TEXT FILE

To create a text file from a report or label format, first activate the database, if necessary (by highlighting its name in the Data panel of the Control Center, pressing ←┘, and selecting Use File). To export only certain records or to sort the database, activate the appropriate query.

Highlight the name of the report format in the Reports panel, press ←┘, and select Print Report. Select Destination and press the space bar to change the setting to DOS File. Select Name of DOS File and note the suggested file name (or change the drive, directory, or suggested file name).

To view the report on the screen as it is stored on disk, select Echo to Screen and press ←┘ to change the setting to Yes. Press **Ctrl-End**. Select Begin Printing. When you get back to the Control Center, select Quit to DOS from the Exit pull-down menu to leave dBASE IV.

You can use the DOS TYPE command to verify that the file exists: Enter **TYPE** *filename* at the DOS prompt. You should see the entire formatted report.

EXAMPLE

Suppose that you created a report format to display totals and subtotals and wish to embed a copy of the report in a document you created with WordStar, WordPerfect, or some other word processing program. In this case, you are exporting printed, formatted data rather than raw data. You need to send the printed report to a disk file (an ASCII text file) and then read that file into a new or existing word processing document.

You can create a text file from the LIST report of the CUSTLIST database (created in Chapter 7). First make sure that CUSTLIST is open (if necessary, highlight its name in the Data panel of the Control Center, press ←┘, and select Use File).

Highlight LIST in the Reports panel, press ←┘, and select Print Report. Select Destination and press the space bar to change the setting to DOS File.

Select Name of DOS File and note the suggested file name, LIST.PRT. To view the report on the screen as it is stored on disk, select Echo to Screen and press ←┘ to change the setting to Yes. Press **Ctrl-End** and then select Begin Printing.

When you get back to the Control Center, select Quit to DOS from the Exit pull-down menu. To verify that the file exists, use the DOS TYPE command: Type **TYPE LIST.PRT** (and press ←┘) at the DOS prompt. You should see the entire formatted report.

READING THE REPORT INTO WORDSTAR

To read the printed report into a WordStar word processing document, first log on to the WordStar directory that contains the WordStar document into which you want to insert the report. Run WordStar in the usual manner (that is, type **WS** at the DOS prompt and press ←┘).

Type **D** to select Document and then enter the name of a new or existing document file. If you are inserting the report into an existing document, move the cursor to exactly the place where you want the incoming report to be inserted.

Press **Ctrl-KR** and, when prompted, type the full path and file name of the file to insert (**C:\DBASE\LIST.PRT** in this example). Press ←┘.

You will see the formatted report appear in your document. Use the **PgUp** and **PgDn** keys to scroll and make changes as necessary. After inserting the report, save the document as usual with the **Ctrl-KD**, **Ctrl-KS**, or **Ctrl-KX** keystrokes.

READING THE REPORT INTO WORDPERFECT

To read the formatted report into a WordPerfect document, log on to the directory that contains WordPerfect or the document into which you want to insert the formatted report.

If you want to read the formatted report into a new document, run WordPerfect by entering the command **WP** at the DOS prompt.

If you want to read the report into an existing WordPerfect document, start WordPerfect by entering the command **WP** *filename*, where *filename* is the name of the existing document.

Move the cursor to the location where you want the inserted report to appear. Press **Ctrl-F5**. Select option 1 and then option 2. Enter the full path and file name of the formatted report (**C:\DBASE\LIST.PRT** in this example) and press ←┘.

You will see the formatted report embedded in the document. Use the usual scrolling keys to verify that the entire file was inserted and to make any changes, if necessary. Save the document by pressing **F7**.

Exporting to WordStar MailMerge Files

You can use dBASE IV to manage names and addresses and WordStar to print form letters. To do so, you need to export records from the dBASE IV database to an ASCII text file that delimits each field with a comma. Then you need to use the WordStar MailMerge dot commands in a form letter to read in the exported data.

EXAMPLE

This example exports data from the CUSTLIST database to a WordStar MailMerge file named CUSTLIST.MRG in a directory named C:\WS4. From the dBASE IV Control Center, press Menus (**F10**) and select Export from the Tools pull-down menu. Highlight Character Delimited and press ⏎ to accept the double quotation mark (ASCII character number 34) as the delimiter. Select CUSTLIST.DBF. When dBASE is done, select Quit to DOS from the Exit pull-down menu.

At the DOS prompt, you can verify that the exportation was successful by entering the command **TYPE CustList.TXT**. You should see the CUSTLIST database records, with Character data surrounded by quotation marks and commas between each field. A sample record is shown here.

    1001,"Smith","John","ABC Co.","123 A St.","San Diego",
    "CA","92067","(619)555-1234",19881115,Y

To store a copy of this exported file in a directory named WS4 (where WordStar is stored) and to change its name to CUSTLIST.MRG, enter this command at the DOS prompt:

    COPY CUSTLIST.TXT C:\WS4\CUSTLIST.MRG

After you press ⏎ and the copy operation is complete, you can log on to the C:\WS4 directory by entering the command **CD\WS4**. Now you need to create a form letter. At the DOS prompt, enter the usual command for running WordStar (usually **WS**). Select D and enter a name for the form letter (for example, **FORMLET.TXT**). Press **Ctrl-O** and then **S1** to set line spacing to 1.

Figure 14.25 shows a sample form letter for printing letters using the exported data in the CUSTLIST.MRG file. Note that the .DF dot command specifies the name of the file containing the data to merge, and the .RV command assigns a variable name to each field in the merge file. You must include a variable name for each field in the merge file, whether or not you plan to actually use the field in the letter, and you must use the same order, left to right, as the fields in the merge file.

```
      C:FORMLET.TXT      P01 L17 C04 Insert Align
L----!----!----!----!----!----!----!----!----!----!--------R
.MT 8
.DF CustList.MRG
.RV CustNo,Last,First,Company,Address,City,State,Zip,Phone,Start,Paid
.OP
.LS1

June 11, 1990

&First& &Last&
&Company/o&
&Address&
&City&, &State&   &Zip&

Dear &First&:

This is a sample WordStar form letter.  The name and address
above were exported from a dBASE IV database to a delimited text
file, which in turn was used as a mailmerge file to print these
letters.

(etc.. etc...)

.PA
```

FIGURE 14.25: Sample WordStar form letter, which can be merged with data exported from a dBASE IV file of names and addresses. The exported file must be in ASCII delimited format, and the order of the fields must match the order of variable names next to the .RV command. Also, this form letter assumes that the ASCII delimited file is named CUSTLIST.MRG.

To place data from the merge file onto the printed letter, use the variable name assigned in the .RV command surrounded by ampersands. If you think that a particular field may sometimes be blank (as COMPANY occasionally is in the CUSTLIST database), type **/o** to the right of the variable name, as in the example *&Company/o&*. Doing so ensures that WordStar will close the gap left by this empty variable, rather than printing a blank line.

After creating the form letter, save it using the WordStar **Ctrl-KD** command. Then select M (for Merge Print) and type the name of the form letter file, **FORMLET.TXT**. Press **Esc** (or **F10** if using WordStar version 5) to bypass other options and begin printing.

Changing Environment Settings

SEQUENCE OF STEPS

From the Control Center, to access the Settings menu:

> Menus (**F10**)
> Tools/Settings [◄─┘]

USAGE

This section discusses the features of the submenus available from the Settings menu, which is available from the Control Center Tools pull-down menu. Changing the settings from this menu affects only the current dBASE IV session. When you exit and then return to dBASE IV later, the original settings will be in effect. (To change a setting permanently, so that it affects all future dBASE IV sessions, use the DBSETUP program, discussed in Chapter 19.)

Options for Changing the Display

SEQUENCE OF STEPS

From the Control Center:

> Menus (**F10**)
> Tools/Settings/**O**ptions [◄─┘]
> make changes
> **Ctrl-End**

USAGE

When you first select Settings, you will see the Options pull-down menu, which displays a list of the most commonly used settings, as shown in Figure 14.26. Table 14.1 summarizes the effects of changing each of the settings. To make changes, move the highlight to the option of interest. Press the space bar or ◄─┘ to change Off to On, or On to Off. For settings in braces, press ◄─┘, enter a number, and press ◄─┘ again. Press **Ctrl-End** to save your settings.

CHANGING THE DISPLAY COLORS — 505

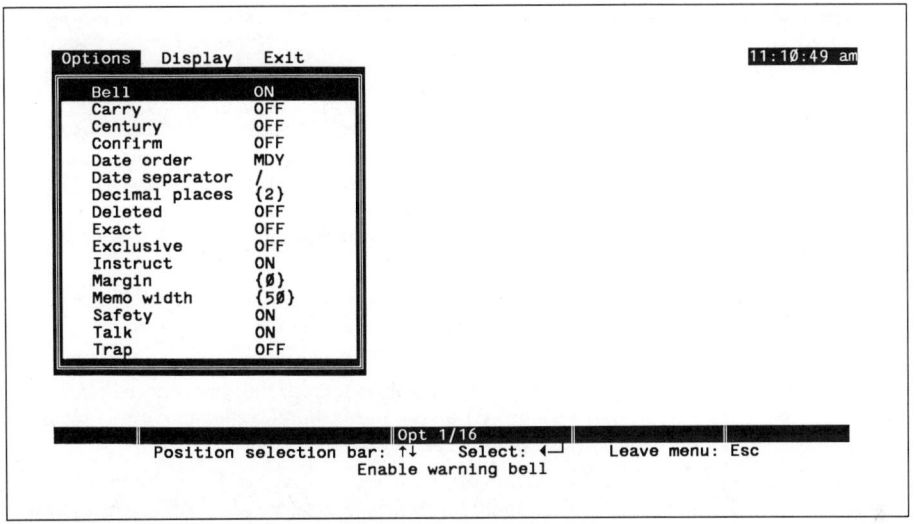

FIGURE 14.26: From the Settings Options menu, you can change a variety of dBASE's default settings to suit your needs. The purpose and effect of each setting is explained in Table 14.1.

OPTION	DESCRIPTION
Bell	When on, beeps whenever a field on an edit screen or custom form is filled or whenever an error occurs. When off, does not beep.
Carry	When on, copies all information from the current record to the next new record when you are entering new data. When off, starts each new record with blank fields.
Century	When off, displays dates with two-digit years (for example, 12/31/90). When on, displays dates with four-digit years (for example, 12/31/1990).
Confirm	When off, automatically moves the cursor to the next field when you fill a field during data entry or editing. When on, keeps the cursor in the current field until you press ⏎.
Date Order	Determines the order of month, day, and year in date displays. Press the space bar to scroll through the options, which are MDY (12/31/89), DMY (31/12/89), and YMD (89/12/31).

TABLE 14.1: Environment Settings Options

OPTION	DESCRIPTION
Date Separator	Determines the character used in date displays. Press the space bar to scroll through the options. Slash (/) displays dates as 12/31/89, hyphen (-) displays dates as 12-31-89, and period (.) displays dates as 12.31.89. Can be used in conjunction with Date Order to create various international date formats (for example, 89.12.31).
Decimal Places	Determines the number of decimal places, in the range 0 to 18, displayed in the results of calculations. The default setting is 2.
Deleted	When off, displays records that are marked for deletion. When on, hides marked records from view and from all operations.
Exact	When off, matches strings of different lengths in a search; for example, a search for **"AB"** locates *ABC Co.* When on, matches strings only of the same length.
Exclusive	When off, lets other network users access the file you are currently using. When on, does not let other network users access the file you are currently using.
Instruct	When on, prompt boxes appear when you select a file name from one of the panels in the Control Center. When off, the prompt box is not displayed. The first option in the prompt box is selected automatically.
Margin	Adjusts the left margin, in characters per inch, for all printed output. For example, **10** adds a 1-inch margin to the left side of the page (assuming that the current font prints ten characters to the inch).
Memo Width	Adjusts the default width of Memo field displays during certain operations. Will accept a value in the range 5 to 250. (Widths defined in custom forms and reports override this setting.)
Safety	When on, displays a warning before dBASE overwrites an existing file and provides an option to cancel the operation. When off, displays no warning and immediately overwrites the existing file.
Talk	When on, displays results of various dBASE operations on the screen. When off, does not display results on the screen. Used mainly for programming.
Trap	Determines whether the dBASE IV debugger is activated when an error occurs in a program. Used for programming.

TABLE 14.1: Environment Settings Options (continued)

Changing the Display Colors

SEQUENCE OF STEPS

From the Control Center:

> Menus (**F10**)
> Tools/**S**ettings/**D**isplay [⏎]
> select an area to color
> select foreground and background colors
> **Ctrl-End**

USAGE

If you have a color monitor, you can use the options on the Display pull-down menu to change the colors displayed on your screen. The Display pull-down menu provides a list of areas to color. When you select an area, you will see a list of possible foreground and background colors for that area, as shown in Figure 14.27. Note that the color options available to you depend on the type of color monitor you have.

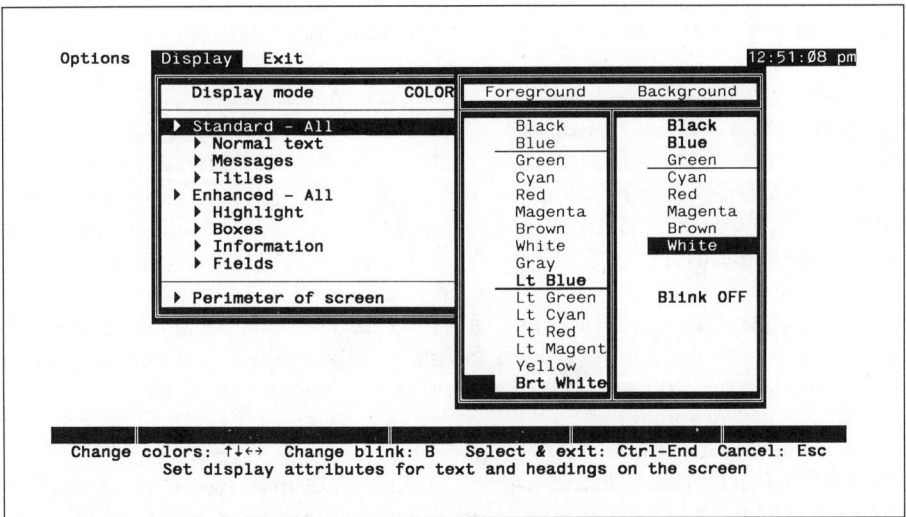

FIGURE 14.27: The Settings Display menu and the foreground and background color options. You can use the arrow keys to scroll through the possible color combinations; dBASE displays the various color combinations as you do so.

The Standard—All option affects the general color of text and background on normal (that is, unhighlighted) sections of the screen. The Enhanced—All option sets the general color for all highlighted text, such as text in the menu, status bar, and input fields of a custom form. You can color more specific areas by selecting options under Standard—All and Enhanced—All. Figure 14.28 shows examples of such specific areas.

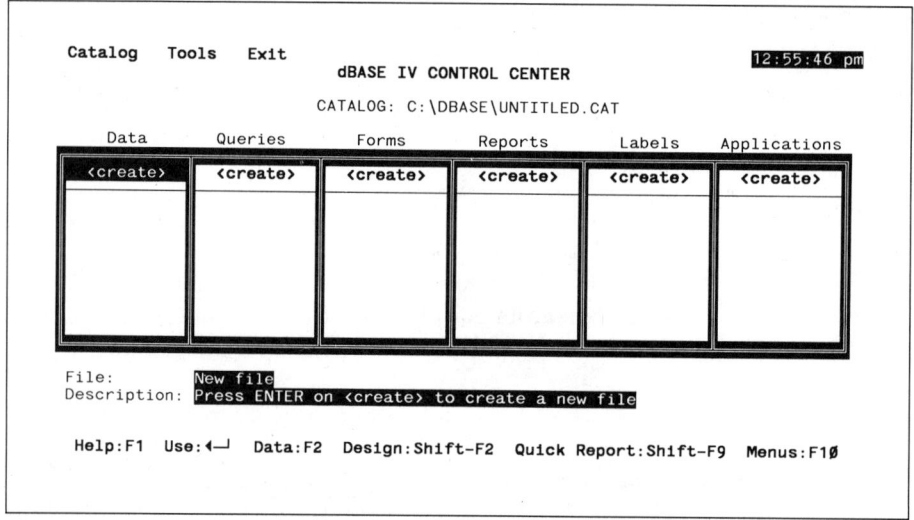

FIGURE 14.28: Some examples of areas of the screen that you can color by using the Settings Display menu.

After you select an area to color, the menu of foreground and background color options appears. A small square indicates the current foreground color. You can use the ↑ and ↓ keys to scroll up and down and select a different foreground color.

After selecting a foreground color, press → to move to the background options. Once again, you can scroll through the options using the ↑ and ↓ keys. As you scroll through foreground and background colors, the screen adjusts to show the different color combinations.

For example, if you select Lt Cyan as your foreground color and then scroll through the background colors, you will see light cyan displayed with all possible backgrounds in the Background column and the currently highlighted background color behind all foreground colors in the Foreground column.

You can switch back and forth between the Background and Foreground columns and try different combinations until you find one you like. Press **Ctrl-End** when you have colored as many areas as you want. To leave the menu and return to the Control Center, select Exit to Control Center from the Exit pull-down menu, or press **Esc**.

Tips and Traps

- To avoid confusing *catalogs* and *directories*, remember that a directory (or subdirectory) is a place on the disk where files are stored, and a catalog is simply a list of file names.
- Before you delete all marked or displayed files on the DOS Utilities screen, use **PgDn** and **PgUp** to scroll through the file list and make certain that you know exactly which files will be deleted.
- Make backup copies of all your database files from time to time. That way, if you ever inadvertently lose any files from your hard disk, you can just copy the backup files from the floppy disks back onto your hard disk.
- When you import data into dBASE IV, do not make any changes to the database structure (such as renaming, adding, or deleting fields) until dBASE has imported all the data. Otherwise, dBASE may become confused when copying backup data into the database and will probably lose some of your data.
- dBASE IV can read dBASE III and dBASE III PLUS database files without translation.
- Adding a file name to a catalog does not *copy* the file to the current drive or directory.
- Whenever you select Go to DOS, be sure to return to dBASE IV and exit dBASE before turning off your computer.
- Colors that you select from the Settings submenu of the Tools pull-down menu affect only the current dBASE session.

Summary

This chapter discussed how to use dBASE IV catalogs as well as most of the options on the Tools pull-down menu. The DOS utilities provide a way of using DOS without exiting from dBASE IV. The import and export features let you translate files to and from other software products and combine dBASE files with those of other products. You can use the Settings menu to customize the screen to your liking.

To select colors for custom forms:

- Chapter 10, "Creating Custom Forms"

To use the DBSETUP program to permanently change a setting (including colors) for all future dBASE IV sessions:

- Chapter 19, "Using DBSETUP"

For a guide to basic DOS concepts and commands:

- Appendix B, "Commonly Used DOS Commands"

Part V

Developing Applications

Chapter 15: Creating Application Objects
Chapter 16: Assigning Actions to Application Objects
Chapter 17: Generating and Using an Application

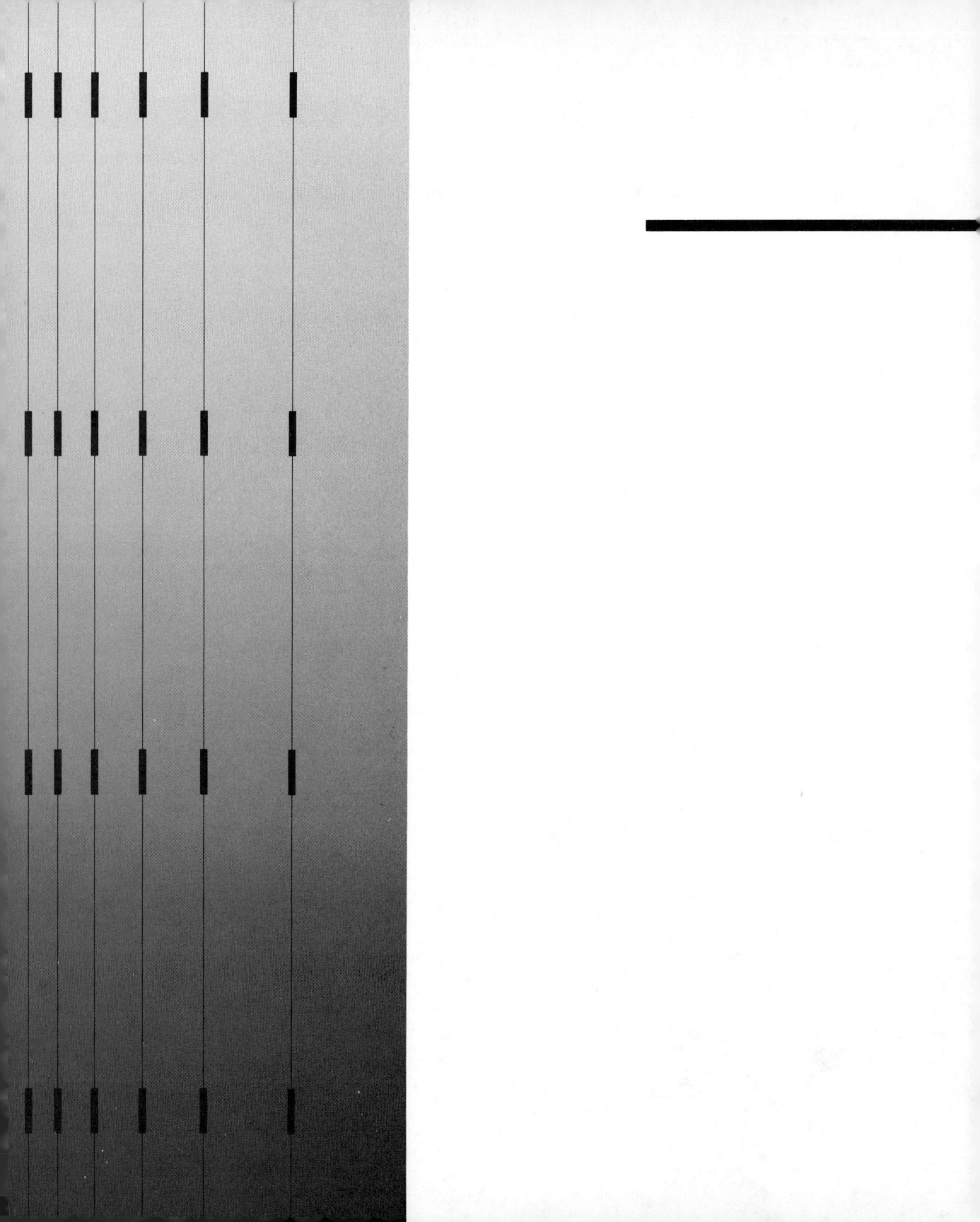

CHAPTER 15

CREATING APPLICATION OBJECTS

Starting the Applications Generator. 517
Creating a New Application. 518
Using the Application Design Screen. 521
    Using the Applications Generator Menus. 524
Modifying the Application Default Settings. 524
    Changing the Application Name and Description. 525
    Changing the Main Menu Type and Name. 526
    Changing the Program Header. 528
    Modifying the Application Environment. 528
        Changing Display Options. 529
        Changing Environment Settings. .530
        Setting a Search Path. 533
        Changing the Default Database, Index, and Sort Order. 534
    Creating a Sign-On Banner. 535
    Saving the Application Definition. 538
Developing a Quick Application. 539
Using the Design Menu. 541
Creating a Horizontal Bar Menu. 543
Creating a Pop-Up or Pull-Down Menu. 544
Creating a Files List. 547
Creating a Structure List. 550
Designing a Values List. 553
Creating a Batch Process. 556
Using the Menu, List, and Batch Pull-Down Menus. 557
    Changing the Object Name and Description. 558
    Overriding the Database or View. 558
    Modifying Display Options. 562
    Embedding Program Code in an Application. 564

  Saving the Current Object. 565
  Putting Away the Current Object. .565
  Clearing the Work Surface. 566
Tips and Traps. 567
Summary. 567

Creating Application Objects

This chapter is a guide to the dBASE IV Applications Generator. It discusses how to define the application environment and how to create the *application objects*, such as bar menus, pull-down menus, lists, and batch processes. Chapter 16 discusses the next phase of application development: assigning actions to application objects. Chapter 17 discusses the final phases of application development: generating the code and running the application. In addition, Appendix F presents a complete hands-on example that demonstrates all the steps involved in designing, creating, generating, and using an application.

Starting the Applications Generator

Before you even enter the Applications Generator, you should create all the necessary database objects, such as databases, report formats, and custom screens, and store them in a unique directory. You also should first sketch out a menu system for the application. Appendix F discusses these preliminary steps in detail.

Before you enter the Applications Generator, make sure that the directory containing the application's database objects is current. Then run dBASE in the usual manner. If you have created a unique catalog for the application, be sure to make that catalog current as well, so that the Control Center displays the application's database objects. Now you are ready to use the Applications Generator to create or modify the application.

SEQUENCE OF STEPS

From the Control Center:
    To create a new application:

        highlight <create> in the Applications panel

        ⏎

        Applications Generator [⏎]

    To modify an existing application:

        highlight the application name

        ⏎

518 CH. 15 CREATING APPLICATION OBJECTS

USAGE

To create a new application, select <create> from the Applications panel in the Control Center. From the prompt box that appears, select Applications Generator.

To modify an existing application, highlight its name in the Applications panel of the Control Center and press Design (**Shift-F2**), or press ↵ and select Modify Application from the dialog box.

CREATING A NEW APPLICATION

If you are creating a new application, you'll first see the Application Definition dialog box, shown in Figure 15.1.

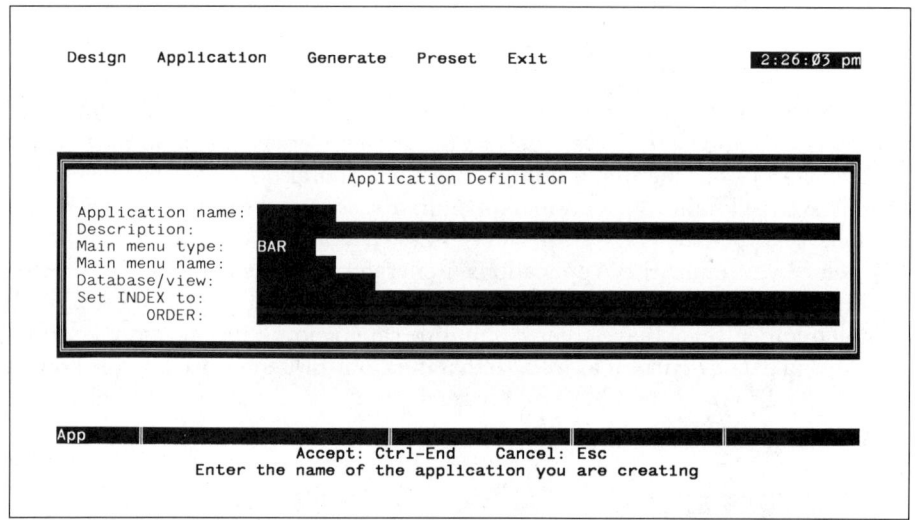

FIGURE 15.1: The Application Definition dialog box appears only when you are creating a new application. After filling in the dialog box, press **Ctrl-End** to access the application design screen.

SEQUENCE OF STEPS

From the Application Definition dialog box:

    type an application name ↵

    type an application description ↵

    press the space bar to select Bar *or* Pop-Up *or* Batch as the main menu type ↵

    type a main menu name ↵

type a database *or* view name (or press Pick (**Shift-F1**)) ↵
type an index name (or leave blank to use the default name) ↵
type the name of the controlling index ↵
Ctrl-End

USAGE

You can freely scroll through the Application Definition dialog box using the usual arrow keys. The purpose of each entry in the dialog box is described in the sections that follow.

Specifying the Application Name   Each application must have a unique name. Enter a valid DOS file name (eight characters maximum, no spaces or punctuation). Use a name that will be easy to remember and that reflects the purpose of the application, such as INVMGR for an inventory manager or PAYROLL for a payroll system. The name you assign here is the one that appears in the Control Center Applications panel after you create the application.

Entering an Application Description   The application description is optional and is provided mainly to help you remember what the application does. The description appears near the bottom of the Control Center screen whenever the application's name is highlighted in the Applications panel. Enter any text up to 76 characters; do not use double quotation marks.

Choosing the Main Menu Type   Press the space bar to scroll through options for the application main menu (the first menu to appear when the user runs the application). Your options are as follows:

OPTION	EFFECT
Bar	Presents a horizontal bar menu as the main menu
Pop-Up	Presents a vertical pop-up menu as the main menu
Batch	Executes a batch process as soon as the user runs the application (not reliable in version 1.0 of dBASE IV and therefore better avoided)

Naming the Main Menu   Assign a valid DOS file name to the main menu for the application (up to eight letters maximum length, no spaces or punctuation).

Later, you must create either a horizontal bar menu or a pop-up menu using the name you enter here. (See "Using the Design Menu" later in this chapter for information about creating menus.)

Selecting the Default Database or View   Enter the name of the database or view that you want to open as soon as the user runs the application. This database is used in all operations that the application later performs, except when you use the Override Assigned Database or View option on the Menu, List, Batch, or Item pull-down menu to override the default selection.

Entering the Default Index File Name   At the Set Index To prompt, enter the name of the index file to use as the default selection for the application. If you leave this option blank, the Applications Generator uses the production index file, which has the same name as the database, but the extension .MDX. (dBASE creates the production index file automatically when you first create a database on the database design screen.)

You can also press Pick (**Shift-F1**) to view a list of single-index files, which have the .NDX extension. Typically, .NDX index files are those created by earlier versions of dBASE, such as dBASE III PLUS.

Specifying the Default Sort Order   At the Order prompt, you can enter the name of the index that will determine the default sort order (as well as the field that can be searched via an index). This must be an existing index that you previously created on the database design screen. Alternatively, you can leave the option blank, in which case database records will be displayed in natural order (that is, the order in which they were entered into the database file).

If you do select an index, you can override this selection for specific application actions later in the application development process, using the Reassign Index Order option on the Item pull-down menu.

This last option completes the Application Definition dialog box. When you have finished specifying options, press **Ctrl-End** to access the application design screen.

EXAMPLE

Figure 15.2 shows a sample application definition. The application name is MEMMGR. The application uses a horizontal bar menu named MEMMAIN as the main menu. A database file named MEMBERS.DBF is specified as the default database. No index file was specified at the Set INDEX To prompt, so

USING THE APPLICATION DESIGN SCREEN

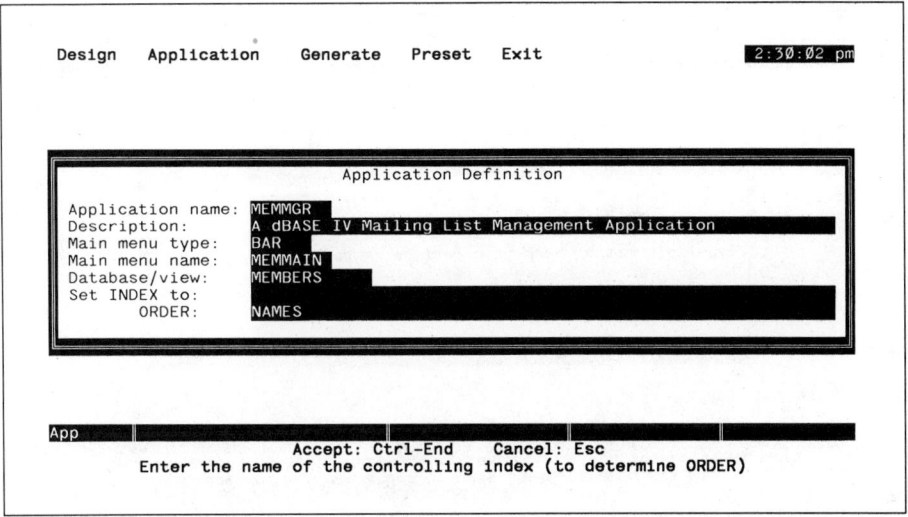

FIGURE 15.2: A sample application definition for a new application. The application is named MEMMGR. It uses a horizontal bar menu named MEMMAIN as the main menu for the application. The default database and index files are MEMBERS.DBF and MEMBERS.MDX, respectively, and the default index for controlling the sort order is NAMES.

dBASE uses the MEMBERS.MDX production index file. The NAMES index in the MEMBERS.MDX index file is specified as the default index for controlling the sort order.

After you've filled in the application definition dialog box, press **Ctrl-End**. You'll be taken to the application design screen.

USING THE APPLICATION DESIGN SCREEN

The application design screen is where you create the objects that make up the application. The application objects include the menus, lists, batch processes, and optional sign-on banner.

The application design screen is shown in Figure 15.3. It has a menu bar, a status bar, a navigation line, and a clock. The main work area in the middle of the screen contains an application object that you can convert into a sign-on banner—that is, a greeting to your user or other information about the application.

Table 15.1 summarizes all the navigation and function keys used in the application design screen. In the table, note that the term *object* refers to the current object (its border will be highlighted). The term *editing frame* refers to a text frame, such as the type of frame used to create custom help screens for the application.

522 — CH. 15 CREATING APPLICATION OBJECTS

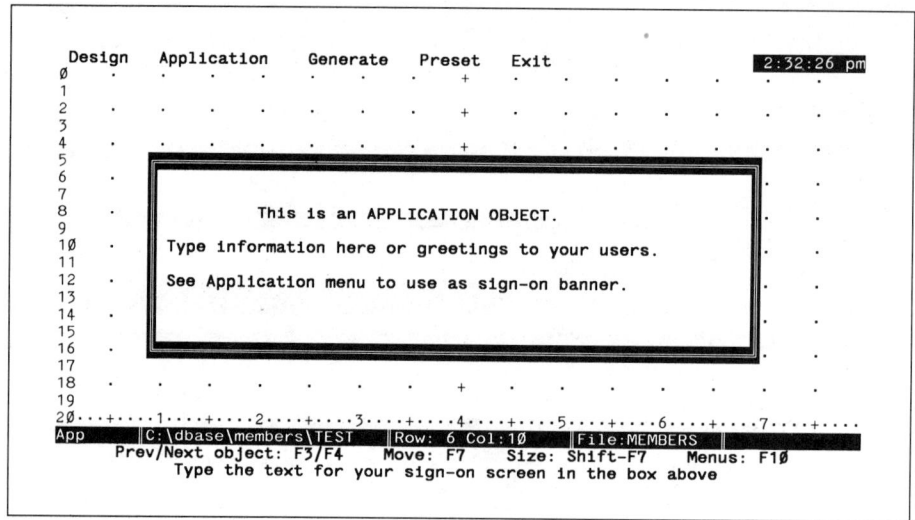

FIGURE 15.3: The application design screen. This is where you create the various application objects, such as menus, lists, and batch processes, and assign actions to menu items.

→	Moves the cursor one character to the right in any object, editing frame, or dialog box.
←	Moves the cursor one character to the left in any object, editing frame, or dialog box.
↑	Moves the cursor one line up in any editing frame or dialog box. Moves the highlight up one line in a pop-up menu.
PgDn	Moves to the next item in a menu or batch process when you are assigning actions with the Item pull-down menu.
End	Moves to the end of the line in an editing frame or to the last option in a dialog box.
Home	Moves to the start of the line in an editing frame or to the first option in a dialog box.
Del	Deletes the character over the cursor.
Backspace	Erases the character to the left.
Ins	Turns insert mode on and off.
Tab	In an editing frame, moves the cursor to the next tab stop. In a dialog box, moves the cursor to the next option.

Table 15.1: Keys Used in the Applications Design Screen

Key	Description
Shift-Tab	In an editing frame, moves the cursor to the previous tab stop. In a dialog box, moves the cursor to the previous option.
←	Selects the currently highlighted option from a menu. In a dialog box, editing frame, or object, completes the entry and moves to the next line or option.
Esc	In an editing frame or dialog box, cancels all current changes and returns you to the design screen. Pressing **Esc** while you are using the Applications Generator menus cancels the current selection. Pressing **Esc** while you are creating an object cancels all unsaved changes. If you are not currently using a menu option or dialog box, pressing **Esc** allows you to leave the application design screen without saving changes.
Ctrl-End	In a dialog box or editing frame, saves all changes and returns you to the design screen. From a menu, saves all changes and returns you to the design screen. From the sign-on banner, saves all current changes and returns you to the Control Center.
F1	Accesses the dBASE IV help system.
F3	Moves the cursor to the previous object on the application design screen and makes that object current.
F4	Moves the cursor to the next object on the application design screen and makes that object current.
F5	Marks the beginning of a new item being added to a horizontal bar menu. Finish entering the item by pressing **F5** again or by pressing ←.
F7	If an object frame is highlighted, lets you move that object to a new location on the design screen. If an item within a frame is highlighted, lets you choose between moving the entire object or just the currently highlighted item.
Shift-F7	Lets you change the size of the currently highlighted object.
F8	Lets you copy an item to another location in the current object or to a different object of the same type.
F9	Removes (or restores) the application design screen menu and message lines.
Shift-F1	Allows you to select options from a list when you are creating an object that supports such selections.

Table 15.1: Keys Used in the Applications Design Screen (continued)

As in all dBASE IV design screens, the navigation line near the bottom of the screen always summarizes the special editing keys currently available.

Using the Applications Generator Menus

The application design screen, like other dBASE screens, has a menu bar at the top, pull-down menus, and submenus. You select menu options using the same techniques as in other dBASE screens.

USAGE

The Applications Generator main menu is somewhat different from other dBASE IV menus, partly because it changes with the type of object with which you are working. For example, when you are working with the sign-on banner, the main menu presents the options Design, Application, Generate, Preset, and Exit. When you are developing a menu for your application, the Applications Generator main menu displays the options Menu (to change the menu) and Item (to assign actions to menu items), and the Application option is removed.

If several application objects are on the screen at the same time, you can scroll through these options using the **F3** key (to move to the previous object) or **F4** key (to move to the next object). The border surrounding the current object is always highlighted, and the main menu is adjusted to match the current application object.

A second difference between standard dBASE IV menus and Applications Generator menus relates to the identical options on many menus. For example, the Preset, Application, Menu, and Item pull-down menus on the Applications Generator main menu each let you define display options (such as colors). At first, these options may appear to be redundant. However, each actually has a unique effect because it defines a setting for a particular *level* within the application. The four levels of an application are Preset, Application, Menu (or List or Batch), and Item. The levels are summarized in Table 15.2.

MODIFYING THE APPLICATION DEFAULT SETTINGS

You can modify the default settings assigned to an application, including those you assigned in the Application Definition dialog box when you first created the application and those defined on the Preset pull-down menu. To modify default settings, you use options on the Application pull-down menu on the application design screen.

Options on the Application pull-down menu affect the default settings for the entire application, except for settings that are redefined by options on the lower-level Menu, Batch, List, and Item pull-down menus.

Preset	Assigns default settings for all future applications
Application	Assigns settings only to the current application, overriding any settings defined on the Preset pull-down menu
Menu, List, or Batch	Assigns settings only to the current menu, files list, structure list, values list, or batch process, overriding settings defined on the Preset and Application menus
Item	Assigns settings only to the current menu item or batch process operation, overriding settings defined on the Preset, Application, Menu, List, and Batch menus

Table 15.2: Levels for Assigning Application Settings

The Application pull-down menu is available on the application design screen only when the sign-on banner is the current object. (If some other object is current, press **F3** or **F4** until the sign-on banner border is highlighted. You will see the Application option in the application design screen main menu.) Press **F10** and move the highlight to the Application option to view the Application pull-down menu. Options on this menu affect the entire application, as discussed in the sections that follow.

Changing the Application Name and Description

The Name and Describe option on the Application pull-down menu lets you view and optionally change the application name and description.

SEQUENCE OF STEPS

From the application design screen:

> press **F3** or **F4** until the sign-on banner is the current object
> **F10**
> Application/Name and Describe

USAGE

You can view and change the name and description that you assigned to an application when you first filled in the Application Definition dialog box. You do this by

526 — CH. 15 CREATING APPLICATION OBJECTS

selecting Name and Describe from the Application pull-down menu. A dialog box containing the application name and description will appear on the screen.

You can change either the name or description. If you change the application name, be sure to use a valid DOS file name if changing the application name. Press **Ctrl-End** to save any changes or **Esc** to abandon them.

EXAMPLE

Figure 15.4 shows the Name and Describe dialog box for a sample application.

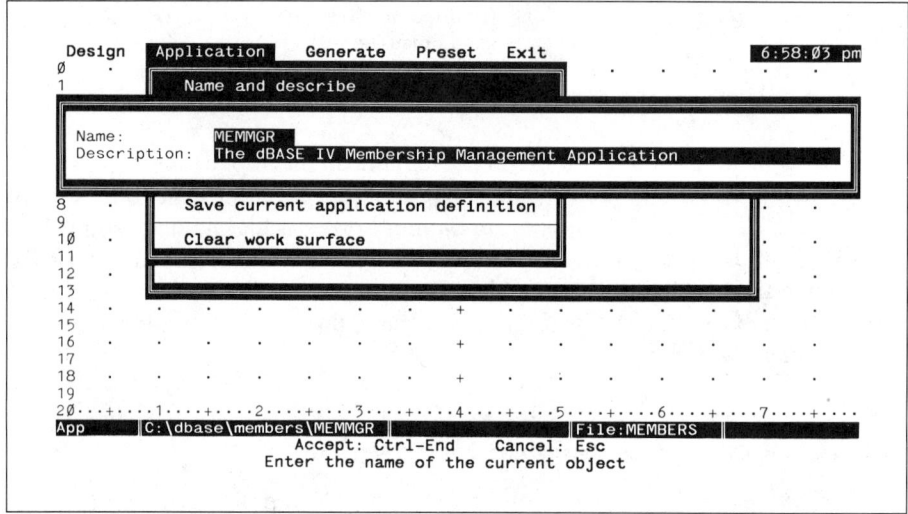

FIGURE 15.4: The Name and Describe dialog box for a sample application. The name is a valid DOS file name (eight letters maximum length, no spaces or punctuation).

Changing the Main Menu Type and Name

The Assign Main Menu option on the Application pull-down menu displays, and optionally lets you change, the type and name of the application's main menu.

SEQUENCE OF STEPS

From the application design screen:

    press **F3** or **F4** until the sign-on banner is the current object
    F10
    Application/Assign Main Menu

USAGE

To view or change the application main menu type or name, first make sure that the sign-on banner is the current object by pressing **F3** or **F4** until the Application option appears in the application design screen main menu. Then press **F10** and move the highlight bar to the Application option. Select Assign Main Menu.

A dialog box will appear showing the currently defined main menu type and name. Press the space bar to scroll through valid main menu types and ↵ to select the current type. When the cursor is in the Main Menu Name box, you can press Pick (**Shift-F1**) to view a list of existing menus.

You can change the menu name or type, but remember that you must use a valid file name for the main menu name. Also, before generating the application code, you must create a menu of the appropriate type with the name you've assigned. Press **Ctrl-End** to save any changes or **Esc** to abandon them.

EXAMPLE

Figure 15.5 shows a dialog box for a sample application. This application uses a bar menu named MEMMAIN as the main menu type. The developer of this application must be sure to create a horizontal bar menu named MEMMAIN before generating the application code.

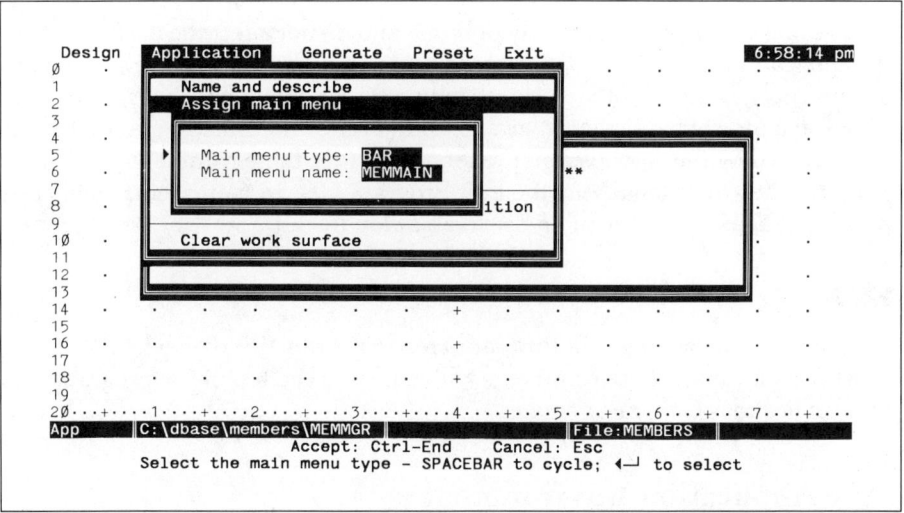

FIGURE 15.5: The Assign Main Menu dialog box for a sample application. Once the main menu type and name are defined in this dialog box, it is up to the application developer to design the menu, using options on the Design pull-down menu.

Changing the Program Header

The Edit Program Header Comments option lets you modify the heading in the generated application program. This option receives its initial setting from the Preset pull-down menu on the application design screen. Changing this setting on the Application pull-down menu affects only the current application. See Chapter 17 for information about the Preset menu.

If you plan to distribute your completed application to others and want to retain the copyright, you should fill in the dialog box with your name, a copyright notice, and the version of dBASE used to generate the application.

Note that these program comments appear only in the code generated by the Applications Generator. The user will not see these comments on the screen.

SEQUENCE OF STEPS

From the application design screen:

> press **F3** or **F4** until the sign-on banner is the current object
> **F10**
> Application/Edit Program Header Comments

USAGE

Heading comments are entirely optional and do not affect the performance of the application in any way. Comments are placed at the top of the generated program simply to inform others who the author is and who has the right to make and distribute copies of the program. Only users who directly manipulate the code created by the Applications Generator will see these comments.

After filling in or modifying the Edit Program Header Comments dialog box, press **Ctrl-End** to save them or **Esc** to abandon them.

EXAMPLE

Figure 15.6 shows the Edit Program Header Comments dialog box filled with some sample data. These comments will appear at the top of the programs that the Applications Generator creates.

Modifying the Application Environment

The Modify Application Environment option on the Application pull-down menu lets you alter some basic assumptions about the application environment. The default settings displayed by the Modify Application Environment option

MODIFYING THE APPLICATION ENVIRONMENT — 529

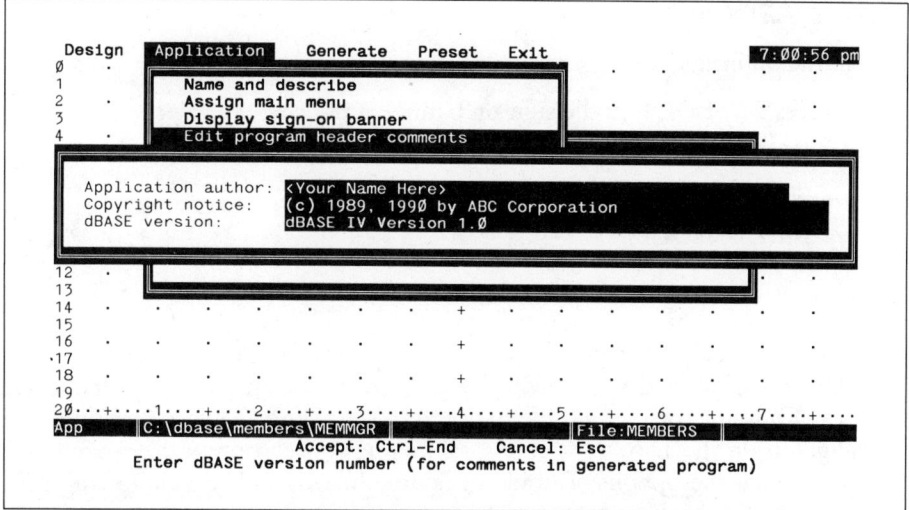

FIGURE 15.6: A sample Edit Program Header Comments dialog box including a copyright notice and dBASE version number. Only users who directly access the application's source code will see these comments.

were initially defined on the Preset pull-down menu (discussed in Chapter 17). Changing these default settings on the Application pull-down menu affects only the current application.

When you select Modify Application Environment from the Application pull-down menu, the following submenu appears:

Display Options
Environment Settings
Search Path
View/Database and Index

Any options that you select from this submenu affect the entire application, unless you specifically override them in a particular menu or menu item. The following sections describe each option.

CHANGING DISPLAY OPTIONS

When you select Display Options, you'll see a submenu that lets you change the border style and colors of the sign-on banner.

SEQUENCE OF STEPS

From the application design screen:

> press **F3** or **F4** until the sign-on banner is the current object
> **F10**
> Application/Modify Application Environment
> Display Options

USAGE

To modify the border style or colors used by the application as a whole, select Modify Application Environment from the Application pull-down menu and Display Options from the submenu that appears. When Object Border Style is highlighted on the Display Options submenu, you can press the space bar to scroll through the options: Double (a double-line frame), Single (a single-line frame), Panel (a wide frame), and None (no frame).

The remaining options on the Display Options let you color the screen. The techniques you use to select colors are identical to those used to select screen colors in the dBASE IV Control Center (see Chapter 14).

After selecting a border style and color scheme, press **Ctrl-End** to return to the Modify Application Environment pull-down menu.

EXAMPLE

Figure 15.7 shows the application design screen with the Display Options pull-down menu and the dBASE IV electronic palette for selecting screen colors displayed. Because the electronic palette was accessed from the Application pull-down menu, the color combinations selected at this stage will affect the entire application. (However, you can override the color scheme defined at this level for any individual menu.)

CHANGING ENVIRONMENT SETTINGS

The Environment Settings option displays a submenu of dBASE IV settings that affect the entire application.

SEQUENCE OF STEPS

From the application design screen:

> press **F3** or **F4** until the sign-on banner is the current object
> **F10**

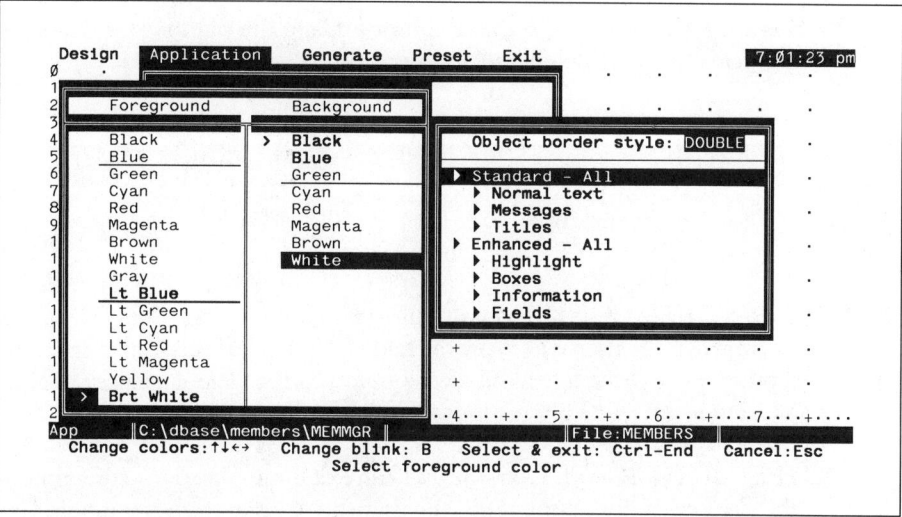

FIGURE 15.7: The dBASE IV electronic palette for determining screen colors is displayed after you select Modify Application Environment, Display Options, and a screen area to color from the Application pull-down menu. Color schemes selected at this point become the default colors for the entire application.

Application/Modify Application Environment
Environment Settings

USAGE

To alter some of the default environment settings for the application, select Modify Application Environment from the Application pull-down menu and Environment Settings from the submenu that appears. You'll see a dialog box of options with the settings summarized in the following paragraphs.

Set BELL If Set BELL is on, the computer's bell rings when dBASE IV detects an error while the user is using the completed application. If this option is off, the bell does not sound. If this option is on, you can determine the frequency and duration of the bell. The frequency can be from 18 to 10,001 cycles per second, and the duration can be from 2 to 20 ticks (where a single tick is approximately 0.055 seconds). If you do not specify the frequency or duration, dBASE uses the default frequency of 512 cycles per second and the default duration of 2 ticks.

Set CARRY If Set CARRY is off, data from one record is not automatically carried to the next record when the user adds new data to a database. If Set

CARRY is off, each new record that the user adds to the database is initialized with all the fields blank. The default setting is Off.

Set CENTURY If Set CENTURY is off, dates are shown in MM/DD/YY format (for example, 12/31/90). If this option is on, dates are displayed in MM/DD/CCYY format (for example, 12/31/1990). The default setting is Off.

Set CONFIRM If Set CONFIRM is off, the cursor automatically leaves a field on a custom form when the user types past the end of the field. If this option is on, the user must press ⏎ to leave a field on a custom form. The default setting is Off.

Set ESCAPE If Set ESCAPE is on, the user can exit the application at any time by pressing the **Esc** key. If this option is off, the user can exit the application only via a menu item that provides an exit option. The default setting is On. (You should leave this option at its default setting until you've perfected the application, in case you, the developer, need to interrupt processing to escape the application.)

Set SAFETY Set SAFETY determines whether or not the application warns the user when an action will overwrite an existing file. If this option is on (the default setting), dBASE displays a warning and an option to cancel the operation. If this option is off, the action will overwrite the existing file without warning.

Set DELIMITERS If Set DELIMITERS is on, fields in custom forms are surrounded by delimiters. If this option is off (the default setting), dBASE displays fields in custom forms without delimiters. If you set this option to On, you can determine the characters used as delimiters. For example, if you specify [ ] as the delimiters, all fields on all custom forms that the application uses are enclosed in square brackets.

After you finish selecting environment settings for the application, press **Ctrl-End** to save them or **Esc** to abandon them.

EXAMPLE

Figure 15.8 shows the environment settings dialog box for a sample application. Most of the default settings have been used in this example, except that the frequency of the bell has been changed to a pitch of 1000, and the duration has been set to 1 (which produces a higher, briefer bell than the default settings of 512 and 2).

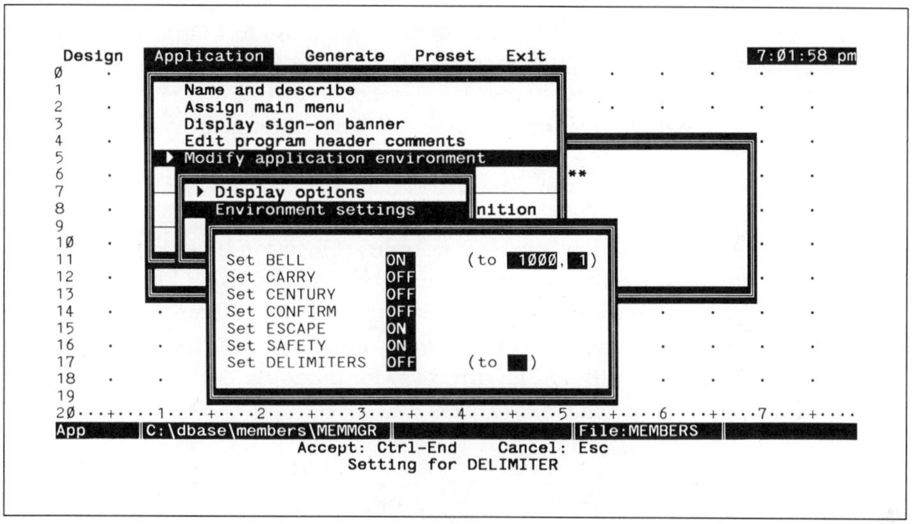

MODIFYING THE APPLICATION ENVIRONMENT — 533

```
     Design  Application   Generate   Preset   Exit              7:01:58 pm
   0
   1          Name and describe
   2          Assign main menu
   3          Display sign-on banner
   4          Edit program header comments
   5        ▶ Modify application environment
   6                                                  **
   7           ▶ Display options
   8             Environment settings         nition
   9
  10
  11           Set BELL          ON      (to  1000, 1)
  12           Set CARRY         OFF
  13           Set CENTURY       OFF
  14           Set CONFIRM       OFF
  15           Set ESCAPE        ON
  16           Set SAFETY        ON
  17           Set DELIMITERS    OFF     (to  ▮)
  18
  19
  20···+····1····+····2····+····3····+····4····+····5····+····6····+····7····+····
  App     C:\dbase\members\MEMMGR                   File:MEMBERS
                    Accept: Ctrl-End      Cancel: Esc
                           Setting for DELIMITER
```

FIGURE 15.8: An Environment Settings dialog box for a sample application. This dialog box selects default settings except for the bell frequency and duration specifications, which have been changed to 1000 and 1, respectively.

SETTING A SEARCH PATH

The Search Path option lets you determine a disk drive and directory in which the completed application searches for database files, report formats, and other database objects. The Drive option determines the disk drive name (for example, B or C), and the search path specifies the path to the files.

SEQUENCE OF STEPS

From the application design screen:

> press **F3** or **F4** until the sign-on banner is the current object
> **F10**
> Application/Modify Application Environment

USAGE

The easiest way to determine the drive and directory that run an application is to create a directory and then always make that directory current when you create the database and application objects and when you modify or run the application.

Alternatively, you can store the generated code for the application in one directory and the database objects (such as database files, reports, and custom forms) in a different directory. If you use this second technique, you must change the default search path to include the directory that contains the database objects.

EXAMPLE

Figure 15.9 shows a dialog box for a sample application in which the database objects are stored in a subdirectory named \DBASE\OBJECTS on drive C. Presumably, the application programs are stored in a different directory. The user must run the application from its own directory, but the application will search the C:\DBASE\OBJECTS directory for database, index, report format, custom form, and other database objects.

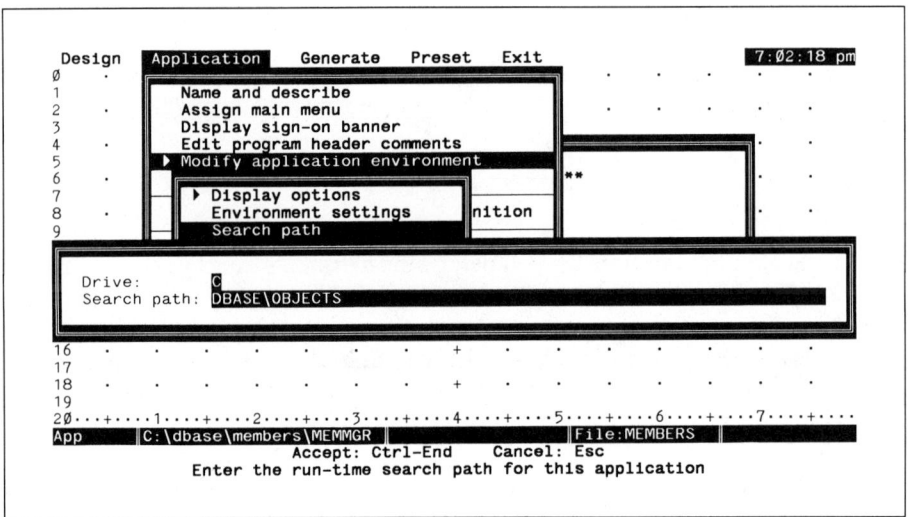

FIGURE 15.9: A search path defined for a sample application. In this example, the application searches the C:\DBASE\OBJECTS directory for the application's database objects, such as databases, index files, report and label formats, and custom forms.

CHANGING THE DEFAULT DATABASE, INDEX, AND SORT ORDER

The View/Database and Index option lets you view and optionally change the default database, index file, and sort order for the application.

SEQUENCE OF STEPS

From the application design screen:

> press **F3** or **F4** until the sign-on banner is the current object
> **F10**
> Application/Modify Application Environment
> View/Database and Index

USAGE

When you select View/Database and Index, the screen displays the current names for the default database, index file, and sort order (as you specified in the Application Definition dialog box when you first entered the Applications Generator). The only reason you would want to change these values from the Application pull-down menu would be if you made a mistake when you first entered them into the Application Definition dialog.

If you select the Database/View option (by highlighting and pressing ←┘), you can also press Pick (**Shift-F1**) to view a list of database file names in the current directory. To select one of those databases, highlight its name and press ←┘.

After filling in the dialog box, press **Ctrl-End** to save your changes or **Esc** to abandon them.

EXAMPLE

Figure 15.10 displays the View/Database and Index dialog box for a sample application. In this example, the default database is named MEMBERS.DBF, and the default index is the production index file, MEMBERS.MDX. The default sort order is an index named NAMES within the production index file.

Creating a Sign-On Banner

The sign-on banner is always displayed in the center of the application design screen. You can modify the text in the sign-on banner and use it to display any information to the user when he or she first runs the application.

SEQUENCE OF STEPS

From the application design screen:

> press **F3** or **F4** until the sign-on banner is the current object
> modify the text in the sign-on banner

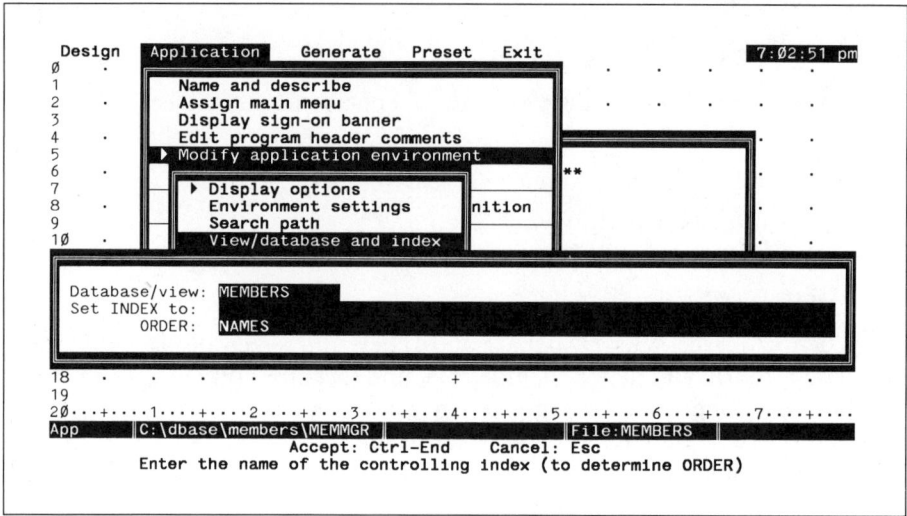

FIGURE 15.10: The View/Database and Index dialog box for a sample application. Because the Set INDEX To option is left blank, dBASE uses the production index file, MEMBERS.MDX. The NAMES index in the production index file is selected as the default controlling index.

F10

Application/Display Sign-On Banner

Yes *or* No

↵

USAGE

The sign-on banner that always appears in the middle of the application design screen initially receives its text from options determined on the Preset pull-down menu (discussed in Chapter 17). You can change any of the text displayed in the sign-on banner whenever the cursor is within the sign-on banner border. However, *do not* include any double quotation marks ('').

To delete a line from the sign-on banner, use the **Ctrl-Y** key. To insert a new blank line into the sign-on banner, position the cursor where you want the new line to appear and press **Ctrl-N**.

You can also resize and move the frame that contains the sign-on banner. To change the size of the frame, press the Size (**Shift-F7**) key. The border will blink. Use the arrow keys to expand or reduce the frame; then press ↵. To move the sign-on banner, press Move (**F7**), use the arrow keys to move the frame, and press ↵ when you are done.

CREATING A SIGN-ON BANNER — 537

By default, the sign-on banner is not displayed when the user runs the application. To have the application display the sign-on banner to the user, select Display Sign-on Banner from the Application pull-down menu. When you select this option, you'll see a dialog box with the options Yes and No. If you select Yes, the sign-on banner will appear as soon as the user runs the application, with the instruction *Press ⏎ to continue* centered at the bottom of the screen. After the user presses ⏎, the application main menu appears on the screen.

If you select No, the user does not see the sign-on banner. Instead, when the user runs the application, he or she is taken directly to the application main menu.

EXAMPLE

Figure 15.11 shows a sample sign-on banner for an application.

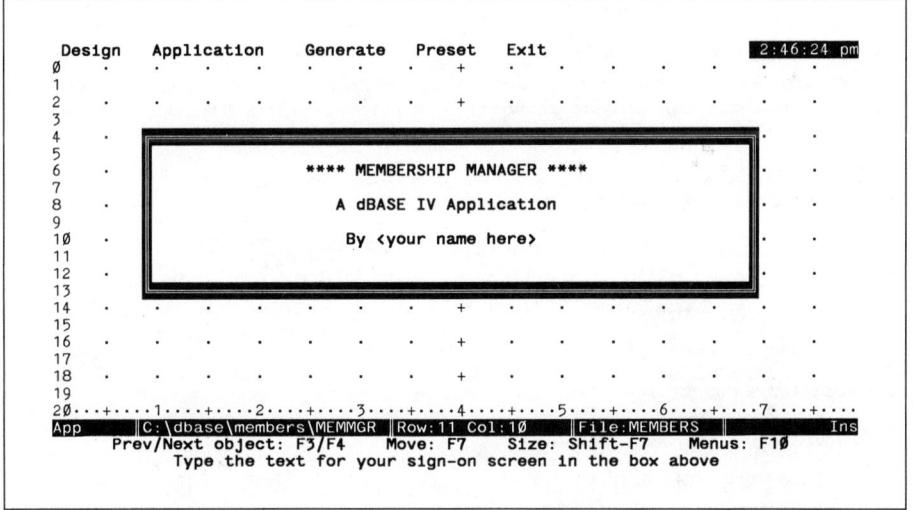

FIGURE 15.11: A sample sign-On banner for an application. If you set the Display Sign-On Banner option on the Application pull-down menu to Yes, the sign-on banner will be the first object that the user sees upon running the application.

Figure 15.12 shows a sign-on banner from the user's perspective. This is the first screen that the user sees upon running the application. If the application developer had not set the Display Sign-On Banner option to Yes, the user would not have seen this screen. Instead, the user would be taken directly to the application's main menu.

538 — **CH. 15** CREATING APPLICATION OBJECTS

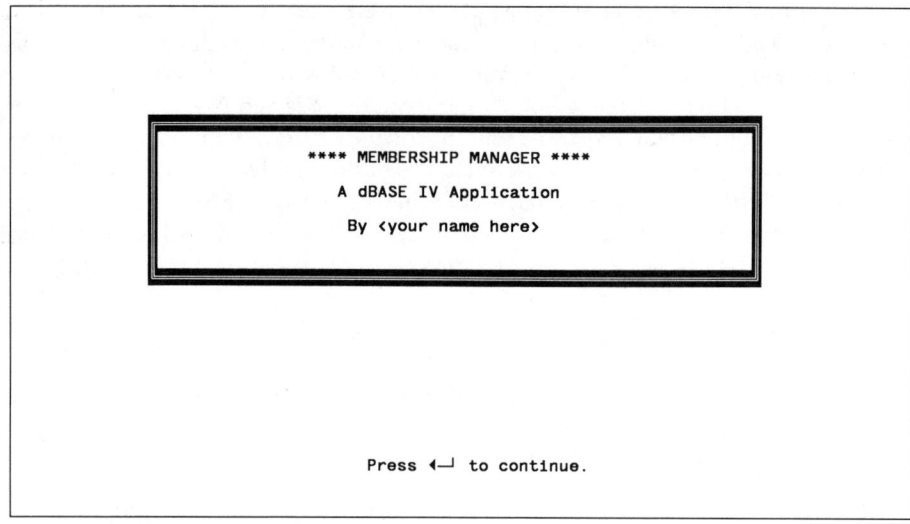

FIGURE 15.12: An application sign-on banner from the user's perspective. If the application developer had not set the Display Sign-On Banner option to Yes, the user would not see this sign-on banner.

Saving the Application Definition

If you change any default settings for the current application, you can select Save Current Application Definition from the Application pull-down menu to save those new settings.

SEQUENCE OF STEPS

From the application design screen:

    press **F3** or **F4** until the sign-on banner is the current object
    F10
    Application/Save Current Application Definition

USAGE

After you have changed any of the default settings or the sign-on banner for the current application using options on the Application pull-down menu, save the new settings by selecting Save Current Application Definition from the Application pull-down menu. The Applications Generator will save the new settings to disk.

If you want to regenerate an existing application with new settings, you first need to save all objects on the design screen by selecting Clear Work Surface from the Application pull-down menu. Then activate the MENU.GEN template by selecting the Select Template option from the Generate pull-down menu. Select Begin Generating from that same menu (as discussed in Chapter 17). When the Applications Generator is finished generating the code, you can select Save Changes and Exit from the Exit pull-down menu to return to the Control Center.

DEVELOPING A QUICK APPLICATION

The Generate Quick Application option on the Application pull-down menu creates a simple application that uses a single database file, sort order, custom screen, report format, and mailing label format. This option presents a menu that allows the user to edit, browse, append, and pack a database file. If you specify an index file, the option also allows the user to reindex the database. If you specify a report or label format, the menu includes options to print either or both of these items.

SEQUENCE OF STEPS

From the application design screen:

> press **F3** or **F4** until the sign-on banner is the current object
> **F10**
> Application/Generate Quick Application

USAGE

Select Generate Quick Application from the Application pull-down menu. Fill in the quick application form using the names of a single database file, report format, label format, and index order (these must have already been created using the appropriate Control Center panels). Rather than typing file names, you can press Pick (**Shift-F1**) to select them from a submenu. (This is the preferred method, as it avoids the possibility of misspelling a file name.)

You can also fill in an author name and menu heading for the application. Press **Ctrl-End** after filling in the quick application form. Select Yes from the dialog box that appears. After the Applications Generator writes the program for the application, you'll see the prompt *Generation is complete. Press any key....* Press any key to proceed.

540 — CH. 15 CREATING APPLICATION OBJECTS

To leave the Applications Generator and return to the Control Center, select Save All Changes and Exit from the Exit pull-down menu. When you return to the Control Center, you'll see the name of the new application in the Applications panel.

You can run the quick application using the usual techniques (described in Chapter 17). In brief, highlight the application's name in the Application panel of the Control Center and press ←┘. Select Run Application and Yes from the options that follow. After a few seconds, the application main menu appears on the screen.

The quick application technique does not create a menu bar with pull-down menus. Instead, it presents a smaller sign-on banner at the top of the screen and a single pop-up menu centered on the screen. The pop-up menu is identical to a pull-down menu, except that it is not directly attached to a menu-bar option.

EXAMPLE

Figure 15.13 shows a Generate Quick Application dialog box that develops a quick application named MEMQUICK using the following files from the current directory:

    MEMBERS.DBF   (Database file)
    MEMFORM.FMT   (Custom screen)

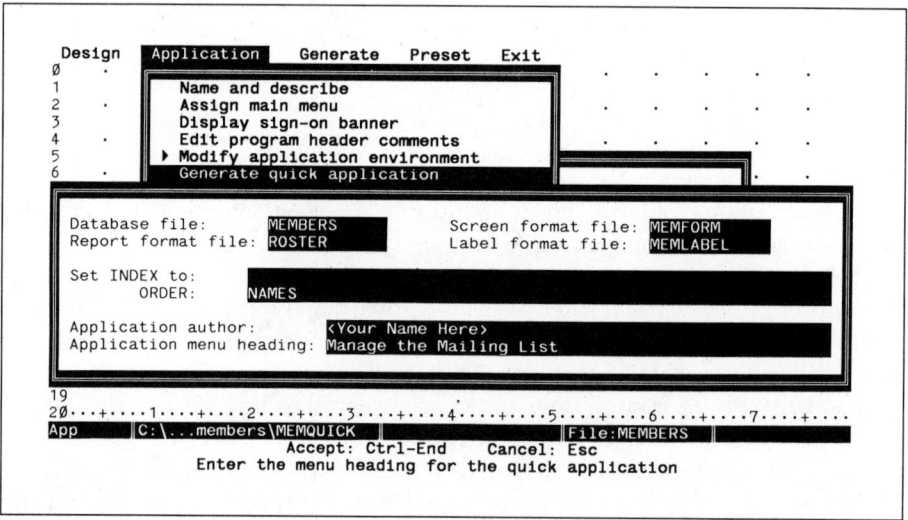

FIGURE 15.13: A sample Generate Quick Application dialog box. After completing the dialog box, press **Ctrl-End** and select Yes from the options that appear. The Applications Generator will begin generating the application code immediately.

ROSTER.FRM   (Report format)
MEMLABEL.LBL   (Label format)
MEMBERS.MDX   (Production index file)
NAMES   (Index of last and first names)

After filling in the dialog box, press **Ctrl-End** and select Yes from the options that appear. The message at the bottom of the screen will inform you when generation is complete, and you will be prompted to press any key.

To use the generated application, select Save All Changes and Exit from the Exit pull-down menu. Then highlight the application's name in the Applications panel in the Control Center and press ←┘. Select Run Application and Yes. You will see a screen like the one in Figure 15.14, which uses the format the Applications Generator uses for all quick applications.

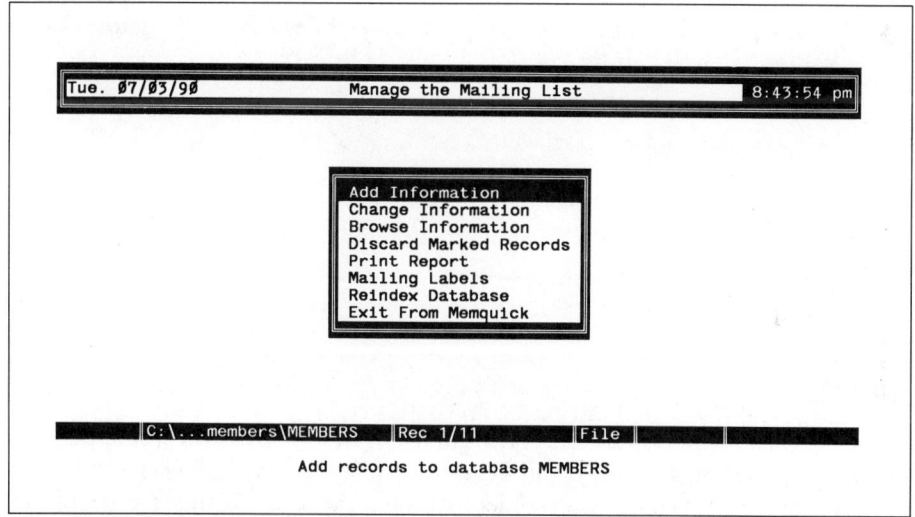

FIGURE 15.14: A sample quick application from the user's perspective. Quick applications use a pop-up menu as the main menu. The user can select options from the menu as usual, by highlighting and pressing ←┘.

For more information about running applications, see Chapter 17.

USING THE DESIGN MENU

The Design option is always available on the application design screen main menu. When you pull down the Design menu, the following options for creating and modifying application objects appear:

    Horizontal Bar Menu
    Pop-Up Menu
    Files List
    Structure List
    Values List
    Batch Process

SEQUENCE OF STEPS

From the application design screen main menu:

    F10

    Design

    Horizontal Bar Menu *or* Pop-up Menu *or* Files List *or* Structure List *or* Values List *or* Batch Process

    highlight <create> *or* an object name ↵

To create a new object:

    type a file name ↵

    type a description ↵

    type a message-line prompt ↵

    Ctrl-End

USAGE

Select the type of object that you want to create. A submenu will appear displaying the option <create> and the names of any existing objects of that type. Select <create> to create a new object (or select the name of an existing object to modify it).

If you are creating a new object, a dialog box will appear asking for a name, description, and message-line prompt (batch processes do not request a message-line prompt). Enter a valid DOS file name, without an extension, after the *Name* prompt.

You can enter any text after the *Description* prompt (but no quotation marks), or you can leave the option blank. The text you enter after the *Message Line* prompt will appear centered at the bottom of the screen when the user runs the application. Note, however, that any message-line prompts that you specify at the Item level override any message-line prompts you specify here.

After filling in the dialog box, press **Ctrl-End.** What happens next depends on the type of object you are creating, as discussed in the sections that follow.

You can also use the Design pull-down menu to modify any existing object that you previously saved and hid using the Put Away Current <object> selection. To do so, select the type of object that you wish to modify from the Design pull-down menu and the name of the object from the list that appears. The object will be displayed on the application design screen with its border highlighted.

CREATING A HORIZONTAL BAR MENU

If you are creating a new horizontal bar menu, an empty menu bar appears at the top of the screen with the cursor inside it.

SEQUENCE OF STEPS

From the application design screen:

F10
Design/Horizontal Bar Menu
select <create> *or* an object name ↵

USAGE

If you specified BAR as the main menu type on the initial application definition screen, you must create a horizontal bar menu on the application design screen. You also must assign the name you specified as the main menu name on the application definition screen to at least one horizontal bar menu.

If you forget the main menu name, press **F10** and select Assign Main Menu from the Application pull-down menu before you begin to design the main menu. If you wish, you can change the main menu name at this point as well.

To create a horizontal bar menu, press **F10** and select Horizontal Bar Menu from the Design pull-down menu. Select <create>. Then type the menu name and, optionally, a description and message-line prompt. Press **Ctrl-End**.

The screen will display an empty horizontal bar menu. To enter menu items (options), press **F5,** type the option, and then press **F5** again. Use the space bar or → key to enter some space, press **F5,** type the next option, and then press **F5** again. Repeat this process for as many options as you wish to place in the menu.

You can move an option by highlighting it and pressing Move (**F7**). Select Item Only from the dialog box, use the arrow keys to move the item, and then press ↵.

To insert a new item, position the cursor at a blank space where you want the new item to appear. Make sure insert mode is on. Then press **F5,** type the new item, and press **F5** again. To insert blank spaces, position the cursor where you want the spaces to appear, make sure insert mode is on, and press the space bar.

To delete a menu option, move the cursor to the first character in the option name and press the **Del** key repeatedly or press **Ctrl-T.**

To change the size of the horizontal bar menu, press Size (**Shift-F7**) and use the arrow keys to resize the menu. Press ← when you are done. To move the bar menu, press Move (**F7**), reposition the menu with the arrow keys, and press ←.

To view the horizontal bar menu without the application design screen menu and messages in the background, press Zoom (**F9**). Then press Zoom (**F9**) again to bring back the application design screen main menu and message lines.

The horizontal bar menu inherits the default settings, such as screen colors and the default database, defined on the Application pull-down menu. If you want to change any of these default settings so that they affect the horizontal bar menu only, first make sure that the bar menu is the current object by pressing the **F3** or **F4** key until the menu border is highlighted. Press **F10** and pull down the Menu menu. Then refer to the section "Using the Menu, List, and Batch Pull-Down Menus" later in this chapter.

When you've finished designing the horizontal bar menu, press **F10** and move the highlight to the Menu option on the main menu. Then select Save Current Menu to save the menu or Put Away Current Menu to save the menu and remove it from the design screen.

EXAMPLE

Figure 15.15 shows an example horizontal bar menu on the application design screen. This menu offers the options Maintain, Update, Print, Utilities, and Exit. The menu uses the default size and position suggested by the Applications Generator.

CREATING A POP-UP OR PULL-DOWN MENU

The Pop-up Menu option on the Design menu is used to create both pop-up and pull-down menus.

SEQUENCE OF STEPS

From the application design screen:

    F10
    Design/Pop-Up Menu
    ←

CREATING A POP-UP OR PULL-DOWN MENU — 545

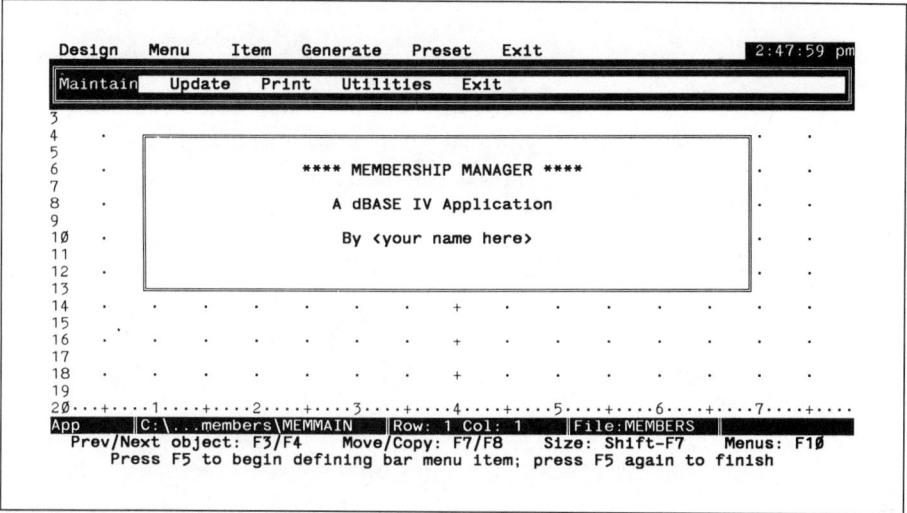

FIGURE 15.15: A sample horizontal bar menu on the application design screen. This menu uses the default position and size initially suggested by the Applications Generator.

To create a new menu: highlight <create>

To modify an existing menu: highlight the menu name

←┘

USAGE

An application can contain any number of pop-up menus. If you specified POP-UP as the main menu type in the initial Application Definition dialog box, you must create a pop-up menu with the name specified in the main menu name box in the Application Definition dialog box.

To create a new pop-up menu, press **F10** and select Pop-up Menu from the Design pull-down menu. Type a DOS file name for the menu and, optionally, a description. You can also type a message-line prompt, which appears at the bottom of the screen when the the menu is displayed. Note that any message-line prompts that you assign to individual items in the menu override the message-line prompt you specify here. After filling in the dialog box, press **Ctrl-End**.

An empty pop-up menu will appear in the center of the screen, as in Figure 15.16. You can use the Size (**Shift-F7**) key to enlarge the menu's frame at any time. You can use the Move (**F7**) key to move the menu at any time.

546 — CH. 15 CREATING APPLICATION OBJECTS

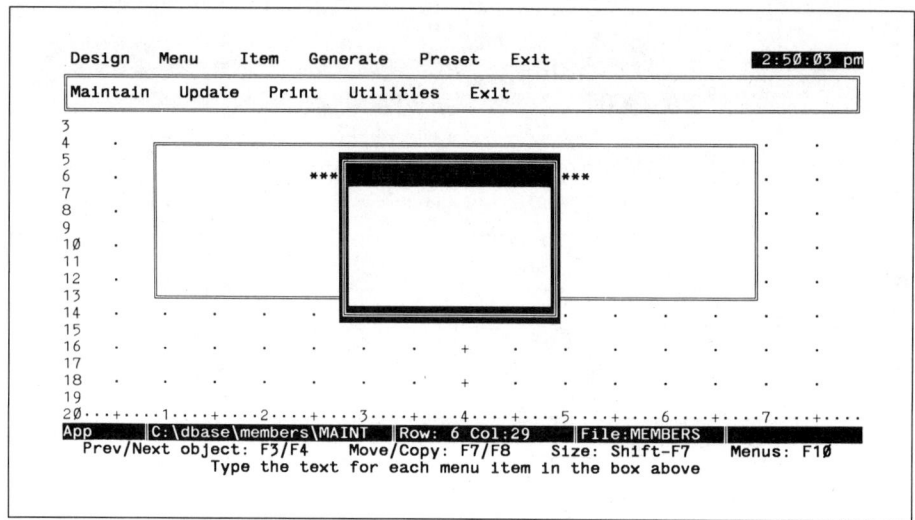

FIGURE 15.16: An empty pop-up menu on the application design screen. You can type options into the empty menu, resize the menu (using **Shift-F7**), and move the menu (using **F7**).

To add items to the menu, just type the item and press the ← key. Be sure to place each menu item on a separate line. If an item is too long to fit within the frame, press **Shift-F7**, use the → key to widen the frame, and then press ←. After filling in all the menu items, you can once again use the Size key (**Shift-F7**) to tighten the frame around the menu items if you wish.

If you need to change an item in the menu, move the highlight to that item and retype the text. To insert a new option, enlarge the frame, if necessary, to make room for the option. Move the highlight to where you want the new option to appear and press **Ctrl-N**. Then type the new option. To delete an option, highlight it and press **Ctrl-Y**.

After creating and positioning your pop-up menu, press **F10** and select either Save Current Menu or Put Away Current Menu (to remove the menu from the design screen) from the Menu pull-down menu.

The pop-up menu inherits default settings, such as screen colors and the default database, defined on the Application pull-down menu. If you want to change any of these default settings so that they affect the current menu only, or if you want to convert the pop-up menus to pull-down menus, refer to the section "Using the Menu, List, and Batch Pull-Down Menus" later in this chapter.

EXAMPLE

Figure 15.17 shows a sample pop-up menu aligned below the Maintain option on a horizontal bar menu. In this example, the pop-up menu contains the options Add

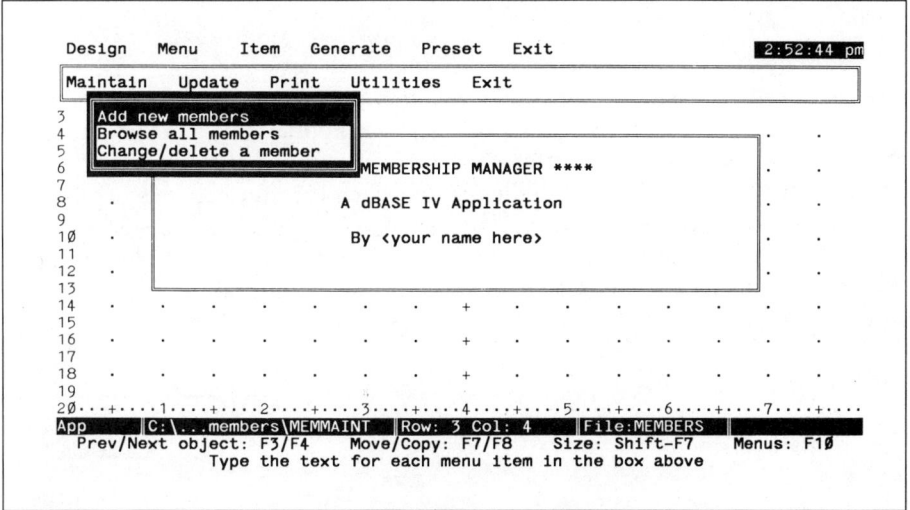

FIGURE 15.17: A pop-up menu aligned below the Maintain option on a horizontal bar menu. To convert the pop-up menu to a pull-down menu, press **F3** or **F4** until the horizontal bar menu is the current (highlighted) object. Then press **F10**, select Attach Pull-Down Menus from the Menu menu, and select Yes.

New Members, Browse All Members, and Change/Delete a Member.

If you do not convert pop-up menus to pull-down menus, the user will see the example pop-up menu *only* after highlighting the Maintain option and pressing ↵. On the other hand, if you do convert pop-up menus to pull-down menus, the user will see the menu as soon as the highlight is on the Maintain option.

CREATING A FILES LIST

A files list is an application object that presents a list of file names to the user. Use this object when you create an application that allows the user to select a file name.

SEQUENCE OF STEPS

From the application design screen:

> **F10**
> Design/Files List
> To create a new files list: highlight <create>
> To modify an existing files list name: highlight a menu
> ↵

USAGE

To create a files list, starting from the application design screen, press **F10** and select Files List from the Design pull-down menu. In the dialog box that appears, enter a valid DOS file name for the files list and, optionally, a description. You can also add a message-line prompt, up to 76 characters long (with no quotation marks), that will appear beneath the files list when the user runs the application.

After you fill in the dialog box and press ←┘, an empty frame appears centered in the screen with a series of X's highlighted, as shown in Figure 15.18. You cannot enter information into this frame, because the application uses the frame to present file names.

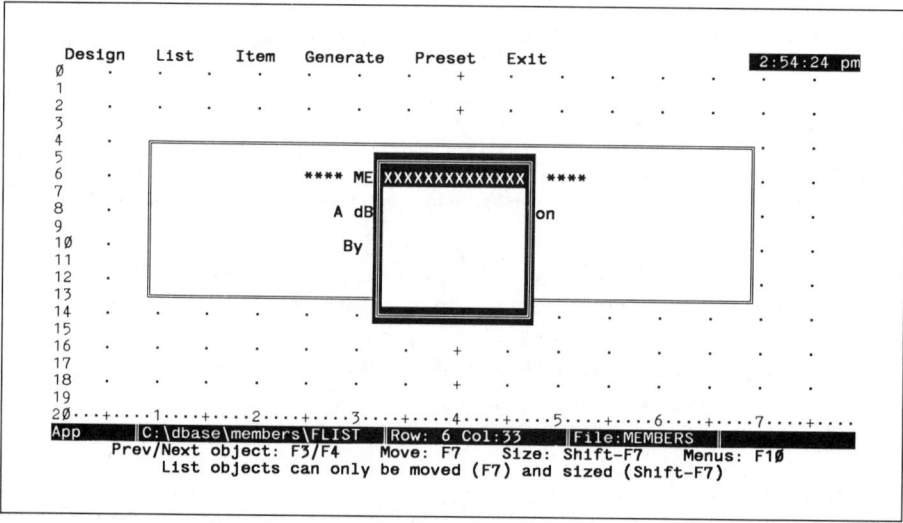

FIGURE 15.18: An empty files list displayed on the application design screen. You can move the frame using the **F7** key and size it using the **Shift-F7** key. However, you cannot make the frame narrower than the contents that it will display (as indicated by the string of X's).

You can, however, resize the object using the Size (**Shift-F7**) key and move the object using the Move (**F7**) key. Keep in mind that the maximum width of a file name is 12 characters, so you cannot make the frame any narrower.

To determine the types of files to be displayed in the files list, first make sure that the files list is the current object. If necessary, press the **F3** or **F4** key until the list's frame is highlighted. Then press **F10** and pull down the List menu from the application design screen main menu.

Next, select Identify Files in List. You will be prompted to enter a file specification. You can use the file name wildcard character **?** to stand for any single character and the wildcard character ***** to stand for any group of characters. Some examples of file specifications follow:

.	Displays the names of all files in the current directory
*.DBF	Displays the names of all database files in the current directory
*.FRM	Displays the names of all report format files in the current directory
*.LBL	Displays the names of all label format files in the current directory
*.FMT	Displays the names of all custom screen files in the current directory
QTR?.FRM	Displays the names of all files that begin with the letters *QTR*, followed by any single character, followed by the extension .FRM

If you leave the *File Specification* prompt blank, the files list will display the names of all files in the directory (as if you had specified ***.***). After typing a file specification, press **Ctrl-End** to return to the List pull-down menu.

For information about other options on the List pull-down menu, see the section "Using the Menu, List, and Batch Pull-Down Menus" later in this chapter.

You can determine when the user sees the files list by assigning the action Open a Menu, and the menu type VALUES to any menu item, batch process operation, or other list in the application (as discussed in Chapter 16). To determine what happens *after* the user selects a file name from the files list, assign an action to the files list itself (again, as discussed in Chapter 16).

The name of the file that the user selects from the list is stored in the variable &LISTVAL. You can use &LISTVAL in the dialog box that defines the action assigned to the file list. For example, if the action to take place after the user selects an option from the files list prints a report, specify &LISTVAL as the name of the file that contains the report format used to print the report.

Be aware that when the user selects a report format file name, dBASE has no way of knowing which database is associated with that report. If you attempt to print a report using fields that are not in the current database (or view), dBASE displays a list of the nonexistent fields, and an error occurs.

EXAMPLE

This example demonstrates the use of a files list in a completed application from the user's perspective. In Figure 15.19, the sample pull-down menu includes the option Select a Report Format. The application developer has assigned the action Open a Menu and the menu type VALUES to this action. When the user selects the option, the values list appears on the screen, as shown in Figure 15.19.

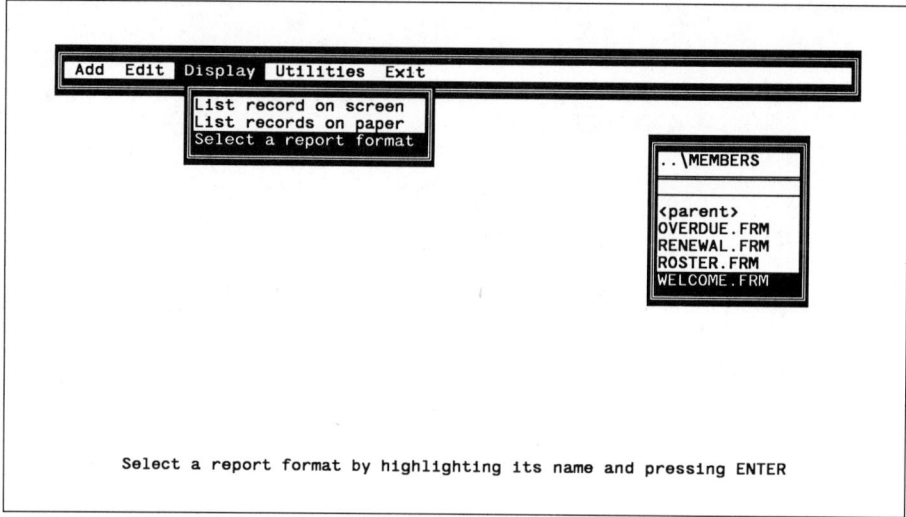

FIGURE 15.19: A values list from the user's perspective. The user sees the values list because the application developer has assigned the action Open a Menu and the menu type VALUES to the Select a Report Format option on the application pull-down menu shown on the screen.

After the user selects a file name, the application prints the selected report. dBASE prints the report because the application developer has assigned the action Print a Report to the values list application object and specified &LISTVAL as the name of the report to print in the Print a Report dialog box.

CREATING A STRUCTURE LIST

A structure list lets your application display a list of field names from the current database. Use this object when you want the user to select field names from a database, such as when he or she is displaying database records or browsing.

SEQUENCE OF STEPS

From the application design screen:

> **F10**
>
> Design/Structure List
>
> To create a new structure list: highlight <create>
>
> To modify an existing structure list name: highlight the structure list name ↵

USAGE

When you first create a structure list, you will be prompted to assign a name, an optional description, and a message-line prompt to the list. You must specify a valid DOS file name, without an extension. The description is optional. The message-line prompt can be up to 76 characters long and cannot contain double quotation marks (''). If you assign a message-line prompt, it is displayed at the bottom of the screen as soon as the user sees the structure list. After filling in the dialog box, press **Ctrl-End**.

Next you will see a frame centered on the screen with a series of highlighted X's to help you determine the width of the frame. You can change the width of the frame using the Size (**Shift-F7**) key and move the frame using the Move (**F7**) key. Keep in mind that the frame must be wide enough to accommodate the largest possible field name (10 characters, as indicated by the X's).

To determine which field names are to be included in the list, first make sure that the structure list is the current object on the design screen. If in doubt, press the **F3** or **F4** key until the structure list's frame is highlighted and it's file name appears in the status bar near the bottom of the screen.

Next press **F10** and select Identify Fields in List from the List pull-down menu. You will be prompted to provide a list of field names that the user can access. If you leave the prompt blank, the user will have access to all field names. To limit the user's access to specific fields, press **Shift-F1** and select field names by highlighting them and pressing ←. Selected field names will be marked by a triangle.

After specifying the field names that the user can have access to, press **Ctrl-End**. If you select too many field names, the Applications Generator will beep and display the message *Selections won't fit in field -- UNselect some entries*. You will need to use the arrow keys to highlight some field names and press ← to unselect them. To cancel all selections, you can press **Esc**.

For information about other options on the List pull-Down menu, see the section "Using the Menu, List, and Batch Pull-Down Menus" later in this chapter.

To determine when the user sees the structure list, attach the action Open a Menu and the menu type STRUCTURE to a menu item, batch process operation, or another type of list (as discussed in Chapter 16). When prompted, specify the name of the structure list.

To determine what happens *after* the user selects field names from the structure list, you need to assign an action to the structure list itself (as discussed in Chapter 16). The &LISTVAL variable stores the field names the user selects. The action you assign to the structure list should be one that supports a FIELDS statement (such as Browse or Display/List). You can use the &LISTVAL variable in the FIELDS option of the dialog box in place of specific field names, so that the action displays only those fields that the user selected from the structure list.

If you attach a structure list directly to a horizontal bar menu and convert pop-up menus to pull-down menus, the user will be allowed to select only one field name from the list. To avoid this, have an option from one of the application's pull-down or pop-up menus activate the structure list.

EXAMPLE

Figure 15.20 shows a sample structure list from the application user's perspective. In this example, the structure list was attached to the Browse Selected Fields option on the pull-down menu shown. After selecting that option, the user sees a list of field names and an empty box, as shown in the figure.

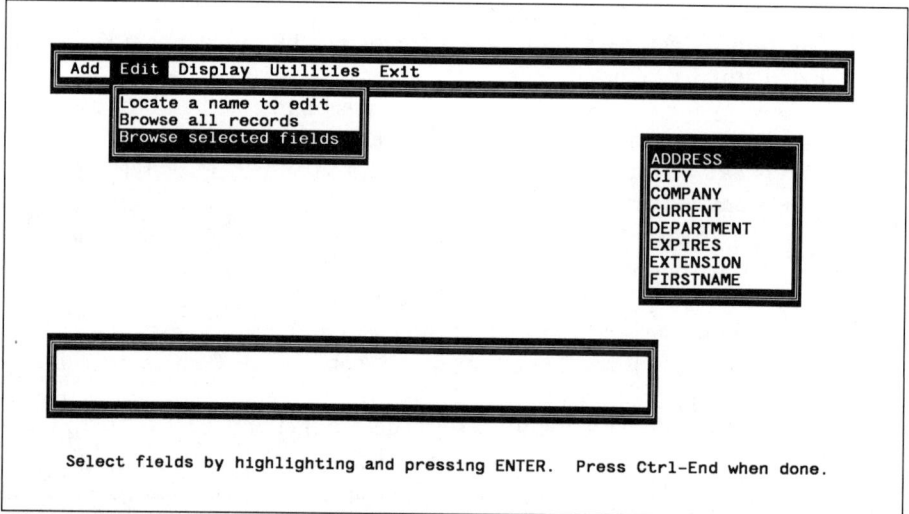

FIGURE 15.20: A structure list displayed on the screen as the user would see it. The user can select a field from the list by highlighting the field and pressing ↵. As the user selects field names, they are copied to the empty box near the lower-left corner of the screen. When the user is finished selecting field names, he or she can press **Ctrl-End**.

The user can now scroll through the structure list and select field names by highlighting the names and pressing ↵. Each time the user selects a field name, it appears in the box near the lower-left corner of the screen.

After selecting a field name, the user presses **Ctrl-End**. Whatever action the developer assigned to the structure list is then activated. For example, if the application developer assigned the action Browse to the structure list and specified &LISTVAL as the field to browse in the Browse a Database File or View dialog box (as discussed in Chapter 16), the user will then see a browse screen containing only those fields selected from the structure list.

DESIGNING A VALUES LIST

A values list is an application object that presents a list of values from a single database field to the user. Use this option when you want your user to select an existing value from a database.

SEQUENCE OF STEPS

From the application design screen:

F10
Design/Values List
To create a new values list: highlight <create>
To modify an existing values list: highlight a list name
↵

USAGE

When you first select <create> to create a values list, you'll be prompted to assign a valid DOS file name to the list. You can also enter a description and a message-line prompt, which will appear beneath the values list whenever this list appears on the screen.

After you assign a name and, optionally, a description and message-line prompt, press **Ctrl-End**. A blank frame for displaying values from the current database appears on the screen. You can size this frame using the Size (**Shift-F7**) key and move it using the Move (**F7**) key. When sizing the frame for the values list, make sure that the frame is wide enough to accommodate the data in the field. For example, if the list displays a field named LASTNAME that is 20 characters wide, the frame too should be at least 20 characters wide.

To determine which field from the current database (or view) the values list displays, first make sure that the files list is the current object. If necessary, press **F3** or **F4** until the files list frame is highlighted and its file name appears in the status bar near the bottom of the screen.

Next press **F10** and select Identify Field Values in List from the List pull-down menu. You will see a message asking you to enter the field to list values for. Press Pick **(Shift-F1)** to see a list of field names in the current database file. Select the name of a Character, Numeric, Float, or Date field by highlighting the name and pressing ↵ (the Logical and Memo data types cannot be used in a values list). Press **Ctrl-End** to return to the List pull-down menu.

The index currently in use determines how the fields are displayed in the values list. For example, suppose you decide to list values in the STATE field of a database, and that database currently contains the records AZ, CA, WA, CA,

AZ, and WA (in that order). If no index is in use, the fields list will display

AZ
CA
WA
CA
AZ
WA

If an index of the STATE field is active when the user views the values list (and the Duplicate Keys option is set to No), the values list will display all the states, in alphabetical order, as follows:

AZ
AZ
CA
CA
WA
WA

If an index of the STATE field with the Duplicate Values option set to Yes is active when the user views the values list, only unique states will be listed, in alphabetical order, as follows:

AZ
CA
WA

To determine which index is in control when the values list is displayed, make sure that the files list is still the current object. Then pull down the Item pull-down menu and select Reassign Index Order. You will see the prompt *Set ORDER To:* If you leave this option blank, the default index order that you defined during the original application definition will be used to display the values list. alternatively, you can type the name of a different index order to use, but you must specify the name of an existing index. Press **Ctrl-End** after you specify the index name.

To determine when the values list is displayed to the user, assign the action Open File and the menu type VALUES to a menu item, batch process operation, or another list in the application (as discussed in Chapter 16). Then, to determine what happens *after* the user selects a value from the values list, assign an action to the values list itself. That action will be activated immediately after the user makes a selection from the values list.

The value that the user selects from the values list is stored in the &LISTVAL variable, which you can use in the dialog box for the action assigned to the values list. For example, suppose your application uses the values list to display data from a field named LASTNAME. If you attach the action Edit Form to the values list, you can then enter the filter condition **LASTNAME = "&LIST-VAL"** in the FOR or FILTER box of the Append/Edit via Form File dialog box (as discussed in Chapter 16).

When using the &LISTVAL variable in an Applications Generator dialog box, you must use appropriate delimiters for the data type of the field being displayed in the values list. For example, if the values list displays a Character field named LASTNAME, then the FOR or FILTER condition expression would be **LASTNAME = "&LISTVAL"**. If the values list displays a Numeric or Float field named QTY, then the filter expression would be **QTY = &LISTVAL**. If the values list displays a Date field named STARTDATE, then the filter expression would be **STARTDATE = {&LISTVAL}**.

EXAMPLE

Figure 15.21 shows a sample values list, which is activated when the user selects Locate a Name to Edit from the pull-down menu displayed on the screen. In this example, the action assigned to the values list allows the user to edit a record and uses the FOR expression **LASTNAME = "&LISTVAL"** to limit editing to records that have the last name that the user selected from the values list.

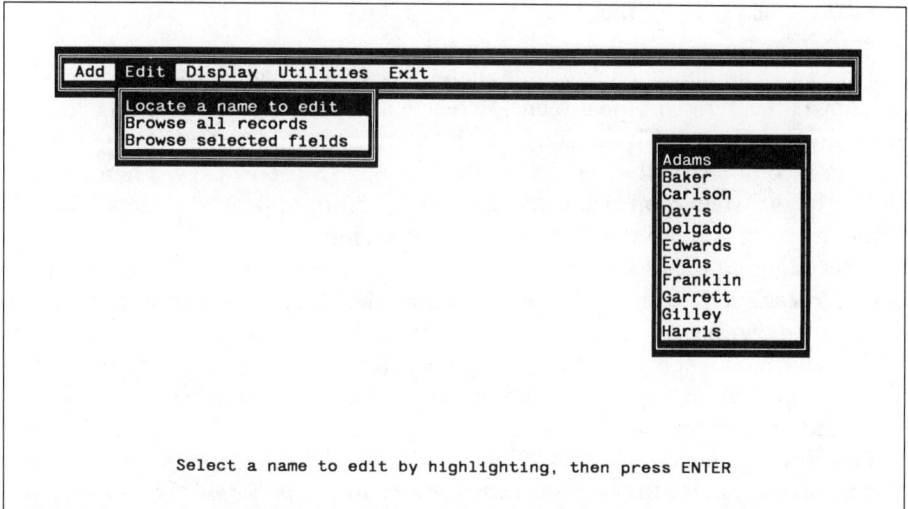

FIGURE 15.21: A sample values list from the user's perspective. In this example, the values list is activated when the user selects Locate a Name to Edit from the pull-down menu shown on the screen. After the user selects a value, the application looks up the record that contains that last name and displays an edit screen for that record.

CREATING A BATCH PROCESS

A batch process is an application object that performs a series of operations for the user.

SEQUENCE OF STEPS

From the application design screen:

> **F10**
>
> Design/Batch Process
>
> ↵
>
> To create a new batch process: highlight <create>
>
> To modify an existing batch process: highlight the batch process name
>
> ↵

USAGE

When you create a new batch process, a dialog box prompts you first to assign a valid DOS file name to the process and, optionally, a description. After you fill in the dialog box and press **Ctrl-End**, you'll see an empty frame centered on the screen. Type a plain-English description of each operation in the batch process. (The user will never see these descriptions, but you'll eventually assign an action to each item.)

If you are modifying an existing batch process, that batch process description will appear centered on the screen. To delete an operation, highlight its description and press **Ctrl-Y**. To insert a new operation, first enlarge the frame, if necessary, to accommodate the new item using the Size (**Shift-F7**) key. Then position the highlight where you want the new operation to appear and press **Ctrl-N**. Type the plain-English description of the operation.

After filling in the descriptions of each step in the process, you can assign an action to each step in the batch process using the Change Action option on the Item pull-down menu, as discussed in Chapter 16.

To determine when the batch process is activated, assign the action Execute Batch Process to an application menu item, another batch process, or a list, as discussed in Chapter 16.

Whenever you are working with the Batch pull-down menu, the second option on the application design screen main menu is Batch. Options on the Batch pull-down menu are described in the following section, "Using the Menu, List, and Batch Pull-Down Menus."

USING THE MENU, LIST, AND BATCH PULL-DOWN MENUS — 557

EXAMPLE

Figure 15.22 shows a sample batch process that performs four operations (these operations are the same as those defined for the sample application presented in Appendix F of this book).

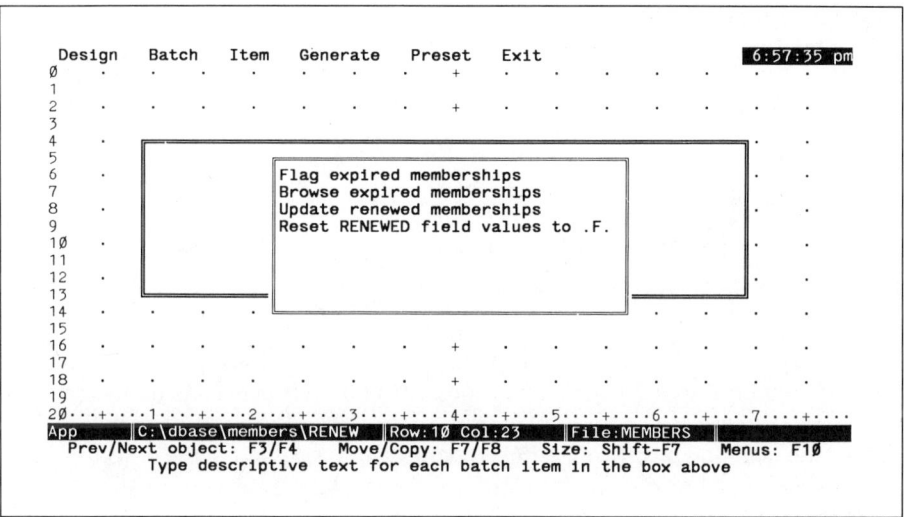

FIGURE 15.22: A sample batch process with plain-English descriptions. After entering in the plain-English descriptions, you can assign an action to each description by highlighting the description and selecting options from the Item pull-down menu.

USING THE MENU, LIST, AND BATCH PULL-DOWN MENUS

Whenever you create or modify a horizontal bar menu, pop-up menu, list, or batch process, the second option on the Applications Generator screen changes to reflect the type of object you are creating at the moment: Menu, List, or Batch.

If several application objects are currently displayed on the screen, you can select the object to work with by pressing the **F3** and **F4** keys. The frame surrounding the currently selected object will be highlighted, and the file name assigned to the object appears in the status bar near the bottom of the screen.

This section discusses those options that the Menu, List, and Batch options have in common. (Options that are unique to each pull-down menu are discussed in the preceding sections, which discuss each object separately.)

Changing the Object Name and Description

The Name and Describe option on the Menu, Batch, or List pull-down menu lets you change the name, description, or message-line prompt assigned to the current object.

SEQUENCE OF STEPS

From the application design screen:

> press **F3** or **F4** until the desired object is current
> **F10**
> Menu *or* List *or* Batch
> Name and Describe

USAGE

The Name and Describe option displays the file name, description, and message-line prompt for the current object (a batch process has no message-line prompt, since it does not display options to the user). When you select Name and Describe, a dialog box displays the current values assigned to the object. You can change any of these assignments and then press **Ctrl-End**.

The description and message-line prompt are optional. If you define a message-line prompt, it appears at the bottom of the screen when the user activates the object (unless you override the object's message-line prompt at the Item level, as discussed in Chapter 16).

EXAMPLE

Figure 15.23 shows the Name and Describe dialog box for a menu in a sample application. Note that this dialog box includes a message-line prompt. (The menu that the dialog box refers to is obscured by the dialog box in this figure.)

Figure 15.24 shows where the message-line prompt appears from the user's perspective. In this example, message-line prompts were not assigned to individual items on the menu, so the same message-line prompt appears at the bottom of the screen regardless of which menu item the user highlights.

Overriding the Database or View

The Override Assigned Database or View option lets you assign a new database, view, index, or sort order to the current application object.

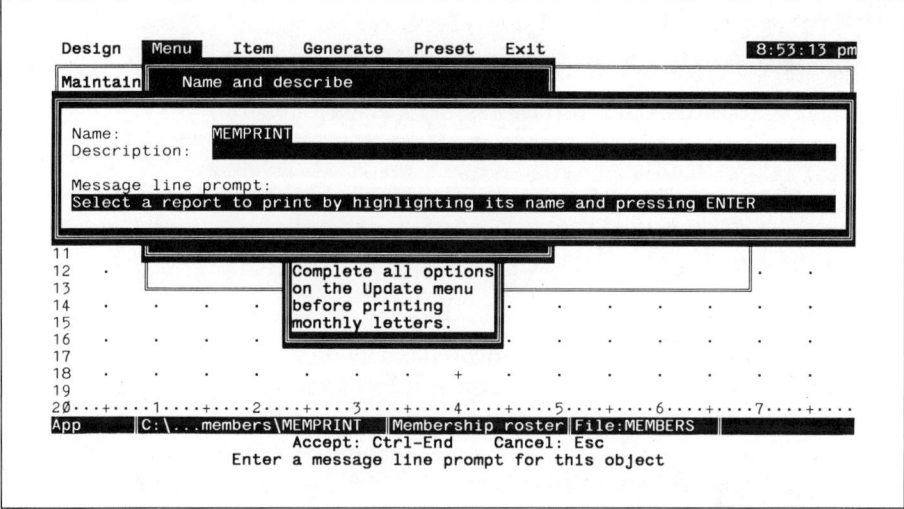

FIGURE 15.23: The Name and Describe dialog box for a sample menu named MEMPRINT. A message-line prompt appears on the screen when the user interacts with the MEMPRINT menu, unless this prompt is overridden by message-line prompts assigned to individual items on the menu.

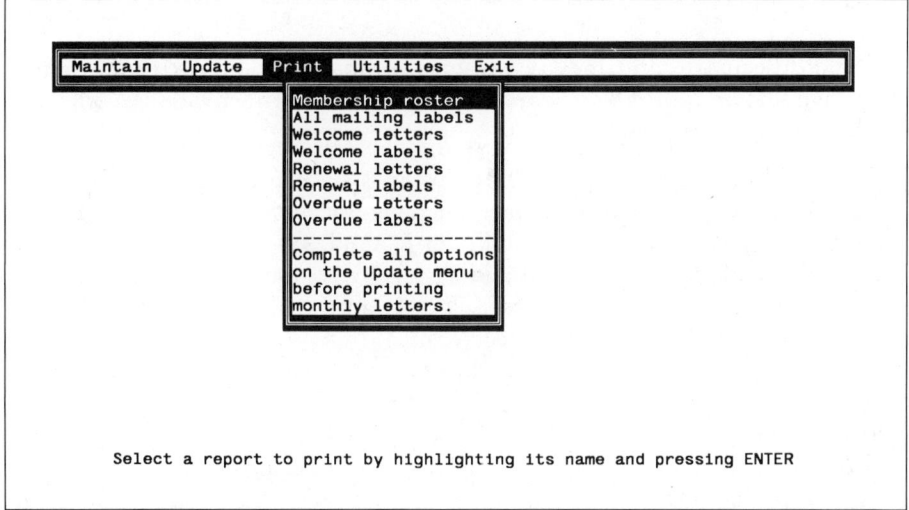

FIGURE 15.24: A sample menu from the user's perspective with the menu's message-line prompt displayed. If any individual item on the pull-down menu is assigned its own message, that item's message-line prompt replaces the message-line prompt for the menu as a whole when the item is highlighted.

SEQUENCE OF STEPS

From the application design screen:

> press **F3** or **F4** until the desired menu is current
> **F10**
> Menu *or* List *or* Batch
> Override Assigned Database or View

USAGE

When you select Override Assigned Database or View, you'll see a dialog box with the name of the current database and index. To change the assigned database or view for use with the current object, move the cursor to the For This Menu, You May Use Values option and press the space bar to scroll through its options. The options are as follows:

OPTION	EFFECT
Above	This object will use the database, index, and sort order specified above.
Entered Below	The object will use the database, index, and sort order specified below.
In Effect at Run Time	The object will use whatever database, index, and view are in use when the user activates the object.

The last option, In Effect at Run Time, tells the application to use whatever database file and index happen to be open when the user activates the current object. You can use this feature to create a generic application that lets the user manage more than one database file. For example, your application could display a list of all database files (stated as ***.DBF**) before displaying the current menu. Whatever database the user selects from the files list would be used by actions assigned to the current object.

If you specify Below, the current object uses the database, index file, and sort order specified at the bottom of the dialog box. If you leave any options blank at the bottom of the dialog box, dBASE uses the default values.

Note that changing the default values at this level affects the current object only. When the user is done with the current object, the default database and index defined at the application level are put back into effect.

Pull-down menus automatically use the database and view assigned to the associated horizontal bar menu. To override the database, view, or index order for a pull-down menu option, you must use the Item menu, rather than the Menu menu.

EXAMPLE

Figure 15.25 shows the Override Assigned Database or View dialog box for a single menu named MEMPRINT in a sample application. The menu's file name appears in the status bar near the lower-left corner of the screen.

The MEMPRINT menu in this example uses the MEMBERS database and ZIP index order when carrying out actions assigned to items within the menu. When the user leaves the MEMPRINT menu, the default database and index order, as defined at the application level, is reinstated.

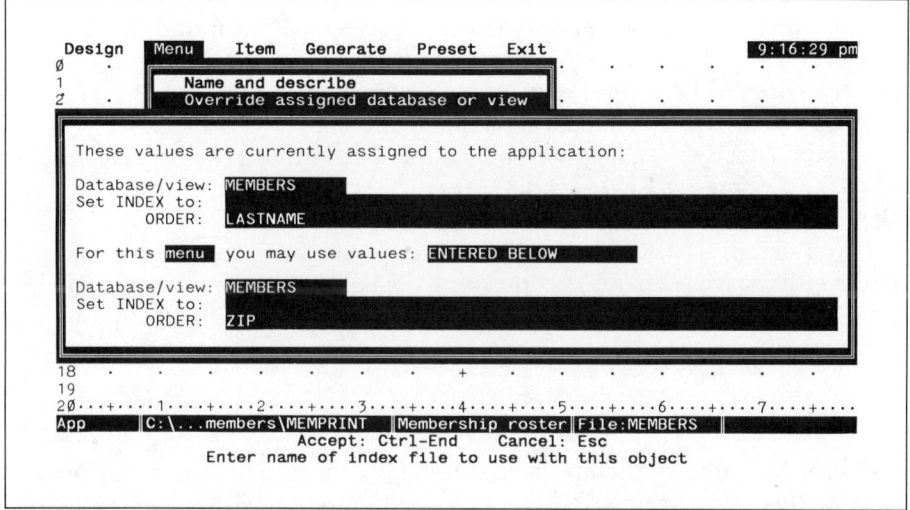

FIGURE 15.25: The Override Assigned Database or View dialog box for a menu named MEMPRINT in a sample application. All options on the MEMPRINT menu assume that the MEMBERS database and ZIP index order are the default selections for all items, except those that override this default at the Item level.

Writing Help Text

The Write Help Text option on the Menu and List pull-down menus lets you write a custom help screen for the current application object.

SEQUENCE OF STEPS

From the application design screen:

    press **F3** or **F4** until the desired object is current
    F10

Menu *or* List
Write Help Text

USAGE

You can assign help text to any menu or list. The user will see this text if he or she presses **F1** while the menu or list is displayed on the screen. (You cannot assign help text to a batch process, because the batch process is never actually displayed to the user.) To assign help text to a menu or list, make sure the object is current and then select Write Help Text from the Menu or List pull-down menu.

The Applications Generator presents a full-screen editing frame. You can type whatever text you wish into this frame and make changes and corrections using the usual dBASE IV editing keys. After creating your custom help screen, press **Ctrl-End** to return to the application design screen.

If you do not define a help screen for a menu or list, then no help is displayed when the user presses **F1**. Instead, the user will see only the message *No help found for <object name>*.

If you design a custom help screen for a specific item on a menu, that help screen is displayed when the user presses **F1**. That is, the help screens you design using the Item menu override the help screens you design using the Menu pull-down menu.

EXAMPLE

Figure 15.26 shows a sample help screen for a menu in a sample application. Because this help screen is assigned to a menu, it describes the purpose of each item on the application menu. The user will see this help screen when the associated menu is displayed on the screen and the user presses **F1**.

Modifying Display Options

The Modify Display Options option on the Menu and List pull-down menus let you assign colors and a border style to the current object. The options are the same ones displayed by the Display Options option on the Application menu, except that they affect the current menu or list only.

SEQUENCE OF STEPS

From the application design screen:

    press **F3** or **F4** until the desired object is current

MODIFYING DISPLAY OPTIONS ━━ 563

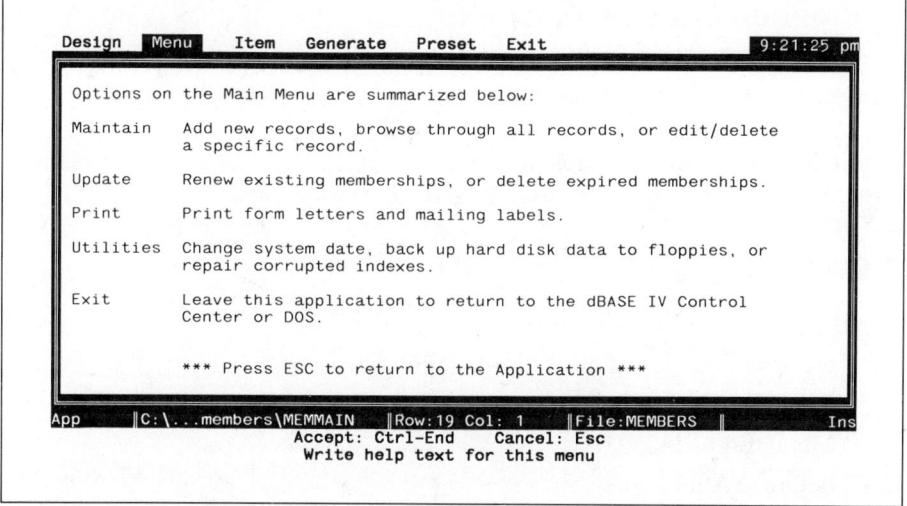

FIGURE 15.26: A sample help screen created for the MEMMAIN menu (the menu's name appears in the status bar near the lower-left corner of the screen). The application user presses **F1** to view custom help screens.

F10

Menu *or* List

Modify Display Options

USAGE

To assign a unique color scheme to an individual menu or list in an application, make that object current and then pull down the Menu or List menu and select Modify Display Options. Select a border style by pressing the space bar to scroll through the options. To select specific colors, select one of the areas to color. The dBASE IV electronic coloring palette will appear, and you can select a color scheme using the usual techniques (as described in Chapter 14). Press **Ctrl-End** to save the new settings.

If you do not assign a unique color scheme border to an individual menu, the menu uses the display characteristics assigned to the application as a whole.

Note that pull-down menus always inherit the color scheme and border assigned to the horizontal bar menu. Even if you change the color scheme or border of a specific pull-down menu, pull-down menus still will use the border and color style of the horizontal bar menu.

Embedding Program Code in an Application

The Embed Code option allows you to add dBASE IV programming language code to a menu, list, or batch process. The code can be executed either before or after the object is activated. This option should be used only by experienced dBASE IV programmers who are thoroughly familiar with the dBASE IV programming language and programming techniques.

SEQUENCE OF STEPS

From the application design screen:

>   press **F3** or **F4** until the desired menu is current
>   **F10**
>   Menu/Embed Code
>   Before *or* After

USAGE

When you select Embed Code, dBASE displays a full screen in which you can write your program. The general keys for composing and editing program code are the same as those used in the dBASE IV program editor. When embedding code above or below an application object, however, you are limited to 19 command lines. Press **Ctrl-End** after writing your code to return to the application design screen.

EXAMPLE

Suppose that, as a programmer, you develop a procedure file containing custom procedures and user-defined functions for use with an application. You name this procedure file BUSPROCS.PRG.

If you want that procedure file to be opened as soon as the user runs the application (just before the application main menu is displayed), first make the application's main menu the current object on the application design screen. Then select the Embed Code and Before options from the Menu pull-down menu. Enter the commands necessary to open the procedure file, as shown in Figure 15.27. Press **Ctrl-End** after entering your programming commands. When the user runs the application, the SET PROCEDURE TO command will be executed before the user sees the application's main menu, and the procedure file will remain open for the entire application session.

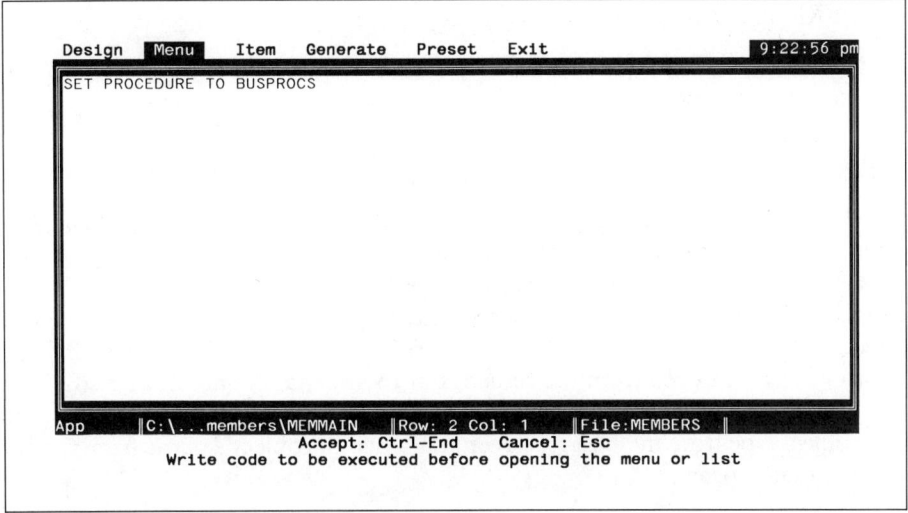

FIGURE 15.27: In this example, a programmer has already developed a procedure file named BUSPROCS.PRG that contains custom procedures and user-defined functions to be used by the application.

Saving the Current Object

The Save Current <object> option saves the current object and leaves it on the design screen.

USAGE

After creating or modifying a menu, list, or batch process, select Save Current <object> from the object's pull-down menu. The object will be saved with the file name you originally specified. You'll then be returned to the Menu pull-down menu.

Putting Away the Current Object

The Put Away Current <object> option removes the current object from the design screen.

SEQUENCE OF STEPS

From the application design screen:

> press **F3** or **F4** until the desired object is current
>
> **F10**

Menu *or* List *or* Batch
Put Away Current <object>
Save Changes *or* Abandon Changes

USAGE

To remove an object from the application design screen, select Put Away Current <object> from the Menu, List, or Batch pull-down menu. If the object is new or has been modified recently, the screen displays the options Save Changes and Abandon Changes. If you select Save Changes, the object is saved with recent changes and removed from the screen. If you select Abandon Changes, the object is removed from the screen, but recent changes are not saved.

If you need to bring back an object that you've put away, select the appropriate object type from the Design screen, and then the object's name from the submenu that appears.

Clearing the Work Surface

SEQUENCE OF STEPS

From the application design screen:

F10
Application *or* Menu *or* List *or* Batch
Clear Work Surface

USAGE

The Clear Work Surface options on the Application, Menu, List, and Batch pull-down menus are identical. The option puts away all objects currently on the design screen. Before saving any new or modified objects, the Applications Generator asks for permission. You can select Save Changes to save the object, or Abandon Changes to abandon changes made to the object since it was last saved.

All objects except the sign-on banner will be removed from the design screen. To access a saved object in the future, select the object type from the Design pull-down menu and then the object's file name from the submenu that appears.

EXAMPLE

Before generating the code for an application, you need to save all new and modified objects and make the sign-on banner the current object. The easiest way to do this is to select Clear Work Surface from the Application, Menu, List, or Batch pull-down menu. When all objects have been saved and put away, you can generate the application code (as discussed in Chapter 17).

TIPS AND TRAPS

- To simplify the process of developing an application, create all the database objects in a unique directory and sketch out a menu structure, as in the example shown in Appendix F.
- The Preset, Application, Menu, Batch, List, and Item menus on the application design screen offer many similar options that affect the application at increasing levels of specificity.
- After creating the objects for an application, you need to assign actions to those objects using the Item pull-down menu (discussed in Chapter 16).
- After creating application objects and assigning actions, you need to generate the code for the application, as discussed in Chapter 17.
- The Application Definition dialog box allows you to select BATCH as the main menu type, but this option is best avoided in version 1.0 of dBASE IV due to unpredictable behavior.

SUMMARY

This chapter discussed the Applications Generator and application design screen in general, as well as application objects that you can add to your own applications.

For information about assigning actions to application objects:

- Chapter 16, "Assigning Actions to Application Objects"

For information about generating the code for an application:

- Chapter 17, "Generating and Using an Application"

For information about the Preset pull-down menu in the applications design screen:

- Chapter 17, "Generating and Using an Application"

For an example of beginning-to-end procedures for designing, creating, and using an application:

- Appendix F, "Designing and Developing an Application"

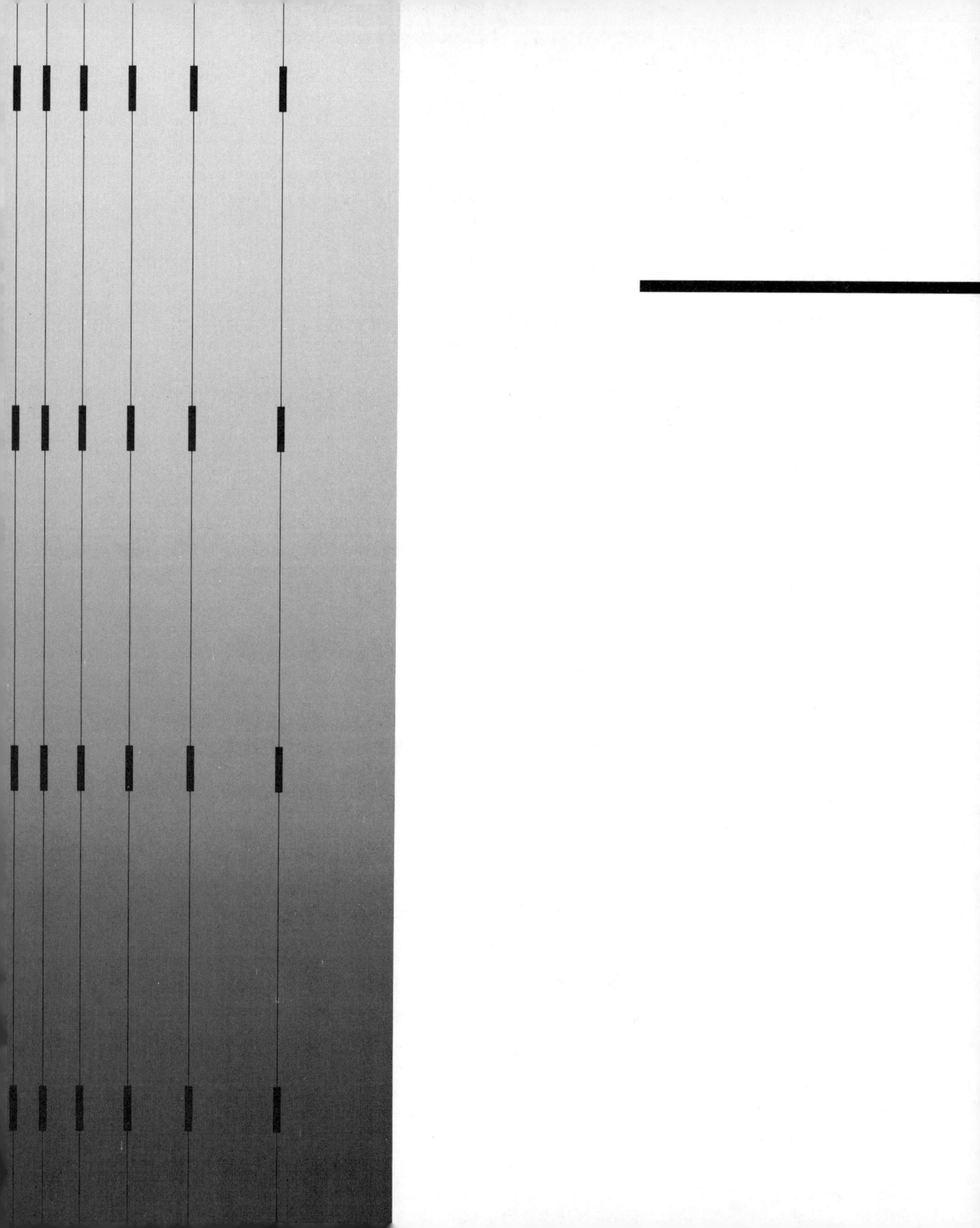

CHAPTER 16

ASSIGNING ACTIONS TO APPLICATION OBJECTS

The Item Menu. 571
Viewing the Action Assigned to an Item. 572
Assigning and Changing Actions. .573
Notes on Assigning Actions. 575
    Filtering Records in an Action. 575
    Using Complete Expressions. 575
    Using AND, OR, and NOT Logic. 576
    Refining Filter-Condition Logic. 577
    Using FILTER, FOR, SCOPE, and WHILE. 577
        FOR Conditions. 577
        FILTER Conditions. 578
        SCOPE Conditions. 578
        WHILE Conditions. 579
Using the Change Action Submenu. 579
    Assigning No Action. 579
    Opening a Menu. 581
    Displaying Data on a Browse Screen. 582
    Displaying Data in a Custom Form. 585
    Displaying or Printing Data. .588
        Printing Reports. 588
        Printing Labels. 589
        Displaying Records without a Report Format. 591
    Performing File Operations. .595
        Copying Files. 595
        Adding Records from a File. 596
        Copying Records to a File. 598
        Substituting Field Values. 599

Marking Records for Deletion	602
Unmarking Records	602
Discarding Marked Records	603
Generating an Index	605
Reindexing a Database	607
Sorting a Database	608
Importing Files	609
Exporting Files	611
Running Programs	612
Executing a dBASE Program	613
Executing a Batch Process	615
Inserting dBASE Code	615
Running a DOS Program	616
Executing a Binary File	618
Playing Back a Keystroke Macro	619
Exiting an Application	620
Overriding the Default Database for a Single Item	621
Attaching Code to an Item	622
Dimming Application Menu Items	623
Positioning the Record Pointer	624
Selecting an Index for an Item	628
Displaying a Window	628
Writing Help Text for an Item	632
Assigning a Message-Line Prompt	632
Tips and Traps	635
Summary	635

Assigning Actions to Application Objects

This chapter discusses all the Applications Generator options that involve assigning actions to application objects. The actions that you assign to objects are performed when the user runs the application and makes selections, as summarized here:

- Actions assigned to individual menu items in an application are performed when the user selects that menu item.
- Actions assigned to plain-English descriptions in a batch process are performed sequentially, starting with the description listed first and progressing toward the description listed last.
- The action assigned to a list object is performed after the list is displayed and the user makes a selection.

All the tools for assigning actions to objects are on the Item pull-down menu. All settings and options on the Item pull-down menu affect a single item only.

THE ITEM MENU

The Item pull-down menu is available on the Applications Generator main menu whenever you are working on a menu, list, or batch process. This menu is used to assign *actions* and attributes to specific menu options, batch processes, and lists in your application.

SEQUENCE OF STEPS

From the application design screen:

>   press **F3** or **F4** until the desired object is current
>   **F10**
>   Item [⏎]

USAGE

To use the Item menu, first make the object to which you want to assign an attribute or action current. If the object is a menu, highlight the option to which you want to assign an action or attribute in your custom menu. Then press Menu (**F10**) and scroll to the Item pull-down menu.

You'll notice that the option from your custom menu appears centered in the status bar near the bottom of the screen. If you are working on a batch process, the operation description appears in the status bar. If you are currently working on a list object, X's appear in the status bar. You can assign one action to this object, which will be performed after the user selects an item from the list.

Although some options on the Item pull-down menu are identical to options on the Menu pull-down menu, options on the Menu menu affect the menu as a whole, whereas options on the Item menu affect individual menu options.

Each option on the Item pull-down menu shown in Figure 16.1 is discussed in the sections that follow.

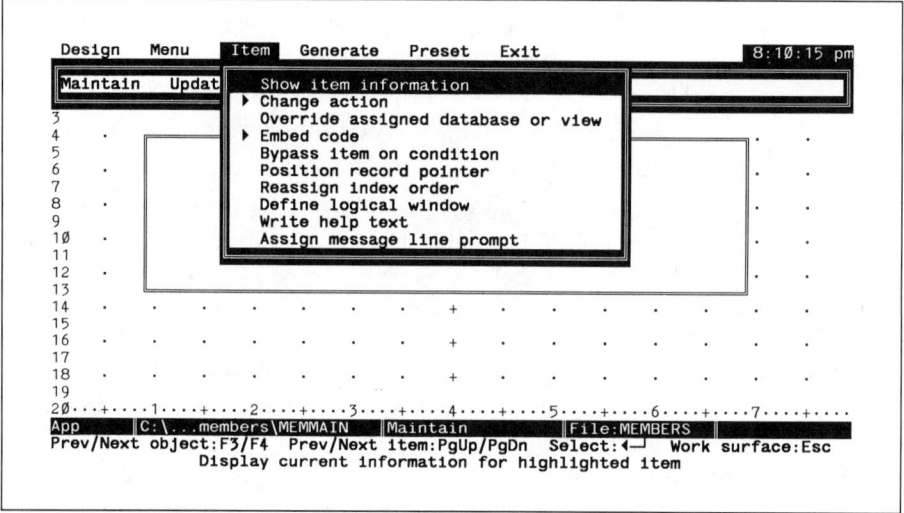

FIGURE 16.1: Item pull-down menu on the application design screen. This menu is available only when an application menu, list, or batch process is on the application design screen.

VIEWING THE ACTION ASSIGNED TO AN ITEM

The Show Item Information option displays the name of the current object, the item that is currently highlighted within that object, the database or view in use, and the action that is currently assigned to the item. You can use this option only to view the action currently assigned to an item. You cannot use it to make changes (you need to use the Change Action option to change the action assigned to an item).

SEQUENCE OF STEPS

From the application design screen:

>press **F3** or **F4** until the desired object is current
>**F10**
>Item/**S**how Item Information [←]

USAGE

To view the database, index order, and action assigned to a menu option, move the highlight to the menu option and select Show Item Information from the Item pull-down menu. After viewing the item information, press ← or **Esc** to return to the Item pull-down menu.

If you want to change the database, view, or index that the item uses, use the Override Assigned Database or View option on the Item pull-down menu. If you want to change the controlling index only, to specify a different sort order, use the Reassign Index Order option on the Item pull-down menu. If you want to change the action assigned to the item, use the Change Action submenu on the Item pull-down menu.

EXAMPLE

Figure 16.2 shows the item information for the Add New Members option on a pop-up menu named MEMMAINT. (Notice that the item Add New Members appears centered in the status bar near the bottom of the screen.) As the screen shows, the item uses the MEMBERS database file and performs an action that allows the user to edit the current database using a custom form.

ASSIGNING AND CHANGING ACTIONS

The Change Action option is the tool you use to assign and change actions that your application performs. When you create an application, you use Change Action to assign (or modify) an action for each option on a menu and each operation in a batch process. You can also assign a single action to each values list, structure list, and fields list. The action you assign to a list occurs immediately after the user selects an item from the list.

SEQUENCE OF STEPS

From the application design screen:

>press **F3** or **F4** until the desired object is current

574 — CH. 16 ASSIGNING ACTIONS TO APPLICATION OBJECTS

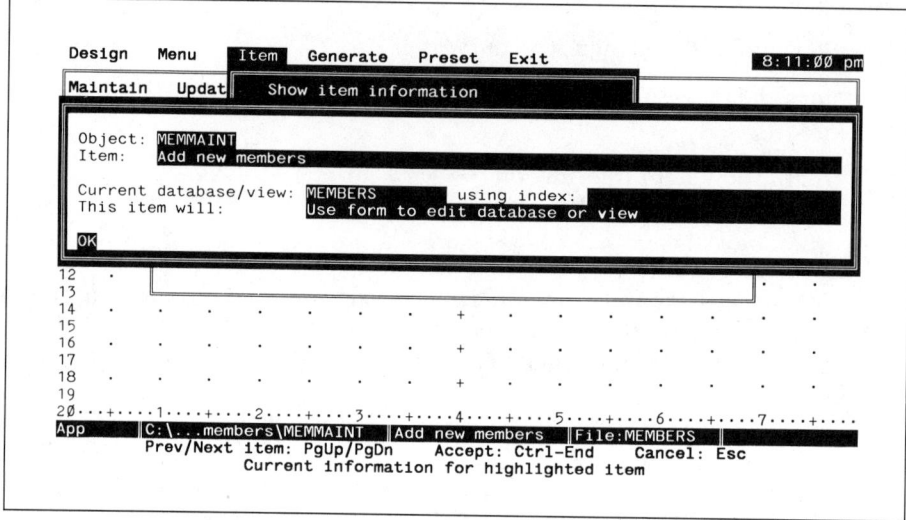

FIGURE 16.2: Item information for the Add New Members option on a menu named MEMMAINT. This screen allows you only to view the current action. To make changes, you must use other options on the Item pull-down menu.

F10

Item/Change Action [↵]

USAGE

Make the menu, batch process, or list the current object on the design screen. For a menu or batch process, highlight the option or plain-English description for which you want to assign (or change) an action. Press **F10** and highlight the Item pull-down menu. Select Change Action. Then select an action and use submenus and dialog boxes to define it.

To move to another option in a menu or another operation in a batch process, press **PgDn** or **PgUp** until the option or operation appears in the status bar. Optionally, press **Esc** to return to the design screen.

When you first select the Change Action option, you'll see the submenu that follows. (The uppercase options to the right of the menu options are the dBASE IV commands that the application will use. For more information about a particular command, refer to the dBASE IV *Language Reference* that came with your dBASE IV package. However, you need no additional information to use the options.)

Text (No Action)
Open a Menu   ACTIVATE MENU

>   Browse (Add, Delete, Edit)   BROWSE
>   Edit Form (Add, Delete, Edit)   EDIT
>   Display or Print
>   Perform File Operation
>   Run Program
>   Quit

We will return to the Change Action options, discussing each one in turn, after discussing some general features of actions that you can assign to menu items.

NOTES ON ASSIGNING ACTIONS

Many options on the Change Action submenu use dialog boxes that allow you to specify how an action is to be performed and the records the action is to include. The dialog boxes have several features in common. These are described in the sections that follow.

Filtering Records in an Action

Many actions that you assign to options in your application allow you to filter records from the database. In the Applications Generator, you need not use the query design screen to do this. Instead, you can enter filter conditions directly into dialog boxes that appear as you create the application.

The rules for defining data types in Applications Generator filter conditions are similar to those applicable to the query design screen and discussed in Chapter 5. You must enter Character data enclosed in quotation marks, Date data enclosed in curly braces, and Numeric data without any delimiters. You can use the same operators in dialog boxes that you use in the query design screen. Similarly, you can use any dBASE function in a filter condition.

However, there are a few differences between the filter conditions you enter into the query design screen and those that you enter into Applications Generator boxes. These are discussed in the sections that follow.

Using Complete Expressions

In an Applications Generator dialog box, you must use a *complete expression* as the filter condition. A complete expression is one that returns either a true or a false result.

On the query design screen, if you want to isolate records that have CA in the State field, you place **"CA"** in the State box in the query.

In an Applications Generator dialog box, the expression "CA" alone would not return a true or false result. (In fact, it would return an error that would cause the application to stop running.) Instead, you use the filter condition **State = "CA"**. This filter condition does indeed return either a true or a false result, because a particular database record either *does* have CA in the State field (true), or it *does not* have CA in the State field (false). Similarly, the filter conditions **StartDate < {12/31/89}** and **Qty > 100** can return only a true or a false result.

Note that each of these filter conditions consists of three components: a field name, an operator, and a comparison value. For example, in the filter condition **Qty > 100**, Qty is the field name, > is the operator, and 100 is the comparison value. The one exception to the rule that a complete expression requires all three components is the Logical field, which does not require an operator or comparison value in order to be evaluated as true or false. We'll discuss this exception in a moment.

Using AND, OR, and NOT Logic

Unlike the query design screen, dialog boxes do not allow you to align or stagger expressions in rows to create AND and OR conditions. Instead, you use the operators .AND. and .OR. In addition, you can use the .NOT. operator to specify conditions that are not true (or Logical fields that contain .F. rather than .T.).

When using .AND., .OR., and .NOT. expressions, you must use complete expressions on both sides of the operator. This rule is to forget, because people generally don't think in terms of complete expressions. For example, suppose StartDate is a Date field, and you want to isolate records from the first quarter of 1989. You might think that you could use the filter condition **StartDate > = {01/01/89} .AND. < = {03/31/89}** to isolate the appropriate records.

However, this expression will cause an error when you run the application, because the expression on the right side of the .AND. operator, < = {03/31/89}, is incomplete. dBASE can't determine that you probably mean **StartDate < = {03/31/89}**, so it doesn't know *what* to compare to {03/32/89}. (You and I can figure this out, but dBASE isn't so smart.) To isolate records from the first quarter of 1989, you must enter the expression **StartDate > = {01/01/89} .AND. StartDate < = {03/31/89}**.

Logical fields do not require an operator or comparison value in a filter condition. The field name in itself is a complete expression, because it refers to a value that is already .T. or .F. For example, if Current is the name of a Logical field, then the expression **Current** is identical to the expression **Current = .T.** To isolate records that have .F. in a Logical field, use the .NOT. operator before the field name. For example, the expression **.NOT. Current** is identical to the expression **Current = .F.**

Refining Filter-Condition Logic

You can use parentheses to refine the meanings of .AND. and .OR. in filter-condition expressions. For example, suppose a database contains State as a Character field and Paid as a Logical field, and you want to isolate the records of New York and New Jersey residents who have paid.

If you use the filter condition **State = "NY" .OR. State = "NJ" .AND. Paid**, you are actually requesting records of all New York residents (regardless of whether they've paid) and only New Jersey residents who have paid.

By default, dBASE interprets all .NOT. expressions first, then .AND. expressions, and then .OR. expressions. Thus, it evaluates **State = "NJ" .AND. Paid** as a complete expression before looking at the .OR. half of the filter condition. To get dBASE to interpret this condition correctly, you must change the order of interpretation. You can do so by using parentheses to group parts of the condition. dBASE always interprets an expression from the innermost parentheses outward. For example, the filter condition **(State = "NY" .OR. State = "NJ") .AND. Paid** isolates the .OR. portion of the filter condition and executes that first. If the State field holds either NY or NJ, then the next condition, the member has Paid, must also be met for the record to be selected.

When you use parentheses to refine the logic of a filter condition, be sure the parentheses are *balanced*. That is, an expression must contain an equal number of opening and closing parentheses. Unbalanced parentheses will cause an error.

Using **FILTER, FOR, SCOPE, and WHILE**

When you begin developing your application, many of the actions you assign will provide up to four different conditional operators you can use to filter records: FOR, FILTER, SCOPE, and WHILE.

FOR Conditions

In most situations, you will want to place your application filter condition after the FOR prompt. FOR accepts any valid filter condition, so long as it fits in the space provided. For example, if you enter the filter condition **State = "NY"** in the FOR section of a Print a Report dialog box, the report will print letters for only New York residents.

FILTER CONDITIONS

The FILTER option, which is available in some dialog boxes, is virtually identical to the FOR option. You can place any valid filter condition in the FILTER section, and the condition will limit the operation to records that meet the filter criterion. For example, if you enter **MONTH(StartDate) = 12** as the FILTER condition in the Print a Report dialog box, the printed report includes only records that have December start dates.

If you use both a FOR and a FILTER condition in a dialog box, the filter conditions are combined using .AND. logic. For example, if the FILTER condition in a Print a Report dialog box is **State = "NJ"** and the FOR condition in that same dialog box is **MONTH(StartDate) = 12**, then the report prints only records with NJ in the State field and December start dates.

Note that you could achieve the same results by placing the filter condition **State = "NJ" .AND. MONTH(StartDate) = 12** in either the FOR or the FILTER section.

SCOPE CONDITIONS

The SCOPE option in an Applications Generator dialog box lets you define the number of records an operation includes. Your options are summarized in Table 16.1.

OPTION	EFFECT
ALL	The operation includes all records in the database.
RECORD *n*	The operation includes only a single record, where *n* is the record number. For example, the scope **RECORD 5** limits the operation to the fifth record in the database.
NEXT *n*	The operation includes only the current record and the specified number of records that follow the current record, where *n* specifies the number of records. For example, if record number 11 is the current record, the scope **NEXT 3** performs the indicated operation on records 11, 12, and 13. If an index is active, **NEXT 3** refers to the current record and the next three records in the sort order determined by the index.
REST	The operation includes current record and all remaining records to the end of the database. If an index is active, REST refers to the current record and all records that follow it in the sort order determined by the index.

Table 16.1: SCOPE options.

The default scope for most operations is ALL. Three exceptions are Substitute Field Values, Mark Records for Deletion, and Unmark Records, which operate only on the current record unless you specify an ALL or FOR scope condition in the dialog box.

WHILE CONDITIONS

The WHILE condition limits an operation to a group of records that are adjacent in the database and meet a filter condition. dBASE executes WHILE operators faster than FOR or FILTER operators, but WHILE operators can be used only if two criteria are met. The database must be indexed (or sorted) on the field being searched, and the current record in the database must already meet the filter condition.

To meet these criteria, an application must perform two steps before the WHILE condition is executed. First, it must make sure the appropriate index is in use (using the Reassign Index Order option on the Item menu if necessary). Second, the application must move the record pointer to the first record that meets the filter condition (using the Position Record Pointer option on the Item pull-down menu).

WHILE is faster than FOR and FILTER because both FOR and FILTER look at every record in the database and isolate records that meet the filter conditions. A WHILE condition, on the other hand, begins with the first record in an index that matches the filter condition and then looks at records *until* it encounters a record that does not meet the filter condition; it wastes no time looking at other records.

USING THE CHANGE ACTION SUBMENU

To assign an action to an item or change the action currently assigned to an item, you need to make sure that the item is current. If you are assigning an action to a menu item or to an operation in a batch process, you should make sure that the item is highlighted on the design screen. (The highlight should appear on that item when you select Change Action from the Item pull-down menu.) The sections that follow describe each action and dialog box available from the Change Action submenu.

Assigning No Action

If you assign the Text (No Action) action to a menu option, the user cannot highlight the option when he or she runs the application.

SEQUENCE OF STEPS

From the application design screen:

> press **F3** or **F4** until the desired object is current
> **F10**
> Item/Text (No Action)

USAGE

Text (No Action) is the default setting initially assigned to all menu items, batch process operations, and list objects. The only time that you would want to leave Text (No Action) assigned to an item is when you want the item only to display information to the user.

EXAMPLE

Figure 16.3 shows a sample pull-down menu on the application design screen. The text below the dashed line is provided as information to the user and is not intended to be selected. Leaving the Text (No Action) action assigned to the dashed line and the text that follows prevents the user from moving the highlight into that area of the menu.

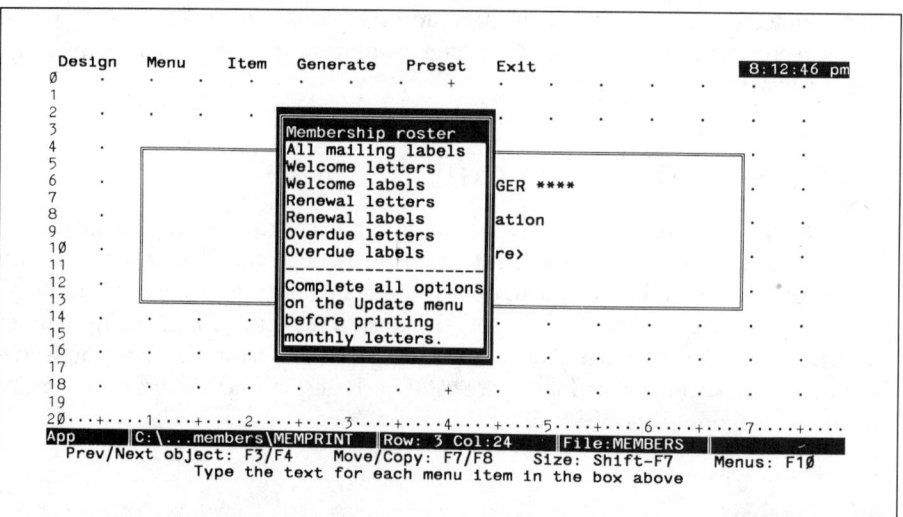

FIGURE 16.3: In this sample menu, the text below the dashed line is intended only to provide information to the user. Leaving the action Text (No Action) assigned to the dashed line and the text that follows it prevents the user from moving the highlight below the actual menu items (which appear above the dashed line).

Opening a Menu

SEQUENCE OF STEPS

From the application design screen:

    press **F3** or **F4** until the desired object is current

    F10

    Item/**C**hange Action/**O**pen a Menu [↵]

USAGE

The Open a Menu option on the Change Action submenu tells the application to display another menu or a list when the user selects the item to which you've assigned this action. When you select the Open a Menu option, you'll see a small dialog box that allows you to define the type and name of a menu to open.

You can press the space bar to scroll through the menu type options: Bar (a horizontal bar menu), Pop-Up (a pop-up or pull-down menu), Files (a file list), Structure (a structure list), and Values (a value list).

After you select the menu type, move the cursor to the Menu Name option and type the name of the menu (or list) that you want the option to display. You can also press Pick (**Shift-F1**) to see a submenu of existing object names and then select the appropriate name.

When the user later runs the application and selects the option to which you've assigned the Open a Menu action, he or she will see the menu (or list object) that you've specified. Note that if a menu option displays a list, you will also need to assign an action to that list. The action you assign will occur immediately after the user makes a selection from the list.

EXAMPLE

Figure 16.4 shows the prompt box asking for the type and name of the menu to open when the user selects the current menu item. In this example, the Maintain option on the horizontal bar menu is assigned the action Open a Menu. The dialog box tells the application to open a pop-up menu named MEMMAINT when the user selects Maintain from the horizontal bar menu.

If you convert pop-up menus to pull-down menus, the MEMMAINT menu is displayed as soon as the Maintain option is highlighted; the user need not press ↵ to view the MEMMAINT menu.

582 — CH. 16 ASSIGNING ACTIONS TO APPLICATION OBJECTS

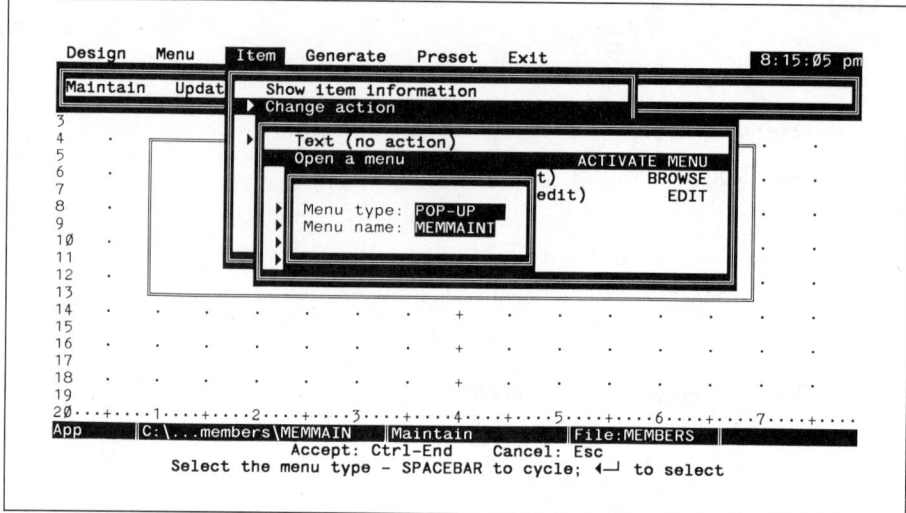

FIGURE 16.4: A sample Open a File dialog box that tells dBASE to open a menu named MEMMAINT when the user selects the associated menu item (the Maintain option on the horizontal bar menu in this example).

Displaying Data on a Browse Screen

The Browse (Add, Delete, Edit) action displays data from the current database or view on a browse screen.

SEQUENCE OF STEPS

From the application design screen:

> press **F3** or **F4** until the desired object is current
> **F10**
> Item/**C**hange Action/**B**rowse (Add, Delete, Edit) [◄─┘]

USAGE

If you want a menu item in your application to display data on a browse screen, assign the action Browse (Add, Delete, Edit) to that menu item. To do so, select the Browse (Add, Delete, Edit) option from the Change Action submenu. You'll first see a dialog box with a list of options. The options in the dialog box are described in the following sections.

After completing the browse screen dialog box, press **Ctrl- End** to return to the Item pull-down menu.

Fields If you do not specify fields, the browse screen displays all fields from the database or view. If you want, you can specify that only certain fields be displayed. The order in which you specify the fields determines the order the browse screen uses when you specify multiple fields. Separate field names with commas. You can also select field names from a submenu by pressing Pick (**Shift-F1**).

Filter If you do not specify any filter conditions, the browse screen displays all records in the database or view. If you enter a valid filter condition, only records that meet this condition are displayed.

Fields to Lock Onscreen You can enter a number indicating how many adjacent fields at the left side of the browse screen you want to remain stationary as the user scrolls to the right. If you use the default setting, zero, for the Fields to Lock Onscreen option, no fields are locked on the screen.

Freeze Edit Field If you do not specify a field to freeze, the user can move the highlight to any field in the browse screen. If you enter (or pick) a field name, the highlight will be confined to the field you specify, and the user can change data only in that field.

Maximum Column Width If you do not specify the maximum column width, all fields are displayed in columns that match their widths as defined in the database structure. If you enter a number, no column will be wider than the number you specify. Fields that are longer than the maximum column width will be truncated on the browse screen.

Format File If you do not specify a format file, the browse screen imposes no restrictions on data entered into the database. If you enter the name of a custom form, then field templates, default values, and other special features of the custom form are applied to the browse screen. To select a valid format file name, press Pick (**Shift-F1**), highlight the name on the list that appears, and press ↵.

Allow Record Add? If you specify Yes for this option, the user can add new records through the browse screen. If you specify No, the user cannot add new records. Use the space bar to select Yes or No.

Allow Record Edit? If you specify Yes for this option, the user can change any data on the browse screen. If you specify No, the user can view data through the browse screen, but cannot make any changes. Use the space bar to select Yes or No.

Allow Record Delete? If you specify Yes for this option, the user can mark records for deletion through the browse screen (using **Ctrl-U**). If you specify No, the user cannot mark records for deletion. Use the space bar to select Yes or No.

Keep Image on Exit? If you specify No for this option, the browse screen disappears when the user exits. If you specify Yes, an image of the browse screen remains on the screen. (It will be tucked behind your application's custom menus.) Use the space bar to select Yes or No.

Display Browse Menu? If you specify Yes for this option, the user can access the Browse menu by pressing **F10**. If you specify No, the user cannot access the Browse menu. Use the space bar to select Yes or No.

Use Previous Browse Table? If you specify No for this option, a new browse screen is constructed each time the user browses records. If you specify Yes, settings from the previous browse screen are used on the current browse screen. Use the space bar to select Yes or No.

Follow Record after Update? If you specify Yes for this option, the highlight follows a record to its new position in a database if a change affects the sort order. If you specify No, the highlight does not follow a record to its new sort-order position. (This option is effective only when an index is in use.) Use the space bar to select Yes or No.

Compress Display? If you specify No for this option, the standard browse screen is used, displaying 17 records at a time. If you specify Yes, some text surrounding the standard browse screen is removed, and the browse screen displays 19 records. Use the space bar to select Yes or No.

EXAMPLE

Figure 16.5 shows a completed sample dialog box for an action that displays a browse screen. In this example, the browse screen displays all fields and all records in

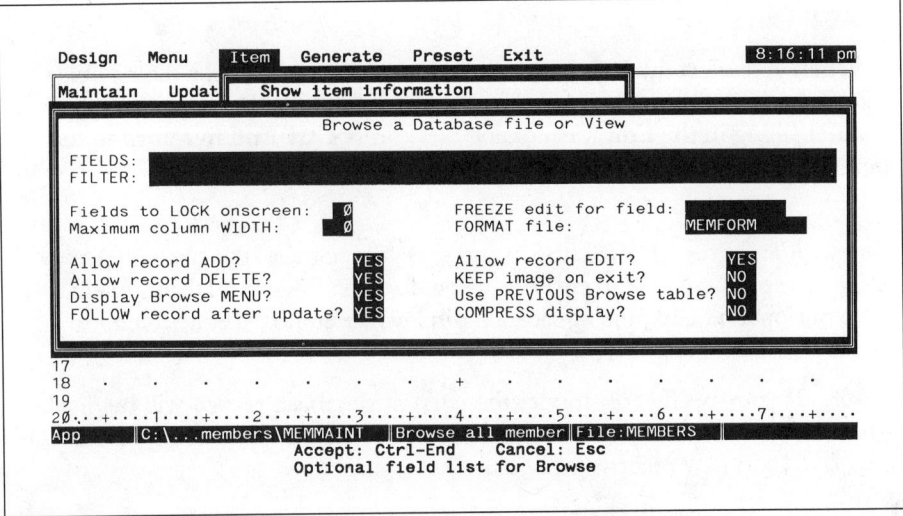

FIGURE 16.5: A sample dialog box for the Browse (Add, Delete, Edit) action. The user can add, edit, and delete records. The picture functions, picture templates, and edit options defined in a custom form named MEMFORM will be used on the browse screen.

the current database. The cursor will not be locked into any particular field, nor will any field be frozen on the screen. No maximum column width is defined. The browse screen will use picture templates, picture functions, and edit options defined in a custom screen named MEMFORM. The user will be able to add new records, edit records, and delete records, using the browse screen.

Displaying Data in a Custom Form

Assign the Edit Form action to a menu option, values list, or batch process operation when you want a menu item to display a single record from the database on a custom form.

SEQUENCE OF STEPS

From the application design screen:

    press **F3** or **F4** until the desired object is current

    F10

    Item/**C**hange Action/**E**dit Form (Add, Delete, Edit) [←]

USAGE

When you select the Edit Form (Add, Delete, Edit) action, a dialog box with a list of options appears. The following sections describe these options.

After filling in the Edit form dialog box, press **Ctrl-End** to return to the Item pull-down menu.

Format File   Press Pick (**Shift-F1**) and select the name of the custom form to use. You can select <create> to create a custom form on the spur of the moment. If you leave this option blank, the application displays the standard edit screen.

Mode   If you specify edit mode, the current database record will be displayed when the user selects the menu option. If you specify append mode, the user will be able to add new records immediately.

Fields   If a custom form is not in use, you can limit the edit screen display to only certain fields. Press Pick (**Shift-F1**) and select fields to display on the edit screen.

FILTER, SCOPE, and WHILE   For a description of this option, see the section "FILTER, FOR, SCOPE, and WHILE" earlier in this chapter.

Allow Record Add?   If you specify Yes for this option, the user can add new records. If you specify No, the user cannot add new records through this custom form. Press the space bar to select Yes or No.

Allow Record Edit?   If you specify Yes for this option, the user can edit data through this custom form. If you specify No, the user can view but not change data. Press the space bar to select Yes or No.

Allow Record Delete?   If you specify Yes for this option, the user can mark records for deletion (using **Ctrl-U**) through this form. If you specify No, the user cannot mark records for deletion. Press the space bar to select Yes or No.

Keep Image on Exit?   If you specify No for this option, the custom form disappears from the screen when the user finishes with it. If you specify Yes, an image of the form remains on the screen after the user exits. Press the space bar to select Yes or No.

Display Edit Menu? If you specify Yes for this option, the user can access the edit menu by pressing Menu (**F10**). If you specify No, the user cannot access the edit menu by pressing **F10**. Press the space bar to select Yes or No.

Use Previous Browse Table? If you specify No for this option, a new browse table is constructed when the user presses **F2** to switch to the browse screen. If you specify Yes, the previously defined browse screen is reinstated. Press the space bar to select Yes or No.

Follow Record after Update? If you specify Yes for this option and an index is in use, the cursor follows the record to its new position if the user changes a field that affects the sort order. If you specify No, the cursor does not follow the record. Press the space bar to select Yes or No.

EXAMPLE

Figure 16.6 shows a sample completed Edit Form (Add, Delete, Edit) dialog box. This dialog box will display a custom form named MEMFORM to allow the user to append new records to the current database.

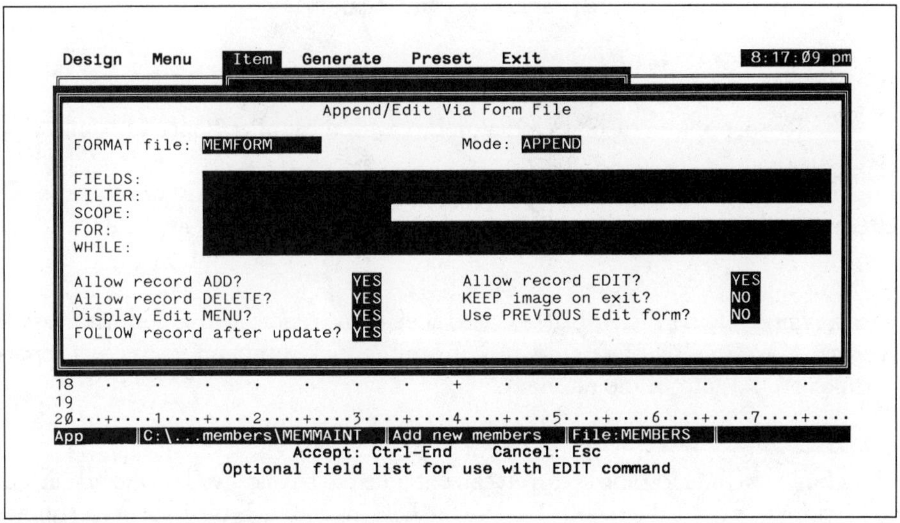

FIGURE 16.6: A sample Edit Form (Add, Delete, Edit) dialog box that allows the user to add new records to the current database, using a custom form named MEMFORM.

Displaying or Printing Data

Selecting the Display or Print option allows you to display data on a screen or printer. When Display or Print is selected, the following submenu appears:

Report	REPORT FORM
Labels	LABEL FORM
Display/List	DISPLAY/LIST

PRINTING REPORTS

The Report option lets you define a report format to use to print data from the database.

SEQUENCE OF STEPS

From the application design screen:

press **F3** or **F4** until the desired object is current
F10
Item/**C**hange Action/**D**isplay or Print/**R**eport [↵]

USAGE

The Report option displays a dialog box with a list of options. The following sections describe these options.

After filling in the Print a Report dialog box, press **Ctrl- End** to return to the Item pull-down menu.

Form Name   Press Pick (**Shift-F1**) and specify the report format for printing the report. You can also select <create> from the Pick submenu to create a report format on the spur of the moment.

Heading   In the Heading box, you can enter text to be displayed on the first line of each printed page of the report. Enclose the heading in brackets ([ ]) or single quotation marks ('). Do not use double quotation marks (") in the report heading.

Report Format Press the space bar to move between the options Full Detail (to print all records used to obtain totals and subtotals) and Summary Only (to print only subtotals and totals, without detail lines).

Heading Format Select Plain (to not print the date and page number in the report heading) or Include Date and Page (to display them).

Before Printing To eject the page currently in the printer before printing a report, select Skip to New Page. Otherwise, press the space bar to scroll to the Do Not Eject option.

Send Output To Press the space bar to scroll through the options Printer, Disk File, Screen, and Ask at Run Time. If you choose Ask at Run Time, the application displays a submenu that allows the user to select the screen, a printer, or a disk file as the output destination.

FILTER, SCOPE, FOR, and WHILE For a discussion of this option, see the section "FILTER, FOR, SCOPE, and WHILE" earlier in this chapter.

EXAMPLE

Figure 16.7 shows a sample completed Print a Report dialog box that displays data from the current database using a report format named WELCOME. The report will be sent to the printer. Only records that have the current month and year in the StartDate field will be printed.

PRINTING LABELS

Assign the Labels action when you want your application to print labels.

SEQUENCE OF STEPS

From the application design screen:

    press **F3** or **F4** until the desired object is current
    F10
    Item/Change Action/Display or Print/Labels [↵]

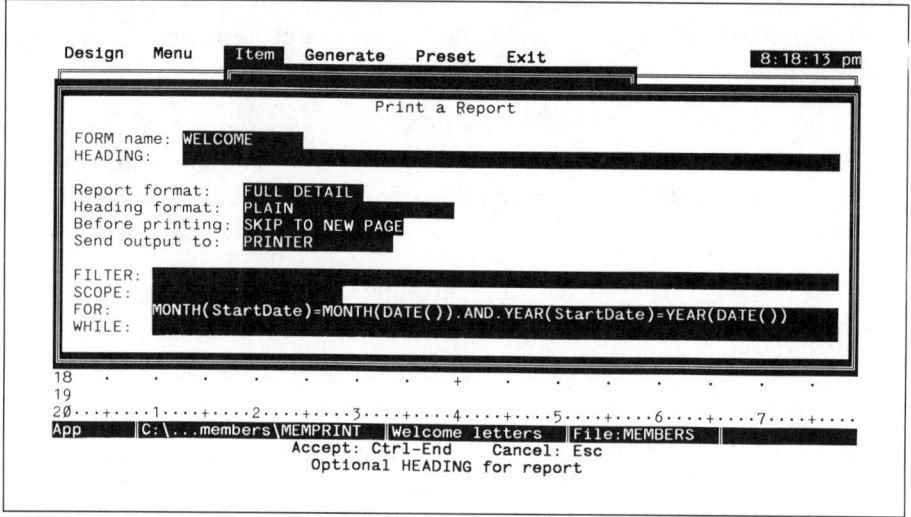

FIGURE 16.7: A sample Print a Report dialog box that prints a report using a report format file named WELCOME. The report will include only records that have the current month and date in the StartDate field.

USAGE

When you select Labels, you'll see a dialog box with a list of options. The following sections describe these options.

After filling in the Print Labels dialog box, press **Ctrl-End** to return to the Items menu.

Form Name To specify the format to use for printing labels, press Pick (**Shift-F1**) while the cursor is in the Form Name box and then select the label format name from the submenu displayed. If no existing format is appropriate, you can select <create> to create a mailing label format.

Send Output To Press the space bar to scroll through the options Printer, Disk File, Screen, and Ask at Run Time. If you choose Ask at Run Time, the application will present the options for printing on the screen, a printer, or a disk file when the user runs the application and opts to print labels.

Print Sample? If you specify Yes for this option, the application prints samples to help the user align the labels in the printer. If you specify No, the application prints labels immediately, without first printing any samples. Press the space bar to select Yes or No.

FILTER, SCOPE, FOR, and WHILE   For a description of this option, see the section "FILTER, FOR, SCOPE, and WHILE" earlier in this chapter.

EXAMPLE

Figure 16.8 shows a sample completed dialog box used to print mailing labels, using a label format file named MEMLABEL. The user will be given the opportunity to print sample labels to make sure the labels align in the printer before printing the actual labels. Labels will be printed only for records that have the current month and year in the STARTDATE field.

DISPLAYING RECORDS WITHOUT A REPORT FORMAT

Choose the Display/List option when you want your application to display database records without using a report or label format.

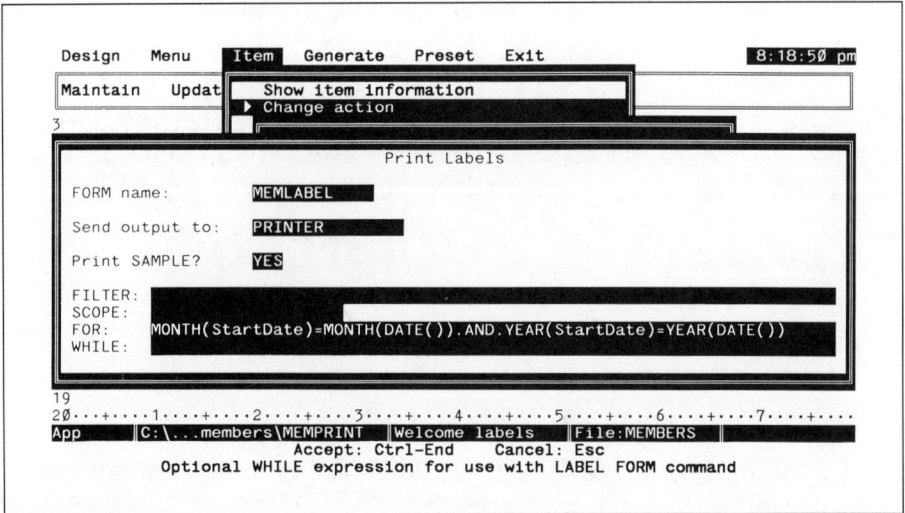

FIGURE 16.8: A sample Print Labels dialog box that prints samples and labels using a label format named MEMLABEL. Labels will be printed only for records that have the current month and year in the StartDate field.

SEQUENCE OF STEPS

From the application design screen:

    press **F3** or **F4** until the desired object is current

    F10

    Item/**C**hange Action/**D**isplay or Print/**D**isplay/List [↵]

USAGE

The Display/List action displays database records using a simple columnar format provided by the DISPLAY and LIST commands in the dBASE IV programming language. The Display/List option presents a dialog box with a list of options. The following sections describe these options.

After completing the Display/List dialog box, press **Ctrl-End** to return to the Item menu.

Pause at Full Page/Screen   If you specify Yes for this option, the display pauses for a keystroke after displaying 20 lines of text. If you specify No, all records are displayed without any pauses. Press the space bar to select Yes or No.

Send Output To   Press the space bar to scroll through the options Printer, Disk File, Screen, and Ask at Run Time. If you choose Ask at Run Time, the application presents options to the user (as shown in the next example).

Include Record Numbers?   If you specify Yes for this option, the record number is printed to the left of each record. If you specify No, record numbers are omitted. Press the space bar to select Yes or No.

Fields   If you do not specify a field, all fields from the database are displayed. To limit the display to specific fields, press Pick (**Shift-F1**) and select fields to display. You can also type field names in the order in which you want them to appear in the display, separating names with a comma.

DISPLAYING OR PRINTING DATA — 593

FILTER, SCOPE, FOR, and WHILE   For a description of this option, see the section "FILTER, FOR, SCOPE, and WHILE" earlier in this chapter.

EXAMPLE

Figure 16.9 shows a sample completed Display/List dialog box. In this example, the user is asked whether to display records on the screen or printer, or to store copies of the records in an ASCII text file. Only the fields LASTNAME, FIRSTNAME, and PHONE are displayed. All records are displayed, however, because no filtering conditions have been specified.

Figures 16.10 and 16.11 show the Display/List action from the user's perspective. In Figure 16.10, the screen asks where to send the output of the display or list (using DOS device names such as CON:, LPT1:, and so forth). Selecting the FILE option sends output to a text file named REPORT.TXT. If a file named REPORT.TXT already exists, the screen asks for permission before overwriting the existing file.

Figure 16.11 shows the resulting output on the screen (assuming that the user selected CON: from the menu of output options). This display uses the simple columnar format of the dBASE IV programming language LIST and DISPLAY commands.

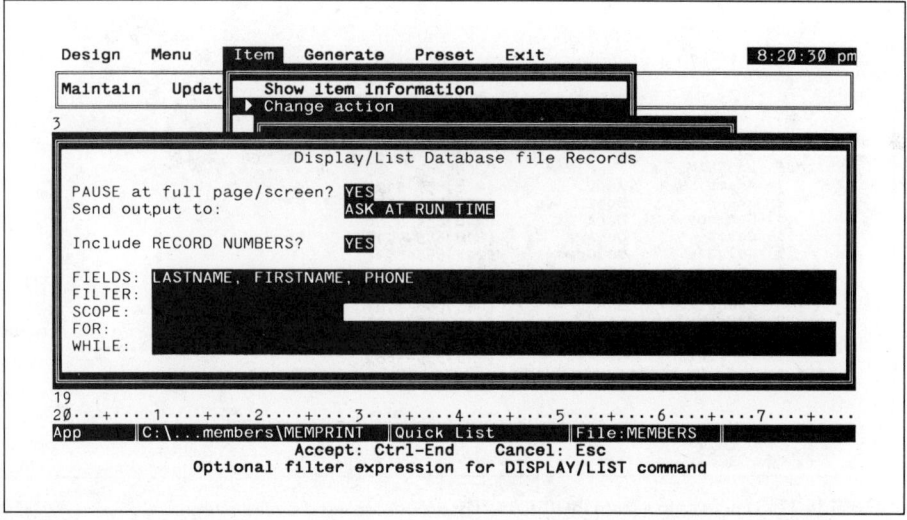

FIGURE 16.9: A sample Display/List dialog box. The menu item to which this action is assigned will ask the user where to display the records. It will then display the LASTNAME, FIRSTNAME, and PHONE fields from the current database.

594 — CH. 16 ASSIGNING ACTIONS TO APPLICATION OBJECTS

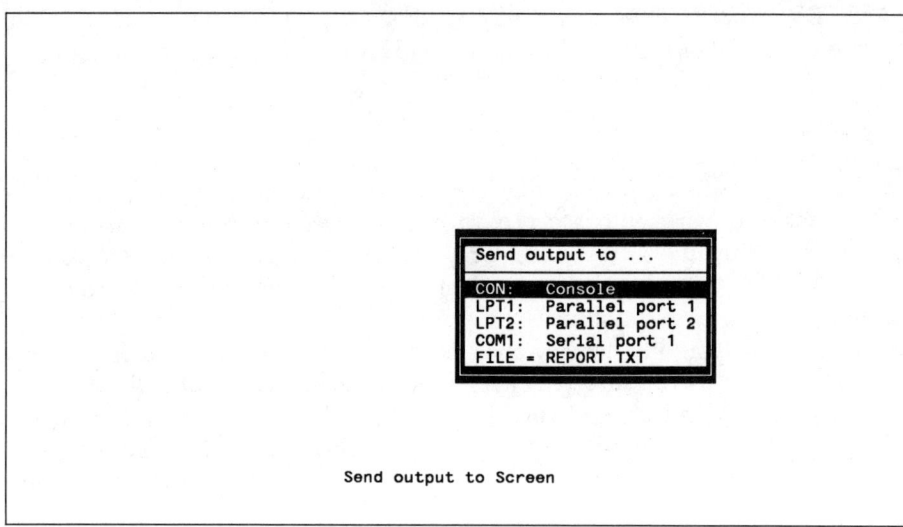

FIGURE 16.10: The application asks the user where to send output from the database.

FIGURE 16.11: Sample output from the Display/List action displayed on the screen.

Performing File Operations

When you select Perform File Operation as the action for an application item, dBASE displays a submenu with the options shown here:

File Copy	COPY FILE
Add Records from File	APPEND FROM
Copy Records to File	COPY TO
Substitute Field Values	REPLACE
Mark Records for Deletion	DELETE
Unmark Records	RECALL
Discard Marked Records	PACK
Generate Index	INDEX ON
Reindex Database	REINDEX
Physically Sort Database	SORT TO
Import Foreign File	IMPORT
Export Foreign File	EXPORT

The following sections discuss the submenu options.

COPYING FILES

Select the File Copy action when you want one of your application's menu options to copy a file. Note that this option can be used to copy any file, but it requires the use of extensions with both the source and destination file names. Wildcard characters are not permitted.

SEQUENCE OF STEPS

From the application design screen:

    press **F3** or **F4** until the desired object is current

    F10

    Item/**C**hange Action/**P**erform File Operation/**F**ile Copy [⏎]

USAGE

When you select File Copy, you are prompted to enter the name of the file to copy from and the name of the file to copy to. If a file with the name specified in the To box already exists, it will be overwritten when the user selects this option from your application.

You can use this option to copy any type of file. Be sure to include the file name extension in both the source and target destinations. DOS wildcard characters are not allowed. (You can use the Run a DOS Program action, discussed later in this chapter, to copy files using wildcards.)

If you want your application to allow the user to pick the name of the file to copy, assign the File Copy option as the action for a files list object. Then specify **&LISTVAL** in the dialog box as the name of the file to copy.

EXAMPLE

Figure 16.12 shows an example of an action that copies the database named MEMBERS.DBF to a file named MEMBERS.BAK. The warning *TO file will be overwritten* is displayed above the file names to remind you that the destination file will be overwritten in the process of copying the source file when the user initiates the action.

ADDING RECORDS FROM A FILE

Select the Add Records from File option when you want your application to add records from one database file to the database in use when the user selects the option.

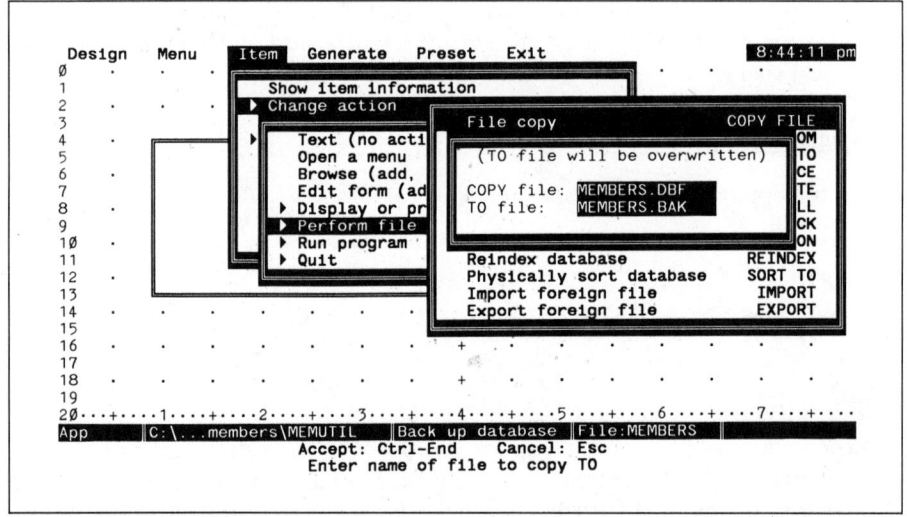

FIGURE 16.12: An example of a Copy File dialog box that copies a database file named MEMBERS.DBF to a file named MEMBERS.BAK.

SEQUENCE OF STEPS

From the application design screen:

> Press **F3** or **F4** until the desired object is current
> **F10**
> Item/Change Action/Perform File Operation/Add Records from File [⏎]

USAGE

When you select Add Records from File, you'll see a dialog box with a list of choices. The following sections describe these choices.

After completing the dialog box, press **Ctrl-End** to return to the Item pull-down menu.

Add Records from File/Array   Enter the name of the file to copy records from, either by pressing Pick (**Shift-F1**) or by typing the file name. An array refers to data stored in RAM. It is a complex structure primarily used by dBASE IV programmers. (Refer to Appendix C for more information about arrays.) The Copy Records to File option, discussed in the next section, lets you copy records to an array. You cannot select an array name from the Pick submenu.

Of Type   Press the space bar to specify the type of file from which records will be copied. Your options are DBF (a dBASE IV database file), dBASE II, FW2 (Framework II), RPD (RapidFile), Delimited (delimited ASCII text file), Array (data in memory), SDF (structured ASCII text file), DIF (data interchange format), SYLK (Multiplan Sylk format), and WKS (Lotus 1-2-3 format).

Delimiter   Specify a delimiter if you are importing a delimited text file that does not use double quotation marks to delimit character strings.

FOR   For a description of this option, see the section "FILTER, FOR, SCOPE, and WHILE" earlier in this chapter.

EXAMPLE

Figure 16.13 shows an example dialog box that copies all the records from a database named NEWDATA.DBF into the current database.

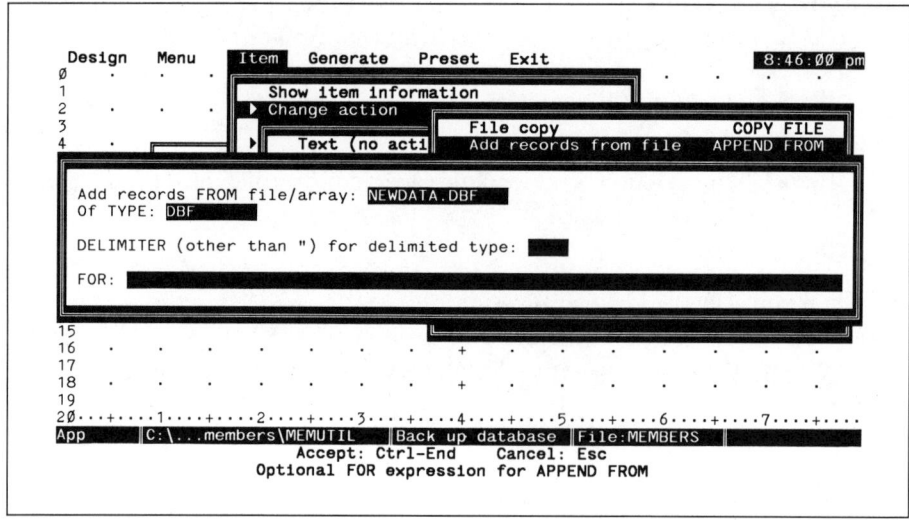

FIGURE 16.13: A sample dialog box that tells the application to copy all records from a database named NEWDATA.DBF into the current database.

COPYING RECORDS TO A FILE

Use the Copy Records to File option when you want your application to copy records from the database file in use (when the user selects the option) to a new file. Note that, unlike the File Copy option discussed earlier, this option copies only database records. Also, this option can isolate specific records for copying, whereas File Copy can copy only an entire file.

SEQUENCE OF STEPS

From the application design screen:

>press **F3** or **F4** until the desired object is current
>**F10**
>Item/**C**hange Action/**P**erform File Operation/**C**opy Records to File [◄─┘]

USAGE

When you select Copy Records to File, you'll see a dialog box with a list of options. The following sections describe these options.

Copy Record to File/Array   Specify the name of the file to copy records to. If you are copying records to an array, do not include a file name extension. Press **Ctrl-End** after completing the dialog box.

Of Type   Select a type of file to copy records to. (See "Of Type" in the preceding section, "Adding New Records to a File.)

Delimiter   If you are exporting copied records to a delimited ASCII file, specify a delimiter (if you want to use a character other than double quotation marks).

Fields   If you do not specify a field, all fields in the database are copied to the new file. You can select specific fields by pressing Pick (**Shift-F1**) or by typing field names, separating them with a comma.

SCOPE, OR, and WHILE   For a description of this option, see the section "FILTER, FOR, SCOPE, and WHILE" earlier in this chapter.

EXAMPLE

Figure 16.14 shows an example of a Copy Records to File dialog box that copies data from the current database file to a Lotus 1-2-3 worksheet file named 123MEMB.WKS.

SUBSTITUTING FIELD VALUES

Select the Substitute Field Values option when you want your application to change the values in a database field. Note that the database in use when the user selects the option from the application is the only database that the operation affects.

SEQUENCE OF STEPS

From the application design screen:

    press **F3** or **F4** until the desired object is current
    F10
    Item/**C**hange Action/**P**erform File Operations/**S**ubstitute Field Values [⏎]

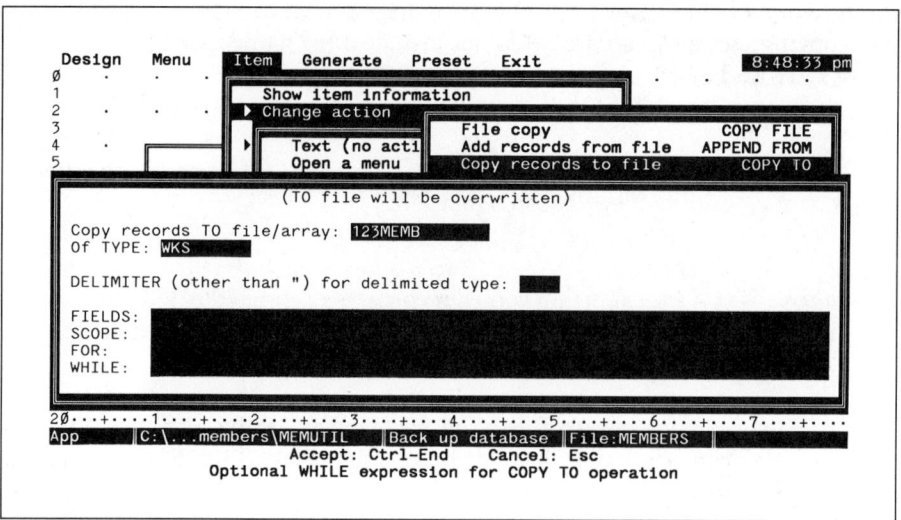

FIGURE 16.14: A sample Copy Records to File dialog box. Data from the current database file is copied to a Lotus 1-2-3 worksheet file named 123MEMB.WKS.

USAGE

When you select Substitute Field Values, dBASE displays a dialog box with a list of options. The following sections describe these options.

Press **Ctrl-End** after completing the dialog box.

SCOPE, FOR, and WHILE If you do not specify any SCOPE, FOR, or WHILE conditions, the substitution is effective only in the current database record. To change values in all database records, specify ALL as the SCOPE condition. To change values in specific records, enter a filter condition in the FOR box. For further information, see the section "FILTER, FOR, SCOPE, and WHILE" earlier in this chapter.

The Field Named Enter the name of each field in which you want to change or replace some value. You can select field names from a submenu by pressing Pick (**Shift-F1**).

With This Value For each field that you specify for a change, enter an expression that defines the new value. For example, to increase a field named UnitPrice by 15 percent, enter the expression **UnitPrice * 1.15**. To change all values in a logical field named UPDATED to .T., specify **ALL** as the SCOPE condition, **UPDATED** as the field to replace the contents of, and **.T.** as the replacement value. Dates must be enclosed in curly braces, and characters must be enclosed in quotation marks.

Additive Option?   This option applies only to Memo fields. If you specify Yes for this option, the value in the With This Value box is added to the end of any existing text in the Memo field. If you leave this option set to No, new text replaces any existing text in the Memo field.

EXAMPLE

Figure 16.15 shows a sample Substitute Field Values dialog box where you enter the scope, field names, and substitute values. In this example, a field named Status is replaced with the word "PAID" in all records that have zero in the AmtDue (amount due) field.

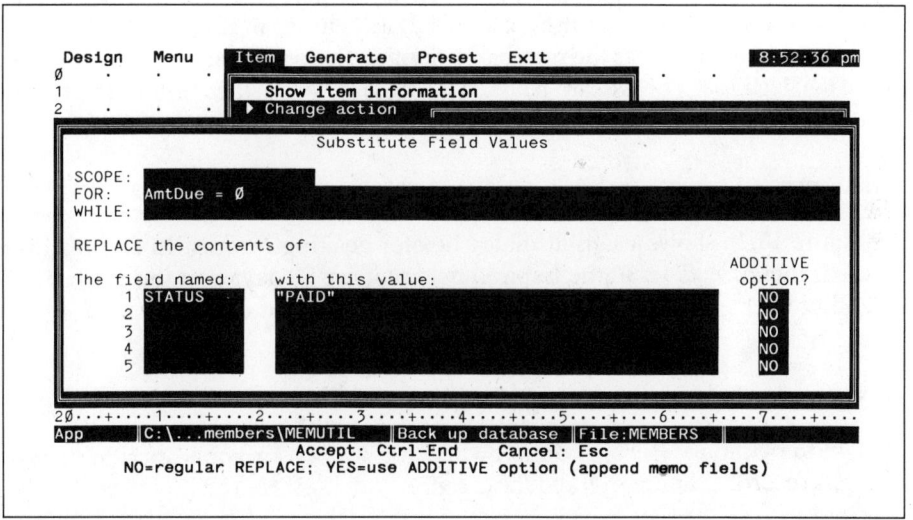

FIGURE 16.15: Substitute Field Values dialog box used to define the field names and their substitute values when the SCOPE, FOR, and WHILE conditions are met. In this example, the Status field is filled with the word PAID in all records where the amount due is zero.

Marking Records for Deletion

Select the Mark Records for Deletion option when you want an application option to mark records for deletion.

SEQUENCE OF STEPS

From the application design screen:

> press **F3** or **F4** until the desired object is current
> **F10**
> Item/Change Action/Perform File Operation/Mark Records for Deletion [←]

USAGE

When you select Mark Records for Deletion, you'll see a dialog box with the options SCOPE, FOR, and WHILE. If you leave all three options blank, only the current record is marked for deletion. To mark all records in the database for deletion, enter **ALL** as the SCOPE condition. To mark specific records for deletion, enter a filter condition in the FOR box. (For more information, see the section "FILTER, FOR, SCOPE, and WHILE" earlier in this chapter.)

This option only marks the records for deletion; it does not actually remove them from the database. The Discard Marked Records option on the Perform File Operations submenu permanently removes marked records from the database.

EXAMPLE

Figure 16.16 shows a sample dialog box for deleting records. In this example, records that have dates in the Expired field that are 60 days past the current date and that have .F. in the Current field will be marked for deletion.

Unmarking Records

Use the Unmark Records option when you want your application to unmark (recall) records that are marked for deletion.

SEQUENCE OF STEPS

From the application design screen:

> press **F3** or **F4** until the desired object is current

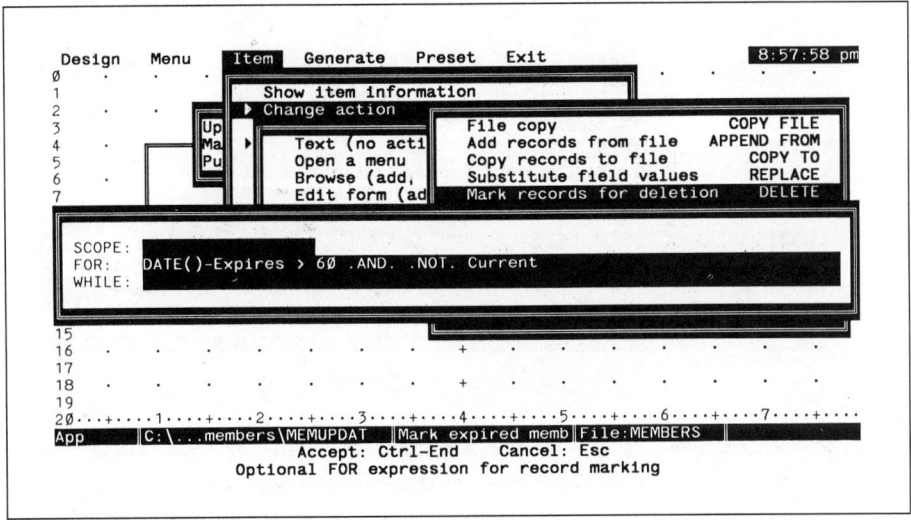

FIGURE 16.16: A sample dialog box for marking records for deletion. Only records that have dates in the Expired field that are 60 days past the current date and that have .F. in the Current field are marked for deletion.

F10

Item/Change Action/Perform File Operation/Unmark Records [↵]

USAGE

When you select the option Unmark Records, dBASE displays a dialog box that presents the options SCOPE, FOR, and WHILE. If you leave all three options blank, only the current record is unmarked. To unmark all the records in the database, enter **ALL** as the SCOPE condition. To unmark records that meet a search criterion, enter a filter condition in the FOR box. (See the section titled "FILTER, FOR, SCOPE, and WHILE" earlier in this chapter.)

EXAMPLE

Figure 16.17 shows the Unmark Records dialog box. In this example, the ALL scope option is used to unmark all marked records in the database.

DISCARDING MARKED RECORDS

The Discard Marked Records option permanently removes all records that are marked for deletion.

604 — CH. 16 ASSIGNING ACTIONS TO APPLICATION OBJECTS

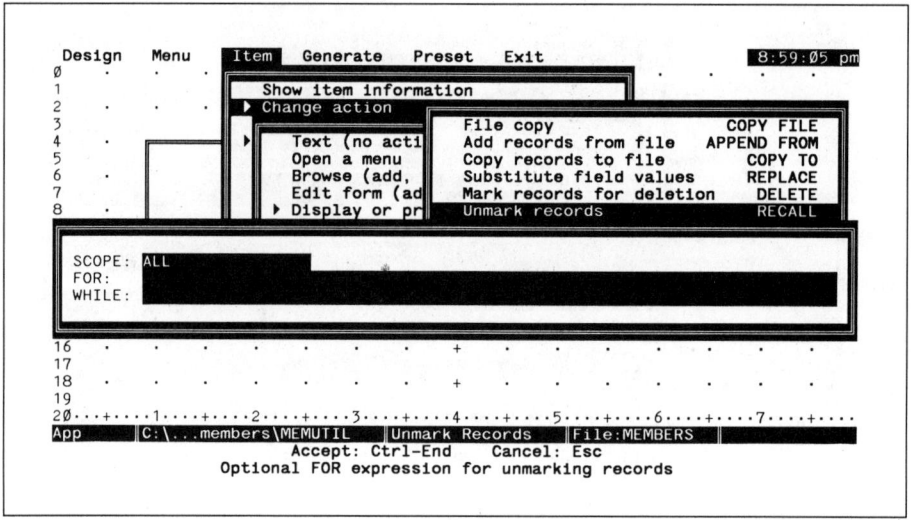

FIGURE 16.17: The Unmark Records dialog box. In this example, the ALL scope option is used to unmark all records in the database that are currently marked for deletion.

SEQUENCE OF STEPS

From the application design screen:

    press **F3** or **F4** until the desired object is current

    F10

    Item/**C**hange Action/**P**erform File Operation/**D**iscard Marked Records [↵]

USAGE

To permanently remove records that are marked for deletion from a database, assign the action Discard Marked Records to a menu item or batch file operation. When you select Discard Marked Records, you'll see the message *This selection will cause all records marked for deletion to be removed from the database. OK*. Press **Ctrl-End** to accept the action or **Esc** if you change your mind.

While the application is deleting records, a counter appears on the screen indicating the number of records remaining as marked records are deleted.

EXAMPLE

Figure 16.18 shows the message displayed when the Discard Marked Records option is selected from the Perform File Operation submenu. If you press

PERFORMING FILE OPERATIONS — 605

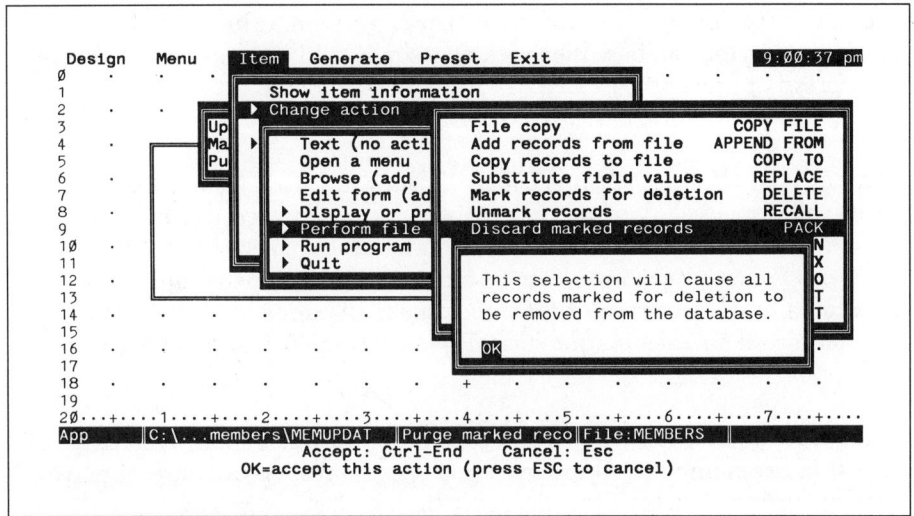

FIGURE 16.18: Discard marked records message. As indicated at the bottom of the screen, you can press **Ctrl-End** to accept this action or Esc to cancel the selection.

Ctrl-End at this point, the action is assigned to the current item. If you press **Esc**, the action is not assigned.

GENERATING AN INDEX

Use the Generate Index option when you want your application to create a new index. (However, it is more efficient to create all indexes through the database design screen *before* you enter the Applications Generator.)

SEQUENCE OF STEPS

From the application design screen:

    press **F3** or **F4** until the desired object is current

    F10

    Item/**C**hange Action/**P**erform File Operation/**G**enerate Index [↵]

USAGE

When you select Generate Index, you'll see a dialog box with a list of options. The following sections describe these options.

Press **Ctrl-End** after completing the dialog box.

Index Key Expression Enter the index key expression, using the rules discussed in Chapter 4. You can base the index on a single field, such as LastName, or on an expression, such as UPPER(LastName + FirstName).

Index First Key Expression Only (Unique)? If you specify No for this option, the index will display all database records when it is activated. If you specify Yes, the index will limit all displays to the first occurrence of each unique value in the database. For example, if you base an index on a field named State and the database contains numerous records for each state, a Unique index will display only the first record for each unique state. Press the space bar to select Yes or No.

Index in Descending Order? If you specify No for this option, records are displayed in ascending sorted order. If you specify Yes, records are displayed in descending sorted order. Press the space bar to select Yes or No.

Generate Index to Index File Enter the name of the index file to create if you are *not* going to use the standard dBASE IV index file (which uses the extension .MDX). The index will be stored under the file name you specify, with the extension .NDX.

Or Tag Use this option to create a standard dBASE IV index, which is stored with other indexes in the .MDX index file. The name can be up to eight characters long and cannot contain any spaces, punctuation, or file name extension.

Of MDX File By default, the dBASE IV production index file is stored in a file with the same name as the database file plus the extension .MDX. To add the new index to the standard index file, enter the database name at this prompt, either with no extension or with the .MDX extension (but do not use .DBF or any other extension in this entry).

EXAMPLE

Figure 16.19 shows the Generate Index dialog box with the index expression based on the uppercase equivalents of the LastName and FirstName fields. The index will be stored with the tag name NAMES in the production index file MEMBERS.MDX.

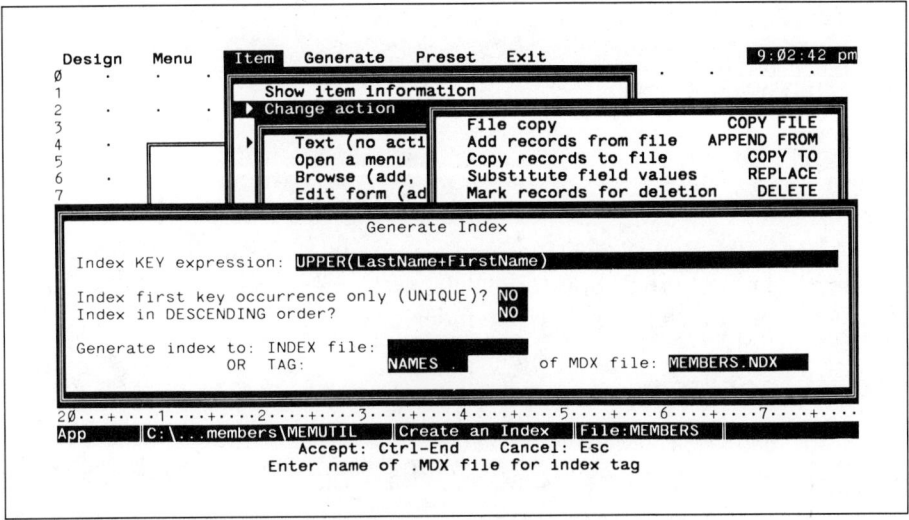

FIGURE 16.19: A sample Generate Index dialog box that tells the application to create an index named NAMES and store that index in the production index file MEMBERS.MDX.

REINDEXING A DATABASE

Use the Reindex Database option when you want your application to allow the user to rebuild indexes. Indexes generally need to be rebuilt only if a power outage or some other problem corrupts index files that are stored in RAM. Because such problems occur from time to time, all applications should provide this option.

SEQUENCE OF STEPS

From the application design screen:

> press **F3** or **F4** until the desired object is current
> **F10**
> Item/**C**hange Action/**P**erform File Operation/**R**eindex Database [↵]

USAGE

When you assign the Reindex Database action to an option in your application, you'll see the message *This selection will cause all active index files for the currently selected database or view to be rebuilt. OK?* Press **Ctrl-End** to accept the action or **Esc** to cancel it.

EXAMPLE

Figure 16.20 shows the message box displayed when the Reindex Database option is selected.

SORTING A DATABASE

Select the Physically Sort Database option when you want your application to create a separate, sorted copy of the database currently in use. (As discussed in Chapter 4, it's much faster to use an index to sort records.)

SEQUENCE OF STEPS

From the application design screen:

    press **F3** or **F4** until the desired object is current

    F10

    Item/**C**hange Action/**P**erform File Operation/**P**hysically Sort Database [⏎]

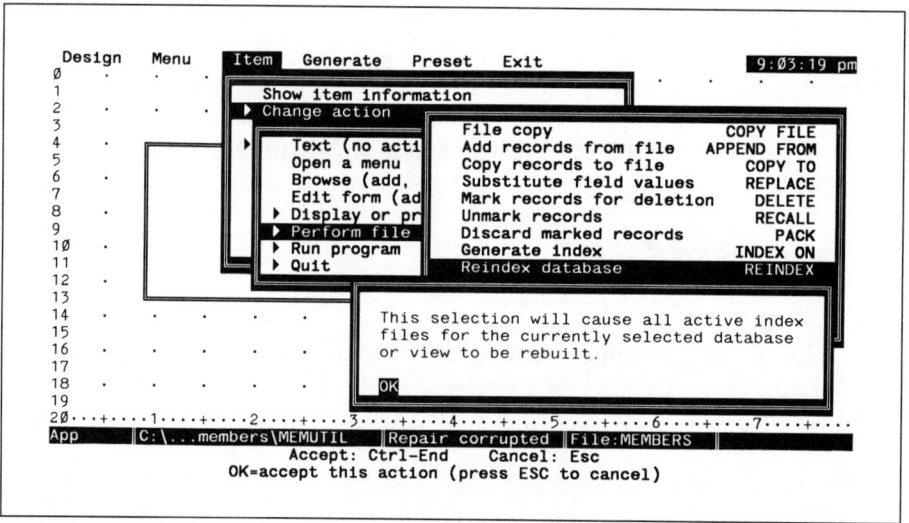

FIGURE 16.20: Reindex Database dialog box displaying the message that all the active indexes for the current database will be rebuilt. As indicated at the bottom of the screen, you can press **Ctrl-End** to accept this action or press **Esc** to cancel the selection.

USAGE

When you select Physically Sort Database, dBASE displays a dialog box with a list of options. The following sections describe these options.

Press **Ctrl-End** after completing the dialog box.

To File   Enter the name of the file you want to copy the sorted records to. If a file of that name already exists when the user selects this option from your application, that file will be overwritten by the new data.

SCOPE, FOR, and WHILE   If you leave the SCOPE, FOR, and WHILE options blank, all records in the current database are copied to the sorted file. To limit the copy to specific records, you can enter a filter condition. (See the section "FILTER, FOR, SCOPE, and WHILE" earlier in this chapter.)

Sort Fields   Enter the names of fields used for sorting in order of importance. For example, to sort records by last name and by first name within identical last names, enter LastName as sort field 1 and FirstName as sort field 2. You can select field names from a submenu by pressing Pick (**Shift-F1**).

Ascending   Press the space bar to select either Ascending (smallest-to-largest order) or Descending (largest-to-smallest order).

Ignore Case   Press the space bar to select either Ignore Case (uppercase and lowercase distinctions do not affect the sort order) or Use Case (all lowercase letters appear after all uppercase letters in the sort order).

EXAMPLE

Figure 16.21 shows a sample Physically Sort a Database dialog box designed to sort the current database file on the StartDate field and store the sorted records in a database named TEMP.DBF.

IMPORTING FILES

Use the Import File option when you want your application to import data from a foreign data format.

610 — CH. 16 ASSIGNING ACTIONS TO APPLICATION OBJECTS

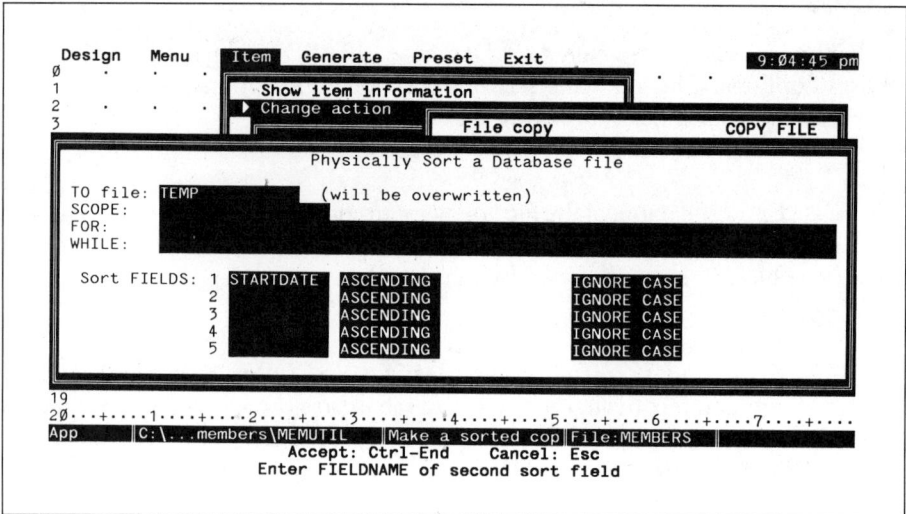

FIGURE 16.21: An example Physically Sort a Database File dialog box that sorts the current database on a field named StartDate and stores the sorted records in a separate database named TEMP.DBF.

SEQUENCE OF STEPS

From the application design screen:

    press **F3** or **F4** until the desired object is current
    F10
    Item/**C**hange Action/**P**erform File Operation/**I**mport Foreign File [←┘]

USAGE

When you select Import File, you'll be given two options in a dialog box; From File and Of Type. These are discussed in the following sections.

Press **Ctrl-End** after completing the dialog box.

From File   Enter the name of the file to import records from in this box. You can press Pick (**Shift-F1**) to select a file name from the current catalog or directory. If you want the application user to select the name of the foreign file, create a files list that displays the appropriate file names. Then assign the Import File action to the files list and enter **&LISTVAL** as the FROM file.

PERFORMING FILE OPERATIONS — 611

Of Type Use the space bar to scroll through foreign file types. Your options are PFS, dBASE II, RPD (RapidFile), FW2 (Framework II), and WK1 (Lotus 1-2-3). (See Chapter 14 for additional information about importing database records.)

EXAMPLE

Figure 16.22 shows a sample dialog box that imports records from a Lotus 1-2-3 file named CUSTOMER.WK1, in the current directory, into the current database file.

EXPORTING FILES

Assign the Export Foreign File action when you want your application to export records from the current database to the format required by a software product other than dBASE IV.

SEQUENCE OF STEPS

From the application design screen:

>   press **F3** or **F4** until the desired object is current
>
>   **F10**
>
>   Item/Change Action/Perform File Operation/Export Foreign File [←]

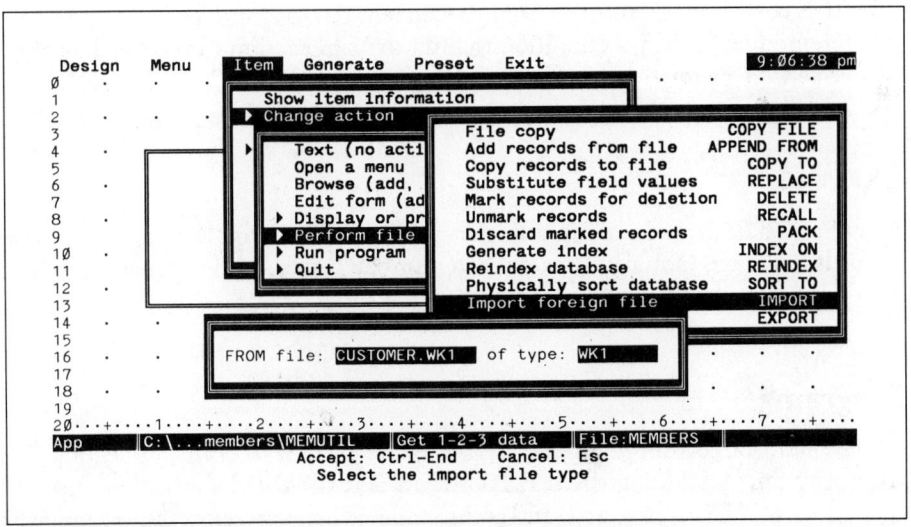

FIGURE 16.22: A sample Import Foreign File dialog box that imports records from a Lotus 1-2-3 worksheet file named CUSTOMER.WK1 into the current database file.

USAGE

When you select Export Foreign File, dBASE displays a dialog box with a list of options. The following sections describe these options.

Press **Ctrl-End** after filling in the dialog box.

To File   Specify the name of the file to export database records to at this prompt. If a file with the name you provide already exists when the user selects this option, that file will automatically be overwritten with new data.

Of Type   Use the space bar to scroll through foreign file formats. Your options are PFS, dBASE II, FW2 (Framework II), and RPD (RapidFile).

Fields   If you do not specify a field, all fields from the current database will be exported to the foreign file. To limit the exportation to particular fields, press Pick (**Shift-F1**) and select fields to export from the submenu that appears. You can also type the names of fields to export, separating names with a comma. Type the names in the order in which you want them to appear in the exported file.

SCOPE, FOR, and WHILE   If you do not specify a SCOPE, FOR, or WHILE condition, all records from the current database file will be exported to the foreign file. Specify a condition to limit the exportation to records that meet some search criterion. (See the section "FILTER, FOR, SCOPE, and WHILE" earlier in this chapter.)

EXAMPLE

Figure 16.23 shows a sample Export Foreign File dialog box used to export records that have January dates (month number 1) in the field named StartDate to a Framework II file named JanCust.

Running Programs

The Run Program option allows you to add actions to your application that run programs (including dBASE III PLUS and dBASE IV programs), batch processes, and DOS programs and commands. When you select this option from the Item pull-down menu, dBASE displays a submenu with the following

RUNNING PROGRAMS — 613

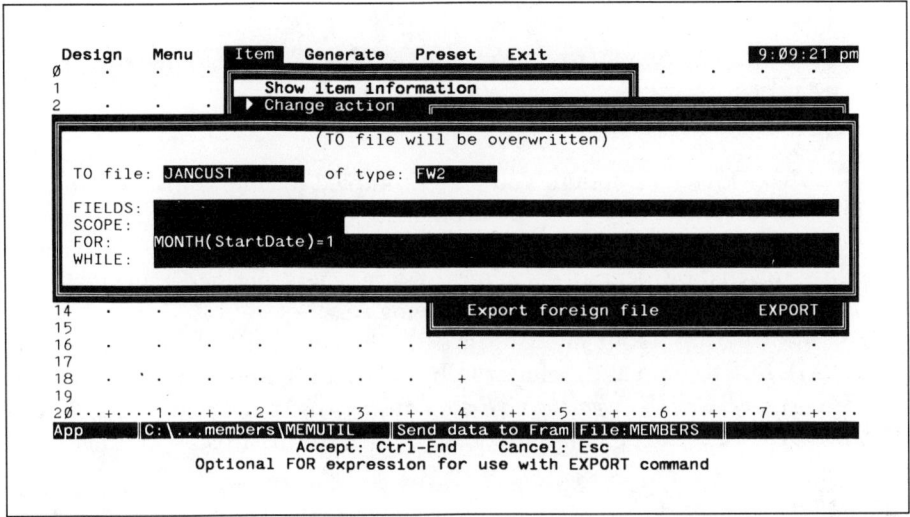

FIGURE 16.23: A sample Export Foreign File dialog box that exports records with January dates in the StartDate field to a Framework II file named JanCust.

options:

Do dBASE Program	DO
Execute Batch Process	
Insert dBASE Code	
Run DOS Program	RUN
Load/Call Binary File	LOAD/CALL
Play Back Macro	PLAY MACRO

Each of these options is discussed in the sections that follow.

EXECUTING A dBASE PROGRAM

Select the Do dBASE Program option when you want your application to execute a custom dBASE program.

SEQUENCE OF STEPS

From the application design screen:

press **F3** or **F4** until the desired object is current

F10

Item/Change Action/Run program/Do dBASE Program [↵]

USAGE

When you select this option, you'll be prompted to enter a dBASE program (command file) name and a list of parameters to pass to it. The name must be that of an existing dBASE III PLUS or dBASE IV command file. The parameters must match the order and data types of parameters specified in the PARAMETERS command in the command file being run.

For information about creating a dBASE command file and about the PARAMETERS command, refer to a dBASE IV programming language reference, such as *dBASE IV Programmer's Reference Guide*, also published by SYBEX, or the dBASE IV *Language Reference* that came with your dBASE IV package.

EXAMPLE

Figure 16.24 shows the dialog box used to execute a dBASE IV program called CALCPAY. In this example, the CALCPAY.PRG command file does not contain a PARAMETERS command, so the Parameters box is left blank.

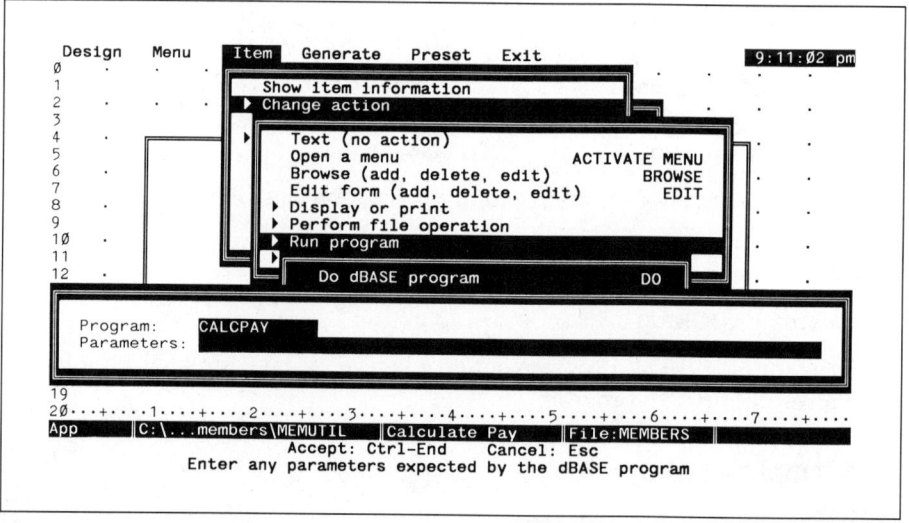

FIGURE 16.24: A sample Run Program dialog box that executes a dBASE command file named CALCPAY.PRG. No parameters are passed to the command file in this example.

Executing a Batch Process

When you want an option in your application to execute a batch process, assign the Execute Batch Process action to the menu item, to the list object, or to a single operation in another batch process.

SEQUENCE OF STEPS

From the application design screen:

> press **F3** or **F4** until the desired object is current
> **F10**
> Item/**C**hange Action/**R**un Program/**E**xecute BATCH Process [⏎]

USAGE

When you select the Execute BATCH Process option from the Run Program submenu, you'll be prompted to enter the name of the batch process to execute. Type the name or press Pick (**Shift-F1**) to select the name from a submenu.

EXAMPLE

Figure 16.25 shows a dialog box used to execute a batch file called RENEW, from the sample application presented in Appendix F in this book.

Inserting dBASE Code

The Insert dBASE Code option lets you create a series of dBASE IV programming commands to be executed when the user selects the attached menu item.

SEQUENCE OF STEPS

From the application design screen:

> press **F3** or **F4** until the desired object is current
> **F10**
> Item/**C**hange Action/**R**un Program/Insert dBASE Code [⏎]

USAGE

When you select the Insert dBASE Code option, you'll be prompted to enter programming commands in a blank window. You can use the same editing keys

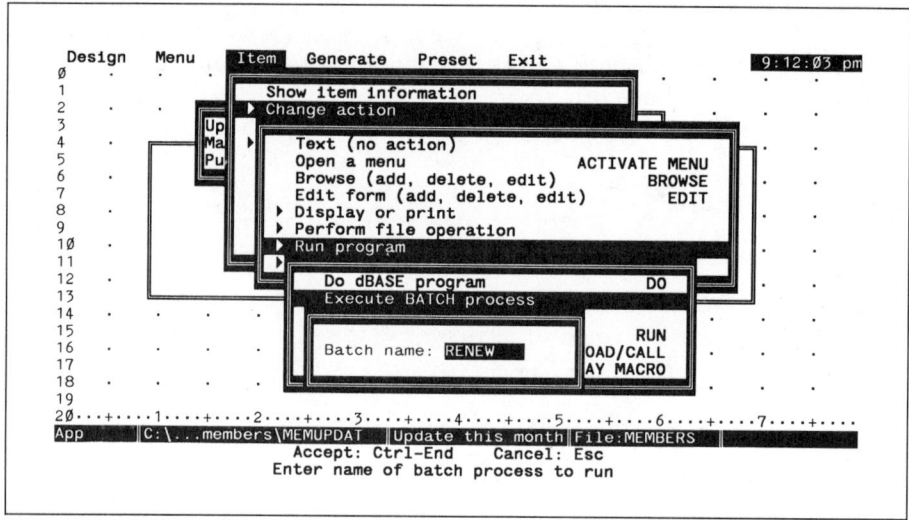

FIGURE 16.25: An example Run BATCH File dialog box that executes a batch process named RENEW. This example is taken from the sample membership management application presented in Appendix F of this book.

as in Memo fields, help text windows, and the dBASE IV program editor. However, when inserting dBASE code into an application, you are limited to 19 lines of text.

For information about creating a dBASE command file and about the PARAMETERS command, refer to a dBASE IV programming language reference, such as *dBASE IV Programmer's Reference Guide*, also published by SYBEX, or the dBASE IV *Language Reference* that came with your dBASE IV package.

EXAMPLE

Figure 16.26 shows a sample Insert dBASE Code editing screen. This screen contains dBASE IV programming language commands to create a window and display the message *Please insert a diskette in drive A:, then press any key to proceed* in it, and then to wait for the user to press a key. After the user presses a key, the RUN COPY commands tell DOS to copy all database (.DBF) and multiple index (.MDX) files from the current directory to the disk in drive A.

RUNNING A DOS PROGRAM

The Run DOS Program action causes dBASE IV to send a command to DOS.

RUNNING PROGRAMS — 617

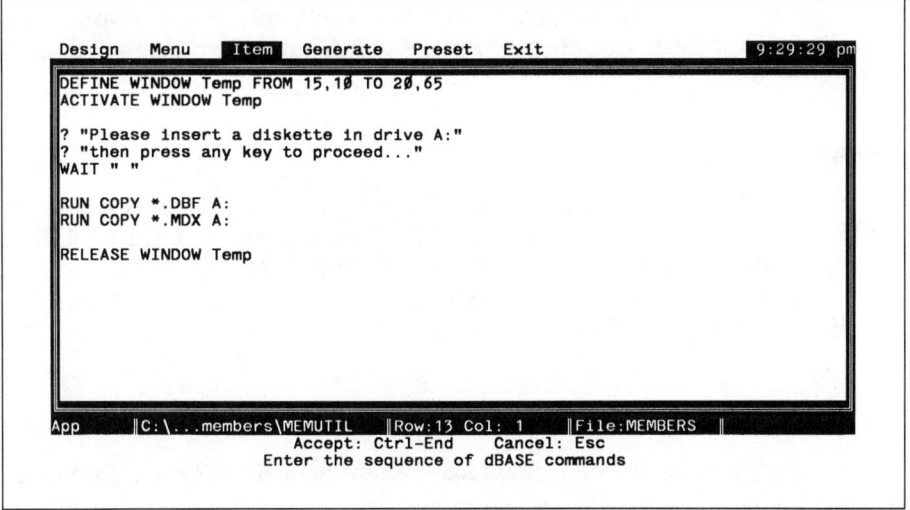

FIGURE 16.26: A sample Insert dBASE Code dialog box that displays a message and waits for the user to insert a disk in drive A. After the user presses a key, the database and multiple index files in the current directory are copied to the disk in drive A. Then the window and message are removed from the screen.

SEQUENCE OF STEPS

From the application design screen:

    press **F3** or **F4** until the desired object is current

    F10

    Item/**C**hange Action/**R**un Program/**R**un DOS Program [↵]

USAGE

When you select the Run DOS Program option, the screen displays the options Program and Parameters. Enter the DOS command or program name in the first box (for example, COPY or DIR). Enter any additional parameters in the Parameters box.

For example, to display the names of all database files in the current directory, you enter **DIR** as the program and ***.DBF** as the parameter. To copy all files with the name JULYGL to the disk in drive A, enter **COPY** as the program name and **JULYGL.*** as the parameter. After the application completes the DOS operation, dBASE returns the user to your custom application.

Note that if you want to execute an external DOS command such as XCOPY, the XCOPY.EXE file must be accessible from the current directory. Otherwise,

618 —— CH. 16 ASSIGNING ACTIONS TO APPLICATION OBJECTS

DOS returns the error message *Bad Command or File Name*. Only directories specified in the DOS PATH command (not the search path you may have assigned using dBASE) are searched.

EXAMPLE

Figure 16.27 shows a sample Run DOS Program dialog box that executes the DOS command XCOPY (the extended COPY command, available in DOS 3.2 and later implementations). The parameters *.DBF A: /M tell XCOPY to copy to the disk in drive A only database (.DBF) files that have been created or modified since the last XCOPY command (/M).

EXECUTING A BINARY FILE

The Load/Call Binary File option loads a binary file into RAM, if it has not already been loaded, and then executes that file.

SEQUENCE OF STEPS

From the application design screen:

press **F3** or **F4** until the desired object is current

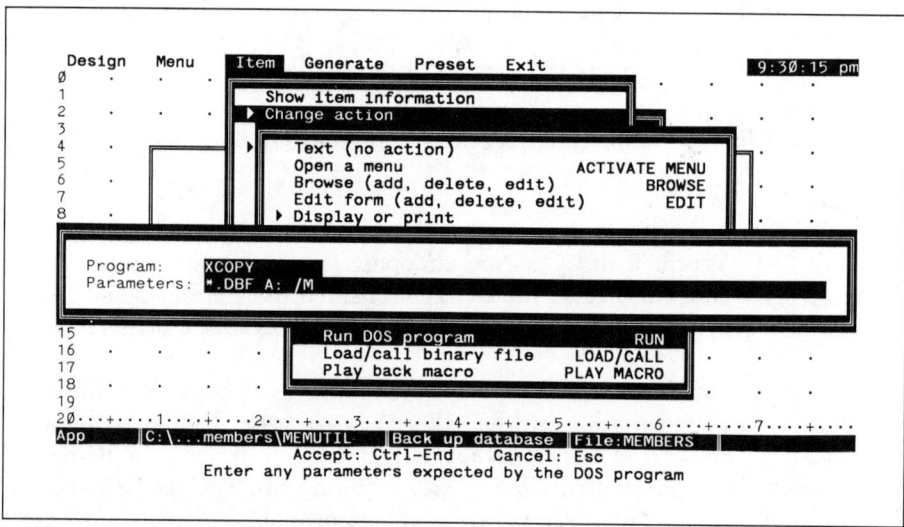

FIGURE 16.27: A sample Run DOS Program dialog box to copy database files from the current directory to the disk in drive A, using the DOS XCOPY command. The /M switch specifies that only new and modified files are to be copied.

F10

Item/Change Action/Run Program/Load/Call Binary File [⏎]

USAGE

The Load/Call Binary File option loads a binary file from the disk into RAM (if it has not previously been loaded) and then executes that binary file. The binary file name must have the extension .BIN. To create a binary file, you must be fluent in assembly language programming.

EXAMPLE

For discussion and examples of how to load binary files and pass parameters to them, refer to the LOAD and CALL commands in a dBASE IV programming language reference, such as *dBASE IV Programmer's Reference Guide*, also published by SYBEX, or the dBASE IV *Language Reference* that came with your dBASE IV package.

PLAYING BACK A KEYSTROKE MACRO

The Play Back Macro action causes your application to play back a series of recorded keystrokes.

SEQUENCE OF STEPS

From the application design screen:

    press **F3** or **F4** until the desired object is current

    F10

    Item/Change Action/Run Program/Play Back Macro [⏎]

USAGE

The Play Back Macro option plays back the keystrokes previously recorded in a keystroke macro. The keystroke macro that you want to play back must be available in the current macro library (as discussed in Chapter 13).

When you select the Play Back Macro option from the Run Program pull-down menu, you will be prompted to enter a macro name. In version 1.0 of dBASE IV, an anomaly occurs at this point. If you press Pick (**Shift-F1**), a window displays a list of all macro *library* names on the current directory. If you select a macro library name, that name appears in the dialog box, but when you run the application later, an error occurs. That's because the dialog box is expecting the name of a single keystroke, *not* the name of an entire macro library.

Executing keystroke macros within an application is further complicated by the fact that dBASE IV holds keystroke macros in memory until a screen that expects keystrokes appears. If several keystroke macros have been loaded up to that point, they are played back in last-in-first-out (LIFO) order, which means that if three keystroke macros have been loaded, the third is played back first, the second is played back next, and the first is played back last.

EXAMPLE

For further information about playing back keystroke macros within an application, refer to the RESTORE MACROS and PLAY MACRO commands in a dBASE IV programming language reference, such as *dBASE IV Programmer's Reference Guide*, also published by SYBEX, or the dBASE IV *Language Reference* that came with your dBASE IV package.

Exiting the Application

The Quit option on the Item submenu allows the user to exit your application either back to dBASE IV or all the way back to DOS.

SEQUENCE OF STEPS

From the application design screen:

 press **F3** or **F4** until the desired object is current
 F10
 Item/**C**hange Action/**Q**uit [⏎]

USAGE

Every application needs an option that allows the user to leave the application. You can have the application exit back to the dBASE IV Control Center or all the way back to the operating system (DOS). You can also create a menu that provides both options, so that the user can choose the exit destination.

The Quit option on the Change Action submenu provides the actions required to leave the application. When you select Quit from the Item submenu, you'll be given two options:

 Return to Calling Program RETURN
 Quit to DOS QUIT

OVERRIDING THE DEFAULT DATABASE FOR A SINGLE ITEM — 621

Select Return to Calling Program if you want the application to return to the dBASE IV Control Center when the user exits. Select Quit to DOS if you want your application to leave dBASE IV and return to DOS when the user exits.

EXAMPLE

Figure 16.28 shows the options available when you select Quit from the Change Action submenu. If you select the first option, the user will be returned to the dBASE IV Control Center after exiting the application. If you select the Quit to DOS option, the user will be returned to DOS, and the entire dBASE IV session is ended.

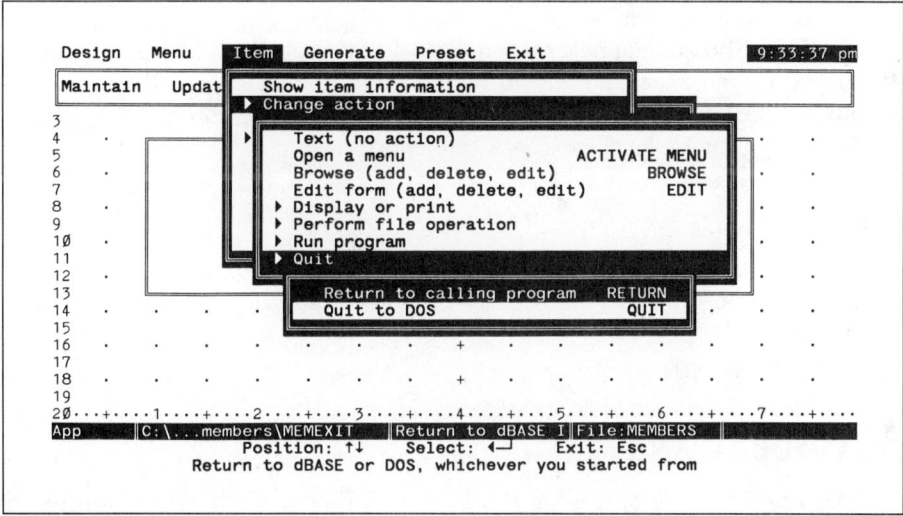

FIGURE 16.28: The two options for exiting an application. These options are displayed when you select Quit from the Change Action submenu.

OVERRIDING THE DEFAULT DATABASE FOR A SINGLE ITEM

The Override Assigned Database or View option on the Item pull-down menu lets you select a new database, view, index file, or index order for a specific menu item, batch process operation, or list object.

SEQUENCE OF STEPS

From the application design screen:

> press **F3** or **F4** until the desired object is current
> **F10**
> Item/**O**verride Assigned Database or View [←]

USAGE

The Override Assigned Database or View option on the Item pull-down menu works in the same manner as the Override Assigned Database or View option on the Menu, List, and Batch pull-down menus (discussed in Chapter 15). However, when selected from the Item pull-down menu, the option affects the current item only, rather than all the items in the menu.

The dialog box that appears when you select this option is identical to the one displayed by the Menu pull-down menu. Note that as soon as the application completes the action, the default database, view, index, and order assigned at the menu or application level goes back into effect.

EXAMPLE

Figure 16.29 shows the dialog box for the Override Assigned Database or View option on the Item submenu. In the example, the index order has been changed to ZIP.

Attaching Code to an Item

The Embed Code option on the Item pull-down menu allows you to add dBASE IV programming language code to a specific menu item, batch process operation, or list.

SEQUENCE OF STEPS

From the application design screen:

> press **F3** or **F4** until the desired object is current
> **F10**
> Item/**E**mbed code [←]
> **B**efore *or* After [←]

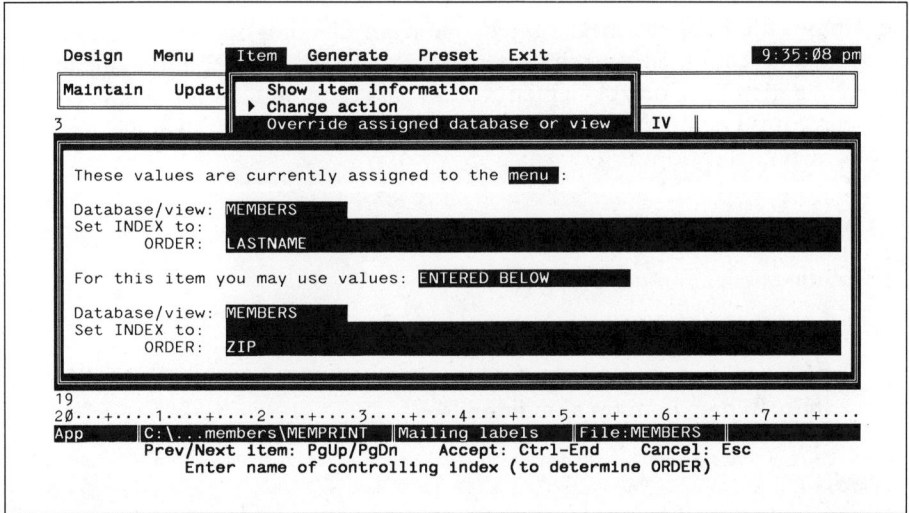

FIGURE 16.29: Override Assigned Database or View dialog box changing the index of the MEMBERS database to zip code order.

USAGE

The Embed Code option on the Item pull-down menu allows dBASE IV programmers to insert dBASE IV commands that will be executed either before or after the current action is executed. When you select Embed Code from the Item pull-down menu, you will be given two options: Before and After. If you select Before, the commands you enter will be executed before the assigned action is performed. If you select After, the commands you enter will be performed immediately after the assigned action.

After you select Before or After, you'll be taken to an editing screen. You can enter up to 19 lines of dBASE IV programming language commands. You use the same editing keys as with the dBASE IV program editor to make changes and corrections. Press **Ctrl-End** after typing your commands.

For more information about the dBASE IV programming language, refer to the *dBASE IV Programmer's Reference Guide*, also published by SYBEX, or the dBASE IV *Language Reference* that came with your dBASE IV package.

DIMMING APPLICATION MENU ITEMS

In your experience with dBASE IV, you've undoubtedly noticed that sometimes menu items are dimmed and unavailable. These items are unavailable because some condition exists that makes the menu option meaningless. For example, the Remove Highlighted File from Catalog option is dimmed and unavailable from the Control Center Catalog pull-down menu if no file name is highlighted in the Control Center. The Bypass Item on Condition option on the Applications Generator Item pull-down menu lets you add a similar feature to your own applications.

SEQUENCE OF STEPS

From the application design screen:

> press **F3** or **F4** until the desired object is current
> **F10**
> Item/**B**ypass Item on Condition [↵]

USAGE

When you select Bypass Item on Condition, a dialog box appears that presents the prompt *Skip this item if:* and a space for entering an expression. The expression you enter must be a valid dBASE IV expression. You can use the Bypass Item on Condition feature only in application pop-up and pull-down menus. Also, you cannot assign this action to menu options that have already been assigned the Text (No Action) action.

EXAMPLE

Figure 16.30 shows a sample Bypass Item on Condition dialog box that dims the current menu item and makes it unavailable if the printer is not ready to accept data. The dialog box uses the built-in dBASE IV function PRINT-STATUS( ) to determine whether the printer is ready.

POSITIONING THE RECORD POINTER

The Position Record Pointer option lets you move the record pointer (that is, locate a specific record in the database file) before the action assigned to an application item takes place. This feature can be useful in an action that allows the user to locate a particular record to edit.

SEQUENCE OF STEPS

From the application design screen:

> press **F3** or **F4** until the desired object is current

POSITIONING THE RECORD POINTER — 625

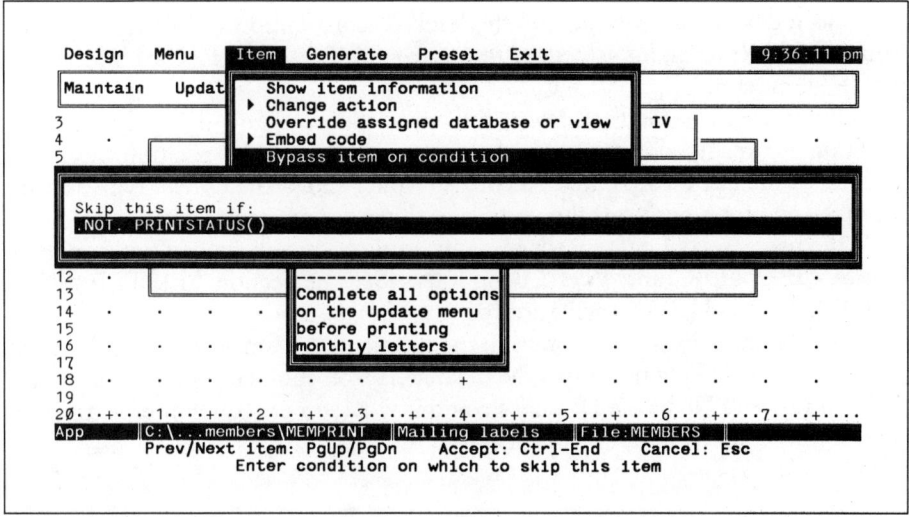

FIGURE 16.30: A sample Bypass Item on Condition dialog box that dims the current menu option and makes it unavailable if the printer is not ready to accept output.

F10

Item/Position Record Pointer [⏎]

USAGE

When you select Position Record Pointer on the Item pull-down menu, you'll see a dialog box with the options summarized in the sections that follow. You can choose any one of the positioning methods.

Press **Ctrl-End** after filling in the dialog box.

Displaying the Positioning Menu at Run Time   At the *Display the Positioning Menu at Run Time?* prompt, use the space bar to select either Yes or No. If you select Yes, when the user selects the menu option to which you've assigned this action, your application automatically displays a list of the first 16 field names and their data types from the current database, plus the name of the current index, if any. A menu below the field names displays these options:

   Seek Record
   GoTo Record
   Locate Record
   Return

If no index is currently active, the Seek Record option will be dimmed and unavailable. If an index is active, the user can select Seek Record and enter a value to search for.

If the user selects GoTo Record, the application presents the options Top (to position the record pointer at the first record), Bottom (to position the record pointer at the last record), and Record # (which allows the user to type a record number and then positions the pointer at the appropriate record).

If the user selects Locate Record, your application will show a submenu with the SCOPE, FOR, and WHILE options. (See the section "FILTER, FOR, SCOPE, and WHILE" earlier in this chapter.)

After the user selects an option from the submenu, the action you assigned to the application menu option through the Change Action submenu will be executed.

If you specify No as the Display Positioning Menu at Run Time? setting, the positioning menu will not be displayed to the user.

Searching for an Index Value   If an index is in use when the user selects the current menu option from your application, you can specify a value to search for in that index. Fill in the Seek First Occurrence of Key option with the starting value that you want to search for. Use proper delimiters for the data type.

Moving the Record Pointer to a Specific Position   Use the GoTo Record option if you want your application to begin the action that follows with the record pointer at a specific position in the database. Your options are Top or Bottom or a particular record number.

Locating a Value in a Field   The Locate (Scope, For, and While) option searches for a value in any field in the database (an index is not required). Enter a scope or filter condition in the FOR or WHILE box. (See the section "FILTER, FOR, SCOPE, and WHILE" earlier in this chapter.)

EXAMPLE

Figure 16.31 shows the Position Record Pointer dialog box with the Display Positioning Menu at Run Time option set to Yes.

Figure 16.32 shows the positioning menu as it appears to the user.

POSITIONING THE RECORD POINTER — 627

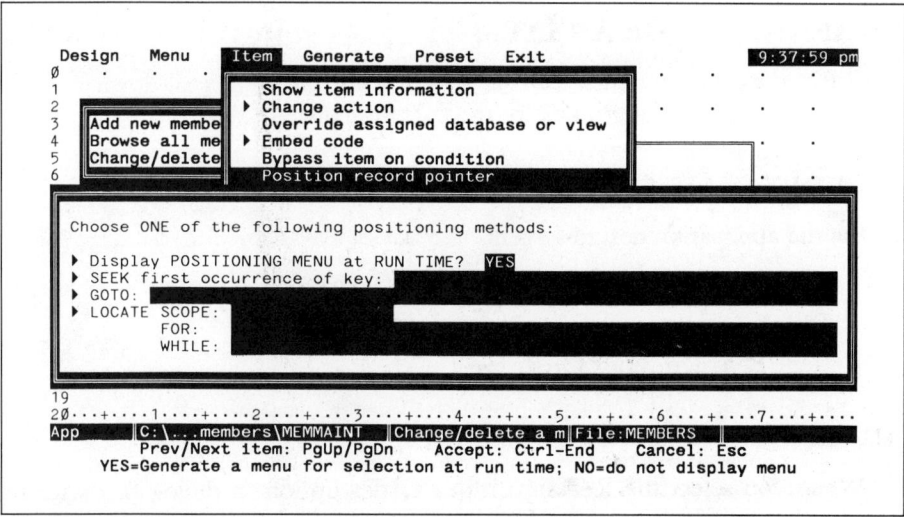

FIGURE 16.31: The Position Record Pointer dialog box with the Display Positioning Menu at Run Time option set to Yes.

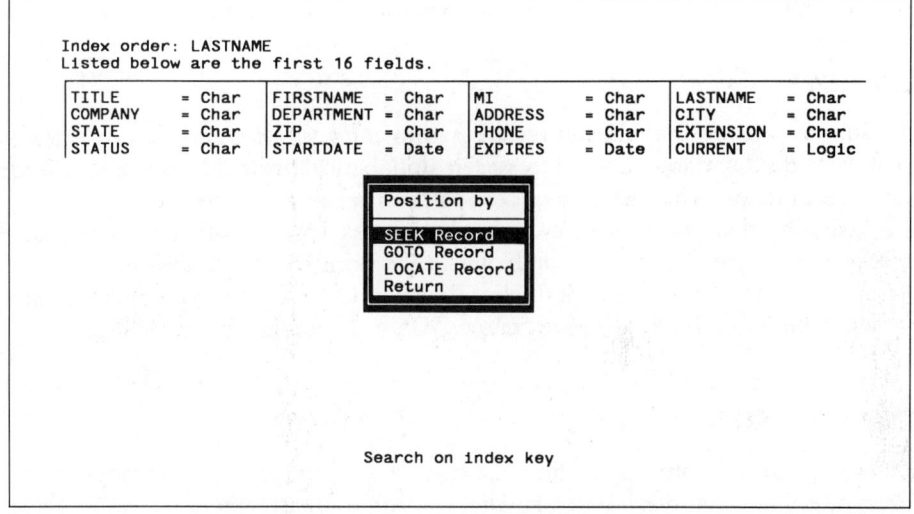

FIGURE 16.32: The positioning menu as it appears to the application user. The index order and field names near the top of the screen are from the currently open database file.

Selecting an Index for an Item

Select the Reassign Index Order option from the Item pull-down menu to specify a new controlling index for the current item.

SEQUENCE OF STEPS

From the application design screen:

>   press **F3** or **F4** until the desired object is current
>   **F10**
>   Item/**R**eassign Index Order [◄─┘]

USAGE

When you select the Reassign Index Order option, a dialog box with the prompt *Set ORDER to:* appears. Enter the name of the index required for the current sort order.

Note that when you select Reassign Index Order for a particular menu item in your application, the new index order is used only while that item performs its action. As soon as that action is complete, dBASE reinstates the default index for the overall application or the index defined for the current menu.

EXAMPLE

Suppose that your application stores names and addresses and uses an index of names to display names and addresses in alphabetical order. However, you want one menu item, Print Mailing Labels, to print labels in zip code order.

Assuming that you previously created an index named ZIP (on the database design screen; see Chapter 4), you highlight the Print Mailing Labels item in your application menu, press **F10**, and select Reassign Index Order from the Item pull-down menu. Then enter the index name **ZIP**, as shown in Figure 16.33.

Displaying a Window

If an action in your application displays data on the screen, you can create a *window* to limit that display to a smaller portion of the screen.

SEQUENCE OF STEPS

From the application design screen:

>   press **F3** or **F4** until the desired object is current

DISPLAYING A WINDOW — 629

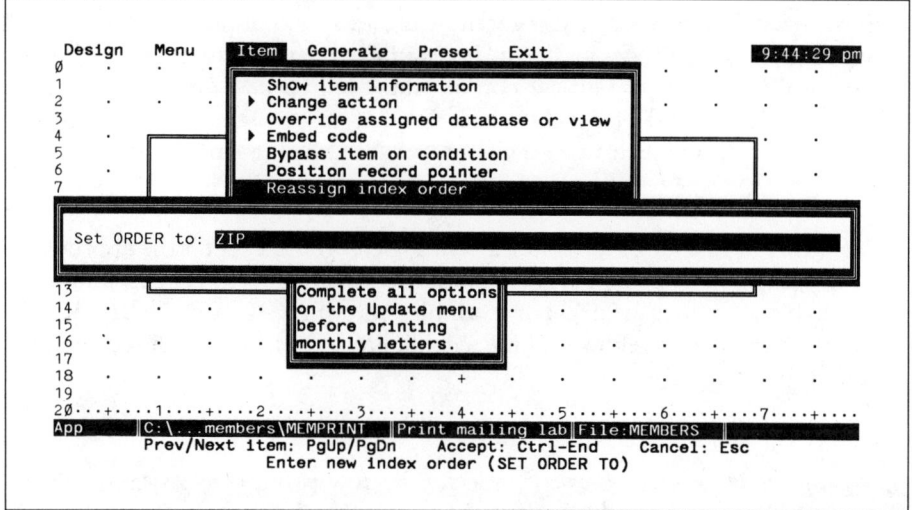

FIGURE 16.33: A sample Reassign Index Order dialog box that makes an existing index named ZIP the controlling index for the current menu item.

F10
Item/**D**efine Logical Window [↵]

USAGE

If the action that you assign to an application menu item displays information on the screen, you can limit that display to a window. When the user runs the application, the window will appear on the screen just before the action is executed. The window remains on the screen during the operation and then is automatically erased when the action is completed.

When you select Define Logical Window from the Item pull-down menu, dBASE displays a dialog box with the options discussed in the following sections.

Entering the Window Name   The name you enter for the window must be a valid DOS file name, with no extension, blank spaces, or punctuation.

Defining a Border Style   The Display Border As option determines the style of the border surrounding the window. Press the space bar to scroll through the options: Single (single-line), Double (double-line), Panel (wide line), Custom (to use characters defined in the Border Characters box), and None.

Using Border Characters If you specify Custom as the display border, you can enter ASCII character codes for the top horizontal border, bottom horizontal border, left vertical border, right vertical border, upper-left corner, upper-right corner, lower-left corner, and lower-right corner (in that order), separated by commas. ASCII characters and their three-digit numbers are listed in Appendix G.

Using Colors To change the colors for the logical window, enter the appropriate color codes (listed in Table 16.2) for the standard, enhanced, border, and background colors (in that order). For example, entering **GR+/B, W/R, BG** displays standard text as yellow on blue, highlighted text as white on red, and the border as cyan.

Specifying the Upper-Left Corner Specify the row (from 0 to 23) and column (from 0 to 78) position of the upper-left corner of the box.

Specifying the Lower-Right Corner Specify the row (from 1 to 24) and column (from 1 to 79) position for the lower-right corner of the box.

EXAMPLE

Figure 16.34 shows the Define Logical Window dialog box for a message window named MSGWNDO that positions the window near the lower-left corner of the screen.

COLOR	CODE	COLOR	CODE
Black	N	Green	G
Blank	X	High intensity	+
Blinking	*	Magenta	RB
Blue	B	Red	R
Brown	GR	White	W
Cyan	BG	Yellow	GR+
Underline	U (monochrome only)		
Inverse	I (monochrome only)		

Table 16.2: dBASE IV Color Codes

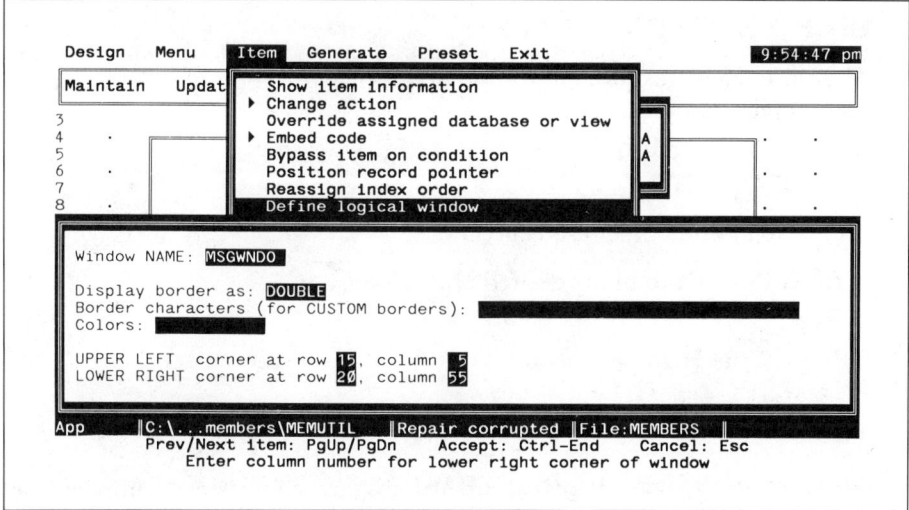

FIGURE 16.34: Define Logical Window dialog box to define a message window near the lower-left corner of the screen.

Figure 16.35 shows how the window appears from the user's perspective. In this example, the window is used with the action Reindex Database. The counter that dBASE displays while reindexing the database is displayed in the window.

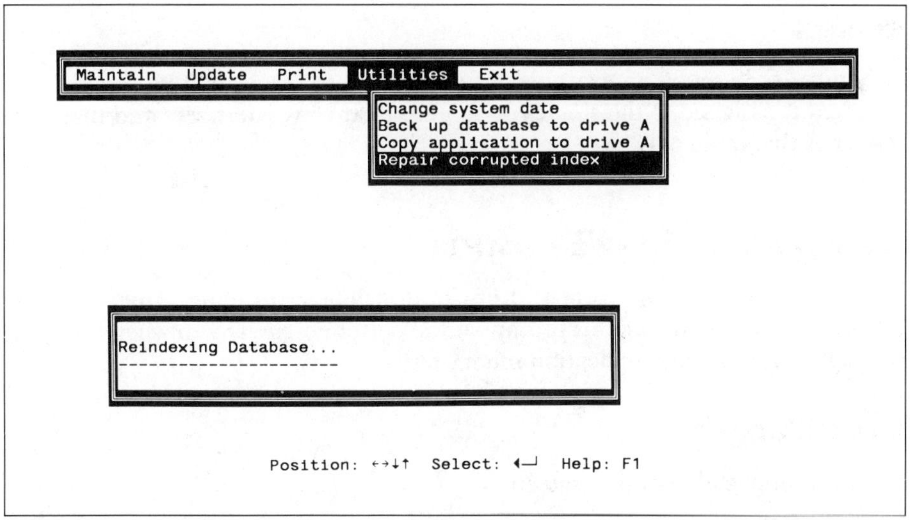

FIGURE 16.35: A sample window from the user's perspective. The action in this example, Reindex a Database, displays its progress inside the window. When reindexing is finished, the window and its contents are removed from the screen.

WRITING HELP TEXT FOR AN ITEM

The Write Help Text option lets you define help text for a specific menu item in your application.

SEQUENCE OF STEPS

From the application design screen:

> press **F3** or **F4** until the desired object is current
> **F10**
> Item/Write Help Text [←]

USAGE

When you select Write Help Text, dBASE displays a full-screen editing frame. Type your help text and use the standard dBASE IV editing keys to make changes and corrections. Press **Ctrl-End** when you are done.

The user will see the help text when he or she highlights the menu item and presses **F1**. If you do not assign help text to a specific menu option, dBASE displays any help text defined for the overall menu when the user presses **F1**. (If you do not define help text for the menu, dBASE displays the message *No help found* when the user presses **F1**.)

EXAMPLE

Figure 16.36 shows an example of help text typed on the editing screen. The help text is assigned to the single menu item Add New Members and therefore discusses that topic only.

ASSIGNING A MESSAGE-LINE PROMPT

The Assign Message Line Prompt option lets you define a message-line prompt. The user will see this prompt at the bottom of the screen when he or she highlights the current application menu item.

SEQUENCE OF STEPS

From the application design screen:

> press **F3** or **F4** until the desired object is current
> **F10**
> Item/Assign a Message Line Prompt [←]

ASSIGNING A MESSAGE-LINE PROMPT — 633

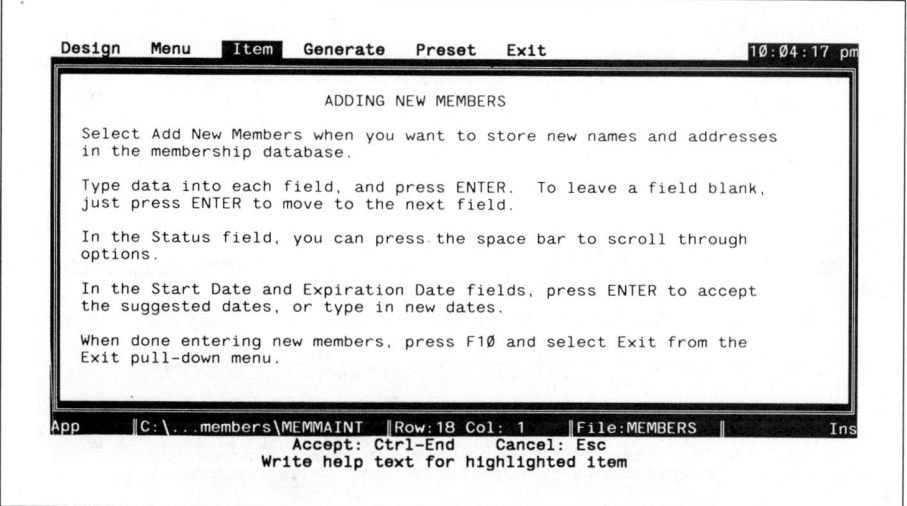

FIGURE 16.36: An example of help text for a single menu option: Add New Members. The user will see the help screen when he or she highlights the Add New Members option in the application and then presses ⏎.

USAGE

When you select the Assign a Message Line prompt option, a dialog box displays the message-line prompt currently assigned to the menu (if any). You'll also be prompted to enter a new message-line prompt.

If you leave the message-line prompt for the current menu item blank, dBASE displays any message-line prompt assigned to the overall menu. If you type a new message-line prompt, dBASE displays that message-line prompt when the user highlights the current menu option.

If you do not assign any message-line prompts on the Menu, Batch, List, or Item menus, the application displays the default message-line prompt:

Position: ← → ↓ ↑   Select: ⏎   Help: F1

EXAMPLE

Figure 16.37 shows an example Assign Message Line Prompt dialog box that tells the user the purpose of the current menu item and also presents a reminder about pressing **F1** to get help.

Figure 16.38 shows the message-line prompt from the application user's perspective, at the bottom of the screen.

634 — CH. 16 ASSIGNING ACTIONS TO APPLICATION OBJECTS

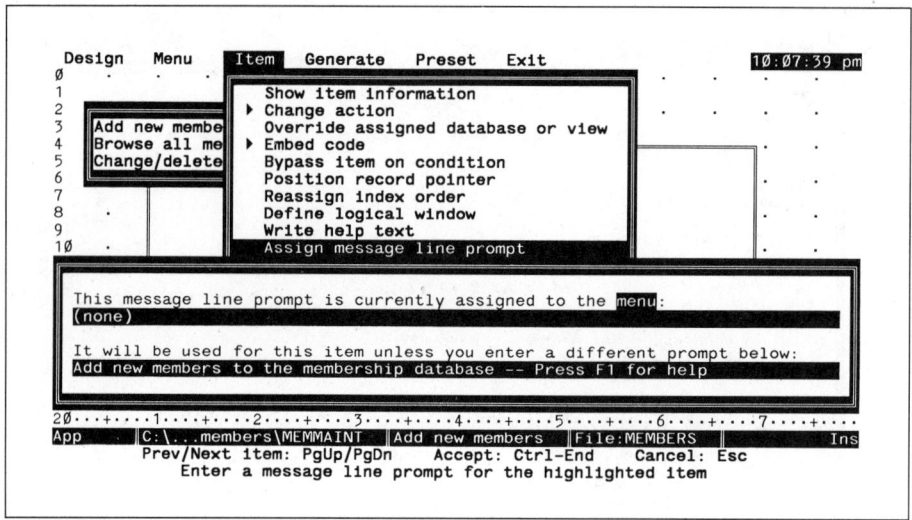

FIGURE 16.37: An example Assign Message Line Prompt dialog box with a custom message-line prompt. This message line is displayed on the screen only when the user highlights the current menu item.

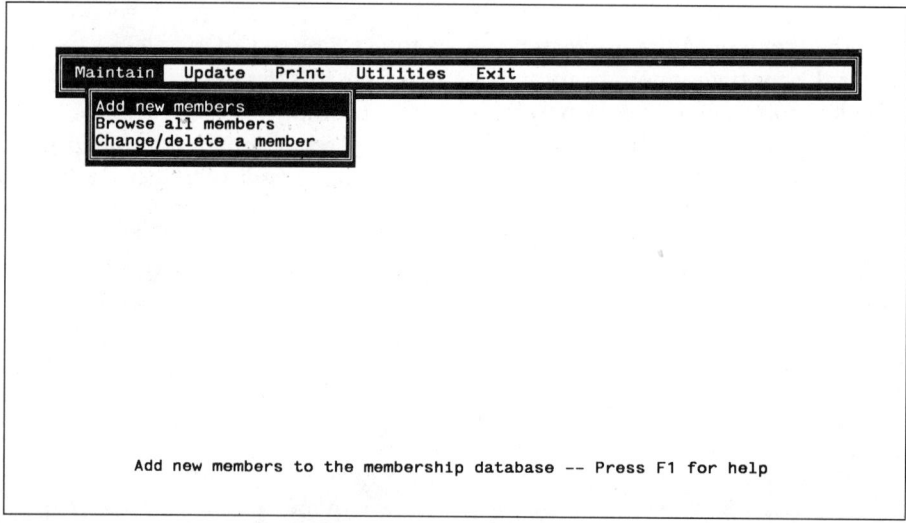

FIGURE 16.38: The message-line prompt assigned to the Add New Members menu item appears at the bottom of the screen whenever that option is highlighted.

TIPS AND TRAPS

- Settings defined by options on the Item pull-down menu override settings defined on the Application, Menu, List, and Batch menus. Settings defined on the Item menu apply to the current item only.
- If you change the action assigned to any menu item, batch process, or list, you must regenerate the application code to incorporate those changes into the application.

SUMMARY

This chapter discussed the second phase of the application development process: assigning actions to application objects.

For an example of the beginning-to-end process of designing, creating, and using an application:

- Appendix F: "Designing and Developing an Application"

For information about creating application objects:

- Chapter 15: "Creating Application Objects"

For information about generating application code and running the completed application:

- Chapter 17: "Generating and Using an Application"

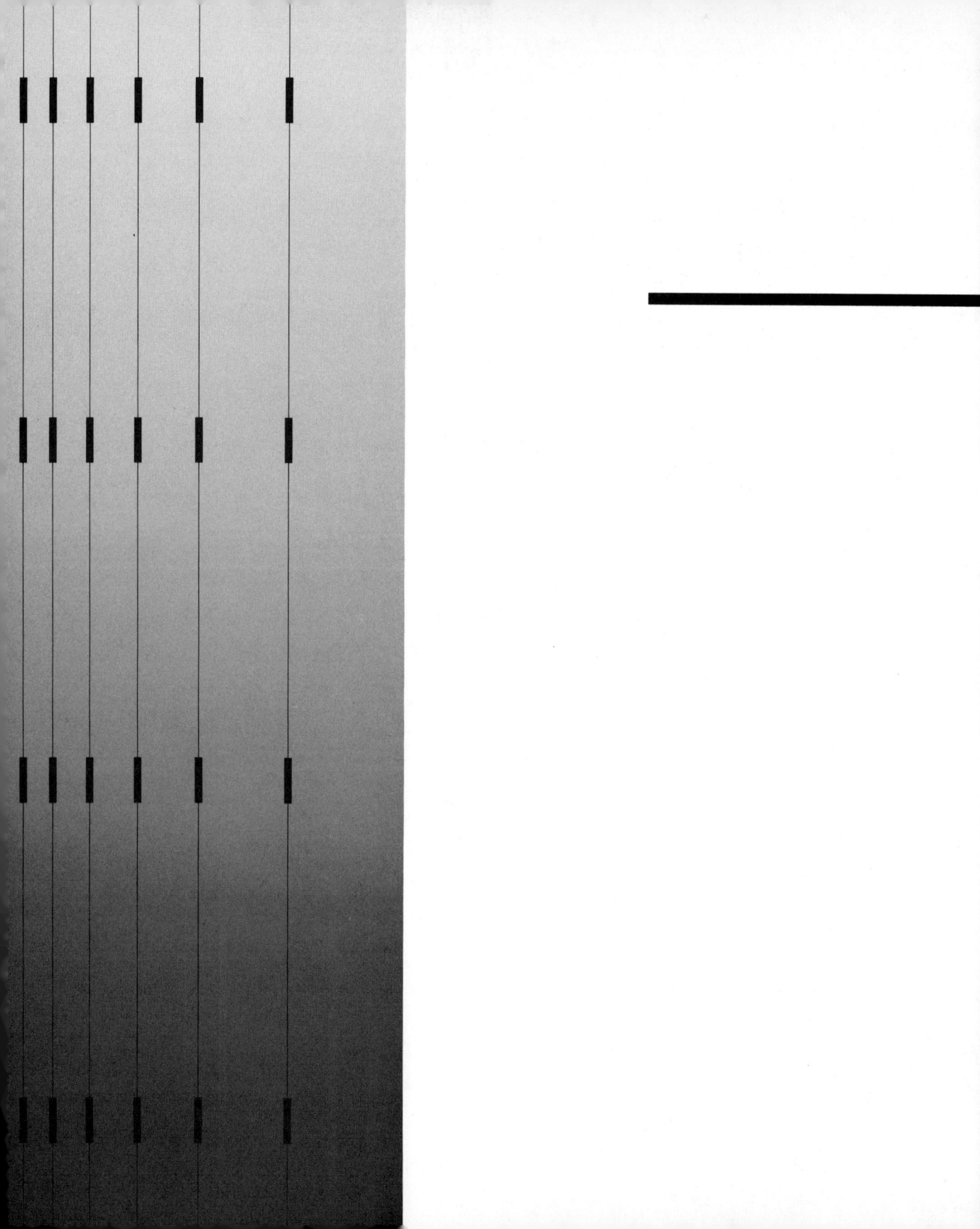

CHAPTER 17

GENERATING AND USING AN APPLICATION

Generating the Application Source Code. 639
    Clearing the Work Surface. 639
    Selecting a Template. 641
    Displaying Code during Generation. 642
    Generating the Source Code. 644
Generating Documentation for an Application. 646
Running the Completed Application. 648
Changing the Applications Generator Default Settings. 652
    Using the Preset Menu. 652
    Specifying Sign-on Default Values. 652
    Determining Default Display Options. .654
    Choosing Environment Settings. 654
    Specifying an Application Drive and Directory Path. 655
Tips and Traps. 656
Summary. 657

Generating and Using an Application

After you have created the objects for an application and assigned actions to those objects, you need to generate the dBASE IV programming language code required to run your application. Also, any time that you make changes to an existing application, you need to regenerate the application code to incorporate those changes into the application.

Once you give the word, dBASE generates the code for your application automatically. Use the Generate pull-down menu in the Applications Generator to tell dBASE to generate the code.

The Applications Generator creates only the *source* code (consisting of dBASE IV programming language commands). The first time you use the completed application, dBASE IV compiles the application code into *object* code (consisting of commands in the language used by your computer).

This chapter discusses the steps for generating an application and addresses several related topics: generating documentation that you or another person can consult if you need to debug or modify the application later, running the completed application, and changing any of the application's default settings.

Generating the Application Source Code

The four basic steps to generating an application's code are as follows:

- Clear the application design screen work surface.
- Select a template.
- Decide whether or not to display the code during generation.
- Instruct dBASE to generate the application code.

These steps are described in sections that follow.

Clearing the Work Surface

You must put away all objects on the application design screen before generating the code for an application.

SEQUENCE OF STEPS

From the application design screen:

F10

From the Application *or* Menu *or* List *or* Batch pull-down menu:

Clear Work Surface [↵]

Save Changes *or* **A**bandon Changes [↵]

USAGE

To clear the application design screen work surface before generating the application code, select Clear Work Surface from the Application, Menu, List, or Batch pull-down menu. If the Applications Generator encounters any new or modified objects on the design screen, it highlights the frame of the object and asks whether you want to save or abandon the new or modified object.

Whenever the Applications Generator encounters a new or modified object on the work surface, that object's frame is highlighted, and the screen displays a prompt asking whether to save or abandon the object, as shown in Figure 17.1.

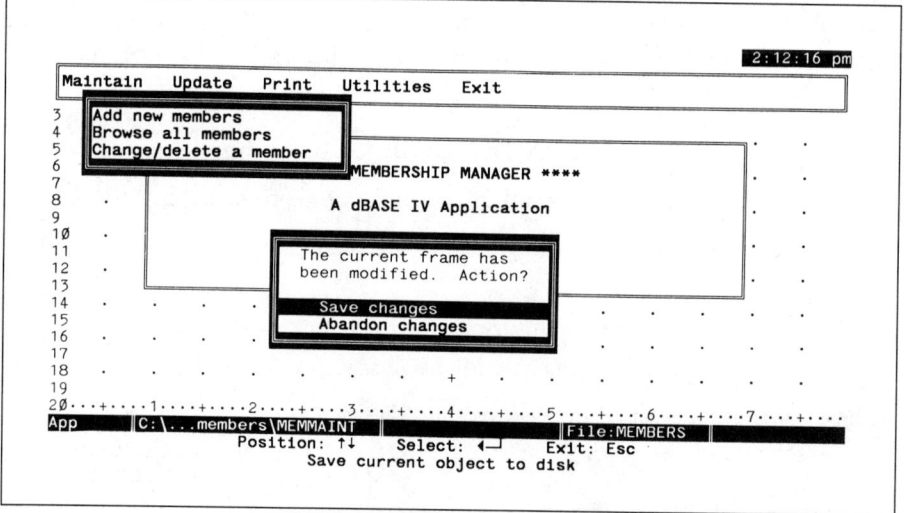

FIGURE 17.1: When you select Clear Work Surface from the Application, Menu, Batch, or List pull-down menu, the Applications Generator asks whether you want to save or abandon new or modified objects.

To save the object, select Save Changes by pressing ⏎. Otherwise, select Abandon Changes by pressing ↓ to highlight that option and then press ⏎. Assuming that you want to save all new and modified objects, select Save Changes each time the prompt appears. After all objects have been put away, you will be returned to the pull-down menus, and only the sign-on banner will remain on the work surface. You must then access the Generate pull-down menu to begin the code generation process.

Selecting a Template

After clearing the work surface, you must select a template for generating the application source code.

SEQUENCE OF STEPS

From the application design screen:

F10
Generate/Select Template [⏎]
MENU.GEN ⏎
⏎

USAGE

After clearing the application design screen work surface, you must select a template for generating the application code. A template is a skeletal version of the application you are developing. When you select Begin Generating, the Applications Generator completes the template to produce your specific application.

The dBASE IV package comes with three templates, summarized here:

MENU.GEN	Used for developing application source code
DOCUMENT.GEN	Used for developing application documentation
QUICKAPP.GEN	Used by the Generate Quick Application option on the Application pull-down menu

In addition to the three templates that came with your dBASE IV package, the dBASE IV Developer's Edition includes a template language that allows you to create your own templates. (See an advanced book about the dBASE IV Developer's Edition for information about the template language.)

To generate the source code for an application, you specify MENU.GEN as the template to use. (QUICKAPP.GEN is used automatically when you generate a quick application. This template should not be used for other applications.)

You must select the Select Template option from the Generate pull-down menu in the application design screen and then type the complete template name, **MENU.GEN**. (You cannot use **Shift-F1** to select a template from a list.)

EXAMPLE

After clearing the application design screen, as discussed in the preceding section, you need to select a template for the Applications Generator to use as a guide in developing the application code. Press **F10**, move the highlight to the Generate option, and select the Select Template option. Then type the template name, **MENU.GEN**, as shown in Figure 17.2, and press ←┘. You will be returned to the Generate pull-down menu.

Displaying Code during Generation

By using the Display during Generation option, you can specify whether you want dBASE to display the application code while it is being generated.

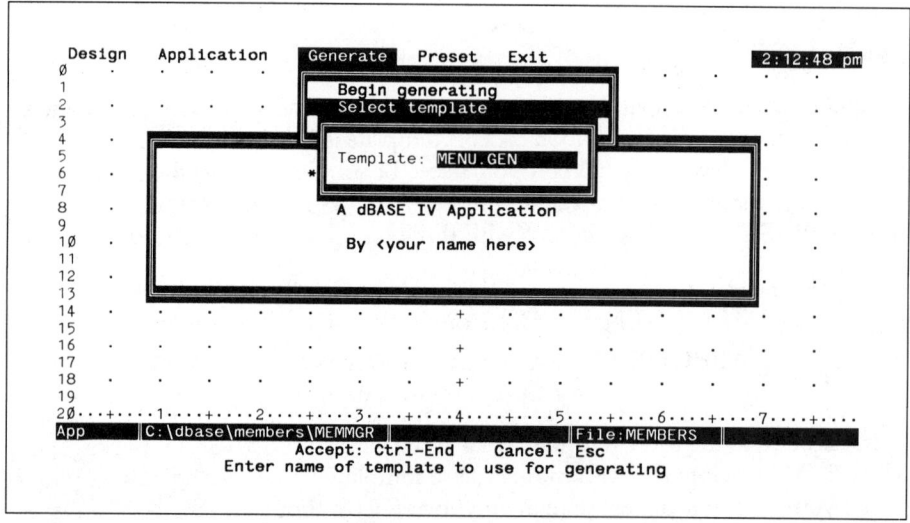

FIGURE 17.2: The MENU.GEN template is specified as the template to use to generate an application. You must type the name of the template correctly and then press ←┘.

SEQUENCE OF STEPS

From the application design screen:

F10

Generate/**D**isplay during Generation [←]

Yes *or* **N**o [←]

USAGE

Normally, the Applications Generator uses a line counter on the status bar near the bottom of the screen to display its progress while generating source code. Optionally, you can view the generated source code as it is being created. Doing so slows down the generation process, but you may find the display interesting if you like to know what's going on behind the scenes.

EXAMPLE

After clearing the application design screen work surface and selecting a template (as discussed in the preceding sections), suppose you want to see the source code on the screen as the Applications Generator creates it. Select the Display during Generation option from the Generate pull-down menu. You'll be given two options, Yes and No, as shown in Figure 17.3.

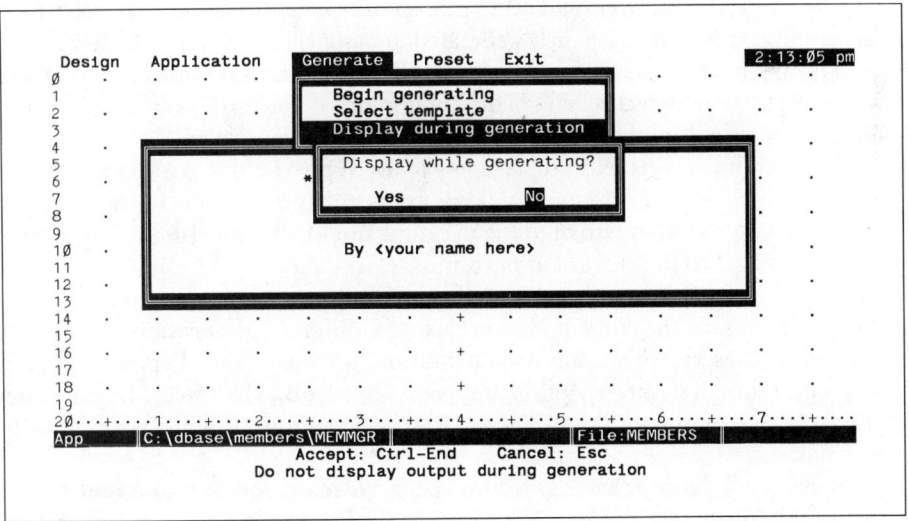

FIGURE 17.3: After you select the Display during Generation option, the Applications Generator provides the options Yes and No.

Select Yes by typing the letter **Y**, or by highlighting the Yes option and pressing ↵. You'll then be returned to the Generate pull-down menu.

Generating the Source Code

The Begin Generating option generates the application code using the template you previously selected via the Select Template option on the Generate pull-down menu.

SEQUENCE OF STEPS

From the application design screen:

F10

Generate/**B**egin Generating [↵]

Y ↵

USAGE

Whenever you create a new application or modify an existing one, you must regenerate the application code. As discussed in the preceding sections, you must first clear the work surface and select a template. You can also decide whether you want to see the generated source code as the Applications Generator creates it.

When you are ready, press **F10** to call up the Generate menu and select Begin Generating. If you've previously generated an application that has the same name as the one you are generating now, the Applications Generator asks for permission to overwrite the previous version of the application. If you are modifying an existing application, type **Y** and press ↵ to proceed with the generation.

Note that if you type **N** and press ↵ to *not* overwrite the existing application when the Applications Generator asks for permission, you'll be prompted to press any key. Do so to return to the previous menu. If you wish to simply abandon all changes to the current application, select Abandon All Changes and Exit from the Exit pull-down menu and Yes from the submenu that appears. Or, if you prefer to save the current changes using a different application name, select Name and Describe from the Application pull-down menu. Type a new name and, optionally, a new description and press **Ctrl-End**. Then select Begin Generating from the Generate pull-down menu to generate an application with the new name.

If you see a prompt asking you to specify a main menu name and type, it means the Applications Generator cannot find a menu of the expected name and/or type. Most likely you have either created a menu with a different name

GENERATING THE SOURCE CODE — 645

than you originally defined (for example, at the definition stage you called it MAIN but at the creation stage you called it FIRST), or defined a name and type but not created the menu. If you simply misnamed the main menu, press the space bar to select a type (Bar, Pop-up, or Batch) and then type the correct file name or press **Shift-F1** and pick the name from the list that appears. If you have not yet created a main menu for the application, press **Esc** to return to the application design screen menus. Then use the appropriate option on the Design pull-down menu to create a menu with the type and name you defined (as discussed in Chapter 15).

dBASE takes some time to develop the source code for an application, so do not attempt to exit the Applications Generator until you see the message-line prompt *Generation is complete -- press any key to continue*. After the application code is generated, you can select Save Changes and Exit from the Exit pull-down menu to return to the Control Center, or you can generate documentation for the application, as discussed in the next section.

EXAMPLE

After you clear the work surface and specify a template (as discussed in the preceding sections), you are ready to generate (or regenerate) your application's source code. To do so, select Begin Generating. Assuming that you are regenerating an application named MEMMGR that you previously created and recently modified, your screen displays the message shown in Figure 17.4.

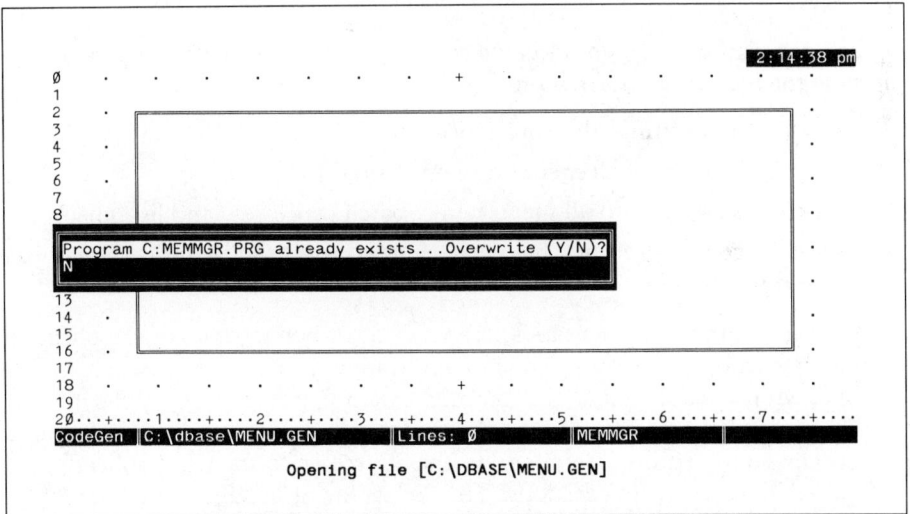

FIGURE 17.4: The Applications Generator asks for permission before overwriting an existing application with the same name. Type **Y** and press ↵ to proceed, or just press ↵ to cancel the generation.

Assuming that you type **Y** and press ⏎ to proceed with the generation, the Applications Generator generates the application's source code. When the Applications Generator is done, the message-line prompt at the bottom of the screen displays *Generation is complete. Press any key....* Press any character key to return to the Applications Generator menus.

GENERATING DOCUMENTATION FOR AN APPLICATION

The Applications Generator also allows you to develop plain-English documentation for your applications.

SEQUENCE OF STEPS

From the application design screen:

> **F10**
>
> Generate/Select Template [⏎]
>
> **DOCUMENT.GEN**
>
> ⏎
>
> **B**egin Generating [⏎]
>
> **Y** *or* **N**

USAGE

You can create documentation for your application. This documentation can include the following information:

- All default settings the application uses.
- Screen images of all menus and other objects.
- Actions assigned to all menu items, batch processes, and list objects.
- Message-line prompts, help text, and settings used by individual objects and menu items.

You can use this documentation as a reference when testing your application, to see what actions are assigned to your application's objects and menu items and to jot down notes about changes you might want to make to the application.

The easiest way to generate the documentation for an application is first to follow the steps required to generate the source code for the application, as described in the preceding sections. Then select the Select Template option from the Generate pull-down menu. Type **DOCUMENT.GEN** as the name of the template to use and press ←. Then select Begin Generating from the Generate pull-down menu.

If you previously developed documentation for the current application, the screen asks for permission to overwrite the existing documentation. Type **Y** and press ← to proceed.

The screen will also ask if you have an IBM-graphics-compatible printer. If you do, type **Y** and press ← to include graphics characters in your documentation. If you do not have an IBM-graphics-compatible printer, press ← to select the default value, No. The documentation will be generated without graphics characters.

The Applications Generator will then create the application documentation. This documentation is stored in the current directory with the same name as the application, plus the extension .DOC. For example, if your application is named MEMMGR, the documentation file will be named MEMMGR.DOC.

When documentation generation is complete, the message-line prompt displays *Generation is complete. Press any key....* Press any character key to return to the application design screen main menu. You can then exit the Applications Generator by selecting Save All Changes and Exit from the Exit pull-down menu. You'll be returned to the dBASE IV Control Center.

You can view or print the application documentation using the Edit option on the dBASE IV DOS Utilities screen. To do so, starting from the Control Center, press **F10** to access the menus, pull down the Tools menu, and select the DOS Utilities option. Highlight the name of the documentation file (which has the same name as the application, plus the extension .DOC) and press ←. Then press **F10**, pull down the Operations menu, and select Edit. The documentation file will appear on your screen in the dBASE IV editor. To print the documentation at that point, press **F10** and select Begin Printing from the Print menu.

You can also print a copy of your application documentation using the DOS COPY, TYPE, or PRINT command (after you exit dBASE IV), as the following example shows.

EXAMPLE

Suppose that you create an application named MEMMGR to manage a membership mailing list (like the example presented in Appendix F of this book). While still in the Applications Generator, you generate documentation using the DOCUMENT.GEN template and then select Save All Changes and Exit from the Exit pull-down menu to return to the dBASE IV Control Center.

To print a copy of the MEMMGR documentation using DOS, select Quit to DOS from the Exit pull-down menu in the Control Center. Then enter any of the following DOS commands at the DOS command prompt (remember that you must press ⏎ after entering *any* DOS command):

    COPY MEMMGR.DOC PRN

or

    TYPE MEMMGR.DOC >PRN

or

    PRINT MEMMGR.DOC

Figure 17.5 shows a portion of the printed documentation for the sample MEMMGR application created in Appendix F.

To return to dBASE IV after printing the documentation, type **DBASE** and press ⏎.

RUNNING THE COMPLETED APPLICATION

To use, or run, a completed application, highlight its name in the Applications panel of the Control Center, press ⏎, and select Run Application. Then select Yes from the options that appear.

SEQUENCE OF STEPS

From the Control Center:

    highlight the application name in the Applications panel

    ⏎

    Run Application [⏎]

    Yes [⏎]

USAGE

After you have successfully generated the source code for an application and exited the Applications Generator, you'll be returned to the dBASE IV Control Center. The name of the application will appear in the Applications Panel.

To run the completed application, highlight its name in the Applications panel and press ⏎. A prompt box presents two options:

    Run Application   Modify Application

```
Page: x  Date: 03-31-90

Layout Report for Popup Menu: MEMPRINT
--------------------------------------

Screen Image:
         0         10        20        30        40        50        60
         >....+....|....+....|....+....|....+....|....+....|....+....|....
    00:
    01:
    02:                     #===================#
    03:                     "Membership roster  "
    04:                     "All mailing labels "
    05:                     "Welcome letters    "
    06:                     "Welcome labels     "
    07:                     "Renewal letters    "
    08:                     "Renewal labels     "
    09:                     "Overdue letters    "
    10:                     "Overdue labels     "
    11:                     "-------------------"
    12:                     "Complete all options"
    13:                     "on the Update menu "
    14:                     "before printing    "
    15:                     "monthly letters.   "
    16:                     #===================#
    17:
    18:
    19:
    20:
    21:
    22:
    23:
    24:
         >....+....|....+....|....+....|....+....|....+....|....+....|....+

Setup for MEMPRINT follows:
---------------------------

  Colors for Menu/Picklist:
  -------------------------
   Color Settings:
      Text         : W+/B
      Heading      : W/B
      Highlight    : GR+/BG
      Box          : GR+/BG
      Messages     : W+/N
      Information  : B/W
      Fields       : N/BG


Bar actions for Menu MEMPRINT follow:
-------------------------------------
Bar: 1
 Prompt: Membership roster
 Action: Run Report Form ROSTER.frm
 Command Options:
   PLAIN
 Print Mode: Send to Default Printer
-------------------------------------------------------------
Bar: 2
 Prompt: All mailing labels
 Action: Run Label Form MEMLABEL.lbl
 Command Options:
   SAMPLE
 Print Mode: Send to Default Printer
 Set Order To ZIP
```

FIGURE 17.5: A portion of the generated documentation for the sample MEMMGR application presented in Appendix F. The documentation provides screen images of all menus, as well as the settings the application uses and the actions assigned to all menu items and batch processes.

```
............................................................
Bar: 3
Prompt: Welcome letters
Action: Run Report Form WELCOME.frm
Command Options:
  FOR MONTH(StartDate)=MONTH(DATE()).AND.YEAR(StartDate)=YEAR(DATE())

Print Mode: Send to Default Printer
Set Order To ZIP

............................................................
Bar: 4
Prompt: Welcome labels
Action: Run Label Form MEMLABEL.lbl
Command Options:
  FOR MONTH(StartDate)=MONTH(DATE()).AND.YEAR(StartDate)=YEAR(DATE())
Print Mode: Send to Default Printer
Set Order To ZIP
............................................................
Bar: 5
Prompt: Renewal letters
Action: Run Report Form RENEWAL.frm
Command Options:
  FOR MONTH(Expires)=MOD(MONTH(DATE()),12)+1

Print Mode: Send to Default Printer
Filter: YEAR(Expires)=YEAR(DATE())+INT(MONTH(Expires)/12)
Set Order To ZIP
............................................................
Bar: 6
Prompt: Renewal labels
Action: Run Label Form MEMLABEL.lbl
Command Options:
  FOR MONTH(Expires)=MOD(MONTH(DATE()),12)+1 SAMPLE
Print Mode: Send to Default Printer
Filter: YEAR(Expires)=YEAR(DATE())+INT(MONTH(Expires)/12)
Set Order To ZIP
```

FIGURE 17.5: A portion of the generated documentation for the sample MEMMGR application presented in Appendix F. The documentation provides screen images of all menus, as well as the settings the application uses and the actions assigned to all menu items and batch processes (continued).

Press ↵ to select Run Application. dBASE IV will display a prompt asking you to confirm your selection. Type **Y** to select Yes (or press ← to highlight the Yes option and then press ↵).

If you assigned a sign-on banner to your application, the sign-on banner will appear on your screen with the message *Press ↵ to continue* displayed at the bottom of the screen. Press ↵ to access the application's main menu (or just wait a few seconds, and the application's main menu will appear).

When the application's main menu appears on your screen, you can use the usual arrow keys to move through menu options, and you can press ↵ to select the currently highlighted option. The application remains in control until you select an option on the application's menus to exit the application or until you press the **Esc** key.

You can also run a dBASE IV application directly from the DOS command prompt by first switching to the directory that stores the application (using the DOS CHDIR or CD command) and then entering the command **DBASE** followed by a space and the name of the application.

You can also run an application from the dBASE IV dot prompt by typing **DO** followed by a space and the name of the application. For example, if you created an application named MEMMGR, and the application's directory is the current directory, you can type the command **DO MEMMGR** at the dBASE IV dot prompt (and then press ◄┘) to run your application.

Remember that, in the future, you always need to switch to the directory that the application is stored in when you want to use the application. The easiest way to do this is by using the CHDIR or CD (Change Directory) command at the DOS command prompt *before* you run dBASE IV. When you enter the command **DBASE** to run dBASE IV, you will see the application's name in the Applications panel of the Control Center, and you can run the application by highlighting its name and pressing ◄┘.

EXAMPLE

Suppose you created an application named MEMMGR. After generating the source code for the application and exiting the Applications Generator, the application's name (MEMMGR in this example) appears in the Applications panel of the Control Center, as shown in Figure 17.6.

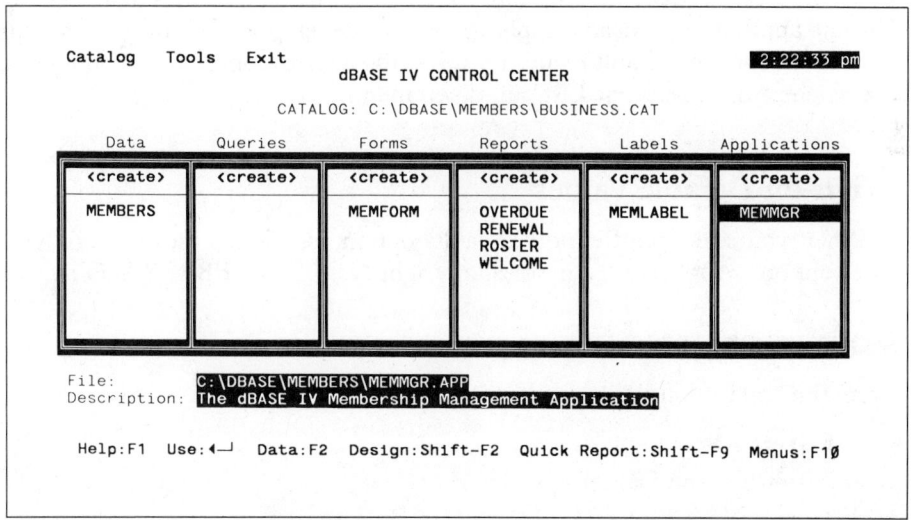

FIGURE 17.6: After creating an application, generating its source code, and exiting the Applications Generator, the application's name (MEMMGR in this example) appears in the Applications panel of the Control Center.

To run the MEMMGR application, highlight its name in the Applications panel and press ↵. From the options that appear, select Run Application (by pressing ↵). Select Yes when dBASE IV asks for verification. The sign-on banner or main menu for the application will appear on your screen.

To run the application directly from DOS, first switch to the application's directory. Then enter the command **DBASE** followed by a space and the name of the application. For example, if your application is named MEMMGR, and it is stored in a directory named \DBASE\MEMBERS, you enter the following commands at the DOS command prompt (be sure to press ↵ after entering each command):

    CD \DBASE\MEMBERS
    DBASE MEMBERS

CHANGING THE APPLICATIONS GENERATOR DEFAULT SETTINGS

After creating and using your first application, you may decide to change some default settings, such as screen colors, for all future applications. To do so, you use options on the Preset menu, as described in the sections that follow.

Using the Preset Menu

The Preset menu provides options for changing default settings that affect the current application and any applications you develop in the future. You can override the Preset default values for a specific application by using options on the Application, Menu, or List pull-down menu.

Specifying Sign-on Default Values

When you select the Sign-on Defaults option, you'll see a dialog box with three options: Application Author, Copyright Notice, and dBASE Version.

SEQUENCE OF STEPS

From the application design screen:

> **F10**
> Preset/Sign-on Defaults [↵]
> To save: **Ctrl-End**

USAGE

When you select Sign-on Defaults from the Preset pull-down menu, dBASE IV displays a dialog box for entering the name of the application author, a copyright notice, and the dBASE version number. You can enter any text (but no quotation marks) after the prompts. Use the usual dBASE editing keys, if necessary, to make changes and corrections. Press **Ctrl-End** after filling in the dialog box.

The text you enter as the sign-on default display will automatically appear in the sign-on banner whenever you create a new application. You can still, however, change the sign-on banner for any new application. Also, remember that your application displays the sign-on banner only if you select Display Sign-on Banner from the Application pull-down menu.

EXAMPLE

To have all future applications display the author name *Andy Adams*, the copyright notice *(c) Andy Adams, 1990*, and the dBASE IV version number *1.0* as the default values, select Sign-on Defaults from the Preset pull-down menu and fill in the dialog box as shown in Figure 17.7. Press ↵ to save your changes.

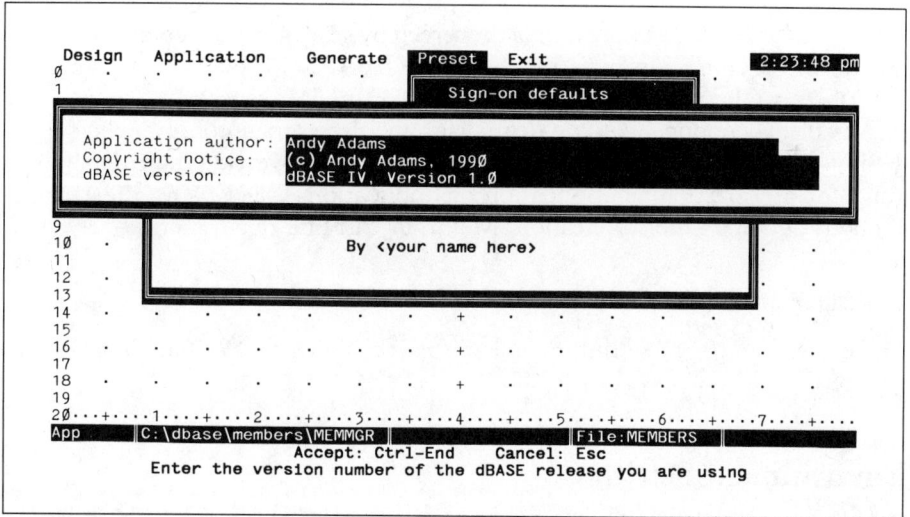

FIGURE 17.7: Default values for the sign-on banner have been modified using the Sign-on Defaults option on the Preset pull-down menu in the Applications Generator.

Determining Default Display Options

SEQUENCE OF STEPS

From the application design screen:

F10
Preset/Display Options [↵]
Object border style *or* screen area to color
To save: **Ctrl-End**

USAGE

The Display Options option on the Preset menu lets you define a default border style and colors for all future applications. You can scroll through the border-style options by pressing the space bar. They are summarized here:

DOUBLE:	Objects borders have a double-line frame
SINGLE:	Object borders have a single-line frame
PANEL:	Object borders have a reverse-video frame with no lines
NONE:	Object borders have no frame

You can also color any portion of the screen by selecting a screen area from the menu and a color combination from the dBASE IV electronic panel (as described in Chapter 14, "Managing Files and the Workspace").

Any display options that you define with the Preset menu become the default settings for all future applications. However, you can override these default settings for any particular application or application object using the Display Options option on the Application, Menu, or List pull-down menu.

EXAMPLE

For an example of setting default display options, see "Changing Display Options" in Chapter 15.

Choosing Environment Settings

SEQUENCE OF STEPS

From the application design screen:

F10

Preset/**E**nvironment Settings [⏎]
To save: **Ctrl-End**

USAGE

The Environment Settings option on the Preset pull-down menu lets you change the default settings used by all applications that you generate in the future. You can override these settings in a particular application by selecting Modify Application Environment from the Application pull-down menu and Environment Settings from the submenu.

For a description and example of application environment settings, see "Changing Environment Settings" in Chapter 15.

Specifying an Application Drive and Directory Path

SEQUENCE OF STEPS

From the application design screen:

F10
Preset/**A**pplication Drive/Path [⏎]
To save: **Ctrl-End**

USAGE

The Application Drive/Path option on the Preset menu lets you define a disk drive and directory path for all future applications. When you select this option, a dialog box appears requesting the name of the disk drive and paths to search.

In the Drive box, enter the name of the drive (for example, B or C) that applications should search for database objects such as the report format, label format, custom screen, database, and index files. Optionally, you can press Pick (**Shift-F1**) and select a drive name from the list of available drive names that appears.

In the Search Path box, enter a valid DOS file search path. If you want the application to search several paths, separate each path with a semicolon. The search path can contain a maximum of 60 characters. Press **Ctrl-End** to save your changes.

You can override the default drive and search path for a specific application by selecting Modify Application Environment from the Application pull-down menu and Search Path from the submenu.

656 ── **CH. 17** GENERATING AND USING AN APPLICATION

EXAMPLE

Figure 17.8 shows the Application Drive/Path dialog box on the Preset pull-down menu. In this example, all future applications will first search the current directory for database objects. If a file cannot be found on the current directory, applications will then search the \DBASE\MEMBERS directory. If the file being searched for cannot be found on \DBASE\MEMBERS, the application will then search the \DBASE\AR directory. If the file does not exist on the last-searched directory, the application will return an error message indicating that the requested file cannot be found.

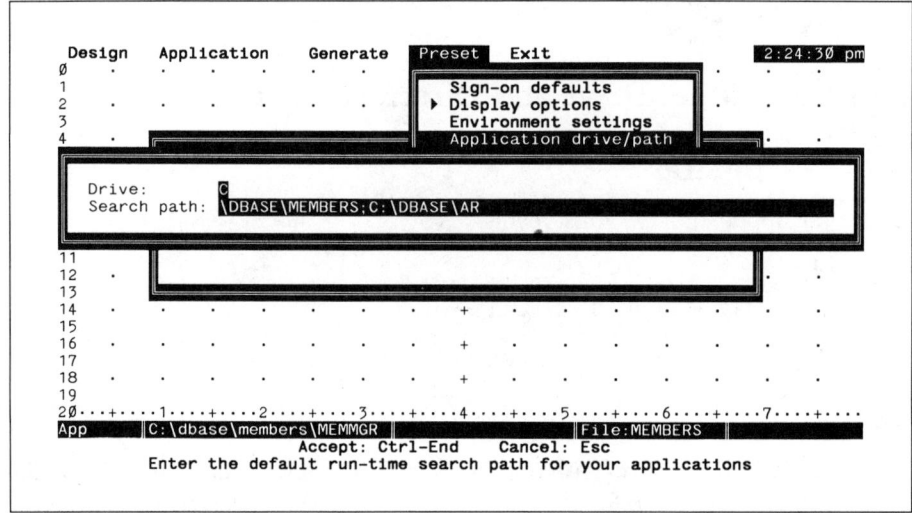

FIGURE 17.8: The Application Drive/Path dialog box on the Preset pull-down menu. When the application cannot find a database object file on the current directory, it searches the paths \DBASE\MEMBERS and \DBASE\AR.

TIPS AND TRAPS

- Remember that whenever you modify an existing application, you must regenerate the source code to incorporate your changes.
- Always clear the application design screen work surface to ensure that all new and modified objects are saved before you generate the code.
- You must name and create a main menu for the application before the Applications Generator will allow you to generate the code.

- Keep a printed copy of the application documentation nearby as you test and refine an application. Use the documentation as a quick reference to settings and actions assigned to each menu item.

Summary

This chapter discussed the final phase of the application development process: generating the application code and using the completed application.

For a complete example of application design, creation, and use:

- Appendix F: "Designing and Developing an Application"

For information about assigning actions to application objects:

- Chapter 16: "Assigning Actions to Application Objects"

For information about creating application objects:

- Chapter 15: "Creating Application Objects"

Part VI

Programming and Configuring dBASE IV

Chapter 18: Introduction to the Programming Language
Chapter 19: Using DBSETUP
Chapter 20: Protecting Data

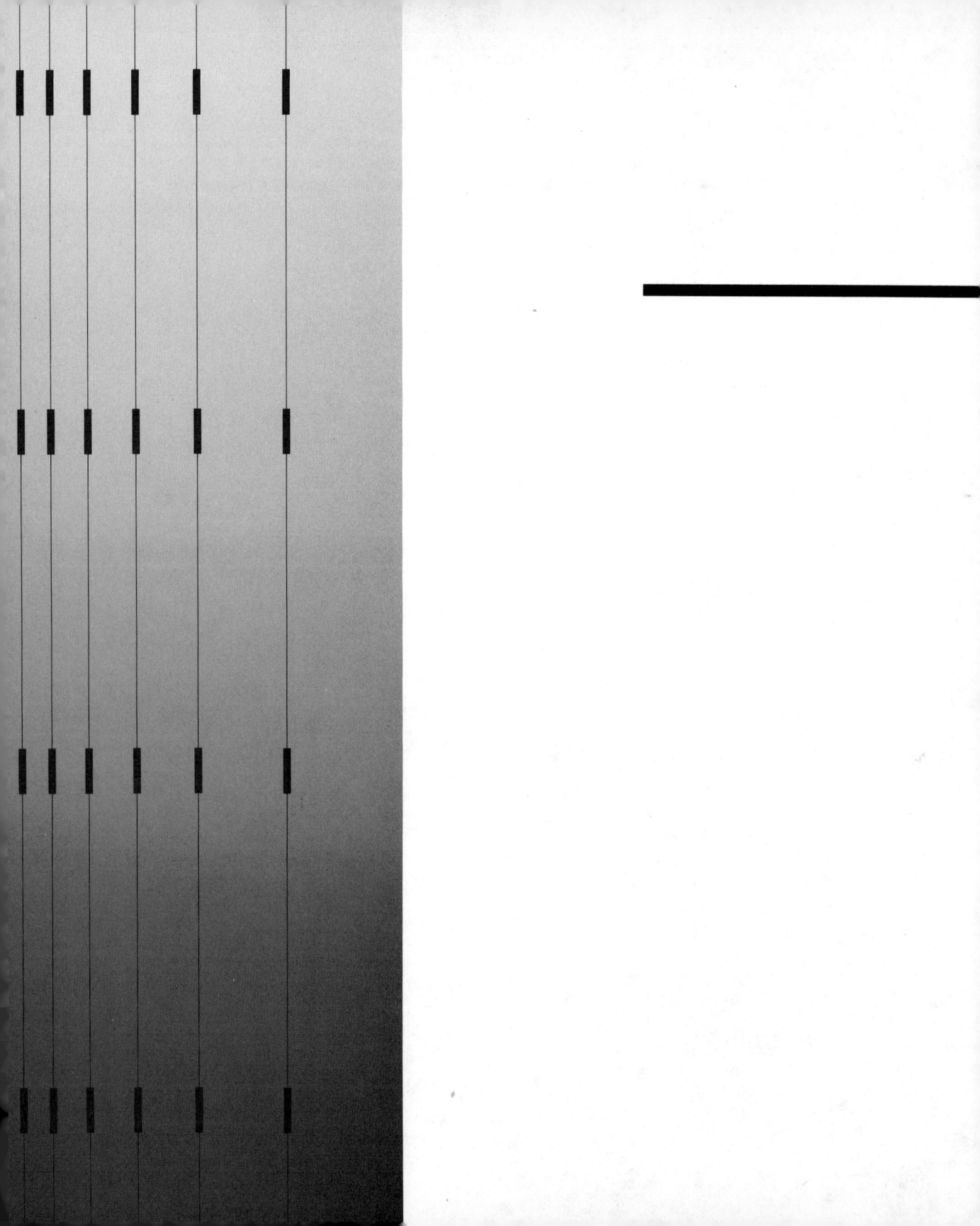

CHAPTER 18

Introduction to the Programming Language

Using dBASE IV Commands from the Dot Prompt. 663
    Handling Errors. 665
Using dBASE IV as a Calculator. 667
Getting Help with Command Syntax. 667
    Using Syntax Charts. 668
Command Files. 670
    Creating Command Files. 671
    Running a Command File. 673
    Command Files That dBASE IV Creates Automatically. 674
Tips and Traps. 676
Summary. 677

Introduction to the Programming Language

As you gain experience using the Control Center, design screens, and Applications Generator, you may find that you need more power and flexibility to achieve some goal, particularly if you want to develop large, complex business applications for jobs like inventory management or accounts payable and receivable. When you need that added power and flexibility, it is available in the dBASE IV *programming language*.

The dBASE IV programming language is the program's most advanced and powerful feature. The programming language consists of *commands,* which tell dBASE specific tasks to perform, and *functions,* which can be used in conjunction with commands. But functions are also used in many operations you perform at the Control Center, and the relevant functions are discussed throughout the first five parts of this book; consult the index to find discussions and examples of individual functions. This chapter provides an introduction to the use of dBASE's commands, both individually, at the *dot prompt,* and combined into *command files,* or *programs.* An in-depth discussion of dBASE programming is beyond the scope of this *User's Desktop Companion;* if you want to learn all about the subject, see *dBASE IV Programmer's Reference Guide* by this author (SYBEX, 1990).

Using dBASE IV Commands from the Dot Prompt

SEQUENCE OF STEPS

To access the dot prompt:

    Menus (**F10**)
    Exit/**E**xit to Dot Prompt [⏎]

or

    Esc
    Yes

To return to the Control Center:

    Data (**F2**)   *or*   **ASSIST** ⏎

USAGE

There are basically two ways to enter dBASE IV programming language commands; either at the dBASE IV *dot prompt,* which executes the command immediately, or in a *command file,* which can store many commands to be run together, at any time, as a single *program* (as discussed later in this chapter). You cannot enter programming language commands from the Control Center.

It's important to understand that the dot prompt and Control Center are basically two alternative techniques for performing dBASE IV operations. The Control Center is *menu driven*; you perform operations by selecting options from menus. The dot prompt is *command driven,* which means you must type in a command when you want dBASE to perform an operation.

The Control Center is usually preferred by beginners and occasional users because it does not require a great deal of memorization. The dot prompt is often preferred by programmers and more advanced users, who have memorized all the commands and intricate details of the programming language, and prefer typing commands to selecting menu options.

To access the dot prompt from the Control Center, you either press Menus (**F10**) and select Exit to Dot Prompt from the Exit pull-down menu, or you press **Esc** and select Yes from the dialog box that appears.

When you get to the dot prompt, you will see only the status bar at the bottom of the screen and a period (dot) with the cursor blinking to the right, as shown in Figure 18.1. You can type any valid dBASE IV command, followed by ⏎,

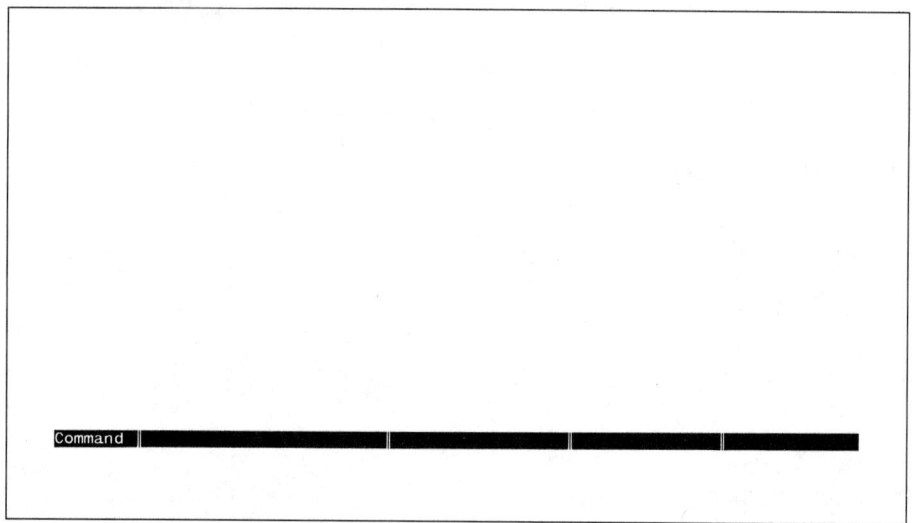

FIGURE 18.1: The dBASE IV dot prompt offers an alternative means of accessing every dBASE IV activity.

whenever you see the dot prompt. Always press ⏎ after typing a dBASE IV command at the dot prompt.

You can leave the dot prompt and return to the Control Center at any time by pressing Data (**F2**), which calls up the dBASE IV ASSIST command. When you press **F2**, dBASE enters the command

    ASSIST

before returning you to the Control Center. An alternative to pressing Data (**F2**) is to type **ASSIST** and press ⏎.

EXAMPLE

To demonstrate how the dot prompt mainly provides an alternative to the Control Center for performing basic dBASE operations, we will perform a couple of tasks now that you are probably already familiar with—opening a database and displaying its contents on a browse screen. From the Control Center, you simply need to highlight the database name in the Data panel, and press Data (F2) to achieve this goal.

From the dot prompt, you need to use two dBASE commands, **USE** and **BROWSE**. Follow the steps below to try this out (the example assumes that you have already created the CUSTLIST.DBF database used in preceding chapters):

1. If the Control Center is currently on your screen, press **F10** and select Exit to Dot Prompt from the Exit pull-down menu.
2. At the dot prompt, type **USE CUSTLIST** and then press ⏎.
3. Type **BROWSE** and press ⏎.

You will be taken to the browse screen, which displays data from the CUSTLIST database. At this point, you can use the BROWSE screen as you normally would; you've simply gotten to it from the command prompt, rather than from the Control Center.

When you leave the browse screen, you'll be returned to the dot prompt (not the Control Center). To try this out, press F10 and select Exit from the Exit pull-down menu. (Remember, if you want to return to the Control Center, type **ASSIST** and press ⏎, or just press the **F2** key.)

Handling Errors

If you make a mistake while typing a command, you can use the **Backspace** key to make changes (before you press ⏎). If you enter a command that dBASE cannot process, you will see a dialog box with an error message that briefly describes the problem and the command you entered and presents the options Cancel, Edit, and Help.

For example, if you enter the command **US CustList** (instead of USE CustList), dBASE displays an error dialog box with the error message *** *Unrecognized command verb*. (The first word in a dBASE IV command is the *verb*, and this error message tells you that dBASE IV does not recognize US as a valid command verb.) Figure 18.2 shows the error dialog box.

You can reenter or edit a previous dot prompt command by pressing ↑ and ↓ at the dot prompt to scroll through the last ten commands entered. You can change any command with the **Backspace** and arrow keys and reenter the command by pressing ⏎.

After the error dialog box appears, you can select Cancel to completely cancel the request and return to the dot prompt. If you select Edit, the cursor will return to the end of the faulty command, and you can use the ←, →, and other standard dBASE IV editing keys to make changes. After making changes, press ⏎ to reenter the command. If you are not sure what an error message means or do not know how to correct an error, select Help and you will be taken to the dBASE IV help system.

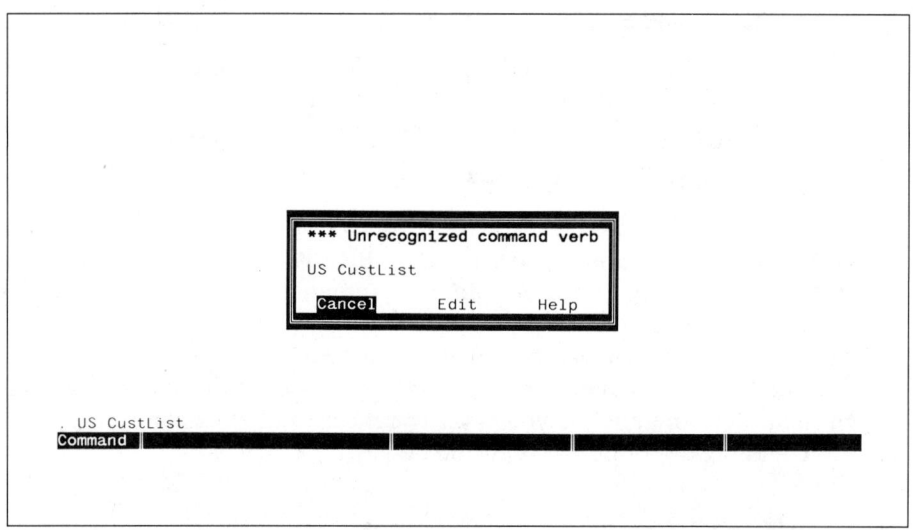

FIGURE 18.2: Sample error dialog box. dBASE displays the error message "*** Unrecognized command verb."

Using dBASE IV as a Calculator

SEQUENCE OF STEPS

To perform a calculation from the dot prompt:

? <calculation expression>

USAGE

One particularly handy feature of the dot prompt that is not available from the Control Center is that it allows you to get immediate answers to questions. You can use the ? command to display information or the results of a calculation. You can think of ? as a kind of PRINT command or WHAT IS? command.

EXAMPLE

If you type the command

? 50*50

from the dot prompt and press ⏎, dBASE displays the results of 50 times 50, which is 2500.

Suppose you need to find the cube root of the number 127. You can ask dBASE for the result of raising 127 to the power (1/3) by entering the command

? 127^(1/3)

dBASE responds with the answer: 5.03.

You can use any dBASE function with the ? command. For example, to find the square root of 81, you can enter the command

? SQRT(81)

and dBASE will respond with the answer: 9.

Getting Help with Command Syntax

SEQUENCE OF STEPS

At the dot prompt:

HELP <COMMAND NAME>

USAGE

dBASE provides about 225 commands (summarized in Appendix E). Information about each of the commands is available in the *dBASE IV Language Reference* manual that came with your dBASE IV package.

To use a command properly, you need to use the correct *syntax*. To get quick help with a command and to see its *syntax chart*, you can enter the command **HELP** at the dot prompt, followed by the name of the command in question. For example, if you enter the command

HELP LIST

dBASE will display a help screen for the LIST command, as shown in Figure 18.3. The top portion of the help screen displays the syntax chart, the second paragraph describes the command, and the bottom portion of the screen describes the various options that the command supports.

Using Syntax Charts

The syntax chart for a command displays the components of the command and the order in which they are to be typed. dBASE uses the following symbols in

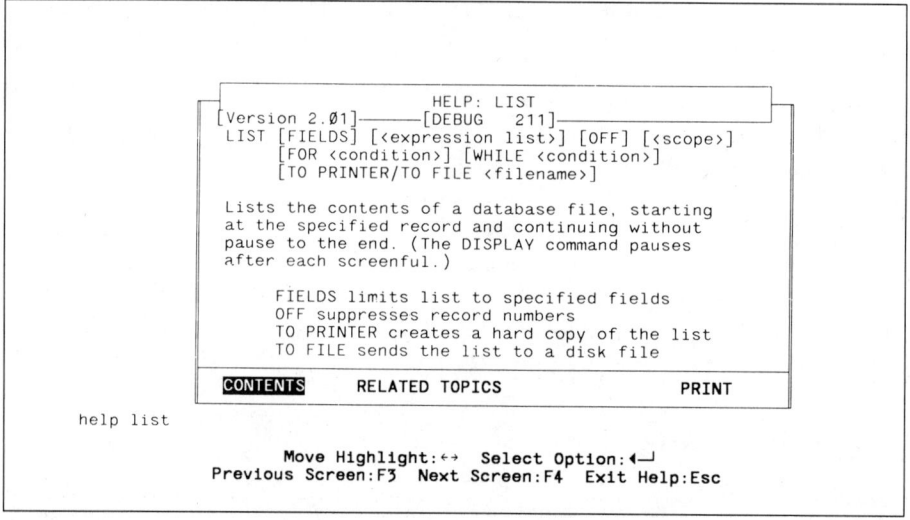

FIGURE 18.3: Help screen for the LIST command, accessed by typing **HELP LIST** at the dot prompt. You can have dBASE display similar help screens for any command.

syntax charts:

[ ] Items in square brackets are optional and can be omitted from the command.

/ When multiple items are separated by slashes, one item or another can be used, but not all.

< > Replace items in angle brackets with specific information.

? In some commands, the question mark can be used in place of specific information in angle brackets to see what objects are available in the current catalog. (For example, **USE ?** displays a menu of database file names.)

The brackets and the slash are used to distinguish different types of command components, but you do not type the brackets or the slash in your commands.

Table 18.1 provides some examples of items that appear in angle brackets in a syntax chart and shows the type of information that would replace those items in a command you enter. Table 18.2 provides examples of valid LIST commands

COMMAND PARAMETER	DATA
<condition>	You must enter a valid filter condition, such as **State = "CA"** or **StartDate > = {01/01/89} .AND. StartDate < = {02/28/89}**.
<expression list>	You must enter an expression, or several expressions separated by commas. The expression can be a field name, variable name, or calculation (such as **Qty*UnitPrice**, where Qty and UnitPrice are field names from the currently open database).
<expC>	You must enter the name of a Character field, actual character data (enclosed in quotation marks), or an expression that results in the Character data type.
<expN>	You must enter the name of a Numeric (or Float) field, actual numeric data, or an expression that results in the Numeric or Float data type.
<expD>	You must enter the name of a Date field, an actual date enclosed in braces, { }, or an expression that results in the Date data type.

Table 18.1: Some Types of Data You Can Include in Commands

SYNTAX	EFFECT
LIST	Lists all fields and records from the current database.
LIST LastName,FirstName	Lists the LastName and FirstName fields from the current database. (**LastName,FirstName** replaces <expression list>.)
LIST FIELDS LastName, FirstName	Same as the preceding command, but includes the optional component FIELDS.
LIST StartDate,StartDate + 30 OFF	Lists the StartDate field and the start date with 30 days added. Record numbers are omitted (because the OFF option is specified).
LIST RECORD 5	Displays the fifth record in the database. (**RECORD 5** replaces <scope>.)
LIST City,State,Zip FOR State = "CA"	Lists the City, State, and Zip fields for records that have CA in the State field. (**State = "CA"** replaces <condition>.)
LIST LastName, FirstName, Company TO PRINTER	Lists the LastName, FirstName, and Company fields, sending output to the printer.

Table 18.2: Examples of Using the LIST Command with the CUSTLIST Database

(assuming that the CUSTLIST database is open). As you can see in the table, the LIST command offers quite a bit of flexibility, as do most dBASE IV commands.

COMMAND FILES

A *command file,* or *program,* is a file that contains a list of commands that dBASE executes in a series. The beauty of command files is that you can enter a few commands or hundreds of commands into a single file and then have dBASE execute them all at any time in response to a single command of yours.

Once again, this discussion is intended simply as an introduction to dBASE programming; there is much more to be said about this topic than can be summarized in a book addressed to users rather than programmers. Consult *dBASE IV Programmer's Reference Guide* (SYBEX, 1990) for more information.

Creating Command Files

SEQUENCE OF STEPS

From the dot prompt:

> **MODIFY COMMAND** <filename>
>
> type each command line for your program ↵
>
> Menus (**F10**)
>
> Exit/Save Changes and Exit   *or*   **Ctrl-End**

USAGE

You can create and edit command files using the dBASE IV program editor. To get to the program editor from the dot prompt, enter the command **MODIFY COMMAND** <filename> (where <filename> is a valid DOS file name, with no extension). For example, to create a program named Test, enter the command **MODIFY COMMAND Test** at the dot prompt.

When you get to the program editor, you can type each command for your program—followed by ↵ to ensure that each command is on a separate line. You can use any of the editing keys in Table 18.3 to make changes and corrections. These are the same keys you use to manage Memo field data.

KEYS	ALTERNATIVE	EFFECT
→	Ctrl-D	Moves the cursor right one character
←	Ctrl-S	Moves the cursor left one character
↓	Ctrl-X	Moves the cursor down one line
↑	Ctrl-E	Moves the cursor up one line
Ins	Ctrl-V	Toggles between insert and overwrite modes: in insert mode, the cursor appears as a blinking square; in overwrite mode, the cursor appears as a blinking underline
Del	Ctrl-G	Deletes the character at the cursor or the block of text that is currently selected with the **F6** key
Ctrl-T		Deletes characters to the right of the cursor up to the first letter of the next word
Ctrl-Y		Deletes the entire line

Table 18.3: Editing Keys Used in the dBASE IV Program Editor

KEYS	ALTERNATIVE	EFFECT
Backspace	Ctrl-H	Moves the cursor left one character, erasing along the way
↵	Ctrl-M	Marks the end of a command; adds a new blank line if insert mode is on
Ctrl-N		Inserts a blank line, regardless of whether Insert mode is on
Home	Ctrl-Z	Moves the cursor to the beginning of the line
End	Ctrl-B	Moves the cursor to the end of the line
Ctrl-→	Ctrl-F	Moves the cursor to the beginning of the next word
Ctrl-←	Ctrl-A	Moves the cursor to the beginning of the previous word
PgDn	Ctrl-C	Scrolls down one screen or to the bottom of the existing text on the current page
PgUp	Ctrl-R	Scrolls up one screen or to the top of the existing text on the current page
Tab		Indents text to the next tab stop
Shift-Tab		Outdents text one tab stop to the left
Select (F6)		Begins the process of marking a block of text. Use the arrow keys to select a block of text, and press ↵ to complete your selection
Move (F7)		Moves a block of text that has been selected with the **F6** key to the current cursor position
Copy (F8)		Copies a block of text that has been selected with the **F6** key to the current cursor position
Ctrl-End	Ctrl-W	Saves changes and exits
Ctrl-Q	Esc	Abandons changes and exits; if a block of text is currently selected (with the **F6** key), pressing **Esc** unselects the block

Table 18.3: Editing Keys Used in the dBASE IV Program Editor (continued)

EXAMPLE

To create a sample command file, type the commands that follow. Be sure to press ↵ after you type each command line. These commands do nothing immediately, because you are just storing them in a file. They will be executed later when you *run* the command file.

```
CLEAR
? "Here are the names in CustList..."
```

USE CustList
LIST LastName,FirstName
?
? "All done!"

When you are done, your screen should look like Figure 18.4.

To save the command file, you press Menus (**F10**) and select Save Changes and Exit from the Exit pull-down menu (or press **Ctrl-End**). You are then returned to the dot prompt. dBASE adds the extension .PRG to the file name you provide, storing the command file in this example as TEST.PRG.

Running a Command File

SEQUENCE OF STEPS

From the dot prompt:

DO <filename>

To edit your program:

MODIFY COMMAND <filename>

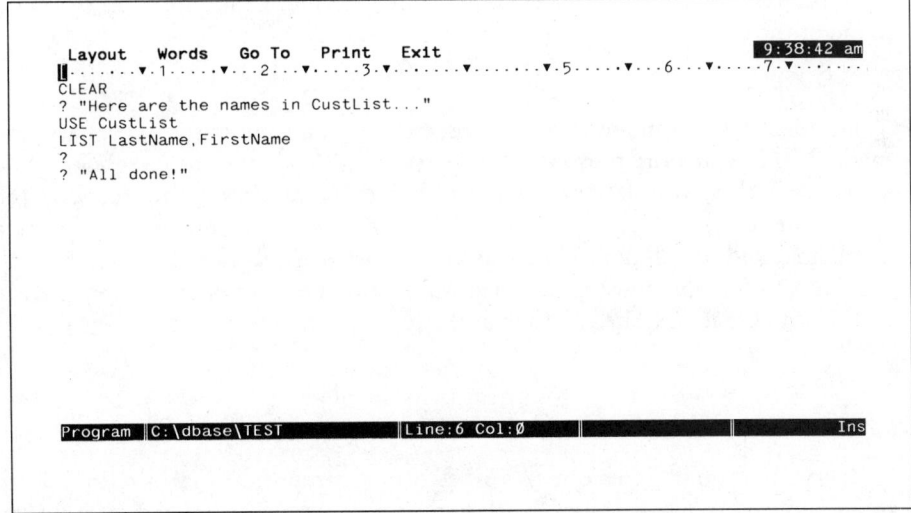

FIGURE 18.4: The Test command file on the dBASE IV program editor screen.

USAGE

To run an existing command file, you use the DO command, followed by the name of the command file. At the dot prompt, enter

DO <filename>

dBASE will take a moment to *compile* the program. When compilation is complete, you will see the results of the command file. When dBASE finishes executing all the commands, it returns you to the dot prompt.

You can run a command file as many times as you wish by entering **DO** <filename> at the dot prompt (or press ↑ at the dot prompt to redisplay the command and then press ↵ to reenter it). On subsequent runs, dBASE will not need to recompile the program, because the compiled version already exists. Therefore, the program will start immediately after you enter the DO

If you need to make changes to your program, enter the command

MODIFY COMMAND <filename>

at the dot prompt. You will be returned to the editor, with the program displayed on the screen. If you make changes, save the program and then rerun it; dBASE will automatically create a new compiled version.

EXAMPLE

To run the Test command file created in the previous example, enter this command at the dot prompt:

DO Test

The CLEAR command clears the screen (except for the status bar). The command **? "Here are the names in CustList..."** displays the message *Here are the names in CustList....* The command LIST LastName,FirstName displays the FirstName and LastName fields from the database. The command **?** prints a blank line, and **? "All done!"** displays the message *All done!*

Figure 18.5 shows how the screen looks after all the commands in the program have been executed. (The message at the top may scroll off your screen.)

Command Files that dBASE IV Creates Automatically

Every time you design a query, a label format, a report format, a custom form or an application using one of the design screens, dBASE uses the information from the design screen to create files that contain all the instructions required to tell the computer what to do.

COMMAND FILES THAT dBASE IV CREATES AUTOMATICALLY — 675

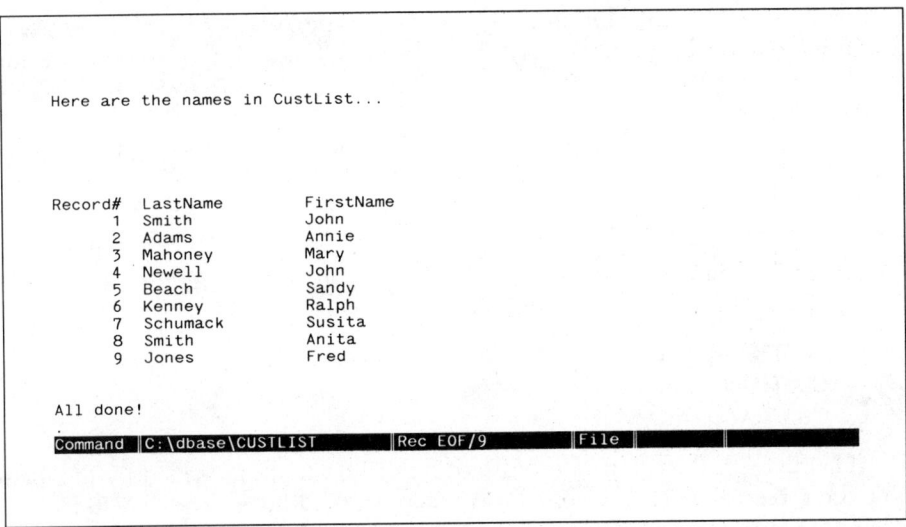

Figure 18.5: Results of running the Test command file

In most cases, dBASE IV creates three files for each object you create, as summarized below:

source code The source code file contains the dBASE IV programming language commands and functions required to perform the operation. This file is provided for programmers who might want to make changes to these commands, outside of the design screen.

object code The object code file contains a *compiled* version of the source code, which the computer can execute very quickly.

design screen file Most design screens also create a file for the design screen itself to use. This file is used when you modify an existing object, such as report format or custom screen, so that the design screen can redisplay your original design.

You can verify for yourself that dBASE IV actually creates two or three files for every object you create, by entering the command

    DIR <filename>.*

at the DOS or dBASE dot prompt, using the name of any dBASE object. This command tells dBASE to display the names of all files on the current directory that have the first name <filename> and any extension. You will see a list of all files with that file name.

For example, if you created the CUSTFORM custom form in Chapter 10, you can enter

DIR CUSTFORM.*

at the DOS prompt for the dBASE directory to see a list of all files with the file name CUSTFORM. You should see the following list:

CUSTFORM.SCR
CUSTFORM.FMT
CUSTFORM.FMO

The file with the extension .SCR contains information needed by the forms design screen to redisplay your form design in the future. The .FMT file contains the source code for displaying the screen. The .FMO file contains the compiled object code.

You can look directly at the contents of any source code file using the dBASE IV program editor. For example, to view the contents of the CUSTFORM.FMT file, enter this command at the dot prompt (remember to press ⏎ after typing the command):

MODIFY COMMAND CustForm.FMT

When the source code appears, you can use the **PgUp** and **PgDn** keys to scroll through the entire file. When you are done, press Menus (**F10**) and select Abandon Changes and Exit from the Exit pull-down menu to return to the dot prompt.

(The .SCR and .FMO files do *not* contain code that you can read directly, so you cannot use the program editor to view their contents.)

Table 18.4 lists the file name extensions for the various files created for each object. You can look at the source code file for any type of object. Note that database files (those with a .DBF extension) contain only data, not code, and so there is no compiled copy of those files.

TIPS AND TRAPS

- You can reenter or edit a previous dot prompt command by pressing ↑ and ↓ at the dot prompt to scroll through the last ten commands entered. You can change any command with the **Backspace** and arrow keys and reenter the command by pressing ⏎.

TYPE OF OBJECT	DESIGN SCREEN FILE	SOURCE CODE	OBJECT CODE
Queries	<None>	.QBE	.QBO
Labels	.LBL	.LBG	.LBO
Reports	.FRM	.FRG	.FRO
Forms	.SCR	.FMT	.FMO
Applications	.APP	.PRG	.DBO

Table 18.4: File Name Extensions for Various dBASE IV Objects

- If you are using a laser printer, you can enter the command **EJECT** at the dot prompt to eject the page.
- Using the dot prompt, and programming, require an in-depth knowledge of the dBASE IV programming language. Refer to a more advanced scource that focuses on dBASE IV programming before attempting any serious work with the programming language.

SUMMARY

This chapter has provided an introduction to the dBASE command language from the user's point of view. In addition to demonstrating a general technique for using commands at the dot prompt, it has presented two of the most useful commands: the question mark, for using dBASE as a calculator; and HELP, for getting on-screen information about any command. It has also shown how to create and run command files, and how to examine the command files that dBASE generates automatically when you create database objects.

For a summary of all dBASE IV functions:

- Appendix D, "dBASE IV Functions"

For a summary of all dBASE IV commands:

- Appendix E, "dBASE IV Commands"

For a complete reference to the dBASE IV programming language:

- *The dBASE IV Programmer's Reference Guide* (Alan Simpson, SYBEX, 1990)

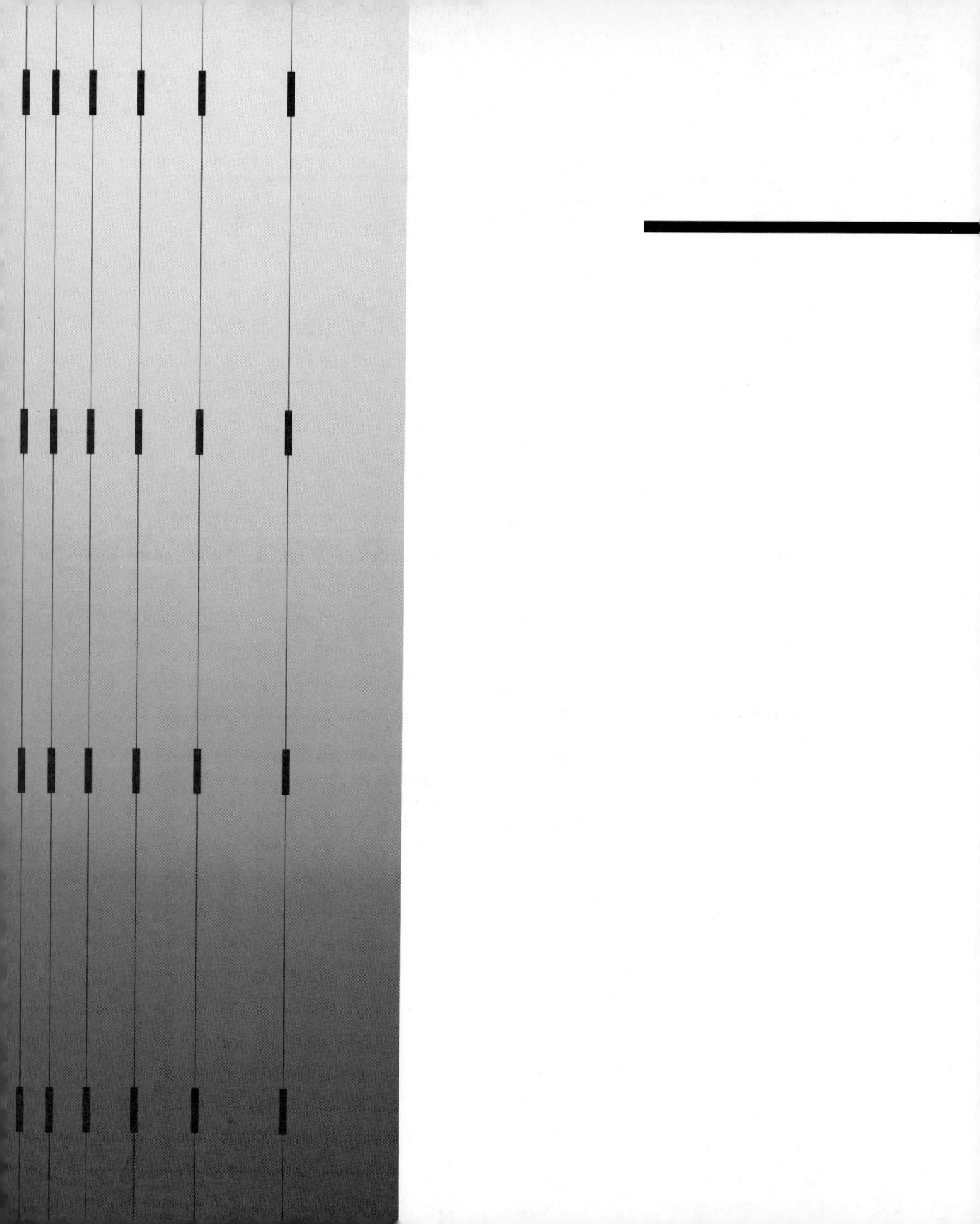

CHAPTER 19

USING DBSETUP

Running and Using DBSETUP. 681
Changing Your Hardware Setup. .683
Accessing dBASE IV from Any Directory. 687
Internationalizing dBASE IV. 689
    Changing the Date Format. .689
    Changing the Currency Format. 690
    Changing the Clock Format. 693
Changing the Default Display Colors. 695
Changing the Default Printer Margin. 698
Summary of DBSETUP Options. .699
DBSETUP Install Menu. 700
    Modify Hardware Setup. 700
    Install dBASE IV. 700
    Transfer Other Files. 700
        Sample Files. 701
        Tutorial Files. 701
        AutoExec.bat. 702
        Config.Sys. 702
        RunTime. 702
        dBASE Template Language Toolkit. 702
    Uninstall dBASE IV. 703
DBSETUP CONFIG.DB Menu. .703
    Modify Existing CONFIG.DB. 703
    Create New CONFIG.DB. 704
    CONFIG.DB Main Menu. 704
        Database Pull-Down Menu. 704
        General Pull-Down Menu. 704
        Display Pull-Down Menu. 708
        Keys Pull-Down Menu. .709

  File Pull-Down Menu. 710
  Memory Pull-Down Menu. 711
  Output Pull-Down Menu. 712
  Exit Pull-Down Menu. 712
DBSETUP Tools Menu. 714
  Display Disk Usage. 714
  Test Disk Performance. 715
  Review System Configuration. 716
DBSETUP DOS Menu. 717
  Go To DOS. 717
  Set Default Drive:Directory. 717
DBSETUP Exit Menu. 718
Tips and Traps. 718
Summary. 718

Using DBSETUP

The initial procedure for installing dBASE IV on your computer (discussed in Appendix A) allows you to define certain characteristics of your computer hardware, such as the screen display mode and the available printers. The installation procedure then configures dBASE to use your selected hardware, copies the dBASE program files to your hard disk, and sets some default settings (such as screen colors and date formats).

If you change your computer's hardware (for example, if you upgrade from a color monitor to an EGA), you need to use the DBSETUP program to reconfigure dBASE IV for the new equipment. You can also use DBSETUP to change the default settings that the installation procedure initially defines.

Chapter 14 discussed how to change the default settings using the Settings option on the Tools pull-down menu. However, that technique changes the default settings for the current dBASE session only. When you use DBSETUP to change the default settings, all future dBASE IV sessions use the new default settings.

Running and Using DBSETUP

The DBSETUP program is separate from dBASE and must be executed directly from the DOS command prompt. The DBSETUP program is stored in a file named DBSETUP.EXE, which in turn needs to have access to DBSETUP.RES, DBSETUP.OVL, DBSETUP.PRD, and DBSETUP.HLP. During the installation process, all of these files are copied to the same drive and directory that stores the DBASE IV programs (usually C:\DBASE).

SEQUENCE OF STEPS

From the DOS command prompt (assuming that dBASE IV is installed on the \DBASE directory of disk drive C):

    C: ↵
    CD \DBASE ↵
    DBSETUP ↵
    ↵

USAGE

When you first run DBSETUP, it displays a main menu and the Install pull-down menu, as shown in Figure 19.1. You use these menus the same way you use the dBASE IV menus: you use the ↑, ↓, →, and ← keys to move the highlight, and press ↵ to select the currently highlighted option. Also, as with other dBASE menus, some options are multiple-choice, and you can press the space bar to cycle through the options.

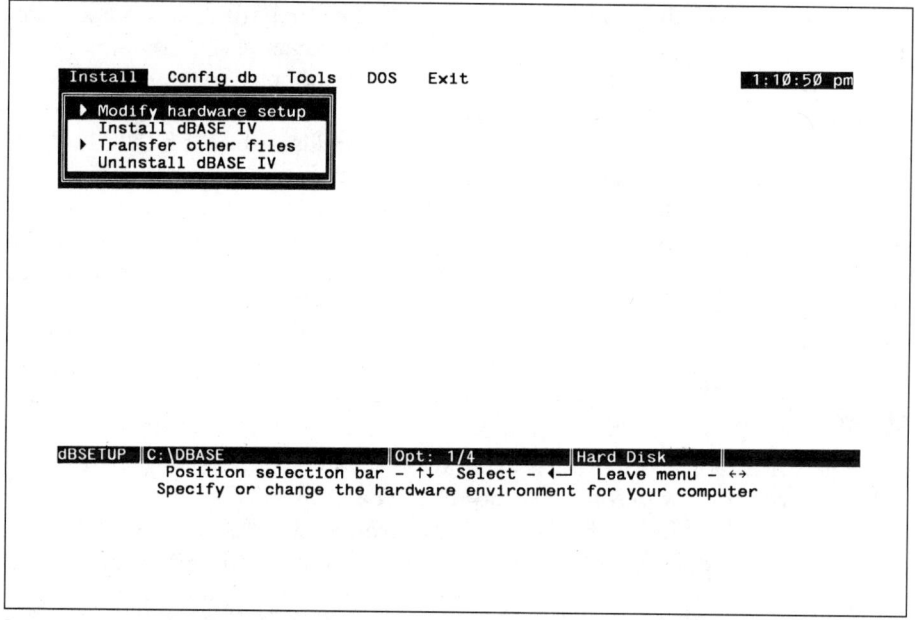

FIGURE 19.1: The DBSETUP menus with the Install menu pulled down. You can use the Modify Hardware Setup option from the Install menu when you need to change your hardware setup after you have installed dBASE IV.

One feature that is unique to the DBSETUP menus, however, is their use of the **Del** key. Many DBSETUP menu options allow you to either change a default setting or return to the original default setting by pressing the **Del** key. As usual, the message line at the bottom of the screen tells you what keys are available for each menu that is displayed.

The purpose of each option on the horizontal menu is summarized here:

Install   Allows you to change existing hardware settings, install dBASE IV, copy additional dBASE IV files from disks to

	the hard disk, or uninstall (remove) dBASE IV from your hard disk.
Config.db	Allows you to change default settings, which are stored in a file named CONFIG.DB on the same drive and directory that stores the dBASE IV program. This option is similar to the Settings option on the Tools pull down menu, available at the Control Center (see Chapter 14), but it provides more options. (Most of the additional options that DBSETUP provides are of interest only to advanced dBASE programmers.)
Tools	Provides information about disk use, performance, and overall system configuration. (These tools assume an in-depth knowledge of computer hardware and DOS and are provided for advanced programmers.)
DOS	Allows you to send a command directly to DOS, to temporarily exit to DOS, or to change the current drive and directory.
Exit	Leaves the DBSETUP program and returns to the DOS command prompt.

Sections that follow provide examples of how to use DBSETUP to change current hardware selections and some of the default settings.

CHANGING YOUR HARDWARE SETUP

SEQUENCE OF STEPS

From the DOS prompt for the \DBASE directory:

    insert System Disk 2 into drive A

    DBSETUP ←

    ←

    Modify Hardware Setup [←]

    change selected equipment

    Ctrl-End

USAGE

To add or change hardware for use with dBASE IV, you first need your copies of your original dBASE IV disks (the ones that came with your dBASE IV package). Put the disk labeled System Disk 2 into disk drive A of your computer.

Next, from the DOS command prompt, access the drive and directory where dBASE IV and DBSETUP are stored (usually C:\DBASE) and run the DBSETUP program (as discussed in the previous section). Press ⏎ to select Modify Hardware Setup from the Install pull-down menu. dBASE displays the Hardware Setup menu. Select the appropriate option for the hardware you want to install and follow the instructions on the screen (as demonstrated in the examples that follow).

EXAMPLES

To change your computer's current display mode, follow the sequence of steps to access the DBSETUP Hardware Setup menu. Then move the highlight to the Display Mode option and press the space bar repeatedly to scroll through its options. When you see the display mode that your monitor uses, press ↓.

To optimize the speed of your display screen, move the highlight to the Optimize Color Display option and press ⏎. dBASE will display the information box shown in Figure 19.2. Press ⏎ to select Proceed.

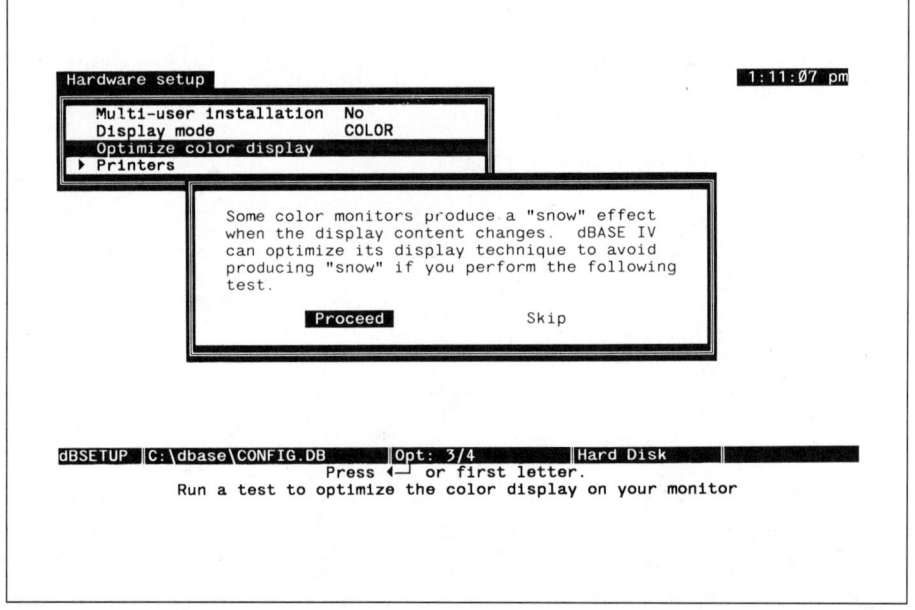

FIGURE 19.2: dBASE optimizes color displays by checking for a snow effect when you select Optimize Color Display from the DBSETUP Hardware Setup menu.

CHANGING YOUR HARDWARE SETUP — **685**

The screen will ask if you see "snow" (interference) on your screen. Type **Y** if you see snow; type **N** if you do not. (Typing **Y** prevents snow from appearing when you use dBASE IV, but slows down the screen speed slightly.) As prompted on the screen, press any key to continue. You'll be returned to the Hardware Setup menu.

If you wish to install a printer (or printers), press ↓ to move to the Printers option. Press ↵. dBASE displays a printer table, as shown in Figure 19.3. Press Pick (**Shift-F1**) to display the list of available printer manufacturers (though your screen may display previously installed printers). Use ↓ to scroll through the list of printers and press ↵ to select yours. (Figure 19.4 shows Epson selected from the list.) A submenu of printer models then appears. Use ↓ to scroll through the printer models and select yours by pressing ↵ when your model is highlighted. (Figure 19.5 shows the first screenful of Epson printer models.)

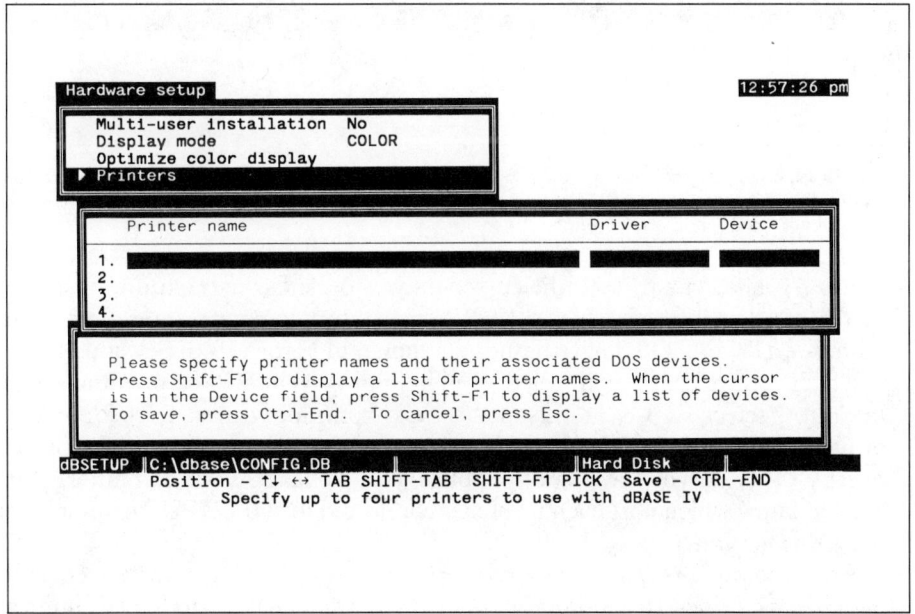

FIGURE 19.3: A printer table appears when you select Printers from the DBSETUP Hardware Setup menu. You fill in the printer name, driver, and device by selecting from menus with Pick (**Shift-F1**). Repeat the procedure to list additional printers.

If you do not see your printer name or model listed, you can select the Generic Driver option. This option supports all printers, but only for basic text; it does not support custom fonts or graphics characters.

686 — CH. 19 USING DBSETUP

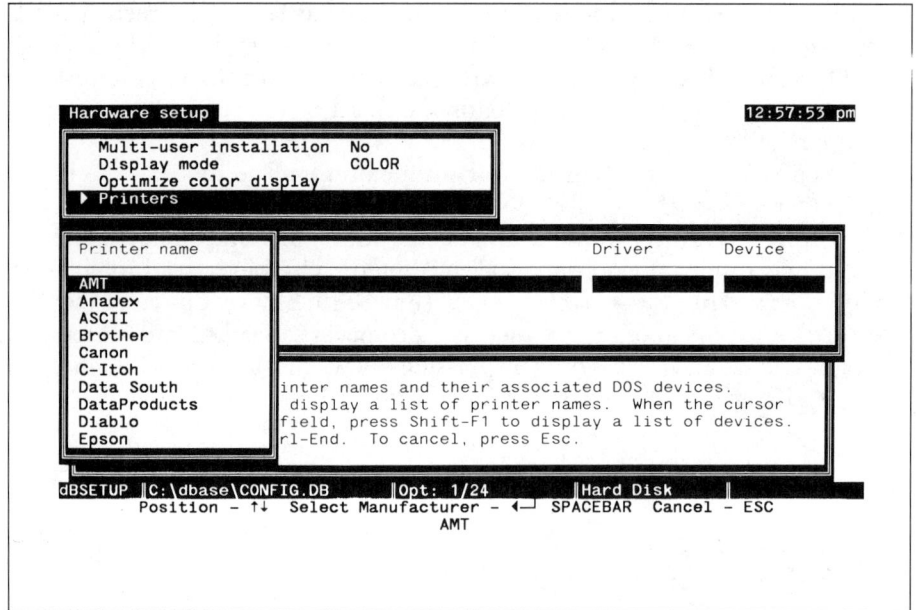

FIGURE 19.4: The first page listing printers you can configure for dBASE IV. If your printer manufacturer is not displayed, select Generic Printer from the next page of this list (press **PgDn** to scroll to the next page where the Generic Printer option is listed.)

After you select a printer, the cursor moves to the Device column, where you specify the port through which dBASE sends output to your printer. Press **Shift-F1** to see a list of DOS device names, as shown in Figure 19.6. Select the device to which your printer is connected by highlighting its name and pressing ←. (If in doubt, select LPT1, as this is the most commonly used port for parallel printers. If you are certain that you have a serial rather than a parallel printer, select COM1. If you have multiple printers attached to your computer, you'll need to know which port each printer is connected to; DBSETUP cannot determine this for you.)

After you press ←, the cursor moves to the next line. Here you can repeat the basic steps outlined in the preceding paragraphs to install up to four printers, or print modes. For example, if you have a Hewlett-Packard Laserjet printer, you can select 100 dots per inch (dpi) mode as one print mode and landscape (horizontal) mode as a second print mode. Be sure to use the same port name for both "printers" when selecting different modes for the same printer.

After selecting a printer (or printers), press **Ctrl-End**. The screen will display a list of the driver names you selected. Select one of these as the default driver (the one automatically used when you first start dBASE IV) by highlighting its name

ACCESSING dBASE IV FROM ANY DIRECTORY

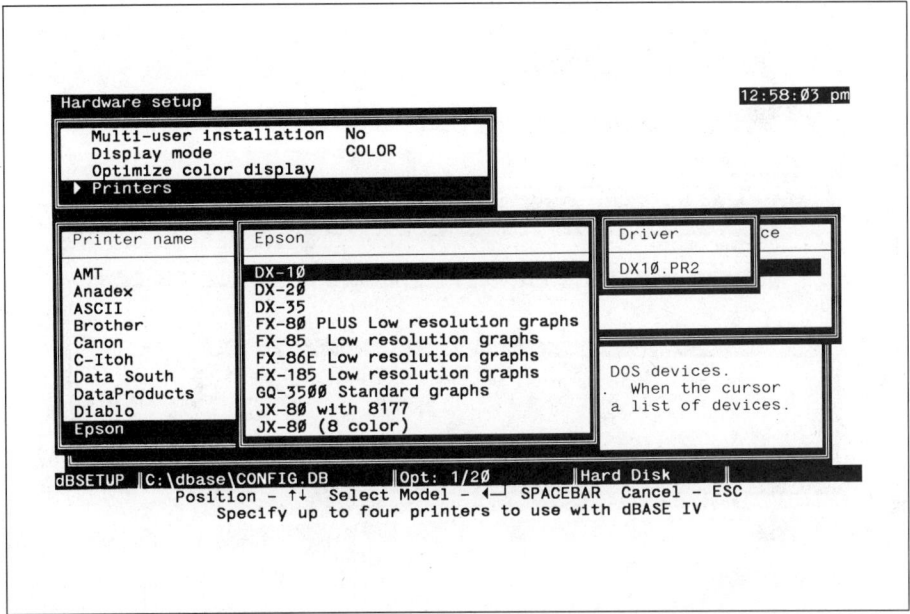

FIGURE 19.5: List of Epson printer models, displayed after you select Epson from the printer name list.

and pressing ←┘. Later, when you actually use dBASE IV, the Print menu (discussed in Chapter 9), will allow you to select one of your other print drivers if you wish to do so.

After selecting the default driver, you'll be returned to the Hardware Settings menu. Type **Ctrl-End** to save your selected settings. You'll see a message asking which drive and directory contain dBASE IV, and a suggested drive and directory (most likely C:\DBASE). Press ←┘ to select the suggested drive and directory.

ACCESSING dBASE IV FROM ANY DIRECTORY

SEQUENCE OF STEPS

At the DOS prompt for the \DBASE directory:

    DBSETUP ←┘

    ←┘

    Install/Transfer Other Files

    AutoExec.BAT

    ←┘

688 — CH. 19 USING DBSETUP

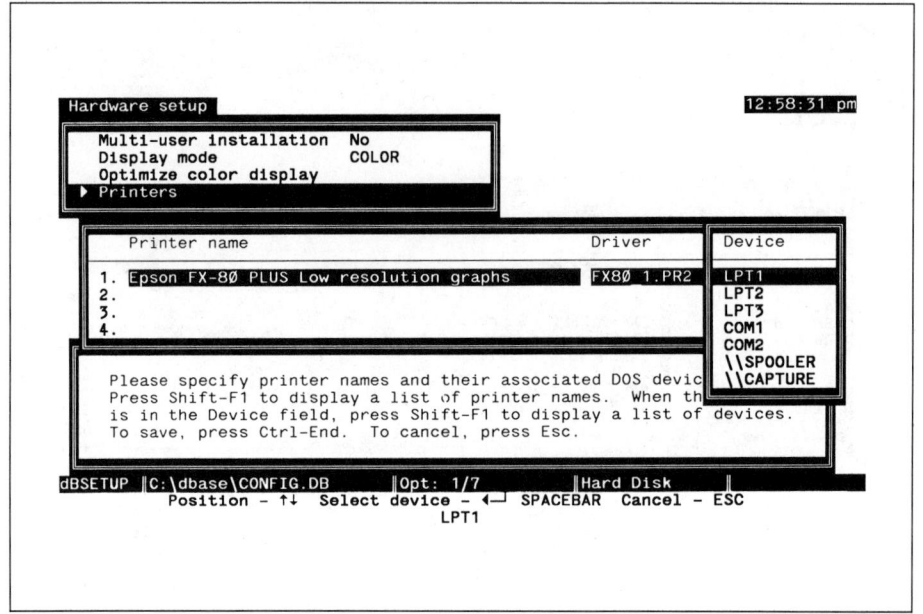

FIGURE 19.6: List of available printer devices. Most systems use a parallel printer connected to LPT1 as the primary printer. A secondary printer may be connected to a second parallel port (LPT2).

Proceed

Esc

USAGE

If you want to start dBASE IV from a directory other than the C:\DBASE directory, you can modify the AUTOEXEC.BAT file to include the correct DOS PATH setting. Note that you need only perform this procedure if you neglected to choose this option during the initial installation procedure and therefore can run dBASE IV only from its home directory (usually C:\DBASE).

At the DOS prompt for the \DBASE directory, type **DBSETUP** and press ← to access DBSETUP. Press ← at the copyright screen. Select Transfer Other Files from the Install pull-down menu. Select AutoExec.BAT from the submenu. Press ← to accept the default drive and directory and then select Proceed. Press **Esc** to leave the submenu. Then select Exit to DOS. The new PATH setting will not take effect until the next time you start the computer or run the AUTOEXEC.BAT file from the DOS command prompt.

INTERNATIONALIZING dBASE IV

dBASE IV initially comes configured to display dates and currencies in American formats. You can change the formats of currencies and dates using the DBSETUP program.

Changing the Date Format

SEQUENCE OF STEPS

At the DOS prompt for the \DBASE directory:

DBSETUP ↵

↵

Config.DB/Modify Existing Config.DB [↵]

↵

General/Date

press the space bar to scroll through the options

Ctrl-End

↵

↵

Exit/Exit to DOS [↵]

To display the year with four digits:

General/Century

Press the space bar to scroll through options

Ctrl-End

↵

↵

To exit DBSETUP:

Exit/Exit to DOS [↵]

USAGE

By default, dBASE displays dates in the format MM/DD/YY. You can use DBSETUP to change to a different date format, which will then be used in all future dBASE IV sessions. Table 19.1 shows the date format for each of the options available. As you can see, many of the options present essentially the same format. You can also convert any date format so that it accepts and displays the year as a four-digit number (for example, 1989) rather than a two-digit number (for example, 89).

OPTION	FORMAT	EXAMPLE
American	MM/DD/YY	12/31/90
ANSI	YY.MM.DD	90.12.31
British	DD/MM/YY	31/12/90
French	DD/MM/YY	31/12/90
German	DD.MM.YY	31.12.90
Italian	DD-MM-YY	31-12-90
Japanese	YY/MM/DD	90/12/31
USA	MM-DD-YY	12-31-90
MDY	MM/DD/YY	12/31/90
DMY	DD/MM/YY	31/12/90
YMD	YY/MM/DD	90/12/31

Table 19.1: International Date Formats for dBASE IV

At the DOS prompt for the \DBASE directory, type **DBSETUP** and press ↵. The copyright screen appears. Press ↵. Select Modify Existing Config.DB from the Config.DB pull-down menu. Press ↵ to accept the suggested drive and directory. On the General pull-down menu, highlight Date, as shown in Figure 19.7. Press the space bar to scroll through the options.

To display the year with four digits, highlight Century on the General pull-down menu. Press the space bar to change the setting to On. Press **Ctrl-End** to save the setting. Press ↵ to accept the displayed drive and directory. Press ↵ when dBASE prompts *This file already exists. Ok to overwrite?* To exit DBSETUP, select Exit to DOS from the Exit pull-down menu.

Changing the Currency Format

SEQUENCE OF STEPS

From the DOS prompt for the \DBASE directory:

    DBSETUP ↵

    ↵

CHANGING THE CURRENCY FORMAT — 691

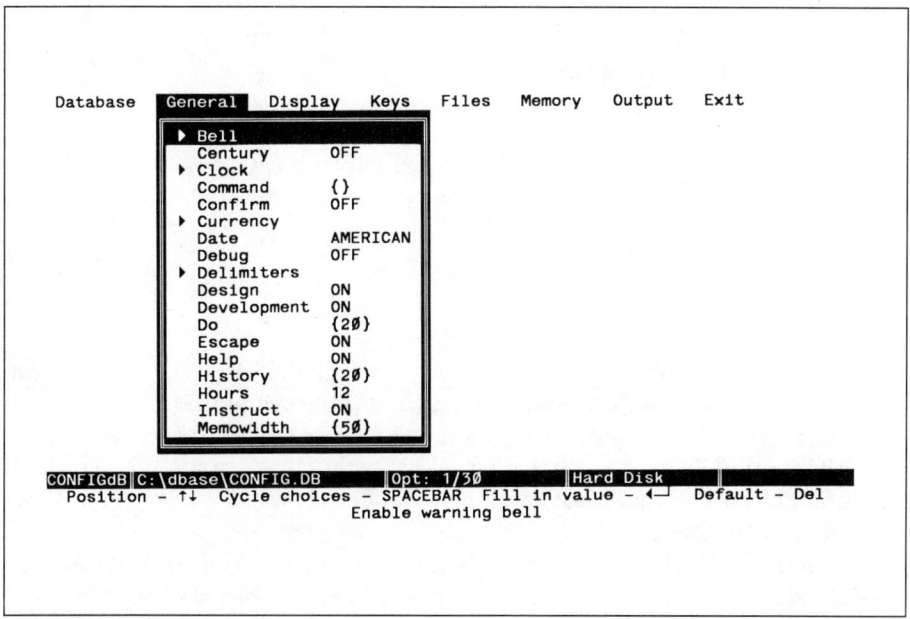

FIGURE 19.7: The DBSETUP General submenu allows you to change many of dBASE IV's default settings. You access this screen of pull-down menus by selecting Modify Existing Config.DB from the DBSETUP Config.DB pull-down menu.

    Config.DB/**M**odify Existing Config.DB [←]
    [←]

To change the currency symbol:

    General/**C**urrency [←]

    Symbol [←]

    press the space bar and type the symbol you want [←]

To display the currency symbol to the right of a number (rather than to the left):

    General/**C**urrency [←]

    Right [←]

To use a character other than a period as the decimal point:

    General/**P**oint [←]

    type the character to use [←]

To use a character other than a comma to separate thousands:

> **G**eneral/**S**eparator [←]
>
> type the character you wish to use as the separator ←

To exit DBSETUP from the General pull-down menu:

> **E**xit/**S**ave and Exit [←]
>
> **E**xit/**E**xit to DOS [←]

USAGE

By default, dBASE IV prints currency amounts that use currency templates or picture functions with a leading dollar sign (for example, $123.45). You can use DBSETUP to modify the display of these currency amounts. You can change the currency symbol, the position of the currency symbol, the character used for the decimal place, and the delimiter character that separates thousands from hundreds.

From the DOS prompt for the \DBASE directory, type **DBSETUP** and press ←. The copyright screen appears. Press ←. Select Modify Existing Config.DB from the Config.DB pull-down menu. Press ← to accept the drive and directory.

To change the currency symbol, select Currency from the General pull-down menu. Select Symbol from the submenu that appears. dBASE prompts for a character string. Press the space bar, type the symbol you want, and press ←.

Why insert a space before the symbol? The currency symbol that you enter can be up to ten characters long. However, to prevent the symbol from being repeated when dBASE displays numbers using the $ picture function (that is, to display $123.45 rather than $$$$123.45), you should make the first character a blank space by pressing the space bar.

To use any of the five currency symbols that are included in ASCII but are not available from the keyboard, hold down the **Alt** key and type the three-digit ASCII code for the symbol from Table 19.2. Use the numeric keypad, not the

ASCII CODE	SYMBOL	MEANING
155	¢	Cent
156	£	Pound
157	¥	Yen
158	PT	Peseta
159	*f*	Franc

Table 19.2: ASCII Codes for International Currency Symbols

numbers at the top of the keyboard. The selected symbol appears on the screen after you type all three digits and then release the **Alt** key.

To display the currency symbol to the right of a number (rather than to the left), select Currency from the General pull-down menu. Press the space bar to scroll through the justification settings, Left and Right.

To use a character other than a period as the decimal point, select Point from the General pull-down menu. dBASE prompts for the character to use. Type the character or the **Alt**-*key* combination and press ↵. Press **Ctrl-End** to save the current settings.

To use a character other than a comma to separate thousands, select Separator from the General pull-down menu. dBASE prompts for a separator character. Type the character you want to use as the separator and press ↵.

To exit DBSETUP from the General pull-down menu, select Save and Exit from the Exit pull-down menu and then select Exit to DOS from the Exit pull-down menu.

Regardless of the format you define while in Config.DB, you still must enter numeric values in the usual manner (for example, **12345.67**) when storing data in the database. However, when you design a custom form or report format to print the data, the number will be formatted according to the template or picture function you define at that time.

For example, suppose you define £ as the currency symbol, Right as the currency justification, the comma (,) as the decimal point, and the period (.) as the separator for thousands. If you design a report or custom form and use the Financial Format picture function and the template 999,999.99 to display the field, the number 12345.67 will be displayed as 12.345,67£.

Changing the Clock Format

SEQUENCE OF STEPS

DBSETUP ↵

↵

Config.DB/**M**odify Existing Config.DB [↵]

↵

General/**C**lock [↵]

To turn the clock off:

To turn the clock off:

    Clock Off

To change the position of the clock:

    Screen Row

    type a number for the row ⏎

    Screen Column

    type a number for the column ⏎

To change the clock display to 24 hour:

    Hours 24

To save your changes and exit DBSETUP:

    Exit/**S**ave and Exit [⏎]

    Exit/**E**xit to DOS [⏎]

USAGE

The Control Center always displays a clock in the upper-right corner of the screen. You can use DBSETUP to remove the clock, change its position, or change its format. (To reset the time, for Daylight Savings Time or any other reason, use DOS.) To move the clock to the upper-left corner of the screen, choose row 0 and column 0. You can also display the time in 24-hour format. If you change the clock display from a 12-hour clock to a 24-hour clock, 1300 will appear, for example, rather than 1:00 P.M.

At the DOS prompt for the \DBASE directory, type **DBSETUP** and press ⏎. The copyright screen appears. Press ⏎. Select Modify Existing Config.DB from the Config.DB pull-down menu. Press ⏎ to accept the suggested drive and directory.

To turn the clock off, select Clock from the General pull-down menu. A submenu appears with Clock highlighted. Press ⏎ to change the setting to Off.

To change the position of the clock, highlight Screen Row, type a number for the row, and press ⏎. Then highlight Screen Column, type a number for the column, and press ⏎.

To change the clock display to 24 hour, select Hours from the DBSETUP Config.DB General menu. Press the space bar to change the setting to 24.

To save your changes and exit DBSETUP, select Save and Exit from the Exit pull-down menu. Then select Exit to DOS from the Exit pull-down menu.

Changing the Default Display Colors

SEQUENCE OF STEPS

From the DOS command prompt and directory that dBASE IV is stored on:

DBSETUP ↵

↵

Config.db/Modify Existing CONFIG.DB

↵ (to accept the default drive and directory)

Display

select a display mode (if this option is available)

select an area to color

select a foreground color

select a background color

Ctrl-End

Save and Exit [↵]

↵ (to accept the default drive and directory)

OK

Exit

USAGE

If you have a color monitor, you can use DBSETUP to change the default colors displayed on your screen when you first start dBASE IV. (Note that some EGA and VGA monitors cannot be configured through DBSETUP.) First you must run the DBSETUP program (as described at the beginning of this chapter) and then select Modify Existing CONFIG.DB from the Config.db pull-down menu. Press ↵ to accept the suggested drive and directory, or change the suggested drive and directory if you have installed dBASE IV elsewhere. On the next menu that appears, move the highlight to the Display option.

The Display pull-down menu provides a list of areas to color, as shown in Figure 19.8. The Display Mode option is available only with certain display adapters that offer more than one mode of operation. For example, if you are using an EGA or VGA monitor, you can switch between EGA25 (for 25-line screens) and EGA43 (for 43-line displays) by pressing the space bar while the option is highlighted.

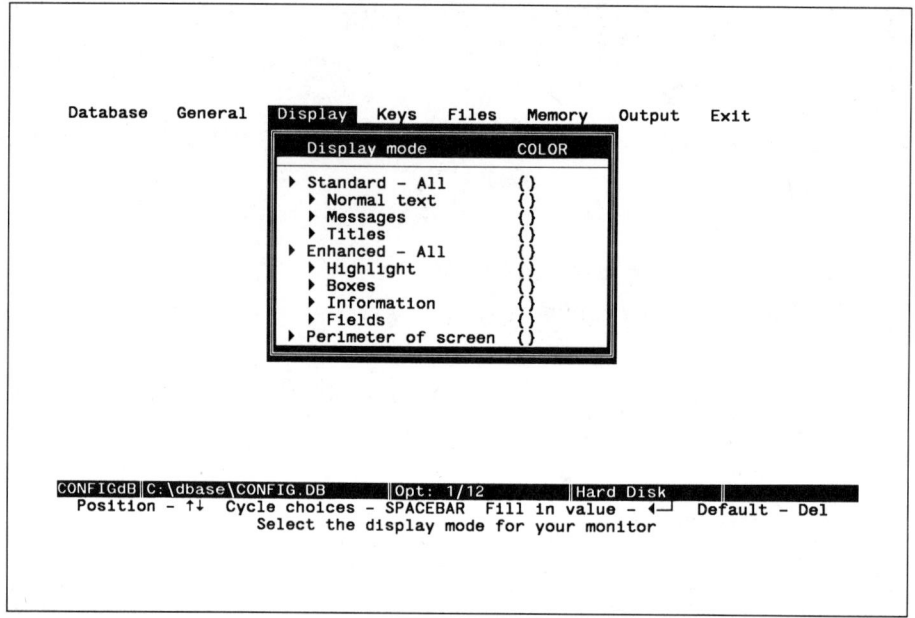

FIGURE 19.8: The Display pull-down menu in DBSETUP. You can select any area of the screen to color by highlighting its name and pressing ⏎. Depending on your type of display, you may also be able to switch between display modes.

Figure 19.9 shows the various areas on the screen that can be colored, using the Control Center as an example. The Fields option affects prompt-box entry areas, the selected field in browse mode, and fields displayed on custom forms.

Select an area of the screen to color by highlighting the appropriate option and pressing the space bar. You will see a color palette, as in Figure 19.10.

To select a color combination, use the ↑ and ↓ keys to move the box symbol up and down through the options. The foreground color will change as you do, so that you can immediately see how the color looks against the current background color.

After positioning the box at the foreground color you prefer, press →. The currently selected foreground color will have a > symbol to the left. Now you can use the ↑ and ↓ keys to scroll through color options for the background, to see how each one looks behind the currently selected foreground color. You can experiment as much as you wish using the ↑, ↓, →, and ← keys.

When you are satisfied with the currently selected color combination, press **Ctrl-End**. You will be returned to the Display pull-down menu. From there, you can select another area to color, or you can select Save and Exit to save the current colors. (Optionally, you can select Abandon and Exit to abandon your changes and retain the default color settings.)

CHANGING THE DEFAULT DISPLAY COLORS — 697

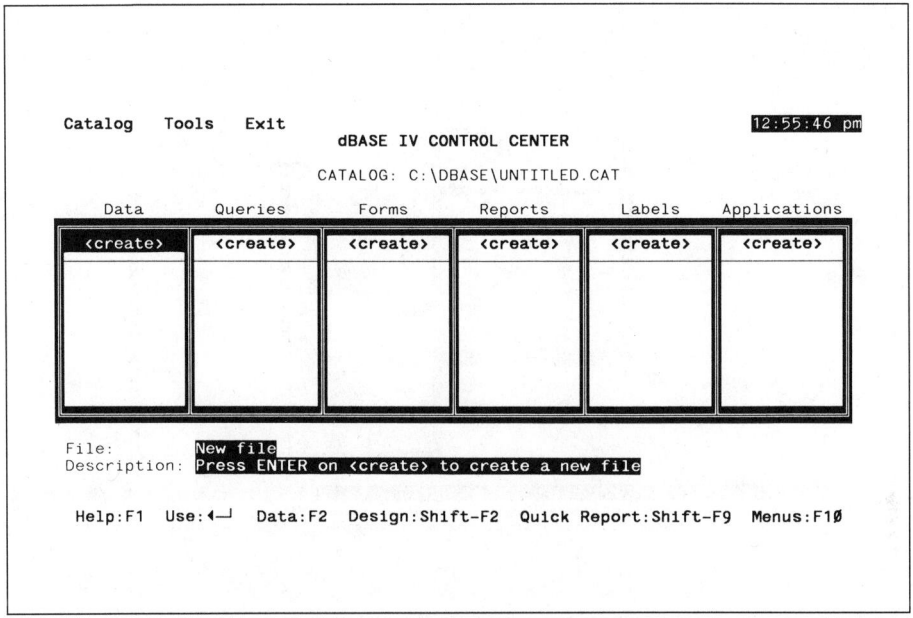

FIGURE 19.9: Areas that can be colored on the screen, using the Control Center as an example. The Standard option affects all standard text (shown as dark letters against a light background in the figure). The Enhanced option affects all enhanced (light-on-dark) areas.

If you opt to save your changes, dBASE will prompt you for the location of the CONFIG.DB file. Press ↵ to accept the default drive and directory, or change the drive and directory if you have stored dBASE IV elsewhere on your hard disk. Select Ok when prompted for permission to overwrite the existing CONFIG.DB file.

EXAMPLE

Suppose you decide to use bright white letters against a red background as the general color combination for standard text. After running DBSETUP and getting to the Display pull-down menu, highlight the Standard—All option and press the space bar.

Press ↑ or ↓ until the box aligns next to the Brt White option; then press →. Press ↑ or ↓ to move the box to align with the Red option. Note that the option is displayed using the selected color combination (bright white letters against a red background).

Press **Ctrl-End** to accept the color combination. (Optionally, you can press the **Del** (or delete) key to go back to the default setting.) Next, select Save and Exit

698 — CH. 19 USING DBSETUP

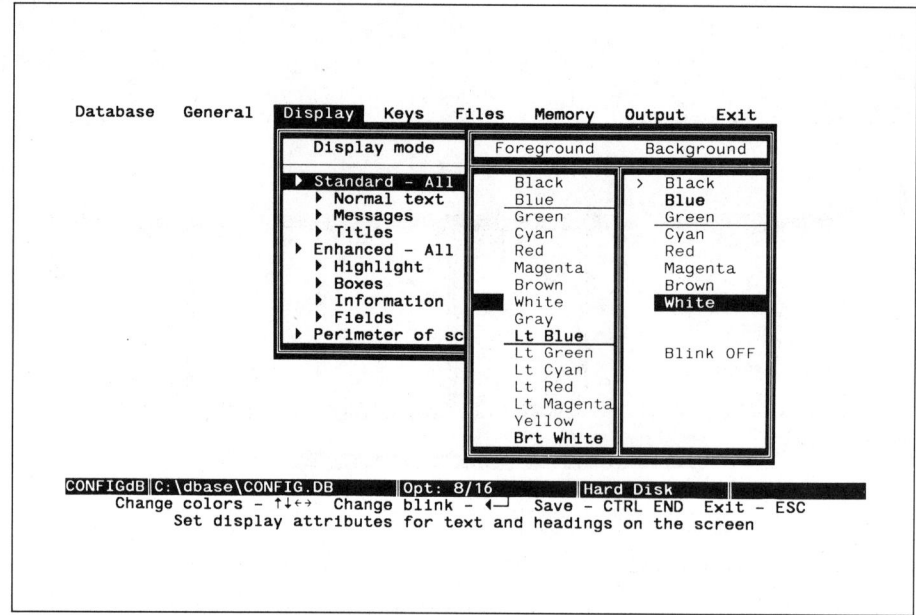

FIGURE 19.10: The color palette for selecting foreground and background color combinations. Pressing ⏎ turns blinking on or off.

from the Exit pull-down menu. Press ⏎ to accept the suggest drive and directory for the Config.DB file (or change it, if you have stored dBASE IV elsewhere, and then press ⏎). When prompted for permission to overwrite the existing CONFIG.DB file, press ⏎ to select Ok.

To leave DBSETUP, select Exit to DOS from the next menu that appears. Whenever you use dBASE IV in the future, it will use the color combination you have specified.

CHANGING THE DEFAULT PRINTER MARGIN

SEQUENCE OF STEPS

From the DOS command prompt and the directory that dBASE IV is stored on:

    DBSETUP ⏎

    ⏎

    Config.db/**M**odify Existing Config.db [⏎]

    ⏎

Output/Margin [↵]
↵
enter the number of columns for the left margin
↵
Ctrl-End
↵
↵

USAGE

You can specify a default left margin for all printed output from dBASE IV using the DBSETUP program. This default setting will be used for all printed output, unless you specify a different margin for a particular report using the Page Dimensions option on the Print pull-down menu.

EXAMPLE

Suppose that your printer leaves no left margin when it prints dBASE IV data, so you wish to set a default margin of 1 inch. To do so, run the DBSETUP program from the directory that stores dBASE IV (usually C:\DBASE). Then move the highlight to the Config.db option on the DBSETUP main menu and select the Modify Existing Config.db option.

When the screen prompts you for a directory to store the modified CONFIG.DB on, press ↵ to select the default directory, C:\DBASE. Then move the highlight to the Output option on the Config.db main menu.

Next move the highlight to the Margin option and press ↵. You can then enter any number in the range 0 to 254. Note that the number represents the number of characters. For example, if your printer prints ten characters to the inch, entering the number 10 will leave a 1-inch left margin on your printed output. Press ↵ after entering a number.

To save the new default setting, press **Ctrl-End**. Then press ↵ to accept the suggested drive and directory for storing the CONFIG.DB file. When prompted for permission to overwrite the existing CONFIG.DB file, press ↵ to select Ok. You can then exit the DBSETUP program by selecting Exit to DOS from the Exit pull-down menu.

SUMMARY OF DBSETUP OPTIONS

The sections that follow provide summary information about all of the DBSETUP menus and options. Many of these are provided for advanced programmers and applications developers. For additional information about these options, refer to the *Language Reference* manual that came with your dBASE IV package or to a more advanced book that focuses on the dBASE IV programming language.

DBSETUP INSTALL MENU

The Install pull-down menu in DBSETUP allows you to install dBASE IV and to change individual settings from a previous installation. Each menu option is summarized in the sections that follow.

Modify Hardware Setup

When the Modify Hardware Setup option is displayed, you can press the space bar to scroll through the options No and Yes. This setting determines how dBASE IV is installed later when you select the Install dBASE IV option from the Install pull-down menu.

Network installation requires planning and a knowledge of how the overall network is configured. Therefore, network installation is best left to the network administrator (the person in charge of the network). The *Network Installation* manual that came with your dBASE IV package discusses network installation for a variety of networks.

The Display Mode, Optimize Color Display, and Printers options let you define the display type and printers attached to your computer. See the section "Changing Your Hardware Setup" earlier in this chapter for examples.

Install dBASE IV

The Install dBASE IV option performs the entire installation process. Before selecting this option, insert the disk labeled "Installation Disk" that came with your dBASE IV package into drive A. This option will guide you through the installation procedure, as discussed in Appendix A of this book.

Transfer Other Files

When you select the Transfer Other Files option, DBSETUP displays the following options:

> Sample Files
> Tutorial Files

Autoexec.bat
Config.sys
RunTime
dBASE Template Language toolkit

Before selecting one of these options, insert one of the disks that came with your dBASE IV package into drive A (any of the dBASE IV disks will do). When you select one of these options, the screen will ask where dBASE IV is installed and suggest the default C:\DBASE. Press ↵ to accept the default drive and directory, or modify the suggested drive and directory to match your dBASE IV drive and directory.

Depending on the option you select, dBASE may then ask for the name of the directory on which to store the transferred files. As usual, you can press ↵ to accept the suggested drive and directory, or you can change the drive and directory name if you wish. The following sections describe the files transferred by each option.

Sample Files

The Sample Files option copies sample dBASE IV database and SQL files from the Sample Programs disks that came with your dBASE IV package to the \DBASE\SQLHOME and \DBASE\SAMPLES directories, unless you specify other directory names. These files are used in examples in the manuals that came with your dBASE IV package.

Tutorial Files

The Tutorial Files option copies the dBASE tutorial program from the Tutorial Disk that came with your dBASE IV package to a directory named \DBASE\DBTUTOR (unless you specify a different directory name). When copying is complete, you'll be returned to the DBSETUP main menu.

To use the dBASE IV tutorial, select Exit to DOS from the DBSETUP main menu. Then, at the command prompt, enter the command **CD DBTUTOR** to switch to the \DBASE\DBTUTOR directory. Then enter the command **INTRO** (and press ↵) to begin the tutorial. The tutorial program is self-explanatory. It leads you step by step through lessons about using dBASE IV.

When you've finished using the tutorial program, press **F5** to exit and type **Q** (to select Quit) when prompted. You'll be returned to the DOS command prompt. To return to the \DBASE directory, type **CD..** and press ↵.

AutoExec.bat

The Autoexec.bat option creates or modifies the DOS AUTOEXEC.BAT file, stored on the root directory of drive C. This option adds the directory that dBASE IV is stored on to the DOS PATH setting, so that you can run dBASE IV from any directory (see "Accessing dBASE IV from Any Directory" earlier in this chapter for additional information).

Config.sys

The Config.sys option creates or modifies the DOS CONFIG.SYS file on the root directory of drive C. Two commands in the CONFIG.SYS file, FILES and BUFFERS, are examined and, if necessary, changed to the following settings:

```
BUFFERS = 15
FILES = 40
```

These settings tell DOS to allow a maximum of 40 files to be opened simultaneously and to set aside 15 disk buffers in RAM. If the FILES setting in CONFIG.SYS is too small, dBASE displays the message *Too many files are open*. The buffers setting affects the speed at which dBASE IV operates. If the BUFFERS setting is too high or too low, dBASE's speed may be compromised.

RunTime

The RunTime option is used only with the dBASE IV Developer's Edition. It copies the programs in the RunTime package from the RunTime disks that came with your dBASE IV package to the drive and directory that stores dBASE. The RunTime package is used by programmers and application developers to create applications that can be distributed to customers who do not own dBASE IV.

dBASE Template Language Toolkit

The dBASE Template Language Toolkit option is available only to owners of the dBASE IV Developer's Edition. It copies the files in the dBASE Template Language from the Template Language disks that came with your dBASE IV package to a directory named \DBASE\DTL (unless you specify a different directory name). The template language allows advanced programmers to develop their own templates, which dBASE uses to generate source code files for reports, screens, labels, and applications.

Uninstall dBASE IV

The Uninstall dBASE IV option is used to remove dBASE IV from the hard disk, as discussed in the section "Uninstalling dBASE IV" earlier in this chapter.

DBSETUP CONFIG.DB MENU

The Config.db option on the DBSETUP menu allows you to change the dBASE IV CONFIG.DB file, which dBASE IV automatically reads when you first run dBASE IV to determine settings for use in the current session. Examples of various CONFIG.DB settings for determining screen colors and internationalizing dBASE IV were presented earlier in this chapter.

dBASE always reads the current directory for the CONFIG.DB file. If it cannot find this file on the current directory, dBASE will search the dBASE IV home directory (usually C:\DBASE) for the CONFIG.DB file. For example, if only your C:\DBASE directory contains a CONFIG.DB file, dBASE will use the settings in that CONFIG.DB file, regardless of which directory is the current directory when you first start dBASE IV.

However, if you store one CONFIG.DB file on the C:\DBASE directory and another on the C:\DBASE\SQLHOME directory, dBASE will use the settings specified on the C:\DBASE\SQLHOME\CONFIG.DB file when (and only when) you start dBASE IV from the C:\DBASE\SQLHOME directory. When you start dBASE IV from any directory other than C:\DBASE\SQLHOME, the settings in the C:\DBASE\CONFIG.DB file are used in the current session.

Modify Existing CONFIG.DB

The Modify Existing CONFIG.DB option lets you change the settings defined in the CONFIG.DB file. When selected, this option displays the dBASE IV default directory, C:\DBASE, as the suggested location of the CONFIG.DB file you wish to modify. You can press ↵ to use the suggested location, or you can enter a different drive and directory location. Then press ↵.

After you modify the existing CONFIG.DB file using options on the CONFIG.DB main menu (discussed in the section "CONFIG.DB Main Menu" later in this chapter), select Save and Exit from the Exit pull-down menu to save any changes. dBASE will ask where to store the modified CONFIG.DB file. Again, you can press ↵ to accept the suggested destination, C:\DBASE, or you can type a different destination and press ↵.

If the destination you specified already contains a CONFIG.DB file, dBASE will ask for permission before overwriting the existing file with the modified settings. Select Ok to overwrite the existing CONFIG.DB file or Cancel to retain the existing, unmodified file.

Create New CONFIG.DB

The Create New CONFIG.DB option allows you to create an entirely new CONFIG.DB file. When you select this option, you'll be taken directly to the CONFIG.DB main menu (discussed in the next section). To save the new settings, select Save and Exit from the Exit pull-down menu.

You'll be prompted to enter a drive and directory on which to store the new CONFIG.DB file, with C:\DBASE as the suggested destination. Press ↵ to store the new CONFIG.DB file on the suggested directory, or enter a new drive and directory. If the drive and directory you specified already contains a CONFIG.DB file, you will be asked for permission to overwrite that file. Select Ok to replace the existing CONFIG.DB file with the new one or select Cancel to cancel the operation.

CONFIG.DB Main Menu

The following sections summarize the options on the CONFIG.DB main menu that appears after you select Modify Existing CONFIG.DB or Create New CONFIG.DB. For additional information about these settings, refer to the chapter on SET commands in the *Language Reference* manual that came with your dBASE IV package or to a more advanced book that focuses on programming with the dBASE IV programming language.

Note that these menus work like those at the Control Center. You can select an option by highlighting it and pressing ↵. With multiple-choice items, you can press the space bar repeatedly to cycle through options. Pressing the **Del** key resets an option to its original default setting. As usual, the message line at the bottom of the screen provides instructions and a brief description of what the option does.

DATABASE PULL-DOWN MENU

Options on the Database pull-down menu are summarized in Table 19.3. These options provide settings that define how dBASE IV handles databases.

GENERAL PULL-DOWN MENU

The General pull-down menu provides access to general settings that affect the dBASE IV environment. The purpose of each option is summarized in Table 19.4.

OPTION	EFFECT
Autosave	Instructs dBASE to save data to disk after each change to the record. With Autosave off, changes are saved in a buffer and written to disk only after the buffer is filled.
Blocksize	Determines the block size of Memo fields and multiple index (.MDX) files in multiples of 512 bytes, in the range 1 to 128. A larger block size may increase the speed of some operations, but only the default, 1, is compatible with dBASE III PLUS files.
Carry	Instructs dBASE to carry data from one record to the next record when you enter new records. When Carry is off, the data from each record entered is not carried forward.
Deleted	When on, instructs dBASE to hide any records that are marked for deletion. Otherwise, such records ae displayed as usual.
Encryption	In a network environment, instructs dBASE to automatically encrypt newly created database files if PROTECT is used. If off, newly created database files are not encrypted.
Exact	Turned off, allows a shorter search string to match a longer one if the first letters of the longer character string match all the characters in the shorter string. Turned on, requires the search to find only strings that have the same characters and the same length.
Exclusive	Turned on, makes database files opened in a network environment accessible only to the user who opened the file. Turned off, allows multiple users in the network to access the file simultaneously.
Expsize	Specifies the amount of memory used to compile expressions, in the range 100 to 2000 bytes. If you encounter the *EVAL work area overflow* error message in your work, you can increase Expsize to some value greater than 100.
FullPath	If on, instructs dBASE functions that return file names to include the drive, path, and file name. With FullPath off, only the drive and name are returned. On is the default setting for dBASE IV, but off provides compatibility with the dBASE III PLUS functions, which do not return path names.
Indexbytes	Specifies the amount of memory for storing index file nodes (where each node points to a database record). Acceptable values are in the range 2 to 128. A higher setting than the default of 63 can speed index searches for large database files that use complex index expressions, but may slow processing on files that use simple index expressions.

Table 19.3: Options on the Database Pull-Down menu for CONFIG.DB

OPTION	EFFECT
Lock	If on, enables automatic record locking for database files in a network environment. Otherwise, automatic record locking is not enabled.
Near	Turned on, allows an index searches to locate the next closest value if an exact match cannot be found. Otherwise, index searches attempt to find exact matches only.
Unique	Turned on, instructs dBASE to include only unique values in new indexes. Duplicate values are excluded. Otherwise, newly created indexes include all records.

Table 19.3: Options on the Database Pull-Down menu for CONFIG.DB (continued)

OPTION	EFFECT
Bell	If on, dBASE sounds a warning bell whenever a field is filled or an error occurs. You can set the frequency (pitch) of the bell to any value between 19 and 10,000, and the duration to any value between 2 to 19 ticks, where a tick is approximately 0.055 seconds. If off, no warning bell is sounded.
Century	If off, dates are displayed without the century (for example, 12/31/90). If on, the century is displayed in dates (for example, 12/31/1990).
Clock	If off, the clock is not displayed on the dBASE IV screens. If on, the clock is displayed on the screens. You can set the row position for displaying the clock to any value between 0 and 24, and the column position to any value between 0 and 68.
Command	Specifies the first command to be executed when dBASE IV is started. By default, the first command is ASSIST, which displays the Control Center screen. If omitted, dBASE IV starts at the dot prompt.
Confirm	If off, the cursor leaves a field on edit screens as soon as the user fills the field. If on, the cursor does not leave a field until ↵ is pressed.
Currency	Determines whether the currency symbol is displayed to the left or right of a number displayed in $ format. Can also be used to specify a currency sign (see "Internationalizing dBASE IV" earlier in this chapter for examples).

Table 19.4: Summary of Options on the DBSETUP General Pull-Down Menu

OPTION	EFFECT
Date	Specifies the date format, as discussed in the section "Changing the Date Format" earlier in this chapter.
Debug	Used by programmers to determine where SET ECHO on output is channeled. If off, the output is sent to the screen. If on, the output is sent to the printer.
Delimiters	If off, fields on data editing screens are not surrounded by delimiters. If on, delimiters are displayed around those fields. You can also specify the characters used for delimiters. For example, by specifying [ ] as the delimiter symbols, you surround fields with square brackets.
Design	If on, full access to the dBASE IV design screens is provided. If off, the design screens are not accessible (that is, the user can use existing objects, but not create new objects).
Development	If on, instructs dBASE to automatically compile modified objects before using them. If off, modified objects must be compiled using the COMPILE command.
Do	Specifies the maximum number of nested DO loops in command files, in the range 1 to 256.
Escape	If on, dBASE IV programs can be interrupted by pressing the **Esc** key. If off, the **Esc** key is disabled.
Help	If on, help is provided automatically when an error occurs at the dot prompt. If off, help is not provided automatically.
History	Specifies the number of dot prompt commands stored in the HISTORY buffer, in the range 0 to 16,000.
Hours	If 12, the time is displayed in 12-hour clock format (for example, 1:00:00 PM). If 24, the time is displayed in 24-hour clock format (for example, 13:00:00).
Instruct	If on, instructs dBASE to display prompt boxes when you highlight a file name in the Control Center and press ←┘. If off, prompt boxes are not displayed.
Memowidth	Specifies the number of columns used to display Memo fields, in the range 8 to 32,000.
Point	Specifies the character used as a decimal point in numbers.
Precision	Sets the number of digits used in mathematical operations involving the numeric data type, in the range 10 to 20.
Prompt	Specifies the character used to display the dot prompt.
Separator	Specifies the character used to separate thousands in numbers of four or more digits.

Table 19.4: Summary of Options on the DBSETUP General Pull-Down Menu (continued)

OPTION	EFFECT
SQL	If off, SQL command syntax is disabled. If on, SQL command syntax is supported as soon as dBASE IV is started.
Status	If on, the status bar is displayed beneath the dot prompt. If off, the status bar is not displayed beneath the dot prompt.
Step	Used by programmers to help in the debugging process. If on, commands in programs are executed one at a time, with options to proceed, suspend, or cancel after each command is executed. If off, program execution proceeds normally.
Talk	If on, feedback from commands such as APPEND FROM, COPY, PACK, STORE, and CALCULATE is displayed automatically on the screen during dot prompt interaction. If off, feedback is omitted.
Tedit	Specifies a text editor to use in lieu of the dBASE IV program editor. If used, the command required to start the external editor must be provided. For example, entering **WS** as the Tedit setting automatically runs the WordStar program when you enter the MODIFY COMMAND command at the dot prompt (assuming that the directory that the WordStar program is stored on is included in the current DOS PATH setting).
Trap	If off, program errors display the usual options to cancel the program, ignore the error, or suspend program execution. If on, the debugger is activated as soon as an error occurs in a program.
Typeahead	Specifies the number of characters stored in the typeahead buffer, in the range 0 to 32,000.
Wp	Specifies an external text editor to use for editing Memo field text. If used, the entry should be the command used to start the external editor from DOS (for example, **WP** for WordPerfect). The text editor's home directory should be included in the current DOS PATH setting.

Table 19.4: Summary of Options on the DBSETUP General Pull-Down Menu (continued)

DISPLAY PULL-DOWN MENU

The Display pull-down menu lets you determine the default screen colors for use in all future dBASE IV sessions. See the section "Changing the Default Directory Colors" earlier in this chapter for an example.

Keys Pull-Down Menu

The Keys pull-down menu lets you assign text to function keys and to function key combinations, such as **Ctrl-F1** or **Shift-F1**. When you first select this option, the default function key assignments for keys **F2** through **F10** are displayed, as shown in Figure 19.11. Function key combinations from **Ctrl-F9** to **Shift-F10** are scrolled off the screen, but can be accessed using the ↓ or **PgDn** key.

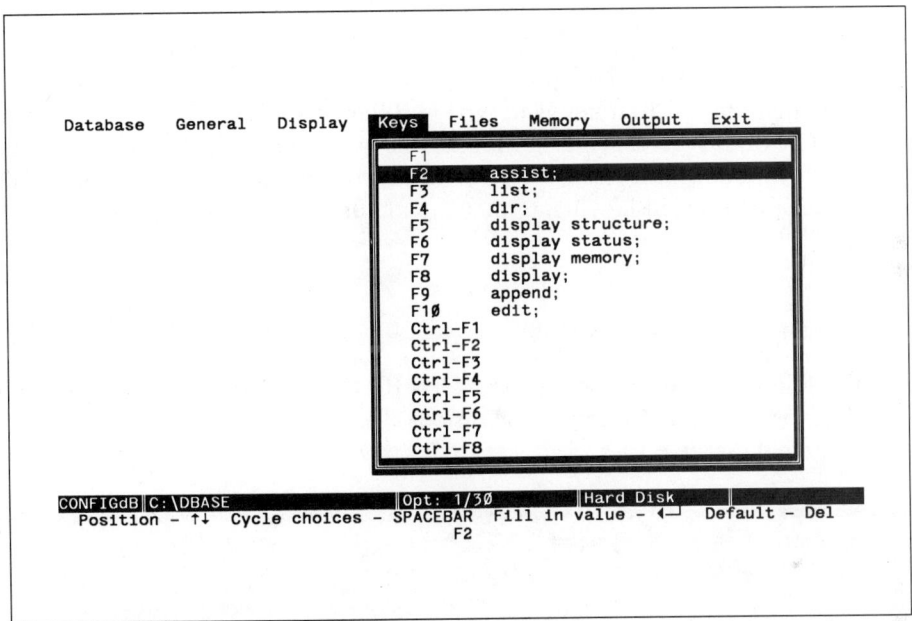

FIGURE 19.11: The Keys pull-down menu in DBSETUP. The default function key assignments assigned in the CONFIG.DB file are displayed. The semicolon (;) represents a press on the ↵ key.

The **F1** function key is reserved for accessing the dBASE IV help system, and **Shift-F10** is reserved for the keystroke macro menu; these keys cannot be modified. The **F11**, **F12**, and **Alt**-*function* key combinations are not programmable.

If you plan to use a function key at the dot prompt, the text you assign to the function key must be a valid dBASE command. You can assign plain-English text to function keys used in design screens; for example, you might want a function key to type your company name and address for use in form letters that you create on the reports design screen.

The semicolon (;) tells dBASE when to press the ↵ key. If you want to assign multiple commands to a function key or to have a key type multiple lines, separate each command or line with a semicolon. For example, the function key assignment

    ABC Co.;123 A St.;Del Mar, CA 92046

types a company name and address in the format

    ABC Co.
    123 A St.
    Del Mar, CA 92046

You can assign a maximum of 33 characters to a single function key. To assign text to a function key, highlight the function key's name and press ↵. Type the text that the function key is to type and then press ↵. (Note to programmers: The SET FUNCTION command allows you to assign up to 238 characters to a function key. Also, the ON KEY command in any command file overrides the function key assignments made using CONFIG.DB or the SET FUNCTION command.)

FILES PULL-DOWN MENU

The Files pull-down menu on the CONFIG.DB main menu provides default settings for names and locations of various dBASE IV files. These options are summarized in Table 19.5.

OPTION	EFFECT
Alternate	Specifies a default file for capturing output from commands that display information on the screen (excluding the @ command). If Alternate is left blank, output is not captured in a file. If you specify a file name, all output is automatically captured in the named file.
Catalog	Specifies a default catalog to activate as soon as dBASE IV is started. If Catalog is left blank, dBASE IV activates the last-used catalog automatically at startup.
Default	Specifies the default disk drive for storing dBASE object files. If Default is left blank, the current drive is assumed.
Files	Specifies the maximum number of files that can be open simultaneously when dBASE IV is in use, in the range 15 to 99. The setting specified in the DOS CONFIG.SYS file overrides this setting.

Table 19.5: Summary of Options on the CONFIG.DB Files Pull-Down Menu

OPTION	EFFECT
Path	Specifies the default directory path for dBASE file searches. If Path is left blank, the current directory is assumed.
Safety	If on, dBASE always asks for permission before overwriting an existing file. If off, existing files are overwritten automatically.
SQLdatabase	Specifies the directory for the dBASE IV sample files. Change this setting only if you specified a directory other than \DBASE\SAMPLES when you transferred the dBASE IV sample files from the dBASE IV disks to your hard disk.
SQLhome	Specifies the default directory for SQL operations. By default, dBASE uses the directory name \DBASE\SQLHOME. Change this setting only if you specified a different directory when you transferred the SQL files from the dBASE IV disks to your hard disk.
View	Specifies a view to open when dBASE IV is first started. The view must already exist, or an error occurs during dBASE IV startup.

Table 19.5: Summary of Options on the CONFIG.DB Files Pull-Down Menu (continued)

MEMORY PULL-DOWN MENU

The Memory pull-down menu lets you change the amount of memory (RAM) allocated to various dBASE IV operations. The default settings are adequate for most dBASE IV operations and should be changed only by programmers knowledgeable about dynamic memory allocation, memory variables, run-time symbols, and compile-time symbols. Table 19.6 summarizes the options on the Memory pull-down menu.

OPTION	EFFECT
Bucket	Specifies the amount of memory, in kilobytes, allocated to @...GET...PICTURE commands in custom forms. The acceptable range is 1 to 31 kilobytes.
Ctmaxsyms	Specifies the maximum number of compile-time symbols allocated to program or procedure file compilation. The acceptable range is 1 to 25,000. Used only when the *Exceeded maximum number of compile time symbols* error message is generated during object compilation.

Table 19.6: Summary of Options in the CONFIG.DB Memory Pull-Down Menu

OPTION	EFFECT
Gets	Specifies the maximum number of @...GET commands that can be active at any time, in the range 35 to 1023.
Mvblksize	Specifies the size of the block in memory, in bytes, for storing memory variables. Acceptable values are in the range 25 to 1000 bytes.
Mvmaxblocks	Specifies the maximum number of blocks in memory set aside for storing memory variables. The acceptable range is 1 to 25 blocks.
Refresh	Specifies the number of seconds between screen updates in a multiuser (network) environment. The acceptable range is 0 to 3600 seconds.
Reprocess	Specifies the maximum number of attempts to execute a command in a network environment, in the range 1 to 32,000.
Rtblksize	Specifies the amount of memory, in bytes, used for storing memory variables in a run-time session. The acceptable range is 25 to 1000 bytes.
Rtmaxblocks	Specifies the maximum number of blocks used for storing memory variables during a run-time session, in the range 1 to 25 blocks.

Table 19.6: Summary of Options in the CONFIG.DB Memory Pull-Down Menu (continued)

OUTPUT PULL-DOWN MENU

The Output pull-down menu on the CONFIG.DB menu lets you determine general settings for dBASE IV output and screen displays. These options are summarized in Table 19.7.

EXIT PULL-DOWN MENU

The Exit pull-down menu on the CONFIG.DB menu lets you save or abandon changes made to new or modified CONFIG.DB files. If you select Abandon and Exit from this menu, all changes are abandoned, and you are returned to the main DBSETUP menu.

If you select Save and Exit from the Exit menu, dBSETUP will prompt you for the location to store the modified CONFIG.DB file. You can press ← to accept the suggested location C:\DBASE, or you can type a new location and

OPTION	EFFECT
Console	If on, output is displayed on the screen normally. If off, the screen displays no output (output is sent to the DOS NUL device: that is, nowhere).
Decimals	Specifies the default number of decimal places for displaying numbers on the screen. The acceptable range is 0 to 18 bytes.
Device	Specifies the default output for @ commands. Press the space bar to scroll through the options SCREEN and PRINT (for the printer).
Echo	Determines whether the SET ECHO command for displaying commands in command files before executing them is initially on or off. The default setting is off (commands are not displayed before execution).
Fastcrt	Allows fast screen updating on screens that support it. This option is also set by the Optimize Color Display option on the Modify Hardware Setup option on the Install pull-down menu.
Headings	If on, field names are displayed above records viewed with the DISPLAY and LIST commands. If off, field names are omitted.
Intensity	If on, fields on data entry and editing screens are displayed in reverse video. If off, fields are displayed in normal video.
Margin	Determines the default number of columns for the left margin in printed output, in the range 0 to 254. For example, to print a 1-inch left margin in printed output with a printer that prints 10 characters to the inch, change this setting to 10.
Noclock	If off, the clock is displayed above all menus. If on, the clock is not displayed above menus.
Odometer	Determines how frequently the progress odometer is updated during operations such as packing, or copying a database. The acceptable range is 1 to 200 records.
Pause	If off, the screen does not automatically pause for a keystroke after each screenful of information. If on, the screen does pause for a keystroke after each screenful of information.
Printer	If off, all output is sent to the screen rather than the printer. If off, output is sent to the screen, unless the printer is specifically requested. Also allows you to specify available printers, the default printer, and optional fonts.

Table 19.7: Summary of Options In the CONFIG.DB Output Pull-Down Menu

OPTION	EFFECT
Scoreboard	(See the section "Changing Your Hardware Setup" earlier in this chapter for information about printers.)
	If on, key indicators and other messages are displayed at the top of the screen if the status bar is disabled. If off, these messages are displayed near the bottom of the screen when the status bar is disabled.
Space	If on, inserts a blank space between expressions that are separated by commas in ? and ?? commands. If off, blank spaces are omitted.
Tabs	Specifies the initial value of the −TABS system memory variable used in PRINTJOB...ENDPRINTJOB blocks in command files.

Table 19.7: Summary of Options In the CONFIG.DB Output Pull-Down Menu (continued)

press ⏎. If the modified CONFIG.DB file will overwrite an existing CONFIG.DB file, dBASE asks for permission before overwriting the existing file. Select Ok to overwrite or select Cancel to cancel overwriting.

If you select Cancel, you'll be returned to the CONFIG.DB menu. At that point, you can select Save and Exit, if you wish, and then specify a different drive and directory to store the modified CONFIG.DB file.

DBSETUP TOOLS MENU

The Tools pull-down menu in CONFIG.DB menu provides information about the computer system. This information is useful primarily to advanced programmers and consultants who require information about disk use, disk performance, and memory use. Examples of the information that each of these options displays are presented in the sections that follow.

Display Disk Usage Option

The Display Disk Usage option on the DBSETUP main menu Tools options displays information about the current version of DOS in use, how DOS has allocated disk space, and the amount of space allocated to various disk areas. The statistics displayed are for the current drive only, even if the hard disk is partitioned into several separate drives.

Figure 19.12 shows an example of the display presented by the Display Disk Usage option for a computer that uses PC-DOS version 3.3 as the operating system. After viewing this information, press any key to return to the DBSETUP main menu.

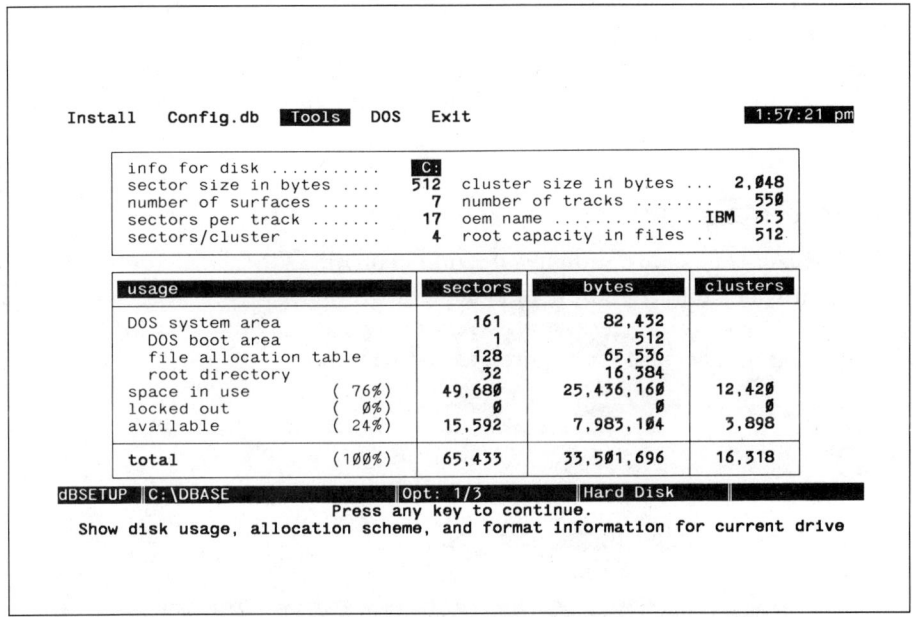

FIGURE 19.12: A sample display from the Display Disk Usage option on the Tools pull-down menu in DBSETUP. This information is primarily useful for advanced programmers who need information about current disk space allocation.

Test Disk Performance

The Test Disk Performance Option on the DBSETUP Tools pull-down menu tests the speed performance of writing data to, and reading data from, the current drive and directory. This option often is used by knowledgeable programmers and consultants to determine how severely the DOS file allocation table (FAT) is fragmented.

If you use the Test Disk Performance option to test the read/write performance on an empty directory, you can determine a base performance level for disk input and output (I/O). If you then test the performance on a crowded directory, and the performance is severely impaired, you can be sure that the impaired performance is due to fragmentation in the FAT.

To bring the performance of an impaired directory up to maximum speed, you'll need to defragment the FAT. You can use any commercial defragmenting program to do so. Since dBASE IV is not copy protected, you need not uninstall it before defragmenting.

However, if your defragmenting program insists on defragmenting the entire hard disk and is not cautious about saving the locations of hidden files and directories that are used for copy protection, you should uninstall copy-protected programs before using your defragmenting program. In general, you should back up the entire hard disk before using any defragmenting program.

Review System Configuration

The Review System Configuration option on the DBSETUP Tools pull-down menu provides information about the computer's general configuration. This information includes the system's microprocessor, available memory, video mode, and parallel and serial ports, as shown in Figure 19.13.

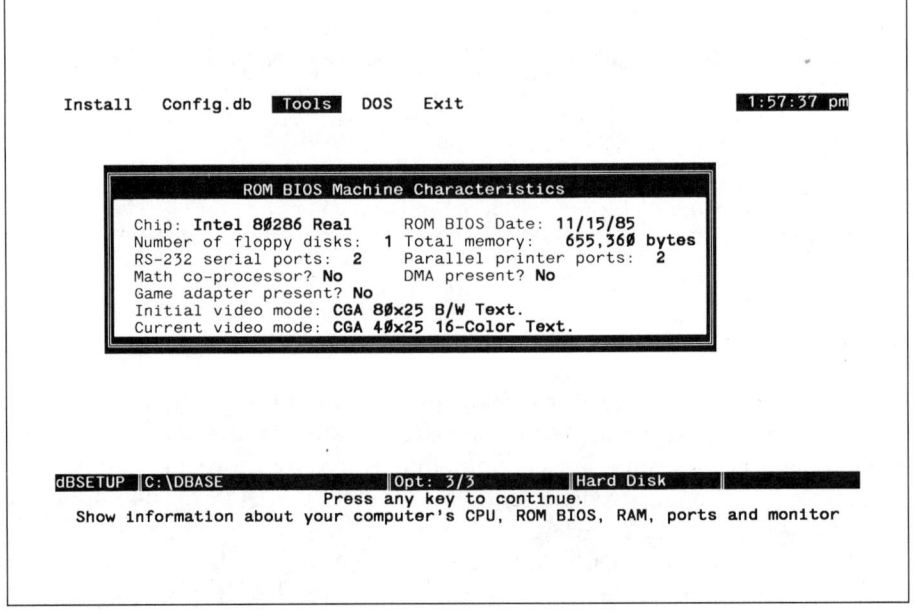

FIGURE 19.13: Sample output specifying the computer's current configuration. This screen was displayed by selecting Review System Configuration from the DBSETUP Tools pull-down menu.

Note that the Total Memory specification refers to the total number of bytes available in conventional memory (RAM) and does not take extended or expanded memory into consideration.

After viewing the system configuration screen, press any key to return to the DBSETUP main menu, as indicated in the message-line prompt near the bottom on the screen.

DBSETUP DOS Menu

The DOS option on the DBSETUP main menu lets you interact with DOS without leaving DBSETUP. The options on that menu are discussed in the sections that follow.

Perform DOS Command

When you select Perform DOS Command from the DOS pull-down menu in DBSETUP, dBASE prompts you to enter a DOS command. You can enter any valid DOS command up to 115 characters long. Then press ←. DBSETUP will send the command to DOS, and the command's output will be displayed on your screen followed by the message *Press any key to return to DBSETUP*. Press any key, and you'll be returned to the DBSETUP main menu.

Go To DOS

When you select the Go To DOS option from the DOS pull-down menu in DBSETUP, the DBSETUP option is suspended, and the DOS command prompt is displayed. You can enter any valid DOS commands as you normally would while at the DOS command prompt. To return to DBSETUP, type the command **EXIT** and press ←.

Set Default Drive:Directory

The Set Default Drive:Directory option on the DOS pull-down menu in DBSETUP allows you to change the default directory for reading and writing files. When you select this option, the screen displays the current drive and directory. You can type a new drive and directory to use as the default setting, or you can press Pick (**Shift-F1**) to view a directory tree. When the directory tree is displayed, you can select a default drive and directory by highlighting its name and pressing ←.

DBSETUP EXIT MENU

The Exit pull-down menu in DBSETUP offers the single option Exit to DOS. When selected, this option leaves the DBSETUP program and returns you to the DOS command prompt. If you've changed and saved any settings on the CONFIG.DB pull-down menus, the new settings will be in effect in all dBASE IV future sessions. If you abandoned any changes that you made on the CONFIG.DB pull-down menus, those changes will not be saved when you exit the DBSETUP program.

TIPS AND TRAPS

- If you find that you use the Settings option on the Tools pull-down menu often (from the Control Center), consider using DBSETUP to change the default setting to the one you use most often.
- Remember that you must exit dBASE IV and return to the DOS command prompt in order to use the DBSETUP program.
- The CONFIG.DB file configures dBASE IV at system startup and *must* be stored on the same drive and directory as dBASE IV.
- The CONFIG.SYS and AUTOEXEC.BAT files are used by DOS during startup (when you first turn on your computer), and these must be stored on the root directory of your startup drive.
- Some EGA and VGA monitors may make DBSETUP *appear* to change the default screen colors used in dBASE IV. But when you later run dBASE, you will see that it still uses the default color scheme.

SUMMARY

When you need to make changes to your hardware setup after you have installed dBASE IV, you should use the DBSETUP program to do so. This chapter discussed a number of changes you can make to hardware settings and also some changes you can make to display settings, including those required to internationalize dBASE IV. Some of the other options on the DBSETUP menus are duplicated in the dBASE IV menus and are described in Chapter 14.

To change a variety of other display options and to use the color palette:

- Chapter 14, "Managing Files and the Workspace"

To install dBASE IV:

- Appendix A, "Installing dBASE IV"

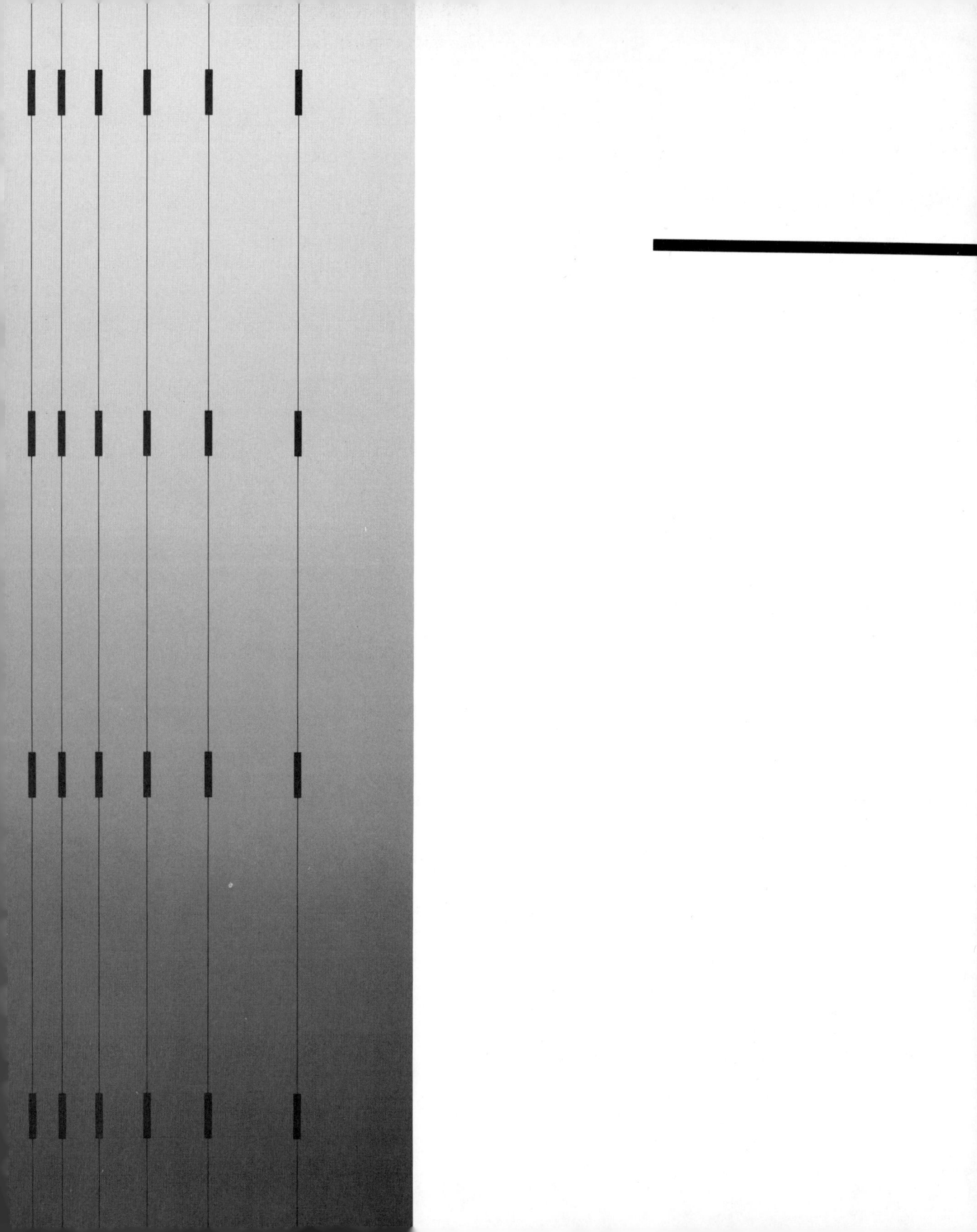

CHAPTER 20

Protecting Data

Designing a Protection Scheme. 723
    Designing User Profiles. 723
        Login Names. 723
        User Passwords. 723
        User Profile Group Names. 724
        User Access Levels. 724
    Designing the File Privilege Scheme. .724
        Database File Groups. 724
        Database File Access Privileges. 725
        Database Field Privileges. 726
Using the dBASE IV Protect System. 728
    Entering the Security System Password. 728
Creating the User Profiles. 730
    Assigning the Login Name. 731
    Assigning the Password. 731
    Assigning the Group Name. 732
    Assigning the Full Name. 734
    Assigning the Access Level. 735
    Saving the User Profile. 736
    Changing a User Profile. 737
    Deleting a User Profile. 739
Creating the File Privilege Schemes. 741
    Selecting the Current Database File. .741
    Assigning the File to a Group. 743
    Establishing File Access Privilege Levels. 743
    Establishing Field Privileges. 745
    Saving the File Privilege Scheme. 748
    Canceling the Current Entry. 748
    Changing File Privilege Scheme. 748

Printing Protection Scheme Reports. 749
    Printing the User Profile Report. .749
    Printing the File Privilege Scheme. 750
Exiting the Protect System. 751
Using Protected dBASE IV Files. 752
Locking Files and Records. 753
    Locking Files. 754
    Locking Records. 754
Tips and Traps. 754
Summary. 755

Protecting Data

If several people in a company use the same computer or have access to the same databases through a local area network (LAN), you may want to protect some databases. For example, you may not want to give all users unrestricted access to databases that contain employee salaries, employee reviews, or corporate bookkeeping records.

To protect databases, you use the dBASE IV Protect system. However, it's a good idea to first design the protection scheme on paper, as discussed in the first section of this chapter.

DESIGNING A PROTECTION SCHEME

Whether you use dBASE IV on a network or on a single computer that requires data protection, you need to design a protection scheme. You can do so by designing *user profiles* and a *file privilege scheme* for each protected database.

Designing User Profiles

You design a user profile scheme by assigning login names, passwords, group names, and an access level to each dBASE IV user on the network or computer, as discussed in the sections that follow.

LOGIN NAMES

A login name is the name the user enters when first logging on to dBASE IV. This name need not be cryptic; the user's actual first or last name or initials are sufficient. Up to eight characters are allowed, and uppercase and lowercase letters are equivalent.

USER PASSWORDS

Each user's password should be unique and confidential to the user. Users should select their own passwords, up to 16 characters long. Whenever the user logs on, he or she will have to enter this password. The password will not appear on the screen as it is typed, to prevent bystanders from seeing the user's password.

User Profile Group Names

Group names let you organize users by application, such as payroll or accounts receivable, or if you prefer, by department, such as sales or marketing. A group name can be up to eight characters long. Once a group name has been assigned to a database file, only users that are assigned to that group can access the database file.

To give a user access to more than one group, enter a separate user profile for each group name. For example, if you want Jones to have access to both payroll and accounts receivable, you must define two user profiles for Jones, each with the appropriate group name.

User Access Levels

Each user should also be assigned an access level. This level can be any value in the range 1 (most privileges) to 8 (least privileges). This number corresponds to the file access privileges you define later in the file privilege schemes.

EXAMPLE

Figure 20.1 shows a sample paper-and-pencil form (which you can create yourself) for creating user profiles. The example shows how the form might be filled in for a hypothetical company. Note that several users are assigned to more than one group, because they have access to more than one application. The network administrator (B. King in this example) has assigned herself unrestricted access (1) to all the groups in the entire network system, so that she can have full control over all files.

Designing the File Privilege Scheme

You need to design a privilege scheme for each protected database in the system. The purpose of designing a privilege scheme is basically to control who has access to what in the system. If you do not create a protection scheme for a database file, all users on the system will have unrestricted access to that file.

Database File Groups

Each protected database file needs to be assigned to a group. The group name you assign here corresponds to a group name in the user profiles. Only users who are assigned to the group will have access to the database file. Keep in mind that

DESIGNING THE FILE PRIVILEGE SCHEME

```
ABC Company

dBASE ADMINISTRATOR User Profiles

Employee      Login                    Group       Access
Name          Name      Password       Name        Level

B. King       King      Honcho         Payroll       1
B. King       King      Honcho         Payables      1
B. King       King      Honcho         Ledger        1
A. Adams      Abigail   Kitten         Payroll       1
A. Adams      Abigail   Kitten         Payables      1
B. Jones      Bait      Pluto          Payroll       8
C. Smith      Chuck     Banana         Ledger        4
K. Watson     Kay       Sky            Payroll       4
K. Watson     Kay       Sky            Ledger        4
R. Yokem      Ron       Tree           Payables      8
R. Yokem      Ron       Tree           Ledger        1
```

FIGURE 20.1: A suggested form for listing user profiles. Filling in a form like this before using the Protect program can make creating user profiles easier.

a group is a group of files, not a group of users. As discussed in the section "Creating the User Profiles" later in this chapter, any particular user may be assigned to (have profiles for) more than one group.

DATABASE FILE ACCESS PRIVILEGES

You can assign access privileges to four types of database operations, as summarized here:

PRIVILEGE	MEANING
Read	User can read (view) the file.
Update	User can change data in the file.
Extend	User can add new records to the file.
Delete	User can delete records from the file.

To each of these access operations, you assign a privilege level, numbered 1 through 8, that corresponds to the access privilege levels assigned to users in their user profiles. For each operation, users whose access level is equal to or *lower* than the access number for that operation will be granted the privilege of performing the operation. That is, the "highest" privilege level (8) is actually the most restricted, and the "lowest" level (1) is the least restricted.

For example, employee C. Smith has an access level of 4 in his user profile, and so he will be allowed to perform operations to which you assign an access level of 4, 5, 6, 7, or 8, but not operations to which you assign an access level of 1, 2, or 3.

Or suppose that you assign the access levels shown here to the current database file:

Read privilege level	8
Update privilege level	6
Extend privilege level	4
Delete privilege level	2

Any user with an access level of 1 (as established in their user profiles) has complete access to the database file, including the ability to read, update, extend, and delete records. A user with an access level of 7 or 8 can only read the file. A user with an access level of 5 or 6 can read and update the file, but not add or delete records from the file.

Because the Protect system requires a separate user profile for each file group to which a user is assigned, you can assign a particular individual different access levels for different groups. For example, notice in Figure 20.1 that employee R. Yokem has full access (level 1) to the Ledger group but can only read (level 8) the Payables files.

DATABASE FIELD PRIVILEGES

You can also assign privileges to individual fields in each database file. These privileges can be used to further refine the protection scheme by adding further restrictions to individual fields.

For each user access level (1 to 8), you can assign a different set of field access privileges. For example, you can hide a particular field from individuals with an access level of 6 or higher, but display that field to individuals with an access level of 5 or lower. You can assign any one of three access privileges to each field, as summarized here:

LEVEL	PRIVILEGES
FULL	User can read and write data in the field.
R/O	Read only; user can read but not write data in the field.
NONE	User can neither read nor write data in the field.

Field privileges take precedence over file privileges *only* when a file privilege is less restrictive. For example, if the file privilege states that the user can only read data in the file, even if the field privilege says that the user has full access to a particular field, the user will be allowed only to read data in the file.

In other words, if the user can only read the file, the only valid field options are R/O (equal access) and NONE (less access).

EXAMPLE

Figure 20.2 shows a sample paper-and-pencil form for designing a file privilege scheme. In this example, the form has been filled in for a sample database file named PAYMAST.DBF. The database name and the group name (Payroll in this example) are filled in near the top of the form.

```
                    File Privilege Scheme Worksheet

       Database file name:  PayMast
       Group name         :  Payroll
```

File Privilege	<-- Least restrictions				Most restrictions -->			
Access level	1	2	3	4	5	6	7	8
Read								X
Update				X				
Extend	X							
Delete	X							

FIELD PRIVILEGES

Field Name	1	2	3	4	5	6	7	8
Emp-No	F	F	F	F	R	R	R	R
Emp-LName	F	F	F	F	R	R	R	R
Emp-FName	F	F	F	F	R	R	R	R
Emp-Addr	F	F	F	F	R	R	R	R
Emp-City	F	F	F	F	R	R	R	R
Emp-State	F	F	F	F	R	R	R	R
Emp-Zip	F	F	F	F	R	R	R	R
Hire-Date	F	R	R	R	R	R	R	R
Salary	F	R	R	R	R	R	R	N
Pr-Rate	F	R	R	R	R	R	R	N
Exemptions	F	R	R	R	R	R	R	N

F = FULL   R = R/O   N = NONE

FIGURE 20.2: A sample form for defining a file privilege scheme for a single database file. The file and group names are at the top of the form. File privilege levels 1 to 8 are listed in the middle of the form. Individual fields in the database and their access levels are listed near the bottom of the form.

The middle section of the form defines file privileges. As you can see by the X's, users who have an access level of 8 are allowed only to read data in the PAYMAST database. Users who have an access level of 4 or higher are allowed to update the file and read it.

The only users who have the right to add new records (extend) or delete records in the PAYMAST database are those who have an access level of 1.

At the field level, notice that users with an access level of 8 cannot even view the contents of the SALARY, HR_RATE, or EXEMPTIONS fields, because these privileges are set to NONE for users at that access level. Users with access levels in the range of 2 to 7 can read these three fields, but only users with an access level of 1 have full access to them.

USING THE dBASE IV PROTECT SYSTEM

After you've designed the user profiles and file privilege schemes, you can put them into action using the Protect system.

SEQUENCE OF STEPS

From the Control Center:

F10
Tools/Protect Data [↵]
Proceed *or* **Cancel** [↵]

USAGE

After designing user profiles and a file privilege scheme, you can use the Protect system in dBASE IV to create the protection scheme. Be forewarned that once you develop a protection scheme, all future access to all files included in the scheme will be under control of the Protect system. Thus, be sure to design your protection scheme carefully on paper.

If you change your mind about developing a protection scheme after selecting Protect Data from the Tools pull-down menu, select Cancel to return to the Control Center. Otherwise, select Proceed to move into the Protect system.

Entering the Security System Password

The first prompt that the Protect system displays asks for a password for the entire protection scheme. This password controls access not to files protected within the system, but to the protection scheme itself. It allows the password holder to add and delete users and files and to change their status. Only the person responsible for maintaining the protection scheme should know this password.

SEQUENCE OF STEPS

From the first prompt of the Protect system:

    type a password (it will not appear on the screen)
    ↵

    retype the password for verification (again, it will not appear on the screen)
    ↵ (*or* **Esc** to cancel)

USAGE

When you first access the Protect system, it displays the prompt shown in Figure 20.3. At this prompt, you can type a password up to 16 characters long (uppercase and lowercase letters are equivalent). The password does not appear on the screen as you type. *It is absolutely essential that you remember this password and store a written copy in a secure place. If you forget the password, you will not be able to access the Protect system in the future.*

FIGURE 20.3: The first prompt to appear when you enter the Protect system asks for the security system password. You can type a password up to 16 characters long. This password will not appear on the screen as you type.

If you type a password that uses the maximum 16 characters, you will automatically be taken to the next screen. Otherwise, you will need to press ↵ after you type the password.

If you are entering the Protect system for the first time, the screen will ask you to type the password again for verification. The screen will not display the password as you type. If the password is less than 16 characters long, you must press ↵ after typing it.

If the second password does not match the first, you'll hear a beep and see the message *Password and Confirmation Mismatch*. Press **Esc** to return to the Control Center and start over. If you type the password correctly the second time, you'll be taken to the Protect system. Figure 20.4 shows how the Protect system appears on the screen when you first access it.

The Protect system screen presents four menus: Users, Files, Reports, and Exit. The Users pull-down menu lets you manage user profiles, the Files pull-down menu is for managing file privilege schemes. The Reports option lets you print information about the protection scheme. Exit allows you to return to the Control Center.

CREATING THE USER PROFILES

Once you are in the Protect system, you can use options on the Users pull-down menu to design or modify user profiles. If you are creating the protection

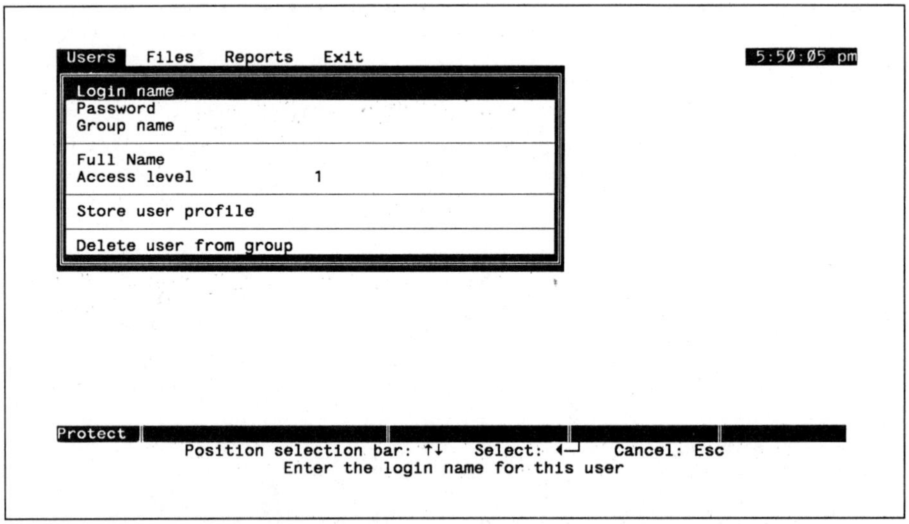

FIGURE 20.4: The Protect system when you first enter it.

scheme for the first time, you should be working from a paper-and-pencil user profile plan, as shown in Figure 20.1 in this chapter. However, you can also add new users and delete existing users via the Users pull-down menu.

The basic procedure for adding a single user profile is as follows: Select each option on the menu (by highlighting and pressing ⏎), fill in a value, and then press ⏎. When you have filled in all the information for one user (that is, when you have filled in one row from the user profile plan), select Store User Profile. Then move on to the next user profile and repeat the procedure. Each option is described in more detail in the sections that follow.

Assigning the Login Name

SEQUENCE OF STEPS

From the Protect system:

    Users/Login name [⏎]
    type a login name
    ⏎

USAGE

The Login Name option on the Users pull-down menu lets you enter one user Login name. This name should be identical to one login name from the user profile list (except that uppercase and lowercase letters are equivalent; in fact, the Protect system converts all login names to uppercase). Press ⏎ after typing the login name.

EXAMPLE

Figure 20.5 shows a single login name typed into the Users pull-down menu. This example corresponds to the first user profile in Figure 20.1.

Assigning the User Password

SEQUENCE OF STEPS

From the Protect system:

    Users/**P**assword [⏎]
    type the user's password
    ⏎

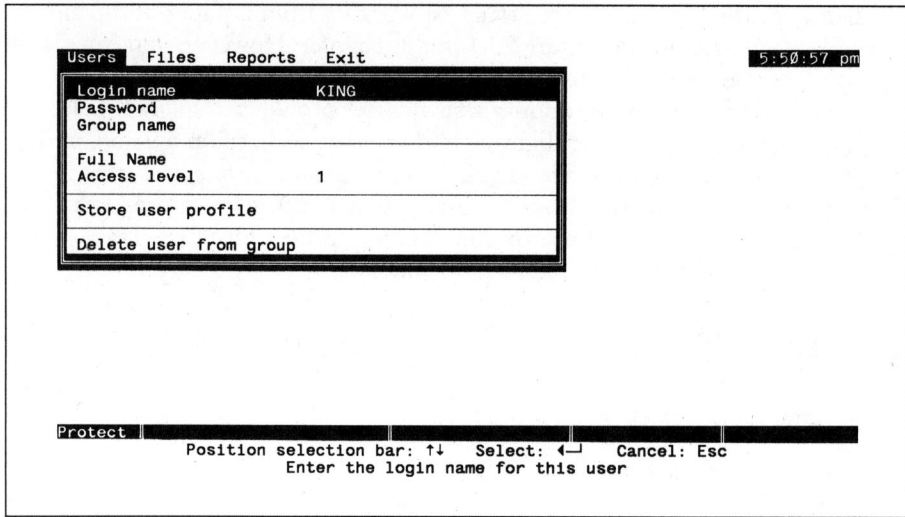

FIGURE 20.5: A single login name entered on the Users pull-down menu in the Protect system. This login name refers to the first user in the sample user profile shown in Figure 20.1.

USAGE

After typing the user's login name, select the Password option by highlighting it and pressing ↵. Then type the password, using either uppercase or lowercase letters (or both). Press ↵ after typing the name.

EXAMPLE

Figure 20.6 shows the user password entered for a single user. In this example, the user password from the first user profile in Figure 20.1, Honcho, has been entered.

Assigning the Group Name

SEQUENCE OF STEPS

From the Protect system:

    Users/**G**roup name [↵]

    type a group name

    ↵

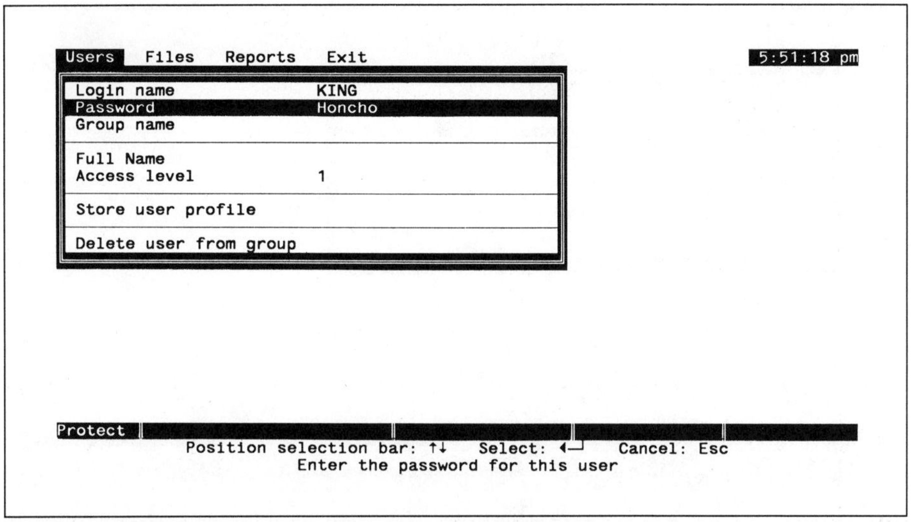

```
 Users  Files  Reports  Exit                           5:51:18 pm
   Login name              KING
   Password                Honcho
   Group name

   Full Name
   Access level            1

   Store user profile

   Delete user from group




 Protect
           Position selection bar: ↑↓   Select: ↵    Cancel: Esc
                    Enter the password for this user
```

FIGURE 20.6: The user password for user King has been entered on the Users pull-down menu. This password corresponds to the first user profile shown in Figure 20.1.

USAGE

Assigning a group name to a user limits that user's access to files assigned to that group. Typically, a group name is a particular application, such as payroll, or a particular department within a company. If a user needs access to files in more than one group, he or she must have a separate profile for each of those groups. For example, in the user profile form shown in Figure 20.1, employees King, Adams, Watson, and Yokem all have profiles for more than one group.

Be sure to type the group name correctly, as previously defined in the user profiles. You can use either uppercase or lowercase letters (lowercase letters are automatically converted to uppercase). Press ↵ after typing the group name.

EXAMPLE

Figure 20.7 shows the Users pull-down menu with a group name added. Notice that the group name shown corresponds to the first user profile listed in Figure 20.1.

```
┌─────────────────────────────────────────────────────────────────────┐
│  Users  Files  Reports  Exit                            5:55:34 pm  │
│       ┌────────────────────────────────────────┐                    │
│       │ Login name           KING              │                    │
│       │ Password             Honcho            │                    │
│       │ Group name           PAYROLL           │                    │
│       │                                        │                    │
│       │ Full Name                              │                    │
│       │ Access level         1                 │                    │
│       │                                        │                    │
│       │ Store user profile                     │                    │
│       │                                        │                    │
│       │ Delete user from group                 │                    │
│       └────────────────────────────────────────┘                    │
│                                                                     │
│                                                                     │
│                                                                     │
│  Protect                                                            │
│          Position selection bar: ↑↓   Select: ←┘   Cancel: Esc      │
│              Enter a new or existing group name for this user       │
└─────────────────────────────────────────────────────────────────────┘
```

FIGURE 20.7: The group name filled for the first user profile. This group name corresponds to the first user profile shown in Figure 20.1.

Assigning the Full Name

SEQUENCE OF STEPS

From the Protect system:

> Users/Full Name [←┘]
>
> type a complete name
>
> ←┘

USAGE

The full name assigned to a user can be up to 24 characters long and should (if possible) be that user's complete name. The user's full name is not actually used in the protection scheme, but it is useful for identifying users in reports printed by the Protect system (as discussed later in this chapter).

After typing the user's complete name, press ←┘.

EXAMPLE

Figure 20.8 shows a sample user's full name entered on the Users pull-down menu. In this example, Barbara King is the full name for B. King, the first listed employee name in the user profile.

```
┌─────────────────────────────────────────────────────────────────────┐
│  Users  Files   Reports   Exit                        5:55:51 pm    │
│   ┌─────────────────────────────────────────────┐                   │
│   │ Login name          KING                    │                   │
│   │ Password            Honcho                  │                   │
│   │ Group name          PAYROLL                 │                   │
│   ├─────────────────────────────────────────────┤                   │
│   │ Full Name           Barbara King            │                   │
│   │ Access level        1                       │                   │
│   ├─────────────────────────────────────────────┤                   │
│   │ Store user profile                          │                   │
│   ├─────────────────────────────────────────────┤                   │
│   │ Delete user from group                      │                   │
│   └─────────────────────────────────────────────┘                   │
│                                                                     │
│                                                                     │
│                                                                     │
│  Protect                                                            │
│             Position selection bar: ↑↓   Select: ⏎   Cancel: Esc    │
│                   Enter a name to further identify this user        │
└─────────────────────────────────────────────────────────────────────┘
```

FIGURE 20.8: A sample user's full name entered on the Users pull-down menu. The full name in this example refers to B. King, the first user listed in the user profiles shown in Figure 20.1.

Assigning the Access Level

SEQUENCE OF STEPS

From the Protect system:

 Users/Access level [⏎]

 ↑ to increase the level number *or* ↓ to decrease the level number

 ⏎

USAGE

 The Access Level option on the Users pull-down menu lets you define the access level for the current user (or user and group combination, if the current user has access to multiple groups). Initially, the user is assigned an access level of 1. To change that level, highlight the option and press ⏎. You can press ↑ repeatedly to increase the number or ↓ repeatedly to decrease the number. The acceptable range is 1 (fewest restrictions) to 8 (most restrictions). Press ⏎ when the desired access level is displayed.

EXAMPLE

Figure 20.9 shows the access level for the current user set to 1 (fewest restrictions). At this point, the first user profile shown in Figure 20.1 has been defined (but not yet saved). Now is a good time to double-check to make sure all options you've entered so far are filled in correctly.

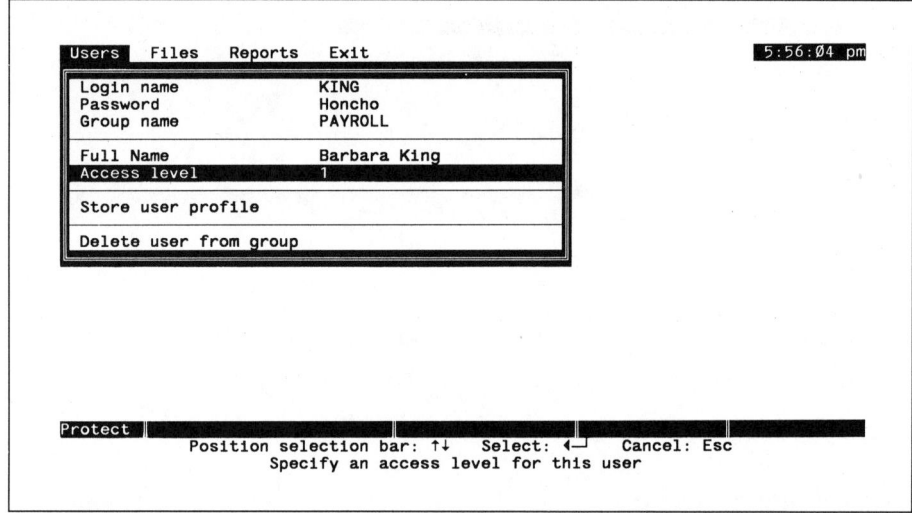

FIGURE 20.9: The current user has been assigned an access level of 1. This step completes the first user profile shown in Figure 20.1.

If you notice a mistake, use the ↑ and ↓ keys to move the highlight to the option that needs correcting. Then press ←. You can then make corrections using the **Backspace**, ←, →, and other standard editing keys. Press ← after making your corrections.

Saving the User Profile

SEQUENCE OF STEPS

From the Protect system:

    Users/**S**tore user profile [←]

USAGE

Once you've defined a single user's profile and verified its accuracy, select the Store User Profile option to save it. This option saves the user profile and clears all current profile information from the menu. At that point, you can repeat the entire process, starting with the Login name for the next user profile. You must select Store User Profile for each user profile that you define.

At any time, you can save all existing user profiles by first selecting Save from the Exit pull-down menu. If you want to leave the Protect system and return to the Control Center, you then select Exit from the Exit pull-down menu.

Changing a User Profile

SEQUENCE OF STEPS

From the Protect system:

    Users/**L**ogin name [⏎]

    type an existing login name

    ⏎

    Users/**P**assword [⏎]

    type an existing password

    ⏎

    Users/**G**roup name [⏎]

    type an existing group name

    ⏎

    Yes [⏎]

USAGE

To change an existing user profile, you must enter the existing login name, password, and group name exactly as when you originally stored that information (except, of course, you need not worry about uppercase and lowercase distinctions). When you fill in the information correctly, the following message appears:

    User already exists, do you want to edit?
      Yes   No

738 — CH. 20 PROTECTING DATA

Select Yes if you wish to change this user's profile or No to start over and enter a different user profile.

If you select Yes, the full name and access level assigned to the current user is displayed on the screen. You can use the ↑ and ↓ keys to move the highlight to any option. Then press ↵ to select that option. Make the required changes using the usual editing keys.

When you've finished making changes, select the Store User Profile option from the Users pull-down menu. To save those changes permanently, select Save from the Exit pull-down menu. To return to the Control Center, select Exit from the Exit pull-down menu.

EXAMPLE

Figure 20.10 shows the prompt displayed after you type King as the login name, Honcho as the password, and Payroll as the group name. Because a user profile has already been saved with these characteristics, the Protect system displays a message indicating that such a profile already exists and asks if you want to edit the existing profile.

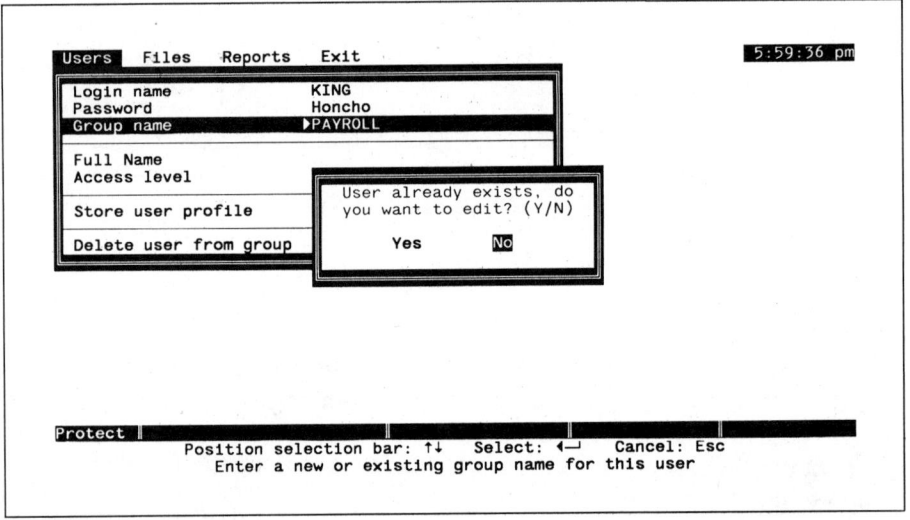

FIGURE 20.10: Message displayed by the Protect system after you fill in a login name, password, and group name that matches an existing user profile. Select Yes to edit the existing profile or No to return to an empty Users menu.

Deleting a User Profile

SEQUENCE OF STEPS

From the Protect system:

    Users/**L**ogin name [←]
    type an existing login name
    ←
    Users/**P**assword [←]
    type an existing password
    ←
    Users/**G**roup name [←]
    type an existing group name
    ←
    Yes [←]
    User/**D**elete user from group [←]

USAGE

To prevent a user from having future access to a particular group, you must first enter the user's login name, password, and group name on the Users pull-down menu in the Protect system. When the screen asks if you want to edit the existing user profile, select Yes.

All of the information for the user profile will be displayed on the screen on the Users pull-down menu. To delete the current user from the group, highlight the Delete User from Group option and press ←. The options on the Users menu will be reset to blank.

Keep in mind that the Delete User from Group option prevents future access to only a particular group of files. For example, if K. Watson has access to both the Payroll and Ledger file groups and you delete her access to the Payroll group, she will still have access to the Ledger group of files.

If you want to completely remove a user from the system, as when an employee leaves the company, you must perform the Delete User from Group operation for each login name, password, and group name assigned to that user.

After deleting one or more user profiles, select Save from the Exit pull-down menu. If you want to return to the Control Center, then select the Exit option from the Exit pull-down menu.

EXAMPLE

Suppose that employee A. Adams is currently granted access privileges to the database files stored in two groups, named Payroll and Payables (as in the fourth and fifth user profiles listed in Figure 20.1). Suppose also that you have already created the entire protection scheme for your system. Now A. Adams leaves the company. You need to remove her privileges to both groups of files.

First you need to access the Protect system and fill in the first three options on the Users pull-down menu for one of A. Adams' user profiles, as shown in Figure 20.11. If you filled in these options correctly, the prompt box asking if you want to edit the user profile appears on the screen (as also shown in the figure).

When you select Yes from the prompt box, all the information for the current user is displayed on the screen. To delete the user profile, select Delete User Profile from the Users pull-down menu. The user profile will be deleted, and the Users pull-down menu will be reset to the default values (blanks, and 1 as the user access level).

To delete the second user profile assigned to A. Adams, you must fill in the login name, password, and group name for her second user profile. Once again, the screen will ask if you want to edit the existing profile. Select Yes and then select Delete User from Group.

To save the deletions, select Save from the Exit pull-down menu. To return to the Control Center, select Exit from that same menu.

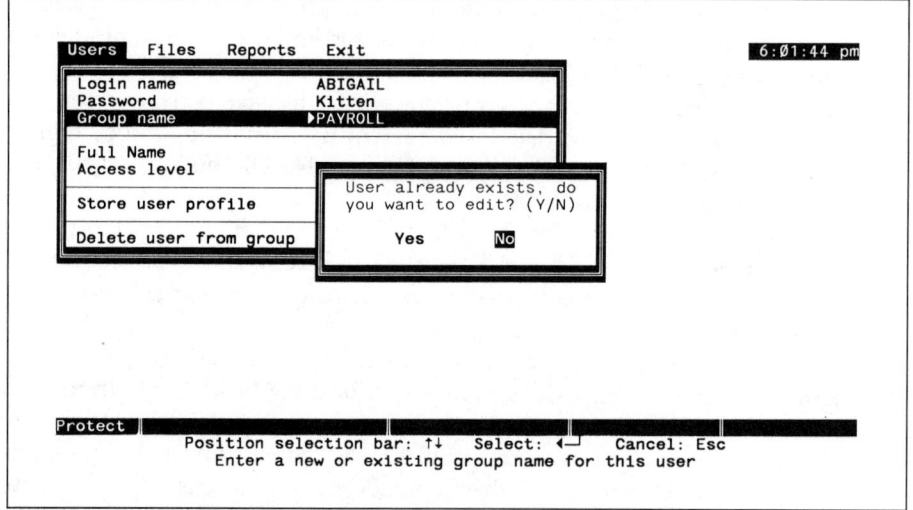

FIGURE 20.11: The Users pull-down menu filled in to edit an existing user profile. The prompt box asks if you want to edit the currently defined profile.

CREATING THE FILE PRIVILEGE SCHEMES

After you have created the user profiles, you can begin developing the file privilege schemes for each individual dBASE IV database. These schemes let you relate the access levels assigned to each user profile to individual database files.

The Files menu on the Protect screen (shown in Figure 20.12) lets you assign a database file to a group, up to eight access levels to each file, and field access privileges for each file access level.

Individual items on the Files pull-down menu in the Protect system are described in more detail in the sections that follow.

Selecting the Current Database File

SEQUENCE OF STEPS

From the Protect system:

    Files/New file [◄─┘]
    highlight a file name ◄─┘

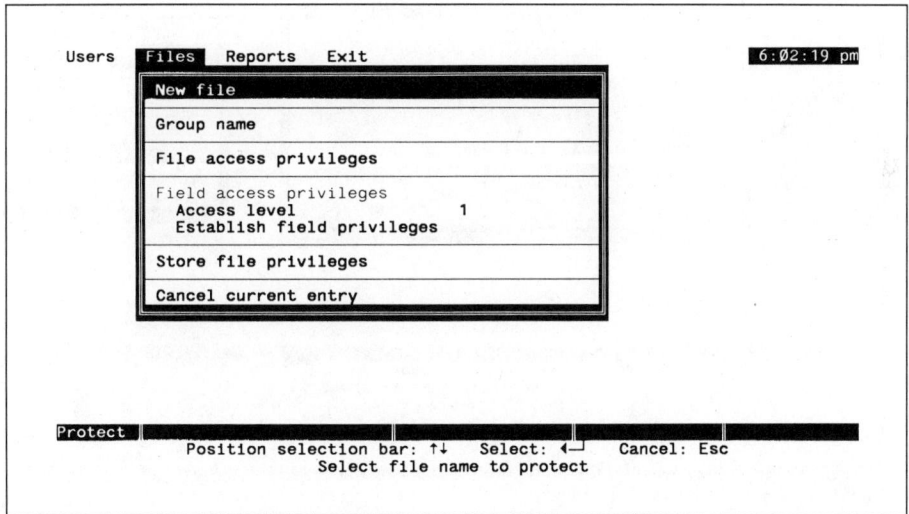

FIGURE 20.12: The Files pull-down menu in the Protect system lets you create a file privilege scheme for any single database file in the current directory.

USAGE

The first option on the Files menu, New File, lets you select a database file to assign a privilege scheme to. When you highlight this option and press ⏎, a list of the names of all database files in the current directory appears, as in Figure 20.13.

Use the ↑ and ↓ keys to highlight the database file you want to use and then press ⏎ to select that database file. The database file name will appear next to the New File option, and all remaining changes will affect only that database file.

You can assign access levels for up to nine database files during a single session with the Protect system. After assigning access privileges to the ninth database file, move the highlight to the Exit menu option and select Save. Then select Exit to return to the Control Center.

If you need to assign access privileges to more database files, you can reaccess the Protect system at any time by selecting Protect Data from the Tools pull-down menu and entering the password when requested to do so. Press → to access the Files pull-down menu and resume your work by selecting New File from the Files pull-down menu.

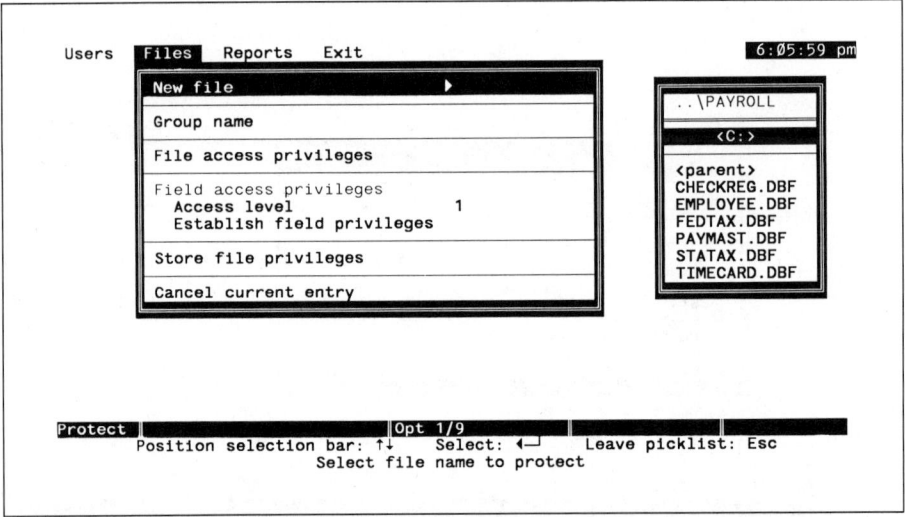

FIGURE 20.13: An example of a file name list that appears when you select New File from the Files pull-down menu in the Protect system.

Assigning the File to a Group

SEQUENCE OF STEPS

From the Protect system:

    Files/Group name [↵]
    type a name
    ↵

USAGE

The Group name option on the Protect system Files pull-down menu lets you assign the currently selected database file to a group. The group name can be up to eight characters long and should refer to a group defined in the user profiles. Typically, the group name refers to a particular application, such as payroll, or a particular department, such as sales.

You can use either uppercase or lowercase letters to type the group name, but the Protect system automatically converts all lowercase letters to uppercase. Press ↵ after typing the group name.

A database file can be assigned to only one group. Only those users who have profiles that permit access to the specified group will have access to the database file. Because a single user profile gives access to only one group of databases, the user who needs access to files in more than one group must have a separate profile for each group to which he or she needs access.

EXAMPLE

Figure 20.14 shows the Files pull-down menu for the PAYMAST.DBF database. In this example, the PAYMAST.DBF database is assigned to the group named Payroll.

Establishing File Access Privilege Levels

SEQUENCE OF STEPS

From the Protect system:

    Files/File access privileges [↵]
    highlight an option ↵

744 —— CH. 20 PROTECTING DATA

```
 Users  Files   Reports   Exit                              6:06:22 pm
        ┌─────────────────────────────────────────┐
        │ New file                    PAYMAST.DBF │
        │ Group name                  PAYROLL     │
        │ File access privileges                  │
        │ Field access privileges                 │
        │   Access level              1           │
        │   Establish field privileges            │
        │ Store file privileges                   │
        │ Cancel current entry                    │
        └─────────────────────────────────────────┘




 Protect  C:\...payroll\PAYMAST                    ReadOnly
          Position selection bar: ↑↓   Select: ↲   Cancel: Esc
          Enter the name of the user group to access this file
```

FIGURE 20.14: The PAYMAST.DBF database has been assigned to the group named Payroll. Only those users with profiles that provide access to the Payroll group are granted access to the PAYMAST.DBF database.

↑ and ↓ to change the level
↲

USAGE

The File Access Privileges option on the Files pull-down menu in the Protect system lets you establish privilege levels for four types of access, as discussed in the section "Database Access Privileges" earlier in this chapter.

To fill in the appropriate numbers on the menu, move the highlight to a field name option and press ↲. Then either type a number (1 to 8) or use the ↑ or ↓ key to increase or decrease the number. When the correct value is displayed, press ↲.

After you assign an access privilege to each of the four file access levels in the submenu, press ← to return to the Files pull-down menu.

EXAMPLE

Figure 20.15 shows the file access privileges for the PAYMAST database defined in the submenu, as indicated by the file privileges defined in Figure 20.2. All users who have access to the Payroll group are allowed to read (view) the contents of the file. Of those users, only those with access levels in the range 1 to 4 are

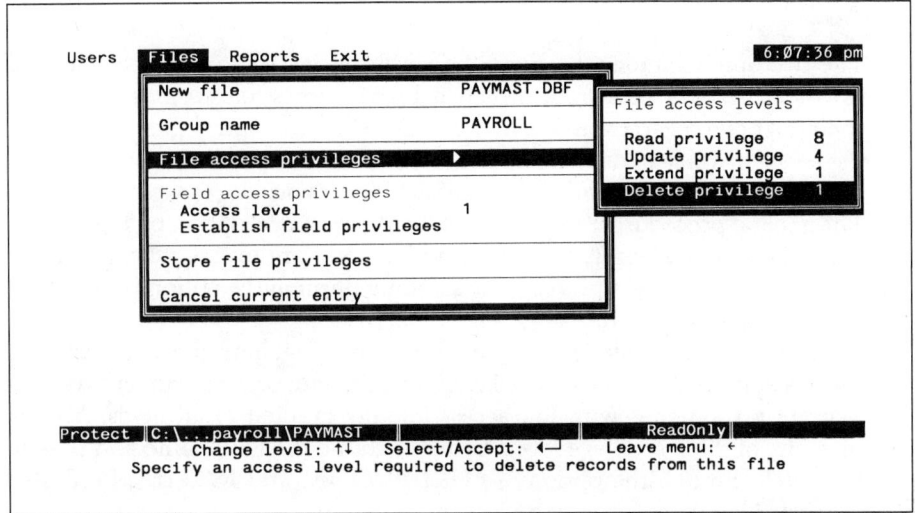

FIGURE 20.15: File access privileges defined for the PAYMAST.DBF database. The access privileges defined here refer to the access levels assigned to individual user profiles.

permitted to update the file. Only users with an access level of 1 are allowed to add and delete records in the PAYMAST.DBF database.

Establishing Field Privileges

SEQUENCE OF STEPS

From the Protect system:

    Files/Access level [◄─┘]
    type a number ◄─┘   *or*   press ↑ and ↓ to scroll ◄─┘
    Files/Establish field privileges [◄─┘]
    ↑ *or* ↓ to highlight the field name
    ◄─┘ to scroll through options
    repeat steps for each field
    ←
    repeat steps for each file access level

USAGE

The two options under the Field Access Privileges option on the Files pull-down menu let you determine which fields are accessible to individual users beyond their overall access to the file. The Access Level option lets you select an access level for which to define field privileges. For each possible user access level (1 to 8), you can assign a different set of field access privileges.

The general procedure is to first select the Access Level option by highlighting it and pressing ←┘. Next, type the access level you want to assign field privileges to, or select the file access privilege by scrolling through the options (1 to 8) with the ↑ and ↓ keys. Then press ←┘.

After you select the file access privilege to use, highlight the Establish Field Privileges option and press ←┘. A list of all field names in the current database appears in a submenu, with full access initially granted to all fields. You can change any of these privilege levels by highlighting the field name and pressing ←┘ to scroll through the options—FULL, NONE, and R/O (read only)—as summarized here:

LEVEL	PRIVILEGES
FULL	User can read and write data in the field.
R/O	Read only; user can read but not write data in the field.
NONE	User can neither read nor write data in the field.

Keep in mind that file privileges take precedence over field privileges. If the file privilege states that the user can only read data in the file, a field privilege of FULL makes no sense. Therefore, if the user can only read a file, the valid field options are only R/O and NONE.

After you have defined the appropriate settings for each field at the current access level, press ← to leave the field name submenu. Then select another file access level to work with (2 to 8) and repeat the process of assigning the FULL, R/O, or NONE access level to each field. Make sure that you assign field privileges to all eight access levels before you save your work. dBASE IV differs from earlier versions in that menu fields in a protected database are now also encrypted to prevent unauthorized access.

EXAMPLE

Figure 20.16 shows field privileges assigned to file access level 1 for the PAYMAST.DBF database. Notice that the Access Level option specifies level 1, and that the FULL field privilege is assigned to every field in the file privilege scheme designed in Figure 20.2.

ESTABLISHING FIELD PRIVILEGES — 747

Figure 20.17 shows field privileges assigned to file access level 4 for the same database, PAYMAST.DBF. Once again, the field privileges defined here relate to those defined for access level 4 in the file privilege scheme defined in Figure 20.2.

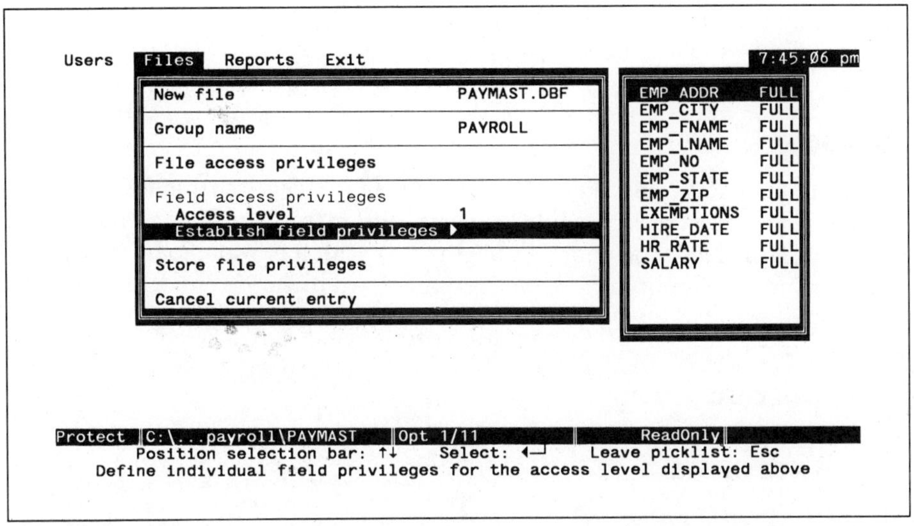

FIGURE 20.16: Field privileges assigned to access level number 1 for the PAYMAST database, as defined in the file privilege scheme shown in Figure 20.2.

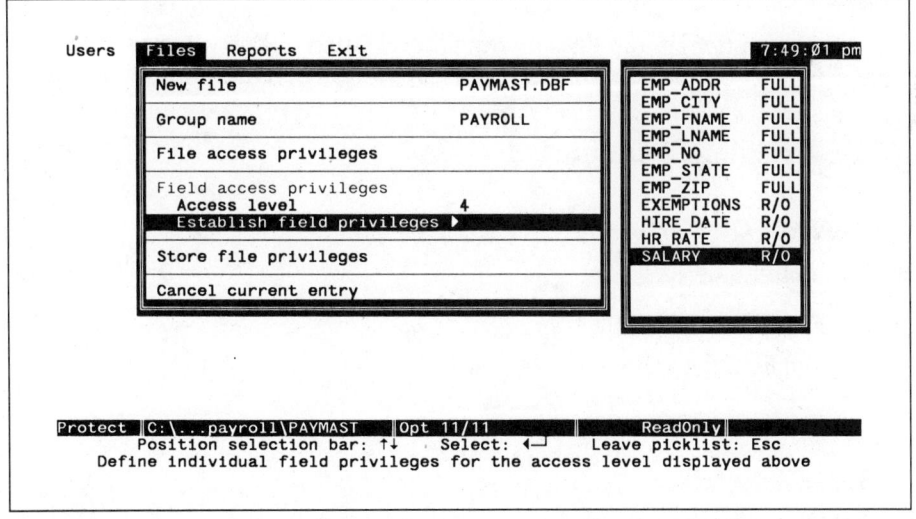

FIGURE 20.17: Field privileges assigned to file access level 4 for the PAYMAST database. Again, these field privileges relate to those defined on paper in Figure 20.2.

Saving the File Privilege Scheme

SEQUENCE OF STEPS

From the Protect system:

    Files/Store file privileges [⏎]

USAGE

When you are satisfied with the file and field privilege scheme for the current database file, select the Store File Privileges option from the Files menu. You can then select the New File option to begin work with a new database file or select the Save and Exit options from the Exit pull down menu to return to the Control Center.

Canceling the Current Entry

SEQUENCE OF STEPS

From the Protect system:

    Files/Cancel current entry [⏎]

USAGE

The last option on the Files menu, Cancel Current Entry, lets you delete the file privilege scheme that you are currently working on and start all over again.

Changing File Privilege Schemes

SEQUENCE OF STEPS

From the Protect system:

    Files/New file [⏎]
    highlight the file name
    ⏎

USAGE

To change an existing file privilege scheme, select New File from the Files pull-down menu in the Protect system and select the name of the database file. The

Protect system will display the current protection scheme on the menu. You can then use the same techniques to make changes that you used to create the file privilege scheme.

After you make your changes, be sure to select Store File Privileges. To return to the Control Center, select Save from the Exit pull-down menu. Then select Exit from that same menu.

PRINTING PROTECTION SCHEME REPORTS

The Protect system lets you print copies of the user profiles and the privilege scheme assigned to any protected database file. You can compare these reports to your original user profiles and file privilege schemes to check for possible errors after you create or change the protection scheme. Note that the user profile report includes user passwords and therefore should be stored in a safe place to prevent users from discovering each others' passwords.

Printing the User Profile Report

SEQUENCE OF STEPS

From the Protect system:

Reports/User Information [↵]
Yes *or* No [↵]

USAGE

To print the user profiles for a protection scheme, select the User Information option from the Reports pull-down menu. The screen will ask if you want to send the report to the printer. Select Yes to print the report or No to display the report on the screen.

EXAMPLE

Figure 20.18 shows a sample user profiles report printed by the Protect system. This report was printed after defining all the user profiles shown in Figure 20.1.

```
User name  Password          Group      Fullname              Level
=========  ================  =========  ====================  =====
KING       Honcho            PAYROLL    Barbara King          1
KING       Honcho            PAYABLES   Barbara King          1
KING       Honcho            LEDGER     Barbara King          1
ABIGAIL    Kitten            PAYABLES   Abigail Adams         1
ABIGAIL    Kitten            LEDGER     Abigail Adams         1
BART       Pluto             PAYROLL    Bart Jones            8
CHUCK      Banana            LEDGER     Chuck Smith           4
KAY        Sky               PAYROLL    Kay Watson            4
KAY        Sky               LEDGER     Kay Watson            4
RON        Tree              PAYABLES   Ron Yokem             8
RON        Tree              LEDGER     Ron Yokem             1
```

FIGURE 20.18: A sample user profiles report printed by the Protect system.

Printing the File Privilege Scheme

SEQUENCE OF STEPS

From the Protect system:

    Reports/File Information [⏎]

    select a file name

    type a group name

    ⏎

    Yes or No [⏎]

USAGE

To print the privilege scheme for a protected file, select the File Information option from the Reports pull-down menu in the Protect system. Then select the name of the protected file from the list that appears, by highlighting its name and pressing ⏎.

When prompted, type the name of the group that the file is assigned to and press ⏎. Then select Yes to print the report or No to display the report on the screen.

EXAMPLE

Figure 20.19 shows a sample file privilege scheme printed by the Protect system. This example shows the privilege scheme for the PAYMAST.DBF database defined in Figure 20.2.

```
Filename    C:\DBASE\PAYROLL\PAYMAST.DBF
Group Name    PAYROLL
Read privilege      8
Update privilege    4
Extend privilege    1
Delete privilege    1

Fieldname       1      2      3      4      5      6      7      8
==========    =====  =====  =====  =====  =====  =====  =====  =====
EMP_NO         FULL   FULL   FULL   FULL   R/O    R/O    R/O    R/O
EMP_LNAME      FULL   FULL   FULL   FULL   R/O    R/O    R/O    R/O
EMP_FNAME      FULL   FULL   FULL   FULL   R/O    R/O    R/O    R/O
EMP_ADDR       FULL   FULL   FULL   FULL   R/O    R/O    R/O    R/O
EMP_CITY       FULL   FULL   FULL   FULL   R/O    R/O    R/O    R/O
EMP_STATE      FULL   FULL   FULL   FULL   R/O    R/O    R/O    R/O
EMP_ZIP        FULL   FULL   FULL   FULL   R/O    R/O    R/O    R/O
HIRE_DATE      FULL   R/O    R/O    R/O    R/O    R/O    R/O    R/O
SALARY         FULL   R/O    R/O    R/O    R/O    R/O    R/O    NONE
HR_RATE        FULL   R/O    R/O    R/O    R/O    R/O    R/O    NONE
EXEMPTIONS     FULL   R/O    R/O    R/O    R/O    R/O    R/O    NONE
```

FIGURE 20.19: A sample File Information report printed by the dBASE IV Protect system. This example shows the privilege scheme for the PAYMAST.DBF database, originally defined in Figure 20.2.

EXITING THE PROTECT SYSTEM

SEQUENCE OF STEPS

From the Protect system:

> Exit/**S**ave or **A**bandon [←]
> Exit/**E**xit [←]

USAGE

The last menu item at the top of the Protect screen is Exit. When you select this option, you'll be given three options: Save, Abandon, and Exit.

Selecting the Save option saves all new and modified privilege schemes. The user profiles are saved in a file named DBSYSTEM.DB. File privilege schemes are stored in the database file structure. When the file privilege scheme is saved, the associated database file and its index files are automatically encrypted to prevent access by unauthorized users.

Selecting the Abandon option cancels all new or modified user profiles and file privilege schemes. Any previous settings defined before the current Protect session are restored.

Selecting Exit from the Exit pull-down menu saves current changes (unless you previously selected Abandon) and returns control to the dBASE IV Control Center.

USING PROTECTED dBASE IV FILES

After a protection scheme has been created for dBASE IV, all users must go through a logging-in procedure before gaining access to the dBASE IV Control Center.

SEQUENCE OF STEPS

From the DOS command prompt:

DBASE ↵

type a group name ↵

type a login name ↵

type a password ↵

USAGE

Once a protection scheme has been created for dBASE IV, users can still start dBASE IV in the usual manner (by entering the command **DBASE** at the DOS command prompt). Before gaining access to the Control Center, however, all users will see a screen that presents these prompts:

```
dBASE IV Login
Enter group name:
Enter your name:
Enter password:
```

The user must type a valid group name, login name, and password. The password does not appear on the screen as it is being typed. Press ↵ after typing each entry.

When all three items have been entered, dBASE checks to verify that they match one of the defined user profiles. If they do, the dBASE IV copyright notice appears, followed by the Control Center.

If the group name, login name, and password do not match a user profile, the entries are erased, and all three items must be reentered. If, after three attempts to log in, the user still does not enter a valid group name, login name, and password, control returns to the operating system.

EXAMPLE

Figure 20.20 shows a sample login screen filled in for a user defined in the user profiles. The password is never displayed on the screen, but must be entered.

FIGURE 20.20: A sample login screen filled in by a user. The password is not displayed on the screen at any time.

LOCKING FILES AND RECORDS

In a network environment, dBASE IV uses *file locking* and *record locking* to maintain the integrity of data in the database. Files and records are locked on an as-needed basis only, to ensure that all users have maximum access to all databases. When a particular operation requires a file or record to be locked for one user, other users can view data in that file or record, but not change it. As soon as the operation that requires the lock is completed, dBASE automatically releases the lock.

The sections that follow describe these operations in more detail.

Locking Files

Operations that act upon the database as a whole automatically lock the entire database file. The person performing the operation has *exclusive use* of the file, and other users can view, but not modify, data in that database. Exclusive use of a file is granted during execution of queries that perform calculations or updating. Exclusive use also is granted while the user is printing a report or mailing labels. As soon as the operation is done, dBASE automatically unlocks the file.

If you attempt to perform an operation that requires file locking, but the file is already locked by another user, the screen displays the message *File is in use by* <login name>. *Retrying lock, press Esc to cancel*. You can wait for dBASE IV to gain access to the file or press **Esc** to stop trying.

Locking Records

Whenever a user is modifying an individual record in a database (via the edit or browse screens), that record is locked. Other users can still view the record, but they cannot make changes to it. As soon as the user moves on to another record, the lock is automatically released.

If you attempt to edit a record that is already locked by another user, the screen displays the message *Record is in use by* <login name>. *Retrying lock, press Esc to cancel*. You can either wait for the other user to finish with the record or press **Esc** to stop trying and then move on to another task.

Under normal circumstances, simply viewing a record on a browse or edit screen does not lock the record. But you can lock the record if you want to prevent other users from changing it while you are viewing it. To do so, press **Ctrl-O** or select Lock Record from the Records pull-down menu on either the edit or browse screen. The message *RecLock* will appear in the status bar while the record is locked. To unlock the record, press **Ctrl-O** again.

TIPS AND TRAPS

- Be sure to write down the security system password and store it in a safe place before creating a protection scheme. If you forget and lose this password, you will never be able to access the Protect system again.
- Before using the dBASE IV Protect system, plan your user profiles and file privilege schemes on paper.
- If you do not use the Protect system to create a privilege scheme for a database file, all users in the system will have unrestricted access to that database.

SUMMARY

This chapter discussed general techniques for creating a file protection scheme.

For general information about using the browse and edit screens:

- Chapter 3, "Adding, Changing, and Deleting Data"

For further information about performing calculations:

- Chapter 6, "Performing Calculations"

For more information about update queries:

- Chapter 11, "Managing Groups of Records"

For information about printing reports and labels:

- Chapter 9, "Printing Reports and Labels"

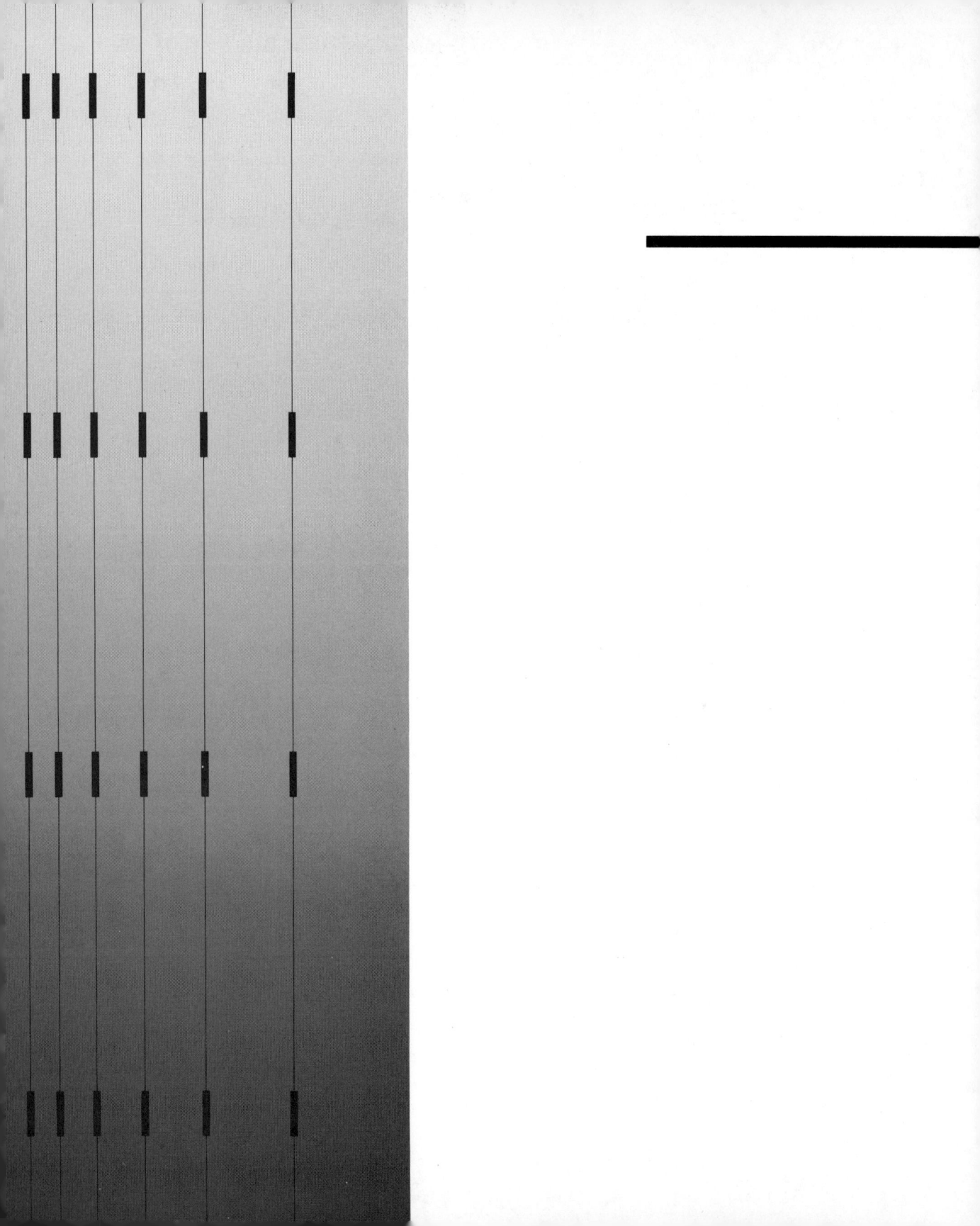

APPENDIX A

INSTALLING dBASE IV

Hardware Requirements. 759
Uninstalling Previous Versions. 759
Installing dBASE IV. 760
    Registering Your Software. 760
    Specifying Your Hardware Setup. 761
        The Multi-User Installation Option. 761
        Selecting a Display Mode. 762
        Optimizing a Color Display. 762
        Selecting Printers. 763
        Making Changes. 767
        Selecting a Drive and Directory. .767
    Copying the dBASE IV Program Files. 768
    Modifying the AUTOEXEC.BAT File. 768
    Modifying the CONFIG.SYS File. 770
    Copying Optional Files. 770

INSTALLING dBASE IV

Before you can use dBASE IV on your computer, it needs to be installed. Installation involves providing dBASE with essential information about the computer setup with which you'll be using the program, as well as filling out the dBASE registration form and copying dBASE onto your hard disk.

You need only go through the installation process once. If your copy of dBASE is already installed on a computer and working, you can safely ignore the information presented here.

This appendix discusses general techniques for installing dBASE IV on a single-user computer. If you want to install dBASE IV on a network, refer to the network installation manual that came with your dBASE IV package. If you change any of the equipment in your computer setup, you should *reconfigure* dBASE, using the DBSETUP program discussed in Chapter 19.

If you have never used a computer before and are unfamiliar with such terms as *drive*, *directory*, and *subdirectory*, you should read Appendix B to learn a little about DOS before installing dBASE IV. Reading Appendix B will help you understand some of the questions that the installation program asks you.

HARDWARE REQUIREMENTS

dBASE IV requires the following minimum hardware and operating system:

- An IBM PC, AT, PC/XT, or PS/2 model 30, 50, 60, or 80; a Compaq Deskpro 386; or any 100-percent compatible personal computer.
- IBM DOS or MS-DOS version 2.0, or a more recent version, for the DOS version of dBASE IV; or OS/2 for the OS/2 version of dBASE IV.
- At least 640K of RAM.
- A hard disk with at least 4 megabytes of available disk space.

UNINSTALLING PREVIOUS VERSIONS

If you have an earlier version of dBASE on your computer, such as dBASE III PLUS, and wish to save it, you should uninstall the earlier version before installing dBASE IV. Use the original disks and the UNINSTALL program that came with the earlier version.

If you want to keep a copy of dBASE III PLUS on your hard disk, be aware that the dBASE IV installation procedure will attempt to install dBASE IV on the \DBASE directory on hard disk drive C, the same directory that stores dBASE III. Thus, to keep both dBASE III PLUS and dBASE IV, you'll need to use two separate directories. For example, you can move all the files for dBASE III PLUS to a directory named \DBASE3 and then store all the dBASE IV files on a directory named \DBASE.

INSTALLING dBASE IV

Before beginning the installation process, make sure you have the dBASE IV disks from the dBASE IV package available. Write down the serial number from dBASE IV System Disk 1. Also note your printer make, model, and type (either parallel or serial). If you are in doubt, consult the manual that came with your printer.

To begin the installation process, follow these steps:

1. Turn on your computer in the usual manner to get to the DOS command prompt (usually C>).
2. Insert the dBASE IV Installation disk in drive A.
3. Switch to drive A by typing the command **A:** and pressing ↵. (You should see the A> prompt on your screen.)
4. Type the command **INSTALL** and press ↵.

Throughout the installation procedure, you will occasionally be asked to insert a different disk from the dBASE IV package into drive A: (the exact disks requested depend on whether you are using 5¼-inch or 3½-inch disks). Each time the screen asks you to insert a different disk, remove the disk currently in drive A, insert the requested disk, and press ↵ to proceed, as the screen instructs.

Registering Your Software

If you are installing dBASE IV for the first time, you will be prompted to complete the software registration form shown in Figure A.1. Type your name, the name of the company you work for (if any), and the serial number printed on dBASE IV System Disk 1. Be sure to check your spelling, as you will not be able to modify this information later. You can move the cursor using the ↑, ↓, →, and ←, and **Backspace** keys to make corrections, or you can type over existing text as necessary.

```
┌─────────────────────────────────────────────────────────────────┐
│ Install                                                         │
│  ┌────────────────────────────────────────────────────────┐     │
│  │ Software Registration                                  │     │
│  │   User Name       ...................  ▓▓▓▓▓▓▓▓▓▓▓▓▓▓ │     │
│  │   Company Name    ...................  ▓▓▓▓▓▓▓▓▓▓▓▓▓▓ │     │
│  │   Serial Number   ...................  ▓▓▓▓▓▓ - ▓▓▓▓▓ │     │
│  └────────────────────────────────────────────────────────┘     │
│                                                                 │
│       ┌──────────────────────────────────────────────────┐      │
│       │  Before using this product for the first time,   │      │
│       │  you must fill in this registration form.  Once  │      │
│       │  you save the form, it cannot be changed.        │      │
│       │                                                  │      │
│       │  Use Ctrl-End to save this form once you have    │      │
│       │  provided the requested information.             │      │
│       └──────────────────────────────────────────────────┘      │
│  Dev Ed    A:\                              360K Floppy         │
│                          Reading . . .                          │
│        Enter registration information.  Save - CTRL-END  Cancel - ESC │
└─────────────────────────────────────────────────────────────────┘
```

FIGURE A.1: The software registration form appears the first time you install dBASE IV on a hard disk. The requested serial number is printed on dBASE IV System Disk 1.

When you have completed the software registration form, press **Ctrl-End** (hold down the **Ctrl** key and press the **End** key) after responding to the prompts on the screen. The installation program will take a few moments to store the software registration information. It will then present the two options Proceed and Exit. Press the ⏎ key to proceed.

Specifying Your Hardware Setup

The next phase of the installation process requires you to describe your computer hardware. A menu will appear on the screen, with one option highlighted, as shown in Figure A.2. Note that you can use the ↑ and ↓ keys to move the highlight. (If the arrow keys don't work, press the **NumLock** key once and then try again.)

The Multi-User Installation Option

Press ↓ to leave this option set to No.

(This appendix discusses only single-user installation. If you are installing dBASE IV on a network, refer to the network installation manual that came with your dBASE IV package for installation instructions.)

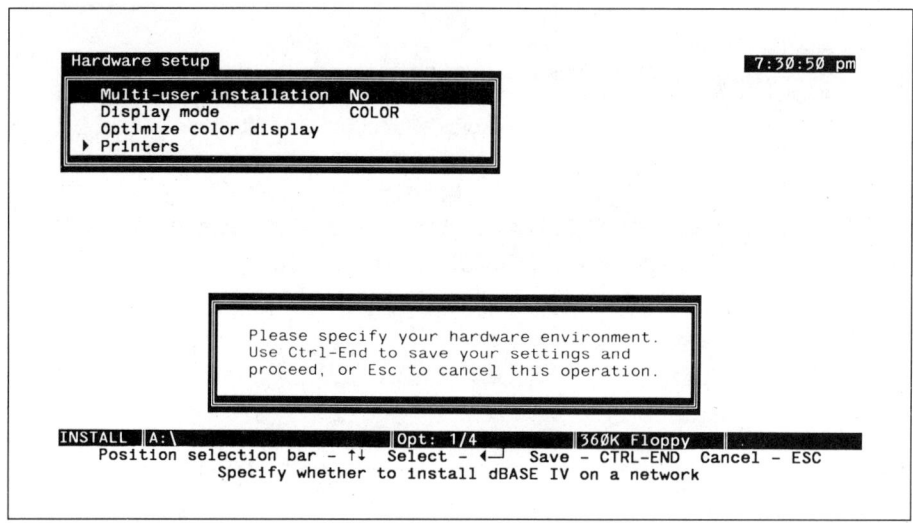

FIGURE A.2: Menu displayed by the dBASE IV installation program. Use the ↑ and ↓ keys to move the highlight and press ↵ to select the currently highlighted option.

SELECTING A DISPLAY MODE

The installation program automatically detects the type of display adapter installed in your computer and lists it next to the Display Mode option on the menu. In most cases, you will want to use the suggested display mode.

However, if you have multiple monitors attached to your computer, or if you use an EGA or VGA adapter, you may want to select an option other than the one suggested. Press the space bar repeatedly to scroll through the options, listed here:

MONO	For monochrome monitors
MONO43	For 43 lines on a monochrome display
COLOR	For the color graphics adapter (CGA)
EGA25	For a 25-line display with EGA or VGA
EGA43	For a 43-line display with EGA or VGA

When the appropriate display option for your computer is displayed next to the Display Mode option, press ↓ to move to the Optimize Color Display option.

OPTIMIZING A COLOR DISPLAY

dBASE IV will write to your screen as quickly as possible, but it cannot determine how quickly your screen can accept information without interference

SPECIFYING YOUR HARDWARE SETUP

("snow"). When the highlight is on the Optimize Color Display option, press ← to test your screen.

A brief message will appear, describing the purpose of the test. Press ← to select the Proceed option and proceed with the test. The next screen will ask if you see "snow" (screen interference). If the screen is clear, type the letter **N** (for no). If you do see snow, type the letter **Y**.

In either case, the screen will then indicate that dBASE IV is optimized for use with your screen. Press any character key (or the space bar or ←) to return to the menu.

SELECTING PRINTERS

The next step in the installation process is to tell dBASE about the printer (or printers) attached to your computer. Press ↓ until the highlight is on the Printers option. Then press ←.

You will see a screen with space for entering up to four printers, as shown in Figure A.3. When the blinking cursor is in the Printer Name column, press **Shift-F1** (hold down the **Shift** key and press the **F1** key).

You will see a list of some printer manufacturers. Only manufacturers with names starting with the letters A through E are shown initially, as in Figure A.4. You can press ↓ repeatedly to scroll through additional manufacturers. Xerox is the last manufacturer listed.

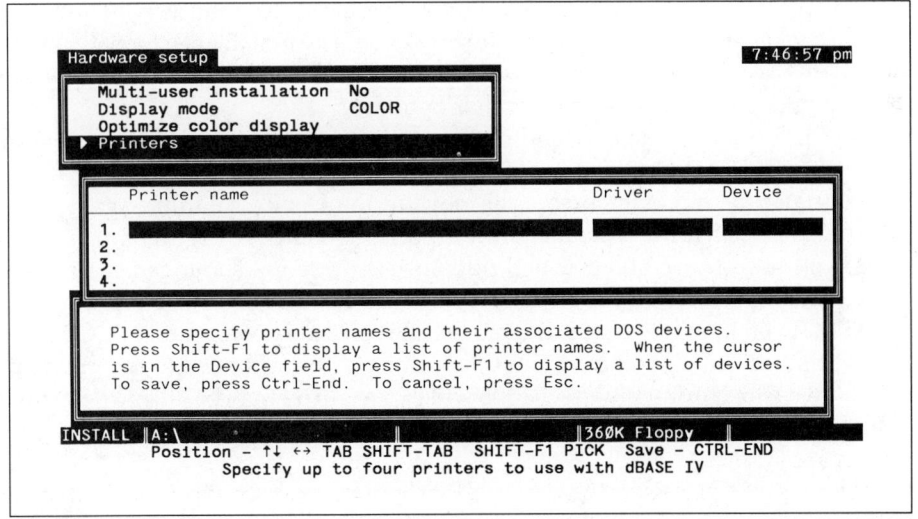

FIGURE A.3: The installation program displays this screen to let you define up to four printers. For a list of some possible printers, you can press **Shift-F1** at any time.

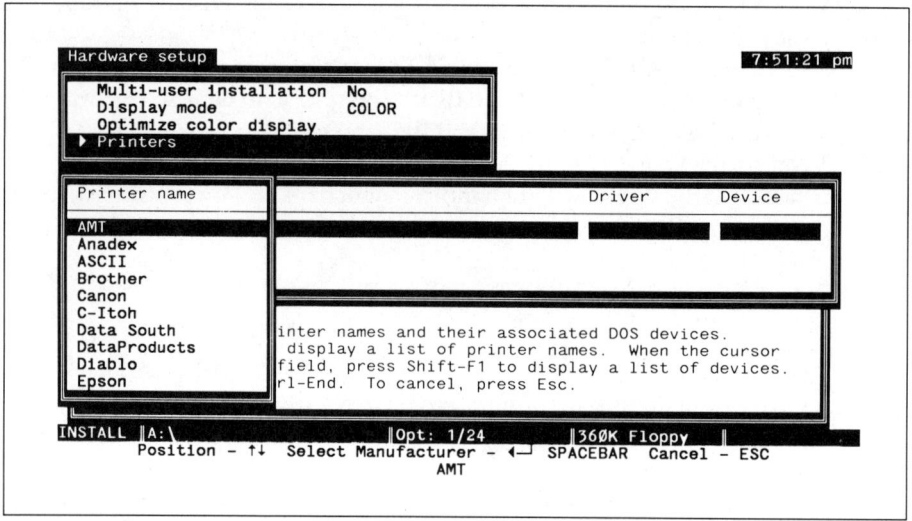

FIGURE A.4: Partial list of printer manufacturers, which actually extends to Xerox. Press the ↓ and ↑ keys to scroll through options. Press ↵ to select a manufacturer.

Use the ↑ and ↓ keys to highlight the name of the company that manufactures your printer. (If you are not sure what printer you have or do not see your printer manufacturer listed, highlight Generic Driver.) If you make a mistake, press the escape key (**Esc**).

If you select a manufacturer that offers several printer models, you will see a list of available models. Figure A.5 shows the list of available models for the Hewlett-Packard option. Again, you can use the ↑ and ↓ keys to highlight any option and then press ↵ to select that option.

The printer manufacturer and model and a *driver name* (a driver is a program that dBASE IV later uses to send information to the printer) will appear on the screen, and the blinking cursor will move to the Device column. Again, press **Shift-F1** to see a list of available printer ports, as shown in Figure A.6.

If you are unsure about which port to use, here are some general rules of thumb to follow. If you have only one printer, and it is a parallel printer, select LPT1. If you have only one serial printer, it is probably connected to COM1, so select that option. If you have multiple printers, you will need to determine on your own which printer is attached to which port. (You may be able to determine this by following the cables from each printer to the back of the computer, *if* the ports are labeled.)

The \\SPOOLER and \\CAPTURE options are used for network installation only.

SPECIFYING YOUR HARDWARE SETUP — 765

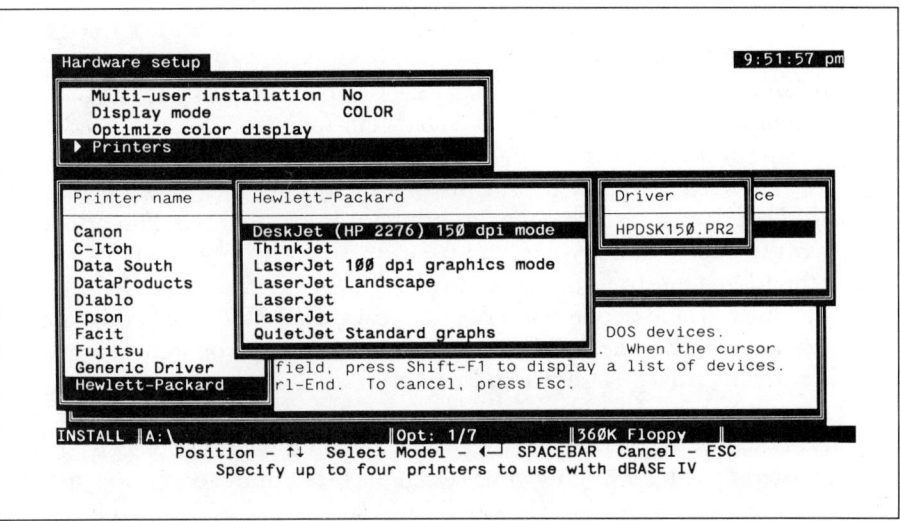

FIGURE A.5: A list of available models for the Hewlett-Packard printers. Use the ↑ and ↓ keys to scroll though options and press ↵ to select the currently highlighted option.

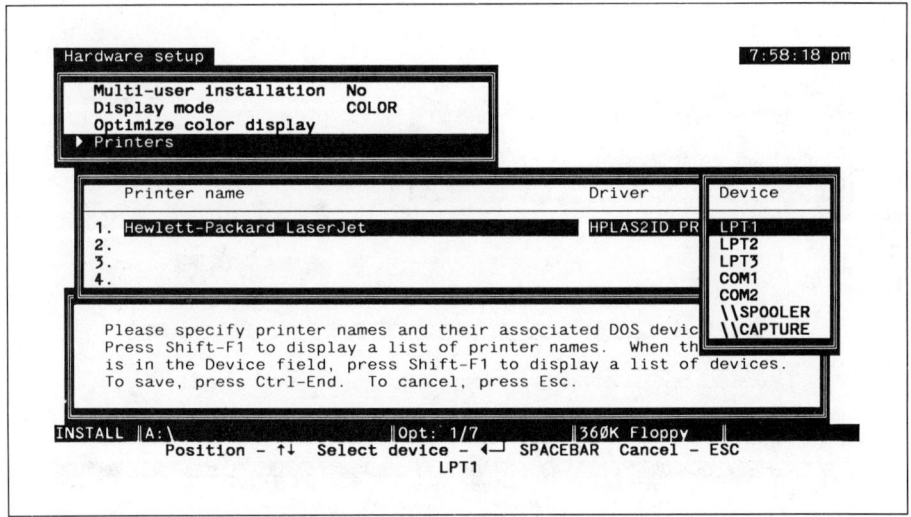

FIGURE A.6: A list of available printer ports. Select the option that describes the port your printer is connected to by highlighting its name and pressing ↵.

Select a printer port by positioning the highlight with the ↑ and ↓ keys and then pressing ↵. The name of the selected port appears in the Device column, and the highlight moves down to the next row. You can press ↑ to move back to the first line, if necessary, to make corrections (again using the **Shift-F1** key to display a list of available choices).

You can use these same techniques to specify up to four printers. If you have a printer that supports multiple modes, you can install the same printer more than once, using a different mode each time. For example, you can install the Hewlett-Packard LaserJet printer as printer number 1, and the Hewlett-Packard LaserJet Landscape option as printer number 2 (this option prints sideways on the page). Later, when you use dBASE IV to print, you can choose either the normal portrait, or vertical, mode, or the landscape mode.

After filling in at least one printer option, press **Ctrl-End** (hold down the **Ctrl** key and press the **End** key). The next screen displays the options you selected, plus the generic driver, as shown in Figure A.7.

You can select any of the listed drivers as the default driver, which dBASE IV will use unless you specify otherwise when printing data. GENERIC.PR2 is always listed first, following by your selections listed in the order you specified them on the previous screen. (If you are not sure which driver name refers to which printer, press **Esc** and then ← to review the printer and driver names. Then press **Ctrl-End**.) Select an option by positioning the highlight and pressing ←. You will be returned to the initial menu.

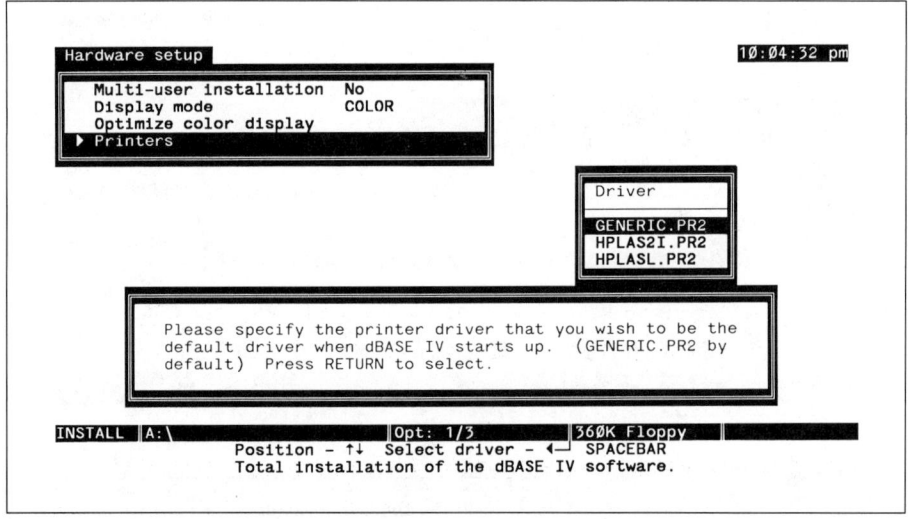

FIGURE A.7: After describing your printers, the installation program asks which one to use as the default driver (that is, the driver dBASE should use if you do not specify otherwise). Select an option by highlighting it and pressing ←.

Making Changes

If for any reason you want to change any of your previous selections, use the ↑ and ↓ keys to highlight any option on the menu and press ⏎ to select the option. In making new selections, use the same techniques you used to make your original selections. When you are done, press **Ctrl-End**.

Now you can start the process of copying the dBASE IV program files from the software package disks onto your hard disk. You will see a screen of options, including Proceed, Modify Hardware Setup, and Exit. Press ⏎ to select Proceed and continue with the installation.

Selecting a Drive and Directory

The next screen asks you to specify the disk drive and directory on which to install dBASE IV. The screen suggests using a directory named \DBASE on hard disk drive C (that is, C:\DBASE), as Figure A.8 shows.

You can specify any drive and directory combination simply by typing over the suggested drive and directory names. If you have multiple hard disks, named C, D, E, and so forth, you can use any of these disks. Do not specify a disk drive name (A or B) or the name of a virtual disk (or RAM disk).

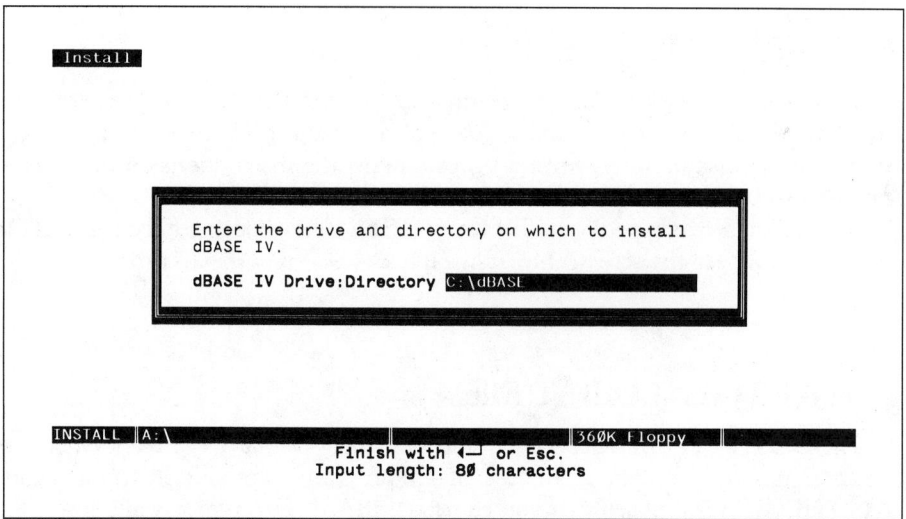

FIGURE A.8: The screen requests a drive and directory for storing dBASE IV and suggests C:\DBASE. You can use any valid drive and directory name, but if you use one other than C:\DBASE, you will later need to adjust your startup procedure accordingly.

You can use any valid DOS directory name: up to eight letters maximum length, no spaces or punctuation other than the underscore (_) or hyphen(-) allowed. The name must be specified in correct DOS syntax (for example, **F:\DB4** for a directory named DB4 on hard disk drive F).

Keep in mind that all of the dBASE IV manuals, as well as examples presented in this book, assume that dBASE IV is installed on the C:\DBASE directory. If you change this default specification, you will need to make adjustments accordingly when first starting dBASE (discussed in Chapter 1 of this book) and when changing default configurations (discussed in Chapter 19 of this book).

After filling in the drive and directory (or, to accept the default location C:\DBASE, doing nothing), press ← to proceed. If the directory you specified does not exist yet, the screen will ask for permission to create it. To proceed, press ← while Proceed is highlighted.

You will then be prompted to enter a directory for storing dBASE IV structured query language (SQL) system files. The screen will suggest SQLHOME, a subdirectory of the directory that stores dBASE IV. There is no particular reason to use a different directory, so just press ← to accept the suggestion.

If the subdirectory does not exist yet, the screen will ask for permission to create the subdirectory. Press ← to select Proceed.

Copying the dBASE IV Program Files

The installation program will begin copying the dBASE IV program files from the disks to your hard disk. You will be asked to change the disk in the source drive (disk drive A) several times. Follow the instructions on the screen, pressing ← once each time you change the disk in drive A.

After all of the main program files for dBASE IV have been copied from all the disks, you will see the screen shown in Figure A.9. Press ← to proceed.

Modifying the AUTOEXEC.BAT File

The DOS AUTOEXEC.BAT file stores instructions that DOS reads whenever you first start your computer. The installation program automatically changes your AUTOEXEC.BAT file so that you can start dBASE IV automatically from any drive or directory. When you see the screen shown in Figure A.10, press ← to proceed with the operation.

MODIFYING THE AUTOEXEC.BAT FILE — 769

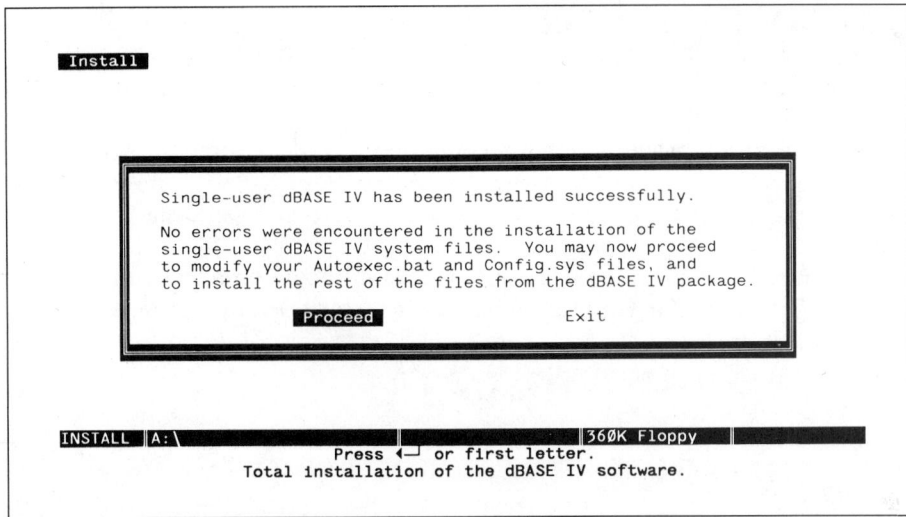

FIGURE A.9: Screen displayed after the installation has successfully copied all the main program files from the dBASE IV disks to your hard disk. Press ⏎ to select Proceed and continue the installation process.

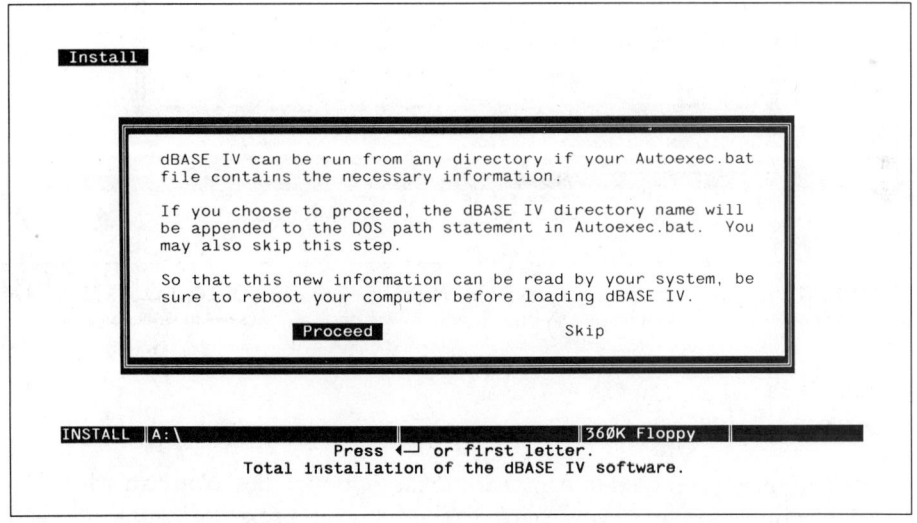

FIGURE A.10: The installation program asks for permission to alter your AUTOEXEC.BAT file so that dBASE IV can be started from any directory. Press ⏎ to select Proceed.

Modifying the CONFIG.SYS File

The DOS CONFIG.SYS file contains information that DOS uses to configure itself to your equipment. This file needs the following minimal settings for dBASE IV to run properly on your computer:

```
FILES = 40
BUFFERS = 15
```

The installation program will ask if you want it to automatically update your CONFIG.SYS file for you, displaying the screen shown in Figure A.11. Press ← to select Proceed.

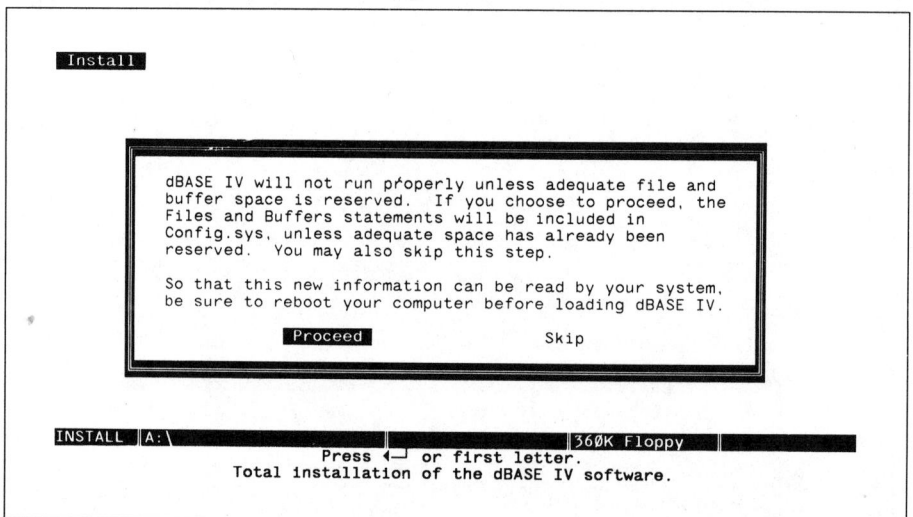

FIGURE A.11: The installation program asks for permission to modify the DOS CONFIG.SYS file, so that DOS can handle as many simultaneously open files as dBASE permits. Press ← to select proceed.

Copying Optional Files

You are next prompted to copy additional, optional files. You can select Proceed to copy those files to your hard disk, or you can press → to move the highlight to Skip and then press ← to skip copying those files at this time. The files that the screen will ask to copy are summarized in the following list (you will be asked if you want to copy the RunTime and template language files only if you are installing the dBASE IV Developer's Edition):

Sample files	Sample databases, sample reports, and other files used in examples in the manuals that came with your dBASE IV package
Tutorial files	The dBASE IV tutorial program, named INTRO, stored on DBTUTOR, a subdirectory of the dBASE home directory (for example, C:\DBASE\DBTUTOR)
RunTime files	The dBASE IV Developer's Edition Run-Time programs, which allow developers to distribute their applications to customers who do not own dBASE IV
Template language files	The dBASE IV Developer's Edition template language files, which allow advanced programmers to develop their own templates for creating forms, report formats, and applications

Note that if you choose not to install any group of files at this time, you can still do so later using the DBSETUP program discussed in Chapter 19.

Each time you select Proceed to copy a group of files to your hard disk, you'll be asked for a subdirectory to store those sample files on and will be given a suggested name. As usual, you can just press ↵ to select the suggested drive and directory and select Proceed if the screen asks for permission to create the directory. To complete the remaining steps, you simply follow the instructions that appear on the screen.

After you have determined which files you want to copy and followed the instructions on the screen for doing so, you will see a screen asking you to insert the Installation disk in drive A. Do so and then press ↵. Your last options are Exit to DOS and Transfer to DBSETUP. (The DBSETUP program is discussed in Chapter 19.) For now, press ↵ to select Exit to DOS.

You will be returned to the DOS A> prompt. Type **C:** and press ↵ to return to hard disk drive C. Now you can begin using dBASE IV, starting in Chapter 1 of this book. Remember: You need not repeat this installation procedure in the future. If you decide later that you want to change some of the selections you made during the installation process, you can use the DBSETUP program, discussed in Chapter 19 of this book.

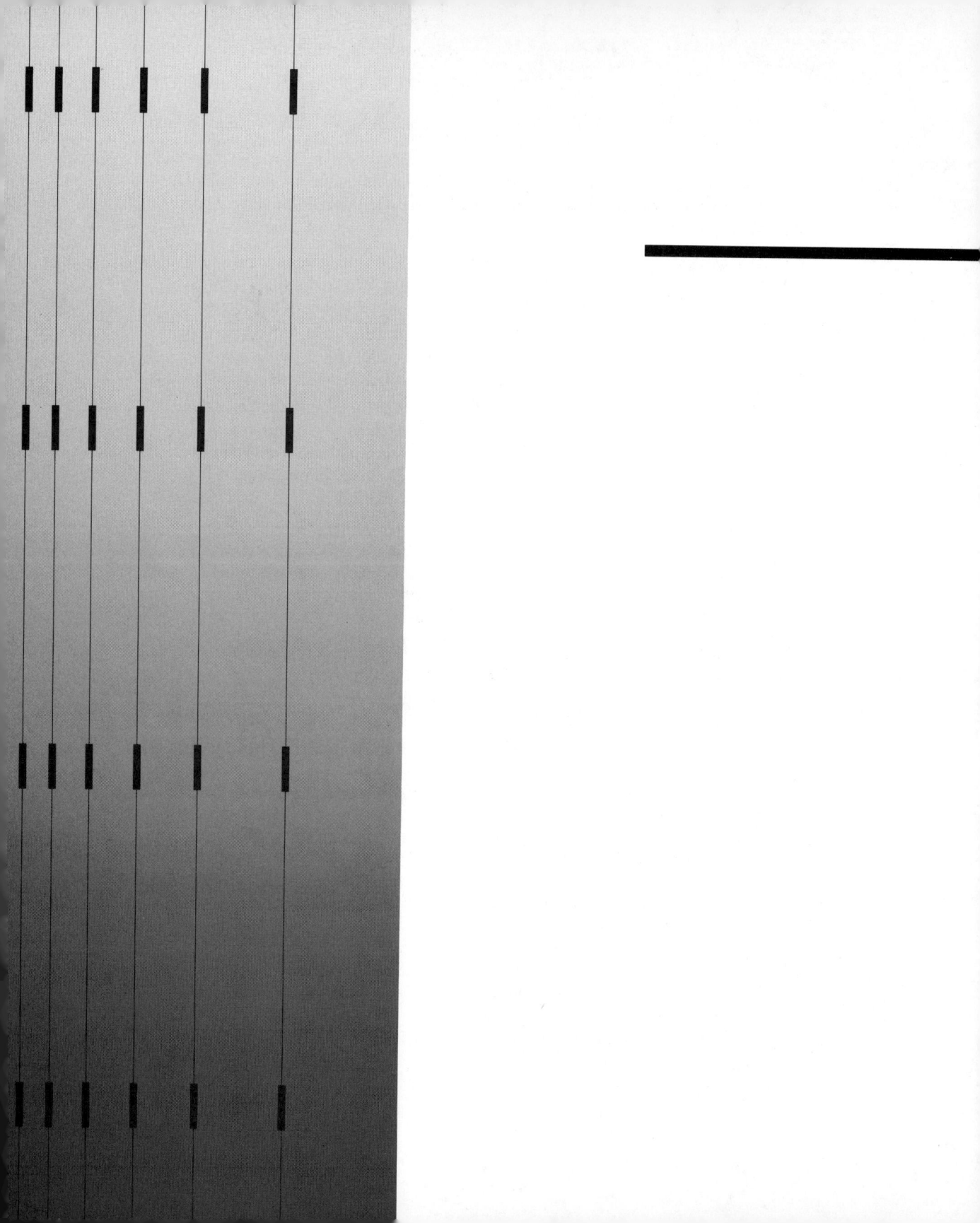

APPENDIX B

USING DOS

Disks and Disk Drives. 775
    Floppy Disks. 776
    Hard Disks. 777
Disk Drive Names. 777
Directories and Files. 778
    Directory Names. 778
    Subdirectories. 779
    Directory Trees. 779
File Names. 779
The DOS Prompt. 782
Setting the Date and Time. 783
Selecting a Disk Drive to Use. 784
Selecting a Directory. 784
Viewing the Current Directory Name. 784
Viewing File Names. 785
Viewing the Directory Tree. 785
Creating Directories. 786
Running Programs. 786
File Search Paths. 787

Using DOS

Most people reading this book will have some experience using at least one computer software package, dBASE IV; and anyone who has worked with a computer at all has used (directly or indirectly) the computer's *operating system*. At the very least, you've called up dBASE into your computer's active memory by entering the program's name at the DOS (or OS/2) prompt. But even many relatively experienced computer users know less than they would like to know about their operating system, and many others might find ways to work more efficiently if they knew more. Even though you are probably ready to start putting dBASE IV to work now, the time you spend learning about your computer's operating system will be well spent. The more you know about the operating system, the more easily you will get along with your computer, and with dBASE IV as well. This appendix offers a brief overview of your computer's operating system and shows how to perform some of its more commonly used operations.

The operating system acts as a sort of a middleman between the *hardware* of the computer and the *software* that you are using. The fact that you are reading this book indicates that your hardware is probably an IBM or compatible microcomputer. The operating system that you are using is probably DOS, or perhaps OS/2. *DOS* is an acronym for *disk operating system*. *OS/2*, which stands for *operating system 2*, is a newer version of DOS. The specific software package, or program, that this book discusses is dBASE IV.

Note that even though there are some differences between DOS and OS/2, both use identical commands for performing the types of operations used in this book. Therefore, this book refers to the operating system simply as DOS.

DISKS AND DISK DRIVES

Information that you store in the computer, whether it be a sales report, customer list, graph, or letter, is *written* in a *file*. Programs, such as dBASE IV, are also stored in files. Each file is stored on a disk, similar to the way that a song is stored on a compact disk or cassette tape. Your tape or disk player lets you hear your cassette tapes and compact disks; your computer lets you *read* the contents of a file on your computer disk.

Most computers can use at least two types of disks for storing files. One type is removable and is called a *flexible disk*, *floppy disk*, or *diskette*. The other type of disk is a *hard disk* or *fixed disk*. A hard disk cannot be removed.

Floppy Disks

Removable disks come in two sizes: 5¼-inch minifloppy disks and 3½-inch microfloppy disks. Your computer might accept one size or both. Figure B.1 illustrates 5¼-inch and 3½-inch disks.

To access the files stored on a disk, you first have to put the disk into the *disk drive* of your computer. Always insert the disk with the label facing upward and toward you. Most 5¼-inch disk drives have a latch or door that you must close after inserting the disk. To remove the disk, open the drive door or latch. The disk will pop out slightly. Gently pull the disk out of the drive to remove it.

The 3½-inch disk drives do not have a door or latch. Instead, you push the disk in until it clicks and pops into the drive. To remove a 3½-inch disk, you press the eject button, which is usually slightly below and to the right of the slot where you insert the disk. The disk will pop out slightly. Gently pull the disk the rest of the way out of the slot.

The write-protect notch on a 5¼-inch disk lets you protect the files stored on the disk. When the notch is uncovered, you have full access to the files on that

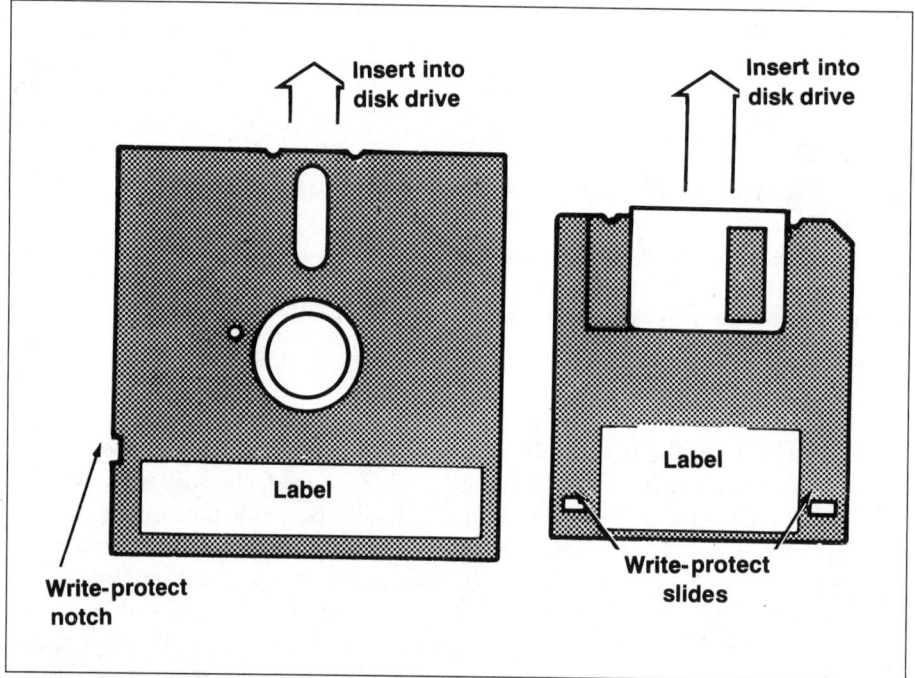

FIGURE B.1: A 5¼-inch and a 3½-inch disk. Insert disks into a drive with the label facing up and toward you, as the figure shows.

disk. That is, you can read and copy information from the disk, change files on the disk, copy new files to the disk, and erase files from the disk.

If you cover the notch with one of the tabs that comes with a box of disks, you can only read or copy files from the disk; you cannot add, erase, or change any of the files that are already stored on the disk.

The 3½-inch disks use a sliding tab to protect files. (Some have two sliding tabs, others have only one.) When the sliding tab is closed, you have full access to the files on the disk. You can read, copy, change, erase, and add new files to the disk. When the sliding tab is open, you can only read or copy files from the disk; you cannot add new files or erase or change existing ones.

Hard Disks

To use dBASE IV, your computer must be equipped with at least one hard disk (or fixed disk) drive as well as a floppy disk drive. You can't see the hard disk because it's inside the main unit of the computer. The hard disk has certain advantages over a floppy disk. For instance, a single hard disk can hold much more information than a floppy disk; it can hold perhaps as much as 100 floppy disks. A hard disk is also much faster than a floppy disk, which makes all your work on the computer faster.

The reason the computer has both hard and floppy disk drives is that you need some way to transport files from one computer to another. The removable floppy disks provide that capability. For example, when you buy dBASE IV, it comes to you on floppy disks. Before using the program, you *install* it, which includes copying dBASE IV from the disks on which it was delivered to the hard disk in your computer.

Floppy disks are also useful for making backup copies of important information. For example, if you store all your accounting data on a hard disk, you might also want to make an extra copy and store it on a floppy disk. You can store that extra copy in a safe place. If someone accidentally erases the accounting data from your hard disk, you can then recopy it from the backup disk onto your hard disk.

You might also want to copy information from your hard disk to a floppy disk for use on another computer. For example, you might want to give a copy of the accounting data to someone else for use elsewhere. Or if you have computers both at home and in your office, you might want to copy data from the hard disk on one computer for use on the other.

Disk Drive Names

DOS identifies each disk drive on your computer with a single letter. Typically, if your computer has one floppy disk drive and one hard disk, the floppy disk drive is named A and the hard disk is named C. If you have two floppy disk drives and one hard disk, the floppy drives are named A and B, with A usually being the one on the top or at the left. The hard disk is still named C.

Your computer might have additional hard disks named D, E, F, and so on. For example, if you share a computer with other users in a network, you might work on a hard disk named E or F. The network administrator (that is, the person in charge of the computer) can tell you the letter assigned to the drive that you are using.

Directories and Files

A single hard disk can store many thousands of files. To help keep all of these files organized, you can create separate work areas, called *directories* (or *subdirectories*). Each directory holds its own set of files, just like each department in a company has its own set of files.

Directory Names

Each directory on a disk has a name, which you assign. The name can be up to eight characters long, but it cannot contain any blank spaces or punctuation. You can use numbers and the underline character (_) in a directory name. Table B.1 lists examples of valid and invalid directory names.

DOS often precedes a directory name with a backslash (\) to distinguish it from a file name. For example, the DBASE directory might be identified as \DBASE. To pinpoint the *exact* location of a particular directory, DOS often precedes the directory name with the drive name, followed by a colon (:) and a backslash. For example, C:\DBASE identifies a directory named DBASE on disk drive C.

DIRECTORY NAME	STATUS
DBASE	Valid
ACCOUNTS	Valid
JAN1989	Valid
GL	Valid
ACCT_REC	Valid
FIRST QTR	Invalid (contains a blank space)
RECEIVABLES	Invalid (too long)
ACCT:REC	Invalid (colon not allowed)

Table B.1: Examples of Valid and Invalid Directory Names

Subdirectories

You can also create subdirectories on your disk. The name of a subdirectory can also be up to eight characters long. A subdirectory name is always preceded by the names of higher-level directories and a backslash. For example, suppose you create a directory named SALES to store information for the sales department of your company. Also suppose you want to keep the accounting data and personnel data for the sales department on separate subdirectories. To do so, you could create one subdirectory named SALES\ACCTNG and another subdirectory named SALES\PERSONNL. Note that the directory and subdirectory names are separated by a backslash.

Directory Trees

You can envision the directory structure (or directory *tree,* as it's sometimes called) on a disk as a hierarchy. The *root* directory (which every computer has) is the highest-level directory. The root directory is always named simply \. There can be any number of directories and subdirectories beneath the root directory. Figure B.2 shows a sample directory tree (the directory on your computer is probably much different).

The terms *parent* and *child* are often used to describe the hierarchical relationships between directories and subdirectories. For example, in Figure B.2 the SALES (or \SALES) directory is the *parent* to both \SALES\ACCTNG and \SALES\PERSONNL. The \SALES\ACCTNG subdirectory is a *child* to the \SALES directory, as is \SALES\PERSONNL.

Be aware that the terms *directory* and *subdirectory* are used interchangeably in most computer literature. For example, it is not unusual to see a phrase such as "switch to the \SALES\ACCTNG directory" or even "the \SALES subdirectory."

The reason for this loose terminology stems from the fact that, from the computer's standpoint, directories and subdirectories are pretty much the same thing: Each is just a place on the disk where files are stored. Subdirectory names, such as \SALES\ACCTNG, are for human convenience. That is, when you see the subdirectory name \SALES\ACCTNG, you can quickly recall that the sales department's accounting information is stored in that work area. But the computer just sees a work area named \SALES\ACCTNG (and has no idea that the information stored there has anything to do with your sales department or with accounting).

File Names

Each directory (and subdirectory) on a disk may contain many files, such as a file containing a customer list; another file containing a parts list; and other files

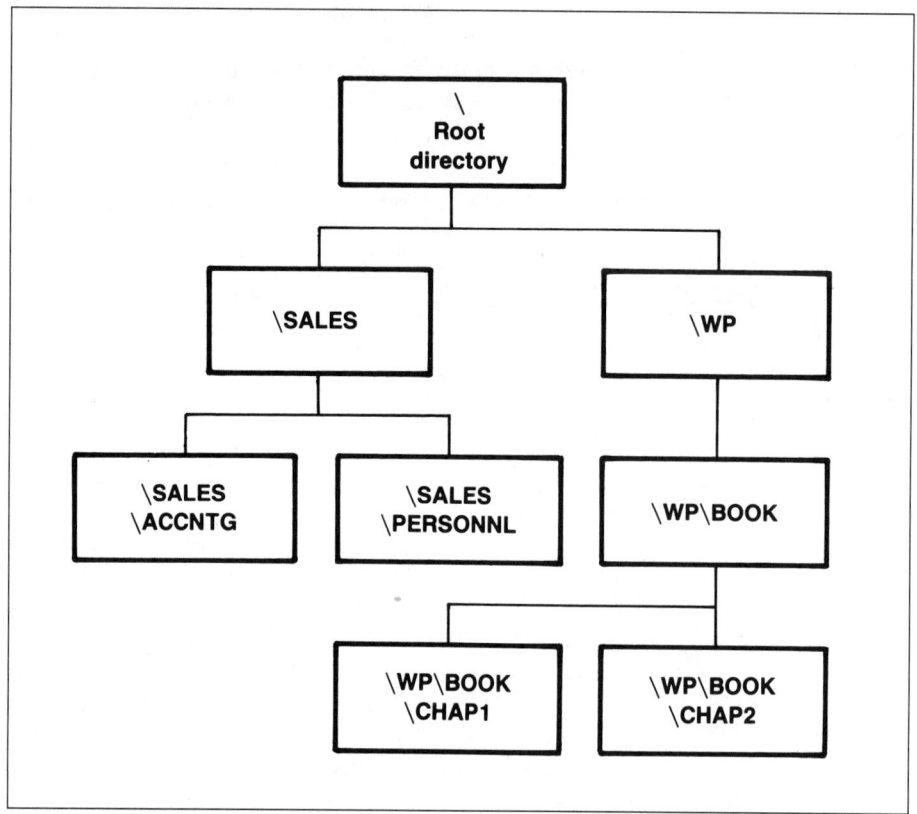

FIGURE B.2: A sample directory tree. Directories are used to organize files on a disk into related groups. The highest-level directory is called the *root directory,* and it always has the name \.

containing letters, graphs, and programs such as dBASE IV. Each file has a name that, like a directory name, can be up to eight letters long and cannot contain spaces. Numbers and the underline character (_) are allowed.

A file name can also have an *extension* (or last name). The extension can be up to three letters long and is always preceded by a period. Usually, the file name identifies the contents of a file, and the extension identifies the type of information in the file. (When using dBASE IV, you usually provide the file name, and dBASE automatically adds the extension.)

Table B.2 lists examples of valid and invalid file names. Table B.3 lists examples of file name extensions and indicates the type of data stored in the files.

The exact location of specific information filed on a disk is often displayed by DOS (and dBASE IV) as a combination of the disk drive, directory (and subdirectory) names, and the file name preceded by a backslash. For example, the

FILE NAME	STATUS
MYREPORT.TXT	Valid
ACCTREC.DAT	Valid
QRT1.89	Valid
1989TAX.FRM	Valid
JAN_1989.DBF	Valid
MAIL LIST.DAT	Invalid (contains a space)
1989SUMMARY.REP	Invalid (file name too long)
MAILIST.DATA	Invalid (extension too long)

Table B.2: Examples of Valid and Invalid File Names

EXTENSION	TYPE OF INFORMATION
.TXT	Text (such as a letter, report, or document)
.BAK	Backup copy of another file
.DBF	dBASE database file
.COM	Program
.EXE	Another extension used for programs

Table B.3: Examples of File Name Extensions

complete name C:\DBASE\MYDATA.DBF identifies a database file named MYDATA.DBF stored on the \DBASE directory on disk drive C. The complete name C:\SALES\PERSONNL\NAMELIST.TXT identifies a text file named NAMELIST.TXT on the \SALES\PERSONNL subdirectory on disk drive C.

Now suppose that, while using dBASE IV, you create a database containing customer names and addresses. You assign the name CUSTLIST to this database and store it on a directory named \DBASE on drive C. Because dBASE automatically adds the extension .DBF, the customer names and addresses will actually be stored in a file named CUSTLIST.DBF. To completely identify the location and name of the customer list, DOS (and dBASE) use C:\DBASE\CUSTLIST.DBF. Figure B.3 illustrates how the CUSTLIST database is stored on a disk.

Another term that you may encounter while using DOS or dBASE IV is *path*. The path refers to the disk drive, directory, and subdirectory name (if any) that describes the location of a file. Figure B.4 shows an example of a path, using a file named FORMLET.TXT stored on the \WP\LETTERS subdirectory of drive C.

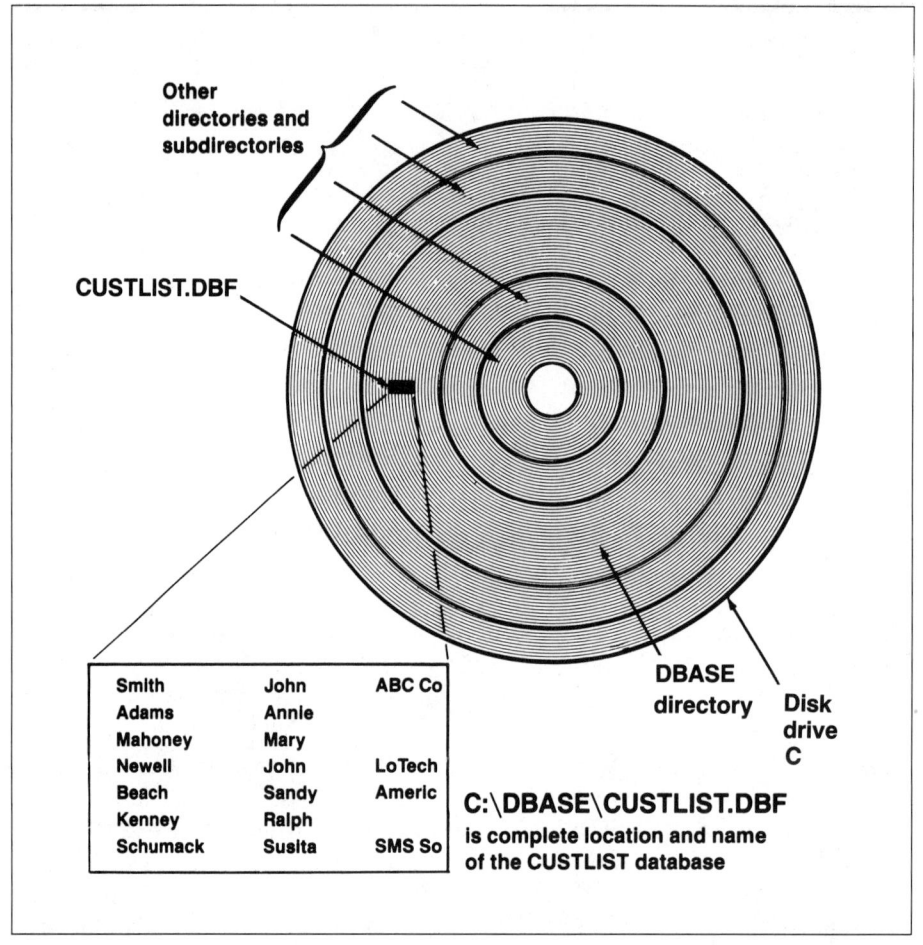

FIGURE B.3: CUSTLIST.DBF database stored on a disk. The complete path name, **C:\DBASE\CUSTLIST.DBF**, tells the computer that the CUSTLIST.DBF database is stored on a directory named DBASE on hard disk drive C.

THE DOS PROMPT

When you first turn on your computer, DOS automatically *boots* (starts) the system and takes control. Your screen shows the *DOS prompt,* which consists of the name of the current disk drive, followed by the > sign. The DOS prompt will probably be C > on your computer (if you boot from a hard disk) or A > (if you boot from a floppy disk).

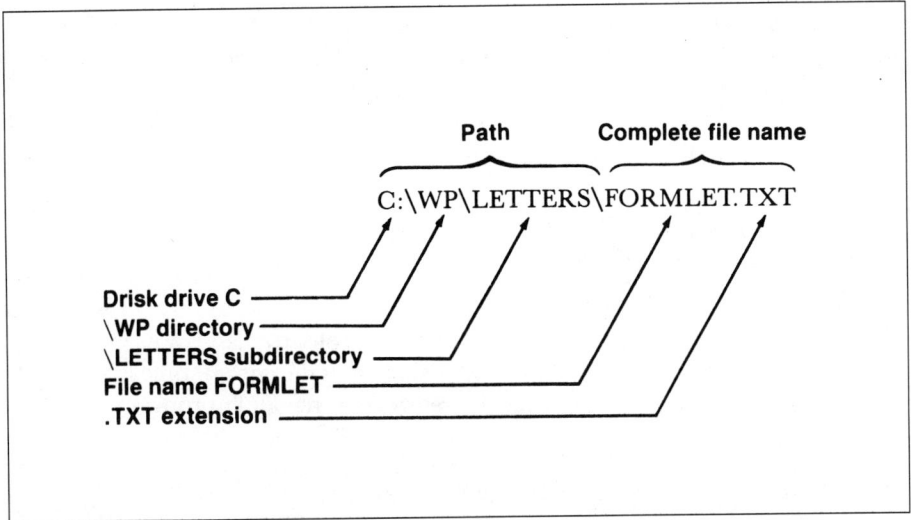

FIGURE B.4: A file name, preceded by its path. The disk drive name precedes the directory (and subdirectory) names. The file name and extension are always listed last. Backslashes separate the various components.

If you are using DOS version 4.0 or the OS/2 operating system, you may not see the command prompt right away. DOS 4 users can access the command prompt by pressing the **F3** key until the command prompt appears. OS/2 users (with Presentation Manager) can access the command prompt by pressing **Alt-Esc** until the command prompt appears.

When the DOS prompt appears, the computer is ready to accept certain *DOS commands*. The following sections discuss some basic DOS commands that can help you use your computer more effectively. For a more complete discussion of DOS commands, refer to the manual that came with your copy of DOS (or OS/2).

SETTING THE DATE AND TIME

Your computer stores the current date (sometimes called the *system date*) in its memory, and dBASE IV can access that date. To see if the date is correct, type the command **DATE** next to the DOS prompt. (If you make a mistake, you can back up by pressing the **Backspace** key.) After typing the DATE command, press ↵ (called the **Enter** or **Return** key on some keyboards).

Your screen will display a prompt such as this one:

    Current date is Sat 12/31/1989
    Enter new date (mm-dd-yy)

If the date shown on your screen is not correct, type a new date in *mm-dd-yy* format (for example, **11/15/89** for November 15, 1989). Press ← after typing the new date, and you'll be returned to the DOS prompt.

To check and correct the system time, type the command **TIME** and press ←. The screen will display the current time and a prompt for entering the correct time, as follows:

```
Current time is 12:26:15.92
Enter new time:
```

If the current time shown is not correct, type the new time using a 24-hour clock format. (You need not enter seconds or hundredths of seconds.) For example, if the current time is 8:30 A.M., type **8:30** and press ←. If the current time is 2:15 P.M., type **14:15** and press ←. You'll then be returned to the DOS prompt.

SELECTING A DISK DRIVE TO USE

To switch to a particular disk drive, type the letter of that drive followed by a colon and press the ← key. (You can switch to a floppy disk drive only if the drive contains a disk and the drive door, if any, is closed.) For example, if you are currently using disk drive A and want to switch to hard disk drive C, you enter the command **C:** and press ←. (This command works, of course, only if your computer has a hard disk named C.)

SELECTING A DIRECTORY

To select a directory or subdirectory, use the DOS change directory command, CHDIR, or its abbreviation, CD. For example, after you have installed dBASE on your computer, you can switch to the \DBASE directory by typing the command **CD \DBASE** and pressing ←. (Be sure to use the backslash (\ ) rather than the forward slash (/) when specifying directory names.)

To switch to a subdirectory, enter both the parent and child directory names. For example, if your computer has a directory named \DBASE\SAMPLES, you switch to that subdirectory by typing the command **CD \DBASE\SAMPLES** and pressing ←.

VIEWING THE CURRENT DIRECTORY NAME

If you switch to a new directory and its name does not appear next to the DOS command prompt, you can see the directory name by typing the command

PROMPT PG and pressing ⏎. The name of the current disk drive and directory will appear at the DOS prompt. For example, if the \DBASE directory on drive C is current, the DOS prompt will be appear as C:\DBASE>. This procedure is handy for keeping track of which directory is current.

VIEWING FILE NAMES

To view the names of files stored on the current directory, you can enter the directory command, DIR, at the DOS prompt. If the directory contains many files, you can enter the command **DIR /W** to display the file names in a wide (columnar) format, or you can enter the command **DIR /P** to have DOS pause after it presents each screenful of file names. (Press any key after each pause to view the next screenful.)

When DIR displays file names, it does not show a period between the file name and the extension. Instead, it displays the name and extension in separate columns. If you do not use the /W option for a wide display, DIR also shows the size of each file and the date and time that the file was created or last changed. DIR also shows the names of directories that are children to the current directory. These have <DIR>, rather than a file size, in the third column of the list.

Here is a sample DIR display (your computer's display will be completely different):

Directory of C:\

ASSIGN	COM	1536	2-11-89	12:00p
DBASE		<DIR>	3-31-89	8:00a
DISKCOPY	COM	39456	2-11-89	12:00p
FIND	EXE	27424	2-11-89	12:00p
PRINT	COM	28492	2-11-89	12:00p

The first row shows that there is a file named ASSIGN.COM on the current directory and that this file occupies 1536 *bytes* of disk space. (A byte is the same as a character; for example, the word *CAT* contains 3 bytes.) ASSIGN.COM was created (or last changed) at 12:00 P.M. on 2/11/89 in this example.

The second row shows that a directory named \DBASE exists on the disk. That directory was created on 3-31-89 at 8:00 A.M.

VIEWING THE DIRECTORY TREE

To view the names of all directories and subdirectories on the current disk drive, switch to the root directory and enter the TREE command. For example, to see the names of directories on disk drive C, you enter these commands (press ↵ after typing each command):

```
C:        ↵
CD\       ↵
TREE      ↵
```

The C: command takes you to drive C. The CD\ command then takes you to the root directory, which is always named \. The TREE command runs a DOS program named TREE, which displays the directory tree. Note that if the TREE.COM program is not on the root directory, DOS displays the message *Bad command or file name*. Don't worry about this; you can still use the other commands discussed in this chapter.

If a particular directory has child directories beneath it, these are listed separately. For example, suppose your TREE display includes

Path: \DBASE

Sub-directories: SQLHOME
                 DBTUTOR
                 SAMPLES

This display informs you that the hard disk includes a directory named \DBASE, with subdirectories \DBASE\SQLHOME, \DBASE\DBTUTOR, and \DBASE\SAMPLES.

To switch to the \DBASE directory, you enter the command **CD \DBASE**. To switch to the \DBASE\SAMPLES subdirectory, you enter the command **CD \DBASE\SAMPLES**. Then you can use the DIR command to see the names of files on the directory (or subdirectory).

CREATING DIRECTORIES

To create a new directory (or subdirectory) on your hard disk, you use the DOS Make directory command, MKDIR, or its abbreviation, MD. Include the full directory name and a preceding backslash. For example, to create a directory named \DBASE\MEMBERS, you enter the command **MD \DBASE\MEMBERS** at the DOS prompt. (You need not create any new directories right now.)

RUNNING PROGRAMS

All programs are stored in files that have the extension .COM, .EXE, or .BAT. To run a program, you usually need to switch to the directory that stores the program and then type the program name (without the extension).

For example, after you install dBASE IV (according to the instructions in Appendix A), the dBASE IV program and its associated files will be stored in a directory named \DBASE. The main dBASE IV program is named DBASE.EXE. Therefore, to run dBASE IV, you will need first to switch to the \DBASE directory on drive C and then enter the command DBASE at the DOS prompt. The exact commands you enter at the DOS prompt are

```
C:         ↵
CD\DBASE   ↵
DBASE      ↵
```

If you attempt to run a program that is not on the current disk drive and directory, DOS will respond with the message *Bad command or file name* (or something similar, depending on the version of DOS that you are using).

There is an exception to the rule that requires a program to be on the current directory. The next section discusses this exception.

FILE SEARCH PATHS

Normally, when you ask DOS to run a program (such as dBASE IV), that program must be stored in the current directory. However, DOS offers a command, PATH, that tells the computer to search other directories if it cannot find a particular program on the current directory.

When you install dBASE IV on your computer (as discussed in Appendix A), dBASE will ask if you want to be able to start dBASE IV from any directory. If you answer yes to this question, the installation program automatically creates the appropriate path so that you can run dBASE IV from any directory.

You can check the current path at any time by entering the command **PATH** at the DOS prompt. After you have installed dBASE IV, you should see C:\DBASE as one of the paths displayed on the screen. For example, you might see PATH = C:\DBASE. If other directories are included in the path, you'll see these as well, each separated by a semicolon. For example, if the root directory, a directory named \WP, and the \DBASE directory are all included in the search path, you'll see PATH=C:\;C:\WP;C:\DBASE.

If for some reason you cannot start dBASE from directories other than the \DBASE directory, you can alter the DOS path using the DBSETUP program, discussed in Chapter 19.

Note that the PATH command searches only for program files, which have the .COM, .EXE, or .BAT extension. If you have version 3.3 or 4 of DOS, you can use the DOS APPEND command to have DOS search multiple directories for nonprogram files. (The equivalent command in OS/2 is DPATH.) Refer to your DOS or OS/2 manual for information about these commands.

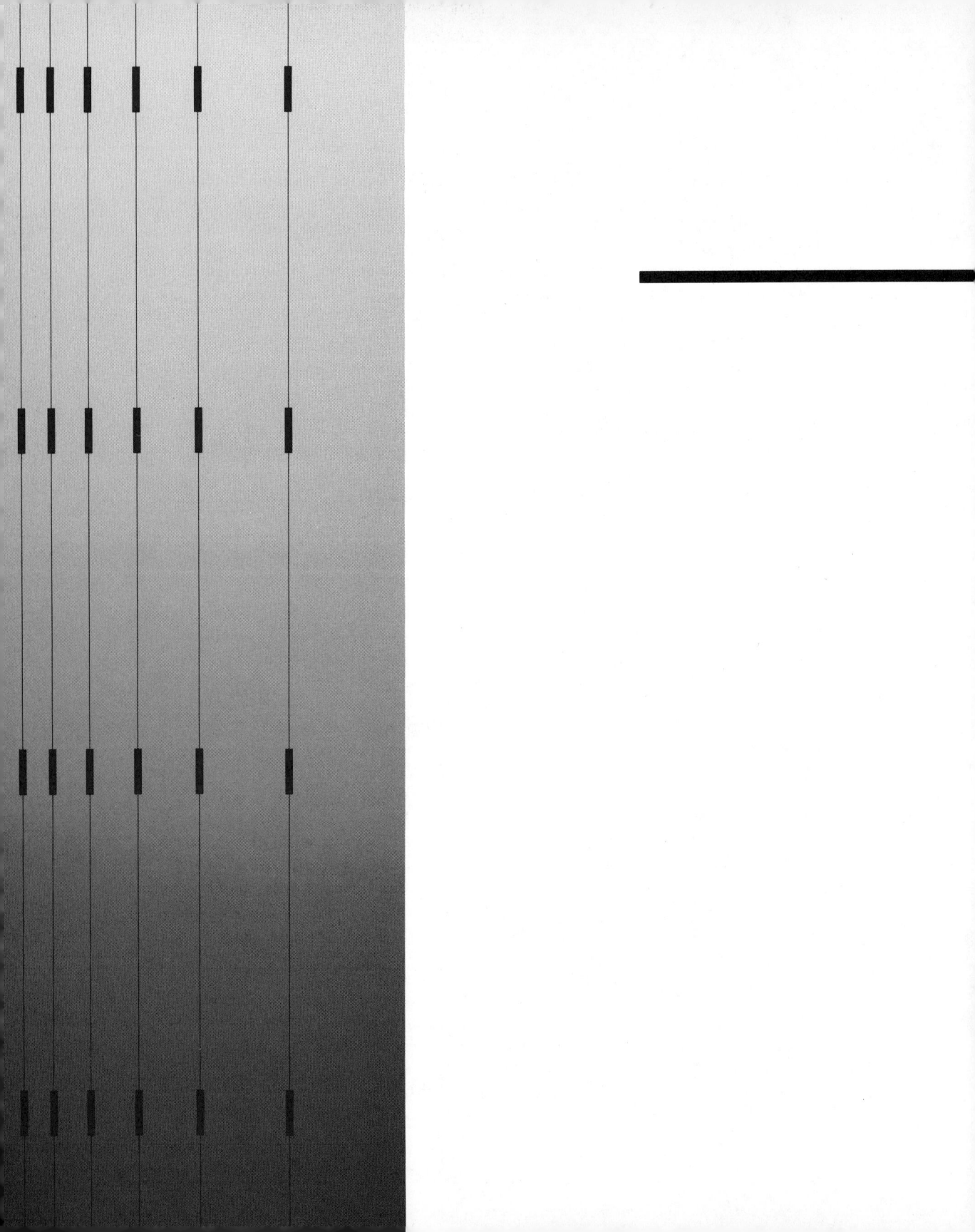

APPENDIX C

SUMMARY OF CHANGES FROM dBASE III PLUS TO dBASE IV

The Control Center. 791
Improved Help System. 791
Increased Limit Values. 791
New Data Type. 792
Improved Date Handling. 792
Improved Memo Fields. 792
Improved Index Management. 792
Improved Browse and Edit Modes. 793
Query by Example. 793
Improved Reports and Labels. 793
Improved Forms. 794
Keystroke Macros. 794
Improved Applications Generator. 794
Windows. 795
New Financial Functions. 795
Improved Programming Language. 795
    Multiple Child Files per Parent. 795
    Automatic Compilation. 795
    SEEK( ) and LOOKUP( ). 795
    SCAN...ENDSCAN Loop. 796
    User-Defined Functions. 796
    Arrays. 796
dBASE IV Developer's Edition. 797

Summary of Changes from dBASE III PLUS to dBASE IV

For experienced dBASE III and dBASE III PLUS users, dBASE IV offers many new and exciting features. This appendix highlights some of the more impressive new features and, where applicable, provides references to further information in this book. (Some of the new features are for programming only and are discussed in more advanced books such as the forthcoming *dBASE IV Programmer's Reference Guide*, by this author and also published by SYBEX.)

The Control Center

The dBASE III PLUS Assistant menu has been replaced by the more functional and easier-to-use Control Center. The Control Center provides access to all design screens and data, and displays the names of all files in a catalog. Unlike earlier versions of dBASE, the Control Center provides access to nearly all dBASE IV features (see Chapter 1).

In addition, the Control Center offers the DOS utilities screen for managing files and directories. This screen allows you to perform most DOS operations in an interactive fashion without leaving dBASE or entering DOS commands (see Chapter 14).

Improved Help System

Context-sensitive help is now available at all times. In addition, the built-in help system provides a table of contents, with various levels of specificity, to simplify the search for related information (see Chapter 1).

For a quick reminder of the syntax and options for a particular dBASE IV command or function, enter the command **HELP <command/function>** at the dot prompt, where <command/function> is the name of the command or function for which you need help (see Chapter 18).

Increased Limit Values

The allowable values for several dBASE III PLUS limitations have been increased in dBASE IV. A single database record can contain up to 255 fields, with a maximum combined length of 255 characters. Up to 99 files can be opened simultaneously, 10 of which can be database files.

NEW DATA TYPE

dBASE IV includes the new data type, Float, for storing floating-point decimal numbers (see Chapters 2 and 6).

IMPROVED DATE HANDLING

You no longer need to use CTOD( ) and DTOC( ) to manage dates. To define the Date data type, just enclose the date in curly braces, as in {01/01/89}.

To index a database to display dates sorted on a date field, you can use the DTOS( ) function in an index expression. DTOS( ) converts a date to a character string in YYYYMMDD format (that is, it converts 12/31/88 to 19881231), which ensures proper sort order (see Chapter 4).

IMPROVED MEMO FIELDS

Memo fields, which were unwieldy in earlier versions of dBASE, are much improved:

- Memo fields can now be displayed in windows on custom forms (see Chapter 10).
- Queries can now search Memo fields (see Chapter 5).
- Deleting and packing database records now deletes and packs Memo fields as well, thereby preventing the Memo field file from growing too large.

IMPROVED INDEX MANAGEMENT

dBASE III PLUS stored all indexes in separate database files and made the user responsible for keeping them current. dBASE IV stores all indexes in a single production index file that has the same name as the database file, but the extension .MDX. As soon as you open a database file, the production index file is automatically opened, and all indexes are instantly adjusted to accommodate changes in the database as they are made. dBASE IV also supports both ascending and descending index sort orders (see Chapter 4).

Improved Browse and Edit Modes

You can now switch between the browse and edit screens simply by pressing the Data key (**F2**). In addition, both screens provide pull-down menus for immediate access to operations such as adding new records, deleting records, searching for a record, and undoing recent changes (see Chapter 3).

Any special features used in a custom form, including templates and picture functions, multiple-choice options, and data validation, can be carried over to a browse screen, giving you equal control over data entry and editing in a custom form and on the browse screen (see Appendix F).

Query by Example

The dBASE III PLUS query form has been replaced by a much-improved query design screen, which provides an interactive query-by-example technique for searching and isolating database records (see Chapter 5).

The query design screen also lets you perform calculations such as those for totals, subtotals, averages, and statistical operations on the fly (see Chapter 6).

Queries can also perform global replacement operations, such as increasing prices by 10 percent in any or all records (see Chapter 11).

Improved Reports and Labels

The dBASE III PLUS Report Generator has been replaced by a much improved reports design screen. New features of the reports design screen include these:

- A WYSIWYG (what-you-see-is-what-you-get) work surface with *bands* defining page headers and footers, as well as report and group (subtotal) introductory and summary bands.
- Unlimited levels of subtotaling.
- Easy access to printer features such as boldfacing, underlining, and special fonts and pitches.
- Word-wrap and search-and-replace editing for easy creation and editing of form letters.
- A form layout, which makes stacking fields in printed reports easy.
- Seven summary operators for calculations: AVERAGE, COUNT, MAX, MIN, SUM, STD (standard deviation), and VAR (variance).
- Improved techniques for moving and copying field templates.

The labels design screen is also greatly improved and offers many of the same features that the reports design screen does (see Chapters 6 through 8).

Improved Forms

The dBASE III PLUS Screen Painter has been replaced by a much-improved forms design screen. New features of the forms design screen include these:

- Automatic layout of all database fields to speed form design.
- Coloring of individual fields and boxed areas on the form.
- Easier access to custom graphics characters.
- Calculated fields.
- Multiple-choice fields that allow a user to scroll through options.
- Edit options that support conditional editing (permit edit if…), data validation, on-screen calculations, custom navigation-line messages for each field, and carry-forward for individual fields.

The forms design screen is discussed in Chapter 10.

Keystroke Macros

dBASE IV offers a keystroke macro feature, which means you can store any series of keystrokes and play them back at any time by pressing a single key (see Chapter 13).

Improved Applications Generator

dBASE IV provides a much improved, more functional Applications Generator, which you can use to build applications of any complexity using pull-down menus, pop-up menus, and windows. Many applications can be developed without any programming whatsoever.

Experienced programmers and application developers need not write all the tedious code for managing menus, windows, or complex custom forms. Instead, the developer can focus on developing a few procedures and user-defined functions to handle the complex data processing components of an application and call the procedures from the application design (see Chapters 15 through 17 and Appendix F).

Windows

dBASE IV supports windowing, which you can use to enhance the appearance of applications (see Chapter 15).

New Financial Functions

dBASE IV includes three new financial functions: FV( ) (future value), PV( ) (present value), and PAYMENT( ) (payment on a loan). (See Appendix D.)

Improved Programming Language

The dBASE programming language includes many new features, summarized in the following sections.

Multiple Child Files per Parent

A single database file can now be related to multiple related "child" files simultaneously.

Automatic Compilation

To maximize processing speed, dBASE IV automatically compiles all programs into a format that the computer can more quickly execute. All objects that you create, including report formats, label formats, custom screens, queries, and calculations, are converted to dBASE IV source code, which you can modify or embed in your own custom programs. All of the objects are also compiled automatically for maximum execution speed.

SEEK( ) and LOOKUP( )

The SEEK and LOCATE commands now have counterparts as functions: SEEK( ) and LOOKUP( ). These functions return .T. if a value is found and .F. if a value is not found. These functions are particularly handy in custom forms that require data to be looked up in a separate database for validation.

SCAN...ENDSCAN Loop

The SCAN...ENDSCAN loop now provides a compact and efficient alternative to the DO WHILE .NOT. EOF( ) loop. For example, the DO WHILE loop

```
USE AnyFile
GO TOP
DO WHILE .NOT. EOF( )
    IF PartNo = "A-111"
        REPLACE UnitPrice WITH 1.10*UnitPrice
        ? PartNo,UnitPrice
    ENDIF
    SKIP
ENDDO
```

can be converted to a simpler SCAN...ENDSCAN loop:

```
USE AnyFile
SCAN FOR PartNo = "A-111"
    REPLACE UnitPrice WITH 1.10*UnitPrice
    ? PartNo,UnitPrice
ENDSCAN
```

User-Defined Functions

You can now create your own dBASE IV functions and use them in commands, report columns, custom forms, and any other place where you normally use the standard built-in functions. You can also attach a user-defined function to a field in a custom form to add sophisticated validation and on-screen calculation capabilities.

Arrays

Like most programming languages, dBASE IV offers arrays. An array is a collection of *subscripted memory variables,* each with the same name, but a different subscript. For example, an array with the name PartName might consist of the array *elements* PartName[1], PartName[2], and PartName[3] (pronounced "part name sub-one, part name sub-two, and part name sub-three").

An array can have either one dimension or two. A one-dimensional array has one subscript, as in the preceding PartName example. A two-dimensional array has two subscripts, such as Score[1,1]. You can envision a two-dimensional array as a table with rows and columns. The first subscript represents the row number, and the second subscript represents the column. For example, you can envision the arrangement of elements in an array named Score that has three rows and four columns as follows:

```
Score[1,1]   Score[1,2]   Score[1,3]   Score[1,4]
Score[2,1]   Score[2,2]   Score[2,3]   Score[2,4]
Score[3,1]   Score[3,2]   Score[3,3]   Score[3,4]
```

dBASE IV Developer's Edition

The dBASE IV Developer's Edition provides additional tools, including a template language, a run-time package, and network management, for advanced applications developers. For more information, refer to a more advanced book that focuses on the dBASE IV programming language and the Developer's Edition.

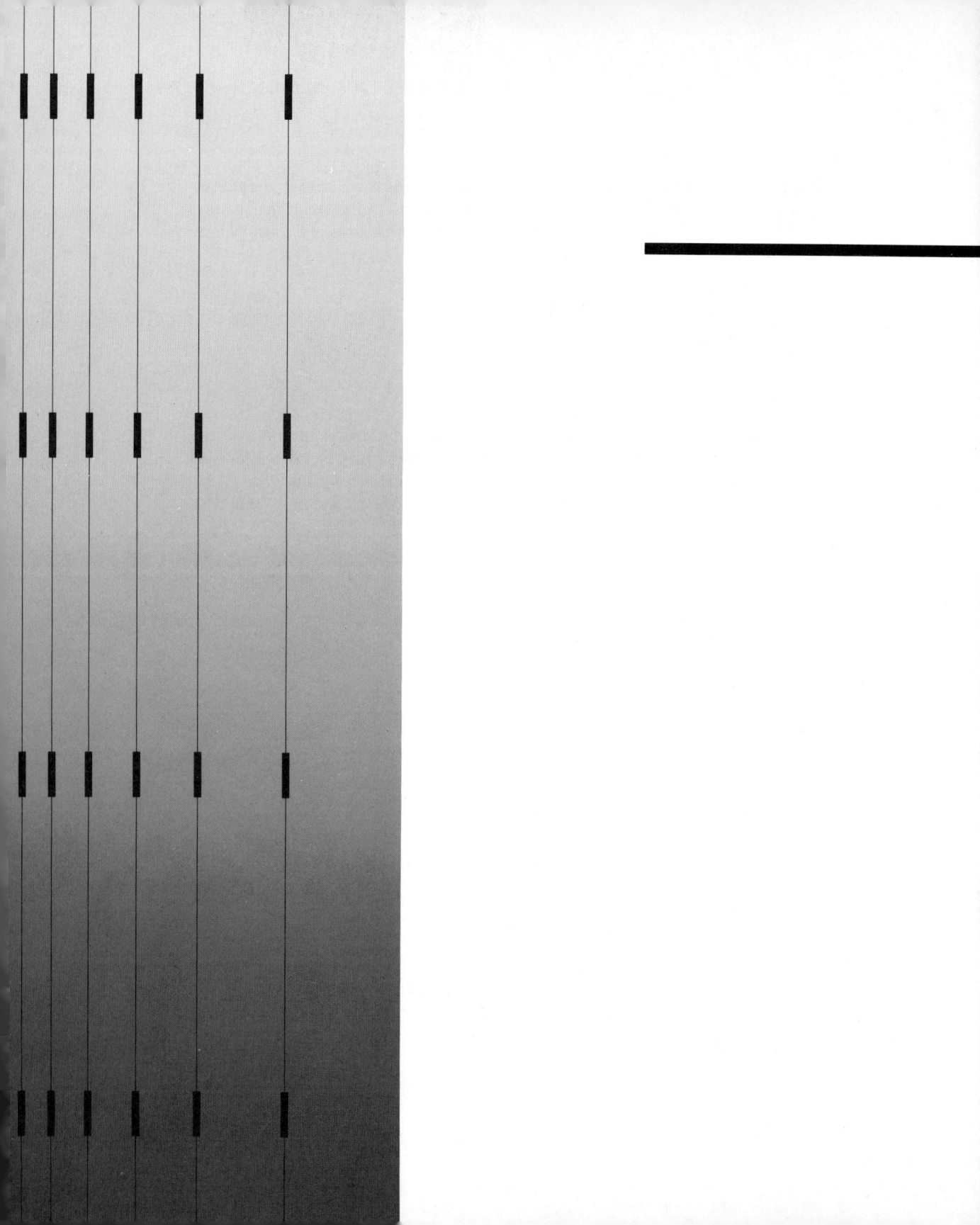

APPENDIX D

dBASE IV Functions

Date Functions. 801
String Functions. 802
Memo Field Functions. 803
Numeric Functions. 803
Financial Functions. 803
Trigonometric Functions. 804
Data Type Conversion Functions. 805
Keystroke Functions. 805
Memo Functions. 805
Identification and Testing Functions. 806
Lookup Functions. 808
Network Functions. 808

dBASE IV FUNCTIONS

This appendix categorizes and summarizes all dBASE IV functions. Functions can be used in any dBASE IV expression and with any command. Each function must use the appropriate syntax and operate on the appropriate data type.

For this and other important information about a function, you can refer to Ashton-Tate's *dBASE IV Language Reference*, which came with your dBASE IV package, or a book such as this author's *dBASE IV Programmer's Reference Guide* (SYBEX, 1990). For a quick reference, you can use the help system: Press **F1** to access the help screen and then select CONTENTS to get to the table of contents. Press **F3**, as necessary, to get to the most general level of contents and select Dot Prompt Commands and Functions from the screen. You can then type the first letters of the function you need help with or use the arrow keys to highlight the function name. Press ⏎ to view the help screen.

DATE FUNCTIONS

The date functions operate upon the Date data type and return Numeric, Date, or Character results.

CDOW( )	Returns the day for the week as a character string (for example, Monday)
CMONTH( )	Returns the month as a character string (for example, April)
DATE( )	Returns the current system date
DAY( )	Returns the day of the month as a number
DMY( )	Returns a date converted to date, month, year format (for example, 31 December 89)
DOW( )	Returns the day of the week as a number.
DTOS( )	Converts a date to a character string in the format "19891231"
MDY( )	Returns a date converted to month, date, year format (for example, December 31, 89)
MONTH( )	Returns the month as a number (1 to 12)

TIME( )	Returns the current system time
YEAR( )	Returns the year of a date

STRING FUNCTIONS

The string functions allow you to manipulate data stored as the Character data type. The term *string* refers to any Character data. For example, "XYZ" is a string of 3 characters, and "Hello there" is a string of 11 characters (spaces always count as characters).

Many functions manipulate *substrings*. A substring is any string embedded in a larger string. For example, the letters "ABC" are a substring of the sentence "Now I know my ABC's..." because ABC appears in the larger sentence.

&	indicates macro substitution
ASC( )	Returns the numeric ASCII code for a character
AT( )	Returns the position of a substring within a string
CHR( )	Returns the ASCII character for a number
DIFFERENCE( )	Returns the difference between two soundex codes
LEFT( )	Returns a substring of the leftmost characters
LEN( )	Returns the length (number of characters) of a string
LOWER( )	Returns the lowercase equivalent of a string
LTRIM( )	Trims leading blanks
REPLICATE( )	Repeats a string
RIGHT( )	Returns a substring of the rightmost characters
RTRIM( )	Removes trailing blanks
SOUNDEX( )	Returns the soundex code of a string
SPACE( )	Generates blank spaces
STUFF( )	Replaces or inserts a substring in a string
SUBSTR( )	Returns a substring from a larger string
TAG( )	Returns the tag name of an index
TRANSFORM( )	Displays data in a predefined format
TRIM( )	Removes leading and trailing blanks
UPPER( )	Returns the uppercase equivalent of a string

Memo Field Functions

The Memo field functions return information about Memo fields.

MEMLINES( )	Returns the number of lines required to print a Memo field
MLINE( )	Returns the current line of Memo field

Numeric Functions

The numeric functions return the results of calculations on Numeric and Float data types.

ABS( )	Returns the absolute (positive) value
CEILING( )	Returns the smallest integer that is greater than or equal to the specified number
EXP( )	Returns the exponential (value of e^x)
FLOOR( )	Returns the largest integer that is less than or equal to the specified number
INT( )	Returns the integer value with any decimal value truncated
LOG( )	Returns the natural logarithm
LOG10( )	Returns the common log to the base 10
MAX( )	Returns the larger of two numbers
MIN( )	Returns the smaller of two numbers
MOD( )	Returns the modulus (remainder) of dividing two numbers
PI( )	Returns π (approximately 3.14159265)
RAND( )	Returns a random number between 0 and 1
ROUND( )	Rounds a number to the specified decimal place
SIGN( )	Returns 1 for a positive number, −1 for a negative number, and 0 for zero
SQRT( )	Returns the square root of the specified number

Financial Functions

The financial functions perform common financial calculations. When using the financial functions PAYMENT( ), FV( ), and PV( ), you must make sure that all parameters refer to the same time period. For example, if you want to determine the *monthly* payment on a loan given the *annual* percentage rate and a term expressed in *years*, then you must divide the annual interest rate by 12 to obtain the monthly rate and multiply the term of the loan by 12 to determine the number of months.

For example, suppose you want to calculate the *monthly* payment on a loan given an *annual* interest rate of 6.75 percent and a term of 30 *years*. First you need to convert the percentage rate, 6.75 percent, to the decimal value 0.0675 by dividing by 100. Then you need to divide the resulting annual decimal rate by 12 to obtain the monthly percentage rate. Finally, you need to convert the *years* for the loan to months by multiplying by 12.

You can perform all of the appropriate conversions directly in the expression used to calculate the payment. If the loan principal is stored in a field (or variable) named PRINCIPAL, the annual interest is stored in a field (or variable) named APR, and the term is stored in a field (or variable) named YEARS, then the expression to calculate the monthly payment is **PAYMENT(Principal,APR/1200,YEARS*12)**.

FV( )	Returns the future value of equal, regular deposits into an investment
NPV( )	Returns the net present value of a series of future cash flows (used only with the CALCULATE command)
PAYMENT( )	Returns the periodic payment on a loan.
PV( )	Returns the present value of equal, regular deposits into an investment

TRIGONOMETRIC FUNCTIONS

The trigonometric functions assume that their arguments are expressed in radians. You can use the DTOR( ) function to convert degrees to radians. For example, **COS(DTOR(45))** returns the cosine, in radians, of a 45-degree angle. The RTOD( ) function converts radians to degrees. The expression **RTOD-(COS(DTOR(45)))** returns the cosine, in degrees, of a 45-degree angle.

ACOS( )	Returns the arcsine, in radians, of a cosine expressed in radians
ASIN( )	Returns the arcsine, in radians, of a sine expressed in radians
ATAN( )	Returns the arctangent, in radians, of any tangent

ATN2( )	Returns the two-quadrant arctangent of a sine
COS( )	Returns the cosine, expressed in radians, of an angle expressed in radians
DTOR( )	Converts degrees to radians
RTOD( )	Converts radians to degrees
SIN( )	Returns the sine, in radians, of an angle expressed in radians

DATA TYPE CONVERSION FUNCTIONS

The functions described in this section all convert values from one data type to another.

CTOD( )	Converts Character data to Date data
DTOC( )	Converts Date data to Character data in MM/DD/YY format
FIXED( )	Converts Float data to Numeric data
FLOAT( )	Converts Numeric data to Float data
STR( )	Converts Character data to Numeric data
VAL( )	Converts Character data to Numeric data

KEYSTROKE FUNCTIONS

The keystroke functions return information regarding the most recent keystroke.

INKEY( )	Returns the numeric code of a keystroke without interrupting program execution
LASTKEY( )	Returns the ASCII numeric value of the most recent keystroke
READKEY( )	Returns the ASCII code used to exit a full-screen editing session

MENU FUNCTIONS

The menu functions return information about horizontal bar, pop-up, and pull-down menus used in applications.

BAR( )	Returns the number of the last-selected option from a pop-up or pull-down menu
MENU( )	Returns the name of the currently active menu

PAD( )	Returns the name of the currently selected horizontal bar menu option
POPUP( )	Returns the name of the currently active pop-up menu
PROMPT( )	Returns the prompt of the most recently selected menu option

IDENTIFICATION AND TESTING FUNCTIONS

The identification and testing functions return information about the current environment.

ALIAS( )	Returns the alias assigned to a work area
BOF( )	Returns .T. when the record pointer is at the beginning of a database file
COL( )	Returns the current column position of the cursor on the screen
COMPLETED( )	Returns .T. if a transaction has been completed
DBF( )	Returns the name of the database file currently in use
DELETED( )	Returns .T. if the current record is marked for deletion
DISKSPACE( )	Returns the amount of available disk space
EOF( )	Returns .T. when the record pointer is past the last record in a database file
ERROR( )	Returns the number generated by an ON ERROR command
FIELD( )	Returns the name of a field in a database file
FILE( )	Returns .T. if the specified file exists
FKLABEL( )	Returns the name of a function key
FKMAX( )	Returns the number of function keys on the keyboard
FOUND( )	Returns .T. if the record being searched for is found
GETENV( )	Returns information about the operating system environment

IDENTIFICATION AND TESTING FUNCTIONS

IIF( )	Immediate IF, embedded inside command lines or report columns; selects one of two alternatives
ISALPHA( )	Returns .T. if the first character is a letter
ISCOLOR( )	Returns .T. if a color monitor is in use
ISLOWER( )	Returns .T. if the first character is a lowercase letter
ISMARKED( )	Returns .T. if a database is in a state of change
ISUPPER( )	Returns .T. if the first character is an uppercase letter
KEY( )	Returns the index expression associated with an index file or tag
LIKE( )	Compares a value to a wildcard string and returns .T. if they match
LINENO( )	Returns the line number of the next command to be executed in a command file
LUPDATE( )	Returns the date of the most recent change to a database file
MDX( )	Returns the name of the currently open production index file
MEMORY( )	Returns the amount of available RAM, in kilobytes
MESSAGE( )	Returns the error message that triggered an ON ERROR condition
NDX( )	Returns the name of the active index (.NDX) file
ORDER( )	Returns the name of the index currently controlling the sort order
OS( )	Returns the name of the operating system in use
PCOL( )	Returns the current printer column position
PRINTSTATUS( )	Returns .T. if the printer is ready to accept data
PROW( )	Returns the current printer row position
RECCOUNT( )	Returns the number of records in a database file
RECNO( )	Returns the number (position) of the current record
RECSIZE( )	Returns the size of each record in database file
ROLLBACK( )	Returns .T. if the most recent transaction rollback was successful
ROW( )	Returns the current cursor position on the screen

SELECT( )	Returns the number of the highest unused work area (between 1 and 0)
SET( )	Returns the current status of a SET command
TYPE( )	Returns the data type of the current field or variable
VARREAD( )	Returns the name of the highlighted field or memory variable being edited
VERSION( )	Returns the version number of the dBASE program in use

LOOKUP FUNCTIONS

The following functions search an index or database file for data.

SEEK( )	Searches an index for a value and returns .T. if the value is located
LOOKUP( )	Searches any field for a value and returns .T. if the value is located

NETWORK FUNCTIONS

The network functions can be used when developing applications that run on a network. (Note that the Applications Generator always develops applications that are ready for use on either a single-user system or a network.)

ACCESS( )	Returns the level of access for the last logged-in user
CHANGE( )	Returns .T. if a value has been changed by a network user
FLOCK( )	Locks a database file
LKSYS( )	Returns the time, date, and user name for a locked file
LOCK( )	Locks a database record
NETWORK( )	Returns .T. if dBASE is currently installed on a network
RLOCK( )	Same as LOCK( )
USER( )	Returns the log-in name of a network user

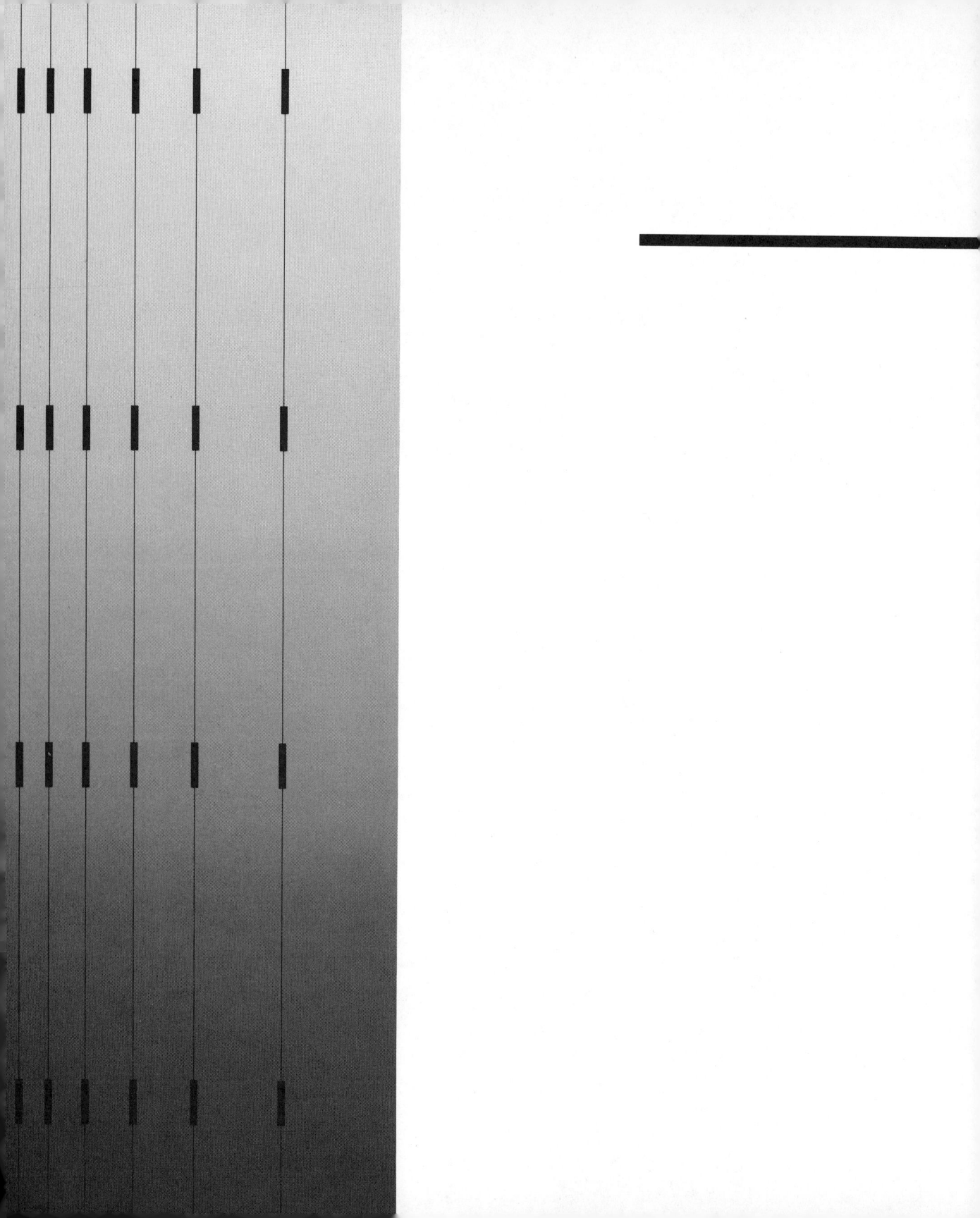

APPENDIX E

dBASE IV Commands

Commands to Create and Use Database Files. 813
Commands to Enter and Edit Database Data. 814
Commands to Sort and Index. 815
Commands to Locate a Record. 815
Commands to Display Data. 816
Commands to Calculate Data. 816
Commands to Copy and Move Data. 817
Commands to Manage Memo Fields. 817
Commands to Create New Objects. 817
Commands to Modify Existing Objects. 818
Commands to Manage Disk Files. 818
Commands to Manage Keystroke Macros. .819
Commands to Import or Export Data. 819
Commands to Get Assistance. 819
Commands to Create and Control Command Files. 820
Commands for Procedures and User-Defined Functions. 821
Commands to Add Comments to Command Files. 822
Commands to Manage Memory Variables and Arrays. 822
Commands for Interfacing with Users. 823
Commands to Control the Screen and Windows. 823
Commands to Manage Menus. 824
Commands to Control the Printer. 825
Commands to Interface with External Programs. 825
Commands to Aid Debugging. 825
Commands to Control the dBASE Environment. 826
Commands for Networking. 830

dBASE IV Commands

This appendix categorizes and summarizes all dBASE IV commands. Remember that you need be concerned with these commands only if you want to go beyond the capabilities of the Control Center and Applications Generator to develop highly sophisticated custom programs and applications, or if you want to work from the dot prompt.

You can use any of the commands in a dBASE IV command file or as Applications Generator embedded code. You can also enter most commands directly at the dot prompt (exceptions are programming clause commands such as DO WHILE...ENDDO, DO CASE...ENDCASE, IF...ENDIF, SCAN...ENDSCAN, and TEXT...ENDTEXT).

Each command must be entered on a single line and must use proper syntax. For the exact syntax of a command, refer to the dBASE IV language reference manual that came with your dBASE IV package or type the command **HELP** followed by the command at the dot prompt. For example, to get help regarding the BROWSE command, you type **HELP BROWSE** at the dot prompt and press ←┘.

Chapter 18 provides additional information about entering commands, creating command files, and interpreting syntax charts. However, an in-depth discussion of all programming commands and techniques is beyond the scope of this book, and therefore you should refer to a more advanced book such as the forthcoming *dBASE IV Programmer's Reference Guide*, by this author and also published by SYBEX.

Commands to Create and Use Database Files

CLOSE DATABASES	Closes all open database files, saving their contents to disk.
SELECT	Specifies a work area, from A to J or 1 to 10, in which to open a database file. Also used to switch among currently open database files.
SET RELATION	Defines the relationship between two or more open database files based on a common field, which must be indexed in the nonselected database file.
USE	Opens a database file for use.

COMMANDS TO ENTER AND EDIT DATABASE DATA

APPEND	Adds new records to the bottom of the current database through the edit or browse screen. If a custom form has been activated through the SET FORMAT command, that form is used instead of the edit screen.
APPEND BLANK	Adds a new blank record to the end of a database file.
APPEND FROM	Copies records from a separate or foreign database file or an array to the currently open database file.
BEGIN TRANSACTION	Records changes to a database file, permitting ROLLBACK to undo those changes.
BROWSE	Calls up the browse screen for entering or editing database data.
CHANGE	Same as EDIT.
DELETE	Marks records for deletion.
EDIT	Allows data in the currently open database to be edited, using either the default edit screen or a custom form opened with the SET FORMAT command.
END TRANSACTION	Marks the end of a BEGIN TRANSACTION block and commits any changes to the database.
INSERT	Inserts new data into a database at a specified record position.
PACK	Permanently removes from a database records that have been marked for deletion with the DELETE, CHANGE, EDIT, or BROWSE command.
RECALL	Reclaims records that have been marked for deletion.
REPLACE	Replaces the data in a database field with a new value.

	ROLLBACK	Undoes all changes to a database file since the last BEGIN TRANSACTION command.
	ZAP	Erases all records from a database file, but leaves the structure intact.

COMMANDS TO SORT AND INDEX

	COPY TAG	Converts production indexes to individual index (.NDX) files.
	DELETE TAG	Removes an index from a production (.MDX) index file.
	INDEX	Creates an index if TAG is specified. If TO is specified, creates an index file with the .NDX extension.
	REINDEX	Rebuilds all indexes in the current production index file.
	SET ORDER	Selects an index from the production index file to determine the sort order and the field that can be used for SEEK and FIND searches.
	SORT	Creates a new, sorted database file from the currently open database file.
	USE...ORDER	Through the ORDER option, specifies a controlling index for the database being opened.

COMMANDS TO LOCATE A RECORD

	CONTINUE	Used in conjunction with the LOCATE command to find the next record matching the search criteria.
	FIND	Locates a value in an index (.NDX) file.
	GO or GO TO	Moves the record pointer to a specific record according to its position or record number (that is, TOP or BOTTOM or a specified record number).
	LOCATE	Positions the record pointer at the first record in the database that matches the search criteria.
	SEEK	Locates a value in the current index (the one that controls the sort order).
	SKIP	Moves the record pointer forward or backward relative to its current position.

COMMANDS TO DISPLAY DATA

@...SAY	Specifies a row and column position on the screen or printer and displays data.
@...TO	Draws a line or box.
?	Prints information starting on a new line. When used alone, prints a blank line.
??	Prints information at the current cursor or printer position.
???	Sends special characters to the printer without changing the printing position.
DISPLAY	Displays the contents of a database record or of several records.
LABEL FORM	Prints mailing labels in the format specified by the CREATE LABEL command.
LIST	Displays database records.
REPORT FORM	Prints a report with the format specified by the CREATE REPORT command.

COMMANDS TO CALCULATE DATA

AVERAGE	Calculates and displays the average of a numeric field in a database.
CALCULATE	Calculates the sum, average, count, highest value, lowest value, net present value, standard deviation, or variance, using numeric fields.
COUNT	Counts the number of records in a database that meet some criterion.
REPLACE	Replaces the contents of specified database records with a new value.
SUM	Calculates and displays the sum of a numeric field in a database.
TOTAL	Creates a summary of an existing file containing totals of specified numeric fields.
UPDATE	Changes the values of fields in one database based upon the fields in a separate, related database.

Commands to Copy and Move Database Data

APPEND FROM	Adds records from a separate or foreign database file to the end of the currently open database file.
COPY	Copies the currently open database to another database or to a foreign file format.
COPY STRUCTURE	Copies a database structure to a new database file.
JOIN	Combines the fields from two related databases into a new database.

Commands to Manage Memo Fields

APPEND MEMO	Copies external data to a Memo field.
COPY MEMO	Copies a Memo field to another file.
SET WINDOW OF MEMO	Uses a defined window for editing a Memo field during browse and edit operations.

Commands to Create New Objects

CREATE	Calls up the database design screen to create a new database file.
CREATE APPLICATION	Calls up the Applications Generator to create a new application.
CREATE LABEL	Calls up the labels design screen to create a new label format for the currently open database.
CREATE QUERY	Calls up the query design screen to create a new query for the currently open database.
CREATE REPORT	Calls up the reports design screen to create a new report format for the currently open database.
CREATE SCREEN	Calls up the forms design screen to create a new custom form for the currently open database.

	CREATE VIEW	For compatibilty purposes, creates a dBASE III PLUS view file from the currently selected database files and relationships.
	MODIFY COMMAND	Creates or modifies a command file (or program) with the file extension .PRG.

COMMANDS TO MODIFY EXISTING OBJECTS

	MODIFY APPLICATION	Calls up the Applications Generator to modify an existing application.
	MODIFY COMMAND	Calls up the editor to create or modify a command file or procedure file.
	MODIFY LABEL	Calls up the labels design screen to modify a label format.
	MODIFY QUERY	Calls up the query design screen to modify an existing query.
	MODIFY REPORT	Calls up the reports design screen to modify an existing report format.
	MODIFY SCREEN	Calls up the forms design screen to modify an existing custom form.
	MODIFY STRUCTURE	Calls up the database design screen to modify the current database file.

COMMANDS TO MANAGE DISK FILES

	COPY FILE	Copies any file to another file name, drive, or directory.
	DELETE FILE	Erases a disk file.
	ERASE	Erases a file from the directory (same as DELETE FILE).
	RENAME	Changes the name of any file.
	SET ALTERNATE	Activates the screen-capture file defined by the SET ALTERNATE TO command.
	SET ALTERNATE TO	Creates a file to capture all screen activity.

COMMANDS TO MANAGE KEYSTROKE MACROS

PLAY MACRO	Executes a keystroke macro.
RESTORE MACROS	Copies recorded keystroke macros from a disk file into memory.
SAVE MACROS	Saves recorded keystroke macros to a disk file.

COMMANDS TO IMPORT OR EXPORT DATA

APPEND FROM	Appends data from foreign software to the currently open database file.
COPY	Copies data from the currently open database file to a foreign file format.
COPY INDEXES	Copies dBASE III PLUS .NDX index files to dBASE IV production (.MDX) index files.
EXPORT	Exports dBASE data to a new foreign file.
IMPORT	Imports data from a foreign file format to a new dBASE IV database file.

COMMANDS TO GET ASSISTANCE

ASSIST	Switches from the interactive dot-prompt mode to the Control Center.
DIR	Displays the names of files in a directory.
DISPLAY STATUS	Displays information about the database files currently in use and other dBASE environmental parameters.
DISPLAY STRUCTURE	Displays the structure of the currently open database file.
HELP	Provides on-line assistance for specific dBASE commands as well as other information.
TYPE	Displays the contents of an ASCII text file.

Commands to Create and Control Command Files

CANCEL	Terminates command-file processing and returns control to the dot prompt.
CASE	Begins an option within a DO CASE clause (must be placed between DO CASE and ENDCASE commands).
COMPILE	Converts a command (.PRG) file to an executable object-code (.DBO) file.
DO	Executes a command file or procedure.
DO CASE	Begins a block of several mutually exclusive routines (must be terminated with an ENDCASE command).
DO WHILE	Begins a loop in a command file (must be terminated with an ENDDO command).
ELSE	Used within an IF clause as the alternate path when the IF expression is false (must be enclosed between IF and ENDIF commands).
ENDCASE	Marks the end of a DO CASE clause.
ENDDO	Marks the end of a DO WHILE loop.
ENDIF	Marks the end of an IF clause.
ENDSCAN	Marks the end of a SCAN...ENDSCAN loop.
ENDTEXT	Marks the end of a TEXT block.
EXIT	Passes control outside of a loop.
IF	Makes a decision based on a single expression (must be terminated with an ENDIF command).
LOOP	Passes control to the beginning of a DO WHILE loop.
OTHERWISE	Used as an alternative path in a DO CASE clause when no CASE statement evaluates to true (must be enclosed between DO CASE and ENDCASE commands).

ON ERROR	Executes a specified command when an error occurs.
ON ESCAPE	Executes a specified command when the **Esc** key is pressed (the SET ESCAPE parameter must be on).
ON KEY	Executes a specified command when the user presses any key.
QUIT	Terminates command file processing, closes all open files, and leaves dBASE IV.
RETURN TO MASTER	Returns control to the first calling program in a series of DO commands.
SCAN	Marks the beginning of a loop to process database records.
TEXT	Begins a block of text in the command file to be displayed on the screen or printer.

COMMANDS FOR PROCEDURES AND USER-DEFINED FUNCTIONS

CLOSE PROCEDURE	Closes a procedure file.
DO...WITH	Calls a command file or procedure and passes parameters to it.
FUNCTION	Marks the beginning and defines the name of a user-defined function.
PARAMETERS	Specifies internal names for values passed to a procedure, user-defined function, or command file.
PROCEDURE	Marks the beginning of and assigns a name to a procedure.
RETURN	Marks the end of a procedure or user-defined function, passes control back to a calling command file or procedure, and resumes processing at the next line.
SET PROCEDURE TO	Opens a procedure file.

COMMANDS TO ADD COMMENTS TO COMMAND FILES

*	Specifies a programmer comment when used as the first character in a line.
&&	Specifies a programmer comment to the right of a command line in a program.
NOTE	Marks a programmer comment in a command file (same as *).

COMMANDS TO MANAGE MEMORY VARIABLES AND ARRAYS

APPEND FROM ARRAY	Copies data from an array to a database file.
DECLARE	Defines the name and dimensions of an array.
CLEAR ALL	Closes all open database files and removes all windows, menus, and memory variables from memory.
CLEAR MEMORY	Erases all current memory variables.
DISPLAY MEMORY	Displays the names, data types, and contents of all currently active memory variables and arrays.
PRIVATE	Specifies that a memory variable is local to a given command file or procedure.
PUBLIC	Makes a memory variable global to all levels of command files and procedures.
RELEASE	Erases memory variables.
RESTORE	Brings memory variables that have been stored on disk in a .MEM file back into memory.
SAVE	Saves memory variables and arrays in a memory (.MEM) file on disk.
STORE	Creates a memory variable and assigns a value to it.

COMMANDS FOR INTERFACING WITH USERS

@...SAY...GET	Displays a message and the current contents of a field or memory variable for editing.
ACCEPT	Stores user input in a Character memory variable.
INPUT	Waits for user entry and stores input in a Numeric memory variable.
READ	Allows data to be entered via the @...SAY...GET command.
WAIT	Waits for the user to press a single key and optionally stores that keystroke in a Character memory variable.

COMMANDS TO CONTROL THE SCREEN AND WINDOWS

@...COLOR	Colors an isolated portion of the screen.
ACTIVATE SCREEN	Sends all output to the entire screen, covering, but not removing, active windows.
ACTIVATE WINDOW	Activates and displays an existing window.
CLEAR	Clears any windows, menus, custom forms, or pending GET commands on the screen.
DEFINE BOX	Defines the border and location of a box.
DEACTIVATE WINDOW	Removes a window from the screen, but leaves its definition intact for future use.
DEFINE WINDOW	Defines the name, border type, and screen position of a window.
MOVE WINDOW	Moves a window to a new screen location.
READ	Allows data to be entered through a custom form if one has been activated by SET FORMAT.
RELEASE WINDOW	Removes a defined window from memory.

SAVE WINDOW	Saves a window definition to a disk file.
SET COLOR	Determines colors used in screen displays.
SET FORMAT TO	Determines the format file to be used with APPEND, EDIT, and READ commands.
SET WINDOW OF MEMO	Uses a defined window for editing a Memo field during browse and edit operations.

Commands to Manage Menus

ACTIVATE MENU	Activates an existing horizontal bar menu.
ACTIVATE POPUP	Activates an existing pop-up menu.
DEACTIVATE MENU	Deactivates a bar menu and erases it from the screen.
DEACTIVATE POPUP	Deactivates a pop-up menu and removes it from the screen.
DEFINE BAR	Defines an option in a pop-up menu.
DEFINE MENU	Defines a horizontal bar menu.
DEFINE PAD	Defines an option in a horizontal bar menu.
DEFINE POPUP	Defines a pop-up menu.
ON SELECTION	Assigns an action to a horizontal bar menu option (PAD) or pop-up menu option (POPUP), to be executed when the option is selected.
RELEASE MENUS	Removes defined horizontal bar menus from memory.
RELEASE POPUP	Removes defined pop-up menus from memory.
SHOW MENU	Displays a horizontal bar menu without activating it.
SHOW POPUP	Displays a pop-up menu without activating it.

Commands to Control the Printer

EJECT	Ejects the page in the printer.
EJECT PAGE	Similar to the EJECT command, but can be sent to any device, such as a disk file or the screen.
ENDPRINTJOB	Marks the end of a print operation.
PRINTJOB	Marks the beginning of a print operation.
SET PRINTER	Sets printing on or off for commands that display data.
SET DEVICE	When DEVICE is set to PRINT, @...SAY, output is directed to the printer rather than to the screen.

Commands to Interface with External Programs

CALL	Runs an assembly language (binary) subroutine that has already been loaded into memory.
LOAD	Copies an assembly language subroutine into memory.
RELEASE MODULE	Removes a loaded assembly language subroutine from memory.
RUN	Runs an external DOS program and automatically returns control to the dot prompt.
!	Same as RUN.

Commands to Aid Debugging

DEBUG	Activates the dBASE IV debugger.
DISPLAY HISTORY	Displays commands stored in the history file (the SET DOHISTORY parameter must be on to record command-file lines).
LIST HISTORY	Same as DISPLAY HISTORY, but does not pause after each screenful of information.
RESUME	Resumes command-file processing after temporary suspension.
SET DEBUG	Sends the results of the SET ECHO command to the printer rather than the screen.

SET ECHO	Displays command lines from command files on the screen before executing them.
SET HISTORY	Specifies the number of lines to be recorded in the history file.
SET STEP	Pauses execution after every line in a command file.
SET TRAP	If on, tells dBASE to activate the debugger as soon as an error occurs in a command file.
SUSPEND	Temporarily suspends processing of a command file and returns control to the dot prompt.

Commands to Control the dBASE Environment

SET	Displays a menu for interactively changing dBASE environment settings.
SET AUTOSAVE	Determines whether database changes are saved immediately.
SET BELL	Determines whether the bell sounds during data entry and editing.
SET BELL TO	Determines the pitch and duration of the bell tone.
SET BLOCKSIZE TO	Defines the block size for storing memory variables.
SET BORDER	Defines the border for menus and windows.
SET CARRY	Determines whether data from the previous record is carried over to the next record during data entry.
SET CATALOG	Determines whether new files are added to an active catalog.
SET CATALOG TO	Creates, opens, or closes a catalog file.
SET CENTURY	Determines whether the century appears in dates.
SET CLOCK	Determines whether the clock appears on the screen.

SET CLOCK TO	Determines the position of the clock on the screen.
SET COLOR	Automatically set at startup, depending on whether a monochrome or color monitor is in use.
SET COLOR TO	Determines colors (or shading) for the screen.
SET CONFIRM	Determines whether a carriage return is required after a data entry field is filled in.
SET CONSOLE	Turns the screen on or off.
SET CURRENCY	Determines whether currency symbols are displayed to the left or right of numbers.
SET CURRENCY TO	Defines the currency sign.
SET DATE	Sets a format for displaying dates.
SET DECIMALS TO	Determines the number of decimal places displayed in the results of mathematical calculations.
SET DEFAULT TO	Specifies the disk drive used to store and retrieve files.
SET DELETED	When on, does not display records that are marked for deletion.
SET DELIMITERS	Determines whether delimiters appear around fields in screen displays.
SET DELIMITERS TO	Specifies the characters to use as delimiters around fields in screen displays.
SET DESIGN	Determines whether design screens can be accessed from the dot prompt or Control Center.
SET DEVELOPMENT	Turns automatic compilation and recompilation on or off.
SET DISPLAY	Sets the screen display mode to monochrome, color, EGA, or VGA.
SET DOHISTORY	Retained in dBASE IV for compatibility with dBASE III PLUS, but performs no action (the DEBUG command is used for debugging).

SET ECHO	Determines whether command-file lines are displayed on the screen before execution.
SET ESCAPE	Determines whether pressing the **Esc** key interrupts command-file processing.
SET EXACT	Determines whether exact matches are required in character-string searches.
SET FIELDS	Activates or deactivates the most recent SET FIELDS command.
SET FIELDS TO	Determines which fields from a database or from multiple related databases are displayed and edited.
SET FILTER TO	Hides database records that do not match a specified search criterion.
SET FIXED	Determines whether a fixed number of decimal places is displayed (use in conjunction with SET DECIMALS).
SET FUNCTION TO	Assigns tasks to function keys.
SET HEADING	Determines whether field names appear at the beginning of the output from LIST and DISPLAY commands.
SET HELP	Determines whether the message *Do you want some help?* appears on the screen after an error occurs.
SET HISTORY	Determines whether commands are recorded in the history file.
SET HISTORY TO	Determines the number of lines to be recorded in the history file.
SET HOURS	Determines whether the clock display uses 12-hour or 24-hour format.
SET INDEX TO	Opens index (.NDX) files for the database currently in use.
SET INSTRUCT	Determines whether Control Center prompt boxes appear on the screen.
SET INTENSITY	Determines whether enhanced display with reverse video is used for full-screen operations.

SET MARGIN TO	Adjusts the left margin setting on the printer.
SET MARK	Changes the separator used in dates.
SET MEMOWIDTH TO	Determines the display width of Memo fields.
SET MENU	Retained in dBASE IV to maintain compatibility with dBASE III PLUS, but performs no function (replaced by SET INSTRUCT).
SET MESSAGE TO	Displays a message centered at the bottom of the screen (if SET STATUS is on).
SET ODOMETER TO	Determines the frequency of updating on the odometer displayed with COPY and other commands (when SET TALK is on).
SET ORDER TO	Determines which index in a production index file is used for the sort order and for SEEK searches.
SET PATH TO	Specifies a path of directories to search for files.
SET POINT	Determines the character used as the decimal point in numeric values.
SET PRECISION	Determines the decimal accuracy used in fixed-point arithmetic.
SET PRINTER TO	Directs printing to a specified device or file.
SET SAFETY	Determines whether the overwrite warning appears on the screen.
SET SCOREBOARD	Determines whether dBASE messages appear in the status bar (or in row zero on the screen, if SET STATUS is off).
SET SEPARATOR	Determines the character used to separate thousands in numeric displays.
SET SKIP TO	Determines the order in which multiple related database files are changed during update operations.
SET SPACE	When on, prints a blank space between fields displayed with ? and ?? commands.

SET SQL	When on, dBASE IV accepts SQL commands.
SET STATUS	Determines whether the status bar appears near the bottom of the screen.
SET STEP	Determines whether dBASE pauses before processing each line in a command file.
SET TALK	Determines whether the results of commands and calculations are displayed on the screen.
SET TITLE	Determines whether the SET CATALOG command prompts for file names as new files are added to the catalog.
SET TRAP	When on, the dBASE IV debugger is activated whenever an error occurs during program execution.
SET TYPEAHEAD TO	Specifies the number of keystrokes stored in the typeahead buffer.
SET UNIQUE	Determines whether an index includes only unique records.
SET VIEW TO	Opens multiple database files and sets up their relationships based upon a previous CREATE VIEW or MODIFY VIEW command.

COMMANDS FOR NETWORKING

CONVERT	Adds a field to a database for multiuser lock detection.
DISPLAY USERS	Displays the names of all currently logged dBASE network users.
LIST STATUS	Displays information about the current status of dBASE IV in the network.
LOGOUT	Logs a user off of the network, allowing a new user to log on.
PROTECT	Activates the dBASE IV file security system.
RETRY	Returns to a calling program and executes the same line.

SET ENCRYPTION	Determines whether protected files are encrypted when copied.
SET EXCLUSIVE	Sets a file open attribute to either exclusive or shared mode.
SET LOCK	Determines whether automatic record locking is activated.
SET PRINTER	Selects a printer on the network.
SET REFRESH	Determines the interval for checking multiuser database changes and updating user screens.
SET RETRIES	Sets the number of times dBASE reexecutes a command before quitting.
UNLOCK	Removes record and file locks.

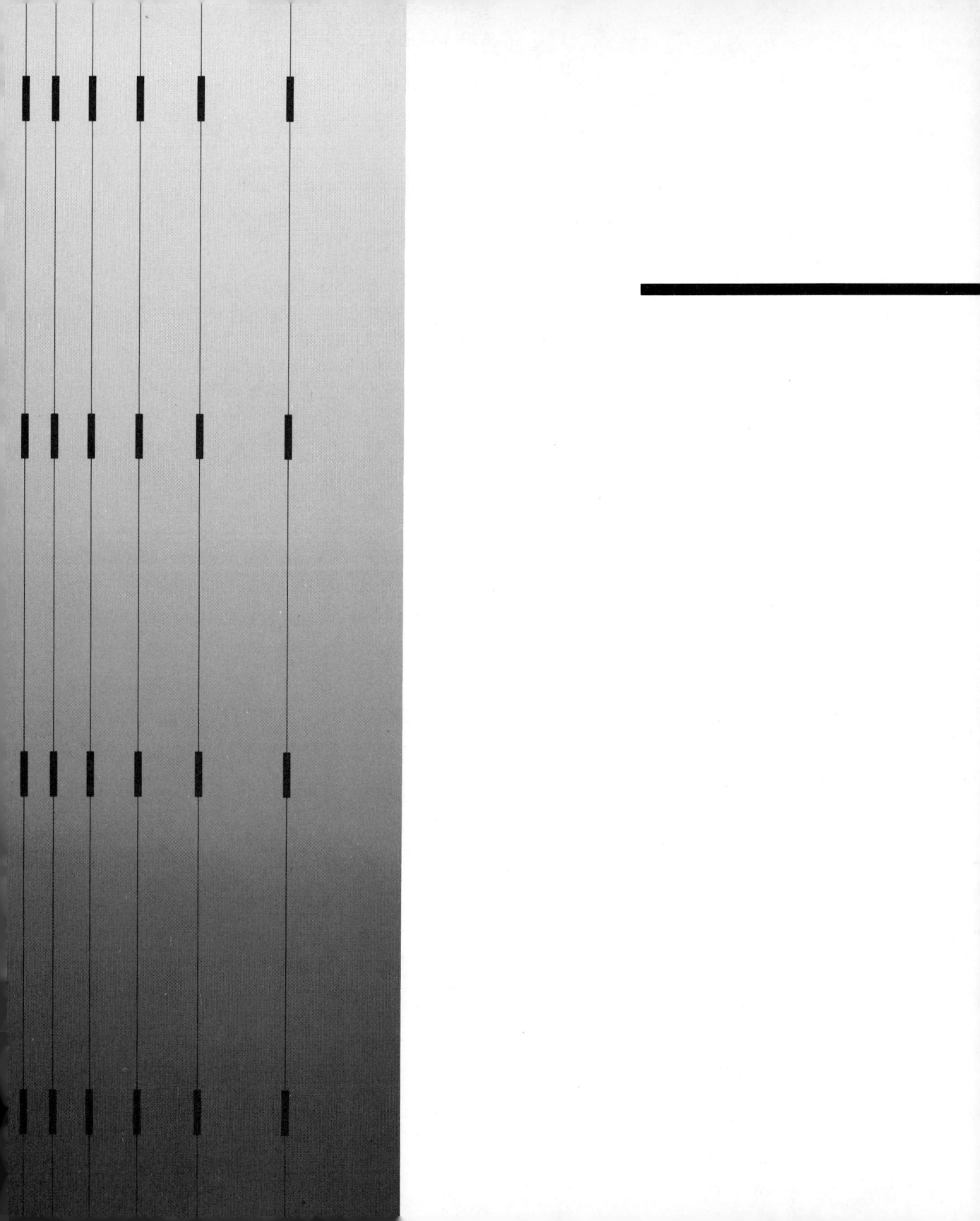

APPENDIX F:

DESIGNING AND DEVELOPING AN APPLICATION

What Is an Application?. 837
Designing an Application. 840
Defining the Goals of the Application. 840
Creating a Directory for the Application. 842
Designing the Database Objects. .843
    Designing the Membership Database. 843
    Creating an Alphabetical Sort Order. 844
    Creating a Custom Form for the Membership System. 845
    Creating the Membership Application Reports. 847
    Creating a Mailing Label Format. 849
Designing the Application Objects. 851
    Designing the Membership Application Menus. 852
Designing the Application Batch Processes. 853
    Operation 1: Flag Expired Memberships. 856
    Operation 2: Browse Expired Memberships. 856
    Operation 3: Update Renewed Memberships. 857
    Operation 4: Reset RENEWED Field to False. 857
Other Design Considerations. 858
Developing the Application. 859
Defining the Application. 959
Using the Application Design Screen. 861
    Developing the Membership Sign-on Banner. 861
    Developing the Membership Horizontal Bar Menu. 862
    Developing the Membership Pull-Down Menus. 863
        Creating the Maintain Pull-Down Menu. 864
        Creating the Update Pull-Down Menu. 865
        Creating the Print Pull-Down Menu. 866

  Creating the Utilities Pull-Down Menu. 867
  Creating the Exit Pull-Down Menu. 868
 Selecting the Current Object. 869
 Putting Away the Membership Application Objects. 870
 Taking a Break. 870
Assigning Actions to Membership Menu Options. 870
 Attaching Menu-Bar Actions. 871
  Assigning an Action to the Maintain Option. 871
  Assigning an Action to the Update Option. 871
 Converting Pop-Up Menus to Pull-Down Menus. 872
 Attaching Items to the Maintain Menu. 873
  Add New Members. 873
  Browse All Members. 873
  Change/Delete a Member. 874
 Assigning Actions to the Update Menu. 875
  Update This Month's Renewals. .875
  Mark Expired Memberships for Deletion. 876
  Purge Marked Records. 877
 Assigning Actions to the Print Menu. 878
  Membership Roster. 878
  All Mailing Labels. 878
  Welcome Letters. 879
  Welcome Labels. 880
  Renewal Letters. 880
  Renewal Labels. 883
  Overdue Letters. 883
  Overdue Labels. 884
 Assigning Actions to the Membership Utilities Menu. 885
  Change System Date. 885
  Back Up Database to Drive A. 885
  Copy Application to Drive A. 886
  Repair Corrupted Indexes. 886

- Assigning Actions to the Exit Menu. 886
  - Return to dBASE IV. 887
  - Exit to DOS. 887
- Building the Batch Process. 887
  - Listing the Operations in the Batch Process. 888
  - Assigning Actions to the Batch Process. 888
    - Flag Expired Memberships. 889
    - Browse Expired Memberships. 889
    - Update Renewed Memberships. 890
    - Reset RENEWED Field to False. 890
- Defining Membership Sort Orders. 892
- Generating the Membership Application. .893
  - Generating Documentation. 893
- Testing the Completed Application. 894
  - Running the Membership Application. 894
  - Adding New Members. 894
  - Changing Member Data. 896
  - Updating the Membership Roster. 896
    - Check the System Date. 897
    - Update This Month's Renewals. 897
    - Delete Expired Memberships. 897
  - Printing the Membership Roster. 898
  - Printing All Mailing Labels. 898
  - Printing Renewal Letters and Labels. 898
  - Printing Overdue Letters and Labels. 899
  - Printing Welcome Letters and Labels. .899
  - Testing the Utilities. 899
  - Exiting the Application. 900
- Modifying the Membership Application. 900
  - Printing the Documentation. 900
  - Returning to the Applications Generator. 901
  - Saving Your Changes. 901

  Refining the Membership Application. 902
    Adding Message-Line Prompts. 902
    Adding Custom Help Screens. 903
  Using the Membership Application. 903
  Tips and Traps. 904
  Summary. 905

Designing and Developing an Application

dBASE IV includes a special feature, called the Applications Generator, that allows you to develop *custom applications*. You can create custom applications to allow inexperienced users to use your databases, forms, reports, and other features that you design, without having to provide in-depth training. Part V of this book presents a complete reference to the Applications Generator, including all of its design screens and menu options.

Developing an application, however, is not simply a matter of using the various design screens in a step-by-step manner. There are literally thousands of steps involved in creating an application. While the chapters in Part V are designed to serve as a reference for anyone who needs quick answers to questions that may arise while working with the Applications Generator, this appendix offers less experienced developers the exercise of designing and developing a complete application.

Developing an application is a creative process, like creating music or art. The composer must understand the basic concepts of music, such as rhythm, beat, and harmony, and must be skilled at playing an instrument before he or she can write and perform a piece of music. Similarly, a dBASE IV applications developer must understand the basic concepts of database management and be fluent in using the Control Center and design screens before he or she can develop an application. Whereas the composer writes and then performs a musical piece, the dBASE IV applications developer *designs* and then *develops* an application.

This appendix focuses on the design phase of creating an application, using an example application that helps an inexperienced user manage a membership database. The latter part of this appendix shows how to use the initial design to actually develop the completed application.

What Is an Application?

An *application* is a customized menu system that simplifies access to a set of related database files, forms, reports, queries, and other database objects. Unlike the Control Center, which simply displays the names of files in a catalog, an application lets you build a menu system that is based on *actions* rather than file names.

For example, suppose you develop several databases, forms, report formats, and so forth to manage a mailing list, and you include them in a single catalog. Figure F.1 shows how the file names might appear in the Control Center. If you, personally, had created all these files, managing the mailing list might be easy because of your knowledge of how to select items from the Control Center, what each file in the panels contains, how to use dBASE menus, and so on.

But suppose you want someone else, perhaps an employee, to use all the files in the catalog to manage the mailing list. If this person (the *user*) has no prior computer experience, you might need to spend considerable time teaching him or her the basics of dBASE IV and the purpose of each item in the Control Center.

An application, on the other hand, would be much easier for the novice to learn. To start with, your application could bypass the Control Center altogether and display a personalized *sign-on banner*, as in Figure F.2.

After pressing ←┘, the novice user would see a custom menu (that you designed) dedicated to managing the mailing list. This custom menu system would replace the dBASE IV menus and provide options specifically geared toward managing the mailing list. Figure F.3 shows a menu for the sample application.

Notice that the application menu clearly defines specific jobs involved in managing the mailing list. From the Maintain pull-down menu, currently displayed on the screen, the user can add new members, browse through the list of

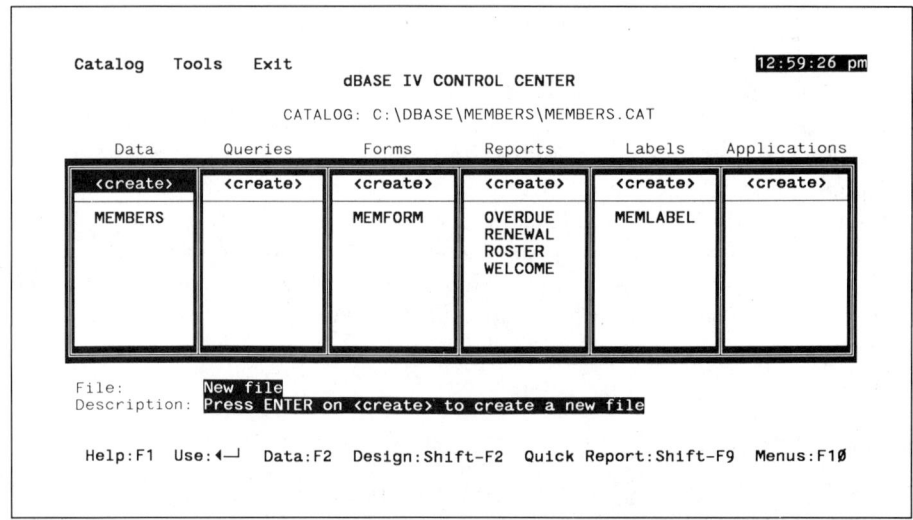

FIGURE F.1: A sample catalog for managing a mailing list. An experienced dBASE IV user could easily manage the mailing list from the Control Center, but a complete novice would probably need some training in using the Control Center.

WHAT IS AN APPLICATION — 839

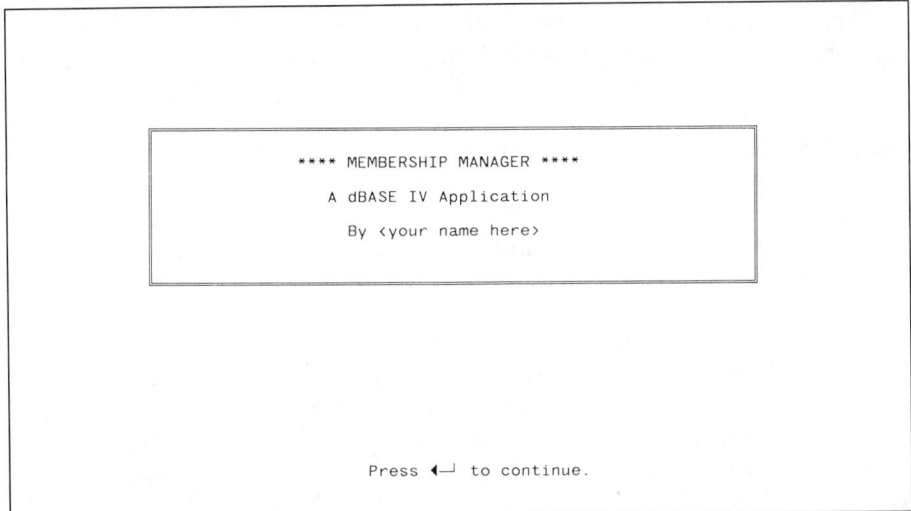

FIGURE F.2: Sign-on banner for a mailing list application. An application can be designed so that the user need never see the dBASE IV Control Center, but instead immediately sees the customized sign-on banner.

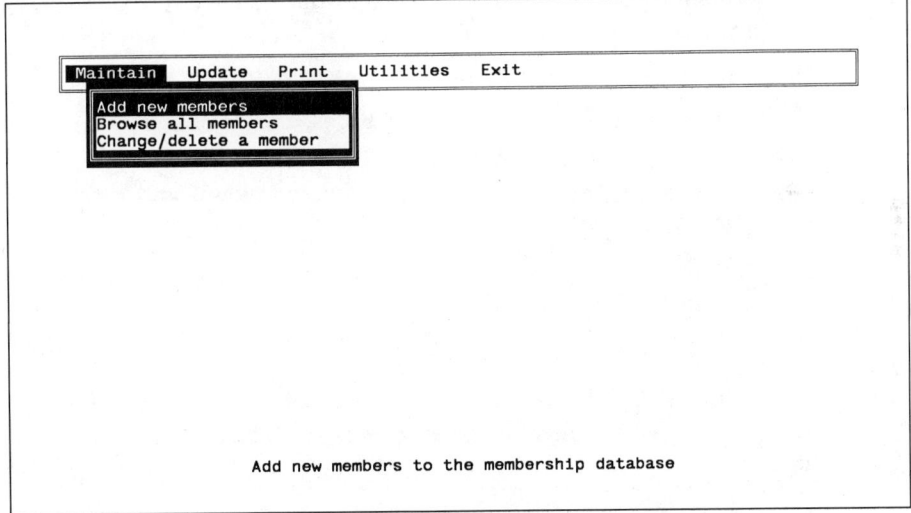

FIGURE F.3: Custom menu for managing the mailing list. To use this application, the user need only know how to use pull-down menus.

members, and change and delete member data. The Update, Print, Utilities, and Exit options on the horizontal menu bar all have pull-down menus associated with them as well.

The user does not need to know anything about the underlying files, forms, reports, or queries, or even that such things exist. All the user needs to know is how to move through the menus and how to select items. The application menus operate like the dBASE IV menus. That is, the user can move the highlight across the menu bar or up and down a pull-down menu to highlight any option. Pressing ← selects the currently highlighted option.

You can also create custom help screens for your application, which the user displays by pressing Help (**F1**), and you can customize the messages that appear at the bottom of the screen as the user scrolls through menu options and makes selections.

When the user is finished using the mailing list management application, he or she can select Exit from the menu bar to return to the DOS prompt without ever seeing the Control Center. In fact, the user need not even know that dBASE IV is involved or that dBASE IV even exists. From the user's perspective, only the mailing list management application exists.

DESIGNING AN APPLICATION

Developing an application can be a big job, so it is best approached with a little planning and design work in advance. You can think of the application design process as several separate steps, as follows:

- Define the goals of the application.
- Design and create the *database objects* (that is, the databases, forms, and reports) of the application, in a separate directory.
- Design the *application objects*, such as menus, windows, and batch processes, for the application.

Designing and creating the database objects requires the use of the design screens and techniques described in Parts I through IV of this book. To develop the application objects, you use the dBASE IV Applications Generator, described in this appendix and in Part V.

The sections that follow describe the basic steps involved in designing an application, using a membership mailing list management system as an example. To better illustrate the exact techniques used in each step of the process, the general steps are broken into small, detailed steps.

DEFINING THE GOALS OF THE APPLICATION

The first step in building an application is simply to jot down some notes about what you want the application to do. If you are automating an existing manual

DEFINING THE GOALS OF THE APPLICATION — 841

system, analyze the manual system and get copies of the forms and reports currently used in the system. Note what information is currently stored in manual files (such as Rolodexes, index cards, forms, and so forth). This information will help you design the databases.

As you make notes, start with a broad description of your goal, such as this:

Develop an application to manage a membership list.

Then break this broad goal into smaller, specific goals and list key features the aplication must have, focusing on the fundamental aspects of database management: database structure, sorting and searching requirements, types of reports needed, and specific types of tasks required. For example, you can refine the description of the membership management application as follows:

- Store members' names and addresses, membership starting and expiration dates, and other useful information.
- At any time during the month,
  —Add, change, and delete members' records.
  —Print a current membership roster, alphabetized by name.
  —Print mailing labels, sorted by zip code, for each active member.
  —Update records when a membership is renewed.
- At any time during the month, perform the following basic housekeeping tasks:
  —Change the system date.
  —Make a backup copy of the database.
  —Copy the entire application to a disk.
  —Repair corrupted indexes.
- Automate printing of the following monthly form letters:
  —Welcome letters and mailing labels for new members.
  —Renewal reminders and labels for memberships that expire next month.
  —Overdue notices and labels for memberships that expired in the previous month.

At this point, you might want to start refining each feature of the application by sketching on paper database and form designs and draft form letters. However, in this appendix we'll design and create simultaneously to save some space and time.

CREATING A DIRECTORY FOR THE APPLICATION

When you develop an application, the Applications Generator creates many files. To prevent these files from cluttering the \DBASE directory, you should develop each application in a unique directory on your hard disk. To create a new directory, you use DOS, rather than dBASE IV. If dBASE is currently in control of your computer, you must exit dBASE and return to the DOS command prompt to create a new directory.

SEQUENCE OF STEPS

From the DOS command prompt:

   type **MD** \ followed by the name of the directory you want to create

To switch to the new directory:

   type **CD** \ followed by the name of the new directory.

USAGE

To create a new directory for an application, you must access the DOS command prompt and use the DOS MKDIR or MD command. The directory name can be up to eight characters long and cannot contain any blank spaces or punctuation. If you want the new directory to be a subdirectory of an existing directory, precede the new directory name with the parent directory name (for example, **MD \DBASE\NEWDIR**).

To make the new directory the current directory, use the DOS CHDIR or CD command. Note that you will be able to run dBASE from this new directory only if the current PATH command includes the dBASE directory. During the installation process, dBASE automatically adds the DBASE directory to the PATH command in your DOS AUTOEXEC.BAT file, so you should be able to run dBASE from the new directory without any problem.

However, if DOS displays the error message *Bad command or file name* when you enter the command **DBASE** to run dBASE IV from the new directory, then you will need to modify your AUTOEXEC.BAT file. See "Running dBASE from Any Directory" in Chapter 19 of this book for details. (Appendix B also discusses DOS commands and directories in more detail.)

EXAMPLE

We will store the sample membership management application discussed in this chapter and the next on a directory named \DBASE\MEMBERS. If you are currently running dBASE IV, select Quit to DOS from the Exit pull-down menu above the Control Center.

At the DOS prompt, type **MD\DBASE\MEMBERS** and press ⏎ to create the new directory. Then type the command **CD \DBASE\MEMBERS** and press ⏎ to switch to the new directory.

If the subdirectory name \DBASE\MEMBERS does not appear next to the DOS command prompt, type the command **PROMPT PG** and press ⏎. This DOS command displays the directory name and helps you keep track of which directory is current when you operate at the DOS level.

Remember that whenever you want to use the membership system in the future, you must switch to the \DBASE\MEMBERS directory. To do so, enter the command **CD\DBASE\MEMBERS** at the DOS prompt before you run dBASE. If dBASE is already running, you can switch to the \DBASE\MEMBERS directory by selecting DOS Utilities from the Tools pull-down menu at the Control Center. From the DOS Utilities DOS menu, select Set Default Drive:Directory and type **C:\DBASE\MEMBERS** as the new default directory.

Designing the Database Objects

Designing the database objects requires the use of the dBASE IV Control Center and design screens, as discussed in Parts I through IV. In fact, you should be able to use all of the design screens before you even attempt to use the Applications Generator, because the Applications Generator itself assumes that you already possess these skills. Therefore, the sections that follow assume that you are already familiar with the Control Center and design screens, and that you are capable of creating database objects on your own. To focus on the design concepts involved, the sections that follow discuss only the essential keystrokes required to access a design screen and save your work.

Designing the Membership Database

One of the first goals of the mailing list management application is to store members' names and addresses and other useful information. Also, we want to be able to display names and addresses in zip code order or in alphabetical order by name. Thus, our first step is to design a database file to store the required data.

In your own work, you will probably want to sketch out the database design on paper first and experiment with various possibilities. In this example, however, we will actually create the database at the same time. We will name this database MEMBERS.DBF. You can create this database structure now by selecting <create> from the Data panel in the Control Center. Type the field information as shown in Figure F.4 (of course, you can't type the description of each field).

```
Num  Field Name  Type       Width  Dec  Index  Description
  1  TITLE       Character     4         N     Mr./Mrs. title
  2  FIRSTNAME   Character    12         N     First name
  3  MI          Character     2         N     Middle initial
  4  LASTNAME    Character    12         N     Last name
  5  COMPANY     Character    25         N     Company
  6  DEPARTMENT  Character    25         N     Department
  7  ADDRESS     Character    32         N     Address
  8  CITY        Character    20         N     City
  9  STATE       Character     2         N     State
 10  ZIP         Character    10         Y     Zip code
 11  PHONE       Character    13         N     Phone number
 12  EXTENSION   Character     4         N     Phone extension
 13  STATUS      Character     8         N     Membership status
 14  STARTDATE   Date          8         N     Starting date
 15  EXPIRES     Date          8         N     Next expiration date
 16  CURRENT     Logical       1         N     Is memberhip current?
 17  RENEWED     Logical       1         N     Renewed this month?
```

FIGURE F.4: Structure of the MEMBERS database, used in the sample membership management application. You can create this database using the usual database design screen available from the Control Center.

Note that only the ZIP field is marked Y for indexing. The name fields aren't marked, because they are used together in an index expression, to create an alphabetical sort. After completing the structure, select Save Changes and Exit from the Exit pull-down menu and assign the file name MEMBERS to the database.

Creating an Alphabetical Sort Order

To create a complex index for alphabetizing names, move the highlight to the MEMBERS database name in the Control Center and press Design (**Shift-F2**). Select the Create New Index option from the Organize pull-down menu to create a complex index with these characteristics:

Name of index	LASTNAME
Index expression	LASTNAME + FIRSTNAME + MI
Order of index	ASCENDING
Display first duplicate key only	NO

After defining the index, press **Ctrl-End**. Then select Save Changes and Exit from the Exit pull-down menu to return to the Control Center.

Creating a Custom Form for the Membership System

A second goal of the membership application is to allow the user to add new members, make changes, and delete members as necessary. A custom form will accomplish this goal.

Once again, rather than sketching out the form on paper, we will just create it. First make sure that the MEMBERS database is open. Then select <create> from the Forms panel. Use the usual editing techniques to arrange the fields as in Figure F.5. (Note that a small portion of the custom form is below the bottom of the screen; you'll see the missing portion in the next figure.)

Some of the fields in the form can be improved by specialized templates or picture functions. These fields are listed in Table F.1 (those not listed use the default template and picture function and do not need to be changed). Remember: To change a template or picture function, move the cursor into the field template and press **F5**.

The STARTDATE, EXPIRES, and CURRENT fields use Edit Options to display default (suggested) values. To assign a default value, move the cursor to the field template, press **F5**, select Edit Options, and then select Default Value. Type the default value and press **Ctrl-End**. The STARTDATE field uses the default value DATE( ) to display the current date. The EXPIRES field uses

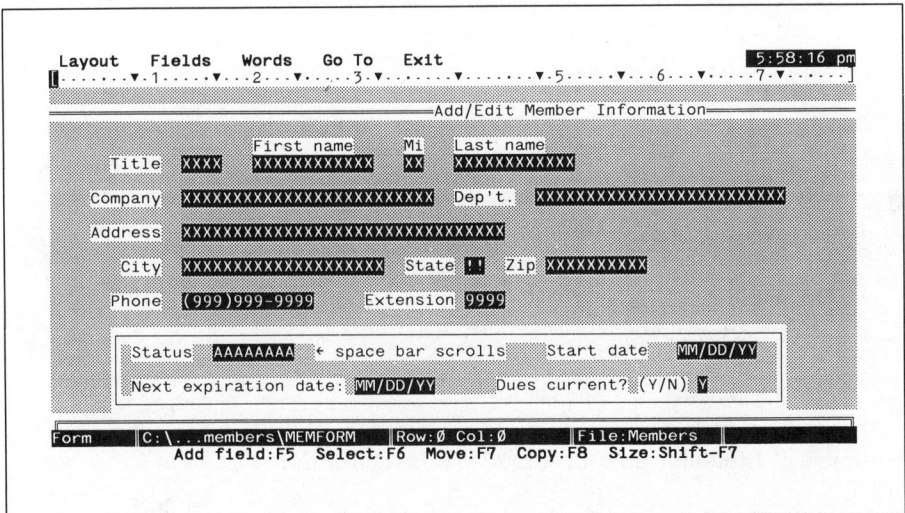

FIGURE F.5: MEMFORM form for the membership application. You can create this form using the usual forms design screen, available from the Control Center. Table F.1 shows templates and picture functions assigned to the various fields on the form.

FIELD	TEMPLATE PICTURE	FUNCTION
STATE	!!	
PHONE	(999)999-9999	
EXTENSION	9999	
STATUS	AAAAAAAA	Multiple choice {M} with options REGULAR, OFFICER
CURRENT	Y	

Table F.1: Templates and Picture Functions Used in the MEMFORM Sample Custom Form Shown in Figure F.6.

the current date plus one year, DATE( ) + 365, as the default value. Because most members pay immediately when they join, the CURRENT field uses a default value of .T. (for true).

Note that the RENEWED field is not included on the form. This field is used in a browse screen to *flag* (identify) members who have renewed their membership. You will see the RENEWED field put to use later.

After you create the form, save it and name it **MEMFORM**. When you get back to the Control Center, highlight MEMFORM in the Forms panel and press Data (**F2**). You should see the form appear on the screen, as in Figure F.6. Note that the default starting date on your screen will match the current date, and the default expiration date will be one year beyond the current date.

To test the form, let's add a sample record. When entering data in the STATUS field, you should be able to switch from REGULAR to OFFICER and back again by pressing the space bar. Enter the following record (enter the start and expiration dates in the example shown here, regardless of the suggested start and expiration dates that appear on your screen):

```
Mr. Andy A. Adams
ABC Technology
Engineering Dep't
13307 Artesia Ave
Los Angeles      CA        90165
(818)555-0101       Extension 123
Status: REGULAR                    Start date: 01/01/89
Next expiration date:01/01/90    Dues current? Y
```

After entering the sample record, select Exit from the Exit pull-down menu to return to the Control Center. Now you can begin developing the reports that the application will use.

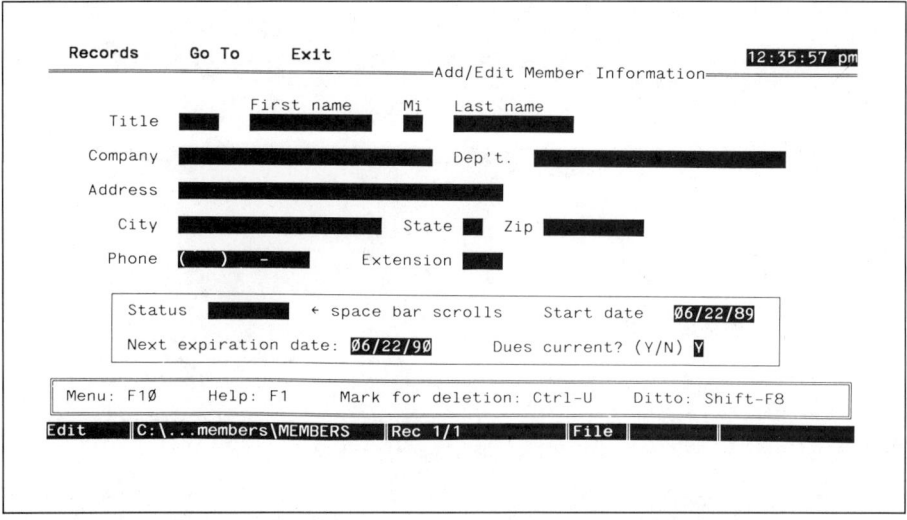

FIGURE F.6: Sample MEMFORM custom form ready to accept data. You should test the form, using it to add at least one sample record to the database, before developing your application, as doing so simplifies testing the completed application later.

Creating the Membership Application Reports

Another goal of the mailing list management application is to allow users to print a membership roster and form letters. Once again, we will create these now, rather than first designing them on paper. Make sure that the MEMBERS database is open. Then select <create> from the Reports panel to access the reports design screen to develop the report formats.

The first report format, named ROSTER, displays a list of all members. Use the usual editing techniques on the reports design screen to format the report to your liking. Figure F.7 shows an example, with the fields arranged as shown here:

```
LASTNAME, TITLE FIRSTNAME MI
   COMPANY DEPARTMENT
   ADDRESS
   CITY, STATE ZIP PHONE EXTENSION
   Status: STATUS Current?: CURRENT
   Start Date: STARTDATE Expiration Date: EXPIRES
```

The Detail band includes a single blank line to separate printed records. Select Save Changes and Exit from the Exit pull-down menu after completing the format.

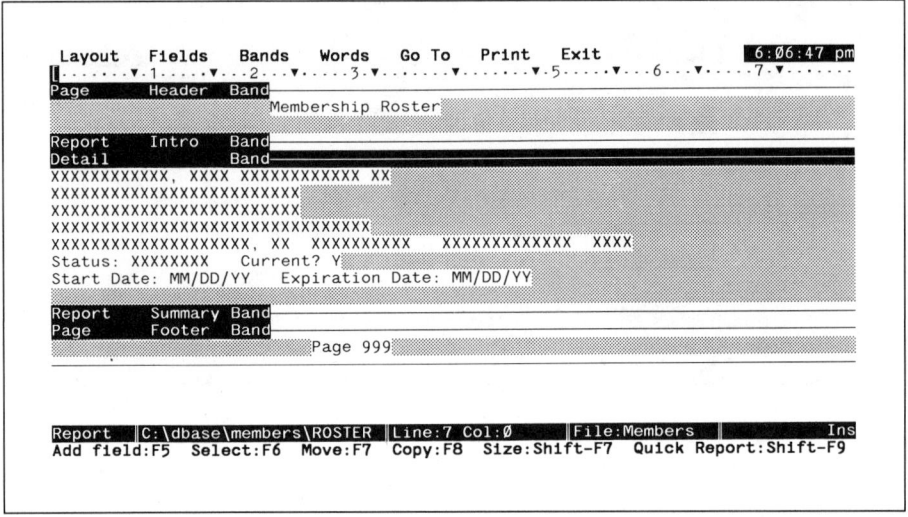

FIGURE F.7: Format of the ROSTER report used in the sample membership management application. You can use the usual reports design screen directly from the Control Center to develop report formats for your application.

The other three reports are form letters, each of which uses an identical name and address format near the top of the letter. To speed the development of the form letters, first select <create> from the Reports panel in the Control Center. Then select Quick Layouts and Mailmerge Layout from the Layout pull-down menu. Using the usual techniques, arrange the fields as shown in the next example. (The MM/DD/YY template is for the current date, which you can place by pressing **F5** and selecting Date from the PREDEFINED column of the menu that appears.)

```
MM/DD/YY
TITLE FIRSTNAME MI LASTNAME
COMPANY
DEPARTMENT
ADDRESS
CITY, STATE ZIP
```

Dear FIRSTNAME:

After arranging the fields as shown, make three copies of the current format by following these steps:

1. Select Save This Report from the Layout pull-down menu.
2. Enter **WELCOME** as the report name and press ↵.

3. Select Save This Report from the Layout pull-down menu.
4. Use the **Backspace** key to erase WELCOME.FRM and then type **RENEWAL** as the report name and press ←┘.
5. Select Save This Report from the Layout pull-down menu.
6. Use the **Backspace** key to erase RENEWAL.FRM and then type **OVERDUE** as the report name and press ←┘.
7. Select Abandon Changes and Exit from the Exit pull-down menu.

When you return to the Control Center, you can complete each form letter by highlighting its name in the Reports panel and pressing Design (**Shift-F2**). Figures F.8, F.9, and F.10 show examples of three form letters. (Most of each letter is scrolled off the bottom of the screen, but you'll undoubtedly want to create your own form letters anyway.)

After creating each report format, you can print a test copy by highlighting the report name in the Control Center and pressing ←┘. Then select Print Report and either Begin Printing or View Report on Screen from the Print submenu.

Creating a Mailing Label Format

The application also needs a format for printing labels. Select <create> from the Labels panel in the Control Center and arrange the fields as follows:

```
TITLE FIRSTNAME MI LASTNAME
COMPANY
```

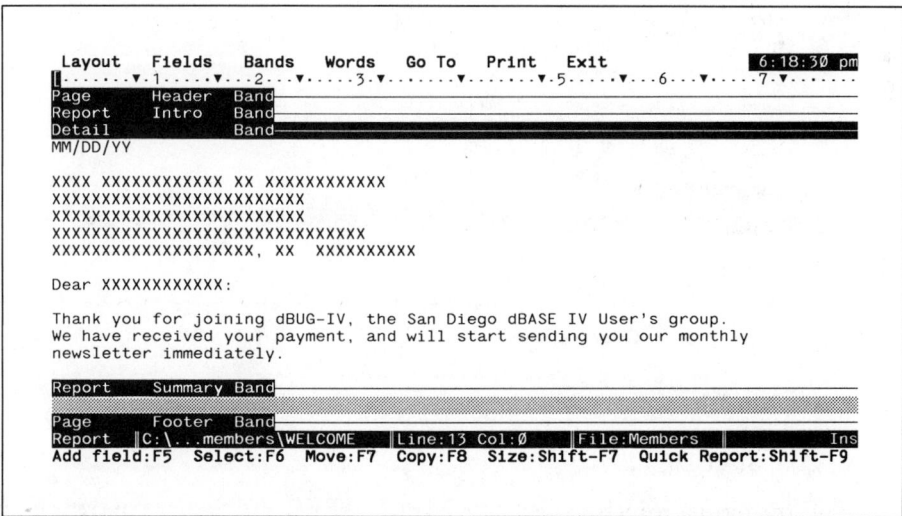

FIGURE F.8: Format for the WELCOME letter.

850 DESIGNING AND DEVELOPING AN APPLICATION

FIGURE F.9: Format for the RENEWAL letter.

FIGURE F.10: Format for the OVERDUE letter.

```
DEPARTMENT
ADDRESS
CITY, STATE ZIP
```

Save the format using the file name MEMLABEL and then test it by printing a label, using the same basic technique you use to print reports.

DESIGNING THE APPLICATION OBJECTS

After you have designed and created the database objects, it's time to exit dBASE, turn off the computer, and start thinking about how you want to link these objects together into an application. The application objects available to you through the Applications Generator include these:

- Sign-on banner
- Horizontal bar menus
- Pop-up and pull-down menus
- Batch processes
- Help screens and messages
- Windows
- Lists

Earlier in this appendix, Figure F.2 showed an example of a sign-on banner. Figure F.3 showed an example of a horizontal bar menu (across the top of the screen) and of a pull-down menu (beneath the Maintain option on the horizontal bar menu). A pop-up menu is essentially the same as a pull-down menu, except that rather than simply highlighting an option on a horizontal bar menu, you need to press a key to see a pop-up menu.

A *batch process* is an application object that performs several operations automatically. A batch process is typically assigned to a menu option so that, when the application user selects a menu option, the application performs several tasks rather than one. You'll see an example as you develop the sample membership management application.

The help screens and messages that you can create for your application operate in the same manner as help screens and messages in the dBASE IV program. That is, when the user highlights a particular menu option, a message appears at the bottom of the screen to provide brief instructions or help. To access a larger help screen, the user must press the Help (**F1**) key.

The only difference between your application's messages and help screens and dBASE IV's is that *you* determine what each displays. Help screens and messages are optional; they are not required in an application. However, it's generally a good idea to include them, since the overall goal of an application is to make database operations accessible to less experienced users. To simplify the design phase of applications development, you may want to leave out the messages and help screens until you've developed and finalized the application. Then you can go back and refine the application by adding these objects. At the end of this appendix you'll see how to add these refinements to our application example.

A *window* displays information on the screen by temporarily overwriting, rather than replacing, existing text. It can be used to display progress reports (such as the number of files copied during a copy operation), small help screens, or other useful information. Like help screens and messages, windows are not required in applications, but are instead refinements in the application.

The Applications Generator also allows you to include three types of *list* in your application: a files list, a structure list, and a values list. These are specialized types of windows that allow the application user to select items from a window by highlighting an item and pressing ←⏎.

You have already seen examples of many lists in your work with dBASE IV. For example, when you select Add File to Query from the Catalog pull-down menu at the Control Center, dBASE IV displays a files list, as shown in Figure F.11. You can then select any file name from this list by highlighting its name and pressing ←⏎.

A structure list displays the names of fields in a database, and a values list displays a list of values (data) in a single field of a database. Examples of all three lists are presented in Chapter 15.

The sections that follow show how to design an application using some of the application objects just described. Again, this phase of the design process is actually a pencil-and-paper task and does not require any interaction with the computer.

Designing the Membership Application Menus

As mentioned earlier, the Applications Generator automatically creates many files when you develop an application. Every horizontal bar menu and

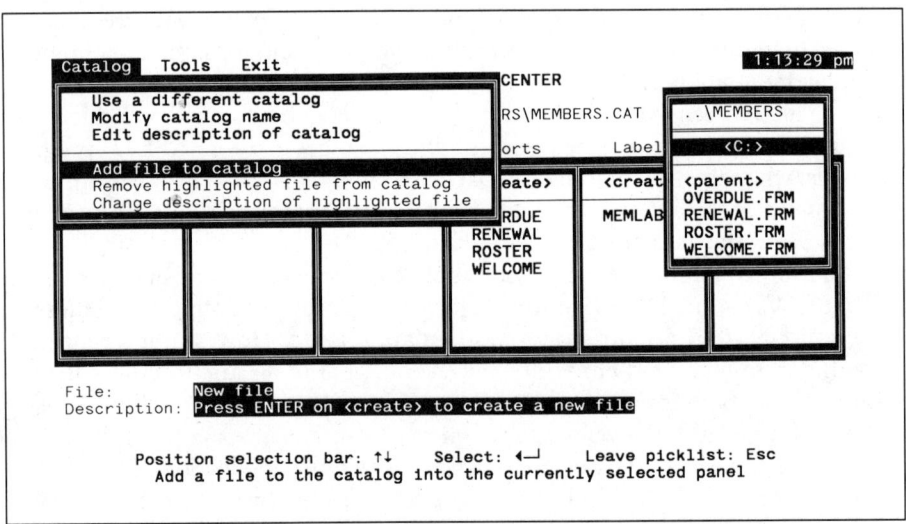

FIGURE F.11: A files list displayed at the dBASE IV Control Center. You can add similar lists to your own applications when you use the Applications Generator.

pull-down (or pop-up) menu needs a unique file name in your application (and each name must conform to the DOS rules for file names: eight letters maximum length, no spaces, and no punctuation other than the underscore or hyphen). The Applications Generator automatically adds its own extensions to these file names, so you should not add your own extensions.

Figure F.12 shows the menu structure for the membership application, including the file names that will be used later when creating the application. Sketching out the menu design and specifying file names on paper in this manner will help you keep track of the menus later when you create the application.

Each option on every menu will later be assigned an *action* that is to be performed when the application user selects that option. Many options will also use database objects that you've created earlier. For example, the Add New Members option in the sample membership management application will use the MEMFORM custom form (a database object) to allow the application user to add new records (an action) to the database.

You may want to make an extra copy of your application's menu structure and jot down some notes about the action each will perform and the database object (if any) required to perform the action. You can also make notes about any sort orders and filter conditions (such as "new members" or "expired members") that each action requires.

For example, Figure F.13 shows the menu structure for the sample membership management application. Although it is complex, it will facilitate remembering which actions and database objects to assign to each application menu option later in the development process. (The next section discusses the RENEW.BCH batch process shown in Figure F.13.)

DESIGNING THE APPLICATION BATCH PROCESSES

A batch process is a group of several operations assigned to a single menu selection. The purpose of a batch process is to allow the user to perform several smaller operations by selecting a single option from one of the application menus.

The sample membership application uses a single batch process, named RENEW.BCH, to help the user renew memberships (dBASE automatically adds the .BCH extension). The batch process performs four operations to automate the task of updating memberships each month. To see what each operation in the process does, assume that the current date is February 28, 1991, and the database contains the four records shown here (only relevant fields are used in this example). Note that Andy Adams' CURRENT field is already marked .F.,

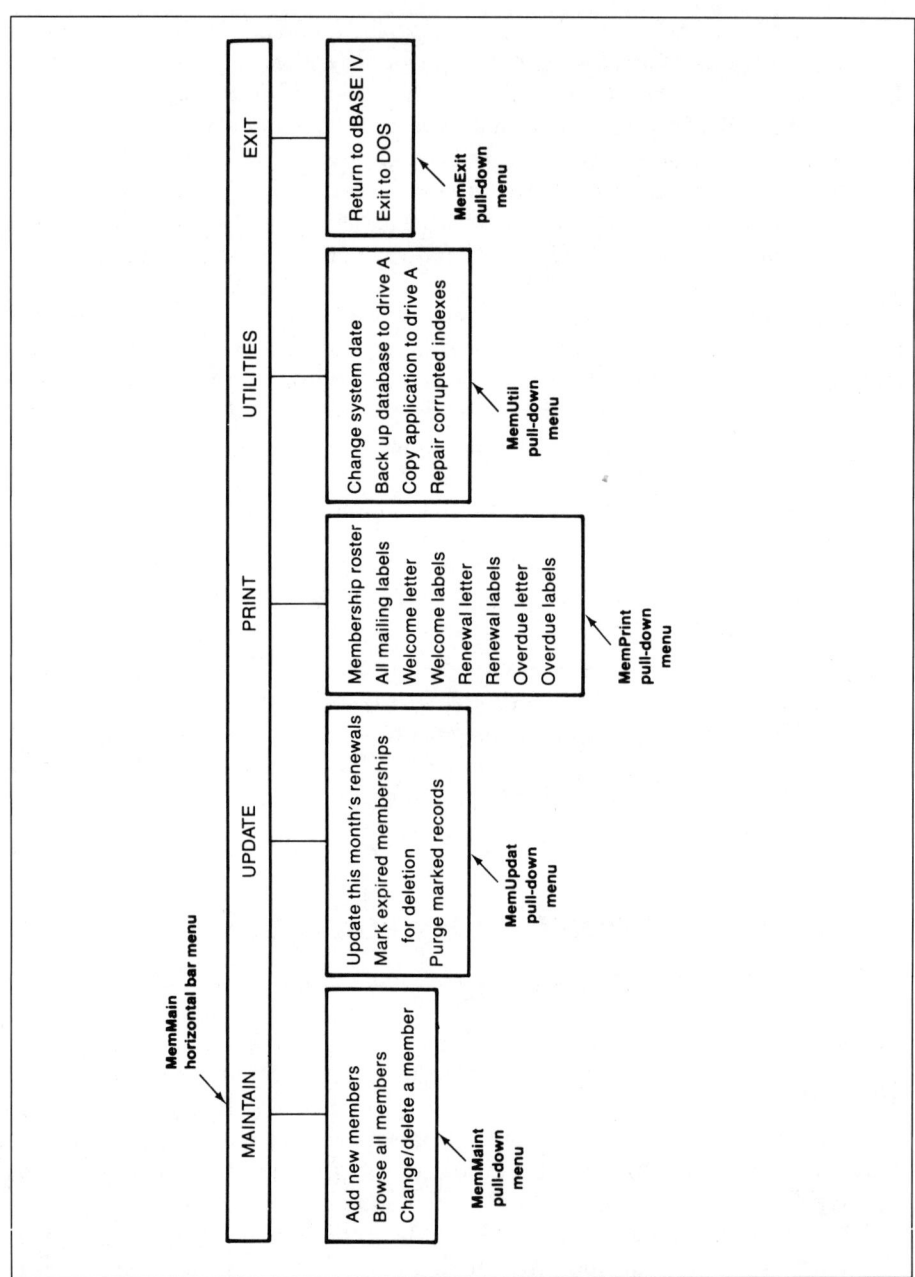

FIGURE F.12: Menu structure for the membership application, including the file name assigned to each menu. Planning the menu structure and determining file names for each menu on paper simplifies later stages of the application development process.

DESIGNING THE APPLICATION BATCH PROCESSES — 855

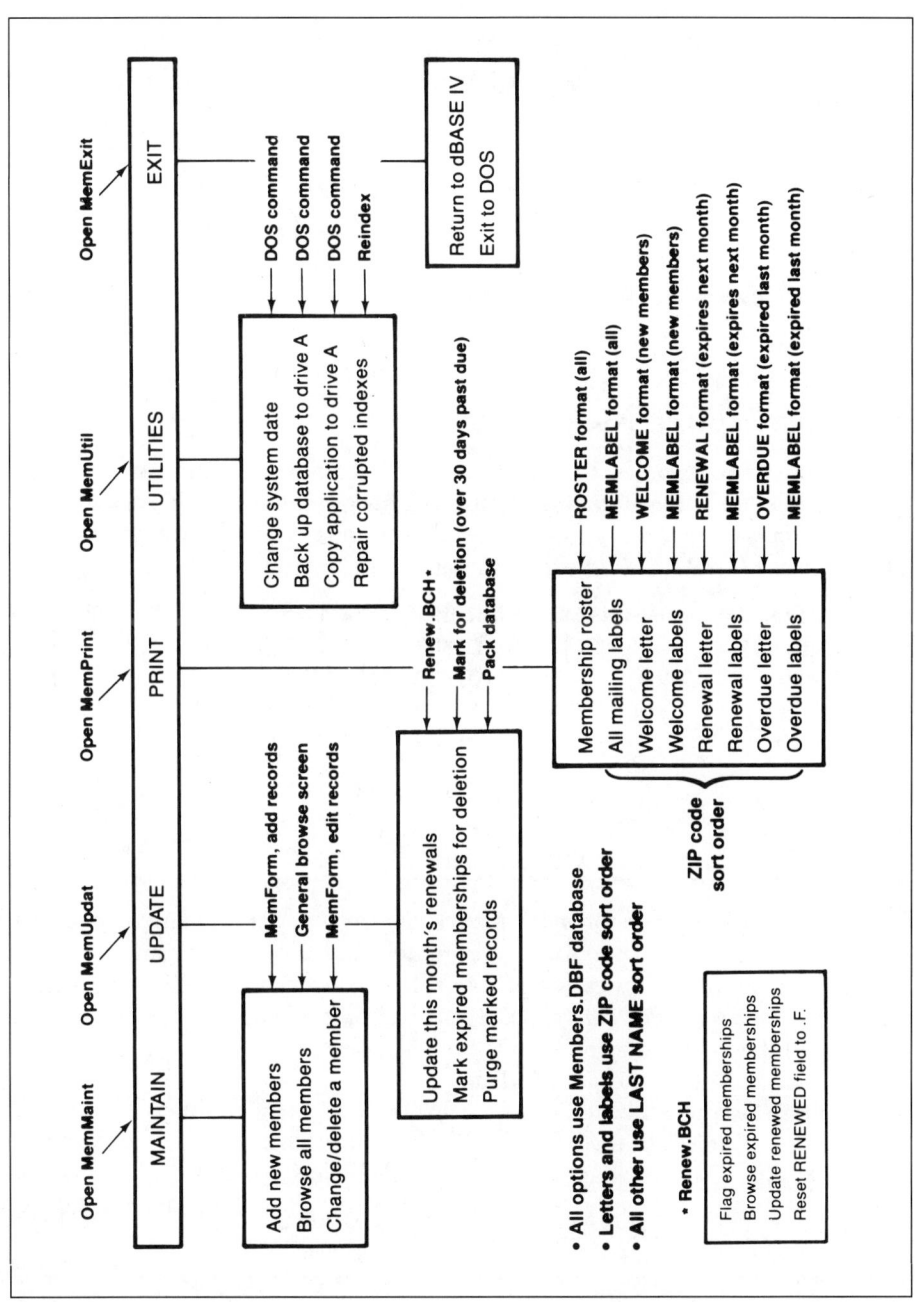

FIGURE F.13: The membership application menu structure with notes about actions and the names of database objects assigned to each option. You can also add notes about sort orders, filter conditions, or any other information to help you later in the application development phase.

because his membership expired last month:

LASTNAME	FIRSTNAME	STARTDATE	EXPIRES	CURRENT	RENEWED
Adams	Andy	01/01/89	01/01/90	.F.	.F.
Baker	Bob	02/01/89	02/01/90	.T.	.F.
Carlson	Cara	02/28/89	02/28/90	.T.	.F.
Davis	Deedra	03/31/89	03/31/90	.T.	.F.

The batch process performs four operations, as summarized in the following sections.

Operation 1: Flag Expired Memberships

The first operation in the batch process automatically changes the CURRENT field to .F. for all memberships that have expired. Again, given that the current date is 02/28/90, this operation will modify two of the four records, bringing the CURRENT field up to date in all records, as follows:

LASTNAME	FIRSTNAME	STARTDATE	EXPIRES	CURRENT	RENEWED
Adams	Andy	01/01/89	01/01/90	.F.	.F.
Baker	Bob	02/01/89	02/01/90	.F.	.F.
Carlson	Cara	02/28/89	02/28/90	.F.	.F.
Davis	Deedra	03/31/89	03/31/90	.T.	.F.

Operation 2: Browse Expired Memberships

The next operation in the batch process displays only expired memberships on a browse screen. The user, who presumably has payments from all renewed members, can then change the RENEWED field from .F. to .T. for members who have renewed. For convenience, the cursor is locked into the RENEWED field, and the field is displayed to the left of other fields. Figure F.14 shows the browse screen with some sample data.

Suppose Adams and Baker have renewed their memberships. The user can change the .F. to .T. in the RENEWED field for each person's record and save these changes. The database then contains the following data:

LASTNAME	FIRSTNAME	STARTDATE	EXPIRES	CURRENT	RENEWED
Adams	Andy	01/01/89	01/01/90	.F.	.T.
Baker	Bob	02/01/89	02/01/90	.F.	.T.
Carlson	Cara	02/28/89	02/28/90	.F.	.F.
Davis	Deedra	03/31/89	03/31/90	.T.	.F.

OPERATION 4: RESET RENEWED FIELD TO FALSE   857

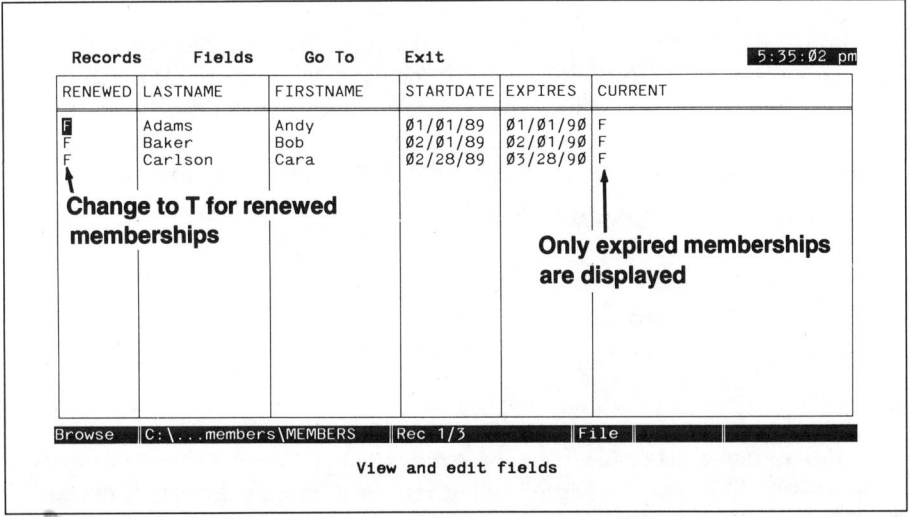

FIGURE F.14: Browse screen for indicating renewed memberships. Only expired memberships are displayed, and the cursor is locked into the RENEWED field. The user can then easily mark renewed memberships simply by changing the appropriate F (false) values to T (true).

Operation 3: Update Renewed Memberships

Now that the database has been saved with renewed memberships marked with a .T., the third operation in the batch process automatically marks the appropriate CURRENT fields with .T. and extends the expiration dates by one year (to 1991) as follows:

LASTNAME	FIRSTNAME	STARTDATE	EXPIRES	CURRENT	RENEWED
Adams	Andy	01/01/89	01/01/91	.T.	.T.
Baker	Bob	02/01/89	02/01/91	.T.	.T.
Carlson	Cara	02/28/89	02/28/90	.F.	.F.
Davis	Deedra	03/31/89	03/31/90	.T.	.F.

Operation 4: Reset RENEWED Field to False

All records with renewed memberships now have .T. in the CURRENT field and have had their expiration dates extended by a year. The user can now deposit the payments and need not be concerned about these memberships for another year. (They won't even appear on the updating browse screen for another year.)

However, the batch process is not quite complete, because even though the third operation in the batch process completed the renewal process, the records still have .T. in the RENEWED field. If the user were to run this batch process again, those records would have their expiration dates extended by *another* year (in this case, to 1992). To prevent this mistake, the fourth operation in the batch process resets all the values in the RENEWED field to .F., as follows:

LASTNAME	FIRSTNAME	STARTDATE	EXPIRES	CURRENT	RENEWED
Adams	Andy	01/01/89	01/01/91	.T.	.F.
Baker	Bob	02/01/89	02/01/91	.T.	.F.
Carlson	Cara	02/28/89	02/28/90	.F.	.F.
Davis	Deedra	03/31/89	03/31/90	.T.	.F.

Now the database is accurate for the current month and ready for next month's updates. Memberships for Adams and Baker need not be renewed again until next year. In March when the user repeats the batch operation, Carlson and Davis will appear on the browse screen for possible renewal. The user will identify those members (if any) that have renewed by placing .T. in the RENEWED field, and the the batch process will once again update all appropriate memberships for the month of March.

At this point, you have finished designing the application, and you have also created all the database objects that the application will use. Later in this appendix, you will use the dBASE IV Applications Generator to develop the completed application.

OTHER DESIGN CONSIDERATIONS

The sample application designed in this appendix is, of course, just an example. You can link any set of database objects, even if they already exist, into an application. However, if the existing application objects are stored in the dBASE IV home directory (usually C:\DBASE), you should move the database objects to a new directory and use the new directory to store all the application objects that the Applications Generator will produce.

As mentioned earlier, using a unique directory for each application prevents the many files the Applications Generator generates from cluttering the dBASE home directory. It also makes copying the completed application to disk easier, because all the necessary files are stored on a single directory.

Another potential design consideration is modularity. For example, the database objects for bookkeeping fall logically into three separate modules: accounts receivable, accounts payable, and general ledger. Should you develop a single application that supports all three modules, or should you develop three separate applications?

In general, creating a single application that supports all three modules is easiest, because the Applications Generator assumes that the current directory stores all files the application uses. Using such an application also is easier for the user, because all modules are readily available from a single main menu.

DEVELOPING THE APPLICATION

After you've designed the application and created its database objects, you are ready to begin using the Applications Generator to develop the application. The basic steps required to develop an application at this stage are summarized here:

1. Define the application name and default settings.
2. Create a sign-on banner for the application (this step is optional).
3. Create the application menus and other application objects.
4. Assign *actions* to each application menu item.
5. Generate the application *code* (programs).
6. Save all changes and exit.

The Applications Generator provides all the tools you need to perform each step. You can also modify any existing application using the Applications Generator, so you are free to build any application in a piecemeal manner, experiment with the various tools and options the Applications Generator provides, and refine your application as you go along.

Remember that we've stored all the database objects for the membership application in a subdirectory named \DBASE\MEMBERS. If you've exited dBASE, you should enter the command **CD \DBASE\MEMBERS** at the DOS command prompt to return to that directory. Then, as usual, enter the command **DBASE** to run dBASE IV.

When you get to the Control Center, you should see the names of the various database objects (MEMBERS, MEMFORM, WELCOME, and so forth) that you've created for the application in the Control Center panels. To get to the Applications Generator to start developing the application, follow these two steps:

1. Select <create> from the Application panel in the Control Center.
2. Select Applications Generator from the submenu.

DEFINING THE APPLICATION

The first dialog box to appear when you enter the Applications Generator asks for the application definition. You need to name the application, using a valid

DOS file name. For this example, we'll use the name MEMMGR (an abbreviation for Membership Manager). You also need to enter a file name for the main menu—MEMMAIN in this example.

At this step, you also need to assign a default database, index file, and sort order. These default settings will be used by all menu selections, except those that you specifically change. For example, the membership application will use the default alphabetical sort order for edit screens, browse screens, and the membership roster. However, menu options that print form letters and mailing labels will override the default setting and use zip code order.

Figure F.15 shows the completed application definition for the membership application. The Set INDEX To option is left blank, which tells the application to use the production index file that dBASE creates automatically. (The production index file has the same first name as the database, but the extension .MDX.) The ORDER option is set to LASTNAME, which specifies the LASTNAME index (created when you initially designed the database) as the default sort order. The main menu type is BAR (for a horizontal bar menu), and the name assigned in this example is MEMMAIN.

After filling in the application definition dialog box, press **Ctrl-End**.

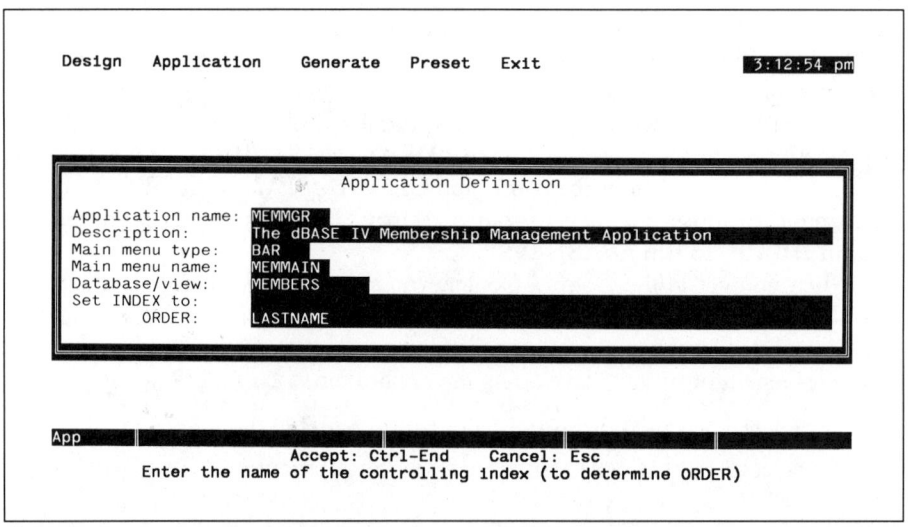

FIGURE F.15: The first dialog box to appear when you create a new application asks for an overall application definition. The example in this figure shows the definition for the membership application.

Using the Application Design Screen

After you have saved the application definition, dBASE takes you to the application design screen. Here is where you create the *application objects* that make up the application. The application objects include the menus, batch processes, and optional sign-on banner. The sign-on banner is centered on the design screen, as shown in Figure F.16.

Like other dBASE IV design screens, the application design screen has a menu bar at the top and pull-down menus. However, unlike other dBASE IV menus, this menu bar changes from time to time to reflect the type of object you are creating at the moment. At first, this can be a little confusing, but as you develop the sample membership application, you will see how and when changes occur.

Developing the Membership Sign-on Banner

If you want, you can use the application object currently on the design screen as a sign-on banner. This banner will then appear each time the user runs the completed application. Use **Ctrl-Y** to delete the text currently in the box and then type your own sign-on information. You can type the application title, a description, the name of the application author, a copyright notice, or any other

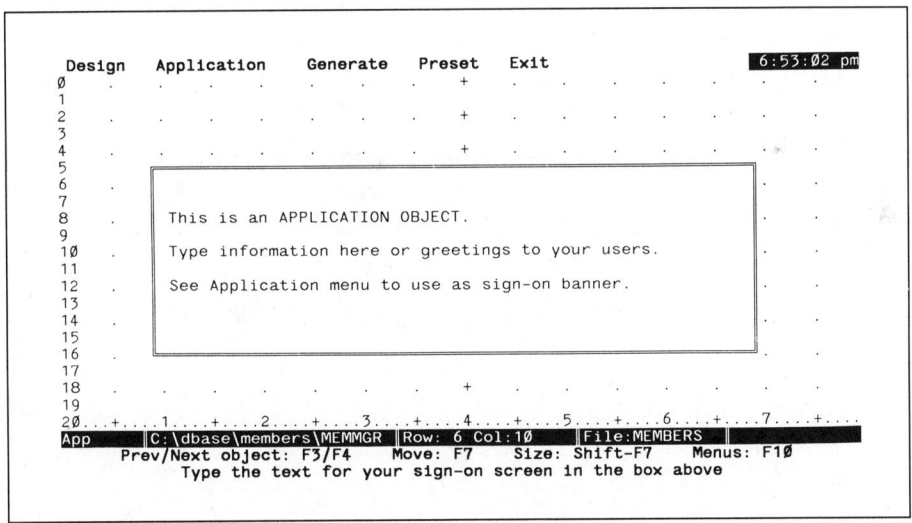

FIGURE F.16: The application design screen is where you design the application objects. The sign-on banner application object is always displayed on this screen (surrounded by a double-line border). Unlike other dBASE IV menus, the menu at the top of this screen changes as you develop the application.

text in the sign-on banner. You can use the usual editing keys to make changes if necessary.

You can also resize and move the sign-on banner frame (as well as most other objects that you create). To change the size of the frame, press Size (**Shift-F7**). The border will blink. Use the arrow keys to expand or reduce the size of the box; then press ↵ when you are done. To move the box, press Move (**F7**) and then use the arrow keys to move the box to a new location. Press ↵ to complete the move operation.

Figure F.17 shows a suggested sign-on banner for the membership application. In this example, the box has been reduced slightly in size and moved up a few rows.

After you complete the banner, make a few menu selections to ensure that the banner appears when the user starts the application. To do so, press Menus (**F10**) and select Display Sign-on Banner from the Application pull-down menu. Then select Yes from the options that appear.

Developing the Membership Horizontal Bar Menu

Next you can create the horizontal bar menu (the main menu, which we earlier decided to name MEMMAIN) that appears across the top of the screen

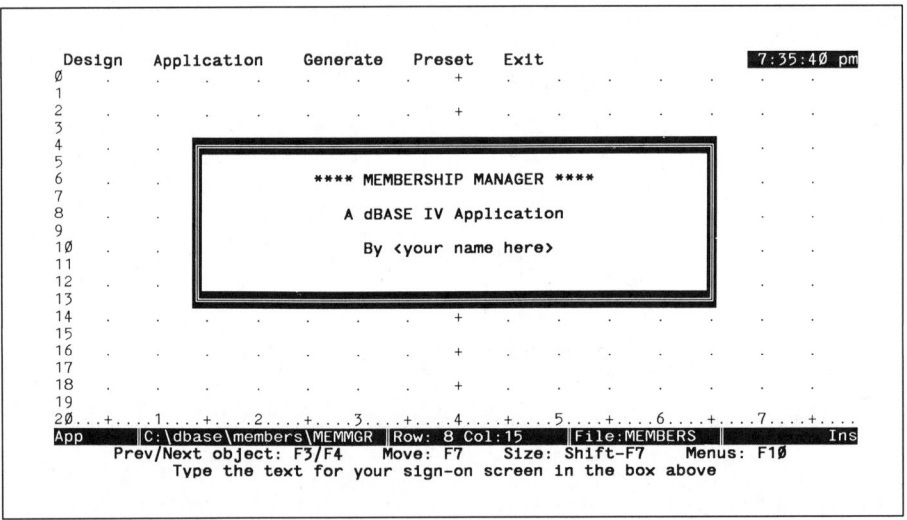

FIGURE F.17: Sign-on banner for the membership application. You can replace the section that reads *<your name here>* with your own name, so that your name is displayed when the user first starts the application.

when the user runs the application. To create the menu, follow these steps:

1. Select Horizontal Bar Menu from the Design pull-down menu.
2. Select <create> from the submenu that appears.
3. In the dialog box that appears, enter **MEMMAIN** as the menu name.
4. Enter **Membership application main menu** as the description.
5. Leave the message-line prompt blank for now.
6. Press **Ctrl-End** when you are done.

Note that after you have created the horizontal bar menu, it becomes the current object, and the second option in the Application Design menu changes from Application to Menu.

Now you can place menu options inside the menu bar. To enter an option, press **F5**, type the option text, and then press **F5** again. Here are the steps to enter the menu options Maintain, Update, Print, Utilities, and Exit, which we defined earlier in the design phase:

1. Press **F5**, type **Maintain**, and press **F5** again.
2. Press the space bar three times, press **F5**, type **Update**, and press **F5** again.
3. Press the space bar three times, press **F5**, type **Print**, and press **F5** again.
4. Press the space bar three times, press **F5**, type **Utilities**, and press **F5** again.
5. Press the space bar three times, press **F5**, type **Exit**, and press **F5** again.

You've now finished the membership application main menu. To see how the menu will appear when the user actually runs the application, you can remove the application design screen menu and status bar by pressing Zoom (**F9**). After you do so, your screen should look like Figure F.18. (To bring back the application design screen menu and status bar, press **F9** again.)

Developing the Membership Pull-Down Menus

Creating the pull-down menu for each main menu option is the next step in developing the membership application. The general procedure for creating each pull-down menu is the same: You start with a blank pop-up menu, increase its size as necessary, and then type menu options and optional text. You can then resize the menu to tighten the frame around the options and move the menu to where you want it to appear when the user runs the application.

864 — DESIGNING AND DEVELOPING AN APPLICATION

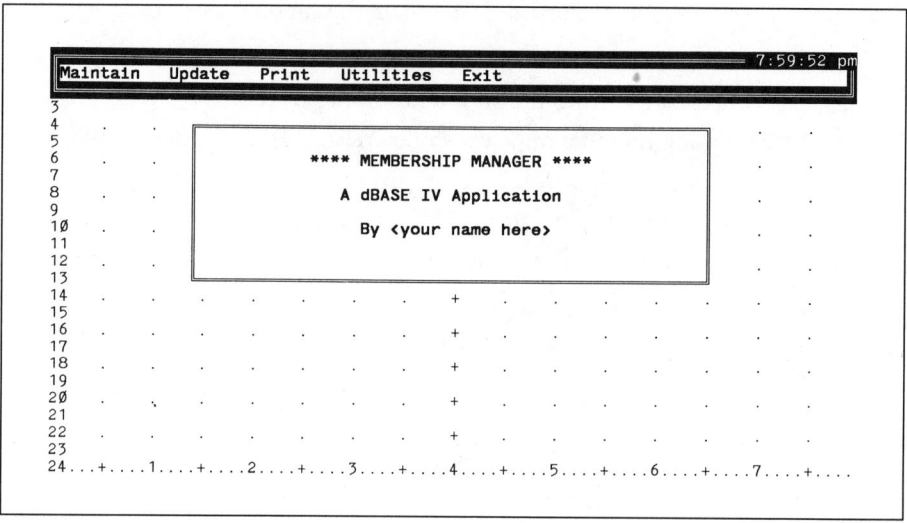

FIGURE F.18: Horizontal bar menu for the membership application, displayed on the application design screen after pressing Zoom (**F9**) to temporarily remove the design screen menus. Press **F9** again when you are ready to bring back the design screen menus.

CREATING THE MAINTAIN PULL-DOWN MENU

Follow these steps to create the pull-down menu for the application's Maintain option:

1. Press **F10** and select Pop-up Menu from the Design menu.
2. Select <create> from the submenu.
3. Enter **MEMMAINT** as the menu name.
4. Leave the other options blank for the time being.
5. Press **Ctrl-End**.
6. Press Size (**Shift-F7**) and press → five times to widen the box. Then press ←.
7. Type the option **Add new members** and press ←.
8. Type **Browse all members** and press ←.
9. Type **Change/delete a member**.
10. Press Size (**Shift-F7**) again and press ↑ five times to remove blank lines in the box. Press ←.
11. Press Move (**F7**) and select Entire Frame to begin moving the menu.
12. Use the arrow keys to move the menu to beneath the Maintain option, as in Figure F.19. Press ← after completing the move.

DEVELOPING THE MEMBERSHIP PULL-DOWN MENUS — 865

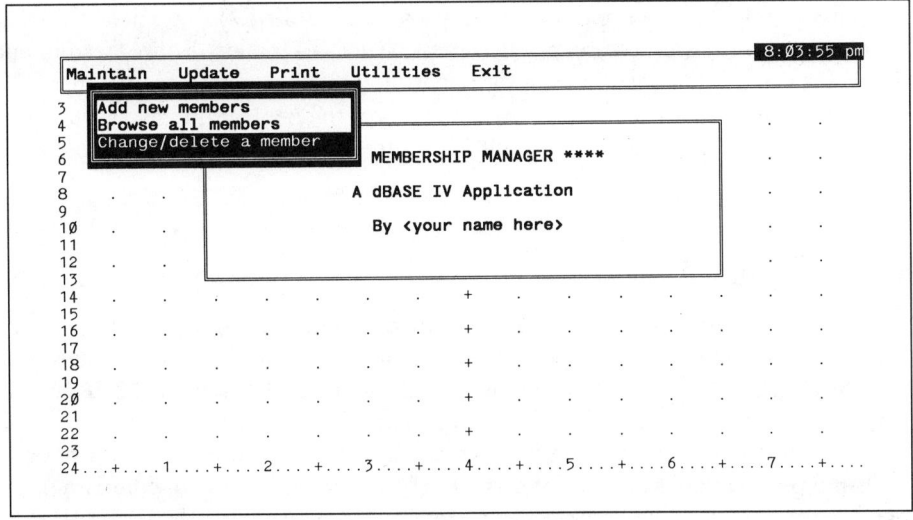

FIGURE F.19: The Maintain pull-down menu for the sample membership application is in place. In this figure, the design screen menus were removed temporarily to present an uncluttered view of the Maintain menu.

After completing the MEMMAINT pull-down menu, save it and put it away (hide it temporarily to reduce screen clutter) by selecting Put Away Current Menu from the Menu pull-down menu. When prompted, select Save Changes.

CREATING THE UPDATE PULL-DOWN MENU

To begin creating the pull-down menu for the application Update option, use the same general techniques as you used to begin creating the Maintain option. That is, select Pop-Up Menu from the Design pull-down menu and <create> from the submenu. Enter **MEMUPDAT** as the name of the update menu. You can leave the description and message-line prompt blank for the time being and just press **Ctrl-End**.

When the menu frame appears, you will need to enlarge it (using **Shift-F7**) to accommodate all the options. (You can resize the menu frame at any time, so don't worry about getting the frame size right the first time.) Then type the following items:

    Update this month's renewals
    Mark expired memberships for deletion
    Purge marked records

After typing the three options, you can use Size (**Shift-F7**) to tighten the frame around the options if necessary. Then press Move (**F7**), select Entire Frame, and align the completed menu beneath the application Update option, as in Figure F.20.

Once again, to reduce screen clutter and save the new menu, select Put Away Current Menu from the Menu pull-down menu and select Save Changes when prompted.

CREATING THE PRINT PULL-DOWN MENU

Now you can create the pull-down menu for the membership application Print option. Start with the usual steps: Select Pop-Up menu from the Design pull-down menu, select <create> from the submenu, and enter **MEMPRINT** as the name of the menu. Press **Ctrl-End** to leave other options blank.

Use **Shift-F7** to enlarge the initial frame to accommodate the menu options. Then type the options and text shown here (use hyphens for the dividing line):

    Membership roster
    All mailing labels
    Welcome letters
    Welcome labels
    Renewal letters

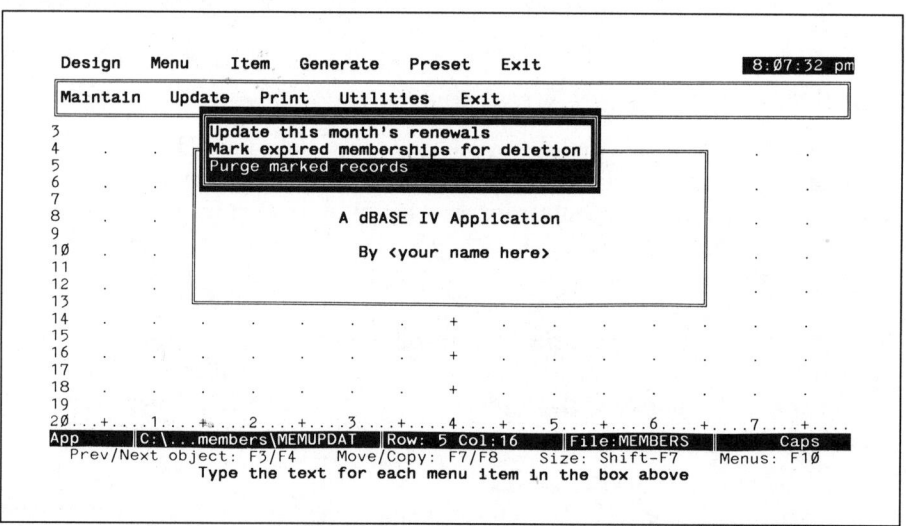

FIGURE F.20: The membership Update pull-down menu in place beneath the Update option on the horizontal bar menu.

DEVELOPING THE MEMBERSHIP PULL-DOWN MENUS

Renewal labels
Overdue letters
Overdue labels

Complete all options
on the Update menu
before printing
monthly letters.

After completing the pull-down menu, resize it (using **Shift-F7**) to tighten the frame around the options. Then move it (using **F7**) so that it appears beneath the Print option on the application horizontal bar menu, as shown in Figure F.21.

After completing the MEMPRINT pull-down menu, select Put Away Current Menu from the Menu pull-down menu. Then select Save Changes from the submenu.

CREATING THE UTILITIES PULL-DOWN MENU

To create the pull-down menu for the application Utilities option, select Pop-Up Menu from the Design pull-down menu and <create> from the submenu. Enter **MEMUTIL** as the menu name and press **Ctrl-End** to leave the other

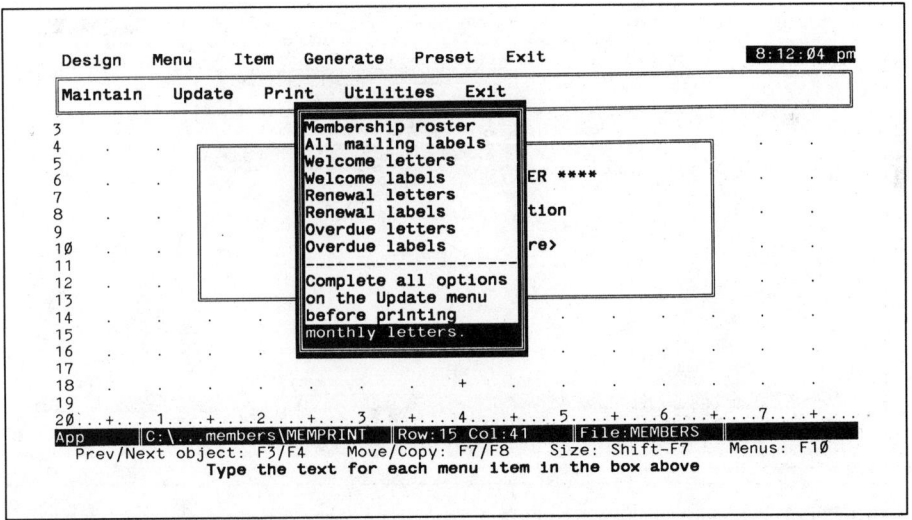

FIGURE F.21: The membership Print pull-down menu is in place beneath the Print option on the horizontal bar menu. This particular menu includes some text, which is separated from the actual menu options by a string of hyphens.

options blank. Use **Shift-F7** to widen the blank frame and then fill in the options as follows:

    Change system date
    Back up database to drive A
    Copy application to drive A
    Repair corrupted index

When you are done, use **Shift-F7** again, if necessary, to tighten the frame around the menu options and then use Move (**F7**) to reposition the menu beneath the Utilities option, as shown in Figure F.22.

Select Put Away Current Menu from the Menu pull-down menu and Save Changes from the submenu to save your work and clear some work space.

CREATING THE EXIT PULL-DOWN MENU

Finally, use the usual techniques to create the pull-down menu for the application Exit option: Select Pop-Up Menu from the Design pull-down menu and <create> from the submenu. Enter the name **MEMEXIT** and press **Ctrl-End** to leave all other options blank for the time being. Fill in the box with these two

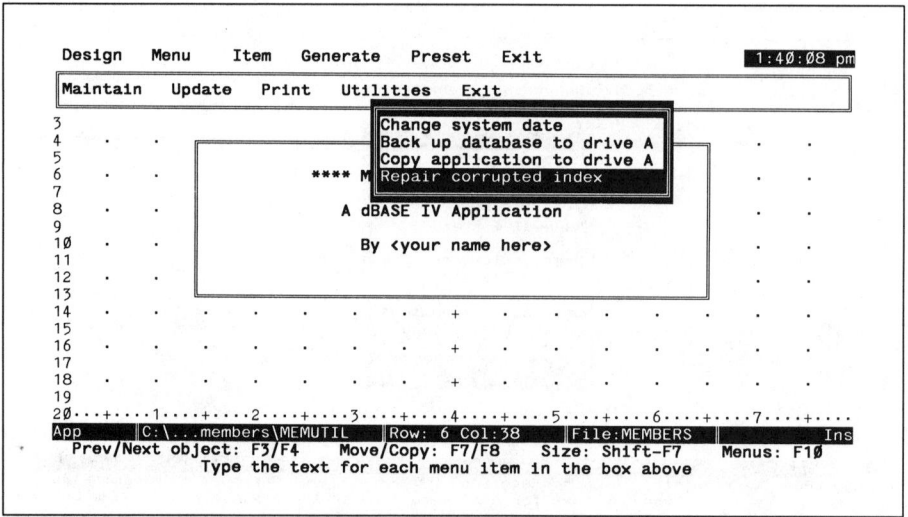

FIGURE F.22: The Utilities pull-down menu is in place beneath the Utilities option on the horizontal bar menu.

options:

> Return to dBASE IV
> Exit to DOS

Size the frame for a tight fit and move the frame to the appropriate location beneath the Exit option on the menu bar, as in Figure F.23.

Selecting the Current Object

Before putting away the Exit menu, you might want to experiment with the Previous (**F3**) and Next (**F4**) keys for a moment. Whenever there are multiple objects on the applications design screen, these keys allow you to scroll from one application object to the next.

If you press either of these keys repeatedly now, you will see the current object switch among the pull-down menu, the horizontal bar menu, and the sign-on banner. The *current object* always has its frame highlighted and overlays any other objects on the screen.

To restore a hidden object (one that you've already put away) to the design screen, select the type of object you want to restore from the Design pull-down menu and then select the object name from the submenu. For example, to restore the MEMPRINT pop-up menu to the design screen, press **F10** and

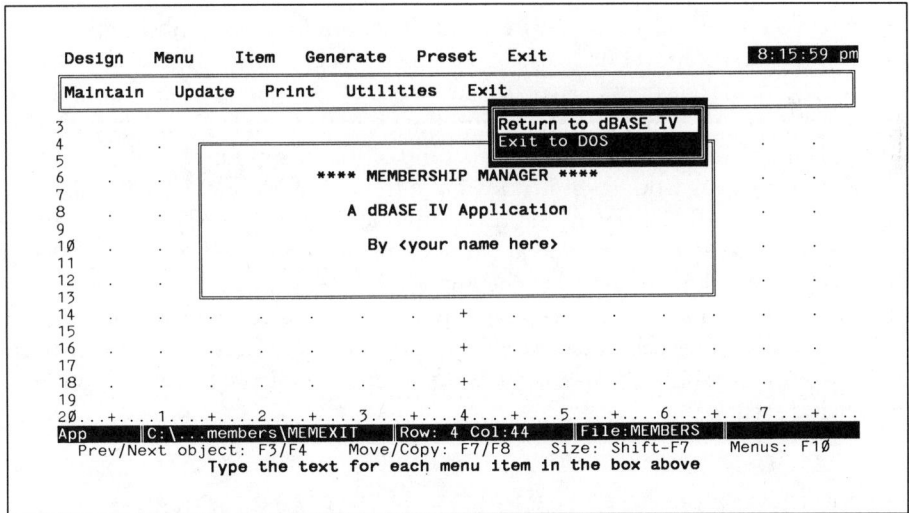

FIGURE F.23: The membership Exit pull-down menu is in place beneath the Exit option on the horizontal bar menu.

select Pop-Up Menu from the Design pull-down menu and MEMPRINT from the submenu. The MEMPRINT menu appears on the design screen and automatically becomes the current object.

You can resize, move, or change the current object at any time, using the same keys you used to create the object. If the current object is a pop-up (or pull-down) menu, you can delete an option by highlighting it and pressing **Ctrl-Y**. To insert a new option, increase the size of the box as necessary, position the highlight at the place where you want to insert an option, and press **Ctrl-N**. You may want to experiment with these options now and correct any mistakes you made while developing the menus.

Putting Away the Membership Application Objects

You can save and put away all of the objects in an application by selecting the Clear Work Surface option from the Menu pull-down menu (or the Application pull-down menu). Select that option now. dBASE will ask whether you want to save any changes made to each unsaved object before dBASE puts the object away. In this case, select Save Changes for each object. Note that the sign-on banner is always displayed on the design screen and cannot be put away.

Taking a Break

Now you have created the entire menu structure for the membership application. Your next step will be to assign actions to each menu option. But first you might want to take a break. To do so, select Save Changes and Exit from the Exit pull-down menu. You'll be returned to the Control Center, where you can exit dBASE in the usual manner before turning off the computer.

To resume your work later, first log on to the C:\DBASE\MEMBERS directory; then run dBASE IV in the usual manner. Highlight MEMMGR in the Application panel at the right side of the Control Center and then press Design (**Shift-F2**). You'll be returned to the application design screen, with the sign-on banner displayed in the center of the screen. Other objects will be hidden.

You can use the techniques discussed here to take a break and then resume your work at any time as you complete the sample membership application in the following sections.

ASSIGNING ACTIONS TO MEMBERSHIP MENU OPTIONS

Your next step is to attach actions to each menu option (also called a *menu item*) in the application. The general procedure is to highlight the option to which you want to attach an action, select Change Action from the Item pull-down menu, and then select an appropriate action. Because each option on the horizontal bar menu displays a pull-down menu, each has the same action: opening a menu. The individual items on the pull-down menus, however, need to be assigned more specific actions, such as adding records and printing reports, that manipulate data.

Attaching Menu-Bar Actions

We will first attach actions to the options in the application horizontal bar menu. Make the horizontal bar menu display the current object by selecting Horizontal Bar Menu from the Design pull-down menu and then selecting MEMMAIN from the submenu that appears.

Now you can assign actions to each option on the horizontal menu, starting with the Maintain option.

ASSIGNING AN ACTION TO THE MAINTAIN OPTION

When the user selects the Maintain option from the horizontal bar menu, you want the application to display the MEMMAINT pull-down menu. Here are the steps to assign the appropriate action:

1. Press **F10** and select Change Action from the Item pull-down menu.
2. Select Open a Menu as the action.
3. Press the space bar until the Pop-Up option appears; then press ↵.
4. Type the name of the appropriate pull-down menu (**MEMMAINT**) or press Pick (**Shift-F1**) and select MEMMAINT from the submenu that appears.
5. Press **Ctrl-End**.

At this point, you'll be returned to the Item pull-down menu. Take a moment to look at the status bar near the bottom of the screen. Notice that in the center it displays the current menu option: Maintain. Whenever you assign an action to a menu option, check the status bar to make sure you are working with the correct menu option.

ASSIGNING AN ACTION TO THE UPDATE OPTION

When the user selects Update from the application main menu, you want the application to display the MEMUPDAT pull-down menu. Here are the steps to assign the appropriate action:

1. Press **PgDn** so that the Update option is current (update appears centered in the status bar near the bottom of the screen).
2. Select Change Action.
3. Select Open a Menu.
4. Press the space bar until the Pop-Up option is displayed; then press ↵.
5. Press Pick (**Shift-F1**) and select MEMUPDAT as the menu to attach.
6. Press **Ctrl-End**.

Repeat steps 1 through 6 for the Print, Utilities, and Exit menu options. For each bar menu option, substitute the appropriate menu option in step 1 and, in step 5, the pull-down menu name, as listed here:

MENU OPTION (STEP 1)	PULL-DOWN MENU NAME (STEP 5)
Print	MEMPRINT
Utilities	MEMUTIL
Exit	MEMEXIT

When you are finished, press **Esc** to leave the Item menu and return to the application design screen.

Converting Pop-Up Menus to Pull-Down Menus

Even though pop-up menus and pull-down menus are formatted identically, they behave in slightly different ways. Pop-up menus are not displayed until the user *selects* the higher-level menu item by highlighting it and pressing ↵. Pull-down menus, on the other hand, are displayed as soon as the higher-level menu option is highlighted (the user need not press ↵ to see the pull-down menu).

To convert the pop-up menus below the membership application bar menu to pull-down menus, select Attach Pull-Down Menus from the Menu pull-down menu. Then select Yes from the submenu that appears. This tells the Applications Generator that any pop-up menu that is attached to the bar menu via the Open a Menu action is to be treated as a pull-down menu.

When you attach pull-down menus to a menu bar, the pull-down menus automatically inherit many characteristics of the menu bar, including the database, index, index order, and colors in use. You can, however, override some of these inherited characteristics, as you'll see later.

Attaching Items to the Maintain Menu

Now you need to begin attaching actions to the pull-down menus. To attach actions to the Maintain pull-down menu, first take the menu out of hiding by selecting Pop-Up Menu from the Design pull-down menu. Then select MEM-MAINT from the submenu.

The Maintain pull-down menu appears on the screen with its frame highlighted, indicating that it is the object currently in use. Now you can assign an action to each menu option.

ADD NEW MEMBERS

The Add New Members option allows the user to add (*append*) new records to the MEMBERS database, using the MEMFORM custom screen you created earlier. Follow these steps:

1. Press Menu (**F10**) and select Change Action from the Item pull-down menu.
2. Select Edit Form (Add, Delete, Edit) from the submenu.
3. Press Pick (**Shift-F1**) and select MEMFORM as the form to use for adding records.
4. When the cursor is in the Mode box, press the space bar, if necessary, to change the option to APPEND.
5. Leave all other options at their default values, as in Figure F.24.
6. Press **Ctrl-End**.

BROWSE ALL MEMBERS

The second option on the Maintain pull-down menu, Browse All Members, allows the user to change the membership data through a browse screen. Here are the steps to attach the appropriate action to the menu option:

1. Press **PgDn** to move to the next menu option (Browse All Members should appear in the center of the status bar).
2. Select Change Action.
3. Select Browse (Add, Delete, Edit).
4. Press ⏎ five times to move to the FORMAT file option.
5. Press Pick (**Shift-F1**) and select MEMFORM as the related format file.
6. Press **Ctrl-End** to leave all other settings at their default values.

874 DESIGNING AND DEVELOPING AN APPLICATION

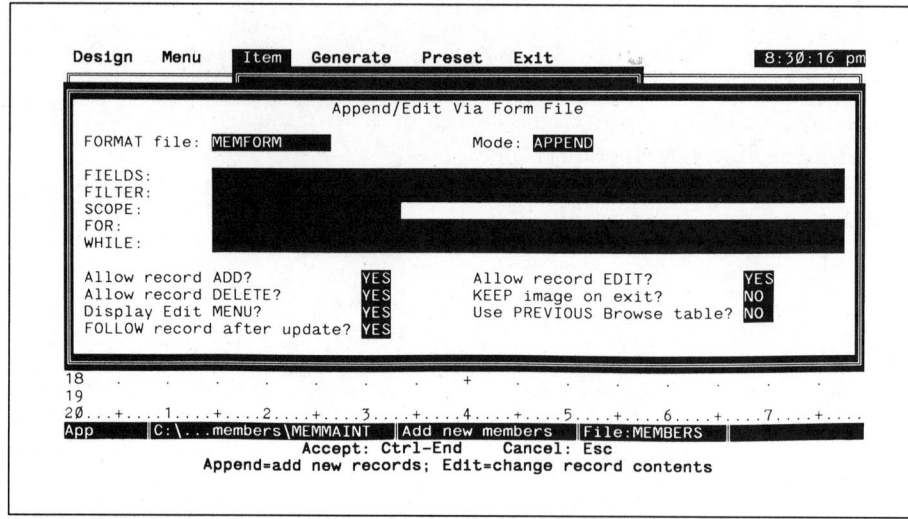

FIGURE F.24: Append/Edit form for the Add New Members option specifies MEMFORM as the name of the custom form used for adding (appending) new records to the membership application database.

In the previous steps, you directed the Applications Generator to display the data on a browse screen when the user selects Browse All Members. However, steps 4 and 5 told the Applications Generator to use the MEMFORM custom screen. This creates a contradiction, because the browse screen displays multiple database records in rows and columns, and the MEMFORM screen displays a single record at a time.

dBASE resolves this contradiction by displaying the browse screen as usual, but using any special templates, picture functions, and edit options defined for the MEMFORM custom form. For example, even though the data is displayed on a browse screen, the user will still be able to press the space bar to scroll through the Regular and Officer options in the STATUS field, because you defined status as a multiple-choice field in the MEMFORM custom form (see Table F.1 earlier in this appendix.)

All other features that you added to the MEMFORM custom form, such as default dates, will also be carried over to the browse screen, because you specified MEMFORM as the FORMAT file for the browse screen. You can test this screen later when you use the completed application.

CHANGE/DELETE A MEMBER

Now you need to assign an action to the third item on the Maintain menu, Change/Delete a Member. This option displays a single record from the MEM-

BERS database on the MEMFORM custom screen and allows the user to make changes. Here are the steps to assign the menu action:

1. Press **PgDn** to display Change/Delete in the status bar.
2. Select Change Action.
3. Select Edit Form (Add, Delete, Edit).
4. Type or select (using Pick, **Shift-F1**) MEMFORM as the form to use.
5. In the Mode box, specify Edit as the mode (pressing the space bar if necessary).
6. Press **Ctrl-End** to complete the operation and leave all other settings at their default values.

Now you have assigned actions to all three items on the Maintain pull-down menu. You can save and put away that menu now by first selecting Put Away Current Menu from the Menu pull-down menu. When prompted, select Save Changes from the submenu.

Assigning Actions to the Update Menu

Now you need to assign actions to the application Update pull-down menu. First, take that menu out of hiding and make it the current object by pressing **F10** and selecting Pop-Up Menu from the Design pull-down menu. Then select MEMUPDAT from the submenu that appears.

The Update pull-down menu appears on the application design screen, and you are ready to assign actions to its options.

Update This Month's Renewals

The Update This Month's Renewals option automates the steps involved in updating renewed memberships. When the user selects this option, the application executes a batch process named RENEW.BCH (dBASE adds the file extension .BCH). We'll create the actual batch process later, but you can assign the action to the menu option. Here are the steps:

1. Make sure that the Update This Month's Renewals option is highlighted in the pull-down menu.
2. Press **F10** and select Change Action from the Item pull-down menu.
3. Select Run Program.
4. Select Execute Batch Process.
5. Type the batch process name **RENEW** and press ⏎.

Now you can assign the action to the next menu option.

Mark Expired Memberships for Deletion

The Mark Expired Memberships for Deletion option marks for deletion all records of members whose membership expired 60 or more days ago (and was never renewed). The option performs this task automatically for the entire database, so that the user need not scroll through and mark these records one at a time. Here are the steps to assign the appropriate action to the menu option:

1. Press **PgDn** to move to the Mark Expired Memberships for Deletion option.
2. Select Change Action.
3. Select Perform File Operation.
4. Select Mark Records for Deletion.
5. Enter the expression **DATE( ) – Expires > 60 .AND. .NOT. Current** as the FOR option, as shown in Figure F.25.

The expression that you entered as the FOR option acts as a filter condition, just like the filter conditions you created in queries in Chapter 5. As with queries, the expression must result in a true or false verdict, as with the expression **PartNo = "A-111"** or **Qty < 10**. However, when using the Applications Generator, you do not stagger filter conditions onto separate rows to create AND and

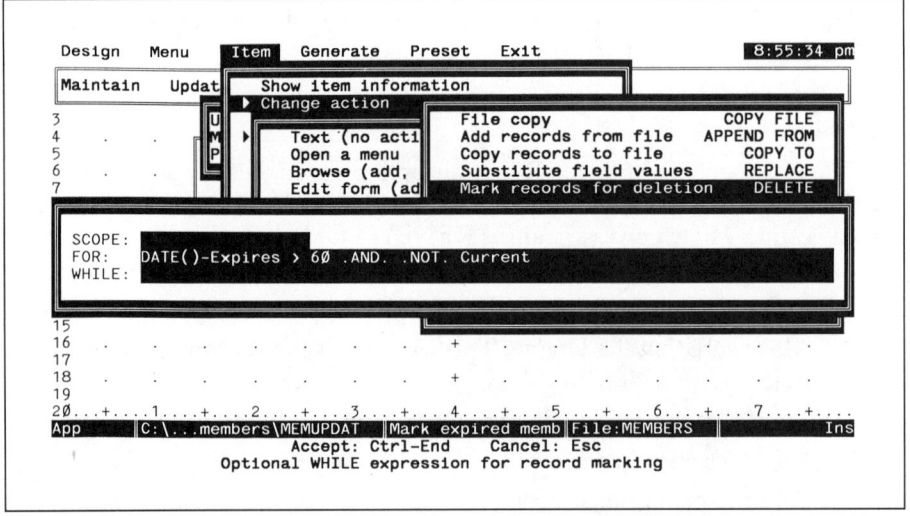

FIGURE F.25: FOR condition for marking expired memberships. Unlike the query design screen discussed in Chapter 5, applications use the dBASE IV programming syntax for filtering records, where .AND. specifies an AND search and .OR. specifies an OR search.

OR queries. Instead, you use the operator .AND. for an AND condition and the operator .OR. for an OR condition.

You can also use the .NOT. operator. When you use .NOT in an expression, dBASE isolates records that do not match the expression. For example, **.NOT PartNo = "AA-111"** displays all records that do *not* have A-111 in the PartNo field.

Logical data types always contain either a true or a false value, so you need not use a complete expression to test this particular data type. Just using a logical field name, such as CURRENT, implies the expression CURRENT = .T. Using the .NOT. operator in front of a Logical field name, as in the expression .NOT. CURRENT, is the same as using the expression CURRENT = .F.

To make complex expressions more readable, it is common practice to type function names, such as DATE( ), in all uppercase letters and to type field names, such as Expires, with only the first letter capitalized. However, you can use whatever uppercase and lowercase conventions you wish.

In this particular example, the filtering expression used as the FOR condition, **DATE( ) – Expires > 60 .AND. .NOT. Current**, specifies records with membership expiration dates that are 60 or more days "less than" (earlier than) the current date and in which membership has not been renewed (that is, the CURRENT field contains .F.). When the user selects this menu option, the application automatically marks such records for deletion.

To permanently delete records that are marked for deletion, the user needs to select the next menu option, Purge Marked Records. Before moving on to the next menu option, however, press **Ctrl-End** to save the current menu action.

PURGE MARKED RECORDS

The next item on the Update menu is Purge Marked Records. This option permanently removes all records that are marked for deletion. This purging includes records that were marked in the previous operation, as well as any that were marked by the user (using **Ctrl-U**) while editing or browsing. To assign an action to this option, follow these steps:

1. Press **PgDn** to move to the Purge Marked Records option (check the status bar to be sure you have the correct option).
2. Select Change Action.
3. Select Perform File Operation.
4. Select Discard Marked Records.
5. Select OK when prompted.

This completes the actions for the Update pull-down menu for the time being, until later when we create the RENEW.BCH batch process. For now, select Put

Away Current Menu from the Menu pull-down menu and Save Changes from the submenu.

Assigning Actions to the Print Menu

The Print pull-down menu in the membership application presents options for printing reports and mailing labels. To assign actions to these menu options, first make the Print menu the current object by selecting Pop-Up Menu from the Design pull-down menu. Then select MEMPRINT from the submenu that appears.

MEMBERSHIP ROSTER

The Membership Roster option allows the user to print a list of all members, using the format you created earlier and named ROSTER. To assign the appropriate action to this menu, follow these steps:

1. Press **F10** and select Change Action from the Item pull-down menu.
2. Select Display or Print.
3. Select Report.
4. Press Pick (**Shift-F1**) and select ROSTER.
5. Press ↵ to leave the HEADING box blank.
6. Complete other print options as follows (all are multiple-choice options that you can scroll through by pressing the space bar):

    Report format: FULL DETAIL
    Heading format: INCLUDE DATE AND PAGE
    Before printing: SKIP TO NEW PAGE
    Send output to: PRINTER

7. Press **Ctrl-End** when you are done.

ALL MAILING LABELS

The second option on the Print menu lets the user print all mailing labels. It uses the MEMLABEL format that you created earlier. Here are the steps to assign the action:

1. Press **PgDn** to scroll to the All Mailing Labels menu option.
2. Select Change Action.

3. Select Display or Print.
4. Select Labels.
5. Press Pick (**Shift-F1**) and select MEMLABEL.
6. Set the Send Output To option to PRINTER.
7. Set the Print Sample? option to Yes.
8. Press **Ctrl-End**.

Welcome Letters

The Welcome Letters option on the Print menu prints the WELCOME form letter for new members who joined in the current month. To assign the action to this menu option, use these steps:

1. Press **PgDn** to move to the Welcome Letters option.
2. Select Change Action.
3. Select Display or Print.
4. Select Report.
5. Press Pick (**Shift-F1**) and select Welcome from the Pick menu.
6. Fill in other options as shown in Figure F.26.

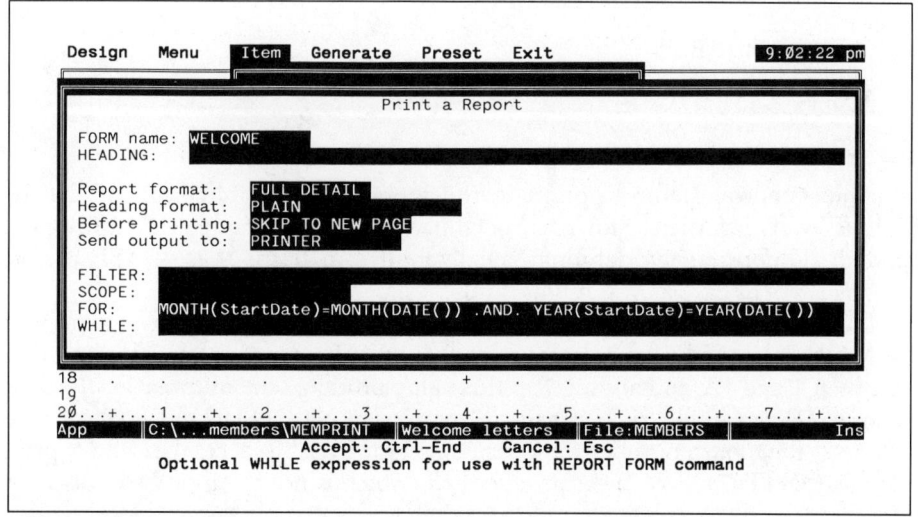

FIGURE F.26: Dialog box for printing welcome letters using the WELCOME report format created during the design phase. The FOR condition in the box limits printing welcome letters to members whose start date is the current month and year (that is, to new members).

Note the filter condition used with the FOR box:

MONTH(StartDate) = MONTH(DATE( )) .AND.
YEAR(StartDate) = YEAR(DATE( ))

This filter condition limits printing of the welcome letters to members who joined in the current month of the current year (that is, to this month's new members). Press **Ctrl-End** after filling in the dialog box.

WELCOME LABELS

The Welcome Labels option prints a mailing label for each letter that the Welcome Letters option printed. It uses the MEMLABEL format and the same filter condition that the Welcome Letters option uses. To assign the action, follow these steps:

1. Press **PgDn** to move to the Welcome Labels option.
2. Select Change Action.
3. Select Display or Print.
4. Select Labels.
5. Press Pick (**Shift-F1**) and select MEMLABEL as the label format.
6. In the FOR box, enter the filter condition

    MONTH(StartDate) = MONTH(DATE( )) .AND.
    YEAR(StartDate) = YEAR(DATE( )).

7. Press **Ctrl-End**.

RENEWAL LETTERS

The Renewal Letters option in the membership application prints the RENEWAL form letter for each person whose membership will expire next month. Unfortunately, defining "next month" in terms that dBASE understands is not as easy as you might think.

For the months January through November, "next month" can be expressed as MONTH(DATE( )) + 1, because the MONTH( ) function returns a number between 1 and 12, and adding 1 to this value produces the number for the next month. (For example, in January, the expression MONTH(DATE( )) + 1 produces 2, the month number for February.) However, in December, the expression MONTH(DATE( )) + 1 produces 13, which is not the month number for January.

To solve this problem, you can divide the month number by 12 and then add 1 to the *modulus* (the remainder after division, if you exclude decimal results) to determine the next month. This approach works because dividing any number less than 12 by 12 produces a modulus that equals the current month. For example, dividing month 1, January, by 12 (1/12) produces zero and a modulus of 1. Dividing February, month 2, by 12 produces zero and a modulus of 2. Dividing the twelfth month, December, by 12 (12/12) produces 1 and a modulus of zero; adding 1 to zero produces 1, the month after December.

The dBASE MOD( ) function returns the modulus of one argument divided by a second argument. Hence, the expression

MOD(MONTH(DATE( )),12)+1

always returns the number of the next month, even in December. But this does not solve all problems for the membership application, because renewal letters should be sent only to people whose memberships expire in the next month of the current year.

Once again, however, you cannot use the simple expression YEAR(DATE( )) to specify the current year, because in December, next month is also next year (that is, the month following December 1990 is January 1991). But if you divide any month number from January through November (month numbers 1 through 11) by 12, the integer portion of the division is zero (for example, 11/12 = 0, if you exclude the decimal portion of the result). Dividing month 12 (December) by 12 (12/12), however, produces 1. If you add the integer portion of the division results to the current year, the result will be the appropriate year.

To isolate the integer portion of a number (with the decimal value completely removed), you use the dBASE INT( ) function. Hence, the complete expression for isolating appropriate years in the EXPIRES field is

YEAR(Expires) = YEAR(DATE( )) + INT(MONTH(Expires)/12)

Actually, there is a third problem to contend with. The space allotted for a FOR filter condition in the Applications Generator does not provide enough room for the complete expression that renewal letters require:

MONTH(Expires) = MOD(MONTH(DATE( )),12+1 .AND. YEAR(Expires)
= YEAR(DATE( )) + INT(MONTH(Expires)/12).

However, there is a way around this limitation too, as you'll see in a moment.

Let's get back on track now and assign the appropriate action to the Renewal Letters menu option, following these steps:

1. Press **PgDn** until Renewal Letters appears in the status bar.
2. Select Change Action from the Item menu.
3. Select Display or Print.

DESIGNING AND DEVELOPING AN APPLICATION

4. Select Report.
5. Type the report format name **RENEWAL** or press Pick (**Shift-F1**) and select RENEWAL from the Pick submenu.
6. Fill in the rest of the Print a Report dialog box as shown in Figure F.27.

As you can see in the dialog box, both the FILTER and FOR options contain filter conditions. The FILTER condition

YEAR(Expires) = YEAR(DATE( )) + INT(MONTH(Expires)/12)

isolates records that have the appropriate expiration year (the current year for months January through November and the next year for December). The FOR condition

MONTH(Expires) = MOD(MONTH(DATE( )),12) + 1

isolates records that have expiration dates in the next month. The FOR and FILTER options are additive, so placing filter conditions in both is equivalent to placing the single long filter condition

YEAR(Expires) = YEAR(DATE( )) + INT(MONTH(Expires)/12) .AND. MONTH (Expires) = MOD(MONTH(DATE( )),12) + 1

into the FOR (or FILTER) condition box.

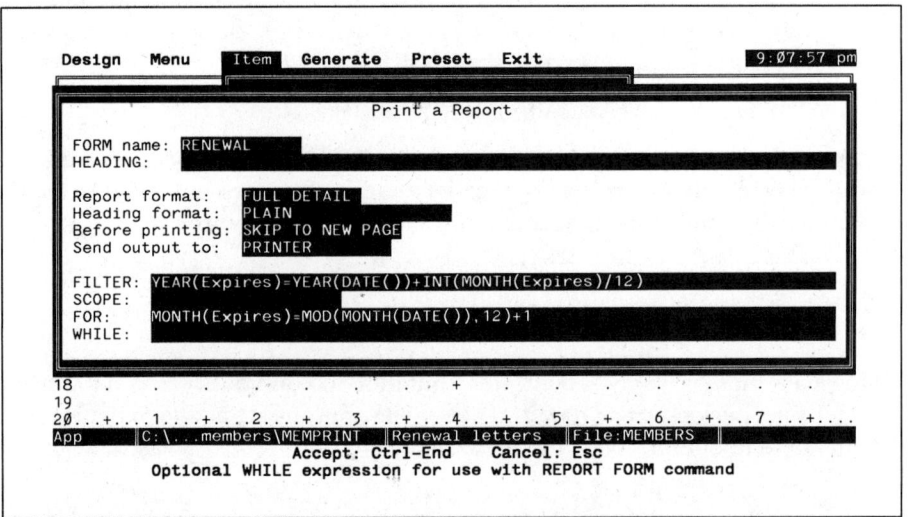

FIGURE F.27: Dialog box for printing renewal letters using the RENEWAL report format created during the design phase. The combined FILTER and FOR conditions limit printing of the letter to people whose memberships expire next month.

After filling in the dialog box (paying close attention to parentheses in the expressions), press **Ctrl-End**.

RENEWAL LABELS

Mailing labels for the renewal letters can be printed using the usual MEM-LABEL format and the same filter condition as is used to print renewal letters. Follow these steps to assign an action to the Renewal Labels menu option:

1. Press **PgDn** to move to the Renewal Labels menu option.
2. Select Change Action.
3. Select Display or Print.
4. Select Labels.
5. Fill in the Print Labels dialog box as shown in Figure F.28.
6. Press **Ctrl-End** after filling in the dialog box.

OVERDUE LETTERS

The Overdue Letters option prints the OVERDUE form letter for people whose memberships expired 30 or more days ago, and who still have not

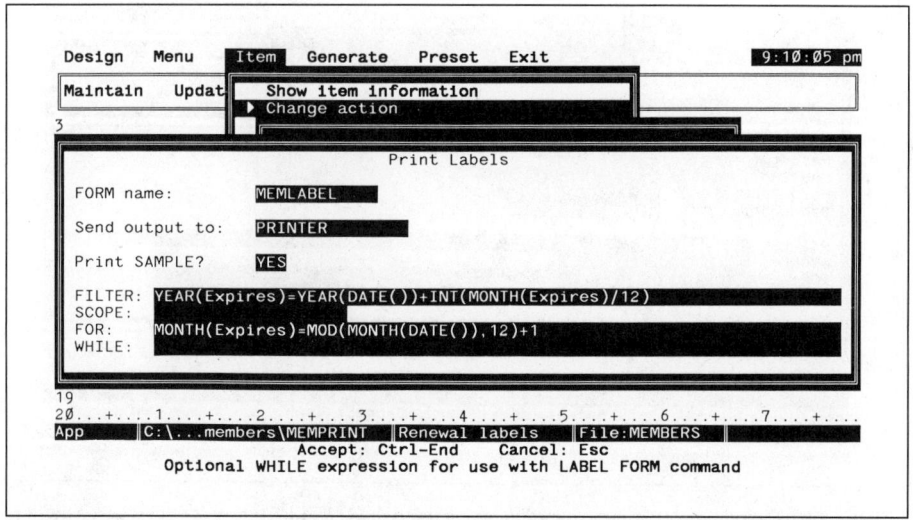

FIGURE F.28: Dialog box for printing renewal labels in conjunction with renewal letters. The dialog box specifies the MEMLABEL mailing label format. It also specifies the same FILTER and FOR conditions as the dialog box for printing the renewal letters.

renewed. Here are the steps to assign the action to the menu option:

1. Press **PgDn** to make Overdue Letters the current menu option.
2. Select Change Action.
3. Select Display or Print.
4. Select Report.
5. Fill in the screen as shown in Figure F.29.
6. Press **Ctrl-End**.

OVERDUE LABELS

The Overdue Labels option prints mailing labels for the overdue letters. It uses the MEMLABEL format and the same filter condition as the overdue letter. Here are the steps to assign the action:

1. Press **PgDn** to make Overdue Labels the current menu option.
2. Select Change Action.
3. Select Display or Print.
4. Select Labels.

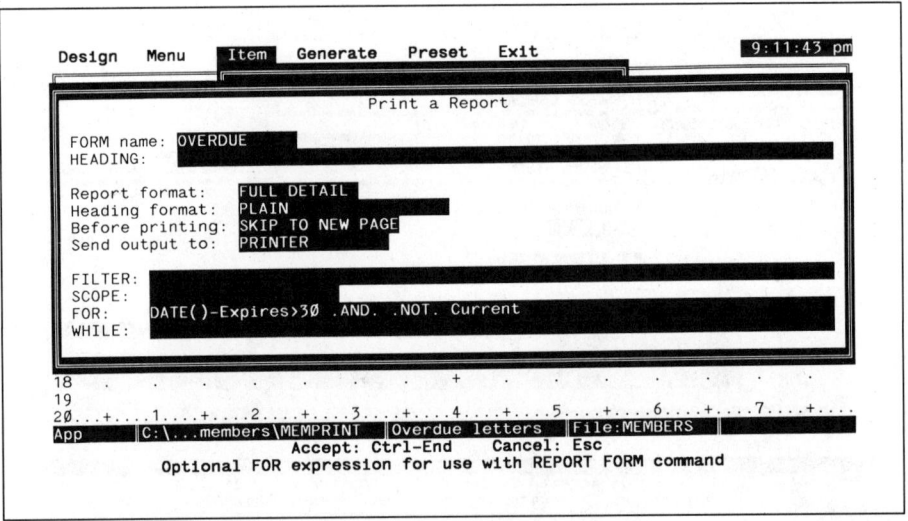

FIGURE F.29: Dialog box for printing overdue letters using the OVERDUE report format created during the design phase. The FOR condition limits printing of letters to people whose memberships expired more than 30 days ago, and who have not yet renewed.

5. Enter **MEMLABEL** as the label format.
6. Enter **DATE( ) – Expires > 30 .AND. .NOT. Current** as the FOR condition.
7. Press **Ctrl-End**.

This completes the menu options for the Print menu. To save the menu and put it away, select Put Away Current Menu from the Menu pull-down menu and Save Changes from the submenu.

Assigning Actions to the Membership Utilities Menu

To assign actions to the Utilities menu, first make it the current menu by pressing **F10** and selecting Pop-up Menu from the Design menu. Then select MEMUTIL from the submenu that appears. Now you can assign actions to the Utilities menu options.

Change System Date

The Change System Date option allows the user to change the current (system) date without exiting the application. It does this by running the external DOS command DATE. Here are the steps to assign the action to this option:

1. Press **F10** and select Change Action from the Item menu.
2. Select Run Program.
3. Select Run DOS Program.
4. Next to the prompt "Program:" enter the command **DATE**.
5. Press **Ctrl-End**.

Back Up Database to Drive A

The Back Up Database to Drive A option uses the DOS command COPY MEMBERS.* A: to copy MEMBERS.DBF and MEMBERS.MDX to a disk in drive A. Here are the steps to assign the action:

1. Press **PgDn** to move to the Back Up Database menu option.
2. Select Change Action.
3. Select Run Program.
4. Select Run DOS Program.
5. In the dialog box, enter **COPY** as the program name.

6. Enter **MEMBERS.* A:** in the parameters box.
7. Press **Ctrl-End**.

COPY APPLICATION TO DRIVE A

The Copy Application to Drive A command copies all files on the \DBASE \MEMBERS directory to a floppy disk in drive A. This option can be used both for making backup copies and for making extra copies to give to others to use. Here are the steps for assigning the action:

1. Press **PgDn** to move to the Copy Application to Drive A option.
2. Select Change Action.
3. Select Run Program.
4. Select Run DOS Program.
5. Enter **COPY** as the name of the program to run.
6. Enter ***.* A:** as the parameters.
7. Press **Ctrl-End**.

REPAIR CORRUPTED INDEXES

Repair Corrupted Indexes helps the user recover from power outages and other situations that can corrupt indexes. To assign the action to this menu option, follow these steps:

1. Press **PgDn** to move to the Repair Corrupted Indexes menu option.
2. Select Change Action.
3. Select Perform File Operation.
4. Select Reindex Database.
5. Select OK.

This completes the actions for the Utilities menu. Select Put Away Current Menu from the Menu pull-down menu and Save Changes from the submenu.

Assigning Actions to the Exit Menu

The Exit menu provides two options: Return to dBASE IV, which leaves the application and returns the user to the Control Center, and Exit to DOS, which returns the user to DOS. Make the Exit menu the current object by following the usual steps:

1. Press **F10** and select Pop-Up Menu from the Design pull-down menu.
2. Select MEMEXIT from the submenu.

RETURN TO dBASE IV

To assign the action to the Return to dBASE IV option, follow these steps:

1. Press **F10** and select Change Action from the Item menu.
2. Select Quit.
3. Select Return to Calling Program.
4. Select OK.

EXIT TO DOS

To assign the action to the Exit to DOS option, follow these steps:

1. Press **PgDn** to move to the next menu option.
2. Select Change Action.
3. Select Quit.
4. Select Quit to DOS.
5. Select OK.

Now you can select Put Away Current Menu from the Menu pull-down menu and Save Changes from the submenu.

You have now assigned an action to every menu option in the membership application. However, you still need to perform a few steps to complete the application.

BUILDING THE BATCH PROCESS

As you probably recall, the membership application uses a batch process to update memberships. You assigned the action Execute Batch Process to the Update This Month's Renewals menu option earlier and specified RENEW as the name of the batch process. Now you need to create that batch process. Two steps are involved: First you list the operations in the batch process, and then you assign an action to each operation. Let's create RENEW.BCH now.

Listing the Operations in the Batch Process

The first step is to list each operation (or step) in the batch process in plain English. This procedure is similar to writing options into a pop-up menu frame. Here are the steps:

1. Press **F10** and select Batch Process from the Design pull-down menu.
2. Select <create> from the submenu.
3. Enter **RENEW** as the batch-process name.
4. Enter **Automate monthly renewals** as the description.
5. Press **Ctrl-End**.
6. Press Size (**Shift-F7**) and widen the frame by at least two spaces. Then press ↵.
7. Type plain-English descriptions of each operation in the batch process, as shown in Figure F.30.

Assigning Actions to the Batch Process

Now you need to assign an action to each operation in the batch process, using a technique similar to that used to assign actions to menu options.

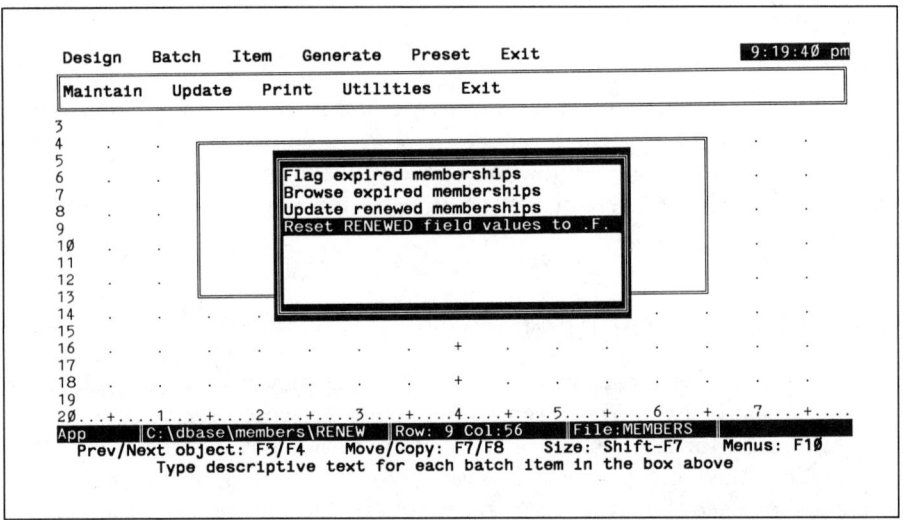

FIGURE F.30: Descriptions of batch-process operations typed into a batch process box. After typing the plain-English descriptions, you can assign an action to each description in much the same manner that you assign actions to menus.

Flag Expired Memberships

The Flag Expired Memberships operation in the batch process places .F. in the CURRENT field for all memberships that have expired. Follow these steps to assign the appropriate action:

1. Press ↑ until the topmost item in the box, Flag Expired Memberships, is highlighted.
2. Press **F10** and select Change Action from the Item pull-down menu.
3. Select Perform File Operation.
4. Select Substitute Field Values.
5. Fill in the Substitute Field Values dialog box as shown in Figure F.31.
6. Press **Ctrl-End** when you are done.

Browse Expired Memberships

The second operation in the batch process displays all expired memberships on a browse screen so the user can quickly and easily identify renewed memberships. To simplify matters further, the cursor is locked into the RENEWED field,

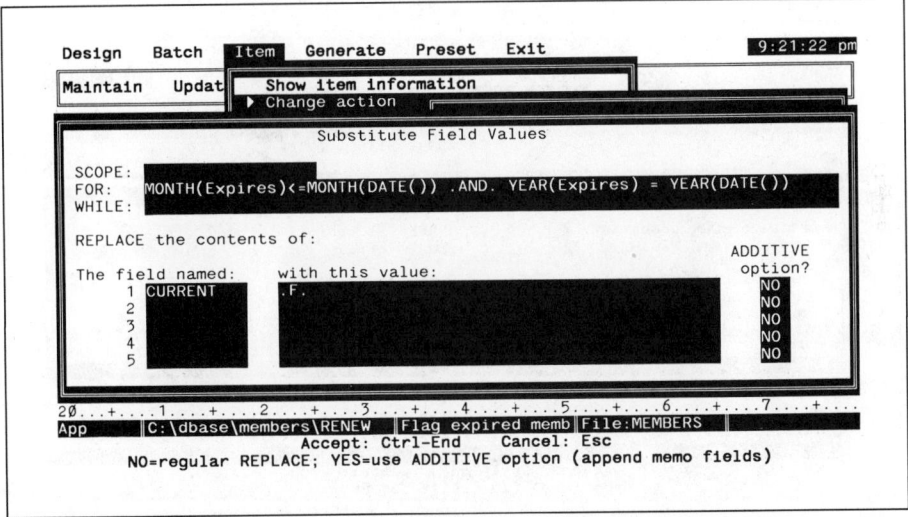

FIGURE F.31: The Substitute Field Values dialog box used for the first batch-process operation, Flag Expired Memberships. This action replaces the value in the field named CURRENT with an .F. for all people whose memberships expired in the current or previous month of the current year.

which is displayed in the leftmost column of the browse screen. Furthermore, the browse screen displays only selected, relevant fields.

To assign the appropriate action to this second batch-process operation, follow these steps:

1. Press **PgDn** to move to the next step, Browse Expired Memberships.
2. Select Change Action.
3. Select Browse and fill in the form as in Figure F.32.
4. Press **Ctrl-End**.

In Figure F.32, the FIELDS box lists the fields that are to be displayed on the browse screen, in the order in which they are to be displayed. The FILTER box indicates that only records with .F. in the CURRENT field are to be displayed. The maximum column width of 15 allows all the fields to fit on the screen (only the first 15 letters of the COMPANY field will be visible on the screen; all other fields are less than 15 characters wide).

The FREEZE Edit for Field: RENEWED option locks the cursor into the RENEWED field, thereby making it easier to scroll up and down from record to record without scrolling left and right. (You'll see this feature in action later when we test the application.)

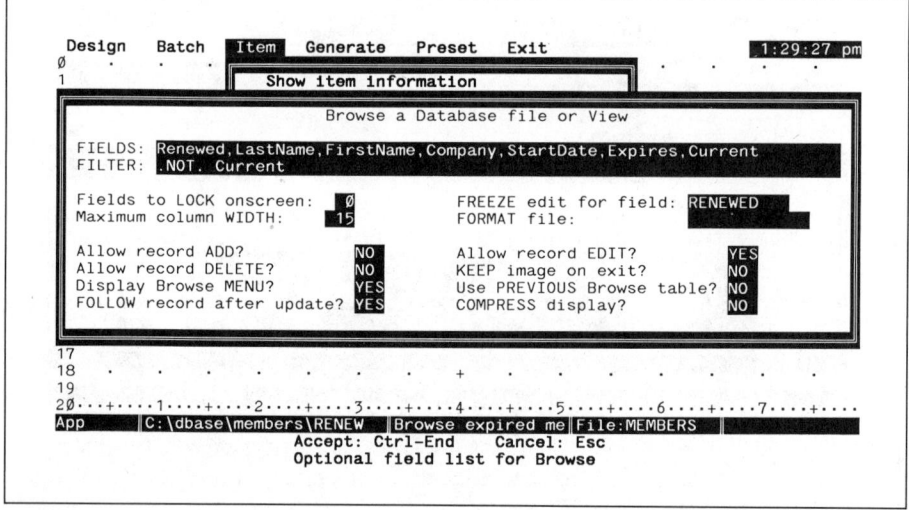

FIGURE F.32: The Browse a Database File or View dialog box is used for the second batch-process operation, Browse Expired Memberships. This dialog box tells dBASE to display the RENEWED, LASTNAME, FIRSTNAME, COMPANY, STARTDATE, EXPIRES, and CURRENT fields on a browse screen and to lock (freeze) the cursor into the RENEWED field.

Update Renewed Memberships

The third operation in the batch process changes the CURRENT field for all renewed memberships to .T. and increments their expiration dates by one year. Here are the steps to assign the appropriate action:

1. Press **PgDn** to move to the next batch operation.
2. Select Change Action.
3. Select Perform File Operation.
4. Select Substitute Field Values.
5. Fill in the dialog box as shown in Figure F.33.
6. Press **Ctrl-End**.

In Figure F.33, the FOR condition limits the operation to records that have .T. in the RENEWED field. For each of these renewed memberships, the date in the EXPIRED field is replaced with its current value plus 365 (thereby adding one year to the expiration date). The CURRENT field is changed to .T., indicating that the membership is now current.

Reset RENEWED Field to False

The fourth operation in the batch process resets the RENEWED field in all database records to false so that expiration dates are not accidentally extended by

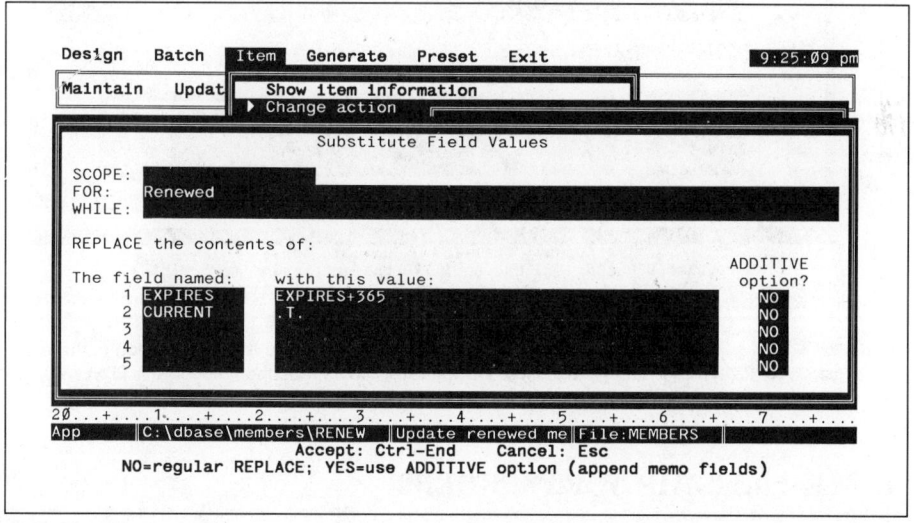

FIGURE F.33: The Substitute Field Values dialog box is used for the third operation in the batch process, Update Renewed Memberships. In this dialog box, we tell dBASE to change the CURRENT field to .T. and to add 365 days (one year) to the EXPIRED field for each renewed membership.

another year the next time the user updates memberships. To assign the action to this operation, follow these steps:

1. Press **PgDn** to move to the next batch operation.
2. Select Change Action.
3. Select Perform File Operation.
4. Select Substitute Field Values.
5. Fill in the Substitute Field Values form as in Figure F.34.
6. Press **Ctrl-End**.

In Figure F.34, the SCOPE box indicates that the operation should include all records in the database, and that the RENEWED field needs to be set to .F.

You have now completed the RENEW.BCH batch process. To put away the batch process application object, select Put Away Current Batch Process from the Batch pull-down menu. When prompted, select Save Changes.

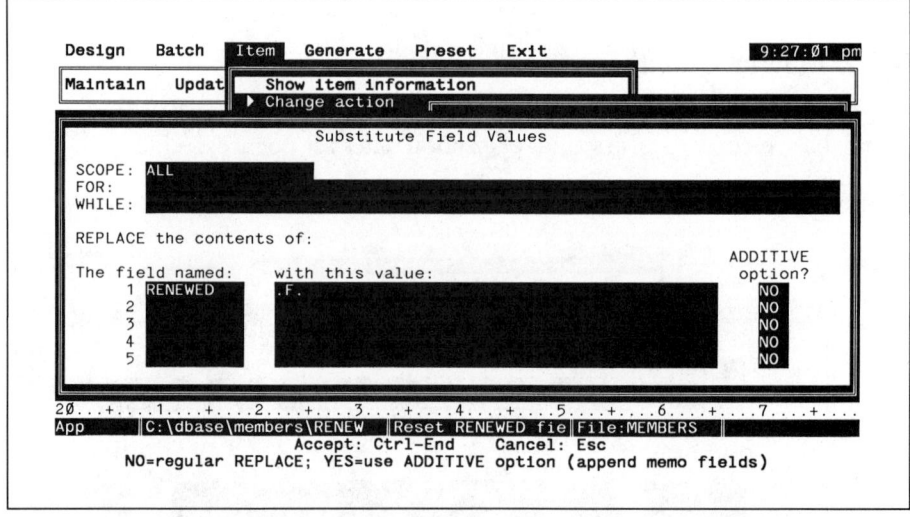

FIGURE F.34: The Substitute Field Values dialog box is also used for the fourth operation in the batch process, Reset RENEWED Field to False. Here we tell dBASE to change the value of the RENEWED field in all database records to .F.

DEFINING MEMBERSHIP SORT ORDERS

As you may recall, when we began developing the membership application, we defined MEMBERS as the default database and LASTNAME as the default index order. All options that display data (such as edit and browse options and the options for various reports) use these default settings. However, we want letters and mailing labels to be printed in zip code order, so we need to override the default settings for a few menu options.

1. Select Pop-Up Menu from the Design pull-down menu.
2. Select MEMPRINT from the submenu.
3. Press ↓ to highlight All Mailing Labels.
4. Press **F10**.
5. Select Reassign Index Order from the Item pull-down menu.
6. When the prompt *Set ORDER to:* appears, type **ZIP** and press ↵.
7. Press **PgDn** to move to the next menu option.

Repeat steps 5 through 7 six times to assign the ZIP index order to the remaining report and label options. When you are done, select Put Away Current Menu from the Menu pull-down menu and select Save Changes.

GENERATING THE MEMBERSHIP APPLICATION

The membership application is now complete, but before you can use it, you need to *generate* the application program (or *code*). This step is not automatic when you develop an application, as it is with forms and reports. Follow these steps to generate the application program:

1. Press **F10** and select Select Template from the Generate pull-down menu.
2. If MENU.GEN is not already displayed, press **Ctrl-Y** to delete the current file name. Then type **MENU.GEN** and press ↵.
3. Select Display during Generation from the same Generate pull-down menu and Yes from the submenu that appears. (This step allows you to watch dBASE generate the application on the screen.)
4. Select Begin Generating.

You will see the program code that the Applications Generator creates pass by in a window on the application design screen. When program generation is complete, you'll see the message *Generation is complete—press any key to continue*. Press any key and proceed.

Generating Documentation

The Applications Generator can also create written documentation that shows each menu in the application, the action assigned to each menu item, and various settings such as screen colors and indexes used. (An example appears in the section "Printing the Documentation" later in this appendix.) You can use this documentation later when modifying and refining your application.

Follow these steps to create this written documentation:

1. Choose the Select Template option from the Generate pull-down menu.
2. Enter **DOCUMENT.GEN** as the template to use.
3. Select Begin Generating.
4. Enter either **Y** or **N** when asked if you have an IBM graphics or compatible printer (enter **N** if you are not sure).

When the document is completed, you'll again be prompted to press any key. Press any key and then leave the Applications Generator. Press Menus (**F10**) and select Save All Changes and Exit from the Exit pull-down menu. You'll be returned to the Control Center. Now you are ready to test the completed application.

TESTING THE COMPLETED APPLICATION

Before you give your completed application to a user (or before you use the application for serious work, if *you* are the user), you need to test it thoroughly. Use the application with some sample data and try every menu option. This section describes how to use the finished application and also provides a few examples for testing the application.

Running the Membership Application

To run the membership application, highlight MEMMGR in the Control Center Application panel, press ←┘, and select Run Application. Select Yes from the dialog box that appears. After a few seconds, you'll see the sign-on banner. Press ←┘ to move on to the menus. You'll see the application's horizontal menu bar and the Maintain pull-down menu on the screen.

You can use the arrow keys to scroll through menu options in the usual manner. Note, however, that the highlight will not land on text within a menu. Figure F.35 shows the application menu bar and Print pull-down menu on the screen.

Now test each option to make sure the application works as expected.

Adding New Members

To add new members to the database, select Add New Members from the Maintain menu. dBASE displays a blank form for entering new records. The

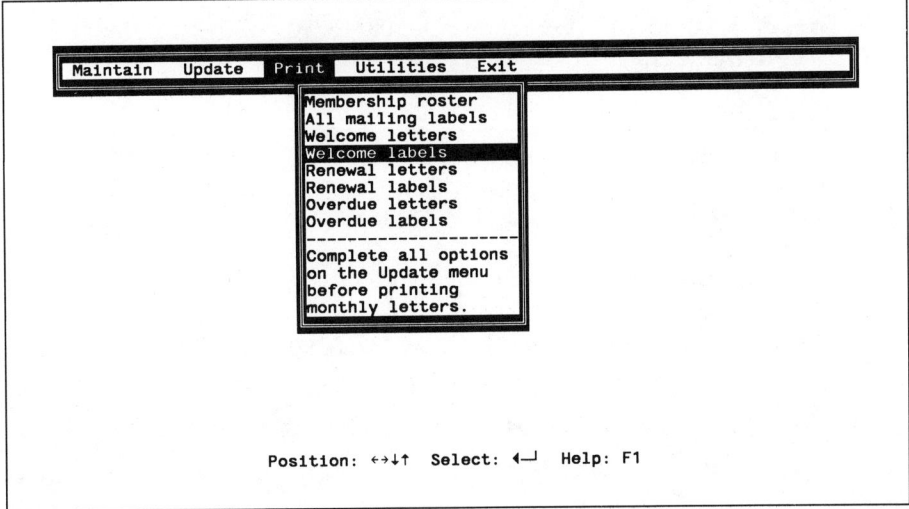

FIGURE F.35: Print menu in the membership application displayed on the screen. Note that you cannot move the highlight to the menu text, because you assigned no action to the text. (The text is displayed in the menu for information only.)

default starting date should match the current system date, and the default expiration date should be one year beyond the starting date.

For testing purposes, enter the following three records, using the dates specified in the samples rather than the default dates shown on your screen:

```
Mr. Bob B. Baker
Boeing International
Ballistics Dep't.
2744 Bering St.
El Monte, CA 91704
(818)555-1232   Ext. 999
Status: REGULAR
Start date: 02/01/89    Expiration date: 02/01/90
Dues Current?: Y

Miss Cara C. Carlson
Cookie Haven
Purchasing Dep't.
3211 Cantamar
Cucamonga, CA 91655
(818)555-9988
```

Status: OFFICER
Start date: 03/15/89   Expiration date: 03/15/90
Dues Current?: Y

Dr. Deedra D. Davis
Doctor's Hosptal
15th Floor
8843 Donga Dr.
Duarte, CA 91555
(818)555-9910   Ext. 8851
Status: REGULAR
Start date: 04/30/89   Expiration date: 04/30/90
Dues current? Y

After entering the sample records, select Exit from the Exit pull-down menu to return to the application menu.

Changing Member Data

The application offers two options for editing membership data: Browse All Members and Change/Delete a Member. Test each method now (but don't change any starting or expiration dates). Note that records should be displayed in alphabetical order by last name.

You should be able to perform an index search from either the custom form or the browse screen. To test this, press Menu (**F10**) and select Index Key Search from the Go To pull-down menu. Enter a valid last name, such as Carlson (with proper upper- and lowercase letters), and press ⏎.

You can mark (and unmark) any record for deletion using the usual **Ctrl-U** keystroke. (The *Del* indicator appears in the status bar.) For the current test session, however, do not leave any records marked for deletion yet.

After testing each option, select Exit from the Exit pull-down menu to return to the membership application main menu.

Updating the Membership Roster

Suppose now that you are the application user, and you want to update the membership database to show renewed memberships and to delete records where memberships have expired. The following sections present the steps you need to take (performing these steps also tests the application).

CHECK THE SYSTEM DATE

First, make sure that the current (system) date is accurate. For testing purposes, assume that the current date is March 30, 1990. Select Change System Date from the Utilities pull-down menu. The following DOS prompt appears on the screen (with the actual system date displayed in place of Mon 1-02-90):

```
Current date is Mon 1-02-90
Enter new date (mm-dd-yy): _
```

Type the test date 3-31-90 and press ⏎. Then press any key to return to the menu.

UPDATE THIS MONTH'S RENEWALS

Next, select Update This Month's Renewals from the Update pull-down menu. You'll see a brief message as the application places F in the CURRENT field of expired memberships. Then a browse screen will appear showing the expired memberships, as in Figure F.36.

Mark the record for Carlson with a **T** (assume that hers is the only renewed membership). Note that the cursor stays locked into the RENEWED field, even if you press ← or →.

After updating the one record, select Exit from the Exit pull-down menu. You'll see some brief messages as the application updates the records with renewed memberships. Then you'll be returned to the application main menu.

To verify that the update was accurate, select either Browse All Members or Change/Delete a Member from the Maintain pull-down menu. You should see Carlson's membership extended to 1991, and the CURRENT field for the record marked T. Select Exit from the Exit pull-down menu to return to the membership application main menu.

DELETE EXPIRED MEMBERSHIPS

Now it's time to test deleting memberships that expired 60 or more days ago and have not been renewed. Select Mark Expired Memberships for Deletion from the Update pull-down menu. You'll see a brief message as the application marks one record for deletion (Andy Adams' record). Next, select Purge Marked Records from the Update menu. Again, you'll see a message as the application packs the database.

To verify that the deletion was performed correctly, select Browse All Members from the Maintain pull-down menu. You'll see that Andy Adams' record has been permanently deleted.

```
┌─────────────────────────────────────────────────────────────────────┐
│  Records      Fields     Go To     Exit                 3:25:54 pm  │
│ ┌────────┬─────────┬──────────┬───────────────┬─────────┬─────────┬─────────┐
│ │RENEWED │LASTNAME │FIRSTNAME │COMPANY        │STARTDATE│EXPIRES  │CURRENT  │
│ │   F    │ Adams   │ Andy     │ ABC Technology│ 01/01/89│ 01/01/90│ F       │
│ │   F    │ Baker   │ Bob      │ Boeing Internat│02/01/89│ 02/01/90│ F       │
│ │   F    │ Carlson │ Cara     │ Cookie Haven  │ 03/15/89│ 03/15/90│ F       │
│ │        │         │          │               │         │         │         │
│ └────────┴─────────┴──────────┴───────────────┴─────────┴─────────┴─────────┘
│  Browse    C:\...members\MEMBERS    Rec 1/4      File                │
│                         View and edit fields                         │
└─────────────────────────────────────────────────────────────────────┘
```

FIGURE F.36: Expired memberships ready for renewal in the sample membership application. Only expired memberships are displayed, and you can mark renewed memberships with a T.

Printing the Membership Roster

At any time during the month, the user can print a list of all members by selecting Membership Roster from the Print pull-down menu. If you test this capability now, the application will print a list of all members currently in the MEMBERS database. These should be in alphabetical order.

Printing All Mailing Labels

If you select All Mailing Labels from the Print pull-down menu, the application should print a sample mailing label and display the message *Do you want more samples? (Y/N)*. Type **Y** if you want to test the label alignment again or **N** to begin printing labels. The application should print three mailing labels in zip code order and then return you to the application menus.

Printing Renewal Letters and Labels

Each month the user can print letters and labels, reminding members whose memberships expire next month that it's time to renew. Select Renewal Letters from the Print pull-down menu. The application should print a letter for Deedra Davis, whose membership expires next month (April 1990). Select Renewal Labels, and the application will print a label for this member.

Printing Overdue Letters and Labels

Each month the user can print overdue letters and labels, reminding late payers that their memberships expired last month, and that they still have not renewed. Currently, Bob Baker is the only member who meets this description (his membership expired in February 1990, and he has not renewed yet).

Select Overdue Letters from the Print pull-down letter. You should see a single letter printed for Bob Baker. Select Overdue Labels from the Print pull-down menu to print a mailing label for this letter.

Printing Welcome Letters and Labels

Each month, the user can print a batch of welcome letters and matching mailing labels for all new members (those who joined in the current month and year). Currently, no records in the test database meet this description, so you'll need to alter the current date to test-print at least one letter. Select Change System Date from the Utilities pull-down menu and change the current date to **3-31-89**. (This procedure is for testing purposes only; you would use real dates when actually putting the membership application to work.)

Select Welcome Letters from the Print pull-down menu. You should see a welcome letter printed for Cara Carlson. Select Welcome Labels. After printing samples, you should see a single label, again for Cara Carlson.

You may now want to reset the date to the actual current date.

Testing the Utilities

You've already had a chance to test the Change System Date option on the Utilities menu. Now you can test the other three options on that menu. If you have a blank, formatted disk available, place it in drive A of your computer and select Back Up Database to Drive A from the Utilities pull-down menu. You should hear the disk drive whir and see the file names MEMBERS.DBF and MEMBERS.MDX on the screen as the application makes the backup copy.

Next, select Copy Application to Drive A from the Utilities menu. Once again, you should hear the disk drive and see the names of all files being copied on the screen as the application copies the entire \DBASE\MEMBERS subdirectory to the disk in drive A.

Finally, select Repair Corrupted Indexes from the Utilities menu to test that option. (Even though the indexes are probably not corrupted at the moment, the option still will rebuild them.) You'll see several messages on the screen as the indexes are rebuilt.

Exiting the Application

If you select Return to dBASE IV from the Exit pull-down menu, you'll be returned to the Control Center. Selecting Exit to DOS from the Exit pull-down menu returns you to the DOS prompt.

MODIFYING THE MEMBERSHIP APPLICATION

If you discovered an error during your testing phase, or if you wish to refine the application, use the Applications Generator to make changes. This section discusses general techniques for modifying an existing application.

Printing the Documentation

We used the Applications Generator to generate some documentation earlier in this appendix. You might want to make a printed copy of this document now, as it can be handy when you are making changes. The document is always stored with the same name as the application, but with the extension .DOC (the documentation is stored as MEMMGR.DOC in this example). To print this documentation, first exit dBASE IV and return to the DOS prompt. Be sure you are logged on to the \DBASE\MEMBERS directory and then type the command

```
TYPE MEMMGR.DOC >PRN
```

Press ↵ after typing the command. If you have a laser printer that won't eject the last printed page, enter the following command at the DOS prompt (hold down the **Ctrl** key and press the letter **L** where you see **<Ctrl-L>**):

```
ECHO <Ctrl-L> >PRN
```

The command will appear on the screen as ECHO ^L >PRN. Press ↵ after entering the command.

The documentation will provide pictures of all menus and descriptions of the actions and objects assigned to each menu option. For example, page 9 of the MEMMGR application documentation displays this information for the Print menu Welcome Letters option:

```
-------------------------------------------------------------
Bar: 3
Prompt: Welcome letters
Action: Run Report Form WELCOME.frm
Command Options:
FOR MONTH(StartDate) = MONTH(DATE( )).AND.
```

```
YEAR(StartDate) = YEAR(DATE( ))
Print mode: Send to default printer
Set Order to: ZIP
```

If any options in your application are not working as expected, the first place you should check is the printed documentation to see what the action *is* doing. Then you can return to the Applications Generator and make changes if necessary.

Returning to the Applications Generator

When you are ready to modify your application, follow these steps to return to the Applications Generator:

1. Highlight the application name in the Application panel of the Control Center.
2. Press ⏎ and select Modify Application from the dialog box.

When you get back to the application design screen, you can select a particular menu by selecting the type of object from the Design pull-down menu (for example, by selecting Horizontal Bar Menu or Pop-Up Menu) and then, from the submenu that appears, the name of the object you wish to use (for example, MEMPRINT).

As discussed previously, you can resize or move the menu using the Size and Move keys. You can delete options by pressing **Ctrl-Y** and insert options pressing **Ctrl-N**. (If the frame is already tightened around the menu options, you'll need to expand it to make room for an insertion.)

To change all or any part of an action assigned to a menu option, highlight the menu option and select Change Action from the Item pull-down menu. The action currently assigned to the menu option will be highlighted in all submenus. You can keep or change the current action on any submenu.

Saving Your Changes

Remember that any changes you make to an application will *not* be reflected in the actual application until you save those changes and regenerate the entire application. Therefore, any time that you make a change to an application, you should follow these exact steps before leaving the Applications Generator design screen:

1. Select Clear Work Surface from the Menu, Batch, or Application pull-down menu.

2. When prompted, select Save Changes.
3. Choose Select Template from the Generate pull-down menu and make sure MENU.GEN is in use.
4. Select Begin Generating from the Generate pull-down menu.
5. Enter **Y** when asked whether to overwrite the existing application.
6. If you want to regenerate the documentation, choose Select Template and use DOCUMENT.GEN.
7. From the Generate menu, select Begin Generating.
8. Enter **Y** when asked whether to overwrite the existing documentation.
9. Select the Save All Changes and Exit option from the Exit pull-down menu.

REFINING THE MEMBERSHIP APPLICATION

When we created the membership application, we did not add help screens or message-line prompts. If you want to add some of these now, highlight MEMMGR in the Application panel of the Control Center, press ↵, and select Modify Application.

Adding Message-Line Prompts

Currently, the application always displays the prompt *Position:* ← → ↓ ↑ *Select:* ↵ *Help: F1* on the message line. You can replace this default prompt with your own prompt. In fact, you can assign a different message-line prompt to each menu option in your application to provide further instructions or information about each option to your user. (A message-line prompt appears when a menu option is highlighted.)

To add message-line prompts, follow these general steps (this example uses the Add New Members option from the Maintain menu):

1. Select Pop-Up Menu from the Design pull-down menu.
2. Select MEMMAINT.
3. Highlight Add New Members.
4. Select Assign Message Line Prompt from the Item pull-down menu.
5. Type the message-line prompt **Add new members to the membership database** and press ↵.

You can press **PgDn** to scroll to the next item and then add a message-line prompt for that menu item. After assigning prompts to all items, select Put Away

Current Menu from the Menu pull-down menu and Save Changes from the dialog box.

You can repeat the preceding steps for each menu and menu option in the application, substituting appropriate text. You can make up your own message-line prompt for each menu option.

Adding Custom Help Screens

You can also add a custom help screen to each menu option, which the user will see when he or she presses **F1** when the option is highlighted. To add custom help screens to your application, use the same basic steps as for adding message-line prompts, but rather than selecting Assign Message Line Prompt from the Item pull-down menu, select Write Help Text. You'll be given an entire screenful of space in which to type your help text. (Press **Ctrl-End** when you are done.) Again, remember to select Put Away Current Menu and Save Changes after adding help screens.

Don't forget to regenerate the entire application after adding message-line prompts and help screens.

Using the Membership Application

If you have actual data to store in the membership database, delete the example records by selecting Browse All Members from the Maintain pull-down menu. Mark each record for deletion using **Ctrl-U** and exit from the browse screen. Then select Purge Marked Records from the Update pull-down menu.

Next, type at least some portion of your real data. When you start using the membership system with real data, keep in mind these points:

- When you first run the application, select Change System Date from the Utilities menu and correct the current system date, if necessary.
- Always print monthly letters on the same day each month (preferably on the last day of the month).
- If for some reason you miss a month and want to print the previous month's letters in the current month, change the system date to the month for which you are printing the letters. For example, if you don't print February's letters until March 2, change the system date to February 28, so that the application behaves as though the month were still February. Be sure to restore the correct system date when you are done.
- Before printing any monthly letters, always perform all the operations on the Update menu in the order they are presented. That is, update the

month's memberships, mark the expired memberships, and purge the marked records. This will ensure that your mailing is based on current, accurate data.

- Back up the database to a disk in drive A at least once a month, using the Back Up Database to Drive A option on the Utilities pull-down menu. The best time to make this backup copy is after you print monthly letters, when the database is up to date.

- You can designate renewed memberships by placing **T** in the RENEWED field when using the Browse All Members option on the Maintain pull-down menu. However, don't change the expiration date if you do so. The next time you select Update This Month's Renewals from the Update menu, the expiration date will be extended by one year (so long as the RENEWED field still contains .T.).

If you were previously using a manual technique to manage your membership records, you may want to use both the manual technique and the membership application for a few months to make sure the application performs the way you want it to. This is called running the application in parallel with the existing system and is one of the most common techniques for testing all types of applications.

TIPS AND TRAPS

- Storing all the files for an application on a unique directory prevents the dBASE IV home directory from becoming cluttered with file names. This method also helps the application more easily find its own files.

- Before you use the Applications Generator to create an application, you should create all the database objects, such as databases, report formats, and custom forms, and sketch out a menu structure for the application.

- When you convert pop-up menus to pull-down menus, the pull-down menus inherit characteristics, such as colors and the default database, from the horizontal bar menu.

- Whenever you change an application, your changes are not incorporated into the application until you choose the Select Template option from the Generate pull-down menu, specify MENU.GEN as the template to use, and then select Begin Generating.

- The DOCUMENT.GEN template creates written documentation about your application, for your future reference.

SUMMARY

This appendix has provided an example of using the dBASE IV Applications Generator to create an application. The basic steps presented here hold true for all applications that you develop. That is, you first create the various menus, attach actions to each item on each menu, and then generate the application programs.

For information about creating database files:

- Chapter 2, "Creating a Database File"

For more information about indexing:

- Chapter 4, "Sorting the Database"

For more information about creating custom forms:

- Chapter 10, "Creating Custom Forms"

For more information about creating report formats:

- Chapter 7, "Designing Formatted Reports"

For more information about creating and using directories:

- Appendix B, "Commonly Used DOS Commands"

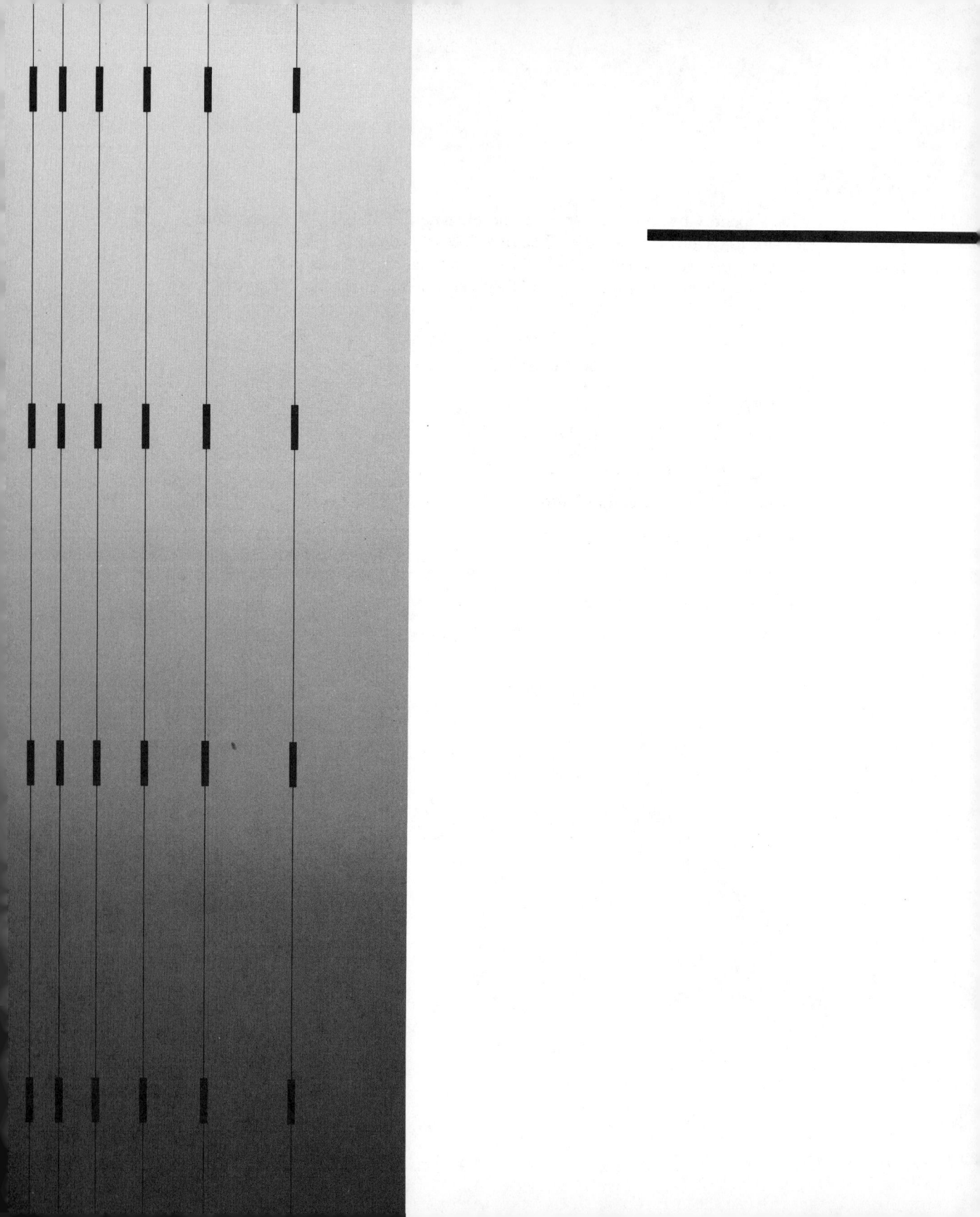

ASCII Table

APPENDIX G

ASCII Table

ASCII VALUE	CHARACTER	ASCII VALUE	CHARACTER
000	(null)	037	%
001	☺	038	&
002	●	039	'
003	♥	040	(
004	♦	041	)
005	♣	042	*
006	♠	043	+
007	(beep)	044	,
008	■	045	-
009	(tab)	046	.
010	(line feed)	047	/
011	(home)	048	0
012	(form feed)	049	1
013	(carriage return)	050	2
014	♪	051	3
015	☼	052	4
016	►	053	5
017	◄	054	6
018	↕	055	7
019	‼	056	8
020	¶	057	9
021	§	058	:
022	▬	059	;
023	↨	060	<
024	↑	061	=
025	↓	062	>
026	→	063	?
027	←	064	@
028	(cursor right)	065	A
029	(cursor left)	066	B
030	(cursor up)	067	C
031	(cursor down)	068	D
032	(space)	069	E
033	!	070	F
034	"	071	G
035	#	072	H
036	$	073	I

ASCII TABLE

ASCII VALUE	CHARACTER	ASCII VALUE	CHARACTER
074	J	113	q
075	K	114	r
076	L	115	s
077	M	116	t
078	N	117	u
079	O	118	v
080	P	119	w
081	Q	120	x
082	R	121	y
083	S	122	z
084	T	123	{
085	U	124	|
086	V	125	}
087	W	126	~
088	X	127	⌂
089	Y	128	Ç
090	Z	129	ü
091	[	130	é
092	\	131	â
093	]	132	ä
094	^	133	à
095	_	134	å
096	`	135	ç
097	a	136	ê
098	b	137	ë
099	c	138	è
100	d	139	ï
101	e	140	î
102	f	141	ì
103	g	142	Ä
104	h	143	Å
105	i	144	É
106	j	145	æ
107	k	146	Æ
108	l	147	ô
109	m	148	ö
110	n	149	ò
111	o	150	û
112	p	151	ù

ASCII TABLE — 911

ASCII VALUE	CHARACTER	ASCII VALUE	CHARACTER
152	ÿ	191	┐
153	Ö	192	└
154	Ü	193	┴
155	¢	194	┬
156	£	195	├
157	¥	196	─
158	Pt	197	┼
159	ƒ	198	╞
160	á	199	╟
161	í	200	╚
162	ó	201	╔
163	ú	202	╩
164	ñ	203	╦
165	Ñ	204	╠
166	ª	205	═
167	º	206	╬
168	¿	207	╧
169	⌐	208	╨
170	¬	209	╤
171	½	210	╥
172	¼	211	╙
173	¡	212	╘
174	«	213	╒
175	»	214	╓
176	░	215	╫
177	▒	216	╪
178	▓	217	┘
179	│	218	┌
180	┤	219	█
181	╡	220	▄
182	╢	221	▌
183	╖	222	▐
184	╕	223	▀
185	╣	224	α
186	║	225	β
187	╗	226	Γ
188	╝	227	π
189	╜	228	Σ
190	╛	229	σ

ASCII TABLE

ASCII VALUE	CHARACTER	ASCII VALUE	CHARACTER
230	μ	243	$\leq$
231	τ	244	$\int$
232	Φ	245	J
233	θ	246	$\div$
234	Ω	247	$\approx$
235	δ	248	°
236	∞	249	•
237	$\emptyset$	250	·
238	ϵ	251	$\sqrt{}$
239	$\cap$	252	n
240	$\equiv$	253	²
241	$\pm$	254	■
242	$\geq$	255	(blank 'F F')

INDEX

\# (pound sign)
  in custom form field templates, 326
  as index indicator, 157, 431
  as relational operator, 132, 175
$ (dollar sign)
  as financial format picture function, 179
  as relational operator, 132
- (hyphen)
  in custom form field templates, 326
  in date displays, 505-506
− (minus sign), as arithmetic operator, 176
\ (backslash), in directory names, 778-779
^ (caret)
  as arithmetic operator, 176
  as exponential format picture function, 179
* (asterisk), as arithmetic operator, 176
** (two asterisks), as exponentiation indicator/operator, 176
*** (three asterisks), as number overflow indicator, 177
{ } (curly braces)
  as date indicators, 130, 170, 337
  as picture function indicators, 330
  as printer escape code indicators, 305
  as special key indicator in macros, 449
+ (plus sign), as arithmetic operator, 176
: (colon), in directory names, 778
; (semicolon), in key assignment commands, 709-710
= (equal sign)
  as relational operator, 132, 175
  use of to form double lines in reports, 188-190
< > (angle brackets or greater/less than symbols)
  in dBASE IV command syntax, 669
  in DOS prompt, 782
  as relational operators, 132, 175
? (question mark), in dBASE IV command syntax, 669

' (apostrophe), in delimited files, 491
, (comma)
  in delimited files, 490-491
  displaying numbers with, 177
  placing in label text, 273
! (exclamation point), in custom form field templates, 326
( ) (parentheses)
  as arithmetic operator, 176
  in custom form field templates, 326
  as negative number symbols, 179
  for refining filter conditions, 577
. (period), 73
  in date displays, 505-506
  in file name extensions, 780
" (quotation marks)
  in custom forms, 349
  in delimited files, 491, 500
  in search conditions, 127, 170
  in sign-on banners, 536
/ (slash)
  as arithmetic operator, 176
  in date displays, 505-506
  in dBASE IV command syntax, 669
[ ] (square brackets)
  in dBASE IV command syntax, 669
  as margin indicators, 66
_ (underline character), in directory names, 778

A

Accept Value When (custom form edit option), 333, 338
access levels
  assigning, 735-736
  for users, 724
actions assignable to application objects, 571-579. *See also* membership management system example

assigning message line prompts, 632–634
dimming menu items, 623–624
discarding marked records, 603–605
displaying data on browse screen, 582–585
displaying data in custom form, 585–587
displaying or printing data, 588–594
displaying windows, 628–631
embedding code, 622–623
exiting application, 620–621
importing/exporting files, 609–612
indexing/reindexing, 605–608
marking/unmarking records for deletion, 602–603
No Action option, 579–580
opening menus, 581–582
overriding default database or view, 621–622
performing file operations, 595–599
positioning record pointer, 624–627
reassigning index order, 628
running programs/batch processes/macros, 612–620
sorting database files, 608–609
substituting field values, 599–601
viewing item assigned, 572–573
writing help text, 632
adding fields, records. *See* fields; records
addition, operator for, 176. *See also* calculations
Additive Option? (Change Action/Perform File Operations/Substitute Field Value submenu option), 601
"Add new records?" message, 37
Add Record from File/Array (Change Action/File Operation/Add Records submenu option), 597
ALL option, for use with SCOPE conditional operator, 578
Allow Record Add?/Edit?/Delete? (Change Action/Browse or Edit submenu options), 583–584, 586
Alternate (DBSETUP/Files menu option), 710
Alt key, in macros, 450, 456
AND/OR logic

searching with, 137–142, 170
using in applications design, 576–577
angle brackets (< >)
in dBASE IV command syntax, 669
in DOS prompt, 782
as relational operators, 132, 175
apostrophes ('), in delimited files, 491
appending groups of records, 390–394
APPEND update operator, 376
.APP file name extensions, 464, 677
Application Definition dialog box, 518–521
application design screen, 521–524
applications. *See also* actions assignable to application objects; Applications Generator; defaults; membership management system example
creating, 518–521
default settings for, 524–535, 538–539, 621–622
designing, 837–841
dimming menu items (making unavailable) in, 623–624
embedding programming language in, 564–565, 622–623
generating documentation for, 646–648
generating source code for, 639–646
naming, 519, 525–526
positioning record pointer in, 624–627
quick development of, 539–541
running, 648, 650–652
Applications Generator. *See also* membership management system example
action assignment in, 870–887
application definition in, 859–860
assigning actions to objects from, 571–572
banner/menu definition in, 861–869
default settings for, 652–656
improved in dBASE IV, 794
object handling in, 869–870
starting, 517–518
using menus of, 524
"Are you sure you want to abandon operation?" message, 52
arguments (in function statements), 216
arithmetic operators, 175–176

arithmetic. *See* calculations
arrays, 796-797
　commands for managing, 822
arrow keys, 73
　for application design screen, 522
　for browse and edit screens, 60
　for database design corrections, 31
　for editing memo fields, 65
　with help screens, 12
　if inoperative, 10, 20
　for labels design screen, 279
　in macros, 450
　for menus, 10
　for reports design screen, 229
A's, in custom form field templates, 325-326
Ascending (Change Action/Perform File Operation/Physically Sort Database submenu option), 609
ascending sort order, 100-102, 104
ASCII
　characters, table of values for, 909-911
　codes for currency formats, 692
　command for typing files in, 819
　for graphics characters on forms, 324
　importing/exporting files in, 490-492, 499-501
　sorting method of, 100, 104
　text/DOS/disk files in, 300, 478-479, 500-501, 818
assembly language, using programs in, 825
asterisks
　*, as arithmetic operator, 176
　**, as exponentiation indicator/operator, 176
　***, as number overflow indicator, 177
attributes, of files, 468
author's name, adding to sign-on banner, 652-653
Autoexec.bat (DBSETUP Install/Transfer Other Files submenu option), 701
AUTOEXEC.BAT file, 688, 768-769
Autosave (DBSETUP/Database menu option), 705
averages
　summary field option for obtaining, 188
　summary operator for obtaining, 205

B

background/foreground colors on screen, 508, 696-698
backslash (\\), in directory names, 778-779
Backspace key
　for erasing character to left, 17, 31, 60, 65, 229, 279, 522
　in macros, 450
backups
　of files, 479-482
　importance of, 52, 394, 509
"Bad command or file name" message, 5-6, 618, 786
bands, 182
　formatting, 243
　group, 191, 357-358, 364-373
　improved in dBASE IV, 793
　opening and closing, 242-243
　for report design, 233-239
banners (sign-on), creating for applications, 535-538, 652-653, 838-839
batch processes, 851
　allowing applications user to execute, 615
　as application objects, 840
　choosing applications options for, 557-567
　creating, 556-557
.BAT file name extensions, 478, 786
.BCH file name extensions, 853
beeps
　setting option for, 505, 531-532
　setting pitch of, 706
　with typematic feature, 10
　when field is filled, 37
Before Printing (Change Action/Display or Print/Report submenu option), 589
Bell (DBSETUP/General menu option), 706
BELL (environment option), 505, 531-532
binary files, allowing applications user to execute, 618-619
blank-delimited files, 490-491
blanks
　displaying for zero values, 179
　inserting between expressions, 714
　placing in label text, 273
　trimming leading and trailing, 249, 251, 329

blocks
    determining size of, 705
    keys for selecting/moving/copying, 66
    specifying number of for storage, 712
    of text for form letters, 257–258
Blocksize (DBSETUP/Database menu option), 705
boldface, printer codes for, 306
booting your computer, 782
borders, 529–530, 629–630
boxes, 251, 322–323
brackets ([ ]), as margin indicators, 66
browse screen
    allowing applications user to display data on, 582–585
    customizing, 77–80
    entering records from, 40–42
    searching for records from, 113–119
Bucket (DBSETUP/Memory menu option), 711
BUFFERS = n command, 479, 770
buffers
    and pausing/cancelling printing, 312
    typeahead, 708
bytes, 785

C

C > symbol (DOS prompt), 5
calculations
    commands for, 816
    conditional, 214–219
    financial functions for, 803–804
    indexing on results of, 219–220
    performing on calculated fields, 183–185, 199–202, 221
    performing on dates, 211–212
    performing in fields in forms, 196–198
    performing from dot prompt, 667
    performing on groups of records, 207–209
    performing in reports, 178–196
    of totals and subtotals, 179–181, 185–188, 190–196
    using numeric fields, 175–177
    using numeric picture functions, 177–178
    using numeric templates, 177
    using queries, 198–219
capitalization. *See* case sensitivity
CapsLock key, 44
CAPTURE (dBASE IV installation process option), 764
caret (^)
    as arithmetic operator, 176
    as exponential format picture function, 179
Carry (DBSETUP/Database menu option), 705
CARRY (environment option), 505, 531–532
Carry Forward (custom form edit option), 333, 336
case sensitivity
    in custom form field templates, 326, 328
    in report/label formats, 249, 284
    in searches, 118–119
    in sorts, 100
Catalog (DBSETUP/Files menu option), 710
catalogs, 16, 461
    adding file names to, 463–464
    changing description for, 463
    creating, 15–18, 462
    current, 7
    naming, 466
    removing file names from, 464–465
    selecting, 462
    specifying default, 710
    vs directories, 509
CD (DOS command), 784
CDOW( ) (record grouping function), 360
Center Align (picture function), 249, 251, 284, 332
centering of text, 249
Century (DBSETUP/General menu option), 706
CENTURY (environment option), 505, 532
character data, global editing of, 376–381
character data type, 27–28,
character delimited files, 490–491, 500
character input symbols, 250, 285
CHDIR (DOS command), 784
child-parent relationship of directories, 779
clearing the work surface, 566–567
clock

format for display of, 693–694
specifying display of, 713
Clock (DBSETUP/General menu option), 706
CMONTH( ) (record grouping function), 360
code. *See also* programming language; programs
  generating/displaying for applications, 639–646
  source and object, 639, 675
colon (:), in directory names, 778
colors
  changing default for, 695–698
  changing on display, 507–509
  on custom forms, 346–347
  defining for windows, 630
  optimizing display of, 762–763
  of sign-on banners, 529–530
columns. *See also* fields
  sizing on browse screen, 79–80
  specifying in report design, 230
.COM file name extensions, 786
COM1/2, 686, 764
comma (,)
  in delimited files, 490–491
  displaying numbers with, 177
  placing in label text, 273
comma-delimited files, 490
Command (DBSETUP/General menu option), 706
command-driven operations, 664
command files, 664, 670. *See also* commands
  commands to create, control and annotate, 820–822
  created automatically by dBASE IV, 674–676
  creating, 671–673
  keys for editing of, 671–672
  running, 673–674
commands. *See also* command files
  for arrays and memory variables, 822
  for calculations, 816
  capturing screen output from, 710
  for command file creation, control and annotation, 820–822

for controlling environment, 826–830
for database files, 813, 817
for data displays, 816
in dBASE IV programming language, 663
for debugging, 825–826
for disk files, 818
for displaying database structure and status, 819
for editing database data, 814–815
handling from dot prompt, 663–666
help with syntax of, 667–670
for importing and exporting data, 819
listing of, 813–831
for macros, 819
for memo fields, 817
for menus, 824
for networking, 830–831
for objects, 817–818
parameters for, 669
for printers, 825
for procedures and user-defined functions, 821
for records, 815
for screens, 823–824
for sorting and indexing, 815
specifying number for storage in buffer, 707
for user interface, 823
common fields, 400–402
compiling programs, 674
  improved in dBASE IV, 795
  specifying maximum symbols allocated during, 711
complete expressions, 575–576
complex indexes, 158–160
Compress Display? (Change Action/Browse submenu option), 584
Condensed type size, 302, 305–306
condition boxes
  for entering search queries, 150
  for marking records for deletion, 74–75
Config.db (DBSETUP menu option), 683, 703–714
Config.sys (DBSETUP Install/Transfer Other Files submenu option), 701
CONFIG.SYS file, 478–479, 770
configuration, providing information about, 716–717

INDEX — 919

Confirm (DBSETUP/General menu option), 706
CONFIRM (environment option), 505, 532
Console (DBSETUP/CONFIG.DB/Output menu option), 713
contains operator ($), 132, 136
context sensitivity of help screens, 11
Control Center, 50. *See also* DOS utilities screen
  accessing DOS commands from, 482-483
  components of, 6-8
  database design/description/modification from, 29-35, 44-50
  database file sorting from, 86-99, 103-108
  dot prompt compared to, 18-19
  environment setting changes from, 504-509
  handling catalogs from, 461-466
  improvements in dBASE IV over previous versions of, 791
  labels design from, 267
  obtaining help on, 13-15
  printing reports and labels from, 289-311
  record addition/deletion from, 68-77
  recording macros from, 437-438
  reports design screen access from, 227
control codes (for printers), 304-305
conversion of data types, functions for, 805
conversion functions, 95-96
COPY (DOS command), 301
copying files, 473, 475-476
copyright notice, 528, 652-653
count of number of records in a group, 188, 205, 362-364
CR as credit number symbol, 179
Create New CONFIG.DB (DBSETUP/CONFIG.DB menu option), 704
creating
  applications, 518-521
  banners (sign-on), 535-538, 652-653, 838-839
  batch processes, 556-557
  catalogs, 15-18, 462
  command files, 671-673
  database files, 25, 29-35
  database structure, 29, 490-492
  directories, 786, 842-843
  envelopes, 267
  file privileges, 741-747
  formats for reports, 181-183
  form letters, 253-261
  labels, 849-850
  macros, 437-442
  menus, 852-853, 862-869
  objects, 542-543
  Rolodex cards, 267
  sign-on banners, 535-538, 861-862
  stickers, 267
  user profiles, 730-736
Ctmaxsyms (DBSETUP/Memory menu option), 711
Ctrl-End key, for saving and returning to design screen or Control Center, 523
Ctrl-N key, for inserting blank line or row, 31, 65, 229, 262, 279
Ctrl-Q key, for abandoning changes and exiting, 66
Ctrl-T key, for removing field or word to right, 65, 229, 279
Ctrl-U key
  for deleting entire records or rows, 31
  for removing deletion marker, 69-70, 72, 74
Ctrl-*x* key
  in macros, 449
  used in dBASE IV Editor, 65
Ctrl-Y key, for deleting entire lines, 60, 65, 229, 279
curly braces ({ })
  as date indicators, 130, 170, 337
  as picture function indicators, 330
  as printer escape code indicators, 305
  as special key indicator in macros, 449
Currency (DBSETUP/General menu option), 706
currency formats, 179, 690-693
current catalog, 7, 462
current file, 7-8
cursor, preventing automatic browse screen positioning of, 80
custom applications, 837
custom forms. *See* forms

D

data. *See also* fields; protecting data
  commands for displaying, 816
  editing, 59–63
  searching for specific information, 114–118
database design screen, 29–33
database files. *See also* database structure; labels; Protect system; records; searching
  adding descriptions of, 33–35
  assigning to application objects, 558–561
  backing up from DOS Utilities screen, 479–482
  changing default in applications, 534–535
  commands for copying and moving, 817
  commands for creating and editing, 813–815
  creating, 25, 29–35
  as database objects, 840
  encrypting, 705
  exporting to other programs, 495–503
  importing from other programs, 483–495
  many-to-many, 406–409
  for membership management system example, 843–844
  one-to-many, 400–406
  opening and closing, 50
  reasons for having multiple, 399–400
  sorting by indexing method, 85–103
  sorting by sorted copy method, 85, 103–108
Database menu (DBSETUP/CONFIG.DB main menu option), 25, 704–706
database structure. *See also* database files; Protect system; records
  ascertaining/creating for imported files, 490–492
  command for displaying, 819
  designing, 29–35
  modifying, 44–50
  saving, 35–36
data screens, 51
data types, 27–29
  changing, 49–50
  conversion functions for, 95–96
  indexing of, 95–97
  selecting, 31–32

date arithmetic, 211
date data type, 27–28, 37
Date (DBSETUP/General menu option), 707
date functions, 801–802
Date Order (environment option), 505
dates
  formatting, 706
  grouping records by, 360–361
  improvements in dBASE IV over previous versions of, 792
  international formats for, 689–690
  performing calculations on, 211–212
  performing comparisons on, 213–214
  setting display options for, 505, 532, 689
  setting in your system, 783–784
Date Separator (environment option), 505–506
.DB2 file name extensions, 495–496
DB as debit number symbol, 179
dBASE III/dBASE III PLUS, dBASE IV's improvements on, 791–797
dBASE IV. *See also* applications; Control Center; database files; database structure; installation; membership management system example; programming language for dBASE IV; Protect system
  accessing from any directory, 687–688
  as calculator, 667
  Developer's Edition, 797
  international date/currency/clock formats in, 689–694
  specifying first command executed by, 706
  specifying version number in applications, 652–653
  summary of changes between versions of, 791–797
  uninstalling, 703
dBASE Template Language Toolkit (DBSETUP Install/Transfer Other Files submenu option), 701
dBASE IV Programmer's Reference Guide, 426, 623, 663
.DBF file name extensions, 34, 549
.DBO file name extensions, 677
DBSETUP
  CONFIG.DB menu of, 703–714

Display menu for, 695–698, 708
DOS menu of, 717
exiting, 718
Exit menu of, 718
Install menu of, 682, 700–703
Keys menu for, 709–710
running, 681–683
Tools menu of, 714–717
DBSETUP.EXE file, 681
DBSETUP.HLP file, 681
DBSETUP.OVL file, 681
DBSETUP.PRD file, 681
DBSETUP.RES file, 681
DBSYSTEM.DB file, 751
DD/MM/YY date format, 690
debit, DB as symbol for, 179
Debug (DBSETUP/General menu option), 707
debugging
  activating on error occurence, 708
  commands to use for, 825–826
  macros, 453–454
  with step-by-step execution, 708
  with Talk and Trap environment options, 506
Decimal Places (environment option), 506
decimals. *See also* currency formats
  in numeric vs float data types, 175
  specifying decimal point character, 707
  specifying precision of, 32, 176–177
Decimals (DBSETUP/CONFIG.DB/Output menu option), 713
Default (DBSETUP/Files menu option), 710
defaults
  for @ command output, 713
  in applications, 524–535, 538–539, 621–622
  in Applications Generator, 652–656
  changing with DBSETUP, 681, 683, 689–699
  for decimals, 713
  for drives and directories, 482, 717
  for margins, 698–699, 713
  for screen colors, 695–698
  specifying for directory paths, 711
Default type size, 302

Default Value (custom form edit option), 333, 336–337
"Delete covered text and fields?" message, 238, 244, 279
Deleted (DBSETUP/Database menu option), 705
Deleted (environment option), 506
deleting fields, records. *See* fields; records
delimited ASCII files, 490–491
Delimiter (Change Action/File Operation/Add or Copy Records submenus options), 597, 599
Delimiters (DBSETUP/General menu option), 707
DELIMITERS (environment option), 532
Del indicator of deletion, 70, 72, 75
Del key
  in DBSETUP, 682
  for deleting character/template/block selected, 60, 65, 229, 263, 279, 285, 522
  in macros, 450
descending sort order, 100–102, 104
Design (DBSETUP/General menu option), 707
designing database files, reports, etc. *See* database files; reports, etc.
Design option, of application design screen, 541–557
design screen, 50
design screen files, 675
Detail band, 233, 236–238
Developer's Edition of dBASE IV, 797
Development (DBSETUP/General menu option), 707
Device (DBSETUP/CONFIG.DB/Output menu option), 713
.DIF file name extensions, 496
dimming menu items (making unavailable)
  in applications, 623–624
DIR (DOS command), 785
directories
  accessing dBASE IV from any/all, 687–688
  changing temporarily, 469–470
  creating, 786, 842–843, 858
  default,

changing, 482
specifying, 655-656, 711
for SQL operations, 711
naming, 778-779
selecting for dBASE IV program and files, 767-768
selecting from DOS, 784
testing I/O performance of, 715-716
vs catalogs, 509
directory tree, 469-470
disk drives, 776. *See also* drives
diskettes, 775
disk files, commands for managing, 818. *See also* ASCII
disks, testing I/O performance of, 715-716
disk use, obtaining information about, 683
display
changing colors of, 507-509
changing options for, 504-506, 529-530
default options for, 654
selecting mode during dBASE IV installation, 762
display attributes, 246-247, 279
Display Browse Menu? (Change Action/Browse submenu option), 584
Display Disk Usage (DBSETUP/CONFIG.DB/Tools menu option), 714-715
Display Edit Menu? (Change Action/Edit submenu), 587
Displaying the Positioning Menu (from Item menu), 625-626
Display menu, for DBSETUP, 695-698, 708
dittoing function
for data entry into custom forms, 336
Ditto key, 60
for records, 705
setting option for, 505
division, operator for, 176. *See also* calculations
documentation, generating and printing for applications, 646-648, 893-894, 900-901
DOCUMENT.GEN template, 641, 646-647
Do dBASE Program (Change Action/Run Program submenu option), 613-614

Do (DBSETUP/General menu option), 707
dollar sign ($)
as financial format picture function, 179
as relational operator, 132
DOS commands
accessing from Control Center, 482-483, 509
allowing applications user to execute, 616-618
examples of, 783-787
invoking from macros, 455-456
presenting prompt for, 717
DOS (DBSETUP menu option), 683, 717
DOS (disk operating system), 775
date and time in, 783-784
directories, subdirectories, trees and files on, 778-779, 784-786
disks and drives on, 775-778, 784
DOS prompt in, 782-783
file names in, 779-782, 785
file search paths on, 787
running programs of, 786-787
DOS files. *See* ASCII
DOS prompt, 5, 717, 782-783
DOS utilities screen, accessing, 466-468
dot prompt, 18-19, 663-666, 707
double-strike, printer codes for, 306
"Do you want more samples?" message, 291
draft quality printing, 302
drivers, 764
drives
default, changing, 482
default specifying, 655-656, 710
selecting for dBASE IV program and files, 767-768
selecting from DOS, 784
duplicate records, hiding, 373-376

E

Echo (DBSETUP/CONFIG.DB/Output menu option), 713
editing, macros, 448-453
Editing Allowed (custom form edit option), 333-334

editing frame, 521
edit options, on customized form fields, 333–339
editor, for memo fields, 64–68
edit screen
　entering records from, 36–40
　searching for records from, 113–118
electronic palette, 346
Elite type size, 302
Embed code option, 622–623
Encryption (DBSETUP/Database menu option), 705
End key
　in macros, 450
　for moving to end of line/menu options/fields, 11, 60, 65, 229, 279, 522
　on reports design screen, 431
"***END RUN dBASE IV" message, 20
Enter key
　for database design corrections, 31
　as end-of-paragraph marker, 65, 67
　for labels design screen, 279
　for reports design screen, 229, 262
　setting option for necessity of, 505, 532
　specifying necessity of, 706
　and value entry, 220
　when not necessary to press, 16, 64, 505
envelopes, creating with labels design screen, 267
environment
　changing settings for, 504–509, 528–535
　choosing setting for, 654–655
　commands for controlling, 826–830
　functions for returning information about, 806–808
Epson printers, 305–306
equal sign (=)
　as relational operator, 132
　use of to form double lines in reports, 188–190
erasing records, 69–77
errors
　handling in command entry, 665–666
　providing help message automatically in case of, 707

trapping in forms input, 325
escape codes for printers, 305
Escape (DBSETUP/General menu option), 707
ESCAPE (environment option), 532
Esc key
　for canceling macro playback, 444
　disabling, 707
　for exiting menus, 10–11, 20, 52
　for exiting without saving changes, 66, 229, 279, 523
　in macros, 450
　for unselecting blocks, 66
Exact option
　DBSETUP/Database menu, 705
　environment, 506
examples (placeholders), 212–214, 221
exceptions, searching for, 136–137
exclamation point (!), in custom form field templates, 326
Exclusive option
　DBSETUP/Database menu, 705
　environment, 506
exclusive use of locked files, 754
Execute BATCH process (from Change Action/Run Program submenu), 615
.EXE file name extensions, 786
Exit (DBSETUP menu option), 683, 711, 714
exiting
　and abandoning changes, 60, 66, 229, 279
　allowed by applications user, 620–621
　browse and edit screens, 169
　dBASE IV, 19
　DBSETUP, 683, 718
　menus, 10–11, 20, 52
　protect system, 751–752
　query mode and views, 169
　setting application options for, 532
exponential notation
　automatic display in, 221
　indicator for, 176
　picture function for, 179
exporting
　commands for, 819

files from dBASE IV, 611-612
Lotus 1-2-3 files, 496-499
Expression Builder, 94-95
expressions
  complete, 575-576
  defining form field edit capability, 334-335
  grouping records by, 359-364
Expsize (DBSETUP/Database menu option), 705
extensions. *See* file name extensions

F

false/true value searches, 130-131, 575-576
Fastcrt (DBSETUP/CONFIG.DB/Output menu option), 713
FAT, determining degree of fragmentation of, 715
feedback, displaying from commands, 708
The Field Named (Change Action/Perform File Operations/Substitute Field Values submenu option), 600
field names
  displaying, 713
  displaying with structure lists, 550-552
  in report design, 236-237
field privileges, establishing, 745-747. *See also* Protect system
fields, 25-26. *See also* calculations; data types; indexes; searching
  adding/deleting, 45-47, 183-185
  adding/deleting/formatting for reports, 245-251
  adding to forms, 196-198
  common (across databases), 400-402
  comparing, 212-219
  displaying after queries on, 162-166
  displaying available values for, 553-555
  in label formats, 271-275, 278-285
  locking/freezing/blanking on browse screen, 77-79
  maximum number of, 26
  moving, 47-48
  naming/renaming, 26-27, 31, 48, 221
  for record numbers, 402-406
  restricting user access to, 77-79, 726-728

specifying delimiters for, 707
summary, 187-188, 192
width of, 32, 49, 176-177, 249-251
Fields to Lock Onscreen (Change Action/Browse submenu option), 583
Fields option
  Change Action/Browse or Edit submenus, 583, 586
  Change Action/Display or Print/List submenu, 592
  Change Action/Perform File Operation/Copy Records submenu, 599
  Change Action/Perform File Operation/Export submenu, 612
field templates
  in customized form design, 319, 325-339
  in label design, 271-275
  in report design, 236-237
field type. *See* data types
field values, allowing applications to change in database fields, 599-601
"File already exists" message, 35, 52
file name extensions
  .APP, 464, 677
  .BAT, 478, 786
  .BCH, 853
  .COM, 786
  .DBF, 34, 549
  .DBO, 677
  .DB2, 495-496
  .DIF, 496
  .EXE, 786
  .FMO, 676-677
  .FMT, 549, 676-677
  .FRG, 677
  .FRM, 464, 549, 677
  .FRO, 677
  .FW2, 496
  .LBG, 677
  .LBL, 464, 549, 677
  .LBO, 677
  .MDX, 792
  .PRF, 311
  .PRG, 478, 677
  .PRT, 478
  .QBE, 464, 677

INDEX 925

.QBO, 677
.RPD, 496
.SCR, 464, 676-677
.TXT, 478, 500
.UPD, 464
.VUE, 464
.WK1, 486
file names. *See also* catalogs; files lists
   adding/removing in catalogs, 464-465
   in DOS, 779-782
   rules for, 17
   sorting, 471-472
file privileges. *See also* Protect system
   changing, 748-749
   creating, 741-747
   deleting, 748
   designing, 724-728
   saving, 748
files. *See also* database files; file name extensions; file names; protecting data
   allowing applications user to access for handling, 595-612
   ASCII (text/DOS/disk), 300, 478-479, 500-501
   copying, 473, 475-476
   deleting, 473-475
   displaying with DOS Utilities screen, 471
   for labels, 276-278
   locking, 753-754
   marking, 472-473
   moving, 473, 476-477
   naming/renaming, 17, 477-478, 779-781
   safety option for overwriting of, 506, 532, 711
   sorting names of, 471-472
   specifying number openable, 710
Files (DBSETUP/Files menu option), 710
file skeleton, 125-126, 162
files lists, 467, 547-550
Files menu, for DBSETUP/CONFIG.DB MENU, 710-711
FILES = *n* command, 479, 770
Filter (Change Action/Browse submenu option), 583
FILTER conditional operator, 578
filter conditions. *See also* queries
   advisability of testing, 378, 394
   with calculated field queries, 202-203
   combining with database links, 419
   combining with sort conditions, 156
   incorporating into applications design, 575
   for isolating records marked for deletion, 74, 386
   refining with parentheses, 577
   removing previous, 170
financial format, picture function for, 179
financial functions, 803-804
first letter, grouping records by, 361-362
fixed disks, 775
fixed-length-field files, 490-491
flexible disks, 775
float data type, 27-29, 175
floppy disks, 464, 775-777
.FMO file name extensions, 676-677
.FMT file name extensions, 549, 676-677
Follow Record after Update? (Change Action/Browse or Edit submenus option), 584, 587
footers, for reports, 233, 239
FOR option
   Change Action/Perform File Operation/Export submenu, 612
   Change Action/Perform File Operation/Physically Sort Database submenu, 609
   Change Action/Perform File Operation/Substitute Field Value submenu, 601
FOR conditional operator, 577
foreground/background colors on screen, 508, 696-698
Format File (Change Action/Browse or Edit submenus option), 583, 586
formats, 8
form letters
   adding descriptions of, 261-262
   creating, 253-261
   saving, 261-262
   viewing, 262
Form Name (Change Action/Display or Print/Report or Labels submenus option), 588, 590

forms
   allowing applications user to display data on, 585-587
   boxes and lines on, 322-323
   calculated fields in, 196-198
   coloring, 346-347
   controlling input to, 325-339
   as database objects, 840
   delimited fields in, 532
   design screen for, 317-319
   graphics characters for, 323-325
   layout specification in reports, 230-231
   memo fields in, 342-345
   modifying, 345-346
   multiple-page, 347-348
   quick layout for, 319
   saving, 339-340
   text and fields for, 319-322
   using, 340-342
   using with multiple related files, 424-431
forms design screen, 317-323, 327-340, 794
Framework II, exporting dBASE IV files to, 496
Freeze Edit Field (Change Action/Browse submenu option), 583
frequency distributions, 209-210
.FRG file name extensions, 677
.FRM file name extensions, 464, 549, 677
.FRO file name extensions, 677
From File (Change Action/Perform File Operation/Import submenu option), 610
FullPath (DBSETUP/Database menu option), 705
function keys
   for application design screen, 523
   assigning text to, 709-710
   for browse and edit screens, 60
   for command file editing, 671-672
   for editing memo fields, 66
   for labels design screen, 279
   in macros, 449
   for queries design screen, 431
   for reports design screen, 229, 263
functions of dBASE IV, 663
   for data type conversion, 805
   for dates, 801-802
   for financial calculations, 803-804
   for identification and testing, 806-808
   for lookups, 808
   for memo fields, 803
   for menus, 805-806
   for most recent keystroke, 805
   for networks, 808
   for numeric fields, 803
   for strings, 802
   trigonometric, 804-805
.FW2 file name extensions, 496

G

General menu (DBSETUP/CONFIG.DB main menu option), 704, 706-708
Generate Index to Index File (Change Action/Perform File Operation/Generate Index submenu option), 606
Generate Quick Application option, 539-541
Generic Driver, 685, 764
Gets (DBSETUP/Memory menu option), 711
global editing
   for appending groups of records, 390-394
   of character data, 376-381
   for marking/unmarking for record deletion, 384-390
   of numeric data, 381-384
Go To DOS (DBSETUP/DOS menu option), 717
graphics characters, for forms, 323-325
greater/less than symbols (>/<)
   in dBASE IV command syntax, 669
   in DOS prompt, 782
   as relational operators, 132, 175
group bands, 191, 357-358, 364-373
grouping (in mathematical operations), indicator for, 176
Group Intro bands, 357
group names, for user/file access, 724, 732-733, 743, 752
groups of records, 357
   by expression value, 359-364
   handling headings at page breaks for, 365
   nesting within groups, 368-373

removing redundant fields from reports of, 365-368
Group Summary bands, 357

H

hard disks, 464, 775, 777
hardware
 changing setup for, 682-687
 required by dBASE IV, 759, 775-777
 specifying setup for, 761-768
headers
 in programs, 528
 for reports, 233, 235
Heading (Change Action/Display or Print/Report submenu option), 588
Heading Format (Change Action/Display or Print/Report submenu option), 589
Headings (DBSETUP/CONFIG.DB/Output menu option), 713
help
 as application object, 851
 commands to obtain, 819
 defining for application objects, 632, 851, 903
 improvements in dBASE IV over previous versions of, 791
 obtaining, 11-15
 table of contents for, 13-15
 writing text for, 561-567
Help (DBSETUP/General menu option), 707
Help key (F1), 11, 60
hidden records, 389
hiding
 deleted records, 71-72, 506
 duplicate records, 373-376
 records marked for deletion, 705
highlighting, restricting user from, 579-580
HISTORY buffer, 707
History (DBSETUP/General menu option), 707
Home key
 in macros, 450
 for moving to first field/menu option/beginning of line, 11, 60, 65, 229, 279, 522
horizontal bar menus, creating, 543-544, 862-863
Horizontal Stretch (picture function), 249-251, 284
Hours (DBSETUP/General menu option), 707
HP Laser-Jet printers, 305-306
hyphen (-). *See also* minus sign
 in custom form field templates, 326
 in date displays, 505-506

I

IBM printers, 305-306
Ignore Case (Change Action/Perform File Operation/Physically Sort Database submenu option), 609
IIF( ) function, 216-217, 221
importing
 commands for, 819
 files into dBASE IV, 483-484, 509, 609-611
 Lotus 1-2-3 files, 484-490
Include Record Numbers? (Change Action/Display or Print/List submenu option), 592
indentation
 of label text, 271
 and "outdentation" with Shift-Tab key, 66
 with Tab key, 66, 229
Indexbytes (DBSETUP/Database menu option), 705
Index in Descending Order? (Change Action/Perform File Operations/Generate Index submenu option), 606
indexes, 85
 activating, 87, 89
 assigning index function actions to menu options, 605-608
 on calculation results, 219-220
 commands for, 815
 complex, 158-160
 default in applications, 520, 534-535

and editing of database files, 102–103
excluding duplicate values from, 706
improvements in dBASE IV over previous
   versions of, 792
modifying, 98–99
for nested groups, 368
on report groups, 359
searching with, 119–123
selecting for, 32
selecting for items, 628
for sorting of records to print, 293–294
sorting on single field, 86–91
sorting within sorts, 91–98
specifying amount of memory for storing,
   705
index expressions, 93
Index First Key Expression? (Change
   Action/Perform File Operations/Generate
   Index submenu option), 606
Index Key Expression (from Change
   Action/Perform File Operations/Generate
   Index submenu option), 606
Insert dBASE Code (Change Action/Run
   Program submenu option), 615–616
insert mode, 59
Ins key
   in macros, 450
   for switching between insert and overwrite
      modes, 44, 59–60, 65, 229, 279, 522
installation. *See also* DBSETUP
   of dBASE IV,
   copying optional files, 770–771
   copying program files, 768–769
   information required for, 760
   with Install option of DBSETUP menu,
      682–683, 700
   making changes to, 767
   modifying AUTOEXEC.BAT file, 768–769
   modifying CONFIG.SYS file, 770
   with multi-user option, 761–762
   optimizing color display, 762–763
   and registering software, 760–761
   selecting display mode, 762
   selecting drive and directory, 767–768
   selecting printers, 763–766
   and uninstalling previous versions of, 703,
      759–760
   of networks, 700
   of printers, 685, 763–766
Instruct option
   DBSETUP/General menu, 707
   environment, 506
Intensity (DBSETUP/CONFIG.DB/Output
   menu option), 713
introductory paragraphs for reports, 233,
   235–236
"Invalid directory" message, 5
italics, printer codes for, 306
Item menu, from Applications Generator,
   571–575

J

justification of text to right, 249

K

Keep Image on Exit? (Change
   Action/Browse or Edit submenus option),
   584, 586
keys. *See also* individual keys
   for browse and edit screens, 59–60
   for command file editing, 671–672
   for database design corrections, 31
   for label format design, 279
   for macro editor, 448–450
   for Memo field editor, 65–66
   for menu navigation, 10–11
   for query design screen, 126
   for reports design screen, 229
   toggle, 44
   for using Control Center, 51
Keys menu, for DBSETUP, 709–710
keystrokes
   functions for analyzing most recent, 805
   recording as macros, 440–442

L

labels
   allowing applications user to print, 589–591

creating for membership management system example, 849–850
designing,
    accessing screen for, 267–269
    placing/editing fields on, 271–275, 278–285
    saving formats for, 275–276
    selecting format for, 269–271
files for, 276–278
improved in dBASE IV, 794
printing, 291–293
viewing designs for, 278
labels design screen, 267–276, 278–285
landscape mode printing, printer codes for, 306
language for programming dBASE IV. *See* programming language for dBASE IV
LaserJet printers, 305–306
laser printers, 291, 293, 303
.LBG file name extensions, 677
.LBL file name extensions, 464, 549, 677
.LBO file name extensions, 677
leading zeroes, displaying, 179
LEFT( ) (record grouping function), 360–362
less/greater than symbols. *See also* greater/less than symbols (>/<)
letter quality printing, 302
letters. *See* form letters; labels
libraries, for macros, 446–447
Like, as relational operator, 132
lines
    adding to customized forms, 322–323
    adding to report formats, 246, 251
    as boxes, 251, 322–323
    of equal signs in row on reports, 188–190
linking of database information, 401, 419–420
LIST command, examples of, 670
lists
    as application objects, 851–852
    choosing applications options for, 557–567
    file, 467, 547–550
    structure, 550–552
    value, 553–555
literals (literal characters), 328, 330–331
Load/Call Binary File (Change Action/Run Program submenu option), 618–619

Locating a Value in a Field (from Item menu), 626
Lock (DBSETUP/Database menu option), 706
locking, files and records, 753–754
logical data type, 27–28
login names, 723, 731, 752
LOOKUP( ) command, 795
lookups, functions for, 808
Lotus 1-2-3 files, importing and exporting, 484–490, 496–499
LPT1/2, 686, 764
L's, in custom form field templates, 326

M

macros, 437
    adding to, 452–453
    allowing applications user to execute, 619–620
    commands for, 819
    copying, 454
    debugging, 453–454
    deleting, 454–455
    editing, 448–453
    improved in dBASE IV, 794
    invoking DOS commands from, 455–456
    invoking other macros with, 452
    libraries for, 446–447
    naming, 439, 445, 456
    pausing, 447–448
    playing back, 442–444, 453–454
    recording from Control Center, 437–438
    recording keystrokes for, 440–442
    recording from macros prompt box, 439
    saving, 445–446
    viewing during playback, 453–454
macros prompt box, 439
mailing labels. *See* labels
mailmerge, specifying in reports, 230
MailMerge (WordStar), 493–494
many-to-many database designs, 406–409
Margin option
    DBSETUP/CONFIG.DB/Output menu, 713
    environment, 506

margins
  defaults for, 713
  setting environment options for, 506
  specifying for all printed reports, 312, 698–699
  specifying in form letters, 255–256
  specifying in report design, 232–233
  specifying when printing, 310
markers, 64, 342
marking
  files, 472–473
  records for deletion, 69–77, 384–390
MARK/UNMARK update operator, 376
mathematical operations. *See* calculations
Maximum Column Width (Change Action/Browse submenu option), 583
maximum value in group, 188, 205
MD (DOS command), 842
.MDX file name extensions, 792
membership management system example
  action-to-menus assignment for, 870–887
  application object creation for, 861–870
  application objects design for, 851–853
  batch processes for, 853–858, 887–892
  code generation for, 893
  creating directories for, 842–843
  custom form design for, 845–847
  database design for, 843–844
  database object design for, 843–850
  developing and defining with Applications Generator, 859–860
  documentation generation for, 893–894
  goals of, 840–841
  index design for, 844
  mailing label design for, 849–850
  making modifications and refinements to, 900–903
  menu design for, 852–853
  reports design for, 847–849
  sort order definition for, 892–893
  testing of, 894–900
  tips and traps for, 904
  using, 903–904
memo data type, 27–28
Memo field editor, 64–68

memo fields, 63–64
  commands for managing, 817
  displaying in reports, 252–253
  in forms, 342–345
  functions for, 803
  improvements in dBASE IV over previous versions of, 792
  maximum size of, 26
  searching, 151
  setting environment options for, 506
  using, 64–68
  width of, 707
memory, specifying allocation to @...GET...PICTURE commands, 711
Memory pull-down menu (in DBSETUP/CONFIG.DB menu), 711–712
memory variables, commands for managing, 822
Memo text field, specifying text editor for, 708
Memowidth (DBSETUP/General menu option), 707
Memo Width (environment option), 506
memo windows, 343–344
menu bar, 6–7
menu-driven operations, 664
MENU.GEN template, 641
menus. *See also* actions assignable to application objects; objects
  allowing applications user to open, 581–582
  as application objects, 840
  in Applications Generator, levels on, 524–525, 652
  choosing in applications design, 519, 526–527
  choosing applications options for, 557–567
  commands for managing, 824
  creating for membership management system example, 852–853, 862–869
  dimming items (making unavailable) in, 623–624
  functions for, 805–806
  horizontal bar, 543–544
  naming in applications design, 519–520, 526–527

INDEX — 931

pop-up or pull-down, 8-9, 544-547
and submenu options, 9-10
Message (custom form edit option), 333, 335
message line prompts, assigning to
  application objects, 632-634, 902-903
message placement on screen, 714
minimum value in group, 188, 205
minus sign (-), as arithmetic operator, 176
MKDIR (DOS command), 842
MM/DD/YY date format, 325, 689
Modify Application Environment option,
  528-535
Modify Existing CONFIG.DB
  (DBSETUP/CONFIG.DB menu option),
  703
Modify Hardware Setup (DBSETUP Install
  menu option), 700
money. *See* currency formats
monitors. *See also* screen
  changing colors on, 507-509
    monochrome and color/EGA and VGA,
    762
Moving the Record Pointer (from Item
  menu), 626
Multiplan SYLK, exporting dBASE IV files
  to, 496
Multiple Choice (picture function), 331-332
multiple database files
  types of, 399-409
  views of, 409-420
multiple-page custom forms, 347-348
multiplication, operator for, 176. *See also*
  calculations
multi-user setup. *See* networks
Mvblksize (DBSETUP/Memory menu
  option), 711
Mvmaxblocks (DBSETUP/Memory menu
  option), 711

N

naming
  applications, 519, 525-526
  catalogs, 463, 465-466
  directories, 778-779
  disk drives, 777-778

fields, 26-27
files, 17, 477-478, 779-781
files when copying, 476
form letters with descriptions, 261-262
groups of users for security purposes,
  732-733
label formats with descriptions, 276
macros, 439, 445, 456
menus in applications design, 519-520,
  526-527
structure lists, 551
subdirectories, 779
users and groups for login purposes,
  723-724
windows, 629
navigation line, 7-8
Near (DBSETUP/Database menu option),
  706
near-letter-quality printing, 302
negative numbers, 176
nesting, groups of records within groups,
  368-373
networks. *See also* protecting data
  commands for, 830-831
  disk drive names in, 778
  functions for, 808
  installing, 700
  locking records in, 706
  restricting access in, 705
  setting options for user access of, 506
  specifying time between screen updates in,
  712
NEXT *n* option, for use with SCOPE
  conditional operator, 578
nines (9999), in custom form field templates,
  326
Noclock (DBSETUP/CONFIG.DB/Output
  menu option), 713
"No help found for <object name>."
  message, 562
NOT logic, using in applications design,
  576-577
N's, in custom form field templates, 326
numbering records within database files,
  402-406
numbers. *See also* currency formats; decimals;

numeric data type
  negative, 176
  sizing of, 176–177
numeric data, global editing of, 381–384
numeric data type, 27–29, 97–98, 175, 707, 792
numeric field functions, 803
numeric fields, calculating with, 175–177
numeric picture functions, calculating with, 177–179
numeric templates, calculating with, 177, 221
NumLock key, 10, 20, 44

O

object code, 639, 675
objects, 7–8. *See also* actions assignable to application objects
  application, 840
    creation examples, 861–870
    design example, 851–853
    putting away, 870
    selection example, 869–870
  commands for creating and modifying, 817–818
  creating from Design option menu, 542–543
  database, 840
    design example, 843–850
  putting away, 565–566, 639–641
  restricting ability to create new, 707
  rules for naming, 17, 558
  saving, 565
Odometer (DBSETUP/CONFIG.DB/Output menu option), 713
Of MDX File (from Change Action/Perform File Operations/Generate Index submenu), 606
Of Type
  from Change Action/Perform File Operation/Add or Copy Records submenus, 597, 599
  from Change Action/Perform File Operation/Import or Export submenus, 611–612
one-to-many database designs, 400–406
operators
  arithmetic, 175–176
  conditional, 577–579
  relational, 132–137, 175
  summary, 203–207
  update, 376
OR/AND logic
  searching with, 137–142, 170
  using in applications design, 576–577
order of precedence of mathematical operations, 176
Or Tag (Change Action/Perform File Operations/Generate Index submenu option), 606
OS/2, 775
Output menu (from DBSETUP/CONFIG.DB menu), 712–714
Override Assigned Database or View, 621–622
overwrite mode, 59

P

packing (of databases), 69
page breaks
  with Eject Page Now option, 299–300
  with New Page option, 303
  when printing group reports, 365
  when printing labels, 293
Page Footer band, 233, 239
Page Header band, 233, 235
page length, 309–310
page numbers, 306–308
pagination, 306–308
panels, 7
parent-child relationship of directories, 779
parentheses (( ))
  as arithmetic operator, 176
  in custom form field templates, 326
  as negative number symbols, 179
  for refining filter conditions, 577

passwords, 723, 728-732, 752
path
   returning entire name of, 705, 787
   specifying for searches, 533-534, 787
Path (DBSETUP/Files menu option), 711
PATH (DOS command), 688, 787
patterns, searching on, 135
Pause (DBSETUP/CONFIG.DB/Output menu option), 713
Pause at Full Page/Screen? (Change Action/Display or Print/List submenu option), 592
pausing
   macros, 447-448
   printing, 311-312, 592
performance of the system, obtaining information about, 683
Perform DOS Command (DBSETUP/DOS menu option), 717
period (.)
   in date displays, 505-506
   in file name extensions, 780
Permit Edit if (custom form edit option), 333-335
PFS:FILE, exporting dBASE IV files to, 496
PgUp/PgDn keys
   for application design screen, 522
   for browse and edit screens, 60
   for labels design screen, 279
   in macros, 450
   for Memo field editor, 65
   for menus, 11
   for reports design screen, 229
Pica type size, 302
picture functions, 248-249, 283-284
   calculating with, 177-178
   for customized forms, 328-333
   for label formats, 283-284
   for report formats, 247-251
placeholders, 212-214, 221
Play Back Macro (Change Action/Run Program submenu option), 619-620
plus sign (+), as arithmetic operator, 176
Point (DBSETUP/General menu option), 707
pop-up menus, 544-547, 851, 872

portrait mode printing, printer codes for, 306
ports, selecting, 686, 764
pound sign (#)
   in custom form field templates, 326
   as index indicator, 157-158, 431
   as relational operator, 132, 175
precedence (order of mathematical operations), 176
Precision (DBSETUP/General menu option), 707
Preset menu, of application design screen, 528-529, 652
.PRF file name extensions, 311
.PRG file name extensions, 478, 677
primary index field, 94
PRINT (DOS command), 300-301
printer codes, 304-305
Printer (DBSETUP/CONFIG.DB/Output menu option), 713-714
printers
   commands for controlling, 825
   controlling, 298-311
   directing output to, 713-714
   Epson, 305-306
   HP LaserJet, 305-306
   IBM, 305-306
   installing, 685, 763-766
   laser, 291, 293, 303
   saving settings for, 311
   tractor-feed, 303, 312
printing
   allowed by applications user, 588-594
   to ASCII files, 300
   with choice of type size, 301-302
   with draft vs near letter quality, 302
   to files, 300
   formatted reports, 290-291
   with line spacing options, 311
   with LIST command, 670
   multiple copies, 308-309
   with page eject, 299-300, 303, 423
   with page length and margin control, 309-311
   pausing/cancelling, 311-312
   profile and privilege reports from Protect system, 749-751

from queries, 297-298
with Quick Report option, 289-290
records selection for, 296-298
reports and documentation from membership management system example, 898-901
subtotaled reports, 195-196
with views, 420-423
Print Sample? (Change Action/Display or Print/Labels submenu option), 590-591
privileges for file access, designing scheme for, 724-728. *See also* Protect system
procedures, commands for, 821
programming language for dBASE IV. *See also* actions assignable to application objects
  advantages of, 425-426
  embedding in applications, 564-565, 622-623
  improved dBASE IV features of, 795
programs, 663-664. *See also* command files; commands; dBASE IV
  compiling, 674
  running from DOS, 786-787
  using in assembly language, 825
prompt boxes, 50, 506, 707
Prompt (DBSETUP/General menu option), 707
PROMPT PG (DOS command), 20, 784-785
prompts
  assigning to application objects, 632-634
  DOS, 5, 717, 782-783
  dot, 18-19, 663-666, 707
  message line, 632-634, 902-903
protecting data, 723. *See also* Protect system
  designing scheme for, 723-728
  implementing dBASE IV Protect system, 728-752
  using protected files, 752-754
Protect system
  entering, 728
  exiting, 751-752
  file privileges for, 724-728, 741-749
  password for, 728-730

printing profile and privilege reports from, 749-751
user profiles for, 723-724, 730-740
using protected files in, 752-754
.PRT file name extensions, 478
PrtSc key, in macros, 450
pull-down menus, 8-9, 544-547, 863-869, 872
putting away objects, 565-566, 639-641

Q

.QBE file name extensions, 464, 677
.QBO file name extensions, 677
Quattro, exporting dBASE IV files to, 496
queries, 123-124. *See also* filter conditions
  for calculations, 198-219
  designing, 125-126
  displaying results of, 162-166
  by example, 124
  improvements in dBASE IV over previous versions of, 793
  for isolating records marked for deletion, 74
  for record searches, 123-149, 160-161
  saving, 166-167
  for selection of records for printing, 296-298
  for sorting of records to print, 294-296
  sorting results of, 151-160, 208-209
  for updating records, 376
query design screen, 123, 126-149
question mark (?), in dBASE IV command syntax, 669
QUICKAPP.GEN template, 641
quick applications, generating, 539-541
quick reports, 179-181
quotation marks ('')
  in custom forms, 349
  in delimited files, 491, 500
  in search conditions, 127, 170
  in sign-on banners, 536

R

ranges
  searching for, 144-145

specifying for custom form field input, 337–338
Rapidfile, exporting dBASE IV files to, 496
READ.ME files, 478
reassigning index order (Item menu option), 628
RECNO( ) function, 403–405
RECORD *n* option, for use with SCOPE conditional operator, 578
records, 25–26. *See also* calculations; groups of records
  adding/deleting, 68–77
  allowing user to display without report format, 591–593
  assigning record handling actions to menu options, 602–605
  blanking on browse screen, 79
  commands for locating, 815
  defining number to be involved in applications operations, 578–579
  entering, 36–42
  hidden, 389
  hiding deleted, 71–72, 506
  hiding duplicates, 373–376
  locking, 80, 753–754
  maximum number of fields/characters in, 26
  numbering within database files, 402–406
  obtaining number of, 188
  positioning pointer for, 624–627
  saving, 43
  searching for, 113–114
  selecting for printing, 296–298
Refresh (DBSETUP/Memory menu option), 711
relational operators
  performing calculations with, 175
  searching with, 132–137
REPLACE update operator, 376
report bands, 233–239, 420–423
Report Format (Change Action/Display or Print/Report submenu option), 589
Report Intro band, 233, 235–236
reports. *See also* form letters
  allowing applications user to print, 588–589
  bands for, 233–239, 420–423
  as database objects, 840
  designing, 227–228, 241–252
  displaying memos in, 252–253
  formats for,
    copying, 244
    creating, 181–183
    generic, 228–232
    moving, 244
    saving, 240
  improved in dBASE IV, 793–794
  margins for, 232–233
  performing calculations in, 178–196
  printing with views, 420–423
  viewing, 241
reports design screen, 227–228
Report Summary band, 233, 238–239
Reprocess (DBSETUP/Memory menu option), 711
REST option, for use with SCOPE conditional operator, 578
retrieval. *See* searching
Reverse Marks option, 473
reverse video, 713
Review System Configuration (DBSETUP/CONFIG.DB/Tools menu option), 716–717
Right Align (picture function), 249, 251, 285, 332
Rolodex cards, creating with labels design screen, 267
root directory, 779
rows. *See* records
.RPD file name extensions, 496
Rtblksize (DBSETUP/Memory menu option), 711
Rtmaxblocks (DBSETUP/Memory menu option), 711
ruler, in editor screen, 66
Run DOS Program (Change Action/Run Program submenu option), 616–618
running
  applications, 648, 650–652
  DBSETUP, 681–683
RunTime (DBSETUP Install/Transfer Other Files submenu option), 701
RunTime files, 771

S

Safety (DBSETUP/Files menu option), 711
SAFETY (environment option), 506, 532
Sample files, 771
Sample Files (DBSETUP Install/Transfer Other Files submenu option), 701, 711
saving
 with autosave, 705
 database structures, 35-36
 file privileges, 748
 form letters, 261-262
 forms, 339-340
 label formats, 275-276
 macros, 445-446
 objects, 565
 queries, 166-167
 records, 43
 report formats, 240
 user profiles, 736-737
SCAN...ENDSCAN Loop, 796
scientific notation. *See* exponential notation
SCOPE conditional operator, 578-579
SCOPE option
 Change Action/Perform File Operation/Export submenu, 612
 Change Action/Perform File Operation/Physically Sort Database submenu, 609
 Change Action/Perform File Operation/Substitute Field Value submenu, 601
Scoreboard (DBSETUP/CONFIG.DB/Output menu option), 714
screens
 commands for controlling, 823-824
 disabling, 713
 eliminating "snow" on, 685, 763
 fast updating of, 713
 pausing after screenful of information, 713
 specifying update intervals in networks for, 712
 used in dBASE IV, 50-52
.SCR file name extensions, 464, 676-677
scrolling through multiple-page custom forms, 347
Scroll Within Display Width (picture function), 331
searching
 case sensitivity and wildcards in, 118-119
 commands for locating records, 815
 with condition boxes, 150
 exact/inexact match options for, 506, 705-706
 forwards and backwards, 114-117
 with indexes, 119-123
 memo fields, 151
 multiple fields, 143-145
 for near matches, 706
 for particular records, 113-114
 with queries, 123-149, 160-161
 for ranges, 144-145
 with relational operators, 132-137
 for relationships, 132-142, 145-149
 for specific information, 114-118
 specifying paths for, 533-534
 for values, 127-131
 with views, 167-169
Searching for an Index Value (from Item menu), 626
secondary index field, 94
SEEK( ) command, 795
"Selections won't fit in field—UNselect some entries" message, 551
semicolon (;), in key assignment commands, 709-710
Send Output To (Change Action/Display or Print/Report or Labels submenus option), 589-590, 592
Separator (DBSETUP/General menu option), 707
Set Default Drive:Directory (DBSETUP/DOS menu option), 717
SET ECHO command, 707, 713
Shift-F8 key (ditto), 60
Shift-Tab key
 in macros, 450
 for moving to previous field/Tab/column, 31, 60, 66, 229, 279, 523

for "outdents", 66
  in queries design screen, 431
  for reformatting paragraphs (in word-wrap editor), 229
sign-on banners, 838-839
  as application object, 851
  creating for applications, 535-538, 861-862
  specifying default values for, 652-653
skeletons, file and view, 126, 162-166
slash (/)
  as arithmetic operator, 176
  in date displays, 505-506
  in dBASE IV command syntax, 669
Smallest/Largest Allowed Value (custom form edit options), 333, 337-338
"snow" on monitor screen, 685, 763
software. *See also* commands; programming language for dBASE IV; programs
  DOS as middleman for, 775
  registering during dBASE IV installation, 760-761
Sort Fields (from Change Action/Perform File Operation/Physically Sort Database submenu), 609
sorting
  allowing applications user to, 608-609
  in alphabetical order, 844
  commands for, 815
  database files by indexing method, 85-103
  database files by sorted copy method, 85, 103-108
  file names, 471-472
  labels for printing, 293-296
  records for printing, 293-296
  results of queries, 151-160, 208-209
  within sorts, 91, 93-98
sort order, selecting as default in applications design, 520, 534-535
soundex technique, 133
Sounds like, as relational operator, 132
source code, 675
  generating for applications, 639-646
source databases, 391
Space (DBSETUP/CONFIG.DB/Output menu option), 714

special characters
  in currency formats, 692
  not allowed in files names, 17
spellings, searching on, 133-134
SPOOLER (dBASE IV installation process option), 764
spreadsheet data, importing/exporting to Lotus 1-2-3, 486-490, 496-499
SQLdatabase (DBSETUP/Files menu option), 711
SQL (DBSETUP/General menu option), 708
SQLhome (DBSETUP/Files menu option), 711
square brackets ([ ])
  in dBASE IV command syntax, 669
  as margin indicators, 66
standard deviation, obtaining, 188
startup
  of applications, 648, 650-652
  of dBASE IV, 5-6
status bar, 43-44, 70, 708
Status (DBSETUP/General menu option), 708
STD, summary field option for obtaining standard deviation, 188
Step (DBSETUP/General menu option), 708
stickers, creating with labels design screen, 267
string functions, 802
strings, 115
structure lists, 550-552, 852
subdirectories, 779
submenus, 9
subscripted memory variables (arrays), 796-797
subtotals
  calculating, 190-194
  printing, 195-196, 220
subtraction, operator for, 176. *See also* calculations
sum
  summary field option for obtaining, 188
  summary operator for obtaining, 205
summary fields, 187-188, 192, 221

summary operators, 203–207
surface for query design, 125
Symphony, exporting dBASE IV files to, 496
syntax of commands
   getting help with, 667–670
   for SQL, 708
"Syntax error" message, 176
system date, 783
system performance and configuration,
   obtaining information about, 683

T

Tab key
   in macros, 449–450
   for moving one column/field/tab
     stop/menu option to right, 31, 60, 66,
     229, 279, 522
   in queries design screen, 431
   for reformatting paragraphs in word-wrap
     editor, 229
Tabs (DBSETUP/CONFIG.DB/Output
   menu option), 714
Talk option
   DBSETUP/General menu, 708
   environment, 506
target databases, 391
Tedit (DBSETUP/General menu option),
   708
Template Language files, 771
Template Language Toolkit (DBSETUP
   Install/Transfer Other Files submenu
   option), 701
templates, 182
   adjusting width of, 249, 284
   for applications source code generation,
     641–642
   for fields in report design, 236–237
   numeric, 177
   placing in form letters, 258–261
Test Disk Performance
   (DBSETUP/CONFIG.DB/Tools menu
   option), 715–716
text
   adding to customized forms, 319–322
   adding to label formats, 273
   adding to report formats, 246
   in blocks for form letters, 257–258
   editing, 59–63
   right-justification/centering of, 249
text editors, 708
text files. *See* ASCII
time
   format of, 693–694, 707
   setting in your system, 783–784
   specifying for on-screen display, 706
titles, for reports, 233, 235–236
To File option
   Change Action/Perform File
     Operation/Export submenu, 612
   Change Action/Perform File
     Operation/Physically Sort Database
     submenu, 609
toggle keys, 44
Toolkit (DBSETUP Install/Transfer Other
   Files submenu option), 701
Tools (DBSETUP menu option), 683,
   714–717
"Too many files are open" message, 479
totals. *See also* calculations
   obtaining on reports, 179–181
   report summary bands for, 238–239
   and subtotals, 185–188, 190–196
tractor-feed printers, 303, 312
Transfer Other Files (DBSETUP Install
   menu option), 700–702
Trap option
   DBSETUP/General menu, 708
   environment, 506
tree (directory structure), 779
trigonometric functions, 804–805
Trim (picture function), 249, 284, 332
true/false value searches, 130–131, 575–576
truncation
   of data in reports, 250
   of numeric data, 177
Tutorial files, 771
Tutorial Files (DBSETUP Install/Transfer
   Other Files submenu option), 701
12-hour clock format, 707
24-hour clock format, 693–694, 707
.TXT file name extensions, 478, 500

Typeahead (DBSETUP/General menu option), 708
typematic feature, 10

U

Unaccepted Message (custom form edit option), 333, 338-339
"Unbalanced parentheses" message, 176
underline character (_), in directory names, 778
underlining, printer codes for, 306
Undo Change to Record option, 62-63
uninstalling dBASE IV, 703, 759-760
Unique (DBSETUP/Database menu option), 706
unmarking files, 473
"Unrecognized command verb" message, 666
UNTITLED.CAT, 7, 16
update operators, 376
update queries, 376
.UPD file name extensions, 464
uppercase conversion
  for customized forms, 329-330
  for reports and labels, 249, 284
Use Previous Browse Table? (Change Action/Browse or Edit submenus option), 584, 587
user access. *See also* Protect system
  denying to fields through structure lists, 551
  restricting, 705
  setting options for networks, 506
  through user passwords, 723
user interface, commands for, 823
user passwords, 723, 728-732, 752
user profiles
  changing, 737-738
  creating, 730-736
  deleting, 739-740
  designing, 723-724
  saving, 736-737

V

values, excluding duplicates from indexes, 706

values lists, 553-555, 852
variance, obtaining, 188
versions of dBASE IV
  specifying in applications, 652-653
  summary of changes between, 791-797
  uninstalling previous, 759-760
Vertical Stretch (picture function), 249-251, 284
video options for color/intensity in custom forms, 346-347
View (DBSETUP/Files menu option), 711
views, 124, 166
  assigning to application objects, 558-561
  changing/deactivating, 168-169
  of multiple databases, 409-420
  overriding default in applications, 621-622
  printing reports with, 420-423
  searching/editing with, 167-168
  selecting as openers in applications design, 520, 711
  using with multiple related files, 424-425
view skeleton, 126, 162-166
VisiCalc, exporting dBASE IV files to, 496
V's (in report format templates), 251, 253
.VUE file name extensions, 464

W

WHILE conditional operator, 579
WHILE option
  Change Action/Perform File Operations/Export submenu, 612
  Change Action/Perform File Operations/Physically Sort Database submenu, 609
  Change Action/Perform File Operations/Substitute Field Value submenu, 601
wildcard characters
  in file backup operations, 480-481
  in file handling from DOS Utilities screen, 473, 476-478
  in file names, 468
  in file selection for displaying with DOS Utilities screen, 471
  in searches, 118-119, 135, 169

windows, 851–852
  as application objects, 840
  displaying in applications, 628–631
  improved in dBASE IV, 795
  naming, 629
With This Value (from Change Action/Perform File Operations/Substitute Field Value submenu), 600–601
.WK1 file name extensions, 486
WordStar files, importing/exporting, 493–495, 501
word-wrap, 64
  in report/label fields, 250, 284
word-wrap editor, 63, 253–254
work space, 7
work surfaces, clearing, 566–567, 639–641
Wp (DBSETUP/General menu option), 708

X

X's
  in custom form field templates, 325–326
  in report/label format templates, 251, 253, 279, 284–285

Y

YEAR( ) (record grouping function), 360
Y's, in custom form field templates, 326
YY.MM.DD (and YY/MM/DD) date format, 690

Z

zeroes (leading), displaying, 179

Selections from The SYBEX Library

DATABASE MANAGEMENT

Mastering Paradox (Third Edition)
Alan Simpson
663pp. Ref. 490-9

Paradox is given authoritative, comprehensive explanation in Simpson's up-to-date new edition which goes from database basics to command-file programming with PAL. Topics include multiuser networking, the Personal Programmer Application Generator, the Data-Entry Toolkit, and more.

The ABC's of dBASE IV
Robert Cowart
300pp. Ref. 531-X

This superb tutorial introduces beginners to the concept of databases and practical dBASE IV applications featuring the new menu-driven interface, the new report writer, and Query by Example.

Understanding dBASE IV (Special Edition)
Alan Simpson
880pp. Ref. 509-3

This Special Edition is the best introduction to dBASE IV, written by 1 million-reader-strong dBASE expert Alan Simpson. First it gives basic skills for creating and manipulating efficient databases. Then the author explains how to make reports, manage multiple databases, and build applications. Includes Fast Track speed notes.

dBASE III PLUS Programmer's Reference Guide (SYBEX Ready Reference Series)
Alan Simpson
1056pp. Ref. 508-5

Programmers will save untold hours and effort using this comprehensive, well-organized dBASE encyclopedia. Complete technical details on commands and functions, plus scores of often-needed algorithms.

The ABC's of dBASE III PLUS
Robert Cowart
264pp. Ref. 379-1

The most efficient way to get beginners up and running with dBASE. Every 'how' and 'why' of database management is demonstrated through tutorials and practical dBASE III PLUS applications.

Mastering dBASE III PLUS: A Structured Approach
Carl Townsend
342pp. Ref. 372-4

In-depth treatment of structured programming for custom dBASE solutions. An ideal study and reference guide for applications developers, new and experienced users with an interest in efficient programming.

Also:

Mastering dBASE III: A Structured Approach
Carl Townsend
338pp. Ref. 301-5

Understanding dBASE III PLUS
Alan Simpson
415pp. Ref. 349-X

A solid sourcebook of training and ongoing support. Everything from creating a first database to command file programming is presented in working examples, with tips and techniques you won't find anywhere else.

Also:

Understanding dBASE III
Alan Simpson
300pp. Ref. 267-1

TO JOIN THE SYBEX MAILING LIST OR ORDER BOOKS
PLEASE COMPLETE THIS FORM

NAME _____ COMPANY _____
STREET _____ CITY _____
STATE _____ ZIP _____

☐ PLEASE MAIL ME MORE INFORMATION ABOUT **SYBEX** TITLES

ORDER FORM (There is no obligation to order)

PLEASE SEND ME THE FOLLOWING:

TITLE	QTY	PRICE
_____	___	___
_____	___	___
_____	___	___
_____	___	___

TOTAL BOOK ORDER _____ $_____

SHIPPING AND HANDLING PLEASE ADD $2.00 PER BOOK VIA UPS _____

FOR OVERSEAS SURFACE ADD $5.25 PER BOOK PLUS $4.40 REGISTRATION FEE _____

FOR OVERSEAS AIRMAIL ADD $18.25 PER BOOK PLUS $4.40 REGISTRATION FEE _____

CALIFORNIA RESIDENTS PLEASE ADD APPLICABLE SALES TAX _____

TOTAL AMOUNT PAYABLE _____

☐ CHECK ENCLOSED ☐ VISA
☐ MASTERCARD ☐ AMERICAN EXPRESS

ACCOUNT NUMBER _____

EXPIR. DATE _____ DAYTIME PHONE _____

CUSTOMER SIGNATURE _____

CHECK AREA OF COMPUTER INTEREST:

☐ BUSINESS SOFTWARE
☐ TECHNICAL PROGRAMMING
☐ OTHER: _____

THE FACTOR THAT WAS MOST IMPORTANT IN YOUR SELECTION:

☐ THE SYBEX NAME
☐ QUALITY
☐ PRICE
☐ EXTRA FEATURES
☐ COMPREHENSIVENESS
☐ CLEAR WRITING
☐ OTHER _____

OTHER COMPUTER TITLES YOU WOULD LIKE TO SEE IN PRINT:

_____
_____

OCCUPATION

☐ PROGRAMMER ☐ TEACHER
☐ SENIOR EXECUTIVE ☐ HOMEMAKER
☐ COMPUTER CONSULTANT ☐ RETIRED
☐ SUPERVISOR ☐ STUDENT
☐ MIDDLE MANAGEMENT ☐ OTHER: _____
☐ ENGINEER/TECHNICAL
☐ CLERICAL/SERVICE
☐ BUSINESS OWNER/SELF EMPLOYED

CHECK YOUR LEVEL OF COMPUTER USE

☐ NEW TO COMPUTERS
☐ INFREQUENT COMPUTER USER
☐ FREQUENT USER OF ONE SOFTWARE
  PACKAGE:
  NAME _____
☐ FREQUENT USER OF MANY SOFTWARE
  PACKAGES
☐ PROFESSIONAL PROGRAMMER

OTHER COMMENTS:

_____
_____
_____
_____
_____
_____

PLEASE FOLD, SEAL, AND MAIL TO SYBEX

SYBEX, INC.
2021 CHALLENGER DR. #100
ALAMEDA, CALIFORNIA USA
94501

SEAL

SYBEX Computer Books are different.

Here is why . . .

At SYBEX, each book is designed with you in mind. Every manuscript is carefully selected and supervised by our editors, who are themselves computer experts. We publish the best authors, whose technical expertise is matched by an ability to write clearly and to communicate effectively. Programs are thoroughly tested for accuracy by our technical staff. Our computerized production department goes to great lengths to make sure that each book is well-designed.

In the pursuit of timeliness, SYBEX has achieved many publishing firsts. SYBEX was among the first to integrate personal computers used by authors and staff into the publishing process. SYBEX was the first to publish books on the CP/M operating system, microprocessor interfacing techniques, word processing, and many more topics.

Expertise in computers and dedication to the highest quality product have made SYBEX a world leader in computer book publishing. Translated into fourteen languages, SYBEX books have helped millions of people around the world to get the most from their computers. We hope we have helped you, too.

For a complete catalog of our publications:

SYBEX, Inc. 2021 Challenger Drive, #100, Alameda, CA 94501
Tel: (415) 523-8233/(800) 227-2346   Telex: 336311
Fax: (415) 523-2373

Operation	Step Sequence	Page
Using Generic Report Formats		
On the reports design screen:	Menus (**F10**)/Layout	228
	Quick Layouts [←┘]	
	Column Layout *or* Form Layout *or* Mailmerge Layout [←┘]	
Editing a Report Format	Highlight the report name in the Reports panel	241
	Design (**Shift-F2**)	
Creating Form Letters	Highlight <create> in the Reports panel [←┘]	253
	Layout/Quick Layouts	
	Mailmerge Layout	

PRINTING REPORTS

Operation	Step Sequence	Page
Printing a Quick Report	Highlight the database or query name	289
	Quick Report (**Shift-F9**)	
	Begin Printing [←┘]	
Printing a Formatted Report	Highlight the report name in the Report panel [←┘]	290
	Print Report [←┘]	
	Begin Printing [←┘]	
To return to the Control Center:	Esc	

USING KEYSTROKE MACROS

Operation	Step Sequence	Page
Recording Keystrokes		
From the Control Center:	Menus (**F10**)/Tools	437
	Macros [←┘]	
	Begin Recording [←┘]	
From anywhere in dBASE IV:	Macros (**Shift-F10**)	439
	Begin Recording [←┘]	
Playing Back Recorded Keystrokes		442–443
From the Control Center:	Menus (**F10**)/Tools	
	Macros [←┘]	
	Play [←┘]	
	Type the letter or function key	
From anyplace in dBASE IV (for letter keys):	**Alt-F10**	
	Press the letter key	
From anyplace in dBASE IV (for function keys):	**Alt**-*function key*	

MANAGING CATALOGS

Operation	Step Sequence	Page
Creating a Catalog	Menus (**F10**)/Catalog	15, 462
	Use a Different Catalog [←┘]	
	<create>	
	Type a name for the catalog [←┘]	
Selecting a Catalog	Menus (**F10**)/Catalog	462
	Use a Different Catalog [←┘]	
	Select a catalog name	